Once again . . .
To MY BROTHER LOUIS
in gratitude for a lifetime
of faith and encouragement

THE NEW
ENCYCLOPEDIA
OF THE OPERA

By David Ewen

Hill and Wang • New York

1 2 3 4 5 6 7 8 9 0

PREFACE

THE WORD to stress in the title of this book is *new*. The present volume is *not* just a revised, updated edition of the *Encyclopedia of the Opera,* originally published in 1955 and reissued in 1963 in an enlarged edition. The plates of that book have been destroyed, and the entire book has been reset to permit a thorough overhauling from A to Z. It is quite true that some of the material of the earlier book has been found still serviceable: the author estimates that about 25 percent, perhaps less, of the older book has been retained. But three-quarters of this volume, perhaps more, contains either completely new entries, earlier entries thoroughly rewritten, or earlier entries greatly expanded. It is hoped that the additional material, as well as certain new approaches and methods, will make this volume even more comprehensive, detailed, and functional than its predecessor. More than 1,500 entries have been added (approximately 75,000 to 100,000 words) to the 3,567 entries (and 300,000 words) of the previous book.

The decision to redo the book completely, rather than compromise by issuing a new edition with essential changes and inclusions, was arrived at by both the author and the publishers in recognition of the fact that the opera scene all over the world has changed radically since 1955. An encyclopedia of the opera that formerly was acceptable, useful, and comprehensive had in fifteen years become sadly outdated. Perhaps the greatest change in the opera world is the expansion of repertory. The public has become aware of operas that were not known to it even by name in 1955. New operas and ignored operas of the past have been made available both in recordings and in the expanded and vitalized repertories of the world's opera houses during the past decade or so. Moreover, several hundred university, conservatory, semiprofessional, and amateur opera groups—as well as new professional opera companies and festivals—have sprung up, and many of them have been most adventurous in placing as much emphasis on modern operas and revivals of rarely heard old operas as on familiar repertory. The opera lover, consequently, has extended the sphere of his interest to embrace operas like *Anna Bolena, Maria di Rohan, La cenerentola,* or *Nabucco,* to mention just a few examples from the operas of the past, together with such modern operas as *Susannah, The Ballad of Baby Doe, Don Rodrigo, Elegy for Young Lovers, King Priam,* or *Vanessa,* to single out a few of the more familiar contemporary works.

Today an encyclopedia that intends to satisfy the basic needs and curiosity of the opera public must deal with many more operas and subjects than in 1955. A comprehensive encyclopedia must discuss the major new operas and their composers thoroughly, explaining and analyzing new idioms and techniques. Some of the older operas that originally received only cursory treatment have since been successfully revived and are now entitled to far more space. Many more opera companies and festivals must be included than was earlier necessary. And, of course, the many new singers, conductors, and composers who have become world famous since 1955 must be dealt with at length.

The basic ingredients of the earlier volume have been retained, though frequently with amplifications. Within this new volume the reader will find the following materials:

STORIES OF OPERA. The most significant operas (well over one hundred) of the past and present are treated in detail, act by act, scene by scene, with descriptions of the principal arias and other important excerpts and information about the composition and performance history. In this new volume, however, accounts of even the more familiar operas have been expanded to include more details of plot and additional arias. In many cases the entries have been completely rewritten.

Several hundred less well-known operas are treated more succinctly, with brief capsule plots and citations of musical highlights and matters of historic interest. Because of the frequency with which they are now performed and recorded, many operas treated in capsule form in the earlier book are here discussed in detail, scene by scene. This is particularly true of the most important works of the twentieth century.

The operas now included in the encyclopedia embrace all the works that are performed most frequently, as well as most of those that make intermittent appearances on the world's opera stages; operas that have special historic importance or interest; the early operas of such masters as Verdi, Puccini, Wagner, Bellini, Donizetti, Rossini, and so forth; operas with unusual technical approaches (atonal operas, quarter-tone operas, monodrama, operas using twelve-tone or serial techniques, electronic operas, and so on) ; operas that were once highly successful and have been retired; and operas that had been discarded but that have been successfully revived. The attempt, in short, has been to provide basic information about any opera in which the present-day operagoer might be interested for one reason or another.

Some of the operas are listed by their original foreign titles, others by titles in English translation. The general practice, in order to make the encyclopedia more functional for English-speaking audiences, has been to use the names most familiar to them. Since *The Jewels of the Madonna* is better known to speakers of English than *I gioielli della Madonna,* the opera is listed under the English title; and since *Il trovatore* is certainly more familiar than *The Troubadour,* the original title is used. Where a title is equally familiar in its original foreign form and in an English translation, the foreign title is preferred: thus *Die Meistersinger* is discussed under that title and not under *The Mastersingers,* and throughout the volume *Tristan und Isolde* is preferred to *Tristan and Isolde* and *Pelléas et Mélisande* to *Pelleas and Melisande.* The music lover consulting this encyclopedia should have no difficulty, however, finding the opera he wants, since there are ample cross references to guide him. These are printed in small capitals.

The capitalization of foreign titles has followed foreign usage.

CHARACTERS OF OPERAS. There will be found here an alphabetical listing of all the principal and some of the minor characters of a hundred or so major operas and of the principal characters of several hundred other operas. The author believes that this is the most complete "who's who" of opera characters to be found anywhere. A departure in this volume from the earlier is to identify the singer who created a major role—but only if that singer is famous enough to warrant having his biography included as well. Where the name of the major character and the title of the opera are the same, as in *Billy Budd,* the name of the singer creating the title role is found in the listing of the characters. This is to avoid an additional, unnecessary entry. In operas treated in capsule form, where the major character and the title of the opera are the same and where no list of characters appears, the creator of the principal role is mentioned in the text but, once again, only if that singer is important. Characters with titles are not listed under the title but under their name: Count Ceprano and Don Basilio appear not under Count or Don but under Ceprano and Basilio.

PASSAGES FROM OPERAS. The most important passages from particular operas—arias, duets, ensemble numbers, choruses, orchestral passages—are found not only in the discussion of the operas themselves but are listed separately in alphabetical order, together with the source. In this volume the dramatic significance of each excerpt is briefly described (something which was not done in the previous encyclopedia).

BIOGRAPHIES. The major figures in every facet of operatic composition and performance are given succinct biographical treatment. These figures include composers, librettists, singers, conductors, stage directors, impresarios, teachers, critics, and musicologists.

HISTORY OF OPERA. The history of opera—its origin, evolution, and development in all the major countries of the world—is discussed in a special article. There are also additional listings for and brief explanations of every form of opera (Masque, Ballad Opera, *Singspiel, Opera Buffa, Opéra Comique,* Music drama, Monodrama, *Opera Semiseria,* and so forth), together with explanations of every major trend and style in opera. In this volume the history is brought up to date to include the avant-garde movement in opera since the middle 1950's.

OPERA IN PERFORMANCE. The history of every major opera house of the world and of every important festival emphasizing opera is to be found here (in a form greatly extended from that found in the earlier book), along with general articles on the history of opera performances in Europe and America. In addition, the articles on opera on radio, television, and recordings have been completely rewritten to make them more complete and up to date, and an additional article, opera in motion pictures, has been added.

LITERARY SOURCES. Listings are made of all the major authors of the world, from Aeschylus to Arthur Miller, whose writings have been a source for opera texts and there are also listings of many of the great classics of literature from which operas have been derived.

SPECIAL ARTICLES. Specific subjects of operatic interest are discussed in special articles. The varied material thus treated includes the aria, the overture, marionette opera, children's operas, painters and paintings in opera, ballet in opera, claque, castrato, and the like. Several additional articles have been added to this volume, notably those on American singers, American opera composers and operas, the Bible in opera, composers as characters in opera, musical quotations and interpolations in opera, and articles on the most important opera grants and foundations.

TERMS IN OPERA. All the important technical terms used in opera are defined.

When the *Encyclopedia of the Opera* was first published, the author explained in his preface that it was "the first book of its kind in any language. The Editor has attempted to make it a comprehensive book about opera and opera performance." Although other encyclopedias of more modest dimensions have appeared since 1955, it is the hope of the author that the present rewritten volume is still the most comprehensive in existence in any language and that no facet of opera has been left untouched.

DAVID EWEN

THE NEW ENCYCLOPEDIA OF THE OPERA

A

Abandon d'Ariane, L', an *opéra minute* by Darius MILHAUD. Libretto by Henri Hoppenot. Premiere: Wiesbaden, Apr. 20, 1928. American premiere: Urbana, Ill., Mar. 6, 1955. This is the second of three miniature operas that the composer completed in 1927. Each takes less than ten minutes to perform; each is on a classical subject; each uses miniature forces both on the stage and in the orchestra; and each calls for a small chorus to serve as commentator and as catalytic agent between episodes. The other two miniature operas are L'ENLÈVE-MENT D'EUROPE and LA DÉLIVRANCE DE THÉSÉE.

Ariane (soprano) comes nightly to a part of the island of Naxos to avoid the advances of Thésée (tenor), who is loved by Ariane's sister, Phèdre. The god Dionysus (baritone), in disguise, arranges for Thésée to become interested in Phèdre (soprano), much to Ariane's relief. Ariane has one more wish: to spend the remainder of her life with Diana in the firmament above. When her wish is granted and the constellation of Ariadne rises behind her, the chorus sings joyously.

Abbado, Claudio, conductor. Born Milan, June 26, 1933. After attending the Verdi Conservatory in Milan and studying conducting at the Vienna Academy of Music, he won first prize in the Koussevitzky Competition at TANGLEWOOD in Lenox, Mass., in 1958 and the Dimitri Mitropoulos Competition in New York City in 1963. Appearances with several major orchestras and at the SALZBURG and HOLLAND festivals followed between 1964 and 1965. In 1965 he led the world premiere of Giacomo Manzoni's opera *Atomtod* at LA PICCOLA SCALA in Milan and in 1966 BELLINI'S I CAPULETTI ED I MONTECCHI at the Holland Music Festival. He was appointed conductor at LA SCALA in 1967 and promoted to permanent music director two years later. He made his debut at the METROPOLITAN OPERA with DON CARLOS on Oct. 7, 1968. In 1971 he was appointed music director of the Vienna Philharmonic.

Abbey, Henry Eugene, impresario. Born Akron, Ohio, June 27, 1846; died New York City, Oct. 17, 1896. He began his career as impresario in Buffalo in 1876 when, with Edward Schoeffel, he acquired and managed the local Academy of Music. In 1880 he produced theatrical presentations in New York, managing such celebrated stage personalities as E. H. Sothern, Henry Irving, Edwin Booth, and Sarah Bernhardt. In 1883 he helped organize the METROPOLITAN OPERA company in New York, assembling a brilliant roster of singers. The company lost close to half a million dollars during the first season and Abbey was replaced by the Metropolitan's second manager, Leopold DAMROSCH. Some years later, from 1891 to 1896, Abbey shared the management of the Metropolitan with Edward Schoeffel and Maurice GRAU, this time with better results. He died a month before the opening performance of the 1896–97 season.

Abbott, Emma, soprano. Born Chicago, Dec. 9, 1850; died Salt Lake City, Jan. 5, 1891. After studying with Achille Errani in New York and Mathilde MARCHESI, Antonio Sangiovanni, and Enrico DELLE SEDIE in Europe, she made her opera debut at COVENT GARDEN in 1876 in THE DAUGHTER OF THE REGIMENT. A year later she made her first appearance in America,

3

in the same opera, at the ACADEMY OF MUSIC in New York. She married Eugene Wetherell in 1878 and helped him organize the Emma Abbott English Grand Opera Company, which he managed and in which she appeared in principal soprano roles. Despite a limited voice, she had an immense audience appeal. She did not hesitate to interpolate popular ballads into operas or to couple a serious opera with a Gilbert and SULLIVAN comic opera on the same evening.

Abduction from the Seraglio, The (Die Entführung aus dem Serail), comic opera in three acts by MOZART. Libretto by Gottlieb Stephanie, adapted from the text by Christoph Friedrich Bretzner for an earlier opera, *Belmont und Constanze* (the music of which was by Johann André). Premiere: Burgtheater, Vienna, July 16, 1782. American premiere: German Opera House, Brooklyn, N.Y., Feb. 16, 1860.

Characters: Constanze (soprano); Blonde, her maid (soprano); Belmonte, Spanish nobleman (tenor); Pedrillo, his servant (tenor); Selim Pasha (speaking role); Osmin, his overseer (bass); a mute; slaves, guards.

The action takes place in Turkey in the sixteenth century.

Act I. A square before the Pasha's palace. A brief overture creates an effervescent mood and a Turkish identity; its main subject is a quotation from Belmonte's air, "Hier soll ich dich denn sehen." Constanze and Blonde have been kidnaped by pirates, brought to Turkey, and sold to the Pasha. Belmonte, Constanze's lover, has followed her. He expresses the hope of a reunion ("Hier soll ich dich denn sehen"). He comes upon Osmin, the fat overseer, who expresses a cynical attitude toward all women ("Wer ein Liebchen hat gefunden") and refuses to help Belmonte. The imminent arrival of the Pasha and Constanze fills Belmonte with joy, since he is about to catch a glimpse of his beloved ("Constanze! Constanze! dich wiederzusehen"). In hiding, Belmonte hears Constanze tell the Pasha she can never be his, since her heart belongs elsewhere ("Ach, ich liebte"). Enraged, the Pasha demands that she change her mind by the morrow.

Act II. The palace garden. Blonde describes the kind of man able to win her heart ("Durch Zärtlichkeit"), but he most certainly is not one like Osmin, whose amatory advances she repulses ("Ich gehe, doch rate ich dir"). After Constanze arrives, she describes her agony at being separated from her beloved Belmonte ("Welcher Wechsel"). She remains defiant toward the Pasha even when he threatens her with torture if she refuses him ("Martern aller Arten"). Blonde now learns that Belmonte has a plan to rescue her mistress and herself. Her joy is unbounded ("Welche Wonne, welche Lust"). The first part of the plan consists of getting Osmin helplessly drunk. After this is accomplished, Belmonte and Constanze exchange words of love ("Sieh die Freudenträne fliessen"), and Blonde and Pedrillo, a young Spanish servant in love with Blonde, join in to form a quartet.

Act III. Before the Pasha's palace. Coming to effect the escape of their women, Belmonte serenades Constanze ("Ich baue ganz auf deine Stärke"), after which Pedrillo sings to Blonde ("Im Mohrenland gefangen war"). The four flee, are apprehended, and brought before the Pasha. Osmin is triumphant ("Ha! wie will ich triumphieren"). The Pasha at first upbraids Constanze for trying to run away. Then he magnanimously forgives her and her lover and the two servants. Belmonte sings a hymn of praise to the generous Pasha ("Nie werd' ich deine Huld verkennen"), and everybody takes up the joyous refrain.

The Abduction from the Seraglio was Mozart's first stage work after he had settled in Vienna in 1781. It was written for the BURGTHEATER, where Emperor Joseph II encouraged domestic productions. Mozart followed the form of the SINGSPIEL, a kind of musical comedy then in vogue in Germany and Austria. His subtle musical characterization, poignant lyricism, and advanced harmonic and orchestral techniques transformed a popular medium into a vehicle for great art and made this work the first important opera in the German language.

Abencérages, Les (or **L'Étendard de Grenade**), opera in three acts by CHERUBINI. Libretto by Étienne de JOUY, based on *Gonzalve de Cordoue,* a novel by J.-P. Florian. Premiere: Paris Opéra, Apr. 6, 1813. The story is centered around the proud family of Spanish Moors known as the Abencérages, headed by the warrior Almansor, and their defeat and final destruction at the hands of the family of Zegris toward the end of the Moslem rule in Granada. This is one of its composer's late operas and is rarely given, but it did enjoy a successful revival at the FLORENCE MAY MUSIC FESTIVAL in 1957. Of special interest are the overture and the tenor aria, "Suspendez à ces mur."

Abends will ich schlafen geh'n, the prayer for protection of Hansel and Gretel in Act II of HUMPERDINCK'S HANSEL AND GRETEL, as they prepare to go to sleep in the woods.

Aber der Richtige, duet of Zdenka and Arabella in Act I of Richard STRAUSS'S ARABELLA. Zdenka tries to interest Arabella in Matteo, while Arabella replies that when the right man comes along she will know who he is.

Abigaille, Nebuchadnezzar's supposed daughter (soprano) in VERDI'S NABUCCO, a role created by Giuseppina STREPPONI.

Abimelech, Satrap of Gaza (bass) in SAINT-SAËNS'S SAMSON ET DALILA.

Abscheulicher! Wo eilst du hin?, dramatic recitative and aria of Leonore in Act I, Scene 2, of BEETHOVEN'S FIDELIO, when she overhears Pizarro's plot to murder her imprisoned husband, Florestan.

Abstrakte Oper No. 1, opera in seven scenes by Boris BLACHER. Libretto by EGK. Premiere: Frankfurt, June 28, 1953 (concert version) ; Mannheim, Oct. 17, 1953 (staged). American premiere: Boston, Mass., Apr. 19, 1956. Egk (himself a famous composer, but in this instance a librettist) explained that this abstract opera had been written for radio but could be performed either on the concert stage or in the opera house. Its cast comprises three solo voices, two narrators, and chorus, accompanied by wind, percussion, and piano. All of the performers are placed in the orchestra pit. Dancers on the stage mime the action, a sometimes absurd and always unrelated series of episodes, such as the shooting of a dressmaker's dummy, negotiations between two diplomats treated satirically, and ironic romantic interludes. The basic mood, however, is that of panic. The text is made up of vocal sounds ("gurru, gurru"; or "adynazit, azit, azant, anitronit"; or "laga, baba, nabuna") together with words whose sequence makes little or no meaning. Each of the seven scenes carries a title to convey the emotion being projected: Fear; Love—I; Pain; Negotiation; Panic; Love—II; and Fear.

When first heard in Frankfurt, the opera created a scandal: laughter, catcalls, whistles, shouts. One critic described it as "the worst opera ever written." The opera, however, proved a substantial success when revived at the BERLIN FESTIVAL in 1957.

Abu Hassan, comic opera in one act by WEBER. Libretto by Franz Karl Hiemer, based on a tale in the ARABIAN NIGHTS. Premiere: Munich, June 4, 1811. American premiere: Park Theater, New York, Nov. 4, 1811. This is early Weber, preceding DER FREISCHÜTZ by a decade. Abu Hassan (tenor) is a beggar deep in debt. He contrives to get money from the Sultan by pretending he is dead and having his wife, Fatima (soprano), get a widow's allowance. Greedily he seeks an allowance for himself by telling the Sultan Omar (bass) that Fatima is dead. This clumsy ruse is uncovered when the Sultan and Sultana visit their humble home to pay their respects. Magnanimously the Sultan not only forgives the culprits but even presents them with enough gold to pay off their debts. The best arias are two sung by Fatima ("Wird Philomene trauern" and "Hier liest welch' martervolles Los") and one by Abu Hassan ("Ich gebe Gastereien"). A duet of Abu Hassan and Fatima is also of interest ("Tränen, Tränen, sollst du nicht vergiessen").

Abul Hassan, the barber (bass) in CORNELIUS' THE BARBER OF BAGDAD.

Académie de Musique, see OPÉRA, L'.

Academy of Music, for over thirty years the principal opera house of New York City. Successor to the Astor Place Opera House, it was situated on Irving Place and Fourteenth Street. Its first manager, Max MARETZEK, opened the theater on Oct. 2, 1854, with NORMA, starring GRISI and MARIO. The Academy of Music continued to present outstanding opera performances until the METROPOLITAN OPERA was founded and became a successful rival.

The Academy was demolished by fire in 1866. It was rebuilt the following year and continued to house opera until the end of the century. During the years 1879–1886 it also housed the concerts of the New York Philharmonic.

Adelina PATTI made her opera debut at the Academy in 1859, Clara Louise KELLOGG in 1861, Emma ALBANI in 1874, and Emma ABBOTT in 1877. Under various managers—John Henry MAPELSON, Ole Bull, Maurice STRAKOSCH, Theodore THOMAS—the Academy of Music presented the American premieres of many outstanding operas, including: L'AFRICAINE; AIDA; ANDREA CHÉNIER; UN BALLO IN MASCHERA; DON CARLOS; MEFISTOFELE; OTELLO; RIENZI; RIGOLETTO; ROMÉO ET JULIETTE; THE SICILIAN VESPERS; LA TRAVIATA; IL TROVATORE.

After its career as an opera house, which ended at the beginning of the twentieth century, the building was used first as a theater, then as a motion-picture house until it was demolished in 1925.

a cappella, unaccompanied choral music. A few striking examples are found in opera: FAUST (the four-measure requiem for Valentin); LA FORZA DEL DESTINO (most of the RATAPLAN).

accompagnato, Italian for "accompanied." The term refers to a recitative, the instrumental accompaniment of which has been written out by the composer. A *recitativo accompagnato* is distinguished from a *recitativo secco* (literally "dry recitative"), in which the declamation is supported by the simplest sort of chords provided by a harpsichord or piano. The earliest example of *accompagnato* is found in the fourth act of MONTEVERDI'S L'ORFEO (1607).

Accusato di furto, Fernando's air in Act II of ROSSINI'S LA GAZZA LADRA.

Acerba volutta, Adriana's agitation brought on by her love for Maurizio in Act II of CILÈA'S ADRIANA LECOUVREUR.

Ach, das Leid hab' ich getragen, Nureddin's ecstatic aria in Act I of CORNELIUS' THE BARBER OF BAGDAD upon learning he is to have a meeting with his beloved Margiana.

Ach, ich fühl's, Pamina's plea for death, convinced as she is that Tamino loves her no longer, in Act I of MOZART'S THE MAGIC FLUTE.

Ach, ich liebte, Constanze's firm avowal to the Pasha that she can never be his since she loves another man, in Act I of MOZART'S THE ABDUCTION FROM THE SERAGLIO.

Achilles, Iphigenia's betrothed (tenor) in GLUCK'S IPHIGÉNIE EN AULIDE.

Ach, so fromm, see M'APPARI.

Acis and Galatea, (1) a MASQUE by HANDEL. Libretto by John GAY and others. Premiere: Cannons, the country home of the Duke of Chandos, 1720. American premiere: Park Theater, New York, Nov. 21, 1842. This work contains several famous arias: Acis' (tenor) "Love in her eyes sits playing" and "Love sounds the alarm," Galatea's (soprano) "Heart, the seat of soft delight" and "As when the dove laments her love," and Polyphemus' (bass) "O ruddier than the cherry." The story is based on the Greek myth in which the shepherd Acis, crushed beneath a rock by the giant Polyphemus, is transformed by his beloved, the sea nymph Galatea, into a bubbling fountain. In Italy, in 1708, Handel produced a serenata entitled *Aci, Galatea e Polifemo*. In 1732 he added some lines from Alexander Pope, John Hughes, and John DRYDEN to Gay's 1720 libretto, combined music of the early Italian serenata and the 1720 masque, and produced the resulting work at the KING'S THEATRE on June 21. This, the *Acis and Galatea* we know today, was called a serenata; it was staged with scenery and costumes but no action. As such it was successfully revived at the ALDEBURGH FESTIVAL in 1966.

(2) Opera (designated by the composer as a *pastorale heroïque*) comprised of a prologue and three acts by LULLY. Libretto by Jean Galbert de Campristron. Premiere: Anent, France, Sept. 6, 1686 (private); Paris Opéra, Sept. 17, 1686 (public). This was the last complete opera by the composer, written a year before his death.

Ackté, Aïno, soprano and impresario. Born Helsinki, Finland, Apr. 23, 1876; died Nummela, Aug. 8, 1944. After completing her music study in Paris, she made her opera debut at the PARIS OPÉRA in 1897 in FAUST. She was a leading soprano of the Paris Opéra for seven years. On Nov. 25, 1904, she made her American debut at the METROPOLITAN OPERA as Micaëla in CARMEN. She remained a member of this company for two seasons; thereafter, until 1910, she sang at COVENT GARDEN, where in 1910 she scored one of her greatest triumphs as SALOME in the first London performance of Richard STRAUSS's opera. Strauss later invited her to appear in this role in Paris and Dresden. In 1911 she founded the Finnish Opera Company at Savonhima, and in 1938 she became manager of the National Opera in Finland—a governmental post in which she supervised all opera within the nation—holding this post only one year.

A consolarmi affretisi, love duet of Linda and Charles in Act I of DONIZETTI'S LINDA DI CHAMOUNIX.

act tune, a term found in English operas of the seventeenth and early eighteenth centuries, denoting music played between the acts, with curtain drawn. Also called *curtain tune*. Modern equivalents are *intermezzo* and *entr'acte*.

Adalgisa, virgin of the Temple of Esus (now usually sung by a mezzo-soprano) in BELLINI'S NORMA.

Adam, Adolphe Charles, composer. Born Paris, July 24, 1803; died there May 3, 1856. He helped establish the form of the OPÉRA COMIQUE. His father, Jean Louis Adam, was a well-known pianist, composer, and teacher. Adolphe attended the Paris Conservatory, where he came under the influence of François BOIELDIEU, then at the height of his success. Adolphe's first dramatic work, the one-act *opéra comique Pierre et Catherine,* was successfully produced at the OPÉRA-COMIQUE in 1829. A year later came the three-act *Danilowa* and, in 1836, LE POSTILLON DE LONGJUMEAU, Adam's best work and one still performed in Europe. Largely due to the success of this opera, Adam was made a member of the Legion of Honor in 1836 and a member of the Institut de France in 1844. In 1847, he organized his own opera company, the Théâtre National, devoted to presenting works by young and unrecognized composers. This venture put Adam heavily in debt. He was able to meet his obligations by writing a number of highly successful comic operas which made him one of the most popular composers of France. He also wrote several ballets, *Giselle* being the most famous. In 1849 he became a professor of composition at the Paris Conservatory. The best of his nearly fifty operas include: *Le Châlet* (1834); *Le Postillon de Longjumeau* (1836); *Le Fidèle Berger* (1838); *Le Brasseur de Preston* (1838); *La Rose de Péronne* (1840); *Le Roi d'Yvetot* (1842); *Le Toréador* (1849); *Giralda* (1850).

Adamastor, roi des vagues profondes (Adamastor, re dell' onde profonde), Nelusko's invocation to the ocean before an impending storm, in Act III of MEYERBEER'S L'AFRICAINE.

Adams, Suzanne, soprano. Born Cambridge, Mass., Nov. 28, 1872; died London, Feb. 5, 1953. She made her debut at the PARIS OPÉRA in 1895 as JULIETTE. After successful appearances at both the Opéra and COVENT GARDEN, she made her American debut at the METROPOLITAN OPERA on Jan. 4, 1899, again as Juliette. She remained at the Metropolitan until 1903 and from 1903 to 1906 was seen at Covent Garden, where she created the role of Hero in STANFORD's *Much Ado About Nothing.* After 1903 she made her home in London. In 1898 she married the celebrated cellist Leopold Stern. His premature death in 1904 led to his wife's retirement from the opera stage only a few years later.

Addio alla madre, Turiddu's farewell to his mother in MASCAGNI's CAVALLERIA RUSTICANA, just before his duel with Alfio, which he senses will prove fatal.

Addio del passato, Violetta's farewell to the world, realizing she is soon to die of tuberculosis, in Act III of VERDI's LA TRAVIATA.

Addio, dolce svegliare, quartet of Rodolfo, Mimi, Marcello, and Musetta in Act III of PUCCINI's LA BOHÈME. Rodolfo and Mimi are bidding each other farewell while Marcello and Musetta are quarreling over her flirtation with a stranger.

Addio, fiorito asil, Pinkerton's farewell to his Nagasaki home that holds for him such tender memories of Cio-Cio-San, in Act III of PUCCINI's MADAMA BUTTERFLY.

Addio Firenze, Gianni Schicchi's mocking farewell to the city of Florence, in PUCCINI's GIANNI SCHICCHI.

Addio Roma, addio patria, Ottavia's farewell to her beloved city, in MONTEVERDI's L'INCORONAZIONE DI POPPEA.

Adele, Rosalinde's maid (soprano) in Johann STRAUSS's DIE FLEDERMAUS.

Adieu, conservez dans votre âme, Iphigenia's farewell to her people as she bravely accepts her own death as a sacrifice to the gods in order to enable the Greeks to proceed to Troy, in Act III, Scene 1, of GLUCK's IPHIGÉNIE EN AULIDE.

Adieu donc, vains objets, the prayer of John the Baptist as he awaits sentence in prison, in Act IV, Scene 1, of MASSENET's HÉRODIADE.

Adieu, Mignon, courage!, Wilhelm's farewell to Mignon after dismissing her as his servant, in Act II, Scene 1, of THOMAS's MIGNON.

Adieu, mon doux rivage, Inez' ballad to the river Tagus, in Act I of MEYERBEER's L'AFRICAINE.

Adieu, notre petite table, Manon's farewell to the table where she and Des Grieux had enjoyed many happy meals, in Act II of MASSENET's MANON.

Adina, wealthy young woman (soprano), the sweetheart of Nemorino, in DONIZETTI's L'ELISIR D'AMORE.

Adina credimi, Nemorino's plea to his beloved Adina to delay her marriage to Belcore, in Act I, Scene 2, of DONIZETTI's L'ELISIR D'AMORE.

Adler, Kurt Herbert, conductor and opera manager (not to be confused with Kurt Adler, chorus master and conductor of the METROPOLITAN OPERA). Born Vienna, Apr. 2, 1905. He conducted in various theaters in central Europe, was one of TOSCANINI's assistants at the SALZBURG FESTIVAL of 1936, then conducted opera and radio concerts in Czechoslovakia. He settled in the United States in 1938 and in 1941 received his American citizenship. Between 1938 and 1943 he conducted at the CHICAGO OPERA. In 1943 he became affiliated with the SAN FRANCISCO OPERA, where in 1952 he was made assistant to Gaetano MEROLA, the artistic director. Upon Merola's death in 1953, Adler assumed his position, which he has held since then.

Under his artistic guidance, the San Francisco Opera became one of the foremost companies in America. Adler has received high decorations from Italy, Germany, and Austria.

Adler, Peter Herman, conductor. Born Jablonec, Bohemia, Dec. 2, 1899. He attended the Prague Conservatory, where one of his teachers was Alexander ZEMLINSKY. At age twenty-two he became musical director of the city of Jablonec. Subsequently, he held various

posts as opera and symphonic conductor, mostly in Czechoslovakia. He came to New York in 1939, making his debut on Jan. 24, 1940, in a special New York Philharmonic symphony concert for Czech relief. In 1944 he became director of the Columbia Concerts Opera Company. From 1949 until its dissolution in 1960 he was artistic and musical director of the NBC-TV OPERA COMPANY, which he had helped to organize. During this period, from 1955 to 1957, he also conducted several works new to the United States with the NEW YORK CITY OPERA, and from 1959 to 1967 he was music director of the Baltimore Symphony Orchestra. In 1967 he became music consultant to National Educational Television, founding the NET Opera in 1969, which presented, during its first season, the American premiere of JANÁČEK'S FROM THE HOUSE OF THE DEAD and the world premiere of Jack BEESON's *My Heart's in the Highlands.*
Admeto, re di Tessaglia, opera in three acts by HANDEL. Libretto by Niccolo Francesco Haym, adapted from Aureli's *L'Antigona delusa da Alceste.* Premiere: Haymarket Theatre, London, Jan. 31, 1727. This was Handel's last opera to be revived during his lifetime (1754). Since then it has received several revivals in Germany, notably in Brunswick in 1925 and in Halle in 1959 in celebration of the bicentenary of the composer's birth in that city.
Admetos, King of Pharae (tenor) in GLUCK'S ALCESTE.
Ad nos, ad salutem, religious hymn sung by three Anabaptists, in Act I of MEYERBEER'S LE PROPHÈTE.
Adolar, Count of Nevers (tenor) in WEBER'S EURYANTHE.
Adone, L', opera in prologue and three acts by MONTEVERDI. Libretto by P. Vendramin, based on a poem by Marini. Premiere: Venice, Dec. 21, 1639. This was one of its composer's late operas, written when he was seventy-two. The music has been lost, but the libretto survives. The opera has historic importance in that it is the first by Monteverdi written for the public stage instead of for the private consumption of nobility in their palaces.
Adorno, Gabriele, Genoese nobleman (tenor) in VERDI'S SIMON BOCCANEGRA.
Adriana Lecouvreur, opera in four acts by Francesco CILÈA. Libretto by Arturo Colautti, based on a play by Eugène SCRIBE and Ernest Legouvé. Premiere: Teatro Lirico, Milan, Nov. 6, 1902. American premiere: New Orleans, Jan. 5, 1907.

Characters: Maurizio, Count of Saxony (tenor); Prince de Bouillon (bass); L'Abate di Chazeuil (tenor); Michonnet, stage director at the Comédie-Française (baritone); Quinault, member of the company (bass); Poisson, another member of the company (tenor); Major Domo (tenor); Adriana Lecouvreur, a star of the company (soprano); Princesse de Bouillon (mezzo-soprano); Mlle. Jouvenot, member of the company (soprano); Mlle. Dagenville, another member of the company (mezzo-soprano); a chambermaid; ladies; gentlemen; servants. The action takes place in Paris in 1730.

Act I. Backstage at the Comédie-Française just before and during the beginning of a performance. The complex plot, based on intrigue and mistaken identities, is set going during a busy first act in which we learn that (a) the leading actress, Adriana Lecouvreur, is in love with an army officer she knows simply as Maurizio but who is really the Count of Saxony; (b) Michonnet is in love with Adriana but does not dare tell her; and (c) the Prince de Bouillon has discovered a letter making an assignation that night for Maurizio with another actress, Duclos, in a villa belonging to the Prince himself. Duclos has long been the Prince's own mistress, but, as he is tiring of her, he gaily invites a party, including Adriana, Michonnet, and others, to surprise the supposed lovers. What he does not know is that the assignation letter is not from Duclos (who never appears in the opera) but from his own wife, the Princesse de Bouillon. The principal numbers include Michonnet's "Michonnet su," Adriana's "Io sono l'umile ancella," and the love duet of Maurizio and Adriana ("La dolcissima effigie").

Act II. Reception hall of the Prince's villa. Maurizio and the Princesse are surprised by the entry of the Prince, but she manages to hide in a dark closet before her husband discovers she is not Duclos. The Prince good-naturedly hints that he would like Maurizio to take the actress off his hands. When Adriana arrives, she discovers Maurizio's real identity for the first time. He tells her passionately that he loves her and confides that he had come to the villa only to consult a woman of high rank (unidentified) on political matters. At Maurizio's request, Adriana goes to the dark closet to help the "woman of high rank" escape, which she does successfully. Neither woman sees the other well enough to recognize her, but both realize they are rivals in love for the same man—Maurizio.

Act III. A sumptuous hall in the palace of Prince de Bouillon. Some months later, the Prince and Princesse de Bouillon entertain a large party and stage a ballet that honors the Princesse. Maurizio, recently returned from Russia on a military-diplomatic mission, is present, and during the byplay the Princesse and Adriana realize that they are each other's rival. To cover her confusion, the Princesse asks Adriana to perform. She creates a sensation by reciting a searing passage from RACINE's *Phèdre* about an adulterous wife and addressing it directly to the Princesse.

Act IV. Adriana's drawing room. Adriana has not returned to the stage for weeks but remains at home pining away for a word from Maurizio. It is her birthday, and Michonnet sadly helps her celebrate. The maid tells him why she is so sad, and he sends a messenger for Maurizio to come. Meantime a quartet of performers from the Comédie-Française comes to sing her a birthday madrigal ("Una volta c'èra un principe"). A box of faded violets arrives with a card signed "Maurizio"—

violets she had presented him in Act I. She interprets the gift as meaning that his love has faded too. What she does not know is that (a) he had presented them to the Princesse in Act II; (b) they come from the Princesse, who has forged Maurizio's name; and (c) they have been poisoned by the Princesse. She embraces the flowers, sings her sad aria ("Poveri fiori"), and lives only long enough to greet the hastily arrived Maurizio and die in his and Michonnet's arms.

Adriana Lecouvreur is an effective late contribution to the GIORDANO-PUCCINI type of VERISMO. After almost seventy years, it still holds the stage well in Italy. Young Enrico CARUSO created the role of Maurizio, and he also sang it at its METROPOLITAN OPERA premiere, Nov. 18, 1907, opposite the beautiful Lina CAVALIERI. Today it is most frequently given outside Italy as a vehicle for a handsome singing actress. Thus it was revived twice at the Metropolitan for Renata TEBALDI, once in the season of 1962–63 and again in 1968–69, when it opened the season.

Adriano, Stefano Colonna's son (mezzo-soprano) in WAGNER'S RIENZI.

Aegisthus, Klytemnestra's beloved (tenor) in Richard STRAUSS'S ELEKTRA.

aegyptische Helena, Die (The Egyptian Helen), opera in two acts by Richard STRAUSS. Libretto by Hugo von HOFMANNSTHAL, based on Greek legend. Premiere: Dresden, June 6, 1928. American premiere: Metropolitan Opera, Nov. 6, 1928. King Menelaus (tenor) and his wife Helen (soprano), on their way home after the fall of Troy, are wrecked on the coast of Egypt. Menelaus has decided he must kill his faithless wife because of the many who have died through her fateful beauty. The magic potion of the Egyptian sorceress Aithra (soprano), however, causes him to forgive her. The vocal highlights include two arias by Helen: "Bei jener Nacht" (Act I) and "Zweite Brautnacht! Zaubernacht" (Act II).

Aelfrida, daughter of the Thane of Devon (soprano) in Deems TAYLOR'S THE

KING'S HENCHMAN, a role created by Florence EASTON.

Aeneas, (1) Trojan hero (tenor) in BERLIOZ' LES TROYENS.

(2) Trojan hero (baritone) in PURCELL'S DIDO AND AENEAS.

Aeneid, The, epic poem by VIRGIL, describing the fall of Troy and the subsequent adventures of Aeneas. Material from this poem is found in BERLIOZ' LES TROYENS and in PURCELL'S DIDO AND AENEAS.

Aeschylus, tragic dramatist. Born Eleusis, Greece, 525 B.C.; died Gela, Sicily, 456 B.C. Some of his dramas have been made into operas. The Orestes trilogy (*Agamemnon, Choëphoroi,* and *Eumenides*) was utilized for MILHAUD'S music for CLAUDEL'S L'ORÉSTIE trilogy, Sergei Taneyev's *Orestes* (1895), and WEINGARTNER'S *Orestes.* PIZZETTI used a part of the Orestes trilogy (and a part of SOPHOCLES' *Elektra*) for *Clitemnestra. Prometheus Bound* was used by Luigi Cortese (*Prometeo,* 1951), Maurice Emmanuel (*Prométhée enchaîné,* 1915), Gabriel FAURÉ (*Prométhée*), and ORFF (*Prometheus*). *The Suppliants* was used by Maurice Emmanuel (*Salamine,* 1929).

Aethelwold, Earl of East Anglia (tenor) in Deems TAYLOR'S THE KING'S HENCHMAN, a role created by Edward JOHNSON.

Africaine, L' (The African Maid), grand opera in five acts by MEYERBEER. Libretto by Eugène SCRIBE. Premiere: Paris Opéra, Apr. 28, 1865. American premiere: Academy of Music, Dec. 1, 1865.

Characters: Vasco da Gama, officer in the Portuguese Navy (tenor); Don Pedro, King's Councilor (bass); Don Alvar, King's Councilor (tenor); Don Diego, King's Councilor (bass); Inez, Don Diego's daughter (soprano); Anna, her attendant (contralto); Selika, an African queen (soprano); Nelusko, her slave (baritone); Grand Inquisitor (bass); priests; soldiers; councilors; tribesmen. The settings are Lisbon and Madagascar; the time is the early sixteenth century.

Act I. Council chamber in the palace of the King of Portugal. Inez is concerned over the fate of Vasco da Gama, gone over two years on one of his expeditions. Tenderly she recalls his beautiful song of farewell ("Adieu, mon doux rivage"). Her concern mounts when her father, insisting that Vasco must be dead, urges her to accept Don Pedro as her husband. The councilors now enter the chamber and acclaim the Grand Inquisitor ("Dieu, que le monde révère"). Unexpectedly Vasco da Gama arrives to inform the councilors about his expedition to a strange new land ("J'ai vu, nobles seigneurs"). He introduces two slaves—Selika and Nelusko—whom he has brought back with him and asks for another ship so that he may return to this land and claim its riches for Portugal. When the councilors refuse, Vasco denounces them violently and is imprisoned.

Act II. The prison. Vasco has been in prison a month, looked after solicitously by Selika, who is in love with him. She sings him a lullaby ("Sur mes genoux, fils du soleil"). Nelusko, jealous, tries to kill Vasco in his sleep but is stopped by Selika. Passionately Nelusko declares that his only allegiance is to Selika, the queen of her realm ("Fille des rois, à toi l'hommage"). After Nelusko departs, Selika tells Vasco of a new secret route to h r land. Vasco is jubilant ("Combien tu m'es chère"). Don Pedro and Inez arrive, and find Selika and Vasco in each other's arms. Don Pedro accuses Vasco of being unfaithful to Inez. Vasco denies this vehemently; he even gives Selika to Inez as her personal slave. Vasco then learns that Inez has bough his freedom by offering to marry Don Pedro who, with the help of the councilors, will undertake an expedition to the land discovered by Vasco.

Act III. Don Pedro's ship. Don Pedro, Inez, Selika, and Nelusko are sailing for Selika's land. The sailors sing a rousing chantey as they attend to their tasks ("Holà! matelots"). Treacherously, Nelusko steers the ship toward a reef, singing of Adamastor, monarch of the seas, who brings ships to their doom ("Adamastor, roi des vagues profondes"). Vasco, meanwhile, overtakes Don Pedro's ship and warns him of impending disaster. The distrustful Pedro orders him seized and executed. Before his command can be carried out, the ship is wrecked. Selika's tribesmen swarm aboard, killing or capturing all the Portuguese. Vasco is protected by Selika.

Act IV. The temple of Brahma on the Island of Madagascar. The prelude is a march in Indian style. Selika is back on her throne, honored by her people. Vasco is enraptured by the beauty of the island ("O Paradis"). The High Priest comes to insist that the remainder of the Portuguese be executed. In order to save Vasco, Selika says she is secretly married to him. Enraptured, Vasco expresses his great love for her and she responds with equal ardor ("O transport, o douce extase"). But as the marriage of Vasco and Selika is to be solemnized by native rites, Vasco hears Inez' distant song of farewell. He had believed her dead. Knowing now that she yet lives, he hopes to save her.

Act V, Scene 1. The queen's garden (this scene is sometimes omitted). When Inez is brought before the queen, Selika is so moved by the intensity of Inez' love that she frees both her and Vasco and orders Nelusko to put them on a ship bound for Portugal.

Scene 2. A promontory above the sea. Watching Vasco's ship recede from sight, Selika addresses the sea, which, she says, is as boundless as her own misery ("D'ici je vois la mer immense"). Then she turns to a poisonous manchineel tree, hoping for peace ("O temple magnifique"). As she lies dying, Nelusko comes to her side to breathe the tree's deadly blossoms and join his beloved. An invisible chorus comments that in death all are equal ("C'est ici le séjour").

L'Africaine was Meyerbeer's last opera. It absorbed him for many years, for he was conscious that he was producing his finest work. He started the first sketches in 1838 and completed the opera twenty-two years later (having, however, composed and produced four other operas in the intervening years). Even then, he continued to make revisions to the last days of his life. He did not live to see the premiere. Like Meyerbeer's other grand operas, L'Africaine shows his predilection for spectacular scenes, but the work shows a more highly developed musical style and more refinement of detail than its predecessors. The best pages of L'Africaine reveal Meyerbeer at the peak of his melodic inspiration.

Afron (or **Aphron**), **Prince,** son of King Dodon (baritone) in RIMSKY-KORSAKOV'S LE COQ D'OR.

Agamemnon, King of the Greeks (baritone) in GLUCK'S IPHIGÉNIE EN AULIDE. *See also* AESCHYLUS.

Agathe, Kuno's daughter (soprano), sweetheart of Max, in WEBER'S DER FREISCHÜTZ.

Agathe's prayer, *see* LEISE, LEISE.

Agenor, King of Thebes (bass) in MILHAUD'S *opéra minute* L'ENLÈVEMENT D'EUROPE.

Agnes, Micha's wife (mezzo-soprano) in SMETANA'S THE BARTERED BRIDE.

Agrippina, opera in three acts by HANDEL. Libretto by Cardinal Vincenzo Grimani. First performance: Venice, Dec. 26, 1709. Herbert Weinstock, Handel's biographer, regards this libretto as "a masterpiece . . . if placed beside any that Handel previously had been privileged to set . . . the most dramatic and beautiful operatic entity he [Grimani] had yet created." The opera, when first produced, was a sensation. It was performed for twenty-seven consecutive nights to capacity audiences, who kept shouting, "Long live the dear Saxon"—the "dear Saxon," of course, being Handel. Handel not only became the idol of Italy because of this opera but his fame spread throughout Europe. Of particular interest is the overture and Poppea's poignant air, "Bel piacer."

Ah! bello a me ritorno, Norma's sorrowful realization in Act I of BELLINI'S NORMA that her people's hatred of the

Romans must result in their hatred for her beloved, the Roman Pollione.

Ah, chacun le sait (Ah, ciascun lo dice), Marie's song of praise to her regiment, in Act I of DONIZETTI'S THE DAUGHTER OF THE REGIMENT.

Ah! che a voi perdoni iddio, *see* MAG DER HIMMEL EUCH VERGEBEN.

Ah! che la morte ognora (Miserere), the celebrated ensemble scene—the prayer for the doomed prisoners—of Manrico, Leonora, and male chorus in Act IV of VERDI'S IL TROVATORE.

Ah che tutta in un momento, duet of Dorabella and Fiordiligi in Act I, Scene 4, of MOZART'S COSÌ FAN TUTTE, in which they lament the absence of their lovers.

Ah! chi mi dice mai, Donna Elvira's bitter aria about having been abandoned by Don Giovanni after he had seduced her, in Act I, Scene 2, of MOZART'S DON GIOVANNI.

Ah, chi tormento, Gianetto's moving aria in Act I of GIORDANO'S LA CENA DELLE BEFFE.

Ah, crudel, Armida's air in HANDEL'S RINALDO.

Ah! di tu pene sparve il sogno, Linda's closing aria, revealing the return of her sanity, in the last act of DONIZETTI'S LINDA DI CHAMOUNIX.

Ah! dolce guidami, one of the most famous arias in DONIZETTI'S ANNA BOLENA, sung by the heroine.

Ah! Du wolltest mich nicht deinem Mund küssen lassen!, Salome's apostrophe to the head of John the Baptist, bitterly denouncing him for having rejected her kisses when he was alive, in Richard STRAUSS'S SALOME.

Ah! fors' è lui, Violetta's realization of her sympathetic response to Alfredo's love—the most celebrated soprano aria in the opera—in Act I of VERDI'S LA TRAVIATA.

Ah! fuggi il traditor, Donna Elvira's bitter denunciation of Don Giovanni for his fickleness, in Act I, Scene 3, of MOZART'S DON GIOVANNI.

Ah! fuyez, douce image, Des Grieux's expression of agitation at his inability to forget Manon, in Act III, Scene 2, of MASSENET'S MANON.

Ah guarda, sorella, duet of Dorabella and Fiordiligi in Act I, Scene 2, of MOZART'S COSÌ FAN TUTTE, in which they give voice ecstatically to their love for their respective men.

Ahi! caso acerbo, La Messaggiera's air in Act II of MONTEVERDI'S L'ORFEO.

Ah! io veggio, Ferrando's ardent song with which he tries to win the interest of Fiordiligi, in Act II of MOZART'S COSÌ FAN TUTTE.

Ah! je respire enfin, Pelléas' expression of relief on leaving the castle vaults, in Act III, Scene 3, of DEBUSSY'S PELLÉAS ET MÉLISANDE.

Ah, je ris de me voir, Marguerite's Jewel Song, as she inspects herself in the mirror while wearing the jewels left her by Méphistophélès, in Act III of GOUNOD'S FAUST.

Ah! je suis seule, Thaïs' monologue on her world-weariness, in Act II, Scene 1, of MASSENET'S THAÏS.

Ah! la paterna mano, Macduff's lament over the murder of his son, in Act IV of VERDI'S MACBETH.

Ah! lève-toi, soleil, Roméo's serenade to Juliette below her balcony, in Act II of GOUNOD'S ROMÉO ET JULIETTE.

Ah! Louise, si tu m'aimes, Julien's plea to Louise to elope with him, in Act II, Scene 1, of CHARPENTIER'S LOUISE.

Ah, madre addio, Manrico's farewell to his mother as he is about to be led to his execution at the close of VERDI'S IL TROVATORE.

Ah, malgré moi, Alceste's response to her people's grief that she is about to sacrifice herself, at the close of Act II of GLUCK'S ALCESTE.

Ah! Manon, mi tradisce, Des Grieux's bitter condemnation of Manon for having betrayed him, in Act II of PUCCINI'S MANON LESCAUT.

Ah, Mimi, tu pìu, duet in which Rodolfo and Marcello express longing for their lost mistresses, Mimi and Musetta, in Act IV of PUCCINI'S LA BOHÈME.

Ah, mon fils!, Fidès' address to her son as an expression of her love and gratitude, in Act II of MEYERBEER'S LE PROPHÈTE.

Ah! mon remords te venge, Hoël's poignant air to Dinorah as he carries her off in his arms after she has swooned, in Act III of MEYERBEER'S DINORAH.

Ah, morir, poetessi adesso, duet of Ernani and Elvira in which they prefer death to separation, in Act I, Scene 2, of VERDI'S ERNANI.

Ah! ne fuis pas encore, love duet of Roméo and Juliette as they reluctantly separate and bid each other goodnight, in Act II of GOUNOD'S ROMÉO ET JULIETTE.

Ah, no, che tu cosi morir, Paolino's assurance to his wife, Carolina, that it is she he loves and nobody else, in Act II of CIMAROSA'S IL MATRIMONIO SEGRETO.

Ah! Non credea mirarti, Amina's sorrowful air in which, believing herself deserted by her beloved Elvino, she laments that her own love has withered like the flowers Elvino had given her the day before and hopes that her tears might revive them. This aria, which many historians regard as the quintessence of BELLINI's bel canto art, appears in Act III of LA SONNAMBULA.

Ah, paventa del furor, Baltasar's bitter denunciation of the king for having abandoned his wife for a mistress, in Act II of DONIZETTI'S LA FAVORITA.

Ah! per sempre io ti perdei, Richard's lament over losing Elvira to Talbot, in Act I of BELLINI'S I PURITANI.

Ah prence, io cado ai vostre piè, Cinderella's plea to the prince to forgive her stepfather and stepsisters, in the closing scene of ROSSINI'S LA CENERENTOLA.

Ah! qual colpo, trio of Rosina, Count Almaviva, and Figaro in Act II of ROSSINI'S THE BARBER OF SEVILLE, in which a misunderstanding between Almaviva and his beloved Rosina has finally been resolved, with asides by Figaro.

Ah! quanto m'è caro, see COMBIEN TU M'ES CHÈRE.

Ah! quel giorno, Arsace's aria in ROSSINI'S SEMIRAMIDE.

Ah, quelle est belle, chorus in which the guests in the Capulet ballroom express their admiration of Juliette when she makes her first entry, in Act I of GOUNOD'S ROMÉO ET JULIETTE.

Ah, quelle nuit, le moindre bruit me trouble, Lady Angela's third-act aria (one of the most famous in the opera) in AUBER'S LE DOMINO NOIR.

Ah! qu'il est loin, Jean's air in Act I of MASSENET'S SAPHO, the most celebrated aria in the opera.

Ah! ritrovarla nella sua capanna, Flammen's aria in Act III of MASCAGNI'S LODOLETTA.

Ah, Seigneur, ah quel supplice, Eurydice's air in the opening scene of Act I of OFFENBACH'S OPÉRA BOUFFE ORPHEUS IN THE UNDERWORLD, a prayer to be freed of her husband Orpheus with whom she has become bored.

Ah! se intorno a quest' urna funesta, elegy of shepherds, shepherdesses, and nymphs at Euridice's grave, in Act I of GLUCK'S ORFEO ED EURIDICE.

Ah, se l'error t'ingombra (The Nuns' Chorus), chorus accompanying Count di Luna's air, "PER ME ORA FATALE," in Act II of VERDI'S IL TROVATORE.

Ah! si, ben mio, Manrico's air of consolation to the distressed Leonora, in the fortress shelter in Act III, Scene 2, of VERDI'S IL TROVATORE.

Ah si, fa core abbracciami, Norma's sympathetic response to Adalgisa, when the latter confesses she has fallen in love with Pollione, in Act II (originally Act I) of BELLINI'S NORMA.

Ah! si la liberté, Armide's aria in Act III of GLUCK'S ARMIDE.

Ah! tu dei vivere, Amneris' plea to Radames to stay alive instead of accepting death, by pleading to the priests for mercy and giving up Aida, in Act IV, Scene 1, of VERDI'S AIDA.

Ah! un foco insolito, Don Pasquale's expression of his conviction that he is deeply in love with the imaginary girl Dr. Malatesta has described to him and of his willingness to marry her, in Act I, Scene 1, of DONIZETTI'S DON PASQUALE.

Ah! viens dans la forêt profonde, Gérald's joy at being in a solitary forest with his beloved Lakmé, who has just nursed him back to health, in Act III of DELIBES'S LAKMÉ.

Ah! viens, Manon, Des Grieux's song

of love to Manon at the close of Act III, Scene 2, of MASSENET'S MANON.

Ah, vivre deux, Hoffmann's aria revealing his love at first sight for Olympia, in Act II of OFFENBACH'S TALES OF HOFFMANN.

Aida, opera in four acts by VERDI. Libretto by Antonio GHISLANZONI, based on a plot by Mariette Bey. Premiere: Cairo, Egypt, Dec. 24, 1871. American premiere: Academy of Music, New York, Nov. 26, 1873.

Characters: The King of Egypt (bass); Amneris, his daughter (mezzo-soprano); Aida, an Ethiopian slave (soprano); Radames, captain of the Egyptian guard (tenor); Ramfis, High Priest (bass); Amonasro, King of Ethiopia, Aida's father (baritone); priests; priestesses; soldiers; slaves; prisoners; Egyptians. The action takes place in Memphis and Thebes during the reign of the Pharaohs.

Act I, Scene 1. A hall in the palace at Memphis. Ramfis informs Radames that the Ethiopian enemy is advancing upon the Nile valley and that the goddess Isis has chosen an Egyptian warrior to lead the defenders. Radames dreams that he will be this warrior and that he will place the fruits of his victory at the feet of the woman he loves, the captured slave, Aida ("Celeste Aida"). Amneris, who wants to marry Radames, suspects that he and Aida are secretly in love. Amneris questions the slave girl ("Vieni, o diletta") but Aida only tells her of her sorrow over the dangers facing her native land, Ethiopia. A fine trio develops as Radames expresses his fear that Amneris has discovered his love. The King of Egypt now enters with his entourage, followed by a messenger announcing the enemy's approach. The King appoints Radames commander of the Egyptian army, calling on his people to rally under their new leader ("Su! del Nilo al sacro lido!"). Aida prays for Radames' victorious return ("Ritorna vincitor!"). Remembering that his victory must spell defeat for her own people, she is torn by inner conflict.

Scene 2. The temple of Vulcan. Ramfis is at the altar, praying with his priests for victory ("Possente, Phthà!"). Priestesses perform a ritual dance. Radames enters to be blessed with sword and armor. The High Priest now prays for divine protection ("Nume, custode e vindice") and the people join in the prayer.

Act II, Scene 1. A hall in Amneris' apartments. Amneris' servants are garbing her in silks and jewels for the imminent victory celebration. Slave girls sing of the joys of love ("Chi mai fra gl'inni e i plausi"). Moorish boys perform a dance. Reclining on her couch, Amneris thinks of her beloved Radames and pines for his return ("Vieni, amor mio"). When Aida arrives, Amneris dismisses her servants and other slaves, hoping to learn the true state of Aida's feelings for Radames. By suggesting that he has been killed in action, then quickly admitting that she had lied, she uncovers Aida's love. Proudly, Amneris insists that only she, the daughter of the Egyptian King, can win Radames. She threatens her slave with death and the latter, though a princess in her own right, is obliged to beg for mercy.

Scene 2. Outside the city walls. The King, Amneris, their courtiers and slaves, the priests, and the people welcome the victorious Egyptian army. The people raise a hymn to victory ("Gloria all' Egitto"), after which the priests thank the gods ("Della vittoria agli arbitri"). Dancing girls perform a ballet symbolizing the victory. The celebration reaches a climax as the Egyptian army arrives to the strains of the celebrated march music. Amneris honors Radames with a laurel wreath. The captive Ethiopians are brought in, among them King Amonasro, who entreats the King to be lenient ("Ma tu, o Re, tu possente"). Aida and Radames join in the plea. At the advice of the High Priest, the King frees the captives but holds Amonasro as a hostage. Then, to reward Radames for his victory, he gives him the hand of

Amneris. The populace sings the praise of Egypt and Isis.

Act III. The banks of the Nile. In a near-by temple priests sing to Isis. Ramfis brings Amneris to invoke divine blessings for her imminent marriage to Radames. After they enter the temple, Aida appears. The slave recalls her beloved homeland ("O patria mia"). Amonasro enters suddenly, enraged over his daughter's love for Radames. He confides to her that the Ethiopians are about to strike back at the Egyptians and that victory would be assured if Radames will name the pass his men are soon to march through. When at first she refuses her father grows angry ("Non sei mia figlia"), renouncing her as his daughter. Then, brokenheartedly, Aida promises to wrest the secret from Radames. At his approach, Amonasro hides. Radames is overjoyed to see Aida again and soon resolves to flee with her to her own land ("Fuggiam gli ardori inospiti"). By asking what route they should take, Aida tricks Radames into revealing what her father wants to know. Amneris, who has come from the temple in time to overhear, denounces Radames as a traitor. Aida and her father flee. Aware of the enormity of his crime ("Io son disonorato"), Radames surrenders his sword to Ramfis.

Act IV, Scene 1. A room in the palace. Torn between love and jealousy, Amneris sends for Radames. She begs him to confess his guilt before the priests and plead for mercy, promising to intercede on his behalf if he will give up Aida ("Già i sacerdoti adunansi"). Radames refuses, preferring death, which leads Amneris to beg him to stay alive ("Ah! tu dei vivere"). Aware she was responsible for Radames' destruction, Amneris gives way to despair ("Ohimè! morir mi sento"). Her despair deepens as she hears the voices of the priests beseeching the gods to punish Radames ("Spirito del Nume sovra noi discendi"). In the judgment chamber the priests gather to pass sentence on him. Three times the High Priest calls on Radames to defend himself, three times Radames remains silent. The priest pronounces the sentence: Radames is to be buried alive ("Radames, è deciso il tuo fato").

Scene 2. The temple of Vulcan. Within his tomb Radames bewails the fact that he will not see Aida again ("La fatal pietra"). But now Aida emerges from the shadows—she has entered the tomb ahead of Radames to share his fate ("Presago il core della tua condanna"). Above the tomb the chanting priests perform a ritual dance. Radames and Aida bid the world farewell ("O terra, addio"), while above, in the temple, Amneris prays to Isis for peace ("Pace t'imploro").

Verdi wrote *Aida* on a commission from the Khedive of Egypt. The opera was meant for performance in a new theater in Cairo as part of a celebration attending the opening of the Suez Canal. The theater and canal were opened, as planned, in 1869, but Verdi did not finish writing *Aida* until 1871. The costumes and scenery, designed and executed in Paris, had to remain there until after the end of the Franco-Prussian War (1871). The premiere was an occasion worth the long delay. The audience included the cream of European and Egyptian society and royalty. Arabian trumpeters, a Cairo military band, and a cast of three hundred participated in the triumphal march in the second act. Verdi himself was absent. He detested publicity and was afraid of ocean travel. His opera did not disappoint. Filled with pageantry, ballets, and dramatic situations, *Aida* was the concluding work of his second creative period. It was not only Verdi's most ambitious work so far, but his most successful attempt at achieving a natural fusion of drama and music. Because of his rich treatment of the orchestra and his avoidance of florid vocal writing, Verdi was accused by some critics of imitating WAGNER. Yet, for all its advanced techniques for that time, *Aida* is pure Verdi throughout—in the beauty of its Italian melodies, in the happy way these melodies lie for the voice, in the emotional intensity of the score, in the felicitous musical characterizations, and in its effective dramatic values.

Aiglon, L' (The Eaglet), opera in five acts by HONEGGER and IBERT. Libretto by Henri Cain, based on the play of the same name by Edmond Rostand. Premiere: Monte Carlo, Mar. 11, 1937. The central character is the tubercular son of Napoleon, dubbed by Victor HUGO the "eaglet" (a role created by Vanni MARCOUX). Honegger wrote Acts I, III, and IV; Ibert, Acts II and V. In addition, an orchestral piece by Ibert was interpolated into the third act as ballet music.

The premiere of this opera was originally scheduled for Naples in Feb., 1937. After it had reached the dress rehearsal, Mussolini ordered that the performance be canceled. The opera was produced the next month at Monte Carlo.

Ai nostri monti, duet of Azucena and Manrico in Act IV, Scene 2, of VERDI'S IL TROVATORE, consoling each other with the hope of returning to the mountain land where they had once been so happy together.

Ainsi que la brise, waltz of the villagers in Act II of GOUNOD'S FAUST.

Air de la poupée (Doll Song), see OISEAUX DANS LA CHARMILLE, LES.

Air du miroir, see DIS-MOI QUE JE SUIS BELLE.

Aithra, an Egyptian sorceress (soprano) in Richard STRAUSS'S DIE AEGYPTISCHE HELENA.

Ai tuoi piedi ci prostriamo, chorus of the people in praise of the Emperor, at the conclusion of Act II of PUCCINI'S TURANDOT.

Aix-en-Provence, one of France's major annual festivals, taking place between July and August. It was founded in 1948 by Gabriel Dussurget and Roger Bigonnet to include outdoor performances of solo, chamber, and orchestral music. Opera has also been represented, usually in an open-air theater in the Archbishop's palace. The opening fes-

tival offered only a single opera, così FAN TUTTE. DON GIOVANNI was performed in the 1949 festival. Both *Così fan tutte* and *Don Giovanni* were conducted by Hans ROSBAUD. For many years it has been the custom to present THE MARRIAGE OF FIGARO at each festival; a newly conceived production was offered in 1968.

Among the operatic novelties featured through the years have been: *La Belle et la bête* (GRÉTRY); *Les Caprices de Marianne* (SAUGUET); IL COMBATTIMENTO DI TANCREDI E CLORINDA; DIDO AND AENEAS; L'INCORONAZIONE DI POPPEA; *Lavinia* (Henry Barraud, b. 1900); LES MALHEURS D'ORPHÉE; IL MATRIMONIO SEGRETO; MIREILLE; *Il mondo della luna* (HAYDN); L'ORFEO; *Platée* (RAMEAU); THE TELEPHONE; LA VOIX HUMAINE. In 1969, the ENGLISH OPERA GROUP presented BRITTEN'S THE BURNING FIERY FURNACE and his THE PRODIGAL SON.

Alain, a shepherd (tenor) in MASSENET'S GRISÉLIDIS.

Albanese, Licia, soprano. Born Bari, Italy, July 22, 1913. She studied singing with Giusepinna Baldassare-Tedeschi, and made an unscheduled debut at the TEATRO LIRICO in Milan in 1934, substituting for an indisposed prima donna in MADAMA BUTTERFLY. In 1935 she won first prize in a national singing contest in Italy. Her formal debut took place at the Teatro Reale in Parma, on Dec. 10, 1935, again in *Madama Butterfly*. Engagements in Milan, London (during the coronation festivities in 1936), and Paris preceded her METROPOLITAN OPERA debut on Feb. 9, 1940, in *Madama Butterfly*. Soon after that, in the same year, she appeared in the first broadcast from the stage of the Metropolitan Opera House, sponsored by Texaco, in THE MARRIAGE OF FIGARO. During World War II she lived in Italy, then returned to New York. In 1945 she married a New York stockbroker and became an American citizen. Except for several months in 1946, when she temporarily lost her voice, she sang at the Metropolitan Opera for a quarter of a century, appearing over one thousand times in forty-eight leading roles. She was one of the few women singers to perform at the Vatican, for Pope Pius XI, and was the first singer of her sex to broadcast over the Vatican radio station. Before World War II she gave command performances at the Italian court. In 1946 she was selected by Arturo TOSCANINI to sing the role of Mimi in his fiftieth anniversary performance of LA BOHÈME with the NBC Symphony. The twenty-fifth anniversary of her debut at the Metropolitan was celebrated on Feb. 9, 1965, with a concert at Carnegie Hall devoted entirely to PUCCINI. Her program consisted of fourteen arias, at least one from each of his operas, presented in chronological order.

Albani, Emma (born Marie-Louise-Cécile-Emma Lajeunesse), soprano. Born Chambly, Canada, Nov. 1, 1847; died London, Apr. 3, 1930. In her eighth year she entered a Montreal convent school, where she first attracted attention to her unusual musical talent. In 1868 she went to Europe, where she studied with Gilbert DUPREZ in Paris and Francesco LAMPERTI in Milan.

She made her opera debut at Messina in 1869 singing the role of Amina in LA SONNAMBULA, and assuming at this time her stage name of Albani. Additional appearances and further study with Lamperti preceded her COVENT GARDEN debut in 1872. This marked the beginning of her twenty-four-year association with Covent Garden, where she was the toast of London's opera public. She gave the first of several command performances for Queen Victoria in 1874. On Oct. 21, 1874, she made her American debut at the ACADEMY OF MUSIC in *La sonnambula*. On Aug. 6, 1878, she married Ernest Gye, then director of Covent Garden. Returning to Covent Garden, she scored major successes as Elsa in LOHENGRIN and Elisabeth in TANNHÄUSER, from which time on she became famous for her interpretation of leading Wagnerian soprano roles. One of the supreme triumphs of

her entire career came as ISOLDE to the TRISTAN of Jean DE RESZKE on June 26, 1896. Meanwhile, in 1883, she was back in America under MAPLESON's direction, and again in 1889 under the direction of Maurice GRAU. On Mar. 24, 1890, she made her debut at the METROPOLITAN OPERA in OTELLO. A year later she became the leading soprano of the company. Her last American appearance in opera took place on Mar. 31, 1892, in DER FLIEGENDE HOLLÄNDER. In July, 1896, she sang at Covent Garden for the last time. She retired from opera in 1906 but continued to sing in concerts. Her farewell appearance took place in London on Oct. 14, 1911, the same year in which she published her memoirs, *Forty Years of Song*. Financial reverses compelled her later to start a new career in music halls. In 1925 she was made a Dame of the British Empire.

Alberich, a Nibelung (baritone or bass) in WAGNER's DAS RHEINGOLD, SIEGFRIED, and GÖTTERDÄMMERUNG.

Albert, (1) officer of the imperial guard (bass) in HALÉVY's LA JUIVE.

(2) Fiancé (baritone) of Charlotte in MASSENET's WERTHER.

Albert, Eugène d', *see* D'ALBERT, EUGÈNE.

Albert Herring, comic opera in three acts by BRITTEN. Libretto by Eric CROZIER, based on a short story by Guy de MAUPASSANT, *Le Rosier de Mme. Husson*. Premiere: Glyndebourne, Eng., June 20, 1947. American premiere: Tanglewood, Lenox, Mass., Aug. 8, 1949. Lady Billows of Suffolk (soprano), producing a May Day festival, offers a prize for a May Queen whose virtue is beyond doubt. Since no such young woman can be found, Lady Billows determines to have a May King, in the person of Albert Herring (tenor). When a practical joker fills Herring's lemonade glass with rum, the May King becomes inebriated and disappears into the night, searching for disreputable pleasures. He returns to the festival the following morning, disheveled and haggard, but proud of his new-won emancipation.

In his first comedy, Britten (while

retaining a modern idiom) often reverts to OPERA BUFFA techniques through frequent deployment of formal arias, duets, and ensemble numbers. He allows himself to lapse into broad burlesque (as in the scene where Miss Wordsworth nervously rehearses school children in singing, "Time to try our festive song") as well as into parody (as when he quotes the love-potion theme from WAGNER's TRISTAN UND ISOLDE as Herring imbibes the lemonade spiked with rum).

This opera has been favored by festivals, performances taking place at EDINBURGH in 1965, CHAUTAUQUA in New York in 1966, and the Stratford Festival in Ontario, Canada, in 1967, among others.

Albine, an abbess (mezzo-soprano) in MASSENET's THAÏS.

Alboni, Marietta (born Maria Anna Marzia), contralto. Born Citta di Castella, Italy, Mar. 6, 1823; died Ville d'Avray, France, June 23, 1894. While she was studying in Bologna, ROSSINI heard her and was so impressed that he coached her in the leading contralto roles of his operas. Her formal debut took place in Bologna on Oct. 3, 1842, in PACINI's *Saffo*. After a successful appearance at LA SCALA in LE SIÈGE DE CORINTHE on Dec. 30, 1842, she made an extensive tour of Germany, Austria, and Russia. She was brought to London in 1847 as a rival attraction to Jenny LIND; her appearances at COVENT GARDEN were sensational, beginning with her debut there in 1847 in SEMIRAMIDE. In 1848 MEYERBEER wrote for her the Page's Song, "Nobles seigneurs, salut," in LES HUGUENOTS, and in the same year she appeared in the baritone role of Don Carlos in the London premiere of ERNANI. She repeated her triumphs in Paris in 1849 and in 1853 toured North America. She retired in 1863 after marrying Count Pepoli but appeared with PATTI to sing a duet from Rossini's *Stabat Mater* at the master's funeral in 1868 and was heard again in 1871 in a performance of Rossini's *Petite Messe solennelle.*

Alceste, (1) opera in three acts by GLUCK. Libretto by CALZABIGI, based on the tragedy of EURIPIDES. Premiere: Burgtheater, Vienna, Dec. 26, 1767. American premiere: Wellesley, Mass., Mar. 11, 1838.

Characters: Admetos, King of Pharae (tenor); Alceste, his wife (soprano); High Priest (bass); Apollo (baritone); Evander, a messenger (tenor); Hercules (bass); Thanatos, god of death (bass); priests; priestesses; people of Pharae. The setting is Pharae in ancient Thessaly.

Act I. The temple of Apollo. King Admetos is dying. Alceste begs Apollo to spare his life, and the people of Pharae join in the prayer ("Grands dieux du destin"). Apollo responds that Admetos can be saved only if someone dies in his place. The people shrink back in horror. Alceste offers herself as the sacrifice ("Divinités du Styx").

Act II. The King's palace. The King has recovered. The people rejoice with song and dance. When the King tries to learn the reason for his miraculous return to health, he gets evasive answers. Though Alceste is also overjoyed, she cannot conceal her grief at having to leave her husband and children. Though not understanding the reason for her sorrow, Admetos gently comforts her ("Bannis la crainte"). When Alceste finally reveals that she has sacrificed her own life for Admetos, he refuses to consider the idea ("Non, sans toi, je ne puis vivre"). Left to herself, Alceste reaffirms her determination to sacrifice herself ("Ah, malgré moi"), much to the grief of the people when they hear of it. The King entreats the gods to permit him to accompany her to the other world.

Act III. The entrance to Hades. Alceste and Admetos have come to share death. When Thanatos tries to claim Alceste, Hercules, an old friend of Admetos', rescues her. Appeased, Apollo allows both Alceste and Admetos to live. The people rejoice.

Alceste was written five years after ORFEO ED EURIDICE. Gluck's operatic reforms, first realized in *Orfeo,* are achieved even more boldly in the later work. *Alceste* is, indeed, a complete realization of the composer's ideal to make music and drama a single entity, to endow both with human values, and to arrive at simplicity. When *Alceste* was published in 1769, it contained a preface in which the composer explained his ideas. *Alceste* was so far ahead of its time that its premiere was a failure. Only a handful of Gluck's friends realized what he had accomplished. The story goes that when the disheartened composer left the theater, he told a friend: *"Alceste* has fallen." The friend replied: "Yes—fallen from heaven."

(2) Opera (subtitled *Le Triomphe d'Alcide*) in prologue and five acts by LULLY. Libretto by QUINAULT. First performance: Paris Opéra, Jan. 19, 1674. The overture and the arias "La morte barbare" from Act III, Scene 4, and "Il faut passer" from Act V are of special interest. Henri PRUNIÈRES arranged a number of excerpts from Act III into *Scène funèbre,* for solo voices, chorus, and orchestra.

See also ALKESTIS.

Alcina, opera in three acts by HANDEL. Libretto by Antonio Marchi, based on *Orlando furioso* by ARIOSTO. Premiere: Covent Garden, London, Apr. 16, 1735. American premiere: Dallas, Texas, Nov. 16, 1960. Alcina (soprano) is a sorceress who uses her necromantic powers to win the love of Ruggiero (CASTRATO mezzo-soprano). But when her love becomes genuine she is deprived of her powers of sorcery and at the same time she loses Ruggiero to Bradamante (contralto), the woman with whom he has been in love all the time. The overture, the aria "Verdi prati," and the Dream Music are noteworthy.

Alcina has received some notable revivals in the twentieth century, beginning with an outstanding performance by the Handel Opera Society in London on Mar. 19, 1957, starring Joan SUTHERLAND. In 1959 the opera received a handsome production at the STOCKHOLM ROYAL OPERA as part of the bicentennial commemoration of the composer's death. In 1960 ZEFFIRELLI produced an extraordinary presentation of the opera at the TEATRO LA FENICE in Venice, once again with Miss Sutherland—a production given later the same year in Dallas, Texas, in what was probably the opera's American premiere and in which Miss Sutherland made her American debut.

Alcindoro, Musetta's rich admirer (bass) in PUCCINI's LA BOHÈME.

Alda, Frances (born Frances Davis), soprano. Born Christchurch, New Zealand, May 31, 1883; died Venice, Sept. 18, 1952. After studying with Mathilde MARCHESI in Paris she made her debut at the OPÉRA-COMIQUE on Apr. 15, 1904, in MANON, assuming the stage name of Alda. Her first appearance at LA SCALA, in 1908, in the Italian premiere of LOUISE, was a triumph and she was forthwith engaged by the METROPOLITAN OPERA. Her first appearance there took place on Dec. 7, 1908, in RIGOLETTO. On Apr. 3, 1910, she married Giulio GATTI-CASAZZA, the Metropolitan's general manager. Fearing that her marriage might create problems in the company, she resigned. She returned in 1911 and remained for twenty years, a luminous figure in a brilliant operatic era. She appeared in over thirty roles, mostly in the French and Italian repertory, but also created, in English, the roles of Roxanne in DAMROSCH's CYRANO DE BERGERAC, Cleopatra in HADLEY's CLEOPATRA's NIGHT, and Madeleine in Victor HERBERT's opera of the same name. She sang in such significant Metropolitan premieres and revivals as LA CENA DELLE BEFFE, FRANCESCA DA RIMINI, MÂROUF, and PRINCE IGOR. When she appeared in LE ROI D'YS, LALO introduced a new aria in the third act at her request. Alda was divorced from Gatti-Casazza in 1928, and on Dec. 28, 1929, she made a gala last appearance at the Metropolitan Opera in MANON LESCAUT. In 1939 she became an American citizen. Subsequently, she taught singing and was the first important prima donna to make radio appearances. During World

War II, she was active in war-relief work. Her autobiography, *Men, Women, and Tenors,* appeared in 1937.

Aldeburgh Festival, a major English festival held each June in Aldeburgh, Suffolk, where Benjamin BRITTEN makes his home. It was founded in 1948 by Britten, Eric CROZIER, and Peter PEARS, with the Earl of HAREWOOD as president and the Countess of Cranbrook as chairman. This festival, where several of Britten's operas received their world premieres, is dominated by the personality of the composer, who plays a major role in guiding its artistic policies. Originally planned as a home for performances of the ENGLISH OPERA GROUP, which Britten helped to organize, the festival soon expanded its activities to embrace concert music, lectures, art exhibits, and poetry readings. The first Britten opera to get its premiere here was LET'S MAKE AN OPERA, in 1949 (this work for children opened the festival in 1965 in a newly devised production). Other Britten premieres were: NOYE'S FLUDDE, A MIDSUMMER NIGHT'S DREAM, and his three church parables, CURLEW RIVER, THE BURNING FIERY FURNACE, and THE PRODIGAL SON. Additional significant operatic premieres or revivals have included GLORIANA (in the SADLER'S WELLS production); BERKELEY's *A Dinner Engagement;* Harrison Birstwistle's *Punch and Judy;* ACIS AND GALATEA; THE FAIRY QUEEN; and THE BEAR. On June 2, 1967, a new concert auditorium, Snape Hall, was inaugurated in celebration of the twentieth anniversary of the festival, with Queen Elizabeth attending. This auditorium was destroyed by fire two days less than a year after it was dedicated. But it was then rebuilt and reopened on June 5, 1970, with Queen Elizabeth II once again attending.

Aleko, opera in one act by RACHMANINOFF. Libretto by Nemirovich-Danchenko, based on PUSHKIN's *The Gypsies.* Premiere: Moscow, May 9, 1893. American premiere: New York City, Jan. 11, 1926. The text avoids the philosophical implications of Pushkin's poem and concentrates on the unhappy love affair of a young gypsy and Aleko's wife. Rachmaninoff's score is in the style of TCHAIKOVSKY and BORODIN. Two arias are sometimes heard today at concerts, that for bass ("The moon is high in the sky") and the other for tenor ("Romance of the Young Gypsy").

Alerte! alerte!, trio of Faust, Marguerite, and Méphistophélès urging Marguerite to escape from prison, in Act V, Scene 2, of GOUNOD's FAUST.

Alessandro, opera in three acts by HANDEL. Libretto by Paulo Antonio Rolli. Premiere: Haymarket Theatre, London, May 5, 1726. METASTASIO used the same story for one of his most successful librettos, which was set to music by about forty composers. It was in Handel's *Alessandro* that Faustina BORDONI made her brilliant debut, in the role of Rosanne. Because Francesca CUZZONI was under contract to the opera company and Handel had originally written *Alessandro* for her, it was necessary to revise the opera to include two equally important female roles, assigning to each the same number of important arias and duets, thus enabling both Bordoni and Cuzzoni to appear in the opera. Though this arrangement appeared to work for a while, it inevitably inspired a rivalry between the two star singers and also split operatic London into two factions, those favoring Bordoni, and those on the side of Cuzzoni.

Rosanne's aria, "Lusinghe più care," has survived the opera.

Alessandro Stradella, opera in three acts by Friedrich von FLOTOW. Libretto by Wilhelm Friedrich. Premiere: Hamburg, Dec. 30, 1844. STRADELLA was a seventeenth-century composer. An incident in his life provides the story for this opera. Stradella (tenor), here a singer, elopes with Leonora (soprano), whose old guardian, Bassi (bass), wants her for himself. Twice, Bassi hires assassins to murder Stradella, but his singing moves them so deeply that they cannot raise a hand against him. Bassi finally approves of the marriage. The overture is well known, as is Stra-

della's third-act aria, "Jungfrau Maria."
Alessandro, Victor, conductor. Born
Waco, Texas, Nov. 27, 1915. His studies
took place at the Eastman School
of Music and the Accademia Santa
Cecilia in Rome. Between 1938 and
1951 he was principal conductor of the
Oklahoma Symphony and since 1952 of
the San Antonio Symphony. He also
distinguished himself in opera, conducting every performance of the SAN AN-
TONIO GRAND OPERA FESTIVAL since 1951.
In 1969 he directed VERDI's DON CARLOS
while inaugurating a new auditorium in
San Antonio, built in conjunction with
Hemisfair, a World's Fair celebrating
the two-hundred-fiftieth anniversary of
the founding of the city. Alessandro also
led performances at the SAN FRANCISCO
OPERA. On Sept. 23, 1967, he made his
debut with the NEW YORK CITY OPERA
in THE BARBER OF SEVILLE.

Alessio, a peasant (bass) in love with
Lisa in BELLINI's LA SONNAMBULA.

Alexis, Prince, Stephana's lover (tenor)
in GIORDANO's SIBERIA.

Alfano, Franco, composer. Born Naples,
Mar. 8, 1876; died San Remo, Oct. 26,
1954. His music study took place in
Naples and Leipzig. His first operas,
Miranda (1896) and *La fonte di Enschir*
(1898), were failures. But RISURREZIONE,
given in Turin in 1904, was a major
success and made Alfano famous. Later
operas established his position in Italian
opera: *L'ombra di Don Giovanni*
(1914); *La leggenda di Sacùntala*
(1921); *Madonna Imperia* (1927);
CYRANO DE BERGERAC (1937); *Il dottor
Antonio* (1949). Alfano at first combined Italian lyricism and sentiment
with the elaborate harmonic and instrumental textures of the Wagnerian
school; his later writing owes much to
RAVEL. In 1924, when PUCCINI's death
left his TURANDOT unfinished, Alfano
was chosen to write the closing pages.
Alfano held several important directional positions, including those of the
Bologna Liceo Musicale (1919–1923)
and the Turin Liceo Musicale (1923–
1939). Between 1940 and 1942 he directed the Teatro Massimo in Palermo,
and from 1947 to 1954 he was the
director of the Rossini Conservatory in
Pesaro.

Al fato dan legge, duet of Ferrando and
Guglielmo as they bid their respective
sweethearts farewell before supposedly
leaving to fulfill their military duties, in
Act I, Scene 2, of MOZART's COSÌ FAN
TUTTE.

Alfio, a teamster (baritone) in MAS-
CAGNI's CAVALLERIA RUSTICANA.

Alfonso, Don, (1) an old bachelor
(bass) in MOZART's COSÌ FAN TUTTE.

(2) Duke of Ferrara (baritone) in
DONIZETTI's LUCREZIA BORGIA.

Alfonso XI, King of Castile (baritone)
in DONIZETTI's LA FAVORITA.

Alfred, Rosalinde's admirer (tenor) in
Johann STRAUSS's DIE FLEDERMAUS.

Alfredo, *see* GERMONT, ALFREDO.

alfresco, "out-of-doors"; an alfresco performance is one given outdoors.

Alice, (1) Robert's foster sister (soprano) in MEYERBEER's ROBERT LE DIABLE.

(2) *See also* ALISA.

Alice M. Ditson Fund, *see* DITSON FUND.

Alidoro, the Prince's friend (bass) in
ROSSINI's LA CENERENTOLA.

Alim, King of Lahore (tenor) in MAS-
SENET's LE ROI DE LAHORE.

Alisa, Lucia's companion (soprano) in
DONIZETTI's LUCIA DI LAMMERMOOR.

Alkestis, (1) opera by Rutland BOUGH-
TON. Libretto is Gilbert Murray's English
translation of the EURIPIDES drama.
Premiere: Glastonbury, Eng., Aug. 26,
1922.

(2) Opera by WELLESZ. Libretto by
Hugo von HOFMANNSTHAL, based on
EURIPIDES. Premiere: Mannheim, Mar.
20, 1924.

See also ALCESTE.

Alla bella dei re, Fernando's aria upon
learning that Leonora, now his wife, has
been the king's mistress, in Act III of
DONIZETTI's LA FAVORITA.

Alla cà d'oro, chorus of his guests praising Alvise at his ball, in Act III, Scene
2, of PONCHIELLI's LA GIOCONDA.

Alla vita che t'arride, Renato's warning

to Riccardo of imminent rebellion, in Act I, Scene 1, of VERDI's UN BALLO IN MASCHERA.

All' idea di quel metallo, duet of Figaro and Almaviva, with Figaro insisting that nothing in the world is as exciting as gold, in Act I, Scene 1, of ROSSINI's THE BARBER OF SEVILLE.

Allmächt'ge Jungfrau, Elisabeth's prayer that Tannhäuser's sin be forgiven, in Act III of WAGNER's TANNHÄUSER.

Allmächt'ger Vater, blick' herab, Rienzi's prayer in Act V of WAGNER's RIENZI.

Alma del gran Pompeo, Julius Caesar's eloquent tribute to Pompey at the latter's tomb, in HANDEL's GIULIO CESARE.

Almanzor, Emir of Tunis (baritone) in WEBER's OBERON.

Almaviva, Count, (1) a nobleman of Andalusia (baritone) in MOZART's THE MARRIAGE OF FIGARO.

(2) The same (tenor) in ROSSINI's THE BARBER OF SEVILLE, a role created by Manuel GARCÍA.

Almaviva, Countess, wife of the Count (soprano), who is whimsically loved by Cherubino, in MOZART's THE MARRIAGE OF FIGARO.

Almira, opera in three acts by HANDEL. Libretto by Friedrich Feustking, based on an Italian libretto by Giuseppe Boniventi. Premiere: Hamburg Opera, Jan. 8, 1705. Handel's first opera was a success from its initial performance, being heard twenty times in the first seven weeks, despite a silly libretto that was part German and part Italian. Handel's score comprised forty-one German and fifteen Italian airs. Herbert Weinstock points out, however, that the score "is preponderantly German in style and feeling and is truly a German opera despite its Italian-sounding short title," singling out such German arias as "Liebliche Wälder" and "Schönste Rosen." An Asiatic dance of the people in the last act apparently pleased Handel, for he used its melody later for a cantata and for the famous aria, "Lascia ch' io pianga," in the opera RINALDO.

Almirena, heroine (soprano) in HANDEL's opera RINALDO, with whom the hero is in love.

A lonely Arab maid, Fatima's nostalgic air after her flight with Sherasmin, in Act II of WEBER's OBERON.

Alphonse, Camilla's beloved (tenor) in HÉROLD's ZAMPA.

Als Büblein klein, Falstaff's drinking song in Act II of NICOLAI's THE MERRY WIVES OF WINDSOR.

Als du im kühnem Sange, Wolfram's description to Tannhäuser of how deeply Elisabeth has missed him during his long absence, in Act I, Scene 2, of WAGNER's TANNHÄUSER.

Als für ein fremdes Land, Isolde's confession to King Mark of her willingness to follow Tristan to a foreign land, in Act II of WAGNER's TRISTAN UND ISOLDE.

Altair, desert chieftain (baritone) in Richard STRAUSS's DIE AEGYPTISCHE HELENA.

alte Sturm, Der, Wotan's argument with his wife Fricka over whether Siegmund should be spared to fulfill his destiny, in Act II of WAGNER's DIE WALKÜRE.

Althouse, Paul, tenor. Born Reading, Pa., Dec. 2, 1889; died New York City, Feb. 6, 1954. He combined an exhaustive academic education with music study with Perley Dunn Aldrich in Philadelphia, and Oscar Saenger and Percy Richor Stephens in New York. His debut took place with the HAMMERSTEIN Opera Company in Philadelphia. On March 19, 1913, he made his METROPOLITAN OPERA debut as Dmitri in the first American performance of BORIS GODUNOV. During the next decade he appeared in the French and Italian repertory at the Metropolitan and sang in the world premieres of four American operas: DE KOVEN's THE CANTERBURY PILGRIMS, Joseph Breil's The Legend (1919), HERBERT's MADELEINE, and CADMAN's SHANEWIS. During a visit to BAYREUTH, he became fired with the ambition of becoming a Wagnerian tenor. For nine years he studied the leading Wagnerian roles, then sang them in Berlin, Stuttgart, and Stockholm. In

1932 he scored a major success in an all-WAGNER program conducted by TOSCANINI in New York. He made his second "debut" at the Metropolitan Opera—this time as a Wagnerian tenor—on Feb. 3, 1934, as SIEGMUND. Six weeks later he became the first American-born singer to appear there as TRISTAN. Althouse remained at the Metropolitan through the 1939–40 season, singing all the major Wagnerian tenor roles. Thereafter, he devoted himself to teaching and coaching. His students included Eleanor STEBER and Richard TUCKER.

alto, in opera, a term once used as the equivalent of CONTRALTO.

Altoum, Emperor, Turandot's father (tenor) in PUCCINI'S TURANDOT.

Alvar, Don, member of the King's council (tenor) in MEYERBEER'S L'AFRICAINE.

Alvarez, Albert (born Raymond Gourron), tenor. Born Bordeaux, France, 1861; died Nice, Feb. 26, 1933. After studies with A. de Martini in Paris, a debut in Ghent, Belgium, and successful appearances in several French cities, he was engaged by the PARIS OPÉRA in 1892. He became a great favorite there, particularly in the French repertory. He created the leading tenor parts in many new French operas, including THAÏS. On Dec. 18, 1899, he made his METROPOLITAN OPERA debut, on opening night of the season, as ROMÉO. He remained with the Metropolitan several seasons, then appeared with the MANHATTAN OPERA COMPANY.

Alvarez, Marguerite d', *see* D'ALVAREZ, MARGUERITE.

Alvaro, Don, the tragic hero (tenor) of VERDI'S LA FORZA DEL DESTINO, a role created by Enrico Tamberlik.

Alvary, Max (born Maximilian Achenbach), tenor. Born Düsseldorf, May 3, 1856; died Gross-Tabarz, Germany, Nov. 7, 1898. He studied principally with Julius Stockhausen and Francesco LAMPERTI. After appearances in Europe he made his American debut on Nov. 25, 1885, as DON JOSÉ, a performance in which Lilli LEHMANN also appeared at the METROPOLITAN OPERA for the first

time. He remained a principal tenor of the Metropolitan Opera for four years, singing chiefly in the Wagnerian repertory (he became the first singer of Wagnerian hero roles to appear without a beard). He was the first LOGE and the first SIEGFRIED in America. In 1891 he appeared as TRISTAN and TANNHÄUSER at the BAYREUTH Festival. One year later he was heard in the RING cycle at COVENT GARDEN, under Gustav MAHLER; because the role of Siegfried in the music drama of the same name was his favorite, Mahler opened the *Ring* cycle with this work in Alvary's honor. Alvary retired in 1897 due to illness.

Alvise, official of the Inquisition (bass) in PONCHIELLI'S LA GIOCONDA.

Amadis (or **Amadis of Gaul**), a hero in a celebrated medieval romance. He is discarded by his mother in the sea, rescued, and raised at the royal court of Scotland. Following his marriage to Oriana, he is knighted, returns to Gaul, and becomes famous for his exploits.

This legend was the subject of several operas, the most significant being that of LULLY, with text by QUINAULT, produced at the PARIS OPÉRA on Jan. 18, 1684. J. C. BACH'S *Amadis des Gaules* (1779) and MASSENET'S *Amadis* (1902) are also based on the same theme.

Amahl and the Night Visitors, one-act opera by MENOTTI. Libretto by the composer. Premiere: NBC-TV, Dec. 24, 1951; Bloomington, Ind., Feb. 21, 1952 (staged). This is both the first opera ever commissioned for television and the first to have its world premiere sponsored by a business organization. Menotti derived his theme from the painting, *The Adoration of the Magi,* by the Flemish artist Hieronymus Bosch. His story concerns the three Wise Men who, on their way to the manger in Bethlehem, stop at the hovel of a crippled boy, Amahl (boy soprano). When Amahl offers them his crutches as a gift to the Holy Child, he is miraculously healed. The opera contains several delightful choruses and ensemble numbers. For almost a decade, it was performed every Christmas over the NBC-TV network. The opera was also staged by the NEW YORK CITY OPERA and in 1953 at the FLORENCE MAY MUSIC FESTIVAL. All in all it has had well over three thousand productions, including those in schools and colleges.

Amami, Alfredo, Violetta's farewell to Alfredo, whom she is abandoning for the sake of his future, in Act II, Scene 1, of VERDI'S LA TRAVIATA.

Amantio di Nicolao, a lawyer (bass) in PUCCINI'S GIANNI SCHICCHI.

Amara, Lucine, soprano. Born Hartford, Conn., Mar. 1, 1927. When she was eighteen she began studying singing in San Francisco with Stella Eisner-Eyn. After being in the chorus of the SAN FRANCISCO OPERA during 1945–46 and making a public debut in a concert at Memorial Auditorium in San Francisco, she won the Atwater Kent Scholarship in 1948 and in 1949 appeared as soloist with the San Francisco Symphony under MONTEUX. On Nov. 6, 1950, she made her debut at the METROPOLITAN in DON CARLOS. She has remained in the company since then, graduating into such leading roles as MIMI, MICAËLA, AIDA, CIO-CIO-SAN, Eurydice in GLUCK'S ORFEO, Antonia in THE TALES OF HOFFMANN, and leading roles in MOZART'S operas. On Oct. 28, 1957, she starred as Tatiana in the opening-night performance at the Metropolitan Opera of its new production of EUGENE ONEGIN. In 1954 she made her debut at festivals in GLYNDEBOURNE and EDINBURGH, in 1955 at the Stockholm Opera, and in 1960 at the VIENNA STATE OPERA.

Amato, Pasquale, baritone. Born Naples, Mar. 21, 1878; died New York City, Aug. 12, 1942. After attending the Naples Conservatory he made his debut at the Teatro Bellini in Naples in 1900 in LA TRAVIATA. He sang in leading opera houses in Europe and visited Buenos Aires and Egypt before being contracted by GATTI-CASAZZA for the METROPOLITAN. His American debut took place on Nov. 20, 1908, in *La traviata;* his role was the elder Germont. He remained at the Metropolitan over

a decade and was acclaimed for his interpretations of SCARPIA, VALENTIN, RIGOLETTO, Figaro (in THE BARBER OF SEVILLE), IAGO, and BARNABA. He created the title role in DAMROSCH'S CYRANO DE BERGERAC, that of Jack Rance in THE GIRL OF THE GOLDEN WEST, and Napoleon in MADAME SANS-GÊNE. He also appeared in the American premieres of L'AMORE DEI TRE RE, FRANCESCA DA RIMINI, GERMANIA, and LODOLETTA.

Because of illness, he went into retirement in 1924, spending most of his time in Italy. On Feb. 26, 1933, he returned to the Metropolitan to help celebrate Gatti-Casazza's silver jubilee, and on Nov. 20 of the same year he celebrated his own twenty-fifth anniversary of his first appearance in New York by appearing at the Hippodrome Theater in the role of the elder Germont, the role of his American debut. On Apr. 1, 1934, he became director of the Hippodrome Opera Company, but he held this post only briefly. In 1935 he became head of the voice and opera departments at the Louisiana State University School of Music, a position he held until his death.

Amelia, (1) Renato's wife (soprano) in VERDI'S UN BALLO IN MASCHERA.

(2) The daughter (soprano) of Boccanegra, whose real name is Maria, but who is raised under the assumed name of Amelia Grimaldi, in VERDI'S SIMON BOCCANEGRA.

Amelia Goes to the Ball (Amelia al ballo), one-act comic opera by MENOTTI. Libretto by the composer (English translation by George Mead). Premiere: Academy of Music, Philadelphia, Apr. 1, 1937. This was Menotti's first opera as a mature composer and his first success. The setting is Milan, the time 1910. The tongue-in-cheek text concerns Amelia's frantic and seemingly frustrated efforts to go to a ball. Her husband (bass) discovers a letter from her lover (tenor), her lover arrives through the window, the two men quarrel. Amelia (soprano) lands her husband in the hospital by smashing a vase over his head, and her lover goes to jail when she makes a false charge against him of having attacked her husband. With the rivals out of the way, Amelia goes to the ball—escorted by the police officer.

The work was produced by the METROPOLITAN OPERA on Mar. 3, 1938. One month later, on Apr. 4, it received its first performance in Italy at San Remo.

American opera composers and operas. The first work by an American composer that can reasonably be called an opera was Francis Hopkinson's *The Temple of Minerva*, produced in 1781. Hopkinson, a signer of the Declaration of Independence, wrote the words as well as the music for his "oratorial entertainment," as it was called at the time; the music has since been lost. The next American opera, a BALLAD OPERA, set forth the career of the Cherokee chieftain whose name was the production's title: *Tammany*, with libretto by Anne Julia Hatton, music by the popular and prolific James Hewitt, an Englishman. It was produced in New York in 1794 under the auspices of the Tammany Society. In 1796 two more American operas were introduced: Victor Pelissier's *Edwin and Angelina* and Benjamin Carr's *The Archers, or Mountaineers of Switzerland* (a work derived from SCHILLER's drama WILHELM TELL). The first American work of grand-opera proportions was LEONORA, adapted from BULWER-LYTTON's *The Lady of Lyons*, with music by William Henry Fry. In the style of operas by DONIZETTI and BELLINI, *Leonora* has considerable value. It was introduced in Philadelphia in 1845, was well received, and was revived thirteen years later at the ACADEMY OF MUSIC in New York. Fry later wrote another successful work, *Notre Dame de Paris*, based on HUGO's novel. Well received in 1855 was George Frederick Bristow's opera *Rip Van Winkle*, a work using an American subject. An attempt to encourage the writing of operas on American themes was made by Ole Bull in 1855. He had recently become manager of the Academy of Music in New York, and in this ca-

pacity he offered a prize of a thousand dollars for "the best original grand opera by an American composer on an American subject." Unfortunately, Bull did not stay long enough at the Academy to conclude this competition successfully. Another effort in this direction was made thirty years later by Theodore THOMAS, then the director of the American Opera Company. One of the announced aims of the new company was the presentation of authentic American operas, but in the year or so of the company's existence no such works were found that merited performance. Early in 1900 there was talk of producing an American opera at the METROPOLITAN OPERA; the work selected was John Knowles Paine's *Azara*. Nothing came of this project. *Azara* was never performed on the stage, though it received a concert performance in 1903. The first American opera performed at the Metropolitan was Frederick Shepherd CONVERSE's THE PIPE OF DESIRE in 1910. A year later GATTI-CASAZZA announced a competition for American operas. The winner was PARKER's MONA, produced by the Metropolitan in 1912 and awarded a ten-thousand-dollar prize. A number of American composers have written operas that exploited peculiarly American idioms. HERBERT and CADMAN produced operas (NATOMA and SHANEWIS) that featured their conceptions of American Indian music; GRUENBERG (in THE EMPEROR JONES) and GERSHWIN (in PORGY AND BESS) used Negro subjects and musical materials; BLITZSTEIN has used jazz styles and techniques (THE CRADLE WILL ROCK). Many American opera composers have used an eclectic style owing little to American folk or popular sources, and in this vein some notable operas have been written: TAYLOR's THE KING's HENCHMAN, FLOYD's SUSANNAH, and most of the operas by MENOTTI. Since the 1950's, some American composers have made extensive use of ultramodern idioms in their operas, such as serialism, DIRECTIONAL MUSIC, ELECTRONIC MUSIC, and so forth.

See the following American composers, all of whom are discussed in their proper alphabetical order in this encyclopedia: Antheil, Bacon, Barber, Bernstein, Cadman, Copland, Walter Damrosch, Dello Joio, Foss, Gershwin, Vittorio Giannini, Herbert, Douglas Moore, Still, Thomson, Ward, Weill, and Weisgall.

See also the following operas: *Azora, The Canterbury Pilgrims, Cleopatra's Night, A Drumlin Legend, The Dybbuk, Evangeline, The Good Soldier Schweik, The Holy Devil, Merry Mount, Miss Julie, Mourning Becomes Electra, Porgy and Bess, Rip van Winkle, The Tender Land, The Triumph of St. Joan, Trouble in Tahiti, Twelfth Night,* and *The Visitation.*

American opera singers. American-born singers achieving international renown is by no means a post–World War II development. The first artists to receive recognition in Europe as well as America were Clara Louise KELLOGG (whose debut, in RIGOLETTO, took place at the ACADEMY OF MUSIC in New York in 1861); Minnie HAUK, whose operatic debut took place in Brooklyn when she was only fourteen, followed by a career that brought her triumphs at COVENT GARDEN, the Vienna Royal Opera (VIENNA STATE OPERA), and the METROPOLITAN OPERA; and David BISPHAM, one of the first American-born baritones to become famous at home and abroad in the Wagnerian repertory.

Following these singers came Annie Louise CARY, the first American-born woman heard in a Wagnerian opera in the United States, appearing as ORTRUD in 1877; Alwina VALLERIA, the first American-born singer cast in principal roles at the Metropolitan Opera (where she made her debut in 1883 in IL TROVATORE); and Suzanne ADAMS, who made her debuts at the PARIS OPÉRA in 1895 and the Metropolitan Opera in 1899 as Juliette in GOUNOD'S ROMÉO ET JULIETTE. Among the more prominent American-born male opera singers of this period were Charles R. Adams, one of the principals at the Vienna Royal

Opera between 1867 and 1876, and William Candidus, who was featured in leading operatic roles in London, Hamburg, Berlin, and Munich.

The stage was now set for American-born singers to assume a place of equal importance with their most distinguished colleagues in the world's opera houses: stars of the first magnitude, such as Mme. CAHIER, Lillian NORDICA, Louise HOMER, Emma EAMES (born in Shanghai of American parents), Geraldine FARRAR, Rosa PONSELLE, Riccardo MARTIN, Clarence WHITEHILL, and Paul ALTHOUSE (the first American to sing the role of TRISTAN at the Metropolitan). The late 1920's and the 1930's saw the rise to world stardom of Grace MOORE, Dusolina GIANNINI, Helen TRAUBEL (one of the foremost Wagnerian sopranos of her time), John Charles THOMAS, Frederick JAGEL, James Melton, Richard BONELLI, Charles KULLMAN, and Lawrence TIBBETT.

Negro singers in opera. One of the earliest Negroes to be heard in opera in America was Mme. Sisseretta Jones, who, besides appearing in popular musical productions, was a member of the World's Fair Opera Company and the ACADEMY OF MUSIC in New York in the latter part of the nineteenth century. The first Negro to sing roles regularly in opera performances, however, did not appear until many years later: Caterina Jarboro was the first Negro woman singer to star in a white company when she was heard in AIDA at the Hippodrome in New York in 1930; Jules Bledsoe was heard as Amonasro in *Aida* in Cleveland in 1932 and subsequently appeared with the CHICAGO OPERA and in a performance of THE EMPEROR JONES at the New York Hippodrome in 1934. In the 1930's two American operas were written which were given with all-Negro or nearly all-Negro casts. These were FOUR SAINTS IN THREE ACTS and PORGY AND BESS. In 1941 Mrs. Mary Cardwell Dawson, a graduate from the New England Conservatory, opened up new opportunities for Negro opera singers by founding the National

Negro Opera Company, which presented standard opera with all-Negro casts in Pittsburgh, Washington, New York, Chicago, and Philadelphia. Out of this company were graduated Camilla Williams and Muriel Rahn. Marian ANDERSON became the first Negro to sing a solo role at the Metropolitan Opera when she appeared as Ulrica in UN BALLO IN MASCHERA in 1955, and in 1957, Leontyne PRICE was the first Negro to appear in principal roles at the SAN FRANCISCO OPERA when she was heard in *Aida* and POULENC's LES DIALOGUES DES CARMÉLITES. The second and third Negroes to appear in important roles at the Metropolitan were Robert McFerrin and Mattawilda DOBBS, making their debuts there in 1955 and 1956 respectively.

Since the middle 1950's, Negro singers have assumed an ever increasing significance in the world of opera, so that within a decade they began to acquire such international stature that their appearances in the world's major opera houses became routine. In 1955 Charles Holland was the first Negro to appear at the OPÉRA-COMIQUE. Among Negro singers who have achieved acclaim the world over for their performances in starring roles at major opera houses and world-famous festivals are Martina ARROYO, McHenry Boatwright, Grace BUMBRY, Reri Grist, George SHIRLEY, Shirley Verrett, William Warfield, and Felicia WEATHERS.

After World War II, American-born singers achieved successes in Europe and America as never before; in fact, some of the world's most widely acclaimed and sought-after stars of the opera were Americans by birth. The following are discussed in alphabetical order in this book: Lucine Amara, Frances Bible, Richard Bonelli, Maria Callas, Phyllis Curtin, Rosalind Elias, Eileen Farrell, Frank Guarrera, Mack Harrell, Margaret Harshaw, Osie Hawkins, Jerome Hines, Helen Jepson, James King, Dorothy Kirsten, Evelyn Lear, George London, John McCracken, Jean Madeira, Robert Merrill, Anna Moffo, Patrice Munsel, Jan Peerce, Roberta Peters, Judith Raskin, Regina Resnik, Eleanor Steber, Risë Stevens, Thomas Stewart, Teresa Stich-Randall, Blanche Thebom, Jess Thomas, Giorgio Tozzi, Richard Tucker, Leonard Warren.

American Opera Society, an organization founded in 1951 (originally named American Chamber Opera Society) by Allen Sven Oxenburg, still its artistic director, for presenting seldom-mounted operas in concert form. The first performance, a revival of MONTEVERDI's IL COMBATTIMENTO DI TANCREDI E CLORINDA, took place on the estate of Mrs. W. Murray Crane, in Westchester, N.Y. In 1952 the company moved to Town Hall, New York City, and since 1957 has performed in Carnegie Hall. Some of its presentations have been counted among the most significant musical events of their seasons: for example, MÉDÉE with Eileen FARRELL in 1955; IL PIRATA with CALLAS in 1959; BEATRICE DI TENDA, in which Joan SUTHERLAND made her New York debut in 1961; SEMIRAMIDE starring Miss Sutherland in 1964; the revival of DOKTOR FAUST in 1966; and the American premiere of HAYDN's ORFEO ED EURIDICE with Sutherland and GEDDA in 1968.

Montserrat CABALLÉ's New York debut in LUCREZIA BORGIA in 1965 made her an overnight sensation in operatic circles. Some of the other singers to make highly successful New York debuts with this company include Teresa BERGANZA, Boris CHRISTOFF, Marilyn HORNE, Gwyneth Jones, Elisabeth SCHWARZKOPF, Giulietta SIMIONATO, and Jon VICKERS.

Besides operas mentioned above, the following American or New York premieres or unusual revivals were of special interest: ANNA BOLENA, LE CADI DUPÉ, I CAPULETTI ED I MONTECCHI, LE DEVIN DU VILLAGE, IL DUCA D'ALBA, LA GAZZA LADRA, *Giovanna d'Arco* (VERDI), GIULIO CESARE, *Hercules* (HANDEL), L' INCORONAZIONE DI POPPEA, IPHIGÉNIE EN TAURIDE, LES MAMELLES DE TIRÉSIAS, MOSÈ, *Otello* (ROSSINI), PARIDE ED ELENA, IL RETABLO DE MAESE PEDRO, *La straniera*

(BELLINI), LES TROYENS, LA VOIX HU-
MAINE, *The Witch of Endor* (PURCELL).

From its inception, the company aimed to present rarely produced operas worthy of a hearing. A minimum amount of costuming, lighting, staging, and props is employed. The society has provided hearings for American singers and also features European stars of the first importance in unusual roles.

Amero sol per te m'era il morire, the closing love duet of Tosca and Cavaradossi in Cavaradossi's prison quarters, in Act III of PUCCINI's TOSCA.

Amfiparnaso, L', designated by its composer, Orazio Vecchi, as a "comedy in music" (*comedia harmonica*) but actually a sequence of accompanied madrigals. Premiere: Modena, 1594. American premiere: New York City, Mar. 13, 1933 (concert version). Written in 1592 and published in 1597, this work consists of fourteen madrigals, all but one for five voices, the whole to be sung with an accompaniment of woodwinds, gambas, and continuo. The theatrical element in this work of Vecchi's and in similar works by other Italian composers of his time is so pronounced that the madrigal comedy is considered an important forerunner of opera. There are two parallel plots in *L'Amfiparnaso.* One, *lirico tragica,* involves the love of Isabella and Lucio; the other, *grottesco comica,* portrays the doings of the buffoons of the *commedia dell' arte.* The work has occasionally been given stage presentations in modern times, in 1950 in Modena to celebrate the four-hundredth anniversary of the composer's birth and at TANGLEWOOD, Lenox, Mass., in 1954.

Amfortas, keeper of the Holy Grail (baritone) in WAGNER's PARSIFAL.

Amfortas! Die Wunde, Parsifal's recollection of Amfortas' suffering that makes it possible for him to resist Kundry's embraces and kisses, in Act II, Scene 2, of WAGNER's PARSIFAL.

amico Fritz, L', opera in three acts by MASCAGNI. Libretto by P. Suardon (pseudonym for N. Daspuro), based on a novel by ERCKMANN-CHATRIAN. Pre-

miere: Teatro Costanzi, Rome, Oct. 31, 1891. American premiere: Philadelphia, June 8, 1892. Fritz Kobus, a rich bachelor (tenor), eventually marries a farmer's daughter, Suzel (soprano), as a result of the machinations of Rabbi David (bass). The opera contains a fine duet, that of Fritz and Suzel in Act II ("Suzel, buon di"), sometimes known as the "Duet of the Cherries." An orchestral intermezzo between the second and third acts; Fritz's aria, "O amore, o bella luce," and Suzel's aria, "Non mi resta che il pianto," both in Act III, are also noteworthy.

Amina, sleepwalking village maiden (soprano) in BELLINI's LA SONNAMBULA, a role created by Giuditta PASTA.

Aminta, an actress (soprano), "wife" of Morosus, in Richard STRAUSS's DIE SCHWEIGSAME FRAU, a role created by Maria CEBOTARI.

Amis, l'amour tendre et rêveur, Hoffmann's *Couplets bachiques* in Act II of OFFENBACH's THE TALES OF HOFFMANN.

Am Jordan Sankt Johannes stand, David's hymm to St. John in Act III of WAGNER's DIE MEISTERSINGER.

Amleto (Hamlet), opera by FACCIO. Libretto by BOITO, based on SHAKESPEARE's HAMLET. Premiere: Teatro Carlo Felice, Genoa, May 20, 1865. One of its soprano arias, "Sortita d'Ofelia," has become a famous concert number.

Amneris, the King of Egypt's daughter (mezzo-soprano) in VERDI's AIDA.

À moi les plaisirs, duet of Faust and Méphistophélès in Act I of GOUNOD's FAUST, expressing their reaction to Faust's magical return to his youth.

Amonasro, King of Ethiopia (baritone), Aida's father, in VERDI's AIDA.

Amor, god of love (soprano) in GLUCK's ORFEO ED EURIDICE.

amore dei tre re, L' (The Love of Three Kings), opera in three acts by MONTEMEZZI. Libretto by Sem BENELLI, adapted from his own verse tragedy of the same name. Premiere: La Scala, Apr. 10, 1913. American premiere: Metropolitan Opera, Jan. 2, 1914.

Characters: Archibaldo, King of Altura (bass); Manfredo, his son (baritone); Avito, a former prince of Altura (tenor); Fiora, Manfredo's wife (soprano); Flaminio, Archibaldo's servant (tenor). The action takes place in an Italian castle; the time is the Middle Ages.

Act I. A hall in Archibaldo's castle. Unable to sleep, Archibaldo recalls the time when he led the barbarian invasion of Italy ("Italia! Italia! é tutto il mio ricordo!"). Flaminio reminds him how Fiora gave up her beloved Avito to marry Manfredo in order to insure peace in the land. When Archibaldo leaves for his chambers, Avito appears, followed by Fiora. They are still in love and they embrace passionately, unmindful of approaching dawn. Archibaldo returns as Avito departs. He demands the name of the person to whom Fiora has been speaking. She insists that she has been talking to herself. The blind King knows that she is lying and he cries out against the affliction which prevents him from reading her face. A flourish of trumpets announces the homecoming of Manfredo from battle. Manfredo is overjoyed with his victory and his return ("O padre mio"). Fiora welcomes her husband frigidly, a circumstance which does not escape the blind King.

Act II. A terrace atop the castle walls. Manfredo, about to return to war, bids his wife a sorrowful farewell ("Dimmi, Fiora, perchè ti veggo ancora"). He asks her to mount the battlement and wave her scarf as he rides down the valley. After Manfredo has left, Avito enters, disguised as a castle guard. Fiora begs him to leave, but cannot resist Avito's plea for a last kiss ("Ho sete! Ho sete!"). They succumb passionately to each other. Archibaldo interrupts this idyll. After Avito manages to escape, Archibaldo bitterly denounces Fiora for her unfaithfulness and demands to know her lover's name. Fiora admits her infidelity but refuses to name Avito. In a fit of rage Archibaldo strangles her. Manfredo unexpectedly returns, worried over Fiora.

Brokenheartedly, Archibaldo reveals that he has murdered her.

Act III. The palace crypt. Mourners sing a dirge before Fiora's bier. After they depart, Avito comes to bid his beloved a desperate farewell ("Fiora ... e silenzio!"). He bends to kiss her lips for the last time. Archibaldo, attempting to trap Fiora's lover, has poisoned her lips. As Avito begins to die, Manfredo, coming to pay his last respects, discovers him. Unable to hate Avito and unable to live on without his wife, he kisses Fiora in order to die. When Archibaldo discovers that his trick has not only destroyed Fiora's lover but also his son, he succumbs to despair.

L'amore dei tre re was Montemezzi's most successful opera. It forged no new trails, but within familiar patterns showing the influences of WAGNER, VERDI, and DEBUSSY, it combined impressive craftsmanship with a powerful story.

amore medico, L' (Doctor Cupid), OPERA BUFFA in two acts by WOLF-FERRARI. Libretto by Enrico Golisciani, based on MOLIÈRE's L'Amour médecin. Premiere: Dresden Opera, Dec. 4, 1913 (under the German title of Der Liebhaber als Arzt). American premiere: Metropolitan Opera, Mar. 25, 1914. The setting is Paris; the time, during the reign of Louis XIV. Lucinda (soprano) is suffering from a prolonged malady that proves to be love, as her father, Arnolfo (bass), objects to her marriage to Clitandro (tenor). She is cured after Clitandro, disguised as a doctor, prescribes a mock marriage which turns out to be real. The score is a skillful amalgam of Mozartean grace and charm with early twentieth-century harmonic idioms and orchestration. The best vocal numbers are Lucinda's opening air, "Voi ci diffuse nell'aria," and Arnolfo's buffa aria, "Io mi compro un bastimento." The orchestral intermezzo is also significant.

Amore o grillo, Pinkerton's confession to Sharpless of his love for Cio-Cio-San, in Act I of PUCCINI's MADAMA BUTTERFLY.

Amor ti vieta, Count Loris' avowal of love for Fedora, in Act II of GIORDANO'S FEDORA.

Amour des trois oranges, L', *see* LOVE FOR THREE ORANGES.

Amour médecin, L', *see* AMORE MEDICO, L'; MOLIÈRE.

Amour! viens aider ma faiblesse, Dalila's appeal to the god of love to help her capture Samson's heart, in Act II of SAINT-SAËNS'S SAMSON ET DALILA.

Amram, David Werner, composer. Born Philadelphia, Nov. 17, 1930. He studied composition with Vittorio GIANNINI at the Manhattan School of Music after attending Oberlin Conservatory. In 1956 he became musical director of the New York Shakespeare Festival for whose performances he wrote incidental music. He has also written music for motion pictures, television, and for jazz combinations, as well as for the concert stage. In 1966–67 he became the first composer to take the post of composer-in-residence with the New York Philharmonic Symphony under a grant from the Rockefeller Foundation. His first opera was *The Final Ingredient,* produced over the ABC-TV network on Apr. 11, 1965. This was followed by the successful premiere of TWELFTH NIGHT by the Lake George Opera Company on Aug. 1, 1968. He published an autobiography in 1968, *Vibrations: The Adventures and Musical Times of David Amram.*

Am stillen Herd, Walther's narrative explaining that all his knowledge came from ancient minstrels and from nature, in Act I of WAGNER'S DIE MEISTERSINGER.

Anacréon ou l'Amour fugitif (The Fugitive Lover), opera in two acts by CHERUBINI. Libretto by R. Mendouze. Premiere: Paris Opéra, Oct. 4, 1803. Cherubini's twentieth opera, it was a miserable failure when first produced and would have been completely forgotten were it not for its remarkable overture, a fixture in the symphonic repertory. This overture is historically important for two reasons: for its use of a ROSSINI-type crescendo for dramatic effect, anticipating Rossini by several years, and for including an English horn in its orchestration, an instrument rarely used in Cherubini's time.

Anatol, (1) a young man (tenor) who has an affair with Erika but marries Vanessa in BARBER'S VANESSA, a role created by Nicolai GEDDA.

(2) Prince Kuragin (tenor), rival of Andrei for Natasha's love, in PROKOFIEV'S WAR AND PEACE.

Ancona, Mario, baritone. Born Leghorn, Italy, Feb. 28, 1860; died Florence, Feb. 22, 1931. Though educated for the law and beginning his career as a diplomat, he decided finally to become a professional singer. He made his debut in Trieste in 1890 and in 1892 appeared in opera at the Olympic Theatre in London. He was engaged for COVENT GARDEN in 1893, where he made his debut as Tonio in the first London performance of PAGLIACCI. He remained with this company until 1903. Meanwhile, on Dec. 11, 1893, he made his debut with the METROPOLITAN OPERA as Tonio, staying with the company for four years. In 1906–07 he appeared with the MANHATTAN OPERA COMPANY. He went into retirement just before World War I, devoting himself subsequently to teaching.

Andersen, Hans Christian, poet and writer of fairy tales. Born Odense, Denmark, Apr. 2, 1805; died Copenhagen, Aug. 4, 1875. Among the operas based on tales by Andersen are: BRUNEAU'S *Le Jardin du paradis;* August Enna's *The Princess on the Pea,* 1900; Niels-Erich Fougstedt's radio opera *The Tinderbox,* 1950; Ebke Hamerik's *The Traveling Companion,* 1946; Stanley Hollier's *The Mother;* MOORE'S *The Emperor's New Clothes;* Margaret Moore's *The Mermaid;* Hermann Reuter's *Die Prinzessin und der Schweinhirt;* Bernard Rogers' *The Nightingale;* Hans Schnazare's *Die Nachtigall;* Bernhard Sekles' *Die zehn Küsse,* 1926; STANFORD'S *The Traveling Companion;* LE ROSSIGNOL; TOCH'S *Die Prinzessin auf der Erbse;* and WAGNER-RÉGÉNY'S *Der nackte Koenig.*

Andersen also wrote *Bruden fra Lam-*

mermoor, a libretto based on SCOTT for the Danish composer Frederik Bredal; a second libretto based on Scott for Christoph Ernst Friedrich's *Kenilworth;* and librettos for operas by Franz Gläser and Johann Peter Hartmann, the one for Gläser being *The Wedding on Lake Como,* derived from MANZONI'S I PROMESSI SPOSI.

Anderson, Marian, contralto. Born Philadelphia, Feb. 17, 1902. She was the first Negro to appear at the METROPOLITAN OPERA in a major role, Ulrica in UN BALLO IN MASCHERA. Her first appearance there on Jan. 7, 1955, also marked the opera debut of this world-famed concert artist. In 1958 she sang in Act II of GLUCK'S ORFEO ED EURIDICE at the CARAMOOR FESTIVAL in Katonah, N.Y. She retired following a concert tour in 1964–65.

Andrea Chénier, opera in four acts by GIORDANO. Libretto by Luigi ILLICA. Premiere: La Scala, Mar. 28, 1896. American premiere: Academy of Music, Nov. 13, 1896.

Characters: Andrea Chénier, a poet (tenor), a role created by Giuseppe BORGATTI; Charles Gérard, revolutionary leader (baritone); Countess de Coigny (mezzo-soprano); Madeleine, her daughter (soprano); Bersi, Madeleine's maid (mezzo-soprano); Roucher, Chénier's friend (bass); Fouquier-Tinville, public prosecutor (bass); Fléville, a writer (baritone); Schmidt, a jailer (baritone); Dumas, president of the Revolutionary Tribunal (baritone); Madelon, an old blind woman (mezzo-soprano); Mathieu, a waiter (baritone); a spy; an abbé; soldiers; revolutionaries; prisoners; servants. The action takes place in Paris before and during the French Revolution.

Act I. Ballroom in the Château de Coigny. A party is about to take place. Gérard, a servant, bitter at social injustice, predicts imminent doom for the aristocracy ("Son sessant' anni"). When Madeleine appears, Gérard remarks on her beauty, for he loves her. Madeleine complains of the tortures suffered by a young lady who must always be dressed fashionably ("Si! io penso alla tortura"). Guests now arrive, one of them Andrea Chénier. A ballet pantomime is performed. The guests sing a pastoral chorus ("O pastore"). Then Chénier recites one of his love poems ("Un dì all'azzurro spazio"), a thinly disguised attack on the rich which horrifies the guests. The embarrassment is relieved by dancing a gavotte. But suddenly beggars, headed by Gérard, burst in and beg for charity ("La notte e giorno"). When Gérard is ordered to send them away, he tears off his livery and announces his sympathy with the poor ("Si, me ne vo, contessa"). The footmen eject Gérard and the beggars, and the dancing continues.

Act II. The Café Hottot. The Revolution is in full swing. Chénier, having denounced Robespierre, is held in suspicion by the revolutionaries. He is sitting at a table when Bersi slips him a note in which an unnamed friend seeks help. Roucher urges Chénier to flee but Chénier refuses ("Credo a una possanza arcana"). Besides, he is eager to help the unknown writer of the note. The writer, who soon comes disguised to the café, is Madeleine ("Eravate possente"). Chénier and Madeleine now realize how much they love each other. They conspire to flee ("Ora soave, sublime ora d'amore"). But before they can escape, Gérard, now an important revolutionary leader, comes for Madeleine. A duel ensues in which Gérard is wounded. Remorsefully, Gérard urges Chénier to escape. When Gérard's friends arrive, he pretends not to know who wounded him.

Act III. The revolutionary tribunal. A mob, gathered to watch the proceedings, sings the revolutionary "La Carmagnole." Gérard learns that Chénier has been caught and arrested. He must now denounce the poet formally. As he does so, he recalls the poet's nobility and loyalty ("Nemico della patria?"). Despite his inner conflicts, Gérard signs the paper dooming Chénier. Madeleine appears to plead for the poet. Gérard tells her that fate has decreed that they belong to one another ("Perchè ciò volle il mio voler possente"). Madeleine tells Gérard of her mother's death ("La mamma morta"), and offers herself to Gérard in return for Chénier's freedom. Gérard promises help. During the trial Chénier defends himself ("Si, fui soldato"), but the mob demands his death, and Gérard cannot help him.

Act IV. Prison of Saint-Lazare. Awaiting execution, Chénier writes a farewell poem ("Come un bel dì di maggio"). Madeleine comes to die with the man she loves; she has bribed a jailer to substitute her name on the death list for that of a victim. Chénier and Madeleine embrace, repeating their devotion for each other ("Vicino a te s'acqueta"). Together, they walk to the guillotine.

Giordano became famous with *Andrea Chénier,* an opera dealing freely with a historical figure, the poet André de Chénier. While he wrote several fine operas after this one, none equaled *Chénier* in power of inspiration, beauty of melody, and sustained dramatic interest. *Chénier* is filled with passionate arias and recitatives, stirring emotional situations and climaxes.

Andrei, (1) son (tenor) of Prince Ivan Khovantsky in MUSSORGSKY'S KHOVANTCHINA.

(2) Prince Bolkonsky (baritone), fiancé of Natasha, in PROKOFIEV'S WAR AND PEACE.

Andrès, Stella's servant (tenor) in OFFENBACH'S THE TALES OF HOFFMANN.

Andresen, Ivar, bass. Born Oslo, July 27, 1896; died Stockholm, Nov. 26, 1940. Following his debut in 1919 as the King in AIDA at the Stockholm Opera, he achieved his first successes at the DRESDEN OPERA. Between 1927 and 1936 he appeared regularly at BAYREUTH, between 1928 and 1931 at COVENT GARDEN, and between 1935 and 1940 at the BERLIN STATE OPERA, specializing in Wagnerian and Mozartean roles. He made his debut at the MET-

ROPOLITAN OPERA on Nov. 1, 1930, as Daland in DER FLIEGENDE HOLLÄNDER and was described by Olin Downes in *The New York Times* as "an artist of first rank." During the two seasons he remained at the Metropolitan he also made distinctive appearances in the roles of KING MARK, POGNER, Hermann (in TANNHÄUSER), King Henry (in LOHENGRIN), and the Sorcerer in ŠVANDA, THE BAGPIPER. In 1935 he scored a major success at the GLYNDEBOURNE FESTIVAL as Sarastro in THE MAGIC FLUTE.

Andreyev, Leonid, author and playwright. Born Orel, Russia, June 18, 1871; died Helsinki, Finland, Sept. 12, 1919. A number of his works have been the source of operas: *The Abyss* (REBIKOV); HE WHO GETS SLAPPED (WARD); *01–01* (Alexander TCHEREPNIN); and *Six Characters in Search of an Author* (WEISGALL).

Ange adorable, love duet of Roméo and Juliette in Act I of GOUNOD'S ROMÉO ET JULIETTE.

Angeles, Victoria De Los, *see* DE LOS ANGELES, VICTORIA.

Angelica, a nun (soprano) in PUCCINI'S SUOR ANGELICA, a role created by Geraldine FARRAR.

Angélique, opera in one act by IBERT. Libretto by Nino. Premiere: Paris, Jan. 28, 1927. American premiere: New York City, Nov. 8, 1937. This was Ibert's first opera. It is a slight comedy in which Boniface, owner of a china shop, is convinced by his friend Charlot that the only way he can get rid of his wife, a shrew, is to put her on sale.

Angelotti, Cesare, a political plotter (bass) in PUCCINI'S TOSCA.

Anges du paradis, Vincent's CAVATINA in Act III of GOUNOD'S MIREILLE.

Anges purs, anges radieux, Marguerite's prayer to be carried to heaven after she dies, in Act V, Scene 2, of GOUNOD'S FAUST. With Faust and Méphistophélès adding their voices in exhortations, this number is customarily referred to as "the Trio" from *Faust.*

Aniara, an opera in two acts designated by its creators as "a revue of mankind

in space time," by BLOMDAHL. Libretto by Erik Lindegren, adapted from a drama of the same name by Harry Martison. Premiere: Stockholm Royal Opera, May 31, 1959.

This is the first opera about the space age; also the first successful opera in which electronic sounds, reproduced on tape, are basic to the musical texture. *Aniara* is a space ship speeding toward Mars following an atomic holocaust that has devastated most of the earth. The passengers cannot forget the cruelty, injustice, and inequality that governed life on earth. On the third day of the journey, *Aniara* veers off course and is destined to travel in space forever. During the years that follow, the oppressiveness of living confined in a vehicle in outer space, the futility of daily life, the increasing boredom of perpetual aimless travel all bring about utter desolation among the passengers. Some of the people become religious zealots. New cults spring up, new fetishes. One group performs a "Repentance Mass," and a blind poetess proclaims "a cult of life." And now twenty years have gone by. Though an attempt is made to celebrate this event in song and dance, the participants are weary beyond description, bereft of all hope for salvation, yet frantically clinging desperately to the straw of a possible miracle. On the last night, one after another of the passengers vanishes. What is left is the voice of the blind poetess praising death.

The text—a bitter indictment of modern society and the motivations and aims of contemporary living—expresses the emptiness governing so much of human existence, as people go through the motions of living in a spiritual void as vast as space itself. Blomdahl's score includes many different elements: folk music, jazz, church hymns, recitatives, SPRECHSTIMME, atonal and polytonal idioms, the TWELVE-TONE TECHNIQUES. Electronic sounds are used throughout to accentuate the growing tensions, to point up the horror that seizes the travelers, to suggest the infinite regions of space, and to reproduce the sounds of ghostly voices come from distant regions.

The North American continent first heard *Aniara* when the STOCKHOLM ROYAL OPERA presented it in Montreal at Expo 67 on May 31, 1967.

Anita, (1) an opera singer (soprano) in KRENEK'S JONNY SPIELT AUF.

(2) A girl from Navarre (soprano) in MASSENET'S LA NAVARRAISE, a role created by Emma CALVÉ.

An jenem Tag, Hans Heiling's aria in Act I of MARSCHNER'S HANS HEILING.

Anna, (1) principal female character (soprano) in BOIELDIEU'S LA DAME BLANCHE—the ward of Gaveston who becomes the wife of the Earl of Avenell.

(2) Inez' maid (contralto) in MEYERBEER'S L'AFRICAINE.

Anna, Donna, the Commendatore's daughter (soprano), beloved of Don Ottavio, in MOZART'S DON GIOVANNI. (This was the only Mozart role ever sung by Adelina PATTI.)

Anna Bolena, opera in two acts by DONIZETTI. Libretto by Felice ROMANI. Premiere: Teatro Carcano, Milan, Dec. 26, 1830. American premiere: New Orleans, Nov., 1839. Anna Bolena (Anne Boleyn, second wife of Henry VIII; soprano) has lost favor with the King, who plans to get rid of her. Anna's first love, Percy (Earl of Northumberland; tenor), returns from exile and is agitated to see Anna again. The King plans to use Percy as a way of disposing of Anna. Anna overhears Percy confessing his love for her. Since he cannot have her he decides to do away with himself. As he is about to kill himself, Anna's page, Smeton (Mark Smeton, a role sung by a mezzo-soprano), rushes in to stop him. Just then the King arrives and orders the arrest of Anna, Percy, and Smeton. Giovanna (Jane Seymour; mezzo-soprano), the King's mistress, tells Anna that the King stands ready to pardon Anna if she is willing to confess she loves Percy; but she refuses to do so, even after Giovanna reveals what her relationship is to the King. At Anna's trial, Smeton lies to save her by saying it was he who was her lover.

After Anna and Percy have been summoned, Giovanna pleads for Anna's life. In the Tower, Percy refuses to accept clemency since that does not include Anna. Within her cell, Anna has lost her mind. She recalls her girlhood and her one-time love for Percy. When the announcement comes that the King is about to embark on a new marriage, Anna prays to heaven to protect the new royal couple.

The opera was a tremendous success when first performed with RUBINI as Percy and PASTA in the title role. In fact, it was so successful that within four years it was given throughout Italy, as well as in London and Paris (the first Donizetti opera heard in those two cities), Graz, Madrid, Brno, Malta, Lisbon, Dresden, and Havana. Then for many years the opera was neglected. On Apr. 14, 1957, LA SCALA gave an extraordinary revival with a cast including CALLAS and SIMIONATO, which became a powerful factor in restoring public interest in this long-forgotten Donizetti opera. It was recorded at the time in its entirety with Callas. The AMERICAN OPERA SOCIETY presented it in New York in a semi-staged production during the season of 1957–58 and performed it again in 1966. Meanwhile it had also been given at the GLYNDEBOURNE FESTIVAL in 1965. The SAN CARLO OPERA in Naples included it in its repertory in 1968.

Ännchen, Agathe's friend (soprano) in WEBER'S DER FREISCHÜTZ.

Anne Truelove, leading female character (soprano) and Tom's beloved in STRAVINSKY'S THE RAKE'S PROGRESS, a role created by Elisabeth SCHWARZKOPF..

Annibale, Don, an aged apothecary (bass), married to the heroine Serafina, in DONIZETTI'S IL CAMPANELLO DI NOTTE.

Annina, (1) Violetta's maid (soprano or mezzo-soprano) in VERDI'S LA TRAVIATA.

(2) Valzacchi's accomplice (contralto) in Richard STRAUSS'S DER ROSENKAVALIER.

Annunzio, Gabriele D', see D'ANNUNZIO, GABRIELE.

Ansermet, Ernest, conductor. Born Vevey, Switzerland, Nov. 11, 1883; died Geneva, Feb. 20, 1969. He was one of the most distinguished conductors of the twentieth century, particularly in modern works and in the French, Russian, and Swiss repertory. Only occasionally did he turn to opera. In 1962 he became the musical adviser of the GENEVA OPERA, where he subsequently led some notable performances, including THE MAGIC FLUTE in 1965. He conducted the American premiere of FALLA'S opera L'ATLANTÍDA (in a concert version) in New York in 1962. On Nov. 20 of the same year, he made his debut at the METROPOLITAN OPERA with PELLÉAS ET MÉLISANDE.

Antheil, George, composer. Born Trenton, N.J., July 8, 1900; died New York City, Feb. 12, 1959. He studied with Constantine von Sternberg, Ernest Bloch, and at the Settlement School in Philadelphia. In 1922 he toured Europe as a pianist. His determination to become a composer made him give up concert work and settle in Paris, where in 1925 he married Elizabeth Markus, niece of the famous Austrian writer, Arthur Schnitzler. In Paris, Antheil began writing music in a revolutionary and provocative vein and for some years was known as an *enfant terrible* of music. The most celebrated of his early works was the *Ballet mécanique,* a pioneer attempt to use nonmusical sounds, such as sirens and motors, for artistic purpose; it was first given in Paris in 1926 and in New York in 1927 (many years later Antheil revised it, and the new version was heard in New York in 1954). He also wrote a JAZZ opera, TRANSATLANTIC, one of the earliest operas by an American-born composer to receive its world premiere in Europe, at the FRANKFURT OPERA in May, 1930, when it was a moderate success. His second opera, *Helen Retires,* written in 1932 to a libretto by John Erskine, was performed at the Juilliard School of Music in New York in Feb., 1934. Though more lyrical than *Transatlantic* and more gracious in manner, *Helen Retires* was a total failure. In

1933 Antheil settled in Hollywood and for a time wrote music for motion pictures. He then entered a new creative period, abandoning his former iconoclasm and writing music in a more conservative idiom. In this vein, he completed a third opera, VOLPONE, well received when introduced at the University of Southern California on Apr. 9, 1953. A later opera, *The Brothers,* was premiered in Denver in 1954; in 1955 *The Wish,* commissioned by a Rockefeller Foundation grant, was first given in Louisville, Ky.; and in 1957 *Venus in Africa* was produced in Denver. Among his last large works was a cantata, *Cabeza de vaca,* televised over the CBS network in 1962. Antheil published his autobiography, *Bad Boy of Music,* in 1945.

Antigone, (1) drama by SOPHOCLES. Daughter of OEDIPUS, Antigone buries her brother Polynices contrary to Creon's commands. For this she is condemned to die. Together with her lover, Haemon (Creon's son), she is shut up in a cave where they commit suicide. Some thirty operas were written on this subject, the most significant being listed below.

(2) Opera by GLUCK (under the title *Antigono*). Libretto by METASTASIO, based on SOPHOCLES. Premiere: Teatro Argentina, Rome, Feb. 9, 1756.

(3) Opera in three acts by HONEGGER. Libretto by Jean COCTEAU, based on SOPHOCLES. Premiere: Théâtre de la Monnaie, Dec. 28, 1927. American premiere: New York City, Apr. 16, 1969.

(4) "Tragic play with music" (under the title of *Antigonae*) in one act by ORFF. Libretto is J. Ch. F. Hölderlin's German translation of the SOPHOCLES tragedy. Premiere: Salzburg, Aug. 9, 1949. This is the first of three musical dramas based on the dramas of Sophocles and AESCHYLUS, the next two being OEDIPUS DER TYRANN and PROMETHEUS. *Antigonae* is in Orff's primitive style, in which rhythmic speech, chants in monotones, and the rhythms of a greatly oversized and highly unorthodox percussion section are predominant. Harmonic,

contrapuntal, and melodic resources are basically dispensed with. Though in a single act, the work requires three hours for performance.

Antonia, Hoffmann's third beloved (soprano) in OFFENBACH's THE TALES OF HOFFMANN.

Antonida, Ivan Susanin's daughter (soprano) in GLINKA's A LIFE FOR THE CZAR.

Antonio, (1) Susanna's uncle, the gardener (bass), in MOZART's THE MARRIAGE OF FIGARO.

(2) Son (tenor) of Michèle, the water carrier, in CHERUBINI's THE WATER CARRIER.

(3) A servant (bass) in THOMAS's MIGNON.

(4) Lodoletta's stepfather (bass) in MASCAGNI's LODOLETTA.

Antonio e Cleopatra, opera in three acts by MALIPIERO. Libretto by the composer, based on SHAKESPEARE's *Antony and Cleopatra.* Premiere: Florence May Music Festival, May 4, 1938. Malipiero explained: "Rather than the typical atmosphere of the play, I have stressed the human drama, reduced to a few essential characters. Even the chorus has a secondary function in the opera; it culminates in the banquet scene on Pompey's galley, where a few brief dances take place. *Antonio e Cleopatra* is really the tragedy of two human beings. Their actions form the central nucleus about which is built the music drama."

Antony and Cleopatra, opera in three acts by BARBER. Libretto is the play of William SHAKESPEARE, adapted by Franco ZEFFIRELLI. Premiere: Metropolitan Opera, Sept. 16, 1966.

This is the opera which the METROPOLITAN OPERA commissioned Barber to write for the opening of its new auditorium at the LINCOLN CENTER FOR THE PERFORMING ARTS. In line with so gala an occasion, an opera in the grand manner was created, calling for grandiose settings and elaborately produced scenes, all designed and directed by Zeffirelli. Zeffirelli took considerable liberties in rearranging the scenes and changing the order of some of the incidents, but he kept the Shakespeare text intact. The production was a lavish one. Unfortunately the complex stage mechanism of the new Metropolitan Opera House was not yet functioning properly in time for opening night, necessitating a hurried change of stage which worked to the opera's disadvantage. Nevertheless, *Antony and Cleopatra* was an impressive spectacle both for eye and ear, though it did not meet with the favor of either critics or public and did not return to the Metropolitan Opera repertory the following season. Barber's score, while mainly in a dramatic recitative style, included several highly effective choral passages and ballet music. The most impressive episodes came at the end of the opera with Cleopatra's narrative just before her suicide, and the lamentation of the people. The role of Cleopatra was created by Leontyne PRICE, that of Antony by Justino DIAZ.

The first two acts are divided into fifteen scenes (seven in the first, eight in the second). The third act has no subdivisions. There is no prelude or overture preceding the rise of the curtain. The people are imploring Antony (baritone) to desert his sybaritic life with Cleopatra (soprano) in Egypt and return to Rome, which he does. The Roman leaders demand from him not only a pledge of loyalty but his consent to marry Octavia, Caesar's sister. When Cleopatra, who is unable to forget Antony, learns of his marriage she gives vent to her anger. On his own part, Antony is still under the spell of Cleopatra; during festivities aboard a royal barge he expresses his determination to return to Egypt.

In the second act, Caesar denounces Antony for having deserted Octavia and betrayed his country. Antony is back with Cleopatra in Alexandria, where they receive the news that Caesar's legions are approaching. In the ensuing battle, the forces of Antony and Cleopatra are defeated. Cleopatra decides to retire to the monument to die. Hearing of this and believing Cleopatra already

dead, Antony stabs himself with his sword and is carried to the monument.

The entire third act takes place at the monument. Cleopatra is still alive; Antony dies in her arms. As his body is being removed for burial, Cleopatra calls for the deadly asp with which she commits suicide. The people grieve at the tragic death of their queen.

Two of the most deeply moving arias in the opera, both sung by Cleopatra, are "Give me some music" and "Give me my robe, put on my crown," the latter heard at her death scene.

Anvil Chorus, *see* VEDI! LE FOSCHE NOTTURNE SPOGLIE.

Aphrodite, music drama in five acts by ERLANGER. Libretto by Louis de Gramont, based on the novel of the same name by Pierre LOUŸS. Premiere: Opéra-Comique, Mar. 23, 1906. American premiere: New York City, Feb. 27, 1920. In Alexandria, the rich sculptor Demetrios (tenor) tries to gain the love of Chrysis (soprano). She will be his on condition that he acquire for her three things: the courtesan Bacchis' mirror, a comb of the High Priest's wife, and a necklace from the statue of Aphrodite. He steals all three and wins Chrysis, but remorse at his crimes turns his love to hatred. He asks Chrysis to appear in public, wearing the three items. The aroused people seize her and put her in prison, where she drinks poison and dies.

Aphron, *see* AFRON.

Apollo, a god (baritone) in GLUCK'S ALCESTE.

L'Apostrophe (The Attack), opera in one act by FRANÇAIX. Libretto by the composer, based on one of BALZAC's *Droll Tales*. Premiere: French Radio, 1947; Holland Music Festival, Amsterdam, July 1, 1951 (staged). The opera concerns the futile love of the hunchback Darnadas for the coquettish Tascherette, and his death at the hands of her jealous husband.

Apotheker, Der, *see* SPEZIALE, LO.

Aprila, o bella, Rafaele's serenade to Maliella in Act II of WOLF-FERRARI'S THE JEWELS OF THE MADONNA.

Apri la tua finestra, Osaka's serenade as

he impersonates the son of the sun-god in a marionette production in Act I of MASCAGNI's opera IRIS.

Aprite un po', Figaro's aria in Act IV of MOZART'S THE MARRIAGE OF FIGARO, expressing his belief that all men are fools where women are concerned, until their eyes are opened.

Arabella, opera in three acts by Richard STRAUSS. Libretto by Hugo von HOFMANNSTHAL, based on his story *Lucidor*. Premiere: Dresden Opera, July 1, 1933. American premiere: Metropolitan Opera, Feb. 10, 1955.

Characters: Count Waldner (bass); Adelaide, his wife (mezzo-soprano); Arabella, his daughter (soprano), a role created by Viorica Ursuleac; Zdenka, another daughter (soprano); Mandryka, a landowner (baritone); Matteo, an officer (tenor); Count Elemer, Arabella's suitor (tenor); Count Dominik, another suitor (baritone); Count Lamoral, a third suitor (bass); the "Fiakermilli" (soprano); Fortuneteller (soprano); servants, card players, a groom, a doctor. The action takes place in Vienna in 1860.

Act I. Salon of a Viennese hotel. There is no orchestral prelude. In financial difficulties, Count Waldner is determined to marry off his daughter Arabella to a rich man. The Count has a second daughter, Zdenka, but since he cannot afford to raise two girls in the style of wealthy bourgeois, he passes her off as a boy. Zdenka is in love with the officer Matteo, who, in turn, is interested in Arabella. Zdenka, out of love for Matteo, forges letters which she says were written to him by Arabella, insisting he keep the letters secret, in view of the fact that Arabella has three suitors. Then, to Arabella, Zdenka nobly promotes Matteo's cause. Arabella insists that when the right man comes along for her she will know who he is ("Aber der Richtige"). Meanwhile, Arabella's father has been trying to get Mandryka, a wealthy out-of-town resident, to become Arabella's husband. Mandryka, upon seeing Arabella's picture, instantly falls in love with her and comes to

Vienna to woo her. The Count is impressed by the size of Mandryka's wallet and gladly accepts Mandryka's offer to help himself to some of its contents ("Teschek, bedien' dich"). Mandryka decides to make his home in a hotel while pursuing Arabella. Meanwhile Arabella has met a new gentleman, Count Elemer, who has made a strong impression on her ("Mein Elemer"). As the act closes, Arabella prepares to go off to a masked ball with her sister Zdenka.

Act II. A ballroom in the Hotel Sperl in the Leopoldstadt district. Mandryka at last meets Arabella and finds her even more fascinating than her photograph. He tells her about himself while revealing the state of his feelings for her ("Ich habe eine Frau gehabt"). Arabella is impressed; a duet of their mutual interest follows ("Und du wirst mein Geliebter"). Mandryka now adds that if she were a Slavonic girl she would follow the Slavonic tradition of giving him a glass of water as a token of her acceptance of his proposal. Arabella requests an hour in which to make her decision. She then enters the ball where she is given a royal welcome by her admirers. Zdenka slips a letter to Matteo, supposedly written by Arabella, arranging a meeting at the hotel in a quarter of an hour. All this is overheard by Mandryka, who is convinced Arabella is deceiving him. He seeks solace with the coquette "Fiakermilli," who has attracted attention. The Count, however, assures Mandryka that he is mistaken about Arabella and will prove her innocence.

Act III. Hall of the hotel. An orchestral prelude describes the coming rendezvous between Arabella and Matteo. Arabella amuses herself by singing a simple folk tune ("Über seine Felder"). When Matteo sees her he becomes ardent and is amazed to find her so cold to him. The arrival of Mandryka and Count Waldner adds to the confusion, particularly after Mandryka challenges Matteo to a duel. Zdenka now breaks down, reveals herself to be a girl, and discloses she is the cause of the whole misunderstanding. Matteo now finds Zdenka to his liking and is ready to ask for her hand in marriage. Arabella then orders a servant to bring a glass of water to her upstairs. When Arabella descends the stairway she offers the water to Mandryka as a token of her acceptance of his proposal ("Das war sehr gut, Mandryka").

Strauss and von Hofmannsthal planned *Arabella* as a Viennese comedy in the style of their earlier DER ROSEN- KAVALIER. As in *Der Rosenkavalier,* this opera uses waltz music throughout the score, but with a good deal of the music also strongly influenced by Slavonic folk- songs. *Arabella* may lack the humanity, compassion, and surpassing eloquence of *Der Rosenkavalier* at its best, but nevertheless, it is a lovable opera, one of Strauss's best, filled with pages of wondrous music that is recognizably Straussian.

Arabella is the last opera in which Strauss worked with von Hofmannsthal. The librettist died only a few days after the opera had been completed.

Arabian Nights, a cycle of stories of Persian or Indian origin. Among the operas based on this tenth-century classic are: Benno Bardi's *Fatme;* THE BARBER OF BAGDAD; Issai DOBROWEN's *A Thousand and One Nights;* MÂROUF; Ernest REYER's *La Statue;* Bernhard Sekles' *Scheharazade;* Victor de SABATA's *Mille e una notte;* ABU HASSAN; Julia Weissberg's *Gulnara.*

ara o l'avello apprestami, L', Rodolfo's vow to kill Luisa and then commit suicide, in Act II of VERDI's LUISA MILLER.

Araquil, a soldier (tenor) in love with Anita in MASSENET's LA NAVARRAISE.

Archibaldo, blind king of Altura (bass) in MONTEMEZZI's L'AMORE DEI TRE RE, a role created by Nazareno DE ANGELIS.

Archy and Mehitabel, concert opera by George Kleinsinger. Libretto by Joe Darion, based on tales by Don Marquis. Premiere: New York, Dec. 6, 1954. The leading characters of this jazzy comedy are a philosophic cockroach, Archy, and an alley cat, Mehitabel. The story con- cerns Archy's attempts to shape Mehita- bel's destiny—a task made thankless by Mehitabel's inborn waywardness.

Arditi, Luigi, composer and conductor. Born Crescentino, Italy, July 22, 1822; died Hove, Eng., May 1, 1903. After attending the Milan Conservatory, he was appointed musical director of the Vercelli Opera in 1843. He left Italy in 1846 for Havana, where he conducted the premiere of his opera, *Il corsaro.* This was followed by appearances as conductor in the United States, where once again he led the premiere of one of his operas, *La spia,* in 1856. In 1858 he was made conductor at HIS MAJESTY's THEATRE in London. Subsequently he also conducted touring opera companies both in England and the United States, including one formed by MAPLESON with PATTI as its star. In 1885 and in 1889 he was conductor at COVENT GARDEN, and in 1891 he conducted a season of opera at Shaftesbury Theatre in London. On Apr. 2, 1892, he made his debut at the METROPOLITAN OPERA with MARTHA. His most famous composition is the vocal waltz, "Il bacio," which several sopranos have interpolated in the lesson scene in ROSSINI's THE BARBER OF SEVILLE.

Ardon gl' incensi, Lucia's "Mad Scene" in Act III, Scene 2, of DONIZETTI's LUCIA DI LAMMERMOOR.

A red-headed woman makes a choochoo jump its track, Crown's cynical blues melody, in Act III of GERSHWIN's PORGY AND BESS.

aria, an extended solo for voice in an opera (or oratorio). The earliest operas of PERI and CACCINI consisted entirely of RECITATIVES. One of the earliest true arias was the famous Lament in MON- TEVERDI's ARIANNA, performed in 1608. This single aria is the only portion of the music that has been preserved. A two-part aria has two contrasting sec- tions (A-B); the three-part, called an *aria da capo,* adds a repetition of the first part after the contrasting middle section (A-B-A). In the early eighteenth century the Italians standardized a num- ber of different styles of aria. The most important were: (1) the *aria canta-bile,* a free-flowing emotional melody in which the singer was permitted to introduce displays of vocal virtuosity through embellishments; (2) the *aria di portamento,* a dignified aria characterized by long notes and smooth delivery; (3) the *aria parlante,* a declamatory kind of song; (4) the *aria di bravura* or *d'agilità,* or *d'abilità,* a highly florid aria intended to display the singer's technique; (5) the *aria d'imitazione,* in which the voice and accompanying instruments imitated the sounds of nature; (6) the *aria di mezzo carattere,* an aria that stylistically is a compromise between an *aria cantabile* and an *aria d'agilità.* In eighteenth-century opera, it was the practice not to have two arias of the same variety follow in succession.

An *arietta* is a short and simple aria; an *arioso* is a vocal number, declamatory in character, which is a cross between a recitative and an aria.

The Italian aria, which dominated the operatic writing of the eighteenth and nineteenth centuries, was characterized by warmth of lyricism and florid passages and achieved an advanced stage of development in the writing of BELLINI, ROSSINI, DONIZETTI, and the earlier VERDI. A more dramatic sort of aria, simpler and more emotional, was evolved by GLUCK and developed further by WEBER. The formal aria was abandoned by WAGNER in his music dramas and by Verdi in OTELLO. The opera score now became a coherent and indivisible whole, without division between recitative and aria. This departure from the formal aria structure is found to an even more marked degree in BORIS GODUNOV, JENUFA, and PELLÉAS ET MÉLISANDE. In WOZZECK and other operas of the Schoenbergian school the aria assumes the inflections of speech (*see* SPRECHSTIMME).

Ariadne, a character in Greek legend, daughter of Minos and Pasphae. She is responsible for saving Theseus from the minotaur's labyrinth by means of a guiding thread. Theseus subsequently deserts her on Naxos, where she marries Dionysos. This subject was used by numerous composers including BENDA, HANDEL, Benedetto Marcello, MASSENET, MILHAUD, and Richard STRAUSS. (*See* ABANDON D'ARIANE, L', ARIADNE AUF NAXOS, and DÉLIVRANCE DE THÉSÉE, LA.)

Ariadne auf Naxos, (1) an early example of SINGSPIEL (1775) by Georg BENDA. MOZART admired it, and it may well have influenced him in the writing of his own *singspiel*-styled operas.

(2) Opera in one act by Richard STRAUSS. Libretto by Hugo von HOFMANNSTHAL. Premiere: Stuttgart, Oct. 24, 1912. American premiere: Philadelphia, Nov. 1, 1928. This is a play within a play. In the prologue an opera company is preparing to perform for a select audience in the private theater of a wealthy eighteenth-century patron. At his request, a serious and comic opera are now performed simultaneously, the story revolving around the lovesick Ariadne (soprano; a role created by Maria JERITZA), whom the frivolous Zerbinetta (soprano) and her three helpers vainly try to cheer and whose joy in life is ultimately reawakened by Bacchus (tenor). Notable numbers in the opera are Zerbinetta's coloratura aria, "So war es mit Pagliazzo" and her air, "Es gibt ob tanzen ob singen"; Ariadne's aria "Es gibt ein Reich"; and the trio of the nymphs, "Töne, Töne."

The Ariadne and Bacchus portion of this opera was originally given as a tail piece to MOLIÈRE's comedy *Le Bourgeois Gentilhomme,* for which Strauss had written the incidental music. But since the opera extended for over an hour and the production required both an opera company and the play company, Strauss and Hofmannsthal soon decided to convert it to a separate and self-sufficient operatic work in one act by adding the prologue. As such it was produced in Berlin in 1913. Though performed in various other cities, it was not successful, leading its authors to revise it once more. Strauss wrote a new overture, and the rest of the opera was revised both in text and music, a version introduced in Vienna on Oct. 4, 1916. Since then it has had many successful revivals.

Ariane, (1) Bluebeard's sixth wife (mezzo-soprano) in DUKAS's ARIANE ET BARBE-BLEUE, a role created by Georgette Leblanc.

(2) Principal female character (soprano) in MILHAUD's *opéra minute* L'ABANDON D'ARIANE.

Ariane et Barbe-bleue (Ariadne and Bluebeard), opera in three acts by DUKAS. Libretto is MAETERLINCK's play of the same name. Premiere: Opéra-Comique, May 10, 1907. American premiere: Metropolitan Opera, Mar. 23, 1911. Dukas's only opera, it is one of the finest French operas after PELLÉAS ET MÉLISANDE, though stylistically it is as derivative from WAGNER as it is from DEBUSSY. The score is marked both by subtlety of detail and massive brilliance. The story concerns Bluebeard's (bass) sixth wife, Ariane (mezzo-soprano), to whom he gives seven keys. Six, of silver, open vaults of precious jewels, and these she may use. But the seventh, of gold, intended for a strange door, is prohibited to her. She opens the door and finds Bluebeard's earlier wives. As Ariane frees them, she decides to leave her husband, but the other wives prefer to stay with him.

In its own time, *Ariane et Barbe-bleue* enjoyed numerous performances and was highly acclaimed. Within four years it was produced in Vienna, Brussels, New York (TOSCANINI conducting), and LA SCALA (in an Italian translation). Since the early 1910's, however, it has rarely been heard outside France. One of those rare occasions took place at COVENT GARDEN in 1937, where it was presented by the company of the PARIS OPÉRA as part of the coronation year festivities in England.

Arianna, opera in prologue and eight scenes by MONTEVERDI. Libretto by Ottavio RINUCCINI. Premiere: Mantua, May 28, 1608. Monteverdi wrote this opera as part of the celebration of Francesco Gonzaga's wedding. The score has been lost except for a few scraps and a single complete number, the Lament of Arianna ("Lasciatemi morire"), one of the most poignant lyric pages in the early history of opera, considered by many historians as the first aria ever written. Monteverdi subsequently rewrote the Lament into a five-voice madrigal, published in his sixth book of madrigals (1614). The contemporary German composer Carl ORFF edited and modernized the Lament.

The opera opened the TEATRO SAN MOÏSE, Venice's third public opera house, in 1640. In the twentieth century the surviving scene was reconstructed and revived in Karlsruhe in 1926 and in Paris in 1931.

Aricie, (1) Phèdre's sister (soprano) and her rival for the love of Phèdre's husband, Theseus, in MILHAUD's *opéra minute* LA DÉLIVRANCE DE THÉSÉE.

(2) Hippolytus' beloved (soprano) in RAMEAU's HIPPOLYTE ET ARICIE.

Arie, Raphael, basso. Born Sofia, Bulgaria, Aug. 22, 1920. He began studying voice when he was eighteen, having previously been trained on the violin. He made his concert debut in 1939. After the end of World War II, he became a member of the Sofia Opera. Winning first prize in a competition held in Geneva in 1946 led to his debut at LA SCALA, where he was heard as Archibaldo in L'AMORE DEI TRE RE in 1947. He has since been heard in most of Italy's leading opera houses. He created the role of Truelove in THE RAKE'S PROGRESS in Venice in 1951.

Ariosto, Lodovico, poet and dramatist. Born Reggio, Italy, Sept. 4, 1474; died Ferrara, June 6, 1533. Often referred to as "the divine Lodovico," he was the author of a masterwork of Renaissance literature, *Orlando furioso,* an epic of Roland. It was the source of numerous operas, including: HANDEL's ALCINA, *Ariodante,* and *Orlando;* MÉHUL's *Ariodante;* Luigi Rossi's *Il Palazzo d'Atlante incantanto;* Georg Caspar Schürmann's

Orlando furioso; and Joseph Touche-moulin's *Fuori di Orlando.* Other operas based on Ariosto's works are Francesca Caccini's *La Liberazione di Ruggiero,* Simone Mayr's *Ginevra di Scozia,* and J. F. REICHARDT's *Bradamante.*

Aristophanes, writer of comedies. Born Athens, Greece, about 450 B.C.; died about 380 B.C. Some of his brilliantly satirical comedies have been used for operas. Among them: *The Birds* (AURIC; BRAUNFELS); *The Frogs* (Granville Bantock); *Lysistrata* (Reinhold Glière; Raoul Gunsbourg; HUMPERDINCK; Victor de SABATA; SCHUBERT's *Der häusliche Krieg*); *Peace* (Marcel Delannoy); and *The Wasps* (VAUGHAN WILLIAMS).

Arkas, captain of the guards (bass) in GLUCK's IPHIGÉNIE EN AULIDE.

Arkel, King of Allemonde (bass) in DEBUSSY's PELLÉAS ET MÉLISANDE.

Arlecchino, Pantalone's servant (baritone), in love with Colombina, in WOLF-FERRARI's LE DONNE CURIOSE.

Arlecchino, oder Die Fenster (Harlequin, or The Windows), one-act opera by BUSONI. Libretto by the composer. Premiere: Zürich Opera, May 11, 1917. American premiere: New York, Oct. 11, 1951 (concert version). Busoni's text is modeled on the *commedia dell' arte.* It is set in Bergamo in the eighteenth century. A five-measure prelude brings on Harlequin (a speaking part) who explains to the audience: " 'Tis not for children, not for gods, this play; for understanding people 'tis designed." Four sections follow entitled "Harlequin as Rogue," "Harlequin as Soldier," "Harlequin as Husband," and "Harlequin as Conqueror." In the first, Harlequin makes love to Matteo's wife; in the second he is a recruiting officer who sends Matteo (baritone) off to war; in the third, he discovers his wife (Columbine; mezzo-soprano) with a rival and slays him with a wooden sword; in the fourth, the rival comes back to life, Matteo returns from the wars, and all the characters take their final bow. Busoni's score is filled with wit, satire, and parody, in which a soldier's march, a lover's serenade, and a love duet are mocked at gaily.

Arlésiana, L' (The Girl from Arles), opera originally in four acts, reduced to three in 1898, by CILÈA. Libretto by Leopoldo Marenco, based on DAUDET's play of the same name, for which BIZET composed the familiar incidental music. Premiere: Teatro Lirico, Milan, Nov. 27, 1897. American premiere: Philadelphia, Jan. 11, 1962. The story concerns the love of Federico (tenor) for Rosa Mamai (mezzo-soprano), a young woman of supposedly questionable reputation. His family stands in the way of their affair and arranges for him to marry a childhood sweetheart, Vivetta (soprano). On the eve of the wedding, Federico commits suicide by throwing himself out of the farmhouse loft. Cilèa's score is noteworthy for its effective use of French folksongs. The most famous aria in the opera is Federico's lament (Lamento di Federico) in Act II, "E la solita storia." Also of interest are the aria of Baldassare (bass), a shepherd, in Act I, "Come due tizzi," and Rosa's third-act prayer, "Esser madre è un inferno."

Armida, (1) the central character in a dramatic poem by TASSO, *La Gerusalemme liberata.* The poem has been the source of several operas. Besides those listed below there are RINALDO, as well as operas entitled *Armida* (or *Armide*) by Benedetto Ferrari, JOMMELLI, SALIERI, and Tommaso TRAETTA.

(2) Opera in four acts by DVOŘÁK. Libretto by Jaroslav Vrchlicky, based on a Czech translation from TASSO. Premiere: National Theater, Prague, Mar. 25, 1904. This, Dvořák's last opera, was described by his biographer Gervase Hughes as a "hotchpotch," partly Wagnerian in style, partly Verdian, partly pseudo-oriental. "The extraordinary thing," says Hughes, "is that there are at the most no more than two or three passages of any length in the whole work which are unmistakably recognizable as being characteristic of Dvořák."

(3) Opera by HAYDN. Libretto by Jacopo Durandi. Premiere: Esterház, Hungary, Feb. 26, 1784. American premiere: New York City, 1969.

(4) Opera in three acts by ROSSINI. Libretto by Giovanni Schmidt. Premiere: San Carlo Opera, Nov. 11, 1817. It was revived at the FLORENCE MAY MUSIC FESTIVAL in 1952, starring Maria CALLAS.

See also ARMIDE; ARMIDE ET RENAUD.

Armide, opera in five acts by GLUCK. Libretto by QUINAULT, based on TASSO's poem. Premiere: Paris Opéra, Sept. 23, 1777. American premiere: Metropolitan Opera, Nov. 14, 1910. The charming ballet music in Act V, accompanying the dances and tableaux with which Armide (soprano) entertains Rinaldo at her palace, is still occasionally heard, particularly in the concert suites arranged by Felix MOTTL and by François Gevaert. Two arias deserve mention: Rinaldo's (tenor) in Act II, "Plus j'observe ces lieux," and Armide's in Act III, "Ah! si la liberté."

Armide et Renaud, opera by LULLY. Libretto by QUINAULT, based on TASSO. Premiere: Paris Opéra, Feb. 5, 1686. American premiere: New York City, Feb. 2, 1953 (concert version). This was Lully's penultimate opera. Its principal aria is that of Renaud in Act II, "Plus j'observe."

Arne, Thomas Augustine, composer. Born London, Mar. 12, 1710; died there Mar. 5, 1778. Originally directed to law, he studied the violin and spinet in secret and acquired such proficiency that his father finally removed all objections to a musical career. In 1733 his first opera, *Rosamond* (libretto by Joseph Addison), was produced and well received. Other operas and MASQUES followed until 1738, when he achieved a triumph with his music for MILTON's *Comus*. In 1740 he wrote the masque *Alfred,* in which the celebrated anthem "Rule, Britannia" appears. Five years later he became the official composer for Vauxhall Gardens. During this period he wrote incidental music for many of

SHAKESPEARE's plays; some of his settings of Shakespeare's lyrics are among his finest creations. In 1759 he received an honorary doctorate in music from Oxford. His last years were darkened by domestic troubles, poor health, and financial problems. His best operas and masques: *Rosamond* (1733); *Dido and Aeneas* (1734); *Comus* (1738); *The Judgment of Paris* (1740); *Alfred* (1740); *Britannia* (1755); ARTAXERXES (1762); *L'Olimpiade* (1764); *The Fairy Prince* (1771).

Arnold, Swiss patriot (tenor) in ROSSINI's WILLIAM TELL, a role created by Adolphe NOURRIT.

Arnolfo, a rich landowner (bass) in WOLF-FERRARI's L'AMORE MEDICO.

Arnould, Sophie, soprano. Born Paris, Feb. 13, 1740; died there Oct. 22, 1802. After studying with Marie Fel and Mlle. Hippolyte Clairon she became a member of the Chapelle Royale. She made her debut at the PARIS OPÉRA on Dec. 15, 1757. For more than twenty years one of the stars of the Opéra, she created the leading soprano role in GLUCK's IPHIGÉNIE EN AULIDE in 1774. She went into retirement in 1778. She is the central character of the opera by Gabriel PIERNÉ, *Sophie Arnould,* introduced at the OPÉRA-COMIQUE in Paris on Feb. 21, 1927.

Arrêtez, ô mes frères, Samson's aria to the Hebrews in Act I of SAINT-SAËNS's SAMSON ET DALILA, urging them to praise God and not to bewail their bondage to the Philistines but to take heart and burst their chains.

Arrigo, a commoner (tenor) in love with Elena in VERDI's THE SICILIAN VESPERS.

Arroyo, Martina, soprano. Born New York City, Feb. 2, 1940. She first attracted attention in 1958 in New York in the American premiere of L'ASSASSINIO NELLA CATTEDRALE. Winning the METROPOLITAN OPERA Auditions the same year brought her a contract from that company, where she made her debut as the off-stage celestial voice in DON CARLOS on Mar. 14, 1959. She continued appearing in minor roles at the Metropolitan

Opera for some years while performing major roles in several European opera houses, including the VIENNA STATE OPERA and the BERLIN DEUTSCHE STAATS-OPER. Since 1963 she has been a principal soprano of the ZÜRICH OPERA. On Feb. 18, 1965, on less than two days' notice, she substituted for Birgit NILSSON in the title role of AIDA at the Metropolitan Opera. By virtue of this highly acclaimed performance she was henceforth assigned such leading roles as Leonora in IL TROVATORE, Elizabeth in DON CARLOS, DONNA ELVIRA, the title roles of MADAMA BUTTERFLY and *Aida,* and her first major Wagnerian part, that of ELSA. Since then she has also appeared in most of Europe's leading opera houses and festivals. In addition she has enjoyed an outstanding career in the concert hall, particularly in the modern repertory, and she was chosen by Karlheinz Stockhausen to sing in the world and American premieres of his avant-garde cantata, *Momente.*

Arsace, young warrior (contralto), son of Semiramis, in ROSSINI'S SEMIRAMIDE.

Artaxerxes, King of Persia in the fifth century, B.C. He is the central character of one of METASTASIO's most celebrated librettos, which was set to music by numerous composers. Thomas ARNE'S *Artaxerxes,* introduced at COVENT GARDEN on Feb. 2, 1762, is considered the only significant serious opera by an English composer in the eighteenth century. Leonardo Vinci was the first composer to write an opera on this Metastasio text, in 1730. Other composers to do so included GLUCK, in 1741, his first opera; also J. C. BACH, CIMAROSA, GALUPPI, GRAUN, HASSE, JOMMELLI, PAISIELLO, and PICCINNI.

Artemis (or **Diana**), goddess (soprano) in GLUCK'S IPHIGÉNIE EN AULIDE.

artists in opera, *see* PAINTERS AND PAINTINGS IN OPERA.

Artôt, Désirée (Marguerite Josephine Désirée Montagney Artôt), mezzo-soprano. Born Paris, July 21, 1835; died Berlin, Apr. 3, 1907. The daughter of a horn professor at the Brussels Conservatory, she studied singing with Pauline VIARDOT-GARCÍA, after which she toured Belgium, Holland, and England in concert appearances. MEYERBEER having engaged her for the PARIS OPÉRA, she made a notable debut as Fidès in his LE PROPHÈTE, Feb. 5, 1858. Despite her success in Paris, she soon embarked on an extensive tour of Italy. Late in 1859 she scored a major success in Berlin, and soon after was a sensation in London, particularly in several ROSSINI operas. During the next decade she sang in Germany and England with outstanding success, though now as a soprano rather than a mezzo-soprano. She visited Russia in 1868. TCHAIKOVSKY proposed marriage to her but she chose, instead, the Spanish baritone Mariano Padilla y Ramos. For the next few years she and her husband appeared in opera performances in Germany, Austria, and Russia. She retired from the stage in 1887, thereafter teaching singing in Berlin and later (after 1889) in Paris.

Arundell, Dennis, producer and director. Born London, July 22, 1898. After studying the piano from childhood on, he attended St. John's College, Cambridge, where he was a pupil in music of Cyril Rootham and Charles Villiers STANFORD and where, after completing his studies, he was made a Fellow. His career as producer of operas began in Cambridge in 1922 with Rootham's *The Two Sisters.* Three years later, also in Cambridge, he produced the first staged version of HANDEL's oratorio *Semele.* From then on he produced or staged major works by HONEGGER, STRAVINSKY, PURCELL, WOLF-FERRARI, WEINBERGER, BENJAMIN, and BRITTEN as well as works from the standard repertory (TOSCA, FAUST, WERTHER, DER FLIEGENDE HOLLÄNDER, etc.) for various opera companies, including SADLER'S WELLS and COVENT GARDEN. He is the composer of two operas, *Ghost of Abel* and *A Midsummer Night's Dream;* translator into English of several opera librettos; and author of a biography of Purcell (1927), *The Critic at the Opera* (1957), and *The Story of Sadler's Wells* (1963).

Arvino, Pagano's brother (tenor), husband of Viclinda, in VERDI'S I LOMBARDI.

Ase, Aelfrida's servant (mezzo-soprano) in TAYLOR'S THE KING'S HENCHMAN.

A Serpina penserete, Serpina's aria in Act II of PERGOLESI'S LA SERVA PADRONA, in which she tries to arouse the jealousy of her employer, Uberto.

Ashby, Wells-Fargo agent (bass) in PUCCINI'S THE GIRL OF THE GOLDEN WEST.

Ashton, Lord Enrico (or Henry), head of the house of Lammermoor (baritone), Lucia's brother, in DONIZETTI'S LUCIA DI LAMMERMOOR.

Aspen Music Festival, a festival held each summer in Aspen, in the Rocky Mountains region of Colorado. It was an outgrowth of the GOETHE Bicentennial, celebrated in Aspen in 1949. Before the festival was officially launched, opera performances were given annually between 1951 and 1953: COSÌ FAN TUTTE (in concert version) in 1951; BASTIEN UND BASTIENNE and the world premiere of Alexander TCHEREPNIN's *The Farmer and the Fairy* (commissioned by the Aspen Institute for Humanistic Studies) in 1952; and a concert version of ROSSINI'S LA CENERENTOLA in 1953.

The music festival came into being in 1954 in conjunction with the founding of a music school, the director of both the school and the festival being Walter F. Paepcke, chairman of the Aspen Institute for Humanistic Studies. Festival performances take place several times a week in an amphitheater. Izler Solomon was director and conductor until the summer of 1962, when he was succeeded by Walter Susskind. Each festival season offers operatic performances at the Wheeler Opera House, produced by the Aspen Opera Workshop. Works from the standard repertory, together with novelties, revivals, and modern works are given. Among the latter have been: THE BEAR; LA CAMBIALE DI MATRIMONIO; COMEDY ON THE BRIDGE; *La Contrebasse* (SAUGUET, an American premiere); *The Country Doctor* (HENZE); *The Diary of a Madman* (SEARLE, an American premiere); LE DOCTEUR MIRACLE; *Un Education manqué* (CHABRIER); HIN UND ZURÜCK; LES MALHEURS D'ORPHÉE; MAVRA;

L'ORFEO (in ORFF's adaptation); *The Pet Shop* (Rieti); *Polifem* (BONONCINI); LO SPEZIALE.

Asrael, opera in four acts by FRANCHETTI. Libretto by Ferdinand Fontana, based on an old Flemish legend. Premiere: Teatro Reggio, Emilia, Italy, Feb. 11, 1888. American premiere: Metropolitan Opera, Nov. 26, 1890 (opening night of season). Asrael and Nefta are angels. Losing Nefta, Asrael searches for her in hell and on earth. After numerous vicissitudes, he is reunited with her in heaven.

Assad, Sulamith's betrothed (tenor) in GOLDMARK'S THE QUEEN OF SHEBA.

Assassinio nella cattedrale, L' (Murder in the Cathedral), opera in two acts and interlude by PIZZETTI. Libretto by the composer, based on T. S. Eliot's poetical drama of the same name, in Albert Castelli's Italian version. Premiere: La Scala, Mar. 1, 1958. American premiere: New York, Sept. 17, 1958. The principal character is Thomas à Becket (bass), the twelfth-century Archbishop of Canterbury appointed by Henry II, who upholds church authority against the interests and ambitions of the king. Because of this, he is assassinated in the Canterbury Cathedral by four knights in the king's service. Though the opera is principally in a recitative style, it has a number of highly emotional arias and several stirring choruses. A musical motive, representing the Archbishop, recurs throughout the opera. This opera is considered the composer's most significant since FRA GHERARDO.

assedio di Corinto, L', *see* SIÈGE DE CORINTHE, LE.

Associated Opera Companies of America, an organization founded in 1967 on a grant from the Martha Baird Rockefeller Fund, with Russell C. Wunderlic as chairman of the board and Aurelio Fabiani as president. Its offices are in Philadelphia, and its aim is to share new sets and costumes (particularly of expensive productions) among various smaller American opera companies. The first production under this arrangement was BORIS GODUNOV by the

BALTIMORE CIVIC OPERA on Nov. 2, 1967.

assoluta, Italian for "absolute." A *prima donna assoluta* is the leading singer of an opera company.

Assur, a prince (baritone) in GOLD-MARK'S THE QUEEN OF SHEBA.

Astaroth, slave (soprano) in GOLD-MARK'S THE QUEEN OF SHEBA.

Astrologer, The, a character (tenor) in RIMSKY-KORSAKOV'S LE COQ D'OR, to whom the prologue and epilogue are assigned, besides a part in the opera itself.

As when the dove laments her love, Galatea's beautiful air in HANDEL'S MASQUE ACIS AND GALATEA.

Atalanta, opera in three acts by HANDEL. Libretto adapted by an unidentified author from Belisario Valeriani's *La caccia in etolia.* Premiere: Covent Garden, May 12, 1736. Handel wrote this opera as part of the celebration of the marriage of the Prince of Wales to Princess Auguste of Saxe-Gotha. One of the most celebrated arias Handel ever wrote is found here, "Care selve," sung by the heroine. Another soprano aria, "Come alla tortella," is also of interest.

A tanto amor, Alfonso's aria as he reluctantly awards Leonora to Fernando, in Act III of DONIZETTI'S LA FAVORITA.

A te, o cara, amor talora, Arthur Talbot's ROMANCE in Act I of BELLINI'S I PURITANI.

A terra! si, nel livido, Desdemona's lament over the loss of her husband's love, in Act III of VERDI'S OTELLO.

Athanaël, a cenobite monk (baritone) in MASSENET'S THAÏS.

Atlantída, L' (Atlantis), a scenic cantata in three parts and prologue by FALLA (completed by Ernesto Halffter). Libretto by the composer, based on Jacinto Verdaguer's poem of the same name. Premiere: Barcelona, Nov. 24, 1961 (concert version); La Scala, June 18, 1962 (staged). American premiere: New York City, Sept. 29, 1962 (concert version). The Catalonian epic poem on which this text is based tells first about the submersion by flood of the continent of Atlantis. It then goes on to describe how Spain is saved from the monster Hercules; how the port of Barcelona came to be built; and finally how Columbus, seeking to solve the mystery of the Atlantic Ocean, comes upon the New World.

This is Falla's most ambitious work for the stage. He labored on it for almost a quarter of a century and was still occupied with it when he died in Argentina, leaving it uncompleted. Unlike so many other Falla compositions, which are characterized by their Spanish national folk idioms, this work has strong liturgical elements. The writing is often modal and considerable stress is placed on polyphony. Choral passages, such as the exalted hymn thanking God for saving Spain that ends the prologue or the Alleluia with which the scenic cantata closes, are remarkably effective. So is the moving aria sung by Columbus, "Supreme night," when, alone on the bridge of his ship, he surveys the sea and the skies about him. The whole work is pervaded with deep religious conviction, mysticism, and an exalted spirituality.

atonality, a term referring to contemporary music in which there is a calculated avoidance of anything suggestive of a normal tonal center and key relationships. Alban BERG'S WOZZECK is probably the most famous opera written in an atonal style. Many other modern operas have been written using TWELVE-TONE or SERIAL TECHNIQUES, two methods that are outgrowths of ATONALITY.

À travers le desert, Mârouf's aria concerning the supposed riches of his caravan, in Act II of RABAUD'S MÂROUF.

Atterberg, Kurt, composer. Born Göteborg, Sweden, Dec. 12, 1887. He combined a training in engineering with musical studies at the Stockholm Conservatory and private lessons with Max von SCHILLINGS. For many years he was employed at the Royal Patent Bureau, while pursuing the careers of music critic, conductor, and composer. A government subsidy finally enabled him to give up his extramusical occupations. In

1940 he became Secretary of the Royal Academy of Music in Stockholm. His music has drawn melodic and rhythmic ideas from Swedish folk sources. His operas: *Härward der Harfner* (1918); *Bäckahästen* (1924); *Fanal* (1932); *Aladdin* (1941); *The Tempest* (1947).

At the Boar's Head, opera in one act by Gustav HOLST. Libretto by the composer, based on SHAKESPEARE's HENRY IV, Parts I and II. Premiere: Manchester, Eng., Apr. 3, 1925. American premiere: New York, Feb. 16, 1935. It was revived in New York in a concert performance on Jan. 27, 1970.

Attila, opera in three acts and prologue by VERDI. Libretto by Temistocle Solera. Premiere: Venice, Mar. 17, 1846. American premiere: Niblo's Garden, New York, Apr. 15, 1850. Its theme is the murder of Attila by Odabella, his intended bride, during the invasion of Italy by the Huns. A number of arias and ensemble numbers have interest: the second-act bass aria, "Dagli immortali vertici," and the third-act trio, "Te sol quest' anima," for example. To some musicologists the tenor aria, "Si, quello io son," is a forerunner of the music in the finale of Act II of LA TRAVIATA. The immense success enjoyed by *Attila* when first produced was not for its melodies but for its capacity to arouse the patriotic ardor of the audience. One of its lines invariably brought down the house: "Avrai tu l'universo, resti l'Italia a me" ("Take the whole universe, but leave Italy to me").

aubade, a French term (derived from *aube,* "dawn") originally applied to music suitable for performance in the morning, as distinct from evening music —nocturnes and serenades. In operatic usage, an aubade is an aria of light, often sentimental nature.

Auber, Daniel François, composer. Born Caen, France, Jan. 29, 1782; died Paris, May 12, 1871. One of the earliest masters of OPÉRA COMIQUE, Auber was trained for business but his passion for music led him to study three years with Luigi CHERUBINI and then undertake composition. His early operas had a lukewarm reception, but in 1820 *La Bergère châtelaine* was a major success in Paris. From then until 1869 Auber wrote over forty operas— both serious and comic—many to librettos by Eugène SCRIBE. His best ones were outstandingly successful, and there were few seasons in which Paris did not see at least one new work by Auber. LA MUETTE DE PORTICI (1828) —also known as *Masaniello*—was his greatest success and set off the Belgian revolution against the Dutch when performed at Brussels in 1830. FRA DIAVOLO (1830) and LE DOMINO NOIR (1837) were close rivals. In 1829 Auber became a member of the French Academy. In 1842 he was appointed director of the Paris Conservatory, a post he held until his death. In 1857 he was made MAÎTRE DE CHAPELLE to Napoleon III. Auber died soon after witnessing the first riots of the Paris Commune in 1871. His best operas after those mentioned above: *Emma* (1821); *Le Concert à la cour* (1824); *Fiorella* (1826); *Le Philtre* (1831); *Le Cheval de bronze* (1835); *Les Diamants de la couronne* (1841); *Au Part du diable* (1843); *La Sirène* (1844); *La Barcarolle* (1845); *Zerline* (1851); MANON LESCAUT (1856); *La Fiancée du Roi de Gerbe* (1864); *Le Premier Jour de bonheur* (1868); *Le Rêve d'amour* (1869).

Au bruit de la guerre (Io vidi la luce nel camp guerir), duet of Sulpizio and Marie describing the joys of regimental life, in Act I of DONIZETTI's THE DAUGHTER OF THE REGIMENT.

Au bruit des lourds marteaux, Vulcan's song in Act I of GOUNOD's PHILÉMON ET BAUCIS.

Aucassin et Nicolette, a French romance of the thirteenth century about Aucassin's love for Nicolette, a captured Saracen girl who turns out to be a princess. Eventually the lovers are united. The story was made into operas by Günther Bialas, CASTELNUOVO-TEDESCO, August Enna, GRÉTRY, John Knowles Paine, Clifton Parker, Johann von

Piszl, and Renzo Rosselini, among others.

Auden, W. H., poet. Born York, Eng., Feb. 21, 1907. In collaboration with Chester KALLMAN, he wrote the librettos for THE RAKE'S PROGRESS, DIE BASSARIDEN, and THE ELEGY FOR YOUNG LOVERS. They also translated into English DON GIOVANNI, THE MAGIC FLUTE, and WEILL's *Die sieben Todensünden*. Without the benefit of collaboration, he provided the text for BRITTEN's first opera, *Paul Bunyan* (which has never been published and was withdrawn after a few performances in New York, 1941).

Auf hohen Felsen lag' ich träumend, Erik's description of his dream in which he sees a strange ship moored in port, in Act II of WAGNER's DER FLIEGENDE HOLLÄNDER.

Au fond du temple, duet of Nadir and Zurga recalling their one-time friendship, broken by their rivalry for Leila, in Act I of BIZET's LES PÊCHEURS DE PERLES. This is one of the most celebrated male duets in French opera.

Aufsteig und Fall der Stadt Mahagonny, *see* RISE AND FALL OF THE CITY MAHAGONNY, THE.

Augusta Tabor, see TABOR, AUGUSTA.

Au Mont Ida, *see* JUGEMENT DE PARIS, LE.

A una fonta afflitto e solo, Elvira's soliloquy in Act III of BELLINI's I PURITANI.

A un dottor della mia sorte, Bartolo's aria in Act I, Scene 2, of ROSSINI's THE BARBER OF SEVILLE, when he takes Rosina to task for trying to deceive a man of his high station.

Auric, Georges, composer and opera manager. Born Lodève, France, Feb. 15, 1899. He was a pupil of Vincent D'INDY and Albert ROUSSEL. He came to prominence in the early 1920's, when his name was linked with those of five other young French composers (including MILHAUD, HONEGGER, and POULENC) in a group called The SIX. Auric later achieved success as a composer of scores for ballets and motion pictures. He wrote only one opera, *Sous le Masque,* in one act (text by Louis Laloy). Between 1962 and 1967 he was the director of both the PARIS OPÉRA and the OPÉRA-COMIQUE. For many years he was also the director of SACEM (the French equivalent of the American Society of Composers, Authors, and Publishers), and in July, 1968, he was elected president of the Congress of International Societies of Authors and Composers meeting in Vienna.

Au secours de notre fille (Ti rincora, amata figlia), chorus of the French soldiers in Act II of DONIZETTI's THE DAUGHTER OF THE REGIMENT, loudly expressing their determination to protect Marie from marrying anybody except the man she loves.

Aus einem Totenhaus, *see* FROM THE HOUSE OF THE DEAD.

Austral, Florence (born Wilson), soprano. Born Melbourne, Australia, Apr. 26, 1894; died Sydney, Australia, May 15, 1968. She attended the Melbourne Conservatory, the London School of Opera, and in 1918 studied privately with Sibella in New York. At this point she was offered a contract with the METROPOLITAN OPERA but refused it, feeling she was not yet ready for such an appearance. Her debut took place at COVENT GARDEN in 1922 when she sang Brünnhilde in DIE WALKÜRE. She was an immediate success. Subsequently she appeared in the entire RING cycle at Covent Garden. In 1925 she made her American debut at the Evanston and Cincinnati festivals, thereafter appearing five successive seasons in song recitals and guest opera appearances. After 1930 she was a leading soprano of the BERLIN STATE OPERA. Her last American tour took place in 1935–1936. She returned to the Berlin State Opera and appeared there until the outbreak of World War II. After the war, and until 1959, she taught singing at the Newcastle Conservatory in Australia.

Autrefois un roi de Thulé (King of Thulé), a folklike ballad sung by Marguerite as she prepares for bed in Part III of BERLIOZ' THE DAMNATION OF FAUST.

Avant de quitter ces lieux, Valentin's aria in Act II of GOUNOD's FAUST, expressing concern over the safety of his sister, Marguerite, since he is about to leave for the army.

Ave Maria, Desdemona's prayer in Act IV of VERDI's OTELLO.

Avis de clochettes, *see* OÙ VA LA JEUNE HINDOUE?

Avito, a former prince of Altura (tenor), lover of Fiora, in MONTEMEZZI's L'AMORE DEI TRE RE.

A woman is a sometime thing, Jake's cynical opinion of woman's fickleness, in Act I of GERSHWIN's PORGY AND BESS.

Azora, opera in three acts by HADLEY.

Libretto by David Stevens. Premiere: Chicago Opera, Dec. 26, 1917. The setting is Mexico in the fifteenth century. Azora is to marry an Aztec general, but she loves Xalca. When Xalca asks for Azora's hand, Montezuma orders both killed. But a beam of light falling on the couple and on a white cross is interpreted as a divine message, and the lovers are freed and allowed to marry.

Azucena, a gypsy (contralto), Manrico's mother. in VERDI's IL TROVATORE.

B

Baba Mustapha, a cadi (tenor) in CORNELIUS' THE BARBER OF BAGDAD.

Babekan, a Persian prince (baritone) in WEBER's OBERON.

Babinsky, a robber (baritone) in WEINBERGER's ŠVANDA THE BAGPIPER.

Baby Doe, principal character (soprano) and wife of the miner in Douglas MOORE's THE BALLAD OF BABY DOE.

Baccaloni, Salvatore, basso. Born Rome, Apr. 14, 1900; died New York City, Dec. 31, 1969. He studied architecture, receiving his degree at twenty-one. Giuseppe Kaschmann directed him to music and taught him singing. Baccaloni made his debut in Rome in 1921 in THE BARBER OF SEVILLE. In 1926 Arturo TOSCANINI engaged him for LA SCALA and advised him to concentrate on *buffo* roles. While a member of La Scala, Baccaloni also sang at other leading European opera houses. In 1934 he was made a Knight of the Crown of Italy. Meantime his American debut had taken place with the CHICAGO OPERA during the 1930–31 season. He first appeared at the METROPOLITAN OPERA on Dec. 3, 1940, in *The Barber of Seville;* three weeks later he was acclaimed in DON

PASQUALE, revived for him. He remained with the Metropolitan Opera until the end of the 1960–61 season, appearing there again in 1962 in L'ELISIR D'AMORE and LA FORZA DEL DESTINO. His last performance at the Metropolitan was in the latter opera on Feb. 14, 1962. During this period he also appeared with most of the world's leading opera companies, toured the United States with his own company, gave concerts, and in the early 1960's appeared in the motion pictures *Fanny* and *The Pigeon That Took Rome.* Baccaloni's repertory included nearly one hundred fifty roles in five languages. He was most famous for his Don Pasquale, Dr. BARTOLO, Dr. DULCAMARA, FALSTAFF, LEPORELLO, OSMIN, and ALFONSO.

bacchanale, an orgiastic dance of no special musical form, performed by a ballet corps. Notable operatic bacchanales are those in SAMSON ET DALILA and TANNHÄUSER, and in the twentieth century in KING ROGER and MOSES UND ARON.

Bacchus, a god (tenor), in Richard STRAUSS's ARIADNE AUF NAXOS, a role created by Hermann JADLOWKER.

Bach, Johann Christian, composer. Born Leipzig, Sept. 3, 1735; died London, Jan. 1, 1782. He is known as the English Bach because of his long residence in England. This youngest son of Johann Sebastian Bach studied with his brother Carl Philipp Emanuel in Berlin and Padre Martini in Italy. His first opera, *Artaserse,* was well received when introduced in Turin in 1761. With two succeeding operas his fame grew so great that he was invited to write an opera for the KING'S THEATRE in London. This was *Orione,* a gratifying success when presented in 1763. The same year Bach was appointed Music Master to Queen Charlotte, a post he held until his death. In 1772 Bach was called to Mannheim to produce a new opera for the Elector Karl Theodor. The work, brilliantly produced, was *Temistocle.* It was a triumphant success. Bach's later operas fared less well. Fashions were changing—the new operas of GLUCK were winning favor—and Bach, though a sensitive orchestrator and a fine melodist, continued to write essentially undramatic works in the older Italian style. Bach's best operas, besides those already mentioned: *Alessandro nell' Indie* (1762); *Lucio Silla* (1776); *La clemenza di Scipione* (1778); *Amadis des Gaules* (1779).

Bacon, Ernst, composer. Born Chicago, Ill., May 26, 1898. His teachers included Ernest Bloch and Eugene GOOSSENS. He has held teaching and directorial posts with various conservatories and colleges, including Hamilton College and the School of Music at Syracuse University. His first operas, both to texts by Paul Horgan, were *A. Lincoln* and *A Tree on the Plains.* The latter was premiered in New York in 1943 and received the David Bispham medal. A DRUMLIN LEGEND, commissioned by the ALICE M. DITSON FUND, was introduced in New York in 1949. Bacon received a Pulitzer Traveling Fellowship in 1932 and Guggenheim fellowships in 1939 and 1942.

Badings, Henk, composer. Born Bandeong, Java, Jan. 17, 1907. After completing his music study with Willem Pijper, in 1934, he became professor of composition at the Music Lyceum in Amsterdam and in 1938 its codirector. He also taught composition at the Rotterdam Conservatory during this period. When the Nazis occupied Holland, he was appointed director of the Conservatory at The Hague. After World War II, he was found guilty of having collaborated with the Nazis and was eliminated from public life in music for two years. Subsequently his case was reexamined, and he was exonerated. Badings has produced important concert works as well as ballets and operas. His first important opera was *The Night Watch* (1942), which had to wait until May 13, 1950, for its premiere in Antwerp. In the early 1950's Badings became interested in ELECTRONIC MUSIC. He had an electronic studio built at Eindhoven, becoming its director in 1960 when the studio became affiliated with the University of Utrecht. Badings has used electronic sounds in his later operas, *Salto Mortale* and MARTIN KORDA, D. P., the latter receiving its world premiere at the HOLLAND MUSIC FESTIVAL on June 15, 1960. Since 1962 Badings has been professor of composition at the Hochschule für Musik in Stuttgart.

Bahr-Mildenburg, Anna (born von Mildenburg), soprano. Born Vienna, Nov. 29, 1872; died there Jan. 27, 1947. After studying voice in Vienna with Rosa Papier and Polini, she made her operatic debut in Hamburg in 1895. Two years later she made her first appearance at the BAYREUTH Festival as ORTRUD. She achieved her first major successes in Hamburg, mainly in the Wagnerian repertory. On June 6, 1906, she made an impressive debut at COVENT GARDEN as ISOLDE, and from 1908 until 1917 she was one of the principal sopranos of the Vienna Royal Opera (VIENNA STATE OPERA). After retiring from the stage, she devoted herself to teaching voice, first in Munich and later in Berlin. Between 1921 and 1926 she was the stage director of the MUNICH OPERA. She was the wife of the famous writer Hermann Bahr, whom she married in 1909 and with whom she wrote *Bayreuth und das Wagner-Theater* (1910).

Bald prangt, den Morgen, the song of the three pages hailing the sun as a dissipator of darkness and superstition, in Act II, Scene 6, of MOZART'S THE MAGIC FLUTE.

Balducci, the Pope's treasurer (bass) in BERLIOZ' BENVENUTO CELLINI.

Balfe, Michael William, composer and baritone. Born Dublin, May 15, 1808; died Rowney Abbey, Eng., Oct. 20, 1870. He went to London in his sixteenth year, earning his living as a violinist and singer. Sponsored by Count Mazzara, he went to Italy to study with Vicenzo Federici and Filippo Galli. Balfe wrote his first ambitious score, a ballet, in Milan (1826). Through his friendship with ROSSINI he became principal baritone of the Italian Opera in Paris, appearing in the French premiere of THE BARBER OF SEVILLE in 1829. In the same year his first opera, *I rivali di se stesso,* was performed in Palermo. In 1835 *The Siege of Rochelle* was given successfully in London. On Nov. 27, 1843, the comic opera by which he is chiefly remembered, THE BOHEMIAN GIRL, started a sensational run in London and was soon given on the Continent in several different languages. Between 1846 and 1856 Balfe traveled widely in connection with various productions of his operas. In 1864 he retired to his estate. After his death his statue was placed in the vestibule of DRURY LANE, the theater in which he had often sung and in which most of his works had first been seen. His principal operas: *The Siege of Rochelle* (1835); *Maid of Artois* (1836); *Joan of Arc* (1837); *Falstaff* (1838); *The Bohemian Girl* (1843); *The Maid of Honour* (1847); *The Armourer of Nantes* (1863); *Blanche de Nevers* (1863); *The Knight of the Leopard* (*Il talismano*) (1874).

ballabile, a popular dance less pretentious than a ballet. A *ballabile* is danced in the triumphal scene, Act II, Scene 2, of AIDA by a small group of girls from the ballet corps.

Ballad of Baby Doe, The, opera in two acts by Douglas MOORE. Libretto by John Latouche. Premiere: Central City, Col., July 7, 1956.

Characters: (Elizabeth) Baby Doe (soprano); Horace Tabor (baritone); Augusta Tabor, his wife (mezzo-soprano); Samantha, her maid (mezzo-soprano); Mama McCourt, Baby Doe's mother (contralto); Father Chapelle, a priest (tenor); Chester A. Arthur, President of the United States (tenor); William Jennings Bryan, Democratic candidate for the Presidency (bass); Silver Dollar, Tabor's daughter (mezzo-soprano); miners and their wives, servants, guests at parties, and so forth. The action takes place in Colorado, in Washington, D.C., and in California, 1880–1899.

Act I, Scene 1. Outside the Opera House. A drunk is boasting that Horace Tabor, mayor of the town, is in the market for a worthless silver mine, the Matchless Mine. Soon Tabor and his cronies emerge from the Opera House, having been bored by the concert (a recital by Adelina PATTI). He is followed by his culture-loving wife, Augusta, who upbraids him severely for his behavior. Meekly, Tabor and his cronies go back into the auditorium but not before a newcomer to town, Baby Doe, has passed by and attracted Tabor's interest.

Scene 2. Outside the Clarendon Hotel. The Tabors, returning home from the concert, are in good spirits. Tabor stops outside the hotel and, through an open window, notices Baby Doe at the piano, accompanying herself in a sentimental ballad. He applauds her performance, which brings her to the window and gives Tabor an opportunity to serenade her.

Scene 3. Living room of the Tabors' apartment in the hotel. Several weeks have gone by. In cleaning Horace's desk, Augusta discovers a canceled check showing he has purchased Matchless Mine; also some verses betraying his interest in Baby Doe. When Tabor defends not only his purchase but even his affection for a young, attractive girl, Augusta is determined to drive the girl out of town.

Scene 4. Lobby of the hotel. Through Augusta's maneuvers, Baby Doe is persuaded to plan to leave Leadville. She writes a letter to her mother informing her of recent developments. When Augusta appears, Baby Doe promises never again to see Horace, whom she praises rhapsodically. Augusta disagrees with Baby Doe's estimation of Horace. This leads Baby Doe to tear up her letter and decide to stay in town. Tabor's arrival sends her into his arms; they sing ecstatically of their love.

Scene 5. A room in Augusta's house in Denver. Tabor has deserted his wife and is living with Baby Doe in the hotel. Augusta's friends try to persuade her to create a scandal and thus destroy Horace's political career. When Augusta discovers that Tabor is planning a secret divorce through a judge he controls, she vows to seek vengeance.

Scene 6. A reception hall at the Willard Hotel in Washington, D.C. The year is 1883. Tabor, now divorced, is seeking an appointment as United States Senator to fill a vacancy. He has just married Baby Doe. At a party celebrating the marriage, Baby Doe enchants the guests until the news leaks out she is a divorcée. Some of the guests are so outraged they prepare to leave the party, when President Chester Arthur arrives and proposes a toast to bride and groom.

Act II, Scene 1. Balcony off the ballroom in Windsor Hotel, Denver. Baby Doe and Tabor have now been married ten years. They are attending the governor's ball. Some of the guests find much to criticize in Tabor's wife, but (as she tells her mother) she is indifferent to their criticism since she loves her husband more than ever. The sudden appearance of Augusta causes apprehension. But Augusta has come merely to warn Baby Doe that Horace is overstretching himself financially by backing silver. Upon questioning from his wife, Horace admits he has suffered serious losses but is convinced that in the end his speculation will prove profitable. Baby Doe expresses implicit belief in his judgment and promises that, come what may, she will always retain Matchless Mine.

Scene 2. A gaming table. The Tabors join some of their friends in a game of poker. Tabor reveals how deeply involved he has become financially because of Matchless Mine and asks for their help not only for himself, but also for the Presidential candidacy of William Jennings Bryan, sponsor of the silver standard. His friends denounce Horace, and he reacts bitterly.

Scene 3. A political rally outside Matchless Mine. It is 1896. Tabor addresses the people in favor of Bryan, who is the next speaker. Bryan is given a tumultuous reception. The scene ends with a victory procession.

Scene 4. A room in Augusta's house in California. Augusta is upset to learn that Bryan has been defeated by McKinley in a landslide. Baby Doe's mother comes to plead with her to use some of her funds to help Tabor, who is now ruined. Augusta refuses. But she cannot forget how deeply she once loved Horace and regrets her inability to be with him during his disaster.

Scene 5. Stage door of the Opera House. Several more years have gone by; we are now in 1899. Tabor is old and impoverished. He is visited by Augusta. At first, in a kind of vision, she appears as young as when he first married her. Also, in a kind of vision, he hears the voices of friends and neighbors describing his one-time rise to fame and fortune. But soon he realizes that all this is fantasy. Augusta is an old woman now, come to warn him that he will die a lonely, forgotten man. A prostitute, a ragtime tune on her lips, accosts two potential customers nearby. She turns out to be Tabor's daughter, now identified as Silver Dollar. More and more Tabor recognizes the extent of his degeneration. When all the figures have left the scene, Baby Doe arrives to take him home and to comfort him with her undying love. Suddenly Matchless Mine comes to view. The curtain comes down as Baby Doe completes her song of love and fidelity.

Commissioned by the KOUSSEVITZKY MUSIC FOUNDATION to help commemorate the bicentennial celebration of Columbia University, *The Ballad of Baby Doe* proved one of the most successful American operas produced in the 1950's. Following its premiere it was given by the NEW YORK CITY OPERA (Apr. 3, 1958) where it became such a box-office attraction that it remained in the repertory for many seasons. On Feb. 10, 1957, the opera was televised over the CBS network. Since then it has been performed both by professional and amateur companies. When the SANTA FE OPERA toured Europe in 1961, it presented this opera in Berlin and Belgrade.

Its success is not hard to explain. Based upon an actual episode and actual characters from America's past, it has a strong, recognizable American identity, with a colorful background that lends itself naturally to attractive production procedures and staging. It is a story (the libretto written in prose rather than verse) with deeply moving situations and a pronounced romantic interest. For it, Moore has produced a score traditional in structure and style and brimming over with appealing melodies that are sometimes popular, sometimes in a folk vein, sometimes operatic. Sentiment is often expressed through waltz rhythms, while the speech of the period is frequently recreated in recitatives that are dramatic and original in structure. For both the eye and the ear, *The Ballad of Baby Doe* is a good show.

Ballad of Queen Mab, *see* MAB, LA REINE DES MENSONGES.

Ballad of the King of Thulé, *see* IL ÉTAIT UN ROI DE THULÉ.

ballad opera, an English theatrical form popular in the eighteenth century. It consisted of a spoken comedy, often satirical, with songs and incidental music. The song texts were written for the occasion; the airs they were set to were chiefly folk and popular songs. The ballad opera was sometimes known as the people's opera, chiefly because of its simple form, its everyday subject matter, and its colloquial speech. The first ballad opera was Allan Ramsay's *The Gentle Shepherd* (1725). The form became famous in 1728 with the production of THE BEGGAR'S OPERA, text by John GAY, the airs arranged by Johann Christoph PEPUSCH. The phenomenal success of this work started a wave of ballad operas. The new craze was largely responsible for the decline of interest in serious opera and the final failure of HANDEL's Royal Academy of Music. The first opera to be performed in the American colonies was the ballad opera *Flora (Hob-in-the-Well)*, presented in Charleston, S.C., in 1735. The first ballad opera performed in New York was *The Mock Doctor* (1750).

Ballata del fischio, Mephistopheles' aria in Act I of BOITO's MEFISTOFELE.

ballatella, a small ballad—a song of no particular form. A noted *ballatella* in opera is Nedda's aria "Stridono lassù" in Act I of LEONCAVALLO's PAGLIACCI.

ballet in opera. From the beginnings of opera, ballets have provided diversion from the dramatic action. In PERI's DAFNE and EURIDICE, the two earliest operas, the ballet offered a change of interest from the succession of recitatives. As Italian opera developed, composers often introduced ballet sequences even when they were not essential for the action. Typical examples of ballet in Italian opera are the finale of LA VESTALE, the minuet in Act I of RIGOLETTO, the oriental dances in Act II of AIDA, and the Dance of the Hours in LA GIOCONDA. While the ballet was an entertaining element in Italian opera, it was rarely an integral feature. In France, however, where ballet was born, the case was otherwise. The earliest opera composers—LULLY and RAMEAU—placed considerable importance on the ballet. Even GLUCK, who tried to free opera of nonessentials, remained faithful to the French tradition by introducing dances in ORFEO ED EURIDICE, ALCESTE, IPHIGÉNIE EN AULIDE, and IPHIGÉNIE EN TAURIDE. In 1767 Jean Jacques ROUSSEAU deplored the irrelevant use of dancing in French opera, but he could not stop the development. MEYERBEER, by whom French grand opera was established, made extensive use of ballet sequences in LES HUGUENOTS, ROBERT LE DIABLE, and L'AFRICAINE. For the remainder of the nineteenth century, ballet continued prominent in French opera. Notable examples are the Indian ballet in LAKMÉ, the waltzes in FAUST and ROMÉO ET JULIETTE, the minuets in MIGNON and MANON, the bacchanale in SAMSON ET DALILA. Even operas which did not originally contain dancing have received ballet scenes to suit the French taste. At the PARIS OPÉRA, music from BIZET's *Arlésienne Suite* has been used for a ballet in the last act of CARMEN. When DER FREISCHÜTZ was given in Paris in 1841, WEBER's *Invitation to the Dance* was orchestrated by BERLIOZ and introduced into the opera. When TANNHÄUSER was first given in Paris, WAGNER had to extend his Venusberg music into a bacchanale for the opening of the first act. VERDI added ballets for the Paris productions of his MACBETH, IL TROVATORE, and OTELLO. The Austrian and German composers generally liked dancing in opera only when it was essential to the dramatic action. The Dance of the Apprentices in DIE MEISTERSINGER, the Dance of the Flower Maidens in PARSIFAL, the Dance of the Seven Veils in SALOME, and the bacchanale in MOSES UND ARON evolve naturally from their respective plots. In Russian opera ballets have been used prominently to contribute pageantry, as in the Polovtsian Dances in PRINCE IGOR and the polonaise in EUGENE ONEGIN. Sometimes the dance is an integral element in the play, as is the polonaise in BORIS GODUNOV and the ballet in the third act of SADKO. Russian folk dances are basic to such early national Russian operas as A LIFE FOR THE CZAR and DARGOMIZHSKY's RUSALKA, just as Slavonic folk dances are essential to the Bohemian folk opera THE BARTERED BRIDE and Polish folk dances to HALKA. **Ballet of the Seasons,** ballet in Act II of VERDI's THE SICILIAN VESPERS.

ballet-opera, a form of opera created in France in the eighteenth century, with restricted dramatic content and almost continuous dancing. LULLY and RAMEAU wrote numerous ballet-operas.

ballo in maschera, Un (A Masked Ball), opera in three acts by VERDI. Libretto by Antonio Somma, based on Eugène SCRIBE's libretto for AUBER's *Gustavus III*. Premiere: Teatro Apollo, Rome, Feb. 17, 1859. American premiere: Academy of Music, Feb. 11, 1861.

Characters: Riccardo, Governor of Boston (tenor); Renato, his secretary (baritone); Amelia, Renato's wife (soprano); Ulrica, a fortuneteller (contralto); Oscar, a page (soprano); Silvano, a sailor (baritone); Samuele and Tommaso, conspirators (basses); courtiers; dancers. The action takes place in Boston in the eighteenth century.

Act I, Scene 1. A hall in Riccardo's residence. The main theme of the orchestral prelude is Riccardo's first-act love song, "La rivedrò." The Governor is hailed by his people and is given a list of guests invited for a ball. Among the names is that of Amelia. The sight of it causes Riccardo to sing of his love for her ("La rivedrò nell' estasi"). The courtiers leave, Renato enters and warns Riccardo of rebellion brewing ("Alla vita che t'arride"), but Riccardo scorns fear. Next comes a judge with a decree of exile for Ulrica, a woman charged with witchcraft. Oscar, the page, pleads for the woman ("Volta la terrea"). Riccardo becomes curious and decides to visit Ulrica's den in disguise, inviting everyone to join him.

Scene 2. Ulrica's hut. Ulrica is at her cauldron performing an incantation ("Re dell' abisso"). Riccardo appears. He hides as a servant announces Amelia. In love with Riccardo, Amelia has come seeking a remedy for her desire. Ulrica tells her about a magic herb that must be plucked near a gallows at midnight

("Della città all' occaso"). With Amelia gone, Riccardo, now joined by his courtiers, asks to have his fortune told (BARCAROLLE: "Di tu se fedele"). Ulrica predicts that he will be murdered by the first man to shake hands with him. The spectators are horrified, but Riccardo laughs ("E scherzo od è follia"). Renato bursts in, and, happy to find Riccardo unharmed, grasps his hand. Riccardo is reassured, doffs his disguise, and throws Ulrica a purse.

Act II. A deserted heath near a gallows. Amelia has come searching for the magic herb that will destroy her great love ("Ma dall' arido"). A clock strikes twelve. She nearly faints as she sees a figure approaching: Riccardo. She entreats him to leave, but their overpowering love throws them into each other's arms ("O qual soave brivido"). They are disturbed by Renato, who has followed Riccardo to warn him of assassins. Amelia veils her face; Renato persuades Riccardo to flee and offers to escort the unknown lady. Samuele, Tommaso, and their accomplices appear and attack Renato. As Amelia rushes to protect him, her veil drops. That a man has a rendezvous with his own wife is a source of infinite merriment to the conspirators. Renato is humiliated and outraged, and he asks Samuele and Tommaso to come to his house.

Act III, Scene 1. A study in Renato's house. Blinded by jealousy and rage, Renato threatens Amelia with death. Unable to convince him of her innocence, she begs for a chance to bid her son farewell ("Morrò, ma prima in grazia"). Alone before Riccardo's portrait, Renato decides to punish not his wife but instead his disloyal friend and sovereign ("Eri tu, che macchiavi"). When the conspirators arrive, he joins them. By lot, he is chosen to assassinate Riccardo at the masked ball.

Scene 2. The palace. Riccardo, at his desk, signs a document sending Renato and his family abroad, and laments the loss of his love ("Ma se m'è forza perderti"). Curtains part, revealing a huge ballroom, and Riccardo joins his guests despite an anonymous warning. He and Amelia bid each other a tender farewell ("T'amo, si, t'amo, e in lagrime"), which Renato interrupts by fatally wounding his erstwhile friend. Dying, Riccardo attests Amelia's innocence and bids his courtiers spare her husband's life.

The locale of *Un ballo in maschera* has repeatedly been shifted. Originally, the setting was Sweden and the opera dealt with the assassination of King Gustavus III at a court ball in 1792. But while Verdi was en route to Naples to supervise the premiere, an attempt on the life of Napoleon III was made in Paris and the Naples government banished the portrayal of regicide from the stage. Rather than carry out the drastic changes in the libretto demanded by the censors, Verdi withdrew the opera and was threatened with a fine and arrest. Neapolitans passionately sided with him and demonstrated in front of his hotel. He became a symbol of independence to patriots striving for the unification of Italy under the House of Savoy. Eventually Verdi left Naples unmolested and produced the opera in Rome after agreeing to shift the locale overseas. So the King of Sweden became a governor of Boston, Mass. Oscar (patterned after Gainsborough's *Blue Boy*) and Amelia were the only characters whose names were left unchanged. However, since the atmosphere of a brilliant eighteenth-century court hardly fits the austerity of colonial New England, the Swedish setting, costumes, and names are restored in many modern productions. Riccardo (Richard, Earl of Warwich) becomes King Gustavus III of Sweden and Renato becomes Anckarström, who really did murder Gustavus III at a masked ball. In Paris, in 1862, when the tenor Mario refused to don Puritan costume, the opera's action was moved to Naples.

Balstrode, Captain, a retired merchant-skipper (baritone) in BRITTEN'S PETER GRIMES.

Baltasar, prior (bass) in DONIZETTI'S LA FAVORITA.

Baltimore Civic Opera, the principal opera company in Baltimore, Md. It started out in 1932 as a workshop but became a professional company in 1950 under the direction of Eugene Martinet. Since then it has given about one hundred twenty performances of just under thirty operas in the standard repertory. It performs in the Lyric Theatre, Baltimore's first building devoted entirely to music. The company is under the artistic direction of Rosa PONSELLE, which honored her on Mar. 10, 1967, on her seventy-fifth birthday with a gala performance of LA FORZA DEL DESTINO. Its production of BORIS GODUNOV on Nov. 2, 1967, represented the first performance given with the cooperation of THE ASSOCIATED OPERA COMPANIES OF AMERICA. In 1963 the Baltimore Civic Opera conducted its first annual contest for new singers, a venture sponsored by the Carling Brewing Company.

Balzac, Honoré de, novelist and short-story writer. Born Tours, France, May 20, 1799; died Paris, Aug. 18, 1850. One of the founders of French realism in fiction, Balzac wrote numerous novels and short stories which were used for operas. Among these operas are: ALFANO's *Madonna Imperia;* FRANÇAIX's L'APOSTROPHE; Boris Koutzen's *The Fatal Oath;* Charles Levadé's *La Peau de chagrin;* Antonio Maggioni's *Il gioco di Soleima;* Jean Nouguès' *L'Auberge rouge* (1910); Val Pattachi's *The Secret;* Othmar SCHOECK's *Massimilia Doni;* and Herrmann Waltershausen's *Oberst Chabert* (1912).

Bampton, Rose, soprano. Born Cleveland, Ohio, Nov. 28, 1909. For five years she was a pupil of Queena MARIO at the Curtis Institute. In the summer of 1929 she appeared with the CHAUTAUQUA OPERA. After three years as a member of the PHILADELPHIA OPERA COMPANY she made her METROPOLITAN OPERA debut on Nov. 28, 1932, as Laura in LA GIOCONDA. She continued in contralto or mezzo-soprano roles until 1936, when she retrained her voice; her debut as a soprano took place at the Metropolitan Opera on May 29, 1937, as Leonora in IL TROVATORE. In 1942 she made the first of several appearances at the TEATRO COLÓN in Buenos Aires. In 1943 she sang the Wagnerian roles of ELISABETH, KUNDRY, and ELSA for the first time. She remained at the Metropolitan until 1950, after which she appeared with the NEW YORK CITY OPERA. Subsequently, she performed in South America, over television in Canada, and in concerts in the United States.

Bannis la crainte, Admetos' gentle aria of comfort to his wife, Alceste, in Act II of GLUCK's ALCESTE.

Banquo, a general (bass) in VERDI's MACBETH.

Barak, a dyer (bass-baritone) in Richard STRAUSS's DIE FRAU OHNE SCHATTEN.

Barbaja, Domenico (or **Barbaia**), impresario. Born Milan, Italy, 1778; died Posilipo, Italy, Oct. 16, 1841. Before becoming interested in opera he earned his living as a coffee-house waiter and became famous by concocting a delicacy henceforth popular in Vienna and Italy: whipped cream on coffee or hot chocolate. He became wealthy through speculations in army contracts during the Napoleonic wars and investments in gambling rooms at LA SCALA. He then turned opera impresario and managed two theaters in Naples and Milan. In 1815 he engaged ROSSINI to write for him two operas a year and assist in their productions; one of these works was *Otello,* produced in 1816. In 1821 Barbaja went to Vienna, where for seven years he directed the KÄRNTNERTHOR-THEATER and the THEATER-AN-DER-WIEN without relinquishing his directorial activities in Italy. In 1821 he brought Rossini to Vienna and then and later introduced many of Rossini's operas there. He commissioned WEBER to write EURYANTHE, produced under his direction in Vienna in 1823. He also commissioned BELLINI to write his first successful operas, and introduced many of DONIZETTI's operas. In 1828 he went into retirement. Some of the greatest singers of the day were in Barbaja's various companies: LABLACHE, GRISI, RUBINI, and SONTAG.

Barbarina, the gardener's daughter (soprano) in MOZART'S THE MARRIAGE OF FIGARO.

Barbarino, an assassin (tenor) in FLOTOW'S ALESSANDRO STRADELLA.

Barbe-bleue, Bluebeard (bass) in DUKAS'S ARIANE ET BARBE-BLEUE.

Barber, Samuel, composer. Born West Chester, Pa., Mar. 9, 1910. His aunt was the celebrated opera singer Louise HOMER. He attended the Curtis Institute in Philadelphia, following which he won several important prizes for instrumental compositions and a Pulitzer Traveling Scholarship. By virtue of numerous distinguished works for orchestra and chamber-music groups, he won an eminent position in American music. His first opera came after he had achieved full maturity as a composer, with VANESSA (1958), one of the most significant American operas of our time. It was introduced by the METROPOLITAN OPERA on Jan. 15, 1958, following which it received the PULITZER PRIZE in music. Barber was the recipient of a second Pulitzer Prize in 1963, this time for a concert work, his *Piano Concerto.* He was commissioned by the Metropolitan Opera to write an opera to open its new auditorium at the LINCOLN CENTER FOR THE PERFORMING ARTS. That opera, ANTONY AND CLEOPATRA, was produced on Sept. 16, 1966. In 1959 Barber was given an honorary doctorate from Harvard University. He has served as vicepresident of the International Music Council of UNESCO in Paris for several years.

Barber of Bagdad, The (Der Barbier von Bagdad), comic opera in two acts by Peter CORNELIUS. Libretto by the composer, based on the story "The Tale of the Tailor" from the ARABIAN NIGHTS. Premiere: Weimar, Ger., Dec. 15, 1858. American premiere: Metropolitan Opera, Jan. 3, 1890. Nureddin (tenor) is in love with Margiana (soprano), the Caliph's daughter. His barber friend, Abul Hassan (bass), assists in arranging a rendezvous. Upon the intrusion

of the Caliph, Nureddin hides in a chest and almost suffocates until discovered. The Caliph finally consents to Nureddin's marriage.

The spirited overture is familiar. It opens with a brass subject representing the barber and follows with quotations of important melodies from the opera, including "Bin Akademiker" and "Komm deine Blumen zu begiessen." The first is the barber's account of his many talents, while the latter is the duet of Nureddin and Margiana's attendant, both in the first act. This act also includes Nureddin's famous aria anticipating his meeting with Margiana, "Ach, das Leid hab' ich getragen." An orchestral tone poem with religious feeling precedes the second act, which opens with the trio, "Er kommt, er kommt," and contains the rapturous love duet of Nureddin and Margiana, "O holdes Bild." The opera closes with an exultant chorus in which the people hail their ruler, "Salaam aleikum."

Barber of Seville, The, or The Vain Precaution (Il barbiere di Siviglia, o La precauzione inutile), (1) OPERA BUFFA in four acts by PAISIELLO. Libretto by Giuseppe Petrosellini, based on BEAUMARCHAIS'S *Le Barbier de Séville.* Premiere: St. Petersburg, Sept. 26, 1782. American premiere: New Orleans, July 12, 1810.

Paisiello's *The Barber of Seville* preceded the far more celebrated opera of the same name by ROSSINI by over a quarter of a century. Before Rossini's came along, Paisiello's comic opera was one of the most celebrated in the *opera-buffa* repertory. Had Rossini never written his opera on the same subject, it is possible that Paisiello's opera would have retained its popularity to the present time. The text is virtually the same as that used by Rossini, which is described in detail in the discussion of Rossini's opera below. Paisiello's music is consistently sparkling, effervescent, filled with charm and wit. Like Rossini's opera, that of Paisiello boasts a delightful serenade, together with a charming improvised aria for Figaro

("Diamo alla noja il bando") with which the opera opens, an effective air for Basilio ("Se il mio nome"), a memorable aria for Rosina ("Lode al ciel"), and a beautifully contrived vocal quintet for the lesson scene.

(2) OPERA BUFFA in two acts by ROSSINI. Libretto by Cesare Sterbini, based on *Le Barbier de Séville* by BEAU-MARCHAIS. Premiere: Teatro Argentina, Rome, Feb. 20, 1816. American premiere: Park Theater, N.Y., May 3, 1819.

Characters: Count Almaviva (tenor); Fiorello, his servant (tenor); Dr. Bartolo, a physician (bass); Rosina, his ward (soprano); Don Basilio, a music teacher (bass); Figaro, a barber (baritone); Berta, a maid (mezzo-soprano). The setting is Seville in the seventeenth century.

Act I, Scene 1. A square in Seville. Count Almaviva is serenading Rosina ("Ecco ridente in cielo"). Figaro appears, describing his vigorous activities as jack-of-all-trades ("Largo al factotum"). Count Almaviva decides to woo Rosina as an impoverished student named Lindoro, since he does not want her to be influenced by his high station. In this he enlists the help of Figaro, who tells Rosina the fiction that he has a poor cousin named Lindoro ("Dunque io son"). As the humble Lindoro, the Count sings her a second serenade in which he regrets he can give her only love in place of wealth ("Se il mio nome"). He offers to pay Figaro well if he will help him meet Rosina. Figaro explains lightly that nothing in the world is so stimulating as gold ("All' idea di quel metallo") and unfolds a plan of action. First, the Count is to pose as a drunken soldier and get quarters in Bartolo's house.

Scene 2. Drawing room in Bartolo's house. Alone, Rosina is reading a love letter from Lindoro ("Una voce poco fa"). Figaro enters but hides as Dr. Bartolo approaches with his friend Don Basilio. Bartolo confides that he intends to marry his ward. Basilio says that Almaviva is often seen in the vicinity, evidently trying to court Rosina, and

that his reputation can readily be demolished by slander ("La calunnia"). Bartolo prefers his own scheme and urges Basilio to draw up a marriage contract without delay. After Basilio and Bartolo leave, Figaro and Rosina reappear. Figaro bears the happy news of Lindoro's love and promises a meeting with him. As soon as Figaro leaves, Bartolo returns and scolds Rosina for trying to deceive a man of his high station ("A un dottor della mia sorte"). No sooner has he finished his tirade than Almaviva enters in his soldier's disguise. Drunkenly, he demands to be quartered. Bartolo objects and there is an uproar which draws an officer and a squad of soldiers from the street. The officer wants to arrest Lindoro but when Almaviva whispers his true name, the officer snaps to attention and salutes --to the amazement of Rosina and Bartolo.

Act II. Again, Bartolo's drawing room. Almaviva returns, this time disguised as a music teacher in order to substitute for the supposedly ailing Don Basilio. He greets Bartolo and his ward unctuously ("Pace e gioia sia con voi"). Bartolo insists on remaining during the singing lesson, yet Almaviva and Rosina manage to exchange hasty words of endearment. When the unsuspecting Basilio arrives, he is bribed by Almaviva and soon leaves. At this point, Figaro insists on shaving Bartolo, making it easy for the lovers to plot their elopement. At last the deception becomes clear to Bartolo. He sends for a notary to draw up a marriage contract and wins Rosina's consent by creating the impression that her supposedly devoted Lindoro is planning to turn her over to the notorious Count Almaviva. During Bartolo's absence Almaviva returns, clears up the misunderstanding, and the lovers express their devotion ("Ah, qual colpo"). Figaro appears and urges haste and silence ("Zitti, zitti, piano, piano"). Basilio returns once more, bringing a marriage contract. A little pressure induces him to alter the husband's name from Bartolo to Almaviva, and when Bartolo enters, his ward has become Almaviva's wife. Bartolo accepts his fate philosophically (particularly when he learns that Almaviva does not want Rosina's dowry).

The Barber of Seville is probably the best loved Italian comic opera, and it is *opera buffa* at its best, turning easily from sentimentality to laughter, from drama to burlesque. The sardonic mockery, sophistication, gallantry, and intrigues of Beaumarchais's plays find their happy equivalent in Rossini's nimble melodies, mercurial rhythms, subtle dynamics, and fleeting patter tunes. Strangely enough, *The Barber* had a disastrous premiere. The Rome audience resented the fact that young Rossini should use a subject previously used by Paisiello and still popular. Organized malice was manifested in whistles, laughter, catcalls. A rather shoddy performance combined with several unforeseeable accidents provided sufficient excuse for the demonstration. The derision grew so great that the second act could scarcely be heard. On the second night, with a few alterations and no organized opposition, it was received much better, and before many years it was established as the most popular of all Italian comic operas. Incidentally, there have been seven settings of the Beaumarchais play besides Paisiello's and Rossini's—two before Paisiello's and one as late as 1929.

The sprightly overture, a staple in the symphonic repertory, is so much in character with the comic text that follows that it must come as a surprise to discover that Rossini had previously used it for two different operas: *Aureliano in Palmira* (1813) and *Elizabetta, Regina d'Inghiliterra* (1815); and our surprise increases when we discover that these two works are not *opera buffa* but OPERA SERIA.

Though the role of Rosina is sung today most frequently by sopranos, it was originally meant for a mezzo-soprano. But in 1826 Henrietta SONTAG, a soprano, was successfully featured in the part and from then on the role

became a favorite with sopranos, though on occasion Rossini's original intention of having a mezzo-soprano for the part is adhered to.

In the famous lesson scene in Act II, it is customary to interpolate music by other composers, since that written by Rossini has been lost. Some of the selections favored by various famous prima donnas for this scene are Arditi's "Il bacio," John Howard Payne's "Home, Sweet Home," and Alabiev's "The Nightingale."

For American opera lovers it is interesting to remark that this opera was the first ever to be sung in Italian in New York (on Nov. 29, 1825). When the opera was given its American premiere at the Park Theater in 1819, it was sung in English.

Barbier, Jules, librettist. Born Paris, Mar. 8, 1825; died there, Jan. 16, 1901. He collaborated with Michel Carré on many French opera librettos, most notably those for GOUNOD'S FAUST, POLYEUCTE, PHILÉMON ET BAUCIS, ROMÉO ET JULIETTE. They also wrote the librettos for MASSÉ'S *Galatée* and *Les Noces de Jeannette,* MEYERBEER'S *Le Pardon de Ploërmel* (DINORAH), Napoléon-Henri Reber's *Les Papillotes de M. Benoît,* and THOMAS'S *Francesca da Rimini* and HAMLET.

Barbieri, Fedora, mezzo-soprano. Born Trieste, June 4, 1920. She studied at the Opera School of the TEATRO COMMUNALE in Florence, making her debut in that city in 1940. After successful appearances at LA SCALA in 1950 and in other major European and South American opera houses, she made her American debut at the METROPOLITAN OPERA on Nov. 4, 1950, in DON CARLOS, the opening performance of Rudolf BING's regime as manager of the Metropolitan. She had previously acquired a reputation in the United States through her recordings. She remained with the Metropolitan until 1957, then returned to Italy, where she sang chiefly at La Scala, though making guest appearances at other Italian opera houses. She has been especially admired as CARMEN,

AZUCENA, AMNERIS, and DAME QUICKLY.
Barbirolli, Sir John, conductor. Born
London, Dec. 2, 1899; died London,
July 28, 1970. Though basically a symphonic conductor, Barbirolli throughout his career appeared intermittently
as conductor of operas. Even before
launching his career in the concert
hall, he gave operatic performances
with the British National Opera Company in 1926 and conducted LA BOHÈME
and MADAMA BUTTERFLY in 1928. He
became music director of the COVENT
GARDEN English Company in 1930. After 1933 he made numerous guest appearances at Covent Garden and also
conducted guest performances at the
VIENNA STATE OPERA. After a hiatus of
thirteen years, Sir John returned to
opera when he recorded *Madama Butterfly* (1967) and OTELLO (1969).

barcarolle, a boat song in 6/8 time and
in a languid tempo, probably originating with the Venetian gondoliers. The
most celebrated example in opera is
"Belle nuit, o nuit d'amour" in THE
TALES OF HOFFMANN. Others are "Di tu se
fedele" in UN BALLO IN MASCHERA, and
"Pescator, affonda l'esca" in LA GIO-
CONDA.

Bardi, Count Giovanni, scholar and
music patron. Born Florence, 1534; died
Rome, 1612. At his palace in Florence
assembled the CAMERATA, the group responsible for the rebirth of ancient lyric
drama and the birth of OPERA. The
seventeenth-century scholar Giovanni
Doni says that Count Bardi made the
suggestions that prompted the rest of
the group to develop the new musical
form. Bardi is thought to have written
the texts for some of the first operas by
members of the Camerata, and it is also
believed that some of these works were
first performed in his home.

Bardolph, one of Falstaff's followers
(tenor) in VERDI'S FALSTAFF.

baritone, the male voice between tenor
and bass. Its normal range is approximately two octaves upward from the A
a tenth below middle C.

Barnaba, a spy (baritone) of the Inquisition in PONCHIELLI'S LA GIOCONDA.

Barrientos, Maria, soprano. Born Barcelona, Mar. 10, 1884; died Ciboure,
France, Aug. 8, 1946. She studied piano
and composition at the Barcelona Conservatory. After only six months of
vocal lessons, she made her opera debut
in Barcelona as SELIKA. Additional study
in Milan was followed by a successful
debut at LA SCALA as LAKMÉ. For fifteen
years she toured Europe and South
America. In 1913 she began a three-year
retirement, then made her North American debut at the METROPOLITAN OPERA
on Jan. 30, 1916, as LUCIA. She remained
at the Metropolitan Opera until 1920,
during which time I PURITANI, *Lakmé*,
and LA SONNAMBULA were revived for
her. She went into final retirement in
1939.

**Bartered Bride, The (Die verkaufte
Braut; Prodaná nevěsta),** comic opera in
three acts by SMETANA. Libretto by Karel
Sabina. Premiere: National Theater,
Prague, May 30, 1866. American pre-
miere: Chicago, Ill., Aug. 20, 1893.

Characters: Kruschina, a Bohemian
peasant (baritone); Kathinka, his wife
(soprano); Marie, their daughter (soprano); Micha, a wealthy landowner
(bass); Agnes, his wife (mezzo-
soprano); Wenzel, their son (tenor);
Hans, Micha's son by a previous marriage (tenor); Kezal, a marriage broker
(bass); Springer, a manager of a circus
troupe (bass); Esmeralda, a dancer
(soprano); Muff, a comedian (tenor);
circus performers; villagers. The setting
is a Bohemian village; the time, the
late nineteenth century.

Act I. A square before an inn. It is the
annual church festival, and people are
singing and dancing to celebrate spring
("See the buds burst on the bush").
Only Hans and Marie are not gay:
Marie has been ordered by her father
to marry the bumpkin Wenzel, a match
arranged by Kezal. Marie tells Hans
where her love truly lies ("Gladly do I
trust you"). After a tender farewell the
lovers part and Marie's parents appear.
They are followed by Kezal, who soon
falls to praising their prospective son-
in-law ("A proper young man"). Marie

reappears and protests that she loves another. Her father angrily insists that she will marry Micha's son, as arranged. The act closes as villagers throng into the square to dance a spirited polka.

Act II. Inside the inn. Hans tells his companions of the joys of true love. Kezal scornfully upholds the view that money is more important. Villagers enter the inn, dance a rousing *furiant* (peasant dance), and leave. Wenzel appears—a timid, well-meaning stutterer ("Ma—Ma—Mamma so dear"). Marie enters and craftily warns Wenzel against the bride Kezal has picked for him: she is a terrible shrew, Marie reveals. After Marie and Wenzel leave the inn, Kezal meets Hans and tries to convince him to give up Marie. Hans talks vaguely of his faraway home ("Far from here do I live"), and Kezal begs him to return there. Hans insists that he will marry Marie. Kezal now describes another attractive girl ("One I know who has money galore"), but Hans is not interested. Hans finally allows himself to be persuaded by a bribe, insisting, however, that Marie's contract specify that she marry only Micha's son. The announcement of this barter causes amazement among the villagers.

Act III. The square before the inn. Wenzel is bemoaning the fact that love has cost him anguish. His cares vanish with the appearance of a circus troupe which performs the famous "Dance of the Comedians." One of its members is Esmeralda, a tight-rope dancer with whom Wenzel instantly falls in love. But his parents soon drag him away to his intended bride. By this time, Marie has learned that Hans has given her up for a bribe ("How strange and dead"). She announces her willingness to marry Wenzel. When Hans tries to explain ("My dearest love, just listen"), Marie turns a deaf ear. Micha finally recognizes Hans as his long-absent son, at which point Hans explains his trick: since ·the contract specifies that Marie must marry the son of Micha, he—the son of Micha—can be Marie's husband. Hans and Marie are reconciled. Only Kezal is heartbroken at the turn of events.

The Bartered Bride is the first important Bohemian folk opera; it is the foundation on which Bohemian national music rests. So popular has it been in its native land that between 1870 and World War II it was performed over one thousand five hundred times in Prague alone. To this day it is one of the finest folk operas ever written, a colorful and spirited picture of village life, filled with catchy songs and dances. The opera originated as an operetta with twenty musical numbers among the dialogues. After three years Smetana added an aria and the popular *Polka* and *Furiant* and a year after that substituted recitatives for the spoken dialogue, thus making it the opera we know today. *The Bartered Bride* was reintroduced in Vienna in 1892, Gustav MAHLER conducting, and was a huge success. When the METROPOLITAN OPERA revived it on May 15, 1936, the opera was performed in English, the translation made by Madeleine Marshall (using the pseudonym of Graham Jones).

Bartók, Béla, composer. Born Nagyszentmiklos, Hungary, Mar. 25, 1881; died New York City, Sept. 26, 1945. He is one of the most significant composers of the twentieth century. Strongly influenced by the folk music of his native land (in which he began his research in 1904, continuing it for many years), he evolved a highly personal style which assimilated some of the characteristics of authentic Hungarian folksongs and dances. Bartók's music derived its muscular strength from irregular rhythms, discords, the declamatory nature of the melodic line, and free tonalities, and its exoticism from its occasional use of modal scales. Bartók wrote an important one-act opera, BLUEBEARD'S CASTLE, in 1911.

Bartolo, an old physician (bass) who appears in MOZART'S THE MARRIAGE OF FIGARO and ROSSINI'S THE BARBER OF SEVILLE.

Basilio, Don, a music master who appears in MOZART'S THE MARRIAGE OF

FIGARO (in which he is a tenor) and in ROSSINI'S THE BARBER OF SEVILLE (in which he is a bass) .

bass (or basso), the lowest male voice, ordinarily ranging two octaves upward from E, an octave and a sixth below middle C. The lowest variety of bass is known as *basso profundo,* while a high bass with a smooth, lyric tone is a *basso cantante.* A bass in a comic role in OPERA BUFFA is referred to as *basso buffo.*

Bassariden, Die (The Bassarids) , opera in one act by HENZE. Libretto by W. H. AUDEN and Chester KALLMAN, freely adapted from *The Bacchae* by EURIPIDES. Premiere: Salzburg, Aug. 8, 1966. American premiere: Santa Fe Opera, N.M., Aug. 7, 1968. Though in a single act (which takes two and a half hours to perform) , this opera is divided structurally into four parts, almost like the four movements of a symphony. The text has been described as "a study of evil, mass hypnosis, and blind, unthinking idolatry." The librettists transfer the center of interest from the chorus of the Greek drama to the principal characters. These characters, as Peter Heyworth explains, "represent a whole range of attitudes to the irrational cult of Dionysus that sweeps the city of Thebes and drives it to destruction. In doing so, they have underpinned the story with a web of psychological motivation that is absent from Euripides but gives the *Bassariden* an essentially contemporary flavor." The opera boasts some arias with a PUCCINI-like lyricism, together with dramatic choruses and some highly descriptive tone painting suggesting WAGNER.

Bastien und Bastienne (Bastien and Bastienne) , SINGSPIEL in one act by MOZART. Libretto by Friedrich Wilhelm Weiskern, based on FAVART'S *Les Amours de Bastien et Bastienne.* Premiere: Vienna, Sept., 1768 (private) . American premiere: New York City, Oct. 26, 1916.

Mozart was twelve when he wrote this gay little musical play at the request of Dr. Anton Mesmer of Vienna Its premiere took place privately in a little theater in the garden of Dr. Mesmer's house. The opera was not heard again for over a century, its first revival taking place at Daly's Theatre in London on Dec. 26, 1894. When first heard in America, it was given in English.

A performance in Paris of a parody of ROUSSEAU'S LE DEVIN DU VILLAGE gave Mozart the idea to write this little comedy. In Mozart's opera there are just three characters—the two named in the title supplemented by Colas, a magician. Bastienne (soprano) , feeling she has lost Bastien's (tenor) love, calls upon Colas (bass) to help her out. He arouses Bastien's jealousy by telling him Bastienne has found a new lover. The ruse works. Bastien and Bastienne are reunited as lovers.

The score comprises an overture (whose main theme is strikingly similar to one used years later by BEETHOVEN in the first movement of the *Eroica Symphony*) and sixteen numbers—arias, duets, and a trio (in 1769 Mozart added recitatives) . A few melodies have characteristic Mozartean charm, notably Bastien's love song, "Meiner Liebsten schöne Wangen," and Bastienne's lament, "Wenn mein Bastien einst im Scherze."

Bat, The, *see* FLEDERMAUS, DIE.

Batti, batti, o bel Masetto, Zerlina's plea to Masetto to forgive her for having flirted with Don Giovanni, in Act I, Scene 4, of MOZART'S DON GIOVANNI.

Battistini, Mattia, baritone. Born Rome, Feb. 27, 1856; died Collebaccaro, near Rome, Nov. 7, 1928. He made his debut at the Teatro Argentina in Rome in 1878 in LA FAVORITA. His first season at COVENT GARDEN (1883) was not particularly successful. He established his reputation in Italy during the next four years and was then acclaimed as an outstanding exponent of bel canto. He was a noted DON GIOVANNI. Returning to London in 1887, he was well received. Subsequently he gathered laurels in Spain and Russia. Because he had a horror of ocean travel, he turned down all offers to appear in the United States. He was heard in song recitals nearly until his death, his voice as agile and beautiful as ever.

Baucis, Philémon's wife (soprano) in GOUNOD's PHILÉMON ET BAUCIS.

Baum, Kurt, tenor. Born Prague, Mar. 15, 1908. After winning first prize in an international competition held in Vienna in 1933, Baum made his debut with the ZÜRICH OPERA in November of the same year in IL TROVATORE. One year later he was a member of the Deutsches Theater in Prague, where he began to assume leading roles in Italian operas. Following further study with Edoardo Garbin in Milan and at the Santa Cecilia Academy in Rome, Baum appeared in several of Europe's leading opera houses. His American debut took place in Chicago on Nov. 2, 1939, as RADAMES. This was followed on Nov. 27, 1941, by his debut at the METROPOLITAN OPERA as the Italian Singer in DER ROSENKAVALIER. Baum remained with the Metropolitan Opera through the 1961–62 season, distinguishing himself in leading roles in the Italian and French repertory. During this period he made his debut at LA SCALA, was heard at major European festivals, and was featured in a command performance of AIDA for Queen Elizabeth II during the coronation festivities in London.

Bavarian State Opera (Bayerische Staatsoper), *see* MUNICH OPERA.

Bayreuth, a city in Franconia, Germany, the home of the Wagnerian Festival Theater and festivals of Wagnerian music dramas. It was in Bayreuth that WAGNER spent the last years of his life, at Villa Wahnfried. Originally King Ludwig II of Bavaria, Wagner's patron, expressed interest in and promised support for a Wagner theater in Munich. When he became aware of the tremendous scope of Wagner's ideas through the plans drawn by Gottfried Semper, he withdrew his support. It was then that the town of Bayreuth provided Wagner with free land for both his theater and his home. Funds for both structures were raised throughout the world by Wagner societies. Additional sums came from concerts conducted by Wagner. When the cornerstone of the theater was laid on May 22, 1872—an event celebrated with a performance of BEETHOVEN's *Ninth Symphony* under Wagner—only one third of the required two hundred fifty thousand dollars was in hand. The construction proceeded as more funds were raised. The theater opened on Aug. 13, 1876, with DAS RHEINGOLD. DIE WALKÜRE was given the following day; SIEGFRIED (the world premiere) on the 16th; and GÖTTERDÄMMERUNG (also the world premiere) on the 17th. The most notable Wagnerian singers of the day were in the casts, including Lilli LEHMANN, Amalia MATERNA, Albert NIEMANN, and Georg Unger. The conductors included Felix MOTTL, Hans RICHTER, and Anton SEIDL. The event attracted world attention. Composers who attended included SAINT-SAËNS, Grieg, RUBINSTEIN, GOUNOD, and TCHAIKOVSKY. Newspapers from all parts of the world sent correspondents. A great deal of excitement and controversy was generated. But for all the attention and interest, the first festival was a financial failure, suffering a deficit of about thirty thousand dollars.

The theater closed until 1882, when it reopened for the world premiere of PARSIFAL. Hermann LEVI conducted and the cast included Herman WINKELMANN as Parsifal, Amalia Materna as Kundry, Theodor REICHMANN as Amfortas, and Emil SCARIA as Gurnemanz. In 1883 and 1884 *Parsifal* was once again the only opera given, while in 1886 *Parsifal* alternated with TRISTAN UND ISOLDE. Between 1888 and 1893 there were five festivals in which TANNHÄUSER and LOHENGRIN were given with *Parsifal*, DIE MEISTERSINGER, and *Tristan und Isolde*. The RING returned in 1896, given five times that season. From then on, with intermissions in 1898, 1900, 1903, 1905, 1907, 1911, and 1913, the festivals were repeated until the outbreak of World War I. They were resumed in 1924 with performances of the *Ring, Parsifal, Tristan,* and *Die Meistersinger* and continued (except in 1926, 1929, and 1932).

From the time of Richard Wagner's death in 1883 up to 1909, the Bayreuth productions were under the artistic direction of his widow Cosima. In 1909 Siegfried WAGNER—son of Richard and Cosima—took over the managerial responsibilities. In 1923–24 Siegfried Wagner toured the United States as conductor to raise funds for the reopening of the festival theater in 1924. When he died in 1930 the direction of the festivals passed to his wife Winifred. After World War II the artistic and financial administration was taken over by the composer's two grandsons, Wieland and Wolfgang WAGNER.

The summer of 1930 marked the first time that a foreign conductor was invited to direct performances. He was Arturo TOSCANINI, who conducted *Tannhäuser* and *Tristan und Isolde* in 1930 and *Tristan und Isolde* and *Parsifal* in 1931. Because of his opposition to the Nazi regime, Toscanini refused to return to Bayreuth during the summer of 1933 (though he had been contracted to do so); his place on the podium was assumed by Richard STRAUSS, with other performances directed by Karl ELMENDORFF. Wilhelm FURTWÄNGLER became principal conductor in 1936 and 1937, while between 1937 and 1944 performances were led by Franz von HOESSLIN, Victor de SABATA, and Karl Elmendorff among others.

There was a seven-year period when no festivals were given. Bayreuth resumed operas during the summer of 1951 with Hans KNAPPERTSBUSCH and Herbert von KARAJAN as conductors. The 1950's saw an increasing number of American singers assuming leading roles, among them being George LONDON, Astrid VARNAY, Regina RESNIK, and Eleanor STEBER.

Tradition was broken several times in the 1960's. In 1960 Lorin MAAZEL (who had never conducted an opera before this) became the first American conductor to appear at the festival, when he led performances of *Lohengrin*. A year later, Grace BUMBRY became the first Negro artist to appear at the festival, scoring a triumph as Venus in *Tannhäuser*. In 1962 the silence customary during the performance was broken by an audience ovation for Irene DALIS, American mezzo-soprano, following her rendition of Ortrud's invocation in *Lohengrin*. And in April, 1967, the Bayreuth festival company made its first appearance outside Europe with performances of the Wieland Wagner productions of *Die Walküre* and *Tristan und Isolde* at the Osaka International Festival in Japan.

With the death of Wieland Wagner in 1966, complete control of the festival passed on to his brother, Wolfgang, under whose direction Bayreuth was led back to some of the more formal and traditional methods of presenting the music dramas than those previously adopted by his brother with his collaboration. Such a more traditional approach became evident in Wolfgang Wagner's production of *Die Meistersinger* in 1968 and, to a large degree, in the production of DER FLIEGENDE HOLLÄNDER in 1969 by August Everding and Josef Svoboda (the latter, the first time a production had been mounted by others than the Wagner brothers since 1952).

Bear, The, a "musical extravaganza" in one act by WALTON. Libretto by the composer and Paul Dehn, based on a play by CHEKOV. Premiere: Aldeburgh, Eng., June, 1967. American premiere: Aspen, Col., Aug. 15, 1968.

Walton here reverts to the satirical vein he had tapped so successfully early in his career with *Façade,* a witty, tongue-in-cheek musical setting of Dadaistic poems by Edith Sitwell. Parody also plays a prominent role in this unpretentious little opera. Walton even parodies the style he used in his opera TROILUS AND CRESSIDA and his *Viola Concerto.*

The plot concerns the efforts of Smirnov, a landowner who looks like a bear, who comes to Popova, a widow, to collect the money due him. A heated argument follows, reaching a climax when each stands ready to shoot the other. It is not long, however, before they realize they are actually in love with each other. The New English Opera Group, which introduced this work, brought it to SADLER'S WELLS in London and then to Expo 67 in Montreal, both in 1967.

Beatrice, (1) heroine (soprano) and wife of the tyrant Filippo in BELLINI's opera BEATRICE DI TENDA, a role created by Giuditta PASTA.

(2) Benedict's beloved (soprano) in BERLIOZ' BÉATRICE ET BÉNÉDICT.

(3) Ottavio's wife (mezzo-soprano) in WOLF-FERRARI'S LE DONNE CURIOSE.

Beatrice di Tenda, opera in two acts by BELLINI. Libretto by Felice ROMANI. Premiere: Teatro la Fenice, Mar. 16, 1833. American premiere: New Orleans, Mar. 5, 1842.

Written between NORMA and I PURITANI, this opera is Bellini's penultimate work. When first produced, it was a failure; nevertheless it was performed in London in 1836, Paris in 1841, New Orleans in 1842, and New York in 1844. From then on to the end of the century, it was performed intermittently in Germany under the title of *Das Castell von Ursino,* as well as in Italy. It has received significant revivals in the twentieth century: at Bellini's birthplace, Catania, in 1935; the Teatro Massimo, in Palermo, in 1959; and in New York on Feb. 21, 1961, on which occasion Joan SUTHERLAND and Marilyn HORNE made their New York debuts. Miss Sutherland again sang the title role when the opera was revived at LA SCALA in May of 1961.

The heroine, though married to the tyrant, Filippo, is in love with Orombello. She has a rival in Agnese who, angered that Orombello has rejected her, informs Filippo about Beatrice's tender feelings for Orombello. Filippo brings his wife to trial and through torture compels Orombello to sign a false confession that he has had an affair with Beatrice. The tyrant then signs a death warrant for both Beatrice and Orombello. But a revolt by Beatrice's supporters and Agnese's confession that she has been lying saves the lives of both Beatrice and Orombello but brings death to Agnese.

Béatrice et Bénédict (Beatrice and Benedict), comic opera in two acts by BERLIOZ. Text by the composer, based on SHAKESPEARE's *Much Ado About Nothing.* Premiere: Baden-Baden, Ger., Aug. 9, 1862. American premiere: New York City, Mar. 21, 1960 (concert version).

In adapting Shakespeare, Berlioz placed more stress on comedy than on intrigue and romance, emphasizing the subplot involving Beatrice and Benedict, while slighting the central love story of Hero and Claudio and their harassment by Don John. The opera opens with the return from war of both Benedict (tenor) and Claudio (baritone), each eagerly awaited by his respective loved one. The love of Beatrice (soprano) and Benedict, however, runs a rough course, since both are hottempered, quarrelsome, and reluctant to betray signs of their tenderness. Through the manipulation of friends, however, each manages to overhear a confession from the other of how deeply he or she is in love. The love affair can now progress smoothly.

The overture has for one of its principal melodies Beatrice's haunting second-act song, "Il m'en souvient." Other distinguished vocal episodes include another air by Beatrice (and one of the most famous musical episodes in the entire opera), "Dieu! viens-je d'entendre," and Hero's aria, "Je vais le voir," in Act II. The score is enlivened with several Sicilian dances and a delightful parody of a sixteenth-century madrigal in "Mourez tendres époux."

Beaumarchais, Pierre Augustin Caron de, dramatist. Born Paris, Jan. 24, 1732;

died there May 18, 1799. His writings did much to precipitate the French Revolution. His most famous plays are the two comedies *Le Barbier de Séville* and *Le Mariage de Figaro,* which have received significant operatic treatment. Both plays are centered around the colorful character of the barber Figaro, who serves as a symbol of middle-class revolt against autocracy. *Le Barbier de Séville* was banned for two years before it was finally given in 1775. The first performance was a failure, but major revisions resulted in success after the second presentation. *Le Mariage de Figaro,* given in 1784, was such a triumph that it ran for eighty-six consecutive performances. Napoleon said of it that it was the "revolution already in action." The most important operas derived from these comedies are ROSSINI'S THE BARBER OF SEVILLE and MOZART'S THE MARRIAGE OF FIGARO. Others include: Friedrich Ludwig BENDA'S *Der Barbier von Sevilla;* DITTERSDORF'S *The Marriage of Figaro;* MILHAUD'S LA MÈRE COUPABLE; PAER'S *Il nuovo Figaro;* and PAISIELLO'S THE BARBER OF SEVILLE.

Beauté divine, enchantresse, Raoul's hymn to Marguerite's beauty, in Act II of MEYERBEER'S LES HUGUENOTS.

Beckmesser, town clerk (bass), who wishes to marry Eva, in WAGNER'S DIE MEISTERSINGER.

Beecham, Sir Thomas, conductor. Born St. Helens, Lancashire, Eng., Apr. 29, 1879; died London, Mar. 8, 1961. He was the son of the prosperous manufacturer of Beecham's Pills. His musical education was haphazard. After leaving Oxford (without a degree), he helped organize an amateur orchestra in Huyton. During a visit of the Hallé Orchestra to that town, Beecham substituted for the regular conductor, Hans RICHTER, who was detained elsewhere. For a while Beecham wandered aimlessly throughout Europe, absorbing musical experiences. In 1902 he became conductor of the Kelson Truman Opera Company that toured the English provinces. Three years later he made his London debut by directing a concert of the Queen's Hall Orchestra. This appearance encouraged him to found the New Symphony Orchestra in 1905. Three years later Beecham created still another orchestra, the Beecham Symphony, which consistently featured English music. In 1910 Beecham organized his own opera company and gave the English premiere of A VILLAGE ROMEO AND JULIET. A year later he took over the management of COVENT GARDEN. Under his direction it became one of the most dynamic and progressive opera companies in Europe. He helped present more than sixty novelties, including a season of Russian operas with CHALIAPIN, a season of OPÉRAS COMIQUES in English, cycles of the Wagnerian music dramas, and English premieres of many Richard STRAUSS operas. The important revivals and premieres included works by Eugène D'ALBERT, Frederick DELIUS, Joseph HOLBROOKE, Nikolai RIMSKY-KORSAKOV, Dame Ethel SMYTH, Charles STANFORD, and Arthur SULLIVAN.

Due to financial reverses, Beecham gave up the direction of Covent Garden in 1919. Four years later he came out of his temporary retirement to conduct symphonic music, appearing with most of the major English orchestras and also becoming a principal conductor at Covent Garden. In 1932 he founded the London Symphony and became artistic director of Covent Garden. Guest appearances took him throughout the world of music. He made his American debut conducting the New York Philharmonic-Symphony in 1928, thus beginning a long and fruitful association with the United States. He first appeared at the METROPOLITAN OPERA on Jan. 15, 1942, conducting a dual bill consisting of LE COQ D'OR and Johann Sebastian Bach's cantata, *Phoebus and Pan,* staged as an opera. He remained at the Metropolitan through the 1943–44 season. After World War II he gave some notable operatic performances at Covent Garden, the EDINBURGH FESTIVAL, GLYNDEBOURNE, Oxford, and Bath, including a revival of THE BOHEMIAN GIRL in 1951, Delius' first opera IRMELIN in 1953, and GRÉTRY's ZÉMIRE ET AZOR in 1955. In 1958 he led a series of operatic performances at the TEATRO COLÓN in Buenos Aires.

Poor health compelled Beecham to cancel many of his performances in the United States in 1960. He was planning to direct ten performances of THE MAGIC FLUTE at Glyndebourne in 1961 when stricken by a fatal heart attack. For his contributions to English music he was knighted in 1914 and received a baronetcy in 1916. He was the author of an autobiography, *A Mingled Chime* (1943).

Beeson, Jack Hamilton, composer. Born Muncie, Ind., July 15, 1921. After attending the Eastman School of Music in Rochester, N.Y., he became composer-in-residence at the American Academy of Rome. Upon his return to the United States he completed his graduate work at Columbia University, where he then became a member of its music faculty. During this period he studied composition privately with Béla BARTÓK. He wrote a number of operas, beginning with *Jonah* in 1950, the most significant being LIZZIE BORDEN, introduced by the NEW YORK CITY OPERA on Mar. 25, 1965. *My Heart's in the Highlands* was premiered by the NET Opera on Mar. 18, 1970.

Beethoven, Ludwig van, composer. Born Bonn, Germany, Dec. 16, 1770; died Vienna, Austria, Mar. 26, 1827. The titan of the symphony, sonata, string quartet, concerto, and the *Missa Solemnis* wrote only a single opera, FIDELIO. It is not difficult to understand why Beethoven waited until age thirty-five to write an opera in an age when Viennese composers naturally gravitated to the theater as a major source of revenue. And it is also not difficult to comprehend why, having written *Fidelio,* Beethoven did not essay a second opera. While Beethoven had a pronounced dramatic gift in his symphonic music, it was "for the interior psychological drama that is alien to

footlights and backdrops," as Robert Haven Schauffler has pointed out. "Beethoven's [thought] was usually too deep for words." Following in the same vein, J. W. N. Sullivan remarked that Beethoven's "most important states of consciousness, what he would have called his 'thoughts,' were not of the kind that can be expressed in language." It can further be noted that Beethoven, while writing some lovely songs, was none too happy in creating for the voice; his thinking was essentially instrumental. We know what an immense struggle it was for Beethoven to set his libretto to music, how much anguish it cost him to impose on himself the restrictions of stage action and the stylized traditions of the SINGSPIEL. Beethoven himself once said that *Fidelio* earned him "the martyr's crown." His inspiration needed the wings of freedom in order to soar. Nevertheless, he did continue for years to search for suitable librettos and to consider a number of subjects seriously, including GOETHE's *Faust.*

Beggar's Opera, The, BALLAD OPERA with dialogue and verses by John GAY, music arranged by John Christopher PEPUSCH. Premiere: Lincoln's Inn Fields Theatre, London, Jan. 29, 1728. American premiere: New York City, Dec. 3, 1750. This was the first successful ballad opera, responsible for the tremendous vogue of the ballad opera in London in the second quarter of the eighteenth century. It had the unprecedented run of sixty-three nights, earning a profit of four thousand pounds for the producer and seven hundred for Gay. It became the model for all future works in this form. It is believed that Gay got the idea for his opera from Jonathan Swift. He called it *The Beggar's Opera* because in the prologue a beggar (representing the author) explains why the work was written; he does not appear in the rest of the play. The hero of the work is Captain Macheath (bass), a highwayman who loves Polly Peachum (soprano). His love affair and betrayal of Polly, his incarceration, and his reprieve on the day of his execution, provide the author with an excuse to embark on a travesty of Italian opera, to poke malicious fun at English politicians, political corruption, English mores, and the pretensions of high society. Pepusch's contribution consisted of an original overture and the figured basses to the songs, the airs of which were English and Scotch ballad tunes and other popular music of the day, including a march from HANDEL's opera RINALDO and a song by Henry PURCELL. In 1729 Gay and Pepusch turned out a sequel, *Polly,* which was not allowed to be staged, though it was promptly published. Both these operas have been successfully revived in the twentieth century. Benjamin BRITTEN is one of the numerous composers who have arranged the songs of *The Beggar's Opera* in recent times. In 1953 *The Beggar's Opera* was made as a motion picture with Laurence Olivier acting and singing the part of Macheath. *See also* THREEPENNY OPERA, THE.

Behüt dich Gott, also known as "Es hat nicht sollen sein," Werner's aria in Act II of NESSLER's DER TROMPETER VON SÄKKINGEN.

Bei jener Nacht, Helen's air to Menelaus as she offers him a cup of wine, one of the two most famous arias in STRAUSS's DIE AEGYPTISCHE HELENA.

Bei Männern, welche Liebe fühlen, duet of Papageno and Pamina in praise of love in Act I, Scene 2, of MOZART's THE MAGIC FLUTE.

Bekker, Paul, writer on music, impresario. Born Berlin, Sept. 11, 1882; died New York City, Mar. 7, 1937. He was a music critic of the *Berliner Allgemeine Zeitung* and the *Frankfurter Zeitung* before becoming intendant of the Prussian State Theater in Kassel in 1925. Between 1927 and 1932 he was director of the Wiesbaden State Theater. The rise of Hitler made him leave Germany for good. He settled in the United States and became the music critic of the *New York Staatszeitung und Herold.* He wrote several books of inter-

est to opera lovers, including biographies of OFFENBACH (1909) and Franz SCHREKER (1919); *The Changing Opera* (1935); and a biography of WAGNER (1931). The last two were published in English in the United States.

Belasco, David, playwright and theatrical manager. Born San Francisco, July 25, 1859; died New York City, May 14, 1931. He was one of the foremost New York theatrical managers in the last two decades of the nineteenth century and the first two of the twentieth. He was also the author and adapter of more than two hundred plays. Two of these—*The Girl of the Golden West* and *Madama Butterfly*—were the sources of operas by PUCCINI.

bel canto, Italian for "beautiful singing." The term is used to distinguish an Italian manner of singing which emphasizes beauty of tone, purity of texture, facility of voice production, agility in ornamental passages, and the lyrical quality of song. This style is contrasted with a more declamatory kind of singing in which the emotional or dramatic element is pronounced.

Belcore, sergeant of the garrison (bass) in DONIZETTI's L'ELISIR D'AMORE.

Belinda, Dido's maid (soprano) in PURCELL's DIDO AND AENEAS.

Bella cosa, amici cari, *buffo* aria of Don Annibale expressing his joy at having just married the lovely Serafina, in DONIZETTI's IL CAMPANELLO DI NOTTE.

Bella è di sol vestita, Chevreuse's aria in DONIZETTI's MARIA DI ROHAN.

Bella figlia dell' amore, the celebrated quartet of the Duke, Maddalena, Gilda, and Rigoletto in Act IV of VERDI's RIGOLETTO. Rigoletto is here contemplating his plan to murder the Duke; Gilda is heartbroken over the infidelity of her lover; and Maddalena is making flirtatious responses to the Duke's overtures.

Bella siccome un angelo, Dr. Malatesta's aria describing to Don Pasquale his beautiful (but nonexistent) sister, in Act I, Scene 1, of DONIZETTI's DON PASQUALE.

Belle, ayez pitié de nous, Laërtes' madrigal about how he is attracted to Philine, in Act II, Scene 1, of THOMAS's MIGNON.

Belle Dulcinée, La, heroine (contralto) and Don Quixote's beloved in MASSENET's DON QUICHOTTE.

Belle Hélène, La (The Beautiful Helen), OPÉRA BOUFFE in three acts by OFFENBACH. Libretto by Henri Meilhac and Ludovic Halévy. Premiere: Théâtre des Variétés, Paris, Dec. 17, 1864. American premiere: Chicago, Sept. 14, 1867.

Here, as in his masterwork ORPHEUS IN THE UNDERWORLD, Offenbach and his collaborators return to mythology for their subject, once again approaching their theme satirically. They borrowed the familiar tale of Helen of Troy and Paris to mock at the Second Empire in France with its emphasis on pleasure and its relaxation of moral and ethical codes. Greek kings appear as unscrupulous opportunists; the soothsayer—a cheat—symbolizes the laxity of the church. Helen is made to rationalize her immorality with specious feminine logic. The ominous doom gaily hovers over the *opéra bouffe* portending the inevitable collapse of a corrupt society in France.

In ancient Sparta, Paris (tenor), son of Priam, has come with a message from Venus demanding that Helen of Troy (soprano) be turned over to him, even though she is about to be married to Menelaus (baritone). After Paris, disguised as a shepherd, wins a competition, Helen crowns him. Menelaus is sent on a war mission so that Paris can make love to Helen. Helen succumbs only after her conscience is placated by convincing herself that what is happening is actually only occurring in a dream. Upon Menelaus' unexpected return, Paris makes his escape. But before long he is back in Sparta, this time disguised as a priest, in order to abduct the all-too-willing Helen.

Perhaps the most famous air is Helen's invocation, "On me nomme Hélène," which became the rage of Paris in the 1880's. Two other airs—both dramatic, both found in the second act, and both sung by Helen—also have interest: "La vrai! je ne suis pas coupable" and "Un mari sage est en voyage"; of interest, too, is Paris' air Le Jugement de Paris, sometimes identified as "Au Mont Ida."

Belle nuit, o nuit d'amour, the famous BARCAROLLE (duet of Giulietta and Nicklausse), praising the beauty of the night and the power of love in Act II, Scene 1, of OFFENBACH's THE TALES OF HOFFMANN. This famous melody had originally been written for an earlier BALLET-OPERA, *Die Rheinnixen* (1864).

Bellezza, Vincenzo, conductor. Born Bitonto, Bari, Italy, Feb. 17, 1888. He received his musical training at the Naples Conservatory, then made his debut at the SAN CARLO OPERA in Naples with AIDA in 1908. After conducting in leading Italian opera houses, he became principal conductor at the TEATRO COLÓN in Buenos Aires in 1920. He made his debut at the METROPOLITAN OPERA with THE JEWELS OF THE MADONNA on Nov. 4, 1926, remaining with this company until 1935; at the same time, between 1926 and 1930 and again in 1935–36, he conducted at COVENT GARDEN. After 1935 he conducted mainly in Rome but in the late 1950's led performances in London.

Bellincioni, Gemma, soprano. Born Monza, Italy, Aug. 17, 1864; died Naples, Apr. 23, 1950. She created the roles of FEDORA, SANTUZZA, and SAPHO. Her debut took place in Naples in 1881 in Carlo Pedrotti's *Tutti in maschera*. She then toured Europe extensively and in 1899 appeared in South America and the United States. Her repertory included over thirty French and Italian roles. She achieved her greatest successes as VIOLETTA, MANON, and CARMEN. In 1890 she appeared in the world premiere of CAVALLERIA RUSTICANA, and in 1897 and 1898 she appeared in the world premieres of MASSENET's *Sapho* and GIORDANO's *Fedora*. She also had a notable career as teacher of singing, first in Berlin and Vienna and after 1932 at the Naples Conservatory.

Bellini, Vincenzo, composer. Born Catania, Sicily, Nov. 3, 1801; died Puteaux, France, Sept. 23, 1835. The descendant of a long line of musicians, Bellini was given an early musical training by his father. A Sicilian nobleman became impressed with his promise and provided the funds for a comprehensive musical education. Bellini now entered the Naples Conservatory; while there he wrote a cantata, *Ismene,* and his first opera, *Adelson e Salvina.* On the strength of this work, Bellini now wrote a second opera, *Bianca e Fernando,* for the impresario Domenico BARBAJA, performed at the SAN CARLO OPERA in Naples in 1826. This brought a second commission from Barbaja, intended for the tenor RUBINI. The new opera, IL PIRATA, introduced at LA SCALA in 1827, was a huge success. Bellini achieved true greatness with LA SONNAMBULA, introduced in Milan on Mar. 6, 1831. It was soon heard throughout Europe, and was introduced to the English-speaking world in an English version featuring Maria MALIBRAN. An even more distinguished work followed, Bellini's masterpiece NORMA, introduced at La Scala on Dec. 26, 1831.

In 1833 Bellini visited London to attend performances of several of his operas. Wherever he went he was the object of adulation, particularly in fashionable salons, where he assisted Giuditta PASTA (creator of Norma) in performances of his best-loved arias. His next destination was Paris. Here, encouraged by ROSSINI, he wrote his last opera, I PURITANI, for the Théâtre des Italiens. After its successful premiere, on Jan. 25, 1835, he withdrew to a secluded villa to work on two new operas. Here he was stricken by intestinal fever which proved fatal. In his delirium he saw before him the great singers of his day—Pasta, Rubini, TAMBURINI—who had appeared in his operas; just before he died he imagined that a performance of *I Puritani* was taking place in his bedroom.

Bellini was one of the masters of Italian opera. His art differed sharply from that of his celebrated contemporaries, Rossini and DONIZETTI. Rossini was essentially the genius of the comic; Donizetti, a master of tragedy as well as comedy. Bellini was primarily the apostle of beautiful lyricism. He did not have a pronounced dramatic feeling, and his skill at harmony and instrumentation was limited. But his gift of song was unrivaled. His melodies were perfect in design and structure, aristocratic in style, varied in expression, and endowed with genuine feelings. Lyricism served his every emotional and dramatic need.

His principal operas: *Il Pirata* (1827); *La straniera* (1829); *Zaira* (1829); I CAPULETTI ED I MONTECCHI (1830); *La Sonnambula* (1831); *Norma* (1831); BEATRICE DI TENDA (1833); *I Puritani* (1835).

Bell Song, see òU VA LA JEUNE HINDOUE?

Belmonte, Spanish nobleman (tenor) in love with Constanze in MOZART'S THE ABDUCTION FROM THE SERAGLIO.

Belle piacer, Poppea's poignant air in HANDEL'S AGRIPPINA. He used the melody again in his opera RINALDO.

Bel raggio lusinghier, Semiramis' coloratura aria in Act I of ROSSINI'S SEMIRAMIDE; the most celebrated aria in the opera.

Ben, Lucy's lover (baritone) in MENOTTI'S THE TELEPHONE.

Benda, Georg (or Jiři), composer. Born Jungbunzlau, Bohemia, June 30, 1722; died Köstritz, Nov. 6, 1795. An early and highly successful composer of SINGSPIELE, Benda was the first composer to have real success with MELODRAMA, a form of entertainment consisting entirely of spoken dialogue with the music merely an accompaniment.

Benda came from a long line of professional musicians, served as a chamber musician in Berlin and Gotha, and became court KAPELLMEISTER in Gotha in 1748. He returned to Gotha after a visit to Italy and wrote his first musical melodrama, ARIADNE AUF NAXOS, in 1774. It aroused considerable excitement. Benda now wrote and produced in Gotha a series of melodramas and *singspiele* that enjoyed considerable vogue. He resigned his post as *kapellmeister* in 1788 and withdrew from professional life. His best operas and melodramas: *Ariadne auf Naxos* (1774); *Medea* (1774); *Der Dorfjahrmarkt* (1776); *Romeo und Julie* (1776); *Der Holzhauer* (1778).

Bender, Paul, bass. Born Driedorf, Westerwald, Ger., July 28, 1875; died Munich, Nov. 25, 1947. His vocal study took place with Luise Ress and Baptist Hoffmann. His debut followed in Breslau in 1900, and his first successes came in Munich, where he appeared in 1903. When he made his debut at COVENT GARDEN in 1914, he was heard as Amfortas in the first stage performance of PARSIFAL in England; he also appeared with outstanding acclaim as HANS SACHS and WOTAN. His METROPOLITAN OPERA debut came on Nov. 17, 1922 in DER ROSENKAVALIER. He remained at the Metropolitan Opera until 1927, while again making appearances at Covent Garden beginning in 1924. After leaving America in 1927, he made his home in Munich, where he taught singing at the State School of Music and where he received the honorary title of Bavarian KAMMERSÄNGER.

Bénédict (or **Benedick**), Béatrice's beloved (tenor) in BERLIOZ' BÉATRICE ET BÉNÉDICT.

Benedict, Sir Julius, composer and conductor. Born Stuttgart, Ger., Nov. 27, 1804; died London, June 5, 1885. In his youth he knew such German and Austrian musicians as Hummel, WEBER, BEETHOVEN, and MENDELSSOHN. On Weber's recommendation, the young man became a conductor at the KÄRNTNERHORTHEATER in Vienna in 1823. Two years later he went to Italy, where he became a conductor at the SAN CARLO OPERA in Naples. There he wrote and produced his first opera, *Giacinta ed Ernesto* (1829). A second opera, *I Portoghesi in Goa,* written for performance in Stuttgart, was not successful there but fared well in Naples. In 1835

Benedict settled in England, his home for the rest of his life. In 1838 he wrote his first English opera, *The Gypsy's Warning.* Soon after this he became a conductor at the DRURY LANE THEATRE, where several of his operas were performed. He accompanied Jenny LIND on her tour of the United States in 1850, directing many of her concerts. Back in England, he became a conductor at HER MAJESTY'S THEATRE. He was knighted in 1871 and four years later was made Knight Commander by the Emperor of Austria. His principal operas: *The Gypsy's Warning* (1838); *The Brides of Venice* (1843); *The Crusaders* (1846); *The Lily of Killarney* (1862); *The Bride of Song* (1864).

Benelli, Sem, dramatist and poet. Born Prato, Italy, about 1875; died Genoa, Dec. 18, 1949. One of the most successful Italian dramatists of his time, his works were the source of two important operas, MONTEMEZZI'S L'AMORE DEI TRE RE and GIORDANO'S LA CENA DELLE BEFFE.

Benjamin, Arthur, composer. Born Sydney, Australia, Sept. 18, 1893; died London, Apr. 10, 1960. He attended the Royal College of Music from 1911 to 1914. After World War I, in which he saw service, he went to Australia to teach piano at the Sydney Conservatory between 1919 and 1921. Returning to London, he began his career as composer with several instrumental works which were published and received important performances. His first stage work was a one-act comic opera, *The Devil Take Her,* introduced at the Royal College of Music in Dec., 1931, and given public performance in London on Nov. 30, 1932. Less than a year later it was televised in several different countries on an exchange plan. *Prima Donna,* his second opera, though completed in 1933, did not get heard until Feb. 23, 1949. But with A TALE OF TWO CITIES, based on DICKENS, Benjamin scored one of his greatest successes. Following a broadcast over the BBC in London on Apr. 17, 1953, it received first prize at the Festival of Britain and was produced in San Francisco in 1960.

Just before his death, he completed his last opera, *Tartuffe,* based on MOLIÈRE's play, which received a posthumous premiere at SADLER's WELLS in London on Nov. 30, 1964.

Bennett, Arnold, novelist. Born Staffordshire, Eng., May 27, 1867; died Eng., Mar. 27, 1931. One of the most popular of early twentieth-century novelists, Bennett wrote the librettos for two operas by Eugene GOOSSENS: *Don Juan de Mañara* and JUDITH.

Bennett, Richard Rodney, composer. Born Broadstairs, Kent, Eng., Mar. 29, 1936. He studied composition with Lennox BERKELEY and Howard Ferguson at the Royal Academy of Music and privately with Pierre BOULEZ in Paris. He emerged as an important composer with a variety of instrumental works, including several string quartets and two symphonies which gained international recognition. In 1951 he wrote a one-act opera, *The Ledge.* A three-act opera followed more than a decade later, THE MINES OF SULPHUR, introduced in London in 1965 with outstanding success, after which it was produced at LA SCALA and in New York. This opera was followed in 1968 by *Victory,* based on the novel of Joseph Conrad, which was commissioned by the Friends of COVENT GARDEN and introduced there on Apr. 13, 1970. In 1970 Bennett served as visiting professor of composition at the Peabody Conservatory in Baltimore, Maryland.

Benois, Nicola, scenic designer. Born St. Petersburg, May 2, 1901. His father, Alexander Benois, was a distinguished painter, critic, and scenic designer, who had been affiliated with DIAGHILEV's Ballet Russe. The son attended the St. Petersburg Academy of Fine Arts. At eighteen he did his first scenic designs, for a production of Glazunov's ballet, *The Seasons.* A prize enabled him to go to Paris in 1924. One year later TOSCANINI engaged him to do the scenic designs for BORIS GODUNOV and KHOVANTCHINA at LA SCALA. Benois was subsequently elevated to the post of principal designer at La Scala, where he has remained since that time. He made his first return to his native country in 1964 when La Scala toured the Soviet Union. His productions of TURANDOT and IL TROVATORE proved so outstanding that he was invited to return the following year to design BRITTEN's A MIDSUMMER NIGHT'S DREAM. In 1967 his productions of *Il trovatore* and NABUCCO, performed by La Scala, were seen at Expo 67 in Montreal, and in Sept., 1968, the SAN FRANCISCO OPERA opened its season with his scenic designs for ERNANI. He has also done scenic designing for the Rome Opera, the TEATRO COLÓN in Buenos Aires, the HAMBURG OPERA, the MONTE CARLO OPERA, and the Parma Opera.

Benoit, a landlord (bass) in PUCCINI's LA BOHÈME.

Benson, Mrs., governess (mezzo-soprano) in DELIBES's LAKMÉ.

Benvenuto Cellini, opera in two acts by BERLIOZ. Libretto by Jules BARBIER and Leon du Wailly. Premiere: Paris Opéra, Sept. 10, 1838. American premiere: New York City, Mar. 22, 1965.

Many composers besides Berlioz have been attracted to the character of Benvenuto Cellini for opera. All these other operas are forgotten, and so are their composers. Berlioz' opera was long remembered mainly because of its remarkable overture, which is in the permanent symphonic repertory. The basic material in this overture is extracted from arias in the opera, such as the Cardinal's monologue ("À tous péchés pleine indulgence") and the ecstatic love duet of Cellini and Teresa ("O Teresa, vous que j'aime"). As for Berlioz' opera itself, it was a fiasco when first heard, receiving only four performances. After that it was given only intermittently in France, England, and Germany. Important revivals in the twentieth century helped to make the opera more popular than it had previously been, notably that given by the CARL ROSA OPERA COMPANY at SADLER'S WELLS in London in 1957, and one at the HOLLAND FESTIVAL in Amsterdam in 1961.

Originally the opera consisted of

spoken dialogue, together with set musical pieces, but in 1852 Berlioz replaced the dialogue with recitatives (dialogue was used in the Carl Rosa Opera revival). The action takes place in Rome in the sixteenth century. Teresa (soprano), daughter of Balducci (bass), Papal Treasurer, is in love with Cellini (tenor), who has been commissioned by the Pope to mold a statue of Perseus. The lovers plan elopement during the height of Carnival, when they can be disguised. This plan is frustrated when Cellini comes in the guise of a monk, gets involved in a brawl with somebody else wearing monk's garb, and stabs him fatally. Cellini manages to escape. Teresa and Cellini are still determined to elope, but Cellini must first complete his statue of Perseus, which he manages to do in a burst of feverish activity. The magnificence of this art work helps absolve Cellini of his crime and leaves him free to pursue his love affair with Teresa without interference from her father.

Some revivals of *Benvenuto Cellini* have interpolated another of Berlioz' celebrated overtures, *Le Carnaval romain,* between Acts I and II.

Benvolio, Roméo's friend (tenor) in GOUNOD'S ROMÉO ET JULIETTE.

Beppe, (1) a clown (tenor) in LEONCAVALLO'S PAGLIACCI.

(2) A gypsy (soprano) in MASCAGNI'S L'AMICO FRITZ.

berceuse, a song or instrumental piece in which the melody has the character of a lullaby. The most celebrated berceuse in opera is found in GODARD'S *Jocelyn:* "Cachés dans cet asile." The aria of Louise's father in LOUISE, "Reste, reposetoi," is also a berceuse, and so is Marie's "Mädel, was fangst du jetzt an?" in WOZZECK.

Berg, Alban, composer. Born Vienna, Feb. 9, 1885; died Vienna, Dec. 24, 1935. A disciple of Arnold SCHOENBERG, Berg wrote two of the most provocative and significant operas of the twentieth century—WOZZECK and LULU. He did not begin formal study of music until his nineteenth year. After becoming a gov-

ernment official in 1905, he devoted his free time to musical interests. His meeting with Schoenberg was a turning point in his life: Berg was profoundly affected by the older man's esthetics and revolutionary ideas of musical composition. After some preliminary creative experiments in which he imitated the styles of WAGNER and the French Impressionists, Berg wrote, in the atonal style, five songs with orchestral accompaniment. He started work on the atonal *Wozzeck* before World War I. During the war he served in the Austrian army. Afterward he returned to his opera, completing it in 1920. On Dec. 14, 1925, the BERLIN STATE OPERA introduced it. It created a sensation and was soon seen throughout Europe. Leopold STOKOWSKI introduced the work to the United States with performances in Philadelphia and New York in 1931.

Berg wrote only one more opera, *Lulu,* left unfinished by his untimely death. In its incomplete state, it was introduced by the ZÜRICH OPERA on June 2, 1937. Where *Wozzeck* had been an atonal opera, *Lulu* was an opera using TWELVE-TONE TECHNIQUES, but arranging the twelve tones of the atonal octave in such a way that they conveyed a certain feeling of tonal structure. This was one of the features that has made his music more readily comprehensible than that of his teacher. Other qualities that Berg's music possesses in marked degree are dramatic power, intensity of emotion, and poignant beauty.

Berganza, Teresa, mezzo-soprano. Born Madrid, Mar. 14, 1934. She studied voice with Lola Rodriguez Aragon at the Madrid Conservatory where, in 1954, she won first prize in singing and the much-coveted award Premio Grande de Lucreza Arana. After making her professional debut in Madrid in 1955, she attracted attention in 1957 at the AIX-EN-PROVENCE Festival as Dorabella in COSÌ FAN TUTTE. A year later she was heard at LA SCALA in LE COMTE ORY; at the GLYNDEBOURNE FESTIVAL, where she was cast as Cherubino in THE MARRIAGE OF FIGARO; and in Dallas, Texas, where she made her American debut as Isabella in L'ITALIANA IN ALGERI. She also sang the part of Neris in MÉDÉE in Dallas the same season. Her New York debut took place in 1962 with the AMERICAN OPERA SOCIETY in the title role of LA CENERENTOLA. In Oct., 1967, she appeared for the first time at the METROPOLITAN OPERA, in *The Marriage of Figaro*. She has since been heard there in THE BARBER OF SEVILLE, *Così fan tutte,* and LA FAVORITA, among other operas. She has been a guest performer at most of the leading opera houses of Europe and has concertized extensively. The Spanish government named her Dame of the Most Noble Order of Isabella La Catolica, making her the youngest artist ever to be thus honored.

Berger, Erna, soprano. Born Dresden, Ger., Oct. 19, 1900. Much of her childhood was spent in Paraguay. In Dresden she worked as a governess for a French family in order to finance her musical education. She applied for a scholarship at the Dresden Opera School, but when Fritz BUSCH heard her sing, he immediately engaged her for the regular company. She subsequently became the principal soprano of the BERLIN STATE OPERA, where she was recognized as one of the leading MOZART interpreters of our time. She has made guest appearances in numerous European opera houses and performed at the BAYREUTH and SALZBURG festivals. On Nov. 21, 1949, she made her American debut at the METROPOLITAN OPERA, on the opening night of the season, as Sophie in DER ROSENKAVALIER. She remained with the Metropolitan Opera company until 1951, distinguishing herself in the French and Italian repertory as well as in Mozart. After leaving the United States she continued to appear in opera in Europe. She retired from the stage in 1955 to teach singing.

Berglund, Joel, bass-baritone. Born Torsaker, Sweden, June 4, 1903. Between 1922 and 1928 he attended the Stockholm Conservatory. Then, after three months of study at the Royal Opera School, he made his debut in 1929 as

Monterone in RIGOLETTO. While affiliated with the STOCKHOLM ROYAL OPERA, he made notable guest appearances with the VIENNA STATE OPERA, TEATRO COLÓN, ZÜRICH OPERA, the BERLIN STATE OPERA, the BUDAPEST STATE OPERA, and at the BAYREUTH Festival, distinguishing himself particularly in the Wagnerian repertory. His debut at the METROPOLITAN OPERA took place on Jan. 9, 1946 as HANS SACHS. He continued to appear at the Metropolitan Opera until 1949, then from 1949 to 1952 served as director of the Stockholm Royal Opera.

Bergmann, Carl, conductor. Born Ebersbach, Ger., Apr. 11, 1821; died New York City, Aug. 16, 1876. A pioneer in promoting WAGNER'S music in America, he came to this country in 1850. After playing the cello in the Germania Orchestra in New York, he was appointed conductor of the New York Philharmonic Orchestra in 1855, a post he held for over two decades. Soon after taking over the baton, he led the first performance in America of a Wagnerian excerpt: the LOHENGRIN Prelude. A year later, he played the TANNHÄUSER Overture for the first time in America, and in 1859 he conducted at the New York Stadttheater the first American performance of a complete Wagner opera: *Tannhäuser.* Though he incurred the wrath of critics and audiences for his continued espousal of Wagner's music, he insisted on performing it as long as he was a conductor.

Bergonzi, Carlo, tenor. Born Polesine-Parmense, Italy, July 13, 1924. He attended the Parma Conservatory, following which he made his opera debut in Lecce in 1948, as a baritone, as Figaro in ROSSINI'S THE BARBER OF SEVILLE. He continued singing baritone roles for the next three years in various Italian opera houses. His debut as tenor took place in Bari in 1950 in the title role of ANDREA CHÉNIER. He has remained a tenor since then, appearing with leading European opera companies in a repertory embracing some thirty principal roles. He made his American debut with the CHICAGO LYRIC OPERA in 1955. On Nov. 13, 1956, he made his first appearance at the METROPOLITAN OPERA (as RADAMES), where he has remained a principal tenor. He is the owner of a hotel-restaurant in Busseto (where VERDI lived in his early life), which he calls I DUE FOSCARI, a Verdi opera in which Bergonzi had appeared over the RAI radio station in Italy in 1951.

Berkeley, Lennox, composer. Born Oxford, Eng., May 12, 1903. He did not begin studying music seriously until 1926, after having completed his academic education at Merton College, Oxford. Between 1927 and 1933 he lived in Paris, where he was a pupil of Nadia Boulanger. He first achieved recognition for a symphony in 1940. After that he produced many concert works strong in lyricism and personal in harmonic language. His first opera, *Nelson* (1951), was a failure when produced at SADLER'S WELLS in London on Sept. 22, 1954. Two one-act operas followed: *A Dinner Engagement,* introduced at the ALDEBURGH FESTIVAL on June 17, 1954, and *Ruth,* produced by the ENGLISH OPERA GROUP in 1956 in London and at LA SCALA.

Berkenfeld, Countess of, Marie's mother (mezzo-soprano) in DONIZETTI's THE DAUGHTER OF THE REGIMENT.

Berkshire Music Festival, presented each summer at Tanglewood, in Lenox, Mass., founded in 1937 by the Boston Symphony Orchestra under Serge Koussevitzky. Since the addition of the Berkshire Music Center on the festival grounds, significant opera performances have been given during the festival season by members of the Opera School. The first opera to be produced was ACIS AND GALATEA in 1940. Since then world and American premieres have included: ALBERT HERRING; L'AMFIPARNASO; *Bad Boys at School* (MEYEROWITZ); *Elephant Steps* (Stanley Silverman); GRIFFELKIN; IDOMENEO; PETER GRIMES; *Port Town* (Meyerowitz); *Il re Teodoro in Venezia* (PAISIELLO); LE ROI D'YVETOT; *The Rope* (Louis Mennini, 1955); *Simoon* (Meyerowitz); *A Tale for the Deaf Ear* (Mark Bucci, 1957). LA CLEMENZA DI TITO received its first

American staged performance at Tanglewood. IL TURCO IN ITALIA, performed in 1948, received its first American hearing since 1826. PIQUE DAME was revived in 1951, RICHARD COEUR DE LION in 1953, and ZAÏDE in 1955. WOZZECK was produced in 1969 in two different stage productions, with two different casts.

Richard STRAUSS's ARIADNE AUF NAXOS was given a concert presentation by the Boston Symphony with soloists as part of the regular festival proceedings in 1968. Other operas receiving concert performances by the Boston Symphony during the festival proper included the 1805 version of FIDELIO, LOHENGRIN (the first time the opera was heard in its entirety in the Western Hemisphere, the performance in 1965 being spread over three concerts), THE MAGIC FLUTE, THE ABDUCTION FROM THE SERAGLIO, and OTELLO.

Berlin Deutsche Staatsoper (Berlin German State Opera), the most significant opera company in Berlin, situated in the Western section. It was an outgrowth of the Charlottenburg Oper (or Deutsches Opernhaus), for many years prominent in Berlin as a progressive opera company. The auditorium of the Charlottenburg Oper was built on the Bismarckstrasse by the municipal council of the Charlottenburg district in 1911–1912, opening on Nov. 9, 1912, with FIDELIO, conducted by Ignaz Waghalter. Georg Hartmann was the first artistic director.

During World War I the Charlottenburg Oper went into artistic decline, and after the war it was closed temporarily. In 1925 the Municipal Council of Berlin provided a regular subsidy for the reorganization of the company. Now named the Berlin Städtische Oper, it reopened on Sept. 18, 1925, with DIE MEISTERSINGER, conducted by the company's new artistic director, Bruno WALTER. Heinz TIETJEN was director between 1925 and 1930; Kurt Singer in 1930–1931; Carl EBERT between 1931 and 1933; Max von SCHILLINGS briefly in 1933 until his death, when he was succeeded by Wilhelm Rode. In 1934, the company reverted to its former name of Deutsches Opernhaus. For the most part it depended upon the standard repertory, but it did present several world premieres including BITTNER's *Mondnacht* in 1928, WEILL's *Die Bürgschaft* in 1932, and SCHREKER's *Der Schmied von Ghent* in 1932. Among its principal conductors were Robert Denzler, Fritz STIEDRY, Hans SCHMIDT-ISSERSTEDT, and Leopold LUDWIG. In 1944 during World War II the theater was destroyed by a bomb during an air attack. The company was reassembled in 1945, called itself the Städtische Oper, and gave performances in the former Theater des Westens in the Kantstrasse. Michael BOHNEN became its musical director. Heinz Tietjen succeeded him in 1948 and was followed by Carl Ebert in 1955 and Lorin MAAZEL in 1965. The conductors included Robert HEGER, Leopold Ludwig, Leo BLECH, Ferenc FRICSAY, and Lorin Maazel among others. It took a number of years for the company to regain its one-time prestige, but it finally succeeded in achieving a place of first importance among the opera houses of Europe. In 1949 it presented the world premiere of EGK's *Circe* and HENZE's *Das Wundertheater;* in 1951, FORTNER's ballet, *Die weisse Rose;* in 1956, Henze's KÖNIG HIRSCH.

A new opera house was built on the site of the old one, in West Germany, opening in the fall of 1961 with a performance of DON GIOVANNI, Ferenc Fricsay conducting. Since then it has extended its repertory to include over sixty-five productions, giving three hundred twenty performances a season (two hundred seventy operas and the rest ballets). Significant world premieres have included: *Americka* (R. Haubenstock-Ramati); DER JUNGE LORD; *König Hirsch;* MONTEZUMA; PREUSSICHES MÄRCHEN; DER PRINZ VON HOMBURG; *Rosamunde Floris* (BLACHER); ULISSE.

These are some of the more notable revivals and novelties produced by the company: *Alkmene* (KLEBE); *Belsazar* (HANDEL); *Boccaccio* (SUPPÉ); LA CENERENTOLA; LE COMTE ORY; DOKTOR FAUST;

FRA DIAVOLO; JENUFA; KAT'A KABANOVÁ; LEONORE 40/45; LULU; MATHIS DER MALER; MÉDÉE; *Mona Lisa* (SCHILLINGS); MOSES UND ARON; NABUCCO; DER PROZESS; THE SAINT OF BLEECKER STREET; VOLO DI NOTTE; DIE ZAUBERGEIGE; *Zweihunderttausend Taler* (Blacher).

The company made its first appearance in the Western Hemisphere in Nov., 1968, as a feature of the Cultural Olympics in Mexico City, and in 1970 it opened the cultural program of Expo 70 in Japan with performances of *Moses und Aron* and six other operas.

Berlin Festival, a festival held in West Berlin each year between September and October, covering opera, ballet, theater, concerts, and art exhibits. It was inaugurated in 1950. Most of the opera performances are given by the BERLIN DEUTSCHE STAATSOPER, which frequently reserves some of its world premieres and unusual revivals for this festival period. These have included the following: ABSTRAKTE OPER NO. 1; *Alkmene* (KLEBE); *Americka* (R. Haubenstock-Ramati, world premiere); *Belsazar* (HANDEL); LEONORE 40/45; MATHIS DER MALER; MÉDÉE; *Mona Lisa* (SCHILLINGS); MONTEZUMA (world premiere); MOSES UND ARON (German premiere); L'ORÉSTIE (MILHAUD, world premiere of entire trilogy); DER PROZESS (German premiere); PREUSSICHES MÄRCHEN (world premiere); DER PRINZ VON HOMBURG (Berlin premiere); *Rosamunde Floris* (world premiere); *Zweihunderttausend Taler* (BLACHER, world premiere).

From time to time operatic activities are enriched with productions by visiting companies. For example, in 1953 the FRANKFURT OPERA presented the new version of CARDILLAC; in 1961 the SANTA FE OPERA from New Mexico introduced to German audiences THE BALLAD OF BABY DOE; in 1966, the Bayerisches Staatstheater revived PURCELL's THE FAIRY QUEEN and the STUTTGART OPERA revived Johann Christian BACH's *Themistokles.*

Berlin State Opera (Staatsoper, now the East Berlin State Opera), the most historic of Berlin's opera companies, its history going back two centuries. Before World War I, it was called the Berlin Royal Opera (Hofoper). Between the two world wars, it was named Berlin State Opera (Staatsoper), and when Berlin was divided into two sectors, the company was designated as the East Berlin State Opera.

It originated as a private theater built by Frederick the Great and was inaugurated on Dec. 7, 1742, with GRAUN's *Cleopatra e Cesare*. In 1756 the house closed down due to the Seven Years' War. For almost two decades it was in a comparatively somnolent state. Operatic activity was renewed in 1775 with Johann Friedrich REICKHARDT as artistic director, but the company failed to realize artistic importance due to the general apathy of the Emperor toward opera. For a long time the major opera activity in Berlin took place at the National Theater in Gendarmenplatz, where MOZART's greatest operas were introduced to the city.

After the turn of the nineteenth century the Royal Opera assumed increasing importance. Count Karl von Brühl became general manager and aimed to develop a significant theater emphasizing the highest artistic values. Since the Emperor Friedrich Wilhelm preferred more meretricious and spectacular productions, Count von Brühl's efforts were greatly hampered. He had to indulge the Emperor's passion for the more ornate Italian operas of the period.

In line with this policy, SPONTINI became musical director in 1819. Under his supervision many of his operas were given lavish presentations. Occasionally von Brühl had his way. Despite Spontini's aversion to, and envy of, WEBER, the world premiere of DER FREISCHÜTZ took place at the Royal Opera and was a success of formidable proportions. (This was one of the few important operas to be introduced by this opera house.) But the Italian vogue continued until the Emperor's death in 1840, when Spontini resigned.

In 1842 MEYERBEER became musical director, NICOLAI one of the principal conductors. A fire demolished the opera house in 1843. A new building was erected on the same site, opening with Meyerbeer's EIN FELDLAGER IN SCHLESIEN, written especially for the new singer Jenny LIND. Meyerbeer not only directed his own operas but produced and conducted EURYANTHE and RIENZI and was responsible for the production of DER FLIEGENDE HOLLÄNDER. In 1849 Nicolai presented the world premiere of his comic opera THE MERRY WIVES OF WINDSOR.

After Meyerbeer's resignation and the appointment of Count Botho von Hülsen as general manager in 1850, an increasingly high level of performances was realized. The level was maintained by Von Hülsen's successor, Count Bolke von Hochberg. With these two general managers, the so-called "classic age of the Royal Opera" unfolded. If the house was comparatively delinquent in presenting new operas of importance—it was particularly negligent in the case of WAGNER—it nevertheless touched a new standard of operatic presentation. Under the later artistic directions of Felix WEINGARTNER (1891–1898), Karl MUCK (1908–1912), and Richard STRAUSS (1918–1919) the Wagnerian dramas came into their own at the Royal Opera.

Meanwhile, in 1896, Emperor Wilhelm II ordered the erection of a new opera house, the old one having outlived its usefulness. The Prussian State Theater bought the Kroll Theater, intending to tear it down and build on the site. But plans were long delayed and were completely disrupted by the outbreak of World War I. After the war, the old opera house was remodeled, reopening in 1924 with DIE MEISTERSINGER conducted by Erich KLEIBER, who served as musical director until 1934, sharing the post between 1926 and 1934 with Leo BLECH, who resigned in 1937. The office of director was shared in turn by Wilhelm FURTWÄNGLER (1933–1934), Clemens KRAUSS (1934–1935), and subsequently, up to 1943, held by Werner EGK, Herbert von KARAJAN, and Karl ELMENDORFF. Under Kleiber's direction, several new operas were introduced including WOZZECK in 1925; SCHREKER's *Der singende Teufel* in 1928; CHRISTOPHE COLOMB in 1930; PFITZNER's *Das Herz* in 1931. Premieres following the Kleiber regime up to the outbreak of World War II included GRAENER's *Der Prinz von Homburg* in 1935, VON KLENAU's *Rembrandt van Rijn* in 1937, and Egk's PEER GYNT in 1938.

Operatic activity, brought to a halt by the war, was resumed in 1945 in the Admiralspalast, Ernst Legal serving as director. On Sept. 4, 1955, the company returned to its former site on Unter den Linden, where a new auditorium had been built. A few months before this new theater was inaugurated, the musical director of the opera company, Erich Kleiber, resigned his post, accusing the East German government of interfering with his artistic plans. With Franz KONWITSCHNY as Kleiber's successor and Max Burghardt as general manager, the new opera house was opened with pomp and ceremony. The 1955–56 season featured, besides the more familiar repertory, significant performances of EUGENE ONEGIN, IPHIGÉNIE EN AULIDE, JENUFA, HALKA, and *Wozzeck;* the season after that witnessed a new production of the Wagner RING together with the first Berlin presentation of Richard Strauss's DIE FRAU OHNE SCHATTEN and revivals of PRINCE IGOR and MONTEVERDI's L'INCORONAZIONE DI POPPEA. Subsequent revivals and novelties included LE COQ D'OR; KEISER's *Masaniello;* DVOŘÁK's RUSALKA; STORY OF A REAL MAN; THE NOSE; THE RISE AND FALL OF THE CITY MAHAGONNY; and BLACHER's *Zweihunderttausend Taler.* The repertory of this company embraces about fifty operas, with Hans Pischner serving as general manager and Otmar Suitner as musical director.

For the history of still another major Berlin opera company *see* KOMISCHE OPER.

Berlioz, Hector, composer and writer on music. Born La Côte-Saint-André, France, Dec. 11, 1803; died Paris, Mar. 8, 1869. He was "the most brilliant and influential of the French Romantic composers and at the same time contributed some of the most brilliant musical journalism of his day," wrote the *Traité de l'instrumentation,* which remains to this day a standard text on orchestration, while his *Mémoires* remains one of the best autobiographies, and certainly the most readable, ever written by a major composer. Some of his symphonic and choral works were recognized at once as works of genius and still form a part of our concert life, especially the *Symphonie fantastique,* the overtures *La Carnaval romain* and *Rob Roy,* the tone poem *Roméo et Juliette,* the *Harold en Italie* symphony, and the oratorio *L'Enfance du Christ.* Although his penchant for bigness, for color, for theatrical effects (in life as well as in his music) might lead one to expect that he was cut out for major success in opera, he never had a real success in that field during his lifetime, and he died bitterly resenting that failure. Ironically, the one work that, long after his death, entered the French repertoire was LA DAMNATION DE FAUST, which he had composed as a cantata to be sung in concert form at the OPÉRA-COMIQUE and which became a major success almost fifty years after its premiere, when it was imaginatively staged as an opera at the MONTE CARLO. The three works he intended for the operatic stage: BÉATRICE ET BÉNÉDICT, BENVENUTO CELLINI, and LES TROYENS.

Berlioz was sent by his parents to Paris to study medicine, but he enrolled in the Paris Conservatory and after seven years won the PRIX DE ROME. When he saw Henrietta Smithson, an Irish girl, perform as Ophelia in English (a language Berlioz did not understand), he fell in love, vowed to marry her, and five years later did. He played no instrument professionally (he was best at the guitar) and supported himself largely through journalism, which he hated. Later, when his standing as a composer was recognized all over Europe, he toured as a conductor. The marriage ended in separation, and after

Henrietta's death Berlioz tried again with no greater success. His last years were marked by illness, disillusionment, loneliness, despair. His wife died, his beloved son died, and he was convinced that his most ambitious, and possibly greatest, work, *Les Troyens,* would never be fully produced as he had composed it. He was almost right. The first uncut staged version of the five-and-a-half-hour opera in Berlioz' original French was mounted in the summer of 1969 at COVENT GARDEN in London.

Bernacchi, Antonio, CASTRATO soprano. Born Bologna, June 23, 1685; died there Mar., 1756. He was taught singing by Pistocchi and G. A. Ricieri, following which he made successful appearances in Venice in 1709–10 and Bologna in 1710–12. His London debut took place in a revival of Alessandro SCARLATTI's *Pirro e Demetrio* in 1716. On Jan. 5, 1717, he was heard in a revival of RINALDO, assuming the role of Goffredo previously sung by female contraltos. In 1717 he returned to Italy. During the next dozen years he appeared with major Italian opera companies, as well as in Munich between 1720 and 1727. He returned to London in 1729 when HANDEL engaged him to replace another popular castrato, SENESINO. Bernacchi created the title role in Handel's *Lotario* in 1729 and that of Arsace in *Partenope* in 1730. Though now past his prime, he continued to sing opera in Italy between 1731 and 1736. He then founded a distinguished singing school in Bologna.

Bernauerin, Die, opera by ORFF. Text by the composer in Bavarian dialect. Premiere: Stuttgart, June 15, 1947. The composer designated this work (which is actually a play with music) as a "Bavarian piece." There are no arias. Unaccompanied spoken dialogue is supplemented by recitatives, while the chorus is often required to hum or chant complex rhythmic spoken passages. The musical accompaniment is provided by a small percussion orchestra. The text is based on a Bavarian legend from the Middle Ages. The hero-

ine, Agnes Bernauerin, daughter of a public bathhouse owner, marries a nobleman. After he has left for the wars, she becomes the victim of local intrigue, is accused of being a witch, and is drowned by her accusers.

Bernstein, Leonard, composer and conductor. Born Lawrence, Mass., Aug. 25, 1918. While he has been essentially a symphonic conductor—for many years the music director of the New York Philharmonic Orchestra, and guest conductor of practically every major orchestra in the world—he has also led distinguished opera performances. His first major opera performance was the American premiere of PETER GRIMES, given in 1946 at Tanglewood, on the grounds of the BERKSHIRE MUSIC FESTIVAL. Also, in 1953 he led the American premiere of POULENC'S LES MAMELLES DE TIRÉSIAS at a festival at Brandeis University in Waltham, Mass. In the same year he became the first American-born conductor to direct a performance at LA SCALA—MÉDÉE; he returned to La Scala a year later to conduct LA SONNAMBULA. In 1961 he made his first appearance at COVENT GARDEN leading FALSTAFF, the same opera with which he made triumphant debuts at the METROPOLITAN OPERA House on Mar. 6, 1964 (a production staged by ZEFFIRELLI) and at the VIENNA STATE OPERA in 1966. About a year later he once again scored a success of major proportions at the Vienna State Opera with his performances of DER ROSENKAVALIER, and in 1969 he led BEETHOVEN's *Missa solemnis* as part of the ceremonies commemorating the centenary of that opera house. At the THEATER-AN-DER-WIEN on May 24, 1970, and at the VIENNA FESTIVAL he led performances of FIDELIO in commemoration of the two-hundredth anniversary of Beethoven's birth. He wrote a one-act opera, TROUBLE IN TAHITI, which was introduced at the Festival of Creative Arts at Brandeis University, Waltham, Mass., on June 12, 1952, and subsequently performed over the NBC television network and by dozens of opera workshops.

Bersi, Madeleine's maid (mezzo-soprano) in GIORDANO'S ANDREA CHÉNIER.
Berta, a maid (mezzo-soprano) in ROSSINI'S THE BARBER OF SEVILLE.
Bertha, John of Leyden's fiancée (soprano) in MEYERBEER'S LE PROPHÈTE.
Bertram, the devil in human form (bass) in MEYERBEER'S ROBERT LE DIABLE.
Bervoix, Flora, Violetta's friend (mezzo-soprano) in VERDI'S LA TRAVIATA.
Bess, Porgy's sweetheart (soprano) in GERSHWIN'S PORGY AND BESS.
Bess, you is my woman now, love duet of Porgy and Bess in Act II of GERSHWIN'S PORGY AND BESS.
betrogene Cadi, Der, see CADI DUPÉ, LE.
Betrothal in a Convent, opera in four acts by PROKOFIEV. Libretto by Mira Mendelson (the composer's wife), based on Richard Brinsley Sheridan's The Duenna. Premiere: Kirov Theater, Leningrad, Nov. 3, 1946. American premiere: New York City, June 1, 1948 (under the title The Duenna). The action of this opera—which is sometimes identified as The Duenna, sometimes as Betrothal in a Monastery, and in Italy as Matrimonio al convento—takes place in Seville in the eighteenth century. The aim of both librettist and composer was to create a comic opera in the style of either MOZART or ROSSINI. Thus, with OPERA BUFFA in the back of his mind, Prokofiev produced a score that emphasizes lyricism and is filled with arias, duets, quartets, large ensemble numbers, and serenades. But the comic is combined with atmospheric writing. As the composer himself explained: "After the comical incidents in the first scene, I tried to give a musical interpretation of the city slowly going to sleep. Since, according to Sheridan, there was a carnival in the city, I composed a large scene for a ballet." He also created a highly effective chorus for the fishwives.

In the preparation of the libretto, what was emphasized was the love of Louise and Antonio and of Clara and Ferdinand, "the two pairs of happy young daydreamers," as the composer described them. He went on to explain

that he also paid attention to "the obstacles their love encountered, their engagements, the poetry of Seville, and the ancient deserted convent." Sheridan's humorous situations were taken into account: "the old Don Xerom who, blinded by his wrath against the old nurse, drives out of the house his own daughter, who was dressed up in the old nurse's clothes, thus helping her to flee to her lover; the avaricious Mendoza, who is so overwhelmed by the large sum of money that he lets himself be deceived, and instead of charming Louise, marries her old nurse; and finally the passionate Ferdinand, who is so jealous of his beloved girl that he is ready to suspect every young woman he sees with a young man of being his unfaithful Clara."
Betz, Franz, baritone. Born Mainz, Ger., Mar. 19, 1835; died Berlin, Aug. 11, 1900. He created the roles of Hans Sachs and of Wotan in SIEGFRIED. He made his debut in Berlin in 1859 in ERNANI, making such a good impression that he was engaged as a permanent member of the Berlin Royal Opera (see BERLIN STATE OPERA). Besides appearing at BAYREUTH, he remained with that company until his retirement in 1897. He distinguished himself particularly in Wagnerian roles, but was also acclaimed in FALSTAFF, DON GIOVANNI, and WILLIAM TELL.
Biaiso, a public letter-writer (tenor) in WOLF-FERRARI'S THE JEWELS OF THE MADONNA.
Bianca al par hermine, see PLUS BLANCHE QUE LA BLANCHE HERMINE.
Bible, the (in opera). From time to time in opera history, up to the present, operas have been based on Biblical subjects and characters. Before the twentieth century, the following are some of the operas of Biblical derivation: HÉRODIADE; JOSEPH; Die Makkaber (Anton RUBINSTEIN); MOSÈ IN EGITTO; Moïse au Sinai (Félicien DAVID); Moses (Rubinstein); THE QUEEN OF SHEBA; SAMSON ET DALILA.

In the twentieth century, these are some of the operas on Biblical themes: Christus (GIANNINI); Comoedia di

Christi Resurrectione (ORFF); DAVID;
DEBORA E JAELE; *I Am the Way* (Hines);
Joseph and His Brethren (ROSENBERG);
Kain und Abel (WEINGARTNER); *Ludus
de Nato Infante Mirificus* (Orff); MARIA
EGEZIACA; MOSES UND ARON; *Ruth* (BERKE-
LEY); SALOME; *Saul* (CASTELNUOVO-
TEDESCO); *The Warrior* (Bernard
Rogers, 1947, based on the story of
Samson and Delilah).

Bible, Frances, mezzo-soprano. Born
Sackets Harbor, N.Y. She attended the
Juilliard School of Music in New York
City, where she studied voice with
Queena MARIO. Her professional debut
took place at CHAUTAUQUA in *The Gondoliers* by Gilbert and SULLIVAN. In 1948
she joined the NEW YORK CITY OPERA,
where she has since remained, appearing in major roles in a highly varied
repertory, including modern works.
The company revived LA CENERENTOLA
specifically for her, and in 1961 featured her in the world premiere of
THE CRUCIBLE. Meanwhile she was engaged by the SAN FRANCISCO OPERA, where
she made her debut as OCTAVIAN on
Sept. 20, 1955, and where she has appeared in numerous productions, including the American premiere of TROILUS
AND CRESSIDA. In 1956, she created the
role of Augusta Tabor in THE BALLAD
OF BABY DOE at the CENTRAL CITY OPERA
FESTIVAL in Colorado. When the NBC
TELEVISION OPERA company toured the
United States in 1956–57, she was heard
as Octavian in DER ROSENKAVALIER.
During the summer of 1961, she was
cast at the Vancouver Festival in the
North American premiere of a MID-
SUMMER NIGHT'S DREAM. A year later
she appeared for nine weeks at the
GLYNDEBOURNE FESTIVAL in England
(where she had previously made her
debut as CHERUBINO); during this en-
gagement she was heard in a revival of
L'INCORONAZIONE DI POPPEA. In 1964 she
made an extensive tour of Australia.

Billy Budd, opera in two acts (originally four) by BRITTEN. Libretto by E. M.
Forster and Eric CROZIER, based on
the story by Herman MELVILLE. Premiere: Covent Garden, Dec. 1, 1951.

American premiere: NBC-TV, Oct. 19,
1952 (abridged); Bloomington, Ind.,
Dec. 5, 1952 (staged).

The central theme (like that of its
distinguished predecessor, PETER GRIMES)
is man's inhumanity to man. Billy
Budd (baritone) is impressed into the British
Navy during the eighteenth century. He
is hated by the master-at-arms, Claggart
(bass), who builds up a false charge of
treason against him. Overwhelmed and
enraged by this unjust accusation, Billy
Budd kills the tyrant, for which he is
court-martialed and hanged. Captain
Vere (tenor) realizes that, while naval
justice has been done, Budd had sufficient justification to commit murder.

There are several unusual points
about this opera. It is written exclusively for male voices. There are few
arias and only a handful of ensemble
numbers. With the exception of a few
chanteys and one or two lyrical pages,
the opera consists entirely of recitatives,
one of the most distinguished of which
is that of Captain Vere, "I could have
saved him," with which the opera ends.
The principal musical interest lies in
the orchestra. Britten's emphasis is on
the drama, and he recruits every musical means at his command to point up
the personal tragedy of his protagonist.

A few years after its premiere (and
after it had been featured at the Exposition of Masterpieces of the Twentieth
Century in Paris in 1952), Britten revised his opera, shortening it to two
acts. In this version, it was produced
at COVENT GARDEN on Apr. 26, 1963, and
in New York on Jan. 4, 1964. It was
also televised over BBC in London. In
commenting on the new version, Irving Kolodin called the opera "one of
Britten's finest and most beautiful
scores," adding: "At present, *Peter
Grimes* is still the most universally admired of Britten's large-scale operas,
but I suspect that, in time, *Billy Budd*
will be recognized as an even finer,
richer score in which the tang of the
sea is evoked with breathtaking power
and subtlety."

An opera on the same subject was

written in 1948 by the Italian composer GHEDINI.

Bin Akademiker, the barber's aria in Act II of CORNELIUS' THE BARBER OF BAGDAD, where he gives a whirlwind account of his multifarious talents as doctor, dentist, chemist, and mathematician, as well as barber.

Bing, Rudolf, opera manager. Born Vienna, Austria, Jan. 9, 1902. Since 1950 he has been the general manager of the METROPOLITAN OPERA. He studied music and art at the University of Vienna. In 1923 he became a manager of concert artists in Vienna. Four years later he went to Germany as head of a unit supplying artists to more than eighty state and municipal opera houses. In 1929 he was appointed musical secretary of the Darmstadt Municipal Theater, and in 1931 he held a similar post with the Charlottenburg Municipal Opera. He left Germany when Hitler came to power. In 1934 Bing helped organize the first season of the GLYNDEBOURNE OPERA company (England), subsequently becoming general manager; he held this post until 1939. He became a British subject in 1946 and helped create the EDINBURGH FESTIVAL in 1947, becoming its general manager. His success in organizing these annual festivals was responsible for bringing him an appointment as general manager of the Metropolitan Opera when Edward JOHNSON resigned in 1949. He assumed this new post on June 1, 1950.

Birds, The, see ARISTOPHANES.

bis, French for "twice," a call equivalent to "encore" and used by audiences desiring repetition of a number.

Bispham, David, baritone. Born Philadelphia, Pa., Jan. 5, 1857; died New York City, Oct. 2, 1921. He was the first American-born opera baritone to win international acclaim. Without any preliminary musical education, he appeared during boyhood in amateur opera performances. When he was twenty-eight, he went to Europe and studied singing with Luigi Vannuccini in Florence and Francesco LAMPERTI in Milan. In 1891 he was selected from fifty applicants for the role of the Duc de Longueville in MESSAGER's *La Basoche,* in London. This was his first professional stage appearance. His first Wagnerian role was that of KURWENAL, in which he appeared under Gustav MAHLER's direction at DRURY LANE in 1892. His success brought him a contract for COVENT GARDEN, where he appeared for the next few years, primarily in Wagnerian roles. On Nov. 18, 1896, he made his American debut as BECKMESSER at the METROPOLITAN OPERA. He appeared there until 1903, singing not only in the WAGNER dramas but also in the American premieres of Ignace Jan Paderewski's *Manru* and Dame Ethel SMYTH's *Der Wald.* After this period Bispham's appearances in opera were few, but he enjoyed great success as a recitalist. He made a point of singing English versions of songs by BEETHOVEN, SCHUBERT, and SCHUMANN. In 1916 he appeared in an English-language production of MOZART's THE IMPRESARIO in New York. This was such a success that it led to the formation of the Society of American Singers, which, with Bispham's inspiration, gave three seasons of light operas in English.

Bispham Memorial Medal Award, an award created by the Opera Society of America, in Chicago, soon after the death of David BISPHAM, for opera in English by American composers. Recipients of the award have been: ANTHEIL, BACON, CADMAN, DAMROSCH, GERSHWIN, GRUENBERG, HADLEY, HANSON, HERBERT, Otto Luening, and TAYLOR.

Biterolf, a minstrel-knight (bass) in WAGNER's TANNHÄUSER.

Bittner, Julius, composer. Born Vienna, Apr. 9, 1874; died there Jan. 19, 1939. For many years he divided his activities between the law (which he practiced successfully up to 1920) and composition. His first opera, *Die rote Gret,* was introduced in Frankfurt in 1907 and was well received. His following operas were successfully performed in Austria and Germany. Bittner arrived at a popular style without sacrificing an original approach; his finest works are graced by an engaging sense of humor. His principal operas and musical plays: *Die rote Gret* (1907); *Der Musikant* (1910); *Der Bergsee* (1911, revised 1922); *Der Abenteurer* (1913); *Der liebe Augustin* (1917); *Die Kohlhaymerin* (1921); *Das Rosengärtlein* (1923, revised 1928); *Mondnacht* (1928); *Der unsterbliche Franz* (1930); *Das Veilchen* (1934).

Bizet, Georges, composer. Born Paris, Oct. 25, 1838; died Bougival, June 3, 1875. The son of a singing teacher, he entered the Paris Conservatory when he was nine years old; his teachers included Antoine MARMONTEL, François Benoist, and Jacques HALÉVY. In 1857 he won the PRIX DE ROME, and in the same year he completed a one-act OPÉRA COMIQUE, LE DOCTEUR MIRACLE. It won first prize in a contest sponsored by Jacques OFFENBACH and was introduced at the Bouffes-Parisiens. Returning to Paris in 1860 after his years in Rome, Bizet embarked on a career as opera composer. His LES PÊCHEURS DE PERLES, given at the THÉÂTRE LYRIQUE on Sept. 30, 1863, was only moderately successful, though after his death it achieved a very wide popularity. LA JOLIE FILLE DE PERTH, in 1867, was a failure; so was a one-act opera given by the OPÉRA-COMIQUE in 1872, DJAMILEH. Meanwhile, in 1869, Bizet married Geneviève Halévy, the daughter of his teacher. He lived the humble existence of an unrecognized composer until 1872, when he was acclaimed for his incidental music to Alphonse DAUDET's *L'Arlésienne,* to this day his most popular orchestral work. His last opera, CARMEN, was completed in 1875 and was introduced at the Opéra-Comique on Mar. 3 of the same year. It received thirty-seven performances that season, an indication that it was no failure, though its great popularity began later. Bizet died exactly three months after the premiere of his greatest work. He brought to French opera a fine feeling for colorful background and exotic atmospheres. His sensuous melodies, vivid harmonies and orchestration, and captivating rhythms were ideally suited to such subjects. He had a keen dramatic sense. His use of recurrent musical themes prompted the criticism that he was being too Wagnerian. But Bizet, for all the Wagnerian influences and oriental subjects, remains a typically French composer in the refinement and sensitivity of his style and the purity of his lyricism.

Bjoner, Ingrid, soprano. Born Kraakstad, near Oslo, Norway, 1929. While studying pharmacy at the University of Oslo she attended the Oslo Conservatory, where she attracted the interest of, and received encouragement from, Kirsten FLAGSTAD. A scholarship enabled Bjoner to study voice with Paul Lohmann in Germany. In 1956 she made her debut over the Oslo Radio in GÖTTERDÄMMERUNG as Gutrune and the Third Norn. Her debut on the operatic stage followed a year later as Donna ANNA. She was an immediate success, with the result that she was engaged as principal soprano of the Wuppertal Opera and invited for guest appearances with the STOCKHOLM OPERA, the VIENNA STATE OPERA, and the BERLIN DEUTSCHE STAATSOPER. In 1959 she was principal soprano of the Düsseldorf Opera. The summer of 1960 marked her debut at the BAYREUTH Festival, where she sang ELSA, a role in which her United States debut took place later the same year, on Oct. 21, with the SAN FRANCISCO OPERA. Her METROPOLITAN OPERA debut took place on Oct. 28, 1961, also as Elsa. From then on she appeared with the leading opera houses of Europe and America, distinguishing herself particularly in the works of WAGNER and Richard STRAUSS. In 1963 she was selected to appear in the title role of Richard Strauss's DIE FRAU OHNE SCHATTEN, which opened the new opera house in Munich, and in 1965 she was called upon to sing the role of Isolde at the one-hundredth anniversary of the production of TRISTAN UND ISOLDE at the MUNICH OPERA. She was awarded the Order of St. Olav, First Class, in 1964, received the title of KAMMERSÄNGERIN by the Bavarian

State in 1965, and was given the Bavarian Order of Merit in 1966.

Björling, Jussi, tenor. Born Stora Tuna, Sweden, Feb. 2, 1911; died Silar Oe, near Stockholm, Sept. 9, 1960. He attended the Stockholm Conservatory. As a boy he joined his father and two brothers in the Björling Quartet which toured Scandinavia in native dress, and then appeared in the United States in 1920–21. In his eighteenth year he entered the Royal Opera School, where his teachers included John Forsell and Tullio Voghera. Immediately after graduation (1929) he made his debut as Don OTTAVIO at the STOCKHOLM ROYAL OPERA. Between 1931 and 1934 he appeared in major European opera houses, making his COVENT GARDEN debut in the spring of 1936 and in 1937 appearing at the SALZBURG FESTIVAL in performances of DON GIOVANNI which were highly acclaimed. He made his American debut over a radio network in 1937. His opera debut took place a month later with the CHICAGO OPERA. On Nov. 24, 1938, he made his bow at the METROPOLITAN OPERA as RODOLFO. He appeared in over fifty leading roles in Italian and French operas at the Metropolitan Opera and in other leading operatic institutions. His last appearance took place at the Metropolitan Opera in CAVALLERIA RUSTICANA on Dec. 2, 1959.

Blacher, Boris, composer. Born Newchang, China, Jan. 6, 1903. He received his early academic and musical schooling in the Far East. When he was nineteen, he went to Berlin, where he attended the Technische Hochschule as a student of architecture and the Hochschule für Musik. Between 1927 and 1931 he was a pupil of Schering and Blume in musicology. Some instrumental compositions and his first ballet, *Fest im Süden,* brought him to the attention of the musical world between 1932 and 1935; the ballet was given in about fifty German theaters. He wrote several more ballets before undertaking his first opera, *Fürstin Tarakanova,* produced in Wuppertal on Feb. 5, 1941. This was followed in 1943 by a CHAM-BER opera, ROMEO UND JULIA, which was introduced in a concert version in 1947 and was produced at the SALZBURG FESTIVAL in 1950; it was heard in America at the Berkshire Music Center at TANGLEWOOD in 1955 (during the composer's first visit to the United States to serve as guest professor of composition). Later operas were DIE FLUT (produced in Dresden on Mar. 4, 1947); PREUSSISCHES MÄRCHEN, given in Berlin in 1952; the provocative abstract opera, ABSTRAKTE OPER NO. I, in 1953; ZWISCHENFÄLLE BEI EINER NOTLANDUNG (Incidents in a Crash Landing), which utilizes electronic sounds extensively, and which received its world premiere in Hamburg in 1966; and *Zweihunderttausend Taler,* whose world premiere was heard at the BERLIN FESTIVAL in Sept., 1969. From 1945 to 1948, Blacher was director of the Berlin Radio, and since 1953 he has been director of the Hochschule für Musik in Berlin. He returned to the United States in 1966 to fill the post of composer-in-residence at the Hopkins Center Congregation of the Arts at Dartmouth College.

Blacher wrote the librettos for EINEM's operas DANTONS TOD and THE TRIAL.

Blanche Dourga, Lakmé's prayer with chorus to the gods, in Act I of DELIBES's LAKMÉ.

Blaze, François-Henri-Joseph (better known as **Castil-Blaze**), writer on music. Born Cavaillon, France, Dec. 1, 1784; died Paris, Dec. 11, 1857. He is frequently described as the father of French music criticism. After completing music study at the Paris Conservatory in 1820, he wrote his first book, the one by which he is most often remembered: *De l'Opéra en France,* a definitive study of the operatic techniques of his day. For a decade he was the music critic of the *Journal des débats.* He translated many librettos into French, including those of DON GIOVANNI, FIDELIO, DER FREISCHÜTZ, and THE MARRIAGE OF FIGARO. His son, Baron Henri Blaze de Bury (1813–1888), wrote biographies of ROSSINI and MEYERBEER.

Blech, Leo, conductor and composer. Born Aix-la-Chapelle, Ger., Apr. 21, 1871; died Berlin, Aug. 24, 1958. He considered making business a career but in 1890 began music study at the Berlin Hochschule für Musik. From 1893 to 1898 he was conductor at the Aix-la-Chapelle Stadttheater, and from 1899 to 1906 at the Deutsches Landestheater in Prague. In 1906 he was appointed principal conductor at the Berlin Royal Opera (BERLIN STATE OPERA). During the next fifteen years he distinguished himself as one of the leading opera conductors in Germany; at the request of Richard STRAUSS, he led the premiere of ELEKTRA in 1909. In 1923 he visited the United States at the head of a German company that performed the Wagnerian repertory, making his American bow on Feb. 12 with DIE MEISTERSINGER. He now became the artistic director of the Berlin Volksoper, and two years later he returned to the Berlin State Opera as principal conductor. He left Germany in 1937 because of differences with the Nazi regime. He conducted opera in Riga in 1939 and after World War II in Stockholm. In 1949 he returned to Berlin and became principal conductor of the BERLIN DEUTSCHE STAATS-OPER. He celebrated his eightieth birthday by conducting in Berlin his opera *Das war ich,* which he had written in 1902 and which had been introduced in Hamburg in 1908. He wrote several other operas early in his career, the most famous being *Versiegelt* (Sealed), introduced in Hamburg in 1908 and produced by the METROPOLITAN OPERA in 1912. His other operas: *Alpenkönig und Menschenfeind* (1903, revised 1917); *Aschenbrödl* (1905).

Blick' ich umher, Wolfram's hymn to pure love, in Act II of WAGNER'S TANN-HÄUSER.

Bliss, Sir Arthur, composer. Born London, Aug. 2, 1891. He attended Pembroke College, Cambridge, from which he received degrees in arts and music. Additional music study took place with Ralph VAUGHAN WILLIAMS at the Royal College of Music. During World War I he served as a commissioned officer and was wounded and gassed. Between 1923 and 1925 he lived in Santa Barbara, Cal. Though he made a number of visits to the United States after that, he settled in London and established his reputation as a nonvocal composer. He did not write his first opera until 1949, THE OLYMPIANS, text by J. B. Priestley. His second opera, *Tobias and the Angel,* was commissioned by BBC, which televised it in 1960; in 1962 it was given the Award of Merit at the SALZBURG FESTIVAL. Bliss was knighted in 1950, in 1952 was appointed Master of the Queen's Music, and in 1963 was awarded the Gold Medal of the Royal Philharmonic Society.

Blitzstein, Marc, composer. Born Philadelphia, Pa., Mar. 2, 1905; died Martinique, Jan. 22, 1964. His formal music study took place at the Curtis Institute, with Alexander Siloti in New York, Nadia Boulanger in Paris, and Arnold SCHOENBERG in Berlin. His earliest works revealed an interest in advanced techniques and unorthodox approaches, but his increasing social consciousness made him abandon this style for a more popular kind of music. He first became famous with an opera in this new vein, THE CRADLE WILL ROCK, introduced in New York in 1937. After receiving a Guggenheim Fellowship in 1940 he completed a second social opera, *No for An Answer.* During World War II he served in the air force, where his duties were mostly of a musical nature. After the war a third opera, REGINA, was introduced on Broadway in 1949. He subsequently made an adaptation of the text of Kurt WEILL'S THE THREEPENNY OPERA (leaving the music intact). After being introduced in Waltham, Mass., in 1952, it came to New York in 1954 to achieve a six-year run; two national companies toured with it in 1960 and 1961. By the time of his death, Blitzstein had almost completed a three-act opera on the subject of Sacco and Vanzetti which he was writing on a FORD FOUNDATION GRANT for the METROPOLITAN OPERA. He had also been working on two one-act operas based on stories by Bernard Malamud, *Idiots First* and *The Magic Barrel*. Blitzstein was on vacation in Martinique when he was beaten to death by three local sailors.

Blomdahl, Karl-Birger, composer. Born Växjö, Sweden, Oct. 19, 1916; died Stockholm, June 16, 1968. He studied composition under Hilding ROSENBERG in Stockholm and under others in Paris and Rome. He subsequently attracted notice with various works in a progressive idiom, including the opera ANIARA, which employs electronic sounds and whose world premiere took place in Sweden in 1959. In 1953 he had been appointed a member of the Royal Academy of Music, where he later assumed the post of professor of composition. He visited the United States in 1955.

Blonde (or Blonda), Constanze's maid (soprano) in MOZART'S THE ABDUCTION FROM THE SERAGLIO.

Bluebeard, *see* BARBE-BLEUE.

Bluebeard's Castle (or Duke Blue-beard's Castle), opera in one act by BARTÓK. Libretto by Béla Balázs. Premiere: Budapest, May 24, 1918. American premiere: Dallas, Texas, Jan. 8, 1946 (concert version); New York City, Oct. 2, 1952 (staged).

The opera opens with a somber prelude. Bluebeard (bass) and his latest bride, Judith (soprano), are seen on a darkened stage at the head of a stairway. She prevails on her husband to give her keys to seven doors in his castle and opens one after another. The first five doors lead respectively to a garden, Bluebeard's armory, a torture chamber, a storehouse of jewels, a splendid view of his realm—all covered with blood. When the sixth door is opened and everything grows dark, Judith is convinced that Bluebeard's earlier wives are lying dead behind the last door. So they are—three in number and each more beautiful than Judith. She then permits her husband to adorn her with jewels and a crown. The text was intended to point up the eternal conflict and the spiritual relationship between man and woman. Most of the opera consists of recitatives, but lyrical passages emphasize the love between Bluebeard and Judith.

Blue Bird, The (L'Oiseau bleu), fairy opera in three acts by Albert WOLFF. Libretto is Maurice MAETERLINCK'S poetic fantasy of the same name. Premiere: Metropolitan Opera, Dec. 27, 1919. The familiar Maeterlinck tale concerns the search of the children Tyltyl (tenor) and Mytyl (soprano) for the bluebird, symbol of happiness. The search carries them to many strange places: the Land of Memory, the Palace of Night, the Palace of Happiness. When they find the bird at last, it is in their humble home.

Blühenden Lebens labendes Blut, the pledge of brotherhood between Gunther and Siegfried at the close of Act I, Scene 1, of WAGNER'S DIE GÖTTERDÄMMER-UNG.

Bluthochzeit, Die (The Blood Wedding), opera in two acts by FORTNER. Libretto by Enrique Beck, based on the drama by Federico García Lorca. Premiere: Cologne, June 8, 1957. With the exception of Leonardo, the characters bear no names. A mother is reluctant to have her son marry a girl who had previously been engaged to Leonardo. Though Leonardo is married, he apparently has not forgotten the girl, for he continually wanders under her window. During the wedding ceremonies of the girl and her fiancé, the bride is nowhere to be found, having fled into the woods with Leonardo. There they are discovered by the wedding guests headed by the bridegroom. In the duel that ensues between Leonardo and the bridegroom both men get killed. The opera ends with Leonardo's wife deep in grief, the bride ready and willing to accept punishment, and the mother convinced that what has happened is the work of destiny.

Though basically in a twelve-tone style, this opera suggests its Spanish background through the prolific use of

Spanish-like folksongs and dances, as well as the rhythm of castanets and the strumming of guitars.

The Lorca drama providing the text had also been used by the composer for a cantata called *Der Wald*. Fortner combined material from *Der Wald* and *Die Bluthochzeit* to create a new opera, *In seinem Garten liebt Don Perlimplin Belisa,* introduced in Schwetzingen on May 10, 1962.

In 1964 a Hungarian composer, Sandór Szokolay, also wrote an opera called *Blood Wedding* based on Lorca. It was introduced by the BUDAPEST STATE OPERA in 1968. Comparing this opera with Fortner's, James H. Sutcliffe wrote: "Though conservative in style, Szokolay's work sticks closer to the play, is musically all of a piece and is tremendously convincing in the theater. Specific Spanish color is avoided except for the wedding scene, but the shimmering orchestral palette—atmospheric and starkly dramatic by turns—carries the opera along."

Blut und Leib der heil'gen Gabe, chorus of the knights describing the Last Supper, in Act I, Scene 2, of WAGNER'S PARSIFAL.

Boatswain's Mate, The, opera in one act by Dame Ethel SMYTH. Libretto by the composer based on a story by W. W. Jacobs. Premiere: London, Jan. 28, 1916. This is the composer's best-known opera. Harry Benn, an ex-boatswain (tenor), is eager to marry Mrs. Waters, a landlady (soprano), but has been turned down consistently. To gain her favor, Harry Benn conspires with Ned Travers (baritone) that Ned should break into the landlady's inn late one night, pretending to be a burglar, and terrorize the landlady; Harry would then rescue Mrs. Waters and earn her gratitude. But Mrs. Waters captures the victim, locks him in a closet, and then releases him while holding him at bay with a gun. Ned Travers confesses to the plot. To punish Harry, Mrs. Waters fires a shot, then with mock hysterics runs to Harry to tell him she has killed a burglar and that they must bury him without delay. Repentant, Harry Benn gives himself up to a policeman (bass), but the whole matter is eventually straightened out. Harry has lost Mrs. Waters for good, and she now seems to look with considerable favor on Ned Travers. The overture, Harry Benn's reminiscences of his wandering years as a youth, and the duet of Ned Travers and Mrs. Waters when first they realize they appeal to each other are some of the highlights of this opera.

Bob, a tramp (baritone) in MENOTTI's THE OLD MAID AND THE THIEF.

Boccaccio, Giovanni, author. Born Florence (?), 1313; died Certaldo, Italy, Dec. 21, 1375. His classic, *The Decameron,* has been the source of several operas including: Cesare Brero's *Novella;* Carlos Chávez's *Panfilo and Lauretta;* Marcel Delannoy's *Ginevra,* 1942; and Rodolphe Kreutzer's *Imogène.* Boccaccio is the central character in a popular comic opera by Franz von SUPPÉ, *Boccaccio.*

Boccanegra, *see* SIMON BOCCANEGRA.

Bodanzky, Artur, conductor. Born Vienna, Dec. 16, 1877; died New York City, Nov. 23, 1939. From 1915 to the time of his death he was the principal conductor of German operas at the METROPOLITAN OPERA. After graduating from the Vienna Conservatory, he became a violinist in the Imperial Opera orchestra. In 1902 he became Gustav MAHLER's assistant at the VIENNA STATE OPERA, and in 1904 he was chosen to lead a performance of DIE FLEDERMAUS in Vienna that was outstandingly successful. After conducting at the PRAGUE OPERA for two years, he became musical director of the MANNHEIM OPERA in 1909. In 1914 he led a performance of PARSIFAL at COVENT GARDEN that so impressed GATTI-CASAZZA that the latter engaged him for the Metropolitan to succeed Alfred HERTZ. Bodanzky's American debut took place on Nov. 18, 1915, with GÖTTERDÄMMERUNG. Except for a brief hiatus in 1928, Bodanzky remained at the Metropolitan for the remainder of his life, distinguishing himself in the fidelity and painstaking thoroughness of his performances. Bodanzky also conducted symphonic and choral music in New York. He prepared new editions of FIDELIO, OBERON, and SUPPÉ's *Boccaccio*, all of them given at the Metropolitan.

Bohème, La, (1) opera in four acts by LEONCAVALLO. Libretto by the composer, based on Henri Murger's novel *Scènes de la vie de bohème*. Premiere: Teatro la Fenice, May 6, 1897. American premiere: New York City, Jan. 31, 1960. Leoncavallo's opera has been thrown completely into the shade by the more popular and more significant opera on the same subject by PUCCINI (*see below*). Both operas were written in the same period, and each composer was aware that the other was setting the Murger novel. A spirited contest developed as to which opera would be performed first. Puccini won. Curiously enough, Leoncavallo's opera was far better received than Puccini's at their premieres. The growing popularity of Puccini's opera, however, spelled doom for Leoncavallo's. Two of Leoncavallo's arias have survived: "Io non ho che una povera stanzetta" and "Testa adorata."

(2) Opera in four acts by Puccini. Libretto by Giuseppe Giacosa and Luigi ILLICA, based on Murger's novel *Scènes de la vie de bohème*. Premiere: Teatro Regio, Turin, Feb. 1, 1896. American premiere: Los Angeles, Oct. 14, 1897.

Characters: Rodolfo, a poet (tenor); Marcello, a painter (baritone); Colline, a philosopher (bass); Schaunard, a musician (baritone); Mimi, a seamstress (soprano); Benoît, a landlord (bass); Parpignol, vendor of toys (tenor); Alcindoro, a state councilor (bass); Musetta, a girl from the Latin Quarter (soprano); customhouse sergeant; students; girls; shopkeepers; soldiers; waiters; vendors. The setting is Paris in the 1830's.

Act I. An attic. On this chilly Christmas Eve in the home of four bohemians, Marcello is about to make a fire by burning a chair; the poet Rodolfo prefers using one of his unpublished manuscripts. Suddenly, Schaunard appears, his arms overflowing with food, drink, and fuel bought with money just acquired from a patron. The friends celebrate; then they decide to continue their merrymaking in a Latin Quarter café; only Rodolfo stays behind. Mimi, a neighbor, comes seeking a light for her candle. Before she leaves she is seized by a coughing fit and begins to faint. Rodolfo revives her and she is about to leave but stops because she seems to have dropped her key. As Rodolfo and Mimi go on their knees to hunt for it, Rodolfo touches Mimi's cold hand. He takes it in his and begins to tell her about himself ("Che gelida manina"). Mimi now reveals to him her hunger for the beauty of flowers and the warmth of springtime ("Mi chiamano Mimi"). From below, in the street, come the voices of Rodolfo's friends urging him to join them. Rodolfo opens the window and moonlight streams into the room. He turns to Mimi and rhapsodizes over her beauty. The two voices join in an ecstatic outpouring of love ("O soave fanciulla"), after which Rodolfo and Mimi go off to join his friends.

Act II. The Café Momus in the Latin Quarter. Rodolfo and Mimi stop off at a milliner's shop to buy her a hat. Then they join their friends at the café. Musetta, one-time sweetheart of Marcello, appears with the wealthy councilor, Alcindoro. Coquettishly she reveals how men are attracted to her (Musetta's Waltz: "Quando m'en vo' soletta"). It is obvious that Marcello, as he listens to her, is seized by his old feeling of love and that Musetta is still responsive to him. She sends Alcindoro to a cobbler's shop, feigning that her shoe is too tight. Then she rushes to Marcello. Mixing in a passing parade, the bohemians escape. The returning Alcindoro finds that he has been not only jilted but left with a large café bill.

Act III. At one of the city's gates. From the adjoining tavern comes the sound of gay voices. Mimi appears, coughing and shivering. She inquires from a policeman where she can find Marcello and is informed that he is now employed as a sign painter in the inn. When she finds Marcello, she confides how difficult life has become with Rodolfo, since he is insanely jealous of her. The appearance of Rodolfo sends Mimi hiding behind a tree, where she overhears his complaints about her, and learns of his concern over her health ("Mimi è una civetta"). When Rodolfo announces his intention to give her up for good, she emerges from hiding. Seeing her revives the poet's ardor. He tenderly takes her in his arms. But Mimi insists that they must separate for his own good ("Donde lieta uscì"). The lovers bid each other farewell while Marcello and Musetta quarrel over her flirtation with a stranger ("Addio, dolce svegliare"), but even now Mimi and Rodolfo realize that they cannot separate. In a renewed wave of tenderness, they depart together.

Act IV. Again the attic. Once more Rodolfo and Marcello have quarreled with their sweethearts. Nostalgically they recall how happy they used to be with Mimi and Musetta. Their reveries are punctuated with food and drink brought by Colline and Schaunard. The bohemians' spirits lift, and a quadrille and a mock duel ensue. The revelry is at its height when Musetta bursts in to say that Mimi, who is outside, is deathly sick. She is brought into the attic and tenderly placed on Rodolfo's bed. Once again the lovers are reconciled. Strains from "Che gelida" and "Mi chiamano Mimi" are briefly recalled. Then Mimi remembers tender episodes of her love for Rodolfo ("Te lo rammenti"). When Rodolfo's friends go to buy medicine for Mimi, the lovers are alone. They repeat their true feelings. When the friends return, Mimi closes her eyes wearily. Rodolfo goes to the window to cover it and obscure the light. But Schaunard notices that Mimi is not asleep—but dead. One glance at his friends, another at Mimi, and Rodolfo knows the tragic truth. He cries out Mimi's name, rushes to her bed, and sobs over her body.

The central interest of the plot lies in the everyday problems, the little joys and sorrows, of several Parisian artists. The opera has no big scenes, the action never gets involved, there are no breathtaking climaxes. Puccini's concern is not so much his story as his characters (particularly the women), and it is the characters who dominate music as well as libretto. Frequently the main arias serve to throw light on the characters who sing them; throughout the opera these recurring melodies are subtly changed to produce new insights into the characters' personalities. The naturalism of the story—combined with the restraint and tenderness of Puccini's music—makes a poignant human drama. It is possibly for this reason that La Bohème has through the years remained Puccini's best-loved work. Possibly for the same reason—since its effect on an audience is subtle rather than overpowering—La Bohème was not at first successful. At its premiere in Turin, the audience was apathetic, the critics outrightly hostile. When La Bohème was given in Rome soon afterward, it was still received coldly. To outward appearances it seemed that Puccini had produced a failure. But its third presentation the same year, in Palermo, was a triumph. There was such an ovation that the entire death scene had to be repeated. From this performance on the opera passed from one triumph to another and to presentations on all the opera stages of the world.

Bohemian Girl, The, comic opera in three acts by BALFE. Libretto by Alfred Bunn, based on the ballet *The Gypsy* by Vernoy SAINT-GEORGES. Premiere: Drury Lane Theatre, London, Nov. 27, 1843. American premiere: Park Theater, New York, Nov. 25, 1844. The setting is eighteenth-century Hungary, where Arline (soprano), daughter of Count Arnheim (baritone), has been kidnaped and raised by gypsies. As a beautiful young woman, she is falsely accused of stealing a medallion and is imprisoned by the Count's men. When she appears before the Count to plead for clemency, he recognizes her by a scar. The opera is noteworthy for such songs as "I dreamt I dwelt in marble halls," "The heart bowed down," and "Then you'll remember," and for its gypsy songs and dances.

Böhm, Karl, conductor. Born Graz, Austria, Aug. 28, 1894. He studied to be a lawyer, but his passion for music led him to attend the Graz Conservatory and to study privately with Eusebius Mandyczewski. He was engaged by the Graz Opera as prompter in 1917, and three years later he became first conductor. On the recommendation of Karl MUCK, he was engaged by the MUNICH STATE OPERA as conductor in 1920, where he remained several years. In 1927 he conducted in Darmstadt, in 1931 became musical director at the HAMBURG OPERA, and in 1933 musical director of the DRESDEN STATE OPERA. In Dresden he led the world premiere of Richard STRAUSS's DAPHNE and SUTERMEISTER's *The Magic Isle,* both of which are dedicated to him. After World War II, Böhm conducted extensively in Europe and South America. In 1954 he received a five-year contract as artistic and musical director of the VIENNA STATE OPERA, inaugurating his regime on Nov. 5, 1955, with FIDELIO. He did not complete that contract, resigning in Mar., 1956, following complaints by the management that he was spending too much of his time abroad. Nevertheless, he continued to appear at the Vienna State Opera as conductor and has since remained there, a strong favorite especially in his performances of MOZART, WAGNER, Richard Strauss, and BERG. Following his debut in DON GIOVANNI on Oct. 31, 1957, he has also appeared extensively at the METROPOLITAN OPERA, as well as in other of the world's major opera houses. For a quarter of a century, he has been a principal conductor at the SALZBURG FESTIVAL. In 1970 Böhm received the Great Golden Medal for his distinguished service to Viennese music.

He was also named General Music Director of Austria, the only conductor to be so honored.

Bohnen, Michael, bass-baritone. Born Cologne, Ger., May 2, 1887; died Berlin, Apr. 26, 1965. He studied voice at the Cologne Conservatory, then made his debut at Düsseldorf in 1910 as Caspar in WEBER's DER FREISCHÜTZ, a part in which he later attained universal success. In 1914 he was heard at the BAYREUTH Festival as HUNDING and DALAND, and from 1913 to 1921 he was a member of the Berlin Hofoper (BERLIN STATE OPERA). He made his METROPOLITAN OPERA debut in the American premiere of SCHILLINGS' *Mona Lisa* on Mar. 1, 1923. Bohnen remained at the Metropolitan until 1932, excelling in baritone as well as bass roles. He went into temporary retirement during World War II in Germany but emerged after the war to become general manager of the Berlin Städtische Oper (BERLIN DEUTSCHE STAATSOPER) between 1945 and 1947, where he occasionally resumed his old roles.

Boieldieu, François Adrien, composer. Born Rouen, France, Dec. 16, 1775; died Jarcy, France, Oct. 8, 1834. He was one of that triumvirate of early OPÉRA COMIQUE composers that includes AUBER and ADAM. After studying with a Rouen organist, he wrote his first opera, *La Fille coupable,* in his eighteenth year. Two years later he went to Paris. A meeting with CHERUBINI was a decisive event in his life. Cherubini accepted him as a pupil and in 1798 appointed him professor of the piano at the Conservatory. In the same year Boieldieu achieved his first success as a theatrical composer with *Zoraïme et Zulnare.* Two years later his LE CALIFE DE BAGDAD was so well received that it ran for seven hundred performances. In 1803 Boieldieu visited Russia, where he was showered with honors. He was appointed KAPELLMEISTER by the Czar and given a contract to write three operas a year. He returned to Paris in 1811, having written numerous works he felt unworthy of presenting in Paris. In 1817 he succeeded MÉHUL as professor of composition at the Conservatory, and a year later he became a member of the Institut de France. His masterwork, and one of the finest works in the *opéra-comique* repertory, was LA DAME BLANCHE, introduced in 1825. It was a sensational success and earned its composer a government pension. After this, Boieldieu produced a failure or two and wrote no more. The fall of the monarchy in 1830 deprived him of his pension; soon after, poor health compelled him to give up his conservatory post. The new government finally came to his help with an annual grant. Boieldieu's principal operas: *La Fille coupable* (1793); *Zoraïme et Zulnare* (1798); *Le Calife de Bagdad* (1800); *Ma Tante Aurore* (1803); *Calypso* (*Télémaque*) (1806); *Jean de Paris* (1812); *Le Petit Chaperon rouge* (1818); *La Dame blanche* (1825).

Bois Épais, air from LULLY's AMADIS DE GAULE.

Boisfleury, Marquis de, brother (bass) of the Marchioness de Serval in DONIZETTI's LINDA DI CHAMOUNIX.

Boito, Arrigo, librettist and composer. Born Padua, Italy, Feb. 24, 1842; died Milan, June 10, 1918. He achieved importance as the composer of MEFISTOFELE and as the librettist of PONCHIELLI's LA GIOCONDA and VERDI's OTELLO and FALSTAFF.

Entering the Milan Conservatory in his fourteenth year, Boito remained there six years. In 1861 he collaborated with Franco FACCIO in writing a cantata which won for both composers a two-year traveling scholarship. Back in Italy after a fruitful stay in Paris, Boito led a movement to reform Italian music by taking into consideration influences and developments—particularly WAGNER's—in the North. To clarify and propagandize his ideas, Boito wrote many brilliant theoretical essays.

While trying to get others to write in the "new" fashion, he began his masterwork, *Mefistofele,* in 1866. The outbreak of war with Austria delayed its composition, Boito joining the Garibaldian volunteers and seeing active service. He completed his opera early in 1868 and on Mar. 5 it was introduced at LA SCALA, the composer conducting. The conflicting opinions on the opera, and the violent demonstrations during its three performances, made it seem that Boito had written a failure. Seven years later, after extensive cutting and revising by the composer, it was produced in Bologna, and this time it found favor. Ever since, it has remained a favorite opera in Italy. He never completed his second opera, NERONE, and it was not performed during his lifetime, but in 1924 Arturo TOSCANINI put in the finishing touches and presented it at La Scala. Its success was limited.

Boito's first important effort at writing librettos came in 1865 when he provided his friend Faccio with the book for *Amleto;* eleven years later he did a similar service for Ponchielli with *La Gioconda.* His major achievements in this direction came in 1886 and 1893 with his librettos for Verdi's last two operas, *Otello* and *Falstaff.* Boito's texts for these works are considered two of the finest librettos in all Italian opera. He was also the author of the excellent Italian translations of RIENZI and TRISTAN UND ISOLDE.

bolero, originally a vigorous eighteenth-century Spanish dance in triple time, later also a dancelike song for solo voice. Boleros were introduced in a number of nineteenth-century operas. Examples occur in MÉHUL's *Les Deux Aveugles,* AUBER's LA MUETTE DE PORTICI, and VERDI's THE SICILIAN VESPERS (Elena's aria "Mercè, diletti amiche").

Bologna Opera. *See* TEATRO COMMUNALE, BOLOGNA.

Bolshoi Theater, (1) leading opera house in Leningrad (also known as the Imperial). It first opened in 1783, then was rebuilt and reopened on Nov. 27, 1836, with A LIFE FOR THE CZAR. It became traditional for the company to open each season with this work, giving it over seven hundred performances before the end of the nineteenth century. Between 1843 and 1846 an Italian opera company occupied the theater. In

1850 a second opera house, the Tsirk, was constructed opposite the Bolshoi. The Tsirk was demolished by fire and was rebuilt in 1860 as the Maryinsky Theater (since come to be known as the Kirov Theater). Among the significant premieres given at both the Bolshoi and the Maryinsky (Kirov) were most of RIMSKY-KORSAKOV's operas, together with THE STONE GUEST, the second version of BORIS GODUNOV, NÁPRAVNÎK's *Francesca da Rimini*, WAR AND PEACE, THE DEMON, and PIQUE DAME. The name "Imperial" was discontinued after the Revolution. It is now known as the Academic Opera.

(2) Leading opera house in Moscow, situated in Revolution Square in the center of the city. It is an outgrowth of the Petrovsky, built in 1780 as the city's first public theater. This theater burned down in 1805 and not until 1825 was a new house built on its site—the Petrovsky Bolshoi (or the Bolshoi, as it has been called since the Revolution), then one of the largest theaters in the world. It was here that there took place the world premieres of A LIFE FOR THE CZAR in 1842 and RUSSLAN AND LUDMILLA in 1846. The opera house had to stop operations between 1853 and 1856 due to reconstruction necessitated by a fire. After 1856 and for the next half century or so, its repertory, besides the basic Italian works, included some of the greatest Russian operas ever written, most of them receiving their world premieres here. These included EUGENE ONEGIN (1881); BORIS GODUNOV (1888); PIQUE DAME (1891); THE SNOW MAIDEN (1893); PRINCE IGOR (1898); THE MAID OF PSKOV (1901); SADKO (1906); KHOVANTCHINA (1912). Lesser known Russian operas were also given, such as SEROV's *Rognyeda* (1868) and TCHAIKOVSKY's *Voyevoda* (1869) and *Oprichnik* (1875).

Since the Revolution the Bolshoi has expanded its activities and its seating space by acquiring a second auditorium, the Filial Bolshoi nearby. The Bolshoi repertory is partly of the standard variety (though WAGNER is rarely given), all sung in Russian. The established classics of Russian opera (in performances of which this company is often unrivaled) are frequently given, together with occasional revivals of such rarely heard works as Tchaikovsky's *Iolanthe* and *Mazeppa* and RUBINSTEIN'S THE DEMON. Among the world premieres have been DZERZHINSKY's THE QUIET DON; KABALEVSKY's *Nikita Veshinin* and *The Armoured Train;* KHRENNIKOV's *Mother* and *In the Storm;* Vano Muradely's *The Great Friendship;* PROKOFIEV's *Semyon Kotko;* Yuri Shaporin's *The Decembrists;* Vissarion Shebalin's *The Taming of the Shrew;* and LADY MACBETH OF MZENSK. Among non-Russian composers, one of the most significant twentieth-century operas produced was BRITTEN's A MIDSUMMER NIGHT'S DREAM.

The first Wagner work given in over a decade (one of the infrequent occasions when Wagner is produced) was the brilliant Sergei Eisenstein presentation of DIE WALKÜRE at the Filial Bolshoi just before World War II. Since the end of the war, the first Wagner opera to get heard at the Bolshoi was DER FLIEGENDE HOLLÄNDER.

In 1967 the Bolshoi Opera paid its first visit to the Western Hemisphere by appearing at Expo 67 in Montreal, Canada, in performances of *Prince Igor* and *Pique Dame.*

Bomarzo, opera in two acts by GINASTERA. Libretto by Mujica Lainez based on his novel of the same name. Premiere: Washington, D.C., May 19, 1967.

Characters: Pier Francesco Orsini, Duke of Bomarzo (tenor); Gian Corrado Orsini, the Duke's father (bass); Maerbale, the Duke's brother (baritone); Girolamo, another brother (baritone); Nicolas Orsini, a nephew of the Duke (tenor); Julia Farnese, the Duke's wife (soprano); Diana Orsini, the Duke's grandmother (contralto); Pantasilea, a courtesan (mezzo-soprano); Silvio de Narni, an astrologer (baritone); a shepherd boy (boy soprano); messenger; prelates; servants; astrologers. The action takes place in Bomarzo, Florence, and Rome during the sixteenth century.

Before working on this opera, both

the composer and librettist had produced a cantata, *Bomarzo,* in 1964 on the same subject as this opera, but with entirely different music.

Both the cantata and the opera came from Lainez' novel, the idea for which occurred to him one day in the gardens of the Duke of Bomarzo, near Rome, which are filled with bizarre, monstrous sculptures. Wondering about the man who could have enjoyed such art work, Lainez conceived the character of the Duke—a hunchback with a warped mind who underwent a lifetime of abnormal and at times hideous experiences.

Ginastera's wife, impressed with the novel, suggested to her husband that he write a cantata, with text prepared by Lainez himself. The finished product suggested to both authors the idea of writing an opera on the same theme. The opera was commissioned by the Coolidge Foundation. Lainez wrote a libretto, and Ginastera conceived entirely new music. The composer explains: "I conceived the flashback idea—a cinema technique still new to opera. Thus I could accomplish the difficult task of making a suite of scenes, a sequence all tied together by the nexus of Bomarzo's life story but not connected in the conventional narrative sense. The scenes come back in the last moments of his life, as though he remembers or dreams them. It is hard to distinguish between what really happened and what he imagines."

The text has a surrealistic, at times expressionist, quality. The opera opens in sixteenth-century Italy as the Duke of Bomarzo is about to die. Images of his life flash through his mind. He remembers how in childhood he is ridiculed by his two brothers, who compel him to put on woman's clothing; how his father makes him stay in a room where he is haunted by a skeleton; how an astrologer promises him an endless life; and how he offers his necklace to a courtesan to have her free him from his surrounding horrors. Later on Bomarzo sees his brother fall to his death from a rock into the sea. He is

prevented from saving the victim by his grandmother. When Bomarzo succeeds his father as Duke, he is haunted by dancing images of women trying to possess him. Then, after a victorious return from battle, he sees a newly painted portrait of himself which makes him tall and handsome and which brings home to him how really hideous he looks.

In the second act, the Duke marries Julia. When the guests depart, he leads his wife through the chambers where he is followed by the face of a devil from one of the art works. On his wedding night, he is terrified by a nightmare, a dance of monsters. The Duke flees from the bridal chamber, trying to find refuge in the ancestral gallery where he embraces the statue of the Minotaur.

Several years have passed. The Duke becomes convinced that his wife Julia has been betraying him with his own brother, Maerbale. Bomarzo arranges to have his brother killed with the aid of the astrologer. In the astrologer's laboratory, figures of ancient alchemists come to life to perform a corybantic, while the astrologer prepares a potion capable of giving the Duke immortality. But the potion is poison. Having drunk it, the Duke is dying. When he lies dead, a passing shepherd bends down to kiss him.

This summary hardly suggests the violence, eroticism, lust, narcissism, and degeneracy depicted in detail throughout the dramatic action. To meet the requirements of such textual material, the composer used every means at his disposal: electronic sounds, serial techniques, tone clusters, aleatoric music, microtonal music. A chorus, placed in the pit, sometimes shrieks its commentary and sometimes utters mere guttural sounds. To emphasize the exoticism of parts of the action, the composer employs unorthodox instruments for fourteen orchestral interludes: a mandolin, harpsichord, viola d'amore, Japanese wood chimes, and a *hyosigo,* a Japanese percussion instrument. Yet once in a while the score is relieved of tensions and torments by affecting arias.

Bomarzo proved powerful theater and was acclaimed as such when introduced in Washington, D.C., and then when given its New York premiere at the NEW YORK CITY OPERA on Mar. 14, 1968. But to Ginastera's native land, Argentina, *Bomarzo* proved too shocking for presentation, and its scheduled performance there on Aug. 8, 1967 was canceled by government order. This created a furor dividing musical Argentina into two camps, those who sided with the municipal authorities and those who resented the censorship of what was already recognized as an important opera.

Bonci, Alessandro, tenor. Born Cesena, Italy, Feb. 10, 1870; died Vitterba, Aug. 8, 1940. He was a master of bel canto and one of the most celebrated tenors of his generation. After five years of study at the Rossini Conservatory in Pesaro with Carlo Pedrotti and Felice Coen he made his debut at the TEATRO REGIO in Parma in 1896 in FALSTAFF. He was an immediate success; before the end of his first season he was engaged by LA SCALA, where he made his debut in I PURITANI. Appearances throughout Europe followed. On Dec. 3, 1906, he made his American debut with the Hammerstein company at the MANHATTAN OPERA House in *I Puritani.* He stayed with this company two seasons, a competitive attraction to Enrico CARUSO. In 1908 Bonci joined the METROPOLITAN OPERA, and in 1914 he became a member of the CHICAGO OPERA. Meanwhile, in 1910–11, he made an extensive transcontinental tour in song recitals. During World War I he served in the Italian army. After the war he toured America for three seasons, appearing at the Metropolitan and with the Chicago Opera during the 1920–21 season. In 1922–23 he was the principal tenor of the TEATRO COSTANZI in Rome. A year later he taught master classes in singing in the United States. After 1925 he went into partial retirement and devoted himself primarily to teaching in Milan. Though his voice lacked volume, it had exceptional beauty of texture and lyrical sweetness. He was a master of phrasing and expression.

Bonelli, Richard (born Richard Bunn), baritone. Born Port Byron, N.Y., Feb. 6, 1894. After studying voice with Jean DE RESZKE, he made his opera debut at the Brooklyn Academy of Music in New York on Apr. 21, 1915, as VALENTIN. This was followed by appearances at the MONTE CARLO OPERA, LA SCALA, and in several major German opera houses. Between 1925 and 1931 he was a member of the CHICAGO OPERA. He made his debut at the METROPOLITAN OPERA on Dec. 1, 1932, as Germont in LA TRAVIATA, remaining with the company through the 1944–45 season. In 1943 he became head of the voice department at the Academy of the West, in Santa Barbara, Cal., serving as chairman of the board at the Academy between 1947 and 1949. Between 1950 and 1955 he taught voice at the Curtis Institute.

Boniface, monastery cook (baritone) in MASSENET'S LE JONGLEUR DE NOTRE DAME.

Bononcini (or Buononcini), Giovanni Battista, composer. Born Modena, Italy, July 18, 1670; died Vienna, July 9, 1747. He is principally remembered for his association and rivalry with HANDEL in London. It was this rivalry that contributed to our language the phrase "tweedledum and tweedledee." It is first found in a satirical poem by John Byrom:

Some say, compar'd to Bononcini,
That Mynheer Handel's but a ninny;
Others aver that he to Handel
Is scarcely fit to hold a candle.
Strange all this difference should be
'Twixt Tweedledum and Tweedledee.

Bononcini came from a long line of professional musicians. He studied first with his father and afterward in Bologna, where he published a volume of masses. In 1690 he was appointed MAESTRO DI CAPPELLA at the Church of San Giovanni in Monte. Four years later he was in Rome, where his first two operas were produced. After some years of success in Berlin and Vienna, he went to London in 1716 to be joint director (with Handel) of the newly organized

Royal Academy of Music, with which he was associated for over half a dozen years. He also wrote many operas for the English stage. London was for a long time divided between two factions: those favoring Bononcini (this group was headed by the powerful Duke of Marlborough, who paid Bononcini an annual stipend of five hundred pounds); and those on Handel's side. In 1731 Bononcini became discredited when a madrigal, submitted by him to the Academy of Ancient Music, was said—quite possibly erroneously—to be by another composer. A year later he left England in disgrace. After living for a time in France he spent several years as court composer in Venice and died in Vienna. He wrote about seventy-five operas, the most successful being: *Polifemo* (1702); *Endimione* (1706); *Turno Aricino* (1707); *Mario fuggitivo* (1708); *Abdolonimo* (1709); *Astarto* (1714); *Ciro* (1722); *Crispo* (1722); *Griselda* (1722); *Erminia* (1723); *Calpurnia* (1724); *Astianatte* (1727); *Alessandro in Sidone* (1737).

Polifemo, text by Ariosti (premiere, Berlin, 1702), was revived by the ASPEN Opera Workshop in Aspen, Col., on July 28, 1961.

Bonze, the (or **Bonzo**), Cio-Cio-San's uncle (bass) in PUCCINI's MADAMA BUTTERFLY.

Bordoni, Faustina, soprano. Born Venice, 1700; died there Nov. 4, 1781. Born to nobility, she studied voice with Gasparini and made a sensational debut in C. F. Pollarolo's *Ariodante* in 1716 in Venice. She achieved such fame in Italy that a medal was struck in her honor in Naples in 1722. In 1724 she was engaged by the court opera in Vienna, where she was heard by HANDEL, who engaged her for his opera company in London. That London debut took place on May 5, 1726 in Handel's ALESSANDRO. After two seasons in London, during which she became involved in a bitter rivalry with Francesca CUZZONI (an intrigue satirized in THE BEGGAR'S OPERA), she returned to Venice, where in 1730 she married the prolific opera com-

poser, HASSE. They established residence in Dresden a year later, and she made appearances there until 1763. Meanwhile she was heard in Paris in 1750 and in Vienna in 1775. After 1775 she and her husband lived in Venice, where she went into retirement.

Borgatti, Giuseppe, tenor. Born Cento, Italy, Mar. 17, 1871; died Reno, Lago Maggiore, Oct. 18, 1950. Completing his vocal studies in Bologna he made his debut in 1892 in Castelfranco Veneto in FAUST. He soon began assuming leading Wagnerian roles and was engaged by TOSCANINI to appear in them at LA SCALA, where he achieved the reputation of being one of Italy's most highly regarded *heldentenore.* He also appeared extensively throughout Europe and South America.

Bori, Lucrezia (born Borja), soprano. Born Valencia, Spain, Dec. 24, 1888; died New York City, May 14, 1960. Until her eighteenth year she was educated in a convent. After deciding to become a singer, she went to Milan for coaching. She made her debut at the TEATRO COSTANZI on Oct. 31, 1908, as MICAËLA. After auditioning for GATTI-CASAZZA and TOSCANINI she was engaged by LA SCALA, where she appeared for the first time in 1910 in IL MATRIMONIO SEGRETO. Her first American appearance took place on the opening night of the METROPOLITAN OPERA's 1912–13 season. The opera was MANON LESCAUT; she was acclaimed. In 1915 a growth in her throat necessitated a delicate operation. It seemed that her career might be over, but she refused to lose faith and kept on working assiduously. She returned to the opera stage in MONTE CARLO in 1918 and to the Metropolitan Opera on Jan. 29, 1921. She remained at the Metropolitan for the next fourteen years, starred in French and Italian operas. Among the important premieres and revivals in which she appeared were: L'AMORE DEI TRE RE, L'AMORE MEDICO, L'ORACOLO, PELLÉAS ET MÉLISANDE, PETER IBBETSON, and LA RONDINE. In 1925 she became one of the first important opera artists to sing on the radio; she was heard in a nation-wide hookup **with** John MC-CORMACK. In 1933, when the Metropolitan Opera faced an economic crisis, she became chairman of a committee "to save the Metropolitan." She helped raise a considerable amount of money and in 1934 once again served as chairman to raise funds.

Her final opera performance at the Metropolitan took place on Mar. 21, 1936, in *La rondine*. A week later the Metropolitan Opera gave a gala concert in her honor, in which she sang excerpts from her favorite operas and was given a twenty-minute ovation. After her retirement, Bori sang occasionally over the radio and became the first woman to be made a member of the board of directors of the Metropolitan Opera Association. In 1942 she was elected president of the Metropolitan Opera Guild.

Boris Godunov, opera in prologue and four acts by MUSSORGSKY. Libretto by the composer, based largely on the drama of the same name by Alexander PUSHKIN. Premiere: Maryinsky Theater, St. Petersburg, Feb. 8, 1874. American premiere: Metropolitan Opera, Mar. 19, 1913.

Characters: Boris Godunov (bass); Xenia, his daughter (soprano); Feodor, his son (mezzo-soprano); Marina, a Polish landowner's daughter (mezzo-soprano); Prince Shuisky, Boris' advisor (tenor); Gregory, a novice, later Dmitri the Pretender (tenor); Varlaam, a monk (bass); Missail, a monk (tenor); Pimen, a monk (bass); Stchelkalov, secretary of the Duma (baritone); Jesuits; monks; boyars: an innkeeper's wife; a police official; a nurse; an idiot. The settings are Russia and Poland; the years 1598 to 1605.

Prologue. Moscow—a square before the Novodievich Monastery. A crowd is kneeling in prayer that Boris Godunov accept the Russian crown ("Why hast thou abandoned us?") Stchelkalov comes out of the monastery to inform the people that Boris has not yet accepted. He urges them to continue their prayers. From the distance is heard the chant of pilgrims approaching to join the people in prayer. Boris finally yields to their plea.

Act I, Scene 1. The square between the Cathedral of the Assumption and the Cathedral of Archangels. A rejoicing crowd fills the square—Boris Godunov is to be crowned (Coronation Scene). The pealing of cathedral bells heralds the approach of a procession of boyars. The people sing the praises of Boris ("To the sun in all splendor"). Boris appears with his two children and promises the people that he will work for their good and for that of Russia. Calling for the help of God, he entreats the people to join him in prayer.

Scene 2. Five years have passed. In a cell in the Monastery of the Miracles, Pimen is chronicling the recent events in Russia (Pimen's Narrative: "Still one more page"). He tells the novice Gregory about the murder of the young Czarevich Dmitri by Boris' men. When Pimen further informs Gregory that the heir to the Russian throne would now have been his age, Gregory is fired with the ambition to impersonate Dmitri and avenge his murder.

Act II, Scene 1. An inn on the Lithuanian border. Gregory and the monks Varlaam and Missail have come here in their flight from the monastery. Gregory is disguised as a peasant, since he is wanted by the police for spreading the false rumor that Dmitri is alive. After a few drinks, Varlaam sings an earthy song ("In the town of Kazan"), then falls into a drunken sleep. Soldiers appear searching for Gregory. Skillfully, Gregory directs their suspicions to the drunken Varlaam; while they are arresting him, Gregory escapes.

Scene 2. The apartment of Czar Boris in the Kremlin. Boris' children, Xenia and Feodor, are with their nurse. She sings them an amusing little ditty (Song of the Gnat). Boris appears, praises his son for the way he has been learning his lessons, and reminds him that some day he will rule Russia. He soliloquizes on the torment of his rule, surrounded as he is by conspirators and blamed by the people for all the evils in the land ("I have attained the highest power"). Boris' anguish is intensified when Prince Shuisky arrives with tidings of the false Dmitri and how the people are rallying under him. Boris is now obsessed with the belief that the dead can arise from their graves and that the false Dmitri is really the true one. After Shuisky departs, panic seizes Boris. He sees the ghost of the murdered Dmitri. Falling on his knees, he prays to God for mercy ("Ah, I am suffocating").

Act III. The garden of a Polish palace. Gregory has come for a rendezvous with Marina, whom he expects to make his queen. Marina and her guests emerge into the garden where a brilliant polonaise is danced. After the guests go back into the palace, Marina meets Gregory, and an ardent love scene follows ("Oh! Czarevitch").

Act IV, Scene 1. The forest of Kromy. Peasants are dragging a captured boyar. They mock him and mock the Czar. A simpleton appears singing a ditty. From a distance the voices of Varlaam and Missail are heard denouncing Boris. Two Jesuits sing the praises of the new Czar, Dmitri. The people attack them, for they do not want the help of the clergy. The emotional climate gets stormy. With a blare of trumpets, Gregory appears, accompanied by his soldiers. The people acclaim him as Dmitri and follow him as he starts for Moscow. Only the simpleton remains to sing mournfully of the coming doom of Russia.

Scene 2. The Kremlin. Stchelkalov reads a message from Boris to the Duma (state council) informing it that a traitor is leading a revolt against the Czar. Shuisky expresses concern over the mental state of Boris, and the boyars are shocked. They are further horrified when Boris appears. He is out of his mind and seems to be fleeing from someone. He soon takes hold of himself, however, ascends his throne, and gives an audience to Pimen. The old monk

relates a strange story about a blind shepherd sent by the voice of Dmitri to his tomb in Uglich Cathedral where, by prayer, the shepherd recovered his vision. The story overwhelms Boris. He cries out for help. Then he summons Feodor. Taking his son in his arms, the Czar bids him farewell ("Farewell my son, I am dying"). He counsels the boy against traitors and blesses him as the new Czar. Bells begin tolling, and the sounds of people in prayer are heard. Boyars and monks fill the room. Boris designates his son as his successor, prays to God for mercy, collapses, and dies.

If any single work can be said to realize the artistic goals of the Russian national school, it is *Boris Godunov*. The Five (Balakirev, BORODIN, CUI, RIMSKY-KORSAKOV, and Mussorgsky) aspired to produce a great musical art by deriving inspiration and subject matter from Russian culture and history; at the same time they aimed at a musical art derived from Russian folksongs and dances. *Boris Godunov* fulfilled these specifications completely. It is a mighty drama of the Russian people taken, in part, from Russian history. It is a drama about the inner torment and anguish of a Czar; it also is a drama about the shifting forces of the Russian people. Mussorgsky produced a score in which the Russian soul speaks out with force and conviction. For his lyricism, Mussorgsky went to Russian folksongs and liturgical music, adapting their individual harmonic and rhythmic traits for his own purposes. He also devised a melody that followed the inflections of the Russian language. To his harmonic and rhythmic language he brought a strength well suited to the personal drama of Boris and the even greater drama of the Russian people.

There exist several different versions of this opera. The first is Mussorgsky's original concept. When *Boris Godunov* received its premiere, however, changes were made to please the opera-house directors; a few pleasing arias and some love interest were interpolated, and the order of some of the scenes was shifted. When the opera was revived in 1904, still a third version appeared, prepared by Rimsky-Korsakov, who refined away much of Mussorgsky's bare harmonic and orchestral styles. It was in this version that *Boris Godunov* (with its greatest interpreter, Feodor Chaliapin, in the title role) achieved its first major success. In 1908 Rimsky-Korsakov decided to revise his version to conform a bit more to Mussorgsky's original intentions. It is this fourth version that is now most often performed in this country and abroad. The act-and-scene division of this version is used as the basis for the synopsis given above. From time to time there have been attempts to revive the opera as Mussorgsky originally wrote it, since it is generally felt that much of the primitive force and cogency of the opera are lost in Rimsky-Korsakov's cultured adaptation. On Feb. 26, 1928, Mussorgsky's first version was introduced at the Bolshoi Opera in Moscow. A year and a half later Leopold Stokowski and the Philadelphia Orchestra gave the American premiere of the original *Boris* in concert version. The original version was produced at COVENT GARDEN on Oct. 31, 1958 (the 1874 version having been heard there in 1948), and was staged for the first time in the United States by the Boston Opera Group on Mar. 10, 1965. Later adapters have tried to make a suitable compromise between Mussorgsky's original version and the Rimsky-Korsakov edition. These include Dmitri SHOSTAKOVICH, whose version was produced by the METROPOLITAN OPERA on Mar. 6, 1953, and that of Karol Rathaus, heard at the Metropolitan Opera on Oct. 27, 1960.

For another version of the *Boris Godunov* theme *see* DIMITRIJ. V. de Joncières also used this subject for an opera, *Dimitri*, produced in Paris in 1876.

Borkh, Inge, soprano. Born Mannheim, Ger., May 26, 1921. She made appear-

ances as an actress in Austria before turning to opera. After a period of vocal study in Italy and at the Mozarteum in Salzburg she made her debut in Lucerne, Switzerland, in DER ZIGEUNERBARON during 1940–41. She scored an outstanding success in Berlin in 1951 in THE CONSUL. Further successes came in Paris (where she sang opposite Alexander Welitch, baritone, whom she married), Bayreuth, and Edinburgh. Her American debut took place with the SAN FRANCISCO OPERA on Sept. 25, 1953, as ELEKTRA in Richard STRAUSS's opera. Later appearances at COVENT GARDEN, the STUTTGART OPERA, LA SCALA, and the METROPOLITAN OPERA (where she made her debut as SALOME on Jan. 24, 1958) added significantly to her fame. In 1959 she returned to Covent Garden. Four years earlier, in 1954, she created the role of Cathleen in IRISCHE LEGENDE at the SALZBURG FESTIVAL.

Borodin, Alexander, composer. Born St. Petersburg, Nov. 11, 1833; died St. Petersburg, Feb. 27, 1887. A member of the Russian nationalist school, Borodin wrote an opera, PRINCE IGOR, that realized the ideals and principles of Russian nationalism. All his life Borodin divided his energies and interests between medicine and music. He was educated at the Academy of Medicine and Surgery in St. Petersburg, becoming there assistant professor of pathology and therapeutics in 1856, receiving his degree in medicine in 1858. After 1859, and up to the end of his life, he did significant research in chemistry and for many years was professor at the Academy. Music, his passion since childhood, he followed seriously for the first time in 1862, when he met and became a pupil of Balakirev. Balakirev inflamed Borodin with his own national ideals, so much so that Borodin eagerly joined him—and MUSSORGSKY, CUI, and RIMSKY-KORSAKOV—in spreading the cult of Russian national music. He completed his first symphony, some songs, and a farcical opera, *The Bogatyrs,* in 1867. Later works—notably the *Second Symphony*, the *Second String Quartet*, the tone poem *In the Steppes of Central Asia*, and the monumental opera that absorbed him on and off for twenty years, *Prince Igor*—made him one of the most significant of the nationalists.

Borodin's health was seriously affected in 1884 by an illness believed to be cholera. Afterward he was frequently in poor health and a victim of mental depressions. He died from a ruptured aneurism while enjoying a party with musical friends. He did not live to finish *Prince Igor*; it was completed by Rimsky-Korsakov and Alexander Glazunov. Besides the earlier opera, *The Bogatyrs*, Borodin also wrote a portion of *Mlada*, a composite opera (never finished) whose other composers were Cui, Mussorgsky, and Rimsky-Korsakov.

Borov, a doctor (baritone) in GIORDANO'S FEDORA.

Borromeo, Carlo, a Cardinal (baritone) in PFITZNER'S PALESTRINA.

Borsa, a courtier (tenor) in VERDI'S RIGOLETTO.

Bostana, Margiana's attendant (mezzo-soprano) in CORNELIUS' THE BARBER OF BAGDAD.

Boston Opera Group. *See* OPERA COMPANY OF BOSTON.

Boston Opera House, a theater built in 1909 as the home for the then newly organized Boston Opera company, directed by Henry RUSSELL. It opened with a splendid performance of LA GIOCONDA, with Lillian NORDICA and Louise HOMER in the cast. The opera company flourished for some years. In 1912 Felix WEINGARTNER was engaged to direct some of the WAGNER dramas, and it was here that Weingartner made his American debut, conducting TRISTAN UND ISOLDE. The company presented the American premiere of Raoul Laparra's *La Habanera* in 1910, and the Boston premiere of PELLÉAS ET MÉLISANDE. In 1914, the year the company expired from lack of support, it visited Paris for a two-month season at the Théâtre des Champs Elysées. Subsequently an effort was made to create another resident

company at the Boston Opera House. This time it was under the direction of Max Rabinoff. The venture was short-lived. The opera house was demolished in 1958.

Boughton, Rutland, composer. Born Aylesbury, Eng., Jan. 23, 1878; died London, Jan. 25, 1960. Before World War I Boughton nursed the ambition to create an English equivalent of BAYREUTH where WAGNER-like music dramas glorifying English traditions would be performed. To realize this mission, Boughton settled in Glastonbury, where, in a small hall and with semiprofessional casts, he produced his own musicodramatic works based on the Arthurian legends. One of these works is his finest opera, *The Immortal Hour*. The Glastonbury performances were interrupted by the outbreak of World War I but resumed afterward. In Aug., 1920, there took place performances of Boughton's *The Birth of Arthur* and *The Round Table*, the first two parts of a projected cycle of Arthurian legends. Boughton now sought to build a special theater with up-to-date equipment. But the needed financial support was not forthcoming, and the entire project collapsed. Boughton's operas: *The Immortal Hour* (1913); *The Round Table* (1916); *Agincourt* (1918); ALKESTIS (1922); *The Queen of Cornwall* (1924); *The Ever Young* (1928); *The Lily Maid* (1934).

Bouillon, Princesse de, Adriana's rival (mezzo-soprano) for Maurice in CILÈA'S ADRIANA LECOUVREUR.

Boulevard solitude, opera in one act (seven scenes) by HENZE. Libretto by the composer and Grete Weil. Premiere: Hanover Opera, Ger., Feb. 17, 1952. American premiere: Santa Fe, N.M., Aug. 2, 1967.

This was Henze's first opera, and it proved sensational. The text was an updated (1950) adaptation of the celebrated MANON LESCAUT story as previously used for opera by MASSENET and PUCCINI. Its setting is a university library. An important change in the plot is making Des Grieux and not Manon the principal character, tracing his disintegration (from the use of drugs) as a result of his relations with Manon. The traditional story is also changed by having Manon shoot her lover.

The seven scenes are made up of twenty-four musical numbers in a variety of styles: formal arias and ensemble numbers; Italian-type lyricism; dance materials (including jazz) ; atonality and SPRECHSTIMME; neoprimitivism. Basically the score is derived from a twelve-tone row.

When introduced, the opera inspired both excessive praise and loud denunciations. The same thing happened when soon thereafter the opera was performed in Naples and Rome, possibly with the dissent far outweighing the approbation. At the American premiere, however, it was well received.

Boulez, Pierre, composer and conductor. Born Montbrison, Loire, France, Mar. 26, 1925. Originally he planned to become an engineer. Intensive music study began in 1944 in Paris with Messiaen. From the beginnings of his career as composer, Boulez embraced avant-garde techniques and idioms, starting off with dodecaphony. With a succession of instrumental works, he became a leading figure in the avant-garde movement, continually extending the horizons of his experiments to include electronic sounds and chance methods. His role in opera has been most influential as a conductor, a career he assumed seriously comparatively late, although for many years he led an orchestra in a Parisian theater. For a while he confined himself to leading his own works. In 1963 he gave a sensational performance of WOZZECK at the PARIS OPÉRA, repeating the performance the following season there. He conducted PARSIFAL at the BAYREUTH FESTIVAL and TRISTAN UND ISOLDE with the Bayreuth Festival company during its visit to Japan. In 1968 he signed an unprecedented contract with the Cleveland Orchestra to appear as guest conductor for several weeks a season, during five consecutive

seasons. In Nov., 1969, he made his COVENT GARDEN debut in PELLÉAS ET MÉLISANDE, and in the same year he was appointed music director of the BBC in London. In the fall of 1970 he succeeded Leonard BERNSTEIN as music director of the New York Philharmonic.

Bourgeois Gentilhomme, Le, see MOLIÈRE.

Bovy, Vina, soprano. Born Ghent, Belgium, May 22, 1900. Her vocal studies took place in Ghent where she made her opera debut as GRETEL in 1917. Appearances in Belgium, France, Italy, and South America followed. On Dec. 24, 1936, she made her debut at the METROPOLITAN OPERA as VIOLETTA. She remained with this company only two seasons. After World War II she appeared at the PARIS OPÉRA and in the Belgian and French provinces. From 1947 to 1955 she was director of the Royal Opera at Ghent.

Bradamante, Ruggiero's betrothed (contralto) in HANDEL'S ALCINA.

Bradford, Puritan clergyman (baritone), "Wrestling Bradford," in HANSON'S MERRY MOUNT.

Braham, John (born John Abraham), tenor. Born London, Mar. 20, 1774; died there Feb. 17, 1856. He was one of the most distinguished interpreters of his time of leading tenor roles in HANDEL'S operas. Leoni was his teacher. Braham was only ten when he made his debut in a concert for the benefit of his teacher. When his voice broke, Braham became a piano teacher. But by 1794 he was able to resume a singing career. In 1796 he became a member of the DRURY LANE company and from 1798 to 1800 of the Italian Opera in London. He appeared at LA SCALA in 1799. Performances with other European opera companies followed. Besides his distinction in Handel, he scored successes as Max in DER FREISCHÜTZ and Sir Huon in OBERON, creating the latter role. Later, when his voice had lowered into the baritone range, he also was an admired WILLIAM TELL and DON GIOVANNI. Between 1840 and

1842 he toured the United States. His last appearance was at a concert in London in 1852.

Brander, Faust's friend (bass) in BERLIOZ' THE DAMNATION OF FAUST.

Brangäne, Isolde's attendant (mezzo-soprano) in WAGNER's TRISTAN UND ISOLDE.

Brangäne's Warning, *see* HABET ACHT.

Branzell, Karin, mezzo-soprano. Born Stockholm, Sept. 24, 1891. Completing her vocal instruction with Thelma Hofer and Enrico Rosati, she made her debut in 1912 with the Stockholm Opera in D'ALBERT's IZEYL. On Feb. 6, 1924, she made her debut at the METROPOLITAN OPERA as Fricka in DIE WALKÜRE. She sang leading mezzo-soprano roles there until 1944, a period during which, for three years, she also appeared at COVENT GARDEN and in BAYREUTH. After leaving the Metropolitan she was a guest performer with various European opera companies, following which she taught voice at the Juilliard School of Music.

Braslau, Sophie, contralto. Born New York City, Aug. 16, 1892; died there Dec. 22, 1935. Her music study took place at the Institute of Musical Art, where she specialized in the piano. After her voice was discovered, she studied singing with Herbert WITHERSPOON, Marcella SEMBRICH, and Mario Marafioti. Her opera debut took place at the METROPOLITAN OPERA on Nov. 27, 1914, as the offstage Voice in PARSIFAL. She did not assume major roles for several years; the first time she did so was on Mar. 23, 1918, when she created the title role in CADMAN's SHANEWIS. For the next two years she continued to appear in important contralto roles. She created for America the parts of Amelfa in LE COQ D'OR and Hua-Quee in L'ORACOLO. Her last opera appearance took place in 1920, at the Metropolitan, after which she devoted herself to concert appearances.

Braunfels, Walter, composer. Born Frankfurt, Dec. 19, 1882. He studied at the Hoch Conservatory in Frankfurt and with Leschetizky and Navratil in Vienna and Thuille in Munich. In 1925 he became codirector (with Herman Abendroth) of the Hochschule für Musik at Cologne but was compelled to relinquish his post when the Nazis came to power. In 1945 he helped reorganize and modernize this school, becoming its president until his retirement in 1950. Braunfels composed a number of operas that were well received in Germany, beginning with *Prinzessin Brambilla,* produced in Stuttgart on Mar. 25, 1909. His later operas were *Ulenspiegel* (1913), *Die Vögel* (1920), *Don Gil von den grünen Hosen* (1924), *Der gläserne Berg* (1928), *Galatea* (1930), *Der Traum ein Leben* (1937), *Die heilige Johanna* (1942), and *Verkündigung* (1948).

Braut von Messina, Die, *see* SCHILLER, FRIEDRICH.

bravo, an Italian word meaning "well done." The term is used as an exclamation of approval, particularly in Italy.

bravour aria, German term for an aria with bravura passages.

bravura, an Italian term (literally: "bravery") applied to a song or passage requiring brilliance and technical adroitness on the part of the singer.

Brecht, Bertolt, poet and dramatist. Born Augsburg, Ger., Feb. 10, 1898; died East Berlin, Aug. 14, 1956. Brecht provided Kurt WEILL with the book for their modern adaptation of THE BEGGAR's OPERA: THE THREE-PENNY OPERA. Other Weill operas with librettos by Brecht are *Der Jasager, Happy Ending,* and THE RISE AND FALL OF THE CITY MAHAGONNY. Brecht's one-act play, *The Trial of Lucullus,* provided the texts for operas by Paul Dessau and Roger Sessions. *The Informer* was made into an opera of the same name by Daniel Sables and *Der Darmwäscher* by WAGNER-RÉGÉNY into *Persiche Episode.* Brecht was the founding theoretician of an esthetic cult popular in Germany in the 1920's—that of GEBRAUCHSMUSIK.

Breisach, Paul, conductor. Born Vienna,

June 3, 1896; died New York City, Dec. 26, 1952. He attended the Vienna State Academy, after which he served as Richard STRAUSS's assistant at the VIENNA STATE OPERA. In 1921 he became conductor of the Mannheim National Theater and in 1924 of the Deutsches Opernhaus in Berlin (BERLIN DEUTSCHE STAATS-OPER). He made his American debut at the METROPOLITAN OPERA on Dec. 12, 1941, conducting AIDA. He stayed at the Metropolitan through the 1945–46 season, when he became principal conductor of the SAN FRANCISCO OPERA until 1952.

Breitkopf und Härtl, one of the world's great music-publishing institutions. It was founded in Leipzig as a general printing establishment by Bernhardt Christoph Breitkopf in 1719. In the middle of the eighteenth century, Johann Gottfried Breitkopf devised a new method for the use of movable musical type. The first significant musical achievement of the firm was the publication of an opera score in 1756. After Gottfried Cristoph Härtl took over the firm from Breitkopf's grandson, it became the leading music-publishing organization in Germany. It published many works of MOZART and HAYDN and, subsequently, monumental complete editions of many of the great German composers.

Bréval, Lucienne (born Berthe Schilling), soprano. Born Berlin, Nov. 4, 1869; died Paris, Aug. 15, 1935. For almost thirty years she was the leading soprano of the PARIS OPÉRA, specializing in Wagnerian roles. Her studies took place at the conservatories of Geneva and Paris. Her debut took place at the Paris Opéra, on Jan. 20, 1892, when she was acclaimed as SELIKA. During the three decades she remained with that company, she created the principal soprano roles in many French operas, including ARIANE ET BARBE-BLEUE, LE CID, GRISÉLIDIS, PÉNÉLOPE, and SALAMMBÔ. In 1899 she made guest appearances at COVENT GARDEN. She made her American debut at the METROPOLITAN OPERA on Jan. 16, 1901, as Chimène in *Le Cid*. She returned to the Metropolitan for the season of 1901–02.

brezza aleggia, La, Arrigo's melodious air to his bride, Elena, in Act V of VERDI's THE SICILIAN VESPERS.

Bridal Chorus, see TREULICH GEFÜHRT.

Bridal Procession, procession in Act III of RIMSKY-KORSAKOV's LE COQ D'OR.

Bride of Abydos, The, see BYRON, GEORGE NOEL GORDON, LORD.

Bride of Lammermoor, The, see SCOTT, SIR WALTER.

brindisi, a drinking or toasting song. Operatic examples include: "Il segreto per essere felice" in LUCREZIA BORGIA; "Viva il vino" in CAVALLERIA RUSTICANA; "O vin, dissipe la tristesse" in HAMLET; "Inaffia l'ugola!" in OTELLO; and "Libiamo, libiamo," in LA TRAVIATA.

British National Opera Company, an important English opera company founded in 1922 under the artistic direction of Percy PITT and including many of the leading singers and instrumentalists who had previously been associated with Sir Thomas BEECHAM. Its first performance (AIDA) took place in Bradford in 1923. Later the same year the company appeared at COVENT GARDEN. Subsequently, it toured England extensively, sometimes with ambitious performances. The company was responsible for the premieres of several English operas, including BOUGHTON's ALKESTIS, HOLST's THE PERFECT FOOL, and VAUGHAN WILLIAMS' HUGH THE DROVER. Frederick Austin succeeded Pitt as artistic director in 1924, and remained in the post until the company was dissolved five years later.

Britten, Benjamin, composer. Born Lowestoft, Suffolk, Eng., Nov. 22, 1913. He is England's most significant composer of operas in the twentieth century and one of the most highly regarded since PURCELL. He demonstrated extraordinary creative talent in childhood, writing his first string quartet when he was nine. At sixteen he had written half a dozen quartets, ten piano sonatas, and a symphony. After studying composition with Frank Bridge he attended the Royal College of Music between 1930 and 1933, where his teachers included John Ireland and Arthur BENJAMIN. His first major success came in 1938 with the orchestral *Variations on a Theme of Frank Bridge,* introduced at a festival of the International Society for Contemporary Music. An avowed pacifist, Britten came to the United States in 1939 and remained in this country during the early years of World War II. He completed several important orchestral works in this country, among them his first opera, *Paul Bunyan.* Given at Columbia University in 1941, the work was severely criticized. While in America, Britten received a commission from the Koussevitzky Foundation to write a second opera. He returned to England in 1942. Exempt from military duty because of his convictions, he helped in the war effort by giving concerts in hospitals and shelters. His commissioned opera, PETER GRIMES, was so successful when introduced in London on June 7, 1945, that it established Britten as one of the major opera composers of our time. He then went on to write THE RAPE OF LUCRETIA, ALBERT HERRING, BILLY BUDD, GLORIANA (written on a commission from the British government for the coronation ceremonies in June, 1953—the first time an opera was ordered for such an event), THE TURN OF THE SCREW, A MIDSUMMER NIGHT'S DREAM, and three church parables (CURLEW RIVER, THE BURNING FIERY FURNACE, and THE PRODIGAL SON). What distinguishes Britten's operas are his natural gift for theatrical effect, his ability in finding the proper musical equivalent for every demand of the stage, and his projection of atmosphere. His gamut is a wide one: he can be passionate and intense, as in *Peter Grimes* and *Billy Budd;* satirical and witty, as in *Albert Herring;* spacious and grandiose, as in *Gloriana;* fanciful, atmospheric, and lyrical, as in *A Midsummer Night's Dream;* religious and spiritual, as in his three church parables.

He can write equally well for large forces in a complex style and for the simple aims of his works for children, LET'S MAKE AN OPERA and NOYE'S FLUDDE.

In 1948 he helped found the ALDEBURGH FESTIVAL in his hometown of Aldeburgh, Suffolk, Eng. In 1953 he received the Companionship of Honor from Queen Elizabeth; in 1964 he was given the first Aspen (Colorado) Award of thirty thousand dollars for his contribution "to the humanities"; and in 1965 he was appointed a member of the Order of Merit, Britain's highest honor.

Brod, Max, author. Born Prague, May 27, 1884. Primarily a literary man, Brod has interested himself in contemporary opera. He translated many of JANÁČEK's operas into English and wrote this composer's biography. He was also the man who discovered WEINBERGER's ŠVANDA THE BAGPIPER and helped get it performed. Celebrated as the literary executor of KAFKA, Brod preserved and brought to publication Kafka's novel *The Trial,* later the source of operas by EINEM and SCHULLER.

Brogny, Cardinal, head of the Council of Constance (bass) in HALÉVY's LA JUIVE.

Brothers Karamazov, The, see DOSTOYEVSKY, FEODOR.

Brownlee, John, baritone. Born Geelong, Australia, Jan. 7, 1901; died New York City, Jan. 10, 1969. As a boy he became a junior naval cadet in the Australian navy, serving during World War I. Following service, he studied accounting. Engaged in the latter profession, he entered a singing competition in Ballarat, and though he had never had a lesson, won first prize. Several singing engagements followed. One of these, a performance of *Messiah,* was attended by Nellie MELBA, who convinced him to go to Paris for serious study with Dinh Gilly. His debut took place at COVENT GARDEN on June 8, 1926, in the performance of LA BOHÈME in which Melba made her farewell appearance. That fall he was engaged by the PARIS OPÉRA, the first time a British subject was made a permanent member of that company;

his Paris debut was in THAÏS in 1927. On Feb. 17, 1937, he appeared for the first time at the METROPOLITAN OPERA. The opera was RIGOLETTO. After that, Brownlee sang at Covent Garden, the Paris Opéra, and the Metropolitan, besides making important guest appearances elsewhere. His greatest successes were in the MOZART repertory, particularly at the GLYNDEBOURNE FESTIVAL; he was also acclaimed in SALOME and PELLÉAS ET MÉLISANDE. He was the head of the opera department of the Manhattan School of Music in New York from 1957 until his death.

Bruch, Max, composer. Born Cologne, Ger., Jan. 6, 1838; died Friedenau, Oct. 2, 1920. His boyhood compositions won him a scholarship at the Mozart Foundation in Frankfurt. His other teachers were Ferdinand Hiller, Carl Reinecke, and Ferdinand Breuning. For a while he taught music in his native city, there completing his first opera, *Scherz, List, und Rache,* performed in 1858. In 1861 he settled temporarily in Munich, where he completed a new opera, *Die Loreley* (whose libretto had been intended for MENDELSSOHN) ; so successful was it when introduced in Mannheim on June 14, 1863, that it was soon repeated in Leipzig. Bruch's third and last opera, *Hermione,* based on SHAKESPEARE's *A Winter's Tale,* was written in 1871 and given in Berlin in 1872. During his long career Bruch held various conducting posts with orchestras in Germany and England. From 1892 to 1910 he was head of the master school in composition at the Berlin Königliche Hochschule. After 1910 he lived in retirement. Among the honors he received were a membership in the French Academy and the Prussian Order of Merit. Bruch is remembered not for his operas but for his G minor violin concerto and his *Kol Nidrei* for cello and orchestra.

Brüderchen, komm tanz' mit mir, Gretel's song (which develops into a duet) as she teaches her brother Hansel to sing and dance, in Act I of HUMPERDINCK's HANSEL AND GRETEL.

Brüderlein, Brüderlein und Schwesterlein, the tongue-in-cheek pledge of brotherhood by Prince Orlofsky's guests at his ball, in Act II of Johann STRAUSS's DIE FLEDERMAUS.

Brüll, Ignaz, composer. Born Prossnitz, Moravia, Nov. 7, 1846; died Vienna, Sept. 17, 1907. He studied in Vienna with Julius Epstein and Felix Otto Dessoff. In 1861 Epstein performed Brüll's *First Piano Concerto* in Vienna. Brüll wrote his first opera, *Der Bettler von Samarkand,* in 1864. His second opera appeared eleven years later: DAS GOLDENE KREUZ. Introduced at the Berlin Royal Opera (*see* BERLIN STATE OPERA) on Dec. 22, 1875, it was such an outstanding success that it was soon performed throughout Europe. It was given at the METROPOLITAN OPERA in 1886. Later operas: *Der Landfriede* (1877) ; *Bianca* (1879); *Königen Mariette* (1883); *Gloria* (1886); *Das steinerne Herz* (1888); *Gringoire* (1892) ; *Schach dem König* (1893) ; *Der Husar* (1898) .

Bruneau, Alfred, composer. Born Paris, Mar. 3, 1857; died there June 15, 1934. After attending the Paris Conservatory, where he won the Prix de Rome, he had one of his orchestral works performed by the Pasdeloup Orchestra in 1884. Turning to the stage, he completed his first opera, *Kérim,* given in Paris in 1887. From then on he specialized in opera. His friendship with ZOLA was a decisive influence. Impressed by Zola's naturalism, he made *naturalisme* the backbone of his own esthetic principles. In this vein he wrote his first important work, *Le Rêve,* based on a Zola story and introduced at the OPÉRA-COMIQUE in 1891. Bruneau adapted other works by Zola, including *L'Attaque du moulin* (1893) and *La Faute de l'abbé Mouret* (1907) . His musical style matched the naturalism of his subjects with its vigor and realism. When the Dreyfus affair placed a temporary stigma on Zola, Bruneau's operas lost favor. Not until 1905 was interest revived in his work, after the premiere of *L'Enfant roi,* his first success in a decade. This was followed by a revival of some of his earlier operas. After World War I Bruneau's work lost favor, the new generation considering it old-fashioned and occasionally crude. For many years, beginning in 1904, Bruneau was the music critic of *Le Matin*. He was made Officer of the Legion of Honor in 1904. Besides the operas mentioned, he wrote: *Messidor* (1897); *L'Ouragan* (1901); *Nais Micoulin* (1907); *Les Quatre Journées* (1916); *Le Roi Candaule* (1920); *Le Jardin du paradis* (1921); *Virginie* (1931).

Brünnhilde, a Valkyrie (soprano), daughter of Wotan, in WAGNER's DIE WALKÜRE, SIEGFRIED, and GÖTTERDÄMMERUNG.

Brünnhilde's Battle Cry, *see* HO-JO-TO-HO.

Brünnhilde! heilige Braut!, Siegfried's farewell to Brünnhilde just before his death, in Act III of WAGNER's GÖTTERDÄMMERUNG.

Brussels Opera, *see* THÉÂTRE DE LA MONNAIE.

Büchner, Georg, playwright. Born Godelau, Ger., Oct. 17, 1813; died Zürich, Feb. 19, 1837. His play WOZZECK was the source of BERG's opera of the same name. Manfred Gurlitt was another composer who made an opera of *Wozzeck* (1926). Another of Büchner's plays, *Dantons Tod,* was made into an opera by EINEM (1947). Other operas based on his dramas include the following: Schwaen's *Leonce und Lena* (1961); WAGNER-RÉGÉNY's *Der Günstling* (1935); and Weissmann's *Leonce und Lena* (1925).

Bucklaw, Lord Arthur (Arturo), Lucia's husband (tenor) in DONIZETTI's LUCIA DI LAMMERMOOR.

Buckley, Emerson, conductor. Born New York City, Apr. 14, 1916. He was educated at Columbia University and at the University of Denver, following which he served as director of the Columbia Grand Opera in Palm Beach, Fla., between 1936 and 1938. From 1943 to 1945 he conducted the SAN CARLO OPERA (U.S.), and between 1954 and 1958 he was director of the Puerto Rico Opera Festival. Since 1950 he has been the musical director of the Miami Opera Guild, Fla., and the CENTRAL CITY OPERA, Col. After 1955 he also gave numerous performances with the NEW YORK CITY OPERA; in 1956 he was musical administrator and conductor of the CHICAGO LYRIC OPERA; and from 1964 on he conducted the SEATTLE OPERA. He has led the world premieres of numerous American operas, including THE BALLAD OF BABY DOE, HE WHO GETS SLAPPED, THE CRUCIBLE, and LADY FROM COLORADO. In 1964 he received the Alice M. Ditson Conductor's Award for distinguished service to American Music. He has also been highly active as a symphonic conductor.

Budapest State Opera (now known as the Budapest Hungarian National Theatre). In actuality it now comprises two opera houses, sharing the same singers, conductors, designers, stage directors, and so forth.

The older opera house dates back to Aug. 22, 1837, with the opening of a new auditorium where one week later the first opera was performed: ROSSINI's THE BARBER OF SEVILLE. For the next forty-seven years, this auditorium was used not only for operas but also for all types of concerts. In opera performances, Ferenc ERKEL was the first principal conductor, subsequently elevated to the post of musical director. Among the more important performances under Erkel's artistic guidance were those of DER FREISCHÜTZ, DON GIOVANNI, Andreas Bartay's *The Stratagem* (Hungary's first comic opera), and Erkel's first opera, *Bátori Mária,* the last produced in 1840. VERDI entered the repertory in 1847 with NABUCCO and ERNANI, and WAGNER's first opera heard in Budapest was given in 1866—LOHENGRIN. Erkel's *Bánk bán,* considered one of the most significant Hungarian operas of the nineteenth century, was heard first in 1861 and after that produced annually. During the last year of operatic performances in this auditorium, the world premiere of a Hungarian opera—Sándor Bertha's *Matthias Corvinus*—was given. The last opera heard on the stage was *The Barber of Seville*, with which the opera company was started.

A new opera house, subsidized by the government, was opened on Sept. 27, 1884, under the artistic directorship of Sándor Erkel, who remained its principal conductor until 1900. In 1884 the company received the official title of Royal Hungarian Opera House. After World War I it was named Royal Hungarian State Opera; following World War II it was renamed the Budapest State Opera; and now it is called the Budapest Hungarian National Theatre. In 1888 Gustav MAHLER became its musical director, and it is from this period that the Budapest Opera achieved international importance. Mahler was succeeded by Artur NIKISCH, who directed from 1893 to 1895 and under whose regime PUCCINI was heard in Budapest for the first time (MANON LESCAUT), with other novel presentations including THE BARTERED BRIDE, DIE MEISTERSINGER, and several new Hungarian operas. Between World War I and 1925, twenty-one new Hungarian operas were introduced.

Meanwhile, in 1911, another opera house came into existence, the Erkel Theatre, which between 1911 and 1917 was called the Folk Opera, between 1917 and 1933 the City Theatre, and after 1937 became a subsidiary of the Budapest State Opera. For many years the Budapest State Opera offered the more sophisticated fare while the Erkel Opera generally leaned toward a more popular repertory; but since the end of World War II, the Erkel Opera has become more ambitious and serious in its programing, such as presenting in a single evening the three stage works by BARTÓK. Both houses perform seven times a week for a ten-month period. Besides the general repertory, the two opera houses have featured various novelties for Hungary (such as PETER GRIMES in 1947 and HENZE's *Undine* in 1969) and numerous new and early operas by Hungarian composers, with emphasis on Bartók, KODÁLY, Ferenc Erkel, and Sándor SZOKOLAY among many others. The world premieres of Szokolay's BLOOD WEDDING (based on FORTNER's BLUTHOCHZEIT) and *Hamlet* were given by the Budapest Hungarian National Theatre in 1968. On Oct. 29, 1969, the State Opera gave the world premiere of a new Hungarian opera, Emil Petrovics's *Bűn és Bünhödés* (Crime and Punishment).

buffa (or **buffo**), Italian for "comic," as in OPERA BUFFA and *basso buffo*. *Buffone* is a jester, as in RIGOLETTO.

Bühnenfestspiel, German for "stage consecration play," a term used by WAGNER for his music drama PARSIFAL.

Bülow, Hans von, conductor and pianist. Born Dresden, Jan. 8, 1830; died Cairo, Egypt, Feb. 12, 1894. World-famous as conductor and pianist, Bülow is of importance in the history of opera through his intimate associations with WAGNER. As a conductor, he promoted Wagner's music. It was a hearing of LOHENGRIN in Weimar in 1850 that convinced Bülow to become a professional musician. He joined Wagner in Zürich and for a year was Wagner's apprentice in conducting. Subsequently, he studied the piano with Franz LISZT, after which he toured extensively as a virtuoso. In 1864 he became principal conductor of the MUNICH OPERA. Later he became famous as the conductor of the Meiningen Orchestra. In 1857 he married Liszt's daughter Cosima. She later became Wagner's mistress and bore him two children before she left Bülow to join Wagner in Switzerland. After her divorce in 1869, she married Wagner. Bülow's adaptations of Wagner's works for the piano include TRISTAN UND ISOLDE.

Bulwer-Lytton, Edward George Earle, novelist and dramatist. Born London, May 25, 1803; died Torquay, Eng., Jan. 18, 1873. Several of Bulwer-Lytton's romances were made into operas. WAGNER's RIENZI came from his novel of the same name. (Another composer, Vladimir Kashperov, also wrote a *Rienzi*.) *The Last Days of Pompeii* was the source of *Le Dernier Jour de Pompéi*, an opera by Victorin de Joncières;

Pompeji, an opera by Marziano Perosi, and Enrico Petrella's *Ione.* The first grand opera by a native American, William Fry's *Leonora,* was based on Bulwer-Lytton's *The Lady of Lyons.* Frederick H. Cowen's *Pauline* was also drawn from this novel.

Bumbry, Grace (Ann), mezzo-soprano. Born St. Louis, Mo., Jan. 4, 1937. Her vocal study took place with Lotte LEHMANN. After winning a Marian Anderson Scholarship and a John Hay Whitney Award, she went to Paris in 1959 to complete her studies. Her debut took place with the PARIS OPÉRA in 1960 as AMNERIS, where she proved a sensation. Engagements in other European opera houses followed. She became the first Negro singer to appear at BAYREUTH where on July 23, 1961, she was cast as Venus in TANNHÄUSER. Early in 1962 she was invited to perform at a formal dinner at the White House for President and Mrs. John F. Kennedy. In 1962–63 she made a coast-to-coast concert tour, beginning in Carnegie Hall. Her American debut in opera took place in 1963 with the CHICAGO LYRIC OPERA, as Venus. On Oct. 7, 1965, she made her METROPOLITAN OPERA debut as PRINCESS EBOLI. In 1964 and in 1966 she was heard at the SALZBURG FESTIVAL as LADY MACBETH and CARMEN respectively. She sang Carmen in a motion-picture production of the opera conducted by KARAJAN and in 1967 in a new Metropolitan Opera production at the LINCOLN CENTER FOR THE PERFORMING ARTS produced by Jean-Louis Barrault.

Bunyan, John, religious writer. Born Elstow, Eng., Nov., 1628; died London, Aug. 31, 1688. His classic *The Pilgrim's Progress* was the source for an early opera by VAUGHAN WILLIAMS, *The Shepherds of the Delectable Mountain,* and also for Vaughan Williams' later opera, *The Pilgrim's Progress.*

buona figliuola, La, *see* CECCHINA, LA.

Buona sera, mio signore, quintet of Rosina, Almaviva, Figaro, Doctor Bartolo, and Don Basilio in Act II of ROSSINI's THE BARBER OF SEVILLE, in which Basilio is edged out of the house.

Buona Zaza, Cascart's aria in Act II of LEONCAVALLO's ZAZA, in which he tries to convince Zaza that her lover, Dufresne, had been unfaithful to her.

Buononcini, *see* BONONCINI.

Bürgschaft, Die (The Pledge), opera in prologue and three acts by Kurt WEILL. Libretto by Caspar Neher, based on a fable by Johann Herder. Premiere: Städtische Oper, Berlin, Mar. 10, 1932. A judge in Africa is called upon to decide the ownership of a bag of money found in a sack of chaff. He solves the problem by ordering the children of the litigants to marry one another, giving them the money as a dowry. Weill's music is primarily in a jazz vein, and his unusual instrumentation calls for two pianos with electric amplifiers.

Burgtheater, the court theater in Vienna where most of the important opera productions took place before the opening of the Vienna Royal Opera in 1869. The Burgtheater was opened on Feb. 5, 1742, with a performance of an Italian opera: Giuseppe Carcano's *Amleto.* Support of opera was so poor that the theater had to close in 1747. It reopened on May 14, 1748, with GLUCK's *Semiramide riconosciuta.* Gluck's career was intimately connected with the theater. First, his operas in the OPERA SERIA vein were successfully performed there, then his first works with which he opened new directions for opera: ORFEO ED EURIDICE, ALCESTE, and PARIDE ED ELENA. Gluck also served as a conductor at the Burgtheater in 1754.

MOZART was the next important composer connected with the Burgtheater. His first opera written in Vienna—and the first important opera in the German language—was introduced there in 1782: THE ABDUCTION FROM THE SERAGLIO. THE MARRIAGE OF FIGARO was given its premiere at the Burgtheater four years later, and COSÌ FAN TUTTE in 1790. In 1792 the Burgtheater gave the premiere of one of the most delightful comic operas in the repertory: CIMAROSA's IL MATRIMONIO SEGRETO.

Ten years after Mozart's death, the Burgtheater gave the first performances in Vienna of CHERUBINI's THE WATER CARRIER and MÉDÉE. In addition, the theater commissioned Cherubini to write a new opera. The work, *Faniska*, was finally given not at the Burgtheater but at the KÄRNTNERTHORTHEATER.

In 1857 the Burgtheater gave the Viennese premiere of LOHENGRIN, under WAGNER's supervision. It was so successful that the theater was emboldened in 1861 to attempt the first performance of TRISTAN UND ISOLDE. But delay followed delay. A full year passed, and though there had been seventy-two rehearsals, no performance was in view. When Luise Dustmann, scheduled to sing Isolde, fell ill in the fall of 1863, the project was abandoned.

In 1869 the Vienna Royal Opera (VIENNA STATE OPERA) was built on the Ring. Henceforth, the most important operatic productions took place there, with the Burgtheater becoming mainly a place for spoken drama.

Burning Fiery Furnace, The, a church parable in one act by BRITTEN. Libretto by William Plomer. Premiere: Aldeburgh, Eng., June 9, 1966. American premiere: Katonah, N.Y., June 25, 1967. This is the second of three stage "parables" by Britten intended for performance in church with limited forces. It was preceded by CURLEW RIVER and followed by THE PRODIGAL SON. The text is an adaptation of the Biblical story from the Book of Daniel in which Shadrach, Meshach, and Abednego, three young Jews in exile in Babylon, go through the fiery ordeal ordered by Nebuchadnezzar and emerge unharmed through the intervention of an angel. Monks, entering and leaving the church chanting a plainsong, are the performers. The processional music and the "Benedicte" sung by the three youths in the furnace are among this work's highlights.

Burr, Aaron, chief conspirator (baritone) in DAMROSCH's THE MAN WITHOUT A COUNTRY.

Busch, Fritz, conductor. Born Siegen, Ger., Mar. 13, 1890; died London, Sept. 14, 1951. He entered the Cologne Conservatory in 1906 and only a year later became musical director of the Riga Stadttheater. After holding various other conductorial posts he became musical director of the STUTTGART OPERA in 1918. Three years later he was engaged for a similar post with the DRESDEN OPERA. There he gave outstanding performances of WAGNER and MOZART and works of twentieth-century composers. Many of Richard STRAUSS's later operas received their world premieres, as did HINDEMITH's CARDILLAC (first version) and WEILL's DER PROTAGONIST, among other works. When the Nazis came to power, Busch (though not a Jew) left Germany because of his antipathy to the new regime. For the next few years he conducted in Scandinavia and served as the musical director of the GLYNDEBOURNE FESTIVAL in England. His first visit to the United States had taken place during the 1927–28 season, when he served as guest conductor of the New York Symphony Society. He returned in 1941 and 1942 to lead various American orchestras and to act as musical director and principal conductor of the adventuresome but short-lived New Opera Company in New York City. From 1942 to 1945 he conducted extensively in South America. In 1945 he became a conductor of the METROPOLITAN OPERA, making his debut there on the opening night of the season (Nov. 26, 1945) with LOHENGRIN. He remained a principal conductor of the Metropolitan until 1949.

Busch, Hans, stage director. Born Aachen, Ger., Apr. 4, 1914. The son of Fritz BUSCH, his education took place in Dresden, at the Geneva University, and at the Reinhardt School in Vienna. In 1937 he assisted TOSCANINI at the SALZBURG FESTIVAL. He came to the United States in 1940 and directed two productions for his father's New Opera Company. While serving in the United States Army in 1942, he acted in an advisory capacity in the rebuilding of LA SCALA. After the war he served as stage director for the METROPOLITAN OPERA. In 1948 he began serving in a similar capacity with the University of Indiana's Opera Workshop, a position he still holds. Here he assisted with the American premiere of BILLY BUDD, the world premieres of DOWN IN THE VALLEY, THE JUMPING FROG OF CALAVERAS COUNTY, *The Ruby* (DELLO JOIO), and AMAHL AND THE NIGHT VISITORS (staged version), together with the presentation of such novelties as ELEGY FOR YOUNG LOVERS, HIN UND ZURÜCK, L'INCORONAZIONE DI POPPEA, THE RAKE'S PROGRESS, and PIQUE DAME, among many other operas.

Busoni, Ferruccio, composer and pianist. Born Empoli, Italy, Apr. 1, 1866; died Berlin, July 27, 1924. He toured Europe as a child pianist, then studied composition with Wilhelm Mayer-Remy. He began his career as teacher by joining the piano faculty of the Helsingfors Conservatory. In 1890 he taught at the Moscow Conservatory, and from 1891 to 1894 at the New England Conservatory in Boston. Returning to Europe, he achieved tremendous success as a piano virtuoso. His first opera, *Die Brautwahl* (The Bridal Choice), was introduced in Hamburg in 1912. Two one-act operas followed during World War I, TURANDOT and ARLECCHINO, both introduced on the same program in Zürich on May 11, 1917. After the war Busoni became a professor of composition in Berlin.

There he worked on his magnum opus, the opera DOKTOR FAUST. He did not live to complete it; it was finished by his pupil Philipp Jarnach and introduced in Dresden in 1925.

Butterfly, *see* MADAMA BUTTERFLY.

Buzzy, a journalist (baritone) in LEONCAVALLO'S ZAZA.

Byron, George Noel Gordon, Lord, poet. Born London, Jan. 22, 1788; died Missolonghi, Greece, Apr. 19, 1824. The epic poems and poetic dramas of Byron have been used for a number of opera librettos. Operas based on Byron's works include the following: Paul Lebrun's *La Fiancée d'Abydos,* 1896 ("The Bride of Abydos"); LATTUADA's *Cain* and Friedrich Schmidtmann's *Kain* ("Cain"); Hans von Bronsart's *Der Corsair* and VERDI's *Il corsaro,* 1848 ("The Corsair"); FIBICH's *Hedy* ("Don Juan"); Natanael Berg's *Leila,* 1912, and Aimé Maillart's *Lara,* 1864 ("The Giaour"); Enrico Petrella's *Manfredo,* 1872, and Carl Reinecke's *König Manfred,* 1867 ("Manfred"); DONIZETTI's *Marino Faliero,* 1835 ("Marino Faliero") and his *Parisina,* 1833 ("Parisina"); Anatal Bogatirev's *The Two Foscari* and VERDI's I DUE FOSCARI ("The Two Foscari").

Robert SCHUMANN began but never completed an opera based on "The Corsair." Byron is the central character of an American opera by Virgil THOMSON.

C

cabaletta, a type of brief aria with several repeats, found in the operas of ROSSINI and some of his contemporaries. In the latter part of the nineteenth century, and particularly in the works of VERDI, the term refers to the final part of an extended aria or duet, the final part being in a quick tempo. The term is derived from *cavallo,* Italian for "horse," suggesting the sound of galloping horses in the orchestral accompaniment. Notable examples of cabaletta are found in Rosina's famous aria in THE BARBER OF SEVILLE, "Una voce poco fa"; the Mad Scene from LUCIA DI LAMMERMOOR; "Come per me sereno" from

LA SONNAMBULA; and "Di quella pira" from IL TROVATORE. STRAVINSKY marked one of the sections of an aria in THE RAKE'S PROGRESS a cabaletta.

Caballé, Montserrat, soprano. Born Barcelona, Spain, Apr. 12, 1933. As a child she attended the Conservatorio del Liceo in Barcelona for six years, where she studied voice with Eugenia Kemeny. After additional training with Maestro Annovazzi and Conchita Baddia, she won the Liceo Conservatory Gold Medal, Spain's most important singing award, in 1954. Her operatic debut took place in Basel, Switzerland, as MIMI in 1957. She remained three years with this company while making extensive guest appearances with other European opera houses. For two years after that she was a principal soprano of the Bremen Opera, which revived DVOŘÁK's ARMIDA for her. Her extensive repertory soon embraced some forty-six roles in Italian, German, and French repertory; in a single week in Bremen she was heard in LA TRAVIATA, TOSCA, THE BARTERED BRIDE, SALOME, and DIE FLEDERMAUS. Her first operatic appearance in the Western Hemisphere took place in Mexico City in MASSENET's MANON in 1964, where she proved such a sensation that she was invited to return the following season to repeat her performance. Meanwhile, during the summer of 1965 she achieved formidable successes at the GLYNDEBOURNE FESTIVAL in the roles of the Countess in THE MARRIAGE OF FIGARO and the Marschallin in DER ROSENKAVALIER. On Apr. 20, 1965, she made her United States debut in New York in an American Opera Society performance of LUCREZIA BORGIA. She proved a sensation. On Nov. 6, 1965, she was acclaimed in *La traviata* at the DALLAS CIVIC OPERA in Texas, and again on Dec. 14, 1965, in New York in a concert performance of DONIZETTI's rarely heard *Roberto Devereux*. One week after that, on Dec. 22, she made her debut at the METROPOLITAN OPERA in FAUST. She helped open a new season for that company on Sept.

18, 1967, in *La traviata,* and in 1968 she was starred in a new production of VERDI's LUISA MILLER. She has appeared with some of the world's leading opera houses and festivals (including SALZBURG) and has come to be recognized as one of the most remarkable and versatile sopranos of her time.

Caccini, Giulio, composer. Born Rome, about 1546; died Florence, Dec. 10, 1618. He was one of the earliest composers to write operas. In Florence, where he spent most of his life, he served as court singer and lutenist to the Grand Duke of Tuscany. He joined the CAMERATA, participating in their discussions on music and art. A direct result of these discussions was his volume of accompanied arias and madrigals for a single voice, called *Le nuove musiche,* published in 1601. This was an epochmaking work, for it marked a major break with the then-existing style of polyphony. There is good reason to believe that the first opera ever written—PERI's DAFNE—contained some music by Caccini. Caccini contributed a few arias to Peri's second opera, EURIDICE (1600). He then wrote an opera of his own on the same text, and this was the first opera score ever to be printed. Later he wrote two operas in collaboration with Peri. Caccini's daughter, Francesca, was a professional singer. She appeared in the role of Euridice in Peri's opera when that work was first performed. She was also the composer of an opera, *La liberazione di Ruggiero* (1625).

Cachés dans cet asile, the celebrated BERCEUSE in GODARD's *Jocelyn.*

cadenza, a term used most frequently for instrumental music but also encountered in vocal music, where it refers to a brilliant, virtuoso passage. In the nineteenth century singers often improvised cadenzas to close arias, but before long began to prepare their cadenzas before performance time.

Cadi dupé, Le (Der betrogene Cadi; The Deceived Cadi), comic opera in one act by GLUCK. Libretto by Pierre René

Lemonnier. Premiere: Burgtheater, Vienna, Dec., 1761. American premiere: Rochester, N.Y., May 16, 1932.

Gluck produced a number of delightful comic operas, of which this is perhaps the most familiar. The text concerns the efforts of the Cadi to inspire the interest and love of Zelmira, who is in love with Nuradin. In order to discourage the Cadi, Zelmira poses as a plain-looking, stammering daughter of Omar the tentmaker. The Cadi loses interest in her, and Zelmira is now free to marry Nuradin. Alfred Einstein commented, in writing about this little opera: "The spirit which Rousseau called 'the return to nature' is to be perceived everywhere: in the orchestra, nature's way is painted by means of figuration and tone color."

Cadman, Charles Wakefield, composer. Born Johnstown, Pa., Dec. 4, 1881; died Los Angeles, Cal., Dec. 30, 1946. He was the first composer to make successful use of American Indian themes and rhythms as a basis for songs and larger works. His interest in Indian music was first aroused by Nelle Richmond Eberhart, who wrote the lyrics for Cadman's song cycle, *Four American Indian Songs,* in which is found "From the Land of the Sky-Blue Water." In 1909 Cadman spent a summer with the Omaha Indians, studying their ceremonials, love calls, dances, and songs. His most ambitious work in this idiom was SHANEWIS, an opera first produced by the METROPOLITAN OPERA in 1918. Cadman later wrote another opera, A WITCH OF SALEM, first performed by the CHICAGO OPERA COMPANY in 1926. American in subject, this opera has no suggestion of Indian influences. Cadman's other dramatic works include the three-act *The Land of Misty Water* and the one-act *The Garden of Mystery.*

Caffarelli (born Gaetano Majorano), CASTRATO soprano. Born Bitonto, Italy, Apr. 12, 1710; died Naples, Jan. 31, 1783. One of the most famous castrati of the eighteenth century, he studied singing with Niccolò Antonio PORPORA, who pronounced him to be the greatest singer in Europe. Assuming his stage name, he made his debut in Rome in 1724 in a female role and was an immediate success. In additional appearances he became the idol of the Italian opera public. He appeared in London for the first time in 1738, singing in HANDEL's *Faramondo.* Later triumphs came in France, Spain, and Austria. He amassed a considerable fortune, enabling him to purchase the dukedom of San Donato.

Cahier, Mme. Charles (born Sarah-Jane Layton Walker), contralto. Born Nashville, Tenn., Jan. 6, 1870; died Manhattan Beach, Cal., Apr. 15, 1951. Her vocal and musical studies took place in Paris with Jean DE RESZKE and in Vienna with Gustav MAHLER, following which she made her debut in opera in Nice in 1904. Between 1907 and 1911 she was principal contralto at the Vienna Royal Opera (VIENNA STATE OPERA). On Apr. 3, 1912, she made her METROPOLITAN OPERA debut as AZUCENA. She subsequently made guest appearances with leading opera houses specializing in Wagnerian contralto roles and as CARMEN before undertaking a highly successful career as concert singer and as a teacher of voice at the Curtis Institute in Philadelphia.

Caius, Dr., intended husband (tenor) of Nanetta Ford in VERDI's FALSTAFF.

Calaf, the Unknown Prince (tenor), in love with Turandot, in PUCCINI's TURANDOT, a role created by Miguel FLETA.

Calchas, high priest (bass) in GLUCK's IPHIGÉNIE EN AULIDE.

Caldara, Antonio, composer. Born Venice, 1670; died Vienna, Dec. 28, 1736. In Vienna, in 1714, he filled the post of imperial chamber composer to Emperor Charles VI, and from 1716 on he was Johann Joseph Fux's assistant as court KAPELLMEISTER. He wrote over sixty operas, none of which has survived, though some of these were performed with outstanding success in his lifetime. He clung to the traditions of the Italian school of his day, but is said to have achieved greater simplicity of structure and greater melodic sobriety than most of his Italian contemporaries.

Calderón de la Barca, Pedro, poet and dramatist. Born Madrid, Jan. 17, 1600; died there May 25, 1681. One of the most notable of Spanish authors, Calderón wrote several plays that were later adapted into operas. These include: Johann Georg Conradi's *Der königliche Prinz,* EGK's *Circe,* GODARD's *Pédro de Zalaméa,* MALIPIERO's *La vita è sogno,* RAFF's *Dame Kobold,* SCHUBERT's *Fierrabras,* Richard STRAUSS's DER FRIEDENSTAG, and WEINGARTNER's *Dame Kobold.*

Calife de Bagdad, Le (The Caliph of Bagdad), OPÉRA COMIQUE in one act by BOIELDIEU. Libretto by Claude Godard d'Aucour de Saint-Just. Premiere: Opéra-Comique, Sept. 16, 1801. American premiere: New Orleans, Mar. 2, 1806.

The setting is ancient Bagdad. The Caliph, Isaaum, enjoys parading around the city in disguise. While wearing the uniform of an officer, he tries to make love to Zeltube. When her mother calls the police, the Caliph has to reveal his identity. He also confesses he is so much in love with Zeltube that he is ready to marry her. Two vocal numbers are of special interest: "D'une flame si belle" and "Depuis le jour ou son courage."

Caliph, The, a character (baritone) in CORNELIUS' THE BARBER OF BAGDAD.

Calkas, High Priest of Pallas (bass) in WALTON's TROILUS AND CRESSIDA.

Callas, Maria Meneghini (born Kalogperopoulou), soprano. Born New York City, Dec. 3, 1923. Of Greek parentage, she was taken to Greece at the age of fourteen. She attended the Athens Conservatory of Music. In her fifteenth year she made her debut at the Athens Royal Opera House. She made her Italian debut in Verona in 1947 in LA GIOCONDA, so impressing the conductor, Tullio SERAFIN, that he coached her for several months. She joined LA SCALA in 1947, scoring triumphs as Elvira in I PURITANI, and as TOSCA, NORMA, and LUCIA.

She also sang the roles of ISOLDE and BRÜNNHILDE. When she appeared at COVENT GARDEN, one critic said she was the "greatest singer, male or female, since Nordica." Between 1951 and 1953 she appeared at the FLORENCE MAY MUSIC FESTIVAL in revivals of ARMIDA and MÉDÉE and the first stage presentation of HAYDN's ORFEO ED EURIDICE. By this time she had become a familiar name in the United States through recordings of her La Scala performances in *Tosca* and *I Puritani.* She turned down an offer from the METROPOLITAN OPERA for "trifling reasons," as she put it, and made her American debut with the CHICAGO LYRIC THEATRE on Nov. 1, 1954, as Norma, creating a sensation. The same season she appeared in LUCIA DI LAMMERMOOR and LA TRAVIATA. She again appeared as Norma when she made her debut at the Metropolitan Opera on Oct. 29, 1956. Between 1950 and 1958 she was one of the principal sopranos of La Scala, where she appeared in significant revivals of I PIRATA, ANNA BOLENA, and *Médée,* among other operas. The extraordinary range and dynamic quality of her voice and her unique dramatic powers were equaled only by the versatility of her repertoire. She became a highly controversial figure because of her tempestuous temperament, often coming into conflict with the directors of leading opera companies. Disagreement with the management led her to make a break with the Chicago Lyric Theatre in 1955 and with both the Metropolitan Opera and La Scala in 1958. In San Francisco she failed to make a scheduled appearance; and in the same year she refused to continue singing Norma at the Rome Opera, walking out of the opera house midway in the performance. Her extraordinary personal appeal, however, made a reconciliation with the leading opera houses inevitable. She returned to La Scala in 1960, and on Mar. 19, 1965, she was back on the stage of the Metropolitan Opera as Tosca. Alan Rich wrote in the *New York Herald Tribune:* "Here we have a woman who, like her or not, is the most important person singing in opera today. . . . For this generation at least Maria Callas is the supreme embodiment of the drama inherent in the romantic Mediterranean operatic language."

Calunnia, La, Don Basilio's description of the pernicious powers of slander to develop from a breeze into a gale, in Act I, Scene 2, of ROSSINI's THE BARBER OF SEVILLE.

Calatrava, Marquis of, Leonora's father (bass) in VERDI's LA FORZA DEL DESTINO.

Calvé, Emma (born Rosa Calvet), soprano. Born Décazeville, France, Aug. 15, 1858; died Millau, France, Jan. 6, 1942. She is most often thought of in the role of CARMEN, a portrayal that gave her her greatest triumphs. For several years she attended a convent in Montpellier, after which she studied singing for two years with Paul Puget. She made her opera debut at the THÉÂTRE DE LA MONNAIE, on Sept. 29, 1882, as MARGUERITE. After an additional year of study with Mathilde MARCHESI, she made a successful first appearance in Paris in 1884. For three seasons she was the principal soprano of the OPÉRA-COMIQUE. In 1887 she appeared at LA SCALA, where she made such a poor impression as OPHELIA that she was hissed off the stage. After another period of study, she returned to La Scala, once again as Ophelia, this time to be acclaimed. In 1890 she created the role of SANTUZZA in Rome. Her first appearance at COVENT GARDEN, in 1892, was a success of the first magnitude. On Nov. 29, 1893, she was acclaimed at her American debut at the METROPOLITAN OPERA as Santuzza. Three weeks later she appeared as Carmen and was a sensation. From this time on she was one of the most celebrated interpreters of that role.

She had a comparatively limited repertory, but her voice had such richness of texture and color and her interpretations were so electric that she maintained a position of first importance among the singers of her time.

She created the title role in MASSENET's SAPHO (Paris, 1897), and that of Anita in his LA NAVARRAISE (1894), a work written for her.

After 1910, and until 1924, she devoted herself primarily to concert appearances. In 1940 she emerged from retirement to appear in a motion picture. She wrote her autobiography, *My Life* (1922), and a volume of reminiscences, *Sous tous les ciels j'ai chanté* (1940).

Calzabigi, Ranieri da, poet and librettist. Born Leghorn, Italy, Dec. 23, 1714; died Naples, July, 1795. He wrote the librettos for three of GLUCK's operas. Before settling in Vienna, in 1761, he had distinguished himself as a historian, literary man, and adventurer. In Vienna he became chamber councilor to the exchequer and allied himself with Gluck and Count Durazzo (director of court theaters) in bringing about a reform in opera based on French dramatic principles, ideas, and culture. Their first collaboration was a ballet, *Don Juan,* given in 1761. A year later they produced ORFEO ED EURIDICE, with which their revolution of opera was finally realized. After writing the librettos for Gluck's ALCESTE and PARIDE ED ELENA, Calzabigi left Vienna, having become involved in a theatrical scandal.

Cambert, Robert, composer. Born Paris about 1628; died London, 1677. After completing harpsichord study with Chambonnières, he wrote, in 1659, the music for a comedy, *La Pastorale d'Issy.* In 1666 he became director of music to the Queen Dowager, Anne of Austria. Three years later he obtained a patent with Abbé Pierre Perrin to establish the Académie Royale de Musique for the purpose of presenting operas; this Académie subsequently became the PARIS OPÉRA. For this theater he wrote in 1671 a work now credited as being the first French opera: *Pomone.* A second opera, *Les Peines et les plaisirs de l'amour,* was written in the same year and later produced in London. In 1671, through the machinations of LULLY, Cambert lost his patent for the Académie. His disappointment driving him out of Paris, he settled in England, where he served as a military bandmaster.

cambiale di matrimonio, La (The Marriage Contract), OPERA BUFFA in one act by ROSSINI. Libretto by Gaetano ROSSI, based on a comedy by Camillo Federici. Premiere: Teatro San Moise, Venice, Nov. 3, 1810. American premiere: New York City, Oct. 14, 1829.

This is Rossini's first opera to be performed. It was written hurriedly on order to fill out a bill of one-act operas planned for the San Moise Theatre when the composer of one of those operas failed to meet his commitment. Rossini completed the opera within a few days, using as an overture an orchestral piece he had written as a student. The text involves the efforts of Mr. Slook, a rich Canadian businessman (baritone), to consummate a business deal with his English agent, Tobia Mill (bass), with the hope of thereby gaining the father's consent to marry Mill's daughter (soprano). The deal falls through, and Mr. Slook does not get the girl, who meanwhile has fallen in love with somebody else. The Rossini score, while obviously the work of an apprentice, has a good deal of the gaiety and effervescence soon to be encountered in his better-known operas. One of its airs, "Come tacer," was used by the composer for the duet "Dunque io son" in THE BARBER OF SEVILLE.

This opera was revived in Vienna and New York City in 1937, in Brussels in 1957, and in a concert performance in New York City in 1961 (the last in a new English translation). On Feb. 23, 1968, it was given at the Piccolo Teatro Municipale in Pesaro in celebration of the centennial of the composer's death.

Cambridge University Musical Society, an organization at Cambridge University, Eng., for the performance of concert music and operas. It was founded in 1843. For many years it devoted itself exclusively to instrumental and choral music. Opera came into its own between 1902 and 1914, when Prof. Edward J. DENT served as director. During this period operas or dramatized oratorios by HANDEL, operas by PURCELL and MOZART (the last in new English translations by Dent) were given frequently. There was a hiatus in its operations during World War II. Performances resumed in 1948 with presentations of a dramatized version of Handel's oratorio *Solomon*, Patrick Hadley's *The Hills*, and Purcell's KING ARTHUR. During the next half dozen years there were given *La rappresentazione di anima e di corpo*, *Athalia* (Handel), L'ORFEO, and PILGRIM'S PROGRESS. In 1954 the Cambridge University Opera Group was founded to extend the operatic activities of the Society, and in 1956 the New Opera Company became affiliated with this organization. Among the more unusual productions mounted since 1954 (many of them English premieres) were: BOULEVARD SOLITUDE; CATULLI CARMINA; *A Dinner Engagement* (Lennox BERKELEY); *Don Procipio* (BIZET); ERWARTUNG; JEANNE D'ARC AU BÛCHER; THE LOVE FOR THREE ORANGES; IL MATRIMONIO SEGRETO; *The Mayor of Casterbridge* (Peter Tranchell); THE POISONED KISS; IL PRIGIONIERO; THE RAKE'S PROGRESS; DER REVISOR; THE SCHOOL FOR WIVES; A TALE OF TWO CITIES.

Camerata, the group of musicians and poets who gathered in Florence in the sixteenth century to discuss music, poetry, and the theater, and who were responsible for the birth of opera. Leaders of the Camerata (literally: the group that meets in a room) were two noblemen, Giovanni Bardi and Jacopo CORSI, and in their homes the fruitful meetings took place. Other members included the composers Vincenzo Galilei (father of the astronomer), Giulio CACCINI, Jacopo PERI, and Emilio de' CAVALIERI, and a poet, Ottavio Rinuccini. For a more detailed account of the Camerata's accomplishments *see* OPERA.

Camille, a character (tenor) in love with Lucile in EINEM'S DANTONS TOD, a role created by Julius PATZAK.

Cammarano, Salvatore, librettist. Born

Naples, Mar. 19, 1801; died there July 17, 1852. After writing several prose dramas, he began writing opera librettos in 1834, and a year later completed LUCIA DI LAMMERMOOR for DONIZETTI. He subsequently wrote librettos for VERDI (including *Alzira, La battaglia di Legnano,* LUISA MILLER, and IL TROVATORE) as well as for other composers, including Giovanni PACINI and Giuseppe MERCADANTE.

Campanari, Giuseppe, baritone. Born Venice, Nov. 17, 1855; died Milan, May 31, 1927. Originally he was a cellist in the orchestra of LA SCALA and later with the Boston Symphony Orchestra. While still in Milan he began to study singing, and in 1893 made his debut in New York with the Gustav Hinrichs Opera Company; during the same year he created for America the role of TONIO. He was immediately acclaimed both for the beauty of his voice and the vitality of his characterizations. On Jan. 7, 1895, he made his debut at the METROPOLITAN OPERA as VALENTIN. He remained at the Metropolitan for three seasons, scoring great successes as Figaro in THE BARBER OF SEVILLE and as Count di LUNA, ESCAMILLO, and FALSTAFF. After abandoning opera he concentrated on concert appearances and teaching.

campana sommersa, La (The Sunken Bell), opera in four acts by RESPIGHI. Libretto by Claudio Guastella, based on Gerhart Hauptmann's play of the same name. Premiere: Hamburg Opera, Nov. 18, 1927. American premiere: Metropolitan Opera, Nov. 24, 1928. Heinrich the bell founder (tenor) comes under the spell of a fairy (soprano). He deserts his people to follow her into the mountains. The death of his wife, Magda (soprano), brings him home, but he cannot forget his sweetheart. On his deathbed, Heinrich calls for the fairy, and she returns to him.

campanello di notte, Il (The Night Bell), OPERA BUFFA in one act by DONIZETTI. Libretto by the composer, based on *La Sonnette de nuit,* a French vaudeville by Brunswick, Troin, and Lherie. Premiere: Teatro Nuovo, Naples, June 6, 1836. American premiere: New York City, May 7, 1917.

Don Annibale Pistacchio, an elderly apothecary, has recently married the young and lovely Serafina. Enrico, long in love with Serafina, seeks revenge. On Annibale's wedding night he continually disturbs the couple by ringing the doorbell, appearing in various disguises to demand medicines—Italian law requiring that an apothecary must be available at all times. Poor Annibale is unable to enjoy the bliss of his wedding night. And to make matters even worse the following morning he is summoned to Rome to settle a will. The most notable aria is that of Don Annibale expressing rapture at being married to one so beautiful ("Bella cosa, amici cari").

This musical farce was successfully revived at the PICCOLA SCALA in Milan in 1957 and at the MANNHEIM OPERA in 1969.

Campanini, Cleofonte, conductor. Born Parma, Italy, Sept. 1, 1860; died Chicago, Dec. 19, 1919. His musical studies took place at the Parma Conservatory. He made his debut as conductor in Parma in 1883 with CARMEN. In the same year he was appointed assistant conductor of the METROPOLITAN OPERA during its inaugural season. Five years later he was brought back to the United States expressly to direct the American premiere of OTELLO at the ACADEMY OF MUSIC. The Desdemona of that performance was Eva TETRAZZINI, who had become Campanini's wife in 1887. After conducting at LA SCALA for three years, he was appointed artistic director and principal conductor of the newly organized Oscar Hammerstein Opera Company at the MANHATTAN OPERA HOUSE. He stayed there three years, finally resigning because of differences with Hammerstein over artistic policies. In 1910 he became first conductor of the CHICAGO OPERA, a post he retained to the time of his death. In 1918 he brought the Chicago company to New York for a four-week season, when the then sensational coloratura soprano,

GALLI-CURCI, made her first New York appearance. Campanini was one of the outstanding conductors of his generation, particularly of the French repertory. Among the operas he introduced to America were HÉRODIADE, THE JEWELS OF THE MADONNA, LOUISE, PELLÉAS ET MÉLISANDE, SAPHO, and THAÏS.

Campanini, Italo, tenor. Born Parma, Italy, June 30, 1845; died Villa Vigatto, Italy, Nov. 14, 1896. He was the brother of the conductor discussed above and one of the most successful opera tenors in the United States before CARUSO. After study in Parma, he made his opera debut in Odessa in IL TROVATORE (1869). After an additional period of study with Francesco LAMPERTI in Milan, he returned to the stage and scored his first major success in Bologna in 1871 in the Italian premiere of LOHENGRIN. He toured the United States in 1873 and 1879–80, and he appeared at the METROPOLITAN OPERA as FAUST in the company's first performance (Oct. 22, 1883). After 1883 he lived principally in New York and was the leading tenor of the Metropolitan Opera. The beautiful texture of his voice and his flawless delivery made him a favorite.

Campièllo, Il (The Piazza), OPERA BUFFA in three acts by WOLF-FERRARI. Libretto by the composer based on GOLDONI's comedy of the same name. Premiere: La Scala, Feb. 12, 1936. The action takes place in Venice about 1750 and concerns an eventful day in the lives of four families inhabiting a Venetian piazza. A climax comes with a street brawl in which two elderly mothers (represented by tenors!) participate.

Il Campièllo was revived by the MANNHEIM OPERA in Germany in Jan., 1969.

Campra, André, composer. Born Aix-en-Provence, Dec. 4, 1660; died Versailles, June 29, 1744. He was one of the early masters to establish the foundations of French opera. After studying with Guillaume Poitevin, he was appointed *maître de musique* of the Toulon cathedral. In 1694 he went to Paris and soon became MAÎTRE DE CHAPELLE at

Notre Dame. At about this time he began writing operas. For fear of losing his ecclesiastical post he presented them as his brother's. The first was *L'Europe galante,* given in Paris in 1697. Two years later he wrote *Le Carnaval de Venise.* The success of these works encouraged him to give up his church post and devote himself exclusively to secular music. From this time on he produced many operas which made him the logical successor to LULLY as the foremost French composer for the theater. His opera *Tancrède,* given in 1702, held the stage in Paris for half a century. In 1718 he received a life pension, and in 1722 he was appointed musical director of the Chapelle Royale and to the Prince de Conti. His principal operas: *L'Europe galante* (1697); *Le Carnaval de Venise* (1699); *Aréthuse* (1701); *Trancrède* (1702); *Iphigénie en Tauride* (1704); *Télémaque* (1704); *Le Triomphe de l'amour* (1705); *Idoménée* (1712); *Les Amours de Mars et Vénus* (1712); *Camille* (1717); *Achille et Déidamie* (1735).

Canio, head of a theatrical troupe (tenor) in LEONCAVALLO's PAGLIACCI.

Canterbury Pilgrims, The, opera in four acts by Reginald DE KOVEN. Libretto by Percy MacKaye, based on CHAUCER. Premiere: Metropolitan Opera, Mar. 8, 1917. The plot concerns the assembling of the Canterbury pilgrims in the courtyard of the Tabard Inn at Southwark, near London, on Apr. 16, 1387. By losing a wager, Chaucer (baritone) must decide to marry Alisoun (contralto); he is finally rescued by legal technicalities. STANFORD wrote an opera with the same title.

Cantiamo, facciam brindisi, the chorus of the peasants celebrating the wedding feast, in the opening of Act II of DONIZETTI's L'ELISIR D'AMORE.

cantilena, a smooth and melodious style of singing or of writing for the voice.

Canzone di cannetella, the light, breezy aria in which Maliella discloses her coquettish ways, in Act I of WOLF-FERRARI's THE JEWELS OF THE MADONNA.

canzonetta, a short song, generally of light, cheerful character.

Caponsacchi, opera in three acts by HAGEMAN. Libretto is Arthur Goodrich's play of the same name, adapted from Robert Browning's poem *The Ring and the Book*. Premiere: Freiburg, Ger., Feb. 18, 1932. American premiere: Metropolitan Opera, Feb. 4, 1937. Caponsacchi (tenor) is accused of having been Pompilia's lover. Pompilia (soprano) is subsequently murdered by her husband, Count Guido Franceschini (baritone). Brought before a papal hearing, Caponsacchi reveals how he has been falsely accused by Guido. The papal court pronounces Caponsacchi innocent and sentences Guido to death.

Capriccio, opera in one act, described as "a conversation piece for music," by Richard STRAUSS. Libretto by the composer and Clemens KRAUSS, based on Abbate Giovanni Battista Casti's libretto for SALIERI's opera *Prima la musica e poi le parole*. Premiere: Munich Opera, Oct. 28, 1942. American premiere: Santa Fe, N.M., Aug. 1, 1958.

Strauss's last opera, *Capriccio* represented to him a kind of valedictory. He wrote it for his own amusement and that of his friends, not intending it for public presentation. He wanted this opera to express his conclusions about opera, specifically about the relative importance in opera of words and music. He also wanted to sum up, so to speak, his musical preferences, and so his score is filled with quotations from MOZART (some of the piano concertos), WAGNER (DIE MEISTERSINGER), VERDI (OTELLO), and several times from some of his own works including ARIADNE AUF NAXOS and several of his songs. Since his setting was Paris and the time 1775, the period during which a good deal of discussion was being exchanged between the supporters of GLUCK and of RAMEAU concerning the relative importance of opera versus music drama, Strauss included in his music a quotation from Gluck (IPHIGÉNIE EN AULIDE) and some from Gluck's Italian rival, PICCINNI.

Strauss did not call this work an opera but "a conversation piece," since its almost actionless libretto is little more than a two-and-a-half-hour discussion as to which is more significant in opera, the words or the music. Flamand, the poet (tenor), becomes the spokesman for the words; Olivier, the musician (tenor), for the music. Both are emotionally involved with the Countess Madeleine (soprano). When La Roche, a producer (bass), plans a series of entertainments to celebrate the Countess' birthday, she suggests that Flamand and Olivier collaborate, using for their material the day's happenings and themselves as principal characters. When they leave to write their "entertainment," the Countess (looking in a mirror) asks herself which man she prefers. She comes to the conclusion that both interest her equally. Her conclusion is Strauss's answer to the problem that opened the opera. In opera, the words and music have equal importance.

Strauss introduced some comic elements into his music, such as a parody of eighteenth-century opera duets. The score also contains a good deal of melodic material that is recognizably Strauss in its eloquence, such as the instrumental sextet with which the opera opens and including Flamand's composition written to honor the Countess ("Kein anders dass mir so im Herzen loht"), Olivier's air, "Tanz und Musik stehn im Bann des Rhythmus," and the Countess' concluding aria, "Ihre Liebe."

Capriccio was a feature of the SALZBURG FESTIVAL in 1950 and the VIENNA FESTIVAL WEEKS in June, 1965.

Capulet, a nobleman (bass), head of the house of Capulet, in GOUNOD'S ROMÉO ET JULIETTE.

Capuletti ed i Montecchi, I (The Capulets and the Montagues), opera in four acts by BELLINI. Libretto by Felice ROMANI, freely based on SHAKESPEARE's *Romeo and Juliet*. Premiere: Teatro la Venice, Mar. 11, 1830. American premiere: Boston, Apr. 4, 1847.

The first act takes place in the courtyard of Capellio's house, Capellio (bass) being the head of the Capulets. Romeo (contralto) has killed Capellio's son and Capellio is determined to get revenge by using his daughter, Giulietta (soprano), as the instrument for Romeo's destruction. The scene then shifts to Giulietta's room to which Romeo comes to tell her of his love. In the second act, Romeo and his men appear in the hall of the Capulets' palace to prevent Giulietta's marriage to Tebaldo (tenor). A struggle ensues during which it is rumored that Romeo is a fatal victim. But in the third act Giulietta learns to her joy that Romeo is alive but has fled. To avoid marrying Tebaldo, Giulietta takes a sleeping potion which when taking effect simulates death. Romeo secretly invades the Capulet palace, finds Giulietta outstretched and is convinced she has committed suicide. In the final act, Romeo poisons himself in the cemetery vault at Giulietta's bier. He dies in her arms as she awakens. Unable to live without Romeo, Giulietta stabs herself.

One of the curious features about this opera is that the role of Romeo was written for a woman's voice, a contralto. (This may be the reason why the opera is given so rarely, though it has been occasionally revived in Italy and was performed in New York City by the AMERICAN OPERA SOCIETY in 1958.) Some of the music in this score was taken by Bellini from one of his earlier operas, *Zaira* (1829).

Caramoor Festival, an annual summer festival of concert music and opera, presented on the grounds of the 180-acre estate of Walter and Lucie Bigelow Rosen in Katonah, N.Y. The Walter and Lucie Rosen Foundation for the Arts was founded in 1946 to give public performances of "things that people cannot get elsewhere, things that not everybody will want to hear." Among the first operas produced were L'INCORONAZIONE DI POPPEA and MÉDÉE. In 1958 an outdoor Venetian theater was erected, opening with a performance of the second act of GLUCK'S ORFEO ED EURIDICE featuring Marian ANDERSON. Since then opera, performed in this theater, has been an integral part of the festival. Between 1958 and 1961 Alfred Wallen-

stein was the musical director and was responsible for the presentation of ACIS AND GALATEA, DIDO AND AENEAS, *Solomon* (HANDEL), and TROILUS AND CRESSIDA, among other works. Between 1961 and 1963, Walter Hendl was musical director. He was succeeded by Julius RUDEL. Among the unusual works presented were: BASTIEN UND BASTIENNE; THE BURNING FIERY FURNACE (American premiere); CARMINA BURANA; CATULLI CARMINA; CURLEW RIVER (American premiere); *Escorial* (David Levy); DIE KLUGE; THE PRODIGAL SON (American premiere); SEMELE; IL SIGNOR BRUSCHINO. In 1968 a new production of *L'incoronazione di Poppea* was given. In 1970 the festival opened its twenty-fifth season with IDOMENEO and presented the American premiere of Malcolm Williamson's *Growing Castle*.

Cara sposa, Rinaldo's famous air in HANDEL'S RINALDO.

Cardillac, opera in three acts by HINDEMITH. Libretto by Ferdinand Lion, based on E. T. A. HOFFMANN's *Das Fräulein von Scuderi*. Premiere: Dresden, Nov. 9, 1926 (original version); Zürich, June 20, 1952 (revised version). American premiere: Santa Fe, N.M., July 26, 1967 (revised version).

The principal character, Cardillac (baritone), is a Parisian goldsmith in the closing decade of the seventeenth century. Unable to separate himself from the masterpieces he has created, he murders his clients. Cardillac's partner warns a prima donna, whose lover has ordered from Cardillac a gold belt, that her life is in danger. The police are warned and catch up with Cardillac outside the opera house where he confesses his crimes. A mob rushes at him and murders him.

In its original version, *Cardillac* was an opera devoid of melody or emotion as well as dramatic interest, in the composer's then rejection of romanticism for pure objectivity. Structurally the opera is reminiscent of WOZZECK in that it utilizes basically instrumental forms for various sections (for example, fugue, canon, passacaglia, and so forth). The writing is in the austere linear style Hindemith then favored.

The purpose of Hindemith's extensive revision of both the libretto and the music a quarter of a century later was to increase the emotional and dramatic interest. Where the orchestra had been all-important in the first version, voices were emphasized in the new one. New recitatives and vocal numbers were added, including a number of highly effective melodic pages and choruses. Linear writing gives way to many passages of deeply moving lyricism or dynamic rhythmic strength. The revised opera became a powerful musical drama where the original version had been consistently dull and static.

Cardinal Brogny, see BROGNY, CARDINAL.

Card Song, see EN VAIN POUR ÉVITER.

Care selve, the most celebrated aria in HANDEL's ATALANTA, and one of the best known from any Handel opera. It was written for the CASTRATO Gizziello, who introduced it.

Carestini, Giovanni, CASTRATO contralto. Born Filottrano, Italy, 1705; died there c. 1760. He made his debut in Rome in 1721 in the principal female role in BONONCINI's *Griselda.* From then to 1733 he established his reputation with appearances throughout Italy. Though originally a soprano, his voice deepened and he acquired what was described by his contemporaries as the finest contralto voice ever heard. In 1723 he was invited to sing at the coronation of Charles VI as King of Bohemia. A decade later he went to London, making his debut in a PASTICCIO. He soon distinguished himself as a member of HANDEL's opera company where he proved to be a rival to FARINELLI, then acknowledged to be the greatest of the castrati. Among Handel's operas in which Carestini appeared in London were ALCINA, *Ariodante,* and *Il pastor fido.* Carestini returned to Italy in 1735. For the next twenty years he was a reigning favorite in Italian, German, and Russian opera houses.

Carlo, Don (baritone), son of the Mar-

quis of Calatrava in VERDI's LA FORZA DEL DESTINO.

Carlos, Don, (1) King of Castile (baritone) in VERDI's ERNANI.

(2) Infante of Spain (tenor) in VERDI's DON CARLOS.

Carl Rosa Opera Company, The Royal, English company which has been producing operas in English for over three-quarters of a century. It was organized in 1873 by Carl Rosa, giving its first performance in Manchester: William Vincent Wallace's *Maritana.* During the first season the company gave operas by BALFE, BELLINI, GOUNOD, MOZART, and VERDI, all in English. The company was reorganized in 1875, and it first appeared in London with THE MARRIAGE OF FIGARO. For the next fourteen years, the company was outstandingly successful, primarily in the provinces but for several seasons also in London. The personnel included many fine American, English, and French artists, including Minnie HAUK and Alwina Valleria from America, Sir John Bentley, and Marie ROZE from France. Seven new British operas were commissioned, and in 1885 the first performance in England of MANON was given. Carl Rosa proved the popularity of opera by amassing a fortune. After his death, in 1889, the management passed to Augustus Harris, while the ownership remained with Rosa's widow. For the next decade the company continued to prosper artistically and financially. In 1891 its performance of CARMEN was so popular that a special company was formed to tour the provinces, with Marie Roze in the title role. In 1893 the company gave a command performance of FRA DIAVOLO at Balmoral Castle, after which Queen Victoria conferred on it the honorary title of "royal." In 1897 PUCCINI helped supervise the first English performances of LA BOHÈME. Operas by English composers were not neglected: during the 1890's seven native works were introduced at COVENT GARDEN, and several others in the provinces.

In 1900 the company was taken over

by Alfred van Noorden, who became its manager, while his brother Walter was principal conductor. Under this regime, the company gave the first English performances of ANDREA CHÉNIER, THE CRICKET ON THE HEARTH, and THE QUEEN OF SHEBA. In 1918 Sir Joseph Beecham's Quinlan Opera Company merged with the Carl Rosa Company, and five years later the manager of the Quinlan Opera, H. B. Phillips, became full owner. He retained control up to the time of his death in 1950, when the ownership passed to his widow, who for several years previously had been artistic director. There was a fifteen-month hiatus in the operations of the company beginning with 1952, but a grant from the Arts Council in Sept., 1954, enabled the company to continue functioning. In 1957 Mrs. Phillips was succeeded by H. Procter-Gregg, who resigned one year later due to serious differences with the board of directors; at the same time the Arts Council stopped its subsidy. Most of the personnel of the company was absorbed by SADLER'S WELLS, and a new and extended scheme of operations was put into effect. An attempt to revive the Carl Rosa Company as an independent unit in 1960 proved unsuccessful.

The Carl Rosa Opera Company presented over one hundred fifty operas between 1875 and 1957, a fourth of which (not including operas by English composers) received their first performances in England. Though the basic repertory comprised the familiar works, the company did present a number of world premieres of English operas (including STANFORD's THE CANTERBURY PILGRIMS) and several significant revivals (including HUBIČKA in its first professional presentation in England and BENVENUTO CELLINI, in its first professional production in England since 1853) .

Carmagnole, La, a popular tune sung during the Reign of Terror in France, mostly at executions. It is quoted in ANDREA CHÉNIER (Act III) and in DANTONS TOD (last act) .

Carmela, Gennaro's mother (mezzo-soprano) in WOLF-FERRARI's THE JEWELS OF THE MADONNA.

Carmelites, The, see DIALOGUES DES CARMÉLITES, LES.

Carmen, opera in four acts by BIZET. Libretto by Henri Meilhac and Ludovic HALÉVY, based on Prosper MÉRIMÉE's story of the same name. Premiere: Opéra-Comique, Mar. 3, 1875. American premiere: Academy of Music, N.Y., Oct. 23, 1878.

Characters: Don José, a guardsman (tenor) ; Carmen, a gypsy (mezzo-soprano) , a role created by GALLI-MARIÉ; Escamillo, a toreador (baritone) ; Micaëla, a peasant girl (soprano) ; Frasquita, a gypsy friend of Carmen's (soprano) ; Mercédès, another gypsy friend (mezzo-soprano) ; Zuniga, captain of the guards (bass); Moralès, an officer (bass); Le Remendado, a smuggler (tenor) ; Le Dancaïre, another smuggler (baritone) ; cigarette girls; gypsies; smugglers; dragoons. The setting is in and near Seville, about 1820.

Act I. A square in Seville. A vigorous prelude alternates between gaiety and foreboding. The principal themes are a bright, gay tune used later for the parade before the bull fight, Escamillo's Toreador Song, and an ominous theme for cellos usually called the "fate" theme. With the rise of the curtain a girl timidly approaches a guardsman to inquire of the whereabouts of Don José. She is informed he will appear with the change of the guards. The guards finally arrive. From a near-by cigarette factory, girls emerge for the noonday respite. One of these, Carmen, makes flirtatious overtures to Don José as she mockingly sings of love (HABANERA: "L'amour est un oiseau rebelle") . Her song ended, she flings a flower at him and rushes back into the factory. Don José picks up the flower and conceals it in a pocket near his heart. The timid girl now reappears. She is Don José's sweetheart, Micaëla, come with news of home. He inquires about and receives tidings about his mother ("Parle-moi de ma mère"). Tenderly they recall their childhood happiness ("Ma mère, je la vois") . Don José then sends her back with a message for his mother. When she has gone, he takes the flower from his pocket and is about to throw it away when he is attracted by noises from the factory. When the women come rushing out, he learns that Carmen has stabbed one of the girls. Carmen is seized and has her hands tied. She is left in Don José's custody while the captain of the guard, Zuniga, goes off to make out a warrant for her arrest. Coyly, with light heart, Carmen insists that she and Don José will soon meet again in the tavern of Lillas Pastia, outside the city walls (SEGUIDILLA: "Près des ramparts de Séville") . Don José is now under her spell. He unties Carmen's hands. When the dragoons come to conduct her to prison, she pushes Don José aside and escapes.

Act II. The prelude is based mainly on the off-stage song Don José sings about the dragoons. In the tavern of Lillas Pastia, gypsies are dancing and singing (Chanson bohème) . Carmen receives the news that Don José, who had been imprisoned for complicity in her escape, has been released. A moment later the famous toreador Escamillo arrives. Proudly he tells his admirers of the excitement of bullfighting (Toreador Song: "Votre toast") , then departs, trailed by the crowd. Carmen and two of her friends are approached by smugglers who want to employ them as lures for the coast guard. Carmen is sympathetic, but before she can accept the offer she wants to await Don José's arrival. Already his voice is heard in the distance. When he appears, Carmen welcomes him passionately. She plays on his emotions; she dances for him. The sudden sound of a bugle call reminds Don José that he must return to his barracks, but he is now so hopelessly in love that he cannot leave Carmen. He removes from his pocket the flower Carmen had once thrown him (Flower Song: "La fleur que tu m'avais jetée") . However, he is also torn by pangs of conscience. He is about to return to duty

when Zuniga appears and mocks Carmen for taking up with a mere soldier when he, an officer, wants her. Don José attacks Zuniga. This act of insubordination makes it impossible for him to return to military duty. He now joins Carmen in her association with the smugglers.

Act III. A brief intermezzo, highlighted by a flute solo, sets the mood for the scene of a mountain pass at night. The smugglers tell of their dangerous trade and how they continually must be on the watch ("Écoute, écoute, compagnon") . Don José is sad and reflective because, as he tells Carmen, he is thinking of his mother. Bitterly, Carmen tells him to go home, a suggestion so upsetting to Don José that he threatens to kill her if she repeats it. Nearby the gypsies Frasquita and Mercédès are reading fortunes with cards. When Carmen begins to read her own, the cards tell of impending disaster (Card Song: "En vain pour éviter les réponses amères") . Her tensions are relieved with the announcement by the smugglers that the time has come for them to carry their contraband through the mountain pass. Don José is left behind to keep guard. When the smugglers are gone, Micaëla comes seeking her lover. Poignantly, she prays to heaven for protection ("Je dis que rien ne m'épouvante") . When a shot rings out, she hides. The shot has come from Don José's gun, fired at the approach of a stranger. Escamillo has come seeking Carmen. Recognizing each other as rivals, Don José and Escamillo fall upon each other with drawn daggers. Only the sudden return of Carmen and the smugglers prevents José's killing the toreador. Saved at the last moment, Escamillo departs with his customary swagger, inviting all the smugglers to be his guests at his next bullfight. Don José insists he will never leave Carmen whatever the cost ("Dût-il m'en coûter la vie") . Micaëla is now discovered by the smugglers. She reveals to Don José that his mother is dying.

Don José must now leave Carmen, but he warns her that they will meet again.

Act IV. Another square in Seville. The festive prelude is alive with Spanish rhythms and melodies, the main melody of which was adapted from an Andalusian folksong. It is the day of the bullfight. Escamillo appears, Carmen with him. They speak of their love in "Si tu m'aimes, Carmen." When the toreador enters the arena, Carmen's gypsy friends warn her that José is lurking nearby to avenge himself for her desertion. The crowd surges into the arena. When Carmen is left alone, José comes to plead for her love. Icily the gypsy tells him she loves him no longer. Don José continues to plead; Carmen remains deaf. Suddenly shouts from the arena hail the victorious Escamillo. Carmen is about to join her hero when José stops her and kills her with a dagger. When the crowd emerges, Don José surrenders, and cries out, "Oh my beloved Carmen!"

Before *Carmen* was universally accepted as one of the finest products of the French lyric theater and before it became one of the best loved operas in the repertory, it had to live down two devastating accusations made against it. When first produced, *Carmen* was criticized by several French writers as being a feeble imitation of the WAGNER dramas. While it is true that Bizet had recourse to the LEITMOTIV technique—though not in the Wagnerian way—and that he had Wagner's respect for the stage and his inventiveness of harmonic and orchestral language, *Carmen* is not the stereotype of a Wagnerian drama by any stretch of the imagination. The essence of Bizet's musical style and dramatic approach was French. Greater familiarity with *Carmen* proved how wrong these Parisian critics were, but hardly had this controversy died down when a new attack was directed against the opera. Several musicologists, particularly Spanish ones, took the opera to task for its supposedly pseudo-Spanish style. But Bizet had no intention of writing national Spanish music. What he wanted to do, and what he succeeded in doing, was to capture the spirit of Spanish song and dance in music essentially his own. Bizet's borrowing from popular melodies and rhythms (as when he expropriated a melody by Sebastian Yradier for his famous Habanera) was used as the Mediterranean spice for his dish, but his dish was still representative of the French cuisine.

While *Carmen* was at first the victim of unjust criticisms, it was by no means the failure that sentimental historians and biographers have led us to believe. Once audiences got over the shock of the sensual story and the lurid characterizations, they began responding enthusiastically to Bizet's wonderful music. Though the premiere took place late in the season, the opera was seen thirty-seven times in its first year. It remained in the repertory the following season, which most certainly would not have been the case had it been a failure. Ludovic Halévy, one of the librettists, recorded that the box-office receipts were "respectable, and generally in excess of those for other works in the repertory."

Originally *Carmen* was an OPÉRA COMIQUE, not a grand opera. In other words, it had spoken dialogue between its musical numbers. However, as seen in the United States and in most European opera houses outside France, *Carmen* is sung throughout, the spoken words having been replaced by recitatives composed by Ernest GUIRAUD.

Carmen, the volatile gypsy girl, is one of the most colorful characters in all opera, and many famous sopranos have distinguished themselves with their vivid, at times highly individual portrayals of the part. Célestine Galli-Marié, the first Carmen, became widely famous in the part.

Carmina Burana (Songs of Beuron), a "scenic cantata" in three parts by ORFF. Text by the composer (partly in Latin, partly in medieval German), based on poems of unknown authorship from the thirteenth century. Premiere: Frankfurt, Ger., June 8, 1937. American premiere: San Francisco, Oct. 3, 1954.

This is the first of a trilogy entitled

Trionfi, of which the subsequent parts are CATULLI CARMINA and TRIONFO D'AFRODITE. In labeling these compositions, the creator took pains to avoid the word "opera," preferring the term "scenic cantata." Although *Carmina Burana* is heard most often as a concert work, it was intended for staging and as such comes within the category of opera. But in line with his ideal of reducing opera to the most basic essentials, Orff did not give any specific instructions as to the kind of costuming, staging, or scenery he preferred, leaving these matters to the discretion of the producer or director. He did specify, however, that he wanted these to be as simple and elementary as possible. He also dispensed completely with plot and dramatic action.

But there is a central theme in all three works, a unifying element. In *Carmina Burana* it is the subject of wandering students, minstrels who hymn the praise of nature, love, freedom, and the tavern. There are three sections: "Springtime," "In the Tavern," and "The Court of Love." The composition begins with a chorus calling upon the goddess of Fortune (this is repeated in the closing section of the work) ; immediately afterward the chorus complains about the blows inflicted on man by Fortune. All this serves as a prelude to the joys of life, in gambling, love, wine, and so forth.

The composition calls for a soprano, tenor, baritone, chorus, and a huge orchestra. In the latter the percussion family is vastly expanded, since rhythm is the composer's prime interest, and it is through rhythm that he achieves his most overpowering effects.

Carmina Burana is Orff's most popular composition. After it was heard for the first time in New York City (in 1959) , it received the New York Music Critics' Circle Award.

Carmosine, *see* MUSSET, ALFRED DE.

Carolina, Paolina's wife (soprano) in CIMAROSA'S IL MATRIMONIO SEGRETO.

Caro nome, Gilda's aria in Act I of VERDI'S RIGOLETTO in which, having met the Duke disguised as a student, she contemplates romantically and tenderly the assumed name with which he introduced himself.

Carré, Albert, impresario. Born Strasbourg, France, June 22, 1852; died Paris, Dec. 12, 1938. He was the director of the OPÉRA-COMIQUE for over a decade. His initiation into the theater was as an actor in Paris. After directing various theaters in France, including the Comédie Française, he was appointed, in 1898, the director of the Opéra-Comique in succession to Léon CARVALHO. He introduced so many fine operas, including LE JUIF POLONAIS, LOUISE, and PELLÉAS ET MÉLISANDE, that the Opéra-Comique became a formidable rival of the OPÉRA. Carré remained director until 1912. After World War I, he was codirector with the Isola brothers until 1925, after which he was made honorary director. He wrote several opera librettos, including that for MESSAGER'S *La Basoche.* His uncle, Michel Carré, collaborated with Jules BARBIER in writing the librettos for eight of GOUNOD'S operas including FAUST and ROMÉO ET JULIETTE, and for MASSÉ's *Paul et Virginie,* MEYERBEER'S *Le pardon de Ploërmel,* DINORAH, THE TALES OF HOFFMANN, THOMAS'S *Hamlet* and MIGNON, among other operas.

Carrosse du Saint-Sacrement, Le, *see* MÉRIMÉE, PROSPER.

Carry Nation, opera in three acts by MOORE. Libretto by William North James. Premiere: Lawrence, Kan., Apr. 28, 1966.

This opera was commissioned to help celebrate the centenary of the University of Kansas, where it was given its world premiere. It was subsequently performed successfully by the SAN FRANCISCO OPERA and the NEW YORK CITY OPERA.

Keeping in mind the occasion for which the opera was written, its authors selected a subject relevant to Kansas history, since Carry Nation, daughter of a Fundamentalist father, began her vigorous campaign against the evils of liquor in Kansas. In the opera she marries Floyd (despite her father's opposition) , a young doctor addicted to drink. The father and his demented mother succeed in separating their daughter from her husband and their child. Floyd dies only a year and a half after his marriage, because of overindulgence in his vice. This tragedy, combined with her own profound religious convictions, is responsible for Carry Nation's subsequent mission to wipe out forever the menace of alcohol through a fanatical crusade that became almost a religion with her. The opera contains a haunting aria by Carry about her terrible loneliness; an affecting love duet between Carry and Floyd; and a vigorous hoedown with a strong American folk identity.

Caruso, Enrico, tenor. Born Naples, Feb. 25, 1873; died there Aug. 2, 1921. One of the greatest operatic tenors of all time, he was the idol of the opera world for over two decades. A musical child, in his ninth year he joined the choir of his parish church. Formal musical training came comparatively late. When he was eighteen he began a three-year period of study with Guglielmo Vergine, completing his training with Vincenzo Lombardi. After several appearances in Naples, he made what he regarded as his official debut there on Nov. 16, 1894, in L'AMICO FRITZ. In 1898 he was engaged by the TEATRO LIRICO in Milan, where he created the principal tenor roles in ADRIANA LECOUVREUR and FEDORA. In 1901 he became a member of the LA SCALA company, where he was featured in leading roles of the Italian and French repertory. Here he created the principal tenor roles in FRANCHETTI's GERMANIA and MASCAGNI's *Le maschere*. Arturo TOSCANINI said, after hearing him in L'ELISIR D'AMORE: "If this Neapolitan continues singing like this, he will make the whole world talk about him." Caruso's international fame began in MONTE CARLO in 1902, where he was so highly acclaimed that he was engaged for three additional seasons and received contracts from COVENT GARDEN and the METROPOLITAN OPERA. His American debut took place at the Metropolitan Opera on Nov. 23, 1903, in RIGOLETTO. This was the opening night of the Metropolitan season. Largely due to his nervousness, Caruso did not make a good first

impression. The critics pointed to his "tiresome Italian mannerisms" (particularly his excessive use of the so-called "Rubini sob"). But before the end of the season he became an outstanding favorite. He achieved a personal triumph as Nemorino in *L'elisir d'amore*. The following season he again appeared at the Metropolitan's opening-night performance maintaining a tradition which lasted seventeen years in all, with only one year skipped. He was now the shining light of the company. When he sang, the box office prospered; his performances brought in close to a hundred thousand dollars a season. He duplicated his Metropolitan Opera triumphs in all the major opera houses, becoming the highest-paid singer and the most adulated in the world. When he sang in Germany and Austria, seats for his performances were often sold at auction. His income from his phonograph recordings totaled almost two million dollars during his lifetime. He appeared successfully in almost fifty roles. His voice was admired for its range, tone, and shading. It was powerful yet supple, exquisite in the upper range, sensuous in the middle tones, extraordinarily expressive in lower registers. "I have never heard a more beautiful voice," Edouard DE RESZKE once wrote to him.

His career ended in 1920. During a performance of *L'elisir d'amore* at the Brooklyn Academy on Dec. 11, he coughed blood. The diagnosis at this time was "intercostal neuralgia" and he continued to sing. His six-hundredseventh and last appearance at the Metropolitan (and his last in opera anywhere) took place on Christmas Eve, when he sang in LA JUIVE while suffering acute pain. After an operation, it seemed certain that Caruso would recover and sing again. However, in Feb., 1921, he developed complications. After more treatment, Caruso returned to Italy for a long rest. During the summer he recovered sufficiently to work with his voice again, but a relapse proved swiftly fatal. His death was mourned throughout the world, which paid a tribute to him such as few other opera singers before or since have received.

Carvalho, Léon (born Carvaille), impresario. Born Port-Louis, France, Jan. 18, 1825; died Paris, Dec. 29, 1897. For many years he was the manager of the OPÉRA-COMIQUE. After attending the Paris Conservatory he sang at the Opéra-Comique, where he met and, in 1853, married the prima donna Marie-Caroline MIOLAN. For a period he was the director of the THÉÂTRE LYRIQUE in Paris, and after that was stage manager of the PARIS OPÉRA. In 1876 he became manager of the Opéra-Comique, holding this post for a decade. In 1887 he was found guilty of negligence in a fire that destroyed the opera house and killed over one hundred people. He was fined and spent some time in prison, being released on appeal. In 1891, restored to good graces, he resumed his management of the Opéra-Comique.

Cary, Annie Louise, contralto. Born Wayne, Me., Oct. 22, 1841; died Norwalk, Conn., Apr. 3, 1921. She was the first American woman to appear in a Wagnerian role in the United States. After preliminary training in America, she went to Europe in 1866 and studied with Giovanni Corsi in Milan. Her debut took place in Copenhagen in IL TROVATORE. During the next few years she combined opera appearances with further study with Pauline VIARDOT-GARCÍA. In 1868 she became a principal soprano of the HAMBURG OPERA and in 1870 made her bow at COVENT GARDEN. After making her American debut in concert, she joined the company at the ACADEMY OF MUSIC where, in 1877, she created for America the role of AMNERIS. Her first Wagnerian role was ORTRUD, sung in 1877. A serious throat ailment compelled her to abandon opera in 1881 at the height of her popularity.

Casanova de Seingalt, Giovanni Jacopo, adventurer celebrated for his picaresque life and amorous exploits described in his *Memoirs.* Born Venice, Apr. 2, 1725; died Dux, Bohemia, June 4, 1798. He was the subject of several operas including Volkmar Andreae's *Abenteur des*

Casanova (1924, four one-act operas), LORTZING'S *Casanova,* and Ludomir Rozycki's *Casanova* (1923). A friend of DA PONTE, he made the trip from Dux to Prague in 1787 to attend the premiere of DON GIOVANNI. Alfred Einstein informs us that apparently Casanova was not satisfied with the libretto, "for among his papers there is preserved a new version for the text of the Sextet in the second act."

Casella, Alfredo, composer. Born Turin, Italy, July 25, 1883; died Rome, Mar. 5, 1947. He attended the Paris Conservatory and first achieved success as a composer with an orchestral rhapsody, *Italia,* in 1909. Though he was in the vanguard of a movement among twentieth-century Italian composers to bring about a renascence of instrumental music, he did not neglect the theater. His first opera, LA DONNA SERPENTE, introduced in Rome in 1932, was in the style of the *commedia dell' arte.* His second was *La favola d'Orfeo* (1932). A one-act opera, *Il deserto tentato,* given at the FLORENCE MUSIC FESTIVAL in 1937, was severely criticized by the outside world for its open espousal of fascism and its glorification of the Italian conquest of Ethiopia. His autobiography, *Music in My Time,* was published in the United States in 1954.

Caspar, a huntsman (bass) in WEBER'S DER FREISCHÜTZ.

Cassel, John Walter, baritone. Born Council Bluffs, Iowa, May 15, 1910. After winning first prize in the Iowa State Music Contest, he served his apprenticeship as singer in radio, musical comedy, and operetta. He made his debut at the METROPOLITAN OPERA on Dec. 12, 1942 as De Brétigny in MANON. He appeared there for many years, starring in principal baritone roles and in such less familiar parts as the Music Master in ARIADNE AUF NAXOS, Abdul in the American premiere of THE LAST SAVAGE, and Count Tomsky in PIQUE DAME. In 1957–58 he opened the season of the NEW YORK CITY OPERA in the New York premiere of THE BALLAD OF BABY DOE in the role of Tabor, which he had created in 1956 at the CENTRAL CITY OPERA, Col.; during the same season he was also heard as Petruchio in the New York premiere of GIANNINI'S THE TAMING OF THE SHREW with the same company. He has been one of a very few singers who have appeared in leading roles in the same season at the Metropolitan Opera and the New York City Opera, besides making guest performances in other major opera houses.

Cassio, Otello's lieutenant (tenor) in VERDI'S OTELLO.

Casta diva, Norma's prayer with chorus, entreating the Moon Goddess for peace, in Act I of BELLINI'S NORMA.

Castagna, Bruna, contralto. Born Bari, Italy, Oct. 15, 1908. She had only three months of vocal instruction before she made her opera debut in Mantua, in her seventeenth year, in BORIS GODUNOV. Tullio SERAFIN thereupon engaged her for the TEATRO COLÓN in Buenos Aires. After singing three years in South America, she was engaged by Arturo TOSCANINI for LA SCALA, where for five years she was a favorite. It was to provide a proper opportunity for her voice that ROSSINI'S L'ITALIANA IN ALGERI was revived there. She first came to the United States in 1934, making her American debut in CARMEN at the Hippodrome Theater in New York. On Mar. 2, 1936, she made her debut at the METROPOLITAN OPERA as AMNERIS. For the next decade she made many successful appearances at the Metropolitan and other major opera houses in such roles as ADALGISA, Amneris, AZUCENA, DELILAH, LAURA, and SANTUZZA. After 1946 she appeared extensively in Europe and South America.

Castelnuovo-Tedesco, Mario, composer. Born Florence, Italy, Apr. 3, 1895; died Hollywood, Cal., Mar. 15, 1968. He studied music at the Cherubini Institute in Florence, then privately with PIZZETTI. His first work of major importance was *Fioretti,* a setting for voice and orchestra of three legends about St. Francis of Assisi, in 1920. This was followed by *La mandragola,* an opera that won the Italian Prize and was introduced in Venice in 1926. In 1931 another opera, *Bacco in Toscana,* was produced at LA SCALA.

AUCASSIN ET NICOLETTE, a puppet show with voices and instruments, was produced at the FLORENCE MAY MUSIC FESTIVAL in 1952. Meanwhile in 1939 he came to America and later established permanent residence in Beverly Hills as a teacher of composition and the creator and orchestrator of motion picture scores. In 1956 he completed two operas based on Shakespeare, *All's Well that Ends Well* and THE MERCHANT OF VENICE. The latter received first prize in 1958 in an international competition sponsored by La Scala. Its premiere took place at the Florence May Music Festival. In 1960 he completed a Biblical opera, *Saul,* and in 1962, *The Importance of Being Earnest,* based on Oscar Wilde's comedy.

Castil-Blaze, *see* BLAZE, FRANÇOIS-HENRI-JOSEPH.

Castor et Pollux, opera in five acts by RAMEAU. Libretto by Pierre Joseph Bernard, based on Greek and Roman mythology. Premiere: Paris Opéra, Oct. 24, 1737. American premiere: Poughkeepsie, N.Y., Mar. 6, 1937 (concert version).

The people of Sparta mourn the death of Castor (tenor), but even greater grief seizes Castor's brother, Pollux (baritone), and the woman Pollux loves, Télaire (contralto). On Télaire's poignant plea, Pollux begs the gods to restore his brother to life. The gods express their willingness to do so on the condition that Pollux replace him in Hades, something which Pollux finally consents to do, after considerable torment and doubt. Because he is willing to sacrifice himself for his brother, Pollux is rewarded with deification. The two brothers then become a constellation in heaven.

The French overture opens with the characteristic slow section followed by a fugue. Perhaps the most celebrated air in the entire opera is Télaire's deeply moving plea to Pollux, "Tristes apprêts," in the first act. Hardly less noble are the death music for Castor, Cupid's eloquent song to Venus, "Plaisirs, ramenez-vous, Venus," Pollux' expression of his inner conflict between duty and self-preservation in "Nature, Amour," the dances of the infernal spirits, and the dances (gavotte, minuet, tambourin) of the gods.

Castor et Pollux received a splendid revival at the FLORENCE MAY MUSIC FESTIVAL in 1935. Subsequently it has been produced intermittently at the PARIS OPÉRA.

castrato, an Italian term for a eunuch with a high-pitched voice. Such singers were extensively employed for opera performances in the eighteenth century. Boys with exceptional voices were castrated to prevent a change of voice at puberty. These eunuchs came to have voices delicate in texture, voluptuous in tone, and flexible in range. Opera composers of the eighteenth century wrote their most florid arias for the castrati, who customarily contributed additional embellishments of their own. MOZART, for example, wrote the part of Idamante in IDOMENEO for the castrato Del Parto; for Welutti, ROSSINI and MEYERBEER created the leading roles in *Aureliano in Palmira* and IL CROCIATO IN EGITTO, respectively. Among the most celebrated castrati were CAFFARELLI, Marchesi, CRESCENTINI, Tenducci, FARINELLI, GUADAGNI, and SENESINO. They were all highly paid and adulated. A journalist reported in 1720 that "women from every grade of society —peeresses incognito, melancholy wives of city merchants, wretched little streetwalkers—all jostled each other . . . hungry for a look or a word" from one of these singers. One woman is reported to have said: "There is only one God and one Farinelli."

Catalani, Alfredo, composer. Born Lucca, Italy, June 19, 1854; died Milan, Aug. 7, 1893. His studies took place with his father, with Fortunato Magi, and at the conservatories of Paris and Milan. A one-act opera, *La falce,* was performed in Milan in 1876. Four years later he wrote his first full-length opera, *L'Elda,* presented in Turin in 1880. His first major success was a revision of *L'Elda,* renamed LORELEY, performed in Turin in 1890. His most popular opera, LA WALLY, was given at LA SCALA in 1892. His other

operas were *Dejanire* (1883) and *Edmea* (1886). In 1886 Catalani succeeded PONCHIELLI as professor of composition at the Milan Conservatory.

Catalani, Angelica, soprano. Born Sinigaglia, Italy, May 10, 1780; died Paris, June 12, 1849. After receiving her education at the Convent Santa Lucia di Gubbio in Rome she made her opera debut at the TEATRO LA FENICE in 1797. Other appearances in Italy, climaxed by performances at LA SCALA in 1801, brought her immense success. In 1804 she became a member of the Italian Opera in Lisbon. Her debut in London in 1806 was brilliant; so great was her drawing power in England that she earned unprecedented sums. She remained in that country seven years (appearing in the first performance in England of THE MARRIAGE OF FIGARO in 1812), then stayed in Paris three years, where she managed, without success, the Théâtre des Italians. Having sung in Russia, Poland, and Germany, and again in England, she retired (after 1828) and directed a singing school in Florence.

Catalogue Song, *see* MADAMINA! IL CATALOGO È QUESTO.

Catherine, (1) a laundress known as Madame Sans-Gêne (soprano) in GIORDANO'S MADAME SANS-GÊNE.

(2) Petruchio's terrible-tempered wife (soprano) in GOETZ'S THE TAMING OF THE SHREW.

Catulli Carmina (Songs of Catullus), "scenic cantata" in three sections by ORFF. Libretto by the composer, based on poems of Catullus. Premiere: Leipzig, Ger., Nov. 6, 1943. American premiere: Los Angeles, Cal., June, 1955 (concert version); Katonah, N.Y., June 26, 1964 (staged).

This is the second of a trilogy entitled *Trionfi,* of which the first is CARMINA BURANA and the last TRIONFO D'AFRODITE. Though heard most often on the concert stage, *Catulli Carmina* is sometimes staged as a dramatic ballet. The three sections are designated as Actus I, II, and III. The libretto begins with a love episode for girls and boys, while they are being reminded by their elders that

Catullus died from love. In the next three scenes the tragic story of Catullus is described. As the chorus sing some of Catullus' verses, a dancer, appearing as Lesbia, leaves Catullus to go to the arms of Caelus. When she repents and tries to return to Catullus, she is rejected.

Except for an instrumental prelude and postlude (performed by four pianos and percussion) the entire score is made up of a cappella choruses.

Cavalieri, Emilio de', composer. Born Rome, c. 1550; died there, Mar. 11, 1602. He was a member of the CAMERATA and wrote several operas, all of them with texts by Laura Guidiccioni. He was one of the first composers to employ the technique of *basso continuo*—a bass part provided with figures and signs indicating the harmonies to be employed in the instrumental accompaniment by the organ, harpsichord, or lute. His most celebrated work was a sacred opera, LA RAPPRESENTAZIONE DI ANIMA E DI CORPO, performed and published in 1600. His other musical works for the stage: *Il satiro* (1590) ; *La disperazione di Fileno* (1590) ; *Il giuoco della cieca* (1595).

Cavalieri, Lina, soprano. Born Viterbo, Italy, Dec. 25, 1874; died Florence, Feb. 8, 1944. She was trained in Paris by Madame Mariani-Masi. In 1901 she made her debut in Lisbon in PAGLIACCI. This was followed by appearances in opera houses in Italy, Poland, Russia, France, and England. On Dec. 5, 1906, she made her American debut at the METROPOLITAN OPERA in the title role of FEDORA. She stayed with the Metropolitan until 1908, after which she joined the MANHATTAN OPERA COMPANY. In 1915–16 she sang with the CHICAGO OPERA. She scored her greatest successes in French opera, particularly in such roles as HÉRODIADE, MANON, and THAÏS. She retired soon after World War I, living first in Paris, then in Florence. She married the celebrated tenor, Lucien MURATORE. She was killed during an air raid in World War II.

Cavalleria rusticana (Rustic Chivalry), one-act opera by MASCAGNI. Libretto by Giovanni Targioni-Tozzetti and Guido Menasci, based on a short story of the same name by Giovanni Verga. Premiere: Teatro Costanzi, Rome, May 17, 1890. American premiere: Grand Opera House, Philadelphia, Sept. 9, 1891.

Characters: Santuzza, a village girl (soprano) ; Turiddu, a soldier (tenor) ; Mamma Lucia, his mother (contralto) ; Alfio, a teamster (baritone) ; Lola, his wife (mezzo-soprano) ; peasants; villagers. The setting is a Sicilian village square; the time, the latter part of the nineteenth century.

The stately overture is descriptive of Easter Sunday. Before the prelude ends, the voice of Turiddu is heard off-stage praising his one-time sweetheart, Lola, who is now Alfio's wife (SICILIANA: "O Lola"). It is Easter morning. Villagers are entering the church. Santuzza meets Mamma Lucia and pleads with her to reveal where the old woman's son, Turiddu, is. Lucia inquires why she is so inquisitive. Santuzza is about to confess that she loves him when Alfio appears, a lusty tune on his lips about his profession as teamster ("Il cavallo scalpita"). When from inside the church the music of the "Regina Coeli" is heard, the villagers assume reverent attitudes and join in the singing. All of them then enter the church, leaving behind only Santuzza and Lucia. It is now that Santuzza can tell Lucia of her love affair with Turiddu ("Voi lo sapete"). Shocked, Lucia rushes into the church to pray for Santuzza. Turiddu now appears, and Santuzza confronts him with his infidelity. They become involved in a bitter quarrel as Turiddu accuses Santuzza of unwarranted jealousy. Their bitter tirades are interrupted by the arrival of Lola. She sings a gay song ("Fior di giaggiolo"), after which the two women exchange harsh words. Lola lightly shrugs off Santuzza's veiled accusations and enters the church. Enraged by this scene, Turiddu curses Santuzza, throws her angrily to the ground, and enters the church. At this critical moment Alfio reappears and Santuzza reveals to him that his wife has been unfaithful. Alfio swears to seek revenge.

The Easter services come to an end. The strains of the "Intermezzo" are heard, contrasting the peace of the holiday with the stormy emotions of the principal characters. The villagers file out of the church. Some of the men fill wine glasses as Turiddu sings a rousing drinking song (BRINDISI: "Viva il vino spumeggiante"). When Turiddu offers a glass of wine to Alfio, the latter turns it down. Insulted, Turiddu challenges Alfio and is accepted. Sensing the approach of doom, Turiddu bids his mother farewell ("Addio alla madre"). His mother tries to follow as he leaves to meet Alfio. Santuzza stops her. Suddenly villagers rush into the square with the dreadful news that Turiddu has been killed.

When *Cavalleria rusticana* won first prize in a contest for one-act operas sponsored by the publishing house of Edoardo Sonzogno, it started a trend in Italian opera known as VERISMO (naturalism). Later examples of *verismo* operas are PAGLIACCI and LA BOHÈME. The premiere of *Cavalleria rusticana* created a sensation equaled by few other operas. An obscure, impoverished composer, Mascagni suddenly became famous. He took forty curtain calls; outside the theater thousands waited to acclaim him. Before many months passed, parades were held in his honor and medals were sold with his picture. By 1892 *Cavalleria* had been seen throughout Europe and in North and South America. This single opera made Mascagni famous and rich. Unfortunately he was never able to duplicate his first success, though he wrote some creditable operas. His own comment was: "It is a pity I wrote *Cavalleria* first. I was crowned before I became king."

Cavalli, Francesco (born Caletti-Bruni), composer. Born Crema, Italy, Feb. 14, 1602; died Venice, Jan. 14, 1676. He was the immediate successor of MONTEVERDI, and a leader in the Venetian school of opera. He assumed the name of his patron, Federico Cavalli, the Podesta of Crema, who was attracted to the boy and took him to Venice in 1616 where he became a singer in the choir of St. Marks

and a pupil of Monteverdi. In 1640 Cavalli was appointed organist at St. Marks, and in 1668, MAESTRO DI CAPPELLA. Meanwhile, in 1639, he wrote his first opera, LE NOZZE DI TETI E DI PELEO, a work of historical importance since it was the first to be designated by its composer an opera (specifically, *opera scenica*) instead of a DRAMMA PER MUSICA. Cavalli wrote over forty operas, the most famous being L'ORMINDO (1644), *Giasone* (1649), *La Calisto* (1651), and *Serse* (1654). (Two of these operas have been revived in the twentieth century: *L'Ormindo* at the EDINBURGH FESTIVAL during the summer of 1966 and at the Juilliard School of Music in New York City in 1968 and *La Calisto* at the GLYNDEBOURNE FESTIVAL in 1970.) In 1660 he was invited to Paris to help produce *Serse* in conjunction with the marriage ceremonies of Louis XIV. He returned to Paris two years later to present another of his operas, *Ercole amante*. Cavalli's significance rests in the tunefulness of his arias and his use of the *recitativo secco* (*see* RECITATIVE).

Cavaradossi, Mario, artist (tenor) in PUCCINI'S TOSCA.

cavatina, Italian term (French: *cavatine*) for a melody simpler in style and more songlike than an aria. MOZART designated both "Se vuol ballare" and "Porgi amor" in THE MARRIAGE OF FIGARO as cavatinas.

Cavatine du page, *see* NOBLES SEIGNEURS, SALUT.

Cebotari, Maria, soprano. Born Kishinev, Bessarabia, Feb. 10, 1910; died Vienna, June 9, 1949. As a child she sang in school and church choirs and at fourteen appeared as a singer and dancer with a traveling company. After a period of study with Oskar Daniel in Berlin she joined the DRESDEN OPERA, where she made her debut as MIMI in 1931, remaining with that company until 1936. In 1932 she scored a major success at the SALZBURG FESTIVAL. After that she appeared with the BERLIN STATE OPERA (1936–1944) and VIENNA STATE OPERA (1946–1949), and made guest appearances at COVENT GARDEN, excelling in such soprano parts as VIOLETTA, Mimi, MADAMA BUTTERFLY, and in several MOZART operas. She also excelled in modern operas, creating the role of Aminta in DIE SCHWEIGSAME FRAU in 1935, Julia in SUTERMEISTER's *Romeo und Julia* in 1942, Lucille in DANTONS TOD in 1947, and Iseut in LE VIN HERBÉ in 1948. She died at the peak of her career of cancer. She made numerous appearances in foreign motion pictures.

Ce bruit de l'or rire, Manon's hymn to gold in Act IV of MASSENET's MA-NON.

Cecchina, La, o La buona figliuola (Cecchina, or The Good Girl), OPERA BUFFA in three acts by PICCINNI. Libretto by Carlo GOLDONI, based on Samuel Richardson's novel *Pamela, or Virtue Rewarded*. Premiere: Teatro delle Dame, Rome, Feb. 6, 1760. American premiere: Madison, Wis., Jan. 6, 1967.

This *opera buffa* was so celebrated in its time that fashions, inns, villas, shops, wines, and so forth were called *alla cecchina*. Soon after its premiere, it was played in all the principal theaters in Rome as well as throughout Italy. The text is typical. Mengotto is in love with Cecchina, a servant girl. Since her master, Tagliaferro, has designs on her, Mengotto realizes that she is out of his own reach. He pursues another servant girl, while Cecchina goes on to marry her master. The best remembered aria is Cecchina's "Una povera ragazza." "Star trompetti" is a popular *buffo* aria, sung by Tagliaferro. Of particular historical importance is the use of extended finales for each act, initiating a tradition that continued in *opera buffa* for many years and was used with the greatest brilliance by MOZART in his comic operas.

Celeste Aida, Radames's rapturous aria about heavenly Aida, with whom he is in love, in Act I, Scene 1, of VERDI's AIDA.

Cellini, Benvenuto, Florentine sculptor, goldsmith, author. Born Florence, Nov. 1, 1500; died there, Feb. 14, 1571. He is the central figure in several operas, the most notable being BERLIOZ' BENVENUTO CELLINI. Others include: *Ascanio* by

SAINT-SAËNS; *Benvenuto* by Eugene Diaz; *Benvenuto Cellini* (1849) by Franz Lachner; *Benvenuto Cellini a Parigi* (1845) by Lauro Rossi.

cena delle beffe, La (The Feast of the Jest), opera in four acts by GIORDANO. Libretto is the play of the same name by Sem BENELLI. Premiere: La Scala, Dec. 20, 1924. American premiere: Metropolitan Opera, Jan. 2, 1926. In fifteenth-century Florence, Gianetto (tenor) —a physically weak poet and painter—is the victim of cruel jests at the hands of Neri (baritone), a captain of mercenaries. When Neri prevents Gianetto's marriage to Ginevra (soprano), Gianetto succeeds in triumphing over Neri by means of trickery until the latter goes mad. Lisabetta's (mezzo-soprano) plea, "Mi chiama Lisabetta," in Act III and Gianetto's first-act aria, "Ah, chi tormento," are popular.

Cendrillon (Cinderella), opera in four acts by MASSENET. Libretto by Henri Cain, based on the fairy tale by Charles PERRAULT. Premiere: Opéra-Comique, May 24, 1899. American premiere: New Orleans, Dec. 23, 1902. *See also* CEN-ERENTOLA, LA; CINDERELLA.

Cenerentola, La (Cinderella), (1) opera in two acts by ROSSINI. Libretto by Jacopo Ferretti, based on the fairy tale by Charles PERRAULT. Premiere: Teatro Valle, Rome, Jan. 25, 1817. American premiere: Park Theater, New York, June 27, 1826. The magical elements of the famous Cinderella story have been omitted in this version. The fairy godmother becomes Alidoro (bass), a practical philosopher employed by the Prince (tenor), who, disguised as a beggar, receives help from Cinderella (contralto) after having been rudely turned down by her stepsisters, Clorinda (soprano) and Tisbe (mezzo-soprano). Though the father of these two girls plans to have one of them marry the Prince, Alidoro contrives to have Cinderella become the fortunate bride.

The opera opens with a beautiful air for Cinderella, "Una volta c'era un re." Two other arias for Cinderella have special appeal: the coloratura air, "Non più mesta accato al fuoco," and her closing song, "Ah prence, io cado ai vostre piè." The opera also boasts an appealing *buffo* aria for Don Magnifico, "Miei rampolli," in the first act.

This same libretto had been previously set to music by Niccolo Isouard and introduced at the OPÉRA-COMIQUE on Feb. 22, 1810.

(2) Opera in three acts by WOLF-FERRARI. Libretto by Pezze-Pescolato, based on the fairy tale by Charles PER-RAULT. Premiere: Teatro la Fenice, Feb. 22, 1900. This was Wolf-Ferrari's first opera.

C'en est donc fait et mon coeur va changer (Me sedur han creduto), Marie's lament that she is being compelled to marry a man she does not love, in Act II of DONIZETTI'S THE DAUGHTER OF THE REGIMENT.

Central City Opera Festival, an annual summer festival (that includes drama and operettas as well as operas) in Central City, Col. The festival was inaugurated in 1932 and has since then given its productions in an opera house built in 1878. The first performance, given under the auspices of the Central City Opera House Association, Inc., was the drama *Camille,* in 1932. For a number of years, drama and operettas were given, until 1940 when THE BARTERED BRIDE brought opera to the festival. One year later THE BARBER OF SEVILLE and ORFEO ED EURIDICE were given. Operations were suspended during World War II and were resumed during the summer of 1946 with LA TRAVIATA and THE ABDUCTION FROM THE SERAGLIO. Since 1946 among the operas given at this festival (besides the more familiar works in the French, Italian, and Mozartean repertory) were AMELIA GOES TO THE BALL, ARIADNE AUF NAXOS, THE BALLAD OF BABY DOE (a world premiere), FIDELIO, THE GIRL FROM THE GOLDEN WEST, L'ITALIANA IN ALGERI, THE LADY FROM COLORADO, MARTHA, and LA PÉRICHOLE. In 1970 Thomas Martin (collaborator with his wife on translations of numerous foreign operas into English) became director of the festival.

Ceprano, a nobleman (bass) in VERDI'S RIGOLETTO.

Cervantes, Miguel de, novelist, dramatist, poet. Born Alcalá de Henares, Spain, 1547; died Madrid, Apr. 23, 1616. He was the author of *Don Quixote.* For operas based on this story, *see* DON QUIXOTE. His story *La Gitanella* was the source of Pius Alexander Wolff's *Preciosa,* for which WEBER wrote an overture, choruses, melodramas, dances, and a song. ORFF'S *Astutuli* and HENZE'S *Das Wundertheater* were derived from Cervantes' *El teatro magico.* Other operas drawn from various works of this author include Henri Barraud's *Numance* (1950), Petrassi's *Il Cordovano* (1949), and GRÉTRY'S *Le Trompeur.*

C'est ici le séjour (Questo sol è il soggiorno), concluding chorus in MEYERBEER'S L'AFRICAINE.

Cesti, Marc' Antonio, composer. Born Arezzo, Italy, Aug. 5, 1623; died Florence, Oct. 14, 1669. A major figure in the Venetian school of opera, he studied with CARISSIMI in Florence and in 1646 became MAESTRO DI CAPPELLA to Ferdinand II de' Medici. Fourteen years later he was appointed tenor to the chapel choir. During the last three years of his life he was assistant KAPELLMEISTER to Emperor Leopold I of Vienna. Cesti returned to Venice just before his death. He wrote eight operas, the first, *L'Orontea* (1649), being so successful that it was performed in several Italian cities besides Venice. Later works were: *Cesare amante* (1651), *La Dori* (1663), and *Semiramide* (1667). Cesti placed great emphasis on lyricism, filling his operas with gracious, flowing melodies charged with feeling.

C'est le dieu de la jeunesse, Gérald's ecstatic reaction to Lakmé when he first sees her, in Act I of DELIBES'S LAKMÉ.

C'est l'histoire amoureuse, an aria known as the Laughing Song, found in AUBER'S MANON LESCAUT. It is sometimes interpolated in the Lesson Scene of ROSSINI'S THE BARBER OF SEVILLE.

Cette nuit, j'ai revue le palais de mon père, Iphigenia's description of her dream in which she learns of her tragic future, in Act I of GLUCK's IPHIGÉNIE EN TAURIDE.

Chabrier, Emmanuel, composer. Born Ambert, France, Jan. 18, 1841; died Paris, Sept. 13, 1894. He received good but erratic training in both music and law, and for eighteen years he served in the Ministry of the Interior, a post he found irksome, for his talents and interests lay entirely in music. Influenced by the vogue for OFFENBACH, he wrote his first stage work, a comic opera, L'Étoile, successfully performed at the Bouffes Parisiens in 1877 (it was revived in New York in 1968). This was followed by Une Education manqué, introduced at the Cercle de la Presse in Paris on May 1, 1879, a one-act opera that was revived at Aspen, Col., in 1959. In March, 1880, he took a three-day leave of absence from his government post to attend a performance of TRISTAN UND ISOLDE in Munich. Then and there Chabrier decided to dedicate himself completely to music. A confirmed Wagnerian, he completed an opera, GWENDOLINE, in the Wagnerian style; it was introduced in Brussels in 1886. LE ROI MALGRÉ LUI, comic opera, was introduced by the OPÉRA-COMIQUE in 1887. His last opera, Briséis, was left unfinished.

chaconne, an old dance in moderately slow ¾ time, presumably of Spanish origin and so similar to another old dance, the passacaglia, that the terms were often used interchangeably. Chaconnes appear frequently in seventeenth- and eighteenth-century operas. There is a chaconne in MONTEVERDI's L'ORFEO; LULLY, RAMEAU, and GLUCK frequently ended their operas with one. The chaconne in Gluck's PARIDE ED ELENA reappears as a passacaglia in IPHIGÉNIE EN AULIDE. One of the most affecting chaconnes in opera is Dido's song "When I am laid in earth," in PURCELL's DIDO AND AENEAS. Other examples of operatic chaconnes are those in HANDEL's Rodrigo, Lully's Cadmus et Hermione, and MOZART's IDOMENEO.

Chaliapin, Feodor (sometimes Shaliapin), bass. Born Kazan, Russia, Feb. 13, 1873; died Paris, Apr. 12, 1938. One of the most celebrated Russian basses and singing actors. The son of a peasant, he was given few opportunities to acquire an education. Without benefit of formal musical training he joined a provincial opera company in 1890. Two years later he studied with Usatov in Tiflis. An engagement followed with the St. Petersburg Opera. In 1896 he joined the company of S. I. Mamontov in Moscow, where he was assigned leading bass roles. He made powerful impressions as BORIS GODUNOV, as IVAN THE TERRIBLE in RIMSKY-KORSAKOV's opera, and as the miller in DARGOMIZHSKY's RUSSALKA. His first appearance outside Russia took place in 1901 at LA SCALA in MEFISTOFELE. He made his American debut in the same opera at the METROPOLITAN OPERA on Nov. 20, 1907. While certain facets of his art were appreciated, he was not acclaimed at this time. Indeed, Henry E. Krehbiel found elements of "vulgarity" in his performance. After further successes in Russia and London, Chaliapin returned to the Metropolitan Opera in Boris Godunov on Dec. 9, 1921. This time his success was unqualified; Krehbiel could now say that only the actor Salvini was Chaliapin's equal. Chaliapin remained at the Metropolitan Opera eight seasons. Roles for which he was famous included Boris, DON BASILIO, Don Quixote (in MASSENET's DON QUICHOTTE), Leporello, and Mephistopheles (in BOITO's Mefistofele). Toward the end of his life he appeared as Don Quixote in a motion picture. He wrote two books of memoirs: Pages from My Life (1926) and Man and Mask (1932).

chamber opera, an opera of modest proportions and intimate character, calling for limited forces and stage paraphernalia. Examples from different periods include ARIADNE AUF NAXOS, BASTIEN UND BASTIENNE, LA FINTA GIARDINIERA, LA FINTA SEMPLICE, DIE FLUT, LE PAUVRE MATELOT, DER SCHAUSPIELDIREKTOR, LA SERVA PADRONA. The ENGLISH OPERA GROUP in England was formed to present chamber operas. For this organization BRITTEN wrote ALBERT HERRING, THE RAPE OF LUCRETIA, and THE TURN OF THE SCREW; BERKELEY, *A Dinner Engagement* and *Ruth*.

Champagne Aria, *see* FINCH'HAN DAL VINO.

Champs paternels, Joseph's aria in Act I of MÉHUL'S JOSEPH.

Chanson bachique, *see* O VIN, DISSIPE LA TRISTESSE.

Chanson bohème, the song and dance of the gypsies in the opening of Act II of BIZET'S CARMEN.

Chanson de la puce (Song of the Flea), *see* PUCE GENTILLE, UNE.

Chanson Hindoue, *see* SONG OF INDIA.

Chanson Huguenote, *see* POUR LES COUVENTS C'EST FINI.

Chantez, joyeux ménestral, the Earl of Avenell's third-act revery with chorus, in BOIELDIEU'S LA DAME BLANCHE.

Chantons, celebrons, notre reine, a chorus in which the people celebrate the marriage of Iphigenia and Achilles in Act II of GLUCK'S IPHIGÉNIE EN AULIDE.

Chappelou, a postillion (tenor) in ADAM'S LE POSTILLON DE LONGJUMEAU.

Charfreitagszauber, *see* GOOD FRIDAY SPELL.

Charles Gérard, *see* GÉRARD, CHARLES.

Charlotte, young woman (soprano) in love with Werther, in MASSENET'S WERTHER.

Charlottenburg Opera, *see* BERLIN DEUTSCHE STAATSOPER.

Charpentier, Gustave, composer. Born Dieuze, France, June 25, 1860; died Paris, Feb. 18, 1956. The librettist and composer of LOUISE, an opera which provoked controversy and won popularity partly by reason of its novel working-class atmosphere. Charpentier attended the Lille Conservatory, where he won several prizes. Entering the Paris Conservatory in 1881, he won the PRIX DE ROME in 1887. During his stay in Rome, he wrote his first successful work for orchestra, *Impressions of Italy*. After his return to Paris he became interested in socialism and wrote songs with a political viewpoint. The writing of *Louise* took him ten years. It was introduced at the OPÉRA-COMIQUE on Feb. 2, 1900. It is still performed there frequently. Charpentier's only subsequent major work was a sequel to *Louise* entitled JULIEN. Produced at the Opéra-Comique on June 3, 1913, it proved a failure.

Charpentier, Marc-Antoine, composer. Born Paris, 1634; died there Feb. 24, 1704. As a young man he studied with CARISSIMI in Italy for several years. Back in Paris he succeeded LULLY as composer of incidental music for MOLIÈRE'S plays, writing numbers for *Le Mariage forcé* in 1672 and *Le Malade imaginaire* in 1673. He held various posts in Paris as *maître de musique* while writing seventeen operas, the most significant of which are *Circe* (1675) and MÉDÉE, the latter, text by Thomas Corneille, produced in Paris on Dec. 4, 1693.

Charton-Demeur, Anne, *see* DEMEUR, ANNE ARSENE.

Chartreuse de Parme, La (The Carthusian Monastery of Parma), opera in four acts by SAUGUET. Libretto by Armand Lunel, based on the novel of the same name by STENDHAL. Premiere: Paris Opéra, Mar. 16, 1939. The opera traces the career of Fabrice del Dongo through wars, political intrigues, and imprisonment until he becomes a priest and enters a monastery. MILHAUD has said that this opera rises "in the last act to genuine heights of emotion."

Chaste fille de Latone, Iphigenia's Hymn to Diane, in Act IV of GLUCK'S IPHIGÉNIE EN TAURIDE.

Chaucer, Geoffrey, (1) poet. Born England about 1340; died there, 1400. Material from his narrative, the *Canterbury Tales,* was used in two operas named THE CANTERBURY PILGRIMS, one by Reginald DE KOVEN, the other by Charles Villiers STANFORD. His poem, *Troilus and Cressida,* was the source of an opera of the same name by William WALTON. Voltaire's *La Fée Urgèle*—made into operas of the same name by Egidio Duni and Ignaz Pleyel—was derived from Chaucer.

(2) The poet (baritone), principal character in Reginald DE KOVEN'S THE CANTERBURY PILGRIMS.

Chautauqua Opera Association, an opera company affiliated with the annual summer music festival at Chautauqua, N.Y. The first opera production, MARTHA, took place on July 19, 1929, conducted by Albert Stoessel, performed in the Norton Memorial Hall, whose construction had been completed one year earlier. In presenting this auditorium to the Chautauqua institution, the Norton family specified all operas were to be given in English; that promising young American singers be given an opportunity to perform; and that acting and staging be given as much importance as singing. Albert Stoessel remained principal conductor between 1929 and 1931, followed by several other conductors, including Julius RUDEL (1958–59) and, since 1966, Evan Whallon. The first artistic director was Alfredo Valenti, who served between 1930 and 1959. Thomas P. Struthers took over this office in 1967.

Among the novelties and highlights since 1929 have been the following: AMAHL AND THE NIGHT VISITORS; LO SPEZIALE; ALBERT HERRING; THE BALLAD OF BABY DOE; LA CENERENTOLA; THE CRUCIBLE; LE DONNE CURIOSE; THE DEVIL AND DANIEL WEBSTER; *Garrick* (1936, Stoessel) ; *In the Name of Culture* (Alberto Bimboni) ; *Jack and the Beanstalk* (GRUENBERG) ; THE JUMPING FROG OF CALAVERAS COUNTY; L'HEURE ESPAGNOL; *Maria Malibran* (Robert Russell BENNETT) ; THE OLD MAID AND THE THIEF; IL MATRIMONIO SEGRETO; LA SERVA PADRONA; SUSANNAH ; and WUTHERING HEIGHTS.

Between 1963 and 1967 a new opera group, The Festival Opera, directed by George Schick, gave annual guest presentations. In 1964 the Ford Foundation endowed the Chautauqua Opera Association with a grant of one hundred thousand dollars for each of five years. In 1968 a special grant from a national foundation provided for an extension of an apprentice program, with special matinee performances offering training for talented students and professionals interested in opera as a career.

Che farò senza Euridice, Orfeo's lament over the loss of his wife, Euridice, in Act III (Act IV in some versions) of GLUCK'S ORFEO ED EURIDICE.

Che gelida manina, Rodolfo's famous "narrative" in Act I of PUCCINI'S LA BOHÈME, where, after touching Mimi's cold hand, he tells her about himself and his profession as poet.

Che il bel sogno di Doretto, Magda's first-act aria in which she embellishes upon a song just completed by the poet, Prunier, in Act I of PUCCINI'S LA RONDINE.

Chekov, Anton, story writer and dramatist. Born Taganrog, Russia, Jan. 17, 1860; died Badenweiler, Ger., July 2, 1904. One of the most distinguished authors of his time, Chekov is represented in the world of opera by the following works drawn from his writings: Valentino Bucchi's *Il contrabasso* (1954); Pierre-Octave Ferroud's *Le Chirugie* (1929) ; Constantine Notara's *Over the Highway;* SAUGUET'S *La Contrebasse;* and WALTON'S THE BEAR.

Ch'ella mi creda libero, Dick Johnson's aria in Act III of PUCCINI'S THE GIRL OF THE GOLDEN WEST, pleading that Minnie not be told he is about to be lynched. This, one of the most famous arias in the opera, was used by the Italian soldiers during World War I as marching music.

Chénier, *see* ANDREA CHÉNIER.

Che puro ciel!, Orfeo's description of the serenity and beauties of Elysium in Act III of GLUCK'S ORFEO ED EURIDICE.

Cherubini, Maria Luigi, composer. Born Florence, Sept. 14, 1760; died Paris, Mar. 15, 1842. Though trained in the Italian school, he was a dominant figure in the development of French opera. He began studying music with his father and between 1773 and 1777 wrote several masses and other church music. The Duke of Tuscany became interested in him and supported his study with Giuseppe Sarti. Cherubini wrote his first opera, *Il quinto Fabio,* in 1780, performed three years later. His first success came with *Armida,* in 1782. After writing five more operas, all in the strict Italian pattern of the time, Cherubini went to London, where he remained two years, producing two more operas without success and serving as composer to the king. In 1780 he settled permanently in Paris. Becoming dissatisfied with the Italian traditions, he aspired to write operas in GLUCK's style, in which drama and musical resources were emphasized. His first work in this new vein, *Démophon,* was a failure in 1788. But in LODOÏSKA, performed in Paris in 1791, his new style became effective. Between 1794 and 1801 he wrote half a dozen operas, including the work generally deemed his finest: LES DEUX JOURNÉES (known in German as *Der Wasserträger,* in English as *The Water Carrier*), first heard in Paris in 1800. Cherubini suffered severe mental depressions after the French Revolution, due primarily to his unhappy marriage and the failures of some of his operas. In 1805 he was invited to Vienna in conjunction with the Viennese premiere of *Les Deux Journées.* For production here, Cherubini wrote a new opera, *Faniska,* an outstanding success. Back in Paris and out of favor with Napoleon, Cherubini devoted himself more to church music than to opera and concentrated on his teaching duties at the Conservatory. From 1822 until just before his death he was one of the Conservatory's directors.

Cherubini's most famous operas: *Armida* (1782); *Adriano in Siria* (1782); *Alessandro nell' Indie* (1784); *Ifigenia in Aulide* (1787); *Lodoïska* (1791); *Elisa* (1794); MÉDÉE (1797); *La Punition* (1799); *La Prisonnière* (1799); *Les Deux Journées* (1800); ANACRÉON (1803); *Faniska* (1806); LES ABENCÉRAGES (1813); *Bayard à Mézières* (1814) —a collaboration with François BOIELDIEU, Charles Catel, and Nicolo Isouard.

Cherubino, Count Almaviva's page (soprano) in MOZART's THE MARRIAGE OF FIGARO.

Che soave zeffiretto, the Letter Duet of Susanna and Countess Almaviva, in which the Countess arranges a rendezvous between her husband and Susanna, in Act III of MOZART's THE MARRIAGE OF FIGARO.

Che vita maladetta, Despina's recitative lamenting the sad lot of a lady's maid, in Act I, Scene 3, of MOZART's COSÌ FAN TUTTE.

Chevreuse, a duke (baritone), secret husband of Maria di Rohan, in DONIZETTI's ope•a MARIA DI ROHAN.

Chiamo il mio ben così, Orfeo's lament at the grave of his wife, Euridice, in the opening scene of GLUCK's ORFEO ED EURIDICE.

Chicago Lyric Opera Company, the leading opera company in Chicago, Ill., and one of the most significant in the United States. Initially called The Lyric Theatre, it was founded in 1954, with Carol Fox as president and general manager. The opening performance was DON GIOVANNI, in Feb., 1954, beginning a three-week season. On Nov. 1, 1954, Maria CALLAS made her American debut there as NORMA, and the first full-scale production of GIANNINI's THE TAMING OF THE SHREW took place the same season. In 1956 following internal dissension, a reorganization took place. It was on this occasion that the company changed its name to Chicago Lyric Opera Company. Thomas Underwood succeeded Carol Fox as president, while the latter retained her post as general manager. In 1958 the Italian government, in an unprecedented move, contributed a subsidy of sixteen thousand dollars to the company. This was the season in which Kiril Kondrashin made his American debut by conducting MADAMA BUTTERFLY, and the company made its first radio broadcast (FALSTAFF, over WBBM-CBS). George PRÊTRE made his American conducting debut one season later in THAÏS, but the highlight of the season was the first revival in America of JENUFA since its American premiere in 1924. In 1960 the company supplemented its own activities with guest performances by the visiting NEW YORK CITY OPERA in presentations of three American works: THE BALLAD OF BABY DOE, SUSANNAH, and WEILL's *Street Scene.* Teresa BERGANZA made her American debut here in 1962 and Nicolai GHIAUROV in 1963. There was a one-year hiatus in its activities in 1967 due to a failure to arrive at a contract satisfactory to the Musicians Union. But in 1968 the company undertook an eleven-week season that opened with SALOME.

The Chicago Lyric Opera Company launched its fifteenth anniversary on Sept. 26, 1969, with a new production of KHOVANTCHINA. It has presented over four hundred opera performances and through the distinction of its repertory and performances is, in the words of *Newsweek,* "among the half dozen best opera companies in the world." Productions of unusual interest (besides those already mentioned above) include: ADRIANA LECOUVREUR, ARIADNE AUF NAXOS, CARMINA BURANA, LA CENERENTOLA, THE FLAMING ANGEL, L'HEURE ESPAGNOL, L'INCORONAZIONE DI POPPEA, MEFISTOFELE, LES PÊCHEURS DE PERLES, PRINCE IGOR, I PURITANI, LE ROSSIGNOL, IL TABARRO, and WOZZECK.

Chicago Opera Company, The, a company organized in Chicago, Ill., in 1910 with members of the then recently disbanded Oscar Hammerstein Opera Company of New York. Under the artistic direction of Andreas DIPPEL and with Cleofonte CAMPANINI as principal conductor, the company opened on Nov. 3, 1910, with AIDA. The following evening Mary GARDEN appeared in PELLÉAS ET MÉLISANDE, and within a few weeks as LOUISE and SALOME. For the next twenty years the personality of Mary Garden dominated the company. With funds provided by social leaders of Chicago, it was able to maintain a standard of artistic excellence found otherwise only at the METROPOLITAN OPERA. The repertory included revivals and premieres. When THE JEWELS OF THE MADONNA received its first American performance in 1912, its composer, Ermanno WOLF-FERRARI, was invited to supervise the production. In 1922, Serge PROKOFIEV led the world premiere of his THE LOVE FOR THREE ORANGES. Several American operas received their first performances, including HADLEY's *Azora* in 1917 (the composer conducting) and CADMAN's *A Witch of Salem* in 1926. GOLDMARK's THE CRICKET ON THE HEARTH and CATALANI's LORELEY

were other operas given American premieres, in 1912 and 1918, respectively. When Campanini died in 1919, the musical direction passed to Gino MARINUZZI. In Jan., 1921, Mary Garden was appointed artistic director (the first time a woman was made head of a major opera house). She spent money with a lavish hand and under her regime the company suffered a deficit of over a million dollars. Two of the most important sponsors, Mr. and Mrs. Harold McCormick, withdrew their support. In the reorganization that followed, the name of the organization was changed to the Chicago Civic Opera Company. The Chicago industrialist, Samuel Insull, became head of a group of businessmen guaranteeing an annual fund of five hundred thousand dollars. Mary Garden returned to her original status as prima donna and the direction of the company passed to Giorgio POLACCO. Under Polacco's regime, the company maintained a high position. Singers bound to it by exclusive contract now included Mary Garden, Lotte LEHMANN, Frida LEIDER, Claudia MUZIO, Rosa RAISA, Alexander KIPNIS, and Tito SCHIPA. In 1929 a new house was built, the magnificent thirty-million-dollar Chicago Opera House on Wacker Drive. The company failed in 1932 because of diminished financial support. Thereafter, other companies tried to fill the gap. The most significant is the CHICAGO LYRIC OPERA.

Chi del gitano i giorni abbella?, the second part of the Anvil Chorus, in Act II, Scene 1, of VERDI's IL TROVATORE.

children's operas. A number of operas have been written for audiences of children, many of them intended for performance by children, some of interest to both adults and children: Wheeler Beckett's *The Magic Mirror* (based on *Snow White*) ; Nicolai Berezowsky's *Babar;* BRITTEN's LET'S MAKE AN OPERA and NOYE'S FLUDDE; COPLAND's THE SECOND HURRICANE; FOSS's GRIFFELKIN; Arnold Franchetti's *The Lion;* GRETCHANINOV's *The Dream of a Little Christmas Tree, The Castle Mouse,* and *The Cat, the Fox and the Rooster;* GRUENBERG's *Jack* and the Beanstalk; HINDEMITH's *Wir bauen eine Stadt;* HUMPERDINCK'S HANSEL AND GRETEL; KABALEVSKY's *The Encounter with a Miracle;* MENOTTI's HELP, HELP, THE GLOBOLINKS!; MILHAUD's *À-propos de Bottes, Un Petit Peu de musique,* and *Un Petit Peu d'exercise;* MOORE's *The Emperor's New Clothes* and *Puss in Boots;* Eduard Poldini's *Aschenbrödel (Cinderella)*, *Dornröschen*, and *Die Knuspershexe* (1927); Francesco Pratella's *La ninna-nanna della bambola* (1923); Vladimir Rebikov's *The Christmas Tree* (1903); ROSSINI's LA CENERENTOLA *(Cinderella)*; Alfred Soffredini's *Il piccolo Haydn* (1889); WEILL's *Der Jasager;* Alec Wilder's *Chicken Little.*

Children's Prayer, *see* ABENDS WILL ICH SCHLAFEN GEH'N.

Chillingworth, Roger, Roger Prynne's assumed name in Walter DAMROSCH'S THE SCARLET LETTER.

Chi mai fra gl'inni e i plausi, chorus of the slave girls in Act II, Scene 1, of VERDI's AIDA.

Chimène, Count de Gormas's daughter (soprano) in MASSENET's LE CID.

Chi mi dira, *see* LASST MICH EUCH FRAGEN.

Chi mi frena, the celebrated sextet of Lucia, Edgardo, Alisa, Arturo, Raimondo, and Enrico in Act II of DONIZETTI's LUCIA DI LAMMERMOOR, in which each gives his reaction to Edgardo's sudden appearance at the wedding ceremony of Lucia and Lord Bucklaw.

Chi servir non brama amor, Fiorilla's air boasting of her talent in the art of love, in Act I of ROSSINI's IL TURCO IN ITALIA.

Chisholm, Erik, conductor and composer. Born Cathcart, near Glasgow, Scotland, Jan. 4, 1904; died Capetown, South Africa, June 7, 1965. He received his doctorate in music at Edinburgh University, where he studied composition with Tovey. For a while he served as organist and teacher in Glasgow, where he founded a society to promote new music. Between 1930 and 1939 he was conductor of the Glasgow Opera, where he mounted numerous novelties, including MOZART's LA CLEMENZA DI TITO and IDOMENEO and BERLIOZ' LES TROYENS. Between 1940 and 1943 he conducted the Anglo-British Ballet. In 1945 he was appointed professor of music at the University of Capetown in South Africa. There, where he remained for the rest of his life, he also wrote music criticism and once again was responsible for producing rarely given operas. His own operas are: *Simoon* (based on Strindberg); *Dark Sonnet* and *Before Breakfast* (based on Eugene O'Neill); *The Inland Woman;* and *Land of Youth.*

Choëphores, Les (The Libation Bearers), play with music in seven sections by MILHAUD. Play by CLAUDEL, translated from AESCHYLUS. Premiere: Paris, Mar. 8, 1927 (concert version); Théâtre de la Monnaie, Mar. 27, 1935 (staged). American premiere: New York City, Nov. 16, 1950 (concert version). This is the second work in the trilogy entitled L'ORÉSTIE, after Aeschylus. The first of the plays is *Agamemnon* and the last *Euménides,* the only drama of the three that is entirely sung. Many critics regard *Les Choëphores* as the finest in the trilogy and one of Milhaud's major works. In this drama ORESTES avenges the death of his father, Agamemnon, by returning to Argos and killing his mother, Clytemnestra, and her lover, Aegisthus. The play opens with a chorus by the libation bearers mourning the death of Agamemnon ("Vocifération funèbre"). Sorrow also suffuses the second section, Electra's "Libation," for solo soprano and mixed chorus. The "Incantation" begins with an invocation of the Fates by sopranos and concludes with a demand for the vengeance for Agamemnon's murder by Orestes, Electra, and the libation bearers. The next two sections are "Présages" and "Exhortation," where the dramatic tensions are intensified, and the work ends with a "Hymn to Justice" for chorus and orchestra and "Conclusion" for voices and percussion.

Remembering that this music was written in 1915, it is significant to point out some remarkable innovations, such as the use of polytonality in the "Libation" section, where different keys are used for male and female voices. Another unusual technique for the time is the introduction of "measured speech" in "Présages" and "Exhortation": the text spoken in rhythm to the music by a woman narrator, juxtaposed with disjointed rhythms in the chorus, which speaks rather than sings, accompanied by percussion and such noisemakers as whistles, a lashing whip, a hammer banging on a board, and so forth.

chorus, a body of singers used for ensemble music. In operas in the sixteenth and seventeenth centuries, the chorus was used to reflect the action, in the manner of Greek drama, but it was seldom required to take part in the plot. GLUCK was one of the first composers to make the chorus a direct participant in the dramatic action.

Chorus of the Bells, see DIN, DON, SUONA VESPERO.

Chorus of the Levites, see SPERATE, O FIGLI.

Chorus of the Swords, see DE L'ENFER QUI VIENT ÉMOUSSER.

Christie, John, founder of the GLYNDE-BOURNE FESTIVAL. Born Glyndebourne, Eng., Dec. 14, 1882; died there July 4, 1962. Having acquired his wealth as an organ builder and having married the singer Audrey MILDMAY in 1931, he founded the Glyndebourne Festival in 1934 on the grounds of his estate in Lewes, Sussex.

Christine Storch, principal female character (soprano) in Richard STRAUSS's INTERMEZZO, a role created by Lotte LEHMANN.

Christmas Eve, see GOGOL, NIKOLAI.

Christoff, Boris, bass. Born Sofia, Bulgaria, May 18, 1918. He was a member of the Gussla Choir in Sofia when he was heard by King Boris, who encouraged him to become a professional singer. Vocal studies followed in Rome with STRACCIARI and in Salzburg with Buratti, leading to his opera debut in Rome in 1946. A year later he was engaged by LA SCALA, where in less than two years he was called upon to sing leading basso roles. He made a sensational debut at COVENT GARDEN in 1949 in one of his most celebrated roles, BORIS GODUNOV; he reappeared at Covent Garden in leading basso roles between 1958 and 1963. As Boris, he was acclaimed at the TEATRO COLÓN in Buenos Aires, at the PARIS OPÉRA, and, in his American debut, at the SAN FRANCISCO OPERA on Sept. 30, 1956. In 1958 he became the principal basso of the CHICAGO LYRIC OPERA and has since also appeared with most of Europe's leading opera companies. He scored a major success in A LIFE FOR THE CZAR at the SAN CARLO OPERA in Naples on Apr. 22, 1967.

Christophe Colomb, opera in two parts by MILHAUD. Libretto by CLAUDEL. Premiere: Berlin State Opera, May 5, 1930. American premiere: New York City, Nov. 6, 1952 (concert version); San Francisco Opera, Oct. 5, 1968 (one act staged).

Milhaud wrote three operas set in the Western Hemisphere. *Christophe Colomb* came first, followed by MAXIMILIEN and BOLIVAR. The life of COLUMBUS is told in a philosophical allegory, mystical and religious in tone. The authors were more interested in offering commentaries on the problems, ideas, and emotions developed during the four centuries following Columbus' discovery of the New World than in his life story. Nevertheless, parts of his story are told by a narrator reading from a huge volume. A chorus (representing the people) provide the commentary.

The two parts of the opera are divided into twenty-seven scenes. Besides experiments previously attempted by the composer in earlier works (such as rhythmic speech and polytonal choruses), several fresh ones are introduced into this opera. One is to combine music and drama with pantomime, ballet, and even motion pictures; another is to produce the work on three different stage levels; and a third is to have the chorus sometimes sing on a single vowel.

Chrysis, Demetrios' beloved (soprano) in ERLANGER'S APHRODITE.

Chrysothemis, Elektra's sister (soprano) in Richard STRAUSS's ELEKTRA.

church parable, a musicodramatic structure developed by BRITTEN, using limited forces, being intimate in character and religious in theme, and intended for performance in churches. Britten's aim in producing such works was a practical one: to gain more performances for his stage works. He wrote three church parables: CURLEW RIVER, THE BURNING FIERY FURNACE, and THE PRODIGAL SON.

Cicilio, a Camorrist (tenor) in WOLF-FERRARI'S THE JEWELS OF THE MADONNA.

Cid, Le, opera in four acts by MASSENET. Libretto by Adolphe d'Ennery, Louis Gallet, and Édouard Blau, based on the historical drama by CORNEILLE. Premiere: Paris Opéra, Nov. 30, 1885. American premiere: New Orleans, Feb. 23, 1890. The central characters are Rodrigo, called Le Cid (the Conqueror, tenor), and Chimène (soprano). Chimène's father (baritone), a Spanish nobleman, is killed in a duel by the Cid. She demands vengeance, but when King Ferdinand (baritone), elated at the news of Rodrigo's victory over the Moors, directs Chimène to pronounce the death sentence, she loses heart and instead embraces the forgiven conqueror.

The ballet music in Act II is particularly famous. It comprises the following Spanish dances: Castillane, Andalouse, Aragonaise, Catalane, Madrilène, and Navarraise. The two principal vocal numbers are Chimène's air, "Pleurez, pleurez, mes yeux," and Rodrigo's prayer, "O Souverain! O Juge! O Père!," both in Act III.

Cieco, Iris' blind father (bass) in MASCAGNI'S IRIS.

Cielo e mar!, Enzo's song of praise to sky and sea as he awaits the arrival of his beloved, Laura, in Act II of PONCHIELLI'S LA GIOCONDA.

Cigna, Gina (born Gina Sens), soprano. Born Paris, Mar. 6, 1900. Her music study took place at the Paris Conservatory. In 1927 she made her opera debut at LA SCALA in the role of FREIA. After becoming a leading soprano at La Scala, she made her debut at COVENT GARDEN in 1933 and her American debut at the METROPOLITAN OPERA as AIDA on Feb. 6, 1937. She was subsequently heard in leading soprano roles in major opera houses in America and Europe, distinguishing herself particularly in such varied roles as Aida, TURANDOT, GIOCONDA, NORMA, and DONNA ELVIRA. Her repertory embraced seventy operas. In 1948 a serious motor accident brought her singing career to an end. She then lived in Milan, devoting herself to teaching. Between 1953 and 1957 she taught voice at the Royal Conservatory in Toronto.

Cilèa, Francesco, composer. Born Palmi, Italy, July 26, 1866; died Verazza, Italy, Nov. 20, 1950. He wrote and produced his first opera, *Gina,* in 1889, while still a student at the Naples Conservatory. It brought him a commission from Edoardo Sonzogno, the publisher, to write *La Tilda,* produced in Florence in 1892. Four years later Cilèa's L'ARLÉSIANA was introduced in Milan. His next work, ADRIANA LECOUVREUR, was first performed in 1902. His last opera, *Gloria,* appeared in 1907. From 1896 to 1904 he was professor of composition at the Musical Institute in Florence. From 1913 to 1916 he was director of the Palermo Conservatory and after 1916 of the Majella Conservatory. About 1930 Cilèa rewrote his opera *Gloria;* this revised version was performed at LA SCALA in 1932.

Cimarosa, Domenico, composer. Born Aversa, Italy, Dec. 17, 1749; died Venice, Jan. 11, 1801. He wrote one of the most celebrated OPERA BUFFAS before those of ROSSINI, IL MATRIMONIO SEGRETO. For eleven years he attended the Conservatorio Santa Maria di Loreto in Naples, where his teachers included Antonio SACCHINI and Nicola PICCINNI. His first opera, *Le stravaganze del conte,* was produced in Naples in 1772. His next, *La finta Parigina,* was a major success. During the next two decades he lived alternately in Rome and Naples, writing operas for both cities. In 1787 he was invited to Russia by Catherine II, where he served as her court composer. He stayed there three years and wrote three operas. Replaced by Giuseppe SARTI in 1792, he went to Vienna, where he succeeded Antonio SALIERI as court KAPELLMEISTER. It was here that he wrote the work for which he is known today, *Il matrimonio segreto,* introduced Feb. 7, 1792, with formidable success. When Emperor Leopold II died, Cimarosa left Vienna and returned to Naples in 1793 to become MAESTRO DI CAPPELLA to the king and teacher of the royal children. When the French Republican army entered Naples in 1799, Cimarosa openly expressed his sympathy for the invaders. For this he was imprisoned and sentenced to death; only his great popularity saved his life. He was finally pardoned by King Ferdinand, on the condition that he leave Naples for good. Broken in health and spirit, he collapsed and died in Venice while en route to St. Petersburg. After *Il matrimonio segreto* his most popular operas were: *La finta Parigina* (1773); *L'Italiana in Londra* (1778); *La ballerina amante* (1782); *Artaserse* (1784); *Cleopatra* (1791); *Penelope* (1794); *L'amante disperato* (1795); *Semiramide* (1799).

Cincinnati Zoo Opera, open-air opera performances produced annually during the summer in an auditorium in the Zoo gardens in Cincinnati, Ohio, usually with performers of first importance. It was founded in 1920 by the Cincinnati Summer Opera Association. Its repertory has for the most part been conservative, though from time to time operas such as COSÌ FAN TUTTE, LA CENERENTOLA, MARTHA, SALOME, and THE MEDIUM are also given. Several important singers either made their debuts here or appeared in roles for which they later became celebrated, including Jan PEERCE, Dorothy KIRSTEN, and James MELTON. The last new opera mounted in the open-air Zoo Pavilion was IL PIRATA in 1969, and on July 12, 1969, a gala farewell was staged there. In 1970 the opera performances moved indoors, into the reconditioned Music Hall in Cincinnati, home of the Cincinnati Symphony.

Cinderella, a fairy tale by Charles PERRAULT (1628–1703), the subject of many operas. A few are: BLECH's *Aschenbrödel;* MASSENET's *Cendrillon;* Eduard Poldini's *Aschenbrödel* (1927); ROSSINI's LA CENE-RENTOLA; and WOLF-FERRARI's *La cenerentola.*

Cio-Cio-San, a geisha girl (soprano) in love with Pinkerton, in PUCCINI's MADAMA BUTTERFLY.

Cioni, Renato, tenor. Born Island of Elba, Italy. Completing his vocal studies with Titta RUFFO at the Conservatorio Cherubini in Florence, he launched his career in opera at the FESTIVAL OF TWO WORLDS in Spoleto in 1959 in IL DUCA D'ALBA by DONIZETTI. He made his first appearances in the United States in 1961 with the CHICAGO LYRIC OPERA and the SAN FRANCISCO OPERA. In Sept., 1968, he opened the season of the San Francisco Opera in ERNANI. His repertory includes some thirty-five roles, with emphasis on the operas of BELLINI and Donizetti. He has appeared both in America and in leading European opera houses opposite so many celebrated sopranos (including SUTHERLAND, CALLAS, Leontyne PRICE, TEBALDI, and SULIOTIS) that he has come to be known as "the tenor of the prima donnas."

Cisneros, Eleanora (born Eleanor Broadfoot), mezzo-soprano. Born New York City, Nov. 1, 1878; died there Feb. 3, 1934. Her initial study of voice took place with Jean DE RESZKE and Muzio-Celli. As Eleanor Broadfoot she made her debut at the METROPOLITAN OPERA on Jan. 5, 1900, at a Sunday evening concert, which was followed by her opera debut in Philadelphia as AMNERIS. In 1901 she married Count Francesco de Cisneros of Havana and temporarily abandoned her stage career to devote herself to further study. Her return debut in opera took place in Turin in 1902. Between 1904 and 1906 she appeared at COVENT GARDEN, from 1907 to 1909 with the MANHATTAN OPERA COMPANY in New York, and in 1911 with the Melba Company in Australia. After a year with the Havana Opera in 1915–16, she went into retirement.

Claggart, John, master-at-arms (bass) in BRITTEN's BILLY BUDD.

Clair flambeau du monde, one of RAMEAU's most beautiful operatic airs.

It is sung by Huascar in LES INDES GA-LANTES.

claque, a group of people engaged to applaud either a performer or a performance and thereby stimulate the audience into audible signs of appreciation, or to voice disapproval and thus create a disturbance. A claque is most often engaged by an individual singer, who instructs it as to when an ovation is to be encouraged. Sometimes opera houses employ claques. The claque originated in France in 1820 when two enterprising Frenchmen organized the *Assurance des succès dramatiques.* The idea took hold immediately; it flourished during the age of MEYERBEER. In the middle of the nineteenth century claques sprouted in most Italian opera houses. They were frequently employed not only to arouse interest in an opera or a singer, but for political purposes, since many operas had texts that could be interpreted as political propaganda. In 1919 the London *Musical Times* reported the fees paid to members of an Italian claque: five lire for each "interruption of bravo" to fifty lire for a "bis [encore] at any cost"; and a special sum for "wild enthusiasm." Claques have also been employed in English and American opera houses. By 1923 claques were used so extensively in America that Walter DAMROSCH complained in his autobiography about the stupidity of singers spending "their money in hiring twenty to fifty husky men, under a well-trained leader, who stand at the side of the balconies and family circle and clap with the machine-like regularity of a steel hammer in an iron foundry in order to produce so and so many recalls after an act." In Vienna in the 1920's, students were hired to serve as claques. In 1954 Rudolf BING, objecting to the number of claquers in the standing-room sections of the METROPOLITAN OPERA, reduced the number of standees allowed for any performance by half. The further reduction of standing-room space at the new auditorium of the Metropolitan Opera at the Lincoln Center for the Performing Arts further diminished the number of claquers employed. But to a certain degree, a claque is still used in many opera houses to help stimulate audience ovations.

Clara, a young mother (soprano) in GERSHWIN'S PORGY AND BESS.

Claudel, Paul, poet, dramatist, and diplomat. Born Villeneuve-sur-Fère, France, Aug. 6, 1868; died Paris, Feb. 23, 1955. He wrote the texts for several French operas, including HONEGGER'S JEANNE D'ARC AU BÛCHER, MILHAUD'S trilogy L'ORÉSTIE and his CHRISTOPHE COLOMB.

Claudio, an officer (baritone), in love with Hero, in BERLIOZ' BÉATRICE ET BÉNÉDICT.

Claudius, King of Denmark (baritone) in THOMAS'S HAMLET.

Claussen, Julia, mezzo-soprano. Born Stockholm, June 11, 1879; died there May 1, 1941. Her musical education took place at the Royal Academy of Music in Stockholm and the Royal Academy of Music in Berlin. She made her opera debut on Jan. 19, 1903, in Stockholm in LA FAVORITA. She remained with the STOCKHOLM OPERA COMPANY for nine years. In 1913 she appeared with the CHICAGO OPERA, after which she made successful appearances at COVENT GARDEN and in Paris. On Nov. 23, 1917, she made her debut at the METROPOLITAN OPERA as DELILAH. She remained with the Metropolitan until 1932, then went into retirement.

Clément, Edmond, tenor. Born Paris, Mar. 28, 1867; died Nice, Feb. 23, 1928. He attended the Paris Conservatory, after which he made a successful debut at the OPÉRA-COMIQUE on Nov. 29, 1889, in *Mireille.* For the next twenty years he was the principal tenor of the Opéra-Comique, where he created the leading tenor roles in many French operas, including BRUNEAU'S *L'Attaque du moulin,* ERLANGER'S LE JUIF POLONAIS, GODARD'S *La Vivandière,* HAHN'S *L'Île de rêve,* and SAINT-SAËNS'S *Phyrné* and *Hélène.* On Dec. 6, 1909, he made his first appearance at the METROPOLITAN OPERA in MANON. Between 1911 and 1913 he was a member of the Boston Opera Company. His art, both as actor and singer, was marked by restraint and understatement.

clemenza di Tito, La (The Clemency of Titus), opera in two acts by MOZART. Libretto by Caterino Mazzolà, adapted from a libretto by Metastasio. Premiere: Prague, Sept. 6, 1791. American premiere: Tanglewood, Lenox, Mass., Aug. 4, 1952. This was Mozart's last opera, written (in eighteen days) for the coronation of Emperor Leopold II as King of Bohemia. One of its principal male roles, that of Sextus, is today sung by a mezzo-soprano because it was originally written for a CASTRATO alto.

The central character, Tito (tenor), is a former tyrant grown benevolent. Nevertheless, Vitellia (soprano) and Sextus conspire to overthrow him. When Sextus sets fire to the palace, it is believed Tito is killed in the flames. However, he has been rescued, and he magnanimously forgives the traitors. GLUCK wrote an opera with the same title using the Metastasio libretto.

Of special historical importance in Mozart's opera is the fact that for the first time he uses a chorus as a background for solo voices. One of the most celebrated arias in the opera is "Parto, parto," sung by Sextus, to whom Mozart also assigned a remarkable recitative ("O Dei, che smania è questo") and an eloquent air, "Deh, per questo istante." Vitellia's aria, "Non, più di fiori," the duettino, "Deh prendi un dolce amplesso," and the terzetto, "Se al volto mai ti senti," are also of special interest.

Cleopatra, Egyptian queen celebrated for her beauty. She is the central character in numerous operas, including: BARBER'S ANTONY AND CLEOPATRA; CIMAROSA'S *Cleopatra;* GRAUN'S *Cleopatra e Cesare;* HADLEY'S CLEOPATRA'S NIGHT; MALIPIERO'S *Antonio e Cleopatra;* MASSÉ'S *Une Nuit de Cléopâtre;* MASSENET'S *Cléopâtre;* and Johann Mattheson's *Cleopatra.*

Cleopatra's Night, opera in two acts by HADLEY. Libretto by Alice Leal Pollock, adapted from Gautier's story *Une Nuit de Cléopâtre.* Premiere: Metropolitan Opera, Jan. 31, 1920. The story concerns

the surrender of Cleopatra to Meïamoun for one night in return for his willing death the following morning.

Cleophas, the name assumed by Joseph in Egypt in MÉHUL'S JOSEPH.

Cleva, Fausto, conductor. Born Trieste, Italy, May 17, 1902. He attended the Trieste Conservatory following which he began his conducting career in Italy. In 1920 he came to the United States (becoming a citizen in 1931), and served as assistant conductor at the METROPOLITAN OPERA. From 1938 to 1942 he was principal conductor of Italian operas there. Between 1942 and 1944 and again from 1949 to 1955, he held a similar post with the SAN FRANCISCO OPERA COMPANY, following which he returned to the Metropolitan Opera. Between 1944 and 1946 he was artistic director of the CHICAGO OPERA.

Clitandro, Lisetta's lover (tenor) in WOLF-FERRARI'S L'AMORE MEDICO.

Cloak, The, *see* TABARRO, IL.

Clorinda, (1) a heathen female warrior (soprano) in MONTEVERDI'S IL COMBATTIMENTO DI TANCREDI E CLORINDA.

(2) One of the two stepsisters of Cinderella in ROSSINI'S LA CENERENTOLA.

Clotilda, Norma's confidante (soprano) in BELLINI'S NORMA.

Cluytens, André, conductor. Born Antwerp, Belgium, Mar. 26, 1905; died Paris, June 3, 1967. Following his music studies in Belgium, he was appointed choral coach at the Royal Belgian Opera when he was sixteen (his father was principal conductor there). He made an unofficial debut by substituting for an indisposed conductor in a performance of LES PÊCHEURS DE PERLES when he was twenty-one. For the next few years he conducted in opera houses in Toulouse, Lyons, and Bordeaux, following which he was appointed first principal conductor, then musical director of the PARIS OPÉRA; he was also musical director of the OPÉRA-COMIQUE. His American debut took place as conductor of the visiting Vienna Philharmonic, in Washington, D.C., on Nov. 4, 1956. In 1955 he substituted for Eugen JOCHUM as conductor of TANNHÄUSER at BAYREUTH, when he was so well received that he was invited to return to the festival for the next few seasons; in 1958 he led there Wieland WAGNER's production of LOHENGRIN. He was scheduled to make his debut at the METROPOLITAN OPERA in DER FLIEGENDE HOLLÄNDER when he died.

Clytemnestra, see KLYTEMNESTRA.

Coates, Albert, conductor and composer. Born St. Petersburg, Apr. 23, 1882; died Capetown, South Africa, Dec. 11, 1953. In 1902 he entered the Leipzig Conservatory, where he studied with NIKISCH, whose assistant he later became at the Leipzig Opera. Coates conducted his first opera, THE TALES OF HOFFMANN, when Nikisch fell ill. In 1906, Coates became the principal conductor of the Elberfeld Opera, where he directed over forty operas. After conducting operas in Dresden, Mannheim, St. Petersburg, and London, he was engaged by Sir Thomas BEECHAM as codirector and conductor at COVENT GARDEN for the first postwar season. He was the first British conductor to conduct at the PARIS OPÉRA. In 1920 he visited the United States for the first time, and three years later he was appointed the musical director of the Rochester Philharmonic Orchestra. In 1928 and 1929 he led opera performances in Italy, including at LA SCALA. For a five-year period he was in charge of a two-month opera season in Barcelona. After that he appeared as guest conductor in most of the leading opera houses of Europe, gave successful opera performances in the Soviet Union, and was director of the British Opera season at Covent Garden. He wrote several operas including: *Sardanapalus* (1916), *Samuel Pepys* (1929), and *Pickwick* (1936).

Cobbler's Song (Schusterlied), see JERUM! JERUM!

Cochenille, Spalanzani's servant (tenor) in OFFENBACH's THE TALES OF HOFFMANN.

Cocteau, Jean, novelist, playwright, and poet. Born Maisons-Lafitte, France, July 5, 1891; died Paris, Oct. 12, 1963. A friend of the French composers known as Les Six, he frequently prepared texts and poems for their works. These include the librettos for *Antigone* (HONEG-GER), LE PAUVRE MATELOT, and LA VOIX HUMAINE. He also wrote the text for OEDIPUS REX. His play *Les Mariés de la Tour d'Eiffel* was made into an opera by Lou Harrison.

Coffee Cantata, a secular cantata by Johann Sebastian Bach (1732), which is sometimes staged as an opera. Picander's text describes how Lieschen (soprano), daughter of Schlendrian (bass), has become addicted to coffee— so much so that she refuses to marry anybody who does not share that passion. Arguments for and against coffee-drinking are presented before the work ends with a choral commentary that since older people are allowed to drink coffee there is no reason why young girls should not. The work is in ten sections opening with the tenor aria, "Schweigt stille, plaudert nicht." The delights of coffee-drinking are described by Lieschen in "Ei! wie schmeckt der Coffee süsse." The composition concludes with the chorus, "Die Katze lässt das Mausen nicht."

Coigny, Countess, see COUNTESS DE COIGNY.

Colas, a magician (baritone) in MOZART's BASTIEN UND BASTIENNE.

Colas Breugnon, opera by KABALEVSKY. Libretto by V. Bragin, based on the novel *Le Maître de Clamecy* by Romain Rolland. Premiere: Leningrad State Opera, Feb. 22, 1938. Colas Breugnon is a Burgundian craftsman of the sixteenth century who approaches every problem of life with laughter. In Kabalevsky's opera, Breugnon is used as a symbol criticizing the social customs and economic problems of the sixteenth century. The score is filled with French folksongs, particularly those originating in Burgundy. The spirited overture, a characterization of Colas Breugnon, is frequently performed.

Colbran, Isabella, soprano. Born Madrid, Feb. 2, 1785; died Bologna, Italy, Oct. 7, 1845. She was the first wife of ROSSINI and a celebrated prima donna. After studying with Girolano CRESCENTINI in Italy, she made her bow in opera in Paris in 1801. Six years later she made a successful debut at LA SCALA. In 1811

Domenico BARBAJA engaged her for his opera company in Naples, where she had a triumph in PAISIELLO's *Nina*. Four years later Rossini wrote *Elisabetta* for her. He fell in love with her, and she soon deserted Barbaja (whose mistress she had been) to live with the composer, who was her junior by seven years. She created the leading female roles in six more of his operas, and they were married on Mar. 15, 1822. Eventually they were estranged, and Rossini deserted her for Olympe Pélissier, whom he married two years after Colbran's death.

Collatinus, Lucretia's husband (bass) in BRITTEN'S RAPE OF LUCRETIA.

colla voce, Italian for "with the voice," a term used to direct an accompanying instrumentalist to follow the voice, often in passages where the rhythm is free.

Colline, philosopher (bass) in PUCCINI's LA BOHÈME.

Cologne Opera (Bühnen der Stadt Köln), principal opera company in Cologne, Ger. Under such musical directors as Otto LOHSE (1911–1912), Otto KLEMPERER (1917–1924), and Eugen SZENKAR (1924–1933) the Cologne Opera achieved distinction for its performances of WAGNER and VERDI, as well as novelties like DIE TOTE STADT (1920), KAT'A KABANOVA (1922), Braunfels' *Galatea* (1930), THE RAPE OF LUCRETIA (1948, a German premiere), and KRENEK's *Tarquinius* (1950). When the old opera house was demolished by bombs in 1943, opera was performed in the hall of the University at Aula until a new auditorium was constructed, opening on May 19, 1957, with OBERON. Fritz Schuch became artistic director in 1959 and Wolfgang SAWALLISCH musical director in 1960. After both resigned in 1963, Istvan KERTESZ became musical director. Since the 1950's the less familiar operas heard include ARABELLA, ARIADNE AUF NAXOS, BLUTHOCHZEIT (a world premiere), LA CLEMENZA DI TITO, THE CUNNING LITTLE VIXEN, EUGENE ONEGIN, THE FAIR AT SOROCHINSK, L'HEURE ESPAGNOLE, DIE KLUGE, NEUES VOM TAGE, I QUATTRO RUSTEGHI, THE RAKE'S PROGRESS, and TROUBLE IN TAHITI.

Colomba, *see* MERIMÉE, PROSPER.

Colonna, Steffano, *see* STEFFANO COLONNA.

Colón Opera, *see* TEATRO COLÓN.

coloratura, Italian for "colored." The term is used in vocal music to denote passages highly ornamented with runs and figures. A coloratura soprano is one who specializes in such music.

Columbine, Arlecchino's wife (mezzo-soprano) in BUSONI'S ARLECCHINO.

combattimento di Tancredi e Clorinda, Il (The Combat of Tancredi and Clorinda), dramatic cantata in one act by MONTEVERDI. Libretto from TASSO's *Gerusaleme libera*. Premiere: Venice, 1624. American premiere: Northampton, Mass., May 12, 1928.

Though identified as a "dramatic cantata" this work is often staged as an opera. The performers on the stage use pantomime, with the singers placed at one side of the stage to sing the roles. A narrator first outlines the theme of the play, then comments upon the action. Tancredi is a Christian knight, in love with Clorinda, a Saracen maiden. She is a warrior, too, dressed as a man. Returning from a victory, during which a Christian fortification has been burnt, she is met by Tancredi, who does not recognize her and kills her in combat as an enemy.

In his orchestration (scored for four viole de braccio and a continuo of harpsichord and violone) Monteverdi uses for the first time such then new technical devices for the strings as tremolos and pizzicati—a style identified as STILE CONCITATO, or agitated or excited style. But he can, of course, also be tranquil and atmospheric, as in the sinfonia, "Invocation of Night."

Combien tu m'es chère (Ah! quanto m'è caro), Vasco da Gama's joyous aria when Selika provides him with a new route to Africa, in Act II of MEYERBEER's L'AFRICAINE.

Com' è bello quanto incanto, Lucrezia Borgia's air, speaking of her love for her son Gennaro, in DONIZETTI'S LUCREZIA BORGIA.

Come due tizzi, the song of Baldassare, the shepherd, in Act I of CILÈA's L'ARLÉSIANA.

Comedy on the Bridge, comic opera in one act by MARTINU. Libretto by J. V. Klicpera. Premiere: Prague Radio, Mar. 18, 1937; Zürich, Mar. 31, 1952 (revised version). American premiere: New York, May 28, 1951 (original version); Aspen, Col., 1958 (revised version). The composer revised this opera extensively, following which it was televised in the United States on a coast-to-coast network. It received the New York Music Critics' Circle Award.

Come in quest' ora bruna, Amelia's aria in Act I, Scene 1, as she views the distant horizon and recalls her past, in VERDI'S SIMON BOCCANEGRA.

Come per me sereno, a brilliant aria in which Amina gives voice to her happiness in loving Elvino, in Act I of BELLINI'S LA SONNAMBULA.

Come rugiada al cespite, Ernani's confession of his love for Donna Elvira, in Act I, Scene 1, of VERDI'S ERNANI.

Come scoglio, Fiordiligi's aria avowing her fidelity to Guglielmo, in Act I, Scene 3, of MOZART'S COSÌ FAN TUTTE.

Come un bel dì di maggio, Chénier's aria in Act IV of GIORDANO'S ANDREA CHÉNIER, his poem of farewell in prison before his execution.

Come vinti, the chorus of the guards in the opening scene of DONIZETTI'S LUCIA DI LAMMERMOOR, confirming Normanno's suspicion that the prowler on the grounds of the castle is Edgardo.

comic opera, a general term for any musicodramatic work of nonserious nature. For particular forms of comic opera, see OPÉRA BOUFFE and OPERA BUFFA. The term OPÉRA COMIQUE means something quite different.

Comme autrefois dans la nuit sombre, Leila's CAVATINA about her love for Nadir, in Act II of BIZET'S LES PÊCHEURS DE PERLES.

commedia per musica, "comedy through music," a term prevailing in eighteenth-century Naples to designate comic operas.

Commendatore, Il, Donna Anna's father (bass) in MOZART'S DON GIOVANNI.

Comme une pâle fleur, Hamlet's arioso in Act V of THOMAS'S HAMLET.

Composer, a character (soprano) in Richard STRAUSS'S ARIADNE AUF NAXOS, a role created by Lotte LEHMANN.

composers as characters in opera. Several operas use composers as characters—some fictional, others drawn from history. Johann Sebastian Bach appears in Emil Ábrányi's *A Tamás templon karnagya* (1947) and Wilhelm Friedemann Bach in GRAENER'S *Friedemann Bach;* LULLY in Nicolo Isouard's *Lulli et Quinault* (1812); MOZART in RIMSKY-KORSAKOV'S *Mozart and Salieri,* in HAHN'S *Mozart,* and in Louis Schneider's 1845 version of Mozart's own comic opera, DER SCHAUSPIELDIREKTOR; Palestrina in PFITZNER'S PALESTRINA; STRADELLA in FLOTOW'S ALESSANDRO STRADELLA; Richard STRAUSS (though identified as Robert STORCH) in his own opera INTERMEZZO. For operas on Chopin see CONSUELO. Fictitious composers appear in two operas by Richard Strauss, ARIADNE AUF NAXOS and CAPRICCIO.

comprimario, Italian for "with the principal," a term applied to secondary or minor roles in opera or to the singers of such roles. The cast of characters of virtually every opera is well populated with *comprimario* roles, CARMEN, for example, providing a half dozen—ZUNIGA, MORALÈS, LE DANCAÏRE, LE REMENDADO, FRASQUITA, and MERCÉDÈS.

comte Ory, Le (Count Ory), OPERA BUFFA in two acts by ROSSINI. Libretto by SCRIBE and Delstre-Poirson. Premiere: Paris Opéra, Aug. 20, 1828. American premiere: New York City, Aug. 22, 1831. This is the last but one of Rossini's operas and one of the two he wrote originally for production in Paris, the last being WILLIAM TELL. The principal character is a licentious count who does not hesitate to employ any means at his command to win young ladies. In his attempt to seduce Countess Adele he assumes various disguises, including those of a hermit and a nun, and is finally exposed as a fraud. Adele's aria, "En proie à la tristesse," the Count's aria, "Dans ce lieu solitaire," and the duet of Adele and the Count, "Ah, respect, Madame," are among its best vocal numbers. The score also boasts an effective drinking song, "Buvons, buvons, soudain," and a charming trio, "A la faveur de cette nuit obscure."

Le comte Ory scored such an extraordinary success when revived at the GLYNDEBOURNE FESTIVAL in 1954 that it has been given numerous performances there in subsequent seasons. The BERLIN GERMAN STATE OPERA also produced it successfully in 1957, and the PICCOLO SCALA in Milan in 1958. The opera has since been given by many other opera companies in Europe and America.

Comus, *see* MASQUE.

Concepcion, Torquemada's wife (soprano), who favors lovers, in RAVEL'S L'HEURE ESPAGNOLE.

Concetta, a Camorrist (soprano) in WOLF-FERRARI'S THE JEWELS OF THE MADONNA.

concitato, Italian for "agitated." In opera the term has been used for a kind of accompaniment first introduced by MONTEVERDI.

congada, an Afro-Brazilian dance, the most famous excerpt from *O contratador dos diamantes,* an opera by Francisco Mignone, produced in Rio de Janeiro on Sept. 20, 1924.

Con morbidezza, *see* MORBIDEZZA.

Connais-tu le pays?, Mignon's autobiographical aria about her adoption by gypsies, in Act I of THOMAS'S MIGNON.

Conner, Nadine, soprano. Born Compton, Cal., Feb. 20, 1914. After studying voice with Armando Fernandez, she was starred on sponsored radio programs for seven years. Between 1939 and 1941 she appeared in an opera company founded and directed by Albert COATES in Los Angeles. On Dec. 22, 1941, she made her debut at the METROPOLITAN OPERA as Pamina in THE MAGIC FLUTE. She was soon elevated there to a position as a leading soprano in a varied repertory, which she occupied until 1958. She made her European debut in 1953 at the HOLLAND MUSIC FESTIVAL in THE MARRIAGE OF FIGARO, following which she appeared with major European opera companies.

Conried, Heinrich (born Cohn), impresario. Born Bielitz, Austria, Sept. 13, 1855; died Meran, Ger., Apr. 26, 1909.

He was the general manager of the METROPOLITAN OPERA for five years. He began his career in the theater as an actor in the Vienna Burgtheater, and with various traveling troupes. In 1887 he was appointed director of the Bremen Stadttheater. In 1888 he came to the United States and became manager of the Germania Theater. He held other managerial posts in this country with various theatrical and opera companies, including the Thalia, Casino, and Irving Place theaters. In 1903 he succeeded Maurice GRAU as manager of the Metropolitan Opera, organizing the Heinrich Conried Opera Company and directing opera performances there for five years. He proved to be an astute and farsighted impresario, combining a feeling for good showmanship with high ideals. He was the recipient of numerous honors from foreign countries, including the Order of the Crown from the German Emperor, the Cross of Knighthood from the Austrian Emperor, and the Order of the Crown from the King of Italy.

Constanze, Belmonte's beloved (soprano) in MOZART'S THE ABDUCTION FROM THE SERAGLIO.

Constanze! Constanze! dich wiederzusehen!, Belmonte's aria expressing delight at the prospect of seeing his beloved again, in Act I of MOZART'S THE ABDUCTION FROM THE SERAGLIO.

Consuelo, a novel about Chopin by George Sand which was adapted for operas by Vladimir Kashperov (1865), Giacomo Orefice (1895), and Alfonso Rendano (1902), all three entitled *Consuelo.*

Consul, The, opera in three acts by MENOTTI. Libretto by the composer. Premiere: Philadelphia, Mar. 1, 1950.

Menotti does not identify the police state in which his present-day text is set. Magda (soprano) is trying to get a visa for another country where her husband, John Sorel, has found refuge. She is relentless and indefatigable in her efforts, persistently haunting the consulate, where a magician is trying to gain attention by performing tricks. All her efforts to meet the consul prove futile, now because of red tape, now through procrastination, now through interruptions. The consul himself never makes an appearance, but his ominous presence is felt. Tragedy stalks Magda. Her child dies from undernourishment; John's mother dies from grief; Magda's husband, John—returned to try to effect her escape—is captured by the police. She can take no more punishment, turns on the gas, and commits suicide. Just before she dies she sees apparitions of figures from the consulate, of John, and his mother, dancing a weird ballet to an eerie tune that had previously been heard as an interlude.

Two vocal excerpts are of outstanding dramatic interest: "I shall find you shells and stars," the lullaby that Magda's mother (contralto) sings to her dying grandchild; and Magda's fiery outburst at her frustrations, "To this we've come." Both are heard in the second act, the last as a closing SCENA.

After coming to New York on Mar. 15, 1950, *The Consul* received the Pulitzer Prize and the Drama Critics' Award as the best play of the year. The opera was mounted in London, Zürich, Berlin, Vienna, and at LA SCALA in Milan in 1951; in Hamburg, in 1952; at SADLER'S WELLS in London in 1954. It was successful everywhere except at La Scala—a failure caused more by political than by musical considerations, since Communists and Fascists both used their influence to discredit it for its obvious attack on a totalitarian society. (Some Italians were resentful because Menotti had become a permanent resident in the United States.)

Contes d'Hoffmann, Les, *see* TALES OF HOFFMANN.

contralto, the lowest voice in the female range, approximating two octaves upward from the F below middle C. The term *contralto* also implies a more strongly developed lower range, with so-called "chest tones" approximating the tone color of a baritone. As this quality was more admired and cultivated fifty and more years ago than it is now, such genuine contralto roles as AZUCENA and ERDA are often undertaken by mezzo-sopranos.

Converse, Frederick Shepherd, composer. Born Newton, Mass., Jan. 5, 1871; died Boston, June 8, 1940. He received his musical training at Harvard University, with George Chadwick in Boston, and at the Munich Conservatory in Germany. After returning to the United States, he taught harmony at the New England Conservatory. In 1904 he became a professor of composition at Harvard. After 1907, he devoted himself exclusively to composition. His opera THE PIPE OF DESIRE, produced at the METROPOLITAN OPERA in 1910, was the first American opera ever performed there. Later operas: *The Sacrifice* (1911); *Sinbad the Sailor* (1913); *The Immigrants* (1914).

Convien partir, o miei compagni d'arme, *see* IL FAUT PARTIR, MES BONS COMPAGNONS.

Cooper, Emil, conductor. Born Kherson, Russia, Dec. 20, 1877; died New York City, Nov. 19, 1960. Of Russian parentage, he attended the Vienna Conservatory and made his conducting debut in 1896 in Odessa. In 1900 he directed opera performances at the Kiev Opera. Four years later he was given a similar post with the Zimin Opera in Moscow. When Feodor CHALIAPIN and a Russian company visited London and Paris with BORIS GODUNOV, Cooper was the conductor. After the revolution in Russia, Cooper helped found the Leningrad Philharmonic Orchestra. In 1923 he made a world tour as conductor of opera and symphonic performances. In 1929 he was the principal conductor of the CHICAGO CIVIC OPERA. In 1934 he conducted special performances of Russian operas at LA SCALA, and in 1944 he joined the conductorial staff of the METROPOLITAN OPERA, where he made his debut on Jan. 26 with PELLÉAS ET MÉLISANDE. Leaving the Metropolitan in 1950, Cooper became principal conductor of the Montreal Opera Guild.

Copland, Aaron, composer. Born Brooklyn, N.Y., Nov. 14, 1900. His music study took place with Victor Wittgenstein and Rubin Goldmarl at the American Conservatory at Fontainebleau and privately with Nadia Boulanger in Paris. After returning to America in 1924 he came to prominence with several orchestral works performed by major organizations. He wrote his first opera, THE SECOND HURRICANE, in 1937, as a "play opera" for performance by high school children. Much more ambitious was his second opera, THE TENDER LAND, introduced by the NEW YORK CITY OPERA COMPANY in 1954. It is through his instrumental music rather than his two operas—and through his achievements as a lecturer, teacher, writer, and promoter of modern music—that he has come to be recognized as one of the foremost musicians America has produced, as well as a leading creative figure in twentieth-century music.

Coppélius, a magician (baritone; his other personalities are Lindorf, Dr. Miracle, and Dapertutto) in OFFENBACH's THE TALES OF HOFFMANN, Act I.

Coq d'or, Le (The Golden Cockerel), opera in three acts by RIMSKY-KORSAKOV. Libretto by Vladimir I. Bielsky, based on a fairy tale by PUSHKIN. Premiere: Moscow, Oct. 7, 1909. American premiere: Metropolitan Opera, Mar. 6, 1918.

The golden cockerel (soprano) has a gift for prophecy. It is brought to King Dodon (bass) by an astrologer (tenor) to protect him from danger. Feeling secure, the king falls asleep but is awakened by the cock's crowing, warning him of imminent danger. The king dispatches his army to ward off the enemy, but the next time the cock crows, the king himself goes off to head his forces. In the field of battle, he finds that his sons have been killed. But he also meets the Queen of Shemakha (soprano), with whom he falls in love and whom he brings back to his kingdom. When the astrologer demands the queen as the price for his cock, the king murders him. The cock in turn avenges the astrologer's death by killing the king—and then flies off.

The most celebrated vocal excerpt in the opera is the "Hymn to the Sun" ("Salut à toi, soleil") sung by the Queen of Shemakha in the second act. Orches-

tral episodes from the opera have been assembled into a four-movement suite often heard at symphony concerts: I. Introduction and Prologue, Slumber Scene, and Warning of the Cockerel; II. Prelude and Scene at the Palace from Act 2; III. Dance of King Dodon and the Queen of Shemakha; and IV. Prelude, Bridal Procession, and Death of King Dodon.

That *Le Coq d'or* was not performed during the composer's lifetime was due to governmental censorship: the officials found too close a similarity between the court of King Dodon and that of Czar Nicolas II and the latter's then recent inept war effort against the Japanese. At the premiere the singers were placed in the box seats while the stage action was performed in pantomime by dancers, a conception of Fokine's. This was the version that introduced the opera to America. Since then the composer's wish to have the singers act as well as sing has been followed. The SAN FRANCISCO OPERA gave a highly successful revival of the opera in 1955 with Erich LEINSDORF conducting and Mattwilda DOBBS appearing as the Queen of Shemakha.

Cordon, Norman, bass. Born Washington, D.C., Jan. 20, 1904; died Chapel Hill, N.C., Mar. 1, 1964. Upon completing vocal studies with Gaetano DE LUCA in Nashville and Hadley Outland in Chicago, he made his opera debut with the SAN CARLO OPERA touring company in 1933 as the king in AIDA. During the season of 1933–34 he appeared with the CHICAGO OPERA. On Mar. 13, 1936, he made his debut at the METROPOLITAN OPERA as MONTERONE. He remained with the company for a decade, appearing in leading bass roles. In 1948 he retired from the stage to become part of a statewide music and opera program developed by the University of North Carolina.

Corelli, Franco, tenor. Born Ancona, Italy, Apr. 8, 1923. Self-taught in singing, he made his opera debut at Spoleto in 1952 in CARMEN. His success there brought him an invitation to appear in Rome, in the same opera, later that year. In 1953 he was heard at the FLORENCE MAY MUSIC FESTIVAL in the first performance of PROKOFIEV'S WAR AND PEACE outside the Soviet Union. Corelli made his debut at LA SCALA on the opening night of the 1953–54 season in LA VESTALE. Since then he has been a leading tenor of that company and has made notable guest appearances in other leading European opera houses. He made a highly successful debut at the METROPOLITAN OPERA as Manrico in IL TROVATORE on Jan. 27, 1961. In appearances in the world's foremost opera houses he has since then established himself as one of the world's foremost Italian heroic tenors.

Corena, Fernando, bass. Born Geneva, Dec. 22, 1923. Having studied with Enrico Romani in Milan and been encouraged by Vittorio GUI, the conductor, he made his debut in Trieste in 1947 as VARLAAM. On Feb. 6, 1954, he made his debut at the METROPOLITAN OPERA as LEPORELLO. He has remained with the company since then, a successor to Salvatore BACCALONI in performance of *basso-buffo* roles. In 1955 he made successful appearances at the EDINBURGH FESTIVAL, and in 1960 he appeared at COVENT GARDEN, where he made his debut as Bartolo in THE BARBER OF SEVILLE.

Corneille, Pierre, dramatist and poet. Born Rouen, France, June 6; 1606; died Paris, Oct. 1, 1684. His dramas *Le Cid, Polyeucte,* and *Robert Devereux* were adapted into operas by many composers. These operas include: CORNELIUS' *Der Cid;* DONIZETTI'S POLIUTO and *Roberto Devereux;* GOUNOD'S *Polyeucte;* HANDEL'S *Flavio* (based partly on *Le Cid*); MASSENET'S LE CID; MERCADANTE'S *Roberto Devereux;* SACCHINI'S *Il Gran Cid;* and Johan Wagenaar's *The Cid* (1916). Pierre Corneille's younger brother, Thomas, was the author of the drama *Médée,* used for operas of the same name by Marc-Antoine CHARPENTIER and Luigi CHERUBINI, among others.

Cornelius, Peter, composer. Born Mainz, Ger., Dec. 24, 1824; died there Oct. 26, 1874. His early musical education was haphazard, since he aspired to be an actor. An unsuccessful stage debut turned him to music. He went to Berlin in 1845, where he studied counterpoint with Siegfried Wilhelm Dehn and wrote his first major works. During a visit to Weimar in 1852 he met Franz LISZT, who became interested in him. Henceforth Cornelius was a Liszt disciple, as well as a champion of WAGNER. It was in Weimar that he wrote his best-known work, the comic opera THE BARBER OF BAGDAD. Its first performance was directed by Liszt on Dec. 15, 1858. The opera was a failure, primarily because there was an organized cabal in the city against Liszt. It was due to the failure of this opera that Liszt decided to resign his post as KAPELLMEISTER. Cornelius became a close friend of Wagner's in 1859. His creative achievements at this time included a second opera, *Der Cid,* performed in Weimar in 1865. A third opera, *Gunlöd,* was left unfinished at his death; it was completed by Eduard Lassen and produced in Weimar in 1891.

Coro delle campane, *see* DIN, DON, SUONA VESPERO.

Coronation March, the march in Act IV of MEYERBEER'S LE PROPHÈTE.

Coronation of Poppea, The, *see* INCORONAZIONE DI POPPEA, L'.

Coronation Scene, the coronation of Boris Godunov in Act I, Scene 1, of MUSSORGSKY'S BORIS GODUNOV.

Corregidor, Der (The Magistrate), opera in four acts by Hugo WOLF. Libretto by Rosa Mayreder-Obermayer, based on Pedro Antonio de Alarcón's novel *The Three-cornered Hat.* Premiere: Mannheim, June 7, 1896. American premiere: New York City, Jan. 5, 1959 (concert version). This is Wolf's only opera. The magistrate, Don Eugenio di Zuniga (tenor), pursues the lovely Frasquita (mezzo-soprano). On one occasion he comes to her door soaked to the skin, having just fallen into a pond. When Frasquita threatens him with a rifle, he falls into a faint, and he must be put to bed. Lucas (baritone), husband of Frasquita, finds the magistrate in his bed and becomes convinced that his wife has been unfaithful. He puts on the magistrate's clothes, now dry, and goes forth to make advances to the magistrate's wife. Both Lucas and the magistrate receive sound thrashings in the confusion that follows, with the result that each wisely decides to confine his lovemaking to his own home. The same story is the basis of Manuel de FALLA's ballet, *The Three-cornered Hat*.

Corsair, The, *see* BYRON.

Corsi, Jacopo, member of the Florentine group that created opera. Born Celano, Italy, c. 1560; died Florence c. 1604. It was at Corsi's palace that the first operas by a member of the CAMERATA were performed: PERI's DAFNE and EURIDICE (1597 and 1600 respectively). Corsi not only assisted in the performances of these first operas, playing the harpsichord, but also contributed some songs to *Dafne;* these are the only numbers to survive from the opera.

Cortigiani, vil razza dannata (Maledizione), Rigoletto's attack on the courtiers who try to keep him from seeing his daughter in the Duke's private chambers, in Act II of VERDI's RIGOLETTO.

cosa rara, Una (A Rare Case), comic opera in two acts by MARTÍN Y SOLER. Libretto by DA PONTE. Premiere: Burgtheater, Vienna, Nov. 17, 1786. This opera was produced through the influence of the Viennese KAPELLMEISTER, SALIERI, in order to check the triumph of the then recently produced THE MARRIAGE OF FIGARO by MOZART. The maneuver worked. *Una cosa rara* proved so popular that Mozart's opera was overshadowed and given only nine performances. *Una cosa rara* contains a waltz whose popularity is believed to have initiated the craze for waltz music in Vienna. Mozart, with tongue in cheek, quoted one of the melodies from Martín's opera in DON GIOVANNI. When *Una cosa rara* was revived in Barcelona in 1936, it proved thoroughly delightful, readily explaining why it was so well received in its own time.

Così fan tutte (So Do They All), comic opera in two acts by MOZART. Libretto by DA PONTE. Premiere: Burgtheater,

Jan. 26, 1790. American premiere: Metropolitan Opera, Mar. 24, 1922.

Characters: Fiordiligi, a lady of Ferrara (soprano); Dorabella, her sister (soprano or mezzo-soprano); Despina, their maid (soprano); Ferrando, an officer in love with Dorabella (tenor); Guglielmo, officer in love with Fiordiligi (baritone); Don Alfonso, an old bachelor (bass); soldiers; servants; musicians; boatmen; guests. The setting is Naples in the eighteenth century.

Act I, Scene 1. A café. While discussing women in general, Ferrando and Guglielmo express the conviction that their respective sweethearts, Dorabella and Fiordiligi, are devoted to them. Their friend Don Alfonso is a cynic. He wagers the soldiers that if their sweethearts were courted by other men they would be unfaithful. To win the wager, the soldiers must follow his instructions to the letter for twenty-four hours. The wager is accepted. Confident of the outcome, the soldiers drink a toast with Don Alfonso.

Scene 2. The garden of Fiordiligi's and Dorabella's villa. Dorabella and Fiordiligi ecstatically sing of the men they love ("Ah guarda, sorella"). Their idyllic mood is shattered when Don Alfonso arrives with sad news: Ferrando and Guglielmo have been recalled to their troops. The two soldiers come to say farewell ("Al fato dan legge"). After the soldiers depart, the sisters withdraw, and Don Alfonso expresses his cynicism regarding the fidelity of women.

Scene 3. An anteroom in the house of Fiordiligi and Dorabella. Despina complains about the lot of a lady's maid ("Che vita maledetta"). Dorabella now enters and bewails her unhappy state ("Smanie implacabili"). Despina is unsympathetic; to her, all men are philanderers ("In uomini, in soldati"). She becomes a willing ally when Don Alfonso seeks her aid in duping her mistresses. Ferrando and Guglielmo appear, disguised as Albanian noblemen. At first, the ladies are cold; Fiordiligi protests her devotion to Guglielmo ("Come scoglio"). Guglielmo continues to woo her ardently ("Non siate ritrosi") only to be again rejected. When the ladies depart, the men express their delight, for their women have proved true. Ferrando even grows sentimental about the course of true love ("Un' aura amorosa"). After he and Guglielmo leave, Don Alfonso and Despina confer about the next move.

Scene 4. Once again in their garden, the two ladies are lamenting the absence of their lovers ("Ah che tutta in un momento") when Ferrando and Guglielmo, still disguised, burst in upon them. They say they are ready to die for love and have taken poison. As they go through "death pangs," the women attend them solicitously. A doctor appears —none other than Despina in disguise. Muttering incantations and flourishing a magnet ("Questo è quel pezzo"), the "doctor" revives the stricken men who then proceed to make love to the women more ardently than ever.

Act II, Scene 1. Within the sisters' villa. Despina tries to convince her mistresses that there is much to be gained by being sympathetic to the attentions of the Albanians, and she describes the art of love ("Una donna a quindici anni"). After Despina leaves, the two women begin to agree that, with their lovers away, a flirtation might prove diverting. Dorabella decides to be receptive to Guglielmo while Fiordiligi expresses preference for the disguised Ferrando ("Prenderò quel brunettino"). Having made their decision, they accompany Don Alfonso to the garden, where, as he has informed them, they are to be pleasantly surprised.

Scene 2. The garden. The "Albanians" are in a flower-bedecked boat, surrounded by musicians and guests. Upon the arrival of the women, the two men sing a serenade ("Secondate, aurette amiche"). The four lovers then pair off. Guglielmo and Dorabella exchange pendants and tender words ("Il core vi dono"). Ferrando is less successful. Rejected, he reiterates his passionate feel-ings for Fiordiligi ("Ah! io veggio") and then departs. Fiordiligi is upset, for she is not altogether immune to temptation ("Per pietà, ben mio, perdona"). With the women gone, the soldiers meet and compare experiences. Ferrando, understandably, becomes furious. Learning that only one of the sisters has proved fickle, Don Alfonso reminds his friends that the test is not yet over.

Scene 3. In the house Fiordiligi expresses disapproval of the way her sister has behaved, while Dorabella, in a more practical vein, insists that it is wisest to follow the dictates of love ("E amore un ladroncello"). Fiordiligi is still unconvinced. She decides to pursue an honorable course: to put on an officer's uniform and go off to fight at the side of her lover. Her good intentions vanish with the appearance of Ferrando, still dressed as an Albanian. Determined to avenge himself on Guglielmo and Dorabella, Ferrando intensifies his advances, then threatens to kill himself. Helplessly, Fiordiligi succumbs. This turn of affairs arouses the fury of both soldiers, since it is now apparent that neither of their sweethearts has remained faithful. But Don Alfonso is more philosophic: he advises the soldiers to marry their sweethearts as they originally planned, since in the matters of the heart all women are unpredictable.

Scene 4. A banquet room. The weddings of the "Albanians" and the sisters are about to be performed. Despina, now disguised as a notary, reads the terms of the marriage contracts. At the last moment a drum roll announces the return of the two soldiers from the war. In the confusion that ensues, the "Albanians" disappear and replace their disguises with their uniforms. They feign surprise at the coldness with which their sweethearts greet them and amazement at the signed marriage contracts. Finally, they reveal that they were the "Albanians." Humiliated, the sisters blame Don Alfonso for their troubles. Don Alfonso convinces them that what has happened has been for the best ("V'inganni, ma fu l'inganno") and advises the lovers to patch up their differences.

Così fan tutte was written in 1790, after DON GIOVANNI and before THE MAGIC FLUTE. It represents Mozart at his fullest mastery as an opera composer. In some respects, *Così fan tutte* is the most remarkable of Mozart's operas. Using as his point of departure an inconsequential comedy of love and infidelity—a text which for all its occasional wit is hardly calculated to make exacting demands on a composer—Mozart produced a miraculous score, subtle in characterization, profound in psychological insight, and traversing a wide gamut of feelings. In his other operas he is at times nobler, more passionate, and more eloquent; but he is never nimbler nor is his touch ever surer. With amazing dexterity, he maintains in *Così fan tutte* a subtle balance between comedy and burlesque, sentimentality and mockery, tenderness and broad satire. The music continually catches the nuances of the play, points them up, brings artistic value to trivialities of stage business. This opera is much more than a succession of wonderful arias and ensemble numbers: it is operatic comedy at its best, with music and libretto equal collaborators in a gay adventure.

countertenor, a high-range male voice, which, though reaching the range of a contralto or soprano, nevertheless retains its masculine identity. Some eighteenth-century operas employed countertenors, and so do one or two operas of our own time, including BRITTEN'S A MIDSUMMER NIGHT'S DREAM.

Countess de Coigny, Madeleine's mother (mezzo-soprano) in GIORDANO'S ANDREA CHÉNIER.

Couplets Bachiques, *see* AMIS, L'AMOUR TENDRE ET REVEUR.

Covent Garden, the leading opera house in England. It is situated in London in the heart of a produce market, on the site of what once was a convent garden and afterward of two theaters destroyed by fire. The first of these theaters opened in 1732. From 1734 to 1737, HANDEL was associated with it, presenting there many of his operas including *Ariodante,* ALCINA, and ATALANTA. He directed the first London performance of *Messiah* there in 1743. This theater also witnessed the premiere of THE BEGGAR'S OPERA. After being destroyed by fire in 1808, it was replaced by a new theater on whose stage took place the English premiere of DER FREISCHÜTZ, the world premiere of OBERON, and the English premiere of AUBER'S LE DOMINO NOIR.

Converted into a luxurious and well-equipped opera house, Covent Garden was opened on Apr. 6, 1847, with ROSSINI'S SEMIRAMIDE. For the first time a formal opera company was established at Covent Garden. This was the Royal Italian Opera, directed by Frederick Beale, with Michael Costa as principal conductor. After 1851, under the direction of Frederick Gye—and with such stars as GRISI, LUCCA, PATTI, and VIARDOT—this company achieved international significance. However, the venture collapsed in 1884. In 1888 a new opera company was organized under the management of Sir Augustus HARRIS. Four years later this company became known as the Royal Opera, and in the same year it presented the first performance in England of the entire RING cycle, under the direction of MAHLER. Under Harris, and after him Maurice GRAU, Covent Garden became the home of some of the most brilliant singing of that day, since the company included Lilli LEHMANN, BATTISTINI, MELBA, CALVÉ, TERNINA, the DE RESZKES, and BISPHAM. During this period, in 1894, MASSENET'S LA NAVARRAISE received its world premiere.

A marked decline of artistic standards took place between 1900 and 1914. Except for a memorable cycle of WAGNER under Hans RICHTER's direction in 1908, the world premiere of LEONI'S L'ORACOLO in 1905, and some stimulating performances under Sir Thomas BEECHAM in 1910 (particularly of ELEKTRA and A VILLAGE ROMEO AND JULIET), presentations at Covent Garden were substandard. During World War I the opera house was closed. It reopened in 1919 for the first of two summer seasons of opera under Beecham. Several different opera companies then occupied Covent Garden for winter seasons, among them the Beecham Opera Company, the CARL ROSA COMPANY, and the British Opera Company. In 1924, the operatic activity at Covent Garden assumed an international character. The German Opera Syndicate presented a season of German opera with Bruno WALTER directing some of the foremost artists from German and Austrian opera houses; this was followed by a season of Italian and French operas with artists from Italy and France. The international character of the performances continued from 1933 to 1939 under the artistic direction of Sir Thomas Beecham.

Once again war closed Covent Garden in 1940, when the auditorium was converted into a ballroom. After World War II the Covent Garden Opera Trust was created under the chairmanship of Lord Keynes. The theater reopened on Feb. 20, 1946, with a performance of PURCELL's THE FAIRY QUEEN. Karl Rankl became music director. During the five years he held this post (1946–1951) he led twenty-two of the thirty operas produced. He and his successors as musical director—Rafael KUBELIK (1955–1958), Georg SOLTI (1958–1969), and Colin DAVIS (since 1969) —developed a repertory and standard of performance which placed Covent Garden with the world's foremost opera houses, a fact officially recognized by the Queen when in 1968 she conferred upon it the title of "Royal Opera." (Covent Garden had once before carried the title of Royal when it was known as Royal Italian Opera, Covent Garden.)

Among the most distinguished revivals, novelties, and new productions of standard repertory since World War II were the following: BENVENUTO CELLINI; LE COQ D'OR; THE DAUGHTER OF THE REGIMENT (with Joan SUTHERLAND); DON CARLOS; FIDELIO (under KLEMPERER); *Der Freischütz; Hamlet* by SEARLE (first British mounting); JENUFA; THE MAKROPOULOS AFFAIR (an English premiere); MOSES UND ARON (an English premiere, Solti conducting); the *Ring* cycle (which under Solti's direction achieved an international renown second only to that enjoyed by BAYREUTH); SALOME (with Dali's scenery); LES TROYENS; and WOZZECK.

The first new opera introduced at Covent Garden after World War II was THE OLYMPIANS, given on Sept. 29, 1949. Notable world premieres since then have included BILLY BUDD (in both its original and revised versions), GLORIANA, KING PRIAM, THE MIDSUMMER MARRIAGE (in both its original and revised versions), and TROILUS AND CRESSIDA.

Covent Garden opened its 1969–70 season on Sept. 17, 1969, with a new production of *Les Troyens,* Colin Davis conducting. It was given, probably for the first time, in its entirety, as BERLIOZ conceived it. In Dec., 1970, Covent Garden presented the world premiere of Sir Michael TIPPETT's *Knot Garden.*

Cradle Will Rock, The, a musical play in two acts by BLITZSTEIN. Libretto by the composer. Premiere: New York City, June 15, 1937. The story takes place in a night court and concerns the efforts of steelworkers to form a union and the attempt of employers and the most influential people of the town to smash it. Mr. Mister, who controls Steeltown, forms a committee of leading citizens to attack the workers' effort, but the union defies these attacks and ultimately proves triumphant.

With *The Cradle Will Rock,* American proletarian opera emerges. The early history of this opera was both dramatic and turbulent. It was written for the Federal Theater, a unit of the WPA. The radical theme of the play impelled several government officials to demand its withdrawal. Just before the opening, and with the first-night audience gathering at the theater, the Federal Theater announced that the production was canceled. A frantic last-minute maneuver transferred both the production and audience to a near-by theater. Denied the support of the Federal Theater, the troupe could not avail itself of costumes, scenery, or orchestra. Consequently the play was performed on a bare stage, with performers dressed in street clothes. The composer performed his score on a piano. Between scenes, he explained to the audience what was about to happen on the stage. This simple, straightforward way of presenting the work added to its force and emotional impact.

Blitzstein's score is in a polyglot style, combining as it does popular tunes, blues, torch songs, parodies, patter songs, chorales, recitatives, mock arias, and occasionally passages in which a modern harmonic language is employed.

The Cradle Will Rock was revived in a concert performance in 1947, performed by the New York City Symphony under Leonard BERNSTEIN. It was fully staged for the first time anywhere on Feb. 11, 1960, by the NEW YORK CITY OPERA.

Credo a una possanza arcana, Chénier's aria in Act II of GIORDANO's ANDREA CHÉNIER expressing his refusal to escape from France and from the threat of imprisonment by the revolutionaries.

Credo in un Dio crudel, Iago's aria voicing the contempt and cynicism with which he regards both man and life, in Act II of VERDI's OTELLO.

Crescentini, Girolamo, CASTRATO soprano. Born Urbania, Italy, Feb. 2, 1762; died Naples, Apr. 24, 1846. He was one of the most celebrated castrati of his generation. He made his debut in Rome in 1783 after having completed vocal studies with Gibelli. His first important engagement took place in Leghorn in CHERUBINI's *Artaserse.* Subsequent successes in Europe's leading capitals earned him the sobriquet of "Orfeo Italiano." CIMAROSA wrote for him the opera *Gli Orazi e Curiazi,* produced in Venice in 1796. During appearances in Vienna in 1805, he was appointed professor of voice to the royal family. In the same year Napoleon decorated him with the Iron Cross and engaged him to sing in Paris between 1806 and 1812. His voice was affected by the northern climate. He returned to Italy, where in 1816 he

became professor of singing at the Royal Conservatory in Naples.

Crespel, Antonia's father (bass) in OFFENBACH's THE TALES OF HOFFMANN, Act III.

Crespin, Regina, soprano. Born Marseilles, France, Mar. 23, 1927. She attended the Paris Conservatory, where she attracted the interest of the management of the PARIS OPÉRA. Following her operatic debut in Mulhouse, France, in 1950 as ELSA, she made her debut at the Paris Opéra in the same role and at the OPÉRA-COMIQUE as TOSCA, both in 1951. Beginning in 1956, she sang leading dramatic soprano roles at the Paris Opéra, including that in the world premiere of POULENC's LES DIALOGUES DES CARMÉLITES in 1957. In 1958 she was heard as KUNDRY at BAYREUTH. A year later she made her LA SCALA debut in a revival of PIZZETTI's FEDRA and appeared at the VIENNA STATE OPERA as SIEGLINDE. This was followed by appearances at the GLYNDEBOURNE FESTIVAL and at the TEATRO COLÓN in Buenos Aires. At the latter house she sang in FAURÉ's PÉNÉLOPE. Her American debut took place with the CHICAGO LYRIC OPERA on Oct. 26, 1962, as Tosca, followed less than a month later, on Nov. 19, by her first appearance at the METROPOLITAN OPERA as the Marschallin in DER ROSENKAVALIER. Besides her seasonal appearances at the Paris Opéra and the Metropolitan Opera, she has been heard regularly in most of the world's leading opera houses and opera festivals. Herbert von KARAJAN selected her to sing Brünnhilde in his production of DIE WALKÜRE that he first presented at SALZBURG, during Easter of 1967, and later in the year at the Metropolitan Opera.

Cressida, daughter (soprano) of the high priest, Calkas, and sweetheart of Prince Troilus in WALTON's opera TROILUS AND CRESSIDA, a role created by Magda LASZLO.

Cricket on the Hearth, The (Das Heimchen am Herd), opera in three acts by GOLDMARK. Libretto by A. M. Willner, based on the story of the same name by

Charles DICKENS. Premiere: Vienna Opera, Mar. 21, 1896. The cricket is the guiding spirit of an English household in the early nineteenth century and extricates its members from various personal difficulties.

Crime and Punishment, see DOSTOYEVSKY; RASKOLNIKOFF.

Crimi, Giulio, tenor. Born Catania, Italy, May 10, 1885; died Rome, Oct. 29, 1939. He created the roles of Luigi in IL TABARRO and Rinuccio in GIANNI SCHICCHI (two of the three operas in PUCCINI's trilogy, IL TRITTICO), and Paolo in ZANDONAI's FRANCESCA DA RIMINI. He made his debut in Treviso in 1912, following this with his first appearance at COVENT GARDEN in 1914 (in LA WALLY) and creating for England the role of Avito in L'AMORE DEI TRE RE. His debut at the METROPOLITAN OPERA took place on Nov. 13, 1918, as RADAMES. He remained with the company for four years, the period in which he participated in the world premiere of *Il trittico*. Between 1916 and 1918 and again between 1922 and 1924 he was a member of the CHICAGO OPERA. After returning to Italy he appeared in Rome and Milan until his retirement in 1928, following which he taught voice.

Cristoforo Colombo, opera in four acts and epilogue by FRANCHETTI. Libretto by ILLICA. Premiere: Genoa, Oct. 6, 1892. American premiere: Philadelphia, Nov. 30, 1913. Franchetti wrote this opera to commemorate the four-hundredth anniversary of the discovery of America by Columbus. In Illica's text Queen Isabella provides Columbus with royal jewels to finance his expedition to the new world. Aboard the "Santa Maria," Columbus' enemy, Roldano, incites the sailors to mutiny. The situation is saved by the sight of land. Roldano continues to intrigue against Columbus until he succeeds in discrediting him and having him sent back to Spain in chains. In the epilogue, Columbus commits suicide at the tomb of Isabella.

Crobyle, a slave girl (soprano) in MASSENET's THAÏS.

crociato in Egitto, Il (The Crusader in Egypt), opera in two acts by MEYERBEER. Libretto by ROSSI. Premiere: Teatro la Fenice, Mar. 7, 1824. This is the last and most successful of Meyerbeer's Italian operas.

Crooks, Richard Alexander, tenor. Born Trenton, N.J., June 26, 1900. He made appearances as a boy singer and continued to appear publicly up to the time of World War I. After the war he studied with Frank La Forge and Sydney H. Bourne. In 1922 he made ten appearances with the New York Symphony Society. His opera debut took place in Hamburg, in 1927, in TOSCA. His American debut took place in Philadelphia, in the same opera, on Nov. 27, 1930. On Feb. 25, 1933, he made his first appearance at the METROPOLITAN OPERA in MANON and was acclaimed. He remained with the Metropolitan for the next decade; after leaving, he specialized in concert appearances, radio concerts, and performances in oratorios. He retired in 1946.

Cross, Milton, radio announcer. Born New York City, Apr. 16, 1897. He attended the Institute of Musical Art, after which he embarked on a career as singer. In 1922 he became a radio announcer. He has been the announcer and narrator for all the broadcasts of the METROPOLITAN OPERA for over three decades. He is the author of *Milton Cross' Complete Stories of the Great Operas* (1947), and co-author (with David Ewen) of *Encyclopedia of Great Composers and Their Music* (1953, thoroughly revised and expanded in 1969). In 1969 Cross received the Handel Medal, the highest award New York City can bestow in the arts, from Mayor Lindsay, who described Cross as "a pioneer in the communication arts."

Crown, a stevedore (bass) in GERSHWIN's PORGY AND BESS.

Crozier, Eric, writer and producer. Born London, Nov. 14, 1914. With E. M. Forster he wrote the librettos for BILLY BUDD and BERKELEY's *Ruth* and, without collaboration, for ALBERT HERRING and

LET'S MAKE AN OPERA. He was one of the founders of the ENGLISH OPERA GROUP and the ALDEBURGH FESTIVAL. As producer he was responsible for the world and American premieres of PETER GRIMES at SADLER'S WELLS and TANGLEWOOD respectively, and THE RAPE OF LUCRETIA at GLYNDEBOURNE. He also produced THE BARTERED BRIDE at Sadler's Wells in a new English adaptation prepared with John Cross.

Crucible, The, opera in three acts by WARD. Libretto by Bernard Stambler, based on MILLER's play of the same name. Premiere: New York City Opera, Oct. 26, 1961.

The opera, like Miller's famous play, has for its theme the Salem witch trials in New England in 1692 which brought to the surface latent lusts, hatred, superstitions, jealousies, and bigotry among the Puritans. When some hysterical girls concoct a story that they had consorted with the devil in a ritual and that the devil has come to take Salem over, the terror-stricken Puritans give way to panic and persecute suspected evil-doers. These include John and Elizabeth Proctor, for their maid, Abigail (who once had an affair with Proctor), spreads the word that her mistress is a witch. Elizabeth Proctor is punished with death and so is her husband, when he refuses to sign a confession that he has had communion with the devil and had been involved in witchcraft.

Since Ward places considerable emphasis on the voice in projecting the powerful drama—mainly recitatives, which Irving Kolodin described as "a kind of melodic sing-song"—he uses only a small orchestra (paired winds, four horns, some strings, and percussion). The vocal parts are used to project the story, while the orchestra contributes a discreet background and at times is called upon to interject a commentary. On occasion, when Ward permits his melodic line to expand, his melody assumes the character of New England psalms.

The Crucible received the Pulitzer Prize in music and a special citation from the New York Music Critics' Cir-

cle. In 1962 the opera received its German premiere in Wiesbaden. On that occasion Ward himself conducted, becoming the first American ever to conduct the premiere of an American opera in Germany.

Cruda sorte, Isabella's opening air in Act I of ROSSINI's L'ITALIANA IN ALGERI, in which she reveals her confidence in being able to capture the heart of any man she wishes.

Crudel, perchè finora, duet of Susanna and Almaviva, in which she upbraids him for being so cruel to her, in Act III of MOZART's THE MARRIAGE OF FIGARO.

Csárdás, see KLÄNGE DER HEIMAT.

Cui, César, composer. Born Vilna, Russia, Jan. 18, 1835; died St. Petersburg, Mar. 24, 1918. A member of the Russian nationalist school, The Five, he wrote ten operas, in some of which he tried to realize the artistic goals set by the nationalists. His first important work in any form was the opera *The Captive in the Caucasus* (1859). An earlier work of the same year, *The Mandarin's Son,* was a failure. His third opera, *William Ratcliffe,* was a major success when introduced in St. Petersburg in 1869. Later operas: *Angelo* (1876); *Le Filibustier* (1894); *The Saracen* (1899); *A Feast in Time of Plague* (1901); *Mlle. Fifi* (1903); *Matteo Falcone* (1908); *The Captain's Daughter* (1911). Cui had a pronounced melodic gift, but he was too derivative to provide sustained interest; all his operas have lapsed into oblivion.

Cunning Little Vixen (Příhody lišby bystroušky), opera in three acts by JANÁČEK. Libretto by Rudolf Tesnohlidek. Premiere: Brünn, Bohemia, Nov. 6, 1924. American premiere: New York City, May 7, 1964. This is a fairy tale, based on a folk fable, in which animals are made to behave like human beings and vice versa. The many animal roles are assigned to sopranos capable of high pitches. The central character, the cunning vixen, is a sensual and coquettish woman symbolizing motherhood. The opera is consistently lyrical and bucolic, betraying the composer's love of nature and animals. It was revived by the HANOVER OPERA in 1968 and by the COLOGNE OPERA, as well as in opera houses in Czechoslovakia in 1969.

Curlew River, a church parable in one act by BRITTEN. Libretto by William Plomer. Premiere: Aldeburgh Festival, Eng., June 13, 1964. American premiere: Katonah, N.Y., June 26, 1966. This is the first of three stage "parables" by Britten intended for performance in church with limited forces. It was followed by THE BURNING FIERY FURNACE and THE PRODIGAL SON. Britten was stimulated into writing *Curlew River* by attending a performance of a Noh play in Japan, a stylized religious presentation. He decided to write a work, similar in aim, but in terms of the Western world. His librettist adapted for him *Sumidagawa,* an early fifteenth-century miracle play. Each role was performed by monks, who enter the church chanting plainsong. After they take their place on stage, seven instrumentalists (also monks) join the chorus. An abbot now announces that there will take place a performance of a miracle that had actually occurred. The parable then describes how a demented mother goes in search of her son who had been kidnapped across Curlew River. What she finds, however, is his grave, which becomes for her a shrine. Her sanity is restored when she receives a vision of her boy in front of her. The monks now leave the stage and march in a procession out of the church, once again chanting plainsong.

Curra, Leonora's maid (mezzo-soprano) in VERDI'S LA FORZA DEL DESTINO.

Curtin, Phyllis (born Smith), soprano. Born Clarksburg, W.Va., Dec. 3, 1927. She attended Wellesley College, majoring in political science but also began to study voice in her junior year. Upon graduating from Wellesley, she continued to study voice and in 1946 made appearances at TANGLEWOOD in Lenox, Mass., and with the New England Opera Theatre, where she was soon assigned feature roles. In 1953 she made her debut with the NEW YORK CITY OPERA

in the American premiere of EINEM'S DER PROZESS (*The Trial*), in which she sang three female roles; she achieved a major success with this company a year later as SALOME. Early in 1955 she created the title role in FLOYD'S SUSANNAH, and later the same year she assumed the title role of MILHAUD'S MÉDÉE at the Festival of Creative Arts at Brandeis University in Waltham, Mass. She subsequently created the principal female roles in two later Floyd operas, Cathy in WUTHERING HEIGHTS at the Santa Fe Opera Festival and Celia in THE PASSION OF JONATHAN WADE with the New York City Opera. Her European debut took place at the World's Fair in Brussels in 1958 in *Susannah.* In 1960–61 she was a principal soprano of the VIENNA STATE OPERA, besides making guest appearances with other European companies, including LA SCALA. She appeared as Cressida in the New York premiere of WALTON'S TROILUS AND CRESSIDA with the New York City Opera. On Nov. 4, 1961, she made her debut at the METROPOLITAN OPERA as Fiordiligi in COSÌ FAN TUTTE.

curtain tune, *see* ACT TUNE.

Curzio, Don, a lawyer (tenor) in MOZART'S THE MARRIAGE OF FIGARO, a role created by Michael KELLY.

Cuzzoni, Francesca, soprano. Born Parma, c. 1700; died Bologna, 1770. After studying voice with Lanzi and making appearances in Venice, she made her debut at the Italian Opera in London in HANDEL'S *Ottone* on Jan. 12, 1723. She enjoyed considerable eminence in London until her bitter rivalry with Faustina BORDONI caused a scandal. She abandoned London for Venice, but was back in England in 1734 to continue making operatic appearances for several seasons. Her career then went into such a sharp decline that she was for a time imprisoned for debt in Holland. She spent her last years in Bologna in utter poverty, supporting herself by making buttons.

Cyrano de Bergerac, (1) a poetic play by Edmond Rostand centering around the poet-soldier Cyrano, who is in love with the beautiful Roxanne. Disfigured by a huge nose which makes him unattractive to women, he makes love to Roxanne through the presentable person of Christian, writing his love letters and making his love speeches. Only when Cyrano is dying does Roxanne realize that Christian has been a front for the poet and that she is really in love with Cyrano.

(2) Opera in four acts by ALFANO. Libretto by Henri Cain, based on Rostand's play. Premiere: Teatro Reale, Rome, Jan. 22, 1936.

(3) Opera in four acts by Walter DAMROSCH. Libretto by W. J. Henderson, based on the Rostand play. Premiere: Metropolitan Opera, Feb. 27, 1913.

Czar's Bride, The, opera in three acts by RIMSKY-KORSAKOV. Libretto by I. F. Tyumenev, based on the play of the same name by Lev Alexandrovich Mey. Premiere: Moscow Opera, Nov. 3, 1899. American premiere: San Francisco, Jan. 9, 1922. Martha, who has been selected by Czar Ivan for his bride, is loved by two other men. One of them, whose love she returns, is the boyar, Lykov. The other, Griaznoy, contrives to win her love by having her drink a love potion; but his mistress substitutes poison. When Martha lies dying in the Kremlin, she learns that her beloved, Lykov, has been beheaded by the Czar on suspicion of having poisoned her. Martha goes mad. Griaznoy kills his mistress. Martha's second-act air, "In Novgorod," and her third-act mad scene ("Ivan Sergeivich, come into the garden") are arias by which this opera is most often represented at concerts.

Czar Has Himself Photographed, The (Der Zar lässt sich photographiren), opera in one act by WEILL. Libretto by Georg KAISER. Premiere: Leipzig, Feb. 18, 1928. This was the first Weill opera in which he made effective use of American jazz idioms. Satirical both in text and in music, it achieved considerable success when first produced, playing in some eighty German theaters soon after its Leipzig premiere.

D

da capo aria, a three-part aria in which the third section, after a contrasting second section, is a repetition with embellishment of the first. The form was developed by the Venetian and Neapolitan schools of opera composers.

Dafne (Italian form of Daphne), (1) in Greek mythology the daughter of Peneus (Thessalian river god) who is pursued by Apollo and is saved when her mother, Gaea, transforms her into a laurel tree. This story was used extensively by the earliest composers of operas. Besides those listed below, operas on this theme were written by CACCINI in 1600, the score of which has been lost; Marco da Gagliano in 1608; and Alessandro SCARLATTI in 1700.

(2) Opera in prologue and six scenes by PERI. Libretto by Ottavio RINUCCINI. Premiere: Corsi Palace, Florence, 1597. This is the first opera ever written. Peri's music has not survived.

(3) Opera by SCHÜTZ. Libretto by Martin Opitz, with material from the Rinuccini libretto. Premiere: Torgau, Ger., Apr. 23, 1627. This work is regarded as the first German opera, since it is the first known opera set to a German text. It was written for the

wedding of Princess Sophie of Saxony and George Landgrave of Hesse. The music has been lost.

See also DAPHNE.

Da Gama, Vasco, officer in Portuguese navy (tenor), in MEYERBEER'S L'AFRICAINE, a role created by Emilio NAUDIN.

Dai campi, dai prati, Faust's aria in Act I of BOITO'S MEFISTOFELE, in praise of virtue.

Daland, a Norwegian sea captain (bass) in WAGNER'S DER FLIEGENDE HOLLÄNDER.

d'Albert, Eugène, composer and pianist. Born Glasgow, Apr. 10, 1864; died Riga, Latvia, Mar. 3, 1932. He entered the National School of Music in London in his twelfth year. Two years later he made his debut as pianist. In 1881 he won the Mendelssohn Prize, which enabled him to study with Hans RICHTER in Vienna and LISZT in Weimar. He lived mostly in Germany but toured extensively. He was a prolific composer. His most successful opera was TIEFLAND, introduced in Prague on Nov. 15, 1903. *Flauto Solo,* heard first in Prague on Nov. 12, 1905, was well received and so was *Die toten Augen,* first heard in Dresden on Mar. 5, 1916, and introduced in the United States in 1923. D'Albert held several musical posts, including that of director of the Hochschule für Musik in Berlin. His most important operas besides those already mentioned: *Der Rubin* (1893); *Die Abreise* (1898); *Kain* (1900); *Der Golem* (1926); *Mister Wu* (1932).

Dalibor, opera in three acts by SMETANA. Libretto by Joseph Wenzig. Premiere: National Theatre, Prague, May 16, 1868. American premiere: Chicago, Apr. 13, 1924. In fifteenth-century Prague, Dalibor (tenor), captain of the guards of the King of Bohemia, is accused of being an insurgent and is imprisoned. Milada (soprano), in love with him, heads a band that storms the prison and frees him. In the flight, Milada is fatally wounded and dies in the arms of her lover, who then stabs himself.

Several arias by Dalibor are notable in this score, including his first-act aria about his friendship for Zdeněk and

his admiration of Zdeněk's violin playing ("When my Zdeněk") and the poignant arias in the second and third acts respectively, "O Zdeněk" and "Ah, where is the spell?" The second act boasts a delightful chorus in "Indeed the world is very gay."

Dalila (Delilah), the High Priest's daughter (mezzo-soprano) in SAINT-SAËN'S SAMSON ET DALILA.

Dalis, Irene, mezzo-soprano. Born San José, Cal., Oct. 8, 1929. She studied voice with Edyth WALKER and Paul ALTHOUSE and, in Milan, with Otto Müller. She made her opera debut in Oldenburg, Ger., in 1953 as Princess EBOLI. In 1954 she became a member of the Städtische Oper in Berlin (BERLIN DEUTSCHE STAATSOPER). Her debut at the METROPOLITAN OPERA took place on Mar. 16, 1957, as Princess Eboli. She has remained with this company since then, appearing in principal mezzo-soprano roles. She has also appeared extensively in major European opera houses and festivals, including COVENT GARDEN in 1958 and the BAYREUTH FESTIVAL in 1961.

Dal labbro il canto estasïato vola, the song of Oberon (Fenton), in Act III, Scene 2, of VERDI'S FALSTAFF.

Dallapiccola, Luigi, composer. Born Pisinio, Istria, Feb. 3, 1904. Having early come to the decision to become a composer, he studied piano and harmony in Istria before attending the Cherubini Conservatory in Florence from which he was graduated in piano in 1924 and composition in 1931. Three years later he was appointed professor of composition. Meanwhile he had gained recognition as composer with a Partita for Orchestra, heard at the festival of the International Society for Contemporary Music in Florence in 1934. Significant choral and instrumental works brought him to the forefront of the younger progressive Italian school. He was one of the first Italians to compose with twelve-tone techniques, using them flexibly until about 1950, when he became more faithful to the dodecaphonic practices as established by Webern. Dallapiccola's first opera was VOLO DI NOTTE, based on the book of St. Exupéry; it was produced in Florence on May 18, 1940. This was followed in 1944 by IL PRIGIONIERO. In 1968 ULISSE received its world premiere at the BERLIN DEUTSCHE STAATSOPER.

Dalla Rizza, Gilda, soprano. Born Verona, Oct. 12, 1892. PUCCINI wrote the role of Magda in LA RONDINE for her. Her vocal studies ended, she made her debut in Bologna in 1910 as Charlotte in WERTHER. Puccini became impressed with her talent and not only wrote the part of Magda for her but had her create the roles of LAURETTA and ANGELICA in Italy and at COVENT GARDEN. TOSCANINI engaged her for LA SCALA in 1923, where she appeared in world premieres of operas by MASCAGNI, ZANDONAI, and others. She went into retirement in 1939 (from which she emerged briefly in 1942 to participate in the Puccini festival at Vincenza by appearing as Angelica), following which she taught singing.

Dallas Civic Opera Company, one of the four opera companies in Texas, and artistically the most significant, even though it offers only three operas a year. It maintains the highest standards of performance and is consistent in its fresh approaches to repertory, staging, and casting. It was founded in 1957 by Lawrence Kelly and Nicola Rescigno, presenting operas at the State Fair Music Hall. Among its notable productions have been several by Franco ZEFFIRELLI: LA TRAVIATA (in which Montserrat CABALLÉ made her American stage debut); HANDEL's ALCINA (with Joan SUTHERLAND in her American debut); and DON GIOVANNI (starring Elena Suliotis, with which the company initiated its 1959 season). Other noteworthy productions included a freshly conceived mounting of RIGOLETTO, in which Alberto Fassini as director and Ferdinando Scarfiotti as designer both made their American debuts, and revivals of Handel's GIULIO CESARE, CHERUBINI's MÉDÉE, and DONIZETTI's ANNA BOLENA. In 1966 the company visited Mexico City with

performances of *La traviata* and *Don Giovanni.*

Dalla stanze, ove Lucia, the aria of Raimondo in Act III of DONIZETTI's LUCIA DI LAMMERMOOR, in which he reveals that Lucia has gone mad.

Dalla sua pace, Ottavio's tender aria in Act I, Scene 3, of MOZART's DON GIOVANNI, in which he reveals that thinking of the woman he loves is the only peace he can find.

Dall' ondoso periglio, Caesar's air in HANDEL's GIULIO CESARE.

Dalmorès, Charles, tenor. Born Nancy, France, Jan. 1, 1871; died Hollywood, Cal., Dec. 6, 1939. He made his opera debut at the Théâtre des Arts in Rouen on Oct. 6, 1899. He subsequently appeared for six seasons at the THÉÂTRE DE LA MONNAIE and for seven at COVENT GARDEN. His American debut took place at the MANHATTAN OPERA HOUSE on Dec. 7, 1906, in FAUST. He remained with the Manhattan company four years, specializing in French roles and creating for America the roles of Julien in LOUISE and Jean Gaussin in SAPHO. In 1910 he joined the Chicago-Philadelphia Opera and in 1917 the CHICAGO OPERA, where he essayed for the first time the roles of PARSIFAL and TRISTAN.

d'Alvarez, Marguerite, contralto. Born Liverpool, Eng., of Peruvian parentage, about 1886; died Alassio, Italy, Oct. 18, 1953. She attended the Brussels Conservatory, after which she made her debut in Rouen, France, as DALILA. She made her American debut with the MANHATTAN OPERA on Aug. 30, 1909, as FIDÈS. After a season in New York, she helped inaugurate Hammerstein's London Opera in 1911, being especially well received in HÉRODIADE and LOUISE. She subsequently appeared at COVENT GARDEN and other leading European opera houses and in America with the CHICAGO OPERA and the BOSTON OPERA. In 1944 she was seen in a motion picture, *Till We Meet Again.* She wrote an autobiography, *Forsaken Altars* (1954).

Dame aux camélias, La, novel by the younger Alexandre DUMAS, the source of VERDI's LA TRAVIATA. Also based on this novel is Hamilton Forrest's *Camille* (1930).

Dame blanche, La (The White Lady), OPÉRA COMIQUE in three acts by BOIELDIEU. Libretto by Eugène SCRIBE, based on two romances by Sir Walter SCOTT, *The Monastery* and *Guy Mannering*. Premiere: Opéra-Comique, Dec. 10, 1825. American premiere: New York City, Aug. 24, 1827 (probable).

La Dame blanche came comparatively late in the composer's career, but when it arrived it proved to be his greatest triumph. It brought the composer a handsome government pension; it was widely parodied and widely performed throughout all of Europe.

"La Dame blanche" is a ghost haunting a Scottish castle in the mid-eighteenth century. The Earl of Avenell, Julius (tenor), having fallen into disrepute, instructs his steward, Gaveston (bass), to conceal his jewels within this castle. Gaveston tries to gain hold of this treasure by purchasing the castle but is thwarted when the Earl (appearing disguised as George Brown) and Gaveston's ward, Anna (soprano), outbid him. It is then that Anna reveals that she is the "white lady" who has been haunting the castle. The Earl and Anna, having reached the decision to get married, decide to make the castle their permanent home.

The overture is a familiar item at "pop" and café-house concerts. It opens with a melody taken from the first-act finale and includes a quotation from a first-act ballad sung by the "white lady," a drinking song, and a quotation of the famous Scottish air, "Robin Adair," which is heard within the opera in both the first and third acts.

The best vocal numbers include two sung by the Earl of Avenell, a CAVATINA, "Viens, gentille dame," and his revery with chorus, "Chantez, joyeux ménestral."

Damian, Werner Kirchhofer's rival (tenor) for Marie, in NESSLER'S DER TROMPETER VON SÄKKINGEN.

Damnation of Faust, The (Le Damnation de Faust), dramatic cantata or "legend" in four parts by BERLIOZ. Libretto by the composer and Almire Gandonnière, based on Gérard de NERVAL's version of GOETHE's drama. Premiere: Opéra-Comique, Dec. 6, 1846 (concert version); Monte Carlo, May 18, 1893 (staged). American premiere: New York City, Dec. 7, 1906 (staged).

The first part is in three scenes and is set on a plain in Hungary. Faust (tenor) is alone in the fields at sunrise, brooding about the sweetness of solitude and the joys of spring. He finds alien to this peaceful setting the dancing and singing of peasants (Scene 2). In the third scene, Faust sees an army on the march, a section that ends with the popular and stirring *Hungarian* or *Rákóczy March* so often played at symphony concerts.

The second part begins with a scene in North Germany. Faust, in his study, is so weary of life that he is ready to take poison. He hears a chorus sing an Easter hymn which reminds him of his past and gives him a new will to live. The scene that follows brings Méphistophélès (baritone), who promises to show Faust new pleasures. They come to Auerbach's Cellar in Leipzig (Scene 3), where students sing a drinking song. One of the revelers, Brander (bass), entertains the guests with a jolly "Song of the Rat" ("Certain rat, dans une cuisine"). Méphistophélès also contributes a mocking tune, the familiar "Song of the Flea" or "Chanson de la puce" ("Une puce gentille"). Faust, bored, is then brought by Méphistophélès to the woods and meadows on the banks of the Elbe (Scene 4). Sylphs lull Faust to sleep. As he dreams of Marguerite (soprano), they dance around him (Dance of the Sylphs). When Faust awakens, Méphistophélès takes him to Marguerite, while soldiers and students join voices in a dramatic final chorus (Scene 5).

In the first scene of Part III, Faust enters Marguerite's chamber and is enraptured at the sight of it. The next scene continues in that chamber. Méphistophélès comes to warn Faust to hide since Marguerite is approaching. When she appears (Scene 3) she prepares for bed as she sings a folklike air, "Ballad of the King of Thulé" ("Autrefois un roi de Thulé"). In the fourth scene, Méphistophélès calls upon the will-o'-the-wisps to beguile Marguerite with a vision of Faust. After they have performed a minuet (Minuet of the Will-o'-the-Wisps), Méphistophélès sings a mocking serenade about man's deceit ("Devant la maison"). The fifth scene is dominated by the first meeting of Faust and Marguerite as they exchange tender words of love. Méphistophélès intrudes in the sixth scene to warn them that the neighbors are suspicious, and the part ends with the sorrowful parting of the lovers.

In the last part, Marguerite gives voice to her sorrow, convinced that Faust has deserted her ("D'amour, l'ardente flamme"). From a distance come the voices of students and soldiers. The second scene is Faust's invocation to nature ("Nature immense"), while in the third, Méphistophélès informs him that Marguerite accidentally killed her mother with poison and that Marguerite, now in prison, is sentenced to die. Méphistophélès offers to help Faust rescue Marguerite, but only if he signs a parchment, which he does. Faust and Méphistophélès then speed off on two black horses (Scene 4) —not to Marguerite, as Faust expected, but to Hell; as they ride they pass peasants intoning the solemn music of a "Sanctus." In Hell, Faust and Méphistophélès are confronted by devils and the damned souls of Pandemonium (Scene 5), all singing in unison a mad ditty made up of unintelligible syllables. Faust has lost his soul. The work ends in Heaven with a chorus of angels welcoming the forgiven Marguerite.

The role of Faust was created by Jean DE RESZKE.

D'amor sull' ali rosee, Leonora's prayer that her love for Manrico will sustain him through his suffering in prison, in Act IV, Scene 1, of VERDI'S IL TROVATORE.

D'amour, l'ardente flamme, Marguerite's grief that Faust has deserted her, in Part IV of BERLIOZ' THE DAMNATION OF FAUST.

Damrosch, Leopold, conductor. Born Posen, Ger., Oct. 22, 1832; died New York City, Feb. 15, 1885. He was the first conductor of German opera at the METROPOLITAN OPERA. In Germany he led the Breslau Philharmonic Society and was a friend of WAGNER's. In 1862 he organized and led the Breslau Orchesterverein. He came to New York in 1871, where he founded the Oratorio Society of New York and the New York Symphony Society, conducting both organizations up to the time of his death. As a guest conductor of the New York Philharmonic Orchestra during 1876–77 he gave the American premiere of the third act of SIEGFRIED. With the New York Symphony he led the American premieres of BERLIOZ' THE DAMNATION OF FAUST and the first act of DIE WALKÜRE. In 1884 Damrosch was chosen principal conductor of the Metropolitan Opera, which was then emphasizing German opera and operas presented in the German language. Damrosch led all the performances—operas by BEETHOVEN, WEBER, WAGNER, and MOZART as well as representative French and Italian operas —in German. Henry Krehbiel spoke of the Damrosch regime as "the beginning of an effort to establish grand opera in New York on the lines which obtain in Continental Europe." On Feb. 10, 1885, Damrosch was stricken with pneumonia. His young son Walter, called upon to assume his father's post, conducted the performance of Feb. 11. The opera was TANNHÄUSER. Leopold Damrosch died four days later.

Damrosch, Walter, conductor and composer. Born Breslau, Ger., Jan. 30, 1862; died New York City, Dec. 22, 1950. He was a major influence in the development of musical culture in America, and he played a significant role in the early history of Wagnerian performances in America. The son of Leopold DAMROSCH, he was nine years old when his father came with his family to America. After preliminary music study with his father and several other teachers, Walter Damrosch returned to Germany to study with Felix Draeske and Hans von BÜLOW. Back in New York, Walter Damrosch helped his father prepare the rehearsals of the New York Symphony, the Oratorio Society, and the German season at the METROPOLITAN OPERA. When Leopold died in 1885, Walter took over his father's various conductorial activities, including the direction of operas at the Metropolitan Opera. In 1885, he enlisted the services of Anton SEIDL to help him carry on his labors at the Metropolitan. He also recruited leading European singers, including Lilli LEHMANN, Emil FISCHER, and Max ALVARY. During the 1885–86 season— Damrosch's first as a full-fledged conductor at the Metropolitan—nine operas were performed, including the American premieres of RIENZI, DIE MEISTERSINGER, and THE QUEEN OF SHEBA. Damrosch remained principal conductor of German opera at the Metropolitan for the next five seasons, during which period he led the American premieres of BRÜLL'S DAS GOLDENE KREUZ, GOLDMARK'S Merlin, and CORNELIUS' THE BARBER OF BAGDAD. The vogue for German opera at the Metropolitan went into a decline after 1890. In 1894 Damrosch founded his own company for the purpose of presenting German operas (see DAMROSCH OPERA COMPANY). After the dissolution of this company he once again became a conductor at the Metropolitan Opera. Serving there in the seasons of 1900–01 and 1901–02, he led all the German operas, including the complete RING cycle. In 1903 Damrosch reorganized the New York Symphony Society, establishing it on a permanent basis. When he retired from the concert field in 1926, he devoted himself to radio work. He was a pioneer in broadcasting symphonic music and music-education programs for children. He appeared as himself in two motion pictures: The Star Maker and Carnegie Hall. He wrote four operas:

The Scarlet Letter (1896); Cyrano de Bergerac (1913, revised 1939); The Man Without a Country (1937); The Opera Cloak (1942).

Damrosch Opera Company, The, a company organized by Walter DAMROSCH in 1894 to present German operas. It was an important force in developing a consciousness of the Wagnerian music dramas in the United States. Damrosch organized it to combat the growing apathy of the opera public in general, and the METROPOLITAN OPERA management in particular, to German opera after 1890. The immediate impetus was Damrosch's success in 1894 with concert versions of GÖTTERDÄMMERUNG and DIE WALKÜRE. He raised the money for his company by selling his New York house. In the summer of 1894 he toured Europe to select his leading singers, returning with contracts with Johanna GADSKI and Rosa SUCHER (both to appear in America for the first time), and Max ALVARY and Emil FISCHER among others. The company opened an eight-week season in New York at the Metropolitan Opera on Feb. 25, 1895, with TRISTAN UND ISOLDE. An extensive tour followed, and the first season netted a profit of $53,000. The company continued five years. In the second season, Milka TERNINA, Katharina KLAFSKY, and David BISPHAM were added to the company, the last making his American debut. In 1896 the company presented the world premiere of Damrosch's first opera, The Scarlet Letter. One season later the company changed its name to the Damrosch-Ellis Company and expanded its activities to embrace Italian and French operas as well as German; at the same time, MELBA and CALVÉ joined the company. The deficits, which started to accumulate after the second season, mounted rapidly, and proved so burdensome that the company had to suspend operations in 1900.

Danae, daughter of Pollux and principal female character (soprano) in Richard STRAUSS'S DIE LIEBE DER DANAE, a role created by Viorica URSULEAC.

Dancaïre, Le, a smuggler (baritone) in BIZET'S CARMEN.

Dance of the Apprentices, dance in Act III, Scene 2, of WAGNER'S DIE MEISTERSINGER.

Dance of the Blessed Spirits, dance in Elysium, in Act III of GLUCK'S ORFEO ED EURIDICE.

Dance of the Buffoons (or **Tumblers**), dance of circus performers in Act III of RIMSKY-KORSAKOV'S THE SNOW MAIDEN.

Dance of the Camorristi, dance in Act III of WOLF-FERRARI'S THE JEWELS OF THE MADONNA.

Dance of the Comedians, dance in Act III of SMETANA'S THE BARTERED BRIDE.

Dance of the Furies, dance in Hades, in Act II of GLUCK'S ORFEO ED EURIDICE.

Dance of the Hours, dance symbolizing the victory of light over darkness and right over wrong, in Act III, Scene 2, of PONCHIELLI'S LA GIOCONDA.

Dance of the Moorish Slaves, dance in Act II, Scene 1, of VERDI'S AIDA.

Dance of the Seven Veils, Salome's voluptuous dance before Herod, in Richard STRAUSS'S SALOME.

Dance of the Sylphs, Sylphs dance as, asleep on the banks of the Elbe, Faust dreams of Marguerite, in Part II of BERLIOZ' THE DAMNATION OF FAUST.

Dandini, a valet (baritone) in ROSSINI'S LA CENERENTOLA.

Daniello, a violinist (baritone) in KRENEK'S JONNY SPIELT AUF.

Daniel Webster, distinguished American statesman and orator, who appears as a character (baritone) in MOORE'S THE DEVIL AND DANIEL WEBSTER and THOMSON'S THE MOTHER OF US ALL.

D'Annunzio, Gabriele, novelist, poet, dramatist. Born Pescara, Italy, Mar. 12, 1863; died Vittoriale, Italy, Mar. 1, 1938. Several of D'Annunzio's dramas have provided effective material for opera texts. One of PIZZETTI's finest operas, FEDRA, is based on D'Annunzio's play of the same name. Others are: FRANCESCA DA RIMINI (ZANDONAI); *La figlia di Jorio* (FRANCHETTI); LA NAVE (MONTEMEZZI); *Parisina* (MASCAGNI); *Il sogno d'una mattina di primavera* (MALIPIERO). D'Annunzio's *Flame of Life* is

of interest to opera goers because it describes an imaginary meeting with WAGNER on a Venetian canal steamer while the master was suffering his last illness. The façade of the Palazzo Vendramin, where Wagner died, bears a plaque with an inscription in which D'Annunzio poetically linked Wagner's dying breath with the waves that touch the building's walls.

Dans ce lieu solitaire, Count Ory's aria in ROSSINI'S LE COMTE ORY.

Danse Slave, dynamic Slavic dance during festivities, in Act II in CHABRIER'S LE ROI MALGRÉ LUI.

Dans la cité lointaine, Julien's serenade to Louise, in Act II, Scene 2, of CHARPENTIER'S LOUISE.

Dans le jardin fleurie, Mârouf's aria in an oriental style, in Act III of RABAUD'S MÂROUF.

Dans le vague d'un rêve, love duet of Gérald and Lakmé, in Act II of DELIBES'S LAKMÉ.

Dante Alighieri, poet. Born Florence, May, 1265; died Ravenna, Sept. 14, 1321. The author of the *Divine Comedy*. The tragic love of Paolo and Francesca (Canto 5 of *The Inferno*) has provided the material for several operas (*see* FRANCESCA DA RIMINI). Dante appears as a character in operas by John Foulds (concert opera), Benjamin GODARD, Jean NOUGUÈS, and Stephen Philpot. An incident from *The Divine Comedy* is referred to by the hero in GIANNI SCHICCHI. The opera is loosely based on this episode.

Dantons Tod (Danton's Death), opera in two parts by EINEM. Libretto by BLACHER, based on Georg BÜCHNER's drama. Premiere: Salzburg, Austria, Aug. 6, 1947. American premiere: New York City Opera, Mar. 9, 1966.

The opera, based on the tragic fall of the Revolutionist Danton during the French Revolution, is written for the most part in dramatic recitative style, sometimes approximating speech, but stirring choral episodes (including quotations of the "Carmagnole" and the "Marseillaise") and expressive orchestral interludes provide welcome contrast. In preparing the libretto, Blacher (who is a distinguished composer in his own right) carried out Büchner's aim to stress political rather than love interest. Danton has become disillusioned with the Revolution, makes fiery antirevolutionary speeches, and is arrested by Robespierre. At first the mob sides with Danton, but it is very soon swayed to demand Danton's death. The climax of the opera comes in the Tribunal Scene, where Danton eloquently pleads his case but in vain. He is executed in the public square, while the mob celebrates with song and dance.

The orchestra plays as important a function as the chorus. The opera begins with a chorale for brass followed by an affecting melody for strings (neither of which is again heard in the opera). After that the orchestra is used to provide a transition from one scene to the next, each self-sufficient, never repeating earlier musical ideas. The composer adapted four of these orchestral interludes into a symphonic suite.

Dantons Tod was its composer's first opera. It achieved an extraordinary success in Europe (though not in America) and was responsible for establishing Einem's reputation on a solid footing.

Danza delle ore, *see* DANCE OF THE HOURS.

Danza della quecas, an orchestral episode accompanying the dance of three geisha girls representing Beauty, Death, and the Vampire, in Act I of MASCAGNI's IRIS.

Dapertutto, the magician (baritone), whose other personalities are Coppélius, Lindorf, and Dr. Miracle, in OFFENBACH's THE TALES OF HOFFMANN, Act II.

Daphne, "bucolic tragedy" in one act by Richard STRAUSS. Libretto by Joseph Gregor. Premiere: Dresden, Oct. 15, 1938. American premiere: Brooklyn, N.Y., Oct. 7, 1960 (concert version); Santa Fe, N.M., July 29, 1964 (staged). William Mann explains that this is an opera "about Nature, mankind amid Nature, man's relation to Nature and to the natural forces which antique civilization worshiped as gods." Daphne (soprano), the heroine, is more in love

with nature than with the shepherd, Leukippos (tenor), much to the young man's distress. Daphne's father, Peneios (bass), a fisherman, convinced that some day the gods will come down to earth, gains justification when Apollo (tenor) arrives disguised as a shepherd. But he is ridiculed by the people. Daphne falls in love with Apollo but refuses to submit to her emotions. At a feast in which Leukippos tries to gain Daphne's affection, Apollo reveals his true identity, kills Leukippos, and transforms Daphne into a laurel tree.

See also DAFNE.

da Ponte, Lorenzo (born Emmanuel Conegliano), librettist and poet. Born Ceneda, Italy, Mar. 10, 1749; died New York City, Aug. 17, 1838. On the occasion of his baptism he acquired the name of da Ponte. He became involved in intrigues and scandals in Venice, resulting in his banishment in 1780. In Vienna he was eventually able to get an appointment as court poet, and he became a favorite of Joseph II. After writing librettos for various composers, he collaborated with MOZART in writing THE MARRIAGE OF FIGARO in 1785. In the next few years he also wrote for Mozart the librettos of DON GIOVANNI and COSÌ FAN TUTTE. After the death of Joseph II, da Ponte lost favor with the court. He went to London in 1793 and for a while worked at the DRURY LANE THEATRE, then a home for opera. Financial difficulties with the threat of imprisonment forced him to leave England secretly, and he came to the United States in 1805. He taught Italian languages and literature for many years, occupying a chair in the Italian language at Columbia College from 1826 to 1837. (In 1929, Columbia established a Lorenzo da Ponte professorship.) During this period he wrote his autobiography. Da Ponte was also active in encouraging the importation of opera to America. In 1825 he aided Manuel GARCÍA, who was one of the first to present Italian opera in the United States. In 1832 he again helped the cause by collaborating with a French tenor, Montresor, in bringing his opera troupe from Europe, and in 1833 he was involved in the erection of the Italian Opera House in New York.

Dardanus, opera in prologue and five acts by RAMEAU. Libretto by Charles Antoine Leclerc de la Bruère. Premiere: Paris Opéra, Oct. 19, 1739. Dardanus (COUNTERTENOR), according to Greek legend, is the founder of the royal house of Troy. He kills his brother Iasus and flees to Samothrace and from there to Phrygia, where he marries Princess Iphise (soprano) and builds the city of Troy. The dances from this opera have been collected into two orchestral suites edited by Vincent D'INDY; the Rigaudon from Act I is popular.

Dargomizhsky, Alexander (sometimes **Dargomijsky**), composer. Born Tula, Russia, Feb. 14, 1813; died St. Petersburg, Jan. 17, 1869. He was Glinka's immediate successor in the writing of national operas. He entered civil service in 1831, remaining there for thirteen years. A meeting with Glinka in 1834 filled him with the ambition to become a composer. After completing his musical training, he wrote an opera, *Esmeralda,* in 1839, which, when produced in 1847, was a failure. He now concentrated on writing smaller pieces and songs, but in 1848 he began working on his most ambitious and most popular work, the opera RUSSALKA. When introduced in St. Petersburg in 1856, *Russalka* was received mildly, but later performances established its popularity. Personal contact with members of the Russian Five fired Dargomizhsky with the ideal of writing national music. Incorporating the ideas of the nationalist school, he composed his last and most important work, THE STONE GUEST, an opera based on PUSHKIN's version of the Don Juan story. His death left the orchestration uncompleted; it was finished by CUI and RIMSKY-KORSAKOV.

Das schöne Fest, Pogner's address to the Mastersingers announcing that his daughter Eva is the prize in the forthcoming song contest, in Act I of WAGNER's DIE MEISTERSINGER.

Das süsse Lied verhallt, love duet of Lohengrin and Elsa, in Act III, Scene 1, of WAGNER's LOHENGRIN.

Das war sehr gut, Mandryka (Staircase Music), the celebrated aria of Arabella as, descending the staircase, she gives Mandryka a glass of water (a Slavonic custom signifying her acceptance of his marriage proposal), in the closing scene of Richard STRAUSS's ARABELLA.

Da tempesta, Cleopatra's song of triumph on discovering that Caesar is victorious and promises to conquer for her the entire world, in Act III, Scene 2, of HANDEL's GIULIO CESARE.

Da-ud, Altair's son (tenor) in Richard STRAUSS's DIE AEGYPTISCHE HELENA.

Daudet, Alphonse, novelist and playwright. Born Nîmes, France, May 13, 1840; died Paris, Dec. 16, 1897. Daudet's plays and novels provided the material for several operas, among them CILÈA's L'ARLESIANA, MASSENET's SAPHO, and Emile Pessard's *Tartarin sur les Alpes.*

Daughter of the Regiment, The (La Fille du regiment; La figlia del reggimento), opera in two acts by DONIZETTI. Libretto by Jean François Bayard and Vernoy SAINT-GEORGES. Premiere: Opéra-Comique, Feb. 11, 1840. American premiere: New Orleans, Mar. 6, 1843.

Characters: Marie, vivandière (canteen manager) of the French 21st Regiment (soprano); the Countess of Berkenfeld, her mother (mezzo-soprano); Ortensio, her servant (bass); Tonio, a peasant (tenor); Sulpizio, a sergeant in the 21st Regiment (bass); a peasant; a corporal; a notary; a duchess; soldiers; peasants; servants; ladies in waiting. The setting is the Tyrol about 1815.

Act I. A mountain pass. The French, under Napoleon, have invaded the Tyrol. Marie, adopted in infancy by the 21st Regiment, has grown to young womanhood and become the regiment's vivandière. She sings of her joy in camp life and battle ("Au bruit de la guerre" —"Io vidi la luce nel camp guerir"). She then discloses that she is in love with Tonio, who is soon afterward dragged in by the French and accused of being a spy. When Marie explains that Tonio once saved her life, the French are kinder to him and hail him as a recruit to their regiment. This inspires Marie to sing a song of praise to the regiment ("Ah, chacun le sait, chacun le dit"—"Ah, ciascun lo dice, ciascun lo sà"), in which the soldiers join. After the soldiers leave, Tonio expresses his love for Marie and insists on his willingness to die for her; Marie, too, speaks of her love and exclaims that for her sake he must live, not die ("Depuis l'instant où dans mes bras"—"Perchè v'amo"). The Countess of Berkenfeld, who has been hiding during the fighting, now reappears and learns from Sulpizio that Marie is her long-lost niece. The Countess insists that Marie return with her to her castle. The French soldiers now appear, singing a stirring song to war and victory ("Rataplan"). Heartbroken, Marie bids farewell to her regiment ("Il faut partir, mes bons compagnons"—"Convien partir, o miei compagni d'arme"). Overwhelmed with grief that he can no longer be with Marie, Tonio angrily tears the regimental colors from his hat and stamps on them.

Act II. A room in the Berkenfeld Castle. Marie is being raised as a lady of nobility. The Countess gives her a singing lesson ("Le jour naissait dans le bocage"—"Sorgeva il dì del bosco in seno"). While Marie is singing the first strains of the song, Sulpizio—who, wounded, has been allowed to stay in the castle—reminds Marie of their regimental song. Almost helplessly, she bursts into the refrain ("Le voilà, le voilà"—"Egli è la"), to the horror of the Countess, who storms out of the room. Since Marie is being compelled to marry the Duke of Crackenthorp, and since she is still in love with Tonio, she laments her misfortune ("C'en est donc fait et mon coeur va changer"—"Me sedur han creduto"). French soldiers suddenly storm into the castle. Tonio is with them. Sulpizio, Marie, and Tonio are overjoyed at their reunion ("Tous les trois réunis"—"Stretti insiem tutti tre"). The Countess, returning, is shocked to find Tonio present; she now discloses that Marie is not her

niece but her daughter, and she insists that it is Marie's duty to obey her mother and marry the Duke. The soldiers reappear from the garden and shout their disapproval of the mother's decision, insisting they will never permit Marie to marry any but the man she loves ("Au secours de notre fille"—"Ti rincora, amata figlia"). After Marie voices her own sentiments ("Quand le destin au milieu"—"Quando fanciulla ancor l'avverso"), the Countess relents and is ready to accept Tonio as a son-in-law. Rejoicing prevails, and the assemblage sings a stirring salute to France ("Salut à la France"—"Salvezza alla Francia").

Donizetti wrote this gay and martial opera for Naples, using his own Italian translation of a French libretto. But another of his operas had antagonized the Neapolitan authorities with its political implications, and Donizetti had to leave Italy for France. He took with him his new opera, and it was in Paris that it was introduced in its original French version. The title role has attracted coloratura sopranos throughout the years, and many famous prima donnas are identified with it. Anna Thillon created the role at the Paris premiere; later sopranos who scored major successes in the part include ALBANI, HEMPEL, Jenny LIND, PONS, PATTI, SEMBRICH, SONTAG, and TETRAZZINI. When the opera was revived by the METROPOLITAN for Frieda Hempel during the 1917–18 season, America was at war and the martial character of the opera had special significance. In keeping with the times, Hempel interpolated the English ballad, "Keep the Home Fires Burning." During World War II—and soon after the Nazis occupied France—the opera again acquired special political interest; Lily PONS draped herself in the flag of the Free French Forces and sang the *Marseillaise*.

David, (1) Biblical opera in five acts by MILHAUD. Libretto by Armand Lunel. Premiere: Jerusalem, June 2, 1954 (concert version); La Scala, Jan. 2, 1955 (staged). American premiere: Los Angeles, Cal., Sept. 22, 1956 (concert version). Milhaud wrote this opera on a commission from the KOUSSEVITZKY MUSIC FOUNDATION. The Biblical story begins with the visit of prophet Samuel to the house of David's father and ends with the anointment of Solomon as King of Israel in succession to David. A chorus, designated as "Israelites of the Year of 1954," dressed in present-day garb, draws parallels between the Biblical tale and modern Israeli history. Sometimes the past and present commingle, as when Biblical youths, returning from the vineyards, are heard singing and dancing to a contemporary Israeli hora.

(2) A rabbi (baritone) in MASCAGNI'S L'AMICO FRITZ.

(3) An apprentice (tenor) to Hans Sachs, in WAGNER'S DIE MEISTERSINGER.

David, Félicien, composer. Born Cadenet, France, Apr. 13, 1810; died St. Germain-en-Laye, Aug. 29, 1876. After four years of music study at the Jesuit College in Aix, he became conductor of a theater orchestra and after that MAÎTRE DE CHAPELLE at the Cathedral. In 1830 he went to Paris for further music study at the Conservatory. A year later he joined a religious brotherhood, the Saint-Simonists, and lived in monastic seclusion. After the brotherhood was dissolved in 1833, David began an extended period of travel in the Near East. His impressions inspired his most famous work, a symphonic ode, *Le Désert*, introduced in 1844 with such success that it created a vogue for compositions with exotic backgrounds. His first successful work for the stage was an OPÉRA COMIQUE, *La Perle du Brésil,* given in Paris in 1851. A second opera, *Herculanum,* won a national prize in 1859. His most celebrated opera, *Lalla-Roukh,* was acclaimed at its premiere at the Opéra-Comique in 1862. Later operas: *Le Saphir* (1865); *La Captive* (not performed). In 1869 David succeeded BERLIOZ as member of the Academy and as librarian at the Conservatory.

Davide, Giovanni, tenor. Born Naples, Sept. 15, 1790; died St. Petersburg, Russia, 1864. The son of an opera tenor (Giacomo Davide), Giovanni studied with his father before making his opera debut in Brescia in 1810. During the next four years he appeared in various Italian opera houses, including LA SCALA, where in 1814 he created the role of Narciso in ROSSINI'S IL TURCO IN ITALIA. Rossini wrote a number of operas for him, including OTELLO and *La donna del lago*. In 1818 and again in 1831, Davide appeared in London. He possessed an extraordinary range (three octaves contained within four B-flats) and technique, but he abused his voice and was compelled to retire in 1841, when he organized a singing school in Naples. He subsequently assumed the post of opera manager in St. Petersburg, where he remained for the rest of his life.

Davis, Colin, conductor. Born Weybridge, Eng., 1927. He attended the Royal College of Music in London, following which he played the clarinet in the orchestra at the GLYNDEBOURNE FESTIVAL. Though self-taught as conductor, he acquired a number of engagements as guest conductor and in 1957 was appointed assistant conductor of the BBC Scottish Orchestra. He first attracted attention when he substituted successfully for Otto KLEMPERER in a concert performance of DON GIOVANNI at the Royal Festival Hall in London in 1959. A year later he became the music director of the SADLER'S WELLS OPERA. From then on he received numerous appointments to appear with major orchestras in Europe and America (making his American debut in 1961 with the Minneapolis Symphony); he also conducted operas at Glyndebourne and COVENT GARDEN. In 1964 he shared the podium with SOLTI and KERTESZ in a world tour of the London Symphony. He made his debut at the METROPOLITAN OPERA during the season of 1967–68 in a new production of PETER GRIMES. In the fall of 1969 he was appointed music director of the Royal Opera, Covent Garden, in succession to Solti.

Dawn on the Moscow River, a celebrated

orchestral prelude to Act I of MUSSORG-SKY'S KHOVANTCHINA describing a bleak winter landscape.

Da zu dir der Heiland (Kirchenchor), the church chorale which brings the services of St. Katherine to a close, at the opening of WAGNER's DIE MEIS-TERSINGER.

Dead City, The, *see* TOTE STADT, DIE.

Deane, Mrs., a widow (mezzo-soprano) in TAYLOR's PETER IBBETSON.

De Angelis, Nazareno, bass. Born Rome, Nov. 17, 1881; died there Dec. 14, 1962. He was one of the most celebrated operatic basses of his time, the creator of the role of Archibaldo in L'AMORE DEI TRE RE, and world renowned for his performances in both the Italian and Wagnerian repertory. In his boyhood he sang with the Sistine Chapel Choir. His opera debut took place in 1903 as Acquila in LINDA DI CHAMOUNIX. From then until 1959 he was heard in the leading opera houses in Italy. In 1910–11 and again between 1915 and 1920 he was a member of the CHICAGO OPERA.

Death of Don Quixote, *see* ÉCOUTE, MON AMI.

Death of Gregory Rasputin, The, opera in three acts by Nicolas Nabokov. Libretto by Stephen Spender. Premiere: Cologne, Ger., Nov. 27, 1959. Commissioned by the Kentucky Opera Association, which presented a premiere in an earlier form, this opera was originally entitled *The Holy Devil,* was in two acts, and concentrated on the last years of Rasputin's life. Following its premiere on Apr. 16, 1958, composer and librettist revised the opera extensively, developing it into three acts, and giving it its new title.

Death of Thaïs, *see* TE SOUVIENT-IL DU LUMINEUX VOYAGE.

De Begnis, Giuseppe, bass. Born Lugo, Romagna, 1793; died New York City, Aug., 1849. He became famous as a *basso buffo* following his opera debut in Modena in 1813 in Stefano Pavesi's *Ser Mercantonio.* ROSSINI called upon him to create the role of Magnifico in

LA CENERENTOLA in 1817. Between 1821 and 1827 he sang in London. In 1823–24 he directed opera in Bath, Eng., and from 1834 to 1837 in Dublin.

Debora e Jaele (Deborah and Jael), opera in three acts by PIZZETTI. Libretto by the composer. Premiere: La Scala, Dec. 16, 1922. This is the first of several Biblical works by Pizzetti and one of his most powerful and passionate operas. The text is a variation of the Biblical story from the Book of Judges. Jaele is accused by the Hebrews of consorting with their enemy, King Sisera. Debora placates them by promising a victory over the king. She convinces Jaele to go to the enemy camp to kill King Sisera, but at the zero hour Jaele is incapable of doing so. The Hebrews launch a battle which puts King Sisera to flight, who seeks refuge with Debora. She kills him to save him from humiliation and torture at the hands of his captors.

De Brétigny, a nobleman (baritone) in MASSENET's MANON.

Debussy, Claude Achille, composer. Born Saint-Germain-en-Laye, France, Aug. 22, 1862; died Paris, Mar. 25, 1918. The father of musical impressionism completed only a single opera; but that work, PELLÉAS ET MÉLISANDE, represents the quintessence of his art and is one of the monuments in post-Wagnerian opera. Debussy attended the Paris Conservatory for eleven years. His teachers included Antoine Marmontel, Emile Durand, and Ernest GUIRAUD. In 1884 he won the Prix de Rome for the cantata *L'Enfant prodigue.* After his sojourn in Rome, Debussy returned to Paris, where he was affected by the Symbolist movement in poetry and the Impressionist school of painting, then flourishing. These influences, combined with his conversations with the iconoclastic French musician, Erik SATIE, crystallized Debussy's thinking about the kind of music he wanted to write and set him off in the direction of musical impressionism. By exploiting a number of characteristic technical devices—including the use of the whole-tone scale; old Church modes; unresolved ninths and eleventh chords; fourths, fifths, and octaves moving in parallel motion; avoidance of formal cadences and tonal centers; exploiting rapidly changing meters and rhythms; and so forth—he achieved a highly personal idiom. In this vein he produced his first songs, his single quartet for strings, pieces for piano, and *L'Après-midi d'un faune* for orchestra. His most ambitious work, the opera *Pelléas et Mélisande*, was begun in 1892 and completed a decade later. The circumstances surrounding the writing and production of this work appear elsewhere. Debussy tried writing another opera even while he was engaged on *Pelléas: Rodrigue et Chimène*, begun in 1892, but abandoned a few years later after the completion of only two acts. He also intended adapting Edgar Allan Poe's *The Fall of the House of Usher* for an opera, but this project never progressed beyond the planning stage.

Decameron, The, *see* BOCCACCIO, GIOVANNI.

Decembrists, The, opera in four acts by SHAPORIN. Libretto by V. A. Rozhdestvensky, based on a play by Alexei Tolstoy. Premiere: Bolshoi Opera, Moscow, June 23, 1953. This opera, one of the most significant to come out of the Soviet Union, took the composer thirty years to write. The theme concerns the uprising in St. Petersburg against Czar Nicholas I on Dec. 14, 1825, and its style follows the traditions of the Russian Five rather than exploiting modern idioms.

Decidi il mio destin, love duet of Silvio and Nedda in Act I of LEONCAVALLO'S PAGLIACCI.

declamation, music in which the voice approximates the inflections of speech and in which the text assumes greater significance than the melody. Declamation is used in opera for dramatic episodes.

décor, French for scenery (and at times misused for stage direction as well).

de Falla, Manuel, *see* FALLA, MANUEL DE.

Degna d'un re, Falstaff's flattery of Mistress Ford during what he hopes will be a liaison, in Act II, Scene 2, of VERDI'S FALSTAFF.

Deh! con te li prendi, Norma's plea to Adalgisa to take care of her children, following her decision to destroy herself, in Act III (in some arrangements Act II) of BELLINI'S NORMA.

de Hidalgo, Elvira, soprano and teacher. Born Barcelona, 1882. She began studying voice at the age of twelve and at sixteen made her debut in Naples as ROSINA. This was followed by an unexpected appearance as Rosina with the MONTE CARLO OPERA in Paris, where she substituted for the ailing Selma KURZ. Once again as Rosina, she made her debut at the METROPOLITAN OPERA on Mar. 7, 1910. For the next thirty years she appeared in leading soprano roles in major opera houses. A highlight of her singing career came in 1916 when she was invited by LA SCALA to appear as Rosina in the centenary celebration of the opera's premiere. She followed her singing career with that of voice teacher in Athens, one of her students being Maria CALLAS. Subsequently she taught at Ankara and at Milan.

Deh! non parlare al misero, Rigoletto's duet with Gilda, in which he tells her about her dead mother, in Act I, Scene 2, of VERDI'S RIGOLETTO.

Deh per questo istande, the famous aria from MOZART'S LA CLEMENZA DI TITO, sung by Sextus in Act II. Though the role of Sextus is male, it is sung by a mezzo-soprano since the part was originally written for a CASTRATO.

Deh placatevi con me, Orpheus' deeply moving plea to the Furies, in Act II of GLUCK'S ORFEO ED EURIDICE.

Deh prendi un dolce amplesso, a twenty-four measure duettino for Sextus and Annio in Act I of MOZART'S LA CLEMENZA DI TITO.

Deh! proteggimi, o Dio!, Adalgisa's moving plea to the gods to free her of her love for Pollione, in Act I of BELLINI'S NORMA.

Deh! tu reggi in tal momento, Ninetta's air in Act II of ROSSINI'S LA GAZZA LADRA.

Deh, vieni alla finestra, Don Giovanni's serenade to Donna Elvira's maid, in Act II, Scene 1, of MOZART'S DON GIOVANNI.

Deh vieni, non tardar, Susanna's invitation to her absent lover to join her in the garden, in Act IV of MOZART'S THE MARRIAGE OF FIGARO.

Deidamia, opera in three acts by HANDEL. Libretto by Paolo Rolli. Premiere: Haymarket, London, Jan. 10, 1740. American premiere: Hartford, Conn., Feb. 25, 1959. Handel's last opera, it proved a total failure when first produced, being removed after only three performances. It received a successful revival (in an English translation by Prof. Edward J. Dent) in London in 1955, following which it was extensively performed throughout Germany. Two arias are of particular interest: that of Deidamia in the first act, "Due bell' alme inamorate"; and Lycomedes' second-act aria, "Nel riposo." Herbert Weinstock considers the music as a whole to be "one of Handel's most charming lighter scores" with "the chorus . . . used in an oratoriolike manner."

Déjà les hirondelles, duet for two sopranos in DELIBES'S LE ROI L'A DIT. It has become a celebrated concert number.

de Jouy, see JOUY, VICTOR DE.

De Koven, Reginald, composer. Born Middletown, Conn., Apr. 3, 1859; died Chicago, Jan. 16, 1920. His music study took place in Germany and Paris. After returning to the United States he wrote several operettas before achieving his first success with the work by which he is today remembered, ROBIN HOOD, introduced in Chicago in 1890. In 1917 he was commissioned by the METROPOLITAN OPERA to write the grand opera, THE CANTERBURY PILGRIMS, performed in 1917. A second grand opera, RIP VAN WINKLE, was introduced in Chicago in 1920. De Koven was the music critic for the *New York Herald* from 1898 to 1900 and again from 1907 to 1912.

de Lara, Isidore, composer. Born London, Aug. 9, 1858; died Paris, Sept. 2, 1935. After appearing as a child-prodigy pianist, he entered the Milan Conservatory in his fifteenth year. His first opera, *The Light of Asia,* an adaptation of a cantata, was given at COVENT GARDEN in 1892. His most successful opera, *Messaline,* was introduced in MONTE CARLO in 1899, and given at the METROPOLITAN OPERA three years later. De Lara's style derived from that of MASSENET. His other operas: *Amy Robsart* (1893); *Moïna* (1897); *Le Réveil de Bouddha* (1904); *Soléa* (1907); *Sanga* (1908); *Naïl* (1911); *Les Trois Masques* (1912); *Les Trois Mousquetaires* (1921).

De l'enfer qui vient émousser, the soldiers' and students' chorus in which they ward off the devil (Méphistophélès) by making crosses with their reversed swords, in Act II of GOUNOD'S FAUST.

Delibes, Léo, composer. Born St. Germain du Val, France, Feb. 21, 1836; died Paris, Jan. 16, 1891. While most famous for his ballets, Delibes is also the composer of LAKMÉ, a staple in the French operatic repertory. He attended the Paris Conservatory and in 1855 wrote an operetta, *Deux Sous de charbon,* introduced in Paris. Between 1862 and 1871 he was organist at the church of St. Jean St. François. In 1865 he became second chorusmaster at the OPÉRA. His first ballet, *La Source,* was a major success when introduced at the Opéra in 1866. His second ballet, *Coppélia,* performed in 1870, was an even greater triumph. In 1873 he wrote his first opera, LE ROI L'A DIT, given at the Opéra-Comique. *Lakmé* came a decade later, bringing its composer to the front rank of French composers for the stage. In 1881 Delibes was appointed professor of composition at the Conservatory and in 1884 member of the Institut de France. Besides the operas mentioned above, Delibes also wrote *Jean de Nivelle* in 1880 and *Kassya,* which was finished by MASSENET after the composer's death.

Delius, Frederick, composer. Born Bradford, Eng., Jan. 29, 1862; died

Grez-sur-Loing, France, June 10, 1934. After working two years in his father's wool establishment, he came to the United States to superintend an orange plantation in Florida which his father bought for him. Here he began to study music intensively by himself, and to compose his first works, including *Appalachia,* for chorus and orchestra. In 1886 he returned to Europe to attend the Leipzig Conservatory. He next went to Paris, where his first works were published. After marrying Jelka Rosen in 1899, he established his home in Grez-sur-Loing. Here he lived the rest of his life, and here he wrote his most celebrated works, including his tone poems for orchestra, and his opera A VILLAGE ROMEO AND JULIET (1900–1902). Soon after World War I, Delius' health failed, and he became a victim of paralysis and blindness. Composition was not abandoned. He dictated his last works, note by note, to an amanuensis. In 1929 he appeared in London to attend a festival of six concerts devoted to his music. His operas: IRMELIN (1892); *The Magic Fountain* (1893); *Koanga* (1897); *A Village Romeo and Juliet* (1900–1902); *Margot la rouge* (1902); *Fennimore and Gerda* (1910).

Délivrance de Thésée, La (Liberation of Theseus), *opéra minute* by MILHAUD. Libretto by Henri Hoppenot. Premiere: Wiesbaden, Ger., Apr. 20, 1928. American premiere: Iowa City, Iowa, May 8, 1961. This is one of three *minute* operas (each requiring about eight minutes for performance, and each on a mythological subject); the other two are L'ENLÈVEMENT D'EUROPE and L'ABANDON D'ARIANE. Phèdre (soprano), though married to Theseus (tenor), is in love with her son Hippolyte (baritone), who repulses her. When Theseus returns from a mission, Phèdre falsely accuses Hippolyte of having made advances to her. Theseus sends Hippolyte into battle in which he is killed. Phèdre is stabbed by a friend of Hippolyte's, who, in turn, is punished by Theseus with hanging.

Della Casa, Lisa, soprano. Born Burg-dorf, Switzerland, Feb. 2, 1919. When she was fifteen she began her vocal training with Margarete Haeser, who remained her only teacher. In 1941 she made her debut as MADAMA BUTTERFLY in Solothurn-Biel, Switzerland. While serving as a member of the ZÜRICH OPERA between 1943 and 1950, she scored a major success as Zdenka in ARABELLA, since become one of her most celebrated roles. She subsequently appeared with extraordinary success at the GLYNDEBOURNE FESTIVAL, MUNICH OPERA, BAYREUTH, EDINBURGH FESTIVAL, LA SCALA, PARIS OPÉRA, COVENT GARDEN, and the VIENNA STATE OPERA, achieving particular distinction in operas by MOZART and Richard STRAUSS. Her debut at the METROPOLITAN OPERA took place on Nov. 20, 1953, as the Countess in THE MARRIAGE OF FIGARO, from which time on she remained a principal soprano of that company. In 1970 she received the Cross of Honor, Austria's highest medal of achievement.

Della città all' occaso, Ulrica's aria in Act I, Scene 2, of VERDI'S UN BALLO IN MASCHERA, describing the powers of a magic herb plucked near a gallows at midnight.

Dell' aura tua profetica, chorus of the Druid priests invoking the help of the gods, in Act I of BELLINI'S NORMA.

Della vittoria agli arbitri, chorus of the priests in Act II, Scene 2, of VERDI'S AIDA, in which they express gratitude to the gods for victory.

Dell' elisir mirabile, Nemorino's air in Act II of DONIZETTI'S L'ELISIR D'AMORE, expressing his confidence in the powers of the love elixir.

delle Sedie, Enrico, baritone and teacher of singing. Born Leghorn, Italy, June 17, 1824; died Paris, Nov. 28, 1907. Before embarking on his musical career he distinguished himself as a soldier, fighting in the war for Italian independence in 1848–49. Taken prisoner by the Austrians during the Battle of Curtatone, he was released, later retiring from the army with the rank of lieutenant and several decorations. He now began the study of singing with various teachers, including Orazio Galeffi, and in 1851 he made his debut in Pistoia, Italy, in NABUCCO. Success came three years later in Florence, after which he appeared in leading baritone roles of the Italian and French repertories throughout Italy, and in Vienna, Paris, and London. In 1867 he abandoned the stage to become a professor of singing at the Paris Conservatory. He wrote a valuable treatise, *L'Art lyrique* (1874), published in the United States as *A Complete Method of Singing*.

Dello Joio, Norman (born Dello Ioio), composer. Born New York City, Jan. 24, 1913. His basic musical training took place at the Institute of Musical Art, the Juilliard Graduate School. He studied the organ with Pietro Yon and composition with HINDEMITH at the Berkshire Music Center. He achieved success as a composer through concert works that gained him two awards from the New York Music Critics' Circle, two Guggenheim Fellowships and, in 1957, the Pulitzer Prize in music for *Meditations on Ecclesiastes* for string orchestra. His first opera was *The Triumph of St. Joan,* introduced at Sarah Lawrence College on May 9, 1950. He abandoned this opera, but used some of its material for a symphony. He wrote a second opera on the subject of St. Joan, originally calling it *Trial at Rouen* (world premiere over the NBC-TV network on Apr. 8, 1956) but later renaming it THE TRIUMPH OF ST. JOAN, though it was a completely different work from the first one of the same name. Later operas: *The Ruby* (first performance in Bloomington, Ind., on May 13, 1955) and *Blood Moon* (introduced in San Francisco on Sept. 18, 1961).

Delmas, Jean-François, bass-baritone. Born Lyons, France, Apr. 14, 1861; died St. Alban de Monthel, Sept. 27, 1933. After studying at the Paris Conservatory, where he won first prize in singing, he made his opera debut at the OPÉRA on Sept. 13, 1886, in LES HUGUENOTS. He became a regular member of the company and for the next four decades distinguished himself in both the French and German repertory. He was particularly impressive in the WAGNER music dramas, creating for France most of the leading Wagnerian baritone and bass roles. He also created the principal bass or baritone parts in ARIANE ET BARBE-BLEUE, *L'Etranger* (D'INDY), MONNA VANNA, SALAMMBÔ, and THAÏS.

Del Monaco, Mario, tenor. Born Florence, July 27, 1915. During boyhood he sang nonprofessionally in MASSENET's *Narcisse* performed at Mondaldo. He then attended the school affiliated with the TEATRO DELL' OPERA in Rome for six months, after which his music study took place mainly through listening to records. After making his professional opera debut in Pesaro as TURIDDU in 1939, he achieved his first success on Jan. 1, 1941, as PINKERTON at the Teatro Puccini in Milan. Appearances in major Italian opera houses took place after World War II. On Sept. 26, 1950, he made his American debut with the SAN FRANCISCO OPERA as RADAMES, and on Nov. 27 of the same year he appeared at the METROPOLITAN OPERA (making his debut as Des Grieux in MANON LESCAUT) and remained with that company as a principal tenor for nine years.

de los Angeles, Victoria (born Victoria Lopez), soprano. Born Barcelona, Spain, Nov. 1, 1923. She attended the Conservatorio del Liceo in Barcelona for three years, after which, in Jan., 1945, she made her professional opera debut as the Countess in THE MARRIAGE OF FIGARO. In 1947 she won first prize in the International Singing Contest in Geneva, which was followed by concert and opera appearances throughout Europe. In 1950 she made highly successful debuts at the PARIS OPÉRA, LA SCALA, and COVENT GARDEN. Her American debut took place in a recital at Carnegie Hall on Oct. 15 of the same year, after which Virgil THOMSON described her as "a vocal delight unique in our time." On Mar. 17, 1951, she made her American opera debut at the METROPOLITAN OPERA as Marguerite in

FAUST. An artist of extraordinary versatility, she has since appeared extensively in opera houses and festivals in the French, German, and Italian repertory, including such roles as MÉLISANDE, EVA, AGATHA, and DESDEMONA. More recently she has confined her operatic work to recordings and to European opera houses, while touring the United States solely in recitals.

Del primo pianto, Turandot's tearful recognition that she is in love with Calaf, in Act III, Scene 1, of PUCCINI'S TURANDOT.

del Puente, Giuseppe, baritone. Born Naples, Jan. 30, 1841; died Philadelphia, Pa., May 25, 1900. As a child he entered the Naples Conservatory to study the cello, but eventually he turned to singing. After only a single year of vocal study he made his opera debut in Jassy. Appearances followed in leading Italian opera houses. In 1873 del Puente made a successful debut at COVENT GARDEN. He was a great favorite in England, where he created for that country the roles of ESCAMILLO and VALENTIN. In 1873 he also made his American debut with the STRAKOSCH Opera Company. He helped make operatic history in this country by appearing in the American premiere of CARMEN and in the performance of FAUST with which the METROPOLITAN OPERA was opened. As a member of the Metropolitan, and subsequently of the Gustav HINRICHS Company, he appeared in the American premieres of L'AMICO FRITZ, LA GIOCONDA, MANON LESCAUT, LES PÊCHEURS DE PERLES, and ROMÉO ET JULIETTE.

Del Tago sponde addio, see ADIEU, MON DOUX RIVAGE.

de Luca, Giuseppe, baritone. Born Rome, Dec. 29, 1876; died New York City, Aug. 27, 1950. For two decades he was the principal baritone of the METROPOLITAN OPERA, appearing more than eight hundred times in about a hundred different roles. After completing his studies at the Schola Cantorum and the Santa Cecilia Academy, both in Rome, he made his opera debut on Nov. 7,

1897, in Piacenza as VALENTIN. Other important opera appearances followed, notably in Genoa, Milan, and Buenos Aires. In the winter of 1903 he was engaged by LA SCALA, where he remained for eight years and where he created the role of SHARPLESS in 1904. He also appeared in the world premieres of ADRIANA LECOUVREUR and SIBERIA. After touring as star in leading opera houses of the world, he made his American debut at the Metropolitan Opera on Nov. 25, 1915, in THE BARBER OF SEVILLE. During the next twenty years he appeared in virtually every important baritone role of the French and Italian repertory and was heard in the world premiere of GOYESCAS and the American premieres of LA CAMPANA SOMMERSA, GIANNI SCHICCHI, and MÂROUF. He was a towering figure in the golden age of opera in America, a master of BEL CANTO.

He left the Metropolitan Opera after the 1934–35 season. The next four years he spent singing in Europe, after which he returned to the Metropolitan on Feb. 7, 1940, in LA TRAVIATA. Back in Italy during World War II, he refused to sing for five years because, as he explained, "I was not in good humor." The ejection of the Nazis from Italy restored his good humor, and he sang for Allied troops at the Rome Opera. Persuaded to return to America, he appeared in a New York recital in Mar., 1946, when he received a tumultuous ovation. On Nov. 7, 1947, his golden jubilee as a singer was also celebrated with a New York recital. In the last two years of his life he devoted himself to teaching voice in New York. He was the recipient of many honors from his native land, including a decoration of the Santa Cecilia Academy and decorations of the Donato First Class, Knights of Malta, Cavalier of the Great Cross, Crown of Italy, and Commendatore of S.S. Maurizio and Lazzaro.

de Maupassant, see MAUPASSANT, GUY DE.

Demetrios, a rich sculptor (tenor) in ERLANGER'S APHRODITE.

Demeur, Anne Arsène (born Charton), soprano. Born Saujon, France, Mar. 5, 1824; died Paris, Nov. 30, 1892. She distinguished herself in performances of BERLIOZ operas, creating the leading soprano roles in BÉATRICE ET BÉNÉDICT and LES TROYENS À CARTHAGE. After studying voice with Bizot, she made her opera debut in Bordeaux in 1842 in LUCIA DI LAMMERMOOR. Following appearances in France, Belgium, and London, she married (1847) a flutist, Jules Antoine Demeur, after which she appeared under the name of Charton-Demeur. In 1849 and again in 1853 she appeared at the OPÉRA-COMIQUE but was poorly received on both occasions. Success came in Italian opera with performances in St. Petersburg, Vienna, Paris, and South America. In 1862 her performance in the premiere of *Béatrice et Bénédict* so delighted the composer that he invited her to create the role of Dido in *Les Troyens à Carthage* in 1863. After she went into retirement, she emerged in 1870 to appear in a Berlioz festival at the PARIS OPÉRA, and again in 1879 to sing in Berlioz' *La Prise de Troie* in a performance by the Pasdeloup Orchestra.

De' miei bollenti spiriti, Alfredo's aria expressing gratitude to Violetta for having taught him the meaning of love, in Act II, Scene 1, of VERDI's LA TRAVIATA.

Demon, The, opera in three acts by RUBINSTEIN. Libretto by A. N. Maikov, revised by Viskotov, based on a poem by Mikhail Lermontov. Premiere: Imperial Opera, St. Petersburg, Jan. 25, 1875. American premiere: San Francisco Opera, Jan. 17, 1922. The demon, eager to capture the beautiful Tamara for himself, provokes the Tartars to kill her betrothed. Although Tamara enters a convent, the demon pursues her. After receiving his first kiss, she dies. Angels put the demon to flight, then carry Tamara off to heaven. Among the distinguished vocal pages are the arias of the Prince of Sinodal (Tamara's betrothed), "On desire's soft, fleeting wing" in Act I, and of Tamara in Act III, "Calm and clear is the night." Tamara's father, Prince Gudal, delivers an effective bass number in Act II, "Do not weep my child," and the demon another one in Act III, "I am he whom you called." *The Demon* was the first opera ever sung in Russian in London (1888).

De mon amie fleur endormie, Nadir's serenade to Leila in Act II of BIZET's LES PÊCHEURS DE PERLES.

Demoni, fatale, chorus of the demons in Act III of MEYERBEER's ROBERT LE DIABLE.

de Musset, Alfred, *see* MUSSET, ALFRED DE.

de Nangis, a conspirator (tenor) against the King of France in CHABRIER's LE ROI MALGRÉ LUI. This is also the name assumed by the king when, disguised, he joins the conspirators.

de Nangis, Raoul, Huguenot nobleman (tenor) in MEYERBEER's LES HUGUENOTS, a role created by Adolphe NOURRIT.

De noirs pressentimento, bass aria of Thoas, the King of Scythia, in Act IV of GLUCK's IPHIGÉNIE EN TAURIDE.

Den sündigen Welten, the chant of the boys' chorus as Amfortas is carried into the Hall of the Holy Grail, in Act I, Scene 2, of WAGNER's PARSIFAL.

Dent, Edward Joseph, musicologist. Born Ribston, Eng., July 16, 1876; died London, Aug. 22, 1957. After being educated at Eton and Cambridge he became, in 1902, Fellow of King's College at Cambridge, and after 1926 professor of music. In 1922 he helped organize the International Society for Contemporary Music, serving as its president for many years. In 1931 he was elected president of the Société Internationale de Musicologie. He was particularly active in the field of opera, both as scholar and as impresario. He edited and produced many old English operas, notably PURCELL's DIDO AND AENEAS. He prepared new English translations of well-known operas. He also wrote many books about opera and opera composers, among them biographies of Alessandro SCARLATTI (1905), BUSONI (1933), and HANDEL (1934), and *Mozart's Operas: A Critical Study* (1913), *Foundations of English Opera* (1928), *Music of the Renaissance in Italy* (1934), and *Opera* (1940).

Deo tuoi figli la madre, Medea's aria in CHERUBINI's MÉDÉE.

De Paolis, Alessio, tenor. Born Rome, Apr. 5, 1893; died New York City, Mar. 9, 1964. Completing his vocal studies with Di Pietro at the Santa Cecilia Academy in Rome, he made his opera debut in Bologna in 1919 in RIGOLETTO. He appeared as FENTON on the opening night of TOSCANINI's new regime at LA SCALA in 1921. For many years thereafter he was a leading tenor at La Scala and in other major opera houses. At the age of forty, he gave up singing leading roles and for thirty years more enjoyed a distinguished career as one of the finest COMPRIMARIO tenors on the stage. His debut at the METROPOLITAN OPERA took place on Dec. 3, 1938, as Cassio in OTELLO. He continued to appear at the Metropolitan Opera in about fifty roles, his last performance being in EUGENE ONEGIN just a few days before his death in an automobile accident. In all he is believed to have appeared in some two hundred roles.

De Paris tout en fête, Julien's ecstatic apostrophe to the city of Paris, in Act III of CHARPENTIER's LOUISE.

de Puiset, Eglantine, Euryanthe's false friend (mezzo-soprano) in WEBER's EURYANTHE.

Depuis le jour, the most famous aria in CHARPENTIER's LOUISE, sung by the heroine in Act III in recollection of the first time she had yielded to her beloved Julien.

Depuis l'instant où dans mes bras (Perchè v'amo), Marie's and Tonio's love duet in Act I of DONIZETTI's THE DAUGHTER OF THE REGIMENT.

Depuis longtemps j'habitais cette chambre, Julien's recollection of the first time he had fallen in love with Louise, in Act I of CHARPENTIER's LOUISE.

de Ravoir, Geronte, Manon's elderly lover (bass) in PUCCINI's MANON LESCAUT.

de Reszke, Edouard, bass. Born Warsaw, Poland, Dec. 22, 1853; died Garnek, Poland, May 25, 1917. One of the most celebrated singers of the late nineteenth century, he was the brother of one of the most adulated tenors of all time, Jean DE RESZKE, and of a famous soprano, Josephine DE RESZKE. Edouard's first singing lessons were given him by his brother Jean. He later studied in Italy with Filippo Coletti and another teacher named Steller. The director of the PARIS OPÉRA was so impressed by his voice that he recommended him to VERDI for the French premiere of AIDA, and on Apr. 22, 1876, de Reszke made his debut in Paris in the role of the king at the Théâtre des Italiens. During the next few seasons he appeared in Paris, Turin, Milan, Lisbon, and at COVENT GARDEN. As a principal bass of the Paris Opéra, he appeared in the five-hundredth performance of FAUST (his brother Jean sang the title role); he also was heard in ROMÉO ET JULIETTE when that work entered the Paris Opéra repertory. His American debut took place during a visit of the METROPOLITAN OPERA to Chicago on Nov. 9, 1891, when he appeared as the king in LOHENGRIN; on this same occasion, Jean de Reszke made his American debut in the title role. A few weeks later, on Dec. 14, Edouard was heard in New York in *Roméo et Juliette*. He remained at the Metropolitan for over a decade. It was here that he started to sing German roles in German (the *Lohengrin* performance in Chicago had been in Italian), beginning with a performance of TRISTAN UND ISOLDE, in which Jean appeared as Tristan in a German-language performance for the first time. A giant figure, Edouard was a commanding personality on the stage; and his voice was like his figure, large and masterful. His last appearance at the Metropolitan took place on Mar. 21, 1903, in *Faust*. For many years thereafter he lived in seclusion on his estate in Poland. The outbreak of war in 1914 proved a disaster to both his health and fortune. During the war years he lived in extreme poverty. An improvement in his personal affairs in 1917 came too late to be appreciated, for by then he was broken in health.

de Reszke, Jean (born Jan Mieczyslaw), tenor. Born Warsaw, Poland, Jan. 14, 1850; died Nice, France, Apr. 3, 1925. One of the foremost tenors of his century, he was the brother of Josephine and Edouard DE RESZKE, soprano and bass. His mother, also a singer, gave him his first music lessons, after which he studied in Warsaw with Ciaffei and in Milan with Antonio Cotogni. He was trained as a baritone, and it was as such, under the name of Giovanni di Reschi, that he made his debut in Venice (Jan., 1874) in LA FAVORITA. During the next few years he continued singing baritone roles without any special success, appearing in Italy, London, Dublin, and Paris. His brother Edouard and the singing teacher Giovanni SBRIGLIA convinced him to change from a baritone into a tenor. After a period of study with Sbriglia, he returned to the opera stage on Nov. 9, 1879, this time as a tenor, in ROBERT LE DIABLE. He was not well received. Regarding himself as a failure, de Reszke withdrew from opera completely for five years, devoting himself to concert appearances. MASSENET induced him to return to opera for the Paris premiere of HÉRODIADE in 1884. De Reszke was a sensation as John the Baptist. From 1884 to 1889 he was the principal tenor of the PARIS OPÉRA, where he created the leading tenor role of LE CID, which Massenet wrote with him in mind. His career now established, it henceforth paralleled that of his brother. With Edouard, he appeared in ROMÉO ET JULIETTE when it entered the Paris Opéra repertory, and he sang in the five-hundredth performance of FAUST. A visit to BAYREUTH in 1888 turned him toward German opera. After an intensive period of study of the Wagnerian repertory, he appeared for the first time in a WAGNER opera in London in 1898, singing the part of TRISTAN in Italian. He followed this with performances as WALTHER and LOHENGRIN (still in Italian) that brought him to the front rank of living Wagnerian tenors. Curiously, when Jean de Reszke was engaged by the METROPOLITAN OPERA in 1891, it was to appear in French and Italian roles; and, more curious still, he, who was destined to become one of the most idolized interpreters of Wagner in America, had been imported by the Metropolitan to defeat the then growing vogue for Wagner in New York. Yet it was the immense personal appeal of Jean de Reszke that was finally instrumental in having the Metropolitan Opera restore the Wagner music dramas to their former prominence in the repertory.

Jean de Reszke's American debut took place in Chicago, during a visit to that city of the Metropolitan Opera, on Nov. 9, 1891. The opera was *Lohengrin,* and it was sung in Italian. (Jean's brother Edouard made his American debut in the same performance.) On Dec. 14, Jean de Reszke appeared for the first time in New York in *Roméo et Juliette,* once again with his brother in the cast, and was only moderately successful. It was only after Jean had begun appearing in the Wagnerian repertory that he became a matinee idol. He appeared for the first time in a German-language performance of *Tristan und Isolde* on Nov. 27, 1895; for the next half dozen years he was considered the ideal Tristan, the standard by which all later Tristans were measured. His last appearance at the Metropolitan Opera took place on Mar. 29, 1901, in *Lohengrin.* After only one other appearance on the opera stage, in PAGLIACCI at the Paris Opéra, he withdrew from an active career. For the next decade and a half he lived in Paris, teaching. Repeated attempts were made to lure him out of his retirement, but they were futile. When his only son died during World War I, he completely lost interest in himself. After 1919 he lived in Nice. Jean de Reszke was one of the greatest tenors of all time. To artistic phrasing, perfect enunciation, and beauty of voice, he brought dramatic power and an arresting stage presence.

de Reszke, Josephine, soprano. Born Warsaw, Poland, June 4, 1855; died there Feb. 22, 1891. She was the sister of the world-famous DE RESZKE brothers, Edouard and Jean. After preliminary studies with her mother and more formal instruction with Mme. Nissen-Salomon, she made her debut at the PARIS OPÉRA on June 21, 1875, singing the role of OPHELIA. She remained at the Opéra for several years, scoring triumphs in the Italian and French repertories and creating the role of Sita in LE ROI DE LAHORE. She turned down a flattering offer to appear in the United States, preferring to remain in Europe. When her brother Jean made his debut as tenor she appeared with him; and in 1884 she appeared with both her brothers in the Paris premiere of HÉRODIADE. At the height of her fame she married Baron Leopold de Kronenberg and retired from opera. Her only further appearances were exclusively for charity, in recognition of which the city of Posen, Poland, presented her with a diamond.

Der Irrnis und der Leiden pfade, Parsifal's description of his search for the Holy Grail, in Act III, Scene 1, of WAGNER'S PARSIFAL.

Der kleine Sandmann bin ich, the Sandman's Song in Act I, Scene 2 (originally Act II), of HUMPERDINCK'S HANSEL AND GRETEL, as he lulls the children to sleep.

Der kleine Taumann heiss' ich, the Dewman's Song in Act II (originally Act III) of HUMPERDINCK'S HANSEL AND GRETEL, as he sprinkles dewdrops on the children.

Der Tag seh' ich erscheinen, Beckmesser's serenade to Eva in Act II of WAGNER'S DIE MEISTERSINGER.

Der Vogelfänger bin ich ja, Papageno's ditty about his life as a bird-catcher, in Act I, Scene 1, of MOZART'S THE MAGIC FLUTE.

de Sabata, see SABATA, VICTOR DE.

de Saxe, Maurice, young man (tenor) loved by both Adriana and the Princesse de Bouillon, in CILÈA'S ADRIANA LECOUVREUR.

Desdemona, Otello's wife in VERDI'S and ROSSINI'S OTELLOS; in Verdi's opera sung by a soprano, in Rossini's by a mezzo-soprano. In the latter opera the role was created by Isabella COLBRAN.

Deserto sulla terra, the troubadour's serenade to Leonora in Act I, Scene 2, of VERDI'S IL TROVATORE.

Des Grieux, Chevalier, young nobleman (tenor) in love with Manon, in MASSENET'S MANON and PUCCINI'S MANON LESCAUT. In the latter opera the role was created by Giuseppe CREMONINI.

Des Grieux, Comte, father (bass) of Chevalier Des Grieux in MASSENET'S MANON.

de Silva, see SILVA, DON RUY GOMEZ DE.

Désiré, an attendant (tenor) in GIORDANO'S FEDORA.

De Siriex, a diplomat (baritone) in GIORDANO'S FEDORA.

de Sirval, Arthur, a nobleman (tenor) posing as a painter in DONIZETTI'S LINDA DI CHAMOUNIX.

De son coeur j'ai calmé la fièvre, Lothario's BERCEUSE in Act III of THOMAS'S MIGNON, as he nurses the ailing Mignon.

Desormière, Roger, conductor. Born Vichy, France, Sept. 13, 1898; died Paris, Oct. 25, 1963. He attended the Paris Conservatory, then for five years conducted the Diaghilev Ballet. In 1937 he was appointed a principal conductor of the OPÉRA-COMIQUE, where he directed the premieres of CHABRIER'S L'ÉTOILE and *Un Education manquée* and revivals of L'HEURE ESPAGNOLE and PELLÉAS ET MÉLISANDE. The last-named opera was one of his specialties, which he conducted (together with other modern works) in various opera houses in Europe. Between 1944 and 1946 he was music director of the Opéra-Comique but was compelled by ill health to resign in 1950, following which he appeared intermittently in guest performances throughout Europe.

Despina, a maid (soprano) in MOZART's COSÌ FAN TUTTE.

Destinn, Emmy (born Kittl), soprano. Born Prague, Feb. 26, 1878; died Budejovice, Czechoslovakia, Jan. 28, 1930. Her music study began with the violin, but the discovery that she had a beautiful voice led to vocal study in Prague with Marie Loewe-Destinn (whose name she assumed). In 1898 Destinn made her opera debut at the KROLL OPERA House in Berlin in CAVALLERIA RUSTICANA. A month later she was engaged by the Berlin Royal Opera (BERLIN STATE OPERA), where she remained for a decade. In 1901 she was chosen by Cosima WAGNER to appear as Senta in the first BAYREUTH production of DER FLIEGENDE HOLLÄNDER; a few years later Richard STRAUSS selected her for the Berlin premiere of SALOME. Meanwhile, on May 2, 1904, she made her debut at COVENT GARDEN as Donna ANNA and was such a success that she returned there for the next ten years, appearing in the first performance in England of MADAMA BUTTERFLY. Her American debut took place at the METROPOLITAN OPERA on Nov. 16, 1908 (the opening night of the season) in AIDA; it was a performance in which TOSCANINI was also making his American debut. Destinn was an instantaneous success. In *The New York Times*, Richard Aldrich described her voice as "of great power, body, and a vibrant quality, dramatic in expression, flexible and wholly subservient to her intentions." She remained a principal soprano of the Metropolitan for the next decade, appearing in the world premiere of THE GIRL OF THE GOLDEN WEST and the American premieres of GERMANIA, PIQUE DAME, and TIEFLAND.

She was a versatile artist. Her eighty or so roles included French, German, Italian, Russian, and Bohemian operas. She was at ease in every style. She had a pronounced histrionic ability as well as a remarkable voice; she was a tragedienne in the grand style.

During World War I she was interned at her Bohemian estate. She returned to opera in 1919 with appearances in Europe and America, retiring in 1921. After opera, her major interest was writing. She wrote a play that was produced, a novel, and a considerable amount of poetry.

Deutsches Staatsoper, *see* BERLIN STATE OPERA.

Deux Journées, Les, *see* WATER CARRIER, THE.

Deux séraphins aux blanches ailes, Thaïs' radiant aria in which, dying, she has a vision of Paradise, in Act III, Scene 3, of MASSENET's THAÏS.

de Valois, Marguerite, Henry IV of Navarre's betrothed (soprano) in MEYERBEER's LES HUGUENOTS.

Devant la maison, Méphistophélès' serenade after having summoned the will-o'-the-wisps to perform a minuet, in Part III of BERLIOZ' THE DAMNATION OF FAUST.

Devant le soleil, Grisélidis' assurance to the Marquis of her love, in Act I of MASSENET's GRISÉLIDIS.

Devil and Daniel Webster, The, opera in one act by MOORE. Libretto by the composer, based on a story by Stephen Vincent Benét. Premiere: New York City, May 18, 1939. Jabez Stone makes a pact with the devil to yield his soul in return for money. When the time comes for Jabez to keep his bargain, Daniel Webster defends him so eloquently before a jury comprising the famous villains of history that Jabez is released from his contract. A folk opera, *The Devil and Daniel Webster* is traditional in structure and style, made up of pleasing arias, many of them derived from popular or folk idioms, and powerful ensemble numbers.

Devil and Kate, The (Čert a Káča), opera in three acts by DVOŘÁK. Libretto by Adolf Wenig. Premiere: National Theater, Prague, Nov. 23, 1899. When Kate fails to get a dancing partner at a country fair she is willing to accept the devil (in the form of Marbuel), who takes her off to hell. Marbuel, annoyed by her garrulity, is only too willing to restore her to George, a shepherd, come to rescue her. Marbuel returns to earth to capture the Queen, but upon espying Kate returns hastily to hell. The overture is made up of two melodies (one of them folk in character) never heard in the opera. Some of the best pages in this score are the folk dances for the villagers in Act I (waltzes and polkas) and the dance of the devils in Act II. Notable vocal episodes include George's autobiographical song, "I'm just a poor shepherd boy," in Act I, and the Queen's aria in Act III, "How tragic fate is."

Devils of Loudon, The (Die Teufel von Loudun), opera in three acts by Penderecki. Libretto by the composer, based on John Whiting's play, *The Devils,* in turn derived from a book by Aldous Huxley. Premiere: Hamburg Opera, June 20, 1969. American premiere: Santa Fe Opera, N.M., Aug. 14, 1969. This is the first opera by one of the most significant composers to come from Poland since World War II. Like many other Penderecki compositions, the opera is based on a religious subject. In Loudon, France, in 1634, Sister Jeanne of the Angels, an hysterical hunchbacked woman, lusts for Father Grandier, a worldly Jesuit priest who has had a number of affairs with Loudon women. When she fails to interest him she accuses him of witchcraft. He is brought to trial and condemned to burn at the stake. The opera ends with curiosity seekers come to Loudon from all over Europe to watch the nuns of the Ursuline Convent curse and expose themselves. When this opera was introduced to Stuttgart on June 22, 1969, directed by Günther Rennert, a mild sensation was caused by staging several scenes with female characters appearing in topless costumes.

Devin du village, Le (The Village Soothsayer), comic opera (or INTERMEZZO) in one act by ROUSSEAU. Libretto by the composer. Premiere: Fontainebleau, Oct. 18, 1752. American premiere: New York City, Oct. 21, 1790. The distinguished French philosopher wrote this opera because of his enthusiasm for LA SERVA PADRONA. Impatient with French operas utilizing texts based on mythology and fables and making extensive use of vocal pyrotechnics and ballets, Rousseau looked upon *La serva padrona* as a welcome antidote to the grand French operas by RAMEAU and LULLY. He became the head of a number of French musicians who set themselves up as staunch advocates of operas such as *La serva padrona* as opposed to the established French tradition. The ensuing verbal battles between these two opposing schools of opera have come to be known as LA GUERRE DES BOUFFONS.

To advance the aims of the school of operatic ideals which he headed, Rousseau wrote a simple pastoral intermezzo about a village girl named Colette (soprano), who seeks the help of a soothsayer (baritone) upon learning that her beloved Colin (tenor) has been unfaithful to her. The soothsayer advises Colette to assume an attitude of utter indifference to Colin, while slyly informing Colin that Colette is in love with another man. The ruse works: Colette and Colin are reunited. The intermezzo is filled with lilting, though frequently slight, tunes such as Colette's "Si des galants de la ville" and "Avec l'objet de mes amours," and Colin's "Je vais revoir ma charmante maîtresse." The opera also contains some delightful orchestral music accompanying a dance pantomime. MOZART set a libretto which is a kind of parody of *Le Devin du village* in BASTIEN UND BASTIENNE.

Dewman, The, a character (soprano) in HUMPERDINCK'S HANSEL AND GRETEL.

Dewman's Song, The, *see* DER KLEINE TAUMANN HEISS' ICH.

Diable Boîteux, Le (The Devil on Two Sticks), chamber OPÉRA COMIQUE by FRANÇAIX. Libretto by the composer, based on a story by Le Sage. Premiere: Paris, 1937. American premiere: New York City, Nov. 19, 1950 (concert version). A limping devil betrays the foibles of man to Don Zambullo in order to liberate himself from the effects of a magician's potion.

Diaghilev, Sergei, impresario. Born Novgorod, Russia, Mar. 19, 1872; died Venice, Italy, Aug. 19, 1929. He is most celebrated as the founder and artistic director of the world-famous Diaghilev Ballet Russe. He was also responsible for introducing Russian opera to Paris, beginning with a presentation of scenes from SADKO, TSAR SALTAN, and RUSSLAN AND LUDMILLA in concert form in 1907. A year later he produced in Paris the first complete stage presentation of BORIS GODUNOV outside Russia (with Feodor CHALIAPIN in the title role) ; in 1909 he introduced Paris to IVAN THE TERRIBLE; and in 1913 he gave the first performance outside Russia of KHOVANTCHINA. He inaugurated two seasons of Russian operas in London in 1913 and 1914. Among the operas he subsequently produced were STRAVINSKY's MAVRA; GOUNOD's LE MÉDECIN MALGRÉ LUI (with SATIE's recitatives) and PHILÉMON ET BAUCIS; and CHABRIER's L'Education manqué (with MILHAUD's recitatives) .

Dialogues des Carmélites, Les (The Carmelites), opera in three acts by POULENC. Libretto by Georges Bernanos, based on Gertrude von le Fort's novel *Die letzte am Schafoot* and a motion-picture scenario by the Rev. Bruckberger and Philippe Agostini. Premiere: La Scala, Jan. 26, 1957. American premiere: San Francisco Opera, Sept. 20, 1957.

Characters: Blanche de la Force (soprano) ; Madame de Croissy, Prioress (mezzo-soprano) ; Madame Lidoine, the new Prioress (soprano) ; Mother Marie (mezzo-soprano) ; Sister Constance (soprano) ; Marquis de la Force, Blanche's father (baritone) ; Chevalier de la Force, his son (tenor) ; Chaplain (tenor); Carmelite nuns; commissioners; a jailer; a doctor; a servant; an officer; crowds. The action takes place in Paris and Compiègne in 1789.

Act I, Scene 1. Library of Marquis de la Force. The Chevalier de la Force brings his father, the Marquis, the disturbing news that the carriage bearing his sister, Blanche, was attacked by a mob. But before long Blanche makes her appearance. She is well, but obviously shaken. Somewhat later she decides to become a Carmelite nun, as a gesture of both renouncing the world and coming closer to God.

Scene 2. Parlor of the Carmelite convent at Compiègne. The Mother Superior explains to Blanche that, in spite of the severity of the rules prevailing at the convent, a heroic life is not the aim of this order. The Carmelites are not interested in self-denial or even the protection of virtue but in prayer and in the testing of one's weakness rather than strength. Blanche, deeply moved, expresses her eagerness to join the Carmelites and assumes the name of Sister Blanche of the Agony of Christ. The Mother Superior blesses her.

Scene 3. A tower in the convent. The Mother Superior is dying. Blanche upbraids the young Sister Constance for indulging in banter during such a tragedy. But Sister Constance cannot take even death seriously, and maintains her lightness of mood by insisting she has always wanted to die young.

Scene 4. A room in the infirmary. Dying, Mother Superior entrusts the care of Blanche to Mother Marie, over whom she is concerned for her weakness of character. Blanche has a tender exchange of words with the Mother Superior, who entreats her to remain true to her own simple and honest nature and to trust her honor to God. After Blanche leaves, the Mother Superior, denied drugs to alleviate her pain, becomes delirious and sees the Carmelite chapel splattered with blood. By the time Blanche returns, the Mother Superior is no longer conscious. She dies with Blanche at her side.

Act II, Scene 1. The nun's chapel. Sisters Blanche and Constance keep a vigil over the body of Mother Superior as they intone a requiem prayer. When Constance leaves to call the next pair of sisters to keep watch, Blanche, left alone, is seized with terror. Mother Marie arrives, consoles her, and suggests that on the morrow Blanche seek God's forgiveness.

Before the curtain rises on Scene 2,

there is a brief interlude during which Sisters Blanche and Constance, carrying flowers to the grave of Mother Superior, discuss the ways of God. To Sister Constance the death of the Mother Superior was a bad one, because it was a "small one." People, she feels, must die for one another or in place of one another.

Scene 2. The chapter room. Madame Lidoine, appointed the new Mother Superior, receives the members of the Carmelite order. She makes a simple address, stressing the importance of humility and prayer rather than martyrdom. Then she joins the sisters in intoning the strains of an "Ave Maria," sung a cappella.

Once more there is an interlude before the curtain. The Chevalier de la Force comes through a secret gate to have an audience with Blanche. The Mother Superior asks Mother Marie to listen to the interview from a hiding place.

Scene 3. The parlor. The Chevalier de la Force has come to warn Blanche that she is in danger and wants her to come home, which she refuses to do.

Scene 4. The sacristy. A Mass is being completed with the singing of the "Ave Verum." The nuns begin discussing the threat facing them, as religious orders are beginning to be suppressed, when mobs attack the convent and demand admission. Four Commissioners are permitted entrance, one of whom explains that all religious orders must be dissolved and all their buildings sold. Mother Marie accepts the verdict with dignity and pride, feeling as she does that in such turbulent times the people need the example of martyrdom. But Blanche is so terrified that she drops the figure of Christ she had been carrying. Outside the convent the people are heard singing the revolutionary "Ça ira."

Act III, Scene 1. The chapel. Mother Marie exacts a vow of martyrdom from her nuns, the first ones called upon to do so being Blanche and Constance. While the others are going through their vows, Blanche flees from the convent.

In an interlude before the curtain the Carmelites are seen in everyday dress, carrying their holy garb in a bundle under their arms. An officer warns them they must make no attempt to resume their calling, a condition Mother Marie accepts as a token of martyrdom.

Scene 2. The library of Marquis de la Force. The proud and luxurious house has been ravaged by the mob and its master guillotined. The house has been taken over by some of the leading revolutionaries, with Blanche as their servant. When Mother Marie comes to take Blanche to a hiding place, Blanche refuses, insisting she must be worthy of the name she has adopted, Sister Blanche of the Agony of Christ.

Scene 3. A prison cell at the Conciergerie. Except for Blanche and Mother Marie, all the nuns are prisoners. After Mother Marie reminds the nuns that they all must be courageous in their martyrdom, the jailer reads an order of the Revolutionary Tribunal condemning all the nuns to die for having betrayed the Revolution.

In an interlude before the curtain the Chaplain informs Mother Marie that the execution is to take place the following morning.

Scene 4. The mob has come to watch the guillotining of the Carmelites. As they progress toward the scaffold, the nuns sing "Salve Regina" (while, at the same time, the loud thump of the guillotine is heard from off-stage). As Sister Constance is about to be guillotined she notices Blanche rushing through the crowd to join her sister nuns. As she mounts the steps of the guillotine, Blanche sings the last verses of "Veni Creator." The guillotine having done its work, the mob disperses.

Les Dialogues des Carmélites is not only its composer's masterwork, but one of the most powerful and emotional operas of the twentieth century. Its success has been universal, not only in some of the world's leading opera houses but also over television (having been televised by the NBC Opera Company over

NBC-TV on Dec. 8, 1957, when it received the New York Music Critics' Circle Award). Possibly it attains its heights of eloquence in its religious music, particularly in the a cappella "Ave Maria," sung almost *sotte voce* at the end of Act II, and the "Salve Regina," which the nuns sing as they make their way to the guillotine. Henri Hell singles out other pages of surpassing grandeur, such as the scene in which Blanche and Constance question each other on the meaning of death, "written musically with a simplicity, a transparency, and a poetry of a really agonizing delicacy of touch"; the speech of the new Prioress as she takes on her duties, unfolding "with all the proper familiarity, like a garland of field flowers"; the duet in which the Chevalier de la Force tries to convince his sister, Blanche, to desert the Carmelites, "a duet of a lyricism that might be called amorous if it did not concern a brother and sister"; and, finally, the prison scene where the Prioress instills courage into the nuns in an aria "intense and poignant," rising "upon a vocal curve in a single outpouring, of an admirable breadth and purity."

Diaz, Justino, bass. Born Puerto Rico, Jan. 29, 1940. He received his musical training at the University of Puerto Rico and at the New England Conservatory with Boris GOLDOVSKY and Frederick JAGEL. His opera debut took place in Puerto Rico in MENOTTI's THE TELEPHONE, when he was seventeen. After appearances with several minor American companies, he achieved his first successes at LA SCALA, at the FESTIVAL OF TWO WORLDS in Spoleto, and at the SALZBURG FESTIVAL. He made his debut at the METROPOLITAN OPERA as Monterone in RIGOLETTO on Oct. 23, 1963. Since then he has appeared with that company in over thirty roles, including that of Antony (which he created) in BARBER's ANTONY AND CLEOPATRA when the Metropolitan Opera inaugurated its new auditorium at the LINCOLN CENTER FOR THE PERFORMING ARTS in 1966. In 1969 he

was acclaimed in the title role of VERDI's *Attila,* which was revived for the first time in the United States in over a century.

Dich, teure Halle, Elizabeth's apostrophe to the Hall of Minstrels, where song has reigned supreme and which once had vibrated with Tannhäuser's melodies, in Act II of WAGNER's TANNHÄUSER.

D'ici je vois la mer immense (Di qui io vedo il mar), Selika's address to the sea, which is as boundless as her own misery, in Act V of MEYERBEER's L'AFRICAINE.

Dickens, Charles, novelist. Born Landsport, Eng., Feb. 7, 1812; died Gadshi'l, Eng., June 9, 1870. Dickens' novels have provided plots for numerous operas. THE CRICKET ON THE HEARTH was adapted by GOLDMARK (*Das Heimchen am Herd*), MACKENZIE, and ZANDONAI (*Il grillo sul focolare*). The Pickwick Papers was the source of Albert COATES's *Pickwick* and Charles Wood's *Pickwick Papers. A Tale of Two Cities* was made into an opera by BENJAMIN and *Barnaby Rudge* by Julian Edwards (*Dolly Varden*).

Dickens also produced an operetta libretto, *The Village Coquettes,* music by John Hullah (1836).

Dick Johnson, *see* JOHNSON, DICK.

Dido and Aeneas, opera in three acts by PURCELL. Libretto by Nahum Tate, based on the fourth book of VIRGIL's *Aeneid.* Premiere: Josias Priest's Boarding School for Girls, Chelsea, in or about 1689. American premiere: New York City, Feb. 10, 1923 (concert version).

Characters: Dido, Queen of Carthage (soprano); Belinda, her maid (soprano); Aeneas, Trojan hero, legendary founder of Rome (baritone); sorceress (mezzo-soprano); attendant; witches; courtiers; sailors. The setting is ancient Carthage.

Act I, Scene 1. The royal palace in Carthage. Dido is tormented because she is in love with Aeneas and senses that disaster awaits her. When Aeneas arrives and reassures her of his great love, her doubts are dispelled. A dance of triumph follows.

Scene 2. A cave. The sorceress and two witches, who hate Dido, plot to destroy her by robbing her of her love. One of them is to assume the form of Mercury and command Aeneas to leave Carthage. The sound of hunting horns reveals that Aeneas and his party are at a hunt. The witches laugh demoniacally as they set forth to put their plan into operation. The scene ends with the Echo Dance of the Furies.

Act II. A grove. Aeneas and his party are on a hunt, and Dido is with them. At Diana's fountain there are festivities, interrupted by a sudden storm. After Belinda has led Dido to shelter, the false Mercury comes to Aeneas to bring him Jove's command to fulfill his destiny by leaving Carthage immediately. Anguished, Aeneas promises to obey. The sorceress and witches sing and dance at the success of their maneuver.

Act III. The harbor. Aeneas' ship is ready to sail. The sailors sing a nautical tune as they prepare to weigh anchor. The sorceress and witches watch with delight, prophesying Dido's death and the destruction of Carthage. Dido arrives and learns for the first time that her lover is about to leave her. After Aeneas has departed, she voices a poignant lament ("When I am laid in earth") and dies in Belinda's arms, while courtiers sing an elegy ("With drooping wings").

Of all seventeenth-century operas, *Dido and Aeneas* remains the one that comes closest to our present-day concept of what a musical drama should be. Surely nowhere else in the operas before GLUCK do we find such integration of music and text, song and dance, into a single artistic entity. One can say more: few operas of any era accomplish so much so economically. There are only three principal characters. The plot is bare, the dramatic action simple to the point of ingenuousness, the conflicts and climaxes direct. The play never lags, never lacks interest, and the famous lament of Dido, "When I am laid in earth," is surely one of the most affecting songs in all opera.

Thomas ARNE also wrote an opera *Dido and Aeneas* (1734), while the sub-ject of the love of Dido and Aeneas is used in the second part of BERLIOZ' opera LES TROYENS.

Dido's Lament, *see* WHEN I AM LAID IN EARTH.

Di due figli vivea, Ferrando's narrative to the soldiers of the Queen about Count di Luna's long lost brother, in Act I, Scene 1, of VERDI'S IL TROVATORE.

Didur, Adamo, bass. Born Sanok, Poland, Dec. 24, 1874; died Katowice, Poland, Jan. 7, 1946. After studying with Kasper Wysocki in Lemberg and Carlo Emerich in Milan, he made his concert debut in Milan as soloist in BEETHOVEN's *Ninth Symphony*. His opera debut took place in Rio de Janeiro in 1894, after which he appeared in major opera houses in Russia, Poland, and London. His American debut took place at the MANHATTAN OPERA House in 1907, and on Nov. 14, 1908, he made his bow at the METROPOLITAN as Méphistophélès in FAUST. In 1913 he created for America the role of BORIS GODUNOV. He remained a principal bass of the Metropolitan for a quarter of a century, making his last appearance there on Feb. 11, 1932, in THE TALES OF HOFFMANN. He then returned to Europe. Two months before the outbreak of World War II he was appointed director of the Lemberg Opera in Poland, but the war made musical activities impossible. After the war Didur taught singing for a brief time at the Katowice Conservatory.

Die Frist ist um, the Dutchman's recitative (followed by the aria "Wie oft in Meeres tiefsten Schlund") describing how he is doomed to travel the seas and how now that seven years have elapsed he is free to go ashore again, in Act I of WAGNER'S DER FLIEGENDE HOLLÄNDER.

Diego, Don, (1) Rodrigo's father (bass) in MASSENET'S LE CID.

(2) Council member (bass) in MEYERBEER'S L'AFRICAINE.

Dies Bildnis ist bezaubernd schön, Tamino's aria to the portrait of Pamina, extolling her beauty, in Act I, Scene 1, of MOZART'S THE MAGIC FLUTE.

Dietsch, Pierre-Louis, composer and conductor. Born Dijon, France, Mar. 17,

1808; died Paris, Feb. 20, 1865. He is remembered for his unhappy part in WAGNER's career. When Pillet, director of the PARIS OPÉRA, turned down Wagner's DER FLIEGENDE HOLLÄNDER on the basis of Wagner's sketches, he bought the libretto for Dietsch. Dietsch's opera, *Le Vaisseau fantôme,* was produced in Paris in 1842 and was a failure. Two decades later, as conductor at the Paris Opéra, Dietsch conducted the Paris premiere of TANNHÄUSER, a fiasco.

Dieu, que le monde révère (Tu che la terra adora), the chorus of the councilors acclaiming the Grand Inquisitor, in Act I of MEYERBEER's L'AFRICAINE.

Dieu, que ma voix tremblante, Eléazar's prayer in the Passover Scene in Act II of HALÉVY's LA JUIVE.

Dieu, qui fit l'homme à ton image, Friar Laurence's prayer after he performs the marriage ceremony of Roméo and Juliette, in Act III, Scene 1, of GOUNOD's ROMÉO ET JULIETTE.

Dieu! viens-je d'entendre, Béatrice's aria in BERLIOZ' BÉATRICE ET BÉNÉDICT, the most famous one in the opera.

Dieux! qui me poursuivez, Orestes' moving aria in Act II of GLUCK's IPHIGÉNIE EN TAURIDE.

Die Zukunft soll mein Herz bewahren, Max's expression of gratitude to the Prince for receiving a year of probation, in the finale of WEBER's DER FREISCHÜTZ.

di Luna, Count, a nobleman (baritone) in love with Leonora in VERDI's IL TROVATORE.

Dimitrij, opera in four acts by DVOŘÁK. Libretto by M. Cervinkova-Riegrova. Premiere: National Theater, Prague, Oct. 8, 1882. This is a continuation of the history treated in MUSSORGSKY's BORIS GODUNOV. In Dvořák's opera Dmitri comes to power following the death of Boris Godunov but is overthrown by Shuisky.

Dimmesdale, Arthur, father (tenor) of Hester Prynne's child in DAMROSCH's THE SCARLET LETTER.

Dimmi, Fiora, perchè ti veggo ancora, Manfredo's farewell to his wife as he is about to leave for battle, in Act II of MONTEMEZZI's L'AMORE DEI TRE RE.

Din, don, suona vespero, Chorus of the Bells as the villagers depart for Vespers, in Act I of LEONCAVALLO's PAGLIACCI.

d'Indy, Vincent, composer. Born Paris, Mar. 27, 1851; died there Dec. 2, 1931. He studied the piano with Louis Diémer and Antoine Marmontel, harmony with Alexandre Lavignac. During the Franco-Prussian War he led a bayonet attack in the battle of Val-Fleuri. After the war he began studying with César FRANCK, whose influence on his work was profound. From 1875 to 1879 D'Indy was chorus master of the Colonne Orchestra (Les Concerts du Châtelet). He received recognition as a composer with a series of orchestral works and an opera, *Le Chant de la cloche,* performed in 1886. His first important opera, *Fervaal,* introduced in Brussels on Mar. 12, 1897, was acclaimed. Later works established him as one of the major figures in French music; these included the operas *L'Etranger* (1901), *La Légende de Saint-Christophe* (1915), and *Le Rêve de Cynias* (1923). D'Indy helped found the Société Nationale de Musique in 1871 and in 1890 succeeded Franck as its president. In 1894 he was one of the founders of the Schola Cantorum, soon to become one of France's most distinguished music schools. D'Indy taught at the Schola for many years. He was also a professor of conducting at the Paris Conservatory. In 1905 and 1921 he visited the United States, conducting performances of his works in New York and Boston.

Dinorah (Le Pardon de Ploërmel), opera by MEYERBEER. Libretto by Jules BARBIER and Michel Carré. Premiere: Opéra-Comique, Apr. 4, 1859. American premiere: New Orleans, Mar. 4, 1861. A sorcerer reveals to Hoël, a goatherd (baritone), the location of a buried treasure, but warns him that the first to touch it must die. Dinorah (soprano), in love with Hoël, goes mad in the belief that Hoël has left her for good. She is almost drowned, but is rescued by her lover. On seeing Hoël, Dinorah recovers her sanity, while Hoël promises to abandon his quest. This opera is nowadays rarely performed. It is remembered for its fine overture and one aria, the Shadow Dance aria ("Ombre légère"), one of Meyerbeer's most brilliant coloratura arias. Other excerpts include Dinorah's lullaby to a goat, "Dors, petite, dors," in Act I; her legend of the treasure, "Sombre destine," in Act II; and Hoël's third-act aria, "Ah! mon remords te venge."

Dio, che nell'alma infondere, the duet of Don Carlos and Rodrigo, vowing eternal friendship, in Act II, Scene 1, of VERDI'S DON CARLOS.

Dio di giustizia, Fedora's prayer for Loris' safety, in Act III of GIORDANO'S FEDORA.

Dio di guida, Nabucco's prayer to God to save the life of Fenena, in Act IV of VERDI'S NABUCCO.

Diomede, Prince of Argos (baritone), rival of Troilus for Cressida's love, in WALTON'S TROILUS AND CRESSIDA.

Dio! mi potevi scagliar, Otello's bitter lament that his illusions have been shattered, in Act III of VERDI'S OTELLO.

Dionysos, a god in disguise (baritone) in MILHAUD'S *opéra minute* L'ABANDON D'ARIANE.

Dio ti giocondi, Desdemona's protestations of her innocence, in Act III of VERDI'S OTELLO.

Di pescatore ignobile, Gennaro's aria in Act II of DONIZETTI'S LUCREZIA BORGIA, detailing how he had been raised by a humble fisherman.

Dippel, Andreas, tenor and impresario. Born Cassel, Ger., Nov. 30, 1866; died Hollywood, Cal., May 12, 1932. He studied singing with Julius Hey, Franco LEONI, and Johann Ress. His opera debut took place in Bremen in 1887. While a member of the Bremen Opera he was given leave to appear at the METROPOLITAN OPERA, where he made his American debut on Nov. 26, 1890, in the American premiere of FRANCHETTI'S ASRAEL. Subsequently he sang with the Breslau Opera, MUNICH OPERA, VIENNA OPERA, at COVENT GARDEN and BAYREUTH; from 1898 to 1908 he was a principal tenor of the Metropolitan Opera. His

extensive repertory of about a hundred and fifty roles made him one of the most valuable members of the company, since he could always be counted on to make a last-minute substitute appearance for an indisposed tenor. For the 1908–09 season of the Metropolitan he was appointed joint manager (with GATTI-CASAZZA) in charge of the German repertory. He left the post in the spring of 1910, and from then until 1913 he was general manager of the Philadelphia-Chicago Opera Company. After that he managed his own light-opera company.

Di Provenza il mar, the aria of the elder Germont, recalling the joys of his Provençal home, a place blessed by sun and sea, as he urges his son to leave Violetta and rediscover the pleasures of his childhood, in Act II, Scene 1, of VERDI'S LA TRAVIATA.

Di qual amor, duet of Don Carlos and Elizabeth of Valois in which they first reveal their love for each other, in Act I of VERDI'S DON CARLOS.

Di quella pira, Manrico's dramatic aria where he vows to save the gypsy Azucena, in Act III, Scene 2, of VERDI'S IL TROVATORE.

Di qui io vedo il mar, *see* D'ICI JE VOIS LA MER IMMENSE.

directional (or spatial dimension in) music. This is an avant-garde technique in twentieth-century music, occasionally used in opera, to gain a stereophonic effect by having the music converge on the audience from all parts of the auditorium, either by scattering the musical forces or electronically by distributing loudspeakers throughout the theater. BADINGS' MARTIN KORDA, D.P., BLACHER'S ZWISCHENFÄLLE BEI EINER NOTLANDUNG, GINASTERA'S DON RODRIGO, and SCHULLER'S THE VISITATION are some contemporary operas utilizing this technique.

Dir Göttin der Liebe, Tannhäuser's ecstatic Hymn to Venus and to the sensual life he had enjoyed on the Venusberg, in Act II of WAGNER'S TANNHÄUSER.

Di rigori armato, a serenade sung by an Italian tenor to entertain the Marschallin as she attends to her interviews, in Act I of Richard STRAUSS'S DER ROSEN-KAVALIER.

Dir töne Lob, Tannhäuser's ecstatic hymn of sensual love to Venus, in Act I of WAGNER'S TANNHÄUSER.

di Signa, Betto, Buoso Donati's brother-in-law (baritone) in PUCCINI'S GIANNI SCHICCHI.

Dis-moi que je suis belle, THAÏS' song in Act II, Scene 1, of MASSENET'S THAÏS, where she entreats her mirror to tell her she is still beautiful.

Di sposa di padre, a beautiful aria from the now forgotten opera *Salvator Rosa* by Carlos GOMES, first produced in Genoa on Mar. 21, 1874.

Disprezzata regina, Ottavia's moving air in MONTEVERDI'S L'INCORONAZIONE DI POPPEA.

di Stefano, Giuseppe, tenor. Born near Catania, Italy, July 24, 1921. Completing his vocal studies with Montesanto in Milan, he made his debut in 1946 at the Reggio Emilia as Des Grieux in MANON. On Feb. 25, 1948, he made his debut at the METROPOLITAN OPERA as the Duke in RIGOLETTO. He remained with the company through the 1951–52 season, then returned for an additional season in 1964–65. Meanwhile he had appeared in some of the world's other major opera houses. In the earlier part of his career he assumed such lighter roles as ELVINO, Wilhelm Meister, NADIR, and so forth, but after 1953 he added to his repertoire such heavier roles as DON JOSÉ, CANIO, RADAMES, and TURIDDU.

Di tanti palpiti, one of ROSSINI'S most beautiful duets, sung by Tancredi and Amenaide in Rossini's TANCREDI. During the final rehearsal, Malanotte, who played the role of Amenaide, refused to sing the first-act aria Rossini had written for her. That very evening Rossini had to write a new number, and he complied with "Di tanti palpiti." It has been said he composed this duet while boiling rice, the reason why it is sometimes referred to as "the rice aria." This melody is sometimes used in the Lesson Scene in THE BARBER OF SEVILLE.

Dite alla giovine, one section of the long duet of Violetta and the elder Germont in Act II, Scene 1, of VERDI'S LA TRAVIATA, in which she finally yields to the old man's demand she desert her beloved Alfredo.

Ditson Fund, Alice M., a fund established at Columbia University in 1944 to commission and produce American operas. Among the works sponsored by this fund have been BACON'S A DRUMLIN LEGEND and *A Tree on the Plains;* Normand Lockwood's *The Scarecrow* (1945); Otto Luening's EVANGELINE; THE MEDIUM; THE MOTHER OF US ALL; Bernard Rogers' *The Warrior* (1947); Bernard Wagenaar's *Pieces of Eight* (1943); and WEISGALL'S *Six Characters in Search of an Author.* The Ditson Fund also provided the funds for the recordings of MOORE'S CARRY NATION and Weisgall's *The Tenor.*

Dittersdorf, Karl Ditters von (born Karl Ditters), composer and violinist. Born Vienna, Nov. 2, 1739; died Neuhof, Bohemia, Oct. 24, 1799. In 1761 he toured Italy with GLUCK, appearing as a violinist. Between 1764 and 1769 he was KAPELL-MEISTER for the Bishop of Grosswardein, in Hungary, for whom he wrote his first comic opera. In 1769 he was employed in a similar capacity by Count Schaff-gotsch, who subsequently appointed him Overseer of Forests and after that Chief Magistrate, a post which carried with it a patent of nobility. He visited Vienna in 1773, where his oratorios *Esther* and *Job* were produced successfully. Emperor Joseph II offered him the post of *kapellmeister* but Dittersdorf declined it. The death of his patron and employer in 1795 brought about a sharp reversal of fortune. Dittersdorf's pension was so meager that he was now frequently in want. Only when Count von Stillfried took his family into his own household was the composer's plight alleviated. Dittersdorf continued composing up to the end of his life. His voluminous output included numerous symphonies, concertos, string quartets, and piano sonatas. He wrote some twenty-eight operas, the best being: THE DOCTOR AND THE APOTHECARY (1786); *Orpheus the Second* (1787); *Hieronymous Knicker* (1789); *The Merry Wives of Windsor* (1796).

Di tu se fedele, Riccardo's BARCAROLLE in Act I, Scene 2 (or in a later arrangement, Act II), of VERDI's UN BALLO IN MASCHERA, asking the fortuneteller Ulrica to prognosticate his future.

diva, Italian for "goddess." This term is used in opera for the principal soprano or sopranos of a company. Like PRIMA DONNA, it is often used satirically.

Divine Comedy, The, *see* DANTE ALIGHIERI; FRANCESCA DA RIMINI.

Divinités du Styx, Alceste's dramatic aria in Act I of GLUCK's ALCESTE, offering herself to the gods as a sacrifice in order to save her husband's life. TOSCANINI introduced this aria in the Hades scene of Gluck's ORFEO when that opera was revived by the METROPOLITAN OPERA in 1910.

Djamileh, OPÉRA COMIQUE in one act by BIZET. Libretto by Louis Gallet, based on MUSSET's *Namouna*. Premiere: Opéra-Comique, May 22, 1872. American premiere: Boston Opera, Feb. 24, 1913. The heroine is a slave to a Turkish nobleman, Prince Haroun (tenor), with whom she is in love. Wearying of her, the prince plans to sell her, but Djamileh (soprano) evolves a plan (in league with the prince's secretary, Splendiano, tenor).

She disguises herself and comes to the prince in a group of girls displayed by a slave dealer. The prince becomes enchanted with her, particularly after she has performed a seductive dance. Only then does Djamileh reveal her true identity, explaining she went through this ruse because of her great love for the prince, who is now willing to restore her to his good graces.

Notable musical excerpts include the orchestral ballet music; the duet of Haroun and Splendiano, "Que l'esclave soit brune ou blonde"; the aria known as Djamileh's Lament; and the chorus, "Quelle est cette belle?"

Not until the twentieth century did *Djamileh* get general recognition, following a brilliant and highly successful revival by the VIENNA Royal (STATE) OPERA under MAHLER in 1898. It has since been performed by many leading opera houses in numerous translations. It was revived by the OPÉRA-COMIQUE on Oct. 27, 1938, to celebrate the centenary of Bizet's birth. On Dec. 7, 1959, it was performed in New York City in a concert version by the Little Orchestra Society under Thomas Scherman.

Dmitri, pretender to the Russian throne (tenor) in MUSSORGSKY's BORIS GODUNOV.

Dobbs, Mattawilda, soprano. Born Atlanta, Ga., July 11, 1925. Her voice teachers were Naomi Maise, Willis James, and Lotte Leonard. She concluded her studies at the Mannes School of Music and at the Berkshire Music Center. On a John Hay Whitney fellowship, she studied for two years in Paris with Pierre Bernac. Her training ended, she won first prize in the International Music Competition in Geneva. In 1952 she made her opera debut at the HOLLAND FESTIVAL in the title role of STRAVINSKY's LE ROSSIGNOL. After appearing in various opera houses in Sweden, England, Austria, and Italy, she made her debut at LA SCALA as Elvira in ROSSINI's L'ITALIANA IN ALGERI and at GLYNDEBOURNE as Zerbinetta in ARIADNE AUF NAXOS, both in 1953. She scored a triumph as QUEEN OF SHEMAKHA at COVENT GARDEN on Jan. 7, 1954, repeating this performance in her American opera debut at the SAN FRANCISCO OPERA in 1955. On Nov. 9, 1956, she made her debut at the METROPOLITAN OPERA as GILDA; she has since remained one of its principal sopranos, scoring major successes in such roles as OLYMPIA, ROSINA, and in the MOZART repertory with PAMINA being one of her most effective roles.

d'Obigny, Marquis, a nobleman (bass) in VERDI's LA TRAVIATA.

Dobrowen, Issai, conductor. Born Nishni-Novgorod, Russia, Feb. 27, 1893; died Oslo, Norway, Dec. 9, 1953. He attended the conservatories in Moscow and Vienna, after which, in 1917, he was appointed professor at the Moscow Conservatory. In 1919 he made his debut as opera conductor at the Moscow BOLSHOI THEATER. Three years later he became a principal conductor of the DRESDEN OPERA, in charge of Russian operas, scoring a major success with his conducting of BORIS GODUNOV. From 1924 to 1927 he was first conductor of the Vienna Volksoper, and in 1927–28 he was general music director of the Royal Opera in Sofia, Bulgaria. In 1932 he settled in Norway and became conductor of the Oslo Philharmonic Orchestra, holding this post until the Nazi occupation. He then went to Sweden and became conductor of the STOCKHOLM OPERA. Between 1949 and 1951 he led performances of Russian operas at LA SCALA. In the United States he was known exclusively as a symphony conductor. He made his debut with the San Francisco Symphony in 1930, subsequently appearing as guest conductor of major American orchestras. Dobrowen wrote one opera, *A Thousand and One Nights,* produced in Moscow in 1921.

Doch eh' ich in des Todes Tal, Sulamith's air with chorus, in Act III of GOLDMARK'S THE QUEEN OF SHEBA.

Docteur Miracle, Le (Dr. Miracle), comic opera in one act by BIZET. Libretto by Leon Battu and Ludovic Halévy. Premiere: Bouffes-Parisiens, Paris, Apr. 9, 1857. American premiere: New Haven, Conn., July 14, 1962. This was Bizet's first produced opera. He had submitted it for a competition sponsored by Jacques OFFENBACH, then the impresario of the Bouffes-Parisiens in Paris, and shared first prize with Alexandre Lecocq.

Doctor and the Apothecary, The (Doktor und Apotheker), comic opera in two acts by DITTERSDORF. Libretto by Gottlieb Stephanie. Premiere: Kärntnerthorthheater, Vienna, July 11, 1786. American premiere: Charleston, S.C., Apr. 26, 1796. Gotthold, son of a doctor, and Leonore, daughter of an apothecary, are in love, but they are thwarted because their respective fathers are enemies. To make matters even worse, Leonore's father wants her to marry Captain Sturmwald. Gotthold resorts to various ruses and disguises to try to elope with

his beloved, but in vain; he also performs various tricks to dampen Sturmwald's enthusiasm for Leonore. Love wins out in the end—but only after Leonore's mother becomes the ally of the lovers and helps effect a reconciliation between the two former enemies. Leonore's poignant aria, "Wie kann ich Freude noch in meinem Blicken zeigen," the comic duet of the doctor and the apothecary, "Sie sind ein Charlatan," Gotthold's aria "Wann hörst du auf," and an orchestral intermezzo between the first and second acts are of musical interest.

Dodon, the king (bass) in RIMSKY-KORSAKOV'S LE COQ D'OR.

Doktor Faust (Doctor Faust), opera in three scenes with two prologues and an interlude by BUSONI (completed by Philip Jarnach). Libretto by the composer, based on the FAUST legend and on *Dr. Faustus* by Christopher MARLOWE. Premiere: Dresden Opera, May 21, 1925. American premiere: New York City, Dec. 1, 1964. This "epic of disillusionment and disenchantment," as the composer described it, avoids theatrical values, love interest, or characterization and places its stress on ideas. The opera is poised almost completely on a spiritual plane. It is a work of large proportions, requiring an immense cast of singers and a greatly expanded orchestra, and makes exacting demands not only on the performers but also on the mechanics of staging. To Edward J. DENT, the character of Faust was meant to represent Busoni himself, surrounded by his students and disciples, using the symbol of Faust, the magician, as a symbol of his own powers at the piano and Faust the idealist, begging for "genius," as Busoni the creator.

The opera opens with two prologues and an interlude. In the first prologue, a magic book is brought to Faust (baritone) in his study, while in the second, Faust derives from the book the means of invoking Mephistopheles to help him enjoy to the full life's experiences in return for a lifetime of service. The interlude describes the murder of a young soldier in a cathedral chapel through Mephistopheles' diabolical powers.

The main part of the opera opens with the marriage ceremony of the Duke (tenor) and Duchess (soprano) of Parma. Faust helps amuse the guests by evoking images, each of whom resembles either Faust or the Duchess. Subsequently Mephistopheles (tenor) arrives to bring the Duke the news that Faust and the Duchess have eloped.

The second scene is at an inn in Wittenberg. Faust is telling some students how he had made love to the Duchess on the day of her wedding to the Duke. Mephistopheles once again becomes the bearer of sad tidings: the Duchess is dead. This tragedy so overwhelms Faust that he, too, yearns for death. Then three dark figures come to Faust demanding the return of the magic book, which he refuses to give up.

The final scene finds Faust confronted in the street by a beggar woman and a child. To his amazement and horror the beggar woman turns out to be the Duchess and the child a dead corpse. Gently, Faust puts the dead child on the ground, then prays for his revival, offering his own life in exchange. After Faust dies, a naked young man arises from the corpse of the dead child.

In his score, Busoni creates a harmonious marriage between the old and the new: the old, in Bach-like choral passages such as the off-stage "Credo," sung when Faust comes to an agreement with Mephistopheles in the second prologue, and the "Gloria" which the students sing in the Wittenberg inn; the new, in his anticipation of HINDEMITH's linear counterpoint and (like BERG in WOZZECK) his use of instrumental forms (variations, rondo, suite, and so forth) within his operatic framework.

Doktor Faust is Busoni's masterwork. He labored on it for many years but did not live to complete it—a chore accomplished from sketches by Philip Jarnach. When first heard, *Doktor Faust* was a total failure. It took decades for the world of music to recognize its strength,

originality, and even profundity. Revivals at the FLORENCE MAY FESTIVAL in 1942, in Berlin in 1955, in New York City in 1964 and 1966, and in Hanover in 1968 all helped to place *Doktor Faust* where it belonged: with the most significant operas of the twentieth century.

Doll Song, *see* OISEAUX DANS LA CHARMILLE, LES.

Dolores, La, opera in three acts by Tomás Bretón. Libretto by the composer, based on a tale by Salares. Premiere: Madrid Opera, Mar. 16, 1895. This is one of the most prominent and successful operas of the Spanish nationalist school. The plot revolves around a waitress, the seductive Dolores, who captures the heart of many men in the small town of Calatayud. The tenor madrigal, "Henchido de amor santo," and a jota for solo voices, chorus, and orchestra are of interest.

Dôme épais, le jasmin, BARCAROLLE sung by Lakmé and her slave girl as they are about to bathe, in Act I of DELIBES's LAKMÉ.

Domgraf-Fassbaender, Willi, baritone. Born Aachen, Feb. 19, 1897. His vocal studies and his opera debut took place in Aachen, the latter in 1922. Following engagements in several German opera houses, he became principal lyric baritone of the BERLIN STATE OPERA, where he remained until the end of World War II. On the opening night of the first season of the GLYNDEBOURNE FESTIVAL in 1934, he appeared as FIGARO in the MOZART opera, returning to that festival several times after that, mainly in Mozartean roles. After World War II he was frequently heard at the HANOVER OPERA, the VIENNA STATE OPERA, and the MUNICH OPERA. He subsequently assumed the post of principal resident producer at the Nuremberg Opera. His reputation in America has been gained through his recordings.

Domingo, Placido, tenor. Born Madrid, Spain, Jan. 21, 1941. His earliest musical experience came through his parents, both of them ZARZUELA singers. His formal training, both in music and in academic subjects, took place in Mexico City, where he made his operatic debut as ALFREDO. On Feb. 22, 1966, when the NEW YORK CITY OPERA COMPANY inaugurated its new home in Lincoln Center with the premiere of GINASTERA's DON RODRIGO, Domingo took the title role with such striking success that he became an overnight star at twenty-five. He continues as a principal tenor with the New York City Opera and serves the same function with the METROPOLITAN OPERA across the plaza. There he made his debut on the opening night of the 1968–69 season as Maurizio opposite Renata TEBALDI in a revival of CILÈA's ADRIANA LECOUVREUR. He made his LA SCALA debut Dec. 7, 1969, as ERNANI in the opening night performance of the 1969–70 season. He was extremely well received there for his beautiful and finely controlled voice, as well as for his tall, dark, handsome appearance. Domingo has had similar triumphs in Vienna, Hamburg, Berlin, and London.

Domino noir, Le (The Black Domino), OPÉRA COMIQUE in three acts by AUBER. Libretto by Eugène SCRIBE. Premiere: Opéra-Comique, Dec. 2, 1837. American premiere: New Orleans, 1838.

At a masked ball, Horatio (tenor) meets Lady Angela (soprano) and is enchanted by her. At the midnight hour, when guests are supposed to unmask, she flees to the convent where she is a sister preparing to become Lady Abbess. The late hour makes it impossible for her to gain admission, and so she finds refuge at the home of Claudia, the housekeeper of one of Horatio's friends. Upon Horatio's appearance there, Lady Angela assumes the part of a peasant girl. Even as a peasant girl she manages to win Horatio's fascinated interest. When next he sees her, she is wearing the robes of the Lady Abbess, though she has not as yet taken her vows. Lady Angela and Horatio are finally united when the Queen of Spain compels the girl to desert her office at the convent and seek out a husband. To Angela, the composer assigned two of the most beautiful arias in this opera, "Une fée, un bon ange" in the first act and in the last act, "Ah, quelle nuit, le moindre bruit me trouble." The score also contains a number of delightful orchestral episodes, including the overture, an entr'acte between the first and second acts, a military march, and the "Ronde aragonaise."

Don Carlos, opera in five acts by VERDI. Libretto by François Joseph Mery and Camille du Locle, based on the SCHILLER tragedy of the same name. Premiere: Paris Opéra, Mar. 11, 1867. American premiere: Academy of Music, New York City, Apr. 12, 1877.

Characters: Philip II of Spain (bass); Don Carlos, Infante of Spain (tenor); Rodrigo, Marquis of Posa (baritone); Elizabeth of Valois (soprano); Grand Inquisitor (bass); Princess Eboli (mezzosoprano); a friar; Countess of Aremberg; Count of Lerma; Theobald, a page; a royal herald; ladies; gentlemen; inquisitors; courtiers; pages; guards; soldiers; magistrates. The setting is France and Spain in the sixteenth century.

Act I (sometimes omitted). Forest in Fontainbleau. Don Carlos has made a secret visit to France to catch a glimpse of the woman selected to be his wife—Elizabeth of Valois. When she appears, he is ecstatic. Posing as Don Carlos' messenger, he offers to be her escort. It is not long before the two realize they are deeply in love with one another, as they reveal in "Di qual amor." But their love is complicated by a change in plans. For reasons of state she must marry Don Carlos' father, Philip II.

Act II, Scene 1. The Convent of San Giusto in Madrid. The monks are praying. Don Carlos arrives, bitter at having lost Elizabeth, and hardly consoled when one of the monks tells him he can find salvation in death alone. At this point, Don Carlos' friend, Rodrigo, appears, having just returned from Flanders. They are overjoyed at their reunion. Don Carlos then reveals his passion for a woman who is now his stepmother.

Rodrigo advises his friend to leave the country. The King and Queen now arrive for prayer. Rodrigo and Don Carlos vow eternal friendship ("Dio, che nell' alma infondere").

Scene 2. A garden outside the monastery. Princess Eboli is in the company of the Queen's ladies. Soon Rodrigo appears with a letter for the Queen from her mother, the Queen of France; at the same time he slips her a secret note from Carlos pleading for a meeting. It is not long before Carlos himself appears to seek the Queen's help in gaining him permission to leave the country. He soon gives vent to his emotions, to which the Queen responds with equal fervor but remains true to her marriage vows. Don Carlos departs in despair, leaving the Queen alone, and when the King arrives, he is at first furious to find the Queen without her ladies-in-waiting. However, he permits Rodrigo to speak to him about granting the people of Flanders more freedom.

Act III, Scene 1. The palace gardens in Madrid. Don Carlos has received a letter arranging a meeting place. Believing it has been sent by the Queen, he arrives at the appointed place in great expectancy. But the letter has come from Princess Eboli. Since she is heavily veiled, Carlos does not recognize her and greets her passionately. It is then only that the Princess Eboli realizes with horror that Carlos is in love with the Queen. She threatens to reveal this to the King, which leads Carlos to draw his dagger and try to kill her; but the Princess is saved by Rodrigo's sudden appearance.

Scene 2. Square in front of the cathedral. The King, his court, and the people are present to witness the immolation of a group of heretics. Carlos arrives, demanding from the King that he be made Viceroy of Flanders. When the King refuses, Carlos draws his sword. Once again it is Rodrigo who saves the situation by holding back Carlos' hand. Don Carlos is arrested for treason. The heretics are set afire; the people rejoice; and a voice from Heaven pronounces pardon for the dying.

Act IV, Scene 1. The King's study. The King, troubled by recent developments, doubts that the Queen loves him ("Ella giammai m'amo"). When the Grand Inquisitor appears, the King tells him about Carlos' act of treason, and they agree he must die. The King, however, is hesitant over the Inquisitor's demand that Rodrigo, too, must be disposed of. After the Inquisitor leaves, the Queen comes seeking her jewel case, which she finds on the King's desk. This upsets her, for the case contains a picture of Don Carlos. When the King finds the picture, he accuses his wife of adultery. The Queen, in turn, convinced that the Princess Eboli has betrayed her, denounces the Princess and orders her to go either to a nunnery or into exile. Contrite and repentant, Princess Eboli expresses grief that her beauty has caused so much harm and vows she will do everything in her power to save Don Carlos ("O don fatale").

Scene 2. A prison. Carlos, in his cell, is visited by Rodrigo come to bid him farewell ("Per me giunto e il di supremo"). He then explains that he has redirected the guilt for the Flemish revolt from Carlos to himself. Carlos refuses to consider such a sacrifice, insisting he will go to the King to explain all. But an assassin's bullet kills Rodrigo who, with his dying breath, informs Carlos that the Queen will be waiting for Carlos on the morrow outside the Monastery of San Giusto ("O Carlo, ascolta"). Rodrigo then dies, happy in the knowledge that Carlos will carry on the fight for freedom. The people, headed by Princess Eboli, rush into the prison seeking revenge, but are calmed by the Grand Inquisitor.

Act V. The Monastery of San Giusto. The Queen has come to the tomb of Charles V to seek consolation ("S'ancor si piange in cielo"). She speaks of the joys she once knew with Don Carlos and her sorrow in leaving him forever ("Tu che le vanita conoscesti del mondo"). When Don Carlos arrives, he informs her he must leave for Flanders to continue the fight for freedom. They bid each other tender farewell, but are interrupted by the sudden arrival of the King and the Grand Inquisitor, together with guards ready to arrest Carlos. Suddenly, a monk, dressed in the former Emperor Charles V's clothes, steps out from the tomb and leads Don Carlos to safety.

Don Carlos belongs to Verdi's productive middle period in which he wrote some of his most famous and best-loved works. Possibly because he wrote this opera for performance in Paris, it has an almost MEYERBEER character, with big ensemble scenes, elaborate settings, spectacular climaxes, and overpowering dramatics. Thus, *Don Carlos* is larger in design and of greater emotional power and visual impact than operas such as RIGOLETTO or LA TRAVIATA, which preceded it; in its emphasis on spectacle, it anticipates its immediate successor, AIDA.

Donde lieta uscì, Mimi's air insisting she and Rodolfo must part for good, in Act III of PUCCINI's LA BOHÈME.

Don Giovanni (Don Juan), DRAMMA GIOCOSO in two acts by MOZART. Libretto by Lorenzo DA PONTE, based on Giuseppe Bertati's libretto for *Don Giovanni Tennorio* (1786) by Giuseppe GAZZANIGA. Premiere: National Theater, Prague, Oct. 29, 1787. American premiere: Park Theater, New York City, May 23, 1826. Characters: Don Giovanni, nobleman (baritone); Leporello, his servant (bass); Don Pedro, the Commandant of Seville (bass); Donna Anna, his daughter (soprano); Don Ottavio, betrothed to Donna Anna (tenor); Masetto, a peasant (baritone or bass); Zerlina, his fiancée (soprano); Donna Elvira, lady of Burgos (soprano); peasants; musicians. The setting is Seville, Spain, in the middle of the seventeenth century.

Act I, Scene 1. Courtyard of the Commandant's palace. The overture opens with thirty measures of dramatic, portentous music that recurs in the banquet scene in Act II, Scene 5. A lighter mood follows presenting vivacious themes that reflect different facets of Don Giovanni's personality and suggest some of his gay

adventures. Leporello, Don Giovanni's servant, is found, at the rise of the curtain, at night in the garden of the Commandant's palace. He is angered at the way in which his master drives him night and day ("Notte e giorno"). Don Giovanni emerges from the palace followed by Donna Anna, whom he has, under cover of night, been attempting to seduce. They exchange angry words. Donna Anna's father appears, and before long he and Don Giovanni are engaged in a duel in which the Commandant (Donna Anna's father) is killed. After the culprit makes his escape, Donna Anna—who has run for help—comes back with her betrothed, Don Ottavio. She is grief-stricken to find her father dead and cannot be consoled by her lover ("Fuggi, crudele, fuggi"). Together they vow vengeance.

Scene 2. A square outside Seville. Don Giovanni, followed by Leporello, comes upon a weeping woman. She turns out to be Donna Elvira, one of Giovanni's former loves, who bitterly denounces the man who has made love to her and then abandoned her ("Ah! chi mi dice mai"). After Giovanni makes a discreet departure, Leporello enumerates to Donna Elvira his Master's conquests (Catalogue Song: "Madamina! il catalogo è questo"). Now it is Donna Elvira who swears she will some day destroy the fickle Don.

Scene 3. A country place near Don Giovanni's castle. The marriage of Masetto and Zerlina is about to be celebrated. Since Don Giovanni finds Zerlina attractive, he has Leporello invite the townspeople into the castle so that he can be alone with her. Zerlina tries her best to resist his charm ("Là ci darem la mano"). Donna Elvira now makes a timely appearance, the Don effects a quick departure, and Elvira denounces Don Giovanni before Zerlina, Donna Anna, and Don Ottavio ("Ah! fuggi il traditor"). After Don Ottavio repeats his intent to avenge the Commandant's death, he sings about his beloved, whose peace of mind alone will bring him happiness ("Dalla sua pace").

In what is usually staged as a separate scene Don Giovanni orders Leporello to gather the villagers for a feast ("Finch' han dal vino").

Scene 4. The garden of Don Giovanni's palace. A party has been arranged. Masetto, jealous of Giovanni's flirtation with Zerlina, quarrels with her but has a change of heart after Zerlina's coy plea for forgiveness ("Batti, batti, o bel Masetto"). Among the guests are Donna Anna, Donna Elvira, and Don Ottavio, all three masked: Don Giovanni invites them, with his other guests, into his palace, which they enter, while praying for help for vengeance ("Protegga il giusto cielo").

Scene 5. Inside the palace. While the guests are dancing to the strains of the famous Minuet and two other tunes all played simultaneously, Don Giovanni draws Zerlina into another room. Her outcries attract the attention of the guests. Suddenly, Don Giovanni enters, dragging Leporello after him and accusing his servant of having made advances to Zerlina. But the guests are not fooled, particularly not Donna Anna, Donna Elvira, and Don Ottavio. Drawing his sword, Don Giovanni forces his way through the crowd and escapes.

Act II, Scene 1. Before Donna Elvira's house. Don Giovanni comes here because he wishes to serenade Elvira's maid. He and Leporello exchange cloaks. Disguised as Leporello, Don Giovanni serenades the girl ("Deh, vieni alla finestra"). Masetto comes on the scene determined to give Giovanni a thrashing, but fails to recognize Giovanni in Leporello's cloak. Being off guard, he is thrashed by Giovanni. Zerlina comes to Masetto to soothe him as he lies stretched out in the street. Masetto confesses he is hurt more grievously in heart than in body, and Zerlina consoles him ("Vedrai, carino").

Scene 2. The garden of the Commandant's palace. When Leporello, still disguised as Don Giovanni, is confronted by Don Ottavio, Donna Anna, Donna Elvira, and Zerlina, he reveals his true identity to escape punishment. Don Ottavio once again speaks of his great love for Donna Anna ("Il mio tesoro").

Scene 3. In a graveyard, Don Giovanni and Leporello meet near a statue raised to the memory of the late Commandant. Don Giovanni mockingly orders Leporello to invite the statue to dinner. To Leporello's horror, the statue nods its head in acceptance.

Scene 4. In the Commandant's palace. When Don Ottavio entreats Donna Anna to marry him, she replies sorrowfully that while she loves him she cannot be his wife as long as she is filled with her terrible grief ("Non mi dir").

Scene 5. Banquet hall in Don Giovanni's palace. While Don Giovanni dines alone, his private orchestra (on stage) plays for him such delightful morsels as the "Non più andrai" aria from THE MARRIAGE OF FIGARO. Donna Elvira comes to prevail on Giovanni to reform. Her quest proving futile, she departs. She quickly returns, screaming, and rushes out another door. Leporello, too, is a victim of terror when he goes to investigate the source of Elvira's fear. For the statue of the Commandant has come to keep his dinner appointment. He is welcomed fearlessly by the proud Don Giovanni. Since Don Giovanni refuses to change his ways, the statue consigns him to the fiery world below. The Don and his palace are consumed in flames. The opera ends with a brief epilogue (sometimes omitted) in which Donna Anna, Donna Elvira, Zerlina, and Ottavio learn from Leporello of Don Giovanni's fate and rejoice over it.

Don Giovanni was the second collaboration of Mozart and the librettist, da Ponte, coming just a year after *The Marriage of Figaro*. *Don Giovanni* was commissioned by the Bondini Opera Company in Prague, which had scored a resounding success with *Figaro*. What that company wanted was another comic opera in like vein, and it is probable that this is what the authors set out to do when they started writing. But, recognizing Mozart's power and passion, da Ponte emphasized the dramatic element in his text, though without abandoning comic and satiric nuances; and Mozart, ever sensitive, alternated the light and comic strokes with darker colors of genuine tragedy. Recognizing that he had produced neither an OPERA BUFFA nor an OPERA SERIA, but a combination of both, Mozart applied to his new opera the designation of *dramma giocoso* or "gay drama." The gaiety is there: in the character of Leporello, in the playful quarrels and reconciliations of Masetto and Zerlina, in the fleet and witty music Mozart wrote for these *opera-buffa* characters. The Italian grace of Don Giovanni's serenade and Don Ottavio's love songs is also in the *opera-buffa* tradition. But it is the tragic element, rather than the comic, that is accentuated, particularly in the characterization of Don Giovanni. And it is with its tragedy that this opera arrives at its highest plane of eloquence: with Donna Anna's terrible grief in the first scene or the cataclysmic music with which Don Giovanni meets his doom in the closing one. That this unconventional alternation of comedy and tragedy did not confuse its first audience speaks volumes for its discrimination. "Connoisseurs and artists say that nothing like this has been given in Prague," reported a contemporary journal. "Mozart himself conducted, and when he appeared in the orchestra, he was hailed by a triple acclamation." Since then, *Don Giovanni* has been generally accepted as Mozart's greatest opera; it is also one of the oldest operas in the permanent repertory of every major opera house.

See also DON JUAN.

Donizetti, Gaetano, composer. Born Bergamo, Italy, Nov. 29, 1797; died there Apr. 8, 1848. He began the study of music with Simon Mayr in Bergamo. All his life he remembered this teacher with esteem and affection. Later, in Bologna, he studied with ROSSINI's teacher, Padre Stanislao Mattei, and aspired to become an opera composer. Since his father objected to this, the young man enlisted in the Austrian army. His military duties did not interfere with his music. In 1818 he completed his first opera, *Enrico di Borgogna,* and it was performed the same year in Venice with moderate success. His first major success came with his fourth opera, *Zoraïde di Granata,* introduced in Rome on Jan. 28, 1822. This triumph brought the composer an official release from the army. Now able to concentrate on music, he produced operas with amazing rapidity—twenty-one between 1822 and 1828. In all these works the influence of Rossini is predominant. The first opera in which Donizetti's own personality asserted itself was ANNA BOLENA, given in Milan in 1830 and soon performed throughout Europe. Donizetti's increasing powers became even more evident in two later works, both of them still in the repertory. One was the comic opera, L'ELISIR D'AMORE, introduced in Milan in 1832; the other was LUCIA DI LAMMERMOOR, first performed in Naples in 1835.

In 1837 Donizetti was appointed director of the Naples Conservatory. He held this post for two years. In 1839, aroused by a bitter feud with the censor over the performance of his opera POLIUTO, Donizetti left Italy and went to Paris. Here he assisted in the performance of some of his operas. Several others were given their premieres here, among them THE DAUGHTER OF THE REGIMENT and LA FAVORITA, both performed in 1840. Donizetti was now one of the most celebrated composers in Europe. He visited Vienna in 1842 for the premiere of LINDA DI CHAMOUNIX and was acclaimed; the Emperor conferred an honorary title on Donizetti. Back in Paris, the composer completed one of his best comic operas, DON PASQUALE, and was present at its highly successful premiere on Jan. 3, 1843. His last opera was *Caterina Cornaro,* given in Naples in 1844. Soon after this, Donizetti began suffering violent headaches and depressions. His mental deterioration necessitated his commitment to an asylum. He made enough improvement to be able to leave it in the custody of his brother at Bergamo. When he died a few months later, he was given a hero's funeral by his native city.

Donizetti was extraordinarily fertile and facile. He wrote sixty-seven operas, most of them now forgotten. Though he produced much that was trite and superficial, he was nevertheless a major figure in Italian opera in the era between Rossini and VERDI. At his best, Donizetti had a wonderful gift of melody and a sound instinct for effective theatricalism. The best pages of his serious operas have power and passion, and his best comic operas are marked by spontaneity, verve, and gaiety.

His finest operas were: *Anna Bolena* (1830); *L'elisir d'amore* (1832); *Parisina* (1833); LUCREZIA BORGIA (1833); *Gemma di Vergy* (1833); *Lucia di Lammermoor* (1835); *Il campanello di notte* (1836); *Roberto Devereux* (1837); *Gianni di Parigi* (1839); *Poliuto* (1840); *La Fille du régiment* (*The Daughter of the Regiment,* 1840); IL DUCA D'ALBA (1840); RITA (1840); *La favorita* (1840); *Linda di Chamounix* (1842); MARIA DI ROHAN (1843); *Don Pasquale* (1843).

Don José, brigadier (tenor) in love with Carmen in BIZET'S CARMEN, a role created by Jean DE RESZKE.

Don Juan, libertine of legend, drama, and poetry. He is the central character of several notable operas. The most celebrated is MOZART'S DON GIOVANNI. Others include ALFANO'S *L'ombra di Don Giovanni;* DARGOMIZHSKY'S THE STONE GUEST; GAZZANIGA'S *Don Giovanni Tennorio* (which preceded Mozart's opera by about a year); GOOSSENS' *Don Juan de Mañara;* GRAENER'S *Don Juans letztes Abenteuer;* LATTUADA'S *Don Giovanni;* MALIPIERO'S *Don Giovanni;* and PURCELL'S *The Libertine.*

See also BYRON, GEORGE NOEL GORDON, LORD.

Donna Diana, comic opera in three acts by REZNIČEK. Libretto by Julius Kapp, based on a comedy of the same name by Moreto y Cavaña. Premiere: Prague Opera, Dec. 16, 1894. The composer's most famous work is now seldom performed, but in its time it was extraordinarily popular throughout Germany. Its vivacious and highly melodious overture, however, has survived. The setting is Barcelona during Catalonia's independence. Don Cesar is in love with Donna Diana, who is cold to him. He uses the ruse of appearing indifferent to her and thus is able to arouse her interest and finally her love. Though the score is basically in a light Viennese idiom (the first-act waltz, for example, and the ballet music in the second act), the composer interpolated some Spanish rhythms and Spanish-type melodies to establish the local color of the setting. Two arias are light and appealing, Viennese in style rather than Spanish: "Mütterchen, wenn's in Schlaf mich sang," and the "Nurren-Lied."

Donna non vidi mai, Des Grieux's romantic aria about his fascination with Manon Lescaut, in Act I of PUCCINI'S MANON LESCAUT.

donna serpente, La (The Serpent Woman), opera in prologue and three acts by CASELLA. Libretto by Cesare Lodovici, based on a comedy by GOZZI. Premiere: Teatro Reale, Rome, Mar. 17, 1932. This is the same story used by WAGNER for his first opera, DIE FEEN.

donne curiose, Le (Die neugierigen Frauen, The Inquisitive Women), OPERA BUFFA in three acts by WOLF-FERRARI. Libretto by Luigi Sugana, based on a comedy by GOLDONI. Premiere: Munich Opera, Nov. 27, 1903. American premiere: Metropolitan Opera, Jan. 3, 1912. In eighteenth-century Venice two women are convinced that their husbands, and another woman that her lover, are carrying on an orgy at their men's club. They manage to gain admission to and to secrete themselves in the club where, to their delight, they discover that all their men are doing is indulging in a lavish meal. One of the most delightful excerpts is the duet of Rosaura (soprano) and Florindo (tenor), "Il cor nel contento," in Act II. In the first scene of Act III Wolf-Ferrari quotes a popular Venetian BARCAROLLE, "La biondina in gondoletta," which, a few years earlier, had been used in the Lesson Scene in

ROSSINI'S THE BARBER OF SEVILLE in some
Italian performances. The best orchestral episodes are the overture, two old-
world dances (a minuet and a forlane),
and a musical setting of the motto of
the club ("No Women Admitted"),
which recurs throughout the opera.

Donner, thunder god (bass) in WAGNER'S
DAS RHEINGOLD.

Don Pasquale, OPERA BUFFA in three acts
by DONIZETTI. Libretto by Giacomo
Ruffini and the composer, based on
Angelo Anelli's libretto for an opera
by Stefano Pavesi, *Ser Marcantonio.*
Premiere: Théâtre des Italiens, Paris,
Jan. 3, 1843. American premiere: Park
Theater, New York City, Mar. 9, 1846.

Characters: Don Pasquale, an old
bachelor (bass), a role created by Luigi
LABLACHE; Ernesto, his nephew (tenor);
Norina, a young widow (soprano); Dr.
Malatesta, a physician (baritone); a
notary; valets; chambermaids. The setting is Rome in the early nineteenth
century.

Act I, Scene 1. A room in Don Pasquale's house. Don Pasquale is opposed
to the love affair of his nephew Ernesto
and the young widow Norina. The
lovers, however, have found an ally in
Dr. Malatesta. Dr. Malatesta rapturously
describes to Don Pasquale his beautiful
and wholly imaginary sister ("Bella siccome un angelo"), and tells the old
bachelor that the girl is in love with him.
Before long, Pasquale is convinced he
loves the girl and expresses the wish to
marry her ("Ah! un foco insolito"). He
is even ready to cut Ernesto out of his
will. Unaware that there is a plot afoot,
Ernesto grows bitter at the betrayal at
the hands of his good friend, Malatesta
("Sogno soave e casto").

Scene 2. In Norina's house. As she
reads a novel, Norina insists she knows
all the tricks of winning a man's love
("So anch'io la virtù magica"). Malatesta comes to Norina and reveals his
plans for fooling Pasquale ("Vado,
corro"). He wants Norina to masquerade as his sister, wed the old man in a
mock marriage, and then so torture him

with her whims and caprices that Pasquale will eagerly seek a way out of his
hasty and unhappy marriage.

Act II. Don Pasquale's house. Aware
that without his uncle's money he will
never be able to marry Norina, Ernesto
once again laments his sad lot ("Cer-
cherò lontana terra"). When he leaves,
Malatesta arrives with the "bride" and
presents her to the handsomely attired
Pasquale. A mock marriage takes place
without further delay during which
Ernesto returns and realizes for the first
time that a fraud is being enacted. The
moment the ceremony ends, Norina becomes a hot-tempered shrew who harasses
her husband with her vicious tongue and
her extravagance.

Act III. Don Pasquale's house. When
Norina, beautifully gowned, brazenly
leaves the house and Pasquale discovers
a love letter addressed to her, he realizes
that he has come to the end of his rope.
In a rage he calls Malatesta, who
promises to set matters right. In Pasquale's garden Ernesto sings a serenade
to his beloved ("Com è gentil"), and
Norina responds ardently. Trapped at
last by old Pasquale, the conspirators
explain their intrigue and that the marriage contract is invalid. Pasquale is so
relieved at being freed from his distress
that he forgives them and readily consents for Ernesto and Norina to marry.

Don Pasquale was Donizetti's last successful opera. He wrote four more, but
they were failures. A good case can be
made for the claim of some writers that
Don Pasquale is Donizetti's finest work.
Certainly it belongs with the greatest
Italian *opera buffas.* Old traditions are
adhered to. The characters belong to
everyday existence and their problems
are the little complications of everyday
life. (As a matter of fact, in Donizetti's
time it was customary to present *Don
Pasquale* in contemporary dress.) This
opera has the inevitable busybody of
opera buffa, who sets the intrigue into
motion. There are the usual amatory
complications, serious and comic, which
are finally straightened out to the satis-

faction of all concerned. But while the formula is a familiar one, the musical treatment gives the work its originality and distinction. The music never lacks sparkle and freshness, and there is also found here wonderful bel-canto writing, together with passages of discreet sentimentality that bring a welcome change of pace.

When the opera was introduced it enjoyed one of the most notable casts ever assembled for an opera premiere. Pasquale was played by Lablache, about whom Ernest Newman has written, "opera has perhaps never seen or heard his like before or since." TAMBURINI was Malatesta; GRISI, Norina; and MARIO, Ernesto. Closer to our own day, two of the most notable of Pasquales have been Salvatore BACCALONI, for whom the METROPOLITAN OPERA successfully revived the opera in 1940, and Fernando CORENA.

Don Pedro, (1) a three-act opera created in 1952 by Hans Erismann from heretofore neglected music by MOZART. A new libretto was written by Oskar Walterlin and Werner Galusser from material by Lorenzo DA PONTE and Abbé G. B. Varesco. The music was derived from two uncompleted operas—*L'oca del Cairo* and *Lo sposo deluso*—and nineteen miscellaneous arias that Mozart wrote about 1783. These fragments were integrated by the Swiss musician Erismann, who added recitatives of his own. *Don Pedro* was introduced at the Zürich Municipal Theater under Erismann's direction in 1952; it was well received.

(2) Councilor (bass) in MEYERBEER'S L'AFRICAINE.

(3) The Commandant (bass) in MOZART'S DON GIOVANNI.

Don Quichotte (Don Quixote), opera in five acts by MASSENET. Libretto by Henri Cain, after a play by Jacques Le Lorrain, based on the novel of CERVANTES. Premiere: Monte Carlo Opera, Feb. 19, 1910. American premiere: New Orleans, Jan. 27, 1912.

Characters: Don Quixote (baritone or bass, a role created by Feodor CHALI-

APIN) ; Dulcinea, courtesan (contralto) ; Sancho Panza (baritone) ; Pedro, a burlesquer (soprano) ; Garcias, another burlesquer (soprano) ; Rodriguez (tenor) ; Juan (tenor) ; valets. The setting is Spain.

Act I. A square in front of Dulcinea's house. Don Quixote arouses the jealousy of one of Dulcinea's admirers by singing her a serenade ("Quand apparaissent les étoiles"). Dulcinea intervenes to prevent a duel, then sends Don Quixote on a fool's errand to retrieve a necklace stolen by a brigand; she promises to marry him if he is successful.

Act II. Before the windmills. In search of the necklace, Don Quixote and his servant Sancho Panza approach some windmills. Mistaking them for giants, the Don attacks them.

Act III. The camp of the brigands. By his knightly manner, Don Quixote is able to win over the brigands to the point that they surrender Dulcinea's necklace.

Act IV. A salon in Dulcinea's house. The Don and Sancho come to Dulcinea's house to turn over the necklace. Dulcinea is overjoyed to receive it, but when Don Quixote demands her hand as his reward ("Marchez dans mon chemin"), she derides him and sends him away.

Act V. A forest path. Don Quixote is dying. He begs Sancho to pray for him (Mort de Don Quichotte: "Écoute, mon ami"). In the distance, the Don hears the voice of Dulcinea, singing to him of love. Transported, he dies, leaving the grief-stricken Sancho.

Don Quixote, the self-styled knight-errant of La Mancha, principal character in CERVANTES' famous romance of the same name. He appears in several operas, including: CALDARA's *Don Chisciotte* and *Sancio Panza;* DONIZETTI's *Il furioso;* Francesco Feo's *Don Chisciotte* (1726) ; FALLA's EL RETABLO DE MAESE PEDRO; Vito Frazzi's *Don Chisciotte* (1951) ; IBERT's *Le Chevalier errant;* KIENZL's *Don Quixote;* NEUENDORFF's *Don Quixote;* MACFARREN's *The Adventures of Don Quixote;* MASSENET's DON QUICHOTTE; MEN-

DELSSOHN'S DIE HOCHZEIT DES CAMACHO; PAISIELLO'S *Don Chisciotte;* SALIERI'S *Don Chisciotte.*

Don Rodrigo, opera in three acts by GINASTERA. Libretto by Alejandro Casona. Premiere: Teatro Colón, July 24, 1964. American premiere: New York City Opera, Feb. 22, 1966. This is the composer's first opera, and it has been hailed as a major work. The setting is eighth-century Toledo, and the hero is the last of the Visigoth kings, who was responsible for the downfall of Spain following his defeat at the battle of Guadalete.

After Rodrigo is crowned king—the scene with which the opera begins—he rapes Florinda, daughter of the Governor of Ceuta. This leads the governor to invade Spain with his troops, where he administers a resounding defeat to Rodrigo's army. Rodrigo seeks penance in a monastery, where he is followed by Florinda come to forgive him. Fatally ill, Rodrigo dies in her arms.

Ginastera followed the example set by BERG in WOZZECK in using instrumental forms for each of his scenes: a rondo, scherzo, suite, canon, nocturne, and so forth; also in making extensive use of ATONALITY and SPRECHSTIMME. The basic idiom of *Don Rodrigo* is the TWELVE-TONE system, a post-*Wozzeck* development. The composer achieves some extraordinary effects through the deployment of DIRECTIONAL MUSIC, particularly in the scene of Rodrigo's death, where the sounds of pealing bells converge on the audience from different parts of the auditorium; a similar stereophonic effect is created in a second-act fanfare for twelve horns.

The opera is remarkable, too, for its structural symmetry. The apex of the structure is the fifth scene, all previous scenes representing an ascent toward it, and all subsequent ones, a descent. Emotional and dramatic contrast is realized by having Scene 1 a contrast to Scene 9; Scene 2 to Scene 8; Scene 3 to Scene 7; and Scene 4 to Scene 6.

Don Rodrigo is the opera with which

the NEW YORK CITY OPERA opened its new auditorium at the LINCOLN CENTER FOR THE PERFORMING ARTS in 1966.

Donzelli, Domenico, tenor. Born Bergamo, Italy, Feb. 2, 1790; died Bologna, Mar. 31, 1873. He created the role of POLLIONE at LA SCALA in 1831. He completed his vocal studies in his native city, where in 1808 he made his opera debut. In 1815 ROSSINI wrote for him the principal male role in *Torvaldo e Dorliska.* For two seasons after that Donzelli appeared at La Scala, following which he was heard in Venice, Vienna, and between 1824 and 1831 at the Théâtre des Italiens in Paris. He made his debut in London in 1829, where he returned in 1832 and 1833. Subsequently he performed in various opera houses in Italy, as well as in Vienna until 1841, when he went into retirement in Verona.

Dorabella, Fiordiligi's sister (soprano), in love with Ferrando, in MOZART'S COSÌ FAN TUTTE.

Dorian Gray, *see* WILDE, OSCAR.

Dormi pur, *see* SCHLAFE WOHL! UND MAG DICH REUEN.

Dorota (or **Dorothea**), Švanda's wife (soprano) in WEINBERGER'S ŠVANDA.

Dorothea, Cinderella's stepsister (mezzosoprano) in MASSENET'S CENDRILLON.

Dors, petite, dors, Dinorah's lullaby to her goat, in Act I of MEYERBEER'S DINORAH.

Dostoyevsky, Feodor, novelist. Born Moscow, Nov. 11, 1821; died St. Petersburg, Feb. 9, 1881. His stories and novels have been used in the following operas: BLACHER'S *Der Grossinquisitor* (based on a chapter from *The Brothers Karamazov*); JANÁČEK'S FROM THE HOUSE OF THE DEAD; Otakar Jeremiáš' *The Brothers Karamazov* (1928); Arrigo Pedrollo's *Delitto e castigo* (1926, based on *Crime and Punishment*); PROKOFIEV'S THE GAMBLER; SUTERMEISTER'S *Raskolnikoff* (based on *Crime and Punishment*); Emil Petrovic's *Crime and Punishment.*

Douphol, Baron, Alfredo's rival (baritone) for Violetta in VERDI'S LA TRAVIATA.

Dove Duo, *see* O HOLDES BILD.

Dove guardi splendono, chorus of the women and children as Desdemona makes her entry, in Act II of VERDI'S OTELLO.

Dove sei, amato bene, King Betarido's exalted air in Act I of HANDEL'S RODELINDA.

Dove son? o qual gioia, *see* O TRANSPORT, O DOUCE EXTASE.

Dove sono, Countess Almaviva's famous aria, in which she recalls how the Count had once been in love with her, in Act III of MOZART'S THE MARRIAGE OF FIGARO.

Down in the Valley, folk opera in one act by WEILL. Libretto by Arnold Sundgaard. Premiere: Bloomington, Ind., July 15, 1948. As the opening words of the Leader explain, this opera is about "Brack Weaver, who died on the gallows one morning in May; he died for the love of sweet Jennie Parsons, he died for the slaying of Thomas Bouche." Brack's story is then told in a series of flashbacks. Weill's score includes five authentic American folksongs: the title song, "The Lonesome Dove," "The Little Black Train," "Hop Up, My Ladies," and "Sourwood Mountain."

dramma giocoso, an Italian term for "gay drama," or an OPERA BUFFA with interpolations of tragic situations. The term is applied to certain eighteenth-century operas; the most celebrated example is DON GIOVANNI.

dramma per musica, Italian for "drama through music," the name by which opera was first designated when the form was created by the CAMERATA in Florence. The word OPERA first replaced *dramma per musica* in 1639 with CAVALLI'S LE NOZZE DI TETI E DI PELEO.

Dream Pantomime, the orchestral interlude in Act II of HUMPERDINCK'S HANSEL AND GRETEL, accompanying the descent of the angels to provide a protective ring for the children as they fall asleep in the forest.

Dreigroschenoper, Die, *see* THREEPENNY OPERA, THE.

drei Pintos, Die (The Three Pintos), an unfinished opera by WEBER. Libretto by Theodor Hell, based on *Der Brautkampf* by Seidel. Weber did not complete this opera because he started working on EURYANTHE in 1821. *Die drei Pintos* was finished and scored by MAHLER, who led its world premiere in Leipzig on Jan. 20, 1888.

Dresden Amen, a famous choral amen, believed to have been written by Johann Gottlieb Naumann (1741–1806). It was used by WAGNER in PARSIFAL. Naumann, a brilliant figure in his day, wrote a number of operas (*Cora* was his most successful) and a great deal of church music.

Dresden Opera (Staatstheater), one of the most important operatic institutions in Germany. Its predecessor was the Royal Opera of Saxony, which up to the middle of the nineteenth century was dominated by the Italian school. When WEBER became director in 1816, a reorganization took place, after which German operas were emphasized. A public opera house for the company was completed in 1841, and it was in this theater that RIENZI was first performed on Oct. 20, 1842. On Jan. 2 of the following year the Dresden Opera gave the premiere of DER FLIEGENDE HOLLÄNDER. In Feb., 1843, WAGNER became the KAPELLMEISTER, a post he held for six years; he was a vital factor in the artistic rehabilitation of the company. In 1869 the theater burned down. Rebuilt from the original plans (with modifications), it reopened in 1878. Under the artistic direction of Ernst von SCHUCH (1889–1914) and Fritz BUSCH (1926–1933), both of whom had been conductors there before becoming artistic directors, the Dresden Opera (renamed the Staatstheater in 1918) became one of the foremost opera houses in Germany, if not all of Europe. Most of Richard STRAUSS'S operas up to 1933 were introduced in Dresden. Other notable premieres included DOKTOR FAUST; D'ALBERT'S *Die toten Augen* and *Christelfein;* Ernst von Dohnányi's *Tante Simona* (1913); GRAENER'S *Hanneles Himmelfahrt;* the first version of CARDIL-

LAC; MANRU (1901); SCHOECK's *Penthesilea;* WEILL's *Der Protagonist;* L'AMORE MEDICO.

With the rise of the Nazi regime, Fritz Busch left the Opera and was replaced by Karl BÖHM. During this period all of Richard Strauss's later operas were introduced (with the exception of *Die Liebe der Danae*), beginning with ARABELLA on July 1, 1933. Other world premieres included a new realization of L'ORFEO by ORFF and the world premieres of SUTERMEISTER's *Romeo und Julia* and *Die Zauberinsel.*

The opera house was partially destroyed during World War II, and performances were given in the Town Hall under the direction of Joseph KEILBERTH. There the world premiere of BLACHER's DIE FLUT took place in 1947. After the opera house was rebuilt, it opened on Sept. 22, 1948, with FIDELIO. Karl von Appen was the new artistic director, while Joseph Keilberth continued as musical director. Keilberth was succeeded in 1950 by Rudolf Kempe (1950–1953), KONWITSCHNY (1953–1955), Lovro von Matačic (1955–1958), and Wilhelm Scheuling (1958–1960). Later musical directors were Otmar Suitner, Kurt Sandering, and Martin Turnovsky. Among the novelties produced by the Dresden Opera since the end of World War II were *Ariadne* (HANDEL); CARMINA BURANA; LA FINTA GIARDINIERA, DER JUNGE LORD; DIE KLUGE; IN THE STORM; *Lucio Silla* (MOZART); *Maître Panthelin* (Rainee Kunad, a world premiere in 1969); SI J'ETAIS ROI; and TIEFLAND.

When the Dresden Opera celebrated its three-hundredth anniversary in 1967, it played host to opera companies from East Berlin, Munich, and Leipzig.

Drinking Song, *see* TRINKE, LIEBCHEN, TRINKE SCHNELL.

Drottingsholm Opera Festival, a summer festival concentrating mainly on sixteenth-, seventeenth-, and eighteenth-century operas. These are performed in an intimate theater in the Drottingsholm Castle, originally built in 1766 and restored in 1912. The festival was inaugurated in 1948. Operas by MONTEVERDI, GLUCK, CIMAROSA, GRÉTRY, SACCHINI, HANDEL, MOZART (and so forth) are presented in the style of their time, with the members of the orchestra dressed in the costume of the appropriate period. The theater celebrated its two-hundredth anniversary in 1966 with a gala presentation of COSÌ FAN TUTTE on May 10 and an excellent performance of L'ORFEO the following August.

Drumlin Legend, A, folk opera in three acts by BACON. Libretto by Helene Carus. Premiere: New York City, May 9, 1949. This opera has an Irish-Scotch folk-music background. The story concerns the conflict of a former aviator between his desire to return to the cockpit and his wish to settle down with a country schoolteacher with whom he is in love. His dilemma is resolved when elves and woodsprites endow him with the power of flying in his imagination, while following his everyday humdrum existence.

Drury Lane Theatre, a theater in London which opened in 1696 and had a long and notable history of operatic productions up to World War I. From 1738 to 1778 Thomas ARNE was its official composer, and many of his operas were here first produced. It is interesting to note that the practice of providing analytical program notes was instituted by Arne at this theater in 1768. In 1833, under the managership of Alfred Bunn, Drury Lane produced Italian operas in English translations. BALFE's THE BOHEMIAN GIRL, William Vincent Wallace's *Maritana* (1845), and BENEDICT's *The Crusaders* were some of the English works written for, and introduced at, Drury Lane during this period. From 1867 to 1877 James Henry MAPLESON used Drury Lane for his annual summer season of opera. In 1870 the theater was under the direction of George Wood when the first performance of a WAGNER opera took place in England: DER FLIEGENDE HOLLÄNDER. In 1882 Hans RICHTER gave here the first performances in England of TRISTAN UND ISOLDE and DIE MEISTER-

SINGER. A year later the CARL ROSA COM-
PANY leased the house, giving the
premieres of several English operas,
including STANFORD'S THE CANTERBURY
PILGRIMS. In 1887 Sir Augustus HARRIS
began a long and distinguished career
as opera impresario at Drury Lane. His
company included the DE RESZKE
brothers, then appearing in England
for the first time. German opera was
seen at Drury Lane in 1892–93, light
opera in 1895, and opera in English in
1896. In 1904 the Moody-Manners
Company occupied the theater for a
season of operas in English, and in 1913
and 1914 Sir Thomas BEECHAM directed
highly successful seasons of Russian
operas, including the English premiere
of BORIS GODUNOV with CHALIAPIN. Opera
returned temporarily to Drury Lane
in 1958 with a two-month season of the
Italian repertory.

Dryad, a character (contralto) in Richard STRAUSS'S ARIADNE AUF NAXOS.

Dryden, John, poet and playwright.
Born Aldwinkle, Eng., Aug. 9, 1631;
died London, May 1, 1700. PURCELL
wrote theater music for many of Dryden's plays, among them *Amphitryon,
Aurengzebe, The Indian Queen, Love
Triumphant,* KING ARTHUR, *Oedipus,
The Spanish Friar,* and *Tyrannic Love.*
Thomas ARNE'S *Cymon and Iphigenia*
and HANDEL'S ACIS AND GALATEA were
both derived from Dryden's works.

Du bist der Lenz, Sieglinde's love song
to Siegmund in Act I of WAGNER'S DIE
WALKÜRE.

Duca d'Alba, Il (The Duke of Alba),
opera in four acts by DONIZETTI (completed by Matteo Salvi). Libretto by
SCRIBE. Premiere: Teatro Apollo, Mar.
22, 1882. American premiere: New
York City, Oct. 20, 1959 (concert version). Donizetti left this opera incomplete, since in 1839 he started working
on LA FAVORITA. This incomplete Donizetti score was recovered in Bergamo
in 1881, at which time Matteo Salvi
filled in the many missing parts. This
Salvi version proved outstandingly successful and was soon produced in vari-

ous cities in Italy and Spain. Scribe had
in the meantime rewritten his libretto
and turned it over to VERDI for THE
SICILIAN VESPERS. *Il Duca d'Alba* then
went into temporary discard. It received
a brilliant revival on June 11, 1959, to
open the season of the FESTIVAL OF TWO
WORLDS at Spoleto. A few months later
it was given its American premiere by
the AMERICAN OPERA SOCIETY. The tenor
aria, "Angelo casto e bel," is an outstanding vocal excerpt from this opera.

Duchess of Towers, Mary, character
(soprano) in TAYLOR'S PETER IBBETSON.

Due bell'alme inamorate, Deidamia's
aria in Act I of HANDEL'S DEIDAMIA. The
accompaniment calls for lute, harpsichord, and cello.

due Foscari, I, (The Two Foscari),
opera in three acts by VERDI. Libretto by
Francesco PIAVE, based on BYRON'S
drama *The Two Foscari.* Premiere:
Teatro Argentino, Rome, Nov. 3, 1844.
American premiere: Boston, May 10,
1847. Loredano, a member of the Venetian Council, vows to destroy the house
of Foscari, believing it responsible for
the death of both his father and uncle.
He is instrumental in having the Council exile Jacopo Foscari for the crime
and finally sees Jacopo's father compelled to abdicate from the Council.
Though the perpetrator of the murders is subsequently proved to be somebody other than Jacopo, Loredano's
vengeance is complete; Jacopo dies on
his way to exile, and his father collapses
after his compulsory abdication. Verdi
wrote some of his finest music for the
bass role of the Doge, the best known
part of which is the aria, "Oh vecchio
cor che batti," in Act I.

This early Verdi opera, which inspired DONIZETTI to proclaim its composer a "genius," is rarely revived, but
it was given a handsome presentation
by the SAN CARLO OPERA in Naples on
May 14, 1968, a production that was
seen in New York the same year.

Duenna, The, see BETROTHAL IN A CON-
VENT.

duet, a piece of music for two voices.

Duet of the Cherries, see SUZEL, BUON DI.

Dufresne, Milio, Zaza's lover (tenor) in LEONCAVALLO'S ZAZA.

Dukas, Paul, composer. Born Paris, Oct. 1, 1865; died there, May 17, 1935. He attended the Paris Conservatory for eight years; his teachers included Théodore Dubois and Ernest Guiraud. Some recognition came to him in 1892 for an orchestral overture, *Polyeucte,* but fame was realized in 1897 with his most celebrated composition, the orchestral scherzo *The Sorcerer's Apprentice* (*L'Apprenti sorcier*). Subsequently, major works, such as the "danced poem" *La Péri* and the opera ARIANE ET BARBE-BLEUE, placed him in the front rank of contemporary French composers. The opera was introduced at the OPÉRA-COMIQUE on May 10, 1907, and a few months later it entered the permanent repertory of the PARIS OPÉRA. After 1910 Dukas wrote little, concentrating on teaching; he was a professor at the Conservatory for a time and wrote criticism for the French journals. In the last year of his life he succeeded Alfred BRUNEAU at the Académie des Beaux-Arts.

Duke Bluebeard's Castle, see BLUEBEARD'S CASTLE.

Duke of Mantua, The, a nobleman (tenor) in VERDI'S RIGOLETTO.

Dulcamara, a quack doctor (bass) in DONIZETTI'S L'ELISIR D'AMORE.

Dulcinée, La Belle, see BELLE DULCINEÉ, LA.

du Locle, Camille, librettist. Born Orange, France, July 16, 1832; died Capri, Italy, Oct. 9, 1903. For many years he was secretary of the PARIS OPÉRA, when Perrin was director, and afterward he served as director of the OPÉRA-COMIQUE. He helped write the texts for VERDI'S AIDA, DON CARLOS, and LA FORZA DEL DESTINO, and he prepared the librettos for Ernest REYER'S SALAMMBÔ and SIGURD.

Dumas, Alexandre (fils), novelist and playwright. Born Paris, July 27, 1824; died there Nov. 27, 1895. Son of Alexandre DUMAS, père, he was the author of the celebrated play *La Dame aux camélias,* the source of VERDI'S LA TRAVIATA. Hamilton Forrest is another composer who made an opera (*Camille,* 1930) of this play.

Dumas, Alexandre (père), novelist and playwright. Born Villiers-Cotterets, France, July 24, 1802; died Puys, France, Dec. 5, 1870. Dumas's works were used for the following operas: CUI'S *The Saracen;* DONIZETTI'S *Gemma di Vergy;* Isidore DE LARA'S *Les Trois Mousquetaires;* FLOTOW'S *La Duchesse de Guise;* HUMPERDINCK'S *Die Heirat wider Willen;* and SAINT-SAËNS'S *Ascanio.*

D'un pensiero, Amina's protestation to Elvino of her innocence of having been unfaithful to him, in Act I of BELLINI'S LA SONNAMBULA.

Dunque io son, duet of Rosina and Figaro, in which he invents the fiction that he has an impoverished cousin named Lindoro interested in her, this in order to further Count Almaviva's amatory pursuit of Rosina, in Act I, Scene 1, of ROSSINI'S THE BARBER OF SEVILLE.

D'un vampiro fatal, chorus in Act III, Scene 2, of PONCHIELLI'S LA GIOCONDA, expressing horror at Laura's supposed death.

Duo de la fontaine, duet of Pelléas and Mélisande in Act II, Scene 1, of DEBUSSY'S PELLÉAS ET MÉLISANDE, in which, during their meeting at a fountain, they realize they are in love with each other.

Duo de la lettre, (1) see J'ÉCRIS À MON PÈRE.

(2) See VOICI CE QU'IL ÉCRIT.

Duprez, Gilbert, tenor, teacher, and composer. Born Paris, Dec. 6, 1806; died Passy, Sept. 23, 1896. Following his study of voice with Choron at the Paris Conservatory, he made an unsuccessful opera debut at the Odeon in 1825 as Almaviva in THE BARBER OF SEVILLE. Further study in Italy followed. In 1835 DONIZETTI selected him to create the role of EDGARDO in Naples. Between 1837 and 1845 he was a principal tenor of the PARIS OPÉRA, where he created several roles including that of BENVE-NUTO CELLINI in BERLIOZ' opera and Fernando in LA FAVORITA. Between 1842 and 1850 he was professor of singing at the Conservatory. In 1853 he founded a singing school of his own. In addition to his activities as singer and teacher, he was the composer of eight now forgotten operas and other music.

Durand et Compagnie, the foremost music publishers of France. The company was founded in Paris in 1870 by Marie Auguste Durand (a professional music critic, organist, and composer) when he acquired the publishing house of Flaxland and altered the name to Durand et Schoenewerk. In 1891 Durand's son Jacques replaced Schoenewerk, and the house became known as Durand et Fils. Still later, the name was changed to Durand et Compagnie. As the principal publishers for MASSE-NET, LALO, SAINT-SAËNS, BIZET, DEBUSSY, RAVEL, among others, the house of Durand issued the famous French operas of the late nineteenth and early twentieth centuries. Among its other significant contributions to opera were a monumental edition of the complete works of RAMEAU, edited by Saint-Saëns, and the first French editions of WAG-NER'S LOHENGRIN, TANNHÄUSER, and DER FLIEGENDE HOLLÄNDER.

Durante, Francesco, composer and teacher. Born Frattamaggiore, Italy, Mar. 31, 1684; died Naples, Aug. 13, 1755. As the director of the Conservatorio San Onofrio from 1718 to 1742 and of the Conservatorio di Santa Maria di Loreto in Naples from 1742 to the time of his death, Durante taught an entire generation of Italian opera composers, including JOMMELLI, PAI-SIELLO, PERGOLESI, PICCINNI, and SACCHINI. His own creative output consisted primarily of religious and choral music.

Durch die Wälder, durch die Auen, Max's bucolic aria in Act I of WEBER'S DER FREISCHÜTZ.

Dusk of the Gods, The, see RING DES NIBELUNGEN, DER.

Dutchman, The, principal character (baritone) in WAGNER'S DER FLIEGENDE HOLLÄNDER.

Dût-il m'en coûter la vie, Don José's insistence he will never leave Carmen, in Act III of BIZET'S CARMEN.

Du und Du Waltzes, music in the finale of Act II of Johann STRAUSS'S DIE FLE-DERMAUS; known also in orchestral transcription.

Dvořák, Antonín, composer. Born Nelahozeves, Bohemia, Sept. 8, 1841; died Prague, May 1, 1904. The Bohemian nationalist composer wrote nine operas (a tenth was abandoned).

Dvořák's music study began with a teacher in Zlonice, Antonin Liehmann, who was the first to recognize his talent. Encouraged by his teacher, Dvořák entered the Organ School in Prague when he was sixteen. His studies ended, he played viola in the orchestra of the National Opera for eleven years; during this period he came under the influence of SMETANA, then conductor at the National Opera, who aroused in him the ambition to write Bohemian national music. Dvořák's first opera, *King Alfred,* written in 1870, was, however, but a pale reflection of a Wagnerian music drama; the composer never allowed it to be published or performed. Smetana's increasing influence made it possible for Dvořák to free himself from Wagnerian influences. He now turned to Bohemian subjects for his operas, filling them with folklike songs and dances. His first venture in this direction was a comic opera, *The King and the Collier,* a failure when produced by the National Opera in 1871. Another comic opera, THE DEVIL AND KATE, given by the National Opera on Nov. 23, 1899, was such a triumph that it immediately entered the permanent Bohemian repertory; it was also performed in Germany and Austria. Another great success came with the national opera RUSALKA, performed in 1901. Dvořák's last opera, ARMIDA, however, was a failure in 1904. It marked Dvořák's return from nationalism to mythology. The composer's disappointment in the reception given *Armida* is believed to have been contributory to the breakdown of his health and his premature death.

For three years, beginning in 1892, Dvořák lived in America, teaching in New York City as director of the National Conservatory, spending his summer vacations in Spillville, Iowa. The fruits of this period were several chamber and orchestral works (including the symphony *From the New World*) containing imitation Negro and American Indian thematic material.

Dvořák's operas, in addition to those already mentioned: *The Pigheaded Peasants* (1874), *Vanda* (1875), *The Cunning Peasant* (1877), DIMITRIJ (1882), and *The Jacobin* (1888).

Dybbuk, The, (1) a famous Yiddish drama by S. Ansky, based on an old Hebrew belief that the spirit of a dead person may enter and obsess the body of a living one. In the play, Chanon, a Chassidic student, becomes absorbed in the mysteries and mysticism of the Kabala. He tries to acquire from the sacred book the power to gain wealth so that he may win Leah, with whom he is in love. He dies, and his spirit enters Leah's body. The play has been used as the basis of several operas.

(2) Opera by Lodovico ROCCA. Libretto by R. Simoni, based on the Ansky play. Premiere: La Scala, Mar. 7, 1934.

(3) Opera by David Tamkin. Libretto by Alex Tamkin (the composer's brother), based on the Ansky play. Premiere: New York City Opera, May 4, 1951.

Dyck, Ernest Van, *see* VAN DYCK, ERNEST.

Dzerzhinsky, Ivan, composer. Born Tambov, Russia, Apr. 9, 1909. His musical education did not begin until his nineteenth year when he entered the Gnessin Music School. From 1930 to 1932 he attended the First State Musical School, and from 1932 to 1934 he was at the Leningrad Conservatory, where one of his teachers, Riazanov, was an important influence in his development. He wrote some piano music from 1932 to 1934 and in the latter year completed the opera that made him famous, THE QUIET DON, produced at the Leningrad Little Opera Theater; within three years the work had two hundred performances in the Soviet Union. He subsequently completed several more operas: *Virgin Soil Upturned* (1937); *In the Days of Volochaiev* (1940); *The Storm* (1941); *The Blood of the People* (1942); *The Blizzard* (1946); *A Man's Destiny* (1961).

E

Eadgar of Wessex, King of England (baritone) in TAYLOR'S THE KING'S HENCHMAN.

Eames, Emma, soprano. Born Shanghai, China, Aug. 13, 1865; died New York City, June 13, 1952. The daughter of American parents, she was brought to the United States when she was five. After study in Boston with Clara Munger, she was encouraged by Wilhelm Gericke, conductor of the Boston Symphony, to go to Paris. She arrived there in 1886 and for two years studied with Mathilde MARCHESI. Her opera debut took place at the PARIS OPÉRA on Mar. 13, 1889, in ROMÉO ET JULIETTE. The composer GOUNOD himself selected her for this performance, and Jean DE RESZKE was the Roméo. She was such a success that she was required to sing the role of Juliette ten times in a single month. She was also called upon to create the roles of Colombe in SAINT-SAËNS's *Ascanio* and Zaïre in Paul de la Nux's *Zaïre*. Intrigues and cabals by envious singers compelled her to leave the Paris Opéra after two seasons. On Dec. 14, 1891, she made her American debut at the METROPOLITAN OPERA, once again as Juliette. For the next eighteen years she was a favorite of the opera public in New York and London. Her voice was not large, but it was used with consummate artistry. Her greatest triumphs came in TOSCA (a performance PUCCINI himself praised ecstatically), DON GIOVANNI, and AIDA. She also appeared in the American premieres of FALSTAFF and WERTHER. Disagreeing with the artistic policies of the then new regime of GATTI-CASAZZA at the Metropolitan Opera, she resigned in 1909, her last appearance taking place in *Tosca* on Feb. 15. She went into temporary retirement from which she emerged in 1911–12 for two performances with the BOSTON OPERA COMPANY as DESDEMONA and Tosca. She subsequently appeared in recitals with her husband, Emilio de Gogorza. She was frequently decorated, her honors including the English Jubilee Medal (presented after a command performance for Queen Victoria in 1896) and the order of Les Palmes Académiques from the French Academy. She wrote her autobiography, *Some Memoirs and Reflections* (1927).

E amore un ladroncello, Dorabella's aria in Act II, Scene 3, of MOZART's COSÌ FAN TUTTE, insisting on the necessity of woman to follow the dictates of her heart in matters of love.

Earl of Avenell (who also appears under the assumed name of George Brown), a character (tenor) in BOIELDIEU's LA DAME BLANCHE.

East Berlin Deutsche Staatsoper, *see* BERLIN STATE OPERA.

Easton, Florence, soprano. Born Middlesbrough-on-Tees, Eng., Oct. 25, 1884; died New York City, Aug. 13, 1955. As a child she made a public appearance as pianist in Canada. In her fourteenth year she entered the Royal Academy of Music in London. After voice coaching with Elliott Haslam in Paris, she made her opera debut in 1903 with the Moody-Manners Opera Company as CIO-CIO-SAN. Two years later she appeared for the first time in America with the Henry SAVAGE Opera Company, singing Kundry and Cio-Cio-San in English versions of PARSIFAL and MADAMA BUTTERFLY. Between 1907 and 1913 she was a member of the Berlin Royal Opera (BERLIN STATE OPERA), where she achieved her first major successes. In 1910 she was heard at COVENT GARDEN in the London premiere of ELEKTRA, and from 1913 to 1915 she was the principal soprano of the HAMBURG OPERA. In 1915 she returned to the United States for two seasons with the CHICAGO OPERA. On Dec. 7, 1917, she made her debut at the METROPOLITAN OPERA in CAVALLERIA RUSTICANA. For twelve consecutive seasons she was one of the most highly esteemed members of the Metropolitan Opera company. She was extraordinarily versatile, her repertory including about a hundred and fifty roles in four languages. Her specialty was German opera, particularly the works of WAGNER, MOZART, and Richard STRAUSS. She also appeared in major world and American premieres, including LA CENA DELLE BEFFE, GIANNI SCHICCHI, JONNY SPIELT AUF, THE KING'S HENCHMAN, and LISZT's oratorio *Die Legende von der heiligen Elisabeth* (given a stage presentation in 1918).

Between 1930 and 1936 Easton sang in England, principally at Covent Garden. She returned to the Metropolitan for a single performance, on Feb. 29, 1936, when she sang Brünnhilde in DIE WALKÜRE. Following this, she went into retirement.

Ebbène, a te ferisci, duet of Arsace and Semiramis in ROSSINI's SEMIRAMIDE.

Ebben? ne andrò lontana, Wally's aria in Act I of CATALANI's LA WALLY, telling the villagers she is off "to the setting sun," having been ejected from her father's house for refusing to marry Gellner.

È ben altro il mio sogno, Giorgetta's

plea to Michele that they settle down to a normal domestic existence, in PUCCINI'S IL TABARRO.

Ebert, Carl, opera manager. Born Berlin, Feb. 20, 1887. He was trained in the theater by Max Reinhardt, after which he had a distinguished career in Germany as actor, becoming the first German actor to receive the honorary title of "professor." He also helped found the first municipally subsidized drama school in Germany. In 1927 he became director of the Darmstadt Theater, where, for four years, he was in charge of operatic as well as dramatic productions. In 1931 he was appointed director of the Städtische Oper in Berlin (BERLIN DEUTSCHE STAATSOPER). When the Nazis came to power he was offered the post of chief of all German opera houses. Unsympathetic to the government, Ebert declined and voluntarily left his native land. In 1934 he helped found the GLYNDEBOURNE FESTIVAL in England, serving as its artistic director from its inception. Two years later, the Turkish government called on him to help establish a Turkish National Theater and Opera. Between 1948 and 1956 he directed the opera department at the University of Southern California; from 1947 to 1959 he was back at Glyndebourne, and from 1956 to 1961 at his former position in Berlin. He also directed operas for the METROPOLITAN OPERA from 1959 to 1962.

Eboli, Princess, Don Carlos' admirer (mezzo-soprano) in VERDI'S DON CARLOS.

È casta al par di neve!, Tonio's song of love to Columbine in Act II of LEONCAVALLO'S PAGLIACCI—Tonio acting the role of Taddeo.

Ecco purch'a voi ritorno, the air Orpheus sings in praise of Euridice's beauty at the beginning of Act II of MONTEVERDI'S L'ORFEO.

Ecco ridente, Count Almaviva's serenade to Rosina in the opening of Act I, Scene 1, of ROSSINI'S THE BARBER OF SEVILLE. Rossini had used the same melody in earlier works: in his opera *Aureliano in Palmira,* where it appears as the address of the Persian king to Isis,

"Spose del grande Osiride," and in his cantata *Ciro Babilonia,* where it is sung by the Roman emperor and his men in an oasis in a Syrian desert.

Echo, a character (soprano) in Richard STRAUSS'S ARIADNE AUF NAXOS.

Écoute, écoute, compagnon, the smugglers' chorus in Act III of BIZET'S CARMEN.

Écoute, mon ami, the death aria of Don Quixote, in Act V of MASSENET'S DON QUICHOTTE.

É deggio e posso crederlo, Leonora's utterance of joy in discovering that her beloved Manrico is still alive, beginning the finale of Act II, Scene 2, of VERDI'S IL TROVATORE.

Edelmann, Otto, bass. Born Brunn-am-Gebirge, near Vienna, Feb. 5, 1917. He attended the Vienna Academy, where he studied voice with Lierhammer and Graarud. In 1938 he made his opera debut in Gera in the role of FIGARO in MOZART'S opera. His career, interrupted by World War II, was resumed in 1947, when he became a member of the VIENNA STATE OPERA. There he achieved international renown for his performances in WAGNER and as Baron OCHS. He made his debut at the METROPOLITAN OPERA as HANS SACHS on Nov. 11, 1954. Since then he has appeared regularly with this company, as well as with the Vienna State Opera and the SAN FRANCISCO OPERA, besides making numerous guest appearances with other leading opera companies.

Edgar, opera in three acts (originally four) by PUCCINI. Libretto by Ferdinando Fontana, based on the poetic drama *La Coupe et les levres* by MUSSET. Premiere: La Scala, Apr. 21, 1889. American premiere: New York City, Apr. 12, 1956 (three scenes only, in concert version). This was Puccini's second opera, and his first full-length one. It was commissioned by the publisher RICORDI on the strength of the composer's maiden effort, LE VILLI, four years earlier. When introduced, it received only three performances. Puccini then revised it into a three-act version that was introduced in Ferrara on Feb.

28, 1892, where it was a huge success, and in other Italian cities with less success. It was well received in Madrid in 1892 with TAMAGNO as Edgar and TETRAZZINI as Fidelia. For this Madrid performance, Puccini wrote a special orchestral prelude describing the birth of spring, in tribute to the Queen of Spain, who was present. Today it is hardly ever heard.

The opera suffers from a poor libretto. The villainess is the village temptress, Tigrana, for whom Edgar betrays his own beloved, Fidelia. This affair ends tragically for all concerned. Tigrana kills Fidelia, for which she is condemned to die; and Edgar, too, meets a gruesome end. Edgar's aria, "O soave vision," Fidelia's arias, "Addio mio dolce amor," and "Nel villagro d'Edgar," and the third-act orchestral intermezzo deserve mention.

Edgardo (or **Edgar**) **of Ravenswood,** Lucia's love (tenor) in DONIZETTI'S LUCIA DI LAMMERMOOR.

Edinburgh International Festival of Music and Drama, one of the most significant European summer music festivals, in which opera plays a prominent role. It was organized in 1947 in Edinburgh, Scotland, by the Glyndebourne Society. Rudolf BING became artistic director. His success in establishing this festival was responsible for his appointment as general manager of the METROPOLITAN OPERA. He was succeeded at Edinburgh by Ian Hunter. For the first half dozen years, the GLYNDEBOURNE OPERA was a major participant in the varied programs, usually in MOZART operas, but occasionally in the presentation of such novelties as the original version of ARIADNE AUF NAXOS, a revival of LE COMTE ORY and MACBETH, and a production of THE RAKE'S PROGRESS. The HAMBURG STATE OPERA gave guest performances in 1952, including in its repertory the first stage performance in Great Britain of MATHIS DER MALER. From then on numerous distinguished visiting opera companies have appeared at the festival, with several additional visits by the Hamburg State Opera, and performances by the PICCOLA SCALA, the STUTTGART OPERA, the STOCKHOLM ROYAL OPERA (in its first visit to Great Britain, presenting the first performance of ANIARA outside Sweden), the Belgrade Opera (in performances of THE GAMBLER, THE LOVE FOR THREE ORANGES, and KHOVANTCHINA), the Prague National Theater (in productions of DALIBOR, RUSALKA, and JANÁČEK'S *Katya Kabanova* and FROM THE HOUSE OF THE DEAD), the BAVARIAN STATE OPERA, the Scottish Opera, and in 1969 the TEATRO COMMUNALE of Florence in performances of operas by DONIZETTI, VERDI, PUCCINI, DALLAPICCOLA, and MALIPIERO.

Unusual operatic revivals at the festival have included Donizetti's *Maria Stuarda;* HAYDN's *Lè Pescatrici* and *Orfeo ed Euridice;* CAVALLI's *L'Ormindo;* IL COMBATTIMENTO DI TANCREDI E CLORINDA; and THE RISE AND FALL OF THE CITY MAHAGONNY. In 1967 ZEFFIRELLI put on a notable production of L'ELISIR D'AMORE; and on Aug. 22, 1968, the festival gave the world premiere of Harrison Birstwistle's *Punch and Judy.* The Earl of HAREWOOD was festival director until 1966, when he was succeeded by Peter Diamond.

Edmondo, a young student (tenor) in PUCCINI'S MANON LESCAUT.

Egk, Werner, composer. Born Auchsensheim, near Augsburg, Ger., on May 17, 1901. After studying the piano with Anna Hirzel-Langenhan in Augsburg and composition with Carl ORFF in Munich, he began his career in Bavaria in 1929 as a conductor. During this period he wrote text and music for several puppet operas. After settling in Munich he completed several operas for radio between 1929 and 1933; he subsequently adapted one of these, *Columbus,* for the stage, its stage premiere taking place at Frankfurt on Jan. 13, 1942. After the rise of the Nazi regime, he succeeded GRAENER as head of the faculty of composition of the Reichskammer. Between 1936 and 1940 he was the conductor of the BERLIN STATE OPERA. His first opera written expressly for the stage was an outstanding success: DIE ZAUBER-GEIGE, produced in Frankfurt in 1935, with the blessings of Nazi officials. Those officials first frowned upon his opera PEER GYNT, produced by the Berlin State Opera on Nov. 24, 1938; but when Hitler himself expressed his enthusiasm, it immediately came into favor. When his ballet *Abraxas* was suppressed on moral grounds following its premiere in Munich in 1948, Egk returned to Berlin, where he was appointed director of the Berlin Hochschule für Musik. But in 1953 he returned to Munich, where he has since been the president of the Association of German Composers. His later operas include *Circe* (1948); IRISCHE LEGENDE (1954); DER REVISOR (1957); *Die Verlobung in San Domingo* (1963); *Casanova in London* (1968). Egk wrote the libretto for BLACHER's opera ABSTRAKTE OPER NO. I.

Eglantine de Puiset, see DE PUISET, EGLANTINE.

Egli è salvo, Don Carlo's fiery aria in which he vows to destroy Don Alvaro, in Act III, Scene 2, of VERDI's LA FORZA DEL DESTINO.

Egyptian Helen, The, see AEGYPTISCHE HELENA, DIE.

È il sol dell' anima, the Duke's love song to Gilda, in Act I, Scene 2, of VERDI's RIGOLETTO.

Einem, Gottfried von, composer. Born Bern, Switzerland, Jan. 24, 1918. While he was still a child, his family settled in Austria, where he began his education and started composing. In 1938 he studied composition in Berlin with Boris BLACHER, after which in 1941 he worked for a while as coach and assistant conductor at the BERLIN STATE OPERA and at BAYREUTH. Suspected of harboring anti-Nazi sentiments, he and his mother were arrested by the Gestapo and confined for four months in a concentration camp. After his release, he wrote several orchestral works that proved successful, together with a ballet, *Prinzessin Turandot*. These were performed in Dresden and Berlin between 1943 and

1945. During this period Einem was Karl ELMENDORFF's assistant at the DRESDEN OPERA. In 1945 Einem settled in Salzburg, where he completed his first opera, DANTONS TOD, a great success when introduced at the SALZBURG FESTIVAL in 1947. His second opera, DER PROZESS, was also introduced at the Salzburg Festival, in 1953. A comic opera, *Der Zerissene,* received its world premiere in Hamburg on Sept. 17, 1964. In 1960 Einem received the Theodor Körner Prize and the Prize of the City of Vienna and in 1965 the Austrian State Prize for music. All his operas have been produced by the VIENNA STATE OPERA, including a new production of *Der Prozess* on Jan. 31, 1970, and the world premiere of *Der Besuch der alten Damen* in 1971.

Ein' feste Burg ist unser Gott (A Mighty Fortress is Our God), a setting by Martin Luther of Psalm 46. It became a battle song of the Reformation and is found in every Protestant hymn book, as well as in the new Roman Catholic hymnal. It is the basis of the overture to LES HUGUENOTS, and is used prominently in the first and second acts. It is also quoted by MENDELSSOHN in his *Reformation Symphony* and by WAGNER in his *Kaisermarsch.*

Ein hübscher Mensch, Christine's monologue (one of the best-known vocal episodes in the opera) in Act I of Richard STRAUSS's INTERMEZZO.

Ein Mädchen oder Weibchen, Papageno's aria expressing his desire for a wife, in Act II, Scene 5, of MOZART's THE MAGIC FLUTE.

Ein Männlein steht im Walde, Gretel's folksong as she rests under a tree, in Act II (or Act I, Scene 2) of HUMPERDINCK's HANSEL AND GRETEL.

Einsam in trüben Tagen, Elsa's aria, known as "Elsa's Dream," in which she describes the champion she dreamt of, in Act I of WAGNER's LOHENGRIN.

Ein Schwert verhiess mir der Vater, Siegmund's narrative about the promise made him by his father that he would find a powerful sword to protect him against his enemies, in Act I of WAGNER's DIE WALKÜRE.

Eisenstein, Baron von, a rich banker (tenor) in Johann STRAUSS's DIE FLEDERMAUS.

E la solita storia ("Lamento di Federico"), Federico's lament in Act II of CILÈA's L'ARLÉSIANA.

Eleanora, Lelio's wife (soprano) in WOLF-FERRARI's LE DONNE CURIOSE.

Eléazar, Jewish goldsmith (tenor) in HALÉVY's LA JUIVE.

electronic music, music composed of electronically generated sounds, sometimes combined with traditional media. Electronic music has been employed extensively in avant-garde operas, among them being: BADINGS' MARTIN KORDA, D. P. and *Salto mortali;* BLACHER's ZWISCHENFÄLLE BEI EINER NOTLANDUNG; BLOMDAHL's ANIARA; KRENEK's *Der goldene Ram;* NONO's INTOLLERANZA 1960; and Bernd Alois Zimmerman's *Die Soldaten.* MENOTTI makes highly effective use of electronic sounds in his children's opera HELP, HELP, THE GLOBOLINKS! Samuel BARBER uses the Ondes Martenot, an electronic instrument, in his orchestration for ANTONY AND CLEOPATRA.

Elegy for Young Lovers (Die Elegie für junge Liebende), opera in three acts by HENZE. Libretto (in English) by W. H. AUDEN and Chester Kallman. Premiere: Schwetzingen, Ger., May 20, 1961. American premiere: New York City, Apr. 29, 1965. A strong libretto, combining vivid characterizations, powerful dramatic episodes, and intellectual and symbolic concepts, and a highly expressive and stylistically varied score has placed this with the more important operas of the twentieth century. The setting is the Austrian Alps; the time, 1910. Gregor Mittenhofer, an egocentric poet, spends his annual vacation at the Schwarzer Adler, where he gets ideas for his writings from the hallucinations of a widow, Hilda Meck. For forty years Hilda Meck has been waiting for the return of her husband, who had disappeared during their honeymoon on the Hammerhorn. When his body is, at

long last, recovered, Hilda is freed from her hallucinations. The poet now seeks inspiration in a love affair between Toni, his stepson, and the poet's own mistress, Elisabeth. The poet sends them to the Hammerhorn to gather edelweiss, where they are fatal victims of a violent storm. Their death provides the poet with the theme for his greatest work, which he calls "Elegy for Young Lovers," and which, at the close of the opera, he reads to the audience.

Henze employs a mixed style in which some of the vocal material has the warmth and lyricism of Italian opera, while other vocal material and the highly dramatic and expressive instrumental background employ advanced idioms and techniques that nevertheless follow operatic tradition by being presented in set arias, duets, and ensemble numbers.

Elektra, music drama in one act by Richard STRAUSS. Libretto by Hugo von HOFMANNSTHAL, based on the tragedy of SOPHOCLES. Premiere: Dresden Opera, Jan. 25, 1909. American premiere: Manhattan Opera House, Feb. 1, 1910.

Characters: Klytemnestra, queen, and widow of Agamemnon (mezzo-soprano); Aegisthus, her lover (tenor); Orestes, her son (baritone); Elektra, her daughter (soprano); Chrysothemis, another daughter (soprano). The setting is Mycenae, in ancient Greece. The action takes place in a courtyard at the rear of King Agamemnon's palace.

Elektra mourns the death of her father, Agamemnon, murdered by his wife Klytemnestra and her lover Aegisthus. Her one consuming passion is to avenge this murder. When her mother comes to her with tales of terrible dreams, Elektra mockingly suggests a cure: the shedding of blood of someone near to her. In a sudden fit of rage, Elektra tells Klytemnestra that the murdered woman will be none other than Klytemnestra herself and that her murderer will have the visage of the dead Agamemnon ("Was bluten muss?"). Klytemnestra's horror is relieved by a messenger's tidings that Orestes is dead. Since Orestes cannot now avenge his father's death, Elektra plans to do so herself with an ax. At this point the messenger reappears, and Elektra recognizes that he is none other than Orestes ("Orest! Es rührt sich niemand!"). Klytemnestra now meets her deserved doom. From within the palace come her shrieks as Orestes kills her. Aegisthus arrives, enters the palace, and is likewise slain. Delirious with joy that vengeance has come, Elektra sings a rapturous song, dances in triumph on her father's grave ("Schweig und tanze"), and sinks lifeless to the ground.

Elektra was the first opera in which Strauss collaborated with the Austrian poet Hugo von Hofmannsthal. This artistic marriage of librettist and composer, destined to yield so many fine operas, was a success from the very beginning. In *Elektra*, as in the operas that succeeded it, we find the sensitivity with which dramatist and musician were attuned to each other's artistic demands. For Hofmannsthal's psychoneurotic play, in which the tragedy of Sophocles becomes filled with morbid lusts and even depravity, Strauss wrote one of his most realistic scores. Music and text are filled with emotional disturbances and demoniac frenzy. The discords are agonizing, the harmonies, oversensual; the flights of melody at times hysterical; the rhythms, nervous and high-tensioned. When *Elektra* was first introduced, many critics condemned it as being the last word in decadence, using such adjectives as "blood-curdling" and "gruesome." Yet many of those who were shocked had to admit the opera's compelling impact. In the half century since its premiere, *Elektra* has lost little of its force—an effective performance is still about as overpowering an emotional experience as the opera stage has to offer. But today we know that *Elektra* is more than just a thunderbolt hurled at an audience by a musical Jove. We recognize its singular power and beauty and find it an opera in which play and music are one in the projection of a mighty drama.

Elemer, Count, Arabella's suitor (tenor) in Richard STRAUSS's ARABELLA.

Elena, Sicilian noblewoman (soprano) and beloved of Arrigo, in VERDI's THE SICILIAN VESPERS.

Elias, Rosalind, mezzo-soprano. Born Lowell, Mass., Mar. 13, 1931. While attending the New England Conservatory she appeared as Poppea in a school performance of L'INCORONAZIONE DI POPPEA and as a soloist with the Boston Symphony. After some additional study at the Berkshire Music Center at TANGLEWOOD, she made her official opera debut with the New England Opera Company in 1948 in RIGOLETTO. She remained with the company until 1952, when she went to Italy to study with Luigi Ricci and Nazareno DE ANGELIS. Appearances at LA SCALA and the SAN CARLO OPERA followed. On Feb. 23, 1954, she made her METROPOLITAN OPERA debut in a minor role in DIE WALKÜRE. During her first season there she made fifty-five appearances in seven minor roles. It was not long, however, before she assumed major parts. In 1958 she created the role of Erika in the world premiere of VANESSA and in 1966 that of Charmian in ANTONY AND CLEOPATRA, with which the Metropolitan Opera opened its new auditorium at the LINCOLN CENTER FOR THE PERFORMING ARTS. Among the other roles in which she achieved major successes have been CARMEN, CHERUBINO, DORABELLA, OCTAVIAN, Emilia in OTELLO, Olga in EUGENE ONEGIN, Fenena in NABUCCO, and ZERLINA (the only mezzo-soprano to sing the last-named role at the Metropolitan).

Elisabeth, the Landgrave's niece (soprano), and Tannhäuser's beloved, in WAGNER's TANNHÄUSER.
See also ELIZABETH.

Elisabeth's Prayer, see ALLMÄCHT'GE JUNGFRAU.

Elisa, Princess, a noblewoman (soprano) at Napoleon's court, in GIORDANO's MADAME SANS-GÊNE.

Elisetta, one of Geronimo's daughters

(soprano) in CIMAROSA'S IL MATRIMONIO SEGRETO.

elisir d'amore, L' (The Elixir of Love), OPERA BUFFA by DONIZETTI. Libretto by Felice ROMANI, based on Eugène SCRIBE's Le Philtre. Premiere: Teatro della Canobbiana, Milan, May 12, 1832. American premiere: Park Theater, New York, May 22, 1844.

Characters: Nemorino, a young peasant (tenor); Adina, a wealthy young woman (soprano); Belcore, a sergeant of the garrison (bass); Dr. Dulcamara, a quack (bass); Gianetta, a peasant girl (soprano); peasants; soldiers; villagers; a notary; a landlord. The setting is an Italian village in the nineteenth century.

Act I. The lawn of Adina's farm. As Adina is reading a book, Nemorino looks upon her longingly and speaks of his love ("Quanto è bella!"). Sergeant Belcore comes to pay court to Adina. When he is rejected, Nemorino becomes encouraged to address her. But he, too, is rudely dismissed. The traveling quack, Dr. Dulcamara, appears with a trunkful of medicines. He proclaims his genius ("Udite, udite"). Desperate for Adina's love, Nemorino gives his last coin for a love elixir. No sooner does the young man drink the potion (which is actually nothing but ordinary Bordeaux wine) than he feels light of heart; he sings and dances. So confident is he of the powers of the elixir that he consciously slights Adina to arouse her jealousy. Piqued, Adina suddenly decides she will marry Belcore and sets the wedding for that very day. Nemorino, having been told that the elixir must have time to work its magic, entreats Adina to delay the wedding ("Adina credimi"). She refuses to do so.

Act II. Interior of Adina's house. Outside, peasants are celebrating ("Cantiamo, facciam brindisi"). While preparations for the wedding are taking place, Dulcamara and Adina sing a BARCAROLLE ("Io son ricco") in which Dulcamara boasts of his popularity in Venice. Nemorino arrives to complain bitterly to Dulcamara of the ineffective-

ness of his elixir. The doctor suggests the purchase of a second bottle. Nemorino acquires the money and drinks the potion ("Dell' elisir mirabile"). Now word comes of the death of Nemorino's uncle. Nemorino has been left a fortune. All the village girls quickly become attentive to the young man, a scene that upsets Adina and Dulcamara no end ("Quanto amore!"). The sight of Nemorino's sudden popularity brings tears to Adina's eyes. He notices her unhappiness and, finding himself alone, sings the most celebrated aria in the opera, "Una furtiva lagrima," in which he insists that he would gladly die to be able to console her. All turns out well, of course, and with Adina and Nemorino in each other's arms, the quack doctor insists that his elixir has brought them together. He finds many new customers for his products.

AUBER'S OPÉRA COMIQUE Le Philtre (1831) also makes use of Scribe's play.

Elizabeth, Philip II's wife (soprano) in VERDI'S DON CARLOS.

See also ELISABETH.

Elizabeth I, Queen of England (soprano) in BRITTEN'S GLORIANA.

Ella giammai m' amo, the poignant aria of Philip II when he realizes that his wife does not love him, in the opening of Act IV, Scene 1, of VERDI'S DON CARLOS.

Ella verra, Scarpia's exultant aria over the prospect of his impending meeting with Tosca, in Act II of PUCCINI'S TOSCA.

Elle a fui, la tourterelle, Antonia's ROMANCE about her absent love, in Act III of OFFENBACH'S THE TALES OF HOFFMANN.

Ellen, the British governor's daughter (soprano) in DELIBES'S LAKMÉ.

Elle ne croyait pas, Wilhelm Meister's ROMANCE as he speaks of his love for Mignon, in Act III of THOMAS'S MIGNON.

Ellen Orford, see ORFORD, ELLEN.

Elles se cachaient!, Marguerite's lament that she has been deserted by Faust, as she sits spinning, in Act IV, Scene 1, of GOUNOD'S FAUST (a scene often omitted).

Elmendorff, Karl, conductor. Born Düsseldorf, Ger., Jan. 25, 1891; died Taunus, Oct. 21, 1962. At first he studied philology, but in 1913 he entered the Hochschule für Musik in Cologne. His apprenticeship as an opera conductor took place in Wiesbaden and Mannheim, after which he became conductor of the MUNICH OPERA, specializing in the Wagnerian repertory. Between 1927 and 1942 he was one of the principal conductors at the BAYREUTH FESTIVAL. During the 1930's he also conducted at the BERLIN STATE OPERA and the FLORENCE MAY MUSIC FESTIVAL and in the 1940's in many leading European opera houses. In 1946 he was appointed musical director of the DRESDEN OPERA and in 1949 of the Cassel Opera.

Elsa, noblewoman of Brabant (soprano), who becomes Lohengrin's wife, in WAGNER'S LOHENGRIN.

Elvino, a young farmer (tenor), betrothed to Amina, in BELLINI'S LA SONNAMBULA.

Elvira, wife (soprano) of Lord Arthur Talbot in BELLINI'S I PURITANI.

Elvira, Donna, (1) former sweetheart (soprano) of Giovanni in MOZART'S DON GIOVANNI.

(2) Noblewoman (soprano) in VERDI'S ERNANI.

Emilia, Iago's wife (contralto) in VERDI'S OTELLO.

Emma, young girl (contralto) in MUSSORGSKY'S KHOVANTCHINA.

Emperor Jones, The, opera in two acts by GRUENBERG. Libretto by Kathleen de Jaffa, based on the play of the same name by Eugene O'NEILL. Premiere: Metropolitan Opera, Jan. 7, 1933.

Characters: Brutus Jones, former Pullman porter (baritone); Henry Smithers, a cockney trader (tenor); native woman; Congo witch doctor; apparitions of soldiers, convicts, planters, slaves. The setting is a West Indian island; the time is the 1920's.

Act I. The throne room of Jones's palace. An escaped convict, Jones has come to a West Indian island and made himself its emperor. He has looted the native people, and now he is making preparations to flee the island with his booty. Henry Smithers reveals to Jones

that he is leaving none too soon: the tribesmen are about to revolt against his rule. When Jones calls his ministers into court nobody appears. Hurriedly, Jones sets about escaping. From the distance comes the sound of chanting and the beating of a tom-tom.

Act II. The forest. As Jones makes his way toward the coast he hears the continual throbbing of the tom-tom, as if pronouncing his doom. At first self-confident and full of bravado, Jones slowly begins to succumb to fright as the tom-tom sounds grow louder and the shadows of the forest lengthen. Hallucinations from his wicked past arise to haunt him, and he shouts at them wildly. Realizing that his pursuers are drawing closer, he falls on his knees and confesses his sins; he begs God for forgiveness and protection ("Standin' in the need of prayer"). But he knows he is doomed. When the witch doctor finds him and calls to his fellow tribesmen, Jones uses his last bullet—a silver one saved for this very purpose—to commit suicide. The tribesmen, finding him dead, dance joyfully around his body. The last word is Smithers'. "Yer died in the grand style, anyhow," he comments.

To convey in his music the ever-growing terror obsessing Brutus Jones, Gruenberg employs modern techniques. In place of arias there is SONG-SPEECH; the harmonic writing is spiced with discords; the rhythmic patterns are complex; the choral writing is at times pierced with agonizing outcries. The opera progresses to the final orgy with relentless movement, and the tension mounts continually, making a great emotional experience in which the listener finds little contrast of mood and little relaxation.

Emperor of China, The, a character (bass) in STRAVINSKY'S LE ROSSIGNOL.

Emperor's New Clothes, The, *see* ANDERSEN, HANS CHRISTIAN.

encore, French for "again." The call has been used mainly by English and American opera audiences since the eighteenth century to demand repetition of a number. In other countries the term BIS is used.

Enfant et les sortilèges, L' (The Child and the Sorceries), a "lyric fantasy" in two acts by RAVEL. Libretto by Colette. Premiere: Monte Carlo Opera, Mar. 21, 1925. American premiere: San Francisco Opera, Sept. 19, 1930. Variously designated a "fantasy," "ballet," and a "comedy of magic," *L'Enfant et les sortilèges* is actually an opera requiring singing, dancing, and pantomime. Colette's play concerns a mischievous boy who, scolded for failing to do his lessons, breaks up furniture and victimizes domestic animals. The furniture comes to life to taunt the boy. A princess emerges from a fairytale book he has torn to say she is through with him. When the boy flees out of the house he is harassed by the animals outside. In the confusion, a squirrel is hurt. The boy nurses him tenderly. This kind act induces the boy's tormentors to forgive him. Ravel's score is one of his wittiest and most satiric, including a provocative duet of cats (in cat language) and a saucy dance of the cups and teapot (an American fox trot).

En fermant les yeux ("Le Rêve"), Des Grieux's aria describing a dream in which he saw himself living with Manon in their own home, in Act II of MASSENET's MANON.

English Opera Group, The, an opera company founded in 1947 by Benjamin BRITTEN, John Piper, and Eric CROZIER for "the creation and performance of new operas" and "to encourage poets and playwrights to tackle the writing of librettos in collaboration with composers," besides reviving chamber operas or operas of the past requiring limited forces. Britten wrote ALBERT HERRING to help launch the first season of the Group and to provide it with a new work for a tour of England and other parts of Europe. The Group has since toured extensively in Europe and Canada, besides being responsible for the formation and artistic direction of the ALDEBURGH FESTIVAL and the creation of an opera studio and the Na-

tional School of Opera. Among the works it commissioned and gave world premieres to are BERKELEY's *Ruth, A Dinner Engagement,* and *Castaway;* LET'S MAKE AN OPERA, THE TURN OF THE SCREW, NOYE'S FLUDDE, as well as Britten's version of THE BEGGAR'S OPERA; Brian Easdale's *The Sleeping Children* (1951); and THE BEAR. Since 1961 COVENT GARDEN has financed this company's activities.

Enlèvement d'Europe, L' (The Abduction of Europa), *opéra minute* in one act by MILHAUD. Libretto by Henri Hoppenot. Premiere: Baden-Baden, July 17, 1927. American premiere: San Francisco, May 18, 1955. This is the first of three "minute operas," each requiring about eight minutes for performance, the other two being L'ABANDON D'ARIANE and LA DÉLIVRANCE DE THÉSÉE. Pergamon is angered that Europe, whom he loves, prefers bulls and cows to men. When Europe appears with a bull, Pergamon attacks it with bow and arrow, but the arrow fails to pierce the bull's tough hide and instead bounces back and kills Pergamon. Europe then departs with her beloved bull.

Enrico Ashton, *see* ASHTON, ENRICO.

En proie à la tristesse, the aria of Countess Adele in ROSSINI's LE COMTE ORY.

ensemble, a group of performers; also unity and balance achieved by a group.

En silence pourquoi souffrir?, Rozenn's and Margared's duet in Act I of LALO's LE ROI D'YS, in which Rozenn questions Margared for the reason for her sorrow on the day of her betrothal.

Entführung aus dem Serail, Die, *see* ABDUCTION FROM THE SERAGLIO, THE.

entr'acte, French term meaning the interval between two acts. In opera usage it denotes the music composed to fill this interval. The term is used interchangeably with INTERMEZZO. Famous entr'actes can be found in GOYESCAS, CAVALLERIA RUSTICANA, and THE JEWELS OF THE MADONNA.

entrada, Spanish for "entrance," denoting music used as a prelude or introduction to an act of an opera.

Entrance of the Gods into Valhalla, The, the closing scene of WAGNER'S DAS RHEIN-GOLD. To the accompaniment of music comprising mainly the motives of the "Rainbow" and "Valhalla," the gods, headed by Wotan, enter their new abode.

entrée, French for "entry." In eighteenth-century opera, an *entrée* was a piece of music in march time accompanying the entry of a procession. Subsequently it came to mean a prelude accompanying the rise of the curtain.

En vain j'ai flagellé ma chair, Athanaël's aria expressing distress over his inability to purge his mind of the vision of Thaïs' beauty, in Act III, Scene 2, of MASSENET'S THAÏS.

En vain pour éviter, Carmen's Card Song, in which she reads in the cards the prognostication of a future disaster, in Act III of BIZET'S CARMEN.

Enzo Grimaldo, *see* GRIMALDO, ENZO.

É possono mai nascere, Carolina's expression of grief upon hearing from her father, Geronimo, that he plans to send her to a convent, in Act II of CIMAROSA'S IL MATRIMONIO SEGRETO.

E pur io torno, Ottone's emotional air in Act I of MONTEVERDI'S L'INCORONAZIONE DI POPPEA.

E quest' asilo ameno e grato, the Spirits' and Euridice's description of the peace and beauty of Elysium, in Act III (or sometimes Act II, Scene 2) of GLUCK'S ORFEO ED EURIDICE (Paris version, 1774).

Era la notte, Iago's fictional revelation to Otello that he had overheard Cassio talking in his sleep about his love for Desdemona, in Act II of VERDI'S OTELLO.

Erckmann-Chatrian, two French novelists who wrote as collaborators. They were: Emile Erckmann (1822–1899) and Alexandre Chatrian (1826–1890). Among the operas derived from their works are: LE JUIF POLONAIS by ERLANGER; L'AMICO FRITZ and *I Rantzau* by MASCAGNI; *L'amico Fritz* by Alexis Roland-Manuel; and *The Polish Jew* (1904) by Karel Weis.

Erda, spirit of the earth (contralto) in WAGNER'S DAS RHEINGOLD and SIEGFRIED.

Erda's Warning, *see* WEICHE, WOTAN, WEICHE!

Erede, Alberto, conductor. Born Genoa, Italy, Nov. 8, 1909. After attending the conservatories of Genoa, Milan, and Basel he became a pupil of Felix WEINGARTNER in conducting. Between 1934 and 1939 he was assistant conductor of the GLYNDEBOURNE FESTIVAL. During much of this period he also conducted the Salzburg Opera Guild, with which organization he first came to the United States in 1937. Two years later he returned to the United States as guest conductor of the NBC Symphony, leading the world premiere of MENOTTI'S THE OLD MAID AND THE THIEF. In 1945 he became artistic director and conductor of the Turin Radio Orchestra, in 1946 of the NEW OPERA COMPANY, London. After this he conducted extensively throughout Europe. On Nov. 11, 1950, he made his debut at the METROPOLITAN OPERA with LA TRAVIATA. He remained a principal conductor of the Metropolitan Opera for five seasons; then from 1958 to 1962 he was the musical director of the Deutsche Oper am Rhein at Düsseldorf-Duisburg.

Erhardt, Otto, director and producer. Born Breslau, Ger., Nov. 18, 1888. He studied music and art at Breslau, Berlin, and Munich, and philosophy at Oxford. After playing the violin in several orchestras, he held the post of stage director at the STUTTGART OPERA between 1920 and 1927, the DRESDEN OPERA between 1927 and 1932 (where he produced the premiere of Richard STRAUSS'S DIE AEGYPTISCHE HELENA), and at COVENT GARDEN between 1934 and 1936. During this period he also produced operas at BAYREUTH (1924) and in Rome and Turin (1925). After directing opera performances for three years at the SALZBURG FESTIVAL, he went to Buenos Aires, where from 1939 until 1956 he was stage director at the TEATRO COLÓN and professor at the Opera Academy. In 1950 he served as stage director of the NEW YORK CITY OPERA. Since 1956 his activity has been confined mainly to Europe. He is the author of a biography of Richard Strauss, published in Buenos Aires in 1950.

Erik, a huntsman (tenor), and Senta's beloved, in WAGNER'S DER FLIEGENDE HOLLÄNDER.

Erika, Vanessa's niece (mezzo-soprano) in BARBER'S VANESSA, a role created by Rosalind ELIAS.

Eri tu, che macchiavi, Renato's aria in which he decides to punish his disloyal friend, Riccardo, for having made love to his wife, in Act III, Scene 1, of VERDI'S UN BALLO IN MASCHERA.

Erkel, Franz (or Ferenc), composer. Born Gyula, Hungary, Nov. 7, 1810; died Budapest, June 15, 1893. He was the creator of Hungarian national opera. In 1838 he became conductor of the National Theater in Budapest, and it was here that his first opera, *Bátori Mária,* was produced in 1840. His most successful opera was *Hunyadi László,* presented in 1844. For many years this was one of the most frequently performed of all Hungarian operas. In 1845 Erkel wrote the Hungarian national anthem. Subsequently he helped direct the Philharmonic concerts in Budapest and was the first professor of piano and instrumentation at the National Academy. Among his later operas: *Erzsébet* (1857); *Kúnok* (1858); *Bánk bán* (1861); *Sarolta* (1862); *Dózsa György* (1867); *Brankovics György* (1874); *King Stefan* (1874).

Erlanger, Camille, composer. Born Paris, May 25, 1863; died there Apr. 24, 1919. He attended the Paris Conservatory, where he won the PRIX DE ROME in 1888. Success came in 1895 with the dramatic legend *Saint-Julien l'Hospitalier,* based on a story by Flaubert, performed at the Concerts de l'Opéra. His most celebrated work was the opera LE JUIF POLONAIS, introduced at the OPÉRA-COMIQUE Apr. 11, 1900. His other operas: *Kermaria* (1897); *Le Fils de l'étoile* (1904); APHRODITE (1906); *Bacchus triomphant* (1910); *L'Aube rouge* (1911); *La Sorcière* (1912); *Le Barbier de Deauville* (1917); *Forfaiture* (1919).

Ernani, opera in four acts by VERDI. Libretto by Francesco PIAVE, based on Victor HUGO's drama *Hernani.* Premiere: Teatro la Fenice, Mar. 9, 1844. American premiere: Park Theater, New York, Apr. 15, 1847.

Characters: Don Carlos, King of Castile (baritone); Don Ruy Gomez de Silva, a Spanish grandee (bass); Donna Elvira, his betrothed (soprano); Juana, her nurse (mezzo-soprano); Ernani, a bandit chief (tenor); nobles; ladies; followers of the King; followers of Don Silva; followers of Ernani. The action takes place in Aragon, Aix-le-Chapelle, and Saragossa, in 1519.

Act I, Scene 1. A mountain retreat in Aragon. Outlawed by the King, Ernani, son of a Spanish duke, has become a bandit. At his retreat, his followers sing a drinking song ("Evviva, beviam"). After giving voice to his love for Donna Elvira in "Come rugiada al cespite," Ernani and his men set about abducting her, since Elvira is about to marry Don Ruy Gomez de Silva.

Scene 2. Elvira's room in the castle. Depressed by the necessity of having to marry a man she does not love, Elvira calls out to Ernani to save her ("Ernani, involami"). Ernani and Elvira insist that death is preferable to their living apart ("Ah, morir, potessi adesso"). Don Carlos comes to her in disguise and tries to make love to her. She resists him and is saved by the sudden appearance of Ernani. The King and Ernani recognize one another, and a conflict seems inevitable. Suddenly Don Silva appears. The King offers a lame excuse for being in Elvira's room, and Ernani makes his escape.

Act II. A hall in Don Silva's castle. Determined to prevent Elvira's marriage to Silva, Ernani comes to the grandee's castle disguised as a pilgrim, and is given shelter and protection. When Elvira appears, dressed as a bride, Ernani discloses his true identity. The laws of hospitality prevent Silva from doing Ernani harm; indeed, he must even protect him when the King comes to capture him. Failing to find Ernani, the King's men take El-vira as hostage. Silva challenges Ernani to a duel; Ernani refuses to accept, since his host has saved his life. Instead, he offers to join forces with Silva to rescue Elvira, promising, once she is saved, to sacrifice himself. As a pledge, Ernani gives his host a hunting horn. When Silva shall blow on that horn, Ernani will kill himself.

Act III. A vault in the cemetery at Aix-le-Chapelle. Don Carlos has come to this solemn tomb because he has been informed that it is the hiding place of conspirators intending to kill him. Then he soliloquizes about the turn of events ("Oh de' verd' anni miei"). Concealing himself, he hears Ernani and Silva plotting against him, with Ernani chosen to do the killing ("Si ridesti, il Leon di Castiglia"). From a secret door, elector and courtiers file in to announce that Don Carlos has just been proclaimed Emperor Charles V. Don Carlos now orders Ernani and Silva put to death. When Elvira pleads for their lives, he rescinds the order and frees them. He even gives his blessings to the union of Ernani and Elvira. This generous gesture moves the assemblage to sing the praises of their Emperor ("O sommo Carlo"). Only Don Silva is bitter at the new turn of events.

Act IV. The terrace of Ernani's palace in Aragon. Elvira and Ernani are together at last, and they are happy. But Silva has not forgotten Ernani's promise. A hunting horn sounds; Don Silva appears and demands that Ernani keep his word. In vain does Ernani plead that his life be spared ("Solingo, errante e misero"). In spite of Elvira's protestations ("Ferma, crudele, estinguere"), Ernani bids his beloved a tender farewell, then kills himself with a dagger.

Ernani was Verdi's fifth opera; it belongs in the first period of his creative development, when he was still uninhibited in his emotional responses, still lavish in his use of musical resources for passionate and melodramatic expression. There is vigor, theatricalism,

and overwhelming feeling in this score, music which lends itself admirably to the ringing phrases of Hugo's eloquent poetry, even in translation. While *Ernani* was Verdi's first opera to make him famous outside Italy, it had a stormy career. When first produced, it ran into censorship trouble. Since Italy was then ruled by Austria, the authorities objected to the conspiratorial nature of the play, and the libretto had to be revised extensively before the opera could be presented. Strange to say, Victor Hugo himself was opposed to the opera; he regarded both the adaptation of his play and Verdi's music as travesties.

Ernani, involami, Donna Elvira's plea to Ernani to save her from marrying a man she does not love, in Act I, Scene 2, of VERDI's ERNANI.

Ernesto, (1) a young man (baritone) long in love with Serafina, who is married to an aged apothecary, in DONIZETTI's IL CAMPANELLO DI NOTTE.

(2) Don Pasquale's nephew (tenor) in DONIZETTI's DON PASQUALE, a role created by Giovanni MARIO.

Erwartung (Expectation), MONODRAMA in four scenes by SCHOENBERG. Libretto by Marie Pappenheim. Premiere: Prague, June 6, 1924. American premiere: New York City, Nov. 15, 1951 (concert version); Washington, D.C., Dec. 28, 1960 (staged).

Erwartung calls for a single character and requires half an hour for performance. The text is a psychological drama exploring the psychological responses and the deep inner emotions of its character rather than unfolding any sort of plot. In a forest, at night, a woman is searching for her lost lover. The next two scenes find her experiencing fears that mount to terror. The final scene takes place outside the forest, where she stumbles over the dead body of her loved one—an experience that evokes from her a wide gamut of feelings, from hope to despair, as well as hallucinations. This little opera anticipates Schoenberg's later development and use of TWELVE-TONE TECHNIQUES by being built from a basic theme made up of all twelve tones of the chromatic scale. Much of the music is dissonant. In spite of the unorthodox methods, the strong presence of WAGNER's influence can readily be detected.

Escamillo, a toreador (baritone) in BIZET's CARMEN.

Eschenbach, Wolfram von, *see* WOLFRAM VON ESCHENBACH.

E scherzo od è follia, quintet of Edgardo, Ulrica, Riccardo, Samuele, and Tommaso in Act I, Scene 2, of VERDI's UN BALLO IN MASCHERA. They express horror on learning from the fortune-teller, Ulrica, that the king will be murdered by the first man to shake his hand.

Es gibt ein Reich, Ariadne's description of a dream about the kingdom of death, in Richard STRAUSS's ARIADNE AUF NAXOS.

Es gibt ob tanzen ob singen, Zerbinetta's air with female chorus, in which they try to brighten Ariadne's spirit, in Richard STRAUSS's ARIADNE AUF NAXOS.

È sogno? O realtà?, Ford's monologue in Act II, Scene 1, of VERDI's FALSTAFF, in which he denounces the fickleness of all women.

Esser madre è un inferno, Rosa's prayer in Act III of CILÈA's L'ARLÉSIANA.

Esterre fatta fisso lo sguardo tuo tremendo, Desdemona's insistence to Otello that he is the only man she loves, in Act III of VERDI's OTELLO.

Esultate!, chorus of the people hailing Otello's victory over the Turks, in the opening scene of VERDI's OTELLO.

Et je sais votre nom, Des Grieux's song of praise to Manon's beauty, in Act I of MASSENET's MANON.

Et la maintenant, Paquillo's hymn of praise to all women, in Act II of OFFENBACH's OPÉRA BOUFFE LA PÉRICHOLE.

Étoile, L' (The Star), comic opera in three acts by CHABRIER. Libretto by Eugène Leterrier and Albert Vanloo. Premiere: Bouffes-Parisiens, Paris, Nov. 28, 1877. American premiere: New York City, Aug. 18, 1890 (under the title *The Merry Monarch*). This was the composer's first work for the stage

and first composition deserving attention. It was revived in a completely new version, under the new title of *The Astrologer,* at the Mannes College of Music in New York City on Jan. 24, 1969.

Étoile du nord, L' (The Star of the North), opera in three acts by MEYERBEER. Libretto by SCRIBE. Premiere: Opéra-Comique, Feb. 16, 1854. American premiere: French Opera House, New Orleans, Mar. 5, 1855. Czar Peter is in love with the village girl, Katherine, who disguises herself as a man and enters the Russian army in place of her brother. She brings the Czar a report about a conspiracy. The conspiracy is quickly rooted out. Disguised as a carpenter, the Czar woos and wins Katherine, who now becomes the Czarina.

Meyerbeer included in *L'Étoile du nord* six numbers from his earlier opera *Ein Feldlager in Schlesien.*

Euch lüften, die mein Klagen, Elsa's aria giving expression to her joy in loving Lohengrin, in Act II of WAGNER's LOHENGRIN.

Eudoxie, Princess, the Emperor's niece (soprano) in HALÉVY's LA JUIVE.

Eugene Onegin, opera in three acts by TCHAIKOVSKY. Libretto by Konstantin Shilovsky and the composer, based on the poem of the same name by PUSHKIN. Premiere: Moscow, Mar. 29, 1879 (student performance); Moscow Opera, Jan. 23, 1881 (public performance). American premiere: New York City, Feb. 1, 1908 (concert version); Metropolitan Opera, Mar. 24, 1920 (staged).

Characters: Eugene Onegin, a young dandy (baritone); Lensky, his friend (tenor); Mme. Larina, a landowner (mezzo-soprano); Tatiana, her daughter (soprano); Olga, another daughter (contralto); Prince Gremin (bass); Triquet, a Frenchman (tenor); Filipievna, a nurse (mezzo-soprano); Petrovitch, a captain (baritone); Zaretski, Lensky's friend (baritone). The setting is St. Petersburg and its environs, the time about 1815.

Act I, Scene 1. A garden adjoining

Mme. Larina's home. There is a brief, atmospheric orchestral prelude. Tatiana and Olga are singing to their mother, Mme. Larina ("Hast thou heard?"). Harvesters are returning from the field ("On the bridge"). Then the nurse of the two girls announces the arrival of Onegin and Lensky. It is not long before Tatiana falls in love with Onegin, while Lensky becomes interested in Olga ("I love you, Olga").

Scene 2. Tatiana's room. Unable to sleep, Tatiana begs her nurse to tell her a story, which she does. Tatiana then reveals to her nurse how much she loves Onegin and impetuously decides to write her beloved a letter telling him of her feelings (Letter Scene).

Scene 3. The garden. Onegin responds to the letter by meeting Tatiana in her garden. He tells her that he is not the man for her and urges her to forget about him ("Written words"). Humiliated, Tatiana runs away.

Act II, Scene 1. A living room in Mme. Larina's home. A ball is taking place, celebrating Tatiana's birthday; it is here that the brilliant and well-known waltz occurs. Overhearing some women gossiping about Tatiana's love for him, Onegin decides to dispel their suspicions by paying attention to Olga. This arouses Lensky's jealousy, since he is in love with Olga, and he challenges Onegin to a duel.

Scene 2. A mill beside a stream. Waiting for Onegin, Lensky recalls his youth (Lensky's Air: "Faint echo of youth"). Onegin appears, the duel takes place, and Lensky is killed.

Act III, Scene 1. A hall in the palace of Prince Gremin. Six years have passed. Tatiana is married to Prince Gremin. Onegin is a guest at their palace during a gay reception. Here occurs the familiar Polonaise. When Onegin arrives, Gremin tells him about how much he loves his wife, Tatiana, and how much happiness she has brought him ("Everyone knows love on earth"). But when Onegin meets Tatiana again he realizes for the first time how much he really loves her himself.

Scene 2. Tatiana's boudoir. Tatiana is awaiting Onegin—he has sent a message that he must talk with her. She is torn with conflicting feelings, for she is still in love with him, yet she wants to be true to her husband. When Onegin arrives, he pleads for her love. For a moment, Tatiana wavers and responds ardently. But she immediately assumes control of herself and sends her distraught lover away forever.

Because it lacks sustained dramatic interest and sharply defined characterizations—and because it does not exploit big emotional scenes and spectacles—*Eugene Onegin* has never been especially popular except in Russia. There it has long been recognized as the composer's finest opera. Tchaikovsky knew he was not writing a popular opera. "It is true that the work is deficient in theatrical opportunities; but the wealth of poetry, the humanity and the simplicity of the story . . . will compensate for what is lacking in other respects," he wrote. The opera was not at first successful, even in Russia. In describing its "weariness and monotony," César CUI was voicing the reaction of most Russian musicians. But repeated performances in Russia brought to the surface the deep humanity of the opera. Audiences began discovering the subtle inner conflicts of the characters, began to respond to the poignancy of Tatiana's unresolved love.

Since 1950 significant revivals of *Eugene Onegin* have gone a long way in establishing its popularity outside Russia: in Vienna in 1950; at SADLER'S WELLS in London in 1952; at the METROPOLITAN OPERA in 1957, presented on the opening night of the season, on Oct. 28.

Eumenides, *see* AESCHYLUS; ORESTES.

È un riso gentil, Dufresne's aria in Act I of LEONCAVALLO's ZAZA, describing Zaza's gentle smile.

Euridice, (1) opera by Jacopo PERI. Libretto by Ottavio RINUCCINI. Premiere: Pitti Palace, Florence, Oct. 6, 1600. Since the music of Peri's DAFNE (the first opera ever written) has been lost, its immediate successor, *Euridice*, is sometimes spoken of as the first complete opera in history. Whereas *Dafne* was described by its librettist as a pastoral fable (*favola pastorale*), *Euridice* was designated a "tragedy." *Euridice* was written for, and performed in conjunction with, the festivities attending the marriage of Henry IV of France to Maria de' Medici. A few arias in this opera were written by CACCINI. The story is a version of the myth concerning Orpheus and Euridice.

(2) The wife of Orfeo (Orpheus) in numerous operas, including: CACCINI's *Euridice;* GLUCK's ORFEO ED EURIDICE; HAYDN's ORFEO ED EURIDICE; LES MALHEURS D'ORPHÉE; L'ORFEO; ORPHEUS IN THE UNDERWORLD; and PERI's *Euridice;* also operas by Johann Christian BACH, CASELLA, GRAUN, KRENEK, and MALIPIERO.

Euripides, dramatist. Born Salamis, Greece, 480 B.C.; died Pella, Greece, 406 B.C. One of the greatest tragic dramatists of classical Greece, Euripides was the author of more than seventy-five plays. Among the operas based on works of Euripides are: BOUGHTON's ALKESTIS; CAMPRA's *Iphigénie en Tauride;* CHERUBINI's MÉDÉE; GHEDINI's *La Baccanti;* GLUCK's ALCESTE, IPHIGÉNIE EN AULIDE, and IPHIGÉNIE EN TAURIDE; HENZE's DIE BASSARIDEN; KRENEK's DAS LEBEN DES OREST; LULLY's ALCESTE; MALIPIERO's *Ecuba;* Martinon's *Hecube;* RAMEAU's HIPPOLYTE ET ARICIE; Alessandro SCARLATTI's *Mitridate Eupatore;* Domenico Scarlatti's *Ifigenia in Aulide* and *Ifigenia in Tauride;* WELLESZ's ALKESTIS and *Die Bacchantinnen.*

Europa, a queen (soprano), former beloved of Jupiter, in Richard STRAUSS's DIE LIEBE DER DANAE.

Europe, daughter (soprano) of King Agenor in MILHAUD's *opéra minute* L'ENLÈVEMENT D'EUROPE.

Euryanthe, romantic opera in three acts by WEBER. Libretto by Helmina von Chézy, based on the thirteenth-century romance *L'Histoire de Gérard de Nevers.* Premiere: Kärntnerthor-theater, Vienna, Oct. 25, 1823. Ameri-can premiere: Metropolitan Opera, Dec. 23, 1887.

Characters: King Louis VI (bass); Adolar, Count of Nevers (tenor); Euryanthe de Savoy, his betrothed (soprano); Lysiart, Count of Forêt (baritone); Eglantine de Puiset, companion of Euryanthe (mezzo-soprano). The action takes place in the Castle of Premery, at the Palace of Nevers, and in a forest. The time is the twelfth century.

Act I, Scene 1. A hall in the Castle of Premery. The overture has become a staple in the symphonic repertory. The court sings the praises of Adolar's betrothed, Euryanthe, to whom Adolar sings a *romanza,* "Unter blühenden Mändelbäumen." Lysiart, jealous of Adolar, insists that all women are not to be trusted; he even boasts that he can win Euryanthe's love. Adolar is willing to wager all his possessions on Euryanthe's constancy. The wager is accepted; Lysiart promises to show Adolar a token of Euryanthe's love.

Scene 2. The garden of the Palace of Nevers. Euryanthe confides to Eglantine a secret entrusted to her by Adolar. Adolar's sister, Emma, a suicide, cannot rest in her grave until a certain ring with which she was buried has been wet by the tears of an innocent accused. Eglantine, also in love with Adolar, realizes that the possession of this ring may be the means of Lysiart's winning his wager. Meanwhile, Euryanthe pines for her beloved Adolar in the CAVATINA "Glöcken im Träne."

Act II, Scene 1. Again the garden at Nevers. Eglantine, having stolen the ring from Emma's grave, gives it to Lysiart, who joins her in a plot to destroy Euryanthe, "Komm, denn unser Leid zu rachen."

Scene 2. The Castle of Premery. Adolar and Euryanthe are on the point of being married and express their feelings in the love duet "Hin nimm die Seele mein." Lysiart now arrives and displays the ring as proof of Euryanthe's infidelity. Since Adolar realizes that nobody but Euryanthe could know of the ring, he is convinced that Lysiart is telling the truth. He gives up his possessions and goes into exile.

Act III, Scene 1. A forest. Euryanthe has followed Adolar. At first he is moved to kill her, but, remembering his love, he merely abandons her. The King's hunting party appears to the strains of a hunters' chorus, "Die Thale dampfen." Euryanthe reveals to the King how Eglantine betrayed her. Realizing that Euryanthe is innocent, the King promises to destroy both Eglantine and Lysiart.

Scene 2. The garden of the Palace of Nevers. Having learned of Euryanthe's innocence, Adolar comes to avenge himself. He arrives just as Lysiart and Eglantine are to be married. As Eglantine confesses her crime, Lysiart kills her. Lysiart is condemned to be executed. Adolar has his property restored to him and is reunited with Euryanthe.

Weber was commissioned to write *Euryanthe* by the Vienna KÄRNTNERTHOR-THEATER, where DER FREISCHÜTZ had recently scored a resounding success. Unfortunately, the new opera was no *Freischütz*. It lacked the original creative power and the strong folk elements of the earlier opera; more important still, it was burdened by a silly libretto. Largely because of this, *Euryanthe* was a failure in Vienna and since then has passed out of the repertory. But it has historical importance as an early example of German romantic opera. Its music has many moments of grandeur and beauty, with occasional anticipations of moods and orchestral colors later to be heard in LOHENGRIN. The parts are finer than the whole; it is only through some of its parts (particularly the wonderful overture) that the opera is remembered.

Eva, Pogner's daughter (soprano), loved by Walther, in WAGNER'S DIE MEISTERSINGER.

Evander, a messenger (tenor) in GLUCK'S ALCESTE.

Evangelimann, Der (The Evangelist), opera in two acts by KIENZL. Libretto by the composer, based on a story by L. F. Meissner. Premiere: Berlin Opera, May 4, 1895. American premiere: Chicago, Nov. 3, 1923. Mathis and Martha are in love, but Martha is also loved by Mathis' brother Johannes. The latter sets fire to a monastery and accuses the innocent Mathis of the crime. Mathis is sent to prison for ten years. During this period, Martha's grief leads her to suicide. Many years later, Mathis becomes an evangelist. Johannes, on his deathbed, is tortured by his conscience. He confesses everything and dies peacefully in the knowledge that his brother Mathis has forgiven him.

Evangeline, opera in three acts by Otto Luening. Libretto by the composer, based on the poem by LONGFELLOW. Premiere: Columbia University, New York, May 5, 1948. The opera follows Longfellow's narrative poem closely, showing the long-frustrated love and the prolonged separation of the heroine and her beloved Gabriel. The music embodies various American references to the period, including Indian calls and Lutheran hymns.

Evans, Geraint, baritone. Born Pontypridd, South Wales, Feb. 16, 1922. He is one of the most distinguished baritones in Europe, celebrated in Wagnerian and Mozartean roles and in contemporary operas by BRITTEN and WALTON. He studied singing in Hamburg with Theo Hermann and in Geneva with Fernando Carpi. His debut took place at COVENT GARDEN in 1948 as the Nightwatchman in DIE MEISTERSINGER. Between 1949 and 1961 he appeared at the GLYNDEBOURNE FESTIVAL. Meanwhile in 1959—the year in which he was awarded a C.B.E. (Commander of the British Empire) —he made his American debut with the SAN FRANCISCO OPERA as BECKMESSER on Oct. 6. During the next few years he appeared at LA SCALA, with the VIENNA STATE OPERA, and at the SALZBURG FESTIVAL. On Mar. 25, 1964, he made his debut at the METROPOLITAN OPERA AS FALSTAFF, where in subsequent years he has been heard in DON GIOVANNI,

PETER GRIMES, and WOZZECK, among other operas. On July 7, 1969, he was knighted by Queen Elizabeth II.

Evening Prayer, see ABENDS WILL ICH SCHLAFEN GEH'N.

Evenings on a Farm near Dikanka, see GOGOL, NIKOLAI.

Evening Star Ode, see O DU MEIN HOLDER ABENDSTERN.

evirato, see CASTRATO.

Evohé, Bacchus m'inspire, Eurydice's spirited hymn to Bacchus, which she sings disguised as a Bacchante, in Act IV of OFFENBACH'S OPÉRA BOUFFE ORPHEUS IN THE UNDERWORLD.

expressionism, a term borrowed from the world of painting and used to describe a music that attempts to express subconscious states and to reduce music to its barest essentials. Its use is almost entirely confined to the works of the Schoenbergian school and consequently to the operas of SCHOENBERG and BERG among others.

F

Faccio, Franco, conductor and composer. Born Verona, Italy, Mar. 8, 1840; died Monza, Italy, July 21, 1891. He attended the Milan Conservatory, where he collaborated with his fellow student Arrigo BOITO in writing a cantata that won a government prize. Faccio's first opera, *I profughi Fiamminghi,* was performed at LA SCALA in 1863. Two years later came AMLETO, libretto by Boito, a major success following its premiere in Genoa. After seeing service in Garibaldi's army, Faccio was appointed professor of harmony at the Milan Conservatory in 1868. In 1871 he was appointed principal conductor of La Scala, where he led the world premiere of OTELLO and the Italian premiere of AIDA.

Fafner, a giant (bass) in WAGNER'S DAS RHEINGOLD and SIEGFRIED. In *Siegfried* he assumes the form of a dragon.

Fair at Sorochinsk, The, opera in three acts by MUSSORGSKY (unfinished). Libretto by the composer, based on GOGOL's tale of the same title. Premiere: St. Petersburg, Dec. 30, 1911. American premiere: Metropolitan Opera, Nov. 29, 1930 (Nicolai TCHEREPNIN version). In this opera Mussorgsky completed only the prelude; the market scene; a portion of the sequel; most of Act II; a ballet sequence adapted from his tone poem *A Night on the Bald Mountain;* a HOPAK for orchestra; and two songs. Four versions now exist, each completed by a different composer: CUI, I. Sakhnovsky, Vissarion Shebalin, and Nicolai Tcherepnin. Liadov orchestrated some of the parts without attempting to complete the opera. The Tcherepnin version is the one most widely favored. The slim thread of the story is used to tie together a series of vignettes depicting the mostly gay and boisterous life and the superstitions of Ukrainian peasants at a fair. Tcherevik (bass), a good-natured peasant, agrees to the marriage of his daughter, Parassia (soprano), to her eligible young admirer, Gritzko (tenor). Khivria (mezzo-soprano), the peasant's wife, however, is opposed to the marriage, for she has not met her prospective son-in-law. At a drunken party, it comes out that Khivria has been carrying on with the bumbling son of the local priest. Exposed and shamed, she consents to the wedding of her daughter to Gritzko. It all ends happily with a dance. These are the most significant excerpts: the orchestral prelude entitled "A Hot Day in Little Russia"; Gritzko's revery in Act I, "Why, my sad heart"; Parassia's daydream in Act III, "Oh banish thoughts of sorrow"; and the orchestral hopak which, in Tcherepnin's version, ends the opera but which Mussorgsky intended for the close of Act I.

Fairy Queen, The, opera (or, more properly, MASQUE) in a prologue and five acts by PURCELL. Libretto probably by Elkanah Settle, adapted from SHAKESPEARE's *A Midsummer Night's Dream.* Premiere: Dorset Gardens, London, Apr., 1692. American premiere: San Francisco, Apr. 30, 1932. Following its premiere, the opera was not heard for over two centuries because the score had been lost. It was finally found by John South Shedlock in the library of the Royal Academy of M⸱⸱sic. He then directed a concert performance in London on June 15, 1901. The first staged presentation since the seventeenth century took place at Cambridge on Feb. 10, 1920. Constant Lambert made a new adaptation that opened the first season of opera at COVENT GARDEN following the end of World War II, in 1946. It was successfully revived at the ALDEBURGH FESTIVAL in England in 1967.

Faites-lui mes aveux (Flower Song), Siebel's aria as he gathers flowers for Marguerite, in Act III of GOUNOD's FAUST.

Falcon, Marie-Cornélie, soprano. Born Paris, Jan. 28, 1812; died there Feb. 25, 1897. She attended the Paris Conservatory and made her debut at the OPÉRA in 1832 as Alice in ROBERT LE DIABLE. She was a principal soprano of the Opéra for the next five years, after which she went into retirement, due to permanent loss of voice. The extraordinary dramatic quality of her voice became known as the "Falcon soprano," and sopranos assuming the roles in which she became famous were thus described.

Falla, Manuel de, composer. Born Cádiz, Spain, Nov. 23, 1876; died Alta Gracia, Argentina, Nov. 14, 1946. He attended the Madrid Conservatory, where his teacher, Felipe Pedrell, was a decisive influence. Pedrell encouraged Falla to become a composer and led him to write Spanish national music based on the foundations of Spanish folksongs. In this vein Falla wrote his first opera, LA VIDA BREVE, which won first prize in a national competition for Spanish operas in 1905. It was introduced in Nice in 1913 and was so successful that the OPÉRA-COMIQUE gave it the following year. In 1915 Falla completed his most famous work, the ballet *El amor brujo.* Seven years later came a charming opera for puppets, EL RETABLO DE MAESE PEDRO. When the Civil War broke out in Spain, Falla at first sided with the Franco nationalist movement. For a while he served as president of the Institute of Spain. But he became disillusioned with the Franco regime and decided to leave his native land for good. In 1939 he settled in South America, and it was here that he died seven years later. He spent his last years working on his most ambitious project, the opera L'ATLANTÍDA, which he did not live to complete.

falsetto, high-pitched notes of female quality produced by male singers singing in the head voice.

Falstaff, (1) the fat, jovial, unprincipled, and endearing knight of SHAKESPEARE's *The Merry Wives of Windsor* and the two parts of HENRY IV. He appears in several operas, the most famous being Verdi's *Falstaff (see below).* Others include: BALFE's *Falstaff;* AT THE BOAR'S HEAD; THE MERRY WIVES OF WINDSOR; SALIERI's *Falstaff;* SIR JOHN IN LOVE.

(2) Lyric comedy in three acts by VERDI. Libretto by BOITO, based on Shakespeare's *The Merry Wives of Windsor* and *Henry IV.* Premiere: La Scala, Feb. 9, 1893. American premiere: Metropolitan Opera, Feb. 4, 1895.

Characters: Sir John Falstaff (baritone), a role created by Victor MAUREL; Ford, a wealthy burgher (baritone); Mistress Ford, his wife (soprano); Nannetta (Anne), their daughter (soprano); Fenton, Nannetta's suitor (tenor); Dr. Caius, a physician (tenor); Mistress Page (soprano); Dame Quickly (mezzo-soprano); Bardolph, one of Falstaff's followers (tenor); Pistol, another follower (bass). The action takes place in Windsor, England, in the fifteenth century.

Act I, Scene 1. A room in the Garter Inn. Falstaff is drinking wine with Pistol and Bardolph, two of his cronies. He has written love letters to two respectable married women, Mistress Page and Mistress Ford, hoping to begin a successful liaison with one of them. He sings the praises of Ford's wife ("O amor! sguardo di stella"). He instructs his cronies to deliver his proposals, but they refuse on the grounds of honor. Falstaff sends his letters by page, upbraids Pistol and Bardolph for their cowardice, and soliloquizes about the virtue of honor ("L'onore! Ladri!").

Scene 2. In Ford's garden. Comparing the notes they have received, Mistress Page and Mistress Ford find them identical. They decide to avenge themselves by collaborating in a plot with Fenton, who is in love with Mistress Ford's daughter. Dame Quickly is dispatched to invite Falstaff to a rendezvous with Mistress Page. At the same time, an arrangement is made for Ford to meet Falstaff under an assumed name. Meanwhile young Fenton and Nannetta, Ford's daughter, exchange amorous words ("Labra di foco!").

Act II, Scene 1. The Garter Inn. After Dame Quickly has arranged with Falstaff for him to meet Mistress Page, Ford appears. He tells Falstaff that his name is Signor Fontana and that his purpose is to bribe Falstaff to speak on his behalf to Mistress Ford, with whom he is very much in love. Falstaff expresses his pride in his powers over women ("Va, vecchio John"). After singing a madrigal in praise of love ("L'amor che non ci dà mai tregue"), Falstaff says he would be delighted to follow Ford's bidding, revealing that he himself has an appointment with the lady. Since Ford knows nothing of the projected meeting, he is suddenly led to suspect that his wife is unfaithful. While Falstaff retires to don his best clothes, Ford denounces all women for their faithlessness ("È sogno? O realtà?"). Falstaff reappears and departs with Ford for the meeting with Mistress Ford.

Scene 2. A room in Ford's house. Dame Quickly announces that arrangements have been made for Falstaff's visit ("Giunta all' albergo"), and Mistress Ford expresses delight at the farce about to be enacted ("Gaie comari di Windsor"). Falstaff, arriving, begins to make love to Mistress Ford and flatters her ("Degna d'un re"). He tells her that though he is now old and fat, once, as a page to the Duke of Norfolk, he was handsome ("Quand' ero paggio del Duca di Norfolk"). Suddenly Ford arrives, fuming because he suspects his wife is entertaining a lover. Confusion prevails as Falstaff hides behind a screen. Ford's feverish search proves futile. When he departs, Mistress Ford and Mistress Page conceal Falstaff in a basket of laundry. Ford returns, remembering the screen, behind which a lover could hide. The women dump the laundry basket out of the window and into the river below. As Falstaff scrambles out of the river, wet and unhappy, Ford sees him and joins in the laughter.

Act III, Scene 1. The Garter Inn. Falstaff is sitting outside the inn, sad and disillusioned, trying to find some comfort in wine ("Mondo ladro"). Dame Quickly revives his spirits by telling him that Mistress Ford regrets what has happened and would like to meet him at midnight in Windsor Park: he is to come disguised as the Black Huntsman.

Scene 2. Windsor Park. In the moonlight Fenton, disguised as Oberon, sings of his lady love ("Dal labbro il canto estasïato vola"). The other conspirators are also present, concealed by the darkness. When Falstaff comes for his rendezvous he hears eerie noises. Convinced that supernatural forces are around, he drops to the ground, terrified, praying for protection ("Questa è la quercia"). The conspirators, dressed as fairies, emerge from hiding, and give him a sound thrashing. Merriment is now at its height, at the expense of poor Falstaff. After Ford consents to have his daughter marry Fenton (a marriage he has all the while opposed) the whole company—even Falstaff—joins in the remark that all the world is but a stage ("Tutto nel mondo è burla").

In writing this, his last opera, Verdi, though at the patriarchal age of eighty, was not afraid to venture in a new direction. *Falstaff* was a comedy, and for fifty years Verdi had written only tragedies. No longer was he concerned with large arias and big scenes. Instead he had to work in smaller dimensions and create a work whose appeal lay in delicacy of expression and wit rather than passion and intensity, in subtlety of detail rather than massive effects, in penetrating characterizations instead of overpowering emotions. Tone painting was required to help create mood and atmosphere. Delicate orchestral effects were employed to accentuate details of stage action. *Falstaff* is a score of the most consummate craftsmanship and artistry. Since Boito's libretto is, at the same time, one of the finest in opera literature, the opera stands with THE BARBER OF SEVILLE, THE MARRIAGE OF FIGARO, and DIE MEISTERSINGER as an outstanding example of comic opera.

The world premiere of a new opera by the grand old man of Italian opera inevitably attracted pilgrims from all parts of the world. The brilliant audience to whom *Falstaff* was introduced at LA SCALA on Feb. 9, 1893, was uninhibited in its enthusiasm; so were the critics. The greatest measure of this success belonged, of course, to the composer, who had produced another masterwork. But a part of the triumph belonged also to the interpreter of the title role, Victor Maurel, one of the world's great baritones. Maurel also played the part when this opera was first introduced in Paris, London, and New York.

fanciulla del West, La, *see* GIRL OF THE GOLDEN WEST, THE.

fandango, a lively Spanish dance in triple time, accompanied by castanets and frequently associated with songs.

MOZART interpolated a fandango in the third act of THE MARRIAGE OF FIGARO.

fanfare, a short flourish for trumpets, used in opera for special festivities or to attract special attention. BEETHOVEN used a fanfare in the second act of FIDELIO to announce the arrival of the Prime Minister. The opening bars of the march in TANNHÄUSER are a fanfare.

Fanget an! So rief der Lenz in den Wald, Walther's improvised love song as a demonstration to the Mastersingers of his skill at song, in Act I of WAGNER'S DIE MEISTERSINGER.

Faninal, a rich merchant (baritone) in Richard STRAUSS'S DER ROSENKAVALIER.

Fantaisie, aux divins mensonges, Gérald's aria speculating on who might be the owner of the jewels he found in the garden of an Indian temple, in Act I of DELIBES'S LAKMÉ.

farandole, a lively dance of Provence and other parts of southern Europe, in 6/8 time. GOUNOD wrote a choral farandole to open the second act of MIREILLE.

Farewell my son, I am dying, Boris Godunov's farewell to his son in Act IV, Scene 2, of MUSSORGSKY'S BORIS GODUNOV.

Farfarello, a devil (bass) in PROKOFIEV'S THE LOVE FOR THREE ORANGES.

Farinelli (born Carlo Broschi), CASTRATO soprano. Born Andria, Italy, Jan. 24, 1705; died Bologna, July 15, 1782. He was the most celebrated castrato of the eighteenth century. After studying with Niccolò PORPORA, he made his stage debut in 1722 in his teacher's *Eumene,* on which occasion he assumed the stage name of Farinelli. In 1727 he engaged the celebrated castrato Antonio BERNACCHI in a test of vocal skill and was defeated; but Bernacchi recognized the younger man's unusual ability and became his teacher. Farinelli now began to enjoy an adulation known by few other singers of his time. He was a sensation in Vienna in 1728 and 1731 and in London in 1734. Women swooned at his performances. In 1737 the Queen of Spain offered Farinelli a lavish salary to become singer to the court. Accepting,

Farinelli stayed in Spain twenty-five years, singing no more in public, and occupying a position of great honor and considerable political power. He was responsible for the long succession of opera productions that made Madrid famous during these years. In 1750 he received the Cross of Calatrava, one of the highest of Spanish orders. When Charles III ascended the throne in 1759, Farinelli was required to leave Spain, but he continued to collect his salary. Surrounded by paintings, harpsichords, and other valuable souvenirs of his court career, he spent the rest of his life in retirement in Bologna. In 1843 the OPÉRA-COMIQUE had a great success with AUBER's La Part du diable (libretto by SCRIBE), which deals with Farinelli's career in Spain. The principal role is written for a female soprano.

Farlaf, Ludmilla's suitor (bass) in GLINKA'S RUSSLAN AND LUDMILLA.

Farlaf's Rondo, Farlaf's PATTER SONG after his visit to the witch for her help, in Act II of GLINKA'S RUSSLAN AND LUDMILLA.

Farrar, Geraldine, soprano. Born Melrose, Mass., Feb. 28, 1882; died Ridgefield, Conn., Mar. 11, 1967. She was the daughter of Syd Farrar, a professional baseball player. She began music study in her fifth year and started appearing publicly when she was fourteen. On the advice of Jean DE RESZKE she studied singing seriously with Emma Thursby in New York, Trabadello in Paris, and Francesco Graziani in Berlin. Later on, as an established opera star in Berlin, she received coaching from Lilli LEHMANN. She made her debut with the Berlin Royal Opera (BERLIN STATE OPERA) in FAUST on Oct. 15, 1901, and was a sensation. She remained with the company three years, appearing in eleven different roles, and giving a command performance for the Emperor. Successes in Monte Carlo and Paris preceded a triumphant return to her native country. On Nov. 26, 1906 (the opening night of the season), she made her American debut at the METROPOLITAN OPERA in ROMÉO ET JULIETTE. For fifteen years,

Miss Farrar was a principal soprano of the Metropolitan Opera, making four hundred and ninety-three appearances in twenty-nine roles. She achieved her greatest successes as CARMEN, CIO-CIO-SAN, the Goose Girl in KÖNIGSKINDER (a role she created), THAÏS, ZAZA, JULIETTE, GILDA, MANON, and TOSCA. She sang in the first performance of MASCAGNI's Amica (Monte Carlo, 1905), and she appeared in the American premieres of ARIANE ET BARBE-BLEUE (1911) and JULIEN (1914). She made her final appearance at the Metropolitan on Apr. 22, 1922, in Zaza. Her striking beauty and personal magnetism were probably more outstanding than the quality of her voice; but when she was at her best she was an artist of compelling force both vocally and personally. While at the height of her fame, Miss Farrar appeared in many silent motion pictures, including Carmen, Joan the Woman, and The Riddle Woman. For a period after her retirement from opera she appeared in song recitals. Some years later she served a single season as a commentator during the Metropolitan Opera broadcasts. In 1938 she published her autobiography, Such Sweet Compulsion.

Farrell, Eileen, soprano. Born Willimantic, Conn., Feb. 13, 1920. She studied singing with Merle Alcock and Eleanor McLellan. She was then heard over the radio, and she toured the United States in song recitals. She appeared in several operas given in concert version, including WOZZECK, LES CHOËPHORES (both as soloist with the New York Philharmonic Orchestra), and in 1955 in MÉDÉE (with the AMERICAN OPERA SOCIETY). In March, 1956, she made her debut in a staged opera in Tampa, Fla., CAVALLERIA RUSTICANA. After that came significant appearances with the SAN FRANCISCO OPERA (where, on Sept. 12, 1958, she opened the season in Médée, in its American staged premiere) and the CHICAGO LYRIC OPERA (where she appeared in IL TROVATORE and LA GIOCONDA). Her debut at the METROPOLITAN OPERA took place on Dec. 6, 1960, in the title role of GLUCK's AL-

CESTE. She has since appeared there in leading soprano roles, with particular distinction in the Wagnerian repertory. She was starred in ANDREA CHÉNIER on opening night of the Metropolitan Opera's 1962–63 season. She has also appeared extensively in Europe both in opera houses and at festivals, having made her first concert appearance there in 1957 to sing at the dedication ceremonies of the Congress Hall in Berlin. In the motion-picture biography of Marjorie LAWRENCE, *Interrupted Melody*, Eileen Farrell did the singing.

Fasolt, a giant (bass) in WAGNER'S DAS RHEINGOLD.

Fassbänder, Zdenka, soprano. Born Tetschen, Bohemia, Nov. 12, 1880; died Munich, Mar. 14, 1954. Following her vocal training in Prague under Sophie Loewe-Destinn, she made her opera debut in Karlsruhe. From 1906 to 1919 she was the leading dramatic soprano of the MUNICH OPERA, where she was acclaimed for her performances in WAGNER and Richard STRAUSS. She was the wife of the celebrated conductor Felix MOTTL.

Fata Morgana, a witch (soprano) in PROKOFIEV'S THE LOVE FOR THREE ORANGES.

Fatima, (1) Mârouf's wife (contralto) in RABAUD'S MÂROUF.

(2) REZIA's attendant (mezzo-soprano) in WEBER'S OBERON, a role created by Lucia VESTRIS.

(3) wife (soprano) of the beggar Abu Hassan in WEBER'S ABU HASSAN.

Fauré, Gabriel, composer. Born Pamiers, France, May 12, 1845; died Paris, Nov. 4, 1924. He attended the École Niedermeyer, after which he served as organist for various Parisian churches, including the Madeleine. He first attracted attention as composer of songs. *Prométhée*, an opera, was introduced in Béziers in 1900. PÉNÉLOPE, another lyric work, was performed with moderate success in Monte Carlo in 1913. Fauré's operas, like his more familiar works, are characterized by beautiful balance, proportion, and purity of expression. In 1905 Fauré succeeded Théodore Dubois as director of the Paris Conservatory,

holding this post fifteen years. In the last years of his life he was a victim of deafness. He was made a member of the Académie des Beaux-Arts in 1909, and in 1922 he received the highest class in the order of the Legion of Honor.

Faure, Jean-Baptiste, baritone. Born Moulins, France, Jan. 15, 1830; died Paris, Nov. 9, 1914. After attending the Paris Conservatory, he made his opera debut at the OPÉRA-COMIQUE in MASSÉ's *Galathée* on Oct. 20, 1852. After eight successful years at the Opéra-Comique, he became the first baritone of the PARIS OPÉRA, remaining there fifteen years, a period during which he appeared in many notable first performances, including those of L'AFRICAINE, DON CARLOS, HAMLET, and FAUST. His greatest successes were in *Faust,* DON GIOVANNI, LES HUGUENOTS, WILLIAM TELL, and LE PROPHÈTE. His last appearance at the Paris Opéra took place on May 13, 1876, in *Hamlet*. After making several appearances in London and Vienna, he retired from opera and was heard only in song recitals. Between 1857 and 1860 he taught singing at the Paris Conservatory. In 1859 he married Caroline Lefebvre, a singer of the Opéra-Comique. He wrote two volumes of songs; one of the songs, "Les Rameaux" ("The Palms") , is very popular.

Faust, (1) aged philosopher and alchemist, the central character of an old German legend treated by many German writers, as well as by Christopher MARLOWE. The most celebrated version is that of GOETHE. The theme of the Faust legend is his exchange of his soul for the return of youth and power. This subject has been treated in several operas, the most famous being that of Gounod (*see below*) . Others include THE DAMNATION OF FAUST; MEFISTOFELE; DOKTOR FAUST; and SPOHR'S *Faust*.

(2) Opera in five acts by GOUNOD. Libretto by Jules BARBIER and Michel Carré, based on Part I of Goethe's drama of the same name. Premiere: Théâtre Lyrique, Paris, Mar. 19, 1859. American premiere: Philadelphia, Nov. 25, 1863.

Characters: Faust (tenor); Méphistophélès (bass); Marguerite (soprano);
Valentin, her brother (baritone); Siebel, young man in love with Marguerite
(mezzo-soprano); Martha Schwerlein,
Marguerite's friend (mezzo-soprano);
Wagner, a student (baritone); soldiers;
students; peasants; priests. The setting
is Germany in the sixteenth century.

Act I. Faust's study. The venerable
Faust, sick of life, is about to take poison when he hears young, gay voices
outside his window. Envious of the
gaiety of youth, he curses the young people and calls on Satan to help him.
Méphistophélès appears. Faust confides
that what he most wants is youth ("Je
veux la jeunesse"). Méphistophélès
makes a bargain with Faust: he will restore Faust's youth in return for his
soul. Faust hesitates until Méphistophélès evokes the image of the lovely Marguerite at her spinning wheel. Then he
acquiesces, drinks a potion prepared by
the devil, and is magically changed into
a young and handsome man, a development hailed by Méphistophélès and
Faust in "À moi les plaisirs." Méphistophélès promises Faust he shall see
Marguerite without delay.

Act II. A public square. Soldiers and
villagers are celebrating the day of the
fair ("Vin ou bière"). Valentin and
Siebel appear. Valentin is confident he
will be protected by a sacred medallion
("O Sainte medaille") but he is greatly
concerned because he must join the
army and leave his sister unprotected
("Avant de quitter ces lieux"). When
Siebel promises to watch over Marguerite, Valentin expresses his gratitude.
Wagner, a student, jumps on a table to
sing a ditty about a rat ("Un rat plus
poltron") but is rudely interrupted by
Méphistophélès, who provides a pleasanter song, a cynical comment on man's
greed for gold ("Le veau d'or"). After
that, the devil delights the crowd with
feats of magic. He prophesies that any
flower touched by Siebel will wither and
die, particularly those he sends to Marguerite; the devil also produces wine by
striking his sword on the sign of the

near-by inn. When Méphistophélès proposes a toast to Marguerite, Valentin
grows furious and rushes at him with his
sword; the sword instantly snaps in
half. Siebel, Wagner, and their friends
now join Valentin. Realizing they are in
the presence of the devil, they raise the
handles of their swords to form crosses
(Chorus of the Swords: "De l'enfer qui
vient émousser"). Méphistophélès, terrified, withdraws. Faust comes seeking
Marguerite. The villagers fill the square
as they dance and sing (Waltz: "Ainsi
que la brise"). Marguerite now passes,
coming from church. Faust offers to
escort her home. Marguerite shyly rebuffs him. As she walks on, Faust sings
of his enchantment with her ("O belle
enfant! Je t'aime"). Méphistophélès is
cynical about Faust's success, and the
townspeople continue their gay waltzing.

Act III. Marguerite's garden. The
orchestral prelude describes a balmy
summer evening. Siebel gathers flowers
for Marguerite and asks them to carry
his message of love ("Faites-lui mes
aveux"). But the flowers die in his
hands. Remembering Méphistophélès'
prophecy, Siebel rushes to a near-by
shrine and dips his hands in holy water.
The flowers he now picks go unharmed,
and he places them tenderly at Marguerite's door. After Siebel leaves, Faust
comes, thinking of Marguerite and paying tribute to her home ("Salut! demeure chaste et pure"). His revery is
disturbed by Méphistophélès, who places
a casket of jewels near Siebel's flowers.
Faust and Méphistophélès hide as Marguerite comes from her house and sits at
her spinning wheel. Musing on the
handsome stranger who greeted her in
the square, she sings a ballad about the
King of Thulé ("Il était un roi
de Thulé"). Suddenly she catches
a glimpse of the flowers and knows they
are Siebel's. Finding the casket, she
opens it and is overjoyed to find it filled
with jewels. Putting them on while inspecting herself joyously in a mirror,
she sings the Jewel Song ("Ah, je ris de
me voir"). As she is doing this, Martha

enters and is amazed at the way the jewels enhance Marguerite's beauty. Faust and Méphistophélès come out from hiding. The devil distracts Martha by telling her that her husband is dead. Faust pursues Marguerite. Night begins to fall. Méphistophélès addresses the night, foretelling that lovers are about to be united ("O nuit, étends sur eux ton ombre") ; then he disappears. Faust and Marguerite reappear in the garden. They reveal their love in two duets: "Laisse-moi contempler ton visage" and "O nuit d'amour." Tearing herself away from Faust, Marguerite promises to meet him the following day. A moment later she appears at the window of her cottage, still thinking of her rapture. Faust rushes toward her, while Méphistophélès laughs mockingly.

Act IV, Scene 1. Marguerite's room. (This scene is often omitted.) Marguerite, at her spinning wheel, is bemoaning her fate ("Elles se cachaient!") : she has been betrayed and deserted. Siebel comes to console her. Marguerite is grateful, but she cannot forget the man she loves.

Scene 2. The cathedral. Marguerite is praying for Faust and their unborn child when Méphistophélès comes to mock her for having yielded to temptation. The church choir sings of Judgment Day ("Quand du Seigneur le jour liura"). Overcome with terror, Marguerite falls into a faint.

Scene 3. The square before the cathedral. (In the original version, this scene came before the preceding one; it is now customary to perform the scenes in the sequence here given.) Soldiers, returning from battle, jubilantly sing of their recent victory and their joy at being home (Soldiers' Chorus: "Gloire immortelle de nos aïeux"). Valentin is with them. Eagerly he questions Siebel about Marguerite. When Siebel is evasive, Valentin rushes into his sister's cottage. Faust and Méphistophélès appear, and the latter sings a mocking serenade beneath Marguerite's window ("Vous qui faites l'endormie"). Valentin emerges and challenges Faust to a duel in which, through the devil's magic, Valentin is fatally wounded by Faust. As the townspeople rush into the square, Faust and Méphistophélès disappear. Bitterly, Valentin condemns his sister and refuses to forgive her. Marguerite watches him die, denouncing her. The townspeople kneel at his side in prayer.

Act V, Scene 1. In the Harz Mountains. (This scene is frequently omitted.) Faust and Méphistophélès come to watch the revels of Walpurgis Night. At the height of the orgy, Faust sees a vision of Marguerite, apparently crushed by a blow from an axe. Shaken, he insists that the devil take him back to his beloved.

Scene 2. A prison. Marguerite has killed her child and is in prison awaiting execution for her crime. At dawn, hearing the voice of her lover, Marguerite becomes delirious with joy ("Sa main, sa douce main"). Faust calls to her to follow him out of the prison, but Marguerite does not seem to hear what he is saying. Impatiently, Méphistophélès urges Faust and Marguerite to make their escape ("Alerte! Alerte!"), but both are deaf to his entreaty. Marguerite, on the threshold of death, prays to be borne heavenward ("Anges purs, anges radieux"), after which she voices her horror of Faust. As she dies, Méphistophélès drags Faust to his doom. Voices of invisible angels sing of Marguerite's redemption ("Sauvée! Christ est ressuscité!").

The early career of Gounod's *Faust* was turbulent. Accepted by the THÉÂTRE LYRIQUE, the opera was repeatedly delayed; when rehearsals finally began, there were new misfortunes: the censors objected to the cathedral scene, and the principal tenor had to withdraw because of ill health. The censors were placated, and a last-minute substitute was found for the tenor. When the opera was at last given, public and critics reacted unfavorably. Not until it was revived by the PARIS OPÉRA on Mar. 3, 1869, did *Faust* begin to enjoy the success it deserved. (It was for this production that Gounod wrote his famous ballet music.) After that the opera proceeded from triumph to triumph. In the next thirty-five years it was seen on the average of once every nine days at the Opéra; during the next forty years it was given an additional thousand performances. In England, where two rival companies competed to give its first performance (1863), the opera became one of the most popular items in the entire repertory. (For one of these English productions, at HIS MAJESTY'S THEATRE on Jan. 23, 1864, Gounod wrote Valentin's famous aria, "Avant de quitter ces lieux"). The opera became a particular favorite of Queen Victoria, who, just before her death, asked to have parts of it sung for her. In the United States, in 1883, Faust was the opera chosen to open the newly founded METROPOLITAN OPERA. Only in Germany was Faust not well received. There it was considered a travesty of the Goethe drama. Nevertheless, under the title of Margarethe, it has long been a part of the standard repertoire of German opera houses.

The success of Faust is as easy to explain as it is difficult to understand why it took a decade for this recognition to arrive. Faust overflows with wonderful melodies of all kinds: rousing choruses; mocking and satiric tunes; sentimental melodies; lilting and heart-warming pages. The music is direct in its emotional appeal, with no attempt at subtlety. It is the wonderful abundance of its lyricism that continues to place Faust in the front rank of the world's most popular operas, even though we have an increasing awareness that its characterizations are stilted, the text is vulgar, and much of the music superficial.

Favart, Charles Simon, librettist and impresario. Born Paris, Nov. 13, 1710; died there Mar. 12, 1792. He was a theater manager in Paris and Brussels before becoming the manager of the OPÉRA-COMIQUE in 1752. For the next twenty-seven years he presented over a hundred plays at both the Opéra-Comique and the Théâtre des Italiens; many of these works influenced the evo-

lution of the OPÉRA COMIQUE form. Favart provided numerous composers with about a hundred and fifty librettos for operas, some of which were GRÉTRY's L'Amitié à l'épreuve, GLUCK's Cythère assiegée, and PHILIDOR's Le Jardinier supposé. The Opéra-Comique was frequently called the "Salle Favart" after his death.

favola del figlio cambiato, La (The Fable of the Changeling), opera in three acts by MALIPIERO. Libretto is the play of the same name by Luigi Pirandello. Premiere: Rome, Mar. 24, 1934. Based on a Sicilian legend, the play concerns the son of a Sicilian peasant woman. In babyhood, the boy is exchanged for an idiot. The idiot turns out to be of royal birth. In the end, the peasant woman gets back her own son and the idiot rightfully becomes a prince. This opera had political repercussions when introduced in Fascist Italy. Mussolini, disturbed by the overtones of the libretto, ordered its removal from the stage two days after the premiere on the grounds that the story had "moral incongruity."

favola d'Orfeo, La, see L'ORFEO.

favola per musica, Italian for "fable through music," one of the names given to opera in the very late sixteenth and early seventeenth centuries. A favola per musica was usually an adaptation of a story on a legendary or mythological subject.

favorita, La, opera in four acts by DONIZETTI. Libretto by Alphonse Royer and Gustave Vaëz, based on the drama Le Comte de Comminges by Baculard-d'Arnaud. Premiere: Paris Opéra, Dec. 2, 1840 (in French). American premiere: New Orleans, Feb. 9, 1843.

Characters: Alfonso XI, King of Castile (baritone); Leonora de Guzman, his mistress (mezzo-soprano); Inez, her confidante (soprano); Fernando, a monastic novice (tenor); Baltasar, prior of the Monastery of St. James (bass); Don Gasparo, the King's officer (tenor). The action takes place in Castile in 1340.

Act I, Scene 1. The cloister of St.

James. Fernando confesses to Baltasar that he has fallen in love with an unknown woman who regularly passes the monastery window (*Romanza:* "Una vergine, un angel di Dio"). The prior, shocked at the revelation, sends the novice away from the monastery. The latter is now free to search for the woman he loves.

Scene 2. The island of Leon. Leonora de Guzman, the King's favorite, has ordered that Fernando be brought to her. She is the unknown woman of whom he dreams; united, they rush to each others' arms. But Leonora knows that Fernando will desert her once he discovers that she is the King's mistress. She gives him a parchment and orders him to leave. Now convinced that Leonora is beyond his reach, Fernando finds that the parchment is his commission as an officer in the King's army. He expresses his satisfaction in "Si, che un tuo solo accento."

Act II. The gardens of Alcazar. The King reveals his love for Leonora in "Vien, Leonora, a' piedi tuoi." He is then beset by Baltasar, who threatens him and his court with excommunication for having abandoned his wife for a mistress. The King is torn between duty and love, as Baltasar denounces him in no uncertain terms ("Ah, paventa del furor").

Act III. A hall of the palace. Now a victorious hero, Fernando is promised by the King any reward he wants. Still not knowing that Leonora is the King's mistress, Fernando asks for her hand in marriage. The King, eager to resolve his personal problems and thus avoid excommunication, is happy to grant this request, though sadly ("A tanto amor"). Knowing that Fernando will have nothing to do with her once he learns of her status, Leonora sings of her anguish and her determination to make any sacrifice for Fernando's happiness ("O, mio Fernando"). She instructs Inez to deliver a letter which tells Fernando the truth, but the interference of the King prevents its delivery. After Fernando and Leonora are married, Baltasar re-turns to the palace and Fernando learns of the sordid deception ("Alla bella dei re").

Act IV. The monastery. Fernando has come back to find peace. The monks comment on the heavenly splendor of religious life ("Splendon più belle in ciel"). Before taking part in the final rites that will make him a monk, Fernando recalls his lost love ("Spirto gentil"). Leonora, disguised as a novice, comes to the monastery to find him. She pleads for his forgiveness ("Pietoso al par d'un Nume"). Fernando and the stricken woman are briefly reunited before she falls dead in his arms.

Feast in Time of Plague, *see* PUSHKIN, ALEXANDER.

Federica, Duchess of Ostheim (contralto) in VERDI's LUISA MILLER.

Federico, principal male character (tenor) in CILÈA's L'ARLÉSIANA, a role created by CARUSO.

Federico's Lament, see E LA SOLITA STORIA.

Fedora, lyric drama in three acts by GIORDANO. Libretto by Arturo Colautti, based on the drama of the same name by Victorien SARDOU. Premiere: Teatro Lirico, Milan, Nov. 17, 1898. American premiere: Metropolitan Opera, Dec. 5, 1906.

Characters: Princess Fedora Romanov (soprano); Countess Olga Sukarev (soprano); Count Loris Ipanov (tenor); De Siriex, a diplomat (baritone); Baron Rouvel (tenor); Grech, a police officer (bass); Borov, a doctor (baritone); Lorek, a surgeon (baritone); Dmitri, a young groom (contralto); Désiré, an attendant (tenor); Cyril, a cook (baritone). The action takes place in St. Petersburg, Paris, and Switzerland in the closing years of the nineteenth century.

Act I. The house of Count Vladimir Andreyevich. Princess Fedora, about to be married to Vladimir, is waiting for him. Seeing his picture, she kisses it and addresses it tenderly ("O grandi occhi"). Suddenly, the Count is carried into his house, fatally wounded. His assassin is believed to be Count Loris Ipanov, a suspected Nihilist. After Vladimir dies, Fedora vows to avenge his death.

Act II. Fedora's house in Paris. As part of her plot to get Count Loris to confess he killed Vladimir, Fedora contrives to have him fall in love with her. He is now a guest at a reception in her house. Finding her alone, Loris tells Fedora of his love for her ("Amor ti vieta") as Fedora leads him on coquettishly. At last, he confesses that he killed Vladimir. Fedora makes plans with the police officer to have Loris seized when her guests have departed. But when the guests are gone, Loris reveals to Fedora the reason for the murder: Vladimir had seduced Loris' wife, Wanda, and had been responsible for her death ("Mia madre"). This information relieves Fedora of the necessity for revenge. Realizing now that she loves Loris, and being reminded by Loris that he is being hounded by spies ("Vedi, io piango"), she helps him escape from the police by staying with her.

Act III. Fedora's villa in Oberland. Fedora and Loris are living happily in Switzerland. A spy, however, has traced Loris' whereabouts. He comes with the news that both Loris' brother and mother have died as a consequence of his crime. Fedora prays for Loris' safety ("Dio di giustizia"). When Loris learns that Fedora was the one who had betrayed him to the police, he becomes blinded by rage and is about to kill her, when she takes poison. As Loris forgives her ("Amor ti vieta") and begs her to live for his sake, she dies in his arms.

Fedra, opera in three acts by PIZZETTI. Libretto by D'ANNUNZIO. Premiere: La Scala, Mar. 20, 1915. Though he had previously made several attempts at opera, some of which he did not finish and others of which he discarded, Pizzetti did not complete this—his first full opera to satisfy him—until 1912; it had taken him three years to write. Here is how CASTELNUOVO-TEDESCO described it: "This was not only his first but, in many respects, his best opera. . . . Based

on a drama by d'Annunzio, it unavoidably contains all the defects of d'Annunzio's theatrical style. At times it is static, often verbose. . . . Apart from certain dramatic effects, it remains, from a musical point of view, a wonderful opera. It possesses perfect coherence and unity of style, dignity and restraint, truly worthy of an ancient Greek tragedy. At the same time, it is full of a nervous energy, of a restrained warmth."

Feen, Die (The Fairies), opera by WAGNER. Libretto by the composer, based on Carlo GOZZI's La donna serpente. Premiere: Munich Royal Opera, June 29, 1888. This was Wagner's first complete opera, written when he was twenty. It was never performed in the composer's lifetime. The principal characters are Prince Arindal of Tramond, and the woman he loves, Ada. She has extracted from him a promise that for eight years he make no effort to uncover her identity. After eight years, the Prince poses the question, and Ada disappears, having been a supernatural being. Unable to forget the Prince, Ada is ready to discard her immortality and become a human. But in the end it is the Prince who becomes supernatural and immortal and is destined to ascend the throne of Fairyland with Ada at his side. An opera on the same text, titled LA DONNA SERPENTE, was written in 1932 by CASELLA, and Gozzi's play was also the basis of Friedrich Himmel's opera Die Sylphen in 1806.

Feldlager in Schlesien, Ein, see ÉTOILE DU NORD, L'.

Feldmarschallin, The, see PRINCESS VON WERDENBERG.

Felsenstein, Walter, producer and director. Born Vienna, May 30, 1901. His music study took place in Graz and Vienna. After a brief apprenticeship in the theater as actor, he became the manager of several opera companies in Germany and Switzerland between 1924 and 1940. From 1940 to 1947 he was a producer of operas at the BERLIN STATE OPERA. Since 1947 he has been the director of the KOMISCHE OPER in East

Berlin. As a result of his meticulous attention to every detail of stage production and his relentless pursuit of perfection of performance regardless of how many rehearsals may be involved, he has elevated this opera company to a place of first importance. Among his notable productions have been JENUFA, THE CUNNING LITTLE VIXEN, OTELLO, THE TALES OF HOFFMANN, ORPHEUS IN THE UNDERWORLD, THE LOVE FOR THREE ORANGES, and THE NOSE. In 1970 he was director of a motion-picture adaptation of *The Tales of Hoffman,* his second opera for the movies (the first being *Otello*).

Fenena, Nebuchadnezzar's sister (soprano) in VERDI'S NABUCCO.

Fenice, La, *see* TEATRO LA FENICE.

Fennimore and Gerda, music drama in "nine pictures" by DELIUS. Libretto (in German) by the composer, based on Jens Peter Jacobsen's novel *Niels Lyhne.* Premiere: Frankfurt-am-Main, Oct. 21, 1919. This was Delius' last opera. The love triangle in the story consists of the poet Niels Lyhne, the painter Erik Refstrup, and Fennimore, a girl they both love. Niels and Fennimore marry. Later, the old love between Erik and Fennimore is revived. After Erik suffers accidental death, Niels finds consolation and happiness in the love of a childhood sweetheart, Gerda.

Fenton, (1) Anna's suitor (tenor) in NICOLAI'S THE MERRY WIVES OF WINDSOR.

(2) Nannetta's (Anne's) suitor (tenor) in VERDI'S FALSTAFF.

Feodor, Boris Godunov's young son (mezzo-soprano) in MUSSORGSKY'S BORIS GODUNOV.

Ferma, crudele, estinguere, Ernani's poignant farewell to his beloved just before he commits suicide at the end of VERDI'S ERNANI.

Fernando, (1) Ninetta's beloved (tenor) in ROSSINI'S LA GAZZA LADRA.

(2) A monastic novice (tenor) in love with Leonora in DONIZETTI'S LA FAVORITA.

(3) Rosario's lover (tenor) in GRANADOS' GOYESCAS, a role created by MARTINELLI.

Fernando, Don, Prime Minister of Spain (bass) in BEETHOVEN'S FIDELIO.

Ferrando, (1) Dorabella's suitor (tenor) in MOZART'S COSÌ FAN TUTTE.

(2) Captain of the guards (bass) in VERDI'S IL TROVATORE.

Ferrier, Kathleen, contralto. Born Higher Walton, Eng., Apr. 22, 1912; died London, Oct. 8, 1953. Following vocal studies with J. E. Hutchinson and Roy Henderson and a successful career as concert singer, she made her opera debut in 1946 in the world premiere of THE RAPE OF LUCRETIA at the GLYNDEBOURNE FESTIVAL. In 1947 and in 1953 she appeared as Orfeo in GLUCK'S ORFEO ED EURIDICE at the Glyndebourne Festival and the HOLLAND FESTIVAL respectively. She toured the United States in 1947–48 and in 1950–51.

Feste e pane!, opening chorus of the holiday crowd in PONCHIELLI'S LA GIOCONDA.

festa teatrale, Italian for "theatrical feast," a type of opera, generally on a mythological or allegorical subject, popular in the eighteenth century. It was written for such occasions as royal weddings and was invariably festive in character.

Festival Internazionale di Musica Contemporanea, *see* VENICE FESTIVAL OF CONTEMPORARY MUSIC.

Festival of Two Worlds, an annual summer festival of the arts held in Spoleto, Italy. It was founded in 1958 by Gian Carlo MENOTTI, who for a decade served as its artistic director. The program of the first festival season included VERDI'S MACBETH. Since then the more significant events in opera have included the following novelties: LE COMTE ORY; *Il furioso all' isola di San Domingo* (DONIZETTI); INTRODUCTIONS AND GOODBYES (a world premiere); *Laborintus II* (BERIO); THE LOVE FOR THREE ORANGES; DER PRINZ VON HOMBURG (first performance outside Germany); *The Scarf* (1958; Lee Hoiby, a world premiere). The first production there of a Menotti opera did not take place until 1968 with THE SAINT OF BLEECKER STREET.

In 1969 Menotti assigned most of his duties to the newly created post of general manager, filled by Massimo Bogiancino. The festival opened its 1970 season on June 20 with a revival of *Il giuramento* by Saverio MERCANDANTE in honor of the centennial of that composer's death.

festivals. The most significant music festivals, featuring opera either exclusively or in part, are discussed in this volume in separate entries. *See:*

United States: Aspen; Berkshire Music Festival; Caramoor; Central City Opera; Chautauqua Festival; Cincinnati Zoo Opera; Lake George Opera Festival; San Antonio Grand Opera Festival; Santa Fe Opera.

Europe: Aix-en-Provence; Aldeburgh; Bayreuth; Berlin Festival; Drottingsholm Opera Festival; Edinburgh; Festival of Two Worlds (Spoleto) ; Florence May Music Festival; Glyndebourne; Handel Festival; Holland; Munich; Prague Spring Festival; Salzburg; Schwetzingen; Settimana Musicale Chigiana; Venice Festival of Contemporary Music; Vienna Festival Weeks; Wiesbaden; Zürich.

Festspiel, German for "festival play." WAGNER called his RING DES NIBELUNGEN a "stage festival play" (*bühnenfestspiel*), and PARSIFAL a "stage consecrating festival play" (*bühnenweihfestspiel*) .

Fête polonaise, an orchestral episode during festivities in Act II of CHABRIER'S LE ROI MALGRÉ LUI.

Feuersnot (Fire-Famine) , one-act opera ("poem for singing") by Richard STRAUSS. Libretto by Ernst von Wolzogen. Premiere: Dresden Opera, Nov. 21, 1901. American premiere: Metropolitan Opera (in Philadelphia) , Dec. 1, 1927. In this opera, Strauss's second, he was strongly influenced by DIE MEISTERSINGER, just as in his first opera, GUNTRAM, he had been affected by the RING DES NIBELUNGEN. In the distant past, during the St. John's Eve celebration in Munich, Diemut (soprano) goes out collecting wood for the solstice fire. She comes to the recluse Kunrad's house, and the moment they meet they fall

in love. But Kunrad (baritone) is presumptuous in kissing her, and Diemut punishes him by making him ridiculous to his fellow villagers. This so enrages the young man that he conjures the *Feuersnot* to take place: all light is extinguished. Diemut repents her hasty act, wins back Kunrad, and the lights are restored. Since Strauss identified himself with the principal male character of Kunrad, he uses themes from his own opera *Guntram.* He also quotes from WAGNER'S DER FLIEGENDE HOLLÄNDER.

Feuerzauber, *see* MAGIC FIRE SCENE, THE.

Février, Henri, composer. Born Paris, Oct. 2, 1875; died there July 6, 1957. He attended the Paris Conservatory, his teachers including MASSENET and FAURÉ. In 1906 his first opera, *Le Roi aveugle,* was performed at the OPÉRA-COMIQUE. Three years later came the opera that made him internationally famous, MONNA VANNA, introduced by the PARIS OPÉRA. Later operas were: *Gismonda* (1918) ; *La Damnation de Blanche-Fleur* (1920) ; *La Femme nué* (1932) .

Fibich, Zdeněk, composer. Born Seborsitz, Bohemia, Dec. 21, 1850; died Prague, Oct. 15, 1900. Influenced by Richard WAGNER's theories regarding the fusion of music and poetry, Fibich developed an operatic form which had been popular in the eighteenth century —the melodrama—in which the spoken dramatic text is provided with an orchestral accompaniment. His teachers at the Leipzig Conservatory included Ignaz Moscheles, Carl Richter, and Salomon Jadassohn. After additional study in Paris and Mannheim, he became a teacher of music in Vilna in 1870. Four years later he returned to his native land and was appointed assistant conductor of the Prague National Theater. After 1881 he concentrated on composition, producing many works influenced by the German romanticists, particularly SCHUMANN and Brahms. His first opera, *Bukovin,* was produced in 1874. He now began evolving the melodrama, producing his first work in this form in 1875, *Christmas Eve.* His most ambitious melodrama was a trilogy entitled HIPPODAMEIA, written between 1890 and 1892. Fibich then returned to writing operas in a more formal and traditional manner and achieved his greatest success with SARKA, a folk opera. His best-known operas and melodramas: *Bukovin* (1874); *Christmas Eve* (1875); *Blanik* (1877); *The Water Sprite* (1883); *Hakon* (1888); the trilogy *Hippodameia: Pelops' Wooing* (1890); *The Atonement of Tantalus* (1891); *The Death of Hippodameia* (1891); *The Tempest* (1894); *Hedy* (1895); *Sarka* (1897); *The Fall of Arcona* (1900).

Fidalma, the aunt (mezzo-soprano) of Carolina and Elisetta in CIMAROSA'S IL MATRIMONIO SEGRETO.

Fidelio, opera in two acts by BEETHOVEN. Libretto by Josef Sonnleithner and George Treitschke, based on a play by Jean Nicolas Bouilly, *Lénore, ou l'amour conjugal.* Premiere: Theater-an-der-Wien, Vienna, Nov. 20, 1805. American premiere: Park Theater, New York, Sept. 9, 1839.

Characters: Florestan, a nobleman (tenor); Leonore, his wife (soprano); Don Fernando, Prime Minister of Spain (bass); Pizarro, governor of the prison (bass); Rocco, chief jailer (bass); Marcellina, his daughter (soprano); Jacquino, Rocco's assistant (tenor); prisoners; soldiers; guards. The setting is a prison near Seville, Spain, in the eighteenth century.

The rise of the curtain is preceded by the playing of the so-called *Fidelio Overture,* made up of two principal themes, one for horn answered by clarinets, the other for strings.

Act I, Scene 1. Rocco's kitchen. (In Beethoven's original version, the entire first act takes place in the prison courtyard. Following an innovation of Gustav MAHLER's, it has been customary to divide the act into two scenes.)

Florestan, a fighter of despotism, has been thrown into prison by his enemy Pizarro, and he is slowly starving to death. Hoping to save him, Florestan's wife, Leonore, disguises herself as a young man, takes the name of Fidelio,

and becomes Rocco's assistant at the jail. Rocco's daughter, Marcellina, falls in love with the disguised woman ("O wär ich schon mit dir vereint"), arousing the jealousy of her suitor, Jacquino. The three of them, along with Rocco, express their reactions to these complications in a quartet ("Mir ist so wunderbar"). Rocco favors marriage, but emphasizes the importance of money ("Hat man nicht auch Gold daneben").

Scene 2. The prison courtyard. Fidelio learns from Pizarro that the Prime Minister is about to inspect the prison. Afraid that the Prime Minister may discover Florestan, Pizarro decides to kill his enemy. The news overwhelms Lenore ("Abscheulicher! Wo eilst du hin?"). She is determined to save her husband ("Komm Hoffnung"). She prevails on Rocco to allow the prisoners to leave their cells for a few minutes. The prisoners emerge haltingly, groping into the blinding sunlight, singing a paean to freedom (Prisoners' Chorus: "O welche Lust!"). Leonore is grief-stricken to find that Florestan is not with them, but is somewhat consoled when Rocco informs her that she will descend with him to Florestan's cell and help with the digging of his grave.

Act II, Scene 1. The dungeon. Florestan is chained to the wall. With anguish he recalls happier days with his beloved wife ("In des Lebens Frühlingstagen"). At this point, Rocco and Leonore enter. She is shocked to see her husband so emaciated, but controls herself lest Rocco become suspicious. Rocco and Leonore dig the grave. Pizarro arrives; with dagger in hand, he rushes toward his victim. Leonore springs between them, declaring she will kill Pizarro with her pistol if he makes another move. A fanfare of trumpets announces the arrival of the Prime Minister. Florestan and Leonore are jubilant; Pizarro is apprehensive, Rocco relieved. When Pizarro departs, Florestan and Leonore rush into each other's arms ("O namenlose Freude!"), after which Leonore leads her husband out of the dungeon.

Scene 2. The courtyard. (It has been customary since Mahler's time to perform the *Leonore Overture No. 3* during this change of scene. This overture contains material from the opera: a theme of Florestan's aria "In des Lebens Frühlingstagen," given by clarinet and bassoon; and the trumpet fanfare announcing the arrival of the Prime Minister. The energetic coda expresses the joy of Leonore and Florestan at their reunion.)

By an edict of the Prime Minister, the prisoners are released. They emerge from their cells, headed by Leonore and Florestan. It is now that the Prime Minister first learns of Florestan's ordeal. The Minister orders Pizarro arrested, then gives Leonore the key to Florestan's chains and asks her to free her husband. Florestan sings a hymn of praise to his devoted wife, and the people join him in this tribute ("Wer ein holdes Weib errungen").

Beethoven's solitary venture in opera is a masterwork—a masterwork with flaws—which is not dwarfed by the stature of his symphonies, sonatas, and chamber music. It is true, as critics have noted, that Beethoven's writing in *Fidelio* is usually more instrumental than vocal, that he was never at his best in vocal music, and that the limitations of the stage constricted his thinking. But after these qualifications are made, *Fidelio* remains a work of outstanding inspiration. It is the only German opera between those of MOZART and WAGNER to survive in the permanent repertory. It has a high-minded nobility, an all-encompassing humanity, and a profundity of feeling found in few other operas. To Beethoven, the story of Leonore and Florestan represented the eternal struggle of man for freedom. Leonore was the symbol of the liberator. This subject inspired the democratic Beethoven. In music as well as text, *Fidelio* is a proclamation of liberty, tolerance, and human dignity. There is probably nothing in German opera more filled with this feeling than

Leonore's celebrated "Abscheulicher!"—Beethoven's outraged defiance of all tyrants; nor can we find many pages more moving than the Prisoners' Chorus, one of the most eloquent musical paeans to freedom ever written. The early performance history of *Fidelio* was stormy. When the opera was introduced, Vienna was experiencing economic depression and political confusion, the aftermath of the French invasion. A new opera was of little interest—even one by Beethoven—and *Fidelio* was a failure. Beethoven revised his opera in 1806, compressing three acts into two, simplifying his writing for the voices, and preparing a new overture. The new version was given in 1806 and was a huge success. (This rarely given 1805 version of *Fidelio* was revived in 1967 in a concert performance by the Boston Symphony under Erich LEINSDORF at the BERKSHIRE MUSIC FESTIVAL.) The opera would now have enjoyed a long and successful run if Beethoven, as the result of a quarrel over money, had not withdrawn it. Not until 1814 was *Fidelio* given again, once more with outstanding success.

Beethoven wrote four different overtures to *Fidelio*. The most famous is the *Leonore No. 3,* one of Beethoven's mightiest orchestral epics, written for the 1806 revival. The *Leonore No. 2* was used at the premiere performance and subsequently discarded. This overture, simplified and concentrated, became the *Leonore No. 1,* intended for a Prague performance that never materialized. The *Fidelio Overture,* which now opens the opera, was written for the 1814 revival.

Ferdinando PAER's opera *Leonora* (1804) is based on the same story as *Fidelio*. *Fidelio* plays an important part both in the text and the music of LIEBERMANN's opera LEONORE 40/45.

Fidès, mother (mezzo-soprano) of John of Leyden in MEYERBEER'S LE PROPHÈTE, a role created by Pauline VIARDOT-GARCÍA.

Fiermosca, sculptor (baritone) in BERLIOZ' BENVENUTO CELLINI.

Fiery Angel, The, see FLAMING ANGEL, THE.

Fiesco, Jacopo, a Genoese nobleman (bass) in VERDI'S SIMON BOCCANEGRA.

Figaro, (1) A former barber, now Count Almaviva's valet (baritone), in MOZART'S THE MARRIAGE OF FIGARO.

(2) A barber (baritone) in ROSSINI'S THE BARBER OF SEVILLE.

Figlia, che reggi il tremulo piè, trio of La Cieca, La Gioconda, and Barnaba in Act I of PONCHIELLI'S LA GIOCONDA. With Barnaba at hand devising his own plans, La Cieca expresses gratitude for her daughter's love, which Gioconda tenderly echoes.

figlia del reggimento, La, see DAUGHTER OF THE REGIMENT, THE.

Filial Bolshoi, see BOLSHOI OPERA.

Filipievna, a nurse (mezzo-soprano) in TCHAIKOVSKY'S EUGENE ONEGIN.

Fille de Madame Angot, La (The Daughter of Madame Angot), OPÉRA BOUFFE in three acts by Lecocq. Libretto by Paul Siraudin, Clairville, and Victor Koning, based on a French vaudeville by A. F. E. Maillot. Premiere: Théâtre Alcazar, Brussels, Dec. 4, 1872. American premiere: New York City, Aug. 25, 1873. This is one of the most celebrated works in the repertory of French *opéra bouffe*. The setting is Paris during the Revolution. The "daughter of Madame Angot" is Clairette, who is in love with the poet Pitou, even though her mother wants her to marry Pomponnet, a hairdresser. To avoid marrying Pomponnet, Clairette gets herself arrested by singing a satirical song about an actress then in favor with the head of the Directory ("Jadis, les rois, race proscrite"). The actress, Mlle. Lange, turns out to be one of Clairette's former schoolmates. Mlle. Lange arranges her release from prison only to discover that in Clairette she has a rival for a man she herself loves, Pitou. In the end Clairette decides to marry Pomponnet and leave Pitou to Mlle. Lange. One of the most beautiful airs in this *opéra bouffe* is Pomponnet's romance ("Elle est tellement innocente") in Act II. The duet of Mlle. Lange and Clairette recalling their past ("Jours fortunes de notre enfance"), a third-act gavotte, and the ballet music are also very good.

Fille des rois, à toi l'hommage (Figlia di re a te l'omaggio), Nelusko's aria in Act II of MEYERBEER'S L'AFRICAINE.

Fille du regiment, La, see DAUGHTER OF THE REGIMENT, THE.

filosofo di campagna, Il (The Country Doctor), an OPERA BUFFA in one act by GALUPPI. Libretto by Carlo GOLDONI. Premiere: Venice, Oct. 26, 1754. American premiere: CBS-TV, Feb. 7, 1960 (half-hour version); Boston, Feb. 26, 1960 (complete staged version). Its composer's masterwork, this little opera is a classic of early Italian *opera buffa*. Don Tritemo is a foolish old man who devises various schemes to keep his daughter Eugenia from marrying Rinaldo. He fails. A secondary plot involves Eugenia's friend Lesbina and a young man named Nardo. Of musical importance are two lovely airs sung by Lesbina, "Quando son gievine" and "Son fresca, son bella"; an aria by Rinaldo, "Anima vile"; and another by Nardo, "Vedo quell'albero." When presented today, this *opera buffa* is usually given in an adaptation by either WOLF-FERRARI OR MALIPIERO.

finale, the concluding number of an opera or of an act of an opera. It is usually a large-scale affair, and it may contain a series of formal arias and ensemble numbers.

Finch'han dal vino, Don Giovanni's light-hearted command to Leporello to gather the girls of the village and spread the table with food, wine, and candles, in Act I, Scene 3, of MOZART'S DON GIOVANNI.

Finita è per frati, see POUR LES COUVENTS C'EST FINI.

Finn, a sorcerer (tenor) in GLINKA'S RUSSLAN AND LUDMILLA.

finta giardiniera, La (The Pretending Gardener), OPERA BUFFA in three acts by MOZART. Libretto by CALZABIGI, altered by Marco Coltellini. Premiere: Munich, Jan. 13, 1775. American premiere: New

York City, Jan. 18, 1927. This gay little opera was a work of Mozart's early manhood, having been written in 1775, when he was nineteen. When Marchesa Violante (soprano) has been slighted by Count Belfiore (tenor), she and her valet disguise themselves as gardeners and gain employment at the palace of the Podesta, ruler of Lagonero. There the Podesta becomes interested in Violante, and the Podesta's maid in the valet. In the end Violante and the Count and the valet and the maid pair off, with only the Podesta left without a mate. Despite the trivial plot, Mozart produced music which W. J. Turner described as "entrancing . . . without reserve," with "inimitable charm and gaiety, tenderness and fertility of invention." Particularly significant are two arias sung by Violante, "Noi donne poverine" and "Geme la tortella," and a duet of Violante and Count Belfiore, "Dove mai son."

finta semplice, La (The Pretending Simpleton), OPERA BUFFA in three acts by MOZART. Libretto by Marco Coltellini, based on a libretto by Carlo GOLDONI. Premiere: Salzburg, May 1, 1769. American premiere: Boston, Jan. 27, 1961, under the title *The Clever Flirt.* This was Mozart's first opera, written when he was only twelve. Since the story involves a philanderer, a woman-hater, and various love intrigues, it is truly a remarkable text for a child to become interested in. The main plot concerns Cassandro (bass) and Polidoro (tenor), two bachelors who try to keep their sister Rosina (soprano) from marrying an officer. Through the machinations of the officer's sister, the bachelors are outwitted. Cassandro's aria, "Ella vuole ed io torrei," and Rosina's aria, "Amoretti," are particularly appealing.

Fiora, Manfredo's wife (soprano) in MONTEMEZZI'S L'AMORE DEI TRE RE.

Fior di giaggiolo, Lola's song in MASCAGNI'S CAVALLERIA RUSTICANA.

Fiordiligi, a lady (soprano) in love with Guglielmo in MOZART'S COSÌ FAN TUTTE.

Fiorilla, the wife (mezzo-soprano) of a Neapolitan nobleman in ROSSINI'S IL TURCO IN ITALIA.

fioritura, Italian for "flourish"—decorative tones, either written by the composer or improvised by the singer, ornamenting the basic notes of the melodic line. The use of *fioritura* was especially common in Italian operas of the eighteenth century.

Firenze è como un albero fiorito, Rinuccio's praise of the origins of the city of Florence in its lovely countryside, in PUCCINI'S GIANNI SCHICCHI.

Fischer-Dieskau, Dietrich, baritone. Born Berlin, May 28, 1925. He is one of the most versatile and most distinguished lieder and opera singers of the twentieth century. He attended the Berlin Hochschule für Musik. His vocal teachers included Georg Walter and Hermann Weissenborn. During World War II he was a prisoner of war in Italy. He made his opera debut in 1948 at the Berlin STÄDTISCHE OPER. From then on he remained there as its leading baritone. He has appeared in the world's leading opera houses and festivals, including BAYREUTH and SALZBURG. He has been acclaimed for his versatility as well as for his artistry, appearing in such diversified parts as MATHIS DER MALER, MACBETH, MANDRYKA, John the Baptist (in SALOME), ALMAVIVA, and in such varied operas as EUGENE ONEGIN, WOZZECK, ELEGY FOR YOUNG LOVERS, CARDILLAC, DOKTOR FAUST, as well as the Wagnerian repertory. In 1968 he appeared at Salzburg in the KARAJAN production of DAS RHEINGOLD (the first time he ever sang Wotan in this music drama). His American debut took place in Cincinnati on Apr. 5, 1955, in a concert featuring a Bach cantata and Brahms's *A German Requiem,* following which he toured the country frequently in recitals and as soloist with orchestras.

Fischer, Emil, bass-baritone. Born Brunswick, Ger., June 13, 1838; died Hamburg, Aug. 11, 1914. Both of his parents were opera singers. They gave their son his vocal instruction prior to his opera debut at Graz in 1857 in BOIELDIEU'S

Jean de Paris. For the next quarter of a century he appeared with major German opera companies, including the DRESDEN OPERA. He broke his contract with the Dresden Opera Company to make his American debut at the METROPOLITAN OPERA on Nov. 23, 1885, in LOHENGRIN. He remained with the Metropolitan Opera for six years, distinguishing himself particularly in the Wagnerian repertory. Though he made a number of appearances with the DAMROSCH OPERA COMPANY in 1895 and 1897, he devoted himself mainly to teaching after 1891. He was given a testimonial performance at the Metropolitan Opera in 1907, in which he was heard in an excerpt from DIE MEISTERSINGER, which yielded him ten thousand dollars.

Fischer, Ludwig, bass. Born Mainz, Ger., Aug. 18, 1745; died Berlin, July 10, 1825. He was one of the most distinguished bassos in Germany of his time, with successful appearances in Mainz, Mannheim, Vienna, Munich, Paris, and London. MOZART wrote for him the role of Osmin in THE ABDUCTION FROM THE SERAGLIO.

Five, The, a group of nineteenth-century Russian composers whose ideal was music grounded in national backgrounds. The group was a leading force in establishing Russian folk opera. The members were César CUI, Alexander BORODIN, Mili Balakirev, Modest MUSSORGSKY, and Nikolai RIMSKY-KORSAKOV.

Flagstad, Kirsten, soprano. Born Oslo, Norway, July 12, 1895; died there Dec. 7, 1962. One of the most distinguished Wagnerian sopranos of the twentieth century, she studied singing with her mother (a coach at the Oslo Opera) and Ellen Schytte-Jacobsen, after which she made her opera debut in Oslo on Dec. 12, 1913, in a minor role in TIEFLAND. She then had additional training with Albert Westwang and Gillis Brant and appeared for several years in operettas and musical comedies as well as opera. After she joined the Gothenburg State Opera in 1927 she concentrated on opera. Two years later she married a wealthy Oslo industrialist, Henry Johansen, following which she went into temporary retirement. But she was soon convinced to return to the opera stage. Until 1933 her opera appearances were confined exclusively to Scandinavia, but in the summer of 1933 she appeared at the BAYREUTH Festival in minor roles. The following summer she was cast as SIEGLINDE. A scout from the METROPOLITAN OPERA heard her and arranged for an audition. This proved successful, and on Feb. 2, 1935, Flagstad made her American debut as Sieglinde. Virtually unknown before she stepped on the stage that day, she created a sensation. The critics were as enthusiastic as the audience. Lawrence Gilman wrote in the *Herald Tribune:* "Yesterday was one of those comparatively rare occasions when the exigent Richard might have witnessed with happiness an embodiment of his Sieglinde. For this was a beautiful and illusive re-creation, poignant and sensitive throughout, and crowned in its greater moments with an authentic exaltation." Three days later Flagstad scored another triumph in her first American appearance as ISOLDE. During the same season she was also heard as Brünnhilde in both DIE WALKÜRE and GÖTTERDÄMMERUNG, and as KUNDRY. As a gesture of honor to its new star the Metropolitan Opera began its 1936–37 season with a German opera (*Die Walküre*) for the first time in thirty-five years. The beauty of Flagstad's voice was matched by the dignity and magnetism of her characterizations. Her voice was extraordinary in power, flexibility, and expressiveness. These qualities were combined with a profound musical understanding and a penetrating insight into the characters she was portraying.

Flagstad's American triumphs were duplicated in Europe, first at COVENT GARDEN and the VIENNA STATE OPERA in 1936, afterward in Zürich, Paris, and Prague. During World War II, she decided to leave the United States and return to her native land. The fact that

Norway was at the time occupied by the Nazis, and that her husband was a Quisling, discredited Flagstad in the eyes of the freedom-loving world. Flagstad insisted after the war that her political conscience was clear: she had never been friendly or cooperative with the Nazis, and her return home was motivated exclusively by the wish of a mother and wife to be with her family in perilous times. The antagonism to Flagstad, however, persisted in America for a long time, and there was opposition to her return appearances in concerts. Eventually, the opposition died down. In 1949 she sang successfully with the SAN FRANCISCO OPERA. A year later she was back with the Metropolitan Opera. She appeared at the Metropolitan Opera for the last time in 1952, singing in ALCESTE. The previous season Flagstad had sung the role of Dido in a London revival of DIDO AND AENEAS. The performance was extraordinarily successful, and during the coronation season of 1953 she sang the role another twenty-seven times, later appearing in the same opera in Norway. She returned to New York in March, 1955, to make two appearances with the Symphony of the Air (formerly the NBC Symphony Orchestra) in all-Wagner programs. During 1959–60 she was director of the Norwegian Opera in Oslo.

Flamand, a musician (tenor) in love with the Countess, symbolic of the role of music in opera, in Richard STRAUSS'S CAPRICCIO.

Flaming Angel, The (or **Angel of Fire**), opera in five acts by PROKOFIEV. Libretto by the composer, based on Valery Briusov's novel. Premiere: Paris Radio, Jan. 15, 1954; Teatro la Fenice, Sept. 29, 1955 (staged). American premiere: New York City Opera, Sept. 22, 1965. In a sixteenth-century highway inn, Renata, a mystic (soprano), is having one of her hallucinations: the Devil is attacking her. The man in the next room, Sir Ruprecht (bass), breaks in, calms her down, and hears her story. Ever since she was a child she had had visions of a flaming angel, whom she loved. At

seventeen, she became convinced that Count Heinrich was the flaming angel's incarnation, lived with him for a year, and then was deserted. Since then she has been wandering aimlessly, having fearful visions. Ruprecht, half falling in love with her, takes her with him to Cologne in search of the Count. When Heinrich is found, he rejects Renata once more, and she insists that Ruprecht challenge him to a duel—only, he must not hurt her angel. After the duel, the Count disappears again and Ruprecht, badly wounded, is nursed back to health by Renata. She has learned to return his love but feels she must be faithful to her flaming angel, and this she does by entering a convent. Ruprecht goes off in the company of Faust and Mephistopheles (who happen to be in Cologne); but Renata so upsets the convent with her hallucinations and apparent dealings with supernatural beings that she is tried by the Inquisitor on the charge of having sexual intercourse with the Devil. She is sentenced, as a witch, to torture and to be burned at the stake.

The Flaming Angel was given in an abridged version at the FESTIVAL OF TWO WORLDS at Spoleto in 1959. A more complete version was seen at the TEATRO DELL' OPERA in Rome in 1965, the NEW YORK CITY OPERA and the CHICAGO LYRIC OPERA in 1966, and the FRANKFURT OPERA in 1969.

Flaminio, King Archibaldo's servant (tenor) in MONTEMEZZI'S L'AMORE DEI TRE RE.

Flammen, French painter (tenor) in love with Lodoletta in MASCAGNI'S LODOLETTA.

Flammen, perdonami, Lodoletta's aria in Act III of MASCAGNI'S LODOLETTA.

Flaubert, Gustave, novelist. Born Rouen, France, Dec. 12, 1821; died Croisset, France, May 8, 1880. Flaubert's novels and stories have been used in operas, the most famous being MASSENET'S HÉRODIADE. *La Légende de Saint Julien l'Hospitalier* is the source of operas of the same name by ERLANGER and ZANDONAI; *Salammbô*, of operas by Eugenius Morawski, REYER, Carl Navratil, Joseph

Hauer, and Franco Casalova; Guido Pannain, Emmanuel Bondeville, and SUTERMEISTER drew on *Madame Bovary* for operas of the same name. *La Tentation de Saint Antoine* is the title of an opera by Cecil Gray.

Flea duet, *see* IL ME SEMBLE SUR MON ÉPAULE.

Fledermaus, Die (The Bat), operetta by Johann STRAUSS THE YOUNGER. Libretto by Haffner and Genée, based on a German comedy by Roderich Bendix, *Das Gefängnis.* Premiere: Theater-an-der-Wien, Vienna, Apr. 5, 1874; American premiere: New York City, Nov. 21, 1874. One of the most popular operettas of all time, *Die Fledermaus* has often been performed in the great opera houses of the world.

The Baron von Eisenstein, a banker (tenor), is supposed to go to jail for eight days for a minor offense but decides instead to attend a ball at Prince Orlofsky's and give himself up in the morning. When, a little later, the governor of the jail comes to take in the Baron, he finds Rosalinde, the Baroness (soprano), entertaining Alfred (tenor), a former suitor. Rosalinde, in order to avoid difficulties, persuades Alfred to say he is the Baron and go off to jail for a night. Then Rosalinde, masked and disguised as a Hungarian countess, goes off to the ball herself, and so does her maid, Adele (soprano), disguised as an actress. At the ball, all sorts of complications evolve, including the Baron's making ardent advances to the unrecognized "Hungarian countess," while Adele attracts the admiration of the Prince (mezzo-soprano), who thinks her talents as an actress are admirable. Next morning, at the jail, everyone arrives, and all confusions are eventually cleared up. The Baron and Rosalinde are reconciled; Alfred is freed from jail; and the Prince takes Adele under his protection. Everyone joins in a chorus in praise of champagne—but Eisenstein must still serve his eight days.

The overture, Drinking Song ("Trinke, Liebchen, trinke schnell"), Laughing Song ("Mein Herr Marquis"), Csárdás

("Klänge der Heimat"), the Hymn to Champagne ("Im Feuerström der Reben"), the Chorus of Guests at Orlofsky's ball ("Brüderlein, Brüderlein und Schwesterlein") are among the operetta's most popular numbers.

Fleurissait une sauge (Légende de la sauge), Boniface's description of the sage flower that sheltered the child Jesus, in Act II of MASSENET'S LE JONGLEUR DE NOTRE DAME.

fliegende Holländer, Der (The Flying Dutchman), opera in three acts by WAGNER. Libretto by the composer, based on an old legend adapted by HEINE. Premiere: Dresden Opera, Jan. 2, 1843. American premiere: Philadelphia Academy of Music, Nov. 8, 1876.

Characters: Daland, a Norwegian sea captain (bass); the Dutchman (baritone); Erik, a huntsman (tenor); Senta, Daland's daughter (soprano); Mary, her nurse (contralto); Steersman (tenor); sailors; maidens; villagers; hunters. The setting is a Norwegian village in the eighteenth century.

The overture, a popular concert number, opens with the motive of the Flying Dutchman in horns and bassoons and includes references to Senta and the Sailors' Chorus.

Act I. In return for his challenge of heaven and hell, the Dutchman is doomed to sail forever on his ship, "The Flying Dutchman," until redeemed through the love of a woman faithful unto death. Once every seven years he is permitted to go ashore to find that love. During one of these periods, he is driven by a storm to a Norwegian harbor. He moors his ship near that of Daland. After the Steersman amuses himself by singing a ballad ("Mit Gewitter und Sturm"), the Dutchman wearily describes how he seeks escape from his doom, driven as he is from shore to shore. Now that seven years have passed, he explains, he can go ashore ("Die Frist ist um," followed by the aria, "Wie oft in Meeres tiefsten Schlund"). Daland is impressed by the Dutchman's wealth, for the latter exhibits a jewel-filled casket. The Dutchman first asks

Daland to give him shelter in his house, then inquires if he has a daughter and whether he would consent to their marriage. Daland has a daughter and, thinking only of the Dutchman's wealth, he gives his consent. When the weather clears, Daland and the Dutchman set sail.

Act II. A room in Daland's house. Senta and her friends are busy spinning (Spinning Chorus: "Summ' und brumm'"). Senta grows impatient with the singing, and when her friends ask her for a better song she sings a ballad about the Flying Dutchman (Senta's Ballad: "Traft ihr das Schiff"). Her lover, Erik, arrives. He begs her to forget the Dutchman and to accept his love. He describes a dream about a mysterious vessel come to shore with a stranger, and Senta's father later walking arm in arm with him ("Auf hohen Felsen lag' ich träumend"). But Senta only points to the picture of the Dutchman hanging on the wall. And now the Dutchman and Daland arrive. Astonished and confused, Senta learns from her father that the Dutchman has asked for her hand in marriage ("Mögst du, mein Kind"). The Dutchman confesses to Senta that she is the woman of his dreams and she is overjoyed ("Wie aus der Ferne").

Act III. The bay near Daland's home. Daland's sailors strike up a chantey (Sailors' Chorus: "Steuermann! Lass die Wacht!"). Erik pursues Senta to beg for her love. He rebukes her for her faithlessness ("Willst jenes Tag's du nicht dich mehr entsinnen"). The Dutchman overhears him. Reasoning that if Senta can be unfaithful to Erik she can also be unfaithful to him, he suspects that his hopes for redemption are again to be shattered. He returns to his ship and, though a storm is raging, sets sail. Senta climbs to the top of a cliff, shouting to the Dutchman that she has always been faithful to him and will continue to be so until death ("Hier steh' ich, treu dir bis zum Tod"). She flings herself into the waters, and "The Flying Dutchman" immediately vanishes beneath the waves.

The Dutchman has, after all, been redeemed. The forms of Senta and the Dutchman are seen embracing as they rise heavenward.

Der fliegende Holländer is one of Wagner's early operas, coming a year after RIENZI and preceding TANNHÄUSER by four. The concept of the music drama had not yet been crystallized by the composer. *Rienzi* had been a work in the style of MEYERBEER. *Der fliegende Holländer* placed little emphasis on ornate scenes or spectacles, but concerned itself with subtle psychological insights into its two principal characters and the drama of their inner conflicts. The music pointed to Wagner's later development, since it was here that he made use for the first time of the *leitmotiv* technique, even though sparingly. The idea for the opera came to Wagner in 1839 when he crossed the North Sea during a storm in which his ship was almost wrecked. Recalling the legend of "The Flying Dutchman" (he had probably read it in Heine's *Memoirs of Herr von Schnabelewopski*), he now identified himself with the character of the Dutchman. He felt that he, too, was fated to wander in misery until he could find redemption through the love of a woman and through the peace and security of a permanent home in his own land. Wagner began writing his opera in Paris. Unable to interest the directors of the PARIS OPÉRA in his music, he sold his libretto to them. They turned it over to Pierre-Louis DIETSCH, who used it for his opera LE VAISSEAU FANTÔME. Produced in 1842, this work was a failure. Meantime, notwithstanding his sale of the text, Wagner continued writing his own opera. The tremendous success enjoyed by *Rienzi* at the DRESDEN OPERA encouraged the director of that company to produce Wagner's new opera. *Der fliegende Holländer* failed to repeat the triumph of *Rienzi*. The opera was too somber, too new in style, too subtle in its portrayal of character and atmosphere to be understood and appreciated at first hearing. However, it was soon appreciated in other German cities and then, like the Dutchman himself, made its way around the world.

Flight of the Bumblebee, a realistic orchestral interlude of a buzzing bee's flight, in Act III of RIMSKY-KORSAKOV'S THE LEGEND OF CZAR SALTAN. It has become familiar in various transcriptions.

Flora, a medium (contralto) in MENOTTI'S THE MEDIUM.

Florence May Music Festival (Maggio Musicale Fiorentino), a music festival held every May in Florence, Italy. Opera is featured prominently, with emphasis on the works of Italians. Performances take place either in the TEATRO COMMUNALE (rebuilt in 1965), the Teatro Pergola, or open-air in the Boboli Gardens. With the exception of the period between 1943 and 1947, the festival has functioned without interruption since it opened with a revival of NABUCCO on Apr. 22, 1933. There have since been numerous premieres as well as revivals of long forgotten operas.

The premieres have included: ANTONIO E CLEOPATRA; AUCASSIN ET NICOLETTE (CASTELNUOVO-TEDESCO); *Il contrabasso* (1954, Valentino Bucchi); *Il diavolo sul campanile* (1935, Adriano LUALDI, new version); *Don Chisciotte* (1951, Vito Frazzi); *Il figliuol prodigo* (MALIPIERO); IL PRIGIONIERO; *The Merchant of Venice* (Castelnuovo-Tedesco); *Rè Lear* (1939, Vito Frazzi); *Vanna Luppa* (PIZZETTI); *Venere prigioniera* (Malipiero).

Unusual revivals have included: LES ABENCÉRAGES; *Agnes von Hohenstein* (SPONTINI); L'AMFIPARNASO; *Antigone* (Traetta); ARMIDA; L'ASSASSINIO NELLA CATTEDRALE; *Le astuzie feminili* (CIMAROSA); *La battaglia di Legnano* (VERDI); *Didone* (CAVALLI); DOKTOR FAUST; *Don Sebastiano* (DONIZETTI); EURIDICE (PERI); GENOVEVA; L'INCORONAZIONE DI POPPEA; JENUFA; *Maria Stuarda* (Donizetti); *La Molinara* (PAISIELLO); *Olympie* (Spontini); L'ORFEO; ORFEO ED EURIDICE (HAYDN); LA PIETRA DEL PARAGONE; LE SIÈGE DE CORINTHE; TANCREDI.

The festival also presented the European premiere of AMAHL AND THE NIGHT VISITORS, the first performances outside the Soviet Union of WAR AND PEACE, and a production of MOSES UND ARON. Leonard BERNSTEIN's *West Side Story* has also been presented.

Florestan, Leonore's husband (tenor) in BEETHOVEN'S FIDELIO.

Floriana, a music-hall singer (contralto) in LEONCAVALLO'S ZAZA.

Floria Tosca, a celebrated prima donna (soprano) in PUCCINI'S TOSCA.

Florindo, young man (tenor) in love with Rosaura in WOLF-FERRARI'S LE DONNE CURIOSE.

Florville, Sofia's beloved (bass) in ROSSINI'S IL SIGNOR BRUSCHINO.

Flosshilde, a Rhine maiden (contralto) in WAGNER'S DAS RHEINGOLD and GÖTTERDÄMMERUNG.

Flotow, Friedrich, Freiherr von, composer. Born Teutendorf, Mecklenburg, Apr. 26, 1812; died Darmstadt, Jan. 24, 1883. His father was a landed nobleman. He studied in Paris with Anton Reicha and Johann Pixis. The 1830 revolution sent him back to Germany, where he completed his first opera, *Peter und Katharina.* Returning to Paris in 1831, Flotow moved with the most distinguished opera composers of the day. For a while he concentrated on writing operettas, but in 1838 a collaboration with a French musician, Albert Grisar, turned him to writing more ambitious works. Flotow became famous as an opera composer with ALESSANDRO STRADELLA, introduced in Hamburg on Dec. 30, 1844. Three years later the Vienna Royal Opera introduced the work by which he is best remembered, MARTHA. Between 1856 and 1863 Flotow served as intendant of the Schwerin Court Theater. The next decade of his life was spent in Paris, Vienna, and Italy. In his last years he settled in Darmstadt. His most successful operas, in addition to those mentioned, were *Rübezahl* (1853); *La Veuve Grapin* (1856); *Zilda* (1866); *L'Ombre* (1870).

Flower Duet, *see* SCUOTI QUELLA FRONDA DI CILIEGIO.

Flower Maidens' Scene, the second scene in Act II of WAGNER'S PARSIFAL, in which the flower maidens in Klingsor's Magic Garden try to entice Parsifal.

Flower Song, *see* FAITES-LUI MES AVEUX.

Floyd, Carlisle, composer. Born Latta, S.C., June 11, 1926. He studied piano with private teachers, then received a piano scholarship at Converse College. Later he studied with Ernst BACON at Syracuse University and with Rudolf Firkušny. In 1947 he was appointed to the music faculty of Florida State University in Tallahassee. He wrote two operas, *Slow Dusk* (1949) and *Fugitives* (1951), before achieving success with SUSANNAH, introduced in Tallahassee, Florida, on Feb. 24, 1955. In 1956 *Susannah* was produced by the NEW YORK CITY OPERA and received the New York Music Critics' Circle Award; in 1958 it was given at the Brussels Exposition in Belgium. WUTHERING HEIGHTS, an opera based on the novel of Emily Brontë, was seen in Santa Fe, N.M., in 1958 and was produced a year later by the New York City Opera. THE PASSION OF JONATHAN WADE, written under the auspices of the Ford Foundation, received its world premiere at the New York City Opera on Oct. 11, 1962. This was followed by *The Sojourner and Mollie Sinclair,* written on commission to commemorate the tercentennial of North Carolina (produced in Raleigh, N.C., on Dec. 2, 1963); MARKHEIM, based on Robert Louis Stevenson's story, heard first in New Orleans on Mar. 31, 1966; and OF MICE AND MEN, based on John Steinbeck's famous novel, whose world premiere was given by the SEATTLE OPERA on Jan. 22, 1970.

Flut, Die (The Tide), chamber opera in one act by BLACHER. Libretto by Heinz von Cramer. Premiere: Berlin Radio, Dec. 20, 1946; Dresden Opera, Mar. 4, 1947 (staged). American premiere: Boston, Mass., Apr. 19, 1956. The setting is a wreck of a ship stranded on a sandbank; the time, "yesterday or today." A banker, his mistress, and a young man are among the travelers brought to the sandbank to see the stranded ship. A sudden rise of the tide leaves them stranded there. The girl flirts with a fisherman. The young man is offered a large sum of money by the banker to swim ashore and get help, but turns it down. When the tide recedes all are saved. The young man is now interested in the banker's money and gets it by killing him. Because of his suddenly acquired wealth, the young man entices the girl away from the fisherman.

Gerhart von Westerman explains that the opera's structure is "broken by choral passages which describe the action and were originally intended for the benefit of a radio audience." However, these choral passages fit easily into a stage presentation. "There is a duality of rhythm and meter in Blacher's music," continues Westerman, "which gives it particular charm without ever clouding the clear simplicity of structure."

Fluth, name for Ford in German-language version of NICOLAI'S THE MERRY WIVES OF WINDSOR.

Flying Dutchman, The, *see* FLIEGENDE HOLLÄNDER, DER.

Fontana, Signor, the name assumed by Ford to conceal his identity in VERDI'S FALSTAFF.

Ford, a wealthy burgher in NICOLAI'S THE MERRY WIVES OF WINDSOR and VERDI'S FALSTAFF. In both operas the role is for a baritone.

Ford, Alice, Ford's wife (soprano) in VERDI'S FALSTAFF.

Ford Foundation Grants for Opera. The Ford Foundation has supported an ambitious program to aid American operas by providing American composers with grants for the creation of new operas and funding four American opera houses (the METROPOLITAN OPERA, the NEW YORK CITY OPERA, the CHICAGO LYRIC OPERA, and the SAN FRANCISCO OPERA) to produce them. These are some of the operas subsidized under this program: ANTONY AND CLEOPATRA; LIZZIE BORDEN; BLITZSTEIN'S *Sacco and Vanzetti* (left unfinished by the composer's death); Abraham Ellstein's *The Golem;* William Flanagan's *The Ice Age;* THE PAS-

SION OF JONATHAN WADE and OF MICE AND MEN; THE HARVEST and THE SERVANT OF TWO MASTERS; GLANVILLE HICKS' *Sappho;* Lee Hoiby's *Natalia Petrovna;* Ezra Laderman's *The Golden Door;* Benjamin Lees's *The Gilded Cage;* MOURNING BECOMES ELECTRA; WINGS OF THE DOVE; ROREM's *Mamba's Daughters* and MISS JULIE; THOMSON's *Lord Byron;* THE CRUCIBLE; and WEISGALLS's *Nine Rivers from Jordan.*

The foundation has also made grants to over fifteen civic opera companies in the United States to lengthen their seasons and stabilize their resources. These grants are made not for the commissioning of new operas but for certain productions already in the repertories of the opera companies.

Ford, Nannetta (or Anne), Ford's daughter (soprano) in VERDI'S FALSTAFF.

Forest Murmurs, *see* WALDWEBEN.

Forge Song, *see* NOTHUNG! NOTHUNG!

Forma ideal, Faust's song of love to the goddess Helen in the last act of BOITO's MEFISTOFELE.

Forsell, John, baritone and opera manager. Born Stockholm, Nov. 6, 1868; died there Nov. 30, 1941. He completed his music study at the conservatories of Stockholm and Paris. In 1896 he made his opera debut at the STOCKHOLM ROYAL OPERA, remaining a permanent member of that company from 1896 to 1901 and again from 1903 to 1909. On Nov. 20, 1909, he made his American debut at the METROPOLITAN OPERA as TELRAMUND, but he stayed with the Metropolitan only one season. He subsequently appeared in leading European opera houses, acclaimed in the German repertory. One of his outstanding interpretations was that of DON GIOVANNI. In 1923 he became intendant of the Stockholm Royal Opera, holding this post until 1938. The list of his many pupils included Metropolitan Opera tenors Jussi BJOERLING and Set SVANHOLM. On his seventieth birthday his extensive career was reviewed in the book *Boken om John Forsell* (1938).

Fortner, Wolfgang, composer. Born Leipzig, Ger., Oct. 12, 1907. After attending the Leipzig Conservatory, he joined the faculty of the Evangelical Church Music Institute in Heidelberg in 1931, where he wrote a school opera. His first professional opera was *Die Witwe von Ephesus,* in one act and for small orchestra, introduced in Berlin on Sept. 17, 1952. In 1954 he was appointed professor of composition at Northwestern Music Academy in Detmold, and in 1957 he became Dozent at the Musikhochschule in Freiburg-im-Breisgau. His numerous compositions in all forms include several more operas: *Der Wald* (1953); DIE BLUTHOCHZEIT (1957); and *In seinem Garten* (1962). *Der Wald* and *In seinem Garten* were revised and combined into a single opera now called *In seinem Garten liebt Don Perlimplin Belisa,* introduced in Schwetzingen, Ger., on May 10, 1962.

Fort Worth Opera Association, one of four opera companies in Texas and the oldest in terms of continuous performances through the years. It was founded in May, 1946, and its first production was LA TRAVIATA on Nov. 25 of that year. In its quarter of a century or so of existence, it has drawn its productions from the standard repertory, many of them sung in English, and the principal roles have usually been assumed by distinguished opera stars. In Oct., 1963, it received a FORD FOUNDATION grant of one hundred thousand dollars for the purpose of increasing its annual budget and to produce at least four operas a season instead of the three produced up to the time prior to the grant; this amount was paid over a period of five years, twenty thousand dollars each year.

Forty Days of Musa Dagh, *see* WERFEL, FRANZ.

forza del destino, La (The Force of Destiny), opera in four acts by VERDI. Libretto by Francesco PIAVE, based on the play *Don Alvaro, o la fuerza de sino* by Angel de Saavedra. Piave's libretto was later revised by Antonio GHISLANZONI. Premiere: St. Petersburg, Nov. 10, 1862. American premiere: Academy of Music, Feb. 24, 1865.

Characters: The Marquis of Calatrava (bass); Leonora, his daughter (soprano); Curra, her maid (mezzo-soprano); Don Carlo, the Marquis' son (baritone); Don Alvaro, a nobleman of Inca origin (tenor); Preziosilla, a gypsy (mezzo-soprano); Padre Guardiano, an abbot (bass); Fra Melitone, a friar (baritone); the Alcalde of Hornachuelos (bass); Mastro Trabuco, a muleteer (tenor); a surgeon; peasants; soldiers; friars. The action takes place in Spain and Italy; the time is the end of the eighteenth century.

The overture is famous. It begins with a passage for trumpet and a tender episode in the minor key. The heart of the overture is Leonora's second-act prayer, "Madre, pietosa Vergine," which is recalled by full orchestra at the conclusion of the overture.

Act I. The home of the Marquis of Calatrava, Seville. Leonora, in love with Don Alvaro, laments that her proud family will never accept him ("Me pellegrina ed orfana"). She plans to elope with him. When Leonora's father discovers the plot, Don Alvaro insists that the proposed elopement was his doing. He demands that the Marquis punish him, not Leonora. As a gesture of submission, Alvaro tosses his pistol aside. It explodes, wounding the Marquis. Cursing his daughter, he dies.

Act II, Scene 1. An inn at Hornachuelos. Leonora, having lost track of Don Alvaro after her father's death, comes seeking him, disguised as a man. In the crowd she discovers her brother, Don Carlo, who has sworn to kill her and Alvaro. She flees.

Scene 2. The monastery at Hornachuelos. Leonora falls on her knees at the monastery door and prays to the Virgin for help ("Madre, pietosa Vergine"). Padre Guardiano offers her a penitent's haven in a mountain cave. The abbot and monks then pray that a curse may befall whoever attempts to harm her. Leonora joins the monks in a prayer to the Virgin ("La Vergine degli angeli").

Act III, Scene 1. A battlefield in Italy.

Don Alvaro, under an assumed name, is with the Spanish army, fighting the Germans. Believing Leonora dead, he recalls her nostalgically ("O tu che in seno"). His thoughts are disturbed by the cries of a wounded man. He proves to be Don Carlo, but the two men do not recognize one another. After Alvaro saves Carlo's life, they swear eternal friendship. The sound of a bugle sends them off to battle.

Scene 2. Headquarters of the Spanish army. Don Alvaro has been seriously wounded in battle. He begs Don Carlo to destroy a certain packet of letters, declaring that he can then die in peace ("Solenne in quest' ora"). While looking for the letters, Carlo comes upon his sister's picture. It is only now that he realizes who his friend is, and he swears to destroy him ("Egli è salvo").

Scene 3. A military camp. Don Alvaro, recovered from his wounds, finds that his friend has now become his enemy. He tries to convince Don Carlo that he is innocent of wrong. Carlo, however, insists that the matter can be settled only in a duel. Forced to fight, Alvaro wounds Carlo seriously. Horrified —for once again he may be responsible for the death of someone dear to Leonora—Don Alvaro decides to seek peace and salvation in holy vows at a monastery.

Act IV, Scene 1. The monastery at Hornachuelos. Five years have passed. As Father Raphael, Don Alvaro has found peace. Carlo, recovered from his wound, has located Alvaro's retreat and comes seeking vengeance ("Invano, Alvaro"). Once again he demands that Alvaro fight until one of them is destroyed. Alvaro refuses and tries to convince Carlo that God alone can bring retribution. In the face of Carlo's bitter insults, however, Alvaro is aroused to a point where he can no longer be compassionate. Seizing a sword, he rushes out of the monastery to fight Carlo.

Scene 2. A wild place in the mountains. Leonora, in her hiding place, prays God to relieve her of her tortured dreams and memories ("Pace, pace, mio

Dio!"). She hears the clashing of swords. This time Don Alvaro wounds his opponent mortally. He summons the inhabitant of the mountain cave—and is overwhelmed to learn that the "hermit" is none other than Leonora. She rushes to her dying brother. He curses her and with his ebbing strength plunges a dagger into her. Leonora, dying, begs Alvaro to find salvation in religion. Alvaro rails against his destiny. Padre Guardiano commands him, rather, to ask forgiveness ("Non imprecare, umiliati").

La forza del destino belongs to the rich middle period of Verdi's creative life, a period that produced LA TRAVIATA, IL TROVATORE, and AIDA. It preceded *Aida*, the last opera of this period, by about a decade. With its pronounced dramatic content and enriched harmonic and orchestral writing, *La forza del destino* represents a gradual departure from the style of *La traviata* toward that of *Aida*. There are many beautiful arias and effective ensemble numbers in *La forza del destino*, but the central point of interest is not in isolated excerpts but in the dramatic feeling that pervades the entire work.

Foss, Lukas, composer. Born Berlin, Ger., Aug. 15, 1922. He came to the United States in 1937 and has since become an American citizen. For a number of years he served as official pianist of the Boston Symphony Orchestra. He achieved his first major success as a composer with a cantata, *The Prairie*, introduced in 1944. He subsequently received a Guggenheim Fellowship and the American Prix de Rome. His first opera, THE JUMPING FROG OF CALAVERAS COUNTY, was successfully introduced in Bloomington, Ind., in 1950 and was subsequently given at the VENICE MUSIC FESTIVAL in Italy. A second opera, GRIFFELKIN, was commissioned by the KOUSSEVITZKY MUSIC FOUNDATION and received its world premiere over the NBC network on Nov. 6, 1955. After that Foss wrote a nine-minute opera, INTRODUCTIONS AND GOODBYES, which received its world premiere in 1959 at the FESTIVAL OF TWO WORLDS in Spoleto. Between

1963 and 1969 Foss was music director of the Buffalo Philharmonic Orchestra in New York. He has become a leading figure in the avant-garde movement in music, both as a conductor and as a composer for the concert stage.

Fouché, a revolutionary patriot (baritone) in GIORDANO'S MADAME SANS-GÊNE.

Four Saints in Three Acts, "an opera to be sung," in four acts by THOMSON. Libretto by Gertrude STEIN. Premiere: Hartford, Conn., Feb. 8, 1934. Miss Stein's beguiling but enigmatic, and at times unintelligible, libretto consists of seemingly random statements and phrases. The action is supposed to take place in Spain at an unspecified time. Thomson's description of the text follows: "It shows Saint Theresa surrounded by women, and Saint Ignatius surrounded by men, all helping and working and studying to be saints. In the first act Saint Theresa is posed in a series of living pictures on the steps of the cathedral at Avila—a sort of Sunday school entertainment showing scenes from her saintly life. The second act is an outdoor party. The third act takes place in a monastery garden, with Saint Ignatius meeting the Holy Ghost ('Pigeons on the grass, alas!') and drilling his Jesuit disciples in military discipline. In an epilogue called Act Four, all the saints hold communion in heaven while the choir sings, 'When this you see remember me.' " For this alogical libretto Thomson wrote a sensitive and melodious score full of delightful American popular, folk, and church-hymn elements.

At the premiere, the opera was given by an all-Negro cast dressed in cellophane costumes. The opera then had a six-week run in New York. It was subsequently heard several times in concert version, was broadcast on a coast-to-coast radio network, was recorded, and in 1952 was given stage presentation in Paris with much of the original cast, the composer conducting. Other revivals include one by the Hollywood High School in Los Angeles in the summer of 1962, in Saratoga, California, in Aug.,

1970, and by the Opera Society of Washington in Washington, D.C., in Nov., 1970.

Four Sea Interludes, the orchestral intermezzi ("Dawn," "The Storm," "Sunday Morning," and "Moonlight") in BRITTEN'S PETER GRIMES.

Fra Diavolo, OPÉRA COMIQUE in three acts by AUBER. Libretto by SCRIBE. Premiere: Opéra-Comique, Jan. 28, 1830. American premiere: Philadelphia, Sept. 16, 1831. Fra Diavolo (tenor) is a notorious bandit who, masquerading as the Marquis of San Marco, compromises an innkeeper's daughter, Zerlina (soprano), in the course of a jewel robbery. Later, betrayed by his henchmen, Fra Diavolo is shot. Facing death, he gallantly absolves the girl of wrongdoing and reunites her with her worthy young lover, Lorenzo (tenor). The best-known arias are two sung by Zerlina: "Quel bonheur!" and "Voyez sur cette roche."

Fra Gherardo, opera in three acts by PIZZETTI. Libretto by the composer, based on the thirteenth-century *Chronicles* of Salimbene de Parma. Premiere: La Scala, May 16, 1928. American premiere: Metropolitan Opera, Mar. 21, 1929. The central character is a weaver who repents having a love affair with Mariola (soprano) and joins a flagellant order to become Fra Gherardo of the White Friars (tenor). He is the spearhead of an attack of the oppressed people of Parma against the nobility. For his part in this fight, he is burned at the stake. Mariola, true to him to the end, is killed by an insane woman. CASTELNUOVO-TEDESCO says this opera "is in parts beautiful, especially in the third act, which, in its choral section, reaches almost the same heights as DEBORA E JAELE." But he adds: "It is not very homogeneous, and it is excessively drawn out."

Françaix, Jean, composer. Born Le Mans, France, May 23, 1912. He attended the Paris Conservatory and made his bow as composer in 1932 with a work for string quartet, heard at the International Society for Contemporary Music in Vienna. His first opera came in 1937: LE DIABLE BOÎTEUX, a one-act chamber opera for two singers and fourteen instrumentalists. Later operas include LA MAIN DE GLOIRE, successfully introduced at the Bordeaux Festival on May 7, 1950; the one-act comic opera, L'APOSTROPHE, performed at the HOLLAND MUSIC FESTIVAL on July 1, 1951; *La Princesse de Cleves* (1953); and *Paris à nous deux,* a lyric fantasy. Françaix made his America debut as soloist with the New York Philharmonic Orchestra in 1938 in his own piano concerto.

France, Anatole (born Jacques Anatole Thibault), author. Born Paris, Apr. 16, 1844; died Tours, Oct. 12, 1924. A dominant figure in French literature, France wrote several novels and stories used for operas. The most notable is MASSENET'S THAÏS. Others include Charles Levadé's *La Rôtisserie de la Reine Pédauque* (1920) and Massenet's LE JONGLEUR DE NOTRE DAME, the latter derived from France's short story "L'Etui de nacre." The American composer Louis GRUENBERG made an opera out of France's comedy *The Man Who Married a Dumb Wife,* but having failed to secure permission from the author he was never allowed to get it performed or published.

Francesca da Rimini, (1) the wife by proxy of the Lord of Rimini. She falls in love with the proxy, her brother-in-law, Paolo, and both are slain after they are caught making love. This tragic romance is referred to by DANTE in Canto V of *The Inferno* in THE DIVINE COMEDY. It has been used in numerous operas, notably ones by Emil Ábrányi, GOETZ, Robert Hernried, MANCINELLI, NÁPRAVNÍK, RACHMANINOFF, THOMAS, and ZANDONAI. Most of these operas bear her name as the title.

(2) Opera in four acts by ZANDONAI. Libretto by T. Ricordi. Premiere: Turin, Feb. 19, 1914. American premiere: Metropolitan Opera, Dec. 22, 1916. The third-act soprano aria, "Paolo, datemi pace," and the fourth-act duet for baritone and tenor, "Tieni, fratello," are among its most interesting passages.

Franchetti, Alberto (Baron), composer.

Born Turin, Sept. 18, 1860; died Viareggio, Aug. 2, 1942. He was born into a wealthy, noble family. He studied with Felix Draeske in Dresden and at the Munich Conservatory and became successful with his first and finest opera, ASRAEL, produced in Brescia in 1888. Having a fortune at his disposal, he produced his later operas under the best possible auspices, but it would be a mistake to say that his success and fame were purchased with coin; they were acquired by means of a fine lyrical gift and a talent for effective theatricalism. His most successful operas were: *Asrael* (1888); *Cristoforo Colombo* (1892); GERMANIA (1902); *Notte di leggenda* (1914). He wrote two operas in collaboration with GIORDANO, *Giove a Pompei* (1921) and *Glauco* (1922).

Asrael was given its American premiere in Hartford, Conn., in Oct., 1966.

Franck, César, composer. Born Liège, Belgium, Dec. 10, 1822; died Paris, Nov. 8, 1890. After attending the Paris Conservatory, he completed his first major work, the eclogue *Ruth,* for solo voices, chorus, and orchestra. This work was performed in 1846. For many years he lived in humble obscurity, serving as organist for various Parisian churches, including Ste. Clotilde, and writing works that met with little recognition during his lifetime. He is most famous today for his orchestral, chamber, and choral works. His three operas were lesser productions, and they are now forgotten. The first, *Le Valet de ferme* (1852), was not published. The others are *Hulda* (1885) and *Ghisèle* (1890).

Frankfurt Opera. The history of the Frankfurt Opera may be said to have begun with the opening of a new opera house in 1880, boasting one of Germany's best equipped stages. Among its earlier conductors were Hans PFITZNER's father, WEINGARTNER, Siegmund von Hausegger, and KRAUSS, the last of whom was also artistic director for several years. STEINBERG was the conductor between 1929 and 1933, followed by Bertil Wetzelsberger (1933–1938) and KONWITSCHNY (1938–1945). Performances were discontinued during World War II and were resumed in the Börsensaal until a new auditorium, the Grosses Haus, opened in 1951. Bruno Vondenhoff was musical director up to 1953. He was succeeded by SOLTI (who resigned in 1961), Lovro von Matačic, and Theodore Bloomfield. Among the operas receiving their world premieres with this company were CARMINA BURANA; *Der ferne Klang* (SCHREKER); DIE GEZEICHNETEN; *Der Golem* (D'ALBERT); DIE KLUGE; *Die Lästerschule* (KLENAU); *Der Schatzgraber* (Schreker); TRANSATLANTIC; VON HEUTE AUF MORGEN; DIE ZAUBERGEIGE.

Frantz, Crespel's servant (tenor) in OFFENBACH's THE TALES OF HOFFMANN.

Fra poco a me ricovero, Edgardo's lament at the seeming fickleness of his loved one, Lucia, in Act III, Scene 3, of DONIZETTI's LUCIA DI LAMMERMOOR.

Frasquita, gypsy friend (soprano) of Carmen in BIZET's CARMEN.

Frau Holde kam aus dem Berg hervor, the shepherd's ditty opening Act I, Scene 2, of WAGNER's TANNHÄUSER, hailing the Goddess of Spring.

Frau ohne Schatten, Die (The Woman Without a Shadow), opera in three acts by Richard STRAUSS. Libretto by HOFMANNSTHAL. Premiere: Vienna State Opera, Oct. 10, 1919. American premiere: San Francisco Opera, Sept. 18, 1959. Performances of this opera since its American premiere have ranked it, in the opinion of some, as one of Strauss's masterpieces, on a level with SALOME, ELEKTRA, and DER ROSENKAVALIER. The text is filled with symbolic and allegorical implications and combines mythology, folklore, and fairy tale. Its main theme is woman's duty to be fertile. Because the Fairy Princess (soprano) has married an Eastern Emperor (tenor), she is no longer either human or fairy. The spirit world decrees that if she cannot find a shadow (symbol of female fertility), the Emperor will be transformed into stone. Her search for a shadow brings her to the humble household of the dyer Barak (bass-baritone), whose wife (soprano) is happy to sell her own shadow for treasure, until her husband makes her realize the tragic consequences of such a barter. In a temple the Empress is told by mysterious voices that she can secure the shadow of Barak's wife by drinking the water of a nearby fountain. But the Empress refuses to bring tragedy to Barak's wife, even at the price of saving her own husband. For this act of unselfishness, the spirit world rewards her with a shadow, and thus she can become fertile.

Just as the shadow represents fertility, so the Empress is symbolic of the necessity of unselfishness and pity for self-fulfillment, and Barak of a simple man whose goodness compensates for his lack of spiritual values.

Barak's soliloquy in Act III, Scene 1, "Mir unvertraut," is one of the peaks in Strauss's musical score. Several orchestral interludes and intermezzi also find the master at the height of his creative powers.

Die Frau ohne Schatten was the first new production in 1966 by the METROPOLITAN OPERA in its new auditorium at the LINCOLN CENTER FOR THE PERFORMING ARTS. It proved the most successful production of the company's inaugural season.

Frazier, a lawyer (baritone) in GERSHWIN'S PORGY AND BESS.

Frédéric, Gérald's friend (baritone) in DELIBES'S LAKMÉ.

Frederick, a young nobleman (tenor or contralto) in THOMAS'S MIGNON.

Frederick of Telramund, *see* TELRAMUND, FREDERICK.

Freia, goddess of youth (soprano), in WAGNER'S DAS RHEINGOLD.

Freischütz, Der· (The Free-Shooter), opera in three acts by WEBER. Libretto by Friedrich Kind, based on a tale in the *Gespensterbuch,* edited by Apel and Laun. Premiere: Schauspielhaus, Berlin, June 18, 1821. American premiere: Park Theater, New York, Mar. 2, 1825.

Characters: Ottokar, a Prince of Bohemia (baritone); Kuno, head ranger to the Prince (bass); Agathe, his daughter (soprano); Ännchen, Agathe's friend (soprano); Caspar, a huntsman (bass); Max, another huntsman (tenor); Samiel, the Black Huntsman (speaking part); Kilian, a peasant (tenor); a hermit; foresters; peasants; musicians; spirits; demons. The setting is Bohemia; the time, the seventeenth century.

The celebrated overture opens with a dignified religious melody for horns, and its core, a mobile theme for violins, is a tonal picture of Agathe.

Act I. A forest shooting range. Kuno has arranged a marksmanship contest to choose his successor as head ranger. Max, in love with Kuno's daughter, is eager to win, but in a preliminary trial, he loses to the peasant Kilian. Disheartened by this setback, Max expresses his anguish ("Durch die Wälder, durch die Auen"). He is now responsive to Caspar, who has a method whereby Max can win. Caspar has sold his soul to Samiel, the Black Huntsman, in return for magic bullets that never miss their mark. Since Caspar must bring Samiel a new victim or lose his life, he is eager to have Max cooperate with the Black Huntsman. Max agrees to go to the Wolf's Glen.

Act II, Scene 1. Agathe's house. Alone and apprehensive, Agathe looks out of the window and marvels at the beauty of the night ("Leise, leise"). When Max comes, he tells her he has shot a stag at the Wolf's Glen and must rush off to bring it back. Agathe knows that the Glen is a haunted place, and she begs Max not to go there. Max, however, is deaf to her pleading.

Scene 2. The Wolf's Glen. Max meets Caspar. Strange apparitions appear; weird incantations are heard. There are flashes of lightning. Samiel creates seven bullets for Max, the last of which may go to Agathe's heart if Samiel wishes.

Act III, Scene 1. Agathe's room. Agathe is getting ready to marry Max. She begs heaven for protection ("Und ob die Wolke sie verhülle"), for she is apprehensive, having had a dream filled with dire omens. Her terror mounts when she receives a bridal bouquet that turns out to be a funeral wreath. She is comforted by her friend Ännchen, following which the bridesmaids appear, singing "Wir winden dir den Jungfern-kranz."

Scene 2. The shooting range. It is the day of the contest. Foresters sing a hymn to hunting (Huntsmen's Chorus: "Was gleicht wohl auf Erden"). The contest begins. Max amazes everyone with his six remarkable shots. The Prince commands Max to hit a passing dove with his seventh bullet. Agathe's voice is heard begging him not to shoot, for she is the dove. But Max fires. His bullet strikes Agathe, but her bridal wreath has caught the bullet and saved her life. Caspar, serving the devil's justice, dies in her place. It is then that Max reveals his pact with Samiel. The Prince first orders Max banished. Eventually, he promises to forgive Max after a year's probation. Max thanks the Prince for his generosity ("Die Zukunft soll mein Herz bewahren"), after which the entire assemblage gives voice to a song of thanksgiving ("Ja! lasst uns zum Himmel die Blicke erheben").

While Der Freischütz is comparatively seldom performed today, being chiefly remembered through a few excerpts, including its dramatic overture, it is historically a most significant opera. With this work romanticism and nationalism came to German opera. From this time on, Italianisms discarded, German opera would have a physiognomy of its own. The text of Der Freischütz is derived from German legend and makes use of German backgrounds and landscapes, as well as the German fascination with superstition and supernatural and diabolical elements. Weber, said Richard WAGNER, "was the most German of German composers." Der Freischütz is one of the few operas that shaped musical history and at the same time was acclaimed by its first audiences. Its premiere was a triumph. The German romantics immediately saw in it the typification of their creed, and they hailed it as a glorification of the German spirit and soul. In Vienna, Dresden, and London it gathered further triumphs; in London the opera was given simultaneously in three different theaters.

Fremstad, Olive, soprano and mezzo-soprano. Born Stockholm, Mar. 14, 1871; died Irvington, N.Y., Apr. 21, 1951. She was one of the greatest Wagnerian sopranos. Brought to the United States at the age of ten, she had already performed in Sweden as a prodigy pianist. She later turned to singing, became soloist in a church choir, and appeared in a production of Patience by Gilbert and SULLIVAN. In 1890 she settled in New York, studying singing with F. E. Bristol, who trained her as a contralto; it was in this range that she made her concert debut, appearing as soloist with various orchestras. She was trained for opera by Lilli LEHMANN in Berlin, and she made her opera debut with the COLOGNE OPERA on May 21, 1895, in IL TROVATORE as Azucena. She remained with the Cologne Opera for three years, appearing in principal soprano roles. She was also seen in BAYREUTH in 1896, and London and Vienna a year after that. After an additional period of study in Italy, she joined the MUNICH OPERA COMPANY for three years, appearing in about seventy different roles. Her American opera debut took place at the METROPOLITAN OPERA on Nov. 25, 1903, in the role of SIEGLINDE (the conductor of the evening, Felix MOTTL, was also making his American debut). The following season she appeared for the first time as KUNDRY, and on Jan. 1, 1908 (an evening when Gustav MAHLER made his American bow), as ISOLDE.

Now one of the most brilliant personalities of the Metropolitan, she appeared in all the major Wagnerian soprano roles, combining a remarkable voice with outstanding histrionic gifts. Her interpretations were a standard by which later Wagnerian sopranos were measured. Besides her success in WAGNER, she scored as SALOME in STRAUSS's opera, a role which she created for New York and Paris, and in the title role of GLUCK's ARMIDE. Her last appearance at the Metropolitan took place on Apr. 23, 1914, as ELSA. She made a few more opera appearances in 1915 with the BOSTON OPERA and the CHICAGO OPERA before withdrawing from the operatic stage. After appearing in song recitals until 1920, she went into complete retirement. Among the many honors given her were appointments as Officer of Public Instruction and Officer of the French Academy, both in Paris. The story of her life was told by Mary Watkins Cushing in *The Rainbow Bridge,* published in 1954.

French Opera House, one of the most important nineteenth-century opera houses in the United States, situated in New Orleans. It was built in 1859 on a site where earlier opera houses had stood, notably the Théâtre St. Pierre, the Théâtre St. Philippe, and the Théâtre d'Orleans. It opened on Dec. 1, 1859, with WILLIAM TELL. During the next few decades some of the most significant of French operas were here introduced to America, including BENVENUTO CELLINI, LE ROI D'YS, DON QUICHOTTE, HÉRODIADE, SALAMMBÔ, SIGURD, and SAMSON ET DALILA.

French Six, The, *see* SIX, LES.

Freni, Mirella, soprano. Born Modena, 1936. Her teachers were Maestro Campogalliani and Leone Magiera, the latter becoming her husband in 1955. Her opera debut took place at the Teatro Communale in Modena on Feb. 3, 1957, as MICAËLA. This was followed by appearances with various Italian opera companies, as well as with the Netherlands Opera in 1959–60, at the GLYNDEBOURNE FESTIVAL between 1959 and 1961, and COVENT GARDEN in 1961. In Jan., 1962, she made her debut at LA SCALA in the role of Nannetta in FALSTAFF; during this same period she was also heard as Romilda in HANDEL'S SERSE at the PICCOLA SCALA. Her greatest success up to that time came on Jan. 31, 1963, at La Scala in the role of MIMI, with KARAJAN conducting, and ZEFFIRELLI as producer, a performance that was both recorded and filmed. In the winter of 1964 she appeared as LIÙ and Mimi with the La Scala Company during its visit to the Soviet Union, and on Sept. 29, 1965, she made her debut at the METROPOLITAN OPERA in New York. Her debut at

the CHICAGO LYRIC OPERA followed the same season and at the SAN FRANCISO OPERA two years after that. Among her other distinguished roles are MARGUERITE, ADINA, JULIETTE, and SUSANNA.

Freudig begrüssen wir die edle Halle, chorus of the knights, noblemen, and ladies as they file into the Hall of the Minstrels in Wartburg Castle, in Act II of WAGNER'S TANNHÄUSER.

Friar Laurence, friar (bass) in GOUNOD'S ROMÉO ET JULIETTE.

Fricka, Wotan's wife (mezzo-soprano) in WAGNER'S DAS RHEINGOLD.

Fricsay, Ferenc, conductor. Born Budapest, Aug. 9, 1914; died Basel, Feb. 20, 1963. After completing his music study with BARTÓK and KODÁLY, he made his conducting debut in Szeged in 1936. In 1945 he became a principal conductor of the BUDAPEST OPERA; in 1947 he led the world premiere of DANTONS TOD at the SALZBURG FESTIVAL; and in 1949 he made appearances with other opera performances in Vienna and Holland. In 1949 he became principal conductor of the RIAS Orchestra in the American sector of Berlin, giving the premieres of LE VIN HERBÉ and ORFF'S *Antigonae.* In 1951–52 he was principal conductor of the Städtische Oper (BERLIN DEUTSCHE STAATSOPER). He resigned because of major differences with the management. His American debut took place with the Boston Symphony on Nov. 13, 1953. For a brief period he was music director of the Houston Symphony. He then returned to Europe, where between 1956 and 1958 he served as principal conductor of the MUNICH OPERA. Between 1961 and 1963 he was again principal conductor of the Berlin Deutsche Staatsoper in West Berlin.

Friedenstag, Der (The Day of Peace), one-act opera by Richard STRAUSS. Libretto by Joseph Gregor, based on CALDERÓN'S play *La redención de Breda.* Premiere: Munich Opera, July 24, 1938. American premiere: Los Angeles, Cal., Apr. 2, 1967. The action of this opera takes place on the day of the Westphalian peace, Oct. 24, 1648, concerns itself with the besieged city of Breda during the Thirty Years' War, and concludes with a culminating hymn to peace. In 1938 the opera had political repercussions. Hitler, who had previously spoken bitterly about the Westphalian peace, was significantly absent from the premiere, and so were most of his henchmen. Despite this obvious official disapproval; the opera enjoyed a huge success, and the composer received many curtain calls.

Fritz Kobus, *see* KOBUS, FRITZ.

Frogs, The, *see* ARISTOPHANES.

Froh, a god of sun, rain, and fruits (tenor) in WAGNER'S DAS RHEINGOLD.

From boyhood trained, Huon's aria expressing delight at being chosen to go to Bagdad to claim Rezia as his wife, in Act I, Scene 1, of WEBER'S OBERON.

From the House of the Dead (Z mrtvého domu), opera in three acts by JANÁČEK (completed by Bretislav Bakala). Libretto by the composer (completed by O. Zitek), based on DOSTOYEVSKY'S *Memoirs from the House of the Dead*. Premiere: Brno, Apr. 12, 1930. American premiere: NET Opera, Dec. 3, 1969 (television). This was Janáček's last opera, left unfinished by his death. The setting is a Siberian penal colony, and the story relates how some of the prisoners came there. The opera is unconventional in that there is no real plot, no arias, and only one female character. It is rarely heard outside Czechoslovakia; nevertheless, successful productions have been given at the EDINBURGH FESTIVAL in 1964, at SADLER'S WELLS in London in 1965, and at the Düsseldorf Opera in 1968. On Dec. 3, 1969, the NET Opera began its existence with the American premiere of this opera, which already had had separate television productions in Czechoslovakia and in Austria.

Fuchs, Marta, soprano. Born Stuttgart, Jan. 1, 1898. She was one of the most distinguished Wagnerian sopranos of her time. After making her opera debut at Aachen in 1928, she appeared with the DRESDEN OPERA between 1930 and 1936, BERLIN STATE OPERA from 1936 to 1942, and the STUTTGART OPERA from

1949 to 1951. She appeared frequently as ISOLDE, BRÜNNHILDE, and KUNDRY at the BAYREUTH Festival.

Fuggiam gli ardori inospiti, Aida's aria suggesting to Radames that he flee with her to her own native land, in Act III of VERDI'S AIDA.

Fuggi, crudele, fuggi, Donna Anna's duet with Don Ottavio in which she expresses grief at the death of her father and her rejection of the consolation Don Ottavio tries to give her, in Act I, Scene 1, of MOZART'S DON GIOVANNI.

Fugitif et tremblant, Lothario's aria telling some merrymakers of his search for his long-lost daughter, in Act I of THOMAS'S MIGNON.

Fuoco di gioia!, chorus in Act I of VERDI'S OTELLO, as a festive bonfire is being lit.

furiant, a lively Bohemian dance. The most famous example in opera is found in Act II of SMETANA'S THE BARTERED BRIDE.

Furtwängler, Wilhelm, conductor. Born Berlin, Jan. 25, 1886; died Eberstein, Ger., Nov. 30, 1954. After an intensive period of study with Joseph Rheinberger, Max Schillings, and Anton Beer-Walbrunn, Furtwängler received his conducting apprenticeship in Zürich, Strassburg, and Lübeck. In 1915 he succeeded Artur BODANZKY as principal conductor of the MANNHEIM OPERA. During the next few years he gained stature with remarkable performances of symphonic music with the BERLIN STATE OPERA Orchestra and at the Museum Concerts in Frankfurt. When Arthur NIKISCH died in 1922, Furtwängler inherited two of the most important conducting posts in Europe: that of the Leipzig Gewandhaus Orchestra and the Berlin Philharmonic. He now advanced to the first position among German conductors. In 1924 he gave highly successful guest performances of the WAGNER music dramas at the Berlin State Opera; during the following years he was to appear there frequently. On Jan. 3, 1925, he made his American debut as a guest conductor of the New York Philharmonic Orchestra. He returned to America during the next three seasons, while filling his regular posts in Germany and making remarkably successful guest appearances in major European cities. His Wagner festivals at the PARIS OPÉRA became a regular feature of the Paris spring music season. In 1931 he made his first appearance at BAYREUTH, directing TRISTAN UND ISOLDE. He subsequently achieved outstanding success in opera performances at the VIENNA STATE OPERA, the Bayreuth and SALZBURG festivals, and at COVENT GARDEN. When the Nazis came to power Furtwängler was appointed deputy president of the Reich Chamber of Music, musical director of the Berlin State Opera, and principal conductor at Bayreuth. A year later he was at odds with the Nazi officials. He was planning the world premiere of HINDEMITH's opera MATHIS DER MALER, at the Berlin State Opera, when government leaders decided that neither the composer nor

his opera was in harmony with the new spirit of Germany. The opera was not performed, and Furtwängler was forced to resign his musical and political posts. Six months later he was again in favor, and he resumed some of his former posts. In 1939 he was made Director of Musical Life in Vienna in a Nazi effort to rehabilitate the musical life of that city. Because of his close association with the Nazi government, Furtwängler became *persona non grata* in the United States. Efforts to give him conductorial assignments with major American orchestras had to be abandoned. In Europe his position as one of the world's great conductors of symphonic music and opera remained unchallenged. It was intended that Furtwängler should lead the Berlin Philharmonic Orchestra during its 1955 tour of the United States, but when his death intervened, Herbert von KARAJAN succeeded to the conductorship.

G

Gabriele Adorno, *see* ADORNO, GABRIELE.

Gadski, Johanna, soprano. Born Anclam, Ger., June 15, 1872; died Berlin, Feb. 22, 1932. She studied with Mme. Schroeder-Chaloupka in Stettin and made her opera debut in 1899 with the KROLL OPERA in the title role of LORTZING's UNDINE. After appearances in various German opera houses, she made her American debut with the DAMROSCH OPERA COMPANY on Mar. 1, 1895, in LOHENGRIN. During the next three seasons she was seen with that company in most of the principal Wagnerian soprano roles and in the world premiere of Walter DAMROSCH's THE SCARLET LETTER. Her first appearance at the METROPOLITAN OPERA took place at a concert

on Dec. 11, 1898. Up to 1904 she appeared, and was acclaimed, in the WAGNER dramas, particularly in the roles of BRÜNNHILDE and ISOLDE. During this period she also appeared at BAYREUTH and COVENT GARDEN. In 1905 and 1906 she appeared at the Wagner festivals in Munich. Returning to the Metropolitan in 1907, she remained there for a decade. During World War I, when her husband, Hans Tauscher (whom she had married in 1892), was deported as an undesirable alien, she left the United States and returned to Germany. During 1929–1931 she sang in America with the Wagnerian Opera Company, but she was then past her prime.

Gailhard, Pierre, bass and opera manager. Born Toulouse, France, Aug. 1, 1848; died Paris, Oct. 12, 1918. After study at the Paris Conservatory, he made his opera debut at the OPÉRA-COMIQUE on Dec. 4, 1867, in THOMAS's *Le Songe d'une nuit d'été.* As a member of that company for the next four years he created several roles, including the principal bass parts in AUBER's *Rêve d'amour* and OFFENBACH's *Vert-Vert.* On Nov. 3, 1871, he appeared for the first time at the PARIS OPÉRA, as Méphistophélès in FAUST. He remained a principal bass there for over a decade. In 1884 he retired as singer and joined Ritt as manager of the Opéra, becoming sole manager of the company from 1905 to 1908. He was responsible for the French premieres of several of the Wagnerian music dramas and for the growing reputations of such singers as the DE RESZKE brothers, EAMES, MELBA, and RENAUD.

Galatea, Acis' beloved (soprano) in HANDEL's pastoral opera ACIS AND GALATEA.

Galitsky, Prince, Prince Igor's brother-in-law (bass) in BORODIN's PRINCE IGOR.

Galitzin, Prince Vassily, a reformer (tenor), member of Young Russia, in MUSSORGSKY's KHOVANTCHINA.

Galli-Curci, Amelita, soprano. Born Milan, Italy, Nov. 18, 1882; died La Jolla, Cal., Nov. 26, 1963. She studied the piano at the Milan Conservatory, but was encouraged by MASCAGNI to specialize in singing. She studied by herself and, without a single formal lesson, made her opera debut at the TEATRO COSTANZI, in 1909, as GILDA. After appearing in many opera houses in Europe and South America, she sang in the United States for the first time on Nov. 18, 1916, as Gilda, in a performance by the CHICAGO OPERA. She was a sensation. On Jan. 28, 1918, during a visit of the Chicago Opera, she appeared in New York for the first time, singing the role of DINORAH, and again was extravagantly acclaimed. Her METROPOLITAN OPERA debut took place on Nov. 14, 1921, as VIOLETTA. For the next three seasons she was one of the few

singers who were simultaneously permanent members of the Metropolitan and the Chicago operas. In 1924 she withdrew from the Chicago company, remaining with the Metropolitan another half dozen years. While her coloratura singing frequently lacked finish, it had great beauty of tone, and her impersonations had warmth and charm. Her finest roles included ROSINA, LAKMÉ, Dinorah, Gilda, JULIETTE, and Elvira in I PURITANI. A throat ailment compelled her to bring her career to a temporary end. She was operated on in 1935, and on Nov. 24, 1936, was able to make a return appearance in Chicago, as MIMI, but it was evident that her singing days were over. She then went into complete retirement in California.

Galli-Marié, Marie Célestine (born de l'Isle), mezzo-soprano. Born Paris, Nov., 1840; died Vence, France, Sept. 22, 1905. She created the roles of CARMEN and MIGNON. Her only teacher was her father, a member of the PARIS OPÉRA company. In 1859 she made her opera debut in Strasbourg, but she did not achieve success until 1862, when, in Rouen, she sang in THE BOHEMIAN GIRL. On Aug. 12, 1862, she made her debut at the OPÉRA-COMIQUE in LA SERVA PADRONA, remaining a principal soprano of that company for over two decades, and appearing in many notable premieres. Though her voice was not exceptional, she brought remarkable dramatic force to her characterizations.

Gallo, Fortune, impresario. Born Torremaggiore, Italy, May 9, 1878; died New York City, Mar. 28, 1970. He came to the United States in 1895 and soon after the turn of the century began his career as impresario by managing several traveling opera companies. In 1909 he founded the company with which his name is chiefly identified, the SAN CARLO OPERA. This company made numerous tours of the United States and Canada and was a vital force in spreading the love of opera. Gallo also supervised many open-air opera performances in stadia, made a film version of PAGLIACCI in 1928, and subsequently was a pioneer in presenting opera in sound motion pictures. His autobiography, *Lucky Rooster,* was published in 1968.

Galuppi, Baldassare, composer. Born Burano, Italy, Oct. 18, 1706; died Venice, Jan. 3, 1785. After studying the violin with his father he earned his living in Venice playing the organ. There he wrote his first opera, *La fede nell' incostanza,* which was such a fiasco that for a while he gave up music. The composer Marcello convinced him to reconsider. After a period of study with Antonio Lotti, Galuppi wrote a second opera, *Dorinda,* which was an outstanding success in 1729. Galuppi went on to write over a hundred operas, presented in the leading Italian opera houses. In 1741 he visited London, where two of his operas, *Scipione in Cartagine* and *Enrico,* were so successful that they influenced a whole school of English opera composers. He became particularly famous for his comic operas, so much so that he is sometimes described as the "father of OPERA BUFFA." His most celebrated work in this vein was IL FILOSOFO DI CAMPAGNA, produced in Venice in 1754. From 1748 to 1762 Galuppi was assistant MAESTRO DI CAPPELLA at St. Mark's in Venice, and from 1762 principal *maestro.* In 1766 he was invited by Catherine II to Russia, where for two years he assisted in producing his operas. He returned to Venice in 1768; there he remained for the rest of his life, active as *maestro* at St. Mark's, as director of the Conservatory, and as composer. His finest operas are: *Dorinda* (1729); *Issipile* (1738); *Adriano in Siria* (1740); *Scipione in Cartagine* (1742); *Enrico* (1743); *Didone abbandonata* (1752); *Il filosofo di campagna* (1754); *Il re pastore* (1762); IFIGENIA IN TAURIDE (1768).

Gama, *see* DA GAMA, VASCO.

Gambler, The, opera in four acts by PROKOFIEV. Libretto by the composer, based on DOSTOYEVSKY's story of the same name. Premiere: Théâtre de la Monnaie, Apr. 29, 1929; American premiere: New York City, Apr. 4, 1957.

The gambler in the title is a general stationed in the German spa of Roulettenburg. Having lost his money at the gambling tables and being heavily in debt, he prays for the death of his wealthy grandmother. But the grandmother is also a gambler, and she, too, loses her fortune at games of chance. To alleviate the situation, the General insists that his daughter, Pauline, marry a French marquis to whom the General is particularly deep in debt. To prevent this marriage, Alexei, an employee of the General and a young man deeply in love with Pauline, takes his chance in the casino and breaks the bank. He offers her all his money as the way out of her undesirable marriage, but to his amazement she flings it back at him contemptuously.

García, Manuel del Popolo Vicente, tenor, composer, and teacher. Born Seville, Jan. 22, 1775; died Paris, France, June 2, 1832. He began singing in the Seville Cathedral choir when he was six, and by the time he was seventeen he was active as actor, singer, conductor, and composer. On Feb. 11, 1808, he made his opera debut in Paris in Ferdinando PAER's *Griselda* and was a great success. In 1811 he went to Italy, where he appeared for five years and profited through contact with Italian singing methods. It was with García in mind that ROSSINI created the principal tenor roles in THE BARBER OF SEVILLE and *Elisabetta.* From 1817 to 1819, in London, and from 1819 to 1824, in Paris, he was the idol of opera-goers; in Paris he created for France the role of Count ALMAVIVA in *The Barber of Seville.* In 1823 he founded a highly successful school of singing in London. Two years later he came to the United States as an opera impresario. From Nov. 29, 1825, to Sept. 30, 1826, he gave seventy-nine performances at the Park and Bowery theaters, including eleven operas new to America. From New York he went to Mexico. On his way back, after a successful year and a half, he was held up and robbed of all his earnings. Returning to Paris, he sang at the Théâtre des Italiens, after which he retired from the stage and devoted himself to teaching. His most celebrated pupils were his daughters Maria MAL-IBRAN and Pauline VIARDOT-GARCÍA, and the tenor Adolphe NOURRIT. García wrote many Spanish, Italian, and French operas, all now forgotten.

García, Manuel Patricio Rodriguez, baritone and teacher, son and pupil of the above. Born Madrid, Mar. 17, 1805; died London, July 1, 1906. At the age of twenty he sang the title role of THE BARBER OF SEVILLE when his father's traveling company (*see above*) opened its season in New York. His father was the Almaviva, his mother Berta, and the Rosina was his sister Maria MALIBRAN. Before he was thirty he retired from the stage in favor of teaching at the Paris Conservatory and the Royal Academy of Music in London. His pupils included Jenny LIND, Henriette Nissen, Mathilde MARCHESI, and his son Gustave (later a successful opera singer). Manuel Rodriguez García invented the laryngo-scope and wrote, in French, the first two scientific studies of physiology of the human voice. He lived to the patriarchal age of a hundred and one.

Garcias, a burlesquer (soprano) in MASSENET'S DON QUICHOTTE.

Garden, Mary, soprano. Born Aberdeen, Scotland, Feb. 20, 1877; died there Jan. 4, 1967. One of the most glamorous prima donnas of the twentieth century, she created the role of MÉLISANDE. While still a child, she was brought to the United States, where she studied singing with Mrs. Robinson Duff. In her sixteenth year she appeared in an amateur performance of the Gilbert and SULLIVAN operetta *Trial by Jury.* Further vocal study took place in Paris with Mathilde MARCHESI. The famous American soprano Sibyl SANDERSON became interested in her and introduced her to Albert CARRÉ, manager of the OPÉRA-COMIQUE. Carré urged her to continue studying until he could find the proper role for her. It was found suddenly and unexpectedly. Some two months after the premiere of LOUISE, Marthe Rioton,

creator of the leading role, was taken ill during a performance. Garden, who had studied the role but had never yet sung before an audience, replaced the indisposed prima donna and was a sensation. She was subsequently invited to sing the role of *Louise* in most of the great opera houses of Europe and America and became identified with it. As a permanent member of the Opéra-Comique company, she was selected by Carré and DEBUSSY in 1902 to create the role of Mélisande in PELLÉAS ET MÉ-LISANDE, this over the vociferous objections of MAETERLINCK, author of the play, who wanted Georgette Leblanc, his common-law wife, to have the role. Mary Garden made the part so completely her own that for many years it was impossible to think of Mélisande without her. She created the principal soprano roles in several other French operas, including ERLANGER'S APHRODITE, MASSENET'S SAPHO, and SAINT-SAËNS'S *Hélène.* Her American debut took place at the MANHATTAN OPERA on Nov. 25, 1907, in the American premiere of THAÏS. Some of the critics remarked that her singing had imperfections, but they could not deny that she was a brilliant personality and that her voice had natural beauty. She remained with the Manhattan Opera company until its dissolution in 1910, scoring a sensation in her first appearance as SALOME in the Richard STRAUSS opera, in which she dispensed with the services of the customary double and herself performed the Dance of the Seven Veils. In 1910, Garden joined the CHICAGO OPERA, remaining with this company until the end of her career in opera. When CAM-PANINI, general manager of the company, died in 1919, Garden was selected as his successor, the first time a woman was called upon to direct a major opera company. She held this post for only one season. As a result of her lavish expenditures and resultant deficits, the company had to be reorganized. The direction passed to other hands, and Mary Garden returned to the company of singers, where she remained until

1931, appearing in several world and American premieres, including those of ALFANO'S RISURREZIONE, Hamilton Forrest's *Camille,* and HONEGGER'S JUDITH.

Oscar Thompson noted that her "work was disturbingly irregular," and that "there was a wide divergence between her best and her most commonplace performances of the same part." But when she was at her best as Mélisande, Louise, or Thaïs, she was an artist of incomparable magnetism and glamour. After her withdrawal from the opera stage, Mary Garden devoted herself to concert work, lectures, and teaching. For a period, she was vocal advisor to Metro-Goldwyn-Mayer in Hollywood. She wrote her autobiography, *Mary Garden's Story,* in collaboration with Louis Biancolli (1951).

Garrick, David, actor and playwright. Born Hereford, Eng., Feb. 19, 1717; died London, Jan. 20, 1779. One of the great theatrical figures of his day, Garrick wrote several plays that were made into operas. One of these, written in collaboration with George Coleman, was *The Secret Marriage,* used by CIMAROSA for his IL MATRIMONIO SEGRETO and by Peter Gast for his less familiar opera *Die heimliche Ehe.* Garrick also wrote the libretto for ARNE'S *Cymon.* He is the central character in the opera by Albert Stoessel *David Garrick* (1936).

Garrido, general in the Royalist army (bass) in MASSENET'S LA NAVARRAISE.

Gasparo, Don, the king's officer (tenor) in DONIZETTI'S LA FAVORITA.

Gastone, Viscount of Letorières (tenor) in VERDI'S LA TRAVIATA.

Gatti-Casazza, Giulio, opera manager. Born Udine, Italy, Feb. 3, 1869; died Ferrara, Italy, Sept. 2, 1940. Though he expected to become an engineer, in 1893 he succeeded his father as director of the Municipal Theater in Ferrara. So brilliant was his work that in 1898 he was offered the most important post of this kind in Italy, the management of LA SCALA. He remained at La Scala for a decade. His regime did much to popularize the Wagnerian music dramas in Italy, many of them receiving their Italian premieres, and also brought about the first Italian productions of such significant operas as BORIS GODUNOV and PELLÉAS ET MÉLISANDE. In 1908 Gatti-Casazza came to the United States to become general manager of the METROPOLITAN OPERA. He held this post with great distinction for over a quarter of a century. Retiring in 1935, he returned to Italy. He was married twice, first to the soprano Frances ALDA, of the Metropolitan Opera, and afterward to Rosina Galli, the Metropolitan Opera ballerina and ballet mistress. Just before his death he completed his autobiography, *Memories of the Opera.*

Gaubert, Philippe, flutist, conductor, and composer. Born Cahors, France, July 4, 1879; died Paris, July 10, 1941. He was the principal conductor of the PARIS OPÉRA for over two decades. He attended the Paris Conservatory, where he won the PRIX DE ROME. Later he appeared throughout France as solo flutist. During World War I he served in the French army, receiving the Croix de Guerre for heroism in the battle of Verdun. From 1919 to 1938 he was the principal conductor of the Paris Conservatory Concerts, and from 1920 to the time of his death, of the Paris Opéra. He wrote two operas: *Sonia* (1913) and *Naïla* (1927).

Gaudenzio, Sofia's guardian (bass) in ROSSINI'S IL SIGNOR BRUSCHINO.

Gaussin, Jean, young man (tenor) in love with Sapho in MASSENET'S SAPHO.

Gautier, Théophile, poet and novelist. Born Tarbes, France, Aug. 31, 1811; died Neuilly, Oct. 23, 1872. His story *Une Nuit de Cléopâtre* was used for two operas, CLEOPATRA'S NIGHT and MASSÉ'S *Une Nuit de Cléopâtre.*

Gaveston, steward (basso) of the Earl of Avenell in BOIELDIEU'S LA DAME BLANCHE.

gavotte, an old French dance in common time and beginning on the third beat. The dance became popular at the court of Louis XIV, and gavottes were used in operas by the early French composers (LULLY and RAMEAU) and by HANDEL. There is a fine specimen in GLUCK's IPHIGÉNIE EN TAURIDE, another in MOZART's IDOMENEO. Perhaps the most popular gavotte of all is that of GOSSEC in his opera *Rosine*. Later instances occur in MANON (Manon's aria "Obéissons quand leur voix appelle") and MIGNON (the orchestral entr'acte before Act II and Frederick's aria "Me voici dans son boudoir"). In ANDREA CHÉNIER the guests dance a gavotte at a party at the Château de Coigny.

Gay, John, poet and playwright. Born Barnstaple, England, Sept., 1685; died London, Dec. 4, 1732. He wrote the texts for HANDEL's ACIS AND GALATEA and for THE BEGGAR's OPERA.

gazza ladra, La (The Thieving Magpie), OPERA BUFFA by ROSSINI. Libretto by Giovanni Gherardini, based on *La Pie voleuse* by D'Aubigny and Caigniez. Premiere: La Scala, May 31, 1817. American premiere: Philadelphia, Sept. 14, 1827. The silly text involves a servant girl, Ninetta, who is accused of stealing a silver spoon. The spoon, however, is found in a magpie's nest, and the girl is exonerated. Ninetta is now free to devote herself to her love affair with Fernando and to avoid the advances of the lecherous old Podesta. The overture is famous; an innovation in its orchestration is the use of two snare drums with which it opens and which caused quite a stir in its time. Among the most distinguished vocal numbers are Ninetta's first-act aria "Di piacer mi balza il cor"; her first-act duet with Fernando, "Come frenare"; and her second-act aria "Deh! tu reggi in tal momento."

Long neglected, this opera is slowly becoming more familiar through revivals: by the AMERICAN OPERA SOCIETY on Mar. 10, 1954; at the Wexford Festival in 1959; at the FLORENCE MAY MUSIC FESTIVAL in 1965.

Gazzaniga, Giuseppe, composer. Born Verona, Oct., 1743; died Crema, Feb. 1, 1818. He wrote fifty operas popular in their own day but since forgotten. He is remembered for *Don Giovanni Tenorio* (1786), an opera familiar to both Lorenzo DA PONTE and MOZART before they wrote their DON GIOVANNI.

Gebrauchsmusik, a German term signifying "functional music," describing a movement in twentieth-century German music. While the term was usually applied to pieces for radio, screen, education, and so forth—particularly such works composed early in his career by HINDEMITH—it also described operas of that period utilizing a functional or popular style. Notable examples are JONNY SPIELT AUF, NEUES VOM TAGE, and THE THREEPENNY OPERA. When the Third Reich came to power, this movement collapsed, since popular and functional elements in art were considered decadent.

Gedda, Nicolai, tenor. Born Stockholm, Sweden, July 11, 1925. He is the son of the choirmaster of the Russian Orthodox Church in Stockholm, who for a number of years was also a member of the famed Don Cossack Chorus. Nicolai Gedda received his academic schooling at the Soedra Latin School in Stockholm and his training in voice from private teachers. In 1952 he made his opera debut with the STOCKHOLM OPERA in LE POSTILLON DE LONGJUMEAU. One year later he appeared for the first time at LA SCALA, in the role of Don Ottavio in DON GIOVANNI. He then made his debut at the PARIS OPÉRA in FAUST, at COVENT GARDEN in RIGOLETTO, and at the VIENNA OPERA in CARMEN. His first appearance at the METROPOLITAN OPERA took place on Nov. 1, 1957, in *Faust*. In 1958 he created there the role of Anatol in VANESSA. He repeated his performance in *Vanessa* the same year at the SALZBURG FESTIVAL, where he was also heard in THE SCHOOL FOR WIVES. Gedda has remained one of the principal tenors of the Metropolitan Opera, besides appearing extensively at other major opera houses and at festivals. His numerous recordings of full-length operas and operettas have further enhanced his international prestige.

Gegrüsst sei hoher Tag, the people's prayer that ends Act I of WAGNER'S RIENZI.

Geliebter, komm, Venus' unsuccessful attempt to reawaken Tannhäuser's ardor for her in the Venusberg scene opening WAGNER'S TANNHÄUSER.

Gellner, Wally's suitor (baritone), Hagenbach's rival, in CATALANI'S LA WALLY.

Geneva Opera. Though the first opera heard in Geneva, Switzerland, was performed in 1766–67 (GRÉTRY'S *Isabelle et Gertrude*), opera did not come to prominence there until 1783 with the erection of a new theater seating twelve hundred and equipped with five permanent stage sets. In the years that followed, THE MARRIAGE OF FIGARO, LE DEVIN DU VILLAGE, and ZÉMIRE ET AZOR were among the operas produced there. A new and greater era began in 1831 with a gala performance of THE BARBER OF SEVILLE, followed by works by BOIELDIEU, ADAM, AUBER, HÉROLD, and MEYERBEER, among others, with a visiting German company presenting TANNHÄUSER. A new theater for opera (a replica of the PARIS OPÉRA) opened on Oct. 2, 1879, with WILLIAM TELL. Six evenings a week were now devoted to opera, including such contemporary operas as CARMEN, FAUST, and MIGNON. On May 1, 1951, this theater burned down, and not until Dec. 10, 1962, did a new opera house arise to replace it. With Marcel Lamy as director and Ernest ANSERMET as musical adviser, the house was inaugurated with DON CARLOS. During this first season of the new opera house, Wieland WAGNER brought from BAYREUTH his production of TRISTAN UND ISOLDE, and two world premieres were given, MONSIEUR DE POURCEAUGNAC and Maurice Yvain's *Corsaire noir*. Herbert GRAF succeeded Lamy as director in 1965, and it was under his regime that the Geneva Opera became one of Switzerland's two leading opera companies. He began his regime with THE MAGIC FLUTE, sets and costumes designed by Oskar Kokoschka, Graf directing, and Ansermet conducting. The same season WOZZECK was produced. In 1968–69 the opera company presented such novelties as revivals of Bloch's *Macbeth* and ROSSINI'S *Mosè*, together with Wagnerian music dramas (completing the presentation of the entire cycle of the RING) and favorites from the Italian repertory. In the fall of 1968, the opera company organized an International Opera Center, a nonprofit organization to provide "talented young opera artists the opportunity of completing their professional training through participation as active apprentice members of the Geneva Opera Company."

Geneviève (contralto), mother of Pelléas and Golaud in DEBUSSY'S PELLÉAS ET MÉLISANDE.

Gennaro, (1) Lucrezia Borgia's son (tenor) in DONIZETTI'S LUCREZIA BORGIA.

(2) A blacksmith (tenor) in WOLF-FERRARI'S THE JEWELS OF THE MADONNA.

Genoveva, opera in four acts by SCHUMANN. Libretto by the composer, based on another libretto by Robert Reinick, in turn derived from dramas by Tieck and HEBBEL. Premiere: Leipzig, June 25, 1850. This is Schumann's only opera, and it is rarely performed. It was revived at the FLORENCE MAY MUSIC FESTIVAL in 1951. The story concerns Siegfried, Count of the Palatinate, who, off to war, entrusts the care of his wife, Genoveva, to his friend Golo. Golo is madly in love with her. When she resists him, his love turns to hate and he desires her destruction. He brings Siegfried false news of his wife's infidelity. Siegfried orders Golo to kill Genoveva, but before the murder can take place, Siegfried learns of Golo's treachery and arrives in time to save his wife. Golo meets his doom by falling over a precipice.

Gentele, Goeran, opera manager. Born Stockholm, Sept. 10, 1917. From 1950 to 1963 he was a producer at the STOCKHOLM ROYAL OPERA and since 1963 he has been that company's general manager. In 1970 it was announced that Gentele would replace Rudolf BING as general manager of the METROPOLITAN OPERA on June 30, 1972.

George, a shepherd (tenor) who rescues

Kate from hell in DVOŘÁK's folk opera THE DEVIL AND KATE.

Gepreisen sei die Stunde, duet of Tannhäuser and Elisabeth reassuring each other of their mutual love, in Act II of WAGNER's TANNHÄUSER.

Gérald, British officer (tenor) in love with Lakmé in DELIBES's LAKMÉ.

Gérard, Charles, a revolutionary leader (baritone) in GIORDANO's ANDREA CHÉNIER.

Gerechter Gott, Adriano's powerful *scena* in Act III of WAGNER's RIENZI.

Germania, lyric drama in prologue, two scenes, and epilogue by FRANCHETTI. Libretto by ILLICA. Premiere: La Scala, Mar. 11, 1902. The setting is Germany in the early nineteenth century. A secret organization is created to fight Napoleon's rising power. Two of its members, Worms (baritone) and Loewe (tenor), are rivals for Ricke's love. Loewe wins Ricke (soprano) and marries her; he and Worms become bitter enemies. Later on, Ricke finds the bodies of both Loewe and Worms on the Leipzig battlefield.

Germont, Alfredo, Violetta's lover (tenor) in VERDI's LA TRAVIATA.

Germont, Giorgio, Alfredo's father (baritone) in VERDI's LA TRAVIATA, a role created by Felice VARESI.

Geronimo, a rich merchant (bass) in CIMAROSA's IL MATRIMONIO SEGRETO.

Geronio, Don, a Neapolitan nobleman (bass), husband of Fiorilla, in ROSSINI's IL TURCO IN ITALIA.

Gershwin, George, composer. Born Brooklyn, N.Y., Sept. 26, 1898; died Hollywood, Cal., July 11, 1937. He became popular as a composer of musical comedies, some of them of more than ordinary quality. One, *Of Thee I Sing,* was the first musical comedy to win a PULITZER PRIZE. After the success in 1924 of his *Rhapsody in Blue* for piano and orchestra he devoted himself to both popular and serious music. His opera PORGY AND BESS was the last and most important of his serious works. An earlier one-act Negro opera, in jazz style, 135TH STREET, was performed one night only in the *George White Scandals of 1922.* (The opera was then called *Blue Monday.*) It has been revived several times since, twice by Paul Whiteman (1925 and 1936), on a television broadcast in 1953, and in Miami in 1970. Gershwin died, aged thirty-eight, after a brain operation.

Gerster, Etelka, soprano. Born Kaschau, Hungary, June 25, 1855; died Pontecchio, Italy, Aug. 20, 1920. While studying with Mathilde MARCHESI at the Vienna Conservatory, she sang for VERDI an aria from LA TRAVIATA. Verdi recommended her to the TEATRO LA FENICE, where she made her opera debut on Jan. 8, 1876, as GILDA. She then toured Italy and Germany with a traveling opera company. In 1877 she married Carlo Gardini, an impresario, and the same year made a successful debut at COVENT GARDEN. A year later she came to the United States with the Mapleson Opera Company, making her American debut in LA SONNAMBULA. She was so successful that she became a rival of Adelina PATTI, then a New York favorite. After 1890 Gerster withdrew from opera and founded a school of singing in Berlin. She also taught for a year in New York. She wrote a treatise on singing, *Stimmführer* (1906).

Gertrude, (1) Juliette's nurse (mezzosoprano) in GOUNOD's ROMÉO ET JULIETTE.

(2) Mother of Hansel and Gretel (mezzo-soprano) in HUMPERDINCK's HANSEL AND GRETEL.

(3) Hamlet's mother (soprano) in THOMAS's HAMLET.

Gerusalemme liberata, La, epic poem by TASSO, the source of numerous operas. *See* ARMIDA; RINALDO.

Gerville-Réache, Jeanne, contralto. Born Orthez, France, Mar. 26, 1882; died New York City, Jan. 5, 1915. She studied in Paris with Rosine Laborde, Pauline VIARDOT-GARCÍA, and Jean Criticos. Her opera debut took place at the OPÉRA-COMIQUE in 1900 in GLUCK's ORFEO ED EURIDICE. During two seasons with that company she created the roles of Catherine in LE JUIF POLONAIS and Geneviève in PELLÉAS ET MÉLISANDE. From 1907 to 1910 she sang with the MANHATTAN

OPERA COMPANY, where her electrifying interpretation of Dalila was largely responsible for making SAMSON ET DALILA popular in America. She married Dr. G. Gibier-Rambeaud, director of the Pasteur Institute in New York. After leaving the Manhattan Opera she appeared for one season with the CHICAGO OPERA.

Gessler, tyrant governor (bass) of Schwitz and Uri in ROSSINI'S WILLIAM TELL.

Gezeichneten, Die (The Stigmatized Ones), opera in three acts by SCHREKER. Libretto by the composer. Premiere: Frankfurt, Apr. 25, 1918. This expressionist drama, set in sixteenth-century Genoa, tells of the fruitless love of a cripple with a beautiful soul for a girl with a beautiful body.

Ghedini, Giorgio Federico, composer. Born Cuneo, Italy, July 11, 1892; died there Mar. 25, 1965. He graduated from the Bologna Conservatory in 1911, after which he taught at the conservatories of Bologna, Turin, and Milan. In 1951 he was appointed director of the Milan Conservatory. After achieving success with several orchestral works, he wrote his first opera, *Maria d'Allesandria,* which was introduced in Bergamo in 1937. His operas: *L'instrusa* (1938), *Re Hassan* (1939), *La pulce d'oro* (1940), *Le baccanti* (1943), *Billy Budd* (1948), *L'iposcrita felice* (1956), and *La via della croce* (1961).

Gherardino, Gherardo's son (mezzosoprano) in PUCCINI'S GIANNI SCHICCHI.

Gherardo, Donati's nephew (tenor) in PUCCINI'S GIANNI SCHICCHI.

Ghiaurov, Nicolai, bass. Born Velimgrad, Bulgaria, 1929. He attended the Moscow Conservatory on a State scholarship, graduating with highest honors in 1955. This was followed by the winning of the Grand Prix in an international competition held in Paris and his opera debut in Sofia as Don Basilio in ROSSINI'S THE BARBER OF SEVILLE. In 1958 he appeared with the BOLSHOI OPERA in Moscow. A year later he scored such a success as Varlaam in BORIS GODUNOV that he was soon elevated to *primo basso.* He has since appeared with the Bolshoi in a wide variety of roles. He achieved world renown when, in the summer of 1965, he helped open the SALZBURG FESTIVAL in the title role of *Boris Godunov,* conducted by KARAJAN. Meanwhile, in 1963 he had made his American debut at the CHICAGO LYRIC OPERA. His debut at the METROPOLITAN OPERA took place on Nov. 8, 1965, in FAUST. This was followed by appearances at Expo 67 in Montreal with the LA SCALA company and by his first appearances with the SAN FRANCISCO OPERA, both in the fall of 1967. He has come to be recognized universally as one of the foremost bassos of our time and the finest interpreter of the role of Boris Godunov since CHALIAPIN and KIPNIS.

Ghione, Francesco, conductor. Born Acqui, Italy, Aug. 26, 1886; died Rome, Jan. 19, 1964. After studying at the Parma Conservatory he played the violin in various Italian opera houses. His debut as conductor took place at the Puglie Opera in 1913. Six years later he directed the Italian repertory at the Barcelona Opera and in 1922 was appointed TOSCANINI'S assistant at LA SCALA. After serving as principal conductor of La Scala for several seasons and appearing with other Italian opera companies, he came to the United States in 1931 as guest conductor of the Detroit Civic Opera. From 1936 to 1939 he was the conductor of the Detroit Symphony. After 1940 he conducted the Italian repertory at the TEATRO COLÓN in Buenos Aires and the Rio de Janeiro Municipal Theater.

Ghislanzoni, Antonio, dramatist and librettist. Born Lecco, Italy, Nov. 25, 1824; died Bergamasco, July 16, 1893. He began his career as a singer but soon turned to writing and editing. For many years he was the editor of the *Gazzetta Musicale* in Milan. He wrote numerous librettos, the most important being the one for AIDA. Others were for CATALANI'S *Edmea;* Vladimir Kashperov's *Maria Tudor;* Enrico Petrella's I PROMESSI SPOSI; PONCHIELLI'S *I Lituani* and *I Mori di Valenza.*

Già i sacerdoti adunansi, duet between

Amneris and Radames in which Amneris promises to intercede for Radames if he will be willing to beg the king for mercy, in Act IV, Scene 1, of VERDI'S AIDA.

Già mi dicon vinal, Scarpia's offer to Tosca to free Cavaradossi in exchange for her favors, in Act II of PUCCINI'S TOSCA.

Già nella notte densa, the love duet of Otello and Desdemona in Act I of VERDI'S OTELLO.

Gianetta, a peasant girl (soprano) in DONIZETTI'S L'ELISIR D'AMORE.

Gianetto, (1) Lodoletta's suitor (baritone) in MASCAGNI'S LODOLETTA.

(2) A poet (tenor), principal character in GIORDANO'S LA CENA DELLE BEFFE.

Giannini, Dusolina, soprano. Born Philadelphia, Pa., Dec. 19, 1902. She studied with Marcella SEMBRICH, after which she made her concert debut in New York in 1923. Four years later her opera debut took place in Hamburg in AIDA. Her success brought her engagements in Europe's leading opera houses. In 1934 she scored a major success as Donna ANNA at the SALZBURG FESTIVAL. On Feb. 12, 1936, she made her debut at the METRO-POLITAN OPERA in *Aida*. She remained at the Metropolitan Opera through the 1940–41 season. In Europe she created the role of Hester Prynne in THE SCARLET LETTER, an opera by her brother, Vittorio. She is the daughter of Ferruccio Giannini, a noted operatic tenor.

Giannini, Vittorio, composer. Born Philadelphia, Pa., Oct. 19, 1903; died New York City, Nov. 28, 1966. He was the son of Ferruccio Giannini, distinguished operatic tenor, and the brother of the soprano Dusolina Giannini (*see above*). He attended the Milan Conservatory on a scholarship, then continued his music study at the Juilliard graduate school. After receiving the grand prize of the American Academy of Rome in 1932, he wrote his first mature opera, *Lucedia*, introduced in Munich on Oct. 20, 1934. Four years later, on June 2, 1938, the HAMBURG OPERA introduced THE SCARLET LETTER, his sister

creating the role of Hester. In 1937, 1939, and 1940 he wrote radio operas on commissions from the Columbia Broadcasting System: *Flora, Beauty and the Beast,* and *Blennerhasset.* On Jan. 31, 1953, the Cincinnati Symphony presented a concert version of THE TAMING OF THE SHREW, an opera he had written for television that was broadcast over the NBC-TV network in 1956, when it received a special award from the New York Music Critics' Circle; it was given a staged public presentation by the NEW YORK CITY OPERA in 1956. His subsequent operas were THE HARVEST, written on a grant from the FORD FOUNDATION and produced in Chicago on Nov. 25, 1961; an OPERA BUFFA, *Rehearsal Call,* introduced in New York City on Feb. 15, 1962; and *The Servant of Two Masters,* his last opera, produced posthumously by the New York City Opera on Mar. 9, 1967. Giannini also wrote a tetralogy of four festival operas collectively entitled *Christus.* He was a member of the faculty of the Juilliard School of Music and the Manhattan School of Music in the departments of theory, composition, and orchestration. Between 1956 and 1964 he was a member of the composition department of the Curtis Institute in Philadelphia, and in 1964 he became president of the North Carolina School of the Arts at Winston-Salem.

Gianni Schicchi, a one-act OPERA BUFFA by PUCCINI. Libretto by Gioachino Forzano, based on the history of a citizen of medieval Florence. Premiere: Metropolitan Opera, Dec. 14, 1918.

Characters: Zita, cousin of Buoso Donati (mezzo-soprano); Rinuccio, her nephew (tenor); Simone, cousin of Buoso (basso); Marco, his son (baritone); La Ciesca, Marco's wife (soprano); Gherardo, Buoso's nephew (tenor); Nella, his wife (soprano); Gherardino, their son (mezzo-soprano); Betto di Signa, Buoso's brother-in-law (baritone); Gianni Schicchi (baritone), a role created by Giuseppe DE LUCA; Lauretta, his daughter (soprano); Spinelloccio, a doctor (bass); Amantio di Nicolao, a lawyer (bass); Pinellino, a shoemaker (bass); Guccio, a dyer (bass). The setting is Florence in the thirteenth century.

Gianni Schicchi is a character from history mentioned in DANTE's *The Inferno* (Canto xxx). The opera text begins with the death of Buoso Donati, a rich Florentine, who has left his fortune to a monastery. The loss of an inheritance disturbs his family. Rinuccio, in love with Lauretta, tries to devise a scheme for acquiring Buoso's wealth. He suggests calling in the wily Gianni Schicchi, dismissing Schicchi's lack of social background by pointing out that even the city Florence has had a humble origin ("Firenze è como un albero fiorito"). Schicchi initially is reluctant to enter into discreditable maneuvers, but his daughter pleads with him ("O mio bambino caro") and effects a change of heart. Schicchi notes that Buoso's death has not yet been made public. This being the case, he offers to impersonate the dead man. The news of Buoso's imminent death is to be spread through Florence, after which Schicchi, as Buoso, will dictate a new will bequeathing his fortune to his family. The plot is set in motion. The family calls in a lawyer to draw up a new will. To the horror of the family, "Buoso Donati" bequeaths his fortune to one Gianni Schicchi. The relatives must remain silent, for to protest would be to incriminate themselves in the fraud. With sardonic overtones, Schicchi bids the city of Florence farewell ("Addio Firenze"). But when the lawyer leaves, the relatives fall upon Schicchi. He drives them away with a stick. As Rinuccio and Lauretta tenderly express their love for one another ("Lauretta mia"), Schicchi remarks that no better use can be made of his new fortune than to help the lovers.

Gianni Schicchi is the third of a trilogy of one-act operas collectively entitled IL TRITTICO (*The Triptych*). IL TABARRO and SUOR ANGELICA are the other operas. Of the three, only *Gianni Schicchi* is a comedy. While tenderness and sentimentality were always Puccini's strongest points, he frequently showed flashes of wit even in his tragic operas. In *Gianni Schicchi* he fully indulged his flair for the comic and succeeded in writing a distinguished *opera buffa*. The character of the crafty Gianni Schicchi is in the best traditions of *opera buffa*, as is the contrast between touching sentiment and broad farce.

Giants in the Earth, opera in three acts by MOORE. Libretto by Arnold Sundgaard, based on a novel by O. E. Rolvaag. Premiere: New York City, Mar. 28, 1951. The text, like the novel by Rolvaag, is based on the settling of the Dakotas by Norwegians. Of Moore's score, Olin Downes wrote: "There is an abundance of concert pieces and dancing, a wedding chorus, a baptismal hymn, and even a fight at the end of the second act which is perfectly legitimate and logical as an incidental feature of the drama. . . . In a number of concerted pieces which call for musical ensemble, Mr. Moore has written dexterously and to the point." This opera was the recipient of the PULITZER PRIZE for music in 1951. Moore and Sundgaard revised it extensively about a decade later.

Giarno, leader of a gypsy band (bass) in THOMAS's MIGNON.

Già ti veggo immorta, Enzo's horrified reaction on hearing of Laura's death, in Act III, Scene 2, of PONCHIELLI's LA GIOCONDA.

Gibichungs, the Gibich's children, Gunther and Gutrune, in WAGNER's GÖTTERDÄMMERUNG.

Gibson, Alexander, conductor. Born Motherwell, Scotland, 1926. He attended the Royal Scottish Academy of Music and the Royal College of Music in London, winning the Tagore Medal at the latter institution as the best student of the year. He made his debut as conductor at SADLER's WELLS in THE BARTERED BRIDE when he was twenty-five. In 1954 he was appointed a full-time conductor at Sadler's Wells, and in 1957 he became the youngest musical director in the history of that company. There he conducted twenty-six operas ranging from MOZART to BARTÓK, including the world premiere of John Gardner's *The Moon and Sixpence*. In 1959 he was appointed conductor of the Scottish National Orchestra. When the Scottish Opera was founded in 1962, he became one of its principal conductors.

Gigli, Beniamino, tenor. Born Recanati, Italy, Mar. 20, 1890; died Rome, Nov. 30, 1957. His formal musical study did not begin until his eighteenth year, when he entered the Santa Cecilia Academy in Rome. There he studied with Antonio Cotogni and Enrico Rosati, after which he made his opera debut in Rovigo, in 1914, in LA GIOCONDA. He now made numerous appearances in leading Italian opera houses and became a great favorite. In 1918 TOSCANINI selected him to sing the role of Faust in a LA SCALA revival of BOITO's MEFISTOFELE during a Boito festival. On Nov. 26, 1920, Gigli made his American debut at the METROPOLITAN OPERA in *Mefistofele* and was acclaimed. He was considered the successor to CARUSO after the latter's death in 1921. The beauty of his voice—its purity of tone, elegance of legato, and suppleness of range—made him an idol of opera-lovers everywhere.

When, during the economic crisis of 1931, Gigli was asked by the Metropolitan Opera management to accept a cut in fee, he refused and withdrew from the company. For the next few years he concentrated his activity in Europe, but returned to the United States in 1938–39 for several concert and operatic appearances. On Jan. 23, 1939, he was back on the stage of the Metropolitan Opera in AIDA and was given an enthusiastic welcome. When he returned to Europe that season, he furnished the European press with some violent opinions about America in general and the Metropolitan Opera in particular. These remarks created a furor in the United States, and Gigli lost favor with many Americans, who were further alienated when he identified himself completely with the Fascist regime in Italy and became an outspoken prop-

agandist for the Axis during World War II. In Europe, however, Gigli's position as one of the world's foremost opera tenors remained unassailable. In 1955 the sixty-five-year-old tenor returned to the United States for a concert tour.

Gil Blas, *see* LE SAGE, ALAIN.

Gil, Count, Suzanne's husband (baritone) in WOLF-FERRARI's THE SECRET OF SUZANNE.

Gilda, Rigoletto's daughter (soprano) in VERDI's RIGOLETTO.

Gillot, Onegin's servant in TCHAIKOVSKY's EUGENE ONEGIN.

Ginastera, Alberto, composer. Born Buenos Aires, Apr. 11, 1916. He is one of the leading composers of Argentina. His musical education took place at the Conservatorio Williams and at the National Conservatory. While attending the latter school he wrote the score for a ballet, *Panambi*, which received the National Prize in 1940. He achieved some measure of recognition as a composer of symphonic music and as a teacher at the Conservatory and the Liceo Militar before paying his first visit to the United States on a Guggenheim Fellowship in 1946–47. Upon returning to his native city he founded, and for several years directed, the Conservatory of Music and Dance. In the years that followed he achieved international renown with his concert music, which received performances at major contemporary music festivals. His String Quartet was the recipient of the prize of the Asociación Wagneriana de Buenos Aires. His first opera was composed when he was in his full maturity. It was DON RODRIGO, written with SERIAL TECHNIQUES and introduced at the TEATRO COLÓN on July 24, 1964. It had been commissioned by the municipality of Buenos Aires and was a formidable success wherever it was performed. So was its successor, BOMARZO, whose premiere was given in Washington, D.C., on May 19, 1967. In 1962 Ginastera became the director of the recently founded Latin American Center for Advanced Musical Studies in Buenos Aires, sponsored by the Rockefeller Foundation.

Gingerbread Waltz, see JUCHHEI, NUN IST DIE HEXE TODT!

Gioconda, La (The Ballad Singer), opera in four acts by PONCHIELLI. Libretto by BOITO, based on Victor HUGO's play *Angelo, tyran de Padoue.* Premiere: La Scala, Apr. 8, 1876. American premiere: Metropolitan Opera, Dec. 20, 1883.

Characters: La Gioconda, a ballad singer (soprano); La Cieca, her blind mother (contralto); Alvise, official of the State Inquisition (bass); Laura, his wife (mezzo-soprano); Enzo Grimaldo, a nobleman (tenor); Barnaba, spy of the Inquisition (baritone); Isepo, a public letter writer (tenor); Zuane, a gondolier (bass); monks; sailors; senators; ladies; gentlemen. The setting is Venice in the seventeenth century.

Act I. "The Lion's Mouth." A street near the Adriatic shore. A brief prelude is built out of part of La Cieca's dramatic aria in Act I. Crowds are milling around and singing ("Feste e pane"). Barnaba, the spy, informs the mob that the regatta will soon begin. When the crowd disperses, La Gioconda arrives, leading her blind mother, La Cieca. The mother is grateful for her daughter's love; the daughter responds with devotion; and Barnaba, from a distance, expresses the hope that he can ensnare the daughter through the mother (Trio: "Figlia che reggi il tremulo piè"). When Barnaba accosts La Gioconda, she brushes him rudely aside. Barnaba determines to destroy her. The crowd now returns from the regatta, bearing aloft the winner. Barnaba maliciously whispers to the loser that he lost because of the diabolical powers of La Cieca. The loser, Zuane, is aroused and attacks the old woman as a witch, but a Genoese nobleman, Enzo Grimaldo, whose ship is harbored in Venice, protects the old woman. The Grand Duke Alvise now emerges from the palace, accompanied by his wife Laura. Laura, once betrothed to Enzo, prevails on the Duke to save La Cieca from mob violence. In gratitude, La Cieca gives Laura a rosary ("Voce di donna"). After the crowd disperses, Barnaba—aware that Enzo is still in love with Laura—slyly tells him that Laura reciprocates and will come to see him that very night on his ship. Enzo is ecstatic ("O grido di quest' anima"). When he leaves, Barnaba dictates a letter to Laura's husband warning him of the projected rendezvous. La Gioconda overhears him; since she herself is in love with Enzo, she is overwhelmed to discover that he is having an affair with another woman. As he reads the letter he has dictated, Barnaba gloats over his powers as a spy ("O monumento"). The crowd returns, and merriment is resumed as they dance *la furlana.* La Gioconda, coming out of the church, distressed at the loss of Enzo, is consoled by her mother.

Act II. "The Rosary." A lagoon near Venice. The sailors of Enzo's ship sing as they work (Marinaresca: "Ho! He! Ho!"). Disguised as a fisherman, Barnaba sings a fisherman's ballad (BARCAROLLE: "Pescator, affonda l'esca"). Since he is awaiting Laura, Enzo sends his sailors away. Alone, he is enraptured by the beauty of the night ("Cielo e mar!"). Barnaba now appears, leading Laura. Laura and Enzo embrace; the old passion is revived; they plan to flee on Enzo's ship. When Enzo orders his sailors to prepare to set sail, Laura falls on her knees and prays God to forgive her ("Stella del marinar"). At this point, La Gioconda appears in disguise and upbraids Laura for stealing her lover ("L'amo come il fulgor del creator"). She is about to stab Laura when a boat appears. Laura realizes with horror that her husband has followed her. She takes her rosary and prays again. Recognizing the rosary as the one her mother gave Laura, La Gioconda now decides to aid her rival, and arranges for her escape. When Enzo returns, he finds not Laura but La Gioconda. Distraught at the loss of the woman he loves and faced with capture by the Duke's men, Enzo orders that his ship be set afire.

Act III. "The House of Gold." Scene 1. A room in Alvise's palace. Realizing that his wife loves another man,

Alvise is planning her murder ("Si, morir ella de"). Upon Laura's arrival, he denounces her for her faithlessness. He then gives her a vial of poison, demands that she drink it, and leaves. Laura is about to take the poison when La Gioconda appears and gives her instead a drug that will induce a deathlike sleep. When Alvise reappears, he is satisfied that his wife has killed herself.

Scene 2. Alvise's ballroom. Alvise is entertaining his guests at a ball. They sing their praises of his palace ("Alla cà d'oro"). There then takes place a spectacular ballet (Danza delle ore: Dance of the Hours). When the dance ends, Barnaba enters, dragging La Cieca after him, accusing her of being a witch. The sound of tolling bells is heard. Barnaba informs one of the masked guests that they are being tolled for Laura. The guests reveal their horror in the chorus "D'un vampiro fatal" and Enzo in "Già ti veggo immorta." When the Duke pulls aside a curtain in order to show his guests the dead body of his wife, Enzo, blinded by sorrow and rage, rushes at him to stab him. Enzo is seized by the Duke's men and taken to prison.

Act IV. "The Orfano Canal." A ruined palace on the island of Giudeca. La Gioconda has brought Laura to a lonely island for safety. Feeling she has nothing more to live for, La Gioconda contemplates suicide ("Suicidio"). Enzo, released from prison, arrives at the island and is reunited with his beloved Laura. The lovers express their gratitude to La Gioconda, bid her a tender farewell ("Sulle tue mani l'anima"), and depart. Barnaba comes to claim La Gioconda, for she has promised her body in return for Enzo's freedom. Before he can take her in his arms, La Gioconda kills herself with a dagger. Bitter with rage, Barnaba shouts into La Gioconda's unhearing ears that he has already had his revenge: he has come from strangling her mother.

La Gioconda is first of all a good show. The many big scenes, the stirring passions, the high tensions make for ex-

cellent theater. It is for this reason that the opera, despite an involved and often confusing libretto, remains a favorite. But *La Gioconda* is an important opera, too. Ponchielli, influenced by WAGNER, brought to Italian opera an orchestral technique, an expressive lyricism, and a dramatic power that were to be influential upon the VERDI of OTELLO and upon Ponchielli's pupil, PUCCINI. *La Gioconda* was the first new opera mounted by the METROPOLITAN OPERA during its first season (1883–84).

gioielli della Madonna, I, *see* JEWELS OF THE MADONNA, THE.

Giordano, Umberto, composer. Born Foggia, Italy, Aug. 27, 1867; died Milan, Nov. 12, 1948. While attending the Naples Conservatory, where he was a student for nine years, he wrote his first opera, *Marina*, which he entered in the Sonzogno competition that was won by CAVALLERIA RUSTICANA. The publisher Edoardo Sonzogno was so impressed with Giordano's opera that he commissioned him to write a new work, *Mala vita*, given in Rome on Feb. 21, 1892. Recognition came to Giordano four years later with his finest and most celebrated work, ANDREA CHÉNIER, introduced at LA SCALA on Mar. 28, 1896. Before the end of the century this opera was performed throughout Europe and in New York City. The most significant of Giordano's later operas were FEDORA, given at the TEATRO LIRICO in 1898; SIBERIA, at La Scala in 1903; MADAME SANS-GÊNE, at the METROPOLITAN OPERA in 1915; and LA CENA DELLE BEFFE, at La Scala in 1920. Among the many honors gathered by Giordano were those of Chevalier of the French Legion of Honor, Commander of the Crown of Italy, and a membership in the Italian Academy.

The centenary of Giordano's birth was commemorated by the SAN CARLO OPERA in Naples in 1967 with a revival of one of his least known operas, *Mese Mariano* (introduced in Palermo in 1910); also by La Scala with a gala presentation of *Madame Sans-Gêne*.

Giorgetta, Michele's wife (soprano) in

PUCCINI'S IL TABARRO, a role created by
Claudia MUZIO.

giorno di regno, Un (A King for a Day),
OPERA BUFFA in two acts by VERDI. Libretto by ROMANI. Premiere: La Scala,
Sept. 5, 1840. American premiere: New
York City, June 18, 1960 (semi-staged).
Verdi's second opera was his first try
at comedy—and his last for half a century. This opera was a dismal failure;
Verdi himself always referred to it as
a "bad opera," realizing that, in truth,
it had very little comedy, was guilty of
inept word setting, and was an unhappy
attempt to imitate ROSSINI and DONI-
ZETTI.

Giorno d'orrore, duet of Semiramis
and Arsace in Act 2, Scene 3, of ROSSINI'S
SEMIRAMIDE.

Giovanna, (1) Jane Seymour, King
Henry VIII's mistress (mezzo-soprano),
in DONIZETTI'S ANNA BOLENA.

(2) Gilda's nurse (mezzo-soprano)
in VERDI'S RIGOLETTO.

Giovanni, Lord of Rimini and Paolo's
deformed brother (baritone) in ZAN-
DONAI'S FRANCESCA DA RIMINI.

**Girl of the Golden West, The (La
fanciulla del West),** opera in three acts
by PUCCINI. Libretto by Guelfo Civinini
and Carlo Zangarini, based on the
David BELASCO play of the same name.
Premiere: Metropolitan Opera, Dec. 10,
1910.

Characters: Minnie, owner of the
Polka Saloon (soprano); Jack Rance,
sheriff (baritone); Nick, bartender
(tenor); Ramerrez, an outlaw, alias
Dick Johnson (tenor); Ashby, Wells-
Fargo agent (bass); Billy Jackrabbit,
an Indian (bass); Wowkle, his squaw
(mezzo-soprano); Jake Wallace, traveling camp minstrel (baritone); José
Castro, member of Ramerrez' gang
(bass). The setting is the foot of Cloudy
Mountain, California, during the Gold
Rush days.

Act I. The Polka Saloon. Miners are
singing and gambling. Ashby tells them
he is hot on the trail of Ramerrez, the
notorious outlaw. When Minnie appears, the atmosphere becomes charged,
for all the men love her—particularly

Jack Rance, who sings of his passion
("Minnie, della mia casa"). When
Rance tries to force his attentions on
Minnie, she repels him with her revolver, reminding him that he is married and that she does not love him.
At this point a stranger enters, introducing himself as Dick Johnson of Sacramento. Minnie and Dick recognize
one another. They have met once before and felt a mutual attraction. Minnie
does not know, however, that Johnson
is really Ramerrez, come to hold up
the saloon. The sheriff, his men, and
the miners depart, searching for Ramerrez. They leave their gold with
Minnie, who announces boldly that she
will protect it with her life. But by now
the outlaw is so much in love with Minnie that he is willing to give up the
gold. Touched, Minnie invites him to
her cabin.

Act II. Minnie's cabin. Minnie and
Johnson are confiding to each other
their love when shots are heard. Before
a posse appears, Minnie hides her lover.
Even when she discovers from the posse
that Johnson is Ramerrez she refuses
to disclose his hiding place. After the
posse leaves, she bitterly attacks Johnson for having failed to tell her the
truth. Johnson confesses all, explaining
the circumstances that led him to become an outlaw, and promising to give
up crime. Minnie, however, sends him
away. No sooner does he step out of
the cabin than he is shot. Minnie drags
him back in and conceals him in the
loft. A falling drop of blood reveals to
the sheriff where the wounded man is
hiding. Desperate, Minnie proposes a
hand of poker—if the sheriff wins, he
can have both the outlaw and herself,
but if he loses, he must give up his
pursuit. Minnie cheats, winning the
game and the life of her lover.

Act III. A forest. Johnson has recovered, has been captured, and is about
to be hanged. He prays that Minnie be
led to believe that he has gone away
to find a new life ("Ch'ella mi creda
libero"). Minnie arrives on horseback,
gun in hand. She entreats the men

to remember their feelings for her and for the sake of those feelings to spare the man she loves. The miners have a change of heart. Minnie and Johnson are free to begin a new life together.

Puccini was commissioned to write this opera by the METROPOLITAN OPERA Association when he visited the United States in 1907 to assist in the first American performance of MADAMA BUTTERFLY. Searching for suitable material, he came upon Belasco's play, then enjoying a huge success on Broadway. "I should think that something stunning could be made of the '49 period," he said at the time. Another thing about the play appealed to him. Its author had been the source of his successful *Madama Butterfly,* and Puccini felt that a revival of this collaboration might promise another success of equal proportions. It took Puccini three years to write his opera. Its premiere was the most brilliant of the season, the cast including CARUSO, DESTINN, and AMATO, with TOSCANINI conducting. Puccini himself was present. The critics and audience were enthusiastic, but later audiences were less satisfied. For a while, the opera was regarded as one of Puccini's lesser accomplishments. His Italian lyricism seemed unsuitable for a text so thoroughly American. Nevertheless, the beauty and harmonic inventiveness of the score have brought the opera back into favor with American audiences.

Giselda, sister (soprano) of Arvino and Pagano in VERDI'S I LOMBARDI.

Giulia, vestal virgin (soprano) in love with Licinius in SPONTINI'S LA VESTALE.

Giulietta, (1) Italian for Juliet, the heroine (soprano) in BELLINI'S I CAPULETTI ED I MONTECCHI, a role created by Giuditta GRISI.

(2) One of Hoffmann's loves (soprano) in Act II of OFFENBACH'S THE TALES OF HOFFMANN.

Giulini, Carlo Maria, conductor. Born Basletta, Italy, May 9, 1914. He attended the Santa Cecilia Academy in Rome, following which he served as music director of Radio Italiana from 1946 to 1951. In the ensuing years he distinguished himself both as a symphony conductor, with appearances with some of the world's foremost orchestras, making his American debut in this capacity in 1955, and in opera. His opera debut took place in 1951 at the Bergamo Festival in LA TRAVIATA, with Renata TEBALDI singing Violetta. Between 1951 and 1956 he was a permanent conductor at LA SCALA, where he has since made guest appearances. Since then he has been conductor first at COVENT GARDEN and subsequently at the TEATRO DELL' OPERA in Rome.

Giulio Cesare in Egitto (Julius Caesar in Egypt), (1) opera in three acts by HANDEL. Libretto by Nicola Francesco Haym. Premiere: Haymarket, London, Feb. 20, 1724. American premiere: Northampton, Mass., May 14, 1927. Though long neglected, *Giulio Cesare* has emerged as Handel's most popular opera during the past quarter of a century or so. "Repeated listening to the complete score," wrote Conrad L. Osborne, "brings one face to face, more closely than ever, with Handel's greatness as a musical dramatist." After its premiere *Giulio Cesare* remained unperformed until 1922, when it was revived at an opera festival in Göttingen, Germany. The opera was often given in Germany after 1942. In July, 1952, it was revived in the ruins of the Teatro Grande of Pompei, when it was declared by one critic to be an "unexpected and intoxicating experience." Revivals in America by the AMERICAN OPERA SOCIETY and most significantly by the NEW YORK CITY OPERA in 1967, as well as the release of the recording of the New York City Opera production, contributed to the growing interest in this opera of the American public.

The opera opens with the arrival of Caesar (CASTRATO mezzo-soprano, now sung by a baritone) in Egypt, where he is hailed as conqueror. Caesar is horrified to learn that Pompey has been murdered by Sextus, brother of Cleopatra, and pays homage at Pompey's tomb. Cleopatra (soprano), rival of Sextus for the throne of Egypt, tries to enlist her beauty to conquer Caesar. At a garden entertainment, where she appears disguised as a goddess, she enraptures him with her singing of "V'adoro, pupille" (one of the most celebrated arias in the opera). But Cleopatra soon becomes enamored of Caesar and is instrumental in having him flee for safety when an avenging mob storms the palace to attack him. Caesar is eventually victorious in battle and thereupon crowns Cleopatra queen.

The most distinguished, at times inspired, arias in the opera are those assigned to Cleopatra, not only "V'adoro, pupille," mentioned above, but also "Tu la mia stella sei," "Piangerò la sorte mia," "Se pietà," "Da tempeste il legno infranto," and "Non disperar."

(2) Opera in three acts by MALIPIERO. Libretto by the composer, based on SHAKESPEARE's tragedy. Premiere: Teatro Carlo Felice, Genoa, Feb. 8, 1936. American premiere: New York City, Jan. 13, 1937 (concert version). This opera was criticized by freedom-loving people in the period preceding World War II because the feeling prevailed that Malipiero wrote it to glorify Mussolini. Malipiero himself explained that he wrote it because "something in the air we breathe today urged me towards a Latin hero."

Giunta all' albergo, Dame Quickly's announcement that arrangements have been completed for duping Falstaff, in Act II, Scene 2, of VERDI's FALSTAFF.

Giuseppe, Violetta's servant (tenor) in VERDI's LA TRAVIATA.

Giusto cielo!, the chorus of the inhabitants of Lammermoor lamenting the death of Lucia in the final scene of DONIZETTI's LUCIA DI LAMMERMOOR.

Give me my robe, put on my crown, Cleopatra's aria in her death scene at the close of BARBER's ANTONY AND CLEOPATRA. The composer adapted it for concert performance.

Give me some music, Cleopatra's aria in Act I of BARBER's ANTONY AND CLEOPATRA. The composer adapted it for concert performance.

Glaives pieux, saintes épées (Nobil ac-ciar, nobili e santi), the "Benediction of the Swords," in which the Catholics are blessed by three monks, in Act IV of MEYERBEER's LES HUGUENOTS.

Glanville-Hicks, Peggy, composer. Born Melbourne, Australia, Dec. 29, 1912. She received her musical education at the Melbourne Conservatory, the Royal College of Music in London (where her teachers included VAUGHAN WILLIAMS in composition), and privately from Egon WELLESZ in Vienna and Nadia Boulanger in Paris. Serious composition began in 1931 with several vocal and orchestral works. Her first opera, *Caedmon,* was completed in 1934. In 1942 she and her husband, Stanley Bate (also a composer), made their permanent home in New York City, where, in 1948, Peggy Glanville-Hicks became an American citizen. In 1953 she received a grant from the American Academy of Arts and Letters; between 1956 and 1958 she was the recipient of a Guggenheim fellowship; in 1960 she was given a Rockefeller grant for research on the music of the Middle East; and in 1961 a Fulbright research grant enabled her to study Hindu folk music and the folk music of the Greek islands.

Her first significant opera was THE TRANSPOSED HEADS, commissioned by the Louisville Orchestra in Kentucky. It was introduced in Louisville on Apr. 3, 1954. Subsequent operas have been *The Glittering Gate* (first performance in New York City on May 14, 1959); *Nausicaa* (introduced in Athens, Greece, on Aug. 19, 1961); *Carlos among the Candles;* and *Sappho,* the last written on a grant from the FORD FOUNDATION.

Glauce, daughter (soprano) of the King of Corinth, wooed by Jason, in CHERUBINI's MÉDÉE.

Glaz, Herta, contralto. Born Vienna, Sept. 16, 1914. After attending the Vienna State Academy she made her debut with the Breslau Opera, in her eighteenth year, as Erda in DAS RHEINGOLD. In 1935 she became the leading contralto of the GLYNDEBOURNE FESTIVAL, and in the same year she sang successfully with the PRAGUE OPERA and at the opera festival in Interlaken, Switzerland. She toured the United States with the Salzburg Opera Guild and made appearances with the SAN FRANCISCO, St. Louis, and CHICAGO OPERA companies. On Dec. 25, 1942, she made her debut at the METROPOLITAN OPERA as AMNERIS. She appeared at the Metropolitan Opera up through the 1955–56 season in a great variety of roles, scoring her greatest successes in the German repertory.

Glinka, Michael, composer. Born Novospasskoye, Russia, June 1, 1804; died Berlin, Feb. 15, 1857. His two operas, A LIFE FOR THE CZAR and RUSSLAN AND LUDMILLA, laid the foundations for Russian national opera. The son of a prosperous landowner, Glinka became strongly conscious of music as a child, but formal study did not come for several years. In 1817 he was sent to St. Petersburg, where he attended the Pedagogic Institute for five years. At the same time he studied piano with John Field and Carl Meyer and violin with Joseph Böhm. Poor health sent him to the Caucasus in 1823. There he studied harmony and orchestration from textbooks and became absorbed with the folksongs and dances of that region. Back in St. Petersburg, he entered civil service and for three years worked in the Ministry of Communications. But music was not neglected. In 1828 he resigned his post and went to Italy, where he developed a passing fondness for Italian opera. Proceeding to Berlin, he studied theory with Siegfried Dehn. His homesickness led him to think of writing national music. "My most earnest desire," he wrote from Berlin, "is to compose music which would make all my beloved fellow countrymen feel quite at home, and lead no one to allege that I strutted about in borrowed plumes." Returning to Russia, he joined a literary and artistic group that included PUSHKIN and GOGOL. He now knew he wanted to produce music of an unmistakable Russian identity, with intimate association with Russian history and the Russian people. With this aim

in mind, he completed his first opera, *A Life for the Czar,* introduced at the Imperial Theater (*see* BOLSHOI THEATER, 1) on Dec. 9, 1836. The opera was a success, and the Czar presented Glinka with a valuable ring. He now began work on a second opera, *Russlan and Ludmilla,* the text derived from a poem by Pushkin. The new opera, introduced in St. Petersburg on Dec. 9, 1842, was at first a failure. It was considered to lack the human interest and dramatic quality of the previous work. Not until a revival three years after Glinka's death did it receive the recognition it deserved. In the closing years of his life, Glinka lived in France and Spain, writing a considerable quantity of symphonic music. His death came suddenly in Berlin. He was buried there, but a few months later his body was taken back to St. Petersburg.

Glinka's significance in Russian music cannot be overestimated. He was the first Russian composer whose music made an impact on the world outside Russia and whose best work has survived. More than this, he was the first Russian composer to realize a national art, setting the stage for DARGOMIZHSKY and the composers grouped as THE FIVE, all of whom admired his operas profoundly.

Globolinks, *see* HELP, HELP, THE GLOBOLINKS!

Glöcken im Träne, CAVATINA in which Euryanthe pines for Adolar, in Act I, Scene 2, of WEBER'S EURYANTHE.

Gloire immortelle de nos aïeux, the Soldiers' Chorus upon their returning home victorious, in Act IV, Scene 3, of GOUNOD'S FAUST.

Gloria all' Egitto, the people's hymn of victory that introduces the triumphal scene of Act II, Scene 2, of VERDI'S AIDA.

Gloriana, opera in three acts by BRITTEN. Libretto by William Plomer, based on Lytton Strachey's *Elizabeth and Essex.* Premiere: Covent Garden, June 8, 1953. American premiere: Cincinnati, May 8, 1956 (concert version). This was the first opera ever commissioned to help celebrate a coronation in England.

Britten wrote it for the coronation of Queen Elizabeth II, who was present at its gala premiere in 1953. Keeping in mind the occasion for which it was created, Britten produced a festive work, filled with pageantry and based on English history. The time is the later years of the reign of Queen Elizabeth I, toward the end of the sixteenth century, and the plot devotes itself to the involvement of the Queen with the Earl of Essex, an involvement that ends tragically for the Earl when the Queen signs a warrant for his death on the charge that he is a traitor. The opera ends with a scene in which episodes from the last period of the Queen's life unfold in montage fashion until her death. Though written in Britten's eclectic style, with a frequent recourse to modern idioms, the opera score intermittently catches the flavor of old English music: in the opening hymn of the crowd in praise of the Queen, "Green leaves are we"; in Essex' lyric, as he accompanies himself on the lute, "Quick music's best when the heart is oppressed"; and in the dance music of "La volta," performed at the Queen's ball by royal request.

Gloriana was revived in 1968 by the SADLER'S WELLS COMPANY in London and at the ALDEBURGH FESTIVAL.

Gloria, o vincitore, chorus of the people acclaiming Calaf for having successfully answered Turandot's three riddles, in Act II, Scene 2, of PUCCINI's TURANDOT.

Gluck, Alma (born Fiersohn, Reba), soprano. Born Bucharest, May 11, 1884; died New York City, Oct. 27, 1938. She studied singing with Arturo Buzzi-Peccia, after which she made her opera debut at the METROPOLITAN OPERA on Nov. 16, 1909, in WERTHER and was a great success. She remained at the Metropolitan Opera for the next three seasons, appearing in about twenty roles. After an additional period of study with Marcella SEMBRICH, she left opera and became a concert singer. For many years she was immensely successful, particularly in joint recitals with

her husband, the violinist Efrem Zimbalist, whom she married in 1914.

Gluck, Christoph Willibald, composer. Born Erasbach, Bavaria, July 2, 1714; died Vienna, Nov. 15, 1787. A giant figure in the history of opera, Gluck helped establish the musical drama, as distinguished from the more formal Italian opera, in works like ORFEO ED EURIDICE and ALCESTE. As a boy he attended Catholic schools, where he studied the violin, organ, and harpsichord. In 1736 he went to Vienna, where he was employed by Prince Ferdinand Lobkowitz. Another patron, Prince Melzi, took him to Italy, where he studied with G. B. Sammartini and wrote his first opera, *Artaserse,* produced in Milan in 1741. He now wrote six more operas, all of them in the Italian tradition, before proceeding to London, where two of his works were staged without success and earned their composer the disapproval of HANDEL. Returning to Vienna by way of Paris, Hamburg, and Dresden, Gluck had his newest opera, *Semiramide riconosciuta,* performed at the BURGTHEATER when that theater reopened on May 14, 1748. The work, with text by METASTASIO, was a success.

In 1754, four years after his marriage to wealthy Marianne Pergin, Gluck was appointed KAPELLMEISTER at the Vienna court theater. In this post he wrote numerous operas. But he was dissatisfied with them. Influenced by the French school, headed by RAMEAU, he felt the need for greater simplicity, naturalism, and dramatic truth; a departure from the mannerisms and pompous artificiality of the Italian tradition. Nor was he alone in these ideas. There were two other figures at the Vienna court who were also devotees of French art and culture. One was Count Giacomo Durazzo, director of the court theaters; the other was Ranieri da CALZABIGI, a poet who had come from Paris in 1761, aroused by the intellectual revolution then sweeping through England and France with ROUSSEAU, VOLTAIRE, and

Diderot as spokesmen. The three kindred spirits combined forces to produce an art that once and for all would overthrow the Italian influence. Their first effort was a ballet, *Don Juan*, produced at the Burgtheater on Oct. 17, 1761. The Calzabigi text was based on the play by MOLIÈRE, the music was by Gluck. This was followed by an even bolder effort to establish their new ideas: the opera *Orfeo ed Euridice*. Given at the Burgtheater on Oct. 5, 1762, the opera was a failure, too plain and neoclassic for Viennese tastes. But the collaborators were not discouraged. They wrote a second opera in their new style, *Alceste*, seen on Dec. 16, 1767, and after that, PARIDE ED ELENA, performed in 1770. Both operas were failures.

Convinced of the truth of his message and discouraged at his failures in Vienna, Gluck decided to go to Paris. There he wrote a new opera, IPHIGÉNIE EN AULIDE. In Paris, as in Vienna, Gluck encountered not appreciation and sympathy, but envy, antagonism, and malice. A powerful clique upheld the Italian tradition, and so much obstruction was placed in Gluck's way that *Iphigénie en Aulide* might never have been produced had not Marie Antoinette herself intervened. It was finally given at the OPÉRA on Apr. 19, 1774, and was a major triumph, the rage of the musical season. *Orfeo ed Euridice*, given its first French performance in 1775, was also an immense success. But the enemies of Gluck, whose leader was Jean François MARMONTEL, would not acknowledge defeat. They brought to Paris one of Italy's most celebrated composers, Niccolò PICCINNI, and had the Opéra commission him to write an opera. An intense rivalry developed between the two composers and their supporters; the musical atmosphere in Paris became charged with bitterness and dissension. The directors of the Opéra stepped boldly into the controversy by commissioning both Piccinni and Gluck to write an opera on the same libretto,

derived from EURIPIDES: IPHIGÉNIE EN TAURIDE. Gluck's opera was seen first, on May 18, 1779, and was so successful that Piccinni tried to withdraw his own work. Though Piccinni's opera had a run of seventeen consecutive performances, it was less well received than Gluck's. The opera war was over. Gluck's last opera, *Echo et Narcisse*, disappointed his Paris following. He now returned to Vienna, rich and honored, and died there of a stroke eight years later.

Gluck was one of the most significant opera composers before MOZART. At a time when opera was growing increasingly formal, stilted, and remote from truth and human experience, Gluck produced a new kind of musico-dramatic work in which music and text were integrated in a coherent whole. "My chief endeavor," as he himself explained, "should be to attain a grand simplicity, and consequently I have avoided making a parade of difficulties at the cost of clearness. I have set no value on novelty as such unless it was naturally suggested by the situation and suited to the expression. In short, there was no rule which I did not consider myself bound to sacrifice for the sake of effect." No one before him brought to opera such touching sentiment, wealth of feeling, realism, and straightforward understanding of text. Gluck's greatest operas represent a revolution that prepared the way for such later works as DON GIOVANNI, DER FREISCHÜTZ, and TRISTAN UND ISOLDE.

glückliche Hand, Die (The Lucky Hand), drama with music in one act by SCHOENBERG. Libretto by the composer. Premiere: Vienna, Oct. 14, 1924. American premiere: Philadelphia, Apr. 11, 1930. A man is lying on the floor on a dark stage, with a mythological monster holding him down with a giant paw. In a chant that is half song and half speech, a chorus comments on the futility of trying to achieve the unattainable. When the man and monster disappear, there follows a series of tableaux in which the man, seeking a woman symbolic of earthly happiness, finds only one who represents wealth and power. This is only the first of several frustrations confronting the man. In the end he is once again found lying on the floor, held down by the monster. The chorus questions: "Must you once again suffer? Don't you know the meaning of sacrifice? Must you go through all this again?" And the final comment of the chorus is the exclamation: "Poor thing!" Schoenberg's music is in the atonal style the composer favored in the early 1910's before he adopted TWELVE-TONE TECHNIQUES.

Glyndebourne Opera Festival, an opera company organized in 1934 by John CHRISTIE and his wife, Audrey MILDMAY, to present MOZART operas in a specially constructed theater on Christie's ancestral estate at Glyndebourne in Lewes, Sussex, Eng. The aim was to achieve a "unity between sight and sound" and a synchronization of "stage time and musical time." Carl EBERT was chosen artistic director; Fritz BUSCH, musical director; and Rudolf BING, general manager. The first festival opened on May 28, 1934, with THE MARRIAGE OF FIGARO, with Audrey Mildmay as Susanna, Aulikki Rautawaara as the Countess, Willi DOMGRAF-FASSBAENDER as Figaro, Lucy Mannen as Cherubino, and Fritz Busch conducting. For two weeks this opera alternated with COSÌ FAN TUTTE, whose principals included Heddle Nash as Ferrando, Ina Souez as Fiordiligi, Luise Helletsgrüber as Dorabella, and Vincenzo Bettoni as Alfonso. A year later the season was expanded to five weeks with THE MAGIC FLUTE and THE ABDUCTION FROM THE SERAGLIO added to the repertory. In 1938 operas by composers other than Mozart were heard when MACBETH and DON PASQUALE were given. During World War II, the festival suspended activity, though the company performed one work, THE BEGGAR'S OPERA. The festival resumed after the war with the world premieres of THE RAPE OF LUCRETIA and ALBERT HERRING, both presented by the newly organized ENGLISH OPERA GROUP. The first postwar production of the Glyndebourne company was GLUCK'S ORFEO ED EURIDICE with Kathleen FERRIER in 1947. In the same year the company appeared for the first time at the EDINBURGH FESTIVAL. There was no opera at Glyndebourne during the summers of 1948 and 1949 (the company confining its activities to the Edinburgh Festival). Operations were resumed at Glyndebourne in 1950, once again with Fritz Busch as principal conductor and Carl Ebert as artistic director. Busch conducted at Glyndebourne for the last time in 1951. Before that—and, of course, subsequently—numerous other conductors led various productions. Among them have been Lamberto Gardelli, Gianandrea Gavazzeni, Vittorio GUI, Rafael KUBELIK, Raymond Leppard, John PRITCHARD, Julius RUDEL, Paul Sacher, Hans SCHMIDT-ISSERSTEDT, Georg SOLTI, Fritz STIEDRY, and Walter Süsskind. In 1952 the Glyndebourne Festival Society was organized to assure the continuance of the annual performances. In 1956, in celebration of Mozart's bicentenary, the company devoted its entire repertory to that master, featuring six operas, two in new productions. With the death of John Christie, its founder and principal supporter, in 1962, the festival began encountering serious financial difficulties. This, however, did not create any interruption of its activities.

When Ebert resigned as artistic director in 1959, he was succeeded by Günther RENNERT, who remained until 1967. A new artistic policy was inaugurated in 1965–66, in which the seasonal repertory was limited to four instead of six operas, but with three instead of two new productions and an extension of the repertory to include more modern works and revivals of early classical operas. In 1967 the season was shortened, but four operas were still given, three of them in new productions.

On Sept. 3, 1969, the Glyndebourne Opera Festival brought its production of *Così fan tutte* to the Festival of Flanders in Ghent.

Besides operas already mentioned in preceding paragraphs the following are some of the more unusual works—modern as well as classical—heard at the festival through the years: ANNA BOLENA, ARIADNE AUF NAXOS, ARLECCHINO, CAPRICCIO, LA CENERENTOLA, LE COMTE ORY, ELEGY FOR YOUNG LOVERS (first performance in English), EUGENE ONEGIN, L'INCORONAZIONE DI POPPEA, L'ITALIANA IN ALGERI, IL MATRIMONIO SEGRETO, ORMINDO, LA PIETRA DEL PARAGONE, THE RAKE'S PROGRESS, and *The Rising of the Moon* (Nicholas Maw, a world premiere).

Gobbi, Tito, baritone. Born Bassano del Grappa, near Venice, Oct. 24, 1915. He was a law student before concentrating on music. After completing his vocal studies with Giulio CRIMI in Rome, he won first prize in an international voice competition in Vienna and made his opera debut in Rome as the elder GERMONT, both in 1938. He soon thereafter became principal baritone of the Rome Opera and in 1942 of LA SCALA, where he scored his first major successes. In 1947 he made his first appearance outside Italy, at the STOCKHOLM OPERA, and one year after that his American debut followed at the SAN FRANCISCO OPERA. Subsequent to a triumphant appearance as DON GIOVANNI at the SALZBURG FESTIVAL in 1950, FURTWÄNGLER conducting, Gobbi made his debut at the METROPOLITAN OPERA as SCARPIA on Jan. 13, 1956. Since then he has been heard in more of the world's leading opera houses, as well as at festivals, his repertory including over ninety roles. He has also appeared extensively in motion pictures, including screen versions of RIGOLETTO, THE BARBER OF SEVILLE, LA FORZA DEL DESTINO, and PAGLIACCI.

Godard, Benjamin, composer. Born Paris, Aug. 18, 1849; died Cannes, Jan. 10, 1895. He attended the Paris Conservatory. His first major work was an "operatic symphony," *Le Tasse,* which won first prize in a competition conducted by the city of Paris in 1878. In the same year he completed his first opera, *Les Bijoux de Jeannette.* Ten years later his opera *Jocelyn* was successfully introduced at the THÉÂTRE DE LA MONNAIE. Even more successful was *La Vivandière,* given by the OPÉRA-COMIQUE in 1895, eleven months after the composer's death. Besides the operas already mentioned Godard wrote *Pedro de Zalamea* (1884); *Le Dante* (1890); *Jeanne d'Arc* (1891); *Les Guelfes* (prod. 1902).

Goethe, Johann Wolfgang von, poet, dramatist, and novelist. Born Frankfurt, Aug. 28, 1749; died Weimar, Mar. 22, 1832. A number of Goethe's dramas and novels were adapted into operas. His masterwork, the epic drama FAUST, was the source of GOUNOD's famous opera of the same name and of operas by BERLIOZ (THE DAMNATION OF FAUST), BOITO (MEFISTOFELE), SPOHR (*Faust*), and several lesser composers. Other of Goethe's works adapted for operas include *Götz von Berlichingen* (GOLDMARK); *Die Leiden des jungen Werthers* (MASSENET's WERTHER and Alberto Randegger's *Werthers Schatten*); *Scherz, List, und Rache* (BRUCH and WELLESZ); *Wilhelm Meister* (Hans Gál's *Requiem für Mignon* and THOMAS's MIGNON).

Goetz (or Götz) Hermann, composer. Born Königsberg, Ger., Dec. 17, 1840; died Hottingen, Switzerland, Dec. 3, 1876. After attending the Stern Conservatory in Berlin, he became organist in Winterthur. His first and most successful opera was THE TAMING OF THE SHREW (*Der widerspänstigen Zähmung*), introduced in Mannheim on Oct. 11, 1874, and soon after that produced in leading German and Austrian opera houses. A second opera, FRANCESCA DA RIMINI, was performed in Mannheim in 1877, after the composer's death.

Gogol, Nikolai, author. Born Poltava, Russia, Mar. 21, 1809; died Moscow,

Mar. 4, 1852. Gogol was a creator of the Russian novel and one of Russia's foremost short-story writers. His material was adapted for numerous operas. Most are based upon stories in *Evenings on a Farm near Dikanka,* which includes *Christmas Eve, The Fair at Sorochinsk,* and *A Night in May. Christmas Eve* is the source of the following operas: Nikolai Afansiev's *Christmas Eve Revels,* RIMSKY-KORSAKOV's *Christmas Eve,* and TCHAIKOVSKY's *Vakula. The Fair at Sorochinsk* is the source of MUSSORGSKY's unfinished opera of the same title. *A Night in May* was used by Rimsky-Korsakov for his opera of the same name and by Lissenko for *The Drowned Woman.* ROSENBERG's opera *The Portrait* is based on a story of the same title, as is SEARLE's *The Diary of a Madman.*

Other operas based on Gogol include *The Inspector General,* or DER REVISOR (EGK, Karel Weis, Jenö Zádor) ; THE MARRIAGE (GRETCHANINOV, MARTINU, Mussorgsky) ; THE NOSE; and *Taras Bulba* (Afansiev, Lissenko) .

Golaud, King Arkel's grandson (baritone) in DEBUSSY's PELLÉAS ET MÉLISANDE.

Golden Cockerel, The, see COQ D'OR, LE.

goldene Kreuz, Das (The Golden Cross), opera in two acts by Ignaz BRÜLL. Libretto by Salomon Hermann MOSENTHAL, based on the play *Cathérine* by MÉLESVILLE and Brazier. Premiere: Berlin Opera, Dec. 22, 1875. American premiere: New York City, July 19, 1879. Christina, heartbroken that her brother Colas must go off to war, offers herself to any man serving as his substitute. A nobleman, Gontran de l'Ancre, acts as the substitute and receives from Christina a golden cross as token of her pledge. Three years later, Gontran returns from the war, wounded. The golden cross becomes the means through which he wins Christina as his wife.

Goldmark, Karl, composer. Born Keszthely, Hungary, May 18, 1830; died Vienna, Jan. 2, 1915. After preliminary study of the violin and composition he attended the Vienna Conservatory. His studies there were aborted by the revolution of 1848, which for a time closed the school. For a while he earned his living playing the violin in Viennese theaters, teaching the piano, and writing music criticism. Two concerts of his works, one in Vienna, the other in Budapest, failed to lift him out of poverty and obscurity. Success finally came with his finest work, the opera THE QUEEN OF SHEBA introduced at the VIENNA (ROYAL) OPERA in 1875 to such acclaim that within a few years it was given almost three hundred times in Vienna alone. By 1885 it had been performed in most of Europe's leading opera houses, as well as at the METROPOLITAN OPERA. Goldmark subsequently wrote several other operas, the most famous being THE CRICKET ON THE HEARTH, in 1896. The others: *Merlin* (1886) ; *Der Fremdling* (1897) ; *Die Kriegsgefangene* (1899) ; *Götz von Berlichingen* (1902) ; *A Winter's Tale (Ein Wintermärchen,* 1908) .

Goldoni, Carlo, dramatist and librettist. Born Venice, Feb. 25, 1707; died Versailles, Jan. 6, 1793. Immensely popular in his day, Goldoni wrote some hundred and fifty plays and opera librettos. Some of the latter were *L'amore artigiano* (Florian Gassmann) ; *L'Arcadia in Brenta* (GALUPPI) ; *Il conte Caramella* (Galuppi) ; IL FILOSOFO DI CAMPAGNA; *Il mondo alla roversa* (Galuppi) ; *Il mondo della luna* (Galuppi; HAYDN) ; LO SPEZIALE; *Il tigrane* (GLUCK) . Comedies of Goldoni from which operas were made include *Il ciarlone* (PAISIELLO) ; LE DONNE CURIOSE; *I due litiganti* (SARTI) ; *Le gelosie villane* (Sarti) ; *La lacondiero* (MARTINU) ; I QUATTRO RUSTEGHI; *The Servant of Two Masters* (Vittorio GIANNINI) ; *Tre commedie Goldoniane: La bottega di caffe, Sior Todero Brontolon, Le baruffe chiozzotte* (MALIPIERO) ; *Vittorina* (PICCINNI) .

Goldovsky, Boris, opera director and teacher. Born Moscow, June 7, 1908. He is the son of the violinist Lea Luboschutz. He attended the Moscow Conservatory and the Budapest Academy. In 1930 he came to the United States, where he studied conducting at the

Curtis Institute and became an American citizen. He has served as head of the opera departments of the Cleveland Institute of Music, the New England Conservatory, and the Berkshire Music Center. Since 1946 he has been head of the New England Opera Theater, a commentator for the radio broadcasts of the METROPOLITAN OPERA, and the founder and director of the Goldovsky Grand Opera Theater, a touring opera company.

Goldsmith, Oliver, poet, playwright, novelist. Born Elphin, Eng., Nov. 10, 1728; died London, Apr. 4, 1774. Goldsmith's famous play *She Stoops to Conquer* was adapted for an opera of the same name by George MACFARREN. Liza Lehmann's *The Vicar of Wakefield* and Victor Pelissier's *Edwin and Angelina* were also derived from Goldsmith's works.

Golem, a ghostly figure representing man, said by legend to have been created in the middle ages by Reb Low of Prague. Two operas have been written on this subject: D'ALBERT's *Der Golem,* introduced in Frankfurt in 1926, and Abraham Ellstein's *The Golem,* performed by the NEW YORK CITY OPERA on Mar. 22, 1962.

Gomes, Carlos, composer. Born Campinas, Brazil, July 11, 1836; died Belem, Sept. 16, 1896. He was Brazil's most famous opera composer in the nineteenth century. His first opera was *A noite do Castelo* in 1861, for which he received official honors; a second opera, *Joana de Flandres* in 1863, won him a scholarship to Italy, where his operatic writing became strongly influenced by Italian traditions and style. His most famous opera was IL GUARANY, which had a spectacular success when introduced at LA SCALA on Mar. 19, 1870. It was subsequently produced throughout the operatic world, reaching the United States (San Francisco) in 1884. Among his other successful operas were *Salvator Rosa* (1874), *Maria Tudor* (1879), and *O escravo* (1889).

Göntest du mir wohl, the song of the forest bird that tells Siegfried about the dragon, Fafner, who guards the Tarnhelm and the Ring, in Act II of WAGNER's SIEGFRIED.

Gonzalve, Concepcion's lover (tenor) in RAVEL's L'HEURE ESPAGNOLE.

Good Friday Spell (Charfreitagszauber), music describing the radiance of the countryside on Good Friday in Act III, Scene 1, of WAGNER's PARSIFAL, as Parsifal is being bathed in preparation for his entrance into the Grail castle.

Good-Night Quartet, *see* SCHLAFE WOHL.

Good Soldier Schweik, The, opera in two acts by Robert Kurka. Libretto by Lewis Allen, based on a novel by Jaroslav Hasek. Premiere: New York City Opera, Apr. 23, 1958. The source of this amusing opera is one of the most celebrated satirical novels published in Eastern Europe in the post-World War I period. Its central character is a humble soldier who is a thorough simpleton, though a kindly fellow, who goes through all kinds of absurd adventures pointing up the stupidity of military bureaucracy and war in general. The brightness and sparkle of Kurka's music, with its frequent exploitation of irony and astringent sounds, make it difficult for us to believe that he could write a score like this while knowing he was dying from leukemia. He expended Herculean energy trying to complete his opera before his death, managing to write the entire vocal score and about three hundred and fifty pages of orchestration (scored exclusively for wind instruments and percussion). He also indicated in red pencil his ideas on how the rest of the work should be orchestrated, a job accomplished for him by his friend Hershy Kay. The high standard established by the composer in this comic opera provides testimony that opera probably lost a highly gifted creator when Kurka died at the age of thirty-five. *The Good Soldier Schweik* was given its first European performance in Oct., 1959, by the DRESDEN (STATE) OPERA. It was mounted soon after that by the STOCKHOLM OPERA and the KOMISCHE OPER in Berlin.

Goose Girl, The, principal female character (soprano) in HUMPERDINCK'S DIE KÖNIGSKINDER.

Goossens, Eugene, composer and conductor, the third conductor of that name. Born London, May 26, 1893; died London, June 13, 1962. The first Eugène Goossens (1845–1906) conducted opera performances in Belgium, France, Italy, and (after 1873) England; he was the first conductor of the CARL ROSA OPERA COMPANY. His son Eugene (1867–1958) was also a conductor of the Carl Rosa Opera. The third Eugene Goossens studied music at the Bruges Conservatory, the Liverpool College of Music, and the Royal College of Music in London. He received recognition as a conductor in 1916, when he led the premiere of Charles STANFORD'S opera *The Critic.* He now appeared as guest conductor with many leading English musical organizations, including the Carl Rosa Opera Company. In 1923 he came to the United States, where for eight years he was musical director of the Rochester Philharmonic and for sixteen years of the Cincinnati Symphony. In 1947 he went to Australia to become conductor of the Sydney Symphony and director of the South Wales Conservatory. He was knighted in June, 1955. He wrote several operas: JUDITH (1929); *Don Juan de Mañara,* produced at COVENT GARDEN on June 24, 1937; and *Gainsborough.* In 1951 he published his autobiography, *Overtures and Beginners: A Musical Autobiography.*

gopak, see HOPAK.

Gorislava, Ratmir's beloved (soprano) in GLINKA'S RUSSLAN AND LUDMILLA.

Gorky (or Gorki), Maxim (born Aleksei Peshkov), author. Born Nizhni-Novgorod (now Gorki), Mar. 28, 1868; died Moscow, June 18, 1936. Raoul Gunsbourg's opera *Le Vieil Aigle,* Giacomo Orefice's *Radda,* and Valery Zhelebinsky's *The Mother* were derived from Gorky's works.

Gormas, Count de, Chimène's father (baritone) in MASSENET'S LE CID.

Goro, marriage broker (tenor) in PUCCINI'S MADAMA BUTTERFLY.

Gossec, François-Joseph, composer. Born

Vergnies, Belgium, Jan. 17, 1734; died Passy, France, Feb. 16, 1829. After serving as chorister at the Antwerp Cathedral and studying the violin, he went to Paris in 1751, where RAMEAU placed him in the employ of La Pouplinière as conductor of his orchestra. His first success as an opera composer came in 1766 with *Les Pêcheurs,* successfully given at the Théâtre des Italiens. In 1770 he founded the Concert des Amateurs; from 1773 to 1777 he conducted the Concert Spirituel; and from 1780 to 1782 he was second conductor at the OPÉRA. He organized the École Royale de Chant in 1784, and eleven years later he became the first director of the Paris Conservatory, as well as a professor of composition. He was a prolific composer, his works including fifteen operas, none of which has survived. (He is remembered chiefly for a trifle, a GAVOTTE, found in his opera *Rosine.*) He was, however, a major figure in the development of symphonic and chamber music and the art of orchestration. His finest operas were *Les Pêcheurs* (1766); *Sabinus* (1773); *Hylas et Sylvie* (1776); *La Fête du village* (1778); *Thésée* (1782); *Rosine* (1786); *Les Sabots et le cerisier* (1803).

Götterdämmerung, see RING DES NIBELUNGEN, DER.

Gottfried, Elsa's brother, transformed into a swan, in WAGNER'S LOHENGRIN.

Gott grüss euch, the King's greeting to his people in the opening scene of WAGNER'S LOHENGRIN.

Gotthold, the hero (tenor) and the beloved of Leonore in DITTERSDORF'S THE DOCTOR AND THE APOTHECARY.

Götz von Berlichingen, see GOETHE, JOHANN WOLFGANG VON.

Gounod, Charles François, composer. Born Paris, June 17, 1818; died there, Oct. 18, 1893. A major figure in French opera of the nineteenth century, he attended the Paris Conservatory, where his teachers included Jacques HALÉVY and Jean François LESUEUR and where, in 1839, he won the PRIX DE ROME. In Italy he became passionately interested in church music. After he returned to

Paris he became a church organist and wrote choral music. During a fortuitous meeting with the opera singer Pauline VIARDOT, he was asked to write an opera. That work was SAPHO, introduced at the OPÉRA on Apr. 16, 1851, with Viardot in the title role. Though it was a failure, Gounod did not lose interest in the stage. He kept on writing operas, and his fourth was the work that made him famous: FAUST, given at the THÉÂTRE LYRIQUE on Mar. 19, 1859. At first only moderately successful, *Faust* became world famous after a triumphant revival at the Opéra in 1869. After *Faust,* Gounod wrote eight operas, only two of which were successful: MIREILLE (1864) and ROMÉO ET JULIETTE (1867).

Between 1852 and 1860 Gounod directed a Parisian choral society, the Orphéon. This association revived his interest in religious choral music, and he wrote a great deal of diversified music in this field, including the celebrated "Ave Maria" and several masses and oratorios. At the outbreak of the Franco-Prussian War, Gounod settled in London, where he lived for five years and appeared as conductor. He returned to Paris in 1875, increasingly absorbed in religious music; he produced little secular music after 1881.

Gounod helped create a restrained and sensitive operatic art that was filled with human values and parted company with the more ornate products of MEYERBEER and his imitators. Unlike his contemporaries BIZET and Halévy, he lacked an instinct for good theater, but he was a fine melodist, the creator of a refined and expressive lyricism supported by a sensitive harmony and orchestration.

His operas: *Sapho* (1851) ; *La Nonne sanglante* (1854) ; LE MÉDECIN MALGRÉ LUI (1858) ; *Faust* (1859) ; PHILÉMON ET BAUCIS (1860) ; LA REINE DE SABA (1862) ; *Mireille* (1864) ; *La Colombe* (1866) ; *Roméo et Juliette* (1867) ; *Cinq-Mars* (1877) ; POLYEUCTE (1878) ; *Le Tribut de Zamora* (1881) ; and *Maître Pierre,* which was left unfinished.

Goyescas, opera in three scenes by GRANADOS. Libretto by Fernando Peri-

quet, suggested by settings and characters in Goya's paintings. Premiere: Metropolitan Opera, Jan. 28, 1916. In 1912 Granados completed two sets of piano pieces entitled *Goyescas,* each piece a musical interpretation of a scene from a Goya painting or tapestry. Almost as soon as he had this work performed, the composer realized that the Goya period in Madrid and some of the piano pieces it had inspired could serve as the basis of an operatic score. He proceeded to write that score before the text was written, and only when his music was completed did Periquet go to work building a libretto for it.

Don Fernando, captain of the guards (a role created by MARTINELLI), is in love with Rosario. When he learns that Rosario has been invited to a ball by a toreador, Paquiro, he is so overcome with jealousy that he decides to invade the ball. There Paquiro challenges him to a duel. Wounded fatally, Don Fernando dies in his beloved's arms.

Granados' music makes skillful use of Spanish dances. One of the instrumental numbers is particularly famous, the INTERMEZZO, which the composer wrote after his score was completed on the suggestion of the directors of the METROPOLITAN OPERA. One of the arias is almost as famous. It is "The Lover and the Nightingale," heard in the second scene. The first staged revival of the opera in the United States took place in New York in 1969 at the Manhattan College of Music.

Gozzi, Carlo, dramatist. Born Venice, Dec. 13, 1720; died Venice, Apr. 14, 1806. He was celebrated for his satires and fairy pieces in Venetian dialect, many of them written to ridicule rival writers. His plays have frequently been adapted as operas, notably LA DONNA SERPENTE (CASELLA; DIE FEEN); *Fiaba dell' amore delle tre melarancie* (THE LOVE FOR THREE ORANGES); *Il re cèrvo* (KÖNIG HIRSCH); and TURANDOT (Antonio Bazzini, BUSONI, Adolph Jensen, PUCCINI, and Karl Reissiger).

Graener, Paul, composer. Born Berlin, Jan. 11, 1872; died Salzburg, Nov. 13,

1944. After studying at Veit's Conservatory in Berlin, he earned his living conducting orchestras in small German theaters. In 1896 he settled in London, conducting the orchestra of the Haymarket Theatre and teaching at the Royal Academy of Music. In 1908 he became head of the New Conservatory in Vienna, and two years later, director of the Mozarteum in Salzburg. In 1920 he was appointed professor of composition at the Leipzig Conservatory, succeeding Max Reger. From 1930 to 1934 he was director of the Stern Conservatory in Berlin. His operas are representative of his style, in which, as Hugo Leichtentritt once wrote, "the naive expression and the simple charm of the folksong has been deeply felt . . . and has been the source of some of his finest inspiration." His operas: *Das Narrengericht* (1913); *Don Juans letztes Abenteuer* (1914); *Theophano*, rewritten as *Byzanz* (1918); *Schirin und Getraude* (1920); *Hanneles Himmelfahrt* (1927); *Friedemann Bach* (1931); *Der Prinz von Homburg* (1935).

Graf, Herbert, stage director. Born Vienna, Apr. 10, 1904. The son of a famous Austrian music critic, Max Graf, he was early directed to music. He attended Vienna University, where he received his doctorate in 1928. He then studied music and stage techniques at the Vienna Academy, following which he became stage director of the Münster Opera. For three years he served in a similar capacity in Breslau and for three additional years in Frankfurt. In 1934 he came to the United States, where he joined the Philadelphia Opera Company. In 1936 he became stage director of the METROPOLITAN OPERA, remaining there until 1960. He also served as stage director for the SAN FRANCISCO OPERA, LA SCALA, VIENNA STATE OPERA, COVENT GARDEN, and for opera performances at such major European festivals as those at SALZBURG, FLORENCE, and HOLLAND. Between 1960 and 1963 he was artistic director of the ZÜRICH OPERA and since 1965 has been artistic director of the GENEVA OPERA. He is the author of *The*

Opera and Its Future in America (1941) and *Producing Opera in America* (1964).

Gralserzählung, *see* IN FERNEM LAND.

Granados, Enrique, pianist and composer. Born Lérida, Spain, July 29, 1867; died at sea, Mar. 24, 1916. He early came under the influence of Felipe Pedrell, who directed him to the writing of Spanish national music. In his twentieth year he went to Paris, where he stayed for two years studying the piano. Back in Spain, he began writing piano music so strongly national in style and technique that he is considered by many the father of modern Spanish music. He wrote his first opera, *María del Carmen,* in 1898, and successfully introduced it in Madrid the same year. GOYESCAS, his most famous opera, was worked up from two volumes of piano pieces. Granados came to America to attend the world premiere of this work at the METROPOLITAN OPERA in 1916. Invited to play for President Wilson at the White House, he delayed his return to Spain by one week. Returning aboard the *Sussex,* he drowned when the ship was torpedoed by a German submarine in the English Channel. Other operas by Granados: *Picarol* (1901); *Follet* (1903); *Gaziel* (1906); *Liliana* (1911).

Grandi, Margherita, soprano. Born Hobart, Tasmania, Oct. 10, 1899. Her principal vocal teacher was Giannina Russ. In 1932 she made her opera debut in Milan in AIDA, subsequent to which she was contracted to appear in opera houses throughout Italy. In 1939 she was starred as Lady Macbeth in a revival of VERDI'S MACBETH at the GLYNDEBOURNE FESTIVAL, and in 1949 she created the part of Diana in BLISS'S OLYMPIANS. She possessed great dramatic powers as well as vocal gifts and is particularly famous for her interpretations of Lady Macbeth and TOSCA.

grand opera, an opera with a serious theme and no spoken dialogue. The distinction is made between grand opera and other types such as light opera, OPÉRA COMIQUE, and OPERA BUFFA.

Grands dieux du destin, the prayer of Alceste to the god Apollo to save the life of her dying husband in Act I of GLUCK'S ALCESTE.

Grane, Brünnhilde's horse in WAGNER'S DIE GÖTTERDÄMMERUNG.

Grassini, Josephina (or GIUSEPPINA), contralto. Born Varese, Italy, 1773; died Milan, Jan. 3, 1850. After studying at the Milan Conservatory, she made her opera debut at the Ducal Theater in Parma in 1789. For the next few years she appeared in Italian comic operas. In 1792 she turned to serious opera, and in 1794 was a triumphant success in Milan. Napoleon heard her in a special concert and engaged her for the PARIS OPÉRA, where she created a furor at her debut on July 22, 1800. She then sang in London and again in Paris. For a number of years she was popular at the French court. She was nearly sixty when Paris heard her for the last time. A highly successful teacher, her pupils included Giuditta PASTA and the sisters Giuditta and Giulia GRISI (the latter were Grassini's nieces).

Grau, Maurice, opera manager. Born Brünn, Moravia, 1849; died Paris, Mar. 14, 1907. He was brought to the United States as a child, and here he received his academic education. In 1872 he became an impresario, managing the first American tour of Anton RUBINSTEIN. Subsequently he managed the American tours of many notable European musical and dramatic personalities, including OFFENBACH, Wieniawski, Salvini, and Bernhardt. In 1890, in collaboration with Henry ABBEY, he produced a season of opera at the METROPOLITAN OPERA, giving twenty-one performances. The following year he joined Abbey and Edward Schoeffel in leasing the Metropolitan Opera House and presenting opera there for the next six years. In 1897 he became sole manager, holding this post with great distinction until 1903. He created such a high standard of performance that his era has since become known as the "golden age of opera." He brought to New York such outstanding personalities as the DE RESZKE brothers, MAUREL, PLANÇON, MELBA, EAMES, and CALVÉ; he helped

make stars of NORDICA, SEMBRICH, and CAMPANARI. He was a pioneer in giving American audiences operas in their original languages, was responsible for the first uncut performances of the WAGNER music dramas in America, and he managed many notable American premieres, one being TOSCA. He retired in 1903 and spent the last years of his life in a small town near Paris.

Graun, Karl Heinrich, singer and composer. Born Wahrenbrück, Saxony, May 7, 1701; died Berlin, Aug. 8, 1759. As a child he studied music at the Dresden Kreuzschule and sang publicly. In 1725 he became principal tenor at the Brunswick Opera, where he was soon elevated to the post of assistant KAPELLMEISTER and where he wrote his first opera, *Pollidoro,* a great success in 1726. In 1735 he became *kapellmeister* to Crown Prince Frederick at Rheinsberg; when Frederick became Emperor, Graun was appointed *kapellmeister* and opera director in Berlin. He secured the services of outstanding artists of Italy and Germany and maintained a high level of performance. Some thirty of his operas were produced in Berlin, making him one of the most celebrated composers of his generation. His best-known operas were *Scipio Africanus* (1732); *Timareta* (1733); *Pharao Tubaetes* (1735); *Rodelinda* (1741); *Catone in Utica* (1744); *Adriano in Siria* (1745); *Mitridate* (1750); *Ezio* (1755); *Montezuma* (1755); *Merope* (1756).

Graupner, Christoph, composer. Born Hartmannsdorf, Saxony, Jan. 13, 1683; died Darmstadt, May 10, 1760. The major part of his music study took place at the Thomasschule in Leipzig. He went to Hamburg in 1706, where he served as accompanist at the Opera. Four years later he went to Darmstadt as KAPELLMEISTER, gaining considerable prestige there both as director of musical performances and as composer. He was extraordinarily fertile, producing over a thousand works of all kinds, including nine operas. In 1722 he was invited to take over the post of cantor at the Thomasschule. Too successful in

Darmstadt to be interested in a change, he turned down the offer, which was then made available to Johann Sebastian Bach. His finest operas: *Dido* (1707); *Hercules und Theseus* (1708); *Bellerophon* (1709); *Simson* (1709); *Berenice und Lucio* (1710); *Telemach* (1711).

Grech, a police officer (bass) in GIORDANO'S FEDORA.

Greek Passion, The, opera in four acts by MARTINU. Libretto by the composer, based on the novel by Nikos Kazantzakis. Premiere: Zürich Opera, June 9, 1961. The text comes from the novel, which Jules Dassin also made into a famous French motion picture entitled *He Who Must Die.* The setting is a Greek village, where a bitter conflict arises between the villagers (many of whom are preparing to appear in a Passion play) and a group of Greek refugees escaping Turkish persecution. The priest and many of the villagers refuse to give these refugees shelter, but some of the Passion players side with the derelicts and thereby themselves become outcasts. The opera ends tragically with the assassination of a shepherd (chosen to play Christ in the play) by a blacksmith (who was to have appeared as Judas).

In his music Martinu skillfully uses both Czech and Greek styles, the better to identify the two conflicting forces in the play. Though the dramatic element is pronounced in Martinu's writing, the opera is richly melodic, with numerous pages of expressive vocal writing for both solo voices and chorus.

Green leaves are we, chorus of the people in praise of Queen Elizabeth I at the opening of BRITTEN'S GLORIANA.

Greensleeves, a celebrated English folksong, used by VAUGHAN WILLIAMS in his opera SIR JOHN IN LOVE.

Gregorio, a kinsman (baritone) of Capulet in GOUNOD'S ROMÉO ET JULIETTE.

Gregory, the Pretender Dmitri (tenor) in MUSSORGSKY'S BORIS GODUNOV.

Gremin, Prince, Tatiana's husband (bass) in TCHAIKOVSKY'S EUGENE ONEGIN.

Grenvil, Dr., a physician (bass) in VERDI'S LA TRAVIATA.

Gretchaninov, Alexander, composer. Born Moscow, Oct. 25, 1864; died New York City, Jan. 3, 1956. His musical education took place at the conservatories of Moscow and St. Petersburg. He made his bow as a composer with a symphony, conducted by RIMSKY-KORSAKOV in 1895. In 1901 he completed his first opera, *Dobrinya Nikitich,* produced in Moscow on Oct. 17, 1903, with CHALIAPIN in the title role. It was well received. In 1925 Gretchaninov left Russia and for several years lived in Paris; during this period he made several concert tours of the United States. In 1939 he settled permanently in New York. He wrote an autobiography, *My Life* (1952). His operas: *Dobrinya Nikitich* (1901); *Sister Beatrice* (1910); *The Dream of a Little Christmas Tree,* children's opera (1911); *The Castle House,* children's opera (1911); *The Cat, the Fox, and the Rooster,* children's opera (1919); *The Marriage* (1946).

Gretel, Hansel's sister (soprano) in HUMPERDINCK'S HANSEL AND GRETEL.

Grétry, André Ernest, composer. Born Liège, Belgium, Feb. 8, 1741; died Montmorency, France, Sept. 24, 1813. He was one of the most significant composers of OPÉRA COMIQUE in the late eighteenth century. While still a boy he heard a performance of LA SERVA PADRONA that so enchanted him that he decided to dedicate his life to writing operas in the style of PERGOLESI. After a period of study with Giovanni Battista Casali in Italy, Grétry wrote his first opera, *La vendemmiatrice,* given successfully in Rome in 1765. Returning to Paris three years later, he acquired the patronage of the Swedish ambassador, with whose help his opera *Le Huron* was put on in 1768. Grétry now wrote operas prolifically: within twenty years more than fifty. When the Revolution broke out, Grétry allied himself with the proletariat and wrote several popular works reflecting the new ideology. The municipality of Paris named a street after him and later placed his statue in the OPÉRA-COMIQUE. When the Paris Conservatory was founded, Grétry became an inspector; with the inauguration of the Institut de France, he was chosen a member. The monarchy restored, Grétry flexibly changed his allegiance and remained a powerful and popular figure in French music. Napoleon III honored him with a pension and with the Legion of Honor. Grétry lived the last years of his life in the home formerly inhabited by Jean Jacques ROUSSEAU, L'Eremitage in Montmorency.

In his theoretical writings Grétry anticipated by a century some of WAGNER's ideas about an opera theater: one with a curved stage so that the action might be visible from all parts of the house; with an orchestra completely concealed from view; with seats of only a single class, and no boxes. Grétry's most successful operas were *Le Tableau parlant* (1769); *Les Deux Avares* (1770); ZÉMIRE ET AZOR (1771); *Céphale et Procris* (1775); *La Fausse magie* (1775); *L'Amant jaloux* (1778); *L'Epreuve villageoise* (1784); RICHARD COEUR DE LION (1784); *La Caravane du Caire* (1784); *Amphitryon* (1788); *La Rosière républicaine* (1793).

Grieve my heart, Rezia's aria in Act III, Scene 2, of WEBER's OBERON, expressing her distress at finding herself a slave in the Emir's palace.

Griffelkin, fantasy in three acts by FOSS. Libretto by Alastair Reid, based on a German fairy tale. Premiere: NBC-TV, Nov. 6, 1955; Tanglewood, Lenox, Mass., Aug. 6, 1956 (staged). Griffelkin is a devil celebrating his tenth birthday. The gift of a magic liquid makes it possible for him to come to earth for a day. This same liquid is able to turn live people to stone and vice versa; with it Griffelkin transforms inanimate stone objects into living beings. He meets and falls in love with a girl, the first one to teach him the meaning of love and pity. Utilizing the last drops of his magic liquid he saves the life of the girl's mother. This is regarded by the other devils as heresy, for which he is banished from hell and forced to lead the life of a normal boy in the household of the mother he had saved and the girl he loves.

This little operatic escapade was commissioned for television by NBC. In the music simplicity is the keynote. Operatic tradition is adhered to through the use of formal arias, duets, and choral numbers. Foss occasionally makes delightful excursions into humor, satire, and parody, as when he parodies MOZART's C major *Piano Sonata* in one of the bravura arias.

Grilletta, a young lady (soprano), the ward of Sempronio, who wishes to marry her, in HAYDN's comic opera LO SPEZIALE.

Grimaldi, Nicola, *see* NICOLINI.

Grimaldo, Enzo, Genoese nobleman (tenor) in love with Laura in PONCHIELLI's LA GIOCONDA.

Grimes, *see* PETER GRIMES.

Grimm, Friedrich Melchior, Baron von, writer. Born Ratisbon, Ger., Dec. 26, 1723; died Gotha, Dec. 18, 1807. Grimm fired the opening shot in the Parisian operatic war known as the GUERRE DES BOUFFONS in 1752. This consisted of a provocative letter published in the *Mercure de France* in which Grimm posed PERGOLESI's LA SERVA PADRONA as an example of true operatic art as opposed to the French operas of LULLY and RAMEAU. Two decades later, however, Grimm sided with GLUCK in that composer's rivalry with PICCINNI in Paris. Grimm was also editor of the *Correspondence littéraire, philosophique et critique.* This circulated in manuscript during the years 1753–1790. Published in sixteen volumes a century later, the *Correspondence* provides valuable information about the history of opera in Paris.

Grimm, Jakob Ludwig, writer and philologist. Born Hanau, Ger., Jan. 4, 1785; died Berlin, Sept. 20, 1863. With his brother Wilhelm he collected, wrote, and published volumes of German fairy tales entitled *Kinder und Hausmärchen* (1812, 1815). These are known and loved throughout the world. HUMPERDINCK's HANSEL AND GRETEL, ORFF's DIE KLUGE and DER MOND, Hugo Kaun's *Der*

Fremde, Theodore Chanler's *The Pot of Fat,* and Leon Stein's *The Fisherman's Wife* are operas derived from these tales.

Grisélidis, opera in prologue and three acts by MASSENET. Libretto by Paul Armand Silvestre and Eugène Morand. Premiere: Opéra-Comique, Nov. 20, 1901. American premiere: Manhattan Opera, Jan. 19, 1910. The setting is Provence in the fourteenth century. The shepherd Alain loves Grisélidis, who is married to the Marquis. When the Marquis goes to war, the devil tries to convince Grisélidis of her husband's infidelity and suggests that she avenge herself by taking Alain as a lover. Grisélidis resists the devil, who then disappears with her child. Back from the war, the Marquis is at first suspicious about his wife's fidelity, but eventually he learns the truth and is able to retrieve their child from the devil. Among the best arias are "Devant le soleil," sung by Grisélidis in Act I; and in Act II, "Il partit du printemps" (Grisélidis), "Loin de sa femme" (the devil), and "Je suis l'oiseau" (Alain).

Grisi, Giulia, soprano. Born Milan, July 28, 1811; died Berlin, Nov. 29, 1869. One of the most celebrated opera stars of her generation, she came from a family of celebrated artists. Her older sister Giuditta and her aunt GRASSINI were celebrated singers; her cousin Carlotta was a famous dancer. After studying singing with various teachers, she made her debut in Milan in 1828 in ROSSINI's *Zelmira.* She was acclaimed, and for the next three seasons she continued to appear in Milan. Dissatisfied with conditions there, she broke her contract and went to Paris. Here she made her first appearance at the Théâtre des Italiens on Oct. 16, 1832, in SEMIRAMIDE under the composer's direction. She remained at the Théâtre des Italiens for the next seventeen years, adored by Parisian opera-goers. In 1833 she visited Venice to appear in I CAPULETTI ED I MONTECCHI, which the composer wrote for her and her sister— Giuditta to sing the role of Romeo and

Giulia that of Juliet. In 1834 she made her London debut in LA GAZZA LADRA; with the exception of a single season she appeared regularly in London for the next twenty-seven years, a reigning favorite. She created the role of Norina in DON PASQUALE in 1843. In 1854 she toured the United States with the tenor MARIO, whom she had married a decade earlier. She went into temporary retirement in 1861, but six years later returned briefly to the opera stage in London. Following this, she sang in concerts. DONIZETTI wrote his *Don Pasquale* for a quartet of singers, one of whom was Grisi. Grisi was also one of four singers for whom BELLINI wrote I PURITANI.

Gritzko, a peasant (tenor) in MUSSORGSKY's THE FAIR AT SOROCHINSK.

Grossmächtige Prinzessin, *see* SO WAR ES MIT PAGLIAZZO.

Gruenberg, Louis, composer. Born Brest-Litovsk, Russia, Aug. 3, 1884; died Los Angeles, June 9, 1964. He came to the United States as an infant. After studying the piano with Adele Margulies, he returned to Europe in 1903 for further music study with Ferrucio BUSONI and at the Vienna Conservatory. Between 1912 and 1913 he wrote two operas, *The Witch of Brocken* and *The Bridge of the Gods,* and a symphonic poem, *The Hill of Dreams,* that won a thousand-dollar prize. In 1919 he returned to the United States and soon completed an opera based on a play by Anatole FRANCE, *The Man Who Married a Dumb Wife.* Failing to secure permission for the use of this play, Gruenberg was denied the rights to have his opera published or performed. In the 1920's he interested himself in the jazz style, producing several serious works in this vein. His most important work is his opera THE EMPEROR JONES, introduced at the METROPOLITAN OPERA on Jan. 7, 1933. He also wrote a radio opera, *Green Mansions,* and two three-act operas, *Volpone* and *Antony and Cleopatra,* the last of which he regarded as one of his most significant achievements. Gruenberg wrote extensively for motion pictures, three of his scores winning Academy Awards.

Guadagni, Gaetano, CASTRATO soprano. Born Lodi, Italy, c. 1725; died Padua, Nov., 1792. After making his debut in Padua in 1747, he went to London and scored a phenomenal success there between 1748 and 1754. During this period he was heard in HANDEL's oratorios *Messiah* and *Samson*. After a period of study with Gioacchino Gizziello in Lisbon, he made several sensational tours of Europe. He was in Vienna in 1762, and there appeared in the first performance of GLUCK's ORFEO ED EURIDICE. After 1770 he sang at the court of the Elector of Munich, and in 1774 he settled in Padua. Gluck rewrote *Telemaco* for him.

Guarany, Il, Brazilian national opera in four acts by GOMES. Libretto by the composer, based on a novel by José Alencar. Premiere: La Scala, Mar. 19, 1870. American premiere: San Francisco, Aug. 27, 1884. This is the only nineteenth-century opera by a South American composer that has appeared in the repertory of several leading opera houses. The central figure of the opera is an Indian of the Guarani tribe. Though the composer utilizes Amazon Indian melodies and rhythms, his style is basically Italian in the tradition of VERDI. The overture and the ballet music are often represented on popular and summer concert programs. The principal vocal numbers are "Gentile di cuore" for soprano and the duet for soprano and tenor, "Sento una forz indomita," in Act I; the soprano *ballata*, "O come e bello il ciel," and the bass aria, "Senza tetto," in Act II.

Guardiano, Padre, an abbot (bass) in VERDI's LA FORZA DEL DESTINO.

Guarrera, Frank, baritone. Born Philadelphia, Dec. 3, 1923. He attended the Curtis Institute on a scholarship, the youngest member ever admitted to the vocal department. His vocal studies were completed at the Berkshire Music Center at TANGLEWOOD, where he appeared in a performance of IDOMENEO. His official debut in opera took place with the NEW YORK CITY OPERA on Oct. 25,

1947, as Silvio in PAGLIACCI. In 1948 TOSCANINI invited him to appear at LA SCALA in a BOITO festival, where he also was heard in operas by other composers. His debut at the METROPOLITAN OPERA took place on Dec. 14, 1948, as Escamillo in CARMEN. He has remained a permanent member of that company, appearing in over twenty leading baritone roles and acclaimed particularly for his interpretations of Figaro in ROSSINI's THE BARBER OF SEVILLE, Count Almaviva in THE MARRIAGE OF FIGARO, Count DI LUNA, ESCAMILLO, and RIGOLETTO.

Gueden, Hilde, soprano. Born Vienna, Sept. 15, 1917. After preliminary music study in Vienna, she received intensive training in singing in Milan, Rome, and Paris. Her debut took place in 1939 at the ZÜRICH OPERA, where she appeared as CHERUBINO. After two years in Zürich, she assumed principal soprano roles at the BERLIN OPERA and the MUNICH OPERA, where she scored major successes in operas of MOZART and Richard STRAUSS. In 1942 she was engaged by the Royal Opera of Rome, making her debut there in the role of Sophie in DER ROSENKAVALIER. During the German occupation of Italy, Gueden withdrew from public appearances, living in temporary retirement in Venice and near Milan. After the war, she was heard at LA SCALA, the VIENNA STATE OPERA, the Royal Opera of Rome, COVENT GARDEN, and at several SALZBURG and EDINBURGH festivals. Her American opera debut took place at the METROPOLITAN OPERA on Nov. 15, 1951, when she sang GILDA; she appeared there in subsequent seasons not only in the traditional repertory but in the American premiere of THE RAKE'S PROGRESS. Elsewhere she has appeared in such other twentieth-century operas as MATHIS DER MALER; ROMEO UND JULIA (she created the role of Julia); THE RAPE OF LUCRETIA; and THE RISE AND FALL OF THE CITY MAHAGONNY. She is universally recognized as a specialist in Mozart and Richard Strauss.

Guerre des Bouffons (The Buffoons' War), a musical war waged in Paris in 1752, precipitated by a performance by a visiting Italian company of LA SERVA PADRONA. Headed by Denis Diderot, Jean Jacques ROUSSEAU, and Friedrich GRIMM, among others, a cult arose proclaiming that PERGOLESI's art was the only true one for opera. The chief target of the attack was Jean Philippe RAMEAU, who had broken with Italian traditions by writing operas that emphasized the dramatic element and utilized advanced harmonic and orchestral writing.

Guglielmo, an officer (baritone) in love with Fiordiligi in MOZART's COSÌ FAN TUTTE.

Guglielmo Ratcliff, *see* WILLIAM RATCLIFF.

Gui, Vittorio, conductor. Born Rome, Sept. 14, 1885. He attended the Academy of Santa Cecilia, after which he made his baton debut in 1907 at the Teatro Adriano with LA GIOCONDA. After appearances in various Italian opera houses, he succeeded CAMPANINI as principal conductor of the SAN CARLO in Naples in 1910. In 1925 he was appointed music director of the Teatro Torino, where he helped inaugurate a vital repertory; under his direction, this opera house achieved national significance. In 1933 he became the principal conductor of the FLORENCE MAY MUSIC FESTIVAL and in 1938 a principal conductor at COVENT GARDEN. Since then he has made numerous appearances in England, including distinguished performances at the GLYNDEBOURNE FESTIVAL, where for several years he was Fritz BUSCH's successor as musical director; since 1951 he has been one of its principal conductors. He has also appeared frequently in guest performances with other leading opera companies.

Guido, commander of the Pisan army (bass) and husband of Monna Vanna in FÉVRIER's MONNA VANNA.

Guidon, Prince, King Dodon's son (tenor) in RIMSKY-KORSAKOV's LE COQ D'OR.

Guillaume Tell, *see* WILLIAM TELL.

Guiraud, Ernest, composer. Born New Orleans, June 23, 1837; died Paris, May 6, 1892. He studied with his father and in his fifteenth year wrote an opera, *Le Roi David,* performed in New Orleans. For several years he attended the Paris Conservatory, where he won the PRIX DE ROME. From 1876 to the time of his death he taught at the conservatory; his many pupils included DEBUSSY, André Gédalge, and Charles Martin Loeffler. In 1875 he was engaged to write accompanied recitatives for the dialogue passages of BIZET's CARMEN; it is in this form, as an opera, that *Carmen* is chiefly known. In France, however, Guiraud's recitatives are not used, and *Carmen* is still performed as an OPÉRA COMIQUE with spoken dialogue. Guiraud was involved in the completion of another world-famous opera: he finished the orchestration of THE TALES OF HOFFMANN when OFFENBACH, through illness, could not go on beyond Act I. Guiraud himself wrote the following operas: *Sylvie* (1864) ; *En Prison* (1869) ; *Le Kobold* (1870) ; *Madame Turlupin* (1872); *Piccolino* (1876); *La Galante aventure* (1882) ; *Frédégonde* (completed by SAINT-SAËNS, 1895) . In 1891 he succeeded DELIBES as a member of the Institut de France.

Gunther, king of the Gibichungs (baritone) in WAGNER's GÖTTERDÄMMERUNG.

Guntram, opera in three acts by Richard STRAUSS. Libretto by the composer. Premiere: Weimar Opera, May 10, 1894. This was Strauss's first opera; it was modeled after the Wagnerian music dramas, particularly those in the RING cycle. The action takes place in a German duchy of the thirteenth century. The tyrant, Duke Robert, is murdered by the minstrel Guntram. For this act Guntram is imprisoned. When Freihild, who is in love with Guntram, becomes ruler of the duchy, Guntram is freed; but because of Freihild's high station, he must renounce his love for her.

Gura, Eugen, baritone. Born Pressern, Bohemia, Nov. 8, 1842; died Aufkirchen, Bavaria, Aug. 26, 1906. After studies at the Munich Conservatory, he made his debut in Munich in 1865 in LORTZING's *Der Waffenschmied.* After two years with the MUNICH OPERA, he appeared with the Breslau Opera, and from 1870 to 1876 with the Leipzig Opera, where he was acclaimed one of the foremost German baritones of the day. In 1876 he appeared in the first complete performance of DER RING DES NIBELUNGEN at BAYREUTH. From 1876 to 1883 he was principal baritone of the HAMBURG OPERA and from 1883 to 1895 of the Munich Opera. He wrote his autobiography, *Erinnerungen aus meinem Leben,* in 1905. His son Hermann was also a noted Wagnerian baritone and served as director of the KOMISCHE OPER in Berlin and the Helsingfors Opera.

Gurnemanz, Knight of the Grail (bass) in WAGNER'S PARSIFAL.

Gustav Hinrichs Opera Company, *see* HINRICHS, GUSTAV.

Gustavus III, *see* RICCARDO.

Gutheil-Schoder, Marie, soprano. Born Weimar, Feb. 16, 1874; died there, Oct. 4, 1935. She studied singing with Virginia Gungl in Weimar, making her opera debut in that city in 1891. Acclaimed, she was immediately engaged by the WEIMAR OPERA, where she remained for nine years. In 1900 she made her debut at the Vienna Royal Opera. For the next twenty-six years she appeared in Vienna with outstanding success, particularly in such roles as SALOME, ELEKTRA, and CARMEN. In 1926 she retired as a singer and for a brief period served as a stage director.

Gut'n Abend, Meister, Eva's address to Hans Sachs in which she suggests coquettishly that if she cannot win Walther's love, she would accept that of Hans Sachs, in Act II of WAGNER'S DIE MEISTERSINGER.

Gutrune, Gunther's sister (soprano) in WAGNER'S DIE GÖTTERDÄMMERUNG.

Guy Mannering, *see* SCOTT, SIR WALTER.

Gwendoline, opera in two acts by CHABRIER. Libretto by Catulle MENDÈS, based on a medieval legend. Premiere: Théâtre de la Monnaie, Apr. 10, 1886. Harald, king of the Vikings, falls in love with Gwendoline, daughter of his captive, the Saxon Arnel. Arnel seemingly consents to their marriage, but arranges for Harald's murder by his bride. At the last moment she refuses to kill her husband. Eventually Arnel kills Harald and Gwendoline commits suicide. Chabrier's score was strongly influenced by WAGNER. The overture has acquired a permanent place in the French symphonic repertory. The core of the overture is the melody from the second-act love duet of Harald and Gwendoline.

Gypsy Baron, The (Der Zigeunerbaron), operetta in three acts by Johann STRAUSS THE YOUNGER. Libretto by Ignaz Schnitzer, based on a libretto by Maurus Jókai, derived from Jókai's story *Saffi.* Premiere: Theater-an-der-Wien, Vienna, Oct. 24, 1885. American premiere: Casino Theater, N.Y., Feb. 15, 1886. This operetta, besides being a staple in the musical theater, is sometimes performed in opera houses. The story concerns Sandor Barinkay (tenor), taken from his ancestral home as a child. Returning to it as a man, he finds it overrun with gypsies. He falls in love with Saffi. The overture is one of the most celebrated in semiclassical literature, combining Hungarian and Viennese styles, as does the rest of the operetta. It opens with gypsy music (used for the arrival of the gypsies in the first-act finale) and includes Saffi's (soprano) gypsy air, "So elend und treu." The climax of the overture is the famous second-act *Schatz,* or Treasure Waltz. The most popular vocal number in the score is Sandor's entrance number, "Ja, das alles auf Ehr'."

H

Hába, Alois, composer. Born Vzyovice, Moravia, June 21, 1893. An experimental composer who has specialized in MICROTONAL MUSIC, and particularly in quarter tones, Hába has written several operas in this idiom. He studied at the Prague Conservatory and after World War I privately with Franz SCHREKER. Hába began writing quartertone music in 1921. He founded a class in quarter-tone music at the Prague Conservatory, devised his own notation, and had instruments built capable of performing his works. His first opera, THE MOTHER, was in quarter tones. It was completed in 1929, and produced in Munich on May 17, 1931. *New Earth* (1935), however, was an opera in the traditional tonal system, and it was never produced. In the opera *Thy Kingdom Come* (1940), singers sing in sixth tones. His class in quarter tones at the Prague Conservatory was discontinued in 1948, and from then until 1953 he taught composition.

habanera, a slow dance in 2/4 time, said to have originated in Havana and long popular in Spain. The most familiar example in opera is Carmen's "L'amour est un oiseau rebelle" in BIZET'S CARMEN. RAVEL'S opera L'HEURE ESPAGNOLE ends with a habanera, a vocal quintet parodying the usual closing scene of Italian operas.

Habanera, La, opera in three acts by LAPARRA. Libretto by the composer. Premiere: Opéra-Comique, Feb. 26, 1908. American premiere: Boston, Dec. 14, 1910. The setting is Spain; Pedro (tenor) has married Pilar (soprano), but Pedro's brother, Ramon (bass), is in love with her. Jealous of Pilar's happiness as she dances a HABANERA with her bridegroom, Ramon kills his brother and escapes before anyone can identify him as the murderer. Haunted by Pedro's ghost, Ramon confesses his crime to Pilar at Pedro's grave. Pilar sinks dead on the grave. Impetuously Ramon plays a snatch from the fateful habanera, then destroys his guitar and flees into the darkness. The prelude to Act III is sometimes given at symphony concerts.

Habet Acht, Brangäne's warning to the lovers Tristan and Isolde in Act II of WAGNER'S TRISTAN UND ISOLDE.

Hab' mir's gelobt, celebrated trio of the Marschallin, Octavian, and Sophie in Act III of Richard STRAUSS'S DER ROSENKAVALIER, in which the Marschallin expresses her willingness to give up her beloved Octavian, while the latter and Sophie reveal their happiness.

Hadji, a Hindu slave (tenor) in DELIBES'S LAKMÉ.

Hadley, Henry, composer. Born Somerville, Mass., Dec. 20, 1871; died New York City, Sept. 6, 1937. After attending the New England Conservatory, he served as conductor with the Schirmer-Mapleson Opera Company. Additional study took place in Vienna with Eusebius Mandyczewski, following which he returned to America and devoted himself to conducting. From 1904 to the end of his life he directed major symphony orchestras in America and Europe, serving at different times as the permanent conductor of the Seattle Symphony, the San Francisco Symphony, and the Manhattan Symphony and as associate conductor of the New York Philharmonic. He was also a founder of the Berkshire Symphonic Festival

288

(BERKSHIRE MUSIC FESTIVAL), where he conducted the first concert in 1933. He composed works in every major form. His first opera to be produced was *The Culprit Fay*, heard in Grand Rapids on May 28, 1909. This was followed by AZORA, mounted by the CHICAGO OPERA on Dec. 26, 1917. A one-act opera, *Bianca*, won the William Hinshaw Prize in 1918 and was introduced in New York City on Oct. 18 of the same year. Hadley's most successful opera, CLEOPATRA'S NIGHT, was given its premiere by the METROPOLITAN OPERA on Jan. 31, 1920. Other operas: *Safie* (1909); *A Night in Old Paris* (1925).

Hageman, Richard, composer and conductor. Born Leeuwarden, Holland, July 9, 1882; died Beverly Hills, Cal., Mar. 6, 1966. His parents were professional musicians, his father the director of the Amsterdam Conservatory, his mother a concert singer. After attending the Brussels Conservatory, he was appointed assistant conductor of the Amsterdam Royal Opera when he was only sixteen; two years later he became its principal conductor. In 1907 he came to the United States, and five years later became a conductor at the METROPOLITAN OPERA. He remained with the Metropolitan nine years, returning for the 1935–36 season. As a composer he is best known for his songs (the most famous being "Do Not Go, My Love" and "At the Well") and his opera CAPONSACCHI, introduced in Freiburg in 1932 and five years later given at the Metropolitan. After leaving the Metropolitan, Hageman went to Hollywood to write music for motion pictures.

Hagen, half brother (bass) of Gunther and Gutrune in WAGNER'S GÖTTERDÄMMERUNG.

Hagenbach, Wally's beloved (tenor) in CATALANI'S LA WALLY.

Hagith, one-act opera by SZYMANOWSKI. Libretto by Felix Dörmann. Premiere: Warsaw Opera, May 13, 1922. This opera is based on an oriental legend in which an old and cruel king tries to regain health and youth by making love to a young girl, Hagith.

Hahn, Reynaldo, composer and conductor. Born Caracas, Venezuela, Aug. 9, 1875; died Paris, Jan. 28, 1947. As a student of the Paris Conservatory he had one of his works published when he was fourteen and some of his orchestral music performed a year later. His first opera, *L'Ile de rêve*, with a Polynesian setting, was introduced by the OPÉRA-COMIQUE on Mar. 23, 1898. Later operas were *La Carmélite* (1902), *Nausicaa* (1919), *La Colombe de Bouddha* (1921), *Mozart* (1925), and *Le Marchand de Venise* (1935). Famous as a song writer, Hahn also conducted opera performances in Paris, Salzburg, and Cannes; in 1945 he was appointed director of the PARIS OPÉRA.

Ha, jetzt erkenne ich sie wieder, Tannhäuser's expression of delight on learning how Elisabeth missed him during his long absence, in Act I, Scene 2, of WAGNER'S TANNHÄUSER.

Halász, Lászlo, conductor and opera manager. Born Debrecen, Hungary, June 6, 1905. He attended the Royal Academy of Music in Budapest and in 1928 made his debut in Budapest as both pianist and conductor. From 1930 to 1932 he was a conductor of the PRAGUE OPERA and from 1933 to 1936 of the Vienna Volksoper. During this period he participated in important festivals in Vienna and Salzburg. He came to the United States in 1936, making his debut as opera conductor in St. Louis with TRISTAN UND ISOLDE. In 1938 he was appointed conductor of the Philadelphia Civic Opera Company, a year later musical director of the St. Louis Grand Opera. When the NEW YORK CITY OPERA was founded in 1943, he became its artistic and musical director. He initiated a vital and progressive artistic program and helped launch the careers of many American singers. Dismissed in Dec., 1951, after a disagreement with the management, he won a court verdict which found that his conduct as director and manager had not constituted a threat to the "prosperity and advancement" of the New York City Opera, as had been charged. He then served for a while as musical director of Remington Records and led operatic performances in Europe and the United States.

Halévy, Jacques Fromental, composer. Born Paris, May 27, 1799; died Nice, Mar. 17, 1862. He entered the Paris Conservatory at age ten; there he won numerous prizes, including the PRIX DE ROME (1819). In Italy he devoted himself to the study and writing of operas. Returning to Paris, he made repeated but futile efforts to get some of his operas performed. However, a new work in a comic vein, *L'Artisan,* was given at the Théâtre Feydeau in 1827. His first success came a year later with *Clari,* performed at the Théâtre des Italiens. His greatest triumph was achieved in 1835 with the opera by which he is today remembered, LA JUIVE, given by the OPÉRA on Feb. 23. In 1836 an unusual comic opera, *L'Eclair,* requiring only four singers and no chorus, was also successful. Though Halévy wrote some twenty more operas, he never duplicated either the inspiration or the popularity of his masterwork, *La Juive.* In 1827 he began a long and successful career as teacher when he was appointed professor of harmony and accompaniment at the Conservatory. Subsequently he became professor of counterpoint, fugue, and advanced composition; his many pupils included GOUNOD and BIZET. In 1830 he became chorus master at the Opéra, a post he retained for sixteen years. In 1836 he was elected a member of the Institut de France, and in 1854 was appointed its permanent secretary. His daughter, Geneviève, married Bizet in 1869. His most successful operas were *Clari* (1828); *La Juive* (1835); *L'Eclair* (1836); *La Reine de Chypre* (1841); *Les Mousquetaires de la reine* (1846); *La Fée aux roses* (1849); *La Dame de pique* (1850); *Le Juif errant* (1852); *L'Inconsolable* (1855); *La Magicienne* (1858).

Halka, Polish folk opera in four (originally two) acts by MONIUSZKO. Libretto by Vladimir Wolski. Premiere: Warsaw Opera, Feb. 16, 1854; American premiere: New York City, June, 1903. This is the most famous opera to come out of Poland and that country's most significant national opera. The plot revolves around the love of Halka for Pan Janusz, who in turn is in love with Sophie. Janusz, however, seduces Halka and then forsakes her. She goes to his castle to denounce him, forces her way inside as Janusz and Sophie are about to be married, and kills herself before their eyes. The Peasants' Ballet in the third act is celebrated. Another Polish composer, Wallek-Valevski, wrote a sequel to *Halka* entitled *Jontek's Revenge.*

Hallelujah to Wine, a vulgar parody sung by the juggler Jean in Act I of MASSENET'S LE JONGLEUR DE NOTRE DAME.

Hallström, Ivar, composer. Born Stockholm, June 5, 1826; died there Apr. 11, 1901. While studying law he collaborated with Prince Gustav of Sweden in writing an opera, *The White Lady of Drottningholm,* produced by the STOCKHOLM ROYAL OPERA in 1847. After completing law study, Hallström became librarian to the Crown Prince Oscar. At the same time he taught the piano and subsequently (1861) became director of Lindblad's Music School. In 1874 he achieved a major success with his opera *The Bewitched,* which, after its introduction in Stockholm, was heard in Munich, Copenhagen, and Hamburg. His operas are so strongly national in character that he has been described as "Sweden's most national scenic composer." Other operas are *Bride of the Gnome* (1875); *Vikings' Voyage* (1877); *Nyaga* (1885); *Per Svinaherde* (1887); *Granada's Daughter* (1892); *Lilen Karin* (1897).

Haltière, Madame de la, Cinderella's stepmother (contralto) in MASSENET'S CENDRILLON.

Hamburg State Opera, one of the oldest opera institutions in Europe. It was founded in 1678 (in Hamburg, Germany) by Johann Adam Reincken and opened with Johann Theile's *Adam und Eva* in a theater (no longer existent) on the Gänsemarkt. Its heyday was between 1695 and 1706, from 1703 under the artis-

tic direction of Reinhard KEISER, who
was responsible for making it the leading opera house in Germany. Keiser
wrote over a hundred operas for the
theater, and it was during his regime
that HANDEL's first opera, ALMIRA, was
written and produced. German opera
went into decline after 1738, and in
1740 Italian opera became ascendant.
For the next century, the Hamburg
Opera assumed a secondary position
among German opera companies. With
the building of the Stadttheater in 1874,
a new era began. B. Pollini was the
first of the new artistic directors. The
company's general musical directors included such outstanding figures as
MAHLER, WEINGARTNER, KLEMPERER, Josef
Stransky, BOEHM, JOCHUM, all of whom
served before World War II and Jochum
until 1944. During this period the first
German productions of OTELLO (1888)
and EUGENE ONEGIN (1892) were given,
the latter with the composer present.

The State Opera building was destroyed in 1943 during an air raid in
World War II but was partially rebuilt
in 1945 and extensively in 1949. Leopold LUDWIG became musical director
in 1950, maintaining his office with distinction for many years. A new opera
house replaced the old one on Oct. 15,
1955, with a performance of THE MAGIC
FLUTE, produced by Günther RENNERT
and conducted by Ludwig; two days
later, came the world premiere of
KRENEK's Pallas Athene weint. Rennert
was general manager of the company
from 1946 to 1956, Heinz TIETJEN from
1956 to 1959. This era saw the production of numerous novelties from
the past and present, including ARIADNE
AUF NAXOS; Aroldo (VERDI) ; CAPRICCIO;
CATULLI CARMINA; DEIDAMIA; IRISCHE
LEGENDE; JENUFA; LULU; MATHIS DER
MALER; MAVRA; TRIONFO DI AFRODITE.

In 1959 Rolf LIEBERMANN became
artistic director, and under his regime
the company became one of the most
progressive in Europe, presenting numerous world premieres, including several operas which have since gained wide
recognition. In Feb., 1961, Liebermann

presented a week of twentieth-century
operas that included the following:
ANIARA; ANTIGONE (HONEGGER) ; LULU;
A MIDSUMMER NIGHT'S DREAM; OEDIPUS
REX; DER PRINZ VON HOMBURG; WOZZECK.
Among the world premieres given dur-
ing the Liebermann regime: Arden mus
sterben (Walter Goehr) ; THE DEVILS OF
LOUDON; Fluchtversuch (BLACHER); Ham-
let (SEARLE); Hamlet (Sandor Szokolay);
HELP, HELP, THE GLOBOLINKS!; Jacobowsky
and the Colonel (KLEBE); THE VISITATION.

During the season of 1968–69 Gian
Carlo MENOTTI conducted several operas,
including DON PASQUALE (a new production which he also staged) and his
own AMAHL AND THE NIGHT VISITORS. In
1969, besides the world premiere of The
Devils of Loudon, the company offered
a week of other twentieth-century operas
it had previously introduced, and in
1970 it gave two world premieres, Milko
Kolemen's State of Siege and Krenek's
That's What Happened.

The Hamburg State Opera paid its
first visit to the Western Hemisphere
in the spring of 1967 with performances
mainly of modern operas both at
Expo 67 in Montreal and in New York
City. In New York it became the first
foreign opera company to appear at the
METROPOLITAN OPERA House at the LIN-
COLN CENTER FOR THE PERFORMING ARTS.

Hamlet, (1) tragedy by SHAKESPEARE,
the source of several operas, the most
famous being Thomas's Hamlet (see
below) .

(2) Opera in five acts by THOMAS.
Libretto by Michel Carré and Jules
BARBIER. Premiere: Paris Opéra, Mar.
9, 1868. American premiere: Academy
of Music, N.Y., Mar. 22, 1872. The story
is essentially the same as Shakespeare's.
Learning that his father has been murdered, Hamlet (baritone) determines
to seek revenge. In order to accomplish
his ends more surely he simulates insanity. He has a group of players perform before the King and Queen a mock
reenactment of the crime. King Claudius,
the murderer, gives himself away, and
Hamlet ultimately kills him. Meanwhile, Ophelia (soprano) , in love with

Hamlet, is so upset by his apparent madness that she truly loses her mind and dies.

While this, the most celebrated operatic treatment of Shakespeare's play, enjoyed enormous popularity in France for over half a century and is still revived there on occasion, *Hamlet* has seldom had much success elsewhere. There is a lack of sustained musical interest, and the libretto is at times confused. However, there are memorable passages in the score: "O vin, dissipe la tristesse," Hamlet's drinking song in the second act; Ophelia's mad scene, "Partagez-vous mes fleurs!" in the fourth act; and Hamlet's beautiful arioso, "Comme une pâle fleur," in the last act. *Hamlet* is the first important opera to use a saxophone in the orchestra.

Hammer Song, *see* HO-HO! SCHMIEDE, MEIN HAMMER.

Hammerstein, Oscar, impresario. Born Stettin, Ger., May 8, 1846; died New York City, Aug. 1, 1919. Coming to America a penniless immigrant of middle-class Jewish parentage, he realized a small fortune from the invention and sale of devices for the manufacture of cigars. He then turned to the theater, wrote several plays, and had a hand in building a number of theaters in New York. He engaged in the managing of opera for the first time in 1906 when he built the MANHATTAN OPERA House and established there a company competitive with the METROPOLITAN OPERA. For four years Hammerstein presented brilliant performances, introducing many world-famous artists to America and emphasizing operatic novelties. In 1908 he built an opera house in Philadelphia where, several nights a week, he brought his New York company; in 1909 he brought opera to Baltimore. In Apr., 1910, Hammerstein sold his operatic interests to the Metropolitan Opera, thus bringing to an end four years of intense rivalry between the two companies. The agreement specified that for the following ten years Hammerstein was not to produce opera in America. Hammerstein, consequently, transferred his activity to London, where, in 1911, he built the London Opera House in Kingsway. When this venture collapsed, he returned to New York and, in 1913, tried to evade his contract by building the Lexington Opera House and attempting to produce operas there. The Metropolitan restrained him by recourse to law. He was still planning to produce opera in New York when he died.

Handel, George Frideric, composer. Born Halle, Saxony, Feb. 23, 1685; died London, Apr. 14, 1759. Handel belongs with the greatest masters in music, for he composed masterworks in virtually every field available to him—chamber music, the orchestral suite, music for keyboard instruments, oratorio, and opera. His operas, however, magnificent music as they are, receive, for reasons to be noted later, comparatively few performances nowadays, while the other compositions maintain a vigorous life in concert halls and churches. Handel began the study of music formally with Friederich Zachow, organist at Halle, who for three years gave the boy a comprehensive training. But academic study was not abandoned. Handel attended the University of Halle for the study of law, at the same time serving as organist at the Dom-Kirche. He left the university in 1703 and went to Hamburg, then the foremost opera center in Europe. There he became a violinist in the opera orchestra. There, too, he wrote his first opera, ALMIRA, produced with outstanding success on Jan. 8, 1705.

Handel left Hamburg in 1706 and went to Italy. An oratorio, *La risurezzione,* introduced in Rome, and an opera, AGRIPPINA, given in Venice, made Handel famous in that country. He attracted the interest of Agostino STEFFANI, a KAPELLMEISTER from Hanover, then visiting Italy. Steffani prevailed on Handel to take over his Hanover post. Handel was not long in Hanover before he asked for and received a leave of absence to visit London. There he arrived in 1710. Within two weeks he had written a new opera, RINALDO. When performed on Feb. 24, 1711, *Rinaldo* was a sensation. It was given fifteen performances to sold-out houses, and Handel became the idol of the English opera public. He now returned to Hanover to fulfill his duties as *kapellmeister,* but did not remain there long. In the fall of 1712 he received a second leave and returned to London. This time he remained, to become one of the most celebrated musicians in England, and one of the most popular opera composers. Queen Anne made him court composer. When the Elector of Hanover succeeded her to the throne, he appointed his Hanoverian *kapellmeister* royal music master. In 1717 Handel went to Cannons, near London, to serve as music master for the Duke of Chandos. He worked here for three years, writing many works, including ACIS AND GALATEA. He was back in London in 1720, filling the important post of artistic director of the newly founded Royal Academy of Music. He gathered some of the leading singers of Europe for his company and wrote some of his most successful operas, the first being *Radamisto,* performed on Apr. 27, 1720.

Handel was now at the peak of his popularity and success, a favorite with royalty and the common man alike. But he also had powerful enemies. There were those who resented him because he was a foreigner, because he was a musical tyrant, because he was a pet of nobility, or because he was a man of boorish manners. The enemies gathered around the powerful figure of the Earl of Burlington, and to offset Handel's popularity, they imported the celebrated opera composer Giovanni Battista BONONCINI. Bononcini's operas, given by the Academy, were enthusiastically received; but when Handel countered with his opera *Ottone,* a triumph, his rival went into permanent retreat. Handel did not long enjoy his victory. In 1728 THE BEGGAR'S OPERA was such a hit that the London public began to lose interest in OPERA SERIA and threw its support to this new type of musical entertainment. The

decline in box office receipts spelled doom for the Academy, and it went into bankruptcy.

Handel now went into partnership with John Jacob Heidegger to organize a new opera company. For this company Handel wrote one opera after another, but none was able to duplicate his earlier successes. When a rival company, sponsored by the Prince of Wales, drew away Handel's best singers and his audiences, Handel had to admit defeat. It was now that he concentrated his enormous energies and gifts in another field, in which he was to be incomparable, that of the oratorio. The greatest of these works, *Messiah,* introduced in Dublin in 1742, rehabilitated Handel's position as a composer. While working on his last oratorio, *Jephtha,* Handel went blind. An operation was unsuccessful. Handel continued to compose, to give organ concerts, and to direct performances of his oratorios. It was while presiding at the organ during a performance of *Messiah* at COVENT GARDEN that he collapsed with his last illness. He died eight days later and was buried in Westminster Abbey.

It is not difficult to understand why Handel saw his operas lose favor with his audiences and why, since his time, they have seldom been performed despite the greatness of some of the scores. Handel was content to write within the Italian patterns and according to traditions which even then were going out of style. Handel's operas are superlative examples of *opera seria,* and this means that they are, in form, largely a series of set arias, with very few concerted numbers and choruses—in effect, song recitals in costume and elaborate scenery. The stories deal with mythology or classical (and usually quite inaccurate) history; the plots are both complicated and stilted; the action formalized; the unbelievability and other absurdities enhanced by women frequently singing the male roles and *castrati* singing either male or female roles. Italian opera became a favorite and quite legitimate target for the brilliant wits of Handel's

London. They almost literally giggled *opera seria* off the local stage. Despite the obvious difficulties, however, periodically in the twentieth century Handel opera scores have been taken from the shelf, the casting and stage direction adapted for modern tastes, and productions put on which have been critically admired and occasionally successful commercially. And individual arias from these operas have always been staples of the recital repertoire, as, for example, "Ombra mai fù" (better known as Handel's "Largo") from SERSE, "Cara sposa" from RINALDO, "Care selve" from ATALANTA, "Caro amore" from *Floridante*, to mention just a few.

The most successful of Handel's forty operas were *Almira* (1705) ; *Rodrigo* (1707) ; *Agrippina* (1709) ; *Rinaldo* (1711) ; *Acis and Galatea* (1720) ; *Radamisto* (1720) ; *Floridante* (1721) ; *Ottone* (1723); GIULIO CESARE (1724); *Tamerlano* (1724) ; RODELINDA (1725) ; *Scipione* (1726) ; ADMETO (1727) ; *Siroe* (1728) ; *Partenope* (1730) ; *Poro* (1731) ; *Ezio* (1732) ; *Arianna* (1734) ; *Ariodante* (1735) ; ALCINA (1735) ; *Atalanta* (1736) ; *Berenice* (1737) ; *Faramondo* (1738) ; *Serse* (1738) ; DEIDAMIA (1740) .

Handel Festival, an annual festival of Handel's operas presented in the German city of Halle, Handel's birthplace. It was inaugurated at the newly built Stadttheater on Mar. 31, 1951, under the musical direction of Hans-Tanu Margraf. Among the significant revivals have been ADMETO, AGRIPPINA (celebrating the sixteenth anniversary of the festival), DEIDAMIA, *Ezio,* GIULIO CESARE, *Otto e Teophano, Poro, Radamisto,* RINALDO, *Siroe,* and *Tamerlano.*

Regular Handel festivals—though not primarily opera festivals, as in Halle—have also been held in London (at intermittent intervals beginning with 1857) and in Göttingen, Ger.

Hanna, a village girl (soprano), the beloved of Levko, in RIMSKY-KORSAKOV'S A MAY NIGHT.

Hanover Opera, an opera company in Hanover, Ger., which has given performances at the Landestheater from 1845 on. The opera house was extensively rebuilt in 1950, and its major significance came as a post-World War II development under the musical direction of Franz KONWITSCHNY, Johannes Schüler, and Günther Wich. They were succeeded by George Alexander Albrecht, with Reinhard Lehmann as artistic director. Among the operas receiving their world premieres here were BOULEVARD SOLITUDE, STANFORD'S *The Veiled Prophet,* and WOLF-FERRARI's *Der Kuckuck in Theben.* In 1968 significant new productions of DOKTOR FAUST and THE CUNNING LITTLE VIXEN were given.

Hans, (1) Marie's sweetheart (tenor) in SMETANA'S THE BARTERED BRIDE.

(2) *See* HANS HEILING.

Hansel and Gretel (Hänsel und Gretel), fairy opera in three acts by HUMPERDINCK. Libretto by Adelheid Wette (the composer's sister), based on the fairy tale of Jakob GRIMM. Premiere: Weimar, Dec. 23, 1893. American premiere: Daly's Theater, New York City, Oct. 8, 1895.

Characters: Peter, a broommaker (baritone) ; Gertrude, his wife (mezzosoprano) ; Hansel, their son (mezzosoprano) ; Gretel, their daughter (soprano) ; the Witch (mezzo-soprano) ; the Sandman (soprano) ; the Dewman (soprano) ; angels; gingerbread children.

The orchestral prelude contains melodies from the opera. It opens and closes with the prayer theme. Other fragments, from the third act, are introduced, including the happy melody of the children at the end of the opera.

Act I. Peter's house. Hansel and Gretel are hungry. To distract her little brother, Gretel teaches him to sing and dance ("Brüderchen, komm tanz' mit mir") . Their mother scolds them for playing instead of working. Now the children must go into the woods to pick strawberries for the evening meal. While they are gone, their father returns from work with a bundle of food under his arm. Learning that the children have gone into the wood, he grows apprehensive and joins his wife in searching for them.

Act II. In the forest. While Hansel is looking for strawberries, Gretel sits under a tree singing a folk song ("Ein Männlein steht im Walde"). Hansel returns with the berries, and since the children are hungry, they yield to the temptation of eating them. Night begins to fall. The darkness brings terror, for the children are now unable to find their way home. The Sandman comes to put the children to sleep with a lullaby ("Der kleine Sandmann bin ich"). The children say their prayers ("Abends will ich schlafen geh'n"). After they fall asleep, angels descend to provide the children with a protective ring (Dream Pantomime).

Act III. The Witch's house. The Dewman sprinkles dewdrops on the children ("Der kleine Taumann heiss' ich"). Waking, the children find themselves in front of a gingerbread house decorated with gingerbread figures of children. The hungry children begin to eat morsels of the house. Suddenly the Witch emerges. Her magic keeps the children rooted to the ground. She locks Hansel in a cage and sets Gretel at housework. The Witch sings a gleeful song about her weird activities (Hexenlied: "Hurr, hopp, hopp, hopp"). Gretel, meanwhile, steals her wand and with it frees her brother. When the Witch orders Gretel to look into the flaming oven, Gretel simulates stupidity and asks the Witch to show her how this is done. When the Witch stands before the open door, Hansel and Gretel push her inside and slam the door. They now express their joy at being free (Gingerbread Waltz: Knusperwalzer—"Juchhei, nun ist die Hexe todt!"). The Witch's oven explodes. This is the signal for all the Witch's previous victims to change from gingerbread back into little children. The parents of Hansel and Gretel appear, find their children free, and a celebration takes place.

With *Hansel and Gretel* Humperdinck helped create the operatic fairy tale. There now arose a school of German opera composers who drew their texts from German folklore and fairy tales and based their music on folk tunes. To this day *Hansel and Gretel* remains the finest product of this school. It is lovable in its simplicity, infectious in its youthful spirit. Humperdinck did not originally plan *Hansel and Gretel* for the opera house. His sister had written a play for children based on the Grimm fairy tale, and she asked her brother to provide an appropriate musical setting. Even after Humperdinck finished this chore, the story continued to appeal to him, and he decided to extend his score to operatic proportions. He sent his finished manuscript to Richard strauss, who accepted it for performance in Weimar. "Truly it is a masterwork of the first rank," Strauss wrote the composer.

Hans Heiling, opera in three acts by marschner. Libretto by Eduard Devrient. Premiere: Berlin Opera, May 24, 1833. The setting is the Harz Mountains in the sixteenth century. Hans Heiling (baritone), son of the Queen of the Spirits (soprano), assumes human form. He falls in love with Anna (soprano), but when she learns of his origin she abandons him for Konrad (tenor). Hans calls on the spirits for revenge. They fail to help him. He sinks into the earth, vowing that never again will any living mortal see him. "An jenem Tag," Hans's aria in Act I, is famous.

Hanslick, Eduard, music critic. Born Prague, Sept. 11, 1825; died Baden, Austria, Aug. 6, 1904. He wrote provocative and influential criticism for the *Wiener Zeitung,* the *Presse,* and the *Neue freie Presse.* A fine pianist, he was trained in law, philosophy, and music and was appointed professor of esthetics at the university in Vienna. He became a devoted champion of Brahms and a bitter antagonist of wagner and the esthetics of the Wagnerian music dramas. It is believed that, when Wagner created the role of beckmesser, he had Hanslick in mind and that he originally even intended calling this character Hans Lick. Hanslick wrote an eight-volume history of opera, *Die moderne Oper* (1875), and a two-volume autobiography, *Aus* *meinem Leben* (1894), among other books. A collection of his critical essays was published in the United States under the title *Vienna's Golden Years of Music* (1950).

Hanson, Howard, composer. Born Wahoo, Neb., Oct. 28, 1896. His musical education took place at Luther College in Wahoo, the Institute of Musical Art in New York, and Northwestern University. He then became professor of theory and composition, and subsequently dean of the Conservatory of Fine Arts, at the College of the Pacific, San José, Cal. In 1921 he became the first Music Fellow to receive the PRIX DE ROME through a competition of the American Academy in Rome. His *Nordic Symphony* was successfully introduced in Italy. In 1924 he returned to the United States and became director of the Eastman School of Music at the University of Rochester, a post he held with great distinction for forty-five years. His opera MERRY MOUNT was introduced by the METROPOLITAN OPERA on Feb. 10, 1934, and his fourth symphony became the first work in that form to receive a PULITZER PRIZE.

Hans Sachs, (1) opera by LORTZING. Libretto by the composer and Philip Reger, based on a play by Johann Ludwig Deinhardstein. Premiere: Leipzig Opera, June 23, 1840. This opera, based on the same historical character as WAGNER'S DIE MEISTERSINGER, preceded Wagner's opera by over two decades.

(2) Cobbler-philosopher (bass or baritone) in WAGNER'S DIE MEISTERSINGER.

Happy Shade, a character (soprano) in GLUCK'S ORFEO ED EURIDICE.

Hardy, Thomas, novelist and poet. Born Upper Brockhampton, Eng., June 2, 1840; died Dorchester, Jan. 11, 1928. BOUGHTON's opera *The Queen of Cornwall* was derived from Hardy's play of the same name. Hardy's novel *Tess of the D'Urbervilles* is the source of ERLANGER's opera *Tess*. *The Three Strangers* served for operas by Hubert Bath and Julian Gardiner; *The Mayor of Casterbridge* was made into an opera by Peter Tranchell.

Harewood, Earl of (born George Henry Hubert Lascelles), critic and director. Born Harewood, near Leeds, Eng., Feb. 7, 1923. He is the first cousin of Queen Elizabeth II. He has served opera faithfully and fruitfully over many years. In 1950 he founded the magazine *Opera* in London. Between 1951 and 1953 he was on the board of directors of COVENT GARDEN, later becoming its controller of opera planning (1953–1960). In 1958 he became director of the Leeds Festival and in 1961, of the EDINBURGH FESTIVAL. He was one of the original sponsors of the ENGLISH OPERA GROUP and the Opera School. In 1954 he brought out an extensively revised edition of KOBBÉ's *Complete Opera Book*.

Harlequin's Serenade, Beppe's serenade (as Harlequin), "O Colombina," in Act II of LEONCAVALLO'S PAGLIACCI.

Harmonie der Welt, Die (The Harmony of the World), opera in five acts by HINDEMITH. Libretto by the composer. Premiere: Munich Opera, Aug. 11, 1957. The principal character is Johannes KEPLER, the renowned astronomer and mathematician, and the plot details the impact the social and political problems of his time (the period of the Thirty Years' War) had upon him. Here is how H. H. Stuckenschmidt summed up the main theme: "Kepler is shown on his eternal wanderings through Prague, Linz, Gueglingen, Sagan, and Regensburg. Three female characters play an important part in his life: his mother, Katharina, a mystical woman well versed in herbology, accused of being a witch, sentenced by court and saved by her own son; his little daughter, Susanna, by his first marriage; and his second wife, also named Susanna, a carpenter's daughter, whom he married against opposition, but who chose to share the life of the great astronomer." Hindemith's style is for the most part polyphonic, with many highly effective fuguelike choruses and other fugato passages. "The magnificent final scene," wrote Stuckenschmidt, "when the very signs of the zodiac come to life and march across the stage, is based on a passacaglia theme with rising and falling fifths—an inspiration of Bruckner-like pathos and majestic grandeur."

Hindemith adapted parts of his opera for a three-movement "symphony," the parts of which are entitled "Musica Instrumentalis," "Musica Humana," and "Musica Mundane."

Haroun, a Turkish prince (tenor) with whom his slave, Djamileh, is in love, in BIZET'S DJAMILEH.

Harrell, Mack, baritone. Born Celeste, Texas, Oct. 8, 1909; died Dallas, Texas, Jan. 29, 1960. His music study began with the violin, but he soon became convinced that his future lay in singing. His vocal studies took place with Robert Lawrence Weer in Philadelphia and Mme. Schoen-René at the Juilliard School of Music. His first public appearance was as soloist with the New York Philharmonic in 1935. This started him off on a concert career, during which he was often heard in concert performances of operas, including LES CHOËPHORES, CHRISTOPHE COLOMB, L'HEURE ESPAGNOLE, L'ORFEO, and WOZZECK. In 1939 he won the METROPOLITAN AUDITIONS OF THE AIR, which led to his debut with the METROPOLITAN OPERA on Dec. 16, 1939, as Biterolf in TANNHÄUSER. He remained with the Metropolitan for almost two decades (through the 1957–58 season), appearing in principal baritone roles in the French, Italian, and German repertories. He was also heard at the SAN FRANCISCO OPERA and at major European festivals.

Harriet, Lady, maid of honor (soprano) to Queen Anne in FLOTOW'S MARTHA.

Harris, Sir Augustus, impresario. Born Paris, 1852; died Folkestone, Eng., June 22, 1896. The son of the stage manager at COVENT GARDEN, he became assistant manager to MAPLESON. In 1879 he leased the DRURY LANE THEATRE, where he produced a highly successful season of Italian opera. A year later he began producing operas at Covent Garden. He was a pioneer in presenting opera in the original language and an influence in popularizing WAGNER in London.

Harshaw, Margaret, soprano. Born Nar-beth, Pa., May 12, 1912. After winning the Metropolitan Opera Auditions in 1942, she made her debut at the METROPOLITAN OPERA as a contralto on Nov. 25, 1942, in the role of the Second Norn in GÖTTERDÄMMERUNG. She continued to sing contralto parts for eight years. In 1950 she began to sing soprano roles, specializing in the Wagnerian repertory. Her first soprano appearance, as Senta in DER FLIEGENDE HOLLÄNDER, took place on Nov. 22, 1950. She remained at the Metropolitan Opera up through the 1963–64 season; there she was heard in the principal soprano roles of the Wagnerian repertory. She has also made appearances at some of the major opera houses and festivals of the world, including the GLYNDEBOURNE FESTIVAL, where she sang the role of Donna ANNA in 1955.

Hartmann, Rudolf, manager and producer. Born Ingolstadt, Ger., Oct. 11, 1900. He studied stage design in Munich and Bamberg, following which he received his first engagement as producer in Altenberg in 1924. Between 1928 and 1934 and again between 1946 and 1952, he was a producer at the Nuremburg Opera and from 1934 to 1938 at the BERLIN STATE OPERA, where he produced the premiere of DIE ZAUBERGEIGE. From 1938 on he was for many years a principal producer at the MUNICH OPERA, where he staged the premieres of Richard STRAUSS'S FRIEDENSTAG and CAPRICCIO besides reviving most of Strauss's earlier stage works. In 1952 he staged the premiere of DIE LIEBE DER DANAE at SALZBURG, and in 1954 he produced the WAGNER RING cycle at COVENT GARDEN.

Harun-al-Rashid, Caliph of Bagdad (bass) in WEBER'S OBERON.

Harvest, The, opera in three acts by Vittorio GIANNINI. Libretto by the composer and Karl Flaster. Premiere: Chicago, Nov. 25, 1961. The setting is an American farm in the first years of the twentieth century. Lora carries on an illicit love affair with her brother-in-law Mark. Her sexual drive leads her then to arouse the carnal desires not only of another brother-in-law but also of their blind father. Lora in the end is strangled by the blind father. Giannini's musical style is in the VERISMO idiom of the Italians, and most noticeably of PUCCINI.

Háry János, opera in five parts with prologue and epilogue (frequently performed in three acts) by KODÁLY. Libretto by Béla Paulini and Zsolt Harsányi, based on a poem by János Garay. Premiere: Budapest Opera, Oct. 16, 1926. American premiere: New York City, Mar. 18, 1960. The central character is the prodigious liar popular in Hungarian folk tales, Háry János. The opera is built around his boastful tales: how Marie Louise, daughter of Emperor Francis and wife of Napoleon, falls in love with him and wants him to join her in Paris, and how she competes for his love with the peasant woman Orzse; how, after Napoleon declares war on Austria as a result of this scandal, Háry defeats the enemy singlehanded; how he is triumphantly welcomed back to Vienna, where he announces his rejection of Marie Louise and his acceptance of Orzse as his wife. Six portions of Kodály's brilliant music are familiar as an orchestral suite, frequently performed at symphony concerts (Prelude: The Fairy Story Begins; Viennese Musical Clock; Song; The Battle and Defeat of Napoleon; Intermezzo; and Entrance of the Emperor and His Court).

Ha, seht, es winkt, the celebrated Schatz, or Treasure Waltz, sung by Sandor, Saffi, and Kalman when they find the hidden treasure in the castle town, in Act II of Johann STRAUSS's THE GYPSY BARON.

Hasse, Johann Adolph, composer. Born Bergedorf, near Hamburg, Mar. 25, 1699; died Venice, Italy, Dec. 16, 1783. He was one of the most prolific composers of his century, producing fifty-six operas and much church and other music. After receiving instruction in music from his father, he was engaged to sing at the HAMBURG OPERA, then directed by KEISER. He remained there four seasons, then joined the company of the opera in Brunswick, where his first opera, Antioco, was produced on Aug. 11, 1721. Convinced his future lay in composition, he went to Naples to study with PORPORA and Alessandro SCARLATTI. There his second opera, Tigrane, was produced on November 4, 1723. With Seostrate, seen first in Naples on May 13, 1726, he enjoyed his first major success. In 1729 he married Faustina BORDONI, the famous singer, who subsequently appeared in the leading female roles of many of his operas, and for whom he wrote two (Artaserse and Dalisa). In 1731 Hasse was made musical director of the DRESDEN OPERA, where his opera Cleofide was given on Sept. 13, with his wife in the principal role. In 1734 he went to London, where his Artaserse, heard on Nov. 10, 1734, was a major success. He was offered the direction of an opera company set in opposition to the one managed by HANDEL, but he rejected the offer. He remained prolific up to 1771, when his last opera, RUGGIERO, was given in Milan. He enjoyed enormous prestige in his own time because of his remarkable gift of melody and his aristocratic style, but he lacked originality, and partly for this reason, his operas lapsed into oblivion.

Hasselmans, Louis, conductor. Born Paris, July 25, 1878; died San Juan, Puerto Rico, Dec. 27, 1947. After attending the Paris Conservatory, he made his conducting debut with the Lamoureux Orchestra. Between 1909 and 1911 he was a conductor at the OPÉRA-COMIQUE. Following engagements with the Montreal Opera and CHICAGO OPERA, he joined the company of the METROPOLITAN OPERA, where he made his debut in FAUST on Jan. 20, 1922. He remained at the Metropolitan until 1936; there he conducted the New York premieres of LA HABANERA and L'HEURE ESPAGNOLE.

Haug, Hans, composer. Born Basel, Switzerland, July 27, 1900. After study at the Basel Conservatory with Egon Petri and Ernst Levy and in Munich with Walter Courvoisier, he began a career as conductor. Between 1928 and 1934 he was one of the conductors of the Basel Municipal Theater. After 1934 he conducted various symphony and radio orchestras in Switzerland, Italy, and France. He has also been a teacher of theory at the Lausanne Conservatory. He has written several operas, the most successful of these being in a comic vein. His operas: *Don Juan in der Fremde* (1930); *Madrisa* (1934); *Tartuffe* (1937) ; *Ariadne* (1943) ; *Le Malade immortel* (1946) ; *Der Spiegel der Agrippina* (1954).

Hauk, Minnie, soprano. Born New York City, Nov. 16, 1851; died Triebschen, Switzerland, Feb. 6, 1929. After only a few months of study with Achille Errani in New York, she mastered the principal soprano roles of half a dozen leading operas. She was only fourteen when she made her debut, in Brooklyn, as Amina in LA SONNAMBULA, on Oct. 13, 1866. When she was fifteen she created for America the role of Juliette in GOUNOD'S ROMÉO ET JULIETTE at the ACADEMY OF MUSIC in New York City, only seven months after the opera's world premiere. Following additional appearances in the United States, she sang in the leading opera houses of Europe, her popularity mounting steadily. In 1877 she made her first appearance as CARMEN, at the THÉÂTRE DE LA MONNAIE. She brought to the role such dramatic vitality and personal animation that she was a sensation. In 1878 she created the role for England and the United States. From this time on, Carmen was to be her most celebrated impersonation (she sang it over six hundred times in English, French, German, and Italian). From 1878 on she divided her operatic activity between America and Europe. For America she created the role of MANON in MASSENET's opera and scored a personal triumph as Selika in L'AFRICAINE. She made her METROPOLITAN OPERA debut in the role of Selika on Feb. 10, 1891. After a season at the Metropolitan, she organized her own opera company and toured the United States. Though now at the height of her fame and ability, she suddenly decided to retire and spend the rest of her life at her beautiful villa near

Lucerne, Switzerland, with her husband, Baron Ernst von Hesse-Wartegg. The death of her husband and the depletion of her fortune during World War I reduced her to poverty. In the last years of her life she suffered the additional affliction of blindness. Her only source of income was a fund created by a group of American opera lovers headed by Geraldine FARRAR. She wrote an autobiography, *Memories of a Singer* (1925).

Hauptmann, Gerhart, dramatist. Born Obersalzbrunn, Silesia, Nov. 15, 1862; died Schreiberhau, Silesia, June 6, 1946. One of the leading dramatists of Germany, and the winner of the 1912 Nobel Prize for Literature, Hauptmann was the author of several dramas which were turned into operas. *Die versunkene Glocke (The Sunken Bell)* was the source of operas by Alexei Davidoff, RESPIGHI, and Heinrich Zöllner. GRAENER made an opera of *Hanneles Himmelfahrt (The Assumption of Hannele)* ; Vit Nejedly, of *Die Weber (The Weavers)* ; and Erwin Lendvai, of *Elga*. Hauptmann also wrote the text for ERLANGER'S *Hannele Mattern*.

Ha! wie will ich triumphieren, Osmin's aria in Act III of MOZART's THE ABDUCTION FROM THE SERAGLIO, expressing joy at the capture of the fleeing Belmonte and Constanze and their servants.

Hawkins, Osie, baritone. Born Phoenix City, Ala., Aug. 16, 1913. He was the recipient of the first scholarship ever given by the METROPOLITAN OPERA. Following a period of voice study and some concert appearances, he made his Metropolitan Opera debut on Jan. 22, 1942, as Donner in DAS RHEINGOLD. When the Metropolitan Opera was on tour that spring, Hawkins twice had to substitute without rehearsals for indisposed singers, first in the role of KURWENAL and then as Wotan in DIE WALKÜRE. He remained a member of the Metropolitan Opera through the 1962–1963 season, appearing in an extensive repertory of French, Italian, and Wagnerian operas and music dramas and earning particular distinction for his interpretation of Wagnerian roles. He has also made numerous appearances with other leading opera companies in America and Europe.

Hawthorne, Nathaniel, author. Born Salem, Mass., July 4, 1804; died Plymouth, N.H., May 19, 1864. His classic *The Scarlet Letter* is the source of operas by Walter DAMROSCH and Vittorio GIANNINI. Other Hawthorne works used for operas include *The Maypole of Merry Mount* (HANSON's MERRY MOUNT); *Rappaccini's Daughter* (CADMAN's *The Garden of Mystery*); *The Snow Image* (ROREM's *A Childhood Miracle*).

Haydn, Franz Joseph, composer. Born Rohrau, Lower Austria, Mar. 31, 1732; died Vienna, May 31, 1809. A giant figure in the development of the symphony, sonata, and string quartet, Haydn was a comparatively negligible influence in opera, though he wrote about twenty works for the stage, including musical puppet plays. As a young composer in Vienna, he achieved a first measure of success with music for a Viennese farce, *Der krumme Teufel,* introduced at the BURGTHEATER in 1752; that success, however, was aborted when a powerful Viennese nobleman interpreted the play as a satire on himself and had it removed. As KAPELLMEISTER of the Eszterházy family, an appointment received in 1761 and continued for thirty years, Haydn directed all the musical performances and wrote innumerable works, among which were operas. Since the theater at the Eszterházy palace was comparatively small and the musical forces limited, these operas have the character of chamber works. They yielded to the prevailing Italian taste and conformed rigidly to the established traditions. Haydn's finest and most ambitious opera, ORFEO ED EURIDICE, was written in 1791 during the composer's first sojourn in London. Because of legal difficulties, a performance was not possible in Haydn's time.

Haydn's operas long suffered total neglect. But beginning with the early 1950's, they began to receive important revivals and to attract world interest. *Orfeo ed Euridice* was heard for the first time anywhere at the FLORENCE MAY MUSIC FESTIVAL in 1951 and received its American premiere fourteen years later. An OPERA BUFFA, IL MONDO DELLA LUNA, forgotten for almost two centuries, was revived at the HOLLAND MUSIC FESTIVAL on June 24, 1959. LO SPEZIALE was given in concert form in New York City in 1959; a staged production followed in 1961, and in it important sections of the opera, long considered lost, were restored. The manuscript of a lost Haydn SINGSPIEL, *Die Feuerbrunst,* was found in the Yale University library and received its first modern performance in Sweden during the summer of 1961. In June, 1962, Haydn's long forgotten *L'infedeltà delusa,* edited by H. C. Robbins Landon, was revived at the Stockholm Festival and in 1970 at the HOLLAND MUSIC FESTIVAL.

Haydn's operas: *La canterina* (1767); *Lo speziale* (1768); *Le pescatrici* (1770); *L'infedeltà delusa* (1773); *L'incontro improviso* (1775); *La vera costanza* (1776); *Il mondo della luna* (1777); *L'isola disabitata* (1779); *La fedeltà premiata* (1780); *Orlando Paladino* (1782); ARMIDA (1784); *Orfeo ed Euridice* (1791).

Heart of Midlothian, The, see SCOTT, SIR WALTER.

Heart, the seat of soft delight, Galatea's radiant aria in Act II of HANDEL's ACIS AND GALATEA.

Hebbel, Friedrich, dramatist and poet. Born Wesselburen, Holstein, Ger., Mar. 18, 1813; died Vienna, Dec. 13, 1863. The father of German social and naturalistic drama, Hebbel was the author of several plays used as the bases of opera librettos. Among the operas are D'ALBERT's *Der Rubin;* Max Ettinger's *Judith;* Joseph Messner's *Agnes Bernauer;* MOTTL's *Agnes Bernauer;* REZNIČEK's *Holofernes;* SCHILLINGS' *Moloch;* SCHUMANN's GENOVEVA.

Hécube, Priam's wife (mezzo-soprano) in BERLIOZ' LES TROYENS.

Hedwig, William Tell's wife (soprano) in ROSSINI's WILLIAM TELL.

Heger, Robert, conductor and composer. Born Strassburg, Alsace, Aug. 19,

1886. After musical study at conservatories in Strassburg, Zürich, and Munich, he received his first assignment as conductor in Strassburg in 1907. Various engagements followed until 1913, when he was appointed principal conductor of the Nuremberg Opera. While holding this post he wrote his first opera, *Ein Fest auf Haderslev.* From 1925 to 1933 he was conductor of the VIENNA STATE OPERA; subsequently, he held conductorial posts with the BERLIN STATE OPERA, COVENT GARDEN, and other major European opera houses. Later operas include: *Der Bettler Namelos* (1932); *Der verlorene Sohn* (1935).

Heil dir, Elsa von Brabant, chorus of the people of Brabant hailing Elsa, the bride, as she makes her way to the cathedral for her wedding, in Act II of WAGNER'S LOHENGRIN.

Heil dir, Sonne!, The love duet of Brünnhilde and Siegfried in the final scene of WAGNER'S SIEGFRIED.

Heil Sachs!, The closing chorus in WAGNER'S DIE MEISTERSINGER, hailing Hans Sachs.

Heimchen am Herd, Das, *see* CRICKET ON THE HEARTH, THE.

Heine, Heinrich, poet and dramatist. Born Düsseldorf, Dec. 13, 1797; died Paris, Feb. 17, 1856. One of the foremost German lyric poets. He was the music critic of the *Allgemeine Zeitung* in Augsburg from 1840 to 1847. His tragedy *William Ratcliff* was the source of many operas, notably by Volkmar Andrae, CUI, LEROUX, and MASCAGNI. Atterberg's opera *Fanal* was based on Heine's ballad *Der Schelm von Bergen.* DER FLIEGENDE HOLLÄNDER was based on Heine's version of an old German legend. DEBUSSY planned making an opera from Heine's *Almansor* but abandoned the project.

Heinrich, König, *see* HENRY THE FOWLER.

Hélas! l'enfant encore, Athanaël's lament, upon his first appearance in Act I, Scene 1, about the corruption of Alexandria, from which he has just returned, in MASSENET'S THAÏS.

Heldentenor, German for "heroic tenor," a tenor with a large voice suitable for dramatic rather than lyric roles.

Helen (or Helen of Troy), legendary beauty for whom Troy was sacked, (1) a character (soprano) in BOITO'S MEFISTOFELE.

(2) Beloved (soprano) of Paris in GLUCK'S PARIDE ED ELENA.

(3) Wife (soprano) of Menelaus in Richard STRAUSS'S DIE AEGYPTISCHE HELENA.

Helle Wehr, Siegfried's oath on his spear that Brünnhilde is a total stranger to him, in Act II of WAGNER'S GÖTTERDÄMMERUNG.

Help, Help, the Globolinks!, opera in one act by MENOTTI. Libretto by the composer. Premiere: Hamburg State Opera, Dec. 18, 1968. American premiere: Santa Fe Opera, Aug. 1, 1969. The composer-librettist describes this four-scene fantasy as "an opera for children and those who love children." It is his first opera to use electronic sounds. They are heard soon after a fugato orchestral prelude is interrupted with a radio announcement of an invasion of Globolinks. "There follows," says James H. Sutcliffe, "seven minutes of theatrical magic during which the creatures arrive [in] ... brilliantly inventive Globolink costumes, utterly inhuman, and resembling seven-foot-high stacks of white elastic top hats ... backed up [by] a kaleidoscopic whirl of colored lights. This gives way to eerie, prismatic reflections from ... revolving towers called 'sonic light-structures.' "

A Globolink has the power not only of robbing a human being of his voice but also, within a day, of transforming him into a Globolink. Children stalled in their school bus try to frighten the Globolinks away by honking the bus horn. Emily, performing on a violin, goes to seek help. Mme. Euterpova, a music teacher at the head of a platoon of teachers playing various musical instruments, helps rescue the children. For, you see, the only thing that frightens a Globolink is tonal music. The only one transformed into a Globolink is Mr. Stone, the principal of the school, a man who hates music.

Hempel, Frieda, soprano. Born Leipzig, June 26, 1885; died Berlin, Oct. 7, 1955. After studying voice for three years with Mme. Nicklass-Kempner in Berlin, she made her opera debut at the BERLIN OPERA in 1905 in THE MERRY WIVES OF WINDSOR. For two years she appeared at the Schwerin Opera, after which she returned to the Berlin Opera, remaining there five years and establishing her reputation. She specialized in the German repertory, scoring major successes in the MOZART operas. In 1911 she was Richard STRAUSS's personal choice for the role of the Marschallin in the Berlin premiere of DER ROSEN-KAVALIER. She also appeared at the BAYREUTH and MUNICH festivals. On Dec. 27, 1912, she made her METRO-POLITAN OPERA debut in LES HUGUE-NOTS. She was a member of the Metropolitan Opera Company seven seasons. Meanwhile, she was acclaimed in the concert hall, particularly for her "Jenny Lind" concerts, which she performed in costume. After leaving the Metropolitan she appeared in recitals in the United States and Europe. Her last recital took place in New York City on Nov. 7, 1951.

Henri de Valois, King of France (baritone), who subsequently is also crowned King of Poland, in CHABRIER's LE ROI MALGRÉ LUI.

Henrietta, Queen, widow (soprano) of Charles I in BELLINI's I PURITANI.

Henry IV, *see* KING HENRY IV.

Henry VIII, opera in four acts by SAINT-SAËNS. Libretto by Leonce Detroyat and Armand Silvestre, based on SHAKES-PEARE. Premiere: Paris Opéra, Mar. 5, 1883. The story is built around the love of Henry VIII for Anne Boleyn, whom he makes queen despite her love for the Spanish ambassador, Gomez, and despite the disapproval of Rome. The popular ballet music in Act II is part of a festival arranged at Richmond by the King to honor the papal legate. Some of the musical material is based on Scottish and Irish tunes. One of the more familiar vocal excerpts is the Kings' first-act aria "Qui donc commande."

Henry the Fowler (König Heinrich), King's first-act aria "Qui donc commande" LOHENGRIN.

Henze, Hans Werner, composer. Born Gütersloh, Ger., July 1, 1926. He attended the Braunschweig (Brunswick) Conservatory. After studying composition with Wolfgang FORTNER and René Leibowitz, the latter a dedicated disciple of TWELVE-TONE TECH-NIQUES, Henze attracted attention with concert compositions in an atonal idiom. In 1948 he served as the musical director of a theater in Constance, and from 1950 to 1952 he was musical advisor for the Wiesbaden State Theater, which produced two of his ballets. Meanwhile, in 1951 his piano concerto received the Robert Schumann Prize. In 1952 Henze left Germany to establish permanent residence in Italy. Nevertheless, his work continued to get performances in Germany—as well as elsewhere. His first full-length opera, BOULEVARD SOLITUDE, aroused considerable controversy when introduced in Hanover in 1952. From then on he began to achieve international renown, not only for his operas but also for his symphonies, and is now numbered with the foremost composers of the twentieth century. His most significant operas since *Boulevard Solitude* have been KÖNIG HIRSCH (1956), DER PRINZ VON HOMBURG (1960), ELEGY FOR YOUNG LOVERS (1961), DER JUNGE LORD (1965), and DIE BASSARIDEN (1966). Henze received the Nordrhein Westphalian Award in 1957, the Berlin Kunstpreis in 1959, and the Grand Prize for Artists in Hanover in 1962. He paid his first visit to the United States in 1963 on the occasion of the world premiere of his Fifth Symphony by the New York Philharmonic. Since 1961 Henze has been professor of composition at the Mozarteum in Salzburg.

Herbert, Victor, composer. Born Dublin, Feb. 1, 1859; died New York City, May 27, 1924. He received an extensive musical education in Germany and became a fine cellist. After marrying Theresa Förster, a singer, he came to the United States in 1886. His wife joined the company of the METROPOLITAN OPERA, and he played in the opera orchestra. He started writing operettas in 1892, scoring his first major success in 1895 with *The Wizard of the Nile.* After 1903 he produced a series of outstanding operetta successes, including *Babes in Toyland, Naughty Marietta,* and *Mlle. Modiste;* but he did not neglect serious music. His first opera, NATOMA, was written on a commission from the MANHATTAN OPERA COMPANY, but this organization ended its career before the opera could be produced. It was first heard in Philadelphia, Feb. 25, 1911, sung by artists of the Philadelphia-Chicago Opera Company. Three days later, performed by the same singers, it was heard at the Metropolitan Opera House. In 1913 Herbert wrote a one-act opera, MADELEINE. It was first performed by the Metropolitan Opera on Jan. 24, 1914. Both these operas were favorably received in their day, but it is as a composer of operettas that Herbert is chiefly remembered.

Hercules, a Greek god (bass) in GLUCK's ALCESTE.

Her (or His) Majesty's Theatre, a theater in the Haymarket (London), known by this name since the accession of Victoria in 1837. Previously called the King's Theatre and earlier the Queen's Theatre, the original structure had a history going back to 1705. It was here that most of HANDEL's operas and oratorios were introduced. Destroyed by fires, the theater was rebuilt in 1790 and 1868. It was pulled down and rebuilt in the 1890's. Many significant opera performances took place on this site, in one or another of the theaters. VERDI's *I masnadieri* was performed here on July 22, 1847. In 1877 MAPLESON used the theater as an opera house and during the next decade gave the first performance in England of WAGNER's entire RING cycle, MEFISTOFELE, and CARMEN (with Minnie HAUK). In 1887

he gave his last season, memorable for performances of FIDELIO with Lilli LEHMANN and LA TRAVIATA with PATTI.

Herman, an army officer (tenor) in love with Lisa in TCHAIKOVSKY's PIQUE DAME.

Hermann, Landgrave of Thuringia (bass) in WAGNER's TANNHÄUSER.

Hero, Claudio's beloved (soprano) in BERLIOZ' BÉATRICE ET BÉNÉDICT.

Hero and Leander, *see* ERO E LEANDRO.

Herod (Hérode), (1) King of Galilee (baritone) in MASSENET's HÉRODIADE.

(2) Tetrarch of Judea (tenor) in Richard STRAUSS's SALOME.

Hérodiade, opera in four acts by MASSENET. Libretto by Paul Milliet and Henri Grémont, based on FLAUBERT's story *Hérodias,* in turn derived from an episode in the New Testament. Premiere: Théâtre de la Monnaie, Dec. 19, 1881. American premiere: New Orleans, Feb. 13, 1892.

Characters: Salomé, daughter of Hérodias (soprano); Herod (Hérode), King of Galilee (baritone); Hérodias, his wife (contralto); Phanuel, a young Jew (bass); John the Baptist (tenor); Vitellius, a Roman proconsul (baritone); the High Priest; merchants, soldiers, priests. The setting is Jerusalem, A.D. 30.

Act I. Courtyard of Herod's palace. Salomé relates to Phanuel how John the Baptist saved her as a child in the desert ("Il est doux, il est bon"). Herod then appears, aroused by his passionate desire for Salomé. His wife, Hérodias, comes to tell him how John the Baptist has denounced her and demanded Herod's death. Knowing of the prophet's hold on the people, Herod is upset. At this point, John the Baptist enters and denounces Herod and Hérodias, who flee in horror. Salomé recognizes John the Baptist as her savior. She falls at his feet adoringly and begs for his love. The prophet advises her to turn to God and find spiritual love.

Act II, Scene 1. Herod's chamber. Slave girls sing and dance for Herod as he lies on his couch, pining for

Salomé. A potion is brought with the promise that it will bring him a vision of the one he loves most. Herod drinks the draught and sees a vision of Salomé, dazzling in her beauty. Rapturously, he sings of his passion ("Vision fugitive"). The vision disappears, leaving Herod more disturbed than ever. Phanuel now brings news that the people are restive against the Roman occupation and want Herod to lead them in rebellion.

Scene 2. A public square. In leading the people against the Romans, Herod gains the support of John the Baptist. But when the Roman Vitellius arrives with his men, Herod once again cringes before the rulers. John the Baptist remains defiant and impresses Vitellius with his courage and dedication. Hérodias warns Vitellius of the malicious influence of the prophet. Fearlessly John denounces the Romans and prophesies their doom.

Act III, Scene 1. Phanuel's house. Hérodias, aware of Herod's passion for Salomé, comes to Phanuel to have him read her future in the stars. Phanuel can find only blood. He also reveals to Hérodias that her long-lost daughter is none other than Salomé.

Scene 2. The temple. John the Baptist has been imprisoned. Salomé comes to the temple to seek him out. Herod tries to make love to her, but she rejects him, declaring she loves another. Herod vows to destroy his rival. When Vitellius demands that John be tried, Herod orders the prophet brought to him. Salomé throws herself upon the prophet with such passion that Herod realizes that it is the prophet with whom Salomé is in love. Disgusted, he orders the death of both Salomé and John the Baptist.

Act IV, Scene 1. A dungeon in the temple. John awaits his sentence, praying for divine guidance ("Adieu donc, vains objets"). Salomé, pardoned by Herod, comes to the prophet, ready to die with him. They fall in one another's arms, conscious of their love ("Il est beau de mourir en s'aimant"). The

priests, coming to take the prophet to his execution, separate them.

Scene 2. A hall in the palace. A brilliant festival is taking place before Herod and Hérodias. Salomé implores Herod to free John the Baptist or, failing this, to allow her to die with him. But it is too late. The executioner comes with the news that the prophet is dead. Horror-stricken, Salomé rushes toward the triumphant Hérodias with a dagger. To save herself, Hérodias reveals to Salomé that she is her mother, whereupon Salomé stabs herself.

Massenet's *Hérodiade* and Richard STRAUSS'S SALOME, based on the same Biblical episode, are in remarkable contrast. In Strauss's opera, both story and music are filled with savage eroticism. Salome's love is made to pass from sensuality to perversion. Massenet's opera is on a more elevated plane. The sensuality is there, but it is treated with refinement and restraint, with noble French lyricism and sweetness. It is never permitted to lapse into decadence. In our time *Hérodiade* lies on the shelf while *Salome* enjoys her seventh decade of vigorous life.

Hérodias, Herod's wife, contralto in MASSENET'S HÉRODIADE and mezzo-soprano in Richard STRAUSS'S SALOME.

Hérold, Louis Joseph Ferdinand, composer. Born Paris, Jan. 28, 1791; died Les Ternes, Jan. 19, 1833. He entered the Paris Conservatory in 1806 and six years later won the PRIX DE ROME. He became interested in opera in Italy and completed his first opera, *La Jeunesse de Henry V,* successfully performed in Naples in 1815. Returning to Paris, Hérold collaborated with BOIELDIEU in writing *Charles de France* and followed it with an OPÉRA COMIQUE of his own, *Les Rosières.* In the next fifteen years he wrote fourteen operas, the finest and the most successful being ZAMPA, in 1831, and LE PRÉ AUX CLERCS, a year later. While none of his *opéras comiques* has survived in the permanent repertory, Hérold was a major figure in the evolution of that form, a link from its early masters, AUBER and Boieldieu, to

OFFENBACH. His most celebrated works were *Les Rosières* (1817); *L'Amour platonique* (1819); *Le Muletier* (1823); *Le Roi René* (1824); *Le Lapin blanc* (1825); *Marie* (1826); *Zampa* (1831); *La Médicine sans médicin* (1832); *Le Pré aux clercs* (1823); *Ludovic* (completed by HALÉVY).

Hertz, Alfred, conductor. Born Frankfurt, July 15, 1872; died San Francisco, Cal., Apr. 17, 1942. After graduating with honors from the Raff Conservatory, he received his first appointment as conductor at the Halle State Theater in 1891. Various engagements followed, leading to his arrival in the United States, where he had come to conduct the German repertory at the METROPOLITAN OPERA. His American debut took place on Nov. 28, 1902, with LOHENGRIN. He remained with the Metropolitan for thirteen seasons, a period in which he directed twenty-seven different operas. In 1903 he led the first stage performance of PARSIFAL outside BAYREUTH. This act, regarded by many Wagnerites as a violation of the master's wish to confine *Parsifal* to Bayreuth, henceforth closed Bayreuth, as well as all leading German opera houses, to Hertz. In 1907 he conducted the American premiere of SALOME and in 1910 the world premiere of DIE KÖNIGSKINDER. He also conducted the premieres of all American operas performed at the Metropolitan in those years. After leaving the Metropolitan in 1915, he served for fifteen years as conductor of the San Francisco Symphony and guest conductor of the SAN FRANCISCO OPERA.

Herzeleide, *see* ICH SAH DAS KIND AN SEINER MUTTER BRUST.

Hester Prynne, *see* PRYNNE, HESTER.

Heure espagnole, L' (The Spanish Hour), one-act comic opera by RAVEL. Libretto by Franc-Nohain (Maurice Legrand). Premiere: Opéra-Comique, May 19, 1911. American premiere: Chicago, Jan. 5, 1920. Ravel described his opera as "a sort of musical conversation." One of two operas by Ravel, it is a jewel of wit and satire in both

text and music. The setting is Toledo, Spain, in the eighteenth century. While Torquemada (tenor), a clockmaker, attends to the clocks of the town, his wife, Concepcion (soprano), entertains a succession of lovers in his shop. As one lover after another arrives, the earlier ones are concealed in grandfather clocks and elsewhere. Torquemada, returning from his work, discovers the various men but is willing to accept their explanation that they are only customers. The complicated situation ends with everybody in gay spirits, the closing HABANERA being a take-off on the traditional closing scenes in Italian operas.

He Who Gets Slapped, opera in three acts by WARD. Libretto by Bernard Stambler, based on Leonid ANDREYEV's play of the same name. Premiere: New York City, May 17, 1956 (under the title *Pantaloon*). The authors reverted to the title originally used by Andreyev when the NEW YORK CITY OPERA revived the opera on Apr. 12, 1959. The opera follows the Andreyev play by describing a circus in which a bareback rider, Consuelo, is being compelled by her guardian to marry a degenerate millionaire. A sad and lonely man joins the circus, and rather than see Consuelo marry a man she does not love, he poisons her and then commits suicide. This text offers the composer ample opportunities to develop his melodic gifts as well as his dramatic powers.

Hexenlied (Witch's Song), *see* HURR, HOPP, HOPP, HOPP.

Hexenritt (Witch's Ride), descriptive prelude to Act II of HUMPERDINCK's HANSEL AND GRETEL.

Hidalgo, Elvira de, *see* DE HIDALGO, ELVIRA.

Hidroat, King of Damascus (bass) in GLUCK's ARMIDE.

Hier liesst welch' martervolles Los, Fatima's aria in WEBER's ABU HASSAN.

Hier soll ich dich denn sehen, Belmonte's aria in Act I of MOZART's THE ABDUCTION FROM THE SERAGLIO, as he hopes for an early reunion with his beloved Constanze.

Hier steh' ich, treu dir bis zum Tod, Senta's avowal of her eternal faith to the Dutchman before committing suicide, in Act III of WAGNER'S DER FLIEGENDE HOLLÄNDER.

Hilbert, Egon, opera manager and director. Born Austria, 1899; died Vienna, Jan. 18, 1968. During World War II he was imprisoned by the Nazis for five years. Between 1946 and 1953 he was appointed administrator of the VIENNA STATE OPERA. In 1953 he went to Italy to serve as president of the Austrian Cultural Institute, but in 1960 he returned to Vienna to become codirector of the State Opera with Herbert von KARAJAN. It was due to violent disagreements between these two directors that Karajan resigned from the Vienna State Opera in 1964, after which Hilbert was its sole director up to the time of his death.

Hiller, Johann Adam, composer. Born Wendisch-Ossig, Prussia, Dec. 25, 1728; died Leipzig, June 16, 1804. He established the operatic form of the SINGSPIEL, forerunner of German comic opera. His music study took place at the Kreuzschule in Dresden. In 1754 he became musical tutor to the household of Count Brühl. Four years later he settled permanently in Leipzig, becoming a major figure of its musical life. He stimulated the revival of musical activity following the Seven Years' War by conducting concerts of orchestral and oratorio music, founding a singing school, establishing the Concerts Spirituels at Leipzig, and serving as cantor of the Thomasschule (the post once held by Johann Sebastian Bach). During this period he wrote numerous musical works, his major contribution being in the field of opera. His most important operas and *singspiele* were *Der Teufel ist los* (1766); *Lottchen am Hofe* (1767); *Der Dorfbarbier* (1770); *Die Jagd* (1770); *Der Krieg* (1772); *Die Jubelhochzeit* (1773); *Das Grab des Mufti* (1779).

Hindemith, Paul, composer. Born Hanau, Ger., Nov. 16, 1895; died Frankfurt, Dec. 28, 1963. After completing his music study at Hoch's Conservatory in Frankfurt, he became concertmaster and eventually conductor of the FRANKFURT OPERA orchestra. During this period (1915–1923) he wrote many chamber works that were successfully given at leading German and Austrian festivals. He also founded and played in the Amar String Quartet. In 1926 the first version of his opera CARDILLAC, introduced in Dresden, made him famous throughout Europe. Even more controversial and more successful was NEUES VOM TAGE (*News of the Day*), first seen in Berlin in 1929. Hindemith was now one of the most highly esteemed of the younger German composers. He combined creative activity with the teaching of composition at the Berlin Hochschule. He was also made a member of the German Academy. Soon after the rise of Hitler, Hindemith's opera MATHIS DER MALER became the center of a political controversy. Hindemith's music was banned in Germany, and the composer was compelled to leave the country. He came to the United States in 1937 and subsequently became a citizen. He joined the faculty of Yale University and gave master classes in composition at the Berkshire Music Center and Harvard University. In 1948 Hindemith became a member of the music faculty at the Zürich University without resigning from Yale, but in 1953 he left Yale to make his home permanently in Zürich. An a cappella mass not only was his last composition but also marked his last public appearance, in Berlin on Nov. 12, 1963. A victim of three strokes, Hindemith died before that year ended. Among the many honors and awards conferred on him were the Sibelius Prize of thirty-two thousand dollars, the Italian Balzan Prize of fifty-two thousand dollars, the NEW YORK MUSIC CRITICS' CIRCLE AWARD (twice), and the Bach Prize of the City of Hamburg.

His operas: *Cardillac* (1926, extensively revised 1952); HIN UND ZURÜCK (1927); *Neues vom Tage* (1929); *Wir bauen eine Stadt,* children's opera

(1931); *Mathis der Maler* (1934); DIE
HARMONIE DER WELT (1952); and THE
LONG CHRISTMAS DINNER (1961). Most
of his important operas, like the bulk
of his prodigious concert-music output,
is in a linear style, contrapuntal music
where the separate voices move independently of harmonic relationships.

In addition to his vast library of
serious compositions, there exist many
pieces for pianola, radio, brass band,
theater, motion pictures, and schools
(the opera *Wir bauen eine Stadt* is an
example of the last), all composed in
the late 1920's, for which the term
GEBRAUCHSMUSIK, "functional music,"
was coined. Another term associated
with the Hindemith of the 1920's is
ZEITKUNST, "contemporary art," which
refers to such operas as *Hin und zurück*
and *Neues vom Tage*.

Hines, Jerome (born Heinz), bass.
Born Los Angeles, Cal., Nov. 9, 1921.
His only voice teacher was Gennaro
Curci, though he subsequently was
coached by Samuel Margolis. He made
his opera debut with the SAN FRANCISCO
OPERA as Biterolf in TANNHÄUSER on
Oct. 24, 1941. Appearances with other
opera companies followed. In 1946 he
won the Metropolitan Opera Auditions,
which led to his debut with the Metropolitan on Nov. 21, 1946, in a minor
role in BORIS GODUNOV. During the next
twenty seasons he was heard in over
thirty bass roles in a highly varied repertory, including PETER GRIMES, *Boris
Godunov* (in which he assumed the
title role in 1954), and a new production of VERDI's MACBETH, in 1960. Meanwhile he appeared in THE RAKE's PRO-
GRESS at the GLYNDEBOURNE and EDIN-
BURGH festivals; in the principal bass
roles of DON CARLOS and MEFISTOFELE in
Buenos Aires; and at the MUNICH OPERA
FESTIVAL of 1954 in the title role of
DON GIOVANNI. In 1958 he became the
first American to assume the role of
GURNEMANZ at BAYREUTH, to which he
returned for several seasons in this and
other Wagnerian bass roles. Also in
1958 he made his LA SCALA debut in a
revival of HANDEL's *Hercules*. He scored

an unprecedented triumph in his first
appearance in Moscow in the title role
of *Boris Godunov* in Sept., 1962. Premier Khrushchev joined the audience
in giving him a standing ovation, an
acclaim all the more remarkable because the performance took place
during the Cuban missile crisis.

Hinrichs, Gustav, conductor. Born
Mecklenburg, Ger., Dec. 10, 1850; died
Mountain Lakes, N.J., Mar. 26, 1942.
He directed the American premieres of
CAVALLERIA RUSTICANA, MANON LESCAUT,
and PAGLIACCI. After completing his
studies in Hamburg, he played in the
Stadttheater orchestra. In 1870 he came
to the United States, and soon after
that became Theodore THOMAS' assistant with the American Opera Company.
In 1886 he organized and subsequently
managed his own opera company in
Philadelphia and for a decade toured
the eastern United States. It was with
this group that he gave the American
premieres of many notable Italian and
French operas. He made his conducting
debut at the METROPOLITAN OPERA on
Feb. 12, 1904, with *Cavalleria rusticana*,
but stayed with the company only a
single season.

Hin und zurück (Here and Back), a
one-act "sketch with music" by HINDE-
MITH. Libretto by Marcellus Schiffer,
based on an English revue sketch. Premiere: Baden-Baden, Ger., July 17,
1927. American premiere: Philadelphia,
Apr. 22, 1928. This is an amusing curiosity written during the period when
Hindemith was interested in ZEITKUNST,
"contemporary art." The first half of
the opera describes how a husband kills
his unfaithful wife, having caught her
with her lover. Midway the plot and
action are put in reverse: the adultress
comes back to life, the husband puts
his revolver back in his pocket, the
lover backs out the front door—until the
opera ends precisely in the same way it
had started.

Hippodameia, a trilogy of operas, or
melodramas, by FIBICH. Written between 1890 and 1892, the three are
Pelops' Wooing (Feb. 21, 1890), *The*

Atonement of Tantalus (June 2, 1891), and *The Death of Hippodameia* (Nov. 8, 1891). This was the most ambitious of Fibich's attempts to modify the musicodramatic art form called MELODRAMA in order to achieve a more complete marriage of poetry and music than had ever been realized in opera.

Hippolyte et Aricie (Hippolytus and Aricia), opera in prologue and five acts by RAMEAU. Libretto by Simon Joseph Pellegrin, based on EURIPIDES. Premiere: Paris Opéra, Oct. 1, 1733. American premiere: New York City, Apr. 11, 1954 (concert version); Boston, Apr. 4, 1966 (staged). Hippolytus is in love with Aricia. Learning that he is loved by his stepmother, Phèdre, Hippolytus plans to flee with Aricia. He is finally destroyed in a sea storm. Ravaged by her conscience, Phèdre commits suicide. Of musical interest are the opening prelude (a march); the tenor aria in the prologue, "A l'amour rendez les armes"; the chorus in the first act, "Rendons un eternal hommage"; and the soprano aria in the fifth act, "Rossignols amoureux."

Hochzeit des Camacho, Die (Camacho's Wedding), opera in two parts by MENDELSSOHN. Libretto by Carl August Ludwig von Lichtenstein, based on an episode from CERVANTES' DON QUIXOTE. Premiere: Berlin, Apr. 29, 1827. American premiere: Boston, Mar. 19, 1885. This was Mendelssohn's first opera, written when he was sixteen. Quitero, though in love with Basilio, is compelled to marry a rich landowner, Camacho. To prevent the wedding, Basilio makes a pretense at stabbing himself. Don Quixote, a wedding guest, urges Camacho to allow Quitero to marry the dying Basilio, since she will soon be a widow and he can then marry her. Camacho agrees to give the dying man his last bit of happiness. But once the marriage ceremony has been performed, Basilio proves very much the healthy young man, and Quitero is far from becoming a widow. Heinrich Eduard Jacob described the work as containing "a wealth of music and

forms," together with "rapid alternations of arias and ensembles . . . the whole thing kept moving at a brisk pace. Tinged in *buffo* colors, it reminded one a little of MOZART."

Hoël, goatherd (baritone) in MEYERBEER'S DINORAH.

Hoesslin, Franz von, conductor. Born Munich, Dec. 31, 1885; died near Site, Sept. 28, 1946. After completing his music study with MOTTL and Reger, he made his debut as opera conductor in St. Gall in 1908. He served his apprenticeship with several opera companies in Germany, then became music director in Dessau in 1923, a post he held for three years. He was one of the principal conductors at BAYREUTH in 1927–28, 1934, and 1938–40. He subsequently conducted operas in France and Spain for a few years, until he was killed in an air crash.

Hoffmann, Ernst Theodor Amadeus, composer, poet, author, critic, conductor. Born Königsberg, Prussia, Jan. 24, 1776; died Berlin, June 25, 1882. Immortalized in THE TALES OF HOFFMANN, he was a man of extraordinary versatility. In addition to his literary creations, including fantasies and fairy tales that inspired musical works (among them CARDILLAC), he wrote ten operas, the most celebrated being *Die lustigen Musikanten* (1805) and UNDINE (1816). He was music director at Bamberg in 1808, and in 1813–14 he conducted operas at Leipzig.

Hofmannsthal, Hugo von, poet, dramatist, librettist. Born Vienna, Feb. 1, 1874; died Vienna, July 15, 1929. He was for many years Richard STRAUSS's librettist. They collaborated upon the following works: ARABELLA, DIE AEGYPTISCHE HELENA, ARIADNE AUF NAXOS, ELEKTRA, DIE FRAU OHNE SCHATTEN, and DER ROSENKAVALIER. Hofmannsthal also wrote the libretto for WELLESZ' ALKESTIS, while his play *Die Hochzeit der Sobeide* was used by Alexander TCHEREPNIN for his opera of the same name.

Hof und Nationaltheater, *see* MUNICH OPERA.

Ho! He! Ho!, the sailor's chorus (Mari-

naresca) in Act II of PONCHIELLI'S LA
GIOCONDA.

Ho-Ho! Schmiede, mein Hammer, the
Hammer Song—Siegfried's narrative in
Act I of WAGNER'S SIEGFRIED.

Ho-Jo-To-Ho!, Brünnhilde's battle cry
in Act II of WAGNER'S DIE WALKÜRE.

Holà! matelots (Su, su, marinar), the
sailors' chorus in Act III of MEYER-
BEER'S L'AFRICAINE.

Holberg, Ludvig, dramatist and writer.
Born Bergen, Norway, Dec. 3, 1684;
died Copenhagen, Jan. 28, 1754. The
works of the founder of Danish literature were the source of several operas,
including Carl Nielsen's *Maskarade,*
SCHOECK'S *Ranudo,* and Julius Weis-
mann's *Die pfiffige Magd.*

Holbrooke, Josef (or Joseph), composer. Born Croydon, Eng., July 5,
1878; died London, Aug. 5, 1958. Educated at the Royal Academy of Music
in London, he received recognition
with *The Raven,* an orchestral work
introduced in 1900. His magnum opus
is an operatic trilogy based on Celtic
legends, entitled *The Cauldron of An-
wyn.* The first opera in this trilogy,
The Children of Don, was introduced
in 1911. The other two, *Dylan* and
Bronwen, were heard in 1913 and 1929.
Holbrooke's other operas: *Pierrot and
Pierrette* (1909); *The Wizard* (1915);
The Stranger (1924).

Holland Music Festival, a festival inaugurated by H. J. Reinink and Peter
Diamant in June, 1947. It has presented
opera as a significant part of its varied
activities and is the only festival of national scope, since performances are
given not only in Amsterdam, but also
in The Hague and other Dutch cities.
Opera is given principally by the
Netherlands Opera, but various visiting groups have also been heard, including the VIENNA STATE OPERA, MUNICH
OPERA, LA SCALA, ENGLISH OPERA GROUP,
Municipal Opera of Essen, and the
Wuppertal Opera. World premieres
have included PHILOMELA, MARTIN
KORDA, D. P., L'APOSTROPHE, and Ton de
Leeuw's *The Dream.* An unusual premiere in 1969 was an ELECTRONIC opera,

Reconstruction, the work of five Dutch
composers.

Novelties from the past and present
have included *Ali Baba* (CHERUBINI),
BENVENUTO CELLINI, BLUEBEARD'S CASTLE,
DOKTOR FAUST, ELEGY FOR YOUNG LOVERS,
FROM THE HOUSE OF THE DEAD, I CAP-
ULETTI ED I MONTECCHI, LA CENEREN-
TOLA, *L'infedeltà delusa* (HAYDN), JE-
NUFA, KAT'A KABANOVÁ, THE LOVE FOR
THREE ORANGES, A MIDSUMMER NIGHT'S
DREAM, IL MONDO DELLA LUNA, MOSES UND
ARON, OBERON, *Le pescatrici* (Haydn),
Platée (RAMEAU), IL PRIGIONIERO, EL
RETABLO DE MAESE PEDRO, IL RITORNO DI
ULISSE IN PATRIA, LA VIDA BREVE, and VON
HEUTE AUF MORGEN.

**Hölle Rache Kocht in meinem Herzen,
Der,** the plea of the Queen of the Night
to Pamina to seek vengeance, in Act II,
Scene 3, of MOZART'S THE MAGIC FLUTE.

Holst, Gustav, composer. Born Chelten-
ham, Eng., Sept. 21, 1874; died London,
May 25, 1934. After completing music
study at the Royal College of Music,
he was appointed musical director of
the St. Paul's Girls' School and professor at the Royal College of Music, retaining both posts for over two decades.
During World War I he was engaged by
the YMCA to organize the musical activities among British troops in Salon-
ika, Constantinople, and points in Asia
Minor. In 1923 he visited the United
States, where he lectured at the University of Michigan. Later, his health
deteriorated, and he was forced to give
up all musical activities except composing. One of the early influences in
his music was Sanskrit literature, a
phase that saw the composition of a
CHAMBER OPERA, SAVITRI, and a grand
opera, *Sita.* Subsequently, English folksong affected his writing; in this vein
he wrote some of his finest works, including an opera, AT THE BOAR'S HEAD.
Toward the end of his life he began
experimenting with nonharmonic counterpoint and free tonalities. His operas:
Sita (1906); *Savitri* (1908); THE PERFECT
FOOL (1921); *At the Boar's Head* (1924);
The Tale of the Wandering Scholar
(1929).

Holy Devil, The, *see* DEATH OF GREGORY RASPUTIN, THE.

Holy Grail, The, a lengendary cup supposed to have been the one used at the Last Supper. It appears in WAGNER's PARSIFAL.

Homer, the traditional blind Greek poet, whose birthplace various Greek cities have claimed to be—at times from the twelfth to the seventh century B.C. His epics, *The Iliad* and *The Odyssey*, were sources for the following operas: HEGER's *Der Bettler Namelos;* Vittorio Gnecchi's *Cassandra;* August Bungert's cycle of six operas *Homerische Welt;* KING PRIAM; GLANVILLE-HICKS's *Nausicaa;* Hermann Reutter's *Odysseus;* PÉNÉLOPE; PENTHESILEA; and ULISSE.

Homer, Louise (born Louise Dilworth Beatty), contralto. Born Sewickley, Pa., Apr. 28, 1871; died Winter Park, Fla., May 6, 1947. For almost two decades she was one of the great stars of the METROPOLITAN OPERA, an imperial figure during the "golden age" of opera in America. The daughter of a Presbyterian minister, she showed marked musical talent as a child. While attending the New England Conservatory, she met and fell in love with the composer Sidney Homer, her teacher in theory and harmony. They were married in 1895. Conscious of his wife's talent, he took her to Paris, where she studied with Mme. Fidèle König and Paul Lhérie. Her opera debut took place in Vichy, in 1898, in LA FAVORITA. She next sang at COVENT GARDEN (1899–1900). Following an engagement at the THÉÂTRE DE LA MONNAIE, she returned to the United States. Her American debut took place on Nov. 14, 1900, in the role of AMNERIS, in San Francisco during a national tour of the Metropolitan Opera. A month later she appeared in the same role in New York City. She was a participant in many of the historic events at the Metropolitan during the early years of the present century. She was the Voice in the first performance of PARSIFAL outside BAYREUTH, in 1903. She was Maddalena in the performance of RIGOLETTO in 1903 in which CARUSO made his American debut. When Arturo TOSCANINI appeared at the Metropolitan Opera for the first time, she was Amneris. Some of the most important premieres and revivals in which she was featured include ARMIDE, LA DAME BLANCHE, THE GYPSY BARON, HANSEL AND GRETEL, DIE KÖNIGSKINDER, MADAMA BUTTERFLY, MANRU, and ORFEO ED EURIDICE (GLUCK).

Her resignation from the Metropolitan Opera in 1919 by no means ended her career. She appeared with other major American opera companies, notably the CHICAGO OPERA, where she sang for three seasons, and on December 13, 1927, she was back on the stage of the Metropolitan for a guest appearance in AIDA. In 1929 she returned there for the last time in a performance of IL TROVATORE. As she closed her career there were few to deny that she had been a worthy partner of the great—that she could indeed be considered among the greatest. She combined the highest artistic integrity with remarkable versatility, beauty of voice and diction with a majestic stage presence. She was a prima donna in the grand manner. After her retirement, she devoted herself to her family. The story of the Homers' happy marriage was told by Sidney Homer in *My Wife and I* (1939).

Home, Sweet Home, a celebrated song with words by John Howard Payne and music by Sir Henry Rowley Bishop. It originated as an aria in Bishop's comic opera *Clari, the Maid of Milan* (1823). Another version of the same melody is found in DONIZETTI's ANNA BOLENA. Some prima donnas have interpolated Bishop's song in the Lesson Scene of ROSSINI's THE BARBER OF SEVILLE.

Honegger, Arthur, composer. Born Le Havre, France, Mar. 10, 1892; died Paris, Nov. 27, 1955. Educated in the conservatories of Zürich and Paris, he did not become known until after World War I, when his name was linked with those of five young French composers (including MILHAUD and POULENC). This avant-garde group was for some years known as LES SIX. Honegger achieved his first substantial success with an oratorio, *Le Roi David,* in 1921. One of his most important works of this period was the opera JUDITH, introduced at MONTE CARLO in 1926. His later works reveal a deep religious feeling and mysticism. He visited the United States for the first time in 1929, appearing as guest conductor of his own works. He remained in Paris during World War II. In 1947 he returned to America to conduct a class in composition at the Berkshire Music Center, but illness prevented him from doing so. Though he never fully recovered, he completed some major symphonic and chamber works in the last years of his life. He was married to Andrée Vaurabourg, a concert pianist, who was often heard in performances of his piano works. His operas: *Judith* (1925); ANTIGONE (1927); *Amphion* (1928); L'AIGLON (1937), a collaboration with Jacques IBERT); *Nicolas de Flue* (1939); *Charles le Tremeraire* (1944). His dramatic oratorio JEANNE D'ARC AU BÛCHER has sometimes been performed as an opera.

Hooker, Brian, dramatist and librettist. Born New York City, 1880; died there Dec. 28, 1946. Best known for his translation of CYRANO DE BERGERAC, Hooker was also the author of librettos for PARKER's operas *Fairyland* and MONA. He also wrote the libretto for GRUENBERG's radio opera, *Green Mansions,* based on the novel of W. H. Hudson.

Hoo-Tsin, a wealthy merchant (bass) in LEONI's L'ORACOLO.

hopak (or **gopak**), a spirited Russian dance with two beats to the measure. A celebrated example in opera occurs in MUSSORGSKY's THE FAIR AT SOROCHINSK.

Hopf, Hans, tenor. Born Nüremberg, Aug. 2, 1916. Vocal study took place principally with Paul BENDER in Munich. In 1936 he made his opera debut at the Bayerische Landesbühnen in Munich. Appearances followed in various opera houses, including the DRESDEN OPERA and the BERLIN STATE OPERA, before he became a permanent member of the MUNICH OPERA in 1949. Between 1951

and 1953 he appeared at COVENT GARDEN. On Mar. 15, 1952, he made his debut at the METROPOLITAN OPERA as Walther in DIE MEISTERSINGER, remaining with that company for three years. A distinguished Wagnerian tenor, he has been heard in BAYREUTH. He has also appeared at the SALZBURG and MUNICH festivals and been acclaimed not only in Wagnerian roles but also in performances in DER FREISCHÜTZ, DIE FRAU OHNE SCHATTEN, and OTELLO, among other operas.

Horace Tabor, *see* TABOR, HORACE.

Horatio, the hero (tenor), in love with a lady of mystery, Lady Angela, in AUBER's LE DOMINO NOIR.

Horch, die Lerche, Fenton's ROMANCE to Anne Page in Act II of NICOLAI's THE MERRY WIVES OF WINDSOR.

Horne, Marilyn, soprano. Born Bradford, Pa., Jan. 16, 1934. She entered the University of Southern California on a voice scholarship, and while there, she studied with William Vennard and attended Lotte LEHMANN's master classes. After some notable appearances on the concert stage, over radio, and on the soundtrack of the motion picture *Carmen Jones* (where she dubbed in the singing voice for Dorothy Dandridge), Horne made her opera debut in the Municipal Opera of Gelsenkirchen, West Germany, in 1957 as Giulietta in THE TALES OF HOFFMANN. During the three years she stayed with this company she was heard in several unusual roles, including Fulvia in HANDEL's *Ezio* and Marie in WOZZECK. At the same time she made guest appearances with other European opera companies. After returning to the United States, she made her official American opera debut with the SAN FRANCISCO OPERA on Oct. 4, 1960, as Marie in *Wozzeck,* and she scored such a triumph that the Los Angeles *Times* nominated her as "the woman of the year." In Feb., 1961, she sang the role of Agnese in BEATRICE DI TENDA in New York in a performance by the AMERICAN OPERA SOCIETY in which Joan SUTHERLAND played the leading female role. She once again appeared with Miss Sutherland in 1964, in a presentation by the American Opera Society of SEMIRAMIDE. Later the same year she gathered further accolades for her performances as Isabella in L'ITALIANA IN ALGERI in San Francisco and as Marie in *Wozzeck* in London, while in Feb., 1965, she was wildly applauded for her appearance in *Semiramide* with the BOSTON OPERA. In 1969, she was starred in revivals in Italy of two ROSSINI operas, LA CENERENTOLA in Turin and LE SIÈGE DE CORINTHE in Milan. The latter performance took place at LA SCALA, where she had made her debut on Mar. 13, 1969, in a new production of OEDIPUS REX. She made her debut at the METROPOLITAN OPERA on Mar. 3, 1970, as Adalgisa opposite Joan Sutherland's NORMA.

Hört ihr Leut', und lasst euch sagen, the call of the watchman proclaiming all is quiet and peaceful, at the close of Act II of WAGNER'S DIE MEISTERSINGER.

Ho sete! Ho sete!, love duet of Avito and Fiora in Act II of MONTEMEZZI'S L'AMORE DEI TRE RE.

Hotter, Hans, baritone. Born Offenbach-am-Main, Ger., Jan. 19, 1909. As a boy he sang in church choirs; as a young man he served as church organist and choir master. He pursued the study of church music at the Munich Academy of Music, after which he decided to enter the operatic field. His initiation took place in Troppau and Breslau, after which he was engaged by the BERLIN OPERA. After a season at the PRAGUE OPERA, he was engaged by the MUNICH OPERA as principal baritone, achieving such success there that he was given the honorary title of KAMMERSÄNGER. He appeared in the premieres of Richard STRAUSS'S DER FRIEDENSTAG and CAPRICCIO. While a member of the Munich Opera, he made guest appearances in Barcelona, Amsterdam, Antwerp, and at COVENT GARDEN. On Nov. 9, 1950, he made his debut at the METROPOLITAN OPERA as the Dutchman in DER FLIEGENDE HOLLÄNDER, remaining with the company through the 1953–54 season, specializing in the Wagnerian repertory. His performances at the BAYREUTH

festival established him as one of the most significant interpreters of the role of WOTAN in the post-World War II era, so much so that it was for him that Covent Garden undertook a new production of the RING cycle in 1961.

Houston Grand Opera, one of the leading opera companies in Texas. It was founded in 1955, financed by Mrs. Louis G. Lobit, with Walter Herbert as its general director. Its first productions were SALOME and MADAMA BUTTERFLY. Walter Herbert, who has remained its director, has relied mostly on the standard repertory (though in 1967 the company did offer Texas performances of DER JUNGE LORD) while expanding the activities of the company from four performances of two operas a season to twenty-five performances of five operas. On Oct. 5, 1967, the company helped inaugurate the Jesse H. Jones Hall for the Performing Arts, part of a forty-million-dollar civic center complex, with a presentation of AIDA.

Hubay, Jenö, violinist and composer. Born Budapest, Sept. 14, 1858; died Vienna, Mar. 12, 1937. After studying with Joachim at the Berlin Hochschule für Musik, he made appearances as violinist throughout Europe. He combined a career as virtuoso with that of teacher, serving as professor of the violin class at the Brussels Conservatory and the Budapest Conservatory; from 1919 to 1934 he was the director of the latter institution. His first opera, *Alienor,* was produced in Budapest in 1891. Two years later his most successful opera, *Der Geigenmacher von Cremona,* was produced in Budapest and acclaimed. Other operas: *Der Dorflump* (1896); *Moosröschen* (1903); *Lavottas Liebe* (1906); *Anna Karenina* (1915). Hubay was knighted in 1907.

Hubička (The Kiss), comic opera in two acts by SMETANA. Libretto by Eliska Krasnohorska, based on a story by Karolina Světlá. Premiere: Prague, Nov. 7, 1876. American premiere: Chicago, Apr. 17, 1921. Though Vendulka is engaged to Lukas, she refuses to allow him to kiss her. Piqued, Lukas goes around kissing every girl he can find—much to the humiliation of Vendulka, who has witnessed the spectacle. The lovers become reconciled, and at long last Vendulka permits her betrothed to kiss her.

Hugh the Drover, BALLAD OPERA in two acts by VAUGHAN WILLIAMS. Libretto by Harold Child. Premiere: London, July 4, 1924. American premiere: Washington, D.C., Feb. 21, 1928. In the Cotswolds, about 1812, Mary is in love with Hugh the Drover, but her father wants her to marry John the Butcher. In a fight to decide who will win Mary, Hugh is the victor, but before he gains his prize he is accused by Mary's father of being a Napoleonic spy. When a sergeant, called to arrest Hugh, recognizes him as a friend and a loyal subject, he absolves him and instead conscripts John the Butcher. Mary's father is now willing to have her marry Hugh.

Hugo, Victor, dramatist, novelist, poet. Born Besançon, France, Feb. 26, 1802; died Paris, May 22, 1885. A leading figure in the French romantic movement, Hugo wrote many novels and dramas that have been effectively adapted as operas. These include *Angelo, le tyran de Padoue* (LA GIOCONDA, CUI's *Angelo,* BRUNEAU's *Angelo, le tyran de Padoue*); *Hernani* (ERNANI); *Lucrèce Borgia* (LUCREZIA BORGIA); *Marie Tudor* (BALFE's *The Armourer of Nantes,* and an opera by Vladimir Kashperov); *Marion Delorme* (operas by Giovanni Bottesini, Carlo Pedrotti, PONCHIELLI); *Mazeppa* (opera by Felipe Pedrell); *Notre Dame de Paris* (BIZET's *Esmeralda,* DARGOMIZHSKY's *Esmeralda,* William Fry's *Notre Dame de Paris,* Felipe Pedrell's *Quasimodo,* Arthur Goring Thomas' *Esmeralda*); *Ruy Blas* (opera by Filippo Marchetti); *Le Roi s'amuse* (RIGOLETTO).

Huguenots, Les (The Huguenots), opera in five acts by MEYERBEER. Libretto by Eugène SCRIBE and Emile Deschamps. Premiere: Paris Opéra, Feb. 29, 1836. American premiere: Théâtre d'Orléans, New Orleans, Apr. 29, 1839.

Characters: Count de St. Bris, a Catholic nobleman (bass); Count de Nevers, another Catholic nobleman (baritone); Raoul de Nangis, a Huguenot nobleman (tenor); Marcel, his servant (bass); Marguerite de Valois, betrothed to Henry IV of Navarre (soprano); Valentine, the daughter of St. Bris (soprano); Urbain, Marguerite's page (soprano or contralto); ladies; gentlemen; citizens; soldiers; students; monks. The action takes place in Touraine and Paris in 1572.

Act I. The House of Count de Nevers. The brief orchestral prelude consists largely of the Lutheran chorale, "Ein' feste Burg," which is quoted throughout the opera as symbolic of militant Protestantism. In an effort to reconcile the Catholics and the Huguenots, the Count de Nevers has invited to his house the Huguenot nobleman Raoul de Nangis to meet his Catholic friends. The men begin to speak about their favorite ladies. Raoul describes one whom that very morning he saved from danger and whose identity is unknown to him (*Romanza:* "Plus blanche que la blanche hermine"). Raoul's servant Marcel then tactlessly sings "Ein' feste Burg," after this a battle ditty, continuing with a song about the Huguenots' ultimate triumph over monks and priests (Chanson Huguenote: "Pour les couvents c'est fini"). Suddenly a veiled lady comes seeking the Count. Raoul recognizes her as the woman he saved earlier. He does not know that she has come to beseech the Count, her fiancé, to release her from her marriage vows since she is now in love with Raoul. After the woman disappears, a page salutes the noblemen (Page's Song: "Nobles seigneurs, salut"). He has come for Raoul and makes the strange request that Raoul accompany him blindfolded to an unspecified destination.

Act II. The garden of Marguerite's castle at Chenonçeaux. Marguerite de Valois, betrothed to Henry IV, rhapsodizes over the beauty of the Touraine countryside ("O beau pays de la Touraine"). Valentine arrives to inform her that Count de Nevers has consented to breaking their engagement, and that she (Valentine) is now free to marry Raoul. Marguerite is delighted, for through this marriage she hopes to cement the friendship of the Catholics and the Huguenots. Raoul enters blindfolded. When he discovers he is in the presence of Marguerite, he sings a hymn to her beauty ("Beauté divine, enchantresse"). He offers her his services and is told that he is to marry Valentine. Raoul consents to do so, even though he does not know who Valentine is. When Valentine is brought to him, Raoul denounces her, for, recognizing her as the veiled lady, he is convinced she is the mistress of Count de Nevers. His behavior outrages the Catholic nobleman, Count de St. Bris; Catholics confront Huguenots menacingly, and bloodshed is avoided only by the intercession of Marguerite.

Act III. A square in Paris. Soldiers are heard singing a RATAPLAN. Valentine, spurned by Raoul, is marrying Count de Nevers. The bridal procession comes to the square to the strains of an "Ave Maria." Marcel brings the Count Raoul's challenge to a duel. Meanwhile, within the chapel, Valentine overhears a Catholic plot to assassinate Raoul. Frantically, she appeals to Marcel to warn his master. A fight between Huguenots and Catholics threatens and is only stopped by the timely arrival of Marguerite. Raoul learns from Marguerite that Valentine is innocent. Too late, he realizes how deeply he has wronged the woman he loves.

Act IV. A room in the castle of Count de Nevers. Valentine is heartbroken over her lost Raoul ("Parmi les fleurs"). Raoul suddenly appears: he has risked his life to see Valentine. When de Nevers, St. Bris, and other Catholic leaders arrive, Raoul hides and overhears their plot to massacre the Huguenots. Only Count de Nevers refuses to be a party to the slaughter, and for this stand, he is taken into custody. Three monks come to bless the Catholics (Benediction of the Swords: "Glaives pieux, saintes épées"). When the Catho-

lics depart, Raoul emerges from hiding, and he and Valentine exchange ardent vows of love ("O ciel où courez-vous?"). He then leads Valentine to the window, and after a signal of tolling bells, the massacre begins. Valentine collapses. (The Italian version of the opera ends at this point, the lovers perishing in a burst of firing from the street.)

Act V. In the original French version the opera continues with scenes showing the course of the St. Bartholomew's Day massacre, the hasty Catholic marriage of Valentine and Raoul, and finally their deaths at the hands of a mob led by St. Bris. Only at the end does St. Bris realize that he has been responsible for the death of his beloved daughter.

In *Les Huguenots* Meyerbeer is a showman par excellence. He has a blood and thunder story, and his music matches the text in drama, splendor, and ceremony. But it would be a mistake to consider the opera only a spectacle, for it combines theatricalism with profound depths of feeling. WAGNER, whose artistic thinking was antithetical to that of Meyerbeer, had to concede that the fourth act (particularly the love duet) was among the finest moments in opera. Others, too, consider this act the high point of Meyerbeer's art. To Arthur Hervey, if Meyerbeer had written nothing else, "he would still be entitled to rank as one of the greatest dramatic composers of all time."

Les Huguenots was Meyerbeer's second French opera, coming five years after ROBERT LE DIABLE. It had a brilliant premiere in Paris and was an outstanding success.

Humming Chorus, the off-the-scene chorus ending Act II, Scene 1, of PUCCINI'S MADAMA BUTTERFLY, as Cio-Cio-San, Suzuki, and Cio-Cio-San's baby await Pinkerton's arrival.

Humperdinck, Engelbert, composer. Born Siegburg, Ger., Sept. 1, 1854; died Neusterlitz, Sept. 27, 1921. He wrote HANSEL AND GRETEL, one of the earliest operatic fairy tales and to this day one of the best. Originally a student of architecture, in 1872 he entered the Cologne Conservatory, where he won the Mozart Prize in 1876. This award enabled him to go to Munich for additional study with Franz Lachner and Josef Rheinberger at the Royal School. The Mendelssohn Prize, in 1879, provided him with funds for travel in Italy. During this trip he met WAGNER, who, from this point on, exerted a powerful influence on the young man. He invited Humperdinck to BAYREUTH to assist him in preparing the first performance of PARSIFAL. Humperdinck served as stage manager and helped write out the orchestral parts of *Parsifal.* He also conducted Wagner's youthful symphony, a performance arranged by Wagner to honor his wife, Cosima, during their visit to Venice.

Humperdinck's career as a teacher began in 1885, when he became a professor at the Barcelona Conservatory. From 1890 to 1896 he taught at Hoch's Conservatory in Frankfurt. It was during this period that he wrote the work that made him famous, *Hansel and Gretel,* introduced in Weimar on Dec. 23, 1893, with phenomenal success. The opera was soon heard throughout Germany, as well as in London and New York. This success enabled Humperdinck to give up teaching and concentrate on composition. But in 1900 he returned to pedagogy as director of the Akademieschule in Berlin. In the same year he was elected to the Senate of the Royal Academy, becoming its president in 1913. During the next few years Humperdinck wrote several more operas, all of them failures. Discouraged, he abandoned opera for a while to write incidental music for various theatrical productions. One of these scores was later augmented into an opera, DIE KÖNIGSKINDER, whose world premiere took place at the METROPOLITAN OPERA in 1910 with the composer present.

His operas: *Hansel and Gretel* (1893); *Dornröschen* (1902); *Die Heirat wider Willen* (1905); *Die Königskinder* (1910); *Die Marketenderin* (1914); *Gaudeamus* (1919).

Hunchback of Notre Dame, The (Notre Dame de Paris), *see* HUGO, VICTOR.

Hunding, Sieglinde's husband (bass), the slayer of Siegmund, in WAGNER'S DIE WALKÜRE.

Hungarian March, *see* RÁKÓCZY MARCH.

Hungarian State Opera, *see* BUDAPEST STATE OPERA.

Hunt and Storm Music, orchestral prelude to Act III of RIMSKY-KORSAKOV'S IVAN THE TERRIBLE, popularized at symphony and semiclassical concerts.

Huntsmen's Chorus, *see* WAS GLEICHT WOHL AUF ERDEN.

Huon de Bordeaux, Sir, Duke of Guienne (tenor) in WEBER'S OBERON, a role created by John BRAHAM.

Hurr, hopp, hopp, hopp, the Witch's Song (Hexenlied) in Act III of HUMPERDINCK'S HANSEL AND GRETEL, describing her weird activities.

Hüsch, Gerhard, baritone. Born Hanover, Feb. 2, 1901. He started singing lessons in his nineteenth year with a local teacher, continuing his studies at the Opera School of the Hanover Conservatory. His opera debut took place in 1923 at the Osnabrück Theater. He then became a member of the Bremen State Theater and the COLOGNE OPERA, distinguishing himself in both places in MOZART's operas. In 1930 he was engaged as leading baritone of the Charlottenburg Opera in Berlin. He subsequently made numerous appearances in the leading opera houses of Europe, including BAYREUTH, where in 1931 he was selected by TOSCANINI for the role of WOLFRAM. Hüsch continued his career in Europe after World War II.

Hymne de joie, the Hebrews' song of victory in Act I of SAINT-SAËNS'S SAMSON ET DALILA.

Hymn to Champagne, *see* IM FEUERSTRÖM DER REBEN.

Hymn to Diane, *see* CHASTE FILLE DE LATONE.

Hymn to the Sun, aria of Queen Shemakha in Act II of RIMSKY-KORSAKOV'S LE COQ D'OR.

Hymn to Venus, *see* DIR GÖTTIN DER LIEBE.

I

Iago, Otello's ensign and adviser (baritone) and the villain in both ROSSINI's and VERDI's OTELLO. The role in the Verdi opera was created by Victor MAUREL.

Ibbetson, Colonel, Peter Ibbetson's uncle (baritone) in TAYLOR's PETER IBBETSON.

Ibert, Jacques, composer and opera director. Born Paris, Aug. 15, 1890; died there Feb. 5, 1962. His study of music was intermittent until his twenty-first year, when he entered the Paris Conservatory. Here his teachers included Roger-Ducasse and FAURÉ, and he won the PRIX DE ROME in 1919. Success came soon after his return from Italy with *The Ballad of Reading Gaol,* a tone poem, introduced in Paris in 1922. His most famous orchestral work, *Escales,* followed two years later. In 1937 Ibert became the first musician appointed as director of the Académie de France in Rome. After World War II he combined this office with that of assistant director of the PARIS OPÉRA. Between 1955 and 1957 he was the artistic director of the Paris Opéra and OPÉRA-COMIQUE. Ibert visited the United States in 1950 to conduct master classes in composition at the Berkshire Music Center at TANGLEWOOD, Mass. In conjunction with this visit, his opera LE ROI D'YVETOT received its American premiere. Ibert's operas: *Andromède et Persée* (1920); ANGÉLIQUE (1927); *Le Roi d'Yvetot* (1930); *Gonzague* (1935); L'AIGLON (1937, written in collaboration with HONEGGER); *La Famille cardinal* (1938); *Barbe-Bleue* (1943); *Le Chevalier errant* (1949).

Ibsen, Henrik, playwright and poet. Born Skien, Norway, Mar. 20, 1828; died Christiana (now Oslo), May 23, 1906. One of the earliest important social dramatists, Ibsen was the author of PEER GYNT, the source of operas by EGK, Leslie Heward, and Viktor Ullmann. Wilhelm Stenhammer's opera *The Feast at Solhaug* is derived from the Ibsen drama of the same name. Karel Moor wrote an opera based on Ibsen's *The Warriors at Helgeland.*

Ice-heart, *see* QUEEN ICE-HEART.

Ich baue ganz auf deine Stärke, Belmonte's serenade to Constanze in Act III of MOZART's THE ABDUCTION FROM THE SERAGLIO.

Ich gehe, doch rate ich dir, duet of Osmin and Blonde as she repulses him, in Act II of MOZART's THE ABDUCTION FROM THE SERAGLIO.

Ich habe eine Frau gehabt, Mandryka's air disclosing to Arabella that he is a widower and revealing his tender feelings for her, in Act II of Richard STRAUSS's ARABELLA.

Ich sah das Kind an seiner Mutter Brust, Kundry's narrative to Parsifal telling him of his mother, in Act II of WAGNER's PARSIFAL.

Ich will deinen Mund küssen, Salome's passionate address to John the Baptist, telling him she yearns for his body and hungers for his kiss, in Richard STRAUSS's SALOME.

Idamante, son (CASTRATO soprano; sung by a tenor in modern performances) of the King of Crete in MOZART's IDOMENEO.

Idomeneo, Rè di Creta (Idomeneo, King of Crete), opera in three acts by MOZART. Libretto by Giambattista Varesco, based on a French libretto by Danchet for an opera by André

Campra, *Idoménée*. Premiere: Munich, Jan. 29, 1781. American premiere: Tanglewood, Lenox, Massachusetts, Aug. 4, 1947. Returning from the Trojan wars, the fleet of the King of Crete (tenor) is ravaged by a storm. Emerging from this crisis, the King vows to sacrifice the first person meeting him when he reaches home. The person turns out to be his son, Idamante (CASTRATO soprano). In an effort to save his child, the King sends him away; but just as Idamante embarks on his ship, a terrible storm erupts. Idomeneo, realizing that the gods are punishing him, confesses everything to the High Priest. At this point, Idamante is ready to sacrifice himself, but his beloved, Ilia (soprano), offers herself in his stead. The gods announce that they will forgive everything if Idomeneo abdicates, if Idamante becomes the new ruler, and if Ilia marries the new king. The opera is rarely performed, but the overture and ballet music are sometimes played at concerts. Among the more significant vocal numbers are Idamante's arias "Non ho colpa" and "Il padre adorato" and Idomeneo's aria "Vedrommi intorno," all in Act I; in Act II, Ilia's aria, "Se il padre perdei," and that of Idomeneo, "Fuor del mar"; and Ilia's aria "Zeffiretti lusinghieri," in Act III, Scene 1.

Idomeneo was Mozart's first important serious opera and his first mature work for the stage.

Ieri son salita, Cio-Cio-San's tender aria in Act I of PUCCINI's MADAMA BUTTERFLY, in which she reveals that she has renounced the faith of her forefathers in order to marry Pinkerton.

Ifigenia in Aulide, *see* IPHIGENIA IN AULIS.

Ifigenia in Tauride, *see* IPHIGENIA IN TAURIS.

I Got Plenty o' Nuthin', Porgy's song in Act II of GERSHWIN's PORGY AND BESS, expressing his happiness with his life, despite his poverty and deformity.

Ihre Liebe, the Countess's concluding aria in Richard STRAUSS's CAPRICCIO, in which she comes to the conclusion that she loves Flamand and Olivier equally.

Il balen del suo sorriso, Count di Luna's revelation to Ferrando that he is in love with Leonora and of his rhapsodic joy in the fact that she may soon be his, in Act II, Scene 2, of VERDI's IL TROVATORE.

Il cavallo scalpita, Alfio's song about his profession as a teamster, in MASCAGNI's CAVALLERIA RUSTICANA.

Il core vi dono, duet of Guglielmo and Dorabella, as they exchange pendants and tender words, in Act II, Scene 2, of MOZART's COSÌ FAN TUTTE.

Il cor nel contento, second-act duet of Rosaura and Florindo, the young lovers in WOLF-FERRARI's LE DONNE CURIOSE.

Il dolce idillio, Gil's assurances to his wife, Suzanne, of his love and devotion, in WOLF-FERRARI's THE SECRET OF SUZANNE.

Il est beau de mourir en s'aimant, duet of John the Baptist and Salomé in Act IV, Scene 1, of MASSENET's HÉRODIADE, as they tell each other of their love, with Salomé insisting she is ready to die with him.

Il est des Musulmans, Mârouf's lament that opens and recurs through Act I of RABAUD's MÂROUF.

Il est doux, il est bon, Salomé's narrative of her childhood in the desert, where she was saved by John the Baptist, in Act I of MASSENET's HÉRODIADE.

Il est un vieux chant de Bohème, Minka's gypsy song in Act II of CHABRIER's LE ROI MALGRÉ LUI.

Il était une fois à la cour d'Eisenach, the legend of Kleinzach about a hunchback jester, Hoffmann's aria in the prologue of OFFENBACH's THE TALES OF HOFFMANN.

Il était un roi de Thulé, Ballad of the King of Thulé, Marguerite's aria as she daydreams about Faust, in Act III of GOUNOD's FAUST.

Il faut partir, mes bons compagnons (Convien partir, o miei compagni d'arme), Marie's farewell to her regiment, in Act I of DONIZETTI's THE DAUGHTER OF THE REGIMENT.

Ilia, beloved (soprano) of Idamante, in MOZART's IDOMENEO.

Iliad, The, *see* HOMER.

Il lacerato spirito, Fiesco's aria revealing his torment at the death of his daughter, in the prologue of VERDI'S SIMON BOCCANEGRA.

Illica, Luigi, librettist. Born Castellarquato, Italy, 1857; died there Dec. 16, 1919. He began his literary career as a journalist in Milan. After 1892 he wrote the librettos for ANDREA CHÉNIER, CRISTOFORO COLOMBO, GERMANIA, and LA WALLY; for MASCAGNI'S IRIS, *Isabeau,* and *Le Maschere* and Gnecchi's *Cassandra,* and for various operas by the composers ALFANO and MONTEMEZZI. In collaboration with Giuseppe Giacosa, he wrote the librettos for four of PUCCINI's operas: LA BOHÈME, MADAMA BUTTERFLY, MANON LESCAUT, and TOSCA.

Il me semble sur mon épaule, the so-called Flea Duet between Eurydice and Jupiter (the latter transformed into a flea), in Act III of OFFENBACH'S ORPHEUS IN THE UNDERWORLD.

Il m'en souvient, Béatrice's haunting song in Act II of BERLIOZ' BÉATRICE ET BÉNÉDICT, her reaction to overhearing Bénédict confess how deeply he loves her. This melody is quoted in the opera's overture.

Il mio sangue, the aria in which Count Walter expresses his ambitions for his son Rodolfo and his determination to have the son marry Federica, the Duchess, in Act I of VERDI's LUISA MILLER.

Il mio tesoro, Don Ottavio's aria about his love for Donna Anna, in Act II, Scene 2, of MOZART'S DON GIOVANNI.

Il padre adorato, Idamante's lament that he had found his beloved father only to lose him again, in Act I of MOZART'S IDOMENEO.

Il real fu dolore, Faust's moody reminiscences of his experiences, in the epilogue of BOITO'S MEFISTOFELE, just before he achieves redemption.

Il segreto per essere felice (BRINDISI), Orsini's drinking song in Act II of DONIZETTI'S LUCREZIA BORGIA.

Imbroglio, an Italian term meaning an intricate or complicated situation. It is used in music to designate a passage whose combination of themes, though actually carefully contrived, suggests confusion. Examples of imbroglios in opera are found at the end of the first and second acts of DIE MEISTERSINGER. Another occurs in Act I, Scene 5, of DON GIOVANNI when, simultaneously, three different dance orchestras play three different dances in three different meters.

Im Feuerström der Reben (Hymn to Champagne), the paean of Orlofsky and his guests to champagne, in Act II of Johann STRAUSS'S DIE FLEDERMAUS.

Im Mohrenland gefangen war, Pedrillo's serenade to Blonde in Act III of MOZART'S THE ABDUCTION FROM THE SERAGLIO.

Immortal Hour, The, opera in two acts by BOUGHTON. The libretto is the play of the same name by Fiona Macleod (William Sharp). Premiere: Glastonbury, Eng., Aug. 26, 1914. American premiere: New York City, Nov. 6, 1926. Etain (soprano), from fairyland, and the dreamer King of Ireland, Eochaidh (baritone), are to be married. Midir (tenor), a fairy prince, kisses Etain's hand and enchants her with his legends and songs. She comes under his spell and follows him to the Land of Heart's Desire. Eochaidh falls dead when he is touched by the Shadow God, Dalua (baritone).

Imperial Theater, *see* BOLSHOI THEATER (1).

Impresario, The, *see* SCHAUSPIELDIREKTOR, DER.

Impressionism, a style of composition in which a sensation or an impression created by a subject is emphasized rather than the subject itself and which is more concerned with subtle nuances and effects than with substance and structure. The style and term originated in the paintings of the Frenchmen Manet, Monet, Pissarro, and Renoir and was applied particularly to the musical style developed by DEBUSSY, whose opera PELLÉAS ET MÉLISANDE is the ideal realization of impressionist writing. DUKAS'S ARIANE ET BARBE-BLEUE and DELIUS' A VILLAGE ROMEO AND JULIET are two other operas written in an impressionist style.

Inaffia l'ugola! (BRINDISI), Iago's drinking song in Act I of VERDI'S OTELLO.

Inbrunst im Herzen, Tannhäuser's Rome Narrative (Romerzählung), in which he describes his futile attempts in Rome to gain absolution, in Act III of WAGNER'S TANNHÄUSER.

incoronazione di Poppea, L' (The Coronation of Poppea), opera in prologue and three acts by MONTEVERDI. Libretto by Francesco Busanello. Premiere: Teatro Santi Giovanni e Paolo, Venice, 1642. American premiere: Smith College, Northampton, Mass., Apr. 27, 1926. This is Monteverdi's last opera and at the same time one of the first operas on a historical rather than a mythological or Biblical subject or a pastoral idyl. Poppea (soprano), in her ambition to become Empress, schemes for Nero (CASTRATO soprano) to divorce his wife, Ottavia (soprano), despite the counsel given her by her friend Seneca (bass). Poppea succeeds in her plot and replaces Ottavia on the throne. Dramatic writing, a fuller orchestration, and efforts at musical characterization all make this one of Monteverdi's most significant operas.

What is believed to have been the first modern staging of this opera took place in Paris in 1913. There were two important revivals in 1937: at the FLORENCE MAY MUSIC FESTIVAL, in an adaptation by Giacomo Benvenuti, and at the OPÉRA-COMIQUE, in a MALIPIERO adaptation. The AMERICAN OPERA SOCIETY presented it in English in 1953 and 1958, while subsequent important productions were given at the AIX-EN-PROVENCE festival in 1961, GLYNDEBOURNE in 1962, the CHICAGO LYRIC OPERA in 1966, and LA SCALA in 1967.

Indes galantes, Les (The Galant Indies), opéra-ballet in prologue and four entrées by RAMEAU. Libretto by Louis Fuzelier. Premiere: Paris Opéra, Aug. 23, 1735. American premiere: New York City, Mar. 1, 1961 (concert version). This, Rameau's third opera, was a major success. The opera narrates four different tales of love, each scene (or entrée, as the composer designated it) taking place in a different and remote part of the world. The first scene describes attempts of the Pasha Osman to win the love of Emilia, a French captive; but in the end he is willing to give her up to her lover, Valère, who had been washed up on the shores of Turkey. This is followed by an episode involving Phani, a member of the royal Incas, in a love affair with Don Carlos. Their love, however, is frustrated through the efforts of the high priest of the sun, Huascar. The third scene is made up mainly of ballets and relates the love of two friends for the other's slaves, in Persia. In the fourth, an American Indian girl, Zima, is being sought after by a Frenchman, a Spanish nobleman, and a native, Adoro. It is the last one she selects.

As an opéra-ballet the work places as much emphasis on dance as on song. Rameau's score consequently is notable for its ballet music, especially for the slave dance in the first scene and the sequence of ballets in the third. But the score is perhaps even more distinctive for its vividly descriptive music, such as the storm music in the first scene, in the second scene the tonal picture of a sun-god festival and the eruption of a volcano, and in many of the accompaniments, in one of which the composer employs a bagpipe. Love's aria, "Ranimez vos flambeaux," in the prologue; Huascar's air, "Clair flambeau du monde," in the second scene; and Zima's song, "Dans ces bois l'amour vole," are a few of the more significant vocal pages.

In des Lebens Frühlingstagen, Florestan's aria recalling his happy days with his wife, Leonore, in Act II, Scene 1, of BEETHOVEN'S FIDELIO.

In diesen heil'gen Hallen, Sarastro's aria in Act II, Scene 3, of MOZART'S THE MAGIC FLUTE.

In dieser feierlichen Stunde, Sophie's

prayer in Act II of Richard STRAUSS's DER ROSENKAVALIER.

Indy, Vincent d', see D'INDY, VINCENT.

Inez, (1) Leonora's confidante (soprano) in DONIZETTI's LA FAVORITA.

(2) Don Diego's daughter (soprano) in MEYERBEER's L'AFRICAINE.

(3) Leonora's confidante (soprano) in VERDI's IL TROVATORE.

In fernem Land, Lohengrin's narrative (Gralserzählung) in which he reveals he is a knight of the HOLY GRAIL and the son of Parsifal, in Act III, Scene 2, of WAGNER's LOHENGRIN.

In Früh'n versammelt uns der Ruf, chorus of the knights, courtiers, and the people hailing Elsa's wedding day, in Act II of WAGNER's LOHENGRIN.

Inghelbrecht, Désiré, conductor and composer. Born Paris, Sept. 17, 1880; died there Feb. 14, 1965. After completing music study at the Paris Conservatory, he began his conducting career with the orchestra of the Société Nationale de Musique. In 1913 he became music director of the THÉÂTRE DES CHAMPS ELYSÉES, where ballets and operas were performed. In 1919 he was engaged as conductor of the newly organized Swedish ballet. Five years later he became a conductor of the OPÉRA-COMIQUE, becoming principal conductor in 1932. After World War II he became principal conductor of the PARIS OPÉRA. He wrote one opera, *La Nuit vénitienne* (1908), and a guide to the conducting of PELLÉAS ET MÉLISANDE, CARMEN, and FAUST.

In grembo a me, see SUR MES GENOUX, FILS DU SOLEIL.

In mia mano alfin tu sei, Norma's duet with Pollione in Act IV of BELLINI's NORMA, where she threatens him with a dagger and claims he is in her power.

Inno al sole, a hymn to the sun, the opening chorus in MASCAGNI's IRIS.

In preda al duol, see PARMI LES FLEURS.

In pure stille, Iris' song as she arranges her flowers in Act I of MASCAGNI's IRIS.

In quelle trine morbide, Manon's aria in which she insists to her brother that wealth is no substitute for love, in Act II of PUCCINI's MANON LESCAUT.

In questa reggia, Turandot's narrative describing her past history and the reason for her determination to destroy any man who falls in love with her, in Act II of PUCCINI's TURANDOT.

Inquisitore, L', the Grand Inquisitor of Spain (bass) in VERDI's DON CALOS.

In seinem Garten liebt Don Perlimplin Belisa, see BLUTHOCHZEIT, DIE.

Inspector General, The, see GOGOL, NIKOLAI.

Intendant, German for "manager" or "director"—the director of a German opera house. The term was applied particularly to opera directors at German courts, these men formerly having been dilettantes of high birth or station.

intermède, French for INTERMEZZO.

intermezzo, (1) in the early Italian theater, a little play with music interpolated between the acts of a serious drama to allow the actors to rest and to permit changes of scenery. The form became increasingly popular and developed into the OPERA BUFFA of the early eighteenth century. Nicola LOGROSCINO was a famous writer in this form. PERGOLESI was another: his LA SERVA PADRONA is an intermezzo.

(2) In the nineteenth century the name "intermezzo" was given to an instrumental interlude played in an opera with the curtain raised, the music denoting a passage of time. Celebrated examples are those in CAVALLERIA RUSTICANA, GOYESCAS, and THE JEWELS OF THE MADONNA.

Intermezzo, opera, or "domestic comedy," in two acts by Richard STRAUSS. Libretto by the composer. Premiere: Dresden Opera, Nov. 4, 1924. American premiere: New York City, Dec. 11, 1963 (concert version). The composer based his text on an actual incident from his own life. A misunderstanding arises between the composer-conductor Storch (baritone) and his wife (soprano) when an unknown female admirer writes him an effusive love letter. Convinced that her husband is unfaithful, Christine Storch announces her intention to seek a divorce. Only when it is discovered that the letter writer had sent her note to the wrong man—she had intended it for one of Storch's colleagues with a similar name, Stroh—is the matter straightened out. At the opera's first performance the two principal characters were made up to look like Herr and Frau Strauss. An episode in the opera involves the card game skat, which was Strauss's favorite.

The opera interpolates quotations from PARSIFAL, FAUST, SCHUMANN'S *Spring Symphony,* and Strauss's own *Ein Heldenleben.* Christine's monologue, "Ein hübscher Mensch," is an important vocal episode.

In the Storm, opera by KHRENNIKOV. Libretto by the composer, based on a novel by Virta, *Solitude.* Premiere: Moscow, May 31, 1939. This successful Soviet opera has for its setting the Kulak rebellion in Tambov in 1919–1921; its basic theme is the love of two young collectivists. The opera is a revision of an earlier work entitled *The Brothers.* The style is melodious and romantic, with the influence of TCHAIKOVSKY evident in such pages as "Maidens' Song," "Lenka's Song," "Natasha's Aria," and the "Partisans' Song" for chorus.

In the town of Kazan, Varlaam's ballad, sung while drunk, in Act II, Scene 1, of MUSSORGSKY'S BORIS GODUNOV.

Intolleranza 1960, opera in two acts by NONO. Text by the composer. Premiere: Venice, Apr. 13, 1961. American premiere: Boston, Feb. 22, 1965. This is an avant-garde opera using strict SERIAL TECHNIQUES and ELECTRONIC MUSIC. Stage action is combined with pictures flashed on a screen at the back of the stage. The opera attacks intolerance, fascism, the atom bomb, segregation, and other contemporary social and political problems in a series of montages. In the end the world is wiped out completely. At its premiere the opera caused a scandal, with fights breaking out between pro-fascists and communists. The police had to be called in to restore order. When Nono made an attempt to come to America for the American premiere in Boston, he was denied a visa by the American Department of State because of his communist affiliation. One week later, however, this decision was reversed and Nono was admitted to the country. The American premiere went without incident, save for a lonely picket marching outside the theater, representing the Polish Freedom Fighters.

Introductions and Goodbyes, opera in one act by FOSS. Libretto by MENOTTI. Premiere: Spoleto, Italy, 1959. American premiere: New York City, May 6, 1960. This is an amusing nine-minute opera whose action takes place at a cocktail party. There is only one solo singer, the host (baritone), supplemented by a chorus representing the guests.

In uomini, in soldati, Despina's complaint that all men are philanderers, in Act I, Scene 3, of MOZART'S COSÌ FAN TUTTE.

Invano, Alvaro, duet of Don Carlo and Alvaro in which the former expresses his desire for vengeance and demands that Alvaro do battle with him, in Act IV, Scene 1, of VERDI'S LA FORZA DEL DESTINO.

Invisible City of Kitezh, The, *see* LEGEND OF THE INVISIBLE CITY OF KITEZH, THE.

Invocation à la nature, L', *see* NATURE IMMENSE.

Io so che alle sue pene, trio of Suzuki, Sharpless, and Pinkerton, when Suzuki comes to realize that Pinkerton has returned to Nagasaki with an American wife, in Act III of PUCCINI'S MADAMA BUTTERFLY.

Io son l'umile ancella, Adriana's aria in which she humbly calls herself not a star of the stage but a mere servant of the arts, in Act I of CILÈA'S ADRIANA LECOUVREUR.

Io son ricco, a BARCAROLLE sung by Adina and Dr. Dulcamara in Act II of DONIZETTI'S L'ELISIR D'AMORE. The melody is repeated at the end of the opera.

Io vidi la luce nel camp guerir, *see* AU BRUIT DE LA GUERRE.

Ipanov, Count Loris, Fedora's lover (tenor) in GIORDANO'S FEDORA, a role created by CARUSO.

Iphigenia in Aulis, tragedy by EURIPIDES, the source of operas by many composers, including CALDARA, GLUCK, GRAUN,

JOMMELLI, and Nicola Zingarelli. For plot, *see* IPHIGÉNIE EN AULIDE.

Iphigenia in Tauris, tragedy by EURIPIDES, the source of operas by GALUPPI, GLUCK, JOMMELLI, and PICCINNI, among others. For plot, *see* IPHIGÉNIE EN TAURIDE.

Iphigénie en Aulide (Iphigenia in Aulis), lyric tragedy in three acts by GLUCK. Libretto by Bailli du Roullet, based on a drama by RACINE, in turn derived from EURIPIDES. Premiere: Paris Opéra, May 19, 1774. American premiere: Philadelphia, Feb. 22, 1935.

Characters: Agamemnon, King of the Greeks (baritone); Klytemnestra, his wife (mezzo-soprano); Iphigenia, their daughter (soprano), a role created by Sophie ARNOULD; Achilles, her betrothed (tenor); Patrocolos (bass); Calchas, high priest (bass); Arkas, captain of the guards (bass); Artemis, or Diana, a goddess (soprano). The action takes place in Aulis after the Trojan War.

The famous overture opens with a majestic subject interpreted by WAGNER as an invocation for deliverance. Two other basic themes represent to Wagner, in turn, an assertion of the will and the maidenly tenderness of Iphigenia.

Act I. The camp of Agamemnon. The goddess Artemis is angered and prevents the Greek fleet from leaving for Troy. To appease her, Calchas demands the sacrifice of Iphigenia. When Iphigenia and her mother arrive at the camp, they are welcomed with song and dance. It is now that Klytemnestra tells her daughter that Achilles, betrothed to Iphigenia, has been unfaithful; but when Achilles arrives, he reassures his beloved.

Act II. Agamemnon's palace. The marriage of Achilles and Iphigenia is being celebrated by the people ("Chantons, celebrons, notre reine"). Achilles is about to lead his bride to the altar when Arkas informs him that she must be sacrificed. Klytemnestra entreats Agamemnon to save Iphigenia, and Achilles makes threats; but the King insists that the sacrifice must take place.

Act III, Scene 1. Agamemnon's tent. With the Greeks demanding that Iphigenia be given up to the gods, Achilles comes to Agamemnon's tent to get her to escape with him. But Iphigenia insists on her own death and bids her people farewell ("Adieu, conservez dans votre âme").

Scene 2. Altar of Artemis. Iphigenia is about to be sacrificed when Achilles, at the head of his own men, arrives to rescue her. Bloodshed is averted when the high priest Calchas announces that the goddess is appeased, and everything ends happily.

Iphigénie en Aulide was the first opera Gluck wrote for Paris after his arrival from Vienna in the fall of 1773. In it he once again carried out the ideals and principles previously established in ORFEO ED EURIDICE and ALCESTE: simplicity, humanity, dramatic truth, and integration of music and libretto. In Paris as in Vienna, Gluck found opponents of his ideas, particularly among adherents of the Italian school. These enemies did everything they could to block the impending premiere of *Iphigénie*. Had it not been for the personal intervention of Marie Antoinette, the opera might not have been produced. Once given, it was a sensation. It became the subject of discussion in all Parisian salons. "We can find nothing else to talk about"— so wrote Marie Antoinette; "you can scarcely imagine what excitement reigns in all minds in regard to this event." Commenting on one of the airs, Abbé Arnaud said: "With that air one might found a religion."

Iphigénie en Tauride (Iphigenia in Tauris), opera in four acts by GLUCK. Libretto by François Guillard, adapted from the drama of EURIPIDES. Premiere: Paris Opéra, May 18, 1779. American premiere: Metropolitan Opera, Nov. 25, 1916. The opera continues the story begun in IPHIGÉNIE EN AULIDE. Iphigenia has become a priestess of the Scythians at Tauris, where the gods, angered, must be appeased with a sacrifice. For this sacrifice, two strangers from Greece are chosen after they have been shipwrecked on the shores of Tauris; they are Orestes (baritone) and Pylades (tenor). Since Iphigenia recalls her Greek origin, she is incapable of sanctioning their deaths. She finally consents to have only one of them sacrificed, and the choice falls on Orestes. Only now does she discover that Orestes is her brother. When a band of Greeks, headed by Pylades, attacks and defeats the Scythians, Iphigenia and Orestes are able, with the approval of Artemis, to return to their native land.

Two of the most celebrated arias in the opera are Pylades' in Act II ("Unis dès la plus tendre enfance") and Iphigenia's Hymn to Diane in Act IV ("Chaste fille de Latone"). Four additional arias deserve attention: Iphigenia's "Cette nuit, j'ai revue le palais de mon père" and "O malheureuse Iphigénie," and Orestes' "Le calme rentre dans mon coeur" and "Dieux! qui me poursuivez."

In this opera the role of Iphigenia was created by Rosalie LEVASSEUR.

Irene, (1) Rienzi's sister (soprano) in WAGNER'S RIENZI.

(2) Jean Gaussin's cousin (contralto) in MASSENET'S SAPHO.

I revel in hope and joy again, Sir Huon's aria expressing his joy at being called upon to rescue Rezia, in Act III, Scene 1, of WEBER'S OBERON.

Iris, opera in three acts by MASCAGNI. Libretto by Luigi ILLICA. Premiere: Teatro Costanzi, Rome, Nov. 22, 1898. American premiere: Philadelphia, Oct. 14, 1902. In Japan, the libertine Osaka (tenor) wants Iris (soprano), daughter of the blind man Cieco (bass). He manages to get her absorbed in a puppet show, then has her abducted. Her father, told that she has entered a house of ill repute, believes she has gone there of her own free will and curses her. In the luxurious setting of Yoshiwara, Iris resists Osaka. Her father comes and, finding her, throws mud at her. Humiliated, Iris jumps out of the window into the sewer below. Dying, she bemoans her fate and

wonders why tragedy should have befallen her. Then, caressed by the rays of the rising sun and embraced by the opening flowers, she is lifted heavenward.

These are the principal musical excerpts: in Act I, the arias of Iris ("In pure stille") and Osaka ("Apri la tua finestra"), the orchestral dance of the geisha girls (Danza della quecas), and the opening chorus, a hymn to the sun ("Inno al sole"); in Act II, arias of Iris ("Un dì, ero piccina") and Osaka ("Or dammi il braccio tuo").

Irische Legende (Irish Legend), opera in five scenes by EGK. Libretto by the composer, based on William Butler YEATS's *The Countess Cathleen*. Premiere: Salzburg, Austria, Aug. 17, 1955. When first introduced, the opera proved so successful that it received twenty curtain calls at its premiere and was regarded as the highlight of the SALZBURG FESTIVAL that season. The setting is Ireland in some future time. The world is dominated by demons, and people, driven by fear and hunger, sell their souls to the devil. Countess Cathleen is no exception. She suffers not only from fear, hunger, and the loss of all her belongings but also from the fact that the man she loves, the poet Aleen, was seduced by the demons and abducted. Cathleen offers her soul to save her land and people, but since her soul belongs to the angels, no pact can be made with the demons. Now repentant, Aleen returns to help Cathleen, but to no avail. The demons are dragged down to hell while Cathleen ascends heavenward to the angels.

Irma, a seamstress (soprano) in CHARPENTIER'S LOUISE.

Irmelin, opera in three acts by DELIUS. Libretto by the composer. Premiere: Oxford, Eng., May 4, 1953. Irmelin is a princess waiting for her true love; Nils, a prince disguised as a swineherd, is in search of a woman he can love. He is told he will find her at the end of a silver stream, which he follows and at whose end he finds Irmelin.

Irving, Washington, author and humorist. Born New York City, Apr. 3, 1783; died Tarrytown, N.Y., Nov. 28, 1859. His famous tale RIP VAN WINKLE, from *The Sketch Book,* was the source of operas by George Frederick Bristow and Reginald DE KOVEN and of an operetta by Jean-Robert PLANQUETTE. SPOHR's opera *Der Alchimist* was derived from another Irving story.

Isabella, (1) a beautiful Italian lady (contralto) in ROSSINI's L'ITALIANA IN ALGERI.

(2) Princess of Sicily (soprano) in MEYERBEER'S ROBERT LE DIABLE.

Isepo, a public letter writer (tenor) in PONCHIELLI's LA GIOCONDA.

I shall find you shells and stars, the lullaby of the grandmother to her dying grandchild in MENOTTI's THE CONSUL.

Ismaele, nephew (tenor) of the King of Jerusalem in VERDI's NABUCCO.

Isolde, Princess of Ireland (soprano), in love with Tristan, in WAGNER's TRISTAN UND ISOLDE, a role created by Malwina Garrigues-Schnorr, wife of SCHNORR VON CAROLSFELD.

Isolde! Tristan! Geliebter!, the ecstatic duet of Tristan and Isolde as they meet in the garden in Act II of WAGNER's TRISTAN UND ISOLDE.

Ist ein Traum, the love duet of Sophie and Octavian at the close of Act III of Richard STRAUSS's DER ROSENKAVALIER.

It ain't necessarily so, Sportin' Life's cynical song about religion in Act II of GERSHWIN's PORGY AND BESS.

It takes a long pull to get there, the worksong of the fishermen as they repair their nets in the opening of Act II of GERSHWIN's PORGY AND BESS.

Italia! Italia! é tutto il mio ricordo!, Archibaldo's recollection of how he led the barbarian invasion of Italy, in Act I of MONTEMEZZI's L'AMORE DEI TRE RE.

Italiana in Algeri, L' (The Italian Woman in Algiers), opera in two acts by ROSSINI. Libretto by Angelo Anelli. Premiere: Teatro San Benedetto, Venice, May 22, 1813. American premiere: New York City, Nov. 5, 1832. The Italian woman of the title is Isabella (contralto), with whom the Mustafa of Algiers (bass) is in love.

Complications arise when Isabella falls in love with Lindoro (tenor), favorite slave of the Mustafa. The Mustafa is distracted by being initiated into a fictional secret society, the Pappatacci, dedicated to good eating and silence. While he goes through the ridiculous rites, Lindoro and Isabella make their escape.

The sprightly overture is often played in concerts. The outstanding vocal numbers include three by Isabella: in Act I, "Cruda sorte, amor tiranno"; in Act II, "Per lui che adoro," accompanied by quartet, and her mock-heroic aria "Pensa alla patria." Lindoro has a fine aria in "Languir per una bella" in Act I.

Italian Opera House, the first theater in New York built especially for opera. It was erected in 1833, sponsored by Lorenzo DA PONTE, on Church and Leonard Streets and opened on Nov. 18 with LA GAZZA LADRA. After two seasons of opera the theater was used for spoken drama. It was destroyed by fire in 1835.

Ivanhoe, (1) romantic novel by Sir Walter SCOTT, the source of several operas, notably, NICOLAI's *Il templario,* DER TEMPLER UND DIE JÜDIN, ROSSINI's *pasticcio Ivanhoe,* and SULLIVAN's only grand opera, *Ivanhoe.*

(2) Opera in five acts by SULLIVAN. Libretto by Julian Sturges, based on SCOTT's novel. Premiere: Royal English Opera House, London, Jan. 31, 1891. This was Sullivan's solitary excursion into grand opera. Though it had a continuous run of one hundred sixty performances, it was a failure. It was the opening production of the newly founded and short-lived English Opera House, created as a home for native English opera.

Ivan Khovantsky, *see* KHOVANTSKY, PRINCE IVAN.

Ivan Susanin, *see* LIFE FOR THE CZAR, A.

Ivan the Terrible, or The Maid of Pskov, opera in four acts by RIMSKY-KORSAKOV. Libretto is the drama of the same name by Lev Mey. Premiere: Maryinsky Theater, St. Petersburg, Jan.

13, 1873. In sixteenth-century Russia, the tyrannical Czar Ivan (bass) inflicts terror on the city of Novgorod. A similar fate awaits Pskov. Its subjects join to fight the Czar, and in the surprise attack that follows, Princess Olga (soprano) and her lover, Michael Toucha (tenor), both natives of Pskov, are killed. Olga turns out to have been the secret daughter of the Czar. The overture and the prelude to Act III, entitled "Hunt and Storm Music," are occasionally performed at concerts.

Ivogün, Maria (born Ilse von Günther), soprano. Born Budapest, Nov. 11, 1891. She studied with Irene Schlemmer in Vienna and in 1913 became principal soprano of the MUNICH OPERA, where she remained for twelve years, specializing in coloratura roles. In 1916 Richard STRAUSS selected her to create the role of Zerbinetta in ARIADNE AUF NAXOS, in which she also made her COVENT GARDEN debut in 1924. From 1925 to 1927 she was principal soprano of the BERLIN STATE OPERA. After this she appeared extensively in leading European opera houses and with the CHICAGO OPERA. She withdrew from opera in the 1930's because of failing eyesight, which soon became total blindness. She thenceforth devoted herself to teaching, joining the faculty of the Vienna Academy of Music in 1948, and the Berlin Hochschule für Musik in 1950.

Ivrogne corrigé, L' (The Reformed Drunkard), comic opera in two acts by GLUCK. Libretto by Louis Anseaume, based on a fable by LA FONTAINE. Premiere: Burgtheater, Vienna, Apr., 1760. American premiere: Hartford, Conn., Feb. 26, 1945, under the title The Marriage of the Devil. Mathurin, a peasant with an extraordinary love for liquor, is cured of this vice by going through an ordeal arranged by his wife and daughter in which he believes he is brought to judgment in hell before Pluto and the Furies.

J

Jackrabbit, Billy, an Indian (bass) in PUCCINI'S THE GIRL OF THE GOLDEN WEST.

Jack Rance, see RANCE, JACK.

Jacquino, assistant (tenor) to Rocco, the jailer, in BEETHOVEN'S FIDELIO.

Ja, das alles auf Ehr', Sandor's entrance aria in Johann STRAUSS'S THE GYPSY BARON, the most famous aria in the operetta.

Jadlowker, Hermann, tenor. Born Riga, Latvia, July 5, 1879; died Tel Aviv, Israel, May 13, 1953. After attending the Vienna Conservatory he made his opera debut in Cologne, in 1899, in KREUTZER'S Das Nachtlager in Granada. For five years he sang principal tenor roles at the BERLIN OPERA and for several seasons after that at the VIENNA OPERA. He made his American debut at the METROPOLITAN OPERA on Jan. 22, 1910, in FAUST. He remained at the Metropolitan for three seasons, creating the principal tenor roles in LE DONNE CURIOSE, DIE KÖNIGSKINDER, and Lobetanz. In 1913 he returned to the Berlin Opera for another six seasons. After leaving the operatic stage, he served as cantor and professor of singing in Riga. For the last fifteen years of his life he taught singing in Israel.

Jaele, one of the two leading female characters (soprano) in PIZZETTI'S DEBORA E JAELE.

Jagel, Frederick, tenor. Born Brooklyn, N.Y., June 10, 1897. After study with Portanova in New York and Cataldi in Italy, he made his opera debut in Leghorn in 1924 in LA BOHÈME, billed under the Italianized name of Federico Jeghelli. During the next four years he appeared frequently in leading Italian opera houses. On Nov. 8, 1927, he made his METROPOLITAN OPERA debut in AIDA. For over two decades he was seen there in a large variety of roles, notably in the world premiere of John Laurence Seymour's *In the Pasha's Garden* and in the American premieres of MONTEMEZZI's *La notte di Zoraima* and MUSSORGSKY'S THE FAIR AT SOROCHINSK. With another company he appeared in the American premiere of Lodovico ROCCA's THE DYBBUK in 1935, and a year or so later he was the first American tenor to appear in a leading role at the TEATRO COLÓN on the opening night of the Buenos Aires opera season. More recently he has been a prominent voice teacher in Boston.

J'ai le bonheur dans l'âme, love duet of Hoffmann and Antonia in Act III of OFFENBACH's THE TALES OF HOFFMANN.

J'ai perdu la beauté, air from LULLY's *Persée.*

J'ai vu, nobles seigneurs (Io vidi, miei signori), Vasco da Gama's description of his expedition to a strange new land, in Act I of MEYERBEER's L'AFRICAINE.

Jake, a fisherman (baritone) in GERSHWIN'S PORGY AND BESS.

Ja! lasst uns zum Himmel die Blicke erheben, concluding chorus of WEBER's DER FREISCHÜTZ, the people's song of thanksgiving.

James, Henry, novelist and playwright. Born New York City, Apr. 15, 1843; died England, Feb. 28, 1916. BRITTEN's THE TURN OF THE SCREW and MOORE's THE WINGS OF THE DOVE are based on novels of the same names by James.

Janáček, Leoš, composer. Born Hukvaldy, Moravia, July 3, 1854; died Prague, Aug. 12, 1928. Sometimes called the "Mussorgsky of Moravia." After music study in Brno and at the College of Organ Playing in Prague, Janáček settled in Brno as a teacher of music. In 1878 he visited Vienna for additional study, after which he assumed a major position in the musical life of Moravia by establishing and conducting public concerts and founding and subsequently directing the Organ School and Conservatory in Brno. In 1896 he paid his first visit to Russia. His interest in the Russian language and literature was now aroused; henceforth their impact on his musical thinking was profound. A second and even more significant influence was that of Moravian folk music, of which he made an intensive study. This study led him to create a musical system of his own, derived from folk elements, in which melody and rhythm were molded after the inflections and rhythms of speech, which he termed "melodies of the language." The crystallization of this new style is found in his greatest work, the opera JENUFA, which took him seven years to write. Janáček wrote orchestral, choral, and chamber works in addition to operas, and he achieved considerable recognition. In 1925 he received an honorary degree from the University of Brno, and on the occasion of his seventieth birthday a cycle of his operas was performed in Brno. Two years after his death, an extensive cycle of his operas was performed throughout Czechoslovakia. His operas: *Šárka* (1887); *Jenufa* (1903); *Fate* (1905); *The Excursions of Mr. Brouček* (1914); KAT'A KABANOVÁ (1921); THE CUNNING LITTLE VIXEN (1923); THE MAKROPOULOS AFFAIR (1924); FROM THE HOUSE OF THE DEAD, completed by Břetislav Bakala (1930).

Janssen, Herbert, baritone. Born Cologne, Sept. 22, 1895; died New York City, June 3, 1965. He studied with J. Daniel in Berlin and in 1924 made his debut with the BERLIN STATE OPERA, where he appeared for several years in principal baritone roles of the German repertory. After successful guest appearances in Europe and South America, he made his American debut on Jan. 24,

1939, at the METROPOLITAN OPERA as Wotan in SIEGFRIED. For the next decade he gave distinguished performances at COVENT GARDEN, the PARIS OPÉRA, and other major opera houses.

Janusz, Halka's beloved (baritone) in MONIUSZKO'S HALKA.

Jaroslavna, Prince Igor's wife (soprano) in BORODIN'S PRINCE IGOR.

Jason, the leader of the Argonauts (tenor) in CHERUBINI'S MÉDÉE.

jazz, a style of American popular music which grew out of the ragtime playing of Negro bands and reached its heyday in the 1920's and 1930's. Significant elements of jazz, distinguishing it from other kinds of American popular music, include its marked syncopations against a steady four-beat rhythm, prominence of certain "blue" notes (compromises between major and minor thirds and the flatted seventh), characteristic "breaks" or comments by solo instruments, and the cultivation of strange tone qualities. During the 1920's there was a vogue in Germany for writing operas in the jazz idiom, and among the works produced there at that time were JONNY SPIELT AUF, NEUES VOM TAGE, THE RISE AND FALL OF THE CITY MAHAGONNY, THE THREEPENNY OPERA, and TRANSATLANTIC.

In a later period, LIEBERMANN used boogie-woogie, a jazz piano idiom, in an episode in PENELOPE. A jazz style can be found in some of the passages of THE CRADLE WILL ROCK and PORGY AND BESS, among other American operas.

Jean, a juggler (tenor or soprano) in MASSENET'S LE JONGLEUR DE NOTRE DAME.

Jeanne d'Arc au bûcher (Joan of Arc at the Stake), dramatic oratorio in prologue and eleven scenes by HONEGGER. Libretto by CLAUDEL. Premiere: Basel, Switzerland, May 10, 1938 (concert version); Zürich, 1942 (staged). American premiere: New York City, Jan. 1, 1948 (concert version); San Francisco Opera, Oct. 15, 1954 (staged). This work is primarily intended for concert performance, but it has often been given with scenery and costumes and presented as an opera—or, in the composer's desig-

nation, as a "mimodrama." Thus presented, it is usually performed on two separate stages: on one, Joan is fastened to the stake throughout the performance, while the action of the play proceeds on the other stage, providing flashbacks into Joan's life, as seen through the saint's eyes. The action involves commentaries by the people; animals performing human judicial functions; potentates symbolizing Ignorance, Avarice, Greed, and so forth; and a card game symbolic of the games of state intrigues and war. Joan's part is exclusively a speaking role. In 1953 the SAN CARLO staged it with Ingrid Bergman, the motion-picture actress, as Joan. It was produced by the Italian motion-picture director (at that time Miss Bergman's husband) Roberto Rossellini.

See also JOAN OF ARC.

Je connais un pauvre enfant (STYRIENNE), Mignon's aria in Act II, Scene 1, of THOMAS'S MIGNON, recalling a gypsy lad she once knew.

J'écris à mon père (Duo de la lettre), duet of Des Grieux and Manon in Act II of MASSENET'S MANON, in which Des Grieux writes a letter to his father asking permission to marry Manon.

Je crois entendre, Philine's aria in Act II, Scene 1, of THOMAS'S MIGNON, boasting of the way all men are attracted to her.

Je crois entendre encore, Nadir's aria in Act I of BIZET'S LES PÊCHEURS DE PERLES, revealing, as if in a dream, his love for Leila. This is the most famous aria in the opera.

Je dis que rien ne m'épouvante, Micaëla's Air in Act III of BIZET'S CARMEN, praying to heaven for protection.

Je dois vous prévenir, the air of the inebriated Paquillo in Act I of OFFENBACH'S OPÉRA BOUFFE LA PÉRICHOLE, in which he is unable to forget the woman he loves.

Je marche sur tous les chemins, Manon's aria describing her devil-may-care attitude toward life and love, in Act III, Scene 1, of MASSENET'S MANON.

Je me souviens, sans voix, Gérald's aria

in Act III of DELIBES'S LAKMÉ, expressing his gratitude to Lakmé for having saved his life and declaring his love.

Jemmy, William Tell's son (soprano) in ROSSINI'S WILLIAM TELL.

Jenufa (Její pastorkyňa), folk opera in three acts by JANÁČEK. Libretto by the composer, based on a story by Gabriela Preissova. Premiere: Brno, Jan. 21, 1904. American premiere: Metropolitan Opera, Dec. 6, 1924. This was the composer's first opera to be staged, but the fourth he composed. It is his masterwork; more than that, it is one of the most significant of all Bohemian folk operas. Jenufa (soprano) is a peasant girl who bears a child to her cousin Stewa (tenor). Stewa no longer loves her, but his stepbrother, Laca (tenor), is willing to marry Jenufa and accept the child as his own. Jenufa's mother (soprano), refusing to let Laca make such a sacrifice, murders the child, then tells Jenufa that it died a natural death and was quickly buried. Jenufa and Laca are married. During the ceremony, the dead body of the child is discovered. The mother confesses her crime and is arrested. The opera's musical style features recitatives shaped from speech patterns, but a more formal lyricism is not abandoned in, for example, Jenufa's "Ave Maria" in Act I. For many years *Jenufa* enjoyed an immense success in European opera houses, following a successful revival at the PRAGUE OPERA in 1916 and a Viennese performance in 1918. Revivals in London in 1956–57, at the CHICAGO LYRIC OPERA in 1959, and in a concert version by the Little Orchestra Society in New York in 1966–67 helped to build its popularity. When the HAMBURG OPERA visited the United States for the first time, one of its most highly acclaimed performances was that of this opera on June 26, 1967, in New York City.

Jepson, Helen, soprano. Born Titusville, Pa., Nov. 25, 1906. A scholarship student, she attended the Curtis Institute in Philadelphia for five years and made her opera debut in 1928 with the Philadelphia Civic Opera as Marcellina in THE MARRIAGE OF FIGARO. After appear-

ances with the Philadelphia Grand Opera and the Montreal Opera, she made her METROPOLITAN OPERA debut on Jan. 24, 1935, in John Laurence Seymour's *In the Pasha's Garden*. She was a featured soprano at the Metropolitan for the next seven years. During this period she also appeared with the Chicago Civic Opera (where she scored a major success as THAÏS, a role she studied with Mary GARDEN) and with the SAN FRANCISCO OPERA. She left the Metropolitan after the 1946–47 season; since 1948 she has appeared as a lecturer about that institution. She has also been a faculty member of Fairleigh-Dickinson College and has taught voice privately.

Jerger, Alfred, baritone. Born Brünn, Austria, June 9, 1889. After studying music in Vienna he made his debut as conductor rather than as singer, in Passau in 1913. Between 1919 and 1921 he was a member of the company of the MUNICH OPERA as singer, and between 1921 and 1953 he was the leading baritone of the VIENNA STATE OPERA. He made appearances in other leading German opera houses, creating the role of MANDRYKA with the DRESDEN OPERA in 1933. He also appeared regularly at the SALZBURG FESTIVAL, being particularly acclaimed for his performances in MOZART'S operas. His later years were spent producing opera at the VOLKSOPER in Vienna and teaching voice at the Vienna Academy.

Jeritza, Maria (born Jedlitzka), soprano. Born Brünn, Austria, Oct. 6, 1887. She studied singing at the Brünn Musikschule and privately with Auspitzer. In 1910 she made her debut with the Olmütz Opera in LOHENGRIN. A year later she appeared with the Vienna VOLKSOPER, where she scored a striking success as ELISABETH. In the summer of 1912 she appeared in a special performance of DIE FLEDERMAUS before the Emperor, and on Oct. 25 of the same year she created the title role in Richard STRAUSS'S ARIADNE AUF NAXOS in Stuttgart. Also in the fall of 1912 she appeared for the first time at the Vienna Royal Opera in an opera written expressly for her, Max von Oberleithner's

Aphrodite. She was so successful that the Royal Opera bought out her contract with the Volksoper. She now became one of the stars of the Royal Opera (later VIENNA STATE OPERA), remaining until 1932, and achieving personal triumphs in operas by PUCCINI, KORNGOLD, and Richard Strauss, as well as in the WAGNER repertory. Puccini regarded her as the ideal TOSCA, and she was Richard Strauss's favorite interpreter of his leading female roles. On Nov. 19, 1921, she made her American debut at the METROPOLITAN OPERA in the American premiere of DIE TOTE STADT. A few days later she created a sensation in *Tosca*. She remained at the Metropolitan ten years, scoring striking successes in THAÏS, TURANDOT, FEDORA, and DER ROSENKAVALIER. She created for America the principal female roles in JENUFA, ALFANO's *Madonna Imperia, Turandot,* and Korngold's *Violanta.* She was featured in revivals of SUPPÉ's *Boccaccio* and *Donna Juanita,* THE GIRL OF THE GOLDEN WEST, DER FLIEGENDE HOLLÄNDER, and *Thaïs.* A woman of striking beauty and great charm, possessed of a voice of singular beauty, she brought to the operatic stage an unforgettable presence. In 1932 she resigned from the Metropolitan and for the next few years made appearances in Europe and America. In 1935 she married the motion-picture executive Winfield Sheehan and withdrew from opera. Several years later, however, she made a few more appearances and sang for a single evening at the Metropolitan in 1951 in *Die Fledermaus.* Her autobiography, *Sunlight and Song,* was published in 1924.

Jerum! Jerum! (Cobbler's Song), Hans Sachs's song as he hammers away repairing a shoe, in Act II of WAGNER's DIE MEISTERSINGER.

Jerusalem Delivered, epic poem by TASSO, the source of numerous operas. *See* ARMIDA; RINALDO.

Jessner, Irene, soprano. Born Vienna, 1909. She attended the Vienna Conservatory, after which she made her opera debut in Teplitz as ELSA. For two years she was a member of the PRAGUE OPERA. On Dec. 25, 1936, she made her American debut at the METROPOLITAN OPERA in HANSEL AND GRETEL. She remained with the Metropolitan Opera company for over a decade, appearing in leading soprano roles in the German, French, and Italian repertories.

Jessonda, opera in three acts by SPOHR. Libretto by Eduard Heinrich Gehe, based on a tragedy by Antoine Martin Lemierre, *La Veuve de Malabar.* Premiere: Cassel, Ger., July 28, 1823. American premiere: Philadelphia, Feb. 15, 1864. Following a custom in India, Jessonda is fated to be burned alive with the dead body of her husband, the Rajah. She is saved by the Portuguese general, Tristan d'Acumba, whom she had loved years before and whom she suddenly meets again when the Portuguese attack her city.

Like EURYANTHE, *Jessonda* is one of the earliest German operas to employ accompanied recitatives instead of spoken dialogue.

Je suis encore tout étourdie, Manon's description of her journey by coach to Amiens, in Act I of MASSENET's MANON.

Je suis l'oiseau, Alain's aria in Act III of MASSENET's GRISÉLIDIS.

Je suis roi, de Nangis' air in Act II of CHABRIER's LE ROI MALGRÉ LUI, asserting he is the real king and his rival a fraud.

Je suis Titania, Philine's POLONAISE in reply to the praises of her admirers, in Act II, Scene 2, of THOMAS's MIGNON.

Je vais le voir, Hero's aria in Act II of BERLIOZ' BÉATRICE ET BÉNÉDICT, anticipating her reunion with her beloved Claudio.

Je veux vivre dans ce rêve, Juliette's waltz song expressing her desire to taste life's joys, in Act I of GOUNOD's ROMÉO ET JULIETTE.

Jewels of the Madonna, The (I gioielli della Madonna), opera in three acts by WOLF-FERRARI. Libretto by the composer, with verses by Carlo Zangarini and Enrico Golisciani. Premiere: Kurfürstenoper, Berlin, Dec. 23, 1911. American premiere: Chicago Opera, Jan. 16, 1912.

Characters: Gennaro, a blacksmith (tenor); Carmela, his mother (mezzo-soprano); Maliella, Carmela's adopted daughter (soprano) ; Rafaele, leader of the Camorrists (baritone) ; Biaisio, a public letter writer (tenor) ; Cicillo, a Camorrist (tenor) ; Rocco, a Camorrist (bass) ; Stella, a Camorrist (soprano) ; Concetta, a Camorrist (soprano); Serena, a Camorrist (soprano) ; citizens of Naples. The action takes place in Naples at the beginning of the nineteenth century.

Act I. A public square. The festival of the Madonna is being celebrated. Gennaro is finishing work on a holy candelabrum while singing a prayer, "Madonna, con sospiri." Maliella coquettishly flirts with Rafaele ("Canzone di cannetella"), who is madly in love with her. He stands ready to meet any test to prove his love—even to stealing the jewels from the Madonna's image that has just been carried through the streets. Gennaro is also in love with Maliella. His mother, fearful of the consequences of his passion, urges him to go to church and pray ("T'eri un giorno"). But when Gennaro overhears Rafaele's rash promise, he realizes he has the information he needs to win for himself the woman he loves.

Act II. A garden. When Gennaro tries to make love to Maliella, he is rudely rejected. He leaves in despair. Rafaele and some of his Camorrist friends now appear. Rafaele sings a serenade ("Aprila, o bella"). He wins over Maliella completely and she promises to run away with him the following day. When Rafaele and his friends depart, Gennaro returns. He has stolen the Madonna's jewels, hoping thereby to gain Maliella's interest. Maliella puts on the jewels and is so taken with them that, in gratitude, she gives herself to Gennaro.

Act III. A Camorrist hide-out. Reveling, the Camorrists dance a tarantella ("Dance of the Camorristi"). When the Camorrists ask Rafaele what he sees in Maliella, the latter replies lightly, "Non sapete" ("I don't know"). Maliella, sobbing wildly, comes to Rafaele and confesses what has happened. Rafaele is furious; he throws her sav-agely to the ground. As she falls, the jewels of the Madonna scatter and superstitious terror grips the Camorrists as they recognize them. When the remorseful Gennaro arrives, Maliella points him out as the thief. A sudden storm blows out the candles. Hysterical in the darkness, Maliella rushes away to drown herself in the sea. The Camorrists disperse. Gennaro gathers the scattered jewels and offers them to an image of the Madonna, then kills himself with a dagger.

While the name of Wolf-Ferrari is most often associated with OPERA BUFFA, a form in which he was an acknowledged master, he succeeded in producing a tragic opera that was a staple of the international repertory for many years. *The Jewels of the Madonna* belongs to the naturalistic school of Italian opera known as VERISMO. Most of the impact of the score comes from the realistic manner in which the music portrays a storm, a carnival, or the suicides of Maliella and Gennaro. It is for its dramatic power, rather than its lyricism, that this work is of paramount interest.

Jewel Song, *see* AH, JE RIS DE ME VOIR.

Joan of Arc, the fifteenth-century French heroine and martyr whose military leadership of the French compelled the English to lift the siege of Orleans, and who finally was burned at the stake by the English. She appears as the principal character in many operas, notably VERDI's *Giovanna d'Arco,* JEANNE D'ARC AU BÛCHER, BALFE's *Joan of Arc,* REZNIČEK's *Die Jungfrau von Orleans,* THE MAID OF ORLEANS, and THE TRIUMPH OF JOAN.

Jobin, Raoul, tenor. Born Quebec, Apr. 8, 1906. His musical training took place in Quebec. He made his opera debut at the PARIS OPÉRA in 1930 as TYBALT. For a decade he assumed leading tenor roles at both the Opéra and the OPÉRA-COMIQUE. On Feb. 19, 1940, he made his debut at the METROPOLITAN OPERA as Des Grieux in MANON. He remained with the company for a decade, while making numerous guest appearances in other opera houses in North and South America. He was a specialist in the French repertory. In 1957 he founded a school for singing in Montreal.

Jochum, Eugen, conductor. Born Babenhausen, Ger., Nov. 1, 1902. He studied music at the Augsburg Conservatory and conducting with Siegmund von Hausegger in Munich. After holding various minor posts as conductor, he became music director of the city of Duisburg in 1930. In 1934 he succeeded Karl MUCK as conductor of the HAMBURG OPERA and Philharmonic. From 1939 to 1949 he was the general music director of the city of Hamburg. He has appeared as conductor in most of the major European opera houses and at the BAYREUTH and MUNICH festivals. In 1949 he helped to reorganize the Munich Radio Symphony, which he conducted for several years. In 1950 he was elected president of the German section of the Bruckner Society. In 1960 he became a principal conductor of the Concertgebouw Orchestra in Amsterdam, with which he made his American debut in 1961.

Johannes Kepler, see KEPLER, JOHANNES.

John, (1) Dot's husband (baritone) in GOLDMARK'S THE CRICKET ON THE HEARTH.

(2) A butcher (bass-baritone) in VAUGHAN WILLIAMS' HUGH THE DROVER.

John of Leyden, leader of the Anabaptists (tenor) in MEYERBEER'S LE PROPHÈTE.

Johnson, Dick, an outlaw (tenor), alias Ramerrez, in PUCCINI'S THE GIRL OF THE GOLDEN WEST, a role created by CARUSO.

Johnson, Edward, tenor and opera manager. Born Guelph, Ontario, Aug. 22, 1881; died there Apr. 20, 1959. For over a decade he was a leading tenor of the METROPOLITAN OPERA and after that its general manager for fifteen years. He began to study music seriously in New York City with Mme. von Feilitsch. For a while he earned his living singing in churches. In 1908 he appeared in New York in the leading role of the Oscar Straus operetta *A Waltz Dream*. He then went to Europe, where for two years he studied with CARUSO's coach, Vincenzo Lombardi. He made his opera debut in Padua in 1912 in ANDREA CHÉNIER, billed as Edoardo di Giovanni. After appearing for two seasons in various Italian theaters, he made his debut at LA SCALA in the first Italian performance of PARSIFAL. Johnson was the leading tenor of La Scala for five seasons, during which time he created the leading tenor roles in FEDRA, LA NAVE, and ALFANO's *L'ombra di Don Giovanni* and appeared in the Italian premieres of GIANNI SCHICCHI and IL TABARRO. His American debut took place in 1920 in FEDORA, with the CHICAGO OPERA. After three years with this company he was engaged by the Metropolitan Opera, making his debut on Nov. 16, 1922, as AVITO. He sang at the Metropolitan Opera for the next thirteen years, featured in the world premieres of THE KING'S HENCHMAN, MERRY MOUNT, and PETER IBBETSON, and in such important American premieres and Metropolitan revivals as FRA GHERARDO, PELLÉAS ET MÉLISANDE, SADKO, and LA VESTALE. The role of Pelléas was considered by many to be one of his most successful interpretations. In 1935 Johnson was appointed director of a special spring season then inaugurated by the Metropolitan. The sudden death of Herbert WITHERSPOON, chosen to succeed GATTI-CASAZZA as general manager, brought the directorial post to Johnson that fall. Johnson remained the general manager of the Metropolitan Opera for the next fifteen years, a regime marked by comparative prosperity at the box office and by many substantial artistic successes. Johnson resigned his post in 1950 and was succeeded by Rudolf BING. On Feb. 28, a gala evening took place at the Metropolitan to honor the departing manager. It was climaxed by an opera pageant in which many of the company's outstanding singers appeared in roles from twelve of the most successful operas produced under Johnson's direction. Twelve days earlier, the last of these important revivals had taken place: KHOVANTCHINA.

John Sorel, see SOREL, JOHN.

John the Baptist, the Prophet (tenor) in MASSENET'S HÉRODIADE.

Jokanaan (John the Baptist), the Prophet (baritone) in Richard STRAUSS'S SALOME.

Jolie Fille de Perth, La (The Fair Maid of Perth), opera in four acts by BIZET. Libretto by Jules-Henri Vernoy de SAINT-GEORGES and Jules Adenis, based on Sir Walter SCOTT'S *The Fair Maid of Perth.* Premiere: Théâtre Lyrique, Paris, Dec. 26, 1867. When first produced, the opera received eighteen performances in Paris and several in Brussels (in 1868), then lay neglected until Nov. 3, 1890, when it was revived by the OPÉRA-COMIQUE. It has been mounted from time to time in Europe, though infrequently, and it was broadcast over BBC in 1956. This opera's neglect is at least partially due to its libretto, which Winton Dean regards as the worst Bizet ever set. The opera, nevertheless, has several interesting numbers for orchestra: the prelude to Act I; the AUBADE, march, and gypsy dance in Act II; and the minuet in Act III, which was used in Bizet's *L'Arlésienne Suite, No. 2.* The better vocal numbers are the tenor serenade "À la voix" and the baritone aria "Quand la flamme de l'amour," both in Act II.

Jommelli, Niccolò, composer. Born Aversa, Italy, Sept. 10, 1714; died Naples, Aug. 25, 1774. His musical studies took place at conservatories in Naples, his teachers including Francesco DURANTE. Before turning to opera he wrote some church music and ballets. His first opera, *L'errore amoroso,* was completed in 1737 and was acclaimed. His second opera, *Odoardo,* was well received in 1738 and brought him a commission from Cardinal Albani to write operas for performance at his palace. Jommelli went to Rome in 1740 and wrote two operas for the Cardinal. A year later another opera, *Merope,* was such an immense success in Venice that the Council of Ten appointed him the director of the Conservatorio degli

Incurabili. In 1745 Jommelli visited Vienna to attend premieres of several of his new operas. He was greatly honored by the Empress and others of high station. After he returned to Rome, he became assistant MAESTRO DI CAPPELLA at St. Peter's, a post he held from 1749 to 1754. He then went to Stuttgart to fill the post of KAPELLMEISTER for the Duke of Württemberg. While in this post (held nearly sixteen years) he wrote twenty operas. In 1769 Jommelli returned to the country of his birth to find that he no longer occupied his former exalted position. His last operas were failures, a circumstance that broke his health and spirit. After writing an occasional cantata and a *Miserere,* he died of apoplexy.

Jommelli wrote over fifty operas. When he adhered to Neapolitan traditions, his works were filled with supple, pleasing melodies and ingratiating harmonies that had an immediate appeal. The works of his German period were in a richer and deeper vein. His harmonic language became so varied, his instrumental coloring so subtle, his dramatic feeling so pronounced that he acquired the sobriquet the "Italian GLUCK." Thus, he wrote his most popular operas while still in Italy, his best operas in the closing years of his life. His most famous operas were *Merope* (1741); *Ezio* (1741, revised 1748 and 1771); *Achille in Sciro* (1745); *Eumene* (1747); *Didone* (1748); *Artaserse* (1749); *Demetrio* (1753); *Alessandro nell' Indie* (1757); *La clemenza di Tito* (1758); ARMIDA (1770); IFIGENIA IN TAURIDE (1773).

Jonas, an Anabaptist preacher (tenor) in MEYERBEER'S LE PROPHÈTE.

Jones, Brutus, ruler of a West Indian island (baritone) in GRUENBERG'S THE EMPEROR JONES.

Jongleur de Notre Dame, Le (The Juggler of Our Lady), opera in three acts by MASSENET. Libretto by Maurice Léna, based on *L'Etui de nacre,* a short story by Anatole FRANCE, derived from a medieval miracle play. Premiere: Monte

Carlo Opera, Feb. 18, 1902. American premiere: Manhattan Opera House, Nov. 27, 1908.

Characters: Jean, a juggler (tenor or soprano); Boniface, the monastery cook (baritone); the Prior (bass); the monk painter (baritone); the monk musician (baritone); the monk poet (tenor); the monk sculptor (bass); citizens of the town. The setting is the Abbey of Cluny, near Paris, in the fourteenth century.

Act I. A square before the abbey. A crowd has gathered to celebrate market day. Jean, a juggler, begs for attention, but the crowd, indifferent to his tricks, persuades him to render a profane song, "Hallelujah to wine." For this offense, Jean is threatened with excommunication. The Prior, having become Jean's ally ("Il pleure"), advises him there is only one way he can find absolution: by entering a monastery. Jean expresses his great love for freedom ("O liberté, ma vie!"). The monastery cook arrives leading a mule laden with food for the glory of the Virgin ("Pour la Vierge"). Starving, Jean is abruptly tempted to follow the Prior's advice.

Act II. A hall within the abbey. A statue of the Virgin is being completed and a hymn to it is being sung ("Ave rosa"). His fellow monks continually mock Jean for his inability to master Latin and the hymns. Jean is mortified at his stupidity. Boniface consoles him by telling him the story of the sage flower that sheltered the child Jesus when the rose feared to ruin its petals. (Légende de la sauge: "Fleurissait une sauge"). Boniface emphasizes that even one so humble as Jean can serve God and be accepted by Him.

Act III. The chapel. Wearing his juggler's clothes, Jean performs his tricks and songs before the altar. The monks discover him in this performance and are outraged at the sacrilege. Boniface restrains them from removing him. Exhausted, Jean collapses at the feet of the Virgin. The face of the image be-gins to shine with a beatific light and the hands stretch out in blessing. Jean dies joyously. A choir of angels receives his soul, as kneeling monks witness the miracle.

Since Massenet intended *Le Jongleur* as a "mystery," he wrote no parts for women in it. When the opera was first produced, the part of Jean was sung by a tenor. Thus the composer who had become famous for his characterizations of women (MANON, HÉRODIADE, THAÏS, SAPHO, and GRISÉLIDIS) produced an effective opera without a woman in a principal role. Subsequently, wishing to appear in the work, Mary GARDEN prevailed on Massenet to adapt the leading role for soprano voice. It was a happy change; the role of Jean became even more effective. When Mary Garden appeared in *Le Jongleur* for the first time (at its American premiere) she scored a sensation; from then on her name was associated with the opera, and since her retirement, performances of *Le Jongleur* have been infrequent.

Jonny spielt auf (Johnny Strikes Up the Band), opera in two parts by KRENEK. Libretto by the composer. Premiere: Leipzig Opera, Feb. 10, 1927. American premiere: Metropolitan Opera, Jan. 19, 1929. Krenek explained that this JAZZ opera (an example of ZEITKUNST, or "contemporary art," then in vogue in Germany) was an interpretation of the "rhythms and atmosphere of modern life in this age of technical science." The story revolves around Jonny (baritone), a Negro jazz-band leader, who steals Daniello's violin. He finds a hiding place for it first in the room of Daniello's girl friend, Anita (soprano), and after that at the home of Max (tenor), a composer who is also one of Anita's boy friends. The four principals come together at a railway station, where Daniello (baritone) is killed by an onrushing train, while Max and Anita depart on a train bound for Amsterdam. Jonny climbs to the top of a railway signal, violin in hand. Suddenly the station clock is transformed into a globe of the world. Jonny creeps to the top of the sphere, bestriding it like a world conqueror, and begins to play jazz tunes. Below, the people dance a Charleston.

Because of its novel subject matter and jazz idioms, *Jonny spielt auf* was turned down by many companies before it was accepted by the Leipzig Opera. Within the next few years it was heard in about a hundred European cities, translated into eighteen languages. New York found it less wonderful—produced by the Metropolitan in 1929, *Jonny* lasted three performances. The opera has now vanished like the frenetic era it celebrated.

Jonson, Ben, dramatist. Born Westminster, Eng., about 1573; died there Apr. 6, 1637. One of the most significant early seventeenth-century dramatists, Jonson wrote several plays that have been made into operas. *Epicoene* was the source of Mark Lothar's *Lord Spleen,* SALIERI's *Angiolina,* and DIE SCHWEIGSAME FRAU, and VOLPONE of operas of the same name by ANTHEIL, GRUENBERG, and Norman Demuth. Sir Edward Elgar wrote an uncompleted opera, *The Spanish Lady,* based on Jonson's *The Devil is an Ass.*

Jontek's Revenge, *see* HALKA.

José, *see* DON JOSÉ.

Joseph, opera in three acts by MÉHUL. Libretto by Alexandre Duval, based on the Bible story. Premiere: Opéra-Comique, Feb. 17, 1807. American premiere: Philadelphia, Oct. 15, 1828. The story of Joseph and of his sale by his brothers to the Egyptians is only partially told in this opera. The work opens in Egypt, where Joseph (contralto) has attained high station through his wisdom in saving that country from famine. He has assumed the name of Cleophas, and rules as governor in Memphis. A famine in Palestine brings Joseph's blind father and brothers to Memphis to plead for food. They do not recognize him, but he knows them instantly.

Eventually he reveals his identity, forgives his brothers, and prevails on his father to do likewise. Joseph's beautiful aria in Act I, "Champs paternels," is famous. WEBER wrote a set of piano variations on a theme from *Joseph,* and melodies from the opera were used by Dame Ethel SMYTH in her one-act opera *L'Entente cordiale.*

Joseph and His Brethren, *see* MANN, THOMAS.

Jour naissait dans le bocage, Le (Sorgeva il dì del bosco in seno), Maria's singing lesson in Act II of DONIZETTI's THE DAUGHTER OF THE REGIMENT.

Journet, Marcel, bass. Born Grasse, France, July 25, 1867; died Vittel, France, Sept. 5, 1933. His music study took place at the Paris Conservatory. In 1891 he made his opera debut at the THÉÂTRE DE LA MONNAIE. Six years later he became a member of the COVENT GARDEN company. On Dec. 22, 1900, he made his American debut at the METROPOLITAN OPERA as RAMFIS. He remained at the Metropolitan eight years. From 1908 to 1914 he made star appearances in leading opera houses of Europe and after 1914 was associated with the CHICAGO OPERA, the PARIS OPÉRA, and LA SCALA. His repertory included sixty-five French, twenty-seven Italian, and eight Wagnerian roles. He appeared in the world premieres of MONNA VANNA, LA NAVARRAISE, NERONE, and THAÏS.

Jouy, Victor Joseph Étienne de, dramatist. Born Jouy, near Versailles, 1764; died St. Germain-en-Laye, Sept. 4, 1846. One of the most successful French dramatists of the early nineteenth century, de Jouy wrote many opera librettos, the most famous being that for ROSSINI's WILLIAM TELL, which he wrote collaboratively with Hippolyte Bis. De Jouy also wrote the librettos for Rossini's MOSÈ IN EGITTO, SPONTINI's *Fernand Cortez* and LA VESTALE, and for various other operas by BOIELDIEU, CHERUBINI, MÉHUL, and Rossini.

Juan, *see* DON JUAN.

Juarez and Maximilian, *see* WERFEL, FRANZ.

Juch, Emma, soprano and opera manager. Born Vienna, July 4, 1863; died New York City, Mar. 6, 1939. She was born while her parents, American citizens, were visiting Vienna. When she was four she was brought to the United States. She studied singing with her father and Mme. Murio-Celli. In her eighteenth year she joined HER MAJESTY's THEATRE in London, then directed by MAPLESON, making her debut as PHILINE. Returning to the United States, she made her American debut with the Mapleson company at the ACADEMY OF MUSIC on Oct. 21, 1881, once again as Philine. She was engaged by the American Opera Company in 1885 and sang many principal roles. When that company was dissolved, she organized the Emma Juch Grand Opera Company. From 1889 to 1891 this company toured the United States, Mexico, and Canada. After 1891 Juch withdrew from opera to devote herself to concert appearances. In 1894 she married Francis L. Wellman, a United States District Attorney, retiring to live in New York City.

Juchhei, nun ist die Hexe todt! (Knusperwalzer—Gingerbread Waltz), duet of Hansel and Gretel as they sing and dance with joy at the witch's death, in Act III of HUMPERDINCK's HANSEL AND GRETEL.

Judith, (1) heroine of the Book of Judith, one of the apocryphal books of the Old Testament. The Israelites, besieged by the Assyrians under Holofernes, are about to surrender when the widow Judith goes to the enemy camp, seduces Holofernes, decapitates him while he is asleep, and returns with his head. The Israelites are so heartened that they issue forth and defeat the Assyrians. Besides the two operas described below, *Judith* has furnished the name and story for operas by Natanael Berg (Stockholm, 1936), Albert Doppler (Vienna, 1870), and A. N. Serov (St. Petersburg, 1863). The same story was used as the basis for the opera *Holofernes* by Emil REZNIČEK (Berlin, 1923)

(2) Opera in one act by GOOSSENS. Libretto by Arnold BENNETT. Premiere: Covent Garden, June 25, 1929. American premiere: Philadelphia, Dec. 26, 1929. Holofernes, oppressor of the Israelites, is taken with Judith's beauty and seeks to win her love. During a bacchanale, Judith feigns acceptance, and at the height of a love scene she kills him.

(3) Opera in three acts by HONEGGER. Libretto by René Morax. Premiere: Monte Carlo Opera, Feb. 13, 1926. American premiere: Chicago, Jan. 27, 1927. This opera is an extension of incidental music for Morax's play, introduced in Switzerland in 1925. Judith goes forth to the conquering Assyrians to plead for her people. The leader, Holofernes, tries to make love to her, and as part of a plan to win him over, she submits. When Holofernes falls into a drunken stupor, Judith cuts off his head. She brings it to her people, who are so inspired that they defeat the enemy. Judith gives thanks to God for the victory and puts on a widow's veil as mourning for the dead.

(4) Bluebeard's bride (soprano) in BARTÓK's BLUEBEARD's CASTLE.

Jugement de Paris, Le, the air sung by Paris in OFFENBACH's OPÉRA BOUFFE LA BELLE HÉLÈNE.

Juif Polonais, Le (The Polish Jew), opera in three acts by ERLANGER. Libretto by Henri Cain and Pierre Barthélemy Gheusi, based on the novel of the same name by ERCKMANN-CHATRIAN. Premiere: Opéra-Comique, Apr. 11, 1900. This is essentially the story in which Henry Irving achieved a triumph on the English stage—his play was called *The Bells.* At an inn, Schmitt tells the story of the murder of a Polish Jew fifteen years earlier. As soon as he finishes his tale, a Polish Jew enters the inn. One of those who has heard Schmitt's story, Mathis, the burgomaster, faints—for it is he who had murdered the Jew years ago, and the present stranger appears to him like an apparition from the grave. Mathis has a nightmare in which he sees himself hanged for the crime. He cries out, then dies of a heart attack. The murderer has been punished.

Juive, La (The Jewess), opera in five acts by HALÉVY. Libretto by Eugène SCRIBE. Premiere: Paris Opéra, Feb. 23, 1835. American premiere: Théâtre d'Orléans, New Orleans, Feb. 13, 1844.

Characters: Cardinal Brogny (bass); Prince Léopold (tenor); Princess Eudoxie, his betrothed (soprano); Eléazar, a Jewish goldsmith (tenor); Rachel, his daughter (soprano); Ruggiero, chief bailiff (baritone); Albert, officer of the imperial guard (bass); courtiers; priests; soldiers; people. The action takes place in the city of Constance, in Baden, in the year 1414.

Act I. The square before the cathedral. The victory of Prince Léopold over the Hussites is being celebrated. However, Eléazar appears oblivious and goes on working. The crowd is angered at his indifference and drags him and his daughter out into the open square. The pair are about to be taken to prison when Cardinal Brogny emerges from the cathedral. He recognizes the Jew: many years before, he had instigated a pogrom in which Eléazar's two sons were killed. Some time after, the Cardinal had also known tragedy when his house mysteriously burned down and his wife and daughter died in the flames. The Cardinal now makes a gesture of friendship, but Eléazar rejects it. The Cardinal prays for all nonbelievers and entreats the crowd to replace hatred with tolerance ("Si la rigueur et la vengeance"). Eléazar and his daughter are let go, and the square becomes empty. Prince Léopold appears, disguised in simple clothes and calling himself Samuel. In love with Rachel, he knows the only way he can hope to win her is by concealing his true identity. Rachel, who returns Léopold's love, invites him to the Passover ceremonies at her house. When the crowd returns and resumes its hostility toward Eléazar, Léopold quickly exerts his authority. Rachel for the first time begins to suspect that her lover is no humble Jewish painter.

Act II. A room in Eléazar's house. The Passover feast, at which Léopold is a guest, is celebrated. A prayer is intoned ("O Dieu, Dieu de nos pères"), after which Eléazar begs for divine guidance and for the ultimate destruction of Israel's enemies ("Dieu, que ma voix tremblante"). Unexpectedly, Princess Eudoxie arrives to order a jewel she wants to present to Léopold the following day. To avoid being recognized, Léopold hides until she leaves. Puzzled by his strange behavior, Rachel insists on an explanation. Léopold confesses the truth. At first Rachel is shocked, but so great is her love that she is soon ready to elope with him. Growing furious, Eléazar rushes at Léopold with drawn dagger. Rachel intervenes and saves her lover. So eloquently does she plead for her right to love that Eléazar's anger turns to compassion. Reluctantly, he gives his consent to her marriage. But Léopold has been contemplating another relationship than marriage. Crying that he cannot wed a Jewess, he rushes out of the house.

Act III. The great hall in the imperial palace. At a royal feast, a ballet pantomime is performed, after which the people hail Prince Léopold ("Sonnez, clairons, que vos chants de victoire"). Eléazar and Rachel arrive to deliver the jewel Eudoxie has ordered. As Eudoxie presents it to Léopold, her betrothed, Rachel furiously denounces Léopold as unworthy, revealing to the startled assemblage that he has made love to her and has promised to marry her. Cardinal Brogny excommunicates Léopold for this offense while cursing him, Eléazar, and Rachel for defying the laws of God ("Vous qui du Dieu vivant outragez la puissance"). Condemned to death, Eléazar, Rachel, and Léopold are imprisoned.

Act IV. A hall in the court of justice. Eudoxie persuades Rachel to change her testimony and assume full responsibility for what has passed between herself and Léopold. Rachel finally consents. The Cardinal arrives, offering to pardon Eléazar and his daughter if they embrace Christianity; defiantly and proudly they both refuse. At this point, Eléazar reveals to the Cardinal that the latter's daughter is alive, having been rescued from his flaming home by a Jew. The Cardinal is deeply moved, but is unable to learn from Eléazar his daughter's whereabouts. After the Cardinal departs, Eléazar quietly contemplates the twist of fate whereby he is compelled to sacrifice Rachel, one whom he has raised as his own and loves dearly ("Rachel, quand du Seigneur").

Act V. A place of execution. A restive crowd eagerly awaits the punishment of Eléazar and Rachel, who are to be boiled in oil ("Quel plaisir, quelle joie!"). Eléazar now learns that Léopold will escape death because Rachel has falsely sworn to his innocence. The old Jew pleads with Rachel to save herself by embracing Christianity, but again she refuses. As she is thrown into the boiling caldron, Eléazar cries to the horrified Cardinal: *"There* is your daughter!" Having had his moment of triumph, Eléazar goes to his death proudly.

Though Halévy wrote over thirty operas, only *La Juive* keeps his name alive. Into this work, one of the finest in the French lyric theater, the composer poured his most expressive lyricism; it is through melody that the dramatic conflicts and crises find expression. Though the central character is a Jew, and one of the scenes reproduces a Jewish ceremony, Halévy made no attempt to write Hebrew music or to enlist Hebraic idioms to give his music authenticity. His melody remains characteristically French throughout in its refinement, objectivity, and sensitivity. The French tenor who created the role of Eléazar, Adolphe NOURRIT, was a constructive influence while the opera was being written. Halévy originally planned the role of Eléazar for a high bass voice, but Nourrit convinced him that a tenor would be more appropriate. It was also Nourrit who convinced Halévy to include in the fourth act the opera's most famous aria: "Rachel, quand du Seigneur." The

role of Eléazar was one of CARUSO's favorites. In his history of the METRO-POLITAN OPERA, Irving Kolodin goes so far as to say that Caruso's performance of this role was "without doubt the most striking artistic triumph of his career. . . . The impersonation he finally presented was the product of more care and study, especially dramatically, than any of the thirty-five other roles he sang during his career in New York."

Julien, (1) a painter (tenor) in love with Louise in CHARPENTIER's LOUISE and *Julien (see below).*

(2) Opera in prologue and four acts by CHARPENTIER. Libretto by the composer. Premiere: Opéra-Comique, June 3, 1913. American premiere: Metropolitan Opera, Feb. 26, 1914. This is a sequel to LOUISE, but it was a dismal failure, receiving only twenty performances in Paris, and it has not been revived since 1914. In this work Louise is dead, but she appears to Julien in a vision, a representation of beauty to reawaken his faith in art and beauty. Julien goes vainly in search of his soul, only to meet frustration and death.

Juliette, daughter of Capulet (soprano) in GOUNOD's ROMÉO ET JULIETTE, a role created by Marie MIOLAN-CARVALHO.

Juliette's Waltz, *see* JE VEUX VIVRE DANS CE RÊVE.

Julius Caesar, *see* GIULIO CESARE IN EGITTO.

Jumping Frog of Calaveras County, The, opera in one act by FOSS. Libretto by Jean Karsavina, based on the story of the same name by Mark Twain. Premiere: Bloomington, Ind., May 19, 1950. A comedy in two scenes (one in a saloon, the other outside), the opera is built around Mark Twain's celebrated jumping contest. The score is made up of cowboy and other Western folk tunes as well as broadly satirical music. It was successfully produced at the VENICE MUSIC FESTIVAL in Sept., 1953.

junge Lord, Der (The Young Lord), comic opera in three acts by HENZE. Libretto by Ingeborg Bachmann, adapted from a tale of Wilhelm Hauff. Premiere: Berlin Deutsche Staatsoper, Apr.

7, 1965. American premiere: San Diego Opera, Cal., Feb. 13, 1967. This is the composer's only comic opera. It is a broad satire on German provincialism, about a man who is idolized in the town of Grünwiesel but who turns out to be a circus ape dressed up as a man. Henze's style is essentially that of OPERA BUFFA, though with modern overtones. One German critic called the opera "the rebirth of *opera buffa.*"

Jungfrau Maria, Stradella's radiant hymn to Holy Mary in Act III of FLOTOW'S ALESSANDRO STRADELLA. It is the most celebrated aria in the opera.

Jungfrau von Orleans, Die, *see* SCHILLER, FRIEDRICH.

Jupiter, (1) a god (baritone) in GOUNOD'S PHILÉMON ET BAUCIS.

(2) A god (tenor) disguised as a bull in MILHAUD'S *opéra minute* L'ENLÈVEMENT D'EUROPE.

Jurinac, Sena, soprano. Born Travnik, Yugoslavia, Oct. 24, 1921. After attending the Zagreb Conservatory, she made her debut at the Zagreb Opera on Oct. 15, 1942. Some three years later she was engaged by the VIENNA STATE OPERA, where she scored her first major successes in a varied repertory of Ital-ian, French, and German operas. In 1947 she appeared for the first time at the SALZBURG FESTIVAL and in the next few years was acclaimed not only at Salzburg but also at the GLYNDEBOURNE and EDINBURGH festivals for her performances in MOZART'S operas. Between 1945 and 1955 she was heard in Vienna at the VOLKSOPER and the THEATER-AN-DER-WIEN and at the Vienna State Opera, where KARAJAN reassigned her the roles in which she had acquired her fame. On Sept. 22, 1959, she made her American opera debut with the SAN FRANCISCO OPERA as CIO-CIO-SAN. In 1961 she appeared at COVENT GARDEN in her first Leonore in FIDELIO. She was given the honorary title of KAMMERSÄNGERIN in Vienna in 1953. Besides her outstanding successes in operas by Mozart, WAGNER, and Richard STRAUSS, she has been acclaimed for her performances as JENUFA, Poppea (in L'INCORONAZIONE DI POPPEA), DESDEMONA, and MADAMA BUTTERFLY. She appeared as Octavian in the motion-picture presentation of DER ROSENKAVALIER in which Elisabeth SCHWARZKOPF appeared as the Marschallin.

K

Kabale und Liebe, *see* SCHILLER, FRIEDRICH.

Kabalevsky, Dmitri, composer. Born St. Petersburg, Russia, Dec. 30, 1904. His music study took place at the Moscow Conservatory and with Miaskovsky. In 1925 he began writing songs and piano pieces, and success came in 1934 with his *Second Symphony*. He extended his reputation with the opera COLAS BREUGNON, introduced in Leningrad on Feb. 22, 1938. Later operas: *Before Moscow* (1942); *The Family of Taras* (1947); *Nikita Vershinin* (1954); *Armoured Train;* and a children's opera, *The Encounter with a Miracle.* In 1939 he was elected a member of the Presidium of the Organizing Committee of the Union of Soviet Composers. A year later he received the Order of Merit, in 1946 the Stalin Prize for a string quartet, and in 1965 the Order of Lenin. He has served as professor of composition at the Moscow Conservatory and as head of the music department of the Institute of Art and History at the Academy of Sciences. In 1959 he paid his first visit to the United States, under the auspices of the American Department of State.

Kafka, Franz, author. Born Prague, July 2, 1883; died Kierling, near Vienna, June 3, 1924. The author of some extraordinary novels and short stories, many of which would have been lost after his death except for the efforts of his literary executor, Max BROD, Kafka is perhaps best known for his haunting tale of persecution, *The Trial (Der Prozess)*, the source of an opera by EINEM and SCHULLER'S THE VISITATION. HENZE's *The Country Doctor* is based on Kafka's story of the same title.

Kahn, Otto H., opera patron and financier. Born Mannheim, Feb. 21, 1867; died New York City, Mar. 29, 1934. A noted banker and member of the New York banking house of Kahn, Loeb and Co., Otto Kahn joined the board of directors of the METROPOLITAN OPERA in 1903. When that organization suffered financial reverses five years later, he was one of fourteen subscribers raising a fund of a hundred and fifty thousand dollars. In 1924 he became president of the board; he held this post seven years. During this time he was a vital force in trying to get a new opera house for the Metropolitan, but his efforts were in vain. After he resigned as president, he remained a member of the board until the end of his life. He was also an honorary director of COVENT GARDEN and the BOSTON OPERA.

Kaiser, Georg, dramatist. Born Magdeburg, Nov. 25, 1878; died Ascona, Switzerland, June 5, 1945. A representative of the German expressionist theater, Kaiser wrote librettos for three operas by WEILL: DER PROTAGONIST, *Der Silbersee,* and THE CZAR HAS HIMSELF PHOTOGRAPHED. BLACHER's opera *Rosamunde Floris* was derived from a play by Kaiser, and he wrote the libretto for Max Ettinger's *Juana.*

Kalidasa, Sanskrit epic poet and dramatist. He lived about the fifth century after Christ and was the author of a drama, *Sakuntala,* that inspired many musical works, including the following operas: ALFANO's *La leggenda di Sacuntala,* Louis Coerne's *Sakuntala,* Ignace Jan Paderewski's *Sakuntala,* and WEINGARTNER's *Sakuntala.*

Kalisch, Paul, tenor. Born Berlin, Nov. 6, 1855; died St. Lorenz am Modensee, Jan. 27, 1946. He was trained to be an architect. Discovering that he had a voice, he went to Italy to study with LEONI and LAMPERTI, subsequent to which he made successful opera appearances in Milan, Rome, Florence, and Munich. From 1884 to 1887 he was a principal tenor of the Berlin Royal Opera (BERLIN STATE OPERA). Following his debut at the METROPOLITAN OPERA on Jan. 30, 1889, in TANNHÄUSER, he remained with the company until 1892, appearing in the American premiere of THE BARBER OF BAGDAD, as well as in the standard Italian and German repertory. In 1888 he married Lilli LEHMANN, and in 1891 he appeared opposite her as MANRICO when she sang an Italian role for the first time.

Kallman, Chester, librettist who has collaborated with W. H. AUDEN. Without Auden's collaboration, he wrote the libretto for Chávez' PANFILO AND LAURETTA.

Kammeroper, *see* CHAMBER OPERA.

Kammersänger (feminine, **Kammersängerin**), German for "chamber singer." This is the highest honorary title bestowed by the German and Austrian governments on opera singers.

Kann ich mich auch an ein Mädel erinnern, the Marschallin's monologue lamenting the loss of her youth, in Act I of Richard STRAUSS's DER ROSENKAVALIER.

Kansas City Lyric Theater, principal opera company in Kansas City, Mo. It was founded in 1958 by Russell Patterson, since then serving as general director, and Morton Walker and opened on Sept. 21 with LA BOHÈME. Its aim is to present opera in English with young American singer-actors at the beginning of their professional careers, these artists chosen by auditions held annually from coast to coast. The company offers each fall a four-week season with performances five nights a week. In its first decade it offered over two hundred performances of thirty different operas. Most of its productions are from the popular repertory, but occasionally it gives novelties such as ARIADNE AUF NAXOS, THE CRUCIBLE, LA SERVA PADRONA, and VANESSA. The 1963 season was preceded by a spring festival of American operas made possible by a FORD FOUNDATION grant. Since 1965, the fall season has been followed by a tour.

Kapellmeister, *see* MAESTRO DI CAPPELLA.

Kappel, Gertrude, soprano. Born Halle, Ger., Sept. 1, 1884. After graduating from the Leipzig Conservatory she joined the HANOVER OPERA, where she made her debut in 1903 in IL TROVATORE. Following a few seasons in Hanover, she appeared in Vienna in leading Wagnerian roles and was so successful that she was engaged as principal soprano of the MUNICH OPERA. For three seasons she appeared with immense success both in Vienna and Munich. On Jan. 16, 1928, she made her American debut at the METROPOLITAN OPERA as ISOLDE. She remained at the Metropolitan through the 1934–35 season, appearing in the Wagnerian repertory and operas by Richard STRAUSS. Meanwhile, in 1933, she became a member of the SAN FRANCISCO OPERA COMPANY. She retired from opera in 1937, establishing her home in Berlin.

Karajan, Herbert von, conductor. Born Salzburg, Apr. 5, 1908. He is one of the world's foremost conductors of symphonic music and opera. He received his musical education in Vienna and his apprenticeship as conductor in Ulm. For five years he was the general music director of the city of Aachen. In 1938 he was appointed a conductor of the BERLIN STATE OPERA, where he remained through the war years. Closely affiliated with the Nazi regime, Karajan was considered an untouchable by the American occupying forces, who refused him permission to give any performances. For a while, Karajan lived in total retirement in Salzburg. Then, through the efforts of Walter Legge, an English recording executive, Karajan received permission from the American authorities to make some recordings with the Vienna Philharmonic. De-Nazification followed, allowing him to resume his conducting career, first with the Vienna Symphony (which he developed from a mediocre into an outstanding organization), then to lead several concerts of the Vienna Philharmonic. In 1948 he was made artistic director of the Gesellschaft der Musikfreunde in Vienna, where his symphonic performances grew so famous they came to be known as "Karajan cycles." He achieved major successes at the festivals of FLORENCE, SALZBURG, and BAYREUTH (at the last, directing the entire RING cycle in 1951 and 1952). He was also made musical director of the newly founded Philharmonic Orchestra of London, with which he toured Europe, and became affiliated with LA SCALA, where he has been responsible for every phase of the productions he has conducted.

In 1955 he was given a lifetime appointment as the musical director of the Berlin Philharmonic in succession to FURTWÄNGLER. When Furtwängler died before he could tour the United States with the Berlin Philharmonic in 1955, Karajan took his place, making his American debut in Washington, D.C., on Feb. 28, 1955. He returned to America the same fall to tour with the Philharmonia Orchestra of London. In 1956 he became the musical director of the VIENNA STATE OPERA (without resigning from his post in Berlin). Because of his dictatorial ways, he often came into conflict with his coworkers, though he was an idol of the Viennese public. Violent disagreements with Egon HILBERT, his codirector, led to Karajan's resignation in 1964 and his vow never again to return to Vienna. But following Hilbert's death in 1967, Karajan had a change of heart and returned in June, 1970, to lead a series of five BEETHOVEN concerts in commemoration of the bicentennial of Beethoven's birth. Since 1957 Karajan has been the artistic director of the Salzburg Festival, where his productions of a varied repertory of operas, including CARMEN and BORIS GODUNOV, have become events of first importance. In 1967 he launched a monumental project to present the *Ring* cycle, one drama a year, with every phase of the productions under his personal supervision; many new concepts, some of them highly controversial were to be incorporated. This venture began in 1967 with DIE WALKÜRE at Salzburg during Easter. DAS RHEINGOLD followed in 1968, SIEGFRIED in 1969, and GÖTTERDÄMMERUNG in 1970. He made his debut at the METROPOLITAN OPERA with the first of these productions, *Die Walküre,* on Nov. 21, 1968.

Kärntnerthortheater, a theater in Vienna, situated behind the State Opera. Originally the home of spoken drama, the Kärntnerthor, which arose on the site of the Stadttheater when the latter burned down in 1761, was frequently used for opera and operetta performances after 1790. In 1820 SCHUBERT's operetta *Die Zwillingsbrüder* was introduced there. The heyday of this theater as a home for opera was between 1821 and 1828, when Domenico BARBAJA was its artistic director. It was here that ROSSINI presented a cycle of his operas during his visit to Vienna in 1822. DER FREISCHÜTZ received its Austrian premiere in this house, and it was for the Kärntnerthor that WEBER wrote EURYANTHE, which received its world premiere here in 1823. LINDA DI CHAMOUNIX, MARIA DI ROHAN, and MARTHA were other operas to be introduced in this theater, in 1842, 1843, and 1847, respectively.

Kat'a Kabanová, opera in three acts by JANÁČEK. Libretto by Vincenc Cervinka, based on Ostrovsky's drama *The Storm.* Premiere: Brno, Oct. 23, 1921. American premiere: Bear Mountain, N.Y., Aug. 2, 1960. Kat'a, though married to Tichon, is in love with Boris, with whom she has a secret rendezvous outside her garden. Conscience-stricken, Kat'a confesses her guilt to her family during a storm, tears herself away from her husband's arms, and commits suicide by plunging into the Volga after bidding farewell to her beloved Boris.

When the opera was first given in Cologne on Nov. 9, 1922, KLEMPERER conducted and Rosa PAULY assumed the title role; a German translation by Max BROD was used. A revival of the opera by the SADLER's WELLS company in 1951 made a star of Amy Shuard, who then became one of the leading sopranos at COVENT GARDEN; another London revival, conducted by KUBELIK, was responsible for his appointment as musical director of Covent Garden in 1955. Since then the opera has received numerous performances throughout Europe. Its American premiere was preceded by an amateur performance in Cleveland on Nov. 26, 1957 (with piano accompaniment).

Janáček's score is filled with realistic representations of sounds of nature. The severity of his melodic line and a powerful harmonic language help to heighten the dramatic impact of the play.

Kate, the garrulous heroine (soprano) in DVOŘÁK's folk opera THE DEVIL AND KATE.

Katerina Ismailova (originally entitled **Lady Macbeth of Mzensk**), opera in four acts by SHOSTAKOVICH. Libretto by the composer and A. Preis, based on a story by Leskov. Premiere: Moscow, Jan. 22, 1934 (original version); Moscow, Jan. 1, 1963 (revised version entitled *Katerina Ismailova*). American premiere: Cleveland, Jan. 31, 1935 (original version); San Francisco Opera, Oct. 10, 1964 (revised version). In nineteenth-century Russia, Katerina Ismailova (soprano) murders her father-in-law and her husband, so that she can marry her lover, Serge (tenor), a workman. When the husband's body is discovered, both Katerina and Serge are arrested, just as they are about to get married. Sentenced to hard labor in Siberia, Serge falls in love there with Sonya (mezzo-soprano), a prostitute. Katerina kills Sonya by throwing her over a parapet into a river and then commits suicide. In the original story by Leskov, Katerina is portrayed as a cruel and ruthless woman. In the opera the composer depicts her as the helpless victim of a callous society, while indicting the provincial middle-class society of the Czarist regime. The opera was produced with great success in Moscow, running two years to packed houses. In 1936 it suddenly became the target for violent attack by the Soviet press. *Pravda* now described it as "the coarsest kind of naturalism. . . . The music quacks, grunts, growls, and suffocates itself in order to express the amatory scenes as naturalistically as possible." Because of this official censure, which continued on and off for about a year, Shostakovich became *persona non grata,* avoided by his fellow composers, looked down upon by others until he became rehabilitated in Soviet music through the success of his *Fifth Symphony.* But the opera was shelved in Russia.

While it was still popular in the early 1930's, the opera was sometimes produced, in various Russian cities, under the title of *Katerina Ismailova,* but most performances, in and out of Russia, retained the title of *Lady Macbeth of Mzensk,* which had been used at the world premiere.

When there took place an easing of governmental pressure on composers and the kind of music they should write during the Khrushchev period, Shostakovich revised his now long-neglected opera, made radical changes in the text to remove some of the more objectional carnal episodes, rewrote some of the music, interpolated two new orchestral ENTR'ACTES, and now named it *Katerina Ismailova* to avoid any confusion with the older opera. The new version was well received when it was first heard in Moscow and also at performances at

COVENT GARDEN, in San Francisco, and in New York City, which followed soon thereafter. It was made into a Soviet motion picture, released in 1968.

Kathinka, Kruschina's wife (soprano) in SMETANA'S THE BARTERED BRIDE.

Keilberth, Joseph, conductor. Born Karlsruhe, Apr. 19, 1908; died Munich, July 7, 1968. His association with opera began in 1925, when he was appointed coach at the Karlsruhe State Theater. Ten years later he assumed the post of principal conductor there and in 1945 was engaged as musical director of the DRESDEN OPERA, where he remained for five years. In 1951 he was made a principal conductor of the MUNICH OPERA, rising to the post of music director in 1959, a post which he held with eminence until his death. In 1952, meanwhile, he made the first of several appearances at the BAYREUTH festival and conducted the HAMBURG OPERA at the EDINBURGH FESTIVAL. He made his American debut with the touring Bamberg Symphony in New York City on Apr. 4, 1954. He appeared extensively as a guest conductor at leading European opera houses.

Keiser, Reinhard, composer and opera director. Born Teuchern, Ger., Jan. 9, 1674; died Hamburg, Sept. 12, 1739. Both as composer and director, he was for over forty years the dominant figure in Hamburg, then the opera capital of Germany. His musical training took place at the Thomasschule in Leipzig. In 1692 he was appointed court musician at Brunswick, and here his first opera, *Basilius,* was performed. Three years later he became chief composer of the HAMBURG OPERA. In the next four decades he wrote over a hundred operas, many of them outstandingly successful in their time; he was probably the most celebrated opera composer of his time in Germany. To formal Italian patterns he brought a rich fund of light and pleasing melodies together with dramatic expressiveness. His most successful operas were *Mahmuth II* (1696); *Ismene* (1699); *Ottavia* (1705); *Almira* (1706); *L'inganno fedele* (1714);

Der Hamburger Jahrmarkt (1725). In 1703 Keiser was appointed director of the Hamburg Opera, an institution he succeeded in raising to a position of first importance. It was while he held this post that HANDEL played the violin in the orchestra and wrote his first opera, ALMIRA, produced by the company. Keiser's extravagance in mounting his productions and his indifference to business matters brought the opera house to the brink of ruin; for a period Keiser had to go into hiding to evade his creditors. His marriage to a wealthy woman in 1709 helped to rehabilitate his fortune. Between 1719 and 1721 he was court composer in Stuttgart, and from 1722 to 1728 he lived in Copenhagen, serving much of this time as royal KAPELLMEISTER. After returning to Hamburg, he was engaged to supervise opera productions in St. Petersburg. He was en route from Russia to Italy, intending to engage singers for St. Petersburg, when he again visited Hamburg. He suddenly decided not to return to Russia, despite his contract, and never left Hamburg again. Not too long after his death his operas disappeared permanently from the stage.

Keller, Gottfried, poet and novelist. Born Zürich, Switzerland, July 19, 1819; died there July 15, 1890. His collection of portraits of Swiss provincial life, *Die Leute von Seldwyla,* contained a story, *Romeo und Julia auf dem Dorfe,* which DELIUS used for his opera A VILLAGE ROMEO AND JULIET. Another Keller story was the source of ZEMLINSKY's opera *Kleider machen Leute.*

Kellogg, Clara Louise, soprano and opera manager. Born Sumterville, S.C., July 12, 1842; died New Haven, Conn., May 13, 1916. Beginning in 1857, she received singing lessons from various New York teachers. After going on a concert tour, she made her opera debut on Feb. 27, 1861, at the ACADEMY OF MUSIC in New York City as GILDA. She established her reputation in the next few years in about fifteen different roles. On Nov. 2, 1867, she made her London debut at HER MAJESTY'S THEATRE in FAUST. She toured the United States between 1868 and 1872. In 1872 she became an opera manager when she joined Pauline LUCCA in founding and directing the Lucca-Kellogg Opera Company, in which both artists starred; the venture was a success. From 1874 to 1876 she traveled throughout the United States with another opera company under her own management, appearing in over a hundred performances in a single season. During 1877 she was a guest artist with many leading European opera companies. The following year she married her manager, Carl Strakosch, and soon after went into retirement in New Haven. Her autobiography, *Memoirs of an American Prima Donna,* was published in 1913.

Kelly, Michael, tenor. Born Dublin, Ireland, Dec. 25, 1762; died Margate, Eng., Oct. 9, 1826. He studied singing in Naples, after which he appeared successfully on the leading Italian opera stages under the name of Occhelli. Moving to Vienna, he came to know MOZART well when, for four years, he sang as a member of the Court Theater. He appeared in the world premiere of THE MARRIAGE OF FIGARO as Basilio and Don Curzio. In 1787 he went to London and became a leading tenor at DRURY LANE, singing there until he retired in 1811. His autobiography, *Reminiscences* (1826), contains valuable information about opera and Mozart.

Kempe, Rudolf, conductor. Born Niederpoyritz, near Dresden, June 14, 1910. Music study took place at the Orchestra School of the Saxon State Orchestra in Dresden. Between 1925 and 1929 he was coach and assistant conductor of the Leipzig Opera, while from 1929 to 1936 he was first oboist of the Leipzig Gewandhaus Orchestra. His debut as conductor took place in 1935 with the Leipzig Opera in LORTZING's *Der Wildschütz.* After conducting assignments in Chemnitz and Weimar, he served as musical director of the DRESDEN OPERA between 1949 and 1952 and the MUNICH OPERA between 1952 and 1954. For two seasons he appeared with the METRO-POLITAN OPERA, where he made his debut with TANNHÄUSER on Jan. 26, 1955. In 1955 he directed PALESTRINA at the SALZBURG FESTIVAL and the RING cycle at COVENT GARDEN. Beginning in 1960 he led the *Ring* cycle for several seasons at the BAYREUTH festival. He has since become the principal conductor of the Royal Philharmonic Orchestra of London and given notable performances at Covent Garden. A distinguished interpreter of German operas, he has proved himself hardly less gifted in the Italian repertory.

Kenilworth, *see* SCOTT, SIR WALTER.

Kepler, Johannes, pioneer astronomer. Born Weil der Stadt, Württemberg, Ger., Dec. 27, 1571; died Regensburg, Nov. 15, 1630. He is the central character (baritone) of HINDEMITH's DIE HARMONIE DER WELT.

Kertesz, Istvan, conductor. Born Budapest, 1929. He studied violin and conducting at the Franz Liszt Academy in Budapest and with Fernando PREVITALI at the Santa Cecilia Academy in Rome, where he received a master's degree with honors in conducting (Premio d'Arti). In 1958 he became the musical director of the Augsburg Opera, following which he made numerous guest appearances at LA SCALA, COVENT GARDEN, the BERLIN STATE OPERA, the HAMBURG OPERA, and the TEATRO COLÓN, besides at some of Europe's leading festivals (SALZBURG, EDINBURGH, VIENNA, SPOLETO). In 1964 he signed a ten-year contract as general music director of the COLOGNE OPERA. Kertesz has also distinguished himself as a symphonic conductor in appearances with most of the major orchestras of Europe and the United States.

Kezal, marriage broker (bass) in SMETANA's THE BARTERED BRIDE.

Khivria, Tcherevik's wife (mezzo-soprano) in MUSSORGSKY's THE FAIR AT SOROCHINSK.

Khovantchina, musical drama in five acts by MUSSORGSKY (completed and revised by RIMSKY-KORSAKOV). Libretto by the composer and Vladimir Stassov. Premiere: St. Petersburg, Feb 21, 1886 (amateur performance); St. Petersburg, Nov. 20, 1911 (professional performance). American premiere: Philadelphia, Apr. 18, 1928.

Characters: Prince Ivan Khovantsky, commander of the Streltsy (bass); Andrei, his son (tenor); Prince Vassily Galitzin, a reformer, member of Young Russia (tenor); Dositheus, leader of the Old Believers (bass); Marfa, a young widow (mezzo-soprano); Emma, a young German girl (contralto); Shaklovity, a boyar (baritone); peasants; slaves; townspeople. The setting is Moscow during the reign of Peter the Great.

Act I. A square within the Kremlin. The orchestral prelude, entitled "Dawn on the Moscow River," consists of a folk melody with five variations. The Streltsy, a band of radicals, are plotting against the Czar's regime. Prince Ivan Khovantsky, their leader, has inflamed them with a speech ("The time of darkness came"). The boyar Shaklovity bribes a letter writer to inscribe an accusation of treason against the Prince. The Prince's son, Andrei, now appears, pursuing the girl Emma. Marfa, a discarded mistress of Andrei, protects the girl, bitterly denounces Andrei, and prophesies a terrible fate for him. When Andrei's father sees Emma, he, too, is taken by her beauty and orders his men to arrest her. She is saved by Dositheus, leader of the Old Believers, who rebukes the men and pacifies them.

Act II. Prince Galitzin's house. Marfa, reading the horoscope of Prince Galitzin, can find only tragedy (Marfa's Divination: "Mysterious powers!"). Terrified, the Prince quarrels with her and secretly orders one of his servants to drown her. When Prince Khovantsky arrives, Galitzin quarrels with him, too, and only the arrival of Dositheus saves the situation.

Act III. A street outside Khovantsky's house. Having been spared, Marfa is sitting outside the Prince's house, recalling her love affair with: Andrei. Night brings peace. Shaklovity passes by and remarks on the sleeping city

("Yes, the Streltsy are sleeping"). But while the city is quiet, its enemies are awake to plot its destruction. The Streltsy enter and are confronted by their women, upset by their husbands' activities. Heated words are exchanged. The letter writer suddenly appears with word that the Czar, with foreign aid, has suppressed an insurrection. The cause of Old Russia is lost; the Streltsy pray for divine help.

Act IV, Scene 1. The country house of Khovantsky. The Prince is being entertained by a lavish spectacle of Persian dances (Dance of the Persian Slaves). Shaklovity comes to summon him to a council of state. As the Prince is dressing, assassins murder him.

Scene 2. A square before the church. This scene is prefaced by a celebrated orchestral ENTR'ACTE describing the bleak landscape of Siberian plains. Prince Galitzin is being led to exile. Dositheus laments the sad fate of Russia. His misery is heightened when Marfa tells him that foreign mercenaries have been enlisted to destroy the Old Believers. The Streltsy are summoned, and they bring axes for their own execution. At the last minute they receive word that they have been pardoned by the Czar. But their cause is lost.

Act V. A wood near Moscow. The Old Believers, true to their principles, are determined to kill themselves. A funeral pyre is built. When Marfa applies the torch, they solemnly march to their deaths in the flames, singing as they go.

In *Khovantchina* Mussorgsky was more concerned with creating a great historical panorama than with emphasizing characters or pointing up dramatic incidents. As Rosa Newmarch wrote: "It reminds us of those early icons belonging to the period when the transport of pictures through the forests, bogs, and wilderness of Russia so restricted their distribution that the religious painter resorted to the expedient of representing on one canvas as many saints as could be packed into it." This is the essential weakness of the opera and accounts for its lack of integration and a focal point of interest. But while not essentially a great opera, made up as it is of a series of vignettes, it is the work of a great composer, with many pages that remind us of the best moments in BORIS GODUNOV. The choral passages, the atmospheric entr'acte, and the poignant closing scene more than compensate for the dramatic shortcomings of the text.

Khovantsky, Prince Ivan, commander of the Streltsy (bass) in MUSSORGSKY'S KHOVANTCHINA.

Khrennikov, Tikhon, composer. Born Elets, Russia, June 10, 1913. He attended the Moscow Conservatory and achieved recognition as a composer with a piano concerto written when he was nineteen. His opera *The Brothers* (1936) added greatly to his reputation, as did his *Second Symphony* (1943). Khrennikov writes in a folk idiom, with a strong emphasis on rhythm and broad Russian melody. *The Brothers,* revised and renamed IN THE STORM, was reintroduced with outstanding acclaim in Moscow on May 31, 1939. *Mother,* a serious opera, was produced in Moscow on Oct. 26, 1957, and an operetta, *100 Devils,* in Moscow on May 16, 1963. He subsequently wrote and had produced a comic opera, *The Son-in-Law without Kith or Kin.*

Kienzl, Wilhelm, composer. Born Waizenkirchen, Austria, Jan. 17, 1857; died Vienna, Oct. 3, 1941. His principal music study was pursued at the Prague Conservatory and with Josef Rheinberger in Munich. A friendship with WAGNER was a decisive and permanent influence. For a number of years Kienzl lived with Wagner at Wahnfried in BAYREUTH and as a result of this personal association absorbed many of the master's ideas and principles. He completed his first opera, *Urvasi,* in 1886. His greatest success came with DER EVANGELIMANN, introduced in Berlin in 1895 and afterward produced with outstanding success throughout Germany and Austria. Kienzl was the director of German opera in Amsterdam and Krefeld, principal conductor of the HAMBURG OPERA from 1889 to 1892, and first conductor at the MUNICH OPERA from 1892 to 1893. In 1893 he settled in Graz and devoted himself principally to composition. His operas: *Urvasi* (1886, revised 1909); *Heilmar der Narr* (1892); *Der Evangelimann* (1895); *Don Quixote* (1898); *In Knecht Rupprechts Werkstatt* (1907); *Der Kuhreigen* (1911); *Das Testament* (1916); *Hassan der Schwärmer* (1925); *Sanctissimum* (1925); *Hans Kipfel* (1928). He also completed Adolph Jensen's *Turandot,* and edited MOZART's LA CLEMENZA DI TITO.

Kiepura, Jan, tenor. Born Sosnowice, Poland, May 16, 1902; died Harrison, N.Y., Aug. 15, 1966. He graduated from the University of Warsaw in 1924. His debut took place a year later with the Warsaw Opera in FAUST. In 1926 he was engaged by the VIENNA STATE OPERA, where he appeared for two years. After 1928 he made successful appearances with leading European opera companies, including LA SCALA, the BERLIN STATE OPERA, and the OPÉRA-COMIQUE. He made his first American appearance with the CHICAGO OPERA in 1931. On Feb. 10, 1938, he made his debut at the METROPOLITAN OPERA in LA BOHÈME. He stayed at the Metropolitan through the 1941–42 season. After that he appeared primarily on the concert stage and in motion pictures.

Kilian, a peasant (tenor) in WEBER's DER FREISCHÜTZ.

King, James, tenor. Born Dodge City, Kan., May 22, 1925. After completing voice studies with Martial SINGHER, he won the American Opera Auditions in Cincinnati in 1961, which brought him engagements at the TEATRO ALLA PERGOLA in Florence and the Teatro Nuovo in Milan, where he made his initial opera appearances. His success brought him a permanent appointment with the BERLIN DEUTSCHE STAATSOPER as leading dramatic tenor and appearances at the SALZBURG FESTIVAL in GLUCK's IPHIGÉNIE EN AULIDE. In 1963 he toured Japan with the Berlin Deutsche Staatsoper. On Jan. 8, 1966, King made his debut at the METROPOLITAN OPERA (in FIDELIO), where he has since remained a principal tenor. He was subsequently heard in the COVENT GARDEN premiere of DIE FRAU OHNE SCHATTEN, as well as at the MUNICH, VIENNA, Salzburg, and BAYREUTH festivals. Though he has achieved his greatest success in WAGNER and Richard STRAUSS, he has also been acclaimed in the Italian and French repertory.

King Arthur, or The British Worthy, a "dramatic opera" in prologue, five acts, and epilogue by PURCELL. Libretto by John DRYDEN. Premiere: Dorset Gardens, London, summer 1691. American premiere: Park Theater, N.Y., Apr. 25, 1800. The Dryden text deals with King Arthur's youth, before he married Guinevere and founded the Round Table. The plot concerns the conflict between the Britons (headed by Arthur) and the Saxons (led by Oswald), and the rivalry of the two leaders for the love of the blind Emmeline. The magic spells of spirits and nymphs enter into the story before Arthur emerges triumphant in love and war. The opera ends with the prophecy that some day Britons and Saxons will merge into a single powerful nation.

The opera was revived on Oct. 29, 1968, as the inaugural presentation of the short-lived Atlanta (Georgia) Opera Company in the newly opened Atlanta Memorial Arts Center.

King Henry IV, Parts I and II, dramas by SHAKESPEARE. The two plays are concerned with the unsuccessful insurrections against the rule of Henry IV, first by the Percys of Northumberland and then by the Earl of Northumberland and the Archbishop of York. In the end, Prince Hal succeeds his father, becoming Henry V. *King Henry IV* was the source for several operas: AT THE BOAR's HEAD; PACINI's *La gioventù di Enrico V;* FALSTAFF (based mostly on *The Merry Wives of Windsor*); SAINT-SAËN's *Henry IV.*

King Lear, tragedy by SHAKESPEARE. Lear, King of ancient Britain, divides his realm between two daughters who ungratefully drive him away. His third daughter, Cordelia, to whom he has given nothing, remains true. Cordelia is wrongfully imprisoned by the wicked general Edmund, and later hanged, whereupon the aged Lear dies of grief. The two ruthless sisters also come to an unhappy end, one of them poisoning the other and then committing suicide. Under the title *Re Lear,* two operas on the subject were produced in Italy during the 1930's—one by Alberto Ghislanzoni (1937) and one by Vito Frazzi (1939). After he finished AIDA, VERDI worked on and off on an opera based on *King Lear,* but he completed only random sketches. At his request, they were destroyed after his death.

King Louis VI, French king (bass) in WEBER'S EURYANTHE.

King Mark, husband of Isolde (bass) in WAGNER'S TRISTAN UND ISOLDE.

King of Clubs, The, a character (bass) in PROKOFIEV'S THE LOVE FOR THREE ORANGES.

King of Egypt, Amneris' father (bass) in VERDI'S AIDA.

King of the Sea, The, a character (bass) in RIMSKY-KORSAKOV'S SADKO.

King of Thulé, Ballad of the, *see* IL ÉTAIT UN ROI DE THULÉ.

King Priam, opera in three acts by TIPPETT. Libretto by the composer, based partly on THE ILIAD. Premiere: Coventry Cathedral, Eng., May 29, 1962. The composer described the theme of his opera as "the mysterious nature of human choice." When Priam and Hecuba hear the prophecy that their baby son, Paris, will some day kill his father, they decide the baby must die. To their relief, the child is abducted to Troy by Hector, to which city, years later, Paris brings Helen from Sparta. When war breaks out between the Trojans and the Greeks, the Trojans are weakened by a long-standing feud between Paris and Hector. Hector is killed by Achilles; and when Priam learns of Hector's death, he begs Achilles for the return of his son. But before this happens, Priam is killed by Achilles' son.

The opera was commissioned by the KOUSSEVITZKY MUSIC FOUNDATION. Following its premiere at the new Coventry Cathedral in England, the opera was produced in June, 1962, at COVENT GARDEN and in Karlsruhe, Ger., in Jan., 1963. Tippett's vocal writing is mostly declamatory. To Peter Heyworth the high point of the opera comes at the end of Act II with the war cry of Achilles piercing through the rejoicing voices of the Trojans, who have just then driven the Greeks back.

King Roger, opera in three acts by SZYMANOWSKI. Libretto by the composer and Jaroslav Iwaszkiewicz. Premiere: Warsaw Opera, June 19, 1926. The theme is the struggle between Western Christianity and Eastern paganism. The setting is medieval Sicily, where the Queen Roxane falls in love with a shepherd-prophet come from India to proclaim a new gospel of beauty and joy. The shepherd is denounced as a heretic. King Roger is finally converted to the new doctrine. The opera closes with a BACCHANALE in the ruins of a Greek temple. The Song of Roxane, in which the Queen pleads with the shepherd for clemency, was once popular in a transcription by Paul Kochanski for violin and piano.

King's Henchman, The, opera in three acts by Deems TAYLOR. Libretto by Edna St. Vincent Millay. Premiere: Metropolitan Opera, Feb. 17, 1927. The setting—England in the tenth century—led one of America's outstanding poets to write her poetic play in archaic language. The story is a variation of the Tristan-Isolde theme. Eadgar of Wessex, King of England (baritone), sends his trusted friend Aethelwold (tenor) to Devon to win for him the princess Aelfrida (soprano). Aethelwold, lost in a forest near Devon, falls asleep. Aelfrida, singing an incantation that will find her future husband, comes upon Aethelwold, and the magic spell makes them fall in love with one another. He sends word to the King that the Devon princess is ugly. After Aethelwold and Aelfrida are married, Eadgar comes to Devon and discovers how beautiful Aelfrida really is. Overwhelmed by his own treachery, Aethelwold kills himself with a dagger in the presence of his wife and King. The King mourns the death of his dear friend ("Nay, Maccus, lay him down"). Among the opera's best pages: the Forest Love Music and the Bardic Song in Act I; the prelude to Act II and the Incantation Song and love duet in that act; and the prelude to Act III.

King Sisera, see SISERA.

King's Theatre, Haymarket, see HER (or HIS) MAJESTY'S THEATRE.

Kipnis, Alexander, bass. Born Zhitomir, Ukraine, Feb. 1, 1891. He was graduated from the Warsaw Conservatory in 1912 as a conductor. He was receiving vocal lessons in Berlin with Grenzebach when World War I began. As an enemy alien he was at first interned, but he was soon permitted to continue his studies. In 1915 he made his debut with the HAMBURG OPERA; from 1916 to 1918 he was a member of the Wiesbaden Opera. After the war he made many successful appearances throughout Europe. He came to the United States for the first time in 1923 as a member of the visiting Wagner Festival Company, making his debut in New York City as POGNER on Feb. 12. He was immediately engaged by the Chicago Civic Opera, where he remained nine seasons. After leaving Chicago, Kipnis became principal bass of the BERLIN STATE OPERA. He also appeared with outstanding success at the BAYREUTH festivals. After the rise of Hitler, Kipnis abandoned Germany and joined the VIENNA STATE OPERA; he was also seen at the PARIS OPÉRA, at COVENT GARDEN, GLYNDEBOURNE, the TEATRO COLÓN, and the SALZBURG FESTIVAL. On Jan. 5, 1940, he made his debut at the METROPOLITAN OPERA as GURNEMANZ. He remained with the Metropolitan through the 1945–46 season, acclaimed in the Wagnerian repertory and in such roles as BORIS GODUNOV, SARASTRO, ARKEL, and ROCCO. Kipnis is also admired as an interpreter of lieder. Since his retirement, he has taught voice privately and at the New York College of Music and the Juilliard School of Music.

Kirchenchor, see DA ZU DIR DER HEILAND.

Kirchhofer, Werner, the trumpeter (baritone) in NESSLER'S DER TROMPETER VON SÄKKINGEN.

Kirov Theater, see BOLSHOI THEATER (1).

Kirsten, Dorothy, soprano. Born Montclair, N.J., July 6, 1917. She studied singing at the Juilliard School of Music while working for the telephone company. Singing over the radio, she attracted the interest of Grace MOORE, who became her sponsor. Kirsten's studies now continued in Italy with Astolfo Pescia. After returning to the United States in 1940, she made her opera debut with the CHICAGO OPERA, following which she was heard in leading soprano roles with the NEW YORK CITY OPERA and the SAN CARLO OPERA COMPANY. On Dec. 1, 1945, she made a successful debut at the METROPOLITAN OPERA as MIMI; she stayed with the Metropolitan through the 1955–56 season. In 1962 she made a triumphant tour of the Soviet Union, the first American ever to sing with the Tiflis Opera. She has also appeared extensively on radio and television and in motion pictures (*Mr. Music, The Great Caruso*).

Kiss, The, see HUBIČKA.

Klafsky, Katharina, soprano. Born St. Johann, Hungary, Sept. 19, 1855; died Hamburg, Sept. 22, 1896. She studied singing with Mathilde MARCHESI in Vienna. After a career in comic opera and in minor opera roles in Salzburg, she went into temporary retirement. She returned to the stage in 1876 and appeared in minor parts in the Wagnerian repertory with the Angelo NEUMANN Company. By 1881 she was appearing in leading parts. From 1886 to 1895 she was the principal soprano of the HAMBURG OPERA and a guest performer at other leading European opera houses. Soon after her marriage to Otto LOHSE, the conductor, she came to the United States and sang the principal Wagnerian roles for the DAMROSCH OPERA COMPANY; her husband appeared with the company as conductor. In the fall of 1896 she again appeared with the Hamburg Opera. On Sept. 11 she sang her final performance—Leonore in FIDELIO—and a week later died.

Klänge der Heimat (Csárdás), Rosalinde's aria with chorus in Act II of Johann STRAUSS'S DIE FLEDERMAUS, in which she poses as a Hungarian countess.

Klebe, Giselher, composer. Born Mannheim, June 28, 1925. After completing his studies with Josef Rufer and Boris BLACHER, he was employed in the program division of the Berlin Radio between 1946 and 1949. He composed a good deal of concert music, most of it either in atonal or dodecaphonic idioms, and attracted wide attention in 1954 with a *Rhapsody* for orchestra that won first prize in the International Festival in Rome. On June 3, 1957, his first opera, *Die Räuber,* based on SCHILLER, was introduced in Düsseldorf. This was followed by *Die tödlichen Wünsche* (Düsseldorf, June 14, 1959); *Alkmene* (Berlin, Sept. 25, 1961); *Figaro lässt sich scheiden,* an OPERA BUFFA (Hamburg, June 28, 1963); *Jacobovsky and the Colonel* (Hamburg, Nov. 2, 1965); and *Märchen der schoenen Lilie* (SCHWETZINGEN Festival, May 15, 1969). *Jacobovsky and the Colonel* received its American premiere in a performance by the visiting HAMBURG OPERA at the LINCOLN CENTER FOR THE PERFORMING ARTS in New York City on June 27, 1967.

Kleiber, Erich, conductor. Born Vienna, Aug. 5, 1890; died Zürich, Jan. 27, 1956. He received a comprehensive academic education in Vienna and Prague while studying music privately and at the Prague Conservatory. In 1911 he became a coach with the PRAGUE OPERA. A year later he was appointed conductor of the Darmstadt Opera, where he remained eight years. He next served as general music director at Mannheim, where a remarkable performance of FIDELIO brought him an appointment as musical director of the BERLIN OPERA. He remained in Berlin for over a decade, distinguishing himself both in the standard repertory and in modern works; among the notable world premieres he conducted were KRENEK'S DAS LEBEN DES

OREST, BERG'S WOZZECK, and MILHAUD'S CHRISTOPHE COLOMB. On Oct. 2, 1930, he made his American debut as guest conductor of the New York Philharmonic. During the next decade he appeared frequently in America as a symphony conductor. After Hitler came to power, Kleiber was permitted to retain his directorship with the Berlin Opera; but after the controversy over the premiere of MATHIS DER MALER he resigned his post. (*See* FURTWÄNGLER.) Between 1934 and 1937 he conducted symphony and opera in Moscow. He also led notable performances at LA SCALA and the SALZBURG FESTIVALS. In 1938 he became the principal conductor of the National Theater in Prague. From 1939 to 1949 he conducted extensively in South America. After 1949 he appeared as guest conductor in leading European opera houses and at major opera festivals in Amsterdam, Zürich, and Prague. In Jan., 1951, he returned to conduct the Berlin State Opera in East Germany. Upon reconstruction of the opera house and the development of plans for a grand reopening in 1955, Kleiber was appointed musical director. However, a few months after the appointment, and before the scheduled reopening, Kleiber resigned his position and moved to West Germany, accusing Communist officials of injecting propaganda into art. He was succeeded by Franz KONWITSCHNY.

Kleist, Heinrich Wilhelm von, author and dramatist. Born Frankfurt-an-der Oder, Oct. 18, 1777; died Wannsee, Nov. 21, 1811. His novelette *Michael Kohlhaas,* one of the finest stories in German literature, was made into an opera by KLENAU. His tragedies *Penthesilea* and *Der Prinz von Homburg* were made into operas, the first by SCHOECK, the second by GRAENER and HENZE. EGK'S opera *Die Verlobung in San Domingo* is also based on a story by Kleist.

Klemperer, Otto, conductor. Born Breslau, May 14, 1885. His music study took place at the Hoch Conservatory in Frankfurt, and in Berlin with Xavier Scharwenka, James Kwast, and Hans

PFITZNER. He held several minor posts as conductor between 1905 and 1907, when he attracted the interest of MAHLER, who recommended him to the National Theater in Prague. Klemperer stayed there three years. Once again with Mahler's recommendation, he now became principal conductor of the HAMBURG OPERA. Several important engagements in various German opera houses preceded his appointment in 1923 as principal conductor of the Berlin Volksoper, where his performances were so outstanding that in 1926 he was made musical director of the BERLIN STATE OPERA on a ten-year contract. During this period Klemperer gave many extraordinary performances, particularly of modern operas by KRENEK, SCHOENBERG, and HINDEMITH. He made his American debut on Jan. 24, 1926, as guest conductor of the New York Symphony Society. He returned to America for several additional seasons besides giving guest performances in Italy, Spain, the Soviet Union, and South America. When the Nazis came to power, Klemperer left his native land for good. In 1933 he was appointed permanent conductor of the Los Angeles Philharmonic Orchestra. Six years later poor health compelled him to resign from this post. After the end of World War II, he made intermittent appearances in Europe, chiefly in symphonic music. From 1947 to 1950 he was the principal conductor of the BUDAPEST OPERA. Once again his career was interrupted when he suffered a serious fall in 1951 and had to be confined to a wheel chair for several years. His physicians were convinced he would never again conduct. Nevertheless, he was able to return to the podium, though compelled to conduct from a seated position. More remarkable still, he began revealing in his interpretations new depths of perception and a new nobility of concept. Still weak and infirm, he led remarkable performances of FIDELIO, THE MAGIC FLUTE, and LOHENGRIN at COVENT GARDEN between 1961 and 1963 and equally extraordinary performances of symphonic and choral music at various major festivals and with leading European orchestras. In 1965, while conducting DON GIOVANNI in Cologne, he became so deeply immersed in the music that he forgot his infirmity and stood upon his feet for the first time in several years. After this, despite his old age and the ravages inflicted by his prolonged illnesses, he resumed his career with guest performances throughout Europe, as well as in recordings, and revealed himself at the height of his interpretative powers. In 1964 he published in London a book of memoirs entitled *Minor Recollections*. In 1970 he established permanent residence in Israel.

Klenau, Paul von, composer and conductor. Born Copenhagen, Feb. 11, 1883; died there Aug. 31, 1946. He studied with Max BRUCH and Karl Halir in Berlin from 1902 to 1904 and after that with Ludwig Thuille in Munich. He was only twenty-one when he wrote *Inferno,* a successful work for orchestra. In 1907 he was appointed conductor of the Freiburg Opera and from 1908 to 1914 he was Max von SCHILLINGS' assistant at the STUTTGART OPERA. In 1913 his one-act opera *Sulamith* was given in Munich. Of his later operas, *Michael Kohlhaas* was the most successful, first given in Stuttgart in 1933. In 1920 he founded the Vienna Singakademie and the Konzerthausgesellschaft. His operas: *Sulamith* (1913); *Kjartan und Gudrun* (1918; revised as *Gudrun auf Island,* 1924); *Die Lästerschule* (1927); *Michael Kohlhaas* (1933); *Rembrandt von Rijn* (1937).

Klingsor, a magician (bass) in WAGNER'S PARSIFAL.

Klose, Margarete, mezzo-soprano. Born Berlin, Aug. 6, 1905; died there Dec. 14, 1968. Her debut on the musical stage took place in Emmerich Kálmán's operetta *Countess Maritza,* at Ulm in 1927. Between 1929 and 1932 she was a member of the MANNHEIM OPERA. From 1932 to 1939 and again from 1958 to 1961 she was a principal mezzo-soprano of the BERLIN STATE OPERA, where she achieved renown in WAGNER and VERDI. Her Wagnerian interpretations were particularly acclaimed at BAYREUTH festivals between

1936 and 1942. In 1935 and 1937 she made notable guest appearances at COVENT GARDEN, while from 1949 to 1958 she was a principal mezzo-soprano of the Berlin Städtische Oper (BERLIN DEUTSCHE STAATSOPER).

Kluge, Die (The Wise One), opera in one act by ORFF. Libretto by the composer, based on a fairy tale by the GRIMM brothers. Premiere: Frankfurt, Feb. 20, 1943. American premiere: San Francisco Opera, Oct. 3, 1958. Subtitled *The Story of the King and the Wise Woman,* the opera deals with a woman who marries a king after being able to answer his riddles. Tired of her wisdom, he asks her to leave him and take anything from the palace she desires. After she has traveled down the road, she opens her trunk to release the king himself—having taken the only thing from the palace she desired. The king is delighted that she has made such a choice, and when she promises never to be clever any longer, he takes her back. The opera includes spoken dialogue, and the music is mainly percussive and rhythmic.

Klytemnestra, (1) wife of Agamemnon (mezzo-soprano) in GLUCK's IPHIGÉNIE EN AULIDE, a role created by Sophie ARNOULD.

(2) Mother of Elektra (mezzo-soprano) in Richard STRAUSS's ELEKTRA, a role created by Ernestine SCHUMANN-HEINK.

Knappertsbusch, Hans, conductor. Born Elberfeld, Ger., Mar. 12, 1888; died Munich, Oct. 25, 1965. His academic studies took place at Bonn University, where he specialized in philosophy; his musical training was completed at the Cologne Conservatory. In 1912 he directed a festival of music dramas in Holland. A year later he became director of opera at Elberfeld, holding this post five years. In 1922, given a lifetime contract, he succeeded Bruno WALTER as musical director of the MUNICH OPERA. He now achieved recognition throughout Europe as an interpreter of WAGNER, MOZART, and Richard STRAUSS. When the Nazis came to power, he refused to join the Nazi party or to subscribe to its political

or musical doctrines. On Hitler's personal decision, he was removed from his Munich post. In 1936 he went to Vienna, where he conducted at the State Opera, becoming its musical director in 1938. After the Anschluss he left Austria and gave guest performances in several European non-Fascist countries. After the end of World War II he directed performances in various major European opera houses and at major festivals. He directed performances at BAYREUTH from 1951 and in Munich from 1954. He was one of the most celebrated conductors of Wagner and Richard Strauss of his time.

Knote, Heinrich, tenor. Born Munich, Nov. 26, 1870; died Garmisch-Partenkirchen, Jan. 15, 1953. After completing his studies with Kirschner in Munich, he joined the MUNICH OPERA in 1892, remaining with that company a dozen years. During this period he appeared in most of the major German opera houses. He made his American debut at the METROPOLITAN OPERA on Dec. 3, 1904, in DIE MEISTERSINGER. He was so successful in this and subsequent Wagnerian performances that during the three seasons he sang at the Metropolitan his popularity rivaled that of Jean DE RESZKE. From 1917 on he was the principal tenor of the CHARLOTTENBURG OPERA. He retired from opera in 1924.

Knusperhäuschen, Das (Gingerbread House), *see* WITCH's HOUSE, THE.

Knusperwalzer (Gingerbread Waltz), *see* JUCHHEI, NUN IST DIE HEXE TODT!

Koanga, opera in four acts (unfinished) by DELIUS. Libretto by Charles Francis Keary, taken from material in *The Grandissimes,* a novel by George Washington Cable. Premiere: Elberfeld Opera, Mar. 30, 1904. The opera was written between 1895 and 1897. Koanga is an African chieftain who is captured and brought to Spain. There, the octoroon Palmyra falls in love with him; they both meet their doom in the jungle after Koanga invokes voodoo and black magic.

Kobbé, Gustav, writer on music. Born New York City, Mar. 4, 1857; died Babylon, L.I., July 27, 1918. His music study was pursued in Wiesbaden with Adolf Tagen and in New York with Joseph Mosenthal. Beginning in 1880 he served successively as music critic for several New York newspapers, including the *Sun, World, Mail,* and *Herald.* He was sent to BAYREUTH in 1883 to cover the first festival there. He wrote several books on opera: *Wagner's Life and Works* (1890) ; *Opera-Singers* (1901) ; *Wagner and His Isolde* (1906) ; *The Complete Opera Book* (1919, revised 1954 by the Earl of HAREWOOD). He also wrote a novel about the world of opera, *Signora, a Child of the Opera-House* (1902).

Kobus, Fritz, principal male character (tenor) in MASCAGNI'S L'AMICO FRITZ, a role created by Paul Lhérie.

Kodály, Zoltán, composer. Born Kecskemét, Hungary, Dec. 16, 1882; died Budapest, Mar. 6, 1967. He entered the Budapest Conservatory when he was eighteen, a fellow student of Béla BARTÓK. He accompanied Bartók on some of his expeditions through Hungary to study and record the folksongs and dances of different regions, and, with Bartók, he was a powerful influence in bringing the folk music of his native land to public notice. This preoccupation had a far-reaching influence on his own music: his works are unmistakably Hungarian. Kodály composed interesting and significant works in many forms. His opera HÁRY JÁNOS (1926) is his best-known composition—not because it is often performed but because of the popular concert suite drawn from its music. His later operas: *The Spinning Room of the Szekelys* (1932) and *Czinka Panna* (1943).

Komische Oper, an opera company established in East Berlin at the request of the Soviet occupation authorities in 1947, replacing the former Scala Theater. Walter FELSENSTEIN has been its artistic director since its founding, and some of his phenomenal productions have not only put the Komische Oper in a place of first importance among German opera companies but have attracted world attention. It opened its 1969–70 season with HANDEL'S DEIDAMIA and in 1970 presented PORGY AND BESS and the Broadway musical *Fiddler on the Roof,* the latter directed by Felsenstein himself.

Komm deine Blumen zu begiessen, duet of Nureddin and Margiana's attendant, Bostana, in Act I of CORNELIUS' THE BARBER OF BAGDAD.

Komm, denn unser Leid zu rachen, Lysiart's duet with Eglantine in Act II, Scene 1, of WEBER'S EURYANTHE, in which he becomes Eglantine's accomplice in destroying Euryanthe. This is sometimes known as the Vengeance Duet.

Konetzni, Anni, soprano. Born Vienna, Feb. 12, 1902; died there June 9, 1968. She was a distinguished Wagnerian soprano who appeared with the BERLIN STATE OPERA between 1931 and 1935, the VIENNA STATE OPERA between 1935 and 1954, and at COVENT GARDEN between 1935 and 1939 and again in 1951. She made her debut at the METROPOLITAN OPERA on Dec. 26, 1934, as Brünnhilde in DIE WALKÜRE, but stayed with the company only one season.

Konetzni, Hilde, soprano, sister of the above. Born Vienna, Mar. 21, 1905. Her voice study took place in the conservatories of Vienna and Prague. In 1929 she made her opera debut at Chemnitz in the role of SIEGLINDE. After four years with the PRAGUE OPERA, she became a principal soprano of the VIENNA STATE OPERA in 1936; there she became such a favorite through the years that she was given the honorary title of KAMMERSÄNGERIN. She also was acclaimed at COVENT GARDEN. Her specialty has been the works of WAGNER, MOZART, and Richard STRAUSS.

Königen von Saba, Die, see QUEEN OF SHEBA, THE.

König Hirsch (later titled *Il re cèrvo,* The King Stag), opera in three acts by HENZE. Libretto by Heinz von Cramer, based on GOZZI's *Il re cèrvo.* Premiere: Berlin Deutsche Staatsoper, Sept. 23, 1956 (original version) ; Cassel, 1963 (revised version, renamed *Il re cèrvo*).

American premiere: Sante Fe Opera, N.M., Aug. 4, 1965. Allegory and fantasy are combined in this fable of Leandro, a prince deserted in the forests who is raised by wild beasts. Upon becoming a man, the Prince returns to his homeland to claim his throne and to seek a bride, but his enemy, Governor Trataglia, contrives to have him sent back to the forests, where he turns into a stag. The Governor, who assumes rule in his kingdom, orders all stags to be killed. The prince-turned-stag, however, is protected by his animal friends. When the prince-turned-stag becomes homesick, he returns to his kingdom, where he reassumes human form and where the despot Governor is assassinated.

The opera adheres to a traditional Italian structure by using formal arias, duets, ensemble numbers, and so forth. It departs from Italian tradition by placing considerable importance on the orchestra, with many sections of symphonic character; in fact, the composer later used the second-act finale as a symphony without changing a note. The first act is basically in TWELVE-TONE TECHNIQUES. The other two acts, while often dissonant and making functional use of various modern idioms, are for the most part romantic and lyrical.

Königskinder, Die (The Royal Children), fairy opera in three acts by HUMPERDINCK. Libretto by Ernst Rosmer (pen name of Elsa Bernstein). Premiere: Metropolitan Opera, Dec. 28, 1910. The Goose Girl (soprano), who lives in the woods with a cruel Witch, meets and falls in love with the King's Son (tenor), who comes to her hut disguised as a beggar. Before he leaves her, he promises she will see him again when a star falls into a certain lily. When this miracle occurs, the Goose Girl and the King's Son meet again, only to die of a poisoned pastry prepared by the Witch.

Konrad, a huntsman (tenor) in MARSCHNER'S HANS HEILING.

Konstanze, see CONSTANZE.

Kontchak, Khan, the Polovtsian chief (bass) in BORODIN'S PRINCE IGOR.

Kontchakovna, Kontchak's daughter (mezzo-soprano) in BORODIN'S PRINCE IGOR.

Konwitschny, Franz, conductor. Born Fulnek, Ger., Aug. 14, 1901; died Belgrade, July 27, 1962. He was a principal conductor in Stuttgart and Freiburg before serving in a similar capacity with the FRANKFURT OPERA between 1938 and 1945, the HANOVER OPERA from 1946 to 1949, and the DRESDEN OPERA from 1953 to 1955. When the State Opera was rebuilt in East Berlin in 1955, he replaced KLEIBER as general music director. He led a distinguished performance of the RING cycle at COVENT GARDEN in 1959.

Konya, Sandor, tenor. Born Sarkad, Hungary, Sept. 23, 1923. Following vocal studies in Budapest and Hanover, he made his opera debut as TURIDDU in Bielefeld in 1951. Engagements in Darmstadt, Stuttgart, and Hamburg led to his appointment as a principal tenor of the Berlin Städtische Oper (BERLIN DEUTSCHE STAATSOPER) in 1955 and at BAYREUTH (as LOHENGRIN) in 1958. In 1960 he made his debuts with LA SCALA and with the SAN FRANCISCO OPERA as Dick JOHNSON. He became a permanent member of the METROPOLITAN OPERA company after his debut there as Lohengrin on Oct. 28, 1961, and since 1963 he has also appeared at COVENT GARDEN.

Körner, Karl Theodor, poet and dramatist. Born Dresden, Sept. 23, 1791; died Gadebusch, Aug. 26, 1831. DVOŘÁK's first opera, *Alfred,* was based on a drama by Körner. Körner's comedy *Die vierjährige Posten* was made into comic operas by GRAENER, Reinecke, and SCHUBERT. FLOTOW's *Die Bergknappen* had a libretto by Körner.

Korngold, Erich Wolfgang, composer. Born Brünn, Austria, May 29, 1897; died Hollywood, Cal., Nov. 29, 1957. The son of a noted Viennese music critic, Julius Korngold, Erich began to study music at an early age. He was extraordinarily precocious. When he was eleven he wrote a pantomime, *Der Schneemann,* performed by the VIENNA STATE OPERA. On Mar. 28, 1916, two one-act operas were introduced in Munich: *Der Ring des Polykrates* and *Violanta;* both were subsequently heard in America. His greatest success came with DIE TOTE STADT, introduced simultaneously in Hamburg and Cologne on Dec. 4, 1920, and soon after given at the METROPOLITAN OPERA. Later operas: *The Miracle of Heliane* (1927) ; *Kathrin* (1937). Korngold came to the United States in 1935 and devoted himself principally to writing scores for motion pictures. In one picture, *Give Us This Night,* he introduced an original one-act opera.

The Miracle of Heliane, which had not been produced for several decades, was revived by the Royal Opera of Ghent in Belgium on Feb. 15, 1970.

Köth, Erika, soprano. Born Darmstadt, Sept. 15, 1927. While studying voice she supported herself by singing with a jazz ensemble. In 1947 she shared first prize with Christa LUDWIG in a competition by the Hessische Opera. Her opera debut followed a year later at Kaiserlautern as Adele in DIE FLEDERMAUS. After three years, she became a permanent member of the VIENNA STATE OPERA and the MUNICH OPERA, where she achieved recognition as one of Europe's leading coloratura sopranos, though she has proved herself hardly less remarkable in lyric roles. LUCIA DI LAMMERMOOR was expressly revived for her in Munich in 1957. She has also distinguished herself in operas by MOZART, ROSSINI, and Richard STRAUSS.

Kotzebue, August Friedrich von, dramatist. Born Weimar, May 3, 1761; died Mannheim, Mar. 23, 1819. He was the author of over two hundred fairy, historical, and social plays, some of which were made into operas, notably LORTZING's *Der Wildschütz* and Ernst Wolf's *Der Eremit auf Formentora.* Kotzebue wrote the libretto for SCHUBERT's opera *Des Teufels Lustschloss* and for Johann REICHARDT's *Das Zauberschloss.* SPOHR's *Der Kreuzfahrer* and BOIELDIEU's *Bieniowski* were based on plays by Kotzebue.

Koussevitzky Music Foundation, a foundation created by Serge Koussevitzky in May, 1942, in memory of his recently deceased wife, Natalie. Its aim was to assist developing creative musical talent by commissioning new works from composers. A permanent endowment was established in Jan., 1950, entitled The Serge Koussevitzky Music Foundation in the Library of Congress, making the library the permanent repository of all original scores commissioned by the foundation. The first opera commissioned by the foundation was PETER GRIMES in 1944. Later commissioned operas were *The Anointed* (Tadeusz Kassern) ; THE BALLAD OF BABY DOE; THE BEAR; *The Blackmoor of Peter the Great* (Arthur Lourié) ; *The Boor* (Ulysses Kay) ; DAVID; KING PRIAM; *Lord Byron* (THOMSON) ; REGINA.

Kraus, Ernst, tenor. Born Erlangen, Bavaria, June 8, 1863; died Wörthersee, Austria, Sept. 6, 1941. After studying with Cesare Galliera in Milan and Anna Schimon-Regan in Munich, he made his debut in Mannheim as TAMINO on Mar. 26, 1893. In 1894 and 1895 he came to the United States and appeared as principal tenor of the DAMROSCH OPERA COMPANY. In 1896 he was appointed leading tenor of the BERLIN OPERA, where he remained for twenty-seven years, distinguishing himself in the German repertory. During this period he appeared as SIEGMUND at BAYREUTH in 1901 and made his debut at the METROPOLITAN OPERA, also as Siegmund, on Nov. 25, 1903. He retired from opera in 1924 and devoted himself thenceforward to teaching.

Kraus, Felix von, bass. Born Vienna, Oct. 3, 1870; died Munich, Oct. 30, 1937. He received a doctorate from the University of Vienna in 1894, but in singing he was mostly self-taught. His debut took place at BAYREUTH in 1899, when he appeared as HAGEN. He was subsequently heard regularly at the Bayreuth festivals and in leading European opera houses, a specialist in the WAGNER repertory. In 1908 he became artistic director of the MUNICH OPERA and a professor at the Munich Conservatory. In 1899 he married the American contralto Adrienne Osborne, who also appeared in the Wagner dramas. He retired from the stage in 1924.

Krauss, Clemens, conductor. Born Vienna, Mar. 31, 1893; died Mexico City, May 16, 1954. As a child he was a member of the Imperial Choir, in which both HAYDN and SCHUBERT had been choristers. His music study took place at the Vienna Conservatory, after which he became chorus master at the Brünn Opera. In 1913 he became second conductor of the Riga Opera. Various appointments followed, and in 1922 he succeeded FURTWÄNGLER as director of the Tonkünstlerverein in Vienna. From 1924 to 1929 he was the artistic director of the FRANKFURT OPERA, where he distinguished himself in performances of operas by MOZART and Richard STRAUSS. Appearances at the MUNICH and SALZBURG festivals extended his reputation. In 1929 he became artistic director of the VIENNA STATE OPERA, and from 1929 to 1934 he was a principal conductor at the Salzburg Festival. He made his American debut in 1929 as a guest conductor of the Philadelphia Orchestra. When Furtwängler was deposed as musical director of the BERLIN STATE OPERA in 1934, following his dispute with the Nazi authorities over the premiere of MATHIS DER MALER, Krauss was selected as his successor. He was not liked in Berlin, and before long he had to shift his activities to Munich. In 1947 he returned to the Vienna State Opera, and after that he directed performances at the BAYREUTH festival. In 1952 he directed the world premiere of DIE LIEBE DER DANAE in Salzburg. He also appeared in South America and Mexico as a conductor of opera, and it was in Mexico that he unexpectedly died. He was the author of the libretto for Richard Strauss's CAPRICCIO.

Krauss, Gabrielle, soprano. Born Vienna, Mar. 24, 1842; died Paris, Jan. 6, 1906. She attended the Vienna Conservatory, then studied singing with Mathilde MARCHESI. In July, 1859, she made her debut at the VIENNA OPERA in WILLIAM TELL. For several years she continued to appear there. On April 6, 1867, she made a strikingly successful debut at the Théâtre des Italiens in Paris in IL TROVATORE. She continued to sing there three seasons. During the next few years she was acclaimed in Italy and Russia. On Jan. 5, 1875, she made her debut at the PARIS OPÉRA, when its new building was inaugurated. She remained a principal soprano of the Paris Opéra for the next dozen years, after which she retired from the stage and devoted herself to teaching. She was a remarkable actress and was often described by her French public as "la Rachel chantante." She appeared in many world premieres, including GOUNOD'S POLYEUCTE and *Le Tribut de Zamora,* HALÉVY's *Guido et Ginevra,* and SAINT-SAËNS'S HENRY VIII.

Krenek, Ernest, composer. Born Vienna, Aug. 23, 1900. After studying with Franz SCHREKER in Vienna and Berlin, he wrote his first opera, *Zwingburg,* in 1922. A second opera, *Der Sprung über den Schatten,* aroused interest when introduced in Frankfurt in 1925. A year later Krenek was named conductor of the Cassel State Theater. While in this post he completed JONNY SPIELT AUF, an opera in the jazz idiom that achieved a sensational success throughout Europe after its introduction at the Leipzig Opera on Feb. 10, 1927. After 1928 Krenek abandoned the jazz idiom to write in the romantic style of Schreker; later he adopted the atonal manner of SCHOENBERG. Krenek first visited the United States in 1937 as conductor of the Salzburg Opera Guild. After the German seizure of Austria, he settled permanently in the United States, becoming a citizen in 1954. He held teaching positions with various universities and conservatories. To celebrate his seventieth birthday, the HAMBURG STATE OPERA commissioned him to write the opera *That's What Happened.* Other operas by Krenek: *Orpheus und Eurydike* (1923); *Der Diktator* (1926); *Das geheime Königreich* (1927); DAS LEBEN DES OREST (1929); *Cefalo e Procri* (1933); *Karl V* (1933); *Tarquin* (1941); *What Price Confidence* (1946); *Dark Waters* (1951); *Pallas Athene weint* (1952);

The Bell Tower (1957). Among his later operas are *Ausgerechnet und verspielt,* a comic opera written for television and produced in Vienna on June 27, 1962, and *Der goldene Bock,* a fantastic CHAMBER OPERA produced in Hamburg on June 16, 1964. In 1963 Krenek received the Grand Prize of Austria. The world premiere of *That's What Happened* took place at the Hamburg Opera on June 27, 1970.

Kreutzer, Conradin, composer and conductor. Born Messkirch, near Baden, Nov. 22, 1780; died Riga, Dec. 14, 1849. He studied law in Freiburg but turned to music in 1800 and completed an operetta which was performed that year. In 1805 he went to Vienna, where for two years he studied with Johann Albrechtsberger and where his opera *Jery und Bätely* was successful when produced in 1810. In 1812 he was appointed court KAPELLMEISTER in Stuttgart, where he wrote eight operas. Five years later he held a similar post at Donaueschingen. He returned to Vienna in 1822. He was, on and off, a principal conductor of the KÄRNTNERTHORTHEATER between 1825 and 1840. From 1833 to 1837 he conducted opera at the Josephstädter Theater. From 1840 to 1846 he was musical director of the city of Cologne. He wrote about thirty operas. The most successful: *Jery und Bätely* (1810); *Libussa* (1822); *Aesop in Phrygien* (1822); *Das Nachtlager in Granada* (1834); *Der Verschwender* (1836).

Kreutzer, Rodolphe, composer and violinist. Born Versailles, Nov. 16, 1766; died Geneva, Jan. 6, 1831. Kreutzer, to whom Beethoven dedicated his *Kreutzer Sonata,* was the composer of many once popular operas. He studied the violin with his father and Anton Stamitz and was only thirteen when he appeared in Paris, playing one of his own concertos. Three years later he was appointed first violinist of the Chapelle du Roi and in 1790 solo violinist at the Théâtre des Italiens. In 1790 his first opera, *Jeanne d'Arc à Orléans,* was introduced at the Théâtre des Italiens, followed a year later by *Paul et Virginie.* He wrote about forty more operas, many of them produced at the OPÉRA, the OPÉRA-COMIQUE, and the Théâtre des Italiens; the most famous was *Lodoïska,* heard in 1791. In 1795 he was appointed a professor of the violin at the Paris Conservatory, where he remained until 1825; in 1801 he was appointed first violinist at the Opéra; and after 1816 he conducted at the Opéra. Several of his operas were performed here under his own direction, notably *Astyanax* (1801), *Aristippe* (1808), and *La Mort d'Abel* (1810). In 1806 he became solo violinist to Emperor Napoleon and in 1815 MAÎTRE DE CHAPELLE to Louis XVIII. He retired from all musical activity after 1826.

Krips, Josef, conductor. Born Vienna, Apr. 8, 1902. After completing his studies in conducting with WEINGARTNER, he was a member of the conducting staff of the Vienna VOLKSOPER from 1921 to 1925, the Dortmund Opera in 1925 and 1926, and the Karlsruhe Opera between 1926 and 1933. Between 1933 and 1938 he was one of the principal conductors of the VIENNA STATE OPERA. The Nazis then compelled him to withdraw from his musical activities, and for the next seven years he earned his living as a day laborer in a food-processing factory. When the war ended, Krips was called up to help rehabilitate the Vienna State Opera and the Vienna Philharmonic by becoming principal conductor. He has since then directed major performances at the Vienna State Opera, being a specialist in the operas of MOZART and WAGNER. From 1949 to 1955 he was the first conductor of the London Symphony. He made his American debut on Feb. 15, 1953, with the Buffalo Philharmonic, and from 1962 to 1969 he was the music director of the San Francisco Symphony. He has, however, continued to conduct opera not only in Vienna but in other major cities, and he is regarded as one of the foremost interpreters of the German repertory of his time.

Kroll Opera, *see* BERLIN DEUTSCHE STAATSOPER.

Kronold, Selma, soprano. Born Cracow,

Poland, 1866; died New York City, Oct. 9, 1920. After studying with Arthur NIKISCH at the Leipzig Conservatory, she made her debut at the Leipzig Opera in 1882 as AGATHE. She then joined the Angelo NEUMANN Opera Company, which toured Europe in the WAGNER dramas. After an additional period of study with Désirée ARTÔT in Paris, she came to the United States in 1888 and appeared in concerts. From 1889 to 1891 she sang with the Berlin Royal Opera, and in 1891 with the Gustav HINRICHS Opera Company in the United States; as a member of the latter company, she created for America the leading soprano roles in CAVALLERIA RUSTICANA, PAGLIACCI, and MANON LESCAUT. She made her debut at the METROPOLITAN OPERA on Feb. 6, 1891, in DIE WALKÜRE. She retired from opera in 1904 and henceforth devoted herself to the Catholic Oratorio Society, which she founded and directed. Subsequently she entered a convent.

Kruschina, a Bohemian peasant (baritone) in SMETANA'S THE BARTERED BRIDE.

Kubelik, Rafael, conductor. Born Bychory, Czechoslovakia, June 29, 1914. He is the son of the famous violin virtuoso Jan Kubelik. He was graduated from the Prague Conservatory in 1933 as violinist, conductor, and composer. Between 1936 and 1939 he was the conductor of the Czech Philharmonic and from 1939 to 1941 first conductor of the Brno National Theater. While serving for six years as artistic director of the Czech Philharmonic, beginning with 1942, he made guest appearances in Europe and the Soviet Union. In 1948 he conducted DON GIOVANNI at the EDINBURGH FESTIVAL. In November, 1949, he made his American debut as a guest conductor of the Chicago Symphony, making such a profound impression that he was appointed musical director of the organization, a post that he held between 1950 and 1953. At the same time he also served as one of the principal conductors of the Concertgebouw Orchestra in Amsterdam, with which he toured the United States in 1954, sharing the podium with

Eduard von Beinum. Between 1955 and 1958 he was the musical director of COVENT GARDEN, where he was responsible for remarkable performances of JENUFA, LES TROYENS, and OTELLO, among many other operas. In 1961 he became the music director of the Bavarian Radio Orchestra of Munich, with which he toured Europe in 1962. He has since appeared frequently as guest conductor of symphony orchestras both in America and in Europe and of opera companies in Europe.

Kullman, Charles, tenor. Born New Haven, Conn., Jan. 13, 1903. He graduated from Yale University in 1924, after which he specialized in music. He received some coaching from local teachers, then won a scholarship at the Juilliard School of Music in New York, where he stayed three years. Another scholarship enabled him to continue his studies at the American Conservatory in Fontainebleau, France. Back in the United States in 1928, he joined the music faculty of Smith College, where he appeared in several opera productions. He also appeared with the American Opera Company in leading tenor roles. After a period of studying the opera repertory in Berlin, he was engaged by KLEMPERER for the KROLL OPERA, at which he made his European opera debut as Pinkerton on Feb. 24, 1931. A year later he joined the BERLIN STATE OPERA. He was so popular there that he had to appear in MADAMA BUTTERFLY twenty-five times in a single season. In 1934 Kullman made his debuts at the VIENNA STATE OPERA and at COVENT GARDEN, and from 1934 to 1936 he appeared at the SALZBURG FESTIVALS in operas conducted by TOSCANINI. Meanwhile, on Dec. 20, 1935, he made his METROPOLITAN OPERA debut in FAUST. He appeared at the Metropolitan in leading Italian, German, and French roles until 1962. In 1955 he received an award from the Metropolitan to celebrate his twentieth anniversary there. He has also been successful in the concert hall, in radio performances, in motion pictures, and as a teacher.

Kundry, an enchantress and penitent

(mezzo-soprano) in WAGNER'S PARSIFAL.

Kuno, Prince Ottokar's head ranger (bass) in WEBER'S DER FREISCHÜTZ.

Kunz, Erich, bass. Born Vienna, May 20, 1909. After studying with Theodore Lierhammer in Vienna, he became an understudy at the GLYNDEBOURNE OPERA in England. He made his official opera debut as OSMIN with the Troppau Opera in Troppau (now Opava), Czechoslovakia. After singing in Plannen and Breslau, he achieved an outstanding reputation at the SALZBURG and BAYREUTH festivals between 1941 and 1944. He subsequently performed in the leading opera houses of Europe and was particularly acclaimed for his MOZART interpretations. His American debut took place at the METROPOLITAN OPERA on Nov. 26, 1952, as LEPORELLO. He remained with the Metropolitan Opera two seasons. He has since appeared in major European opera houses and festivals and become particularly famous for such roles as PAPAGENO, BECKMESSER, and Leporello.

Kurt, Melanie, soprano. Born Vienna, Jan. 8, 1880; died New York City, Mar. 11, 1941. She began the study of singing with Fannie Mütter in Vienna and in 1902 made her debut in Lübeck as ELISABETH. After appearances in Leipzig, she withdrew from the stage to study with Lilli LEHMANN in Berlin. She returned to opera in 1905 with appearances in Brunswick. From 1908 to 1912 she was principal soprano of the Berlin Royal Opera, famous for her Wagnerian interpretations. When the Charlottenburg Opera (BERLIN DEUTSCHE STAATSOPER) opened in Berlin in 1912, she was engaged as principal soprano. On Feb. 1, 1915, she made her American debut at the METROPOLITAN OPERA as ISOLDE; she remained with this company two seasons. Her appearances in opera now grew infrequent as she specialized in concert appearances and teaching. She went into retirement in 1932 and at the outbreak of World War II came to live in New York.

Kurwenal, Tristan's retainer (baritone) in WAGNER'S TRISTAN UND ISOLDE.

Kurz, Selma, soprano. Born Bielitz, Austria, Nov. 15, 1875; died Vienna, May 10, 1933. After studying voice with Hans Pless, she made her debut at the FRANKFURT OPERA. She was so successful that Gustav MAHLER engaged her for the VIENNA STATE OPERA. She remained in Vienna for over a quarter of a century, until 1926, scoring triumphs in most of the famous coloratura roles. In 1930 she was made an honorary member of the Vienna Opera, an honor previously held by only six singers. Shortly before her retirement in 1926, she came to the United States for a few concert appearances. As a member of the Vienna Opera, she appeared in successful guest performances at other major European opera houses, including COVENT GARDEN.

Kyoto, a procurer (baritone) in MASCAGNI'S IRIS.

L

Lablache, Luigi, bass. Born Naples, Dec. 6, 1794; died there Jan. 23, 1858. His music study took place at the Conservatorio della Pietà de' Turchini in Naples. In 1812 he made his debut at the SAN CARLO in Naples in Valentino Fiorávanti's *La molinara*. After an additional period of study he was engaged as principal bass of the Palermo Opera, where he remained for five years. He then made his debut at LA SCALA in LA CENERENTOLA. After many other successful appearances throughout Italy, he appeared in Vienna in 1824, receiving a gold medal. Three years later he sang in a performance of MOZART's *Requiem* performed at BEETHOVEN's funeral services. SCHUBERT came to know Lablache at this time, dedicating his *Three Italian Songs* to him. In 1830 Lablache made his London debut in IL MATRIMONIO SEGRETO, and the following year he appeared for the first time in Paris in the same opera. For several years he appeared alternately in London and Paris, a great favorite in both cities. In 1835 he created the role of Riccardo in I PURITANI and in 1843 that of DON PASQUALE, both in Paris. For a period he was Queen Victoria's singing master. Poor health forced him to retire in 1852. He had a voice exceptional in range and volume. His most famous characterization was that of LEPORELLO.

Labra di foco, love duet of young Fenton and Nanette Ford in Act I, Scene 2, of VERDI's FALSTAFF.

La brise est douce et parfumé, the choral FARANDOLE in Act II of GOUNOD's MIREILLE, during a festival in an arena.

Labyrinth, opera in one act by MENOTTI. Libretto by the composer. Premiere: NBC-TV, May 3, 1963. This is Menotti's second opera commissioned and written expressly for television. Its severe demands for unique camera effects make it virtually impossible to stage. It has been described as "opera's first adventure in photographic surrealism." The symbolic text finds a bride and bridegroom come for their honeymoon to a hotel, the latter intended as a representation of the world. There they encounter a variety of characters, each symbolic of some facet of life. A spy represents science or philosophy; a bellboy, dreams; an old chess player, the past; and so forth. The hotel desk manager is Death, who urges the groom to lie down on a bench, which is rapidly converted into a coffin. But the coffin has no bottom, so that when it is carried away the bridegroom is left lying

on the bench. He opens his hand and finds the key to his room. Menotti's aim in this opera was to penetrate to the essence of life and examine its essentials, but he was also trying to satirize grand opera. His musical style is eclectic, partly VERISMO, and at times utilizes such popular forms as the WALTZ and the tango.

Laca, Jenufa's husband (tenor) in JANÁČEK's JENUFA.

La calunnia è un venticello, Basilio's aria about the malicious powers of slander, in Act I, Scene 2, of ROSSINI's THE BARBER OF SEVILLE.

La Charmeuse, a dancer (soprano) in MASSENET's THAÏS.

Là ci darem la mano, duet of Don Giovanni and Zerlina in which he tries to win her interest and she to resist his charm, in Act I, Scene 3, of MOZART's DON GIOVANNI.

La Cieca, La Gioconda's blind mother (contralto) in PONCHIELLI's LA GIOCONDA.

La Ciesca, Marco's wife (soprano) in PUCCINI's GIANNI SCHICCHI.

Lackland, Sir Gower, fiancé (tenor) of Lady Marigold in HANSON's MERRY MOUNT.

La dolcissima effigie, Maurizio's message of love to Adriana, who still does not know his identity, in Act I of CILÈA's ADRIANA LECOUVREUR.

La donna è mobile, one of the most celebrated tenor arias in Italian opera, in which the Duke of Mantua expresses his belief that all women are fickle, in Act IV of VERDI's RIGOLETTO.

Lady Angela, the heroine (soprano), a lady of mystery with whom Horatio falls in love, in AUBER's LE DOMINO NOIR.

Lady Billows, an elderly autocrat (soprano) in BRITTEN's ALBERT HERRING.

Lady from Colorado, The, opera in three acts by WARD. Libretto by Bernard Stambler, based on a novel by Homer Croy. Premiere: Central City, Col., July 3, 1964. Commissioned by the Central City Opera House Association, this opera boasts numerous musical episodes that are of local Colorado interest, frequently singing the praises of the state and its people. The text is set in Elkhorn, a mountain town; the time is the late nineteenth century. The plot involves the destinies of an Irish immigrant girl and her husband, an expatriate English nobleman.

Lady Macbeth, wife of Macbeth and principal female character (soprano) in VERDI'S MACBETH. This character also appears in Ernest Bloch's *Macbeth* (soprano).

Lady Macbeth of Mzensk, *see* KATERINA ISMAILOVA.

Laërtes, (1) Polonius' son (tenor), in THOMAS'S HAMLET.

(2) An actor (tenor) in THOMAS'S MIGNON.

Laetitia, a servant (soprano) in MENOTTI'S THE OLD MAID AND THE THIEF.

La fatal pietra, Radames' lament in his final duet with Aida, in Act IV, Scene 2, of VERDI'S AIDA.

La Fenice, *see* TEATRO LA FENICE.

La fleur que tu m'avais jetée (Flower Song), Don José's song to Carmen as he removes from his bosom the flower she had once thrown at him, in Act II of BIZET'S CARMEN.

la Fontaine, Jean de, poet and fabulist. Born Château Thierry, France, July 8, 1621; died Paris, Apr. 13, 1695. Famous for his *Contes* and *Fables,* la Fontaine wrote works that were the source for operas by GRÉTRY, HÉROLD, MONSIGNY, PHILIDOR, and numerous other composers, including GLUCK (L'IVROGNE CORRIGÉ), GOUNOD (*La Colombe*), and PIERNÉ (*La Coupe enchantée*).

Lagerlöf, Selma, novelist. Born Mårbacka, Sweden, Nov. 20, 1858; died Mårbacka, Mar. 16, 1940. One of Sweden's most celebrated authors. Lagerlöf wrote stories that have inspired a number of operas. Her masterwork, *Gösta Berling's Saga,* was made into an opera by ZANDONAI, *I cavalieri di Ekebu.* Manfred Gurlitt's *Nordische Ballade* was derived from *Arne's Treasure,* Oskar Lindberg's *Fredlös* from *The Outlaw,* and Franco Vittadini's *Nazareth* from one of the author's short stories.

Laisse-moi contempler ton visage, love duet of Marguerite and Faust in Act III of GOUNOD'S FAUST.

Lake George Opera Festival, the only permanent summer opera repertory company in the eastern part of the United States. It was founded in 1961 by Fred Patrick, with David Lloyd as artistic director. For four seasons it remained on a more or less amateur basis. Since then it has given significant performances in the auditorium of Queensbury High School in Glens Falls, N.Y., where it annually holds a six-week festival with a minimum of five performances a week. In 1968 it offered a SHAKESPEARE festival (five operas, sung in English, based on Shakespeare), which included such novelties as ROSSINI'S OTELLO, BRITTEN'S A MIDSUMMER NIGHT'S DREAM, and the world premiere of David AMRAM'S *Twelfth Night.* In 1969 it offered a festival of comedy that included ALBERT HERRING, ARIADNE AUF NAXOS, and L'HEURE ESPAGNOLE. Since 1965 it has produced several American operas, among them GIANNINI'S THE TAMING OF THE SHREW; THE TELEPHONE; THE BALLAD OF BABY DOE; and THE CRUCIBLE.

Lakmé, OPÉRA-COMIQUE in three acts by DELIBES. Libretto by Edmond Gondinet and Philippe Gille, based on Pierre LOTI'S *Le Mariage de Loti.* Premiere: Opéra-Comique, Apr. 14, 1883. American premiere: Academy of Music, N.Y., Mar. 1, 1886.

Characters: Gérald, a British officer (tenor); Frédéric, his friend (baritone); Nilakantha, a Brahman priest (bass); Lakmé, his daughter (soprano), a role created by Marie VAN ZANDT; Mallika, her slave (mezzo-soprano); Ellen, the Governor's daughter (soprano); Rose, her friend (mezzo-soprano); Mrs. Benson, their governess (mezzo-soprano); Hadji, a Hindu slave (tenor); Hindus; British officers; ladies; sailors; musicians; Brahmans. The setting is India in the middle nineteenth century.

Act I. The garden of an Indian temple. The Brahman priest Nilakantha tells his followers that the English invader will soon be driven from India. From within the temple come the voices of Lakmé and her followers in prayer ("Blanche Dourga"). After the worshipers scatter, Lakmé and her slave girl get ready to bathe in the stream, as they sing the BARCAROLLE "Dôme épais, le jasmin." Then some English sightseers invade the garden, heedless of its sanctity. One of them is Gérald. The visitors espy Lakmé's jewels and are so taken by them that when the others leave, Gérald decides to sketch them ("Prendre le dessin d'un bijou"), at the same time wondering who their owner might be ("Fantaisie aux divins mensonges"). Lakmé catches him in the act. They are immediately attracted to each other, Gérald voicing his own sentiments in "C'est le dieu de la jeunesse." Lakmé begs Gérald to leave the garden. He departs, but only after he has told Lakmé how much he loves her. Nilakantha reappears, perceives that the place has been desecrated by a foreigner, and vows that the criminal must die.

Act II. A public square. Lakmé and Nilakantha are both in disguise, for the priest is searching for the stranger who has profaned the temple. He orders Lakmé to sing, certain that the offender will reveal himself at the sound of her voice. Lakmé renders a haunting exotic melody (Bell Song: "Où va la jeune Hindoue?"). Overcome by his love, Gérald rushes toward Lakmé, and a love duet follows ("Dans le vague d'un rêve"). Nilakantha stabs him and escapes, thinging Gérald dead. Lakmé is overjoyed to find that Gérald's wound is not mortal.

Act III. A forest. The orchestral ENTR'ACTE is in the style of a gentle lullaby. Lakmé is nursing Gérald back to health, singing to him, "Sous le ciel tout étoilé." He greets his savior and lover ("Je me souviens, sans voix") and speaks of his joy in being here with Lakmé ("Ah! viens dans la forêt profonde"). Lakmé goes to get some water from a nearby sacred fountain; those who drink it will remain true in their love. While she is away, Gérald's friend Frédéric arrives and urges him to rejoin his regiment. As Lakmé returns with

the magic water, martial music is heard in the distance. Noting her lover's reaction to it, Lakmé realizes that he will return to his proper place and she will lose him forever. Unable to think of life without him, she plucks a lethal datura blossom and eats it. Gérald is horrified but Lakmé welcomes death ("Tu m'as donné le plus doux rêve"). Her father appears. Incensed at finding the Englishman with his daughter, he orders his men to kill Gérald. Lakmé proudly tells her father that she will placate the gods by dying in his place. Singing of her love for Gérald, she expires.

The only one of Delibes's operas to survive, *Lakmé* is one of the most popular items in the French repertory. Its appeal is not difficult to explain. Its orientalism gives it a delightful flavor, and it boasts one of the most famous coloratura arias in all opera, the "Bell Song."

Lalla Roukh, a poem by Thomas MOORE, consisting of four tales about an Indian princess, Lalla Roukh, who goes to the valley of Kashmir to meet her beloved, the Sultan of Bucharia. Operas inspired by this poem include DAVID's *Lalla Roukh,* RUBINSTEIN's *Feramors,* and STANFORD's *The Veiled Prophet of Khorassan.*

Lalo, Edouard, composer. Born Lille, France, Jan. 27, 1823; died Paris, Apr. 22, 1892. After preliminary studies in Lille, Lalo entered the Paris Conservatory in his sixteenth year. In 1867 he entered his first opera, *Fiesque,* in a competition sponsored by the THÉÂTRE LYRIQUE. While it won only third prize, the director of the PARIS OPÉRA accepted it. Due to a series of misfortunes, including the burning of the opera house, it was not performed. Lalo's recognition as a composer came in the 1870's with two works for violin and orchestra written for the violinist Sarasate: a concerto and the *Symphonie Espagnole.* His most important and most successful opera, LE ROI D'YS, was given at the OPÉRA-COMIQUE in 1888 and entered the permanent repertory of that theater. Lalo began a third opera, *La Jacquerie;* it was finished by Arthur Coquard after Lalo's death.

L'altra notte, Marguerite's contemplation during the prison scene of her imminent execution, in Act III of BOITO's MEFISTOFELE.

La luce langue, Lady Macbeth's dramatic aria in Act II of VERDI's MACBETH, expressing her conviction that anybody who stands in the way of her husband's ambition must be murdered. This aria was written when Verdi revised *Macbeth* for Paris, in 1865.

La mamma morta, Madeleine's aria in Act III of GIORDANO's ANDREA CHÉNIER, informing Gérard of her mother's death.

Lamartine, Alphonse de, poet. Born Macon, France, Oct. 21, 1790; died Paris Mar. 1, 1869. GODARD's *Jocelyn* and Jules Mazellier's *Graziella* were inspired by poems of this author.

Lamento di Federico, *see* E LA SOLITA STORIA.

Lament of Arianna, *see* LASCIATEMI MORIRE.

L'amo come il fulgor del creator, duet of Laura and La Gioconda bitterly condemning each other for stealing Enzo's love, in Act II of PONCHIELLI's LA GIOCONDA.

L'amor mai che non ci da tregue, Falstaff's madrigal in praise of love, in Act II, Scene 1, of VERDI's FALSTAFF.

La mort m'apparait souriante, Eurydice's invocation to death after having been bitten by a snake in Act I of OFFENBACH's OPÉRA BOUFFE ORPHEUS IN THE UNDERWORLD.

L'amour est une vertu rare, Thaïs' hymn of praise to the purity of love in Act II, Scene 2, of MASSENET's THAÏS, as she entreats Athanaël not to destroy the statue of Eros.

L'amour est un oiseau rebelle, Carmen's coquettish HABANERA in Act I of BIZET's CARMEN. Bizet borrowed this melody from Sebastian Yradier's song "El Arreglito," believing it to be a Spanish folksong.

Lamoureux, Charles, conductor. Born Bordeaux, France, Sept. 28, 1834; died Paris, Dec. 21, 1899. His studies were completed at the Paris Conservatory, after which he played the violin in various orchestras and was assistant conductor of the Paris Conservatory Orchestra. In 1876 he conducted at the OPÉRA-COMIQUE, resigning a year later due to differences with the management over matters of interpretation. He then became conductor of the OPÉRA for the next two years, once again leaving after disagreements with the management. He now devoted himself principally to symphonic music, founding the renowned Concerts Lamoureux in 1881, which he directed for the remainder of his life. He was one of the earliest champions of WAGNER in France and led the first performance of a Wagner opera to be heard in Paris after the fiasco of TANN-HÄUSER in 1861. The opera was LOHEN-GRIN, introduced on May 3, 1887.

L'amour se devint maître, Minka's aria expressing her love for de Nangis, in Act I of CHABRIER's LE ROI MALGRÉ LUI.

Lamperti, Francesco, teacher of singing. Born Savona, Italy, Mar. 11, 1813; died Como, May 1, 1892. He attended the Milan Conservatory. Beginning in 1850, he taught there for a quarter of a century. Afterward, he taught privately. The long list of noted singers who were his pupils includes Emma ALBANI, Desirée ARTÔT, Italo CAMPANINI, and Marcella SEMBRICH. His methods adhered to the old traditions of Italian singing; he wrote several valuable treatises. He was made a Commander of the Crown of Italy.

Landgrave of Thuringia, *see* HERMANN.

Languir per una bella, Lindoro's aria in Act I of ROSSINI's L'ITALIANA IN ALGERI.

L'anima ho stanca, Maurizio's aria as he presents a bunch of violets to Adriana, in Act II of CILÈA's ADRIANA LE-COUVREUR.

La notte e giorno, the beggars' chorus in Act I of Giordano's ANDREA CHÉNIER.

Laparra, Raoul, composer. Born Bordeaux, France, May 13, 1876; died Paris, Apr. 4, 1943. He attended the Paris Conservatory, winning the PRIX DE ROME in 1903. He completed his first opera in 1899, *La Peau d'âne.* Success came with his second opera, LA HABANERA, introduced by the OPÉRA-COMIQUE in 1908. He was music critic for *Le Matin* until 1933, after which he concentrated on composition. Later operas: *La Jota* (1911); *Le Joueur de viole* (1925); *Las Torreras* (1929); *L'Illustre Fregona* (1931). Laparra made extensive use of Spanish and Basque folk elements in his operas. He was killed during an air raid.

La Périchole, a gypsy street singer (soprano), heroine of OFFENBACH'S LA PÉRICHOLE.

Lara, Isidore de, see DE LARA, ISIDORE.

Largo, Handel's, the designation by which the aria "Ombra mai fù" from HANDEL'S opera SERSE is most familiar. In the opera it is an andante tenor aria describing the cool shade of a palm tree. It has been retitled "Largo" in countless instrumental transcriptions.

Largo al factotum, Figaro's patter song in Act I, Scene 1, of ROSSINI'S THE BARBER OF SEVILLE, detailing his many functions.

Larina, Madame, a landowner (mezzo-soprano) in TCHAIKOVSKY'S EUGENE ONEGIN.

La rivedrò nell' estasi, Riccardo's aria in expectation of soon beholding the face of the woman he loves, in Act I, Scene 1, of VERDI'S UN BALLO IN MASCHERA.

Larsen-Todsen, Nanny, soprano. Born Hagby, Sweden, Aug. 2, 1884. After completing her studies at the Stockholm Conservatory, she made her debut at the STOCKHOLM ROYAL OPERA in 1907. During her association with this company, she made many guest appearances in major European opera houses. On Jan. 31, 1925, she made her American debut at the METROPOLITAN OPERA as Brünnhilde in GÖTTERDÄMMERUNG. She remained at the Metropolitan Opera three seasons, specializing in Wagnerian roles. She appeared at BAYREUTH for the first time in 1927, singing there in the next four festivals, one of the few Bayreuth sopranos to be heard as Brünnhilde, ISOLDE, and KUNDRY. She was a guest singer at leading European opera houses up to World War II, after which her operatic appearances were few.

La Scala, see TEATRO ALLA SCALA.

Lascia ch'io pianga, Almirena's eloquent air in HANDEL'S RINALDO. This is the most famous aria in the opera. Handel first used this melody for a dance of Asiatics in the last scene of his first opera, ALMIRA; after that he borrowed the melody for a cantata.

Lasciatemi morire, the Lament of Arianna, the only excerpt to survive from MONTEVERDI'S opera *Arianna* (1608). This is one of the most celebrated arias in seventeenth-century opera. For its time it was extraordinary for its chromatic intervals, discordant harmonies, and intervallic leaps in the melody, all intended to heighten the expression of the heroine's emotions on being thwarted by a fisherman in an attempt to commit suicide by drowning. Monteverdi developed this air into four five-voice madrigals, published in his sixth book of madrigals (1614).

Lassale, Jean, baritone. Born Lyons, France, Dec. 14, 1847; died Paris, Sept. 7, 1909. Though originally intent on a mercantile career, he attended the Paris Conservatory and studied singing privately with Novelli. He made his debut in Liège in 1869 as ST. BRIS. In 1872 he was engaged by the PARIS OPÉRA, where he made his debut on June 7 in WILLIAM TELL. For the next twenty years he was an idol of the Paris Opéra audiences. His repertoire included sixty operas in the French, Italian, and German repertories. He created the principal baritone roles in GOUNOD'S *Polyeucte;* LE ROI DE LAHORE; Emile Paladilhe's *La Patrie;* SIGURD; SAINT-SAËNS'S *Ascanio* and HENRY VIII; and THOMAS'S *Françoise de Rimini.* On June 15, 1892, he made his American debut at the METROPOLITAN OPERA as NELUSCO and scored a major success. For the next half dozen years he appeared at the Metropolitan. In 1901 he settled in Paris as a teacher of singing, and in 1903 he became a professor at the Paris Conservatory.

Lasst mich euch fragen (Chi mi dira), the drinking chorus of the farmers in Act III of FLOTOW'S MARTHA.

Last Days of Pompeii, The, see BULWER-LYTTON, EDWARD.

Last Rose of Summer, The (Qui sola,

vergin rosa; Die letzte Rose), Harriet's song in Act II of FLOTOW'S MARTHA, requested by Lionel. It is an old Irish air, "The Groves of Blarney," poem by Thomas MOORE.

Last Savage, The, OPÉRA BOUFFE in three acts by MENOTTI. Libretto by the composer. Premiere: Opéra-Comique, Oct. 21, 1963. American premiere: Metropolitan Opera, Jan. 23, 1964. This is a satire on contemporary civilization and on many of its customs and frailties. During the course of the action, Menotti mocks at such refinements of contemporary life as cocktail parties, beatniks, taxes, the class struggle, SERIAL-TECHNIQUE composers, abstract painters, and so forth. Part of the action takes place in India and part in Chicago. The central character is Kitty, an anthropologist. The daughter of a millionaire, she has the wherewithal to come to India to search for the legendary Abominable Snowman. In India, a love affair develops between her and the son of the Maharajah. The fathers are pleased at the possibility of the two families joining, but each has distracting problems to concern him: Kitty's father is worried about government bureaucracy, mounting taxes, and the growing power of trade unionism; the Maharajah is disturbed by the social reforms taking place in his country. Since Kitty has no intention of marrying until she has found the legendary Snowman, the parents contrive to invent one by transforming a stable boy into the Snowman, or "last savage."

The Last Savage was commissioned by the PARIS OPÉRA (the first time since VERDI that a foreign composer had received a contract from the Opéra for a new work). But because of the lightness of its theme and the *opéra-bouffe* character of Menotti's music, the decision was reached to mount it at the OPÉRA-COMIQUE. Menotti wrote his libretto in Italian for the first time since AMELIA GOES TO THE BALL, his initial opera. For the Paris premiere he translated his text into French, while George Mead, who had also translated *Amelia,* translated it into English for the METROPOLITAN OPERA premiere.

Laszló, Magda, soprano. Born Marosvasarhély, Hungary, c. 1919. Her principal study of voice took place at the Franz Liszt Academy in Budapest and with Irene Stowaser. Between 1943 and 1946 she was a member of the BUDAPEST OPERA. She then made successful appearances in Italy, where in 1949 she created the role of the mother in IL PRIGIONIERO over the radio and in Florence at its first stage presentation in 1950. In 1954 she created the part of Cressida in TROILUS AND CRESSIDA. In 1962 she was heard in L'INCORONAZIONE DI POPPEA at the GLYNDEBOURNE FESTIVAL.

Lattuada, Felice, composer. Born Morimondo, Italy, Feb. 5, 1882. He graduated from the Milan Conservatory in 1911 and four years later completed his first opera, *Sandha,* performed in Genoa in 1924. Recognition came with his *Don Giovanni,* which won a national prize in 1922, and success with his finest opera, LE PREZIOSE RIDICOLE (after MOLIÈRE), first given at LA SCALA in 1929 and soon heard throughout Italy, in Buenos Aires, Berlin, Prague, and at the METROPOLITAN OPERA (1930). His other operas: *La tempesta* (1922); *La caverna di Sálamanca* (1937).

Laubenthal, Rudolf, tenor. Born Düsseldorf, Mar. 10, 1886. He turned to singing after being educated in the sciences. His apprenticeship as an opera singer took place with the BERLIN OPERA, after which he achieved success as a Wagnerian tenor in leading German opera houses and at COVENT GARDEN. On Nov. 9, 1923, he made his American debut at the METROPOLITAN OPERA in DIE MEISTERSINGER. He remained at the Metropolitan for a decade, appearing in all the major Wagnerian dramas, as well as in such important revivals and premieres as DIE AEGYPTISCHE HELENA, THE BARTERED BRIDE, DER FREISCHÜTZ, JENUFA, and ŠVANDA. After leaving the Metropolitan he appeared in the major opera houses of Austria, Germany, and England.

Laughing Song, (1) an aria from AU-

BER'S MANON LESCAUT ("C'est l'histoire amoureuse") frequently interpolated into the Lesson Scene of ROSSINI'S THE BARBER OF SEVILLE.

(2) Adele's aria ("Mein Herr Marquis") in Act II of Johann STRAUSS'S DIE FLEDERMAUS.

Laura, Alvise's wife (mezzo-soprano), in love with Enzo, in PONCHIELLI'S LA GIOCONDA.

Lauretta, Gianni Schicchi's daughter (soprano) in PUCCINI'S GIANNI SCHICCHI.

Lauretta mia, duet of Rinuccio and Lauretta in PUCCINI'S GIANNI SCHICCHI.

Lauri-Volpi, Giacomo, tenor. Born Rome, Dec. 11, 1894. After studying at the Santa Cecilia in Rome and privately with Enrico Rosati, he made his debut in 1920 at the Teatro Costanzi in MANON. Two years later he was engaged by LA SCALA, where he scored a major success. On Jan. 27, 1923, he made his American debut at the METROPOLITAN OPERA in RIGOLETTO and became an immediate favorite. He remained at the Metropolitan for the next decade, during which time he created for America the role of Calaf in TURANDOT, and was heard in two hundred thirty-three performances in twenty-six roles. He toured South America extensively in 1926. After leaving the Metropolitan (1932) he appeared at La Scala and other major opera houses of Europe. Just before and after World War II he confined his appearances to Italy, before going into retirement in Valencia, Spain. He paid a return visit to the United States in conjunction with the ceremonies, on Dec. 18, 1968, for the unveiling of his bust (the work of John Galster, a Danish sculptor) to be placed in Founders' Hall under the main foyer of the Metropolitan Opera House. His autobiography appeared in two volumes: *L'equivoco* (1938) and *A viso aperto* (1953).

Lausanne International Competition, an annual competition for opera singers, organized in Lausanne, Switzerland, in 1950. Winners receive contracts with leading European opera houses. The judges have included Claude Delvincourt, Frederick Jacobi, Toti dal Monte, and Ninon Vallin. Among the winners have been Victoria DE LOS ANGELES, Rita Gorr, Grace Hoffmann, Anne McKnight, and Teresa STICH-RANDALL.

La vendetta, Doctor Bartolo's insistence that Figaro be compelled to marry Marcellina in fulfillment of an agreement, in Act I of MOZART'S THE MARRIAGE OF FIGARO.

La Vergine degli angeli, Leonora's prayer with a chorus of monks that a curse fall on anyone who harms her, in Act II, Scene 2, of VERDI'S LA FORZA DEL DESTINO.

La volta, a vigorous dance popular in Elizabethan England and revived by BRITTEN in GLORIANA for the Queen's ball, in Act II, Scene 3.

La vrai! je ne suis pas coupable, Hélène's dramatic air in Act II of OFFENBACH'S LA BELLE HÉLÈNE.

Lawrence, Marjorie, soprano. Born Deans Marsh, Australia, Feb. 17, 1909. She first studied singing with the local pastor and afterward in Melbourne, where she won first prize in an opera competition. For the next three years she studied with Cécile Gilly in Paris, after which she made her debut in 1932 in MONTE CARLO in TANNHÄUSER. She was immediately engaged by the PARIS OPÉRA for leading Wagnerian roles, appearing there for four years. On Dec. 18, 1935, she made her American debut at the METROPOLITAN OPERA in DIE WALKÜRE. During her next six seasons at the Metropolitan she was recognized as one of the outstanding Wagnerian sopranos.

During a performance of *Die Walküre* in Mexico City in 1941 she was stricken with poliomyelitis. It was feared she would be paralyzed for life. Showing a remarkable will to recover, and aided by her husband, Dr. Thomas King (whom she had married shortly before the tragedy), she fought her sickness with supreme patience. In a few months she could move her muscles again; a few months more and she found she had regained her voice. In the fall of 1942 she appeared in a song recital in Town Hall, New York, seated in a wheel chair. Still unable to walk, she returned to the stage of the Metropolitan Opera on

Jan. 22, 1943, as VENUS, singing the role in a reclining position. A year later, she attempted the role of ISOLDE at the Metropolitan, strapped throughout the performance to a carefully camouflaged wheel chair. In Chicago, on Dec. 11, 1947, she stood throughout an entire performance of ELEKTRA. She then proceeded to fill a complete schedule of concert and opera appearances in America and Europe. She has told the story of her illness and recovery in *Interrupted Melody,* a book published in 1949 and made into a motion picture in 1955. Between 1957 and 1960 she was professor of voice at Newcomb College at Tulane University in New Orleans. She then was made director of the Opera Workshop at Southern Illinois University at Carbondale where, in Feb., 1966, she appeared as Mme. Flora in THE MEDIUM.

Lawrence, Robert, conductor and critic. Born New York City, Mar. 18, 1912. After receiving his diploma in conducting at the Juilliard School in 1936, he served for a time as the music critic of the New York *Herald Tribune,* then appeared as guest conductor of several American orchestras. On Sept. 20, 1942, he led a performance of THAÏS in Montreal with singers from the METROPOLITAN OPERA. In 1944–45 he conducted TOSCA with the Royal Opera of Rome and in 1960 he conducted LES TROYENS for the AMERICAN OPERA SOCIETY. In 1962 he became the artistic director of the Friends of French Opera, which presented annual performances of the French repertory, many of the works rarely given. He has edited and made adaptations of numerous operas and is the author of the *Metropolitan Opera Guide* (1939) and *The World of Opera* (1955). In 1968 he was made director of the opera department of the Peabody Institute at Baltimore. He has made guest appearances with leading symphony orchestras in America and Europe, besides serving as musical director of the Phoenix (Arizona) Symphony between 1949 and 1952 and the Ankara

Symphony in Turkey from 1957 to 1959.

Lazzari, Virgilio, bass. Born Assisi, Apr. 20, 1887; died Castel Gandolfo, Oct. 4, 1953. After studying with Antonio Cotogni in Rome, he joined the Vitale Light Opera Company. He transferred from light to serious opera for a season at the TEATRO COSTANZI. For three seasons he appeared in leading bass roles at the TEATRO COLÓN in Buenos Aires. In 1916 he came to the United States, making his debut with the St. Louis Opera as RAMFIS. From 1918 to 1933 he was a member of the CHICAGO OPERA. On Dec. 28, 1933, he made his METROPOLITAN OPERA debut as Don Pedro in L'AFRICAINE. For the next seventeen years he appeared at the Metropolitan in twenty-two major bass roles, his last appearance there being on Dec. 5, 1950, as LEPORELLO. Besides his appearances at the Metropolitan, Lazzari was heard at the SALZBURG FESTIVALS, COVENT GARDEN, LA SCALA, and the OPÉRA-COMIQUE. One of his most celebrated roles was that of King Archibaldo, which he had the benefit of studying with the composer, MONTEMEZZI.

leading motif, *see* LEITMOTIV.

Leander, the Prime Minister (baritone) in PROKOFIEV'S THE LOVE FOR THREE ORANGES.

Lear, Evelyn, soprano. Born New York City, Jan. 18, 1930. She began her vocal studies at Hunter College and attended the Juilliard School of Music, where she appeared in COSÌ FAN TUTTE and met and married Thomas STEWART (later to become a distinguished operatic baritone). They came to Berlin in 1957 on Fulbright grants, where they continued their vocal education at the Hochschule für Musik. A year later she was engaged by the BERLIN DEUTSCHE STAATSOPER on a three-year contract (her husband having been contracted a year earlier) but remained with the company for a decade. They became the only Americans and the only husband-and-wife team to receive the honorary title of KAMMERSÄNGER. Miss Lear made her debut with the Berlin company as the Composer in

ARIADNE AUF NAXOS in 1959 and soon afterwards was well received as CHERU- BINO. In 1960 she received an offer from the VIENNA FESTIVAL to sing the part of LULU, in a concert version of BERG's mu- sical drama, but only if she could learn the role in three weeks. She did so with such success that in 1962 she was en- gaged for the first staged performance of *Lulu* in Vienna, at the newly re- built THEATER-AN-DER-WIEN. In addition she was called upon to perform lead- ing roles in the world premiere of KLEBE's *Alkmene,* offered during the opening week of the new opera house of the Berlin Deutsche Staatsoper in 1961, and EGK's *Die Verlobung in San Do- mingo,* which reopened the Munich Na- tional Theater in 1963.

Her American debut took place in Kansas City in the Kansas City Arts Foundation presentation of HANDEL's GIULIO CESARE in Oct., 1965, in the role of Cleopatra. In 1966 she made a sensa- tional impression as Marie in WOZZECK at the CHICAGO LYRIC OPERA. At her de- but at the METROPOLITAN OPERA, she cre- ated the role of Lavinia in the world premiere of Marvin David Levy's MOURNING BECOMES ELEKTRA on Mar. 16, 1967. Though her specialty is modern opera, particularly Berg's two master- works, she has appeared in the world's leading opera houses in a wide va- riety of operas, including ARABELLA, DER ROSENKAVALIER, DON GIOVANNI, L'INCORO- NAZIONE DI POPPEA, ORFEO ED EURIDICE (GLUCK), THE ABDUCTION FROM THE SERAGLIO, LES TROYENS, CARMEN, and LA BOHÈME, among others.

Leben des Orest, Das (The Life of Orestes), opera in five acts by KRENEK. Libretto by the composer, based on the *Electra* of EURIPIDES. Premiere: Leipzig Opera, Jan. 19, 1930. While the text follows the plot of the Euripides trag- edy, it is an interesting experiment at modernizing the Greek drama through the application of a jazz style in the ZEITKUNST movement then so popular in Germany.

See ORESTES.

Le calme rentre dans mon coeur, Ores- tes' air in which he reveals he has found peace of mind, in GLUCK's IPHIGÉNIE EN TAURIDE.

Lefebvre, a police sergeant (tenor), later Duke of Danzig, in GIORDANO's MADAME SANS-GÊNE.

Légende de la sauge, *see* FLEURISSAIT UNE SAUGE.

Legend of Kleinzach, The, *see* IL ÉTAIT UNE FOIS À LA COUR D'EISENACH.

Legend (or Tale) of the Czar Saltan, The, opera in prologue and four acts by RIMSKY-KORSAKOV. Libretto by Vladimir Bielsky, based on a poem by PUSHKIN. American premiere: New York City, Dec. 27, 1937. The opera bears a for- midable full title that reads: "The Leg- end (*or* Tale) of the Czar Saltan, of his son, the famous and mighty hero Prince Gvidon Salanovich, and of the beautiful Swan Princess." The Czar Sal- tan marries Militrissa, youngest of three sisters. When he goes off to war, the two envious sisters write him that Militrissa has given birth to a monster. Saltan orders his wife and child put in a casket and thrown into the sea. The casket drifts to an island which becomes the new home for Militrissa and her son. The boy grows up to be a magician. From the bottom of the sea he evokes a kingdom and proclaims himself its Czar. When the Czar Saltan finally discovers that his son is human, he becomes recon- ciled to him and Militrissa. This opera is known in America chiefly for its or- chestral interlude in the third act, "The Flight of the Bumblebee."

Legend (or Tale) of the Invisible City of Kitezh, opera in four acts by RIMSKY- KORSAKOV. Libretto by Vladimir Bielsky. Premiere: Maryinsky Theater, St. Peters- burg, Feb. 20, 1907. American premiere: Ann Arbor, Mich., May 21, 1932 (con- cert version); Philadelphia, Feb. 4, 1936 (staged). Prince Vsevolod, son of King Yury and joint ruler of Kitezh, meets Fevronia in a forest, falls in love with her, and asks for her hand in marriage. They marry in Kitezh. The Tartars descend on the city and capture the bride. Two Tartars fight for her, but the drunkard Grisha helps her escape. Fevronia flees through a forest haunted by dancing devils and goblins. Exhausted, she sinks to the ground. The spirit of the Prince arrives to lead her back to the holy city, where bride and groom are welcomed back by the king and his people. The most familiar excerpts are the bard's song, "By the Banks of the Yar," in Act II, for bass; and the orchestral ENTR'ACTE in Act III, entitled "The Battle of Kerzhenetz."

Légères hirondelles, Mignon's recollection of a land of sunshine and swallows she once knew, in Act I of THOMAS's MIGNON.

Lehl, a shepherd (tenor) in RIMSKY-KORSAKOV's THE SNOW MAIDEN.

Lehmann, Lilli, soprano. Born Würzburg, Nov. 24, 1848; died Berlin, May 17, 1929. One of the greatest Wagnerian sopranos of all time, she was raised in a highly musical atmosphere, started piano lessons when she was six and a few years later studied singing with her mother, the opera singer Marie Loewe. On Oct. 20, 1865, Lilli Lehmann made her debut in Prague as the First Page in THE MAGIC FLUTE. At the next performance of the opera, the leading singer became indisposed, and Lehmann stepped into her role. She gave such a good account of herself that henceforth she was assigned leading roles. After her appearances in Danzig and Leipzig, she was engaged by the BERLIN (Royal) OPERA, where she made her debut on Aug. 19, 1870, as Vielka in MEYERBEER's EIN FELDLAGER IN SCHLESIEN. She remained with that company for many years, distinguishing herself in coloratura roles. After being coached by WAGNER, she appeared at the first BAYREUTH FESTIVAL, creating the roles of the Forest Bird and WOGLINDE. After 1875 she was made a life member of the Berlin Opera, with the title of KAMMERSÄNGERIN, and allowed frequent leaves of absence to appear with other European companies.

She made her American debut on Nov. 25, 1885, at the METROPOLITAN OPERA. Her role was CARMEN, and she made a favorable impression even though Carmen was never one of her outstanding interpretations. A more accurate measure of her art came five days later when she was heard as Brünnhilde in DIE WALKÜRE. Henry Krehbiel described her as "a most statuesquely beautiful Brünnhilde," with a voice "clear and ringing, never out of tune, and full of feeling." Lehmann stayed at the Metropolitan Opera until 1889, an idol. She created for America the roles of ISOLDE and Brünnhilde in SIEGFRIED and GÖTTERDÄMMERUNG. She was also acclaimed in DON GIOVANNI (Donna Anna), EURYANTHE, FIDELIO, and THE QUEEN OF SHEBA. She invested every role with nobility and dramatic fire, just as she brought to her singing a consummate technique and a profound understanding of style. She was one of the most versatile singers of any age, mastering about one hundred and seventy roles in one hundred and nineteen operas of the French, Italian, and German repertories, even including parts in comic operas.

Because she stayed in America beyond her leave of absence from the Berlin Opera, she became for a time *persona non grata* in German opera houses. On her return to Germany, she had to concentrate on song recitals, becoming a preeminent interpreter of *lieder*. In 1891 the Emperor lifted the ban against her. She returned to the Berlin Opera and to the other first-class opera stages of Germany and Austria, and renewed her triumphs. In 1896 she appeared in all three Brünnhilde roles at Bayreuth. After 1905 she was associated with the SALZBURG FESTIVALS both as a leading soprano and as director; her performances in the MOZART operas became a criterion. She returned to the United States in 1891 and during the next eight years appeared at the Metropolitan Opera and with the DAMROSCH OPERA COMPANY. Her last appearance at the Metropolitan took place on Mar. 25, 1899, in LES HUGUENOTS.

Besides her fruitful career as a prima

donna, Lehmann distinguished herself as one of the outstanding singing teachers of her generation. Many notable singers studied with her, including Geraldine FARRAR and Olive FREMSTAD, both of whom received practically their entire training from her.

Lehmann was the author of several books, including a treatise on singing published in English as *How to Sing* (1902); a study of *Fidelio* (1904); an autobiography, published in English as *My Path Through Life* (1914). She translated Victor MAUREL's *Dix Ans de carrière* into German and edited a volume of arias by Mozart.

Lehmann, Lotte, soprano. Born Perlberg, Ger., Feb. 27, 1888. In no way related to Lilli LEHMANN, Lotte Lehmann has occupied an imperial position in concert hall and opera house. Her music study took place at the Berlin Royal Academy of Music and privately with Mathilde MALLINGER. Between 1910 and 1913 she appeared at the HAMBURG OPERA, making her debut there as Freia in DAS RHEINGOLD. In 1914 she was invited to make a guest appearance at the VIENNA OPERA as AGATHE. She was so successful that she was immediately engaged on a permanent basis. It was in Vienna that she first sang the roles which were to spread her fame throughout Europe: SIEGLINDE, the MARSCHALLIN, Leonore in FIDELIO. She became a favorite of Richard STRAUSS, who selected her for the roles of the Young Composer in ARIADNE AUF NAXOS and Barak's wife in DIE FRAU OHNE SCHATTEN in the Vienna premieres of these operas; he wrote ARABELLA for her and invited her to create the role of Christine in INTERMEZZO. From the Austrian government she received the honorary title of KAMMERSÄNGERIN. Engagements in leading opera houses of Europe, and at the SALZBURG FESTIVALS, followed. On Oct. 28, 1930, she made her American debut with the CHICAGO OPERA in the role of Sieglinde. On Jan. 11, 1934, she made her first appearance at the METROPOLITAN OPERA, once again as Sieglinde. She

appeared at the Metropolitan in all her famous roles until 1945, repeating the triumphs she had earned abroad.

When the Nazis came to power, Lotte Lehmann renounced her native land and settled in Austria. After the Anschluss she came to the United States and became an American citizen. She made her last appearance at the Metropolitan on Mar. 29, 1945, in one of her greatest roles, that of the Marschallin. On Feb. 16, 1951, concluding a song recital at Town Hall, New York, she quietly announced to the audience that she was retiring from the concert stage. She then became head of the voice department of the Music Academy of the West in Santa Barbara, Cal. Though she retired from this post in 1962, she continued teaching classes in German *lieder* from time to time; and in 1962 the city of Vienna bestowed on her the Cross of Honor for Science and Art, First Class. In celebration of her eighty-first birthday, in Feb., 1969, a new auditorium at the Music Academy was named after her.

She has written several books, including a novel, *Eternal Flight* (1937), and three autobiographical volumes, *Wings of Song* (1937), *Midway in My Song* (1938), and *My Many Lives* (1948).

Leiden des jungen Werthers, Die, *see* GOETHE, JOHANN WOLFGANG VON.

Leider, Frida (soprano). Born Berlin, Apr. 18, 1888. She studied singing in Berlin and Milan, following which she made her opera debut in Halle, Germany. Successful appearances in opera and song recitals led to her engagement by the BERLIN OPERA, where for many years she appeared principally in the Wagnerian music dramas. In 1924 she appeared for the first time at COVENT GARDEN, as ISOLDE. In 1928, singing for the first time at BAYREUTH, she appeared as BRÜNNHILDE and KUNDRY. She came to the United States in 1928 and for four seasons appeared with the CHICAGO OPERA. On Jan. 16, 1933, she made her debut at the METROPOLITAN OPERA as Isolde, remaining with that company for two seasons. She then appeared with the VIENNA STATE OPERA and other major opera houses in Europe.

Leila, a priestess (soprano) in BIZET's LES PÊCHEURS DE PERLES.

Leinsdorf, Erich, conductor. Born Vienna, Feb. 4, 1912. He attended the Vienna Academy. In the summer of 1934 he became Bruno WALTER's assistant at the SALZBURG FESTIVAL, and the following year he was TOSCANINI's assistant there, besides helping prepare performances for the FLORENCE MAY MUSIC FESTIVAL. In the fall and winter of 1936 he conducted opera and orchestra concerts in Italy. On Jan. 21, 1938, he made his American debut at the METROPOLITAN OPERA with DIE WALKÜRE and was acclaimed. When Artur BODANZKY fell ill just before the opening of the Metropolitan's 1939–40 season, Leinsdorf assumed leadership of the entire WAGNER repertory; upon Bodanzky's death, Leinsdorf became his successor. In 1943 he left the Metropolitan to concentrate on symphonic music. He first became musical director of the Cleveland Orchestra and then, in 1947, of the Rochester Philharmonic. In 1956–57 he served as musical director of the NEW YORK CITY OPERA. During his brief regime the world premiere of HE WHO GETS SLAPPED (or *Pantaloon*), the American premieres of DER MOND and THE TEMPEST, and the New York premiere of SUSANNAH were given. He returned to the Metropolitan Opera in 1957 as "musical consultant" and conductor. In Sept., 1957, he led the American premiere of LES DIALOGUES DES CARMÉLITES with the SAN FRANCISCO OPERA, and in 1959 he conducted performances of DIE MEISTERSINGER at BAYREUTH. In the fall of 1962 he was appointed music director of the Boston Symphony. At the BERKSHIRE MUSIC FESTIVAL at Tanglewood, he conducted the Boston Symphony in concert performances of several operas, including the 1805 version of FIDELIO, THE MAGIC FLUTE, and LOHENGRIN (the last of these being presented in its entirety for the first time in the Western Hemisphere, performed one act an evening).

He resigned from the Boston Symphony in 1969 and devoted himself to appearances as guest conductor. In the fall of 1969 he made fifteen appearances at the TEATRO COLÓN.

Leise, leise, fromme Weise, Agathe's prayer in Act II of WEBER's DER FREISCHÜTZ, as, looking out the window, she contemplates the beauty of the night.

Leitmotiv, German for "leading motif," a melodic, harmonic, or rhythmic pattern or figure recurring throughout an opera to identify some person, thing, situation, feeling, or idea. The music dramas of WAGNER make extensive use of a series of leitmotivs. The device of a recurring musical motif was not new with Wagner. It is found, for instance, in the operas of WEBER, and BERLIOZ used the technique in his *Symphonie fantastique*. However, no one before Wagner used the device so extensively and so adroitly. Wagner frequently built up various melodic, rhythmic, and contrapuntal combinations of leitmotivs into elaborate symphonic textures.

Le jour se lève, Mireille's MUSETTE in Act III of GOUNOD's MIREILLE.

Lélio, Eleanora's husband (baritone) in WOLF-FERRARI's LE DONNE CURIOSE.

Lemnitz, Tiana, soprano. Born Metz, Lorraine, Oct. 26, 1897. Following her music study in her native city, she made her opera debut in Heilbronn in 1921. After being a member of the Aachen Opera from 1922 to 1929, she became the leading soprano of the HANOVER OPERA, serving there from 1929 to 1933. Between 1934 and 1957 she was principal soprano of the BERLIN STATE OPERA. During this time she made guest appearances in European and South American opera houses but never in the United States, despite an invitation to join the METROPOLITAN in 1936. She distinguished herself in an extensive repertory covering German, French, Italian, and Russian operas and was particularly acclaimed for her interpretations of the roles of PAMINA, OCTAVIAN, SIEGLINDE, and JENUFA.

Lemoyne, Jean-Baptiste (born Moyne),

composer and conductor. Born Eymet, France, Apr. 3, 1751; died Paris, Dec. 30, 1796. He studied in Berlin with Johann Philipp Kirnberger. For a while he was conductor for Frederick the Great at the Berlin Court Theater. After returning to Paris he falsely represented himself as GLUCK's pupil and in 1782 produced an opera, *Elektra,* written according to Gluck's ideas and principles. After *Elektra* failed, Gluck repudiated Lemoyne, insisting that he had never been the Frenchman's teacher. Out of revenge, Lemoyne began writing operas in the style of Nicola PICCINNI, Gluck's esthetic rival. The most successful were *Phèdre* (1786) and *Nepthé* (1789) .

Leningrad Opera, *see* BOLSHOI THEATER (1) .

Lensky, Eugene Onegin's friend (tenor) in TCHAIKOVSKY'S EUGENE ONEGIN.

Leo, Leonardo, composer and teacher. Born San Vito degli Schiavi, near Brindisi, Italy, Aug. 5, 1694; died Naples, Oct. 31, 1744. He attended the Conservatorio della Pietà dei Turchini in Naples, where one of his teachers was Alessandro SCARLATTI. His first success as an opera composer came with his *Sofonisba* in 1718. In all he wrote some fifty operas, many of them enormously popular in their time, a number being fine examples of the OPERA-BUFFA form. *Demofoönte* (1735) ; *Farnace* (1736) ; *L'Olimpiade* (1737) ; and *La contesa dell' Amore colla Virtù* (1744) were among his best productions. In 1725 Leo became a teacher at the Conservatorio di Sant' Onofrio in Naples. Here his pupils included Niccolò JOMMELLI, Giovanni Battista PERGOLESI, Nicola PICCINNI, and Antonio SACCHINI.

Leoncavallo, Ruggiero, composer. Born Naples, Mar. 8, 1858; died Montecatini, Italy, Aug. 9, 1919. He was the composer of PAGLIACCI. Soon after his graduation from the Bologna Conservatory he wrote his first opera, *Chatterton.* Hoping to get it produced, he turned his savings over to an irresponsible impresario, who absconded with the money. Leoncavallo now traveled extensively,

earning his way by teaching singing and piano and playing the piano. In Paris he wrote music-hall songs and played the piano in cabarets. Victor MAUREL, the baritone, became interested in him and introduced him to the Italian publisher, Ricordi, who commissioned him to write an operatic trilogy set in the Renaissance. The first opera of the set, *I Medici,* was turned down as too expensive to produce. Leoncavallo decided to write a more modest work in the realistic style of CAVALLERIA RUSTICANA, an opera then achieving a sensational success. Leoncavallo's, written in a space of four months, was *Pagliacci.* When it was introduced in Milan on May 21, 1892, with Maurel as Tonio and TOSCANINI conducting, it was a major triumph. Now famous and prosperous, Leoncavallo had his two earlier works performed. *I Medici* was given by LA SCALA in 1893 and *Chatterton* was given in Rome in 1896. Both were fiascos. Even the composer's later operas were poorly received. Indeed, the composer never achieved a second success remotely equivalent to *Pagliacci's,* which still maintains a secure place in the international repertoire. His LA BOHÈME (1897) was well received and is still very occasionally revived; but it suffered by comparison with PUCCINI's *La Bohème* (produced fifteen months earlier) right from the beginning. ZAZA (1900) was more splashily successful in the first quarter of this century, for it served as a fine vehicle for singing-actresses attracted by the central role of a Parisian music-hall singer with easy-going morals. Today it is very seldom heard, even in Italy. Leoncavallo, who always served as his own librettist, went on producing operas practically to the day of his death —in fact, the last two works, which were operettas, only reached the stage *post mortem.* None of them had any success to speak of, and he died an embittered man. The names and dates of these later works: *Maia* (1910) ; *Malbruk* (1910) ; *I zingari* (1912) ; *La reginetta delle rose* (1912) ; *Are You There?* (1913) ; *La candidata* (1915) ; *Goffredo Mameli*

(1916); *Prestami tua moglie* (1916); *À Chi la giarettiera* (1919); *Edipo Re* (1920); *Il primo bacio* (1923).

Leoni, Franco, composer. Born Milan, Oct. 24, 1864; died London, Feb. 8, 1949. He attended the Milan Conservatory, where he was a pupil of Amilcare PONCHIELLI. His first opera, *Raggio di Luna,* was produced in Milan in 1888. Four years later he settled in England. Here he produced *Rip Van Winkle* in 1897, and in 1905 the opera that made him internationally famous, L'ORACOLO. His other operas: *Ib and Little Christina* (1901); *Tzigana* (1908); *Francesca da Rimini* (1914); *Massemarello* (1920); *Le baruffe chiozzotte* (1920); *Falene* (1920); *La terra del sogno* (1921).

Leonora, (1) opera in three acts by William H. Fry. Libretto by Joseph R. Fry, adapted from BULWER-LYTTON's *The Lady of Lyons.* Premiere: Philadelphia, June 4, 1845. This work is generally now conceded to be the first grand opera by a native American composer. It was patterned after the Italian formula of DONIZETTI, BELLINI, and ROSSINI, with set numbers such as arias, duets, trios, recitatives, big choruses, and ensembles. At its premiere it was sung in English and had a run of twelve nights. An Italian company sang it in its own language at the Academy of Music in New York in 1858.

(2) Stradella's sweetheart (soprano) in FLOTOW's ALESSANDRO STRADELLA.

(3) The Marquis of Calatrava's daughter (soprano) in VERDI's LA FORZA DEL DESTINO.

(4) Manrico's beloved (soprano) in VERDI's IL TROVATORE, a role created by Rosina Penco.

Leonora de Guzman, King Alfonso's mistress (soprano) in DONIZETTI's LA FAVORITA.

Leonore, (1) Florestan's wife (soprano) in BEETHOVEN's FIDELIO, a role created by Anna MILDER-HAUPTMANN.

(2) The heroine (soprano) and Gotthold's beloved in DITTERSDORF's THE DOCTOR AND THE APOTHECARY.

Leonore 40/45, "opera semiseria" in seven scenes, with prologue and prelude, by LIEBERMANN. Libretto by Heinrich Strobel. Premiere: Basel, Switzerland, Mar. 26, 1952.

The heroine is Yvette, a French girl (used as a symbol for European culture). She falls in love with Albert, a German soldier during World War II, who has learned that he is being called into the army during a radio broadcast of BEETHOVEN's FIDELIO. While the war is on, Albert and Yvette meet at a concert. Though they are enemies by nationality, they fall in love. Albert defects from the army; he and Yvette find jobs and get married. A tribunal (symbolic of bureaucracy) refuses to legalize this union until papers carrying heavenly seals sanction the marriage.

The term "opera semiseria" is a Liebermann invention, implying that the opera moves on two levels, satiric and dramatic. Satire is found in a choral episode where concert audiences reject modern music, in the way in which the music of other composers is interpolated into the score, and in the criticism of bureaucracy. Drama comes through the efforts of two lovers to find personal happiness and the efforts of dark, unseen powers to keep them apart. The text employs both the French and German languages, sometimes alternately, sometimes simultaneously. The music is dodecaphonic, though there are some extraordinarily fine lyrical passages, such as the love duet of Albert and Yvette in Scene 2 and Albert's poignant expression of his longing for Yvette in Scene 4.

Leonore Overtures, Nos. 1, 2, 3, *see* FIDELIO.

Léopold, a prince (tenor) in love with Rachel in HALÉVY's LA JUIVE.

Leporello, Don Giovanni's servant (bass) in MOZART's DON GIOVANNI.

Le Rêve, *see* EN FERMANT LES YEUX.

Leroux, Xavier, composer. Born Velletri, Italy, Oct. 11, 1863; died Paris, Feb. 2, 1919. He attended the Paris Conservatory, winning the PRIX DE ROME in 1885. He began writing for the theater in 1890 by composing incidental music for a play by Victorien SARDOU and

Emile Moreau, *Cléopâtre*. Five years later his first opera, EVANGÉLINE, was produced in Brussels. His next opera, *Astarté,* introduced by the PARIS OPÉRA in 1901, was a major success. Two later operas were acclaimed: LA REINE FIAM-METTE, given by the OPÉRA-COMIQUE in 1903 with Mary GARDEN as Orlanda; and *Le Chemineau,* introduced by the Opéra-Comique in 1907. From 1896 to the time of his death Leroux taught harmony at the Paris Conservatory. His other operas: *William Ratcliffe* (1906); *Théodora* (1907); *Le Carillonneur* (1913); *La Fille de Figaro* (1914); *Les Cadeaux de Noël* (1916); *1814* (1918); *Nausithoé* (1920); *La Plus Forte* (1924).

Lert, Ernst, conductor, stage director, opera manager. Born Vienna, May 12, 1883; died Baltimore, Md., Jan. 30, 1955. He received his doctorate from the University of Vienna in 1908. He then became associated with several German and Austrian opera companies as assistant director and coach. From 1920 to 1923 he was general director of the FRANK-FURT OPERA, and from 1923 to 1929 he was the stage director of LA SCALA during Arturo TOSCANINI's artistic direction. He came to the United States in 1929 and for two seasons was stage director of the METROPOLITAN OPERA. Subsequently, he directed opera performances in various American cities and in Paris, Salzburg, Florence, Spain, and South America. From 1936 to 1938 he was head of the opera department of the Curtis Institute of Music in Philadelphia. In 1950 he became director of opera at the Peabody Institute in Baltimore. He is the author of *Mozart auf dem Theater* (1918) and of a biography of the conductor Otto LOHSE (1918).

le Sage, Alain René, novelist and dramatist. Born Sarzeau, France, May 8, 1668; died Boulogne, Nov. 17, 1747. His most celebrated novel, *Gil Blas,* was the source of Théophile Semet's opera of the same name, while an episode from that story was used in LESUEUR's *La Caverne.* Le Sage's drama *Le Diable boiteux* was the source for BALFE's *Satanella,* FRANCAIX's LE DIABLE BOITEUX,

and HAYDN's *Der neue krumme Teufel.* GLUCK's comic opera *La Rencontre imprévue* came from a Le Sage comedy.

Lescaut, (1) cousin of Manon Lescaut, a guardsman (baritone), in MAS-SENET's MANON.

(2) Manon Lescaut's brother (baritone) in PUCCINI's MANON LESCAUT.

Les oiseaux dans la charmille (Air de la poupée, Doll Song), the coloratura aria delivered by Olympia, the mechanical doll, after having been wound up by Spalanzani for the delectation of his guests, in Act I of OFFENBACH's TALES OF HOFFMANN.

Lesueur, Jean-François, composer. Born Drucat-Plessiel, France, Feb. 15, 1760; died Paris, Oct. 6, 1837. He received some musical training in two monasteries, but for the most part he was self-taught. Going to Paris in 1784, he presently became MAÎTRE DE CHAPELLE at Notre Dame, where he inaugurated ambitious performances of church music. He was forced to leave this post in 1788 when he was accused of extravagance in spending church funds for these concerts and of degrading the dignity of the church. Turning to dramatic music, Lesueur wrote his first opera, *La Caverne,* in 1793. It was successful, and so was his second, *Paul et Virginie* (1794). He wrote many operas after this, some of them enormously popular. His best operas, besides those mentioned, were: *Télémaque* (1796); *Ossian* (1804); and *La Mort d'Adam* (1809). He was made an official of the Paris Conservatory at its founding in 1795. In 1804 he became *maître de chapelle* to Napoleon. In 1818 he became a professor of composition at the Conservatory: his pupils included BER-LIOZ, GOUNOD, and THOMAS. He succeeded André GRÉTRY as a member of the Institut de France.

Let not a moon-born elf mislead me, Grimaldi's song in Act II of PURCELL's KING ARTHUR.

Let's Make an Opera, children's opera in two acts by BRITTEN. Libretto by Eric Crozier. Premiere: Aldeburgh Festival, June 14, 1949. American premiere: St.

Louis, Mar. 22, 1950. In this simple and straightforward musical play for children, composer and librettist demonstrate how an opera is written and produced. In the first act are discussed the problems facing composer, librettist, and producer—a discussion in which six children and five adults take part. In the second act, the opera these actors develop is performed. It is called *The Little Sweep*. One of the novel features of *The Little Sweep* is the presence of several choruses to be sung by the audience. The audience is taught its part during the intermission between acts.

Letter Duet, (1) *see* CHE SOAVE ZEFFIRETTO.

(2) *See* VOICI CE QU'IL ÉCRIT.

Letter Scene, Tatiana's aria in Act I, Scene 2, of TCHAIKOVSKY'S EUGENE ONEGIN.

Leukippos, a shepherd (tenor) in love with Daphne, in Richard STRAUSS'S DAPHNE.

Levasseur, Nicolas Prosper, bass. Born Bresles, France, Mar. 9, 1791; died Paris, Dec. 7, 1871. He attended the Paris Conservatory and made his debut in 1813 at the PARIS OPÉRA. After two successful seasons at the KING'S THEATRE in London, he rejoined the Opéra in 1816 and for six years acted chiefly as an understudy. In 1822 he was acclaimed in Milan for his performance in MEYERBEER'S *Marguerite d'Anjou*. This success brought him a five-year contract with the Théâtre des Italiens in Paris. From 1828 to 1853 he was the principal bass of the Paris Opéra, creating the leading bass roles in several important operas including Meyerbeer's ROBERT LE DIABLE (1832), LES HUGUENOTS (1836), and LE PROPHÈTE (1849). In 1841 he was appointed professor of lyric declamation at the Paris Conservatory. After retiring from the opera stage in 1853 he concentrated on teaching, remaining at the Conservatory until a year before his death.

Levasseur, Rosalie, soprano. Born Valenciennes, France, Oct. 8, 1749; died Neuwied-am-Rhein, Ger., May 6, 1826. She created the leading female roles in GLUCK'S ARMIDE and IPHIGÉNIE EN TAURIDE. As Mlle. Rosalie, she made her debut in Paris in 1776 in Gluck's ORFEO ED EURIDICE. As Rosalie Levasseur, she succeeded Sophie ARNOULD as leading soprano of the OPÉRA, where she appeared in world premieres of operas by PHILIDOR, PICCINNI, SACCHINI, and others.

Le veau d'or, Méphistophélès' scornful song about man's greed for gold, to the village crowd in Act II of GOUNOD'S FAUST.

Levi, Hermann, conductor. Born Giessen, Ger., Nov. 7, 1839; died Munich, May 13, 1900. A celebrated conductor of WAGNER, he directed the world premiere of PARSIFAL. After studying in Mannheim with Vincenz Lachner and at the Leipzig Conservatory, he became music director at Saarbrücken, holding this post from 1859 to 1861. For the next three years he conducted German operas in Rotterdam. In 1872 he was engaged as principal conductor of the MUNICH OPERA, where he remained almost a quarter of a century, particularly distinguishing himself in the Wagner dramas. In 1882 he was invited by Wagner to conduct the premiere of *Parsifal* in BAYREUTH. A year later he led the musical performance at Wagner's funeral services in Bayreuth. In 1894 he was appointed music director of the Munich Court Theater, but poor health compelled him to resign two years later. He edited COSÌ FAN TUTTE, DON GIOVANNI, and THE MARRIAGE OF FIGARO, and translated into German the librettos of LES TROYENS and GWENDOLINE.

Levko, the headman's son (tenor) and Hanna's sweetheart, in RIMSKY-KORSAKOV'S MAY NIGHT.

Libiamo, libiamo (BRINDISI), the drinking song of Alfred Germont and Violetta, in Act I of VERDI'S LA TRAVIATA.

libretto, an Italian term, literally "little book," but specifically a term used for the text, or play, of an opera. The earliest librettos for Italian operas were highly standardized, the subjects usually dealing with mythological or historical subjects. Such librettos were written at the beginning of the seventeenth century by the poet Ottavio RINUCCINI for the very first composers of opera: PERI, CACCINI, and MONTE-VERDI. A century later Pietro METAS-TASIO, favoring historical subjects over mythological, wrote some thirty dramatically sound librettos that, being set by composer after composer, made him one of the dominant figures of eighteenth-century Italian opera. The poet Raniero de CALZABIGI, author of the librettos for GLUCK'S ALCESTE and ORFEO ED EURIDICE, was the first influential opera dramatist to break away from the traditional forms established by Metastasio. The revolt was carried further by Lorenzo DA PONTE, author of the librettos for MOZART'S COSÌ FAN TUTTE, DON GIOVANNI, and THE MARRIAGE OF FIGARO. A French libretto tradition was established by Pierre Perrin and Philippe QUINAULT in their texts for operas by Jean-Baptiste LULLY. Important later writers of librettos in France include Eugène SCRIBE, who provided texts for AUBER, MEYERBEER, and HALÉVY; Henri Meilhac (texts for MASSENET and BIZET); and the collaborators Jules BARBIER and Michel CARRÉ (for Meyerbeer, GOUNOD, THOMAS, and OFFENBACH). The important Italian librettists of the nineteenth century include Felice ROMANI (texts for BELLINI and DONIZETTI); Francesco Maria PIAVE (for VERDI); Arrigo BOITO (Verdi and PONCHIELLI); and the collaborators Giuseppe Giacosa and Luigi ILLICA (PUCCINI). The notable figure among German librettists is Hugo von HOF-MANNSTHAL, the author linked with the operas of Richard STRAUSS. The composer who wrote his own texts was, preeminently, WAGNER. Others include CHARPENTIER (LOUISE) and Ruggiero LEONCAVALLO (PAGLIACCI). An outstanding present-day example of a librettist-composer is MENOTTI. Another source for an opera libretto is a spoken drama, set to music with little or no alteration. An instance is DEBUSSY'S PELLÉAS ET MÉLISANDE, using MAETERLINCK'S poetic play of the same name.

Libuše, opera in three acts by SMETANA. Libretto by Joseph Wenzig. Premiere: National Theater, Prague, June 11, 1881. Two brothers, Chrudos and Stahlav, vie for the love of Krasava. They are brought to trial before Libuše, Queen of Bohemia. Chrudos is contemptuous about appearing before a woman and insults her, an incident that has wide repercussions. The Queen descends from her throne in favor of a man who can rule the land with iron hand. She marries such a man, and the new king effects a reconciliation of the two brothers after Chrudos apologizes to Libuše.

Libuše's aria "Eternal Gods" in Act I and her prophecy in Act III are the two best-known vocal excerpts.

Licinius, a general in the Roman army (tenor), in love with Giulia, in SPONTINI'S LA VESTALE.

Liebe der Danae, Die (Danae's Love), opera in three acts by Richard STRAUSS. Libretto by Joseph Gregor. Premiere: Salzburg Festival, Aug. 14, 1952. American premiere: Los Angeles, Apr. 5, 1964. Strauss completed this opera in 1940. Stylistically he reverted to the Wagnerian influences of his youth. The libretto combines two mythological stories, that of Danae and that of Midas. Danae (soprano), daughter of King Pollux, is sought by Midas (tenor) and by Jupiter (baritone); the latter assumes Midas' form in trying to win her. Jupiter threatens Midas with the loss of his golden touch and a return to human status if he does not give up Danae. The latter is ready to share Midas' humble fate and rejects the mighty Jupiter. She becomes a housewife in a dreary hut, where Jupiter reappears to tempt her with wealth and power. But once again she rejects him. Touched by her devotion, Jupiter finally gives the pair his blessing.

Liebermann, Rolf, composer and opera director. Born Zürich, Sept. 14, 1910. He studied with Hermann SCHERCHEN and Vladimir Vogel, after which he conducted various Swiss orchestras. He first came to prominence as a composer with the opera LEONORE 40/45, which excited considerable controversy following its premiere in Basel in 1952. His second opera, PENELOPE, was well received when introduced in Salzburg in 1954. Both works were designated by the composer as "opera semiseria" to indicate that they proceeded on two levels: the humorous and satiric, and the serious and dramatic. The SCHOOL FOR WIVES, commissioned by the Louisville Philharmonic Orchestra, was introduced in Louisville, Ky., in 1957. Here the composer abandons the TWELVE-TONE TECHNIQUES employed in his earlier operas for a consonant, neobaroque style, utilizing economical forces. In addition to his operas, Liebermann has produced a considerable amount of concert music, including the *Concerto for Jazz Band and Orchestra,* which was widely performed in America and Europe following its premiere at the Donaueschingen Festival in Germany on Oct. 17, 1954. After being on the music staff of the Swiss Radio Corporation in Zürich for many years, Liebermann was appointed in 1962 music director of the HAMBURG OPERA, which he developed into one of the most progressive operatic institutions in the world. In 1967 he brought his company for its first appearances across the Atlantic for performances at Expo 67 in Montreal and at the LINCOLN CENTER FOR THE PERFORMING ARTS in New York.

Liebesnacht: O sink' hernieder, Nacht der Liebe, the love duet of Tristan and Isolde in the garden of the castle, in Act II of WAGNER'S TRISTAN UND ISOLDE. **Liebestod: Mild und leise wie er lächelt,** Isolde's farewell to the dead Tristan in her arms, as she presents her last message of love and begs for deliverance in death, in Act III of WAGNER'S TRISTAN UND ISOLDE.

Liebesverbot, Das (Love's Prohibition), opera in two acts by WAGNER. Libretto by the composer, based on SHAKESPEARE'S *Measure for Measure.* Premiere: Magdeburg Opera, Mar. 29, 1836. This, Wagner's second complete opera, was a fiasco. Claudio, an aristocrat, is arrested for fornication (a crime) and is to be executed. His sister, Isabella, arouses a mob against the Governor, who is then forced to abrogate the unreasonable law. Wagner's music is here strongly influenced by BELLINI and ROSSINI.

Liebling, Estelle, singer and voice teacher. Born New York City, Apr. 21, 1884; died there, Sept. 25, 1970. She studied voice with Mme. MARCHESI in Paris and Nicklass-Kempner in Berlin. After making her debut as LUCIA at the DRESDEN OPERA, she appeared with the STUTTGART OPERA, the OPÉRA-COMIQUE, and the METROPOLITAN OPERA, making her debut at the latter on Feb. 24, 1902, as Marguerite in LES HUGUENOTS. She was, however, most celebrated as a teacher of singing, serving as professor at the Curtis Institute from 1936 to 1938, and after that teaching privately. Among her many pupils were Titta RUFFO, Göta LJUNGBERG, Max LORENZ, Maria MÜLLER, Marie Rappold, Irra Pettina, and Beverly SILLS. Her brother, Leonard Liebling, was a noted music critic in New York and editor of *Musical Courier.*

Liederspiel, German for "song-play." This term was sometimes used interchangeably with the more familiar one of SINGSPIEL for a popular musical play combining dialogue and songs in the German and Austrian theater of the eighteenth century.

Life for the Czar, A (or Ivan Susanin), opera in five acts by GLINKA. Libretto by Baron von Rosen. Premiere: Imperial Theater, St. Petersburg, Dec. 9, 1836. American premiere: New York City, Nov. 14, 1871 (concert version); San Francisco, Dec. 12, 1936 (staged).

Characters: Ivan Susanin, a peasant (bass); Antonida, his daughter (soprano); Vanya, Susanin's adopted son (contralto); Bogdan Sabinin, Antonida's betrothed (tenor); Sigismund, the Polish king (bass); a Russian soldier; a Polish messenger; peasants; soldiers; Polish ladies and gentlemen. The action takes place in Russia and Poland in the winter of 1612.

Act I. The village of Domnino, Russia. News arrives of the defeat of the Poles by the Russians. Antonida thinks of her love for Sabinin (Antonida's

CAVATINA: "My gaze is fixed on the fields"). She is ready to marry him as soon as peace returns to Russia.

Act II. The camp of the Poles. A Polish festival is being celebrated with the dancing of a POLONAISE, MAZURKA, and WALTZ. The Polish soldiers vow to fight on until they achieve victory. When they hear that Romanov has been made Czar of Russia they decide to advance against him.

Act III. Susanin's hut. It is Antonida's wedding day, hailed by the bridal chorus "Spring waters flow over the fields." The Poles compel Susanin to lead them to the new Czar. Susanin secretly plans to defend Romanov with his life.

Act IV, Scene 1. Before a monastery. Vanya urges his followers to save Romanov from the Poles. In rushing forth, he rides his horse to its death.

Scene 2. A wood. Susanin is leading the Poles through the snow, not to the Czar but on a false trail. He soon realizes that the Poles have guessed what he is up to ("They guess the truth"). The price of Susanin's heroic deed is his life.

Act V. Before the Kremlin. In a festive ceremony, the new Czar comes to Moscow, hailed by a mighty chorus of the people. He honors Antonida Sabinin and Vanya for their loyalty. He also laments the death of the hero Susanin. The people once again raise their voices in a hymn to their Czar. (The opening and closing choruses of this act are based on the *Slavsia,* old Russian songs of praise).

A Life for the Czar, Glinka's first opera, has greater historic than esthetic interest. Except for two fine arias (those of Antonida in Act I and Susanin in Act IV), several stirring choruses (particularly the closing hymn), and some delightful folk dances, the opera means little to present-day audiences outside Russia. The libretto is diffuse and confusing, the combination of Italian lyric style with Russian national elements is often disturbing, and many of the numbers are banal. But the opera's place in history is secure. As the first Russian national opera, it showed the way for such later masters as DARGOMIZHSKY, MUSSORGSKY, RIMSKY-KORSAKOV, and BORODIN.

The premiere of *A Life for the Czar* was a success. But apparently the audiences of 1836 liked the opera for the wrong things. What they admired was the Italian-influenced arias; the typically Russian portions of the work were largely ignored. Some critics, speaking of Glinka's use of folk songs and dances, sardonically referred to the score as "coachman's music."

Light as fairy feet, the chorus of the elves in the opening of WEBER'S OBERON.

light opera, a term used interchangeably with operetta to designate a romantic play featuring songs (and sometimes dances) and spoken dialogue.

Lincoln Center for the Performing Arts, a center in New York City comprising two opera houses, Philharmonic Hall, theaters, a library of the performing arts, and the Juilliard School of Music. The METROPOLITAN OPERA built here its new auditorium, opening on Sept. 16, 1966, with the world premiere of BARBER'S ANTONY AND CLEOPATRA. The NEW YORK CITY OPERA transferred its production to the New York State Theater at the Center, opening on Feb. 22, 1966, with the American premiere of GINASTERA'S DON RODRIGO.

Lincoln's Inn Fields Theatre, a theater which figured in HANDEL's career. It was built in 1714 by Christopher Rich and opened after his death by his son John. Here, in 1727, THE BEGGAR'S OPERA was first performed. In 1732 John Rich moved his activities to COVENT GARDEN and for two seasons the Lincoln's Inn Fields Theatre was the home for various entertainments. In 1734 Italian opera was produced here in direct opposition to Handel's ventures; Niccolò PORPORA was the leading composer, SENESINO the principal singer. Subsequently, Handel used this theater for performances of some of his operas and oratorios. The building was last used as a theater in 1756. Ninety years later it was demolished and the site used by the College of Surgeons.

Lind, Jenny, soprano. Born Stockholm, Oct. 6, 1820; died Wynd's Point, Malvern, Eng., Nov. 2, 1887. The "Swedish Nightingale" was the most celebrated singer to come from Sweden and one of the most glamorous prima donnas of the nineteenth century. She began the study of singing at the school of the Stockholm Court Theater when she was nine. On Mar. 7, 1838, she made her debut with the STOCKHOLM ROYAL OPERA as AGATHE. Her successes during the next few years were brilliant enough, but in 1841, dissatisfied with her technique, she went to Paris to study with Manuel GARCÍA. MEYERBEER heard her at this time and used his influence to gain her an appointment with the BERLIN OPERA. After making her Berlin debut as NORMA, she appeared in the Viennese premiere of EIN FELDLAGER IN SCHLESIEN in 1846. She was a sensation. Triumphant performances followed in principal German cities, Stockholm, and Copenhagen. In Vienna, where she made her debut as Norma in 1846, she aroused such a pitch of excitement that she had to take some thirty curtain calls; at a benefit performance of LA SONNAMBULA, the Empress tossed a royal wreath on the stage, an act without precedent. In London she was an idol after her first appearance there in ROBERT LE DIABLE in 1849. Though outstanding in dramatic roles, she was particularly famous in coloratura parts, where the purity of her voice and its remarkable range and flexibility aroused the greatest enthusiasm.

After 1849 she withdrew from opera and devoted herself exclusively to concert recitals and appearances in oratorio. She visited the United States in 1850 and for two years made extensive concert tours under the management of P. T. Barnum. In 1852 in Boston, she married Otto Goldschmidt, her concert conductor. After 1856 they lived mostly in England. Jenny Lind made one of her last public appearances in 1870 at the Rhenish Music Festival in Düsseldorf in a performance of her husband's oratorio *Ruth*. In 1883 she became a teacher of singing at the Royal College of Music in London. Two years after her death a memorial medallion was unveiled in Westminster Abbey.

Linda di Chamounix, opera in three acts by DONIZETTI. Libretto by Gaetano ROSSI. Premiere: Kärntnerthortheater, Vienna, May 19, 1842. American premiere: New York City, Jan. 4, 1847. Linda is in love with the young painter, Charles, who is actually a nobleman in disguise. When she thinks herself deserted she goes mad. But the apparent desertion was only a misunderstanding. After Charles returns to Linda and reminds her of their love by singing an old love song, she recovers her sanity. Linda's aria in Act I, "O luce di quest' anima," and her Mad Scene in Act II, "Linda! A che pensato" are famous. So are "A consolarmi affretisi," the Act I love duet of Charles and Linda, and Linda's closing aria, "Ah! di tu pene sparve il sogno." The role of Linda was created by Eugenia Tadolini.

Lindorf, councilor of Nuremberg (bass), in the Prologue and Epilogue of OFFENBACH'S THE TALES OF HOFFMANN. His other identities are Coppélius, Dapertutto, and Dr. Miracle.

Lindoro, (1) the name assumed by Count Almaviva to woo Rosina in ROSSINI'S THE BARBER OF SEVILLE.

(2) A favorite slave (tenor) of the Mustafa in ROSSINI'S L'ITALIANA IN ALGERI.

linear music, *see* HINDEMITH, PAUL.

Linette, a princess (contralto) hidden in an orange in PROKOFIEV'S THE LOVE FOR THREE ORANGES.

Lionel, young man (tenor) in love with Harriet, in FLOTOW'S MARTHA.

Lipton, Martha, mezzo-soprano. Born New York City, Apr. 6, 1915. She was graduated from the Juilliard School of Music in 1940. Following numerous concert appearances, she made her opera debut in COSÌ FAN TUTTE in Mar., 1941, with the New Opera Company in New York. On Nov. 27, 1941, she made her debut at the METROPOLITAN OPERA as Siebel in FAUST. During the next twenty years she was heard in over thirty-five roles in thirty operas, including the American premiere of THE RAKE'S PROGRESS in 1953. She has appeared in such leading opera houses as the TEATRO COLÓN, the VIENNA STATE OPERA, and the PARIS OPÉRA and has sung in operas at several of Europe's leading festivals, including those of HOLLAND and EDINBURGH.

Lisa, (1) an innkeeper (soprano), in love with Elvino, in BELLINI'S LA SONNAMBULA.

(2) The Countess' granddaughter (soprano), for whose love Herman and Prince Yeletsky are rivals, in TCHAIKOVSKY'S PIQUE DAME.

List, Emanuel, bass. Born Vienna, Mar. 22, 1891; died there, June 21, 1967. After appearing as boy soprano and later as a member of a vocal quartet in Europe, he came to the United States and received his first systematic vocal instruction from Josiah Zuro in New York. In 1921 he returned to Europe, and a year later he made his debut at the Vienna VOLKSOPER as Méphistophélès in FAUST. Two years later he was engaged by the BERLIN STATE OPERA, where he remained a decade, successful in leading German bass roles, particularly those of HUNDING and Baron OCHS. He also appeared at the festivals of BAYREUTH, SALZBURG, and MUNICH. On Dec. 27, 1933, he made his debut at the METROPOLITAN OPERA as Hermann in TANNHÄUSER. He remained at the Metropolitan seventeen seasons, appearing in the principal Wagnerian music dramas and Richard STRAUSS operas, among other works. He also made numerous guest appearances with other leading opera houses in America, Europe, and South America.

Liszt, Franz, composer, pianist, and conductor. Born Raiding, Hungary, Oct. 22, 1811; died Bayreuth, July 31, 1886. His significance in opera rests on his encouragement of and sympathy with Richard WAGNER, whose father-in-law he became, as well as on his achievements as KAPELLMEISTER in Weimar, where between 1848 and 1859 he conducted opera performances. He presented the world premieres of THE BARBER OF BAGDAD and LOHENGRIN, together with such novelties as GENOVEVA, *Alfonso und Estrella* (SCHUBERT), BENVENUTO CELLINI, as well as TANNHÄUSER and DER FLIEGENDE HOLLÄNDER. In his youth Liszt had written a one-act operetta, *Don Sanche,* introduced in Paris in 1825, when it received four performances.

Little Sweep, The, *see* LET'S MAKE AN OPERA.

Litvinne, Félia (born Françoise-Jeanne Schütz), soprano. Born St. Petersburg, Russia, 1860; died Paris, Oct. 12, 1936. She studied singing with Victor MAUREL and Giovanni SBRIGLIA. She made her debut in 1882 at the Théâtre des Italiens in Paris in HÉRODIADE. She then appeared for a season with the MAPLESON company in New York. In 1886 she made her debut at the PARIS OPÉRA, establishing herself as a favorite in the Wagnerian music dramas. On Nov. 25, 1896, she made her debut at the METROPOLITAN OPERA in LES HUGUENOTS. She remained at the Metropolitan only one season. Her subsequent career in Europe included appearances at LA SCALA and COVENT GARDEN. After leaving the stage in 1917, she devoted herself to teaching, becoming a professor of singing at the American Conservatory at Fontainebleau in 1927. She wrote an autobiography, *Ma Vie et mon art* (1933).

Liù, a young slave girl (soprano), in love with Calaf, in PUCCINI'S TURANDOT.

Lizzie Borden, opera in three acts by BEESON. Libretto by Kneward Elmslie, based on a scenario by Richard Plant. Premiere: New York City Opera, Mar. 25, 1965. The story is based on the celebrated murder trial in Fall River, Mass., in 1893, which has been retold in several books and a ballet. Lizzie Borden was accused of having murdered her wealthy father and stepmother with an ax. In the trial she was acquitted. The opera text is treated with Freudian insight and, adds Peter G. Davis, "with more than a casual backward glance at the classic Electra tragedies." Mr. Davis finds that Beeson's music "does a splendid job in projecting the smothered, tortuous, and carefully considered intensity that always seems to attend New Englanders when they go berserk: an obsessive, smoldering sense of evil pervades the entire fabric of the drama and becomes all the more terrible when it finally erupts into deed." Davis selects a "florid Victorian genre piece" (Abigaille's "Hirondelle" aria) as one of the highlights of the score.

Ljungberg, Göta, soprano. Born Sundsvall, Sweden, Oct. 4, 1893; died Lidingo, near Stockholm, June 28, 1955. She studied singing at the Stockholm Royal Academy and the Royal Opera School. Her debut took place in 1920 at the STOCKHOLM ROYAL OPERA as ELSA. In 1925 she sang at COVENT GARDEN. Eugene GOOSSENS wrote his opera *Judith* for her. She next appeared for three seasons at the BERLIN OPERA, where she was acclaimed in the Wagnerian repertory. On Jan. 20, 1932, she made her American debut at the METROPOLITAN OPERA in DIE WALKÜRE. She appeared at the Metropolitan through the 1934–35 season, specializing in the WAGNER operas and scoring outstanding success in the world premiere of MERRY MOUNT and in a revival of SALOME in which she herself performed the Dance of the Seven Veils. After leaving the Metropolitan, she appeared extensively in Europe. For several years after 1945 she taught singing in New York, after which she returned to Sweden.

L'oca del Cairo (The Goose of Cairo), an unfinished opera by MOZART consisting merely of several completed vocal numbers. See DON PEDRO.

Lodoïska, opera in three acts by CHERUBINI. Libretto by Claude François Fillette Loraux. Premiere: Théâtre Feydeau, Paris, July 18, 1791. American premiere: New York City, Dec. 4, 1826. Several operas were written on the same subject, one of which, with music by Rodolphe KREUTZER, was given only two weeks after that of Cherubini. Cherubini's opera was the first to make his name known throughout Europe and to present him as a reformer of Italian opera. It was a huge success at its premiere, receiving nearly two hundred performances in its first year. The heroine is in love with Floreski, a prisoner in the castle of Dourlinski, who desires Lodoïska for himself. He forgets about her, however, when the castle is attacked by the Tartars, and Lodoïska is rescued by her lover.

Lodoletta, opera in three acts by MASCAGNI. Libretto by Gioacchino Forzano, based on *Two Little Wooden Shoes*, a children's story by Ouida. Premiere: Teatro Costanzi, Apr. 30, 1917. American premiere: Metropolitan Opera, Jan. 12, 1918. At a birthday party for Lodoletta, a sweet and naive country girl in Holland, she meets a rich and sophisticated Parisian painter. Later she poses for him; she rejects her country swain, and after her stepfather dies, follows the painter, Flammen, to Paris and arrives at his house on New Year's Eve while a party is in progress. She does not have the courage to enter. Aimlessly she wanders in the snow, and dies of cold and starvation. Flammen finds her and takes her in his arms, lamenting that he has always been in love with her. Two arias, both from Act III, have become popular. One is Flammen's "Ah! ritrovarla nella sua capanna," the other Lodoletta's "Flammen, perdonami."

Lodovico, Ambassador to the Venetian Republic (bass) in VERDI'S OTELLO.

Loge, god of fire (tenor) in WAGNER'S DAS RHEINGOLD, a role created by Heinrich VOGL.

Logroscino, Nicola, composer. Born Bitonto, Italy, Oct., 1698; died Palermo, Sicily, about 1765. He studied with Francesco Mancini and Giovanni Veneziano. From 1728 to 1731 he was an organist. After settling in Naples (about 1738) he became a deservedly popular composer of comic operas, his works remaining in vogue until the ascendancy of PICCINNI. His finest operas were: *L'inganno per inganno* (1738); *La violanta* (1741); *Il governatore* (1747); *Tanto bene che male; Il vecchio marito; La furba burlata* (1760), the last a collaboration with Nicola Piccinni.

Lohengrin, opera in three acts by WAG-

NER. Libretto by the composer, based on medieval legends. Premiere: Weimar, Aug. 28, 1850. American premiere: Stadt Theater, New York, Apr. 3, 1871.

Characters: Henry the Fowler, King of Germany (bass); Frederick of Telramund, Count of Brabant (baritone); Ortrud, his wife (mezzo-soprano); Elsa of Brabant (soprano); Lohengrin, Knight of the Holy Grail (tenor); a herald (bass); Gottfried, Elsa's brother (silent role); nobles of Saxony and Brabant; gentlemen and ladies of the court; pages; attendants. The action takes place in and near Antwerp early in the tenth century.

Act I. The banks of the Scheldt River. The orchestral prelude, symbolizing the HOLY GRAIL, is wrought entirely of the Grail theme. King Henry, desiring to build up an army to fight the Hungarians, finds the people of Brabant, whom he greets in "Gott grüss euch," torn apart by dissension. Telramund reveals that much of the trouble arises from the suspicion that Elsa has murdered her young brother in order to make a bid for the throne of Brabant. Called before King Henry to defend herself against this charge, Elsa tells of a strange dream in which a knight appeared to tell her he will be her protector (Elsa's Dream: "Einsam in trüben Tagen"). Telramund insists that his accusations against Elsa are well founded; he is ready to fight anyone who questions his veracity. When the King asks Elsa who her champion is to be, she mentions the knight of her dreams and says she will be his bride ("Des Ritters will ich waren"). The King's herald then twice calls on her champion to appear, but there is no answer. Elsa falls on her knees and prays for her deliverer to come (Elsa's Prayer: "Du trugest zu ihm meine Klage"). There now appears a swan-drawn boat bearing the Knight Lohengrin. After Lohengrin bids his swan farewell ("Nun sei bedankt, mein lieber Schwan"), he approaches King Henry and announces his intention of championing Elsa. Elsa promises her hand in marriage to Lohengrin if he is victori-

ous. In return, Lohengrin extracts from her the promise that she will not attempt to discover his name, who he is, or from where he has come. When Elsa gives the promise, he confides his love to her. After King Henry offers a prayer for the contestants ("Mein Herr und Gott, nun ruf' ich dich"), the duel between Telramund and Lohengrin takes place. Lohengrin, the victor, generously spares the life of the defeated and shamed Telramund. The crowd hails the victor ("O fänd' ich Jubelweisen").

Act II. The courtyard of the fortress of Antwerp. Telramund and his wife Ortrud are in disgrace. They vow to seek vengeance ("Der Rache Werk"). Ortrud conceives a method of defeating Lohengrin and regaining their lost station: Elsa must make the mysterious knight reveal his identity, thus depriving him of his magic powers. At this point Elsa appears on the balcony outside her bedroom and speaks of her happiness ("Euch lüften, die mein Klagen"). Ortrud begs Elsa for forgiveness and Elsa promises to do what she can to gain clemency for her and her husband. At the same time she reaffirms her faith in and love for her champion. Dawn breaks. The square is filled with courtiers and knights who hail the day of Elsa's wedding ("In Früh'n versammelt uns der Ruf"). As Elsa and her retinue make their way from the fortress toward the cathedral, the people acclaim her ("Heil dir, Elsa von Brabant"). Elsa is about to mount the cathedral steps when she is stopped by Ortrud who accuses Lohengrin of being a black magician whose defeat of Telramund was achieved by foul means. Elsa denounces her for this slander, but the seeds of doubt have now been planted in her mind. Telramund creates suspicion among the people by repeating his wife's accusation. Lohengrin insists that the charge against him is false even though he may not reveal his true identity. Elsa now assures Lohengrin that she does not doubt him. The bridal procession continues into the cathedral.

Act III, Scene 1. The bridal chamber.

A vigorous orchestral prelude describes the joy surrounding the marriage of Lohengrin and Elsa. To the strains of the celebrated Bridal Chorus ("Treulich geführt") the bridal procession enters the chamber. When Lohengrin and Elsa are left alone, they embrace and speak of their love ("Das süsse Lied verhallt"). But doubt has entered Elsa's heart, and she longs to know who her husband really is. Lohengrin entreats her to desist from asking, but Elsa is insistent. At this point Telramund and four of his men burst into the chamber to attack Lohengrin. Lohengrin kills Telramund with a single blow of his sword, whereupon the henchmen abandon their evil mission. Sadly, Lohengrin reveals that all his happiness has ended.

Scene 2. The banks of the Scheldt. The king informs his people that the time for battle is at hand ("Wie fühl ich stolz mein Herz entbrannt"). The people select Lohengrin as leader, but he declines; having killed Telramund, he feels his act should be judged. He goes on to denounce Elsa's treachery that compels him now to reveal his identity. He is a Knight of the Holy Grail (Gralserzählung: "In fernem Land"), the son of Parsifal, King of the Grail, and his power is that of destroying evil influences. Having revealed his secret, Lohengrin must return to Monsalvat, home of the Grail. He takes his bride Elsa in his arms and laments the fact that they now must part forever ("O Elsa, was hast du mir angethan?"). Lohengrin's swan appears. Ortrud triumphantly discloses that the swan is none other than Elsa's brother, Gottfried, transformed by her evil magic. Had Elsa kept faith with Lohengrin, she declares, she would not only have had him and his love, she could have saved her brother. Lohengrin rights one more wrong: he restores the boy Gottfried to human form, then departs in his boat, now drawn by the white dove of the Holy Grail.

Lohengrin, written between 1846 and 1848, was Wagner's last "opera." After *Lohengrin* he cut the cord that had tied him to the past; the new esthetics which he was to articulate were to be realized in his very next work, TRISTAN UND ISOLDE, his first music drama. Standing as it does between TANNHÄUSER and *Tristan*, *Lohengrin* looks two ways. We find the past in the emphasis on the voice, which is still a dominating element; in many of the arias, duets, and choral numbers cast in traditional mold; in such formal scenes as the bridal procession. The future is found in the increasingly ingenious use of LEITMOTIVS, in the virtuoso handling of the orchestra, in the oneness of the conception, the singleness of the mood. But for all its glimpses into the future, *Lohengrin* remains a romantic opera. Having proved to his satisfaction that he had written the finest romantic opera of his generation, Wagner could abandon old paths and strike out in new directions.

Since Wagner was *persona non grata* in Dresden after 1849, a political refugee, *Lohengrin* was turned down by the DRESDEN OPERA, which had previously introduced DER FLIEGENDE HOLLÄNDER and TANNHÄUSER. When hoped-for premieres failed to materialize in Paris and London, Wagner sent the score to LISZT, then the KAPELLMEISTER in Weimar. It took courage for Liszt to produce a new work by a revolutionary in exile, and Liszt possessed that courage. The opera at first proved more or less a failure. Partly, it was too long and invited fatigue: partly, it was too new for immediate acceptance. But the opera did not have to wait long for recognition. Within the next few years it was heard in different parts of Germany, achieving an ever-mounting success. By 1860 *Lohengrin* had been performed so often that Wagner, living in exile in Switzerland, once complained that he was the only German alive who had not heard it.

The first *complete* performance of *Lohengrin* in the Western Hemisphere, and possibly anywhere outside BAYREUTH, took place in 1965 at the BERKSHIRE MUSIC FESTIVAL in a concert performance by the Boston Symphony under Erich LEINSDORF, given on three evenings, an act an evening.

Lohse, Otto, conductor. Born Dresden,

Sept. 21, 1859; died Baden-Baden, May 5, 1925. He studied with Hans RICHTER and Felix Draeseke at the Dresden Conservatory. In 1882 he was appointed conductor of the Wagner Society and the Imperial Russian Music Society, both in Riga. Seven years later he was made first KAPELLMEISTER of the Riga Stadttheater. In 1893 he became director of the Hamburg Stadttheater. Here he married the singer Katharina KLAFSKY. In the spring of 1896 he and his wife came to the United States and joined the DAMROSCH OPERA COMPANY. They were back in Germany a year later, and from then on Lohse held important conductorial posts: in Strassburg from 1897 to 1904; in Cologne from 1904 to 1911; with the THÉÂTRE DE LA MONNAIE in 1911–12; and with the Leipzig Stadttheater from 1912 to 1923. From 1901 to 1904 he also directed performances of the Wagnerian music dramas at COVENT GARDEN. In 1916 he received the honorary title of Royal Professor. He wrote one opera, *Der Prinz wilder Willen,* performed in Riga in 1890.

Loin de sa femme, the devil's aria in Act II of MASSENET'S GRISÉLIDIS detailing the benefits of being single.

Lola, Alfio's wife (mezzo-soprano) in MASCAGNI'S CAVALLERIA RUSTICANA.

Lombard, Alain, conductor. Born Paris, Oct. 4, 1940. His music study took place with Gaston Poulet and Suzanne Démarques. In his ninth year, Lombard made his baton debut directing a symphony concert in Paris. In Apr., 1961, he made a guest appearance conducting FAUST with the Lyons Opera, where he served for three seasons first as second, then as principal, conductor in an extensive repertory. In 1963 he made his American debut conducting HÉRODIADE with the AMERICAN OPERA SOCIETY. This was followed in 1965 by his debut with the NEW YORK CITY OPERA with LES DIALOGUES DES CARMÉLITES and at the METROPOLITAN OPERA with ballet. In the same year he won first prize in the Dimitri Mitropoulos Competition for Conductors in New York. One of its rewards was an appointment as assistant to Leonard BERNSTEIN with the New York Philharmonic, with which he made his debut that year, leading a performance of BARTÓK's *The Miraculous Mandarin.* On Dec. 24, 1966, he made his opera debut with the Metropolitan Opera with *Faust.* He has since served as one of the permanent conductors of that company both during its regular season and on tour. Since 1966 he has been music director of the Greater Miami Philharmonic. While retaining this post he served as guest conductor of major orchestras in America and Europe. During the summer of 1969 he led concert performances of MADAMA BUTTERFLY at the Ravinia Festival. He has also led concert performances of BORIS GODUNOV and DIE WALKÜRE with the Greater Miami Philharmonic. In 1971 he was invited to the HAMBURG OPERA in Germany to conduct CARMEN and ORPHEUS IN THE UNDERWORLD.

Lombardi alla prima crociata, I (The Lombards at the First Crusade), opera in four acts by VERDI. Libretto by Themistocles Solera, based on a narrative poem by Tommaso Grossi. Premiere: La Scala, Feb. 11, 1843. American premiere: Palmo's Opera House, New York, Mar. 3, 1847. Under the title *Jerusalem,* its score and libretto both revised to suit French tastes, this opera was produced at the PARIS OPÉRA Nov. 26, 1847. Verdi's distinguished biographer Francis Toye wrote: "It may be doubted whether the annals of opera contain a more uncouth libretto than this." Against a background of the invasion and siege of Jerusalem during the first crusade, its story involves, as the central figure, a mysterious hermit (Pagano, baritone) who tries to murder his brother (Arvino, tenor) out of jealousy and kills his father instead and who, in the end, turns out to be the hero who is mortally wounded leading the attack on Jerusalem. Meantime, his niece (Giselda, soprano) has fallen in love with an enemy soldier (Oronte, tenor), who is also mortally wounded in battle but is converted to Christianity before he dies. Despite the ultraromantic incredibility and complexity of the plot—or maybe because of them—there are many opportunities for striking set numbers, and the powerfully romantic genius of the young Verdi embraced these opportunities. The trio of Giselda, Oronte, and Arvino, "Qui posa il fianco," Giselda's first-act prayer, "Tu vergine santa in voco," the three choruses in the first act (those of the nuns, the conspirators, and the Ambassadors), and the Crusaders' war chorus, "O signore, dal tetto natio," are of particular interest.

I Lombardi was Verdi's first opera to get a hearing in the United States.

London, George (born Burnson), bass-baritone. Born Montreal, May 30, 1921. The son of American parents, he was taken to Los Angeles in his boyhood. Here, while attending public schools, he sang in churches and various amateur productions. In 1947 he toured the United States with the Bel Canto Trio (whose other members were Mario Lanza and Frances Yeend). He made his opera debut in Europe in 1949 with the VIENNA STATE OPERA as AMONASRO. Subsequently he appeared in Vienna as ESCAMILLO, BORIS GODUNOV, and in all the four baritone roles in THE TALES OF HOFFMANN. On Nov. 13, 1951 (the opening night of the season), he made his debut at the METROPOLITAN OPERA as Amonasro. On Jan. 9, 1952, he made his debut at LA SCALA as PIZARRO. After this, besides making appearances at the Metropolitan, he sang in the leading festivals of Europe, including those of BAYREUTH, SALZBURG, MUNICH, HOLLAND, GLYNDEBOURNE, and EDINBURGH. His appearance as Boris Godunov at the Metropolitan in 1953 was an event of particular historic importance, since this was the first time the company was both giving the opera in MUSSORGSKY's original version (though somewhat edited) and in an English translation, and it was the first time an American singer had appeared in the title role. He became the first American, also, to sing the role at the BOLSHOI OPERA in Moscow (1960). In 1955 London was honored by the President of Austria with the title of KAMMERSÄNGER. In 1964 he created for America the title role of THE LAST SAVAGE at the Metropolitan Opera, and in 1968 he was named music administrator of the John F. Kennedy Center for the Performing Arts in Washington, D.C.

Long Christmas Dinner, The, opera in one act by HINDEMITH. Libretto by the composer and Thornton WILDER, based on the play of the same name by Wilder. Premiere: Mannheim, Dec. 17, 1961. American premiere: New York City, Mar. 13, 1963. All the action takes place at a Christmas dinner. However, during the course of the dinner a complete century elapses through the strategic means of placing the "Door of Life" on one side of the room, through which four generations of the family pass to partake of the meal, from early settlers to the latest young rebels. The latter desert the house for good to leave it to a lonely, unmarried cousin. "The score is made up of small closed numbers," writes Peter Heyworth. "Each of these ideas is handled with consummate skill and contrapuntal adroitness."

Longfellow, Henry Wadsworth, poet. Born Portland, Me., Feb. 27, 1807; died Cambridge, Mass., Mar. 24, 1882. Otto Luening's opera EVANGELINE (produced in New York in 1948) was adapted from Longfellow's poem. *The Blind Girl of Castel-Cuille* was the source of operas of the same name by Cornelius Dopper and Earl Ross Drake.

L'onore! Ladri!, Falstaff's contemplations on the virtue of honor, in Act I, Scene 1, of VERDI'S FALSTAFF.

Lorek, surgeon (baritone) in GIORDANO'S FEDORA.

Loreley, Die, (1) opera in three acts by CATALANI. Libretto by Angelo Zanardini and Carlo d'Ormville. Premiere: Teatro Regio, Turin, Feb. 16, 1890. American premiere: Chicago, Oct. 27, 1930. The setting is the banks of the Rhine in medieval times. Walter, Governor of Oberwesel, betrothed to Anna, meets and falls in love with the Loreley. At the marriage ceremony, the Loreley appears. Walter rushes to her, but the Loreley eludes him by sinking into the Rhine. Anna dies of grief. Walter continues to pursue the Loreley and finds her singing atop her rock. When she once again evades him, he commits suicide by jumping into the river. The most famous excerpt from the opera is orchestral, the *Danza delle ondine,* The Dance of the Waves.

(2) An unfinished opera by MENDELS-SOHN written in 1847 on a text by Emanuel von Giebel, based on the legend of the Loreley.

Lorenz, Max, tenor. Born Düsseldorf, May 10, 1901. He studied singing in Berlin with Grenzebach. In 1928 he was engaged by Fritz BUSCH for the DRESDEN OPERA, where he scored a major success in DIE AEGYPTISCHE HELENA. In 1931–32 and again in 1933–34 he appeared at the METROPOLITAN OPERA in leading Wagnerian tenor roles. Between 1933 and 1943 he appeared at the BAYREUTH FESTIVAL; in 1937 he was engaged as principal tenor of the VIENNA STATE OPERA. Just before World War II he appeared in other countries; after the war he sang not only at the Vienna State Opera but at the TEATRO COLÓN, in various Italian opera houses, and at festivals in Paris, Amsterdam, Zürich, and SALZBURG, where he created the leading tenor roles in such operas as DER PROZESS, PENELOPE, and IRISCHE LEGENDE.

Lorenzo, an officer of the carabiniers (tenor), in love with Zerlina, in AUBER'S FRA DIAVOLO.

Loris Ipanov, Count, *see* IPANOV, COUNT LORIS.

Lorsque je t'ai vu, Margared's turbulent air in Act II of LALO'S LE ROI D'YS, upon witnessing Mylio at the head of his army preparing to leave Ys and suspecting him of loving her sister.

Lorsque l'enfant revient, Werther's prayer for strength to stay away from his beloved Charlotte until Christmas and for her happiness until his return, in Act II of MASSENET'S WERTHER.

Lortzing, Gustav Albert, composer. Born Berlin, Oct. 23, 1801; died there Jan. 21, 1851. The son of professional actors, Lortzing spent his boyhood and youth traveling with his parents. His education, consequently, was haphazard, though at one time he did attend the Singakademie in Berlin. He wrote his first operetta, *Ali Pascha von Janina,* in 1822; it was produced two years later.

He subsequently achieved considerable success as a tenor with the Leipzig Stadttheater. It was in this theater, too, that he was recognized as a composer with *Die beiden Schützen* in 1837. His most famous opera, ZAR UND ZIMMERMANN, was an even greater success when introduced in Leipzig a year later and was soon performed extensively throughout Germany and Austria. In 1842 he was again successful with a new opera, *Der Wildschütz.* In 1846 Lortzing was invited to Vienna to conduct the premiere of his *Der Waffenschmied.* Engaged as first conductor of the THEATER-AN-DER-WIEN, he lost the post during the revolutionary period of 1848. From then on he was unable to obtain a satisfactory position. He supported himself first as an actor in small German theaters, then by conducting ballet and vaudeville performances in Berlin. His health and spirit were broken; he died a poor and unhappy man. His most famous operas were in a comic vein, but he also wrote a romantic opera, *Regina.* It was first performed at the BERLIN OPERA in 1899, nearly fifty years after Lortzing's death. His other operas: *Die Schatzkammer des Ynka* (1836); *Caramo* (1839); HANS SACHS (1840); *Casanova* (1841); UNDINE (1845); *Zum Grossadmiral* (1847); *Rolands Knappen* (1849); *Die Opernprobe* (1850).

Los Angeles, Victoria de, *see* DE LOS ANGELES, VICTORIA.

Lo sposo deluso (The Deluded Spouse), unfinished opera by MOZART. *See* DON PEDRO.

Lothario, an aged minstrel (bass), who turns out to be a nobleman, in THOMAS'S MIGNON.

Loti, Pierre (born Louis Marie Julien Vaud), novelist. Born Rochefort, France, Jan. 14, 1850; died Hendaye, France, June 10, 1923. His novels that were made into operas include: *Lakmé* (DELIBES); *Madame Chrysanthème* (MESSAGER); *Ramuntcho* (TAYLOR); and *Le Roman de Spahi* (Lucien Lambert's *Le Spahi*).

Louise, opera in four acts by CHARPENTIER. Libretto by the composer. Premiere: Opéra-Comique, Feb. 2, 1900.

American premiere: Manhattan Opera House, Jan. 3, 1908.

Characters: Louise, a seamstress (soprano); her mother (contralto); her father (baritone); Julien, a painter (tenor); Irma, a seamstress (soprano); an errand girl; King of the Fools; peddlers; housekeepers; working people; street boys; grisettes; Bohemians. The setting is Paris toward the end of the nineteenth century.

Act I. The attic flat of Louise's family. Julien has written to Louise's parents requesting their permission for his marriage to their daughter; from his balcony across the way he urges her to elope with him if permission is denied. Louise is torn between her love for Julien and her duty to her parents. Julien recalls the time when first he fell in love with her ("Depuis longtemps j'habitais cette chambre"). As they are repeating to each other their expressions of love, Louise's mother appears and takes her daughter severely to task for encouraging a worthless Bohemian. When Louise's father comes home, he reads Julien's letter. The mother insists that no consideration be given to Julien, but the father prefers a more cautious approach. This so infuriates the mother that she begins to quarrel with her daughter. The father consoles Louise ("O mon enfant"), and the young woman reluctantly promises not to see Julien again.

Act II, Scene 1. A street in Montmartre. Dawn breaks on Paris. Street cries are heard. Louise and her mother come to the establishment where Louise is employed. When her mother leaves, Julien appears and begs Louise to elope with him ("Ah! Louise, si tu m'aimes"). Once again Louise is torn between love and duty. She rushes into the shop, leaving Julien forlorn.

Scene 2. A dressmaker's workroom (this scene is often omitted). The other seamstresses do not fail to notice how disturbed Louise is. Irma suggests that Louise may be in love, then pronounces a rhapsody over love and Paris ("Une voix mystérieuse"). From outside the window comes Julien's unexpected serenade ("Dans la cité lointaine"). The seamstresses mock Julien, but Louise, unable to resist his appeals, rushes out to join him.

Act III. A cottage. Louise and Julien, now living together, are more in love than ever. Louise recalls the day when first she yielded ("Depuis le jour"). They embrace, and the gathering night envelops them. The beauty of Paris causes Julien to sing the praises of both the city and his beloved ("De Paris tout en fête"). A few moments later a group of Bohemians appear; they call to Julien and Louise, then crown Louise the Muse of Montmartre. The gaiety is at a climax when Louise's mother appears with the news that Louise's father is dying. Julien is willing to let Louise go to her father, but only after the mother promises that she will be free to return.

Act IV. The attic flat. Louise has nursed her father back to health. She is still with him, her mother having refused to let her go back to Julien. The father laments the lot of a workman with ungrateful children. But he soon draws Louise to him and sings her a lullaby as if she were still a child (BERCEUSE: "Reste, repose-toi"). Since Louise is eager to return to her lover, a harsh quarrel erupts. Sternly, the father opens the door and orders her out. After Louise has gone, he cries after her. Then, shaking his fist at the city outside his window, he bitterly exclaims that it is the evil of Paris that has destroyed his home.

Naturalism entered French opera with *Louise,* a story concerned with the lives of everyday people. The central theme—the love affair of the artist and the seamstress—raised the then revolutionary question of a woman's right to live her life without dictation by parents or society. *Louise* was the first opera, moreover, to contain elements of socialist thinking. There is another important element in the work—a symbolic one—Paris. The spell of the city is made tangible through the musical tributes of Julien in the third act and Louise in the fourth, through the cries of street vendors, through the evocative orchestral interludes. It is the inescapable magic of the setting quite as much as the turbulent love of Julien and Louise that has enchanted opera audiences.

Two months after *Louise* was first heard, Marthe Rioton, the creator of the title role, fell ill during a performance. Her understudy, who had never yet sung before an audience, stepped into the part and gained an ovation. Her name was Mary GARDEN and the measure of her triumph was that she sang the role of Louise over two hundred times at the OPÉRA-COMIQUE during the next few years.

On Feb. 28, 1950, the fiftieth anniversary of *Louise* was celebrated in Paris. The composer, now in his ninetieth year, took over the baton for the closing scene. Climaxing the occasion, the President of France conferred on Charpentier the grade of Grand Officer of the Legion of Honor.

Louisville Orchestra Commissions (for opera). A number of American operas have been commissioned by the Louisville Orchestra in Louisville, Ky., as it was their annual practice to commission composers to write works specifically for that organization. Among these operas, all of which received their world premieres in concert performances by the Louisville Orchestra, are: GLANVILLE-HICKS'S THE TRANSPOSED HEADS in 1954; Richard Mohaupt's *Double Trouble* (Dec. 4, 1954) ; ANTHEIL's *The Wish* (Apr. 2, 1955) ; LIEBERMANN's SCHOOL FOR WIVES in 1955; Nicolas Nabokov's *The Holy Devil* (later revised under the title of *The Death of Gregory Rasputin*) in 1958; and Hoiby's BEATRICE (Oct. 23, 1959, premiere over WAVE-TV in Louisville) .

Louÿs, Pierre (born Louis) , poet and novelist. Born Ghent, Belgium, Dec. 10, 1870; died Paris, June 4, 1925. His famous novel *Aphrodite* was the source of ERLANGER's opera of the same name. Another of his novels, *La Femme et le pantin,* was used for ZANDONAI's *Conchita.*

Love for Three Oranges, The, opera in four acts by PROKOFIEV. Libretto by the composer, based on a tale by GOZZI. Premiere: Chicago Opera, Dec. 30, 1921. Prokofiev's opera is a play within a play. A highly demonstrative audience of Cynics, Emptyheads, Glooms, and Joys watches the performance of a burlesque opera about a legendary prince. The young man, dying of gloom, can be cured only by laughter. A wicked sorceress, Fata Morgana, thwarts every attempt to lighten his spirits, but when she takes a ridiculous fall during a scuffle with palace guards, the prince laughs and is cured. The sorceress now decrees that he must find and fall in love with three oranges. When the prince finds the oranges in a desert, he learns that each contains a beautiful princess. Two of the young women perish of thirst. The Cynics of Prokofiev's audience revive the third with a bucket of water. After more trials, the prince and princess are united and the sorceress and her evil cohorts meet suitable justice. In the course of this gay work Prokofiev pokes good-natured fun at various absurdities of conventional plots and romantic operas, with copious quotations from French and Russian operas. The best-known selections are the six movements that the composer gathered into an orchestral suite: *Les Ridicules; Scène infernale; Marche; Scherzo; Le Prince et la princesse;* and *La Fuite.*

Love in her eyes sits playing, aria of Acis, in HANDEL'S ACIS AND GALATEA.

Love of Three Kings, The, *see* AMORE DEI TRE RE, L'.

Lover and the Nightingale, The, the best known aria in GRANADOS' GOYESCAS, heard in Scene 2.

Love sounds the alarm, Acis' dramatic warning of the power of love, in HANDEL'S ACIS AND GALATEA.

Lo vidi e il primo palpito, Luisa's aria, telling of her love for Rodolfo, in the opening scene of VERDI'S LUISA MILLER.

Lualdi, Adriano, composer. Born Larino, Italy, Mar. 22, 1887. After studying with Stanislao Falchi in Rome and WOLF-FERRARI in Venice, he became an opera conductor in 1908. In 1918 he settled in Milan, and from 1923 to 1927 was music critic of the periodical *Secolo*. In 1928 he became head of the music department of the Italian government. For several years he was artistic director of the Florence and Venice music festivals. In 1936 he succeeded CILÈA as director of the Naples Conservatory, holding this post until 1943. Next, he became director of the Cherubini Conservatory in Florence. He did considerable research in old Italian music, which led him in his own compositions to revive old Italian operatic forms and styles. In this vein he wrote *Il cantico*, a lyric intermezzo (1915); *Le furie di Arlecchino*, an intermezzo giocoso for marionettes (1915); *La morte di Rinaldo*, a dramatic scene (1916); and *Guerin meschino*, a medieval legend for marionettes (1920). His more traditional operas are: *Le nozze di Haura* (1908); *La figlia del re* (1922); *Il diavolo nel campanile* (1925); *La Grancèola* (1930); *La luna dei Caraibi* (1953).

Lubin, Germaine, soprano. Born Paris, Feb. 1, 1890. She attended the Collège Sévigné in Paris with the intention of becoming a doctor, but a passion for music made her change her mind. In 1908 she entered the Paris Conservatory, where she won three first prizes in singing. In 1912 she joined the OPÉRA-COMIQUE, where she appeared in the world premiere of Guy Ropartz' *Le Pays*. In 1914 she was engaged by the PARIS OPÉRA, where she has ever since remained, becoming principal dramatic soprano in 1938. She has distinguished herself particularly in the Wagnerian repertory but has also had notable success in contemporary French operas and operas by BERLIOZ, GLUCK, and Richard STRAUSS. In 1938 she was seen at BAYREUTH as KUNDRY. She has also sung in London, Berlin, Vienna, Prague, and at several SALZBURG FESTIVALS.

Luca, Giuseppe de, see DE LUCA, GIUSEPPE.

Lucas, a widower (tenor) in love with Vendulka in SMETANA'S THE KISS.

Lucca, Pauline, soprano. Born Vienna, Apr. 25, 1841; died there Feb. 28, 1908. After studying with Uschmann and Richard Lewy in Vienna she joined the chorus of the VIENNA OPERA. She made her debut in Olmütz on Sept. 4, 1859, in ERNANI and was so successful that she was made a principal soprano of the company. After her sensational performances as NORMA and VALENTINE in Prague in 1860, MEYERBEER called her to Berlin to create for Germany the role of SELIKA. She was immediately engaged as permanent court singer there. From 1863 to 1872 she sang every season in London (except for 1869) and was a great favorite. She terminated her ties with Berlin in 1872 and embarked on a two-year tour of America. After returning to Europe she was associated with the Vienna Opera until 1889, when she retired from the stage.

Lucia, Turiddu's mother (contralto) in MASCAGNI'S CAVALLERIA RUSTICANA.

Lucia di Lammermoor, opera in three acts by DONIZETTI. Libretto by Salvatore CAMMARANO, based on Sir Walter SCOTT's novel *The Bride of Lammermoor*. Premiere: San Carlo, Naples, Sept. 26, 1835. American premiere: Théâtre d'Orléans, New Orleans, Dec. 28, 1841.

Characters: Lord Enrico Ashton of Lammermoor (baritone); Lucia, his sister (soprano); Raimondo, chaplain of Lammermoor (bass); Edgardo, Master of Ravenswood (tenor); Lord Arturo Bucklaw (tenor); Alisa, Lucia's companion (soprano); Normanno, follower of Lord Ashton (tenor); followers of Ashton; inhabitants of Lammermoor. The setting is Scotland toward the end of the seventeenth century.

Act I, Scene 1. A wood. Normanno informs Lord Ashton that there is a prowler on the grounds of Lammermoor Castle and that he suspects the intruder to be Edgardo. His suspicions are substantiated by the guards ("Come vinti"). Normanno further discloses that Lord Ashton's sister, Lucia, has been meeting the intruder. Ashton vows to destroy Edgardo, his mortal enemy.

Scene 2. A park near the castle. Awaiting her lover, Lucia sings of an apparition she believes she has seen of a young woman long ago murdered by one of the Ravenswoods ("Regnava nel silenzio"). Her gloomy mood lightens as she thinks of Edgardo ("Quando rapita in estasi"). When Edgardo appears, it is with the news that he has been ordered to France. He suggests that he visit Lord Ashton and confess that he loves Lucia. Lucia insists such a mission would be futile. The lovers bid each other a passionate farewell ("Verranno a te sull' aure").

Act II, Scene 1. An anteroom in Lammermoor Castle. Lord Ashton is determined to put an end to the love affair of his sister and Edgardo, since he plans to solve his own financial problems by marrying his sister to wealthy Lord Arturo Bucklaw. He shows Lucia a letter he has forged in Edgardo's hand. Reading it, Lucia mistakenly believes that Edgardo has deserted her. Distraught with grief, Lucia consents to marry Bucklaw.

Scene 2. The castle's great hall. Before an assemblage of knights and ladies, Lucia signs the marriage contract that makes her Lord Bucklaw's wife. An armed stranger boldly stalks into the hall. Consternation prevails when he is recognized as Edgardo. Now begins the opera's famous sextet ("Chi mi frena"). Edgardo wonders what restrains him from an act of vengeance; Lucia voices her despair at her brother's treachery; Enrico voices compassion for his sister's plight; Raimondo, the kindly chaplain, invokes the aid of heaven; Alisa, Lucia's companion, and Arturo Bucklaw, her husband, express the hope that there will be no bloodshed. When Edgardo finally realizes how ruthlessly he has been treated, he curses the entire Lammermoor family and rushes away.

Act III, Scene 1 (this scene is usually omitted). The tower of Ravenswood. Lord Ashton, bent on avenging the

honor of his household, comes to Ravenswood Castle to challenge Edgardo to a duel. As a storm rages, both Ashton and Edgardo vow vengeance.

Scene 2. The hall of Lammermoor. The wedding festivities of Lucia and Lord Bucklaw are being celebrated ("Per te d'immenso giubilo"). Raimondo abruptly appears with the ghastly news that Lucia has slain her husband and gone mad ("Dalle stanze, ove Lucia"). As if in confirmation, Lucia enters the hall, dressed in a long white gown. She raves, unconscious of her surroundings (Mad Scene: "Ardon gl'incensi"). She believes that Edgardo is with her and that they are being married. She even mistakes her brother for Edgardo. Pathetically, she begs that a flower be placed on her grave, that no tears be shed ("Spargi d'amaro pianto"). Swooning, she falls into the arms of the faithful Alisa.

Scene 3. The burial ground of the Ravenswoods. Not knowing the fate that has befallen Lucia, Edgardo laments the fickleness of his loved one and longs for death (Tomb Scene: "Fra poco a me ricovero"). Mourners from Lammermoor pass. From them, Edgardo learns of Lucia's madness. He is about to rush to her side when a tolling bell and the grief of the inhabitants of Lammermoor ("Giusto cielo!") announce that she is dead. Aware now that Lucia has never faltered in her love for him, Edgardo promises her spirit that they will never be parted again ("Tu che a Dio spiegasti l'ali"). He then stabs himself and dies.

Donizetti composed this opera with Fanny PERSIANI in mind. It was Persiani, one of the most brilliant coloratura sopranos of her day, who created the role of Lucia not only in Italy but England. Since her time virtually every great coloratura has appeared as Lucia. Containing two of the most famous numbers in all opera, the sextet and Lucia's mad scene, *Lucia* has remained popular with audiences quite as much for the sustained beauty of its lyricism as for the opportunities it affords great coloratura sopranos to exhibit their virtuosity.

Lucieta, Lunardo's daughter (soprano) in WOLF-FERRARI'S I QUATTRO RUSTEGHI.

Lucile, Desmoulins' wife (soprano), loved by Camille, in EINEM'S DANTONS TOD, a role created by Maria CEBATORI.

Lucinda, principal female character (soprano) in WOLF-FERRARI'S L'AMORE MEDICO.

Lucretia, wife (contralto) of Collatinus in BRITTEN'S THE RAPE OF LUCRETIA, a role created by Kathleen FERRIER.

Lucrezia Borgia, opera in three acts by DONIZETTI. Libretto by Felice ROMANI, based on Victor HUGO's play *Lucrèce Borgia*. Premiere: La Scala, Dec. 26, 1833. American premiere: New York City, Nov. 25, 1844. In sixteenth-century Italy, Don Alfonso d'Este, Duke of Ferrara (baritone), suspects that his wife, Lucrezia Borgia (soprano), is carrying on a love affair with young Gennaro. Gennaro (tenor) is actually her own illegitimate son, though nobody but the mother knows this fact. When Alfonso has Gennaro arrested, Lucrezia arranges his escape. Infuriated by the insults of several young aristocrats, she has them poisoned. To her horror, she discovers that one of those whom she has destroyed is her son. The most familiar arias are those of Lucrezia ("Com' è bello quanto incanto"), Gennaro ("Di pescatore ignobile"), and Orsini ("Il segreto per essere felice").

A revival of *Lucrezia Borgia* by the AMERICAN OPERA SOCIETY in 1965 made a star overnight of Montserrat CABALLÉ, appearing in the title role.

Lucy, a young lady (soprano) fond of telephone conversations in MENOTTI'S THE TELEPHONE.

Ludikar, Pavel, bass-baritone and opera manager. Born Prague, Mar. 3, 1882. He turned to music after completing studies in law and philosophy. He made his opera debut in 1904 at the National Theater in Prague as SARASTRO. Important appearances followed in leading European opera houses, including LA SCALA and the DRESDEN (Royal) OPERA. In 1913 he made his first opera appearances in America with the Boston Civic Opera Company. On Nov. 16, 1926, he made his debut at the METROPOLITAN OPERA in the American premiere of PUCCINI'S TURANDOT. He remained at the Metropolitan through the 1931–32 season, singing about eighty roles in a dozen languages. In 1935 he was appointed manager of the National Theater in Prague, and three years later he created the title role in KRENEK's *Karl V* in Prague. During World War II he was actively associated with Germany's musical life. After the war he appeared in Germany and Czechoslovakia. Then he retired in Vienna.

Ludmilla, Svietosar's daughter (soprano) in GLINKA's RUSSLAN AND LUDMILLA.

Ludwig, Christa, mezzo-soprano and soprano. Born Berlin, Mar. 16, 1924. Both her parents were opera singers at the Vienna VOLKSOPER, and her father was the director of the Opera at Aachen. Her own vocal studies took place with her mother and Hueni-Mihaceck. In 1946 she made her opera debut in Frankfurt as Orlofsky in DIE FLEDERMAUS. She made numerous opera appearances before achieving a major success at SALZBURG in 1954 as CHERUBINO, a performance that brought her a contract with the VIENNA STATE OPERA in 1955. She made her debut at the METROPOLITAN OPERA as Cherubino on Dec. 10, 1959, remaining through two seasons. She has since appeared with major opera companies in Europe, scoring successes of the first magnitude in such roles as OCTAVIAN, Leonore in FIDELIO, Princess EBOLI, and major female Mozartean roles.

Ludwig, Leopold, conductor. Born Witkowitz, Austria, Jan. 12, 1908. After completing his music study in Vienna, he held a number of appointments as conductor with several German companies until 1939, when he was engaged by the VIENNA STATE OPERA. He remained there until 1943, returning in later years frequently to give significant guest performances. From 1934 to 1950 he was principal conductor of the BERLIN DEUTSCHE OPER, and since 1950 he has been the musical director and principal conductor of the HAMBURG OPERA. He made his American debut with the SAN FRANCISCO OPERA on Sept. 30, 1958, in THE BARTERED BRIDE, where in 1968–69 he celebrated his tenth consecutive season with a new production of DIE WALKÜRE and a revival of WOZZECK. He has made guest appearances with other world-famous opera companies, as well as at Europe's leading festivals, including those of GLYNDEBOURNE and EDINBURGH.

Luigi, a longshoreman (tenor), Giorgetta's lover, in PUCCINI'S IL TABARRO.

Luisa Miller, opera in three acts by VERDI. Libretto by S. CAMMARANO, based on SCHILLER's play *Kabale und Liebe.* Premiere: Teatro San Carlo, Naples, Dec. 8, 1849. American premiere: Castle Garden, N.Y., July 20, 1852.

Characters: Walter, a count (bass); Rodolfo, his son (tenor); Miller, an old soldier (baritone); Luisa, his daughter (soprano); Federica, Walter's niece and the Duchess of Ostheim (contralto); Laura, a peasant girl (contralto); Wurm (bass). The action takes place in a village in the Tyrols in the first half of the eighteenth century.

Act I. The village square. It is Luisa's birthday. The villagers are celebrating. Luisa tells of her love for Rodolfo ("Lo vidi e il primo palpito"), who is actually the son of a count, but who conceals himself under the identity of a peasant named Carlo. Wurm is also in love with Luisa. He demands of Miller, Luisa's father, that Luisa be compelled to marry him, but this the father refuses to do, insisting he cannot be a tyrant to his own child ("Sacra la scielta"). The Count wants his son Rodolfo to marry Federica, his niece, and is ready to do everything in his power to prevent Rodolfo and Luisa from getting married ("Il mio sangue"), even to the point of threatening Luisa and her father with

prison. But they are kept free by Rodolfo's readiness to reveal that his father has acquired his title and possessions by assassinating his predecessor.

Act II. A room in Miller's house. Luisa's father, nevertheless, has finally been imprisoned. In order to save him, Luisa is ready to put in writing a confession that she has never loved Rodolfo and prefers Wurm. In the aria "Tu puniscimi, O signore" she reveals the pain the writing of this letter has cost her. When Rodolfo sees the letter, his heart is broken, as he reveals in one of the most celebrated arias in the opera, "Quando le sere al placido," and his love now turns to hate. He not only is ready to marry the Duchess, but he is also determined to kill Luisa and then commit suicide ("L'ara o l'avello apprestami").

Act III. A room in Miller's house. Rodolfo comes to Luisa's house, extracting from her the confession that she had written the letter voluntarily and that its contents represent the truth. Overwhelmed, Rodolfo swallows poison. So does Luisa. Just before her death she reveals to Rodolfo that she loves him and him alone. With his last ounce of strength, Rodolfo draws his sword and stabs Wurm.

Lukas, young widower (tenor) in love with Vendulka in SMETANA'S HUBIČKA.

Lully, Jean-Baptiste, composer. Born Florence, Nov. 28, 1632; died Paris, Mar. 22, 1687. Though Italian by birth, Lully was the founder of French opera. He had little formal instruction in music. He was, however, so precocious that in 1646 Chevalier de Guise became interested in him and engaged him as a page for Mlle. de Montpensier, cousin of the King of France. Unattractive and clumsy, Lully was instead assigned to the kitchen. His preoccupation with music soon brought him a post with the house orchestra, and subsequently he was made a leader of a small band of violins. After six years with Mlle. de Montpensier, he was engaged by Louis XIV as ballet dancer, composer of ballet music, and director of the court orchestra. He soon became the king's favorite. A new orchestra was founded for him, "Les petits violons du roi." Under his direction it became one of the finest ensembles in France. In 1664 Lully began collaborating with MOLIÈRE on opera-ballets, beginning with *Le Mariage forcé,* which not only foreshadowed his own later procedures in writing operas but was also a predecessor of the OPÉRA COMIQUE. These opera-ballets—*L'Amour médecin* (1665) and LE BOURGEOIS GENTILHOMME (1670) were two more—were very popular at court and made Lully one of France's first composers. Among the honors conferred upon him were a patent of nobility, an appointment as *secretaire du roi,* and the rank of *maître de musique.* So highly regarded was Lully at court that when, in 1662, he married Madeleine Lambert, the marriage contract was signed by the King, the Queen, and the Queen Mother. Lully now used his power to acquire an exclusive patent to direct opera performances in Paris. For these performances he wrote a pastoral, *Les Fêtes de l'amour,* in 1672. A year later came his first opera, *Cadmus et Hermione,* which can be regarded as the cornerstone on which French opera rests. In collaboration with the librettist Philippe QUINAULT, he now wrote some fifteen operas which established a tradition for French opera, introducing the so-called French overture, French declamation, accompanied recitatives, fully developed arias, and enriched harmonic and rhythmic vocabularies. Lully's best operas held the stage for almost a century after his death. They include: *Cadmus et Hermione* (1673); ALCESTE (1674); *Thésée* (1675); *Atys* (1676); *Isis* (1677); *Psyché* (1678); *Bellerophon* (1679); *Proserpine* (1680); *Persée* (1682); *Phaëton* (1683); AMADIS DE GAULE (1684); *Roland* (1685); ARMIDE ET RENAUD (1686); *Acis et Galatée* (1686). There is a story to the effect that Lully caused his own death from gangrene of the foot, brought on by a misplaced blow of the long stick he used for audible time-beating. It is a story that probably tells us more about how performances were directed at the PARIS OPÉRA than it does about Lully's death.

Lulu, opera in three acts (unfinished) by BERG. Libretto by the composer, a condensation of two plays, *Erdgeist* and *Die Büchse der Pandora,* by Frank WEDEKIND. Premiere: Zürich Opera, June 2, 1937. American premiere: Santa Fe Opera, N.M., Aug. 7, 1963.

Berg did not live to finish *Lulu,* which today, after frequent performances in Europe and America since the 1950's, is regarded as a masterwork, in many respects a more powerful musical drama than his WOZZECK. He managed to complete two full acts, two hundred sixty-eight measures of the third act, and a finale. When *Lulu* was staged for the first time, it was given in its incomplete state, with two acts and two fragments. When produced in Germany in Essen in 1953, the third act was filled out with spoken drama taken out of Wedekind; it was presented the same way at its American premiere, but in English.

The opera begins with a prologue in which the animals of a circus are introduced with their tamer. Each animal symbolizes a character in the play that follows, Lulu being represented by a snake. The opera proper is concerned with the numerous illicit love affairs of Lulu, until she turns into a prostitute, and the shocking consequence of each—murder, suicide. Eventually Lulu is slain by Jack the Ripper. Willi Reich observes that within the actions of Lulu and the tragedies they provoke, "there are the fundamental ethical principles, principles of eternal greatness, which could have been kindled into life only by a poet as gifted as Frank Wedekind was." Berg used a different approach in *Lulu* from the one used in his earlier *Wozzeck.* For one thing, Lulu is written entirely with Schoenbergian TWELVE-TONE TECHNIQUES. The mold is also different. In *Wozzeck* there are many contrasting forms, some of them frankly instrumental in conception. In *Lulu* the style is more operatic and realistic, with a preference for arias, duets, trios, and ensemble numbers.

A five-movement suite for orchestra contains some of the most significant pages in the opera. They are: *Rondo, Ostinato, Song of Lulu, Variations,* and *Adagio.* Impressive vocal episodes include Lulu's *Lied* and the duet of Lulu and Alva, both in Act II; Alva's hymn to Lulu's beauty; and the Countess Geschwitz' tender farewell, "Lulu, mein Engel."

Luna, Count di, *see* DI LUNA, COUNT

Lusinghe più care, Rosanne's aria, the most famous excerpt from HANDEL'S ALESSANDRO.

Lustigen Weiber von Windsor, Die, *see* MERRY WIVES OF WINDSOR, THE.

Luther, a tavern keeper (bass) in OFFENBACH'S THE TALES OF HOFFMANN.

Lyceum Theatre, a theater built in London in 1765. It was intended for opera, but since the necessary license could not be obtained it was first used for other entertainments. In 1809 the license was finally given. When DRURY LANE burned down that year, its opera company moved to the Lyceum and gave four months of opera performances in English. Now named the English Opera House, the Lyceum was torn down and rebuilt in 1815. In the new house DER FREISCHÜTZ received its English premiere in 1824. Destroyed by fire in 1830, the theater was again rebuilt. Ten years later it was again called the Lyceum. Through the years it was used for spoken drama as well as opera. While COVENT GARDEN was being rebuilt in 1856, the Royal Italian Opera Company appeared at the Lyceum. In 1876 and 1877 the Lyceum was used by the CARL ROSA OPERA COMPANY. VERDI'S OTELLO was given its English premiere here in 1889. After 1900 the theater was chiefly a music hall, though in 1919 the Carl Rosa Opera Company again performed here.

Lycidas, *see* MILTON, JOHN.

lyric drama, a synonym for opera in general.

lyric opera, a term sometimes applied to an opera in which the lyrical element is more prominent than the dramatic or in which the arias are the primary interest.

Lysiart, Count of Forêt (baritone) in WEBER'S EURYANTHE.

Lysistrata, *see* ARISTOPHANES.

Lytton, *see* BULWER-LYTTON, EDWARD.

M

Maazel, Lorin, conductor. Born Paris, Mar. 5, 1930. The son of Americans living abroad, he was brought as a child to the United States, where he studied conducting with Vladimir Bakaleinikoff. He gave remarkable guest performances as a child prodigy conductor with leading orchestras in America, including the NBC Symphony, to which he was invited by TOSCANINI. Later he continued his academic education by attending the University of Pittsburgh for three years. From 1948 to 1951 he was a second violinist and apprentice conductor of the Pittsburgh Symphony. He then went to Europe on a Fulbright Fellowship for research in early Italian music. A year later he began his European conducting career through guest appearances at several major festivals and with some of the leading symphony orchestras. Between 1952 and 1960 he averaged fifty performances a year in all parts of Europe. In 1960 he became the youngest conductor and the first American to appear at the BAYREUTH FESTIVAL, where he conducted LOHENGRIN. After that he directed performances at most of the important European opera houses. Maazel made his New York debut as a mature conductor on Oct. 1, 1962, with the visiting L'Orchestre National Français. A month later, on Nov. 1, he made his debut at the METROPOLITAN OPERA with DON GIOVANNI, which he conducted from memory. Between 1965 and 1971 he was musical director of the BERLIN DEUTSCHE STAATSOPER and permanent conductor of the Berlin Radio Orchestra. On Jan. 7, 1968, he led the first Italian performance of DALLAPICCOLA'S ULISSE at LA SCALA.

Mab, la reine des mensonges (The Ballad of Queen Mab), Mercutio's description of his dream about Queen Mab, in Act I of GOUNOD'S ROMÉO ET JULIETTE.

Macbeth, opera in four acts by VERDI. Libretto by Francesco Maria PIAVE, based on SHAKESPEARE's drama. Premiere: Teatro alla Pergola, Florence, May 14, 1847 (original version); Théâtre Italien, Paris, Apr. 21, 1865 (revised). American premiere: Niblo's Garden, New York City, Apr. 14, 1850.

Characters: Lady Macbeth (soprano); Macbeth, a general (baritone), a role created by Felice VARESI; Banquo, a general (bass); Macduff, a nobleman (tenor); Duncan, King of Scotland (mute role); Lady in Waiting (soprano); Malcolm, Duncan's son (tenor); Fleance, Banquo's son (mute role); Doctor (bass).

The action takes place in Scotland and England in the eleventh century.

Act I. A heath. The Prelude uses material from the sleepwalking scene. Witches are singing a chorus prophesying that Macbeth will become thane and king and Banquo, the father of kings, when Macbeth and Banquo arrive. A messenger from King Duncan informs Macbeth he has been appointed Thane of Cawdor. Both Macbeth and Banquo are overcome to see the witches'

prophecy beginning to come true. In the ensuing scene at Macbeth's castle, Lady Macbeth is reading a letter from her husband about the prophecy (Letter Scene: "Vieni, t'affretta"). When Macbeth and Duncan arrive, on Lady Macbeth's urging Macbeth murders the king in his sleep. Macduff discovers the dead body; consternation and horror prevail throughout the household.

Act II. A hall in the castle. Lady Macbeth pleads with Macbeth to forget the past. With Banquo now a threat to Macbeth's throne, Lady Macbeth becomes convinced that he, too, must be murdered ("La luce langue"). Assassins are hired, Banquo is killed, but Banquo's son manages to escape. At a royal banquet in the castle Lady Macbeth sings a drinking song, but suddenly Banquo's ghost appears, occupying Macbeth's chair. Macbeth is terror stricken. The guests are disturbed by Macbeth's obvious show of horror, but they do not know the reason since they cannot see the ghost.

Act III. The witches' cavern. Macbeth returns to the witches to seek their counsel and to get a glimpse into the future. They warn him about Macduff, but promise that Macbeth cannot be vanquished until "Great Birnam wood" come to "high Dunsinane hill." Ghosts and apparitions appear to terrify Macbeth, but the arrival of Lady Macbeth provides him with courage. They vow to destroy anybody who is a threat to them.

Act IV. On the borders of Scotland and England. In a deserted place near Birnam wood, Scottish exiles are lamenting the tyranny that has seized their country ("Patria oppressa"), now that Macbeth is king. Macduff mourns the death of his wife and child, who have been murdered by order of Macbeth ("Ah! la paterna mano"). The English army appears with Malcolm at its head. The soldiers are instructed to break off a bough and carry it with them. In the next scene, in the castle, Lady Macbeth walks in her sleep, holding a lighted candle in hand.

Not all the perfumes of Arabia, she says, can remove from her hands the smell of blood (Sleepwalking Scene: "Una macchia è qui tutt'ora"). In a hall in the palace Macbeth is musing over the death of his wife ("Pietà, rispetto amore"). He is told of the approach of the enemy; each soldier holding a branch gives the impression of a moving Birnam forest. The opposing armies meet in battle, and so do Macbeth and Macduff face to face. Macduff kills Macbeth. The people sing a hymn of joy that their country has finally been freed.

McCormack, John, tenor. Born Athlone, Ireland, June 14, 1884; died Dublin, Sept. 16, 1945. Though a concert favorite for many years, McCormack first achieved recognition in opera. After attending local schools, he was sent to Dublin to prepare for civil service examinations. While there he sang for Vincent O'Brien, director of the Marlboro Cathedral Choir, who urged him to devote himself to music. He gave McCormack some instruction, then engaged him to sing with his choir. In 1904 McCormack won a gold medal at the National Irish Festival in Dublin. After a period of study with Sabbatini in Italy he made his opera debut in Savona in 1905 in L'AMICO FRITZ. He then went to London, where he earned his living singing in hotels and cabarets. An appearance at a Boosey Ballad Concert was so successful that he received several important engagements and an audition for COVENT GARDEN. He made his Covent Garden debut on Oct. 5, 1907, in CAVALLERIA RUSTICANA. Oscar HAMMERSTEIN engaged him for the MANHATTAN OPERA HOUSE and McCormack made his American debut here on Nov. 10, 1909, in LA TRAVIATA. From 1910 to 1912 he was the principal tenor of the BOSTON OPERA, and from 1912 to 1914 of the Philadelphia Opera. Meanwhile, on Nov. 29, 1910, he had made his first appearance at the METROPOLITAN OPERA in *La traviata*. McCormack was again heard at the Metropolitan between 1912 and 1914 and between

1917 and 1919. The exquisite artistry of his phrasing and the purity of his voice made him a favorite, particularly in the operas of PUCCINI. His feeling for the classic style also made him an outstanding interpreter of MOZART.

After World War I, McCormack abandoned opera for the concert stage, becoming one of the most highly acclaimed and best-loved concert singers of the world, particularly admired for Irish songs and ballads. He also made numerous radio appearances and was starred in a Hollywood film, *Song of My Heart*. He went into retirement in 1938, emerged briefly during World War II to sing for the British Red Cross, but he was soon ordered by his physician to give up all singing. Though he had been an American citizen since 1919, McCormack lived the last years of his life in his native Ireland, where he died in 1945 of bronchial pneumonia. Among the many honors that came to him were the Order of St. Gregory the Great, the Order of the Holy Sepulchre, and the vice-presidency of the Irish Royal Academy. On Feb. 23, 1928, he was raised to papal peerage with the title of Count. In collaboration with Pierre Key, he wrote an autobiography, *John McCormack: His Own Life Story* (1919). After his death, his widow wrote his biography, *I Hear You Calling Me* (1949).

McCracken, John Eugene, tenor. Born Gary, Ind., Dec. 16, 1926. Formal music study began following his discharge from the Navy after World War II, when he attended Columbia University and assisted in the production of several operas with the Columbia Theatre Associates. The necessity of earning a living compelled him for several years to sing in the chorus of the Roxy Theater, a motion-picture house in New York, and play minor roles in Broadway plays. He continued, however, to study voice with Wellington Ezekiel, who prepared him for his opera debut with the CENTRAL CITY OPERA in 1952 as Rodolfo in LA BOHÈME. On Nov. 21, 1953, he made his debut at the METROPOLITAN OPERA in a minor role in *La Bohème*. Assigned only small parts for several years, McCracken left the company in 1957 for Europe. He appeared in leading roles in various opera companies in Germany, Switzerland, Greece, and Jugoslavia, while going through an intensive period of vocal study in Milan. Back in the United States in 1960 he made such a highly successful appearance in the title role of VERDI'S OTELLO that he was signed to sing major parts with the VIENNA STATE OPERA and the ZÜRICH OPERA. There he achieved remarkable successes in various French and Italian roles. On Oct. 2, 1962, he made his debut with the SAN FRANCISCO OPERA, where he caused a sensation as Othello. This was followed by his return to the Metropolitan Opera on Mar. 10, 1963, once again as Othello, the first American-born tenor to sing the part in that company's history. He has since appeared not only with the Metropolitan Opera but with most of the world's leading opera houses and at major European festivals.

Macduff, a nobleman (tenor) in VERDI'S MACBETH.

Macfarren, Sir George Alexander, composer. Born London, Mar. 2, 1813; died there Oct. 31, 1887. He completed his music study at the Royal Academy of Music, where in 1834 he became a professor. In 1875 he was appointed professor of music at Cambridge and a year later principal of the Royal Academy. The most notable of his twelve operas: *The Devil's Opera* (1838); DON QUIXOTE (1846); *King Charles II* (1849); ROBIN HOOD (1860); *Jessy Lea* (1863); *She Stoops to Conquer* (1864); *The Soldiers' Legacy* (1864); *Helvellyn* (1864). In 1840 he edited DIDO AND AENEAS. He was knighted in 1883.

Machiavelli, Niccolò, statesman and writer. Born Florence, May 3, 1469; died there June 22, 1527. His powerful comedy, *La mandragola,* a satire on the corruption of Italian society, was the source of operas by CASTELNUOVO-TEDESCO and Ignaz Waghalter.

Ma chi lascia sobborgo, duet of Giorgetta and Luigi recalling their past happy days, in PUCCINI'S IL TABARRO.

Mackenzie, Sir Alexander, composer. Born Edinburgh, Scotland, Aug. 22, 1847; died London, Apr. 28, 1935. He attended the Sonderhausen Conservatory (Germany) and the Royal Academy of Music in London. In 1865 he returned to Edinburgh, where during the next decade he became prominent as violinist, teacher, and conductor. In 1879 he settled in Florence to concentrate on composition. Back in England in 1888, he was appointed principal of the Royal Academy of Music (from which he retired only in 1924) and in 1892 principal conductor of the Philharmonic Society. He was knighted in 1895 and in 1922 made Knight Commander of the Victorian Order. His operas: *Colomba* (1883); *The Troubadour* (1886); *His Majesty* (1897); *The Knights of the Road* (1905); *The Cricket on the Hearth* (1914); *The Eve of St. John* (1925).

Macpherson, James, writer and poet. Born Ruthven, Scotland, Oct. 27, 1736; died there Feb. 17, 1796. He published several volumes of "translations" by a supposed third-century Gaelic poet, Ossian. Though Macpherson was never able to prove the authenticity of this poetry, it had a tremendous vogue, not only in England but on the Continent. Several operas were derived from these poems of "Ossian," notably Edgar L. Bainton's *Oithona*, François Bathelemon's *Oithona*, Jean Georg Kastner's *Oskars Tod*, MÉHUL'S *Uthal*, Edward Sobolewski's *Komola,* Ian Whyte's *Comola,* and Peter von White's *Colmal.* Ossian is the central character of Jean LESUEUR'S opera *Ossian,* produced in 1804.

Ma dall' arido, Amelia's aria as she searches for a magic herb at a gallows at midnight, in Act II of VERDI'S UN BALLO IN MASCHERA.

Madama Butterfly, opera in three acts by PUCCINI. Libretto by Luigi ILLICA and Giuseppe Giacosa, based on a play by David BELASCO, in turn derived from a short story by John Luther Long. Premiere: La Scala, Feb. 17, 1904. American premiere: Washington, D.C., Oct. 15, 1906.

Characters: Cio-Cio-San (Madama Butterfly, a geisha girl, soprano); Suzuki, her servant (mezzo-soprano); B. F. Pinkerton, U.S. Navy lieutenant (tenor); Kate Pinkerton, his wife (mezzo-soprano); Sharpless, U.S. Consul at Nagasaki (baritone); Goro, a marriage broker (tenor); Prince Yamadori, in love with Cio-Cio-San (baritone); the Bonze, Cio-Cio-San's uncle (bass); friends and relatives of Cio-Cio-San. The setting is Nagasaki, Japan, in the early 1900's.

Act I. The exterior of Pinkerton's house. The short prelude is based on a Japanese theme that recurs throughout the opera; it breaks into the first act without pause. Pinkerton tells Sharpless of his infatuation for a Japanese girl and of his intention to marry her for "nine hundred and ninety-nine years," with the privilege of annulment when convenient. Pinkerton's levity upsets Sharpless, who tries to convince the lieutenant of the gravity of a relationship with a Japanese girl. Pinkerton repeats how intensely he loves her ("Amore o grillo"). Laughing voices of Japanese girls are heard and Cio-Cio-San appears. She introduces her relatives and friends to Pinkerton ("Spira sul mare"). Presently, she informs her beloved that for his sake she has renounced her religion ("Ieri son salita"). The marriage ceremony is interrupted when Cio-Cio-San's uncle appears to condemn his niece for renouncing her people. Contemptuously, her relatives spurn the girl and depart. Butterfly bursts into tears but is soon soothed by Pinkerton's tenderness. As night descends, the lovers are happy in each other's arms as they confide their passionate feelings ("Viene la sera").

Act II. Inside Butterfly's house three years later. As Suzuki prays before an image of Buddha, Butterfly chides her gently for appealing to a Japanese god. Butterfly is faithful to Pinkerton, who had left long ago with the American fleet, and she is true to his religion and country, certain that some fine day he will come back to her ("Un bel dì"). Sharpless brings Butterfly a letter which she is about to read when the marriage broker arrives with a wealthy suitor, Prince Yamadori. Butterfly is deaf to all proposals and the Prince leaves. When Sharpless later inquires what Butterfly would do if Pinkerton were to desert her and tries to hint that this has actually occurred ("Ora a noi"), she answers gravely that she would kill herself. She calls in the child, Little Trouble, who is the fruit of her love, and sings to him "Sai cos' ebbe cuore." Sharpless now knows that a terrible tragedy is imminent. Suddenly there comes from the harbor the sound of a cannon shot. Cio-Cio-San seizes a telescope and learns that Pinkerton's ship has returned. In anticipation of her beloved's return, Butterfly helps Suzuki decorate the house with cherry blossoms (Flower Duet: "Scuoti quella fronda di ciliegio"). She then dons her wedding dress. Then as unseen voices are heard in the "Humming Chorus," Cio-Cio-San, her child, and Suzuki await Pinkerton's arrival.

Act III. The same scene. A tender orchestral prelude recalls the love music of the first act. Dawn has come. Weary of her vigil, Butterfly goes to an inner room. While she is absent, Pinkerton and Sharpless arrive. Suzuki is overwhelmed with joy at the sight of Pinkerton, but when she sees an American woman at Pinkerton's side she senses the worst (Trio: "Io so che alle sue pene"). Sharpless persuades Pinkerton to leave without seeing Butterfly. After a tender farewell to the house and his memories ("Addio, fiorito asil"), Pinkerton departs. When Butterfly rushes into the room she finds not Pinkerton, but Sharpless and a strange woman in Western dress. When she sees her servant in tears she begins to understand what has happened. The American woman, Pinkerton's wife Kate, implores Cio-Cio-San to turn over to her Pinkerton's child. At last, Cio-Cio-San is ready to do this—but only on condition that Pinkerton himself makes the request. When Sharpless and Kate leave to call Pinkerton, Butterfly is left alone with Little Trouble. She bids her child farewell ("Tu, tu, piccolo iddio!"), gives him a doll and an American flag to play with, and she blindfolds him. Then she goes behind a screen with her dagger. A moment later she staggers out; by the time Pinkerton appears, she is dead, and the boy, seated on the floor, is waving the flag. Pinkerton is overwhelmed with grief, and Sharpless gently leads the motherless child from the house.

Madama Butterfly, today one of Puccini's best-loved operas, was a fiasco when first performed. The antagonism of the audience was such that the shouting often drowned out the music. Puccini finally appeared on the stage in an effort to restore order. He was jeered into the wings. There is good reason to believe that enemies of Puccini, envious of his mounting success, had helped organize this opposition. If so, they were also aided by the opera itself. Coming from a composer who had already endeared himself to his audiences with MANON LESCAUT, LA BOHÈME, and TOSCA, *Madama Butterfly* was something of a shock. The exotic setting, the love affair of an American and a Japanese girl were not to Italian tastes. A major irritant was the overlong second act (the opera was originally complete in two acts).

Believing that he had written his finest opera, Puccini did not lose faith. However, he allowed himself to be convinced by a few friends (including Arturo TOSCANINI) to revise the work. He deleted some of the more objectionable and exotic vocal passages, made more of the tenor role, and divided the long second act to make a third. Three months after its premiere the opera was heard again. This time it was a triumph. A month later Toscanini introduced it to South America. From then on the opera aroused unqualified enthusiasm and its popularity continues unabated. It has something of the refinement and delicacy of a Japa-

nese print. Puccini's lyricism, mainly Italian, is in his tenderest and sweetest vein, and his characterization of Butterfly is one of the most affecting in his gallery of operatic women. His ability to evoke the proper atmosphere and mood with a few strokes of the pen shows the hand of a master, and the oriental harmonic and instrumental effects no longer startle but provide a welcome suggestion of authenticity.

Madame Sans-Gêne, opera in three acts by GIORDANO. Libretto by Renato Simoni, based on the play of the same name by Victorien SARDOU and Emile Moreau. Premiere: Metropolitan Opera, Jan. 25, 1915. The setting is France during and following the French Revolution. Catherine, a laundress known as Madame Sans-Gêne (soprano), active in the revolution, marries the police sergeant Lefebvre (tenor). After the rise of Napoleon (baritone), Lefebvre becomes Duke of Danzig. Catherine arouses the displeasure of Napoleon's court with her frank and earthy ways, but Napoleon stands by her when she reminds him how she had been faithful to his cause. When Napoleon suspects his Empress of carrying on an affair with an Austrian count, Catherine becomes the means by which Napoleon is reassured of his wife's loyalty.

Madamina! il catalogo è questo, the Catalogue Song in Act I, Scene 2, of MOZART'S DON GIOVANNI, in which Leporello enumerates Don Giovanni's numerous conquests.

Maddalena, Sparafucile's sister (mezzosoprano) in VERDI'S RIGOLETTO.

Madeira, Jean (born Browning), mezzosoprano. Born Centralia, Ill., Nov. 14, 1924. After completing her vocal studies at the Juilliard School of Music she made her debut under her maiden name of Jean Browning at Chautauqua, N.Y. in 1943. On Dec. 2, 1948, she made her debut at the METROPOLITAN OPERA as the First Norn in GÖTTERDÄMMERUNG. She remained with this company for the next two decades, appearing in principal roles in the German, French, and Italian repertory. She scored a triumph with her interpretation of CARMEN. While a member of the Metropolitan Opera Company, she appeared with other leading companies as well as at such celebrated European festivals as those at BAYREUTH, SALZBURG, and AIX-EN-PROVENCE. On Sept. 29, 1968, she created the dual roles of Circe and Melantho in DALLAPICCOLA'S ULISSE at the BERLIN FESTIVAL, and in 1969 she appeared as Erda in a new production of the RING cycle at the MUNICH OPERA.

Madeleine, (1) one-act opera by Victor HERBERT. Libretto by Grant Stewart, adapted from a play by Adrien Decourcelles and L. Thibault, *Je Dine chez ma Mère*. Premiere: Metropolitan Opera, Jan. 24, 1914. The setting is Paris on New Year's Day, 1760. Madeleine Fleury, an opera singer (soprano), is heartbroken because her dinner invitations to various lovers and friends are turned down, all for the same reason: each happens to be dining with his or her mother. Finally, Madeleine takes down the portrait of her own mother from the wall and announces that she, too, will dine with her mother. The role of Madeleine was created by Frances ALDA.

(2) The heroine (soprano) with whom Chapelou is in love in ADAM'S LE POSTILLON DE LONGJUMEAU.

(3) The Countess de Coigny's daughter (soprano) in GIORDANO'S ANDREA CHÉNIER.

(4) A countess (soprano) in Richard STRAUSS'S CAPRICCIO.

Mademoiselle Fifi, *see* MAUPASSANT, GUY DE.

Madonna, con sospiri, Gennaro's prayer to the Madonna as he works on a holiday candelabra honoring a religious festival for the Madonna, in the opening of WOLF-FERRARI'S THE JEWELS OF THE MADONNA.

Madre, pietosa Vergine, Leonora's prayer, with male chorus, to the Virgin, in Act II, Scene 2, of VERDI'S LA FORZA DEL DESTINO.

madrigal comedy or **madrigal opera,** a musical form popular in Italy in the sixteenth century, consisting of a series of madrigals (songs for several voices, usually in a contrapuntal style), so designed as to tell a dramatic story. The most famous example is Orazio Vecchi's L'AMFIPARNASO, published in 1597. The madrigal comedy was a forerunner of opera. In the twentieth century the form was revived by MENOTTI in *The Unicorn, the Gorgon, and the Manticore.*

mad scenes. Italian grand opera has on several occasions made effective dramatic use by having its heroines go mad. Among the most famous mad scenes are those in I PURITANI (*see* QUI LA VOCE SUA SOAVE); LINDA DI CHAMOUNIX; and most celebrated of all, that in LUCIA DI LAMMERMOOR (*see* ARDON GL'INCENSI). Notable mad scenes are also encountered in DONIZETTI'S ANNA BOLENA and THOMAS'S HAMLET.

Maerbale, brother (baritone) of the Duke of Bomarzo, in GINASTERA'S BOMARZO.

maestro, Italian for "master," a title of respect conferred in Italy on composers, conductors, and often on impresarios as well.

maestro di cappella, an Italian term that first meant "master of the chapel," referring to the band of musicians playing or singing in a chapel or church. A *maestro di cappella* might be a choirmaster, a conductor, composer, or all three. The term later narrowed to denote a conductor. The German equivalent is *kapellmeister;* the French, *maître de chapelle.*

maestro di musica, Il (The Music Master), one-act comic opera by PERGOLESI. Libretto by an unknown author. Premiere: Naples, summer of 1731. American premiere: New York City, Apr. 17, 1936. The teacher of a beautiful, female voice student feels she is not ready for a public appearance. The local impresario, attracted to the girl, thinks otherwise and offers her an engagement. The teacher now changes his mind, allows the girl to appear, and even falls in love with her.

Maeterlinck, Maurice, author. Born Ghent, Belgium, Aug. 29, 1862; died

Nice, France, May 6, 1949. He won the Nobel Prize for literature in 1911. Several of his sensitive and at times mystical plays have been made into operas. The most celebrated is *Pelléas et Mélisande*, the text of DEBUSSY's impressionist opera. Others are: *Ariane et Barbe-bleue* (DUKAS); *Monna Vanna* (operas by Henri FÉVRIER and Emil Abrányi); *The Blue Bird* (Albert Louis WOLFF); *Soeur Béatrice* (operas by GRETCHANINOV and François Rasse); *La mort de Tintagiles* (operas by Lawrence Collingwood and Jean NOUGUÈS).

Magda, (1) Ruggiero's beloved (soprano) in PUCCINI's LA RONDINE.

(2) Heinrich's wife (soprano) in RESPIGHI's LA CAMPANA SOMMERSA.

Magdalena, Eva's nurse (mezzo-soprano) in WAGNER's DIE MEISTERSINGER.

Magda Sorel, the heroine and the victim of a totalitarian society (soprano) in MENOTTI's THE CONSUL, a role created by Patricia NEWAY.

Mag der Himmel euch vergeben (Ah! che a voi perdoni iddio), quintet closing Act III of FLOTOW's MARTHA, when Lady Harriet gets Lionel arrested.

Maggio Musicale Fiorentino, *see* FLORENCE MAY MUSIC FESTIVAL.

Maggiorivoglio, Marchioness of, the name for the Countess of Berkenfeld in the Italian version of DONIZETTI's THE DAUGHTER OF THE REGIMENT.

Magic Fire Scene (Feuerzauber), the concluding scene, in which Brünnhilde is surrounded by a circle of flames, of WAGNER's DIE WALKÜRE.

Magic Flute, The (Die Zauberflöte), opera in two acts by MOZART. Libretto by Johann Emanuel SCHIKANEDER. Premiere: Theater-auf-der-Wieden, Vienna, Sept. 30, 1791. American premiere: Park Theater, New York, Apr. 17, 1833.

Characters: Sarastro, High Priest of Isis (bass); Queen of the Night (soprano); Pamina, her daughter (soprano); Tamino, a prince (tenor); Papageno, a birdcatcher (baritone); Papagena, his sweetheart (soprano); Monostatos, a Moor (tenor); attendants of the Queen of the Night; priests; priestesses; slaves; warriors. The action takes place in Memphis, Egypt, in the days of Ramses I.

The three majestic chords that open the overture are restated within the opera before the March of the Priests and Sarastro's air, "O Isis." These chords begin a solemn introduction that in turn leads into a rapid section where the lively main theme is given fugal treatment and an involved development.

Act I, Scene 1. A lonely landscape. Tamino, fleeing from a serpent, faints but is rescued by three attendants of the Queen of the Night. Papageno appears, preceded by his piping. Papageno sings a ditty ("Der Vogelfänger bin ich ja") that explains his preference for girls to birds. Tamino, wakening, believes that it is Papageno who has saved him from the serpent: when he thanks the birdcatcher, Papageno does not disillusion him. Because of this deception, Papageno is punished by the Queen's attendants by having his lips sealed with a padlock. The attendants then show Tamino a portrait of the Queen's daughter, Pamina, whose beauty inspires the prince to rhapsody ("Dies Bildnis ist bezaubernd schön"). Now the Queen of the Night comes to tell Tamino that Pamina is the prisoner of a tyrant, that if Tamino will save her he can have her as his wife ("O zitt're nicht, mein lieber Sohn"). Tamino consents to save her. To help him in his adventure, the Queen provides him with a magic flute which, when played, will safeguard him from harm. Papageno is instructed to accompany Tamino to the palace of the abductor, Sarastro; the lock is removed from his lips, and he is given a set of chimes whose magic property is similar to that of Tamino's flute.

Scene 2. A room in Sarastro's palace. Pamina is being guarded by Monostatos. The Moor flees in terror when Papageno appears, for he thinks the birdcatcher is the devil. Papageno convinces Pamina that she should follow him toward liberation and true love. They both sing the praises of love ("Bei Männern, welche Liebe fühlen").

Scene 3. A grove before the Temple of Isis. Tamino is told by a temple priest that Sarastro is no tyrant but a man of high ideals; someday, the priest declares, the reason for imprisoning Pamina will be made clear. When he hears the ringing of Papageno's chimes, Tamino goes searching for him. Papageno and Pamina have been trapped by Monostatos and his slaves and have been rescued by the magic chimes. Suddenly Sarastro enters. Pamina falls on her knees confessing that she had tried to escape. A moment later Tamino is brought in; he, too, has been seized by the slaves. Seeing each other for the first time, Tamino and Pamina rush toward one another. Sarastro reveals to the pair that they must now perform secret rites. Their heads are covered with veils.

Act II, Scene 1. A palm grove. Sarastro and his priests file in (March of the Priests). Sarastro pleads that Tamino be initiated into the final mysteries of their order, for his marriage to Pamina has been preordained. The priests give their consent. Sarastro then invokes the gods to bring the lovers the courage to meet their trials ("O Isis und Osiris").

Scene 2. The courtyard of the Temple of Isis. Tamino and Papageno are about to undergo several severe tests. For one thing, Tamino is denied the privilege of speaking to Pamina; for another, Papageno must not say a word to the bride selected for him by Sarastro. When the attendants of the Queen of the Night warn him to flee from this place of evil, Tamino turns a deaf ear.

Scene 3. A garden. While Pamina sleeps, Monostatos tries to steal a kiss. He is sent scurrying by the Queen of the Night, who then pleads with Pamina to avenge her ("Der Hölle Rache"). When she gives Pamina a dagger with which to kill Sarastro, Pamina recoils in horror. Later, Pamina appeals to Sarastro to have mercy on her mother. Sarastro replies that in a holy place there is no room for hate or vengeance ("In diesen heil'gen Hallen").

Scene 4. A hall in the Temple of Probation. Unable to hold his tongue, Papageno begins to blabber to an old woman who brings him water. A peal of thunder sends the old woman away in terror. Pages now arrive with a feast. Tamino, however, can think only of his beloved. He summons her with his flute. She appears, full of love, but is bewildered when Tamino refuses to speak to her. Convinced that she is no longer loved, Pamina seeks death ("Ach, ich fühl's"). Tamino and Papageno are summoned to their next test.

Scene 5. A place near the Pyramids. The priests and Sarastro call to the gods to witness the climax of Tamino's trials. Sarastro reassures both Tamino and Pamina that all will turn out well in the end. He then leads Tamino away. Papageno staggers in, tired and thirsty. Magically, a huge goblet of wine appears. Drinking his fill, Papageno becomes inebriated and expresses his wish for a wife ("Ein Mädchen oder Weibchen"). The old woman reappears and insists that she is the wife who has been selected for him. He must accept her—the alternative is a life with only bread and water. When he does so, she is magically transformed into a young and beautiful bird-girl, Papagena. Papageno is about to take her in his arms when a voice warns him that he must first undergo another trial.

Scene 6. A garden. The three pages hail the sun that banishes the superstitions of night ("Bald prangt, den Morgen"). Pamina, convinced that she has lost Tamino's love, is about to kill herself. Her hand is stayed by three pages who reassure her that Tamino is still in love with her.

Scene 7. A wild mountain spot. Just before meeting another test of courage, Tamino is allowed to meet and embrace Pamina. Pamina takes Tamino's hand and conducts him through a cavern of fire as Tamino plays his magic flute for protection. After this the lovers negotiate a water cavern. The priests hail their success.

Scene 8. A garden. Papageno thinks he has lost his beautiful girl. He is so upset that he begins to hang himself. The pages appear and remind him to use his chimes. Eagerly, Papageno tinkles out his magic tune. It brings Papagena, and the two embrace.

Scene 9. A gloomy spot near the Temple of Isis. The Queen of the Night, her three attendants, and Monostatos are making one last attempt to destroy Sarastro and abduct Pamina. A burst of lightning and crash of thunder herald their descent into the depths of the earth.

Scene 10. The Temple. Tamino and Pamina are conducted before Sarastro. He pronounces them ready to serve Isis. Sarastro, supported by his followers, intones the praises of Isis and Osiris.

The Magic Flute, written in the last year of Mozart's life, was commissioned by Emanuel Schikaneder, the impresario of a theater presenting SINGSPIELE. It was with the requirements of the *singspiel* in mind that Mozart wrote his music. Schikaneder wrote the kind of play Viennese liked. It was filled with good and diabolical forces in conflict; it had burlesque characters; it glorified the triumph of love over all obstacles; it had an oriental setting. All this was made to serve as symbolism for the Masonic order of which both Schikaneder and Mozart were members. Confusion set in with last-minute revisions of characters and drastic alterations of plot made necessary by the production in Vienna of another opera with a story similar to Schikaneder's.

The popular character of the play—but certainly not its obfuscation—was carried out in Mozart's music. Interspersed with the dialogue are many tunes, particularly those sung by Papageno, that have the wholesomeness of folksongs. And there are arias that are among the most beautiful written by Mozart. Mozart's feeling for a comic situation was never surer. Yet at other moments he would rise to grandeur and nobility, as in Sarastro's arias. Perhaps in no other of his operas is the full range of his genius so strongly evident as here, in this work intended as popular entertainment but transformed into a wondrous work of art.

When *The Magic Flute* was given a new production at the Grand Theater in Geneva in 1965, the scenery and costumes were designed by Oskar Kokoschka, pioneer of German expressionism in art. Another world-famous artist, Marc Chagall, designed costumes and sets for a new production of *The Magic Flute* by the METROPOLITAN OPERA in 1967.

Magic Garden Scene, the scene in Klingsor's garden in Act II, Scene 2, of WAGNER'S PARSIFAL where the flower maidens dance enticingly about Parsifal while Kundry, transformed into a beautiful woman, makes an unsuccessful effort to seduce him.

magic opera (Zauberoper), a kind of opera popular in Vienna at the close of the eighteenth and the beginning of the nineteenth centuries. The text was usually on some fairy-tale subject and included both broad comedy and elaborate scenic effects. The work was made up of spoken dialogue interspersed with music numbers. THE MAGIC FLUTE and DER FREISCHÜTZ are the most celebrated examples. SCHUBERT'S *Die Zauberharfe* is another.

Magische Töne, Assad's aria in Act I of GOLDMARK'S THE QUEEN OF SHEBA.

Magnifico, Don, Cinderella's stepfather (bass) in ROSSINI'S LA CENERENTOLA, a role created by Giuseppe DE BEGNIS.

Mahabharata, The, a Hindu epic, the source of operas by HOLST (SAVITRI) and MASSENET (LE ROI DE LAHORE). Its theme is the great struggle between the houses of Kauravas and Pandavas for the control of a kingdom.

Mahagonny, *see* RISE AND FALL OF THE CITY MAHAGONNY, THE.

Mahler, Gustav, conductor and composer. Born Kalischt, Bohemia, July 7, 1860; died Vienna, May 18, 1911. Though Mahler wrote two operas in his youth, they were not published, and as a composer he is known only for his symphonies and his songs. However, he was one of the preeminent opera conductors of his time. He entered the Vienna Conservatory in 1875, his teachers including Robert Fuchs (harmony), Julius Epstein (piano), and Franz Krenn (composition). After leaving the conservatory he conducted orchestras of several small-town theaters. In 1882 he was appointed conductor of the Olmütz Opera. This was followed by several other appointments, including one at the PRAGUE OPERA, where Mahler gave notable performances of the RING cycle and several MOZART operas. He was next heard at the BUDAPEST OPERA, where his true stature as conductor was first appreciated. From Budapest, Mahler went on to the HAMBURG OPERA. There he continued to command the respect of discriminating musicians; his work was so outstanding that in 1897 several of Vienna's leading musicians (including Brahms and Guido Adler) recommended him for one of the most important conductorial posts in Europe, that of the VIENNA OPERA.

Mahler served as the music director of the Vienna Opera for a decade, creating one of the great epochs in the history of that company. Relentless in his dedication to perfection, he made the Vienna Opera the first opera house in Europe, if not in the world. He revitalized the repertory; he presented the old operas in new, restudied versions; he was meticulous about every detail of scenery and staging. He beat down mediocrity and opposition. "Certainly no operatic theater was ever directed on a more grandiose plan," wrote the Viennese critic Max Graf. There were those who called Mahler a saint because of his holy dedication to art. But he also had enemies who hated him for one or more reasons: because he was dictatorial, a Jew, lavish in his expenditures, or because they had been the objects of his savage attacks when they were guilty of sloth or indifference. These enemies were indefatigable in putting obstacles in his way and creating intrigues against him. By 1907 Mahler decided he had to leave Vienna. As he explained to his coworkers: "I must keep on the heights. I cannot let anything irritate me or drag me down." He gave his last performance in Vienna, FIDELIO, on Oct. 15, 1907. That winter he came to the United States and on Jan. 1,

1908, made his American debut at the METROPOLITAN OPERA with TRISTAN UND ISOLDE (a performance in which Olive FREMSTAD appeared for the first time as Isolde). He was acclaimed. The following season he combined his activity at the Metropolitan Opera with duties as conductor of the New York Philharmonic Orchestra. He continued dividing his energies between the Metropolitan and the Philharmonic through the 1909–10 season. The following season he devoted himself entirely to the Philharmonic. The strain of continuous work broke his health. He collapsed in New York, returned to Europe, where he led a few concerts of his own works, then died at the age of fifty.

Maid of Orleans, The, opera in three acts by TCHAIKOVSKY. Libretto by the composer, based on a translation of SCHILLER's drama *Die Jungfrau von Orleans.* Premiere: St. Petersburg, Feb. 25, 1881. The opera is based on the story of JOAN OF ARC.

Maid of Pskov, The, *see* IVAN THE TERRIBLE.

Main de gloire, La, opera in four acts by FRANÇAIX. Libretto by the composer, based on a story by Gérard de NERVAL. Premiere: Bordeaux Festival, May 7, 1950. The text is compounded of fantasy, comedy, and tragedy. A young man has cast a spell over his hand so that he may be victorious in a duel. No longer in control of his hand, he finds that it leads him from one crime to another until he is punished with death.

Maintenant que le père de Pelléas est sauvé, Arkel's expression of relief that Pelléas' father has recovered from his illness, in Act IV, Scene 1, of DEBUSSY's PELLÉAS ET MÉLISANDE.

Maison, René, tenor. Born Traumeries, Belgium, Nov. 24, 1895; died Mont-Doré, France, July 15, 1962. He studied singing in Antwerp and at the Paris Conservatory, after which he made his debut in Geneva in 1920 in LA BOHÈME. Appearances followed in Monte Carlo in 1922 and after that elsewhere in Europe and South America. From 1927 to 1932 he appeared with the Chicago

Civic Opera and the SAN FRANCISCO OPERA. In June, 1936, he made a successful debut at COVENT GARDEN as Julien in LOUISE. From 1934 to 1937 he appeared at the TEATRO COLÓN. He made his METROPOLITAN OPERA debut on Feb. 3, 1936, in DIE MEISTERSINGER, remaining at the Metropolitan for the next seven seasons. Between 1950 and 1957 he taught singing at the Julius Hart School in Boston and from 1957 to 1962 at the Chalof School of Music in the same city. He became an American citizen in 1959.

maître de chapelle, see MAESTRO DI CAPPELLA.

Majorano, Gaetano, see CAFFARELLI.

Makropoulos Affair, The, opera in three acts by JANÁČEK. Libretto by the composer, based on Karel Capek's play of the same name. Premiere: Brno Opera, Dec. 18, 1926. American premiere: San Francisco Opera, Nov. 22, 1966. The principal character is a singer, Emilia Marty, who has lived for three hundred and forty-two years, having been kept alive by a magic potion. She has become an evil, decadent woman who spreads her viciousness and cruelty on whomever she comes into contact with. Everybody is eager to get her formula for long life, without realizing that as far as she is concerned life has become intolerable. The opera ends with the formula being burned, and Emilia finally dying. This is one of Janáček's most powerful operas, whose text lends itself to the composer's dramatic declamatory style while the orchestra contributes the mood and atmosphere.

Malatesta, Dr., physician (baritone) in DONIZETTI'S DON PASQUALE, a role created by Antonio TAMBURINI.

Malazarte, Brazilian folk opera in three acts by Oscar Lorenzo Fernandez. Libretto by the composer, based on a play by García Aranha. Premiere: Rio de Janeiro, Sept. 30, 1941. The setting is colonial Brazil; the central character the legendary figure of Malazarte, master of evil arts. Music and text are filled with folk elements. Voodoo rites, magic, native dances play a prominent part. The Afro-Brazilian dance, "Batu-que," with which the first act ends, has been performed at symphony concerts.

Malcolm, Duncan's son (tenor) in VERDI'S MACBETH.

Maledezione, see CORTIGIANI, VIL RAZZA DANNATA; VOUS QUI DU DIEU VIVANT.

Malheurs d'Orphée, Les (The Misfortunes of Orpheus), opera in three acts by MILHAUD. Libretto by Armand Lunel. Premiere: Théâtre de la Monnaie, May 7, 1926. American premiere: New York City, Jan. 29, 1927 (concert version); New York City, May 22, 1958 (staged). Orpheus is here a druggist in an unspecified town where his clients are animals. He falls in love with a gypsy girl, Eurydice, and takes her off to the mountains. Eurydice dies there; not even Orpheus' tender solicitude, the love of his animals, or the power of drugs can save her. This opera has been revived, in London in 1960, by the Aspen School Opera Workshop in Colorado in 1963, and at the AIX-EN-PROVENCE festival in 1968.

Malibran, Maria Felicita (born García), contralto. Born Paris, Mar. 24, 1808; died Manchester, Sept. 23, 1836. She was the daughter of the tenor Manuel GARCÍA and the elder sister of the great mezzo-soprano, Pauline VIARDOT. At the age of five, she appeared in PAER's opera Agnese, in Naples, playing a child's part. She then studied solfeggio with Auguste Mathieu Panseron in Naples and singing with her father. Her official debut took place in London, on June 7, 1825, as ROSINA. She then came to New York, where for two years she appeared with the Manuel García opera company in works by ROSSINI and MOZART and two operas written for her by her father. She went into temporary retirement in New York after marrying the French merchant Malibran. They soon separated. Returning to Paris, the singer made her debut at the Théâtre des Italiens in 1828. Her success was tremendous. She now appeared in opera in most of the major cities of Italy and in London. Later, she toured Europe in joint recitals with the violinist Charles de Bériot, whom she married early in 1836.

A month later a fall from a horse gave her head injuries that she never overcame, and after a few more appearances in concerts her brief life came to an end. The American composer Robert Russell Bennett has made her the central character of his opera *Maria Malibran* (1935).

Maliella, Carmela's adopted daughter (soprano) in WOLF-FERRARI'S THE JEWELS OF THE MADONNA.

Malipiero, Gian Francesco, composer. Born Venice, Mar. 18, 1882. He came from an aristocratic Venetian family that had included several notable musicians. When Malipiero was seven, his family left Italy. For several years father and son played in German and Austrian theater orchestras. In 1896 an Austrian nobleman provided funds for Malipiero's formal study. He now attended the Vienna Conservatory for one year and after that the Liceo Benedetto Marcello in Venice; his studies were completed with Enrico Bossi in Bologna. In 1902 Malipiero began research in old Italian music, the results of which were his editions of the works of such masters as VIVALDI, CAVALLI, Marcello, and MONTEVERDI. In 1913 he went to Paris; that city's musical life stimulated and affected him. At this point he entered five of his works in an Italian competition: he won four prizes. One of the five works was his first opera, *Canossa,* introduced in Rome on Jan. 24, 1914. Just before the outbreak of World War I, Malipiero settled in Asolo. He has since lived there whenever his teaching and editorial duties have allowed him to. He became director of the Liceo Benedetto Marcello in Venice in 1939. He has written numerous works for the stage. His style, classical in its serenity, combines the techniques and spirit of old Italian music with contemporary harmonic thought. His operas: *Canossa* (1913); *L'Orfeide,* a cycle of three operas including *Sette canzoni* (1920), *Orfeo* (1921), and *La morte della maschere* (1922), *Tre commedie goldoniani,* a cycle of three operas including *La bottega di coffe, Sior Todoro Brontolon,* and *Le baruffe chiozzotte* (1923); *Filomela e*

l'infatuato (1925); *Merlino maestro d'organi* (1927); *Il mistero di Venezia,* a cycle of three operas including *Il finto Arlecchino* (1927), *Le Aquile d'Aquileia* (1929), and *I corvi di San Marco* (1929); *Torneo notturno* (1930); *La bella e il mostro* (1930); LA FAVOLA DEL FIGLIO CAMBIATO (1933); *Giulio Cesare* (1936); ANTONIO E CLEOPATRA (1938); *Ecuba* (1939); *La vita e sogno* (1940); *I capricci di Callot* (1941); *L'allegra brigata* (1943); *Mondi celesti e infernali* (1949); *Il figliuol prodigo* (1957); *Venere prigioniera* (1957); *Il capitan Spavento* (1963); *Don Giovanni* (1963); *Le metamorfosi di Bonaventura* (1966); *L'Aredodese* (1967); *Gli eroi di bona ventura* (1969).

Mallika, Lakmé's slave (mezzo-soprano) in DELIBES'S LAKMÉ.

Mallinger, Mathilde (born Lichtenegger), soprano. Born Agram, Croatia, Feb. 17, 1847; died Berlin, Apr. 19, 1920. Her studies took place at the Prague Conservatory, and with Richard Lewy in Vienna. On Oct. 4, 1866, she made her debut in Munich as NORMA. Two years later she created the role of Eva in the world premiere of DIE MEISTERSINGER. During this period she appeared successfully in Austria and Russia. From 1890 to 1895 she was professor of singing at the Prague Conservatory, and after 1895 she taught at the Eichelberg Conservatory in Berlin.

Mal reggendo all'aspro assalto, Manrico's explanation to Azucena of why he spared the life of the Count in a duel, in Act II, Scene 1, of VERDI'S IL TROVATORE.

Malvolio, an assassin (baritone) in FLOTOW'S ALESSANDRO STRADELLA.

Mamelles de Tirésias, Les (The Breasts of Tiresias), an *opéra burlesque* in prologue and two acts by POULENC. Libretto by Guillaume Apollinaire. Premiere: Opéra-Comique, June 3, 1947. American premiere: Waltham, Mass., June 13, 1953. The heroine of this surrealistic text is Theresa, who is tired of being a wife. By releasing her breasts (which in actuality are balloons, exploded with flame from a cigarette lighter), she becomes a man. The husband changes his sex, too, and gives birth to forty thousand children. A good deal of nonsense, with no relevancy to what has happened, follows, including a duel by two characters in which they both get killed (the argument is over whether they are in Zanzibar or Paris). In the end the two main characters revert happily to their original sexes and advise the audience to proliferate in order to rehabilitate France and avoid future wars.

Ma mère, je la vois, duet of Don José and Micaëla in Act I of BIZET'S CARMEN, in which Micaëla brings him news about his mother, reviving recollections of his childhood.

Mamma Lucia, see LUCIA.

Mamma, quel vino è generoso, Turiddu's farewell to his mother in MASCAGNI'S CAVALLERIA RUSTICANA.

Mancinelli, Luigi, conductor and composer. Born Orvieto, Italy, Feb. 5, 1848; died Rome, Feb. 2, 1921. He studied the cello in Florence. After playing in various orchestras he became a conductor. In 1874 he was appointed conductor of the Rome Opera. Seven years later he settled in Bologna as conductor of the Teatro Communale and director of the Liceo Musicale. In 1886 he went to London, where for two years he was principal conductor at COVENT GARDEN during its spring seasons. There he conducted the first German-language performance in England of TRISTAN UND ISOLDE. From 1887 to 1895 he directed opera performances at the Royal Theater in Madrid. He came to the United States in 1893, making his debut at the METROPOLITAN OPERA on Nov. 27 with FAUST. He remained a principal conductor of the Metropolitan through the 1902–03 season, conducting German, Italian, and French operas. He was a distinguished Wagnerian conductor, one of the first in Italy to sponsor the WAGNER music dramas. In 1906 he helped inaugurate the TEATRO COLÓN in Buenos Aires, conducting there until 1912. He then retired to his villa at Lake Maggiore. He wrote the following operas: *Isora di Provenza* (1884); *Ero e Leandro*

(1897); *Paolo e Francesca* (1907); *Sogno di una notte d'estate* (1916).

Mandryka, a wealthy landowner (baritone) in love with Arabella, in Richard STRAUSS'S ARABELLA.

Manfred, see BYRON, GEORGE NOEL GORDON, LORD.

Manfredo, King Archibaldo's son (baritone), husband of Fiora, in MONTEMEZZI'S L'AMORE DEI TRE RE, a role created by Carlo Galeffi.

Manhattan Opera Company, company established by Oscar HAMMERSTEIN at the Manhattan Opera House on Thirty-fourth Street in New York City in 1906. For four years it was one of the great opera institutions of the world. Hammerstein built the Manhattan Opera House to make it a home for opera in English. Before the house was completed, he changed his plans and decided to present great operas in their original languages and with the world's foremost singers. The new company and the new opera house were first seen on Dec. 3, 1906. The opera was NORMA. Cleofonte CAMPANINI was artistic director. A glittering parade of opera stars appeared there, including Nellie MELBA, Lillian NORDICA, Luisa TETRAZZINI, Ernestine SCHUMANN-HEINK, Giovanni ZENATELLO, Lina CAVALIERI, John MCCORMACK, Mary GARDEN, Alessandro BONCI, Charles DALMORÈS, Maurice RENAUD—many of them appearing in America for the first time. The emphasis was on French operas, then being neglected by the competitive METROPOLITAN OPERA, and on provocative novelties. Among the latter were PELLÉAS ET MÉLISANDE with Mary Garden, ELEKTRA, LOUISE, and SAPHO. The success of the Manhattan Opera provided serious, even damaging, competition to the Metropolitan Opera, with the result that Heinrich CONRIED had to resign as director of the Metropolitan, where a drastic reorganization took place. After giving four hundred and sixty-three performances of forty-nine different operas, the Manhattan Opera suddenly closed in 1910. What caused Hammerstein to withdraw from opera was at the time a mystery. Since then, however, it has been revealed that a contractual agreement was made between Hammerstein and the directors of the Metropolitan by which, for a cash sum of over one million dollars, Hammerstein agreed not to stage opera performances in America for a period of ten years.

Mann, Thomas, author. Born Lübeck, Ger., June 6, 1875; died Zürich, Aug. 12, 1955. He won the Nobel Prize for literature in 1929. His monumental series of four novels on the Biblical story of Joseph, *Joseph and His Brethren,* was made into a cycle of four opera-oratorios by ROSENBERG. Mann's story THE TRANSPOSED HEADS was used in an opera of the same name by GLANVILLE-HICKS. Franco Mannino's *Luisiella* (1969) is also based on one of Mann's stories.

Manners, Charles (born Southcote Mansergh), bass and impresario. Born London, Dec. 27, 1857; died Dublin, May 3, 1935. His music study took place at the Royal Irish Academy in Dublin, the Royal Academy in London, and in Florence. He made his stage debut in the premiere of *Iolanthe* by Gilbert and SULLIVAN. Subsequently he joined the CARL ROSA OPERA, and in 1890 he made his COVENT GARDEN debut in ROBERT LE DIABLE. In 1893 he appeared in the United States as vocal soloist with the Anton Seidl orchestra. Three years later he sang in South Africa. In 1897, with his wife Fanny Moody, an opera soprano, he formed the Moody-Manners Opera Company. Its aim was the presentation of opera in English. The company gave successful seasons at Covent Garden, DRURY LANE, and in the English provinces. In 1904 and 1906 Manners directed opera festivals in Sheffield, the proceeds going toward the founding of a university there. He retired from all operatic activity in 1913.

Mannheim Opera, a major German opera company situated in Baden-Württemberg. Performances took place at the National Theater, which opened in 1779 and was destroyed by bombs during World War II in 1943. The company first achieved significance in the nineteenth century under the musical direction of Vincenz Lachner, Felix WEINGARTNER, and August Nassermann. Among its principal conductors from 1900 to World War II were BODANZKY, FURTWÄNGLER, KLEIBER, and ELMENDORFF. The National Theater was rebuilt and reopened in Jan., 1957, with DER FREISCHÜTZ. Horst STEIN became principal conductor in 1963. Among operas receiving world premieres in Mannheim were WELLESZ'S ALKESTIS in 1923; Orff's adaptation of MONTEVERDI'S L'ORFEO in 1925; and the first staging of EGK'S ABSTRAKTE OPER NO. 1 in 1953. Significant novelties included the first German presentations of PRINCE IGOR and LE ROSSIGNOL. In 1969 the company offered among its new productions EUGENE ONEGIN, IL TURCO IN ITALIA, and IL CAMPIELLO.

Manon, opera in five acts by MASSENET. Libretto by Henri Meilhac and Philippe Gille, based on Abbé PRÉVOST's story *L'Histoire du chevalier des Grieux et de Manon Lescaut.* Premiere: Opéra-Comique, Jan. 19, 1884. American premiere: Academy of Music, New York, Dec. 23, 1885.

Characters: Chevalier des Grieux (tenor); Count des Grieux, his father (bass); Manon Lescaut (soprano); Lescaut, her cousin (baritone); Guillot de Morfontaine, Minister of France (bass); De Brétigny, a nobleman (baritone); actresses; travelers; soldiers; townspeople; vendors; gamblers. The action takes place in Amiens, Paris, and Le Havre early in the eighteenth century.

Act I. Courtyard of an inn at Amiens. Lescaut awaits the arrival of his unknown cousin, Manon, a young girl on her way to a convent. She arrives by coach and tells Lescaut of her journey ("Je suis encore tout étourdie"). Lescaut tries to warn her of the ways of the world ("Ne brochez pas, soyez gentille"). The roué Guillot de Morfontaine tries to impress Manon with his wealth. She rebuffs him. Seemingly, she is not interested in men, since she is about to enter a convent; however, the sight of three prettily dressed young women sets her reflecting on the sadness of thus rejecting life and love ("Voyons, Manon, plus de chimères"). Her revery is interrupted by the arrival of the young Chevalier des Grieux. He is struck by her beauty ("Et je sais votre nom"); she is also attracted to him. When Guillot puts his coach at Manon's disposal, hoping she will receive his attentions, Manon impetuously suggests to Des Grieux that they use it to go to Paris together ("Nous vivrons à Paris tous les deux").

Act II. The apartment of Chevalier des Grieux in Paris. With the help of Manon, Des Grieux is writing to his father asking his consent to marry Manon (Duo de la lettre: "J'écris à mon père"). Lescaut arrives, angered that his cousin has been abducted; however, when Des Grieux shows him the letter he is writing, evidence of his honorable intentions, the visitor is placated. De Brétigny, who has apparently known Manon for some time, tries to induce her to go off with him for a life of pleasure and wealth, and to convince Manon, he informs her that Des Grieux's father will shortly have his son forcibly taken from her. Manon wavers as she recalls her happiness with her beloved; but she finally gives in. While Des Grieux is out mailing his letter, she bids farewell to the table where they both have enjoyed so many happy meals ("Adieu, notre petite table"). When Des Grieux returns he finds her in tears. He tries to console her by revealing one of his dreams, in which he lives with Manon in their own home (Le Rêve: "En fermant les yeux"). When Des Grieux goes to the door to answer a knock, he is abducted by his father's men.

Act III, Scene 1. A street in Paris during a festival day. Before the rise of the curtain, a minuet is played as an entr'acte. The festive crowd includes De Brétigny and Guillot de Morfontaine. When Manon appears she is instantly surrounded by her admirers. Gaily she tells them of her devil-may-care life ("Je marche sur tous les chemins"); she also voices her philosophy that life is meant for song and dance (GAVOTTE: "Obéissons quand leur voix appelle"). When Des Grieux's father arrives, he discloses to De Brétigny that his son is at Saint-Sulpice, about to enter the priesthood. The news reawakens Manon's love for the Chevalier. She rushes off to Saint-Sulpice.

Scene 2. A parlor in the Seminary of Saint-Sulpice. Des Grieux's father has come to beg his son not to renounce life; he finds the young man deaf to his pleas. After his father leaves, the Chevalier bids the world farewell, but even while doing this he is unable to free his mind of memories of Manon ("Ah! fuyez, douce image"). Now Manon herself enters. At first Des Grieux rejects her, but Manon's beauty and tenderness are overpowering, and her persuasion irresistible ("N'est-ce plus ma main que cette main presse?"). At last he takes her in his arms, confessing he loves her more than ever ("Ah! viens, Manon"). They rush off together.

Act IV. A fashionable gambling room in Paris. The Chevalier and Manon arrive. Manon extols the joys of gold ("Ce bruit de l'or rire"). Des Grieux begins to gamble, and since his luck is phenomenal, he is accused of cheating. In the ensuing disturbance, the police are summoned. Des Grieux is saved from an unpleasant situation by his father, but Manon is apprehended as a woman of ill repute.

Act V. A lonely spot on the road to Le Havre. Manon is being sent by coach to exile. Des Grieux bribes an officer for permission to speak to her. Passionately, he tries to convince Manon to run away with him, but Manon, ill and exhausted, has lost the will to live. She grows weaker; her mind begins to wander. She falls into Des Grieux's arms, emits a cry, and dies.

Manon is both one of the most popular French operas and one of the most characteristic. It contains delightful dances in antique style which help evoke the background of eighteenth-century France. It is also filled with a lyricism of such grace and refinement that only a Frenchman could have written it. There are some critics who consider this lyric style so characteristic of the composer that they have come to describe it as "Massenetique." But the dramatic element is not sacrificed, and for this reason *Manon* is one of Massenet's most effective works. The climactic scenes, while never aspiring to the grandeur and bigness of those in Italian opera, do not fail to affect audiences everywhere. It was to accentuate the drama that Massenet borrowed from WAGNER the LEITMOTIV technique. And it was also to serve the drama that he resorted to the innovation of utilizing the spoken dialogue traditional to OPÉRA COMIQUE against an effective orchestral background; the dialogue keeps the action fluid, while the accompaniment emphasizes and intensifies the mood of the play. A decade after finishing *Manon* the composer wrote a one-act sequel, to a libretto by Georges Boyer, entitled LE PORTRAIT DE MANON. It has not held the stage.

Manon Lescaut, (1) opera by AUBER. Libretto by Eugène SCRIBE, based on the story of Abbé PRÉVOST. Premiere: Opéra-Comique, Feb. 23, 1856.

(2) Opera in four acts by PUCCINI. Libretto by Luigi ILLICA, Giuseppe Giacosa, Giulio Ricordi, Marco Praga, and Domenico Oliva, based on the story of Abbé PRÉVOST. Premiere: Teatro Regio, Turin, Feb. 1, 1893. American premiere: Philadelphia, Aug. 29, 1894. Characters: Chevalier des Grieux (tenor); Manon Lescaut (soprano), a role created by Cesara Ferrani; Lescaut, her brother, sergeant of the King's Guards (baritone); Géronte de Ravoir, a Parisian gallant (bass); Edmondo, a student (tenor); students; citizens; courtesans; sailors; dancers; police; ladies; gentlemen. The settings are Amiens, Paris, Le Havre, and Louisiana; the time, early in the eighteenth century.

Act I. Before an inn in Amiens. A coach has arrived bringing Manon Lescaut, her brother, and a *bon vivant*, Géronte. The Chevalier des Grieux, who is at hand, is sad. His friends chide him for being in love and he replies with a mocking serenade to all women ("Tra voi, belle"). When he sees Manon, he is struck by her beauty. Upon addressing her, he learns she is about to enter a convent. Manon is called away by her brother. Des Grieux grows rhapsodic over Manon's fascination ("Donna non vidi mai"). The libertine Géronte plans to abduct Manon, but Des Grieux learns of this. Upon Manon's reappearance, Des Grieux implores her to run away with him to Paris, and now, herself in love, Manon agrees. They escape in Géronte's coach, to the humiliation of the old man, who vows to use his wealth to win Manon away from her lover.

Act II. An apartment in Géronte's house. Manon has deserted Des Grieux to live with Géronte. But she has not forgotten her former lover; she complains to her brother that wealth is no substitute for love ("In quelle trine morbide"). A group of singers now entertains her with a madrigal ("Sulla vetta tu del monte"). When Géronte and his friends arrive, Manon dances a minuet for them and expresses her delight in "L'ora, o Tirsi." Des Grieux appears unexpectedly. At first he and Manon exchange bitter words ("Ah! Manon, mi tradisce"), but resentment soon turns to passionate love. When Géronte returns he finds Manon in Des Grieux's arms. He simulates indifference, but as he leaves he mutters a threat. Lescaut bursts into the room to warn Manon that Géronte has gone to the police with a complaint against her. Quickly, Manon gathers her jewels and secretes them under her cloak. When the police arrive to seize her, Manon is so terrified she allows her cloak to fall off her shoulders and the jewels to scatter. The police arrest her.

Act III. A square in Le Havre. A brief orchestral intermezzo recalls Manon's love for Des Grieux and her despair at the tragedy befalling her. Lescaut and Des Grieux have come to save Manon from being deported to Louisiana. They are unable to bribe the guard. Des Grieux pleads with the captain to allow him to accompany Manon ("No! pazzo son! guardate!"). The captain is won over, and Des Grieux rushes up the gangplank.

Act IV. A desolate plain near New Orleans. The countryside is gloomy; night is gathering. Des Grieux and Manon are seeking shelter. Ill and exhausted, she repents having brought such disaster to the man she loves ("Tutta su me ti sposa"). When Manon falls, Des Grieux continues his search alone. In the darkness, Manon grows increasingly terrified ("Sola, perduta, abbandonata"). Returning, Des Grieux finds Manon dying. He takes her in his arms, and there Manon breathes her last.

When we speak of Manon Lescaut, the opera that usually comes to mind is MASSENET'S. While Massenet's is the more popular and the finer work of the two, there is much in Puccini's to recommend it; and it surely would have won a wider and more enthusiastic acceptance if it did not have to compete with one of the finest creations of the French lyric theater. While *Manon Lescaut* is a comparatively early work of Puccini's (it was his third opera), it already presents the qualities that endear Puccini to us: a lyricism of incomparable sweetness and charm which, in the big arias, becomes dominating and commanding; a compassion for the leading characters; a variety of harmony that sustains musical interest throughout the work; a diversity of mood and feeling. No wonder that when George Bernard Shaw first heard *Manon Lescaut* he wrote: "Puccini looks to me more like the heir of VERDI than any of his rivals." It took a strong faith on the part of an obscure and impoverished composer who thus far had written only two minor works to compete with Massenet on his own ground. Massenet's MANON was ten years old and already an established favorite in European opera houses. Yet the act was justified by the results. *Manon Lescaut* was such a triumph at its first performance that Puccini had to take fifty curtain calls. Soon afterwards, it was given throughout Italy, then the rest of Europe. The opera lifted its composer from his obscurity to that pinnacle of prominence which made the premiere of each subsequent opera, successful or not, a matter of international interest.

Manrico, the troubadour (tenor) in love with Leonora in VERDI'S IL TROVATORE.

Manru, opera in three acts by Ignace Jan Paderewski. Libretto by Alfred Nossig, based on *The Cabin Behind the Wood,* a novel by Krazewski. Premiere: Dresden Opera, May 29, 1901. American premiere: Metropolitan Opera, Feb. 14, 1902. Against her mother's wishes, Ulana (soprano) marries the gypsy Manru (tenor). When Ulana feels she is losing her husband's love, she revives it with a love potion prepared by the dwarf Urok (baritone). Asa (soprano), a gypsy girl, lures Manru back to his people. When Ulana commits suicide, Manru, now head of his tribe, is killed by his rival for Asa.

Man Without a Country, The, opera in two acts by Walter DAMROSCH. Libretto by Arthur Guiterman, based on the story of the same name by Edward Everett Hale. Premiere: Metropolitan Opera, May 12, 1937. The story is familiar. Lieutenant Philip Nolan betrays his country by joining Aaron Burr's conspiracy to found a new empire in the United States. He repents and expiates his crime by dying for his country in a naval engagement with the Berber pirates off Tripoli. The original story was changed by the librettist to include a love interest in the person of Mary Rutledge, Philip's sweetheart.

Manzoni, Alessandro, novelist and poet. Born Milan, Mar. 7, 1785; died there May 22, 1873. His masterwork, the novel *I promessi sposi,* was the source of the plot of operas by Franz Gläser, Enrico Petrella, and Amilcare PONCHIELLI. VERDI wrote his famous *Requiem* on the occasion of Manzoni's death.

Maometto II, opera in two acts by

ROSSINI. Libretto by the Duke of Ventignano, based on VOLTAIRE's play. *See* SIÈGE DE CORINTHE, LE.

Mapleson, James Henry, impresario. Born London, May 4, 1830; died there Nov. 14, 1901. After studying at the Royal Academy of Music in London, he sang in opera performances in Verona under the name of Enrico Manriani. His managerial career began in 1861 when he took over the Lyceum Theatre in London and presented Italian operas. From 1862 to 1867 he directed operas at HER MAJESTY'S THEATRE. When this house burned down, he transferred his activities to DRURY LANE. In 1877 he reopened Her Majesty's Theatre. During his career in England, Colonel Mapleson (as he was called) introduced many notable operas, among them THE ABDUCTION FROM THE SERAGLIO, CARMEN, THE DAMNATION OF FAUST, FAUST, LA FORZA DEL DESTINO, UN BALLO IN MASCHERA, MEFISTOFELE, THE MERRY WIVES OF WINDSOR, THE SICILIAN VESPERS, and the complete RING cycle. Singers who made their English debuts under his direction included Italo CAMPANINI, Etelka GERSTER, Lilli LEHMANN, Christine NILSSON, and Jean DE RESZKE.

In 1878 Mapleson became the manager of the ACADEMY OF MUSIC in New York; for the next eight years he helped shape operatic history in America. The extent of his repertory and the brilliance of his productions were not matched by any other opera company in the United States at that time. One after another the world's great operatic stars were introduced to America on the stage of the Academy of Music: Emma ALBANI, Italo Campanini, Etelka Gerster, Minnie HAUK, Clara Louise KELLOGG, Pauline LUCCA, Victor MAUREL, Emma NEVADA, Lillian NORDICA, Adelina PATTI, and many others. During this period Mapleson gave one hundred and sixty-seven performances of nineteen operas. The following were his important American premieres: AIDA, CARMEN, RIGOLETTO, LA TRAVIATA, IL TROVATORE.

The competition offered by the newly opened METROPOLITAN OPERA (1883) spelled doom for the Academy of Music. Receipts fell off; many of Mapleson's stars joined the new company. In 1886 Mapleson left New York to carry on his operatic activities in England. He returned in 1896 for another try at the Academy of Music but was unable to gain a permanent foothold. His autobiography, *The Mapleson Memoirs,* appeared in 1888.

Mapleson's nephew, Lionel S. Mapleson, was librarian of the Metropolitan Opera for nearly fifty years. He left an important collection of letters, autographs, photographs, clippings, scores, and first recordings (made by himself) of Metropolitan Opera performances. This collection is preserved in the Metropolitan's library.

M'appari (Ach, so fromm), Lionel's aria in which he describes how Martha came to him like a vision to assuage his sorrow, in Act III of FLOTOW's MARTHA.

Marcel, Raoul de Nangis's servant (bass) in MEYERBEER's LES HUGUENOTS.

Marcellina, (1) Rocco's daughter (soprano) in BEETHOVEN'S FIDELIO.

(2) Figaro's mother (contralto) in MOZART'S THE MARRIAGE OF FIGARO.

Marcello, a painter (baritone) in PUCCINI'S LA BOHÈME.

march, music used to accompany a parade or march, usually in 4/4 time, though often in 2/4 or 6/8. Since the days of LULLY, opera composers have used marches for scenes of pageantry and as a convenient device to bring large groups on stage or off. Among the most famous marches in opera are the Triumphal March in AIDA, the Coronation March in LE PROPHÈTE, and the March of the Guests in TANNHÄUSER. The best known wedding march in opera is the Bridal Chorus in LOHENGRIN, while the most eloquent funeral march is Siegfried's Funeral Music in GÖTTERDÄMMERUNG. Other interesting examples of marches in opera are found in LA BOHÈME (at the end of the second act) ; LE COQ D'OR (Bridal Procession) ; THE DAMNATION OF

FAUST (Rákóczy March); A LIFE FOR THE CZAR; THE LOVE FOR THREE ORANGES; THE MAGIC FLUTE (March of the Priests); HANDEL's *Scipio* (to this day used by the Grenadier Guards of Britain).

Marche du couronnement, *see* CORONATION MARCH.

Marchesi, Mathilde de Castrone (born Graumann), teacher of singing. Born Frankfurt, Mar. 24, 1821; died London, Nov. 17, 1913. She studied singing with Otto NICOLAI in Vienna and Manuel GARCÍA in Paris. After appearing in concerts, she married the Italian baritone Salvatore MARCHESI in 1852. Together they toured Europe in concert and opera. From 1854 to 1861 and again from 1869 to 1878 she taught singing at the Vienna Conservatory. She was also a member of the faculty of Cologne Conservatory, and taught singing privately in Paris. Many of her pupils became opera stars, including Emma CALVÉ, Emma EAMES, Mary GARDEN, Etelka GERSTER, and Nellie MELBA. Marchesi wrote a vocal method, twenty-four volumes of studies, and an autobiography, *Marchesi and Music* (1897).

Marchesi, Salvatore, baritone and teacher of singing. Born Palermo, Sicily, Jan. 15, 1822; died Paris, Feb. 20, 1908. He combined the study of music (with Francesco LAMPERTI and Pietro Raimondi) with that of law. Involved in the 1848 revolution in Italy, he was exiled. He came to America and made his opera debut in New York in ERNANI. He then returned to Europe for study with Manuel GARCÍA, after which he established himself in London both as singer and teacher. After marrying Mathilde Graumann in 1852 (*see* above), he made opera and concert appearances with her throughout Europe. (Their daughter, Blanche Marchesi (1863–1940), was also a celebrated singer and teacher.) He taught at the conservatories of Vienna and Cologne, translated the librettos of many German and French operas into Italian, and published a vocal method.

Marchez dans mon chemin, Don Quixote's plea to Dulcinea to marry him, in Act IV of MASSENET's DON QUICHOTTE.

Marco, Simone's son (baritone) in PUCCINI's GIANNI SCHICCHI.

Marcoux, Vanni (born Jean Emile Diogene Marcoux), bass-baritone. Born Turin, Italy, June 12, 1877, of French parentage; died Paris, Oct. 22, 1962. He studied voice and law in his native city and was admitted to the bar at Turin. However, he went to Paris to complete his voice studies under Frédéric Boyer, and this led to his opera debut as Frère Laurent in ROMÉO ET JULIETTE at Bayonne on Jan. 28, 1900. Following appearances in France and Belgium, he became a member of the COVENT GARDEN company, where he remained between 1905 and 1912 and where he created for England the role of Arkel in PELLÉAS ET MÉLISANDE and appeared in the world premiere of L'ORACOLO. He made his debut at the PARIS OPÉRA on Jan. 13, 1909, an occasion upon which he created the role of Colonna in MONNA VANNA. At MASSENET's request, he appeared in the title role of DON QUICHOTTE at its world premiere in MONTE CARLO in 1910. In 1912 he made his American debut with the Boston Opera company, and in 1913–14 and again between 1926 and 1932 he was one of the principals of the CHICAGO OPERA. Between 1938 and 1943 he taught voice at the Paris Conservatory, and from 1948 to 1951 he was the director of the Grand Théâtre at Bordeaux.

Maretzek, Max, impresario and conductor. Born Brünn, Moravia, June 28, 1821; died Staten Island, New York City, May 14, 1897. He began his musical career after studying medicine. After playing the violin in and conducting orchestras in Germany and England, he came to the United States to conduct at the Astor Place Opera House. Later, he formed his own company and presented opera. He was forced to suspend operations temporarily when the success of Jenny LIND deflected audiences from his theater. He later continued his activities at the Astor Place Opera House, Niblo's Garden, the Crosby Opera House in Chicago, and in Mexico and Havana. A highly volatile person, intransigent and dictatorial, he was often in violent disagreement with members of his various companies and with the critics. He wrote two operas: *Hamlet* (1843) and *Sleepy Hollow* (1879). He also wrote two books of reminiscences: *Crotchets and Quavers* (1885) and *Sharps and Flats* (1890).

Marfa, a widow (mezzo-soprano) in MUSSORGSKY'S KHOVANTCHINA.

Margared, Rozenn's sister (mezzo-soprano) and rival for Mylio's love, in LALO'S LE ROI D'YS.

Margaretha, the Baron of Schoenau's daughter (soprano) in NESSLER'S DER TROMPETER VON SÄKKINGEN.

Margiana, the Caliph's daughter (soprano) in CORNELIUS' THE BARBER OF BAGDAD.

Marguerite, Faust's beloved in BERLIOZ' THE DAMNATION OF FAUST, BOITO'S MEFISTOFELE, and GOUNOD'S FAUST. In all three operas she is a soprano. In the Berlioz opera, the part was created by Nellie MELBA; in Gounod's, by Marie MIOLAN-CARVALHO.

Marguerite de Valois, the betrothed (soprano) of Henry IV, in MEYERBEER'S LES HUGUENOTS.

Maria, (1) Simon Boccanegra's daughter (soprano) in VERDI'S SIMON BOCCANEGRA.

(2) Werner Kirchhofer's betrothed (soprano) in NESSLER'S DER TROMPETER VON SÄKKINGEN.

Maria di Rohan, opera in three acts by DONIZETTI; original title: *Il Conte de Chalais.* Libretto by Salvatore CAMMARANO, based on a melodrama by Edouard Lockroy. Premiere: Kärntnerthortheater, Vienna, June 5, 1843. American premiere: New York City, Dec. 10, 1849. Maria is secretly married to Chevreuse. When Chevreuse kills Richelieu's nephew, Maria intercedes for him with Riccardo, Count de Chalais, and falls in love with him. Riccardo challenges a young gallant when the latter insults Maria. Maria begs Ric-

cardo not to endanger his life for her sake. Upon learning what has happened, Chevreuse challenges Riccardo to a duel in which Riccardo is killed. Maria now begs for death, but her husband prefers her to live a life of disgrace. Two arias are popular, both sung by Chevreuse: "Bella è di sol vestita" and "Voce fatal." The opera, long neglected, received several important revivals in the 1950's and 1960's, notably at the SAN CARLO in Naples in 1962 and at LA SCALA in 1969.

Maria Egiziaca (Mary of Egypt), opera in three episodes (one act) by RESPIGHI. Libretto by C. Guastalla. Premiere: New York City, Mar. 16, 1932 (concert version); Teatro Colón, July 23, 1933 (staged).

Maria Golovin, opera in three acts by MENOTTI. Libretto by the composer. Premiere: Brussels, Aug. 20, 1958. American premiere: New York City, Nov. 5, 1958. This opera was commissioned by the NATIONAL BROADCASTING COMPANY for the Brussels Exposition of 1958, where it was first heard. Following its premiere in America at the Martin Beck Theatre, it was televised by NBC early in 1959 and presented soon after that by the NEW YORK CITY OPERA. Since then, however, the composer has made a number of significant revisions, and the new version was heard for the first time in Washington, D.C., on Jan. 22, 1965.

The opera is set near a European frontier, a few years after "a recent war." The heroine, Maria Golovin, becomes involved romantically with a blind maker of bird cages, while her husband is serving time as a prisoner of war. When Maria's husband is finally freed, she is forced to leave her blind lover. In despair, the blind man shoots her but unknowingly misses aim. Thus he is left with the delusion that Maria is dead and that nobody will ever again possess her.

Marianne, Faninal's housekeeper (soprano) in Richard STRAUSS'S DER ROSENKAVALIER.

Marie, (1) Wozzeck's mistress (soprano), who is murdered by him, in BERG's WOZZECK.

(2) Vivandière (canteen manager, soprano) of the French 21st Regiment, in DONIZETTI's THE DAUGHTER OF THE REGIMENT.

(3) The Burgomaster's daughter (soprano), who is loved by Peter Ivanov, in LORTZING's ZAR UND ZIMMERMANN.

(4) Hans's beloved (soprano) in SMETANA's THE BARTERED BRIDE.

Marietta, a dancer (soprano) in KORNGOLD's DIE TOTE STADT.

Marina, a Polish landowner's daughter (mezzo-soprano) in MUSSORGSKY's BORIS GODUNOV.

Marinaresca, *see* HO! HE! HO!

Marino Faliero, *see* BYRON, GEORGE NOEL GORDON, LORD.

Marinuzzi, Gino (or **Giuseppe**), conductor and composer. Born Palermo, Sicily, Mar. 24, 1882; died Milan, Aug. 17, 1945. He made his debut as conductor in Catania after graduating from the Palermo Conservatory. He then conducted in many opera houses in Italy and Spain before going to LA SCALA, where he remained three seasons. From 1915 to 1919 he was director of the Liceo Musicale in Bologna. In 1919 he was appointed principal conductor of the TEATRO COSTANZI. In the same year he came to the United States to succeed Cleofonte CAMPANINI as artistic director of the CHICAGO OPERA. After 1921 he confined his conducting to Europe and South America. He wrote two operas: *Barberina* (1903); *Jacquerie* (1918).

Mario (born Giovanni Matteo), tenor. Born Cagliari, Sardinia, Oct. 17, 1810; died Rome, Dec. 11, 1883. Born to a noble family, he was trained for the army. After completing his studies at the Turin Military Academy he joined the Piedmontese Guard, in which his father was general. In 1836 he fled from Italy with a ballet dancer. Reaching Paris, he began the study of singing at the Paris Conservatory. On Nov. 30, 1838, he made his debut at the OPÉRA in ROBERT LE DIABLE. He had signed the single name "Mario" to his contract and from then on was not known by any other. Strikingly handsome and endowed with an exquisitely beautiful voice, he was an immediate success. In 1839 he made a sensational debut in London in LUCREZIA BORGIA, and in 1840 he joined the Italian Opera in Paris. For the next quarter of a century he appeared both in Paris and London, recognized as one of the supreme operatic tenors of his generation, particularly in romantic roles. He frequently appeared with the soprano Giulia GRISI, whom he married in 1844. His last appearance was in LA FAVORITA at COVENT GARDEN in 1871. He then retired to Rome, where he was soon reduced to such poverty that, in 1880, his friends arranged a concert in London for his benefit.

Mario Cavaradossi, *see* CAVARADOSSI, MARIO.

Mario, Queena (born Tillotson), soprano. Born Akron, Ohio, Aug. 21, 1896; died New York City, May 28, 1951. She studied singing with Marcella SEMBRICH and Oscar Saenger in New York and made her debut on Sept. 4, 1918, with the SAN CARLO OPERA COMPANY in New York as OLYMPIA. Her debut at the METROPOLITAN OPERA took place on Nov. 30, 1922, as MICAËLA. She remained at the Metropolitan eighteen years. In 1931 she took over Mme. Sembrich's classes at the Curtis Institute. She also taught singing at the Juilliard School of Music and conducted a summer school and opera workshop at her farm in Bethel, Conn. In 1925 she married Wilfred Pelletier, conductor of the Metropolitan; they were divorced three years later. She wrote several mystery novels, one of them with an opera setting, *Murder in the Opera House.*

Mariola, an orphan (soprano), in love with Fra Gherardo, in PIZZETTI's FRA GHERARDO.

marionette opera. Opera performances with marionettes are believed to have originated in Florence in the seventeenth century, when Filippo Acciajuoli first produced them. The first marionette opera is believed to have been *Il Girello,* music by Jacopo Melani and Alessandro STRADELLA. Acciajuoli gave his marionette performances throughout northern Italy.

London had a puppet theater in the arcade of COVENT GARDEN in 1713 where complete operas were given. Opera was also seen in an open-air marionette theater in Vienna at about this same time. There was a fully equipped marionette theater at the palace of Prince Esterházy, for which HAYDN wrote *Der Götterrat,* a prologue to his opera *Philemon und Baucis.* Subsequently, he wrote three more marionette operas, all now lost.

Notable marionette theaters have flourished in Europe in recent times, and in these theaters operas have been given. Examples are the Théâtre Guignol in Paris, the Teatro dei Piccoli in Rome, the Salzburg Marionette Theater, Ivo Puhonney's Marionette Theater in Germany, and the Swiss Marionette Theater.

Several contemporary composers have written marionette operas. They include CASTELNUOVO-TEDESCO (AUCASSIN ET NICOLETTE); FALLA (EL RETABLO DE MAESE PEDRO); HINDEMITH (*Nuschi-Nusch*); LUALDI (*Le furie di Arlecchino* and *Guerin meschino*); RESPIGHI (*The Sleeping Beauty*); ROSENBERG (MARIONETTES). There is a marionette sequence in MASCAGNI'S IRIS.

Marionettes, a puppet opera in two acts by ROSENBERG. Libretto by the composer, based on a play by Jacinto Benavente. Premiere: Stockholm Opera, Feb. 14, 1939. This is a puppet opera in theme, but it is performed by living actors. It is in the style of the *commedia dell' arte,* its action takes place in some imaginary seventeenth-century country, and it numbers among its characters such stock figures as Harlequin, Columbine, Pantaloon, Polichinelle, together with their friends, families, and enemies. Crispin, a speaking role, is an intriguer who sets the plot spinning, which involves a romance between Leandro, an adventurer, and Silvia. In the prologue Crispin explains to the audience that "this is a little play of puppets, impossible in theme, without any reality at all," and so on. At the end of the play, Silvia also addresses the audience, saying: "You have seen how these puppets have been moved by plain and obvious strings, like men and women in the farces of our lives."

Markheim, opera in one act by FLOYD. Libretto by the composer, based on the story by Robert Louis Stevenson. Premiere: New Orleans, Mar. 31, 1966. The Stevenson story about the murder in cold blood of a pawnbroker by Markheim is altered. The pawnbroker becomes Josiah Creach, a greedy, sadistic man. "This in turn alters Markheim from a premeditated murderer," explains Harry Wells McGraw, "to a pathetic debauchee deliberately goaded past the breaking point." Floyd's score avoids, adds McGraw, "Wagnerian symphonicism, virtuoso vocalism, and any other device that would detract from maximum concentration of dramatic effect.... Floyd's declamatory writing is carefully shaped to the demands of clean enunciation and precise character portrayal."

Marlowe, Christopher, dramatist and poet. Born Canterbury, Eng., Feb. 6, 1564; died Deptford, Eng., May 30, 1593. One of the most distinguished of the Elizabethan dramatists, he appears as the central character in Wilfred Mellers' opera *The Tragical History of Christopher Marlowe.* BUSONI's opera DOKTOR FAUST is based on Marlowe's *Dr. Faustus.*

Marmontel, Jean François, librettist. Born Bort, Limousin, France, July 11, 1723; died Abloville, France, Dec. 31, 1799. He wrote librettos for operas by CHERUBINI, GRÉTRY, MÉHUL, PICCINNI, RAMEAU, and SPOHR, among others, including Cherubini's *Démophon,* Grétry's *Céphale et Procris* and *Zémire et Azor,* and Piccinni's *Atys* and *Didon.* Marmontel was prominent in the clash in Paris between the forces supporting GLUCK's ideas about opera and those on

the side of Italian tradition and PIC-
CINNI; he allied himself with the Italian
group.

Mârouf, comic opera in five acts by
RABAUD. Libretto by Lucien Népoty,
based on a story from the ARABIAN
NIGHTS. Premiere: Opéra-Comique, May
15, 1914. American premiere: Metropolitan Opera, Dec. 19, 1917. The cobbler Mârouf (tenor) escapes from his
humdrum existence with a termagant
wife by taking to sea. He becomes the
solitary survivor of a shipwreck. Reaching the shores of Khaitan, he is rescued
by an old boyhood friend, Ali (baritone), now a wealthy merchant. Ali
dresses Mârouf in silks and finery and
introduces him as the world's richest
merchant. The Sultan (bass) offers
Mârouf the run of his palace and his
daughter (soprano) as wife. Mârouf
takes advantage of this situation by de-
pleting the Sultan's treasury. Day after
day Mârouf promises the Sultan that
his mighty caravans will soon arrive. At
last, Mârouf confesses the truth to the
princess, who continues to love the
cobbler. They elope to the desert. Here
they encounter a peasant who, through
the power of a magic ring, turns into
a genie, while the lovers' abode is transformed into a palace. The Sultan and
his men, pursuing Mârouf, find him
surrounded by wealth. Mârouf is forgiven. Three arias, all sung by Mârouf,
are of special interest: "Il est des Musulmans" in Act I; "À travers le desert"
in Act II; and "Dans le jardin fleurie"
in Act III. One of the most effective
portions in the opera is the ballet in
Act III.

Marquis, The, Grisélidis' husband (baritone) in MASSENET'S GRISÉLIDIS.

Marriage, The, (1) a satirical comedy
by Nikolai GOGOL whose main plot concerns the problems besetting two lovers
contemplating marriage and whose
central theme is that marriage is only
for those emotionally prepared for it.
This play is the source of operas by
GRETCHANINOV, MARTINU, and MUSSORG-
SKY (the Mussorgsky opera was not
finished).

(2) Opera in three acts by Gretchaninov. Libretto by the composer, based
on Gogol's play. Premiere: Paris, Oct.
8, 1950.

(3) Opera in one act by Martinu.
Libretto by the composer, based on
Gogol's play. Premiere: NBC Televi-
sion network, Feb. 7, 1953.

**Marriage of Figaro, The (Le nozze di
Figaro),** OPERA BUFFA in four acts by
MOZART. Libretto by Lorenzo DA PONTE,
based on BEAUMARCHAIS's *Le Mariage
de Figaro.* Premiere: Burgtheater,
Vienna, May 1, 1786. American premiere: possibly as early as 1799 in New
York, though a presentation at the
Park Theater in New York on May 10,
1824, was then claimed to be the first
in America.

Characters: Count Almaviva (baritone); Countess Almaviva (soprano);
Cherubino, the Count's page (soprano); Figaro, the Count's valet
(baritone); Dr. Bartolo (bass); Don
Basilio, a music master (tenor);
Susanna, head waiting woman to the
Countess (soprano); Marcellina (contralto); Antonio, gardener (bass);
Barbarina, his daughter (soprano); Don
Curzio, a counselor-at-law (tenor); peasants; townspeople; servants. The action
takes place at Count Almaviva's chateau
near Seville, Spain, in the eighteenth
century.

Act I. The apartment assigned to
Figaro and Susanna. Figaro is about
to be married to Susanna, and the
Count has assigned them quarters con-
veniently near his own apartment.
When Susanna suggests the reason for
this, Figaro is at first concerned; then
he remarks lightly that he knows how
to handle his master ("Se vuol ballare"). There are other complications
to Figaro's marriage. He has borrowed
money from Marcellina and signed a
contract promising to marry her if he
fails to repay her. Bartolo and Marcellina arrive discussing this contract
and the best way of implementing it.
Bartolo vows the wretch, Figaro, will
have to keep his bargain ("La vendetta"). Susanna, suspicious of Mar-

cellina, makes her feelings known to her rival. They exchange bitter words ("Via resti servita"), after which Marcellina leaves in a huff. Cherubino enters lamenting the fact that the Count is about to send him away for having found him alone with Barbarina. The page, however, is secretly in love with the Countess. He eagerly sings a song about adolescent love ("Non so più cosa son") and snatches away one of the Countess' ribbons now in Susanna's possession. When the Count abruptly appears, Cherubino hides behind a chair. Basilio's arrival sends the Count behind a chair, too. Eventually both are discovered, and the Count angrily orders Cherubino to enlist in his regiment. Figaro mockingly gives Cherubino advice on how to behave as a soldier ("Non più andrai").

Act II. The apartment of the Countess. The Countess laments that the Count no longer loves her and is unfaithful ("Porgi amor"). Susanna and Figaro contrive a plan to revive the Count's interest in his wife by arousing his jealousy. The Count will be made to discover a letter seemingly sent to the Countess; at the same time a rendezvous will be arranged in which Susanna will appear disguised as the Countess. They also plan to make the Count ridiculous by having him meet Susanna at a tryst, with Cherubino dressed as Susanna. Cherubino enters the apartment and, as Susanna accompanies on the guitar, sings a song he has just composed about the meaning of love ("Voi che sapete"). Susanna tries to show him how to dress and act like a girl, but they are interrupted by a knock on the door. It is the Count, and Cherubino is hastily locked in a closet. The Count goes searching for a crowbar with which to force the door. While he is gone, Cherubino escapes out the window and Susanna takes his place. When the Count finds Susanna, he is effusive in his apologies until the gardener comes to tell him that somebody has just jumped out the window and trampled the flower bed. The gardener has also found a piece of paper dropped by the culprit—Cherubino's commission in the Count's regiment. Figaro assuages the Count's suspicions by insisting that he had Cherubino's commission in his own pocket and that he is the man who jumped out the window. Marcellina, accompanied by Dr. Bartolo, now arrives to demand that Figaro go through with his bargain to marry her. The Count says he will adjudge that matter later, but he is still very suspicious of Figaro's explanation about the commission.

Act III. A hall. The Count, seeking a rendezvous with Susanna, threatens that he will insist on Marcellina and Figaro marrying if she declines. Susanna makes a pretense of yielding and the two arrange a meeting ("Crudel, perchè finora"). But, notwithstanding his agreement with Susanna, the Count is bent on punishing Figaro by forcing him to honor his agreement with Marcellina. Negotiations begin between Marcellina and the lawyer, Don Curzio, and Figaro and the Count, during which the astonishing discovery is made that Figaro is actually Marcellina's long-lost son. The obstacle to Figaro's marriage to Susanna has thus been removed. Meanwhile the Countess, alone, recalls the time when the Count was in love with her ("Dove sono"). When Susanna arrives, the Countess dictates a letter arranging a rendezvous between the Count and Susanna (Letter Duet: "Che soave zeffiretto"). The Countess decides to take Cherubino's place in the affair—in other words, to disguise herself as Susanna. The marriage formalities of Figaro and Susanna are now taken care of. Guests enter to the strains of a march. Afterward, they dance a FANDANGO. The Count, receiving the letter from Susanna, happily invites everyone to attend a gala celebration to be held later in the evening.

Act IV. The Count's garden at night. Barbarina quite unwittingly lets Figaro realize that Susanna has a rendezvous with the Count, and he delivers a spirited warning to men that women are not to be trusted ("Aprite un po'"). His suspicions are confirmed when he overhears his own Susanna sing an ecstatic aria about the approach of an unnamed lover ("Deh vieni, non tardar"). Then, what with the darkness and Susanna's having changed costumes with the Countess, there is a whole series of wooings based on mistaken identities. Cherubino starts to make love to Susanna, thinking her to be the Countess; but the Count, imagining he is keeping his rendezvous, sends Cherubino packing and starts his own wooing of Susanna (though it is really his wife). And Figaro, who soon catches on to the disguises, in order to teach Susanna a lesson makes love to her while pretending to think she is the Countess. The confusion is finally resolved as the Count goes down on his knees to beg his wife's readily granted forgiveness, Figaro and Susanna are happily reunited, and even Cherubino and Barbarina are paired off.

The French dramatist Beaumarchais wrote a trilogy of plays in which the central character is Figaro. The first of these, *The Barber of Seville*, was made into operas by PAISIELLO and ROSSINI; the second, *The Marriage of Figaro*, was Mozart's inspiration. Beaumarchais's comedies were a pointed attack against the decadent aristocracy of his day—so much so that Napoleon described them as "the revolution already in action." Consequently, when da Ponte and Mozart decided to collaborate on *The Marriage of Figaro*, the Austrian Emperor was not in favor of the project. Only when da Ponte promised to purge the play of political and social implications did the Emperor give his consent. Thus, da Ponte's libretto became a farce rather than a social satire. Da Ponte scrambled his characters and their amatory designs with a lightness of touch that made for highly effective comedy. Following his librettist's suggestions, Mozart composed one of his most vivacious scores, chameleonlike in its rapidly changing

hues, penetrating in its psychological understanding of the characters. The music is sometimes sentimental and poetic, sometimes noble, sometimes touched with mockery. No wonder, then, that *The Marriage of Figaro* is sometimes called the "perfect *opera buffa.*" It is, as Eric Blom wrote, "Italian comic opera in its final stage of perfection... as great as a whole as it is captivating in detail."

Marschallin, The, the Princess von Werdenberg (soprano) in Richard STRAUSS'S DER ROSENKAVALIER.

Marschner, Heinrich, composer. Born Zittau, Ger., Aug. 16, 1795; died Hanover, Dec. 14, 1861. He studied law at the Leipzig University, but Johann Friedrich Rochlitz convinced him that he should embrace music. After studying with Johann Gottfried Schicht, he wrote his first opera, *Der Kyffhäuserberg,* produced in Vienna in 1816. Settling in Pressburg as a music teacher, he wrote two more operas, one of them, *Heinrich IV und d'Aubigné,* presented by WEBER in Dresden. Largely due to popularity of this opera, Marschner was appointed joint-KAPELLMEISTER in 1823 (with Weber and Francesco Morlacchi) of the DRESDEN OPERA. He rose to the post of music director one year later but resigned when Weber died. He went on to Leipzig, where he became *kapellmeister* of the Leipzig Opera. There he wrote and had produced the opera that spread his fame throughout Europe: DER TEMPLER UND DIE JÜDIN, based on Sir Walter Scott's IVANHOE. In 1831 he was appointed court *kapellmeister* in Hanover. He held this post until his retirement twenty-eight years later, when he was given the honorary title of *generalmusikdirektor.* Marschner wrote his most famous opera in Hanover, HANS HEILING, a triumph at its premiere in Berlin on May 24, 1833. Marschner's operas are significant historically in that they carry on the German Romantic movement launched by Weber. His operas: *Der Kyffhäuserberg* (1816); *Saidar* (1819); *Heinrich IV und d'Aubigné* (1820); *Der Holzdieb*

(1825); *Lucretia* (1826); *Der Vampyr*
(1828); *Der Templer und die Jüdin*
(1829); *Des Falkners Braut* (1832);
Hans Heiling (1833); *Das Schloss am
Aetna* (1835); *Der Bäbu* (1837); *Adolf
von Nassau* (1843); *Austin* (1851);
Hjarne der Sängerkönig.

Martern aller Arten, Constanze's aria
in Act II of MOZART's THE ABDUCTION
FROM THE SERAGLIO, expressing defiance
at the Pasha's advances, in spite of his
threat of physical torture.

Martha, (1) Marguerite's mother (contralto) in BOITO's MEFISTOFELE.

(2) A village girl (soprano) in D'AL-
BERT's TIEFLAND.

(3) Marguerite's friend (mezzo-soprano) in GOUNOD's FAUST.

(4) Opera in four acts by FLOTOW. Alternate title, *Der Markt von Richmond*
(The Market at Richmond). Libretto
by Friedrich Wilhelm Riese, based on
a ballet-pantomime, *Lady Henriette,*
by Vernoy de SAINT-GEORGES, to which
Flotow had contributed a portion of
the music. Premiere: Vienna, Nov. 25,
1847. American premiere: Niblo's Garden, New York, Nov. 1, 1852.

Characters: Lady Harriet, maid of
honor to Queen Anne (soprano);
Nancy, her maid (contralto); Sir Tristan Mickleford, Lady Harriet's cousin
(bass); Plunkett, a wealthy farmer
(bass); Lionel, his foster brother, later
the Earl of Derby (tenor); Sheriff of
Richmond (bass); Lady Harriet's servants; other servants; farmers; pages;
hunters; ladies. The setting is Richmond, Eng., during the reign of Queen
Anne.

The popular overture is made up
of some of the more famous melodies
from the opera, opening with a slow
section in which "Mag der Himmel
euch vergeben" is prominent, continuing with a fast passage quoting the
lively country dances from the opera,
and, after a crescendo, reaching a climax
with a statement of the main theme of
the third-act quintet.

Act I, Scene 1. Lady Harriet's boudoir.
The sound of happy peasant voices outside her window gives Lady Harriet the
idea for an amusing escapade: she will
join the peasants in disguise and accompany them to Richmond Fair. She
and her maid Nancy don appropriate
garb and assume fictitious names: Lady
Harriet becomes Martha, Nancy becomes Julia. Lady Harriet's cousin, Sir
Tristan, goes along as a farmer named
John.

Scene 2. The Fair. Harriet and Nancy
meet two young farmers, Lionel and
Plunkett, who offer to hire them as
servants. In a spirit of fun, the girls
accept, binding themselves to their
masters for a year. They soon regret this
bargain but are unable to break it.

Act II. Plunkett's farm. The two girls
decide to make their employers' lives
intolerable. Meanwhile, Lionel has
fallen in love with Martha. When he
begs her to sing for him, she complies
("The Last Rose of Summer"; "Die letzte
Rose"; "Qui sola, vergin rosa"). Lionel
falls on his knees and confesses his love
and willingness to marry her even if she
is only a servant. The situation is relieved by Plunkett's arrival. He, too,
loves his servant. The four now engage
in a game of coquetry as they bid each
other good night (Good-Night Quartet:
"Schlafe wohl! und mag dich reuen";
"Dormi pur"). After Lionel and
Plunkett retire, Sir Tristan taps at the
window. Learning that he has a carriage
waiting, the ladies escape.

Act III. A hunting park in Richmond
Forest. Lionel and Plunkett are hoping
to see the Queen's hunt. Plunkett and
a group of farmers sing the praises of
British ale ("Lasst mich euch fragen";
"Chi mi dira"). When Nancy arrives
with a company of court ladies, Plunkett
immediately recognizes her as Julia
and insists that she return to his service;
the ladies rudely send him away. Lionel
appears. He is sad, for he is thinking
of his lost love ("Ach, so fromm";
"M'appari"). His reflections are interrupted by the sudden appearance of
Lady Harriet. Lionel is confused at
finding her dressed as a lady; but he is
so overjoyed that he reveals his inmost
feelings. Lady Harriet rejects him scorn-

fully, since she does not want to give way to her true emotions. When Lionel insists that she return to work for him, Lady Harriet has her men arrest him (Quintet: "Mag der Himmel euch vergeben"; "Ah! che a voi perdoni iddio").

Act IV, Scene 1. Plunkett's farm. Lionel has been freed. Meanwhile, his possession of a certain ring has disclosed that he is really the Earl of Derby. Lady Harriet is now willing to concede that she loves him, but Lionel rejects her. Even her attempt to awaken his love by singing "The Last Rose of Summer" is futile. Brushing her aside, he leaves. Plunkett and Nancy, reunited, plan a method whereby Lionel and Lady Harriet will be reconciled.

Scene 2. Richmond Park. Lady Harriet has set up a replica of Richmond Fair. She hopes that if Lionel revisits the scene of their first meeting, his love may be revived. Lady Harriet and Nancy reappear in peasant dress. The strategy works. Seeing Lady Harriet again as Martha, in the setting of the Fair, Lionel is moved to happiness. The two pairs of lovers express their joy in a final rendition of "The Last Rose of Summer."

Martin, Frank, composer. Born Geneva, Sept. 15, 1890. His music studies consisted mainly of private lessons with Joseph Lauber. Between 1923 and 1925 he lived in Paris, where his early style became crystallized, influenced by the French Impressionists. He later adopted a contrapuntal idiom into which a modern harmonic language was integrated. In this style he scored a major success with LE VIN HERBÉ, an oratorio based on the Tristan saga, which has received stage presentations in Europe's leading opera houses. THE TEMPEST, an opera based on SHAKESPEARE, was introduced in Vienna on June 17, 1956, and his oratorio LE MYSTÈRE DE LA NATIVITÉ was staged at the SALZBURG FESTIVAL in 1960, after having been introduced over the Swiss radio on Dec. 24, 1959. A comic opera, MONSIEUR DE POURCE-AUGNAC, based on MOLIÈRE, was given its world premiere in Geneva on Apr. 23, 1963.

Martin, Riccardo (born Hugh Whitfield Martin), tenor. Born Hopkinsville, Ky., Nov. 18, 1874; died New York City, Aug. 11, 1952. He was one of the first American-born singers to appear in leading tenor roles at the METROPOLITAN OPERA. An endowment enabled him to go to Paris in 1901 to study with Giovanni SBRIGLIA and Jean DE RESZKE and later to complete his study with Vincenzo Lombardi in Florence. His debut took place in Nantes in GOUNOD'S FAUST in 1904. Two years later he made his American debut with the SAN CARLO OPERA, then visiting New Orleans. On Nov. 20, 1907, he made his debut at the Metropolitan Opera in MEFISTOFELE, a performance in which Feodor CHALIAPIN made his American bow. Martin remained at the Metropolitan Opera through the 1914–15 season, appearing in leading tenor roles; he returned for the season of 1917–18. He created the leading tenor roles in three American operas: CYRANO DE BERGERAC, MONA, and THE PIPE OF DESIRE. After leaving the Metropolitan he appeared with various opera companies in America and Europe, including three seasons with the Chicago Civic Opera.

Martinelli, Giovanni, tenor. Born Montagnana, Italy, Oct. 22, 1885; died New York City, Feb. 2, 1969. Though musical as a child, he did not begin formal music study until comparatively late. While he was serving in the army in his twentieth year, the bandmaster recognized that he had an unusual voice and arranged for him to go to Milan for an audition. As a result, a sponsor was found to finance his study with Mandolini. After a concert debut in Milan, Martinelli made his bow in opera at the Teatro Dal Verme in Milan in ERNANI on Dec. 29, 1910. PUCCINI was so impressed that he engaged the singer for the European premiere of THE GIRL OF THE GOLDEN WEST (Rome, 1911). After successful appearances throughout Europe, Martinelli made his American debut on Nov. 3, 1913, with the Chicago-Philadelphia Opera Company in TOSCA. On Nov. 20 he appeared for the first time with the METROPOLITAN OPERA. The opera was LA BOHÈME. By the time

CARUSO's career came to its untimely end in 1920, Martinelli was recognized as his successor. During the more than three decades he was associated with the Metropolitan, Martinelli was heard in over fifty leading tenor roles of the French and Italian repertories. He sang in such notable world and American premieres as those of LA CAMPANA SOMMERSA, FRANCESCA DA RIMINI, GOYESCAS, and MADAME SANS-GÊNE. On Nov. 24, 1939, he made one of his rare appearances in German opera when he was none too happily cast by the CHICAGO OPERA as TRISTAN. His own favorite roles were ELEAZAR, OTELLO, and RADAMES. He left the Metropolitan Opera after the 1944–45 season and was then occasionally heard in recitals, as soloist with orchestras, over the radio, and as master of ceremonies for the television program "Opera Cameos." On Nov. 20, 1963, the fiftieth anniversary of his debut at the Metropolitan Opera was celebrated with a "gala evening" devoted to music from operas in which he had appeared with that company. In 1967 he was called upon to make an unannounced appearance as the Emperor in TURANDOT in Seattle, when a member of the local company became indisposed. Martinelli spent much of his time, in his last years, in an unsuccessful effort to save the old building of the Metropolitan Opera House from destruction.

Martin Korda, D.P., opera in three acts by BADINGS. Libretto by Albert von Heyk. Premiere: Holland Festival, June 15, 1960. The setting is a displaced persons' camp, and the plot concerns the futile and tragic attempt of one of these people to obtain release through negotiations with the government. ELECTRONIC SOUNDS, used to create eerie effects, are transmitted through loudspeakers distributed throughout the auditorium.

Martin's Lie, opera in one act by MENOTTI. Libretto by the composer. Premiere: Bristol, Eng., June 3, 1964. American premiere: CBS-TV, May 30, 1965. This is a church opera of modest dimensions. The principal character is a twelve-year-old orphan in medieval England who identifies a heretic, come to find refuge, as his own father and, even at the threat of torture, refuses to disclose where the man is hiding. The orchestra comprises only thirteen instruments.

Martinu, Bohuslav, composer. Born Polička, Czechoslovakia, Dec. 8, 1890; died Liestal, Switzerland, Aug. 28, 1959. He was graduated from the Prague Conservatory in 1913. For ten years he earned his living playing the violin in the Czech Philharmonic Orchestra. During this period he wrote several orchestral works, including a ballet, *Istar,* successfully produced in Prague in 1922. In 1923 he went to Paris, where he remained until 1940. It was in Paris that he began writing operas. His first, *The Soldier and the Dancer,* was introduced at the Brno National Theater in 1928. His most important opera of this period was *The Miracle of Our Lady,* performed in Brno in 1934. Soon after the German invasion of France Martinu came to the United States and made it his permanent home. His orchestral and chamber works have been widely performed in this country. In his later works, Czech influences are combined with French precision and refinement, usually within classical forms. Besides the two already mentioned, Martinu wrote the following operas: *The Day of Charity* (1930); *The Voice of the Forest* (1935); COMEDY ON THE BRIDGE, radio opera (1936); *The Suburban Theatre* (1936); *Alexander bis* (1937); *Juliette* (1938); THE MARRIAGE, television opera (1952); *What Men Live By* (1953); *La locandiera* (1954); *Mirandolina* (1959); *Ariadne* (1961); THE GREEK PASSION, an oratorio sometimes staged as an opera (1961). *The Greek Passion and Ariadne* were produced posthumously: the former in Zürich on June 9, 1961; the latter in Mannheim on Feb. 18, 1964.

Martín y Soler (or Solar), Vicente, composer. Born Valencia, Spain, Jan. 18, 1754; died St. Petersburg, Russia, Jan. 30, 1806. He was at first a choirboy at the Valencia Cathedral, and then an organist in Alicante. His first opera, *I due avari,* was produced in Madrid in 1766. He then visited Italy, where some of his operas were so well received that he became a favorite with Italian audiences, a serious rival to CIMAROSA and PAISIELLO. UNA COSA RARA, produced in Vienna in 1785, was so popular that it succeeded in obscuring MOZART'S THE MARRIAGE OF FIGARO. Mozart later quoted a number from *Una cosa rara* in his DON GIOVANNI: it is one of the little pieces played by the Don's band during the supper scene. From 1788 to 1801 Martín directed Italian operas in St. Petersburg. When the vogue for Italian opera gave way to French, the composer devoted his efforts to teaching. Besides the operas mentioned, Martín wrote the following successful works: *Ifigenia in Aulide* (1781); *La donna festeggiata* (1783); *Ipermestra* (1784); and *L'arbore di Diana* (1787).

Marullo, a courtier (baritone) in VERDI'S RIGOLETTO.

Mary, (1) *see* DUCHESS OF TOWERS.

(2) Senta's nurse (contralto) in WAGNER'S DER FLIEGENDE HOLLÄNDER.

(3) The lifelong sweetheart (soprano) of Peter Ibbetson, in TAYLOR'S PETER IBBETSON, a role created by Lucrezia BORI.

Maryinsky Theater, *see* BOLSHOI THEATER (1).

Masaniello, Neapolitan fisherman (tenor) in AUBER'S LA MUETTE DE PORTICI.

Mascagni, Pietro, composer. Born Leghorn, Italy, Dec. 7, 1863; died Rome, Aug. 2, 1945. As a student of the Cherubini Institute in Leghorn he wrote a symphony and a choral work that were performed. His talent attracted the interest of Count Florestano de Larderel, who financed his further study at the Milan Conservatory. Unhappy at the conservatory, Mascagni left it and supported himself by conducting a traveling opera company. He then settled in the town of Cerignola as piano teacher. In 1889 he wrote his first opera—it was CAVALLERIA RUSTICANA—for the competition sponsored by the publishing house of Sonzogno. The opera not only won the prize but was a sensation at its premiere at the TEATRO COSTANZI on May 17, 1890. The acclaim was repeated wherever the opera was heard; by 1892 it had been performed not only throughout Italy, but also in Paris, Berlin, London, and New York. Mascagni became a household name in Italy, a man of influence and wealth. He wrote fourteen operas after *Cavalleria*. Several were minor successes: L'AMICO FRITZ (1891), IRIS (1898), and LODOLETTA (1917). But Mascagni could never duplicate the the success of his first opera. As the composer himself remarked: "It is a pity I wrote *Cavalleria* first. I was crowned before I became king."

Mascagni combined his career as composer with that of conductor. In 1902 he toured the United States directing performances of his operas; this tour ended disastrously on account of mismanagement. In 1911 he conducted his operas in South America. In 1929 he succeeded TOSCANINI as musical director of LA SCALA. He wrote several works glorifying fascism and Mussolini, notably the opera *Nerone*. During World War II, Mascagni came upon bad times. His property was confiscated, and he himself was held in contempt for his avowed fascist sympathies. The last year of his life was spent in poverty and disgrace in a small room at the Hotel Plaza in Rome.

His operas: *Cavalleria rusticana* (1890); *L'amico Fritz* (1891); *I Rantzau* (1892); *Guglielmo Ratcliff* (1895); *Silvano* (1895); *Zanetto* (1896); *Iris* (1898); *Le maschere* (1901); *Amica* (1905); *Isabeau* (1911); *Parisina* (1913); *Lodoletta* (1917); *Il piccolo Marat* (1921); *Scampolo* (1921); *Nerone* (1935).

Ma se m'è forza perderti, Riccardo's aria in Act III, Scene 2, of VERDI'S UN BALLO IN MASCHERA, as he signs the document exiling Renato and his family.

Masetto, a peasant (baritone) in MOZART'S DON GIOVANNI.

Masked Ball, A, *see* BALLO IN MASCHERA, UN.

masque, an elaborate theatrical entertainment combining song, dance, poetry, and pageantry, most in vogue from the close of the sixteenth to the middle of the eighteenth centuries, and most frequently serving to entertain the aristocracy. The subject matter was usually mythological or allegorical. The form first became popular in Italy, but its heyday was reached in England. Some of England's foremost writers provided the texts, including Beaumont, Fletcher, Dekker, Ford, Ben JONSON, and MILTON. The music was created by such outstanding English composers as Campion, Gibbons, Lawes, Locke, PURCELL, and HANDEL. One of the most celebrated of English masques was John MILTON's *Comus,* with music by Henry Lawes, written for performance at Ludlow Castle in 1634. Later distinguished examples include Matthew Locke's and Christopher Gibbons' *Cupid and Death* (1653), John Blow's *Venus and Adonis* (1680), and Thomas ARNE's *Alfred* (1740).

Masquerade (Maskarade), opera in one act by Carl Nielsen. Libretto by Vilhelm Andersen, based on a comedy by Ludvig Holberg. Premiere: Copenhagen, Nov. 11, 1906. This light and amusing little comic opera, one of the most famous to come out of Denmark, helped to make its composer famous in his own country. The text is based on a trifling episode in eighteenth-century Copenhagen. Two young people meet at a masquerade, fall in love, and then discover that they are the ones their parents had previously matched up, an arrangement they had stubbornly resisted. The gay and sprightly overture, which begins with a dance tune and continues with a lyrical section, is sometimes heard at symphony concerts.

Massé, Victor (born Felix-Marie Massé), composer. Born Lorient, France, Mar. 7, 1822; died Paris, July 5, 1884. He attended the Paris Conservatory, where he won the PRIX DE ROME in 1848. In Rome, he wrote his first opera, *La favorita e la schiava.* Soon after returning to Paris he completed his first French opera, *La chambre gothique,* introduced with acclaim at the OPÉRA-COMIQUE in 1849. His greatest success came with the OPÉRA COMIQUE

Les Noces de Jeannette, given at the Opéra-Comique in 1853. In 1860 he was engaged as chorus master of the OPÉRA, and in 1866 he was appointed professor of composition at the Paris Conservatory. A serious illness compelled him to go into retirement in 1876. Meanwhile, in 1872 he had succeeded Daniel AUBER as a member of the Institut de France. Among his other successful operas were *Paul et Virginie* (1876) and *Une Nuit de Cléopâtre,* performed posthumously at the Opéra-Comique in 1885.

Massenet, Jules Emile Frédéric, composer. Born Montaud, France, May 12, 1842; died Paris, Aug. 13, 1912. The composer of MANON and THAÏS, Massenet was a dominating figure in the French lyric theater of the late nineteenth century. He entered the Paris Conservatory at the age of eleven. Under the sympathetic guidance of such teachers as Napoléon-Henri Reber and Ambroise THOMAS, he won several prizes, including the PRIX DE ROME in 1863. Soon after returning to Paris from Rome, he completed a one-act opera, *La Grand'tante,* produced by the OPÉRA-COMIQUE in 1867. After the Franco-Prussian War, in which he participated as a member of the National Guard, Massenet attracted the limelight with his incidental music for *Les Erinnyes* (it included a section later to become popular as the song "Élégie") and an oratorio, *Marie Magdeleine.* His position in French music became secure with the opera LE ROI DE LAHORE, successfully performed at the OPÉRA on Apr. 27, 1877. In 1879 he was elected to the Académie des Beaux-Arts, the youngest man ever to receive this honor.

Massenet's finest operas were produced between 1880 and 1900. In 1881 there was HÉRODIADE, first seen in Brussels. Then there followed the operas that made Massenet a leading representative of French romantic opera: *Manon* (1884), LE CID (1885), WERTHER (1892), *Thaïs* (1894), and SAPHO (1897). In 1894 the composer wrote a one-act sequel to *Manon,* LE PORTRAIT DE MANON, to a libretto by Georges Boyer. The finest traits of the French lyric theater are found in these works: a deep poetic feeling; tenderness of melody; delicacy of style; irresistible charm. Though Massenet wrote many operas after 1900, he never equaled the quality of his earlier work. Eager to maintain his popularity, he stunted his artistic growth by repeating the mannerisms and imitating the style that had made him famous; he remained a champion of an old and dying romantic tradition while younger composers were finding new approaches and esthetics.

Between 1878 and 1896 Massenet was professor of advanced composition at the Paris Conservatory. His many pupils included Gustave CHARPENTIER, Gabriel PIERNÉ, Florent Schmitt, and Henri RABAUD. Twenty-two years after Massenet's death, his bust was placed in the Opéra-Comique; on that occasion his DON QUICHOTTE was revived with CHALIAPIN in the title role. Massenet's operas, besides those already mentioned: *Don César de Bazan* (1872); *Esclarmonde* (1889) ; *Le Mage* (1891) ; LA NAVARRAISE (1894); *Cendrillon* (1899); GRISÉLIDIS (1901); LE JONGLEUR DE NOTRE DAME (1902) ; *Chérubin* (1905) ; *Ariane* (1906) ; *Thérèse* (1907); *Bacchus* (1909); *Roma* (1912) ; *Panurge* (1913) ; *Cléopâtre* (1914) ; *Amadis* (1924) .

Master Peter's Puppet Show, *see* RETABLO DE MAESE PEDRO, EL.

mastersingers (Meistersinger), the name given to the German guilds of poet-musicians that flourished from the thirteenth century to the sixteenth, with HANS SACHS their most noted figure. The mastersingers carried on the traditions of the earlier and more aristocratic MINNESINGERS, whose troubadour-influenced movement had its beginnings in the twelfth century. The songs of the mastersingers, usually on Biblical subjects, followed strict musical rules. WAGNER's opera DIE MEISTERSINGER is concerned with the lives and activities of some of these musicians.

Mastersingers of Nuremberg, The, *see* MEISTERSINGER VON NÜRNBERG, DIE.

Materna, Amalia, soprano. Born St. Georgen, Styria, July 10, 1844; died Vienna, Jan. 18, 1918. She created the roles of Brünnhilde (in SIEGFRIED and DIE GÖTTERDÄMMERUNG) and KUNDRY. Her singing career began with concert appearances, her opera debut taking place in Graz in 1864. After marrying the actor Karl Friedrich, she was engaged by the Karl Theater in Vienna for appearances in operettas. A period of study with Heinrich Proch preceded her debut at the KÄRNTNERTHORTHEATER in Vienna in 1869 as SELIKA. She was a major success and was engaged by the VIENNA OPERA, where she remained up to the time of her retirement in 1897. Besides appearances in the Italian and French repertory she was preeminently successful in the Wagner dramas. In 1876 WAGNER selected her to sing the three BRÜNNHILDE roles at the first BAYREUTH FESTIVAL. In 1877 she sang under Wagner's direction at a Wagner Festival in London, and in 1882 she returned to Bayreuth to appear in the world premiere of PARSIFAL. In 1882 she visited the United States for the first time, appearing as soloist with the Theodore THOMAS Orchestra in Wagner programs. On Jan. 5, 1885, she made her American opera debut at the METROPOLITAN OPERA as ELISABETH. She returned to the United States in 1894 to appear with the DAMROSCH OPERA COMPANY. After her retirement she devoted herself to teaching singing in Vienna.

Mathilde, daughter (soprano) of the tyrant Gessler and the sweetheart of Arnold, in ROSSINI'S WILLIAM TELL.

Mathis der Maler (Matthias the Painter), opera in seven scenes by HINDEMITH. Libretto by the composer. Premiere: Zürich Opera, May 28, 1938. American premiere: Boston, Feb. 17, 1956. This opera is based on the life of the sixteenth-century painter Matthias Grünewald. The background is the Peasants' War of 1524. Grünewald becomes the spearhead for the peasants' uprising against the Church. But once he becomes involved in the struggle he sees so much oppression and tyranny on his own side that he loses faith in the cause. He escapes with his beloved, Regina, to Odenwald. At first, he is haunted by ugly visions. But then beautiful apparitions come to him, and these succeed in bringing him back to his art. He gives up Regina and the outside world to dedicate himself completely to his artistic mission. This opera figures in the political history of Nazi Germany. Wilhelm FURTWÄNGLER, music director of the BERLIN STATE OPERA, scheduled the premiere for 1934. But the Nazi authorities objected to the portrayal of peasants rising against authority and expressed contempt for a composer who was married to a non-Aryan and whose works were "degenerate." Furtwängler wrote a vehement letter to Goering protesting the ban, insisting that, as music director, he was the sole authority for the repertory of the Berlin State Opera. He also published a heated defense of Hindemith in the *Deutsche Allgemeine Zeitung*. Because of his stand, Furtwängler was relieved of all his official musical duties and sent into temporary retirement. Hindemith was forced to leave the country.

The music of *Mathis der Maler* first became known through a "symphony" adapted from the score by the composer. It is made up of three movements: "The Concert of the Angels" (the overture); "The Entombment" (the sixth scene); and "Temptation of Saint Anthony" (intermezzo of the final scene). These titles are the titles of a triptych painted by Grünewald. In his score Hindemith has successfully combined his own linear writing with music that in style and spirit suggests Gregorian chants and medieval folksongs.

The first time the opera was staged in Zürich in 1938, it was a huge success. Its first presentation in Germany took place in Stuttgart in 1946. Before the 1950's ended, the opera had been produced by LA SCALA, the VIENNA STATE OPERA, the Berlin State Opera, and in

the United States in Boston. A new production of the opera was given at the Zürich Music Festival on June 29, 1965.

Mathisen, an Anabaptist preacher (bass) in MEYERBEER'S LE PROPHÈTE.

Matho, a Libyan mercenary (tenor) in REYER'S SALAMMBÔ.

matrimonio segreto, Il (The Secret Marriage), OPERA BUFFA in two acts by CIMAROSA. Libretto by Giovanni Bertati, based upon *The Clandestine Marriage* by George Colman, the elder, and David GARRICK. Premiere: Burgtheater, Vienna, Feb. 7, 1792. American premiere: Italian Opera House, New York, Jan. 4, 1834. Carolina (soprano), daughter of the rich and greedy merchant Geronimo (bass), is secretly married to the lawyer Paolino (tenor). In order to mollify his father-in-law when he discloses this marriage, Paolino arranges a match between the merchant's older daughter, Elisetta (soprano), and a rich friend named Count Robinson (bass), a development that leads Geronimo to express his delight in "Un matrimonio nobile." But matters become complicated when Elisetta falls in love with Paolino, while the rich friend falls in love with Carolina. The latter does her best to convince her rich suitor she is unworthy of him ("Questa cosa accordar"). After Paolino gives his wife assurances that it is she and she alone he loves ("Ah, no, che tu cosi morir"), they decide to run away. But Geronimo has plans of his own. He intends sending his daughter to a convent, a development that causes Carolina considerable sorrow, to which she gives voice in "È possono mai nascere." Paolino and Carolina run away but are intercepted by Geronimo. Though the -merchant is at first horrified to learn they are already married, he finally gives his belated blessings. And Count Robinson and Elisetta decide they are really meant for each other.

Il matrimonio segreto is a classic *opera buffa,* one of the early successful examples of this form, and an important predecessor of ROSSINI'S THE BARBER

OF SEVILLE. VERDI considered it the model of what an *opera buffa* should be; and it is the only Italian *opera buffa* between that of PERGOLESI and those of Rossini that is intermittently performed. The sprightly overture is often played at symphony concerts.

Matteo, an officer (tenor) in love with Arabella, who eventually realizes he really loves Arabella's sister, Zdenka, in Richard STRAUSS'S ARABELLA.

Ma tu, o Re, tu possente, Amonasro's plea to the King of Egypt for mercy, in Act II, Scene 2, of VERDI's AIDA.

Matzenauer, Margaret, soprano and contralto. Born Temesvar, Hungary, June 1, 1881; died Van Nuys, Cal., May 19, 1963. After studying with Antonia Mielke and Fritz Emerich in Berlin, she made her debut in 1901 in Strassburg in the role of Puck in OBERON. After three years in Strassburg, she was engaged as principal contralto of the MUNICH OPERA, where she remained until 1911. There she scored major successes in the Italian and Wagnerian repertories. During this period she appeared as guest artist in many European opera houses, including the BAYREUTH FESTIVAL, where, in the summer of 1911, she appeared as Waltraute, FLOSSHILDE, and the Second Norn. On Nov. 13, 1911 (the opening night of the season), she made her American debut at the METROPOLITAN OPERA as AMNERIS. Later the same season she was acclaimed when she appeared as KUNDRY for the first time in her career, substituting for Olive FREMSTAD without a single rehearsal. Matzenauer remained at the Metropolitan through the 1929–30 season. During the 1930's she appeared in concerts and as soloist with symphony orchestras and in oratorios. She went into retirement after World War II. Though she had appeared as a contralto in Munich, she was heard in both leading contralto and soprano roles at the Metropolitan. Her greatest successes came in the roles of Leonore in FIDELIO, the three BRÜNN-HILDES, Kundry, ISOLDE, Donna ELVIRA,

SELIKA, ORFEO, CARMEN, DALILA, and Amneris. She appeared in many significant world, American, and Metropolitan premieres, including LISZT's *Saint Elizabeth* (in a stage presentation), JANÁČEK's JENUFA, SPONTINI's LA VESTALE, and VERDI's UN BALLO IN MASCHERA and DON CARLOS.

Maudite à jamais soit la race, call of the High Priest to the Philistines to avenge Abimelech's death at the hands of Samson, in Act I of SAINT-SAËNS's SAMSON ET DALILA.

Maupassant, Guy de, author. Born Château de Miromesnil, France, Aug. 5, 1850; died Paris, July 6, 1893. His celebrated short story *Mlle. Fifi* was made into operas by CUI (*Mam'zelle Fifi*) and Glière (*Rachel*). BRITTEN's opera ALBERT HERRING was derived from Maupassant's *Le Rosier de Mme. Husson.*

Maurel, Victor, baritone. Born Marseilles, France, June 17, 1848; died New York City, Oct. 22, 1923. He first attended the Ecole de Musique in Marseilles and afterward the Paris Conservatory, where he received first prize upon his graduation in 1867. In the same year he made his debut at the PARIS OPÉRA in LES HUGUENOTS. He did not make much of an impression. When he was assigned only minor roles, he left the Opéra and during the next few years appeared at LA SCALA (where he was heard in the world premiere of GOMES' IL GUARANY) and COVENT GARDEN (where he created for England the Wagnerian roles of TELRAMUND, WOLFRAM, and the DUTCHMAN). On Nov. 26, 1873, he made his American debut in the American premiere of AIDA at the Academy of Music in New York. He stayed only a single season in New York, after which he went into temporary retirement. He returned to the Paris Opéra on Nov. 28, 1879, in HAMLET; for the next fifteen years he sang regularly at the Opéra, one of its most brilliant stars. Maurel's greatest triumphs came in 1887 and 1893 when he created the roles of Iago and Falstaff in the world premieres of VERDI's OTELLO and FALSTAFF. Maurel's interpretations of these two roles were regarded as definitive. He was called upon to create the role of Iago in France and England and that of Falstaff in France, England, and the United States. In 1894 and again in 1899 Maurel appeared at the METROPOLITAN OPERA. After 1909 he settled in New York as a teacher of singing. In 1919 he designed the scenery for the Metropolitan production of GOUNOD's MIREILLE. He wrote four books on singing, and an autobiography, *Dix Ans de carrière* (1897). Though Maurel had a comparatively limited voice, he used it with exquisite artistry and combined it with dramatic power.

Maurizio, Count of Saxony (tenor), lover of Adriana and of the Princesse de Bouillon in CILÈA's ADRIANA LECOUVREUR, a role created by CARUSO.

Mavra, one-act opera by STRAVINSKY. Libretto by Boris Kochno, based on Alexander PUSHKIN's poem *The Little House at Kolomna*. Premiere: Paris Opéra, June 2, 1922. American premiere: Philadelphia, Dec. 28, 1934. When Parasha's mother (contralto) laments the loss of her cook, Parasha (soprano) brings a replacement in the form of Vassily, her suitor (tenor), who has assumed woman's disguise and the name of Mavra. The ruse is uncovered when Parasha and her mother find their cook—shaving. The mother faints. Vassily jumps out a window and escapes. Stravinsky has provided the following explanation about this opera: "*Mavra* is in the direct tradition of GLINKA and DARGOMIZHSKY. I wanted merely to try my hand at this living form of OPERA BUFFA." The scoring is for twelve woodwinds, twelve brasses, and a double-bass. The recitative is dispensed with completely, and the emphasis is on a broad, at times a tender, lyricism, and on occasional satirical and burlesque effects in the orchestral accompaniment.

Max, (1) a composer (tenor) in KRENEK's JONNY SPIELT AUF.

(2) A ranger (tenor), principal male character, in WEBER's DER FREISCHÜTZ.

Maximilien, opera in three acts by MILHAUD. Libretto by Armand Lunel, based on Franz WERFEL's drama, *Juarez and Maximilian*. Premiere: Paris Opéra, Jan. 5, 1932. This is one of three major operas by Milhaud on American subjects, the other two being CHRISTOPHE COLOMB and *Bolivar*. This opera depicts the career of Maximilian, the Austrian archduke who became Emperor of Mexico in 1864 and three years later was overthrown and executed by the republican army headed by Juarez.

May Night, A, opera in three acts by RIMSKY-KORSAKOV. Libretto by the composer, based on a story by GOGOL. Premiere: Maryinsky Theater, St. Petersburg, Jan. 21, 1880. This was the composer's second opera, representing a sharp departure from his maiden effort for the stage, IVAN THE TERRIBLE (or *The Maid of Pskov*). Where the first opera was realistic, with strong accent on declamation and polyphony, *May Night* (based on a humorous story) has a marked national identity, influenced to a large degree by GLINKA, with excursions into fantasy which later became Rimsky-Korsakov's forte in his operas. The story finds Levko, son of a headman of a lakeside village, in love with Hanna, a village maiden in whom the headman himself is interested. Levko punishes his father by convincing him that their house is haunted, having organized all kinds of eerie happenings. In the end, Levko gets Hanna, but only after the headman comes to the erroneous conclusion that this is the demand of the Commissar.

The overture is celebrated, opening in a world of fantasy with a fanciful subject. A horn solo then leads to the main part of the overture, which has a national personality, particularly in the main theme. Among the better-known vocal excerpts are Levko's air, "The sun descends," his emotional third-act song, "Sleep, my beauty," and the choral episode in Act I, "Cooper, stop the holes."

Maypole Dances, dances in Act II of HANSON's MERRY MOUNT.

Mayr, Richard, bass. Born Henndorf, Austria, Nov. 18, 1877; died Vienna, Dec. 1, 1935. While attending the University of Vienna, he sang for Gustav MAHLER, who persuaded him to embrace a musical career. Mahler contracted Mayr for the VIENNA OPERA, but Mayr's debut took place in BAYREUTH in 1902 in the role of HAGEN. His Vienna debut took place the same year in ERNANI. For the rest of his career Mayr remained the principal bass of the Vienna Opera, successful in the German repertory, acclaimed particularly for his interpretation of the role of Baron OCHS, probably his most celebrated characterization. It was in this role that he made his COVENT GARDEN debut in 1924. His American debut took place at the METROPOLITAN OPERA on Nov. 2, 1927, in the role of POGNER. He remained at the Metropolitan Opera through the 1929–30 season. He was also a great favorite at the SALZBURG FESTIVALS. Shortly before his death he retired from the Vienna Opera at his own request and received a pension.

Mazeppa, opera in three acts by TCHAIKOVSKY. Libretto by the composer and V. P. Burenin, based on PUSHKIN's *Poltava*. Premiere: Bolshoi Theater, Moscow, Feb. 15, 1884. American premiere: Boston, Dec. 14, 1922. The action takes place in the seventeenth century in the Ukraine, where Mazeppa marries Maria, his godchild, against her parents' wishes. Mazeppa is led to murder Maria's father, and after that her illicit lover, Andrei. Meanwhile he leads an unsuccessful insurrection against the Czar. He is compelled to flee from his homeland, while his wife, Maria, ends up insane.

mazurka, a Polish national dance in triple time, usually with a strong accent on the second or third beat. There is a delightful mazurka in GLINKA's A LIFE FOR THE CZAR.

Measure for Measure, *see* SHAKESPEARE.

Meco all' altar di Venere, Pollione's aria revealing his love for Adalgisa, in Act I of BELLINI's NORMA.

Medea, a sorceress and murderess in Greek legend. She helps Jason gain the Golden Fleece and flees with him to Corinth, where she murders Jason's wife and children and then flees to Athens. Her story appears in several operas, notably the ones by Marc-Antoine CHARPENTIER, CHERUBINI, PACINI, and MILHAUD. *See* MÉDÉE.

Médecin malgré lui, Le (The Doctor in spite of Himself), OPÉRA COMIQUE in three acts by GOUNOD. Libretto by Jules BARBIER and Michel Carré, based on the play of the same name by MOLIÈRE. Premiere: Théâtre Lyrique, Paris, Jan. 15, 1858. American premiere: Cincinnati, Mar. 20, 1900. The text adheres closely to Molière's play. Having received a beating from her husband, Sagnarelle, the wife seeks revenge. She spreads the news that her husband is a miracle-working physician, disguised as a humble woodchopper. When he refuses to serve Lucinde, daughter of the wealthy Geronte, Sagnarelle is beaten by the servants of the household. But Lucinde has only pretended being ill, refusing to marry the man her father had chosen for her and preferring Leander. At last, Sagnarelle is compelled to diagnose Lucinde's supposed illness and prescribe a cure. When the lovers elope, poor Sagnarelle is once again given a thorough beating for being a fraud. All turns out well when Leander inherits a fortune and is accepted happily by Geronte as a worthy son-in-law. And Sagnarelle's wife forgives her husband.

Among the notable pages in Gounod's light and tuneful score are the following: Leander's serenade to Lucinde in Act II, "Qu'ils sont doux"; Sagnarelle's hymn to medicine opening Act III, "Vive la médecine"; and the mock choral hymn to science that closes the opera, "Nous faisons tous ce que nous savons faire."

This work was Gounod's first *opéra comique* and his first success in writing for the stage.

Médée, (1) opera ("tragédie lyrique") in prologue and five acts by Marc-Antoine CHARPENTIER. Libretto by

Thomas Corneille, based on the Greek legend. Premiere: Paris Opéra, Dec. 4, 1693. This opera enjoyed a huge success when first performed, one critic in 1693 considering it the most learned music written since LULLY, but it failed to survive, possibly because of a poor libretto.

(2) Opera in three acts by CHERUBINI. Libretto by François Benoît Hoffmann, based on the tragedy of Corneille. Premiere: Théâtre Feydeau, Paris, Mar. 13, 1797. American premiere: New York, Nov. 8, 1955 (concert version); San Francisco Opera, Sept. 12, 1958 (staged). This is sometimes referred to as the "first modern opera," since it is the first in the tradition of romantic grand opera. In the nineteenth century, recitatives were added by Franz Lachner. Though intermittently revived in France, Germany, and Italy since its premiere, *Médée* did not achieve popularity nor was its true importance appreciated until comparatively recent times, when it has been acclaimed due to the remarkable performances of the exacting title role by such singers as Maria CALLAS, Eileen FARRELL, and Gwyneth Jones. Callas achieved the heights of her artistic career in this role, first at the FLORENCE MAY MUSIC FESTIVAL in 1953; then in 1955 in Dallas, Texas; in 1959 at COVENT GARDEN; and in 1961 at LA SCALA. Eileen Farrell also achieved a triumph when she appeared in the title role in New York in a performance by the AMERICAN OPERA SOCIETY in 1955 and at the SAN FRANCISCO OPERA in 1958. Gwyneth Jones was heard in a performance by the American Opera Society in 1966.

Jason, having won the Golden Fleece in Colchis through the magic powers of Médée, has grown tired of her and has become interested in Glauce, daughter of the King of Corinth. Médée is banished from Corinth, but compelled to leave her two sons behind. When Jason and Glauce get married, Médée interrupts the ceremony and tries to win Jason back. But the king once again orders her banishment. Seeking vengeance, Médée kills Glauce by means of

a poisoned nightgown. She also murders her own two sons by Jason. Then she sets the temple afire.

These are among the principal arias: that of Jason ("Or che più non vedro") and that of Médée ("Deo tuoi figli la madre"). The march music and bridal scene in Act II are also noteworthy.

(3) Opera in one act by MILHAUD. Libretto by Madeleine Milhaud (the composer's wife). Premiere: Antwerp, Oct. 7, 1939.

Meditation, the orchestral ENTR'ACTE with solo violin prefacing Act II, Scene 2, of MASSENET's THAÏS. It expresses Thaïs' renunciation of a life of pleasure for that of the spirit.

Medium, The, "musical drama" in two acts by MENOTTI. Libretto by the composer. Premiere: New York City, Oct. 8, 1946.

Characters: Madame Flora, a medium (contralto); Monica, her daughter (soprano); Toby, a mute; Mrs. Gobineau (soprano), one of Madame Flora's clients; Mr. Gobineau (baritone), another client; Mrs. Nolan (mezzo-soprano), another client. The action takes place at the present time in Madame Flora's parlor.

Act I. Madame Flora is preparing for a séance, with the help of her daughter, Monica, and Toby, a mute she has picked up in the streets and given a home. Two of the clients, the Gobineaus, have come to speak to their dead baby, who had drowned in a pool. A new client, Mrs. Nolan, wants to communicate with the spirit of her daughter. Through Monica's disguised voice manipulated behind a curtain, the clients are made to believe that they are actually contacting their dead loved ones. Suddenly, Madame Flora emits a scream, insisting somebody has tried to choke her. She accuses Toby, who is rescued by Monica, and the girl's singing soothes both the mute and Madame Flora. Terrified, Madame Flora begins to pray.

Act II. A few days later, Toby and Monica are playing games with puppets while Monica sings a waltz, "Monica,

Monica, dance the waltz." It is obvious, as they play, that Toby is in love with her. When Madame Flora appears, she tries to extract from Toby the confession that he tried to choke her, offering him Monica in marriage if he is willing to confess. Toby, refusing to respond, is given a sound beating. When Madame Flora's clients return for a new séance, Madame Flora tells them that the séances have ended, that she is nothing but a fraud, and returns their money. The clients are so convinced that they had communicated with their dead children that they refuse to believe her. Madame Flora finally drives them away. She tries to calm herself by taking a few drinks and then prays to God for forgiveness. Hearing a noise, Madame Flora, losing all reason, begins firing a gun at the drawn curtain, killing Toby who has concealed himself there. Monica rushes out of the house seeking help as Madame Flora begs the dead Toby to confess that he was the one who had tried to strangle her.

The Medium was Menotti's first successful attempt to write music for a tragic text, and it was the first opera in which he revealed his true dramatic powers. It is his most successful serious opera, having been given over one thousand performances in the United States and Europe within a few years' time. In 1955 it toured Europe under the auspices of the American State Department. It was also Menotti's first opera to be recorded in its entirety, and the only one to be made into a motion picture (1951).

Mefistofele, opera in prologue, four acts, and epilogue by BOITO. Libretto by the composer, based on GOETHE's *Faust*. Premiere: La Scala, Mar. 5, 1868. American premiere: Academy of Music, New York, Nov. 24, 1880.

Boito's treatment of Goethe's drama differs markedly from that of GOUNOD: it attempts to incorporate the entire drama instead of merely the first part. It also tries to delve deeply into the inner conflicts and turmoil of the characters, rather than dwell on the plot line, and

to project Goethe's symbolism and philosophic concepts. After Marguerite's death, there are some scenes symbolizing the union of Greek and German ideals by means of the bringing together of Helen of Troy and Faust, and by Faust's ultimate redemption.

The opera's notable arias include the following: those of Faust, "Dai campi, dai prati" in Act I, "Forma ideal" in Act IV, and "Il real fu dolore" in the epilogue; and those of Marguerite, "L'altra notte" and "Lontano, lontano," both in Act III.

When initially performed, *Mefistofele* was a failure. It lacked action; it lasted too long (six hours). Boito's enemies, of whom there were many, saw to it that the failure was magnified into a fiasco. Only after Boito made extensive revisions did the opera begin to take hold. He shortened it, changed Faust from a baritone to a tenor, and interpolated new, pleasing vocal material (including the aria "Lontano, lontano"). Reintroduced this way, in Bologna on Oct. 4, 1875, it proved successful. It was then heard in London and New York, the first times the opera was given outside Italy. The opera was included in the repertory of the METROPOLITAN OPERA in 1883–84. It received a highly successful revival in a new production at the NEW YORK CITY OPERA on Sept. 24, 1969.

Mehta, Zubin, conductor. Born Bombay, India, Apr. 29, 1936. He is the son of Mehil Mehta, a conductor, from whom he received his first music instruction. In 1954 he studied conducting with Hans Swarowsky in Vienna and four years later won first prize in an international competition for conductors in Liverpool. His debut was made with the Vienna Philharmonic in 1959. It proved so successful that he was soon invited to appear with the leading orchestras of Europe and in the Soviet Union. In 1960 he was appointed associate conductor of the Los Angeles Philharmonic, and in 1961 he was elevated to the post of music director, which he has since retained with extraordinary success. For a while he served concurrently as conductor of the Montreal Symphony. His guest appearances, which have been worldwide, included performances of operas. Since Dec. 29, 1965, when he made his METROPOLITAN OPERA debut with AIDA, he has appeared regularly each season with that company. He also has been heard extensively in leading European opera houses and festivals. He brings to opera the same electrifying personality and the same scholarly (though at times highly personal) readings that have made him a significant symphonic conductor of our time.

Méhul, Etienne Nicolas (or Etienne Henri), composer. Born Givet, France, June 22, 1763; died Paris, Oct. 18, 1817. As a boy he studied the organ. A wealthy amateur provided him with funds to go to Paris. There in 1777 he studied with Johann Friedrich Edelmann. He wrote several operas before one was performed: an OPÉRA COMIQUE, *Euphrosine et Coradin,* seen at the Théâtre des Italiens in 1790. The work was such an outstanding success that Méhul became famous. In the next four years he extended his reputation with two more operas: *Stratonice* (1792) and *Horatius Coclès* (1794). During the French Revolution Méhul allied himself with the republicans by writing many patriotic songs, one of which, *Le Chant du départ,* rivaled the *Marseillaise* in popularity. He was now the recipient of many honors. In 1795 he became a member of the Institut de France and an inspector of the Paris Conservatory. In 1800 he was commissioned to write a special work commemorating the storming of the Bastille.

With Napoleon's rise to power, Méhul managed to maintain his eminent position in French music. He was, indeed, a favorite of Napoleon's. His most celebrated work, the opera JOSEPH, was a considerable success when introduced at the Théâtre Feydeau on Feb. 17, 1807. Poems were written in its honor; Napoleon gave Méhul a prize of five thousand francs. The decline of Méhul's fortunes coincided with the fall of Napoleon. Méhul was demoted at the

Conservatory from inspector to professor, with a corresponding reduction in salary. His operas were no longer performed, and his former fame was obscured by the rising popularity of other composers, notably SPONTINI. The last years of his life were unhappy. He died of consumption.

Méhul wrote some thirty operas. His comic operas were significant in helping establish the traditions of *opéra comique;* they are characterized by gaiety, verve, sparkling melodies, and effective ensemble numbers. In his serious operas, of which *Joseph* is the best, Méhul reveals a strong dramatic sense and a dignified, expressive lyricism. Besides those already mentioned, Méhul wrote the following successful works: *Le Jeune Henri* (1797); *Adrien* (1799); *Ariodant* (1799); *Bion* (1800); *Une Folie* (1802); *Le Trésor supposé* (1802); *Joanna* (1802); *Helena* (1803); *Les Deux Aveugles de Tolède* (1806); *Uthal* (1806); *Gabrielle d'Estrées* (1806).

Mein Elemer, Arabella's aria revealing that a young count, Elemer, has attracted her interest, in Act I of Richard STRAUSS's ARABELLA.

Mein Herr Marquis (Laughing Song), Adele's aria as she flirts in disguise with her employer Eisenstein and mocks him for mistaking her for a lady-in-waiting, in Act II of Johann STRAUSS's DIE FLEDERMAUS.

Mein Herr und Gott, nun ruf' ich dich, King Henry's prayer before the duel of Lohengrin and Telramund takes place, in Act I of WAGNER's LOHENGRIN.

Meister, Wilhelm, a student (tenor) in THOMAS's MIGNON.

Meistersinger, *see* MASTERSINGERS.

Meistersinger von Nürnberg, Die (The Mastersingers of Nuremberg), opera in three acts by WAGNER. Libretto by the composer. Premiere: National Theater, Munich, June 21, 1868. American premiere: Metropolitan Opera, Jan. 4, 1886.

Characters: Hans Sachs, cobbler (bass or baritone); David, his apprentice (tenor); Pogner, a goldsmith (bass); Eva, his daughter (soprano); Magdalena, her nurse (soprano); Walther von

Stolzing, a knight (tenor); Beckmesser, a town clerk (bass); MASTERSINGERS; journeymen; apprentices; guildspeople; girls. The setting is Nuremberg in the middle of the sixteenth century.

The stirring orchestral prelude contains five major themes from the opera, beginning with the majestic march of the mastersingers and including the "Prize Song."

Act I. The church of St. Katharine. The chorale ("Da zu dir der Heiland") brings the services to a close. Eva, as she leaves the church, is stopped by Walther von Stolzing. She tells him she will be the wife of the guildmaster who wins the song contest soon to be held. In love with Eva, Walther is determined to win. He has David teach him some of the rules, but David only manages to confuse him. The mastersingers now file into the church for a musical test. Pogner, father of Eva, announces that his daughter is to be the prize in the song contest (Pogner's Address: "Das schöne Fest"). The mastersingers ask Walther where he learned the art of song. He tells them that his knowledge came from nature and the ancient minstrels ("Am stillen Herd"). Walther is now asked to demonstrate his ability, and Beckmesser prepares to mark his errors on a slate. Walther improvises a song ("Fanget an! So rief der Lenz in den Wald"); the frequent scratchings on Beckmesser's slate betray the abundance of errors. Only Hans Sachs senses how much talent there is in Walther's song; the other mastersingers reject him rudely.

Act II. A street. Outside his shop, Hans Sachs soliloquizes on the beauty of Walther's song ("Wie duftet doch der Flieder"). Eva appears; coquettishly, she suggests that since she cannot have Walther for a husband she would accept Hans Sachs ("Gut'n Abend, Meister"). Hans Sachs is in love with Eva, but he knows that he is too old for her. When Walther arrives, he and Eva retire a little to plot elopement. Their planning is interrupted when Beckmesser comes to serenade Eva under her window ("Den Tag seh' ich erscheinen"). As Beckmesser sings his song, Hans Sachs rudely interrupts him with a ditty of his own ("Jerum! Jerum!"), banging loudly with his hammer as he sings. He also maintains that a shoe, like a song, must be fashioned with care ("Mit den Schuhen ward ich fertig schier"). The noise attracts Magdalena to the window, and since Beckmesser mistakes her for Eva, his singing becomes more passionate. The din awakens the townspeople. David, in love with Magdalena, sees Beckmesser serenading her and gives him a sound thrashing. The townspeople pour into the streets, and pandemonium prevails. Walther and Eva decide that this is the moment to make their escape, but they are gently restrained by Sachs. When the din subsides, a watchman passes through the now silent streets proclaiming that all is well ("Hört ihr Leut', und lasst euch sagen").

Act III, Scene 1. Inside Sachs's shop. The orchestral prelude has for its core Sachs's monologue "Wahn! Wahn!" and a quotation from the "Prize Song." It is early morning of the following day. When David enters the shop, Sachs asks him to sing a hymn to St. John, whose festival day is soon to be celebrated. After completing the hymn ("Am Jordan Sankt Johannes stand"), David leaves. Sachs soliloquizes philosophically over the sad state of the world which, to him, has gone mad ("Wahn! Wahn! Überall Wahn!"). Walther now arrives to tell Sachs of a dream in which a song of great beauty came to him. When he sings a portion of it—it is the "Prize Song"—Sachs is impressed and puts it down on paper. Later, when Beckmesser slips into the shop, he finds this paper; thinking it is one of Sachs's songs, he decides to steal it and use it in the contest. After his escape, Eva arrives to have her shoes repaired; while she is present, Walther, Magdalena, and David also appear. Walther sings Eva a part of his dream song. Eva, Magdalena, David, and Sachs join in to express their individual reactions (Quintet: "Selig, wie die Sonne").

Scene 2. A field beside the Pegnitz

River. Here the song contest is to be held. Apprentices dance with their girls ("The Dance of the Apprentices"). The various guilds march in with flying banners. After Hans Sachs is acclaimed by the people ("Wach' auf, es nahet gen den Tag"), he announces the opening of the contest. Beckmesser is called first. Performing from the stolen manuscript, he becomes so confused that he arouses derisive laughter. Sachs now summons Walther, who sings his song ("Morgenlich leuchtend im rosigen Schein"). The people acclaim the singer and his song. Walther is the winner, receiving the golden chain of the Masters Guild. Eva is his. Now that Walther is victorious, Sachs takes pains to point out to him that rules and discipline are important to art. The people now once again acclaim their beloved cobbler, Hans Sachs ("Heil Sachs! Hans Sachs!").

It is a far different Wagner we meet in *Die Meistersinger* from the Wagner of the RING and TRISTAN UND ISOLDE. *Die Meistersinger* is Wagner's only comedy. With his supreme command of musical resources and his infallible instinct for the theater, Wagner created a work whose salient features are humor, gentleness, glowing warmth, joyfulness. In *Die Meistersinger* we are no longer in the world of gods and legendary heroes, but in that of human beings whose problems are those of the real world: the world of success and failure (symbolized by the song contest); a world in which there is both frustration (for Sachs) and fulfillment (for Walther and Eva). There is a human quality here that we find nowhere else in Wagner. It appears not only in the remarkable text but in the radiant score, which often reminds us of old German chorales, of street songs and lute songs. *Die Meistersinger*, completed in 1867, came eight years after *Tristan und Isolde* and more than a decade after the first two dramas of the *Ring* cycle. Thus, it was conceived and completed when Wagner's ideas about the music drama were fully crystallized. In some respects, *Die Meistersinger* represents a retreat from these ideas: it re-

turns to older concepts of opera with its formal arias, ensemble numbers, choral numbers, processional march, dances, and so forth. But the integration of these operatic elements is achieved with such skill and the various elements are so essential to the dramatic context that Wagner's basic concept of opera as a synthesis of the arts is still realized.

In planning *Die Meistersinger*, Wagner wanted to give comic treatment to a song contest, just as he had given it dramatic treatment in TANNHÄUSER. As the idea germinated, he planned to use the contest as a symbol of his own artistic struggle against rules and formal procedures. Thus Beckmesser, the ridiculous advocate of the *status quo* in art, became the symbol of the critics who continually attacked Wagner and his esthetics—in particular, the Viennese critic Eduard HANSLICK. Walther, achieving a new artistic truth by iconoclastically destroying stultifying laws and concepts, arrives at a new freedom of expression, just as Wagner himself did.

Melba, Nellie (born Helen Mitchell), soprano. Born Richmond, near Melbourne, Australia, May 19, 1859; died Sydney, Australia, Feb. 23, 1931. One of the most brilliant coloratura sopranos of her generation, her musical education was comprehensive rather than specialized, including piano, organ, and theory, as well as voice. She sang and played the organ in local churches until her marriage to Captain Charles Nesbit Armstrong in 1882. After that she concentrated on singing, studying in Melbourne and for a year with Mathilde MARCHESI in Paris. On Oct. 12, 1887, Melba made her opera debut at the THÉÂTRE DE LA MONNAIE as GILDA. She was sufficiently impressive for COVENT GARDEN to engage her. She appeared there for the first time on May 24, 1888, in the title role of LUCIA DI LAMMERMOOR and received a tumultuous ovation. The following year she made her debut at the PARIS OPÉRA, where for the next two seasons she was an outstanding attraction. After further European triumphs she came to the United States and made a sensational debut at the

METROPOLITAN OPERA on Dec. 4, 1893, as Lucia. "Her voice is . . . exquisitely beautiful," wrote H. E. Krehbiel. "Added to this . . . she has the most admirable musical instincts." She continued to gather accolades at the Metropolitan during the next three seasons. On Dec. 30, 1896, she made an unfortunate attempt to extend her repertory by appearing as Brünnhilde in SIEGFRIED. This effort taxed her so severely that she was compelled to go into temporary retirement and give her voice a complete rest. She emerged in 1897 appearing with the DAMROSCH OPERA COMPANY. She then continued her dazzling career. In America she sang with the MANHATTAN OPERA from 1907 to 1909 and after that with the CHICAGO OPERA. Her last American appearance took place in the spring of 1920; her farewell opera appearance took place at Covent Garden in 1926. After that she retired to Melbourne, where she became director of the Melbourne Conservatory.

Her voice, exceptional in flexibility, clarity, and precision, was heard to best advantage in such coloratura roles as LAKMÉ, Gilda, Lucia, Violetta, and ROSINA, but she was also an outstanding artist in the more lyrical parts of MIMI, DESDEMONA, and MARGUERITE. In 1918 she was made a Dame of the British Empire. She wrote an autobiography, *Melodies and Memories* (1925), and was the subject for a screen biography starring Patrice MUNSEL, *Melba* (1952).

Melchior, Lauritz, tenor. Born Copenhagen, Mar. 20, 1890. For a quarter of a century one of the world's foremost Wagnerian tenors, he entered the Royal Opera House School in 1912 and on Apr. 2, 1913, made his debut at the Royal Opera in the baritone role of SILVIO. After several appearances in Denmark, he toured Sweden with Mme. Charles CAHIER in IL TROVATORE. Mme. Cahier convinced Melchior to retrain his voice as a tenor. After several years of study Melchior made his return debut in Copenhagen on Oct. 8, 1918, this time as a tenor, in TANNHÄUSER. A year later he sang in London, where the novelist Hugh Walpole urged him to specialize in the Wagnerian repertory. Still another period of study and readjustment took place while he worked on the Wagnerian repertory with Anna BAHR-MILDENBURG. On May 14, 1924, Melchior appeared at COVENT GARDEN as SIEGMUND, from then on specializing in the principal tenor roles of the WAGNER music dramas. On July 23, 1924, he appeared for the first time at BAYREUTH, singing the role of PARSIFAL. On Feb. 17, 1926, he made his American debut at the METROPOLITAN OPERA as Tannhäuser. He remained the principal Wagnerian tenor of the Metropolitan until 1950.

As a Wagnerian tenor Melchior made opera history. He sang the role of TRISTAN over two hundred times (his foremost predecessor, Jean DE RESZKE, had appeared in that role less than fifty times); as Tristan he appeared in sixteen different opera houses and under twenty-two different conductors. On Feb. 22, 1934, his hundredth performance as SIEGFRIED was commemorated on the stage of the Metropolitan. His twentieth year at the Metropolitan was celebrated on Feb. 17, 1946, when he appeared in several scenes from different Wagner dramas. His last appearance at the Metropolitan was in LOHENGRIN on Feb. 2, 1950. While still a member of the Metropolitan, Melchior frequently appeared in motion pictures and on the radio. After retiring from opera, he continued these appearances, also singing in concerts, on television, and in night clubs. Many honors have been bestowed on him, including the Knighthood of Dannebrog, the Knighthood of Bulgaria, the Saxonian Order of Knights, the Silver Cross of Denmark, and the Ingenio et Arti, which has been given to only three men in Denmark. He also received the Carl Eduard Medal, first class, from Saxe-Coburg-Gotha for outstanding services at Bayreuth. He established the Lauritz Melchior Heldentenor Foundation to encourage singers to prepare for careers as heroic tenors, the first recipients, on Feb. 17, 1969, being William Cochran and John Russell.

Melchthal, Arnold's father (bass) in ROSSINI'S WILLIAM TELL.

Mélesville (born Anne Honore Duveyrier), dramatist and librettist. Born Paris, Nov. 13, 1787; died there Nov., 1865. With the collaboration of various writers, including Eugène SCRIBE, Pierre Carmouche, E. C. de Boirie, and J. T. Merle, she wrote numerous librettos for operas by ADAM, AUBER, CHERUBINI, DONIZETTI, LORTZING, and others. The libretto for HÉROLD'S ZAMPA was her work alone, and BRÜLL'S DAS GOLDENE KREUZ was derived from one of her plays.

Mélisande, (1) Golaud's wife (soprano), beloved by her brother-in-law Pelléas, in DEBUSSY'S PELLÉAS ET MÉLISANDE, a role created by Mary GARDEN.

(2) One of Bluebeard's wives (soprano) in DUKAS'S ARIANE ET BARBEBLEUE.

Melitone, Fra, a friar (bass) in VERDI'S LA FORZA DEL DESTINO.

Melodies of the Language, see JANÁČEK, LEOŠ.

melodrama, (1) an operatic passage or scene in which the singer recites his part while a musical commentary on the situation appears in the orchestral accompaniment. Examples of such melodramas are the grave-digging scene in FIDELIO and the bullet-casting scene in DER FREISCHÜTZ.

(2) An operatic form, similar to the above, in which the opera's entire text is spoken, not sung, to an orchestral accompaniment. The form was developed by Georg BENDA in the eighteenth century. Its most ambitious practitioner was Zděnek FIBICH (1850–1900), who wrote a trilogy of melodramas, HIPPODAMEIA, in which he tried to realize a closer unity between poetry and music than had heretofore been achieved.

Melot, a courtier (tenor) in WAGNER'S TRISTAN UND ISOLDE.

Melville, Herman, author. Born New York City, Aug. 1, 1819; died there Sept. 28, 1891. His story *Billy Budd* was made into operas by BRITTEN and GHEDINI; his novel *Moby Dick* into an opera by James Low. KRENEK'S *The Bell Tower* is also based on a Melville story.

Mendelssohn, Felix, composer. Born Hamburg, Feb. 3, 1809; died Leipzig, Nov. 4, 1847. This celebrated composer wrote several operas, none of them significant. As a boy he wrote a comic opera, *The Two Nephews,* whose only performance took place at his home to celebrate his fifteenth birthday. Two years later he completed DIE HOCHZEIT DES CAMACHO, based on an episode in *Don Quixote,* a fiasco when introduced in Berlin on Apr. 29, 1827. In 1829 he completed an operetta, *Die Heimkehr aus der Fremde,* performed privately. Years after the composer's death it was given its first public performance in England, under the title *Son and Stranger.* In his last year Mendelssohn worked on an opera entitled LORELEI, but he completed only a few excerpts: the finale to the first act, an "Ave Maria," and a "Vintage Song." The libretto was subsequently used by Max BRUCH.

Mendès, Catulle, author. Born Bordeaux, France, May 22, 1841; died Saint-Germain, France, Feb. 8, 1909. One of the most distinguished French poet-dramatists of the late nineteenth century, Mendès wrote the librettos for CHABRIER'S GWENDOLINE, ERLANGER'S *Le Fils de l'étoile,* HAHN'S *La Carmélite,* and MASSENET'S *Ariane* and *Bacchus.* His *conte dramatique La Reine Fiammette* was made into an opera by Xavier LEROUX. Mendès wrote a book about WAGNER (1886); in his novel *Le Roi vierge* (1880) Wagner appears as a character.

Menelaus, (1) King of Sparta (baritone) in OFFENBACH'S LA BELLE HÉLÈNE.

(2) King of Sparta (tenor), husband of Helen, in Richard STRAUSS'S DIE AEGYPTISCHE HELENA.

Mengetto, the lover (tenor) of Cecchina, who loses her to Cecchina's master, in PICCINNI'S LA CECCHINA.

Mengono, a young man (tenor), sweetheart of Grilletta, in HAYDN'S LO SPEZIALE.

Menotti, Gian Carlo, composer. Born Cadigliano, Italy, July 7, 1911. Between 1923 and 1928 he attended the Milan Conservatory and was so precocious that after a year there he wrote a three-act opera, *The Death of Pierrot,* libretto as well as music. He came to the United States in 1928 and continued his study at the Curtis Institute of Music. The fruit of this study was a one-act opera, AMELIA GOES TO THE BALL, introduced in Philadelphia and New York by members of the Curtis Institute under Fritz REINER in 1937. It was so successful that the National Broadcasting Company commissioned him to write a radio opera, THE OLD MAID AND THE THIEF, introduced in 1939. Meanwhile in 1938 the METROPOLITAN OPERA presented *Amelia Goes to the Ball.* In 1942 the Metropolitan introduced *The Island God,* which was a failure. After winning a thousand-dollar grant from the American Academy and National Institute of Arts and Letters in 1945 and a Guggenheim Fellowship a year later, Menotti completed THE MEDIUM on a commission from the DITSON FUND. At its premiere in 1946, it received such acclaim that it was decided to produce it on Broadway. Together with Menotti's new one-act opera, THE TELEPHONE, it opened on Broadway on May 1, 1947, and was an outstanding success. Subsequently, *The Medium* received over a thousand performances in this country by various groups; it was made into a motion picture, directed by the composer; and it was heard in leading European opera houses. Menotti's next opera, THE CONSUL, was also a formidable success. Opening on Broadway on Mar. 16, 1950, it was acclaimed by the critics and was a box-office hit. It gathered several honors, including the PULITZER PRIZE and the New York Drama Critics' Award. Subsequently, it was produced in about a dozen countries and in eight different languages. In 1950 it became the first opera written and first produced in America to be performed at LA SCALA. In 1951 Menotti wrote the first opera expressly intended for television transmission, AMAHL AND THE NIGHT VISITORS. It was presented on Christmas Eve, 1951, and since then it

has often been heard as a holiday feature over television, besides receiving successful stage presentations, including one at the FLORENCE MAY MUSIC FESTIVAL in 1953. In 1954 Menotti's THE SAINT OF BLEECKER STREET was introduced on Broadway, winning the composer his second Pulitzer prize. Later operas: MARIA GOLOVIN (1958); *Labyrinth,* a one-act opera for television (1963); THE LAST SAVAGE (1963); MARTIN'S LIE, a one-act church opera (1964); HELP, HELP, THE GLOBOLINKS!, a children's opera 1968); and *The Most Important Man in the World* (1970).

In 1958, Menotti founded the FESTIVAL OF TWO WORLDS at Spoleto, Italy. Menotti wrote the librettos for BARBER'S VANESSA and FOSS'S INTRODUCTIONS AND GOODBYES. In 1968–69 Menotti produced and directed several operatic performances at the HAMBURG STATE OPERA.

Both his librettos and his scores show that Menotti's interests and talents are thoroughly dramatic, often melodramatic. His musical language tends to look back rather than forward—toward PUCCINI most critics point out. He has no taste for SERIAL TECHNIQUES, ELECTRONIC MUSIC, or other late developments, and he has stated his position with clarity and gentle satire in *Help, Help, the Globolinks!* The easy assimilability of his music and his extraordinary feeling for the stage as author, composer, producer and director account for the remarkably wide appeal of his most successful operas.

Me pellegrina ed orfana, Leonora's lament in Act I of VERDI'S LA FORZA DEL DESTINO, because her family refuses to accept her lover, Don Alvaro.

Méphistophélès, the devil (baritone) in BERLIOZ' THE DAMNATION OF FAUST, a role created by Maurice RENAUD; also in BOITO'S MEFISTOFELE and GOUNOD'S FAUST. In the last two the role is for a bass.

Méphistophélès' Serenade, *see* VOUS QUI FAITES L'ENDORMIE.

Mercadante, Saverio, composer. Born Altamura, near Bari, Italy, Sept., 1795; died Naples, Dec. 17, 1870. He attended the Collegio di San Sebastiano in

Naples, where he was one of Niccolo Zingarelli's star students. His first work for the stage was *L'apoteosi d'Ercole,* given with outstanding success at the SAN CARLO in Naples on Aug. 19, 1819. International fame came with an OPERA BUFFA, *Elisa e Claudio,* given at LA SCALA in 1821. During the next forty-five years he wrote another fifty or more operas, in the best of which he instituted some major reforms, especially in the use of the orchestra. His greatest successes, besides those already mentioned, were: *I briganti,* produced in Paris in 1836; *Il giuramento,* given at La Scala in 1837 and revived there in a revised version a century later; and *Il bravo,* introduced in Milan in 1839. His last opera, *Virginia,* was given in Naples in 1866. In 1833 Mercadante was appointed MAESTRO DI CAPPELLA at the Novara Cathedral. While holding this post he lost one eye, an infirmity that in 1862 resulted in complete blindness. In 1839 he became *maestro di cappella* at Lanciano and a year afterward succeeded Zingarelli as the director of the Naples Conservatory, a post held until the end of his life.

Mercédès, Carmen's gypsy friend (soprano) in BIZET's CARMEN.

Mercè, diletti amiche, Elena's joyful BOLERO following her marriage to Arrigo, in Act V of VERDI's THE SICILIAN VESPERS.

Merchant of Venice, The (Il mercante di Venezia), opera in three acts by CASTELNUOVO-TEDESCO. Libretto by the composer, based on the SHAKESPEARE drama. Premiere: Florence, May 25, 1961. American premiere: Los Angeles, Apr. 13, 1966. With this opera, the composer won first prize among sixty-four competitors in a contest sponsored by LA SCALA with funds provided by David Campari. Though the composer used only Shakespeare's words in his text, he reduced the drama to about one-fifth its original size, compressing the five acts into three. The first and third acts take place in Venice, and the second at Portia's home at Belmont. The basic plot, however, is adhered to. The musical style is varied, ranging from the lyrical and romantic to modern techniques, including the use of a twelve-tone chord three times.

Mercutio, Roméo's friend (baritone) in GOUNOD's ROMÉO ET JULIETTE.

Mère coupable, La (The Guilty Mother), opera in three acts by MILHAUD. Libretto by Madeleine Milhaud (the composer's wife), based on BEAUMARCHAIS's *The Barber of Seville.* Premiere: Geneva, Switzerland, June 13, 1966. Milhaud here attempts to interpret in terms of twentieth-century musical idioms a text which had inspired the masterwork by ROSSINI.

Mérimée, Prosper, author. Born Paris, Sept. 28, 1803; died Cannes, France, Sept. 23, 1870. Mérimée's short stories and novels provided subjects for many operas. The most famous is *Carmen,* the source of BIZET's famous opera. Others are *Le Carrosse du Saint-Sacrement* (operas by Henri Büsser and Lord Berners, and OFFENBACH's OPÉRA BOUFFE LA PÉRICHOLE); *Colomba* (operas by PACINI, Henri Büsser, and MACKENZIE); *La Dame de pique* (opera by HALÉVY); *Mateo Falcone* (opera by CUI); *L'Occasion* (opera by Louis Durey); *La Vénus d'Ille* (SCHOECK's *Venus* and Hermann Wetzler's *The Basque Venus*).

Merola, Gaetano, conductor and opera director. Born Naples, Italy, Jan. 4, 1881; died San Francisco, Cal., Aug. 30, 1953. He attended the Royal Conservatory in Naples. In 1899 he came to the United States and became an assistant conductor at the METROPOLITAN OPERA. In 1903 he conducted for the Henry SAVAGE Opera and in 1906 at the MANHATTAN OPERA House. After a period of conducting in London he returned to the United States and in 1923 helped found the SAN FRANCISCO OPERA, which he directed up to the time of his death, helping make it the second leading opera institution in this country.

Merrill, Robert, baritone. Born Brooklyn, N.Y., June 4, 1919. After receiving instruction from teachers in New York, he appeared in hotels and at the Radio

City Music Hall. In 1945 he won the METROPOLITAN AUDITIONS OF THE AIR and on Dec. 15 of that year made his METROPOLITAN OPERA debut in LA TRAVIATA. Since then he has been a principal baritone of the Metropolitan Opera. He has also sung in other leading opera houses of America and Europe. In 1946 he was the singer selected to appear at the Roosevelt Memorial before both houses of Congress. TOSCANINI selected him for the leading baritone roles in his broadcasts of *La traviata* and UN BALLO IN MASCHERA, the latter being Toscanini's last opera broadcast. In 1952 Merrill appeared in the motion picture *Aaron Slick from Punkin Crick,* his defection from the Metropolitan Opera to Hollywood without permission creating a temporary rift between himself and Rudolf BING, the general manager of the Metropolitan, and causing his dismissal from the company. Following his reinstatement, Merrill has come to be recognized as one of the world's foremost baritones in the French and Italian repertory. He is the author of an autobiography, *Once More from the Beginning* (1965).

Merry Mount, opera in five acts by HANSON. Libretto by Richard L. Stokes, based on a New England legend and Nathaniel HAWTHORNE's *The Maypole of Merry Mount.* Premiere: Metropolitan Opera, Feb. 10, 1934. The setting is New England in 1625. Pastor Bradford, a Puritan clergyman, is tortured by sensual dreams and unfulfilled desires. Spurning a Puritan girl, he falls in love with a Cavalier woman, Lady Marigold Sandys. The marriage of Lady Marigold to Gower Lackland is interrupted by the Puritans. There is a battle—the Cavaliers are defeated and some nominally friendly Indians are enraged. Later, Bradford makes advances to Lady Marigold. Attempting to aid her, Gower Lackland is struck by a guard and slain. When Bradford falls asleep, he dreams that he is in hell, that Gower is Lucifer, and that Lady Marigold becomes his. He awakes to

find that the Indians have set fire to the settlement. The Puritans propose to stone Bradford and Lady Marigold, the fancied source of their trouble. Bradford, aghast at the tragedies his lusts have precipitated, sweeps Lady Marigold into his arms and springs into the flaming church. The composer has made an orchestral suite of the overture, the Children's Dance, the love duet of Bradford and Lady Marigold, the prelude to Act II, and the Maypole Dances.

Merry Wives of Windsor, The (Die lustigen Weiber von Windsor), comic opera in three acts by NICOLAI. Libretto by MOSENTHAL, based on SHAKESPEARE's comedy. Premiere: Berlin Opera, Mar. 9, 1849. American premiere: Philadelphia, Mar. 16, 1863. The opera follows the Shakespeare play with minor modifications: Falstaff's followers (Bardolph, Pistol, and Nym) are omitted; the love of Fenton and Anne is touched upon only in passing. The opera emphasizes Falstaff's efforts to make love simultaneously to Mistress Ford and Mistress Page and the comic episodes befalling him in the attempt. The climax, as in the play, is reached in Windsor Park, where Falstaff becomes the victim of playful revenge on the part of the ladies and their husbands.

The overture is a favorite in the semiclassical repertory. There is a slow introduction with an expressive melody in the basses, which other instruments repeat. In the main part of the overture two melodious tunes are heard, the first in strings and woodwinds, and the other in violins, the latter being a tonal portrait of Anne Page.

Among the better-known vocal numbers are Fenton's ROMANCE to Anne Page in Act II, "Horch, die Lerche," and in the same act Mrs. Ford's aria, "Nun eilt herbei," and Falstaff's drinking song, "Als Büblein klein"; and in Act III, Mistress Page's "The Ballad of Herne the Huntsman."

See also FALSTAFF; SIR JOHN IN LOVE.

Mes amis, écoutez l'histoire (Ronde du Postillon), Chapelou's aria, the most famous in ADAM'S LE POSTILLON DE LONG-JUMEAU, heard in Act I. Here he talks about his profession as a postilion.

Me sedur han creduto, *see* C'EN EST DONC FAIT ET MON COEUR VA CHANGER.

Mesrour, chief of the harem guards (speaking part) in WEBER'S OBERON.

messa di voce, a term applied to the singing of a gradual crescendo, followed by a gradual decrescendo, on a long-sustained note.

Messager, André Charles Prosper, composer and conductor. Born Montluçon, France, Dec. 30, 1853; died Paris, Feb. 24, 1929. He attended the Ecole Niedermeyer and concluded his studies with SAINT-SAËNS. He then held various posts in Paris as organist and choirmaster. He first attracted attention as a composer with a symphony that won a gold medal in 1875 and a ballet, *Fleur d'orange,* introduced at the Folies Bergères in 1878. His first success in opera came in 1885 when the Bouffes-Parisiens presented his OPÉRA COMIQUE, *La Béarnaise;* it was soon presented in London, where it had a long run. Later *opéras comiques* established his reputation in France. These included *La Basoche* (1890), *Les P'tites Michu* (1897), and *Véronique* (1898). Messager also distinguished himself as an opera conductor. From 1898 to 1903 he was the conductor of the OPÉRA-COMIQUE where, in 1902, he led the world premiere of PELLÉAS ET MÉLISANDE (which is dedicated to him). From 1901 to 1907 he was artistic director of COVENT GARDEN and from 1907 to 1919 director and principal conductor of the PARIS OPÉRA. He returned to the Opéra-Comique for the single season of 1919–20. He also led the Concerts du Conservatoire after 1908, touring the United States with this orchestra in 1918. In 1926 he was elected a member of the Académie des Beaux Arts. Among English-speaking people, his best-known work was the operetta *Monsieur Beaucaire,* based on Booth Tarkington's novel and first produced in Birmingham, Eng., in 1917.

Besides the operetta and *opéras comiques* already mentioned, he wrote: *La Fauvette du temple* (1885); *Le Bourgeois de Calais* (1887); *Isoline* (1888); *Le Mari de la reine* (1889); *Madame Chrysanthème* (1893); *Miss Dollar* (1893); *Mirette* (1894); *Le Chevalier d'Hermental* (1896); *La Fiancée en loterie* (1896); *Les Dragons de l'impératrice* (1905); *Fortunio* (1907); *Béatrice* (1910).

Metastasio, Pietro (born Trapassi), dramatist, poet, librettist. Born Rome, Jan. 3, 1698; died Vienna, Apr. 12, 1782. His poetic dramas on classical and Biblical subjects were used by an entire century of opera composers; more than any other single influence, they were responsible for maintaining stylistic traditions in Italian opera. As a boy, the poet was adopted and supported by a patron, Gian Vincenzo Gravina, at whose request he changed his name to Metastasio; Gravina ultimately left him his fortune. In 1730 Metastasio went to Vienna and became court poet and dramatist, holding this post until the end of his life more than half a century later. He wrote a great number of poetic dramas in the grand manner favored by the Viennese court. Of particular interest were his twenty-seven DRAMMI PER MUSICI. All of these were set to music, some of them an astonishing number of times. *Artaserse* was made into forty different operas between 1724 and 1823; *La clemenza di Tito* into six operas (one by MOZART). HASSE set all of Metastasio's dramas to music, some of them several times. A few other composers who used his dramas were GLUCK, HANDEL, HAYDN, JOMMELLI, PICCINNI, and PORPORA. These dramas were filled with intricate plots, flowery speeches, and grandiose climaxes, all appealing strongly to eighteenth-century taste. It was against the Metastasio tradition that Gluck rebelled when he produced such operas as ORFEO ED EURIDICE and ALCESTE.

Metastasio's most popular works included: *Achille in Sciro; Adriano in*

Siria; Alessandro nell' Indie; Antigono; Artaserse; La clemenza di Tito; Demetrio; Demofoönte; Didone abbandonata; Ezio; L'isola disabitata; Olimpiade; Partenope; Il rè pastore; Il Ruggiero; Semiramide riconosciuta; Siroe; Il trionfo di Clelia.

Metropolitan Auditions of the Air, a weekly half-hour radio program of the ABC network, instituted in 1936 to audition likely singers for the METROPOLITAN OPERA. A special committee from the Metropolitan Opera selects each season those worthy of appearing with the regular company. The first winner was Thomas L. Thomas, who made his Metropolitan Opera debut on May 16, 1937, in PAGLIACCI. Other singers who have stepped into the ranks of the Metropolitan Opera from these auditions have been: Marilyn Cotlow, Justino DIAZ, Frances Greer, Frank GUARRERA, Margaret HARSHAW, Clifford Harvuot, Thomas Hayward, Raoul Joubin, Robert MERRILL, Patrice MUNSEL, Regina RESNIK, George SHIRLEY, Eleanor STEBER, Risë STEVENS, Teresa Stratas, and Leonard WARREN.

Metropolitan Opera. The former home of the Metropolitan Opera, more properly the Metropolitan Opera Association, was on Broadway between Thirty-ninth and Fortieth streets in New York City. For almost a century the Metropolitan Opera has been the foremost operatic institution of the United States, and one of the great opera organizations of the world. It was founded by several leading New York financiers, who, unable to procure boxes for the operas at the Academy of Music, decided to sponsor a house of their own further uptown. They subscribed eight hundred thousand dollars for the purpose. With Henry E. ABBEY as the first artistic director, the new opera house opened on Oct. 22, 1883, with FAUST, starring Italo CAMPANINI and Christine NILSSON. During the first season there were sixty-one presentations of nineteen operas. Though the rich of New York filled the boxes, the Opera suffered a deficit of six hundred thousand dollars. With the stockholders now taking over the management, Leopold DAMROSCH was made artistic director. The emphasis was on German opera. The few works of non-German origin were sung in appropriate translations. Damrosch's sudden death before the season's end brought his young son Walter as a hurried replacement. For the third season, Anton SEIDL was engaged as principal conductor, with Walter DAMROSCH as his assistant. This regime continued through the 1890–91 season, all performances being heard in German. Important singers of the period included Max ALVARY, Emil FISCHER, and Lilli LEHMANN. The following American premieres took place: DIE MEISTERSINGER, TRISTAN UND ISOLDE, DAS RHEINGOLD, SIEGFRIED, and GÖTTERDÄMMERUNG.

From 1892 to 1898 the Metropolitan was guided by the directorial triumvirate of Henry E. Abbey, Maurice GRAU, and Edward Schoeffel. The German policy was now abandoned. The company sang the French and Italian repertories in the original languages; German operas, given occasionally, were performed in Italian. Notable new singers included Emma CALVÉ, Emma EAMES, Edouard and Jean DE RESZKE, Pol PLANÇON, and Nellie MELBA. A fire ravaged the theater in 1892, necessitating extensive alterations. There was no opera season in the fall and winter of that year. The reconstructed house reopened on Nov. 27, 1893, with *Faust.* There was no 1897–98 season at the Metropolitan, the death of Henry Abbey in 1896 having precipitated a reorganization of the company. Maurice Grau now became manager. A new era was launched with TANNHÄUSER on Nov. 29, 1898. The five seasons of Grau's direction have been described as "the golden age of opera." With some of the greatest singers of that generation in his company—Giuseppe CAMPANARI, Emma Eames, Johanna GADSKI, Louise HOMER, Lilli Lehmann, Victor MAUREL, Lillian NORDICA, Plançon, the de Reszkes, Thomas SALIGNAC, Marcella SEMBRICH, Ernestine SCHUMANN-HEINK, Milka TERNINA, Ernst VAN DYCK

—Grau assembled incomparable all-star casts. The Grau management was an outstanding success both artistically and financially.

When poor health compelled Grau to withdraw, Heinrich CONRIED took over the reins from 1903 to 1908. A new reorganization of the company took place with Conried's arrival. Twelve directors, who assumed all financial responsibility, created the Conried Metropolitan Opera Company on a stockholding basis. The Conried regime saw many brilliant new members added to the company: Alessandro BONCI, Enrico CARUSO, Feodor CHALIAPIN, Geraldine FARRAR, Olive FREMSTAD, and the conductors Gustav MAHLER and Felix MOTTL. Placing less importance on individual singers than on integrated productions, Conried made notable advances in such matters as costuming and staging. Two outstanding events of his era were the American premieres of PARSIFAL and SALOME, each of which attracted considerable publicity and aroused passionate feelings. *Parsifal* came in Conried's first season. It stirred nationwide controversy, since it was the first stage production of the opera outside BAYREUTH, and it was known that WAGNER had intended *Parsifal* for his festival theater alone. When Bayreuth representatives went to court to keep the performance from taking place, New York split into two camps, one siding with Cosima WAGNER, the other feeling that a work of art belonged to the world. Conried won the legal fight, and the announced performance stirred the anticipation of opera lovers throughout the country. A special "Parsifal" train was run from Chicago. The premiere on Dec. 24, 1903, was a tremendous artistic and financial success. For the remainder of the season, *Parsifal* remained the most exciting opera in the repertory, always playing to sold-out houses; its eleven performances brought in almost two hundred thousand dollars. The premiere of *Salome* (Jan. 22, 1907) also brought on a tempest. A righteous-minded citizenry descended on Conried for permitting such a display of obscenity on the stage. The clergy and press joined in the battle. Before a second performance could take place, the Metropolitan directors decided that further performances of the opera were "detrimental to the best interests" of the company, and the work was removed from the repertory.

Other notable events during Conried's regime had happier results. HUMPERDINCK and PUCCINI were invited to attend performances of their operas. Lavish productions were given THE QUEEN OF SHEBA, DIE FLEDERMAUS, and THE GYPSY BARON. Conried resigned in 1908 on the grounds of ill health, but it was no secret that, having come upon evil days at the box office, due to the competition of the newly founded MANHATTAN OPERA COMPANY, the management of the Metropolitan felt that a new deal was called for. The Metropolitan Opera Company was formed in 1908 with Giulio GATTI-CASAZZA of LA SCALA as general manager and Andreas DIPPEL as administrative manager. Gustav Mahler was engaged to conduct German works, and Arturo TOSCANINI was added to the staff of conductors.

Gatti-Casazza remained general manager of the Metropolitan for a quarter of a century. He sensitively gauged the wishes of his audiences and catered to them; his regime was prosperous. Yet the ideals of a great operatic institution were not discarded. He was responsible for over a hundred novelties, many of them world premieres. It was due to him that an American opera was given at the Metropolitan for the first time, CONVERSE'S THE PIPE OF DESIRE (1910), and that the Metropolitan offered a ten thousand dollar prize for another American opera, won in 1912 by PARKER'S MONA. Gatti-Casazza also gave seasonal cycles of the Wagnerian music dramas, frequently without cuts. He enriched every department of the opera house, he made possible the weekly broadcasts, and he maintained the Metropolitan as one of the world's great musical centers.

After the 1934–35 season Gatti-Casazza

retired and was succeeded by Herbert WITHERSPOON. Witherspoon's sudden death, even before his first season began, placed the direction of the Metropolitan in the hands of Edward JOHNSON, for many years a principal tenor of the company and in 1935 the director of a special popular-priced spring season. For the next fifteen years Johnson directed the Metropolitan with great distinction. He helped develop American singers: such outstanding American artists as Mimi Benzell, Dorothy KIRSTEN, Grace MOORE, Patrice MUNSEL, Jan PEERCE, Eleanor STEBER, Blanche THEBOM, Helen TRAUBEL, Richard TUCKER, and Leonard WARREN made their bow. He also inaugurated the METROPOLITAN AUDITIONS OF THE AIR and encouraged the founding of the METROPOLITAN OPERA GUILD. He was responsible for consummating a deal with Columbia Records for the recording of Metropolitan Opera performances. His regime emphasized performances of operas in English, in fresh new translations. He was responsible for many significant American premieres and revivals. When Johnson resigned his post in 1950, he was succeeded by Rudolf BING, artistic director of the GLYNDEBOURNE OPERA and the EDINBURGH FESTIVAL. Bing's long regime has often been subjected to criticism for his failure to pay more attention to significant twentieth-century European operas or to revivals of the less familiar works of the past; for adhering basically to a policy of offering, for the most part, the standard works; and for standing pat too often with outmoded staging and scenery. Nevertheless, much has been accomplished during the Bing regime. He has employed such experienced theatrical figures as Garson Kanin, Margaret Webster, Alfred Lunt, and Cyril Ritchard, among others, to stage various productions. He was the first Metropolitan Opera director to engage Negro singers, some of whom soon achieved world renown. Many more operas than heretofore were given in new English translations.

Some of his innovations were short-lived, but they were tried, even if soon found failing. He attempted to televize operas from the stage of the Metropolitan Opera on a national hookup (*Die Fledermaus* and LA BOHÈME during the 1952–53 season), and by closed circuit to theaters (the opening-night performance of the 1954–55 season, which for the first time in Metropolitan Opera history was made up of acts from different operas). He provided open-air opera performances during the summer at the Lewisohn Stadium in 1962 and 1963 and arranged for the funds to pay for free performances in the public parks of New York in summer beginning in 1967. In the fall of 1960 he helped found the Metropolitan Opera Studio to prepare small-scale programs for presentation in New York City schools. And in 1965 he organized a special company, the Metropolitan Opera National Company, to tour the United States and Mexico for thirty-seven weeks, a venture that collapsed after the spring season of 1967 due to spiraling costs.

Despite the continued objections of some critics to Bing's supposedly static repertory and kind of productions, many unusual operatic presentations have taken place during his regime, both at the old auditorium and at the new one at the LINCOLN CENTER FOR THE PERFORMING ARTS. At the old house, significant revivals of operas long absent from or new to the Metropolitan Opera stage and new productions of exceptional merit included the following: COSÌ FAN TUTTE, staged by Alfred Lunt, in 1951; LA FORZA DEL DESTINO in 1952; *Faust* (in nineteenth-century costuming), BORIS GODUNOV (nearly in its original version), and *Tannhäuser* (in the Dresden version) in 1953; in 1956–57, NORMA, with CALLAS making her Metropolitan debut, and LA PÉRICHOLE; EUGENE ONEGIN in 1957; in 1959, WOZZECK, *The Gypsy Baron,* and VERDI's MACBETH; NABUCCO in 1960; MARTHA in a new English translation in 1960–61; ANDREA CHÉNIER which opened the season of 1962–63, followed by ARIADNE AUF NAXOS and ADRIANA LECOUVREUR; ZEFFIRELLI's production of FALSTAFF, conducted by Leonard BERNSTEIN in 1964; PIQUE DAME in 1965. In addition BARBER's VANESSA was given its world premiere in 1958 and his ANTONY AND CLEOPATRA on the opening night of the new house in 1966. American premieres included THE RAKE's PROGRESS in 1953, ARABELLA in 1955, and THE LAST SAVAGE in 1964. World-famous singers and conductors who appeared at the Metropolitan Opera for the first time included: Victoria DE LOS ANGELES, Leonard Bernstein, Karl BOEHM, Montserrat CABALLÉ, Maria Callas, Franco CORELLI, Eileen FARRELL, Mirella FRENI, Nikolai GHIAUROV, Tito GOBBI, Hilde GUEDEN, Erich KUNZ, Lorin MAAZEL, Zubin MEHTA, Dimitri MITROPOULOS, Birgit NILSSON, Leontyne PRICE, Elisabeth SCHWARZKOPF, Irmgard SEEFRIED, Giulietta SIMIONATO, William STEINBERG, Leopold STOKOWSKI, Joan SUTHERLAND, and Renata TEBALDI.

The last performance at the old auditorium on Broadway and Thirty-ninth Street took place on the evening of Apr. 16, 1966. Fifty-nine of the company's leading singers and eleven conductors were heard in twenty-four selections from operas heard at the Metropolitan. On Sept. 16, 1966, the Metropolitan company entered its new auditorium at the Lincoln Center for the Performing Arts with the world premiere of Barber's *Antony and Cleopatra*, staged by Zeffirelli. Another world premiere by an American composer came in 1967, Levy's MOURNING BECOMES ELECTRA. Among other significant events since the opening of the new auditorium have been Wieland WAGNER's production of LOHENGRIN (for which Wagner had been scheduled to come to America but died before the opera was given) and the first Metropolitan Opera production of Richard STRAUSS's DIE FRAU OHNE SCHATTEN, both in 1966–67; new productions of ROMÉO ET JULIETTE (with Mirella Freni and Franco Corelli, the season's opening-night presentation), THE MAGIC FLUTE (with Marc Chagall's costumes and settings), PETER GRIMES, LUISA MILLER, and DIE WALKÜRE (the last in Herbert von KARAJAN's production, with Karajan making his Metropolitan Opera debut) in 1967–68.

In 1966 the Metropolitan Opera made its first appearance in Europe in over fifty years with performances in Paris at the invitation of the International Festival, "Théâtre des Nations." In 1967 the Metropolitan Opera participated in the summer festival at the Lincoln Center for the Performing Arts.

The following operas had their world premieres at the Metropolitan: *Antony and Cleopatra;* THE BLUE BIRD; THE CANTERBURY PILGRIMS; CLEOPATRA's NIGHT; CYRANO DE BERGERAC; THE EMPEROR JONES; THE GIRL OF THE GOLDEN WEST; GIANNI SCHICCHI; GOYESCAS; *In the Pasha's Garden; The Island God;* THE KING's HENCHMAN; DIE KÖNIGSKINDER; *The Legend;* MADAME SANS-GÊNE; MADELEINE; THE MAN WITHOUT A COUNTRY; MERRY MOUNT; *Mona; Mourning Becomes Electra;* PETER IBBETSON; *The Pipe of Desire;* SHANEWIS; SUOR ANGELICA; IL TABARRO; *The Temple Dancer; Vanessa; The Warrior* (Bernard Rodgers).

Metropolitan Opera Guild, an organization founded in 1935 to help sell subscriptions to the Metropolitan Opera and to increase attendance. Its first president was Mrs. August Belmont. The first year the membership numbered two thousand. The Guild has since extended its membership greatly and expanded its activities to include assistance in the Metropolitan's various fund-raising campaigns and the provision of money for new productions, scenery, and equipment. It also instituted in 1936 a youth series, giving schoolchildren the chance to attend special performances at reduced prices, with the Guild making up the difference. Since 1936 over 300,000 schoolchildren have attended the Guild's performances. During the opera season the Guild publishes *Opera News,* for many years edited by Mrs. John De Witt Peltz, who has been succeeded by Frank Merkling, providing listeners to the Metropolitan's weekly radio broadcasts complete information about the current opera, as well as general information about operas, their composers, and their performers.

Me voici dans son boudoir, Frederick's GAVOTTE in Act II, Scene 1, of THOMAS's MIGNON expressing his joy at being with Philine.

Meyerbeer, Giacomo (born Jakob Liebmann Beer), composer. Born Berlin, Sept. 5, 1791; died Paris, May 2, 1864. Though of German birth and Italian training, Meyerbeer was one of the creators of the French grand-opera tradition. He changed his last name when a rich relative named Meyer left him a legacy; his first name was Italianized when he started writing Italian operas. His wealthy parents encouraged him in his musical interests, and he made remarkable progress. He appeared in concerts as a prodigy pianist. His music study took place with Muzio Clementi, Carl Friedrich Zelter, and Anselm Weber. In 1810 he went to Darmstadt to live with Abbé Vogler as his pupil and household guest. Vogler's intensive training led Meyerbeer to write his first ambitious works, including his first opera, *Jephtha's Vow,* a dismal failure when performed in Munich. In 1812 Meyerbeer left Vogler and went to Vienna. His second opera, *Wirth und Gast,* introduced in Stuttgart, was now performed in Vienna and was such a fiasco that for a while Meyerbeer thought seriously of giving up composing for good. The celebrated composer and court musician Antonio SALIERI convinced him he needed more study. For several years Meyerbeer traveled in Italy, absorbing the Italian tradition, and writing operas in the Italian manner. One of these, *Romilda e Costanza,* was a triumph when introduced in Padua in 1817. He now received commissions from several major Italian opera houses for new works. These operas, including *Semiramide riconosciuta* (1819), *Eduardo e Cristina* (1820), and *Margherita d'Anjou* (1820), made Meyerbeer one of the most popular opera composers in Italy. After a prolonged visit to Berlin, where he wrote IL CROCIATO IN EGITTO, performed with outstanding success in Venice in 1824, Meyerbeer went to Paris in 1826. Acquaintance with such important composers of French operas as HALÉVY, AUBER, and CHERUBINI, and the assimilation of the ideals and techniques of French opera, made Meyerbeer dissatisfied with the kind of music he had written up to now. For a while he stopped writing altogether. When he returned to composition, he completely discarded his Italian identity and became French. His first opera in the French style was ROBERT LE DIABLE, produced at the OPÉRA on Nov. 21, 1831. It created a sensation. LES HUGUENOTS followed in 1836, and LE PROPHÈTE in 1849—operas that made Meyerbeer not only the most famous opera composer in Europe at that time but the outstanding exponent of French opera. Meyerbeer glorified, as had no French opera composer before him, in heroic drama, stage action, ballet, pomp, stunning visual effects, and overpowering climactic scenes. But his passion for stage effects was combined with immense dramatic power, an inspired lyricism, and a remarkable orchestral virtuosity. His ability to dramatize musical writing made Hugo Riemann refer to him as "one of the most important steps to Wagner's art." And WAGNER himself expressed his indebtedness to the best pages in Meyerbeer.

In 1842 the King of Prussia appointed Meyerbeer KAPELLMEISTER in Berlin. There he completed and produced a new opera, EIN FELDLAGER IN SCHLESIEN (1844), written with Jenny LIND in mind (she appeared in the Vienna premiere in 1846). Despite his many activities as conductor and composer in Berlin, Meyerbeer was able to visit different parts of Europe. He was in Paris in 1849 for the premiere of *Le Prophète* and once again there in 1854, when his L'ÉTOILE DU NORD was thunderingly acclaimed at its premiere at the OPÉRA-COMIQUE. In 1859 he completed another successful work produced by the Opéra-Comique, *Le Pardon de Ploërmel,* subsequently famous under its later title of DINORAH. Meyerbeer's last opera, L'AFRICAINE, occupied him for a quarter of a century. Feeling it was his greatest work, he gave it a devotion bestowed on no other opera. Even when the opera was in rehearsal, he kept on making painstaking revisions. He did not live to see it performed. He died May 2, 1864, and *L'Africaine* was introduced at the Opéra almost a year later, on Apr. 28.

Besides the operas already mentioned, Meyerbeer wrote the following works: *Emma di Resburgo* (1820); *L'Esule di Grenata* (1822); *Das Branddenburger Thor* (1823).

Meyerowitz, Jan, composer. Born Breslau, Ger., Apr. 23, 1913. His music study took place at the Berlin Hochschule für Musik and in Rome with RESPIGHI, CASELLA, and MOLINARI. After a period of travel, beginning with 1938, he came to the United States in 1946 for permanent residence, becoming an American citizen in 1951. He has held teaching positions at the Berkshire Music Center at Tanglewood and at Brooklyn College, New York. Writing in the traditions of the Italian and French schools of the nineteenth century, he has produced several operas besides a good deal of concert music. The operas: *Simoon* (1949); *The Barrier* (1950); *Eastward in Eden* (1951); *Bad Boys at School* (1953); *Esther* (1957); *Port Town* (1960). *Simoon, Bad Boys at School,* and *Port Town* were introduced at the Berkshire Music Center in TANGLEWOOD at Lenox, Mass.

mezza aria, literally a "half aria"—that is, an aria having in part the character of a RECITATIVE.

mezza voce, singing with "half voice," the volume and force reduced for quiet utterance.

mezzo-soprano, the female voice intermediate between contralto and soprano, partaking of the qualities of each.

Mia madre, Loris' narrative to Fedora explaining why he killed Vladimir, in Act II of GIORDANO'S FEDORA.

Micaëla, a peasant girl (soprano), in love with Don José, in BIZET'S CARMEN.

Micaëla's Air, *see* JE DIS QUE RIEN NE M'ÉPOUVANTE.

Micha, a wealthy landowner (bass), father of Hans and Wenzel, in SMETANA'S THE BARTERED BRIDE.

Mihael Kohlhaas, *see* KLEIST, HEINRICH WILHELM VON.

Michele, a skipper (baritone) in PUCCINI'S IL TABARRO, a role created by Adam DIDUR.

Mi chiama Lisabetta, Lisabetta's plea in Act III of GIORDANO'S LA CENA DELLE BEFFE.

Mi chiamano Mimi, Mimi's autobiographical aria in Act I of PUCCINI'S LA BOHÈME.

Michonnet, stage director at Comédie-Française (baritone) in CILÈA'S ADRIANA LECOUVREUR.

Mickleford, Sir Tristan, Lady Harriet's cousin (bass) in FLOTOW'S MARTHA.

microtonal music, music made up of intervals smaller than the half tone, such as quarter tones. HÁBA'S THE MOTHER is a microtonal opera. Parts of Georges Enesco's lyric tragedy OEDIPE and GINASTERA'S BOMARZO use microtonal music.

Midsummer Marriage, The, opera in three acts by TIPPETT. Libretto by the composer. Premiere: Covent Garden, Jan. 27, 1955. On their wedding day, Mark and Jennifer quarrel. Only after they have gone through a number of trials and tests (which bring reminders of THE MAGIC FLUTE) can they reconcile their differences and go through with their wedding plans. A subsidiary plot involves the differences between another couple, on a lower social level, Jack and Bella. Magical elements are introduced into the plot through the presence of Sosostris, a clairvoyant, and "two Ancients." The plot is highly complex, symbolical, and filled with philosophical concepts—the reason why the opera originally was a failure. But Tippett's score is one of his richest and finest achievements, "magical and uplifting" in the opinion of Frank Granville Barker, "extolling the ecstasies of human love in an unfailing stream of richly colored, ravishing sound. It reaches its frenzied erotic climax in the Ritual Dances of Act II, then achieves a warm, glowing contentment in the lovers' reunion of Act III." The opera achieved a major success when COVENT GARDEN offered it in a new production in Apr. of 1968.

Midsummer Night's Dream, A, opera in three acts by BRITTEN. Libretto by the composer and Peter Pears, based on SHAKESPEARE's comedy. Premiere: Aldeburgh Festival, June 11, 1960. American premiere: San Francisco Opera, Oct. 10, 1961. Though only half of Shakespeare's play is used for the opera, the libretto remains faithful to Shakespeare's basic plot and intentions. The opera progresses on three different levels, the worlds of fairies, of the lovers, and of the rustics; for each of these Britten provides appropriate music, radically changing his style and musical materials. As Howard Taubman explained: "Fairyland is immersed in the musical devices of Impressionism; the rustics have a kind of arioso style that bursts into full operatic bloom in the final act in a way reminiscent of the Italian lyric theatre of the early nineteenth century; the lovers are delineated in a conventional neo-Romanticism." To Gerhart von Westerman the "Quarrel Music" in Act II involving Helena, Hermia, Lysander, and Demetrius is "perhaps the most operatic music Britten has ever written, and certainly the most fluent and dramatic pages in this opera."

Miei rampolli, Don Magnifico's BUFFA air, recounting his dream about himself as a wealthy ass and then expressing his anger at having been aroused from his sleep by noises, in ROSSINI'S LA CENERENTOLA, Act I.

Mignon, OPÉRA COMIQUE in three acts by THOMAS. Libretto by Michael Carré and Jules BARBIER, based on GOETHE's novel *Wilhelm Meisters Lehrjahre*. Premiere: Opéra-Comique, Nov. 17, 1866. American premiere: Academy of Music, New York, Nov. 22, 1871.

Characters: Mignon, a girl kidnaped by gypsies (mezzo-soprano), a role created by Célestine GALLI-MARIÉ; Philine, an actress (soprano); Wilhelm Meister, a student (tenor); Frederick, another student (tenor); Laërtes, an actor (tenor); Lothario, a wandering minstrel (bass); Giarno, leader of a gypsy band (bass); Antonio, a servant (bass); gypsies; townspeople; peasants; actors; actresses; ladies; gentlemen; servants. The action takes place in Germany and Italy in the late eighteenth century.

The familiar overture is made up of two of the opera's best-known arias: that of Mignon, "Connais-tu le pays?" and Philine's POLONAISE, "Je suis Titania."

Act I. The courtyard of a German inn. Lothario, long bereft of his memory through grief at the loss of his daughter to gypsies, is following the life of a wandering minstrel. He tells a group of merrymakers of his continuing search for his child ("Fugitif et tremblant"). Gypsies arrive and entertain the crowd. Their leader, Giarno, asks Mignon to dance. When she refuses he threatens to strike her. Lothario and Wilhelm Meister leap to her defense. After Mignon thanks them, Wilhelm, a happy-go-lucky student, speaks of his personal philosophy: he wants only to wander in freedom and enjoy pleasures ("Oui, je veux par le monde"). When he asks Mignon about herself, all she can tell him is that she comes from a distant land from which she was taken by gypsies when a child ("Connais-tu le pays?"). Touched by her story, Wilhelm buys her freedom from the gypsies and engages her as his servant. When Lothario approaches Mignon to bid her farewell, she recalls the land of sunshine and swallows ("Légères hirondelles"). Wilhelm Meister, meanwhile, has become acquainted with the actress Philine, to whom he is immediately attracted. She invites him to a party at the castle of Baron Rosenberg.

Act II, Scene 1. A boudoir in the castle. Before the rise of the curtain, there is a delicate GAVOTTE as an ENTR'ACTE. On entering Philine's boudoir, Laërtes sings a madrigal about the way her charms affect his lover's heart ("Belle, ayez pitié de nous"). Soon Wilhelm appears, followed by his gypsy servant. Laërtes informs him that the actors will present *A Midsummer Night's Dream,* with Philine as Titania. With anguish Mignon notices how adoringly Wilhelm regards Philine as the actress puts on her make-up and sings a ditty on how all men are attracted to her ("Je crois entendre"). After Wilhelm and Philine depart, Mignon muses about a gypsy lad she once knew (STYRIENNE: "Je connais un pauvre enfant"). She then tries on one of Philine's gowns and applies Philine's cosmetics. While she is momentarily out of the room, Frederick, who is in love with Philine, enters the boudoir through a window, singing of his joy at being near his sweetheart ("Me voici dans son boudoir"). When Wilhelm returns and finds Frederick, there is a quarrel. Mignon intervenes to stop it. Seeing how attractive she is in Philine's dress, Wilhelm sadly tells Mignon that she can be his servant no longer ("Adieu, Mignon, courage"). Upset that she must lose her master, Mignon tears off Philine's dress and dons her gypsy garb.

Scene 2. The castle gardens. The distraught Mignon is contemplating suicide. The demented Lothario appears and listens to the girl's tale of sorrow and her hope that lightning will strike the castle and spoil the triumph of her rival, Philine. After Lothario wanders off toward the castle, the performers and guests stream into the garden. When Philine is praised by her admirers she sings them a stirring POLONAISE ("Je suis Titania"). Lothario returns and tells Mignon that her vengeance has been realized: he has set the castle afire. When Philine orders Mignon to enter the castle and fetch a bouquet, Mignon meekly obeys. Suddenly the cry is heard that the castle is burning. Wilhelm rushes into the flames and saves Mignon.

Act III. A castle in Italy. Wilhelm and Lothario are nursing the ailing Mignon. Lothario sings her a lullaby (BERCEUSE: "De son coeur, j'ai calmé la fièvre"). Now aware that he loves Mignon, Wilhelm gives voice to his inmost feelings (ROMANCE: "Elle ne croyait pas"). When the girl awakes, Wilhelm convinces her that he loves her alone. Meanwhile, Lothario, finding himself in familiar scenes, has recovered his memory. He is overjoyed to find that this castle to which Wilhelm has brought him is actually his own and that he is Count Lothario ("Mignon! Wilhelm! Salut à vous!"). Then his ancient sorrow returns—the memory of his lost daughter Sperata. The name stirs Mignon's memory, she recognizes her surroundings, and father and daughter are joyously reunited.

Mignon is an opera of which it can be said that its parts are greater than the whole. Several arias and numbers are deservedly famous, for they are representative of the French lyric theater at its best. It is these high points that keep *Mignon* alive and make its performance a rewarding evening. But not even the most enthusiastic admirer of this opera would call it a masterpiece. The libretto is pedestrian, and the music too often descends to the level of the words. Thomas himself thought that it would be a failure. However, the premiere, with Galli-Marié as Mignon, was a triumph. And the composer lived to attend the thousandth performance of *Mignon* at the OPÉRA-COMIQUE. At this institution the original version of *Mignon,* with spoken dialogue, is still given. Other opera houses prefer to use the recitatives which Thomas himself prepared for the English premiere at DRURY LANE in 1870.

Milada, beloved (soprano) of Dalibor in SMETANA'S DALIBOR.

Milanov, Zinka (born Kunc), soprano. Born Zagreb, Jugoslavia, May 17, 1906. She attended the Zagreb Conservatory for five years after which she made her debut at the Zagreb Opera in IL TROVATORE in 1927. After nine years with that company she was engaged by Bruno WALTER for the VIENNA STATE OPERA, where she appeared in the Italian repertory. Guest appearances in Germany, Czechoslovakia, and at the SALZBURG FESTIVAL spread her reputation throughout Europe. On Dec. 17, 1937, she made her American debut at the METROPOLITAN OPERA in *Il trovatore*. She has been a principal soprano of the Metropolitan since that time, one of the few principal singers to inaugurate two successive Metropolitan Opera seasons, those of 1951 and 1952; in 1940 she had also appeared in the opening-night performance at the Metropolitan.

Mildenburg, Anna von, soprano. Born Vienna, Nov. 29, 1872; died there Jan. 27, 1947. After completing her studies at the Vienna Conservatory she made her opera debut in Hamburg in 1895. She was quickly recognized as a leading interpreter of the Wagnerian dramas, and in 1897 she was invited to appear at BAYREUTH. In 1898 she was appointed a member of the VIENNA OPERA, where she remained two decades, achieving great success in the Wagnerian repertory. After her retirement in 1917 she settled in Munich, where for two years she taught singing and dramatics at the State Academy. In 1921 she was appointed stage director of the Munich National Theater, and in 1926 she founded her own singing school. In 1938 she transferred her activities to Berlin, where she taught at the German Institute of Music. Together with her husband, the dramatist Hermann Bahr, whom she married in 1909, she wrote *Bayreuth und das Wagner Theater* (1910).

Milder-Hauptmann, Pauline Anna, soprano. Born Constantinople, Turkey, Dec. 13, 1785; died Berlin, May 29, 1838. BEETHOVEN wrote for her the role of Leonore in FIDELIO. When she was a girl of fourteen Joseph HAYDN found that she had a voice "as big as a house" and gave her some instruction. Then, encouraged by the Viennese impresario Emmanuel SCHIKANEDER, she studied with Tomascelli, a singing master, and Antonio SALIERI, the court KAPELLMEISTER. She made her debut in 1803 in Franz Xavier Süssmayer's opera *Der*

Spiegel von Arkadien and was engaged as principal soprano of the VIENNA OPERA. On Nov. 20, 1805, she appeared in the first performance of *Fidelio*. Between 1816 and 1829 she was the principal soprano of the BERLIN (Royal) OPERA, where she was particularly successful in GLUCK's operas. She left Berlin after differences with the director, Gasparo SPONTINI, and went on a tour of Russia, Sweden, and Denmark. She made her farewell appearance in 1836 in Vienna.

Mildmay, Audrey, soprano. Born Hurstmonceaux, Eng., Dec. 19, 1900; died London, May 31, 1953. As an opera singer she was heard with the CARL ROSA COMPANY in England and with a touring company of THE BEGGAR'S OPERA in the United States in 1931. Her significance in opera rests in the fact that she was responsible for the birth of the GLYNDEBOURNE FESTIVAL in 1934, having urged her husband John CHRISTIE, whom she had married in 1931, to create it on his estate in Lewes, Sussex. At Glyndebourne she was heard as SUSANNA, ZERLINA, and NORINA. With Rudolf BING she also helped to bring about the creation of the EDINBURGH FESTIVAL.

Mild und leise wie er lächelt, *see* LIEBESTOD.

Milhaud, Darius, composer. Born Aix-en-Provence, France, Sept. 4, 1892. His music study took place at the College of Aix and the Paris Conservatory. While still a Conservatory student Milhaud wrote an opera, *La Brebis egarée,* produced a decade later by the OPÉRACOMIQUE. In 1917 Milhaud accompanied Paul CLAUDEL, French Ambassador to Brazil, to South America as an attaché of the Legation. There he became interested in Brazilian folk and popular music and began incorporating elements from it in his compositions. He also had the collaboration of Claudel on several ambitious works which included L'ORÉSTIE, a trilogy of operas based on tragedies of AESCHYLUS: *Agamemnon,* LES CHOËPHORES, and *Les Euménides.* Milhaud returned to Paris in 1919 and became associated with five other young French composers in a group known as

Les SIX. His reputation grew in the era between the two world wars; and after RAVEL's death, it was generally conceded that Milhaud was France's leading composer. His works, in every branch of composition, embraced a wide variety of styles ranging from the popular to the esoteric. Among the most significant of his works is a second trilogy of operas, this time on American subjects, described by Virgil THOMSON as "a monument of incomparable grandeur": CHRISTOPHE COLOMB (1928); MAXIMILIEN (1930); and *Bolivar* (1943). Still another opera, MÉDÉE (1938), was performed at the PARIS OPÉRA just before the Nazi occupation. At that time Milhaud left France and settled in America, teaching at Mills College and writing many symphonic and chamber works. Milhaud returned to Paris after the war, where he became professor of composition at the Conservatory and has since then divided his time between the United States and France, despite a crippling arthritis which interferes neither with his mobility nor his activities as composer and conductor. His seventieth birthday was celebrated with a festival of his music at Mills College. A Biblical opera, DAVID, was introduced in Jerusalem (in Hebrew) in 1954; a one-act opera, *Fiesque,* was given a concert performance by the New York Philharmonic in 1960; and LA MÈRE COUPABLE, based on MOLIÈRE, was given its world premiere in Geneva in 1966. Milhaud was made Commander of the French Legion of Honor and Officer of the Order of the Southern Cross in Brazil.

Besides those already mentioned, Milhaud has written the following operas: LES MALHEURS D'ORPHÉE (1924); *Esther de Carpentras* (1925); LE PAUVRE MATELOT (1927). The following are children's operas: *À propos de bottes* (1932); *Un Petit Peu de musique* (1932); and *Un Petit Peu d'exercise* (1934. He also wrote three *opéra minutes,* or miniature operas, all in 1927: L'ENLÈVEMENT D'EUROPE, L'ABANDON D'ARIANE, and LA DÉLIVRANCE DE THÉSÉE.

Miller, an old soldier (baritone), Luisa's father, in VERDI's LUISA MILLER.

Miller, Arthur, playwright. Born New York City, Oct. 17, 1915. WARD's opera THE CRUCIBLE, which received the PULITZER PRIZE in 1962, and ROSSELLINI's opera A VIEW FROM THE BRIDGE were derived from Miller's plays of the same names.

Milton, John, poet. Born London, Dec. 9, 1608; died there Nov. 8, 1674. His epic, *Paradise Lost,* was the source of an opera by RUBINSTEIN. His MASQUE, *Comus,* was set to music first by Henry Lawes, later by ARNE. He is the central character in an opera by SPONTINI, *Milton.* Spontini planned a sequel, to be titled *Milton's Death,* but it was never completed.

Mime, a Nibelung (tenor) in WAGNER's DAS RHEINGOLD and SIEGFRIED.

Mimi, a maker of artificial flowers (soprano), in love with Rodolfo, in PUCCINI's LA BOHÈME, a role created by Cesira Ferrani.

Mimi è una civetta, Rodolfo's aria expressing concern over Mimi's delicate health, even while he has just announced his intention of leaving her forever, in Act III of PUCCINI's LA BOHÈME.

mimodrama, a musical drama utilizing pantomime. HONEGGER's JEANNE D'ARC AU BÛCHER is an example.

Mines of Sulphur, The, opera in three acts by BENNETT. Libretto by Beverly Cross. Premiere: Sadler's Wells, London, Feb. 24, 1965. American premiere: New York City, Jan. 17, 1968. The setting is a manor house in eighteenth-century England. Its owner is murdered by his mistress and her accomplice, a criminal. Before they escape, strolling players come to the house seeking refuge. Fate deals out punishment to the murderers, using these players as its agency. When the criminal kisses the leading lady he is infected with the plague she is carrying. They are left alone terror-stricken on a dark stage as the curtain descends.

This opera was commissioned by SADLER'S WELLS, which not only introduced it, but also brought it to Paris and Zagreb. The work's success kept mounting with subsequent presentations in Cologne, Marseilles, New York, and especially at LA SCALA, where on Feb. 25, 1966, it was staged by the famous American film director John Huston.

Minka, a bondwoman (soprano) in love with De Nangis, in CHABRIER'S LE ROI MALGRÉ LUI.

Minnesingers, poet-musicians of the twelfth and thirteenth centuries. The German equivalent of troubadours, they specialized in writing love songs (*minnelieder*). The minnesingers were succeeded in the fourteenth century by the MASTERSINGERS. TANNHÄUSER, the central figure in WAGNER's opera of the same name, was a minnesinger.

Minnie, owner of the Polka Saloon (soprano) in PUCCINI'S THE GIRL OF THE GOLDEN WEST, a role created by Emmy DESTINN.

Minnie, della mia casa, Jack Rance's aria about his love for Minnie, in Act I of PUCCINI'S THE GIRL OF THE GOLDEN WEST.

minuet, a dance in triple time, usually of moderate speed, first popular at the court of Louis XIV of France, after which it spread throughout Europe to become easily the predominant dance form of the eighteenth century. Such vast numbers of minuets were turned out that HAYDN is reported to have said that a truly individual piece in this restricted form would be a fair measure of a composer's worth. LULLY (1632–1687) was the first composer to introduce minuets in his operas. Operas by the later masters RAMEAU and HANDEL also contain minuets. One of the most celebrated of operatic minuets is that occurring in MOZART'S DON GIOVANNI (Act I, Scene 5). Later notable examples in operas are Berlioz' MINUET OF THE WILL-O'-THE-WISPS, the opening of the festival scene in Act III of MASSENET'S MANON, and the dance of the courtiers in Act I of RIGOLETTO.

Minuet of the Will-o'-the-Wisps, the music with which Méphistophélès summons evil spirits to surround Marguerite's abode in Part III of BERLIOZ' THE DAMNATION OF FAUST.

Mio caro bene, Rodelinda's song to springtime in HANDEL'S RODELINDA.

Miolan-Carvalho, Marie, soprano. Born Marseilles, Dec. 31, 1827; died Puys, Seine-Inferieure, July 10, 1895. She created the roles of Marguerite in FAUST, Juliette in ROMÉO ET JULIETTE, and MIREILLE. Her vocal studies took place with DUPREZ at the Paris Conservatory. In 1849 she made her opera debut as LUCIA at the OPÉRA-COMIQUE in Paris, remaining with that company until 1855. Between 1856 and 1867 she was a principal soprano of the THÉÂTRE LYRIQUE in Paris, and between 1859 and 1864 and in 1871–72, she made successful appearances at COVENT GARDEN. She was the wife of the opera impresario, Léon CARVALHO.

Miracle, Dr., the magician (baritone) in OFFENBACH'S THE TALES OF HOFFMANN; his other identities in the opera are Dapertutto, Coppélius, and Lindorf.

Mira, o Norma, duet of Norma and Adalgisa in Act III of BELLINI'S NORMA, in which Adalgisa pleads with Norma not to commit suicide.

Mireille, opera in three acts by GOUNOD. Libretto by Michel Carré, based on *Miréio,* a poem by Frédéric MISTRAL. Premiere: Paris Opéra, Mar. 19, 1864. American premiere: Philadelphia, Nov., 1864 (only two acts). In the province of Millaine, in legendary times, Mireille (a role created by Marie MIOLAN-CARVALHO) is in love with Vincent. Complications, particularly the opposition of Mireille's father and the presence of a dangerous rival in Ourrias, a bullfighter, are finally overcome, and the lovers are joyfully reunited.

The overture, pastoral in nature, is popular. The best-known vocal numbers are: in Act I, Mireille's waltz, "O légère hirondelle"; in Act II, the choral FARANDOLE, "La brise est douce et parfumé," and Mireille's love song for Vincent, "Mon coeur ne peut pas changer"; and in Act III, Vincent's CAVATINA, "Anges du paradis," and Mireille's MUSETTE to a shepherd, "Le jour se lève."

When *Mireille* was revived at the AIX-EN-PROVENCE festival in 1954, it was produced in a place called "Val d'Enfer" in the village of Les Baux de Provence (twenty miles or so from Aix-en-Provence), because this is the setting for one of the scenes in Mistral's poem. Gounod's original five-act version was used.

Mir ist so wunderbar, the quartet, written in the form of a canon, of Marcellina, Jacquino, Leonore, and Rocco in Act I of BEETHOVEN'S FIDELIO, with each character giving expression of his or her emotion over the complication of having Marcellina fall in love with Fidelio and arousing the jealousy of her suitor, Jacquino.

Mir unvertraut, Barak's soliloquy about his duty to protect his wife, one of the most famous arias in the opera, in Act III, Scene 1, of Richard STRAUSS'S DIE FRAU OHNE SCHATTEN.

mise en scène, French term for staging, scenery, and stage direction.

Miserere, *see* AH! CHE LA MORTE OGNORA.

Missail, a monk (tenor) in MUSSORGSKY'S BORIS GODUNOV.

Miss Julie, opera in two acts by ROREM. Libretto by Kenward Elmslie, based on the drama by STRINDBERG. Premiere: New York City Opera, Nov. 4, 1965. This opera was commissioned by the FORD FOUNDATION. In preparing the text, the librettist "split the one-act play down the middle," as Rorem has explained, "to make a two-act opera and underplayed the master-slave theme in favor of sensuality." Except for the addition of four subsidiary characters and a chorus, the work is "pure Strindberg." The Strindberg play describes a love affair between Miss Julie, a highborn lady, and a servant. It is now the servant who becomes master, and the highborn lady who becomes a menial servant, so much so that at his command she first robs her own father and then commits suicide.

Mistral, Frédéric, poet. Born Maillane, France, Sept. 8, 1830; died there Mar. 25, 1914. He won the Nobel Prize for Literature in 1904. His epic poem *Miréio,* published in 1859, was the basis for GOUNOD'S opera MIREILLE, while his poem of bygone Avignon, *Nerto,* was the source of an opera by Charles Widor.

Mit Gewitter und Sturm (Steuermannslied), the Steersman's song in the opening of Act I of WAGNER'S DER FLIEGENDE HOLLÄNDER.

Mit mir, mit mir, Baron Ochs's waltz in Act II of Richard STRAUSS'S DER ROSENKAVALIER, as he tries to convince Sophie how fortunate she is to gain him for a husband.

Mitropoulos, Dimitri, conductor. Born Athens, Mar. 1, 1896; died Milan, Italy, Nov. 2, 1960. He attended the Conservatory in Athens, where his opera, *Soeur Béatrice,* based on MAETERLINCK's play, was produced in 1920. In 1940 he became musical director of the New York Philharmonic and on Dec. 5, 1954, he made his debut at the METROPOLITAN OPERA with SALOME. He remained there for several seasons conducting remarkable performances of TOSCA, UN BALLO IN MASCHERA, and MADAMA BUTTERFLY. In 1958 he resigned as musical director of the New York Philharmonic Orchestra. He then made guest appearances with leading opera companies in Europe and the United States. He died of a heart attack while directing a symphonic rehearsal at LA SCALA in Milan.

Mi vendici, Azucena's plea to Manrico to avenge the cruel murder of her mother, in Act II, Scene 1, of VERDI'S IL TROVATORE.

Mizguir, a Tartar merchant (baritone) in love with the Snow Maiden, in RIMSKY-KORSAKOV'S THE SNOW MAIDEN.

Mödl, Martha, soprano. Born Nuremberg, Mar. 22, 1912. Her vocal studies completed in her native city, she made her opera debut as Remscheid in 1942 as CHERUBINO. Between 1945 and 1949 she appeared in mezzo-soprano roles at the Düsseldorf Opera, and in 1949 she became a principal member of the HAMBURG STATE OPERA. She also made significant appearances at the VIENNA STATE OPERA and COVENT GARDEN. Developing her voice for dramatic soprano roles, she appeared at BAYREUTH as KUNDRY in 1951; subsequently she was heard also as ISOLDE, BRÜNNHILDE, and SIEGLINDE. When the reconstructed Vienna State Opera opened on Nov. 5, 1955, she assumed the role of Leonore in FIDELIO. On Jan. 30, 1957, she made her debut at the METROPOLITAN OPERA as Brünnhilde in SIEGFRIED, remaining only a single season with the company. Since then she has been heard in leading European opera houses, principally in Germany.

Moffo, Anna, soprano. Born Wayne, Pa., June 27, 1934. She attended the Curtis Institute on a four-year scholarship, where she studied voice with Mme. Giannini-Gregory. She completed her voice training in Rome on a Fulbright fellowship with Ricci and Favaretto. After several appearances over the Italian radio, she made her debut in opera over Italian television as CIO-CIO-SAN, stage-directed by Mario Lanfranchi, whom she married in 1957. An appearance as Norina in DON PASQUALE followed at the FESTIVAL OF TWO WORLDS in Spoleto, after which she was given leading soprano roles at LA SCALA and in opera houses in Paris and London. In 1958 she made her debut at the VIENNA STATE OPERA, and in 1959 she sang at the SALZBURG FESTIVAL. Meanwhile she had made her first opera appearance in America in 1957 with the CHICAGO LYRIC OPERA as MIMI, returning to that company the following year for a second season. On Nov. 14, 1957, she made her debut with the METROPOLITAN OPERA as Violetta. Since then she has been one of the principal sopranos of the company, giving a remarkable account of herself both as an actress and a singer in the Italian and French repertories. In 1960 she was acclaimed at the SAN FRANCISCO OPERA both in San Francisco and on tour. Her appearances have been worldwide, not only in opera, but also over television and in motion pictures.

Mögst du, mein Kind, Daland's revelation to his daughter that the Dutchman has asked for her hand in marriage, in Act II of WAGNER's DER FLIEGENDE HOLLÄNDER.

Moïse, *see* MOSÈ IN EGITTO.

Molière (born Jean Baptiste Poquelin), playwright. Born Paris, Jan. 15, 1622; died there Feb. 17, 1673. France's master of comedy and satire was a veritable reservoir of opera texts. Among his plays made into operas are: *Les Amants magnifiques* (LULLY); *L'Amour médecin* (Lully, Ferdinand Poise, and WOLF-FERRARI); *Amphitrion* (GRÉTRY); *L'Amour Peintre* (BIZET); *Le Bourgeois Gentilhomme* (Lully, HASSE's *Larinda e Vanesio;* also Richard STRAUSS's ARIADNE AUF NAXOS); *Georges Dandin* (Lully); *L'École des femmes* (LIEBERMANN and Virgilio Mortari); *Le Malade imaginaire* (Marc-Antoine CHARPENTIER, HAUG's *Le Malade immortel*); *Le Mariage forcé* (Lully, Marc-Antoine Charpentier); *Le Médecin malgré lui* (Marc-Antoine Charpentier, GOUNOD); *Monsieur de Pourceaugnac* (DONIZETTI's *Il Giovedi Grasso,* FRANCHETTI, Hasse, Frank MARTIN); *La Princesse d'Elide* (Lully); *Les Precieuses ridicules* (LATTUADA, Otakar Zich); *Le Sicilien* (Lully); *Tartuffe* (BENJAMIN, Haug, and Shaporin).

Molinari-Pradelli, Francesco, conductor. Born Bologna, July 4, 1911. His principal study of conducting took place in Rome with Bernardino Molinari. He made his debut as conductor in symphonic music in 1938. In 1946 he made his debut at LA SCALA, following which he directed opera performances in London, Naples, and other European opera houses. In 1957 he became one of the principal conductors of the SAN FRANCISCO OPERA. On Feb. 7, 1966, he made his first appearance at the METROPOLITAN OPERA conducting UN BALLO IN MASCHERA. He has since been a principal conductor there.

Mona, opera in three acts by PARKER. Libretto by Brian HOOKER. Premiere: Metropolitan Opera, Mar. 14, 1912. This opera won the ten-thousand-dollar prize offered in 1911 by the METROPOLITAN OPERA for an American work. The setting is Britain toward the end of the first century. Mona is a British princess in love with Quintus, son of the Roman Emperor. During the confusion attending the Roman conquest, Mona slays Quintus in the mistaken belief that she is aiding the cause of peace between her people and the conquerors. Critics and public applauded the opera but it was dropped after only four performances.

Mona Lisa, opera in two acts and epilogue by SCHILLINGS. Libretto by Beatrice Dovsky. Premiere: Stuttgart Opera, Sept. 26, 1915. American premiere: Metropolitan Opera, Mar. 2, 1923. In the prologue, a tourist and his wife visit a Carthusian monastery in Florence. They hear from a lay brother the story of Mona Lisa, wife of Giocondo, and her love for Giovanni, this story becoming the core of the opera. In the epilogue, the tourists are revealed to be modern reincarnations of Mona Lisa and Giocondo, while the lay brother is Giovanni. In its day and for some years after the premiere, this opera was very successful but chiefly in Germany.

Mon coeur ne peut pas changer, Mireille's love song to Vincent in Act II of GOUNOD's MIREILLE.

Mon coeur s'élance, Bertha's CAVATINA as she anticipates meeting John in Act I of MEYERBEER'S LE PROPHÈTE.

Mon coeur s'ouvre à ta voix, Dalila's song of love to Samson in Act II of SAINT-SAËNS'S SAMSON ET DALILA, the most celebrated aria in the opera.

Mond, Der (The World), opera in one act by ORFF. Libretto by the composer, based on a tale by GRIMM. Premiere: Munich, Feb. 5, 1939 (original version); Munich, Nov. 26, 1950 (revised version). American premiere: New York City Opera, Oct. 16, 1956. In this fairy-tale opera, Orff combines spoken word, pantomime, comic and satirical episodes, and singable arias with his characteristic complex, unusual rhythmic devices. The little opera requires a narrator, whose desk is the dividing line between the earth and the underworld. He reads about a land that has never known a moon. Out of that country come four boys. Upon seeing the moon they decide to steal it and bring it back home with them. When they do so, their people are delighted, for now their land has light at night, too. When the boys get old, they each want a quarter of the moon to take with them to the grave. They get their wish, and upon their death their land is once again dark. In the underworld the four boys assemble the moon and hang it up as a lamp. This awakens the dead, who cause a tumult, bringing St. Peter down from heaven to investigate what the noise is all about. He removes the moon, advises the dead to return to sleep, and goes back to heaven where he uses the moon as a star so that it can light up the whole world at night.

mondo della luna, Il (The World of the Moon), OPERA BUFFA in three acts by HAYDN. Libretto by Carlo GOLDONI. Premiere: Esterhaź, Hungary, Aug. 3, 1777. American premiere: New York City, June 7, 1949. Buonafede (bass) is an eccentric Venetian millionaire who is determined to keep his daughter, Clarissa (soprano), from making any contacts outside their house. An astrologer, Dr. Ecclittico (baritone), convinces him he has invented a telescope through which the moon and its inhabitants can be seen. Administered sleeping pills and transported to Dr. Ecclittico's garden, the wealthy Venetian, upon awakening, becomes convinced he is on the moon. He is so fascinated with the lunar world that he loses interest in his own domestic problems, to the point where he allows his daughter Clarissa to marry her beloved, Leandro (tenor), and is even indifferent when his own housekeeper, in whom he is interested, marries a rival. Some of the interesting vocal excerpts are: Leandro's "Und liegt auch zwischen dir und mir"; Clarissa's air, "Wind der mich fächelt warm"; and a duet by Leandro and Clarissa, "Am Tor der himmlischen Freude."

This delightful comic opera was revived, for the first time since Haydn's day, at Schwerin, Ger., on Mar. 20, 1932, in a German translation, and in an English adaptation it was first heard at the Greenwich Mews Playhouse in New York City, June 7, 1949. Since the American musicologist H. C. Robbins Landon edited the original complete score in 1958, it has had fairly frequent revivals in Europe.

Mondo ladro, Falstaff's attempts to console himself with wine after the fiasco of his "romance" with Mistress Ford, in Act III, Scene 1, of VERDI'S FALSTAFF.

Monforte, Governor of Sicily (baritone) in VERDI'S THE SICILIAN VESPERS.

Monica, the medium's daughter (soprano) in MENOTTI'S THE MEDIUM.

Monica, Monica, dance the waltz, Monica's waltz tune as she plays games with Toby the mute and some puppets, in Act II of MENOTTI'S THE MEDIUM.

Moniuszko, Stanislaus, composer. Born Ubiel, Poland, May 5, 1819; died Warsaw, June 4, 1872. He studied in Warsaw with August Freyer and in Berlin with Carl Rungenhagen. In 1840 he left Berlin for Vilna, where he became a church organist and taught piano. In 1846 his OPERA BUFFA, *The Lottery,* was successfully performed in Warsaw. Two years later there took place in Vilna a concert performance of his masterwork, the folk opera HALKA; ten years later *Halka* received its first stage presentation at the Warsaw Opera. Between 1868 and 1892 it was acclaimed in leading European opera houses, and in 1905 it was given in the United States. In 1858 Moniuszko settled in Warsaw, where for many years he was director of the Opera and a teacher at the Conservatory. His last two operas were failures, contributing to bring about his untimely death. In all he wrote fifteen operas. Besides those already mentioned, his greatest successes were: *The Raftsman* (1858); *The Countess* (1860); *The Haunted Castle* (1865); *The Pariah* (1869); *Beata* (1872).

Monna Vanna, opera in four acts by FÉVRIER. Libretto is the drama of the same name by MAETERLINCK. Premiere: Paris Opéra, Jan. 13, 1909. American premiere: Boston, Dec. 5, 1913. The setting is Pisa in the middle ages, under siege by the Florentine army. The commander of the invading army, Prinzivalle, offers to lift the siege if Monna Vanna, wife of the Pisan commander Guido, will come to his tent at night. Guido refuses, but Monna Vanna is ready to sacrifice herself for her people. The Florentine commander turns out to be a childhood friend of Monna's; he respects her love for her husband, treats her with courtesy, and orders the siege lifted. For this, his men regard him as a traitor. He escapes with Monna Vanna to Pisa. Guido refuses to believe his wife innocent and orders Prinzivalle thrown into a dungeon. This unjust act turns Monna Vanna against her husband. Now in love with Prinzivalle, she gets the key to his cell and together they effect an escape. The composer Emil Abrányi also wrote an opera derived from this play, using his own libretto.

monodrama, a musical drama for a single character. Monodramas originated in the eighteenth century and were seen chiefly in France and Germany. The single character was usually a woman, the heroine of the dramatic situation in question. Such monodramas were written by ROUSSEAU in France and REICHARDT and BENDA in Germany, among others. BERLIOZ' *Lélio*—for actor, supplemented by solo singers, chorus, piano, and orchestras—was described by the composer as a "lyric monodrama." In the twentieth century the form has been revived by several composers, including Bussotti (*Solo for Karl-Erik Welin*), POULENC (LA VOIX HUMAINE), ROREM (*Last Day*), and SCHOENBERG (ERWARTUNG).

Monostatos, a Moor (tenor) in MOZART'S THE MAGIC FLUTE.

Monsalvat, the castle of the HOLY GRAIL in WAGNER'S PARSIFAL.

Monsieur de Pourceaugnac, comic opera in three acts by MARTIN. Libretto by the composer, based on the comedy of the same name by MOLIÈRE. Premiere: Geneva Opera, Apr. 23, 1963. The opera was commissioned by the Swiss Radio and was the composer's first attempt at writing comedy. Some of the text is spoken, with little or no accompaniment, while the score is filled with infectious vocal episodes in a light vein. Following its premiere, the opera was successfully given at the HOLLAND FESTIVAL in June, 1963.

Monsigny, Pierre-Alexandre, composer. Born Fauquembergue, France, Oct. 17, 1729; died Paris, Jan. 14, 1817. He was one of the earliest masters of the OPÉRA COMIQUE. After receiving his early musical training at the Jesuit College in St. Omer, he went to Paris in his eighteenth year and became a clerk. Hearing PERGOLESI'S LA SERVA PADRONA sent him back to music study. After five months of training with Pietro Gianotti, he wrote his first *opéra comique, Les Aveux indiscrets,* introduced at the Théâtre de la Foire in 1759. His first major success was LE CADI DUPÉ in 1761. During the next fifteen years Monsigny was elevated to a position of first importance among the composers of *opéra comique* of that period, his succession of triumphs including *Rose et Colas* (1764), *Le Déserteur* (1769), *Le Faucon* (1772), *Le Rendezvous bien employé* (1774), and *Félix* (1777). Though at the height of his popularity and creative power when he completed *Félix,* he never wrote another opera. In 1768 he was given the sinecure of *maître d'hotel* in the household of the Duke of Orleans, a post enabling him to live in luxury. When the Duke died in 1785, his son appointed Monsigny administrator of his affairs. The French Revolution wiped out Monsigny's fortune. His poverty was relieved in 1798 when the OPÉRA-COMIQUE gave him an annuity, increased by Napoleon a few years later. In 1800 Monsigny was appointed an inspector of the Paris Conservatory. Proving insufficiently experienced for this post, he relinquished it two years later. In 1813 he succeeded GRÉTRY as a member of the Institut de France.

Montano, Otello's predecessor as Governor of Cyprus (bass) in VERDI'S OTELLO.

Monte Carlo Opera, *see* OPÉRA DE MONTE CARLO, L'.

Montemezzi, Italo, composer. Born Vigasio, Italy, Aug. 4, 1875; died Verona, Italy, May 15, 1952. The composer of L'AMORE DEI TRE RE, he completed his high-school education in Verona and went to Milan intending to enter the University. En route he decided to specialize in music. After three trials he was admitted to the Milan Conservatory, from which he later graduated with honors. His first opera, *Giovanni Gallurese,* was produced in Turin in 1905 with such success that it was repeated seventeen times in one month. A second opera, *Hellera,* was given in Turin in 1909. His third opera, *L'amore dei tre re,* presented at LA SCALA on Apr. 10, 1913, made him world famous; it has since been accepted as one of the finest works of the twentieth-century Italian lyric theater. Montemezzi's LA NAVE, introduced at La Scala in 1918, was also a major success; it was selected by the CHICAGO OPERA to inaugurate its 1919–20 season, a performance the composer conducted. His later operas: *La notte di Zoraima* (1930); *L'incantesimo* (1943). In 1939 Montemezzi settled in California, where he resided for a decade, appearing as guest conductor at the METROPOLITAN OPERA in 1949 for performances of *L'amore dei tre re.* He returned to Italy in 1949.

Monterone, Count, father (baritone) of one of the victims of the Duke of Mantua in VERDI'S RIGOLETTO.

Monteux, Pierre, conductor. Born Paris, Apr. 4, 1875; died Hancock, Me., July 1, 1964. After studying at the Paris Conservatory he played the violin in various orchestras, including that of the OPÉRA-COMIQUE. In 1911 he became the principal conductor of Sergei DIAGHILEV'S Ballet Russe. As such he led the first performances of STRAVINSKY'S *The Rite of Spring* and RAVEL'S *Daphnis and Chloé.* In 1913 and 1914 he was a principal conductor of the PARIS OPÉRA; during this period he was also a guest conductor at COVENT GARDEN and DRURY LANE. He saw action for two years in the infantry during World War I, then was recalled from the front to propagandize the Allied cause in the United States. He visited America for the first time in 1916 as conductor of the Swedish Ballet. In 1917 he was appointed principal conductor of French operas at the METROPOLITAN OPERA, making his debut there on Nov. 17 with FAUST. He remained at the Metropolitan two seasons, leading the first performance of Henry F. Gilbert's ballet *The Dance in Place Congo* and the American premieres of LE COQ D'OR, MÂROUF, and LA REINE FIAMMETTE. Monteux returned to the Metropolitan Opera thirty-five years later, on Nov. 17, 1953, opening the new season with a new production of *Faust*. Best known as a symphonic conductor, Monteux founded and for many years directed the Paris Symphony. Between 1919 and 1924 he was the conductor of the Boston Symphony, and from 1935 to 1953 he was the music director of the San Francisco Symphony. His eightieth birthday was celebrated in 1955 at a concert of the Boston Symphony, featuring two works written in his honor by MILHAUD and Stravinsky. Monteux became Commander of the Order of Orange Nassau of Holland in 1950 and of the French Legion of Honor in 1952.

Monteverdi, Claudio, composer. Born Cremona, Italy, May, 1567; died Venice, Nov. 29, 1643. The first great figure in the history of opera, Monteverdi studied music with Marc Antonio Ingegneri in Cremona. In 1583 he began publishing the first volumes of his vocal compositions. In 1589 he became a violinist and singer at the court of the Duke of Mantua. The Duke took the composer with him on various trips through Europe, which enabled Monteverdi to broaden his musical horizons. A hearing of the Florentine composer PERI'S EURIDICE stimulated Monteverdi's interest in opera. In 1606, now the Duke's MAESTRO DI CAPPELLA, Monteverdi was commissioned to write a work honoring the marriage of the Duke's son to the Infanta of Savoy. For this occasion Monteverdi produced his first opera, L'ORFEO, a work that was to enjoy wide popularity. With his very first opera the composer carried the new art form to artistic significance, producing a wealth of feeling and dramatic power it had not known with Peri. In 1608 Monteverdi wrote a second opera, *Arianna*. The "Lament" from this work (the only fragment that has not been lost) was one of the most celebrated vocal numbers of that day. Monteverdi later arranged it as a madrigal for five voices.

Monteverdi left Mantua in 1612 and in 1613 was appointed *maestro di cappella* of St. Mark's Cathedral in Venice, where he remained for the rest of his life. He kept on writing operas, helping Venice to become the operatic center of Italy. In 1637 the first public opera house was opened in Venice. Between 1641 and 1649 twenty different operas were performed there, many of them by Monteverdi. Of his operas written in Venice the most celebrated is L'INCORONAZIONE DI POPPEA (1642). Written when the composer was seventy-five, it was his last opera. The following year Monteverdi decided to revisit the city of his birth. He never reached his destination. Taken ill en route, he was brought back to Venice, where he soon died. He was given a funeral of the sort usually reserved for princes.

Monteverdi was one of music's most significant pioneers. He endowed the then prevailing style of opera, the recitative, with such expressiveness that it is sometimes said that the aria was born with him. He was the first composer to use ensemble numbers and purely instrumental passages in operas. He extended the resources of the orchestra and made many experiments in matters of orchestration: he claimed as his own discovery the string tremolo and pizzicato. The effectiveness of Monteverdi's operas may be emphasized by pointing out that they still afford pleasure to present-day audiences. Besides operas already mentioned, Monteverdi wrote: *Il ballo delle ingrate* (1608); *La favola di Peleo e di Theti* (1617); *Il matrimonio d'Alceste con*

Admeto (1617); *La vittoria d'amore* (1619); *Andromeda* (1619); *Il commento d'Apollo* (1620); IL COMBATTIMENTO DI TANCREDI E DI CLORINDA (1624); *La finta pazza Licori* (1627); L'ADONE (1639); *Le nozze d'Enea con Lavinia* (1641); IL RITORNO D'ULISSE (1641).

Montezuma, opera in three acts by Roger Sessions. Libretto by G. A. Borgese. Premiere: Berlin Deutsche Staatsoper, Apr. 19, 1964. American premiere: Boston, Oct. 19, 1969. In the sixteenth century Mexico is invaded by the Spanish, led by Cortez. The Spanish conquerors are at first looked upon by the Mexicans as heroes. But when the Spaniards begin to pillage and plunder and murder, driven by their rapacious leader, Alvarado, the Mexicans become so consumed with hate for the invaders that they kill their own emperor, Montezuma. Sessions uses mainly a declamatory style for his voices, while assigning rhythmic or thematic patterns to identify his various characters. There is so little dramatic action that one critic described the work as basically a "monumental chronicle."

Montfleury, an actor (tenor) in Walter DAMROSCH'S CYRANO DE BERGERAC.

Moore, Douglas, composer. Born Cutchogue, N.Y., Aug. 10, 1893; died Greenport, L.I., July 25, 1969. His academic education took place at Yale University, where he took courses in music with David Stanley Smith and Horatio PARKER. He continued his music study in Europe with Vincent D'INDY and Nadia Boulanger. After receiving a Pulitzer fellowship in music in 1925, he became a member of the music department of Columbia University, where he served as head between 1940 and 1962; upon his retirement he was made McDowell Professor Emeritus. His first opera, WHITE WINGS, was completed in 1935, but was not heard until 1949. This was followed by *The Headless Horseman* (1936) and THE DEVIL AND DANIEL WEBSTER, the latter written in 1938 and given a highly successful premiere in New York in 1939. GIANTS IN THE EARTH, introduced in 1951, received the PULIT-

ZER PRIZE in Music. His greatest success in opera came with THE BALLAD OF BABY DOE, its premiere taking place at CENTRAL CITY, Col., in 1957, following which it was extensively performed. His later operas: *Gallantry,* a one-act satire (1957); WINGS OF THE DOVE (1961); and CARRY NATION (1966). He also wrote two operas for children: *The Emperor's New Clothes* and *Puss in Boots*. Between 1946 and 1952 Moore was president of the National Institute of Arts and Letters and from 1960 to 1963, president of the American Academy.

Moore, Grace, soprano. Born Slabtown, Tenn., Dec. 1, 1901; died Copenhagen, Jan. 26, 1947. She studied voice at Ward-Belmont College in Tennessee and the Wilson-Green Music School in Maryland. She made her debut in 1918 in a concert with Giovanni MARTINELLI in Washington, D.C. She then went to New York, where she appeared in night clubs and musical comedies, becoming a star. She abandoned Broadway in 1926 and for eighteen months studied with Richard Barthelmy and Mary GARDEN in Europe. She made her opera debut at the METROPOLITAN OPERA on Feb. 7, 1928, as MIMI. She was received enthusiastically by the audience, but the critics felt she still required more training and experience. On Sept. 29, 1928, she made her debut at the OPÉRA-COMIQUE. Appearances there and in other European opera houses added to her reputation, but it was only after her resounding success in the motion picture *One Night of Love* (1934) that she became world famous as a prima donna. In 1935 she made her debut at COVENT GARDEN in a command performance before Queen Mary. Soon after, she gave twelve command performances, six for kings and six for presidents; four nations decorated her; and she became the only American singer to have her name inscribed on a golden plaque outside the Opéra-Comique.

Although critics were never completely won over by her artistry, her vitality and glamor made her a favorite in opera houses everywhere. One of her greatest artistic successes came on Jan. 28, 1939, at the Metropolitan Opera, when she sang the role of LOUISE, having previously studied it with the composer. She died in an airplane crash at a time when her career was at its peak. She wrote an autobiography, *You're Only Human Once* (1944), and her career was made the subject of a motion picture, *So This Is Love,* starring Kathryn Grayson.

Moore, Thomas, poet. Born Dublin, May 28, 1779; died Bromham, Eng., Feb. 25, 1852. His metrical romance LALLAH ROUKH was the source of operas by DAVID, Daniel Kashkin (*The One-Day Reign of Nourmahal*), RUBINSTEIN (*Feramors*), SPONTINI (*Nurmahal*), and STANFORD (*The Veiled Prophet of Kohrassan*). Arthur Goring Thomas' *The Light of the Harem* was based on Moore's poem of the same name. After 1802 Moore frequently wrote melodies as well as poems, and between 1807 and 1834 he published a collection of Irish tunes to his own words. In 1811 he wrote the text for an opera, *M.P.,* the music by Charles Edward Horn. Produced in London, it was a failure. Moore's poem "The Last Rose of Summer," set to the melody "The Groves of Blarney," was introduced by FLOTOW in his opera MARTHA.

Morales, a sergeant (bass) in BIZET'S CARMEN.

morbidezza, Italian for "delicacy" or "gentleness." *Con morbidezza* is an indication for the singer to sing sweetly; this term is sometimes employed to describe either the sweetness of some of PUCCINI's arias or the sweet manner in which they should be sung.

Morfontaine, Guillot de, Minister of France (bass), in MASSENET'S MANON.

Morgenlich leuchtend im rosigen Schein, the song with which Walther wins the prize in the competition of the mastersingers, in Act III, Scene 2, of WAGNER'S DIE MEISTERSINGER. Also known as "The Prize Song."

Morrò, ma prima in grazia, Amelia's aria begging for the opportunity to bid her son farewell, in Act III, Scene 1, of VERDI'S UN BALLO IN MASCHERA.

Mort de Don Quichotte, *see* ÉCOUTE, MON AMI.

Moscona, Nicola, bass. Born Athens, Sept. 23, 1907. After completing his studies at the Athens Conservatory he made his opera debut at the National Theater in Athens in 1930 as SPARAFUCILE. Between 1931 and 1937 he made many operatic appearances in Greece and Egypt. After additional study in Milan, he made his American debut at the METROPOLITAN OPERA on Dec. 13, 1937 in AIDA. He remained with the company through the 1961–62 season, appearing in principal bass roles in over four hundred fifty performances in New York and in a repertory embracing some hundred operas in seven languages. In addition to his appearances at the Metropolitan, he was heard with major European companies and at leading European festivals.

Mosè in Egitto (Moses in Egypt), opera in three acts by ROSSINI. Libretto by Andrea Tottola. Premiere: San Carlo, Naples, Mar. 5, 1818. American premiere: New York City, Dec. 22, 1832 (concert version); Italian Opera House, New York, Mar. 2, 1835 (staged). While originally a great success in its first form, Rossini rewrote it for Paris, with a French text in four acts by JOUY and Balocchi, and as *Moïse* it was introduced at the PARIS OPÉRA on Mar. 26, 1827, when it proved even more impressive. One reason for its enthusiastic reception was that Rossini had added what is still the most overpowering ensemble number he ever composed, the prayer in the scene in which the Red Sea parts, "Dal tuo stellato soglio." The story of both versions follows the Biblical story of the struggle between Pharaoh and the Jews, the infliction of the plagues on the Egyptians, and the exodus from Egypt, culminating in the destruction of the Egyptian army in the Red Sea. Love interest is introduced between Pharaoh's son and a Hebrew girl, Anaïs, an episode invented to provide a vehicle for the brilliant prima donna Isabella Colbran, Rossini's mistress, later his wife.

The second-act basso aria, "Eterno, immenso," is of interest.

Mosenthal, Salomon Hermann von, novelist, dramatist, librettist. Born Cassel, Ger., Jan. 14, 1821; died Vienna, Feb. 17, 1877. This distinguished German writer contributed librettos to several operas, including BRÜLL's *Das goldene Kreuz* and *Der Landfriede;* FLOTOW's *Albin;* GOLDMARK's THE QUEEN OF SHEBA; Edmund Kretschmer's *Die Folkunger;* Theodor Leschetizky's *Die erste Falte;* and NICOLAI's THE MERRY WIVES OF WINDSOR. MACFARREN's *Helvellyn* was based on Mosenthal's novel *Der Sonnenwendhof.*

Moses und Aron (Moses and Aaron), opera in two acts by SCHOENBERG. Libretto by the composer, based on "Exodus" in the Old Testament. Premiere: Hamburg Radio, Mar. 12, 1954 (concert version); Zürich Opera, June 6, 1957 (staged). American premiere: Boston, Nov. 2, 1966. Schoenberg worked on this TWELVE-TONE opera in 1932 completing at the time text and music for two acts, and just the text for the third act. In 1951, he returned to his opera intending to write the music for the third act, but did not live to do so. He left instructions that, were the opera to be produced, the third act be given as spoken drama. Though a failure when first heard, the opera began to gain in recognition with repeated performances throughout Europe, until by 1965 it came to be regarded by many musicologists as one of Schoenberg's masterworks and one of the foremost operas of the twentieth century. The premiere in England at COVENT GARDEN on June 28, 1965, caused a sensation prior to the performance when the censors refused to permit naked virgins, sexual practices, and the sacrifice of live animals on the stage of Covent Garden in the orgy scene before the Golden Calf. A compromise was reached by dressing the virgins in loincloths, having the sexual scenes take place on a thoroughly darkened part of the stage, and the sacrifice of live animals simulated. Once this problem was solved, the opera went on to receive tremendous acclaim from both audiences and critics.

The opera begins when the voice in the burning bush calls to Moses and ends with the orgy before the Golden Calf. Moses' role is spoken, while that of Aaron is sung. Built on a single twelve-tone row and making extensive use of SPRECHSTIMME, the opera nevertheless achieves highly emotional and spiritual effects through expressive polyphony. Tensions and dramatic climaxes are built up through orchestral sonorities. Hans F. Redlich described the opera as a "mixture of elements of opera, oratorio, and cantata, serving together in the transmission of a tremendous religious experience."

Mother, The (Die Mutter), opera in ten scenes by HÁBA. Libretto by the composer. Premiere: Munich, May 17, 1931. This is the first opera written in quarter tones. The composer ordered a special quarter-tone piano, two quarter-tone clarinets, and two quarter-tone trumpets built to perform his music, explaining: "Harmonically I have used combinations ranging from two to twenty-four different sounds. Melodically I use multiples of quarter-tones: 3/4 tones, 5/4 tones, neutral thirds, sixths, fourths, and sevenths." The vocal parts require quarter-tone singing.

Mother of Us All, The, opera in three acts by THOMSON. Libretto by Gertrude STEIN. Premiere: New York City, May 7, 1947. This was the second collaboration of Thomson and Stein. The first, FOUR SAINTS IN THREE ACTS, had subject matter but no plot. *The Mother of Us All* has for its central character Susan B. Anthony, pioneer in the woman suffrage movement, and the opera traces her career from her initial struggles to her final victory. Other historical characters appear, including Ulysses S. Grant, Daniel Webster, and Andrew Jackson; also two characters identified as Virgil T. and Gertrude S. Thomson wrote this opera on a commission from the Alice M. DITSON FUND. After its premiere, it was given a special citation by the NEW YORK MUSIC CRITICS' CIRCLE; a regular award was prohibited because Thomson was a member of the circle. Thomson's score is pleasing not only for its satirical overtones but also for its skillful use of folklike melodies, ballads, and hymns.

motion pictures (and opera), *see* OPERA PERFORMANCE (6).

Mottl, Felix, conductor. Born Unter St. Veit, Austria, Aug. 24, 1856; died Munich, July 2, 1911. He graduated from the Vienna Conservatory with highest honors. His first important appointment was as conductor of the Akademische Richard WAGNER Verein in Vienna. In 1875 he was Wagner's assistant at BAYREUTH, preparing the first festival. Five years later he became court KAPELLMEISTER in Karlsruhe, rising to the position of general music director in 1893. He distinguished himself there not only in the works of Wagner but in his presentation of a cycle of BERLIOZ' operas, including the complete LES TROYENS. In 1886 he was principal conductor of the Bayreuth Festival. In 1903 he left Karlsruhe and became general music director in Munich; in 1907 he combined this post with that of director of the Court Opera. Mottl was engaged by the METROPOLITAN OPERA in 1903 to direct the American premiere of PARSIFAL. When Bayreuth instituted legal action to prevent this performance, Mottl withdrew and Alfred HERTZ substituted for him. However, Mottl conducted other performances at the Metropolitan Opera that season, making his debut there on Nov. 25 with DIE WALKÜRE. Besides the Wagner dramas, he directed operas by MOZART, BIZET, BOIELDIEU, and GOUNOD. Mottl wrote three operas: *Agnes Bernauer* (1880); *Fürst und Sänger* (1893); and *Ramin*. He edited the vocal scores of all the Wagner music dramas.

Mourning Becomes Electra, opera in three acts by Marvin David Levy. Libretto by Henry Butler, based on Eugene O'NEILL's drama of the same name, which, in turn, is deliberately based on AESCHYLUS' *Oresteia* trilogy. Premiere: Metropolitan Opera, Mar. 16, 1967. The reduction of O'Neill's thirteen-act trilogy to the functional size of a three-act libretto was no minor problem for the librettist, but he solved it with a tightly woven fabric in which the basic strands of O'Neill's plot were retained. Each of the three acts bears a title: "The Homecoming," "The Hunted," and "The Haunted." In the first act, Christine's husband (Ezra) and son (Orin) are returning from the Civil War. She has meanwhile found a lover in Adam. This illicit relationship so disturbs Christine's daughter, Lavinia, that Christine promises to give up Adam for good. But when Ezra returns, Christine poisons him.

In the second act, Christine is overjoyed at the return of her son; at the same time the townspeople are paying their last respects at Ezra's bier. Lavinia suspects how her father was murdered; and Christine betrays herself by her reactions when she notices that bottle of poison that Lavinia has placed on Ezra's coffin. Two days later, Christine joins Adam in Boston, where she confesses she killed Ezra. Adam promises to run off with her. But before this can happen, Adam is fatally stabbed by Orin, who had followed his mother into Boston and had overheard her confession. Orin then discloses to his mother that he has killed Adam. Rushing into the house, she shoots herself. Orin repents having been the cause of his mother's death, but Lavinia feels triumphant that vengeance has taken place.

In the third act, a year has passed. Lavinia and Orin are returning home after a long trip. She urges Orin to forget the past, but Orin locks himself in his room and shoots himself. Lavinia is now left alone, henceforth to lead a solitary, desolate life in the bleak house, crushed under the weight of guilt.

For this somber drama, Levy produced a score made up principally of severe-lined declamations supported by dark-colored harmonies. There is as little relief or variance from the tensions and tragic moods of Levy's music as there is in Butler's text. It became the first American opera ever produced by the Dortmund Opera in Germany when it received its European premiere there in Nov., 1969.

Moussorgsky, *see* MUSSORGSKY.

Mozart, Wolfgang Amadeus, composer. Born Salzburg, Austria, Jan. 27, 1756; died Vienna, Dec. 5, 1791. Like every other branch of musical composition, opera was greatly enriched by the genius of Mozart. His DON GIOVANNI, THE MARRIAGE OF FIGARO, and THE MAGIC FLUTE are milestones in the evolution of opera. Mozart began studying the harpsichord when he was only four, being taught by his father, Leopold, an eminent musician in his own right. The boy immediately revealed sure instincts and a phenomenal capacity to assimilate everything taught him. His gifts for sight-reading and improvisation aroused the awe of all who heard him. Quite as wonderful were his creative powers. He wrote minuets when he was five, a sonata when seven, a symphony when eight. In his sixth year he and his sister (a skilled harpsichord player) were taken by their father to the electoral court in Munich, where the young performers won the hearts of royalty and were showered with gifts. The success of this trip encouraged the father to undertake others. For the next several years he exhibited his children throughout Europe. In Paris, four of Mozart's violin sonatas were published; in London, his first symphonies were performed, and his harpsichord playing amazed and pleased the Queen's music master, Johann Christian BACH.

In Vienna in 1768 the Emperor commissioned Mozart to write an OPERA BUFFA, LA FINTA SEMPLICE. The artists at the opera house (led by GLUCK) refused to participate in a performance of an opera by a child, and they prevented its performance. Another little Mozart opera, BASTIEN UND BASTIENNE, was given privately in the garden theater of Dr. Anton Mesmer, the hypnotist. Mozart and his father embarked on an extended tour of Italy in 1770. In Rome the fourteen-year-old boy gave a remarkable demonstration of his genius

by writing down from memory, after a single hearing, the complete score of Gregorio Allegri's celebrated *Miserere.* In Italy as elsewhere, Mozart received numerous honors and tributes. In Milan he was commissioned to write an opera. The work, *Mitridate, Rè di Ponto,* was introduced on Christmas Day, 1770; it was so successful that it was given twenty times. The following year Mozart's *Ascanio in Alba,* a serenata, was also a major success at its premiere in Milan. The venerable opera composer, Johann Adolph HASSE, remarked prophetically: "This boy will throw all of us into the shade." In 1774 Mozart again returned to Milan to supervise the premiere of his comic opera, LA FINTA GIARDINIERA.

The period between 1772 and 1777 was spent principally in Salzburg, under unhappy conditions. A new Archbishop, Hieronymus von Colloredo, had come to Salzburg. He had little appreciation of Mozart's genius, and the young man was treated as servants were, with imperious authority and personal abuse. The masterworks that Mozart was creating were ignored. A welcome avenue of escape finally came in 1777 when Mozart and his mother set off for Paris hoping to find there some advantageous post; the father, denied a leave of absence by the Archbishop, had to remain behind. The visit to Paris did not prove rewarding. There seemed to be no further interest in Mozart now that he had outgrown the appeal of childhood. A tragic circumstance of the journey was the sudden death of Mozart's mother. Mozart had to return to Salzburg to his drab existence in a post that paid poorly and in which he suffered so many indignities. The insufferable situation was accentuated on Jan. 29, 1781, when, on a trip to Munich, he was acclaimed for his new opera, IDOMENEO, his first work that gave an indication of his coming powers as a stage composer. Mozart now knew he would have to make a permanent break with the Archbishop and make his way elsewhere. That break came in 1782 when Mozart visited Vienna with the Archbishop's entourage. Denied permission to appear at some benefit concerts, Mozart flew into a rage, denounced his employer, and was summarily dismissed. From now on, to the end of his life, Mozart lived in Vienna. He did not have to wait long for recognition. The Emperor commissioned him to write a new opera for the court theater, THE ABDUCTION FROM THE SERAGLIO (*Die Entführung aus dem Serail*). It was given on July 16, 1782, and despite the intrigues organized against it by envious composers, headed by Antonio SALIERI, it was a triumph. One of the best comic operas before those of ROSSINI, *The Abduction* is today the oldest opera in the German language that is still frequently performed.

Confident of his future, Mozart married Constance Weber on Aug. 4, 1782. He expected a profitable post at court but was kept waiting. The Emperor was lavish with praise and commissions but niggardly about opening his purse strings. To earn a living, Mozart gave lessons, which brought him a pittance. Frequently he was subjected to the humiliation of begging friends for loans. But his frustrations and disappointments did not arrest the flow of his compositions: masterworks bringing new dimensions to the symphony, concerto, and string quartet, as well as opera. A few in Vienna recognized the grandeur of this music. One was Joseph HAYDN, then the most celebrated composer in Europe, who described Mozart as "the greatest composer I know, either personally or by name."

A meeting with Lorenzo DA PONTE in 1785—he had recently been appointed poet of the Viennese court theaters—resulted in three of Mozart's greatest operas. Da Ponte wrote admirable librettos for all three. The first was *The Marriage of Figaro* (*Le nozze di Figaro*) , given at the Burgtheater on May 1, 1786. Once again the anti-Mozart forces in Vienna rallied to sabotage the performance; only the personal intervention of the Emperor thwarted this maneuver. The opera was a success of the first magnitude; so many numbers were encored that the length of the first performance was almost doubled. But Mozart's enemies were not defeated. They presented at the Burgtheater a catchy little opera —MARTÍN's UNA COSA RARA—to deflect the interest and enthusiasm of the Viennese from Mozart's new work. They succeeded; *The Marriage of Figaro* closed after only nine performances. The following year Mozart again collaborated with da Ponte. Their new work was *Don Giovanni*, whose premiere in Prague on Oct. 29, 1787, was another triumph. The city went mad over Mozart's melodies. "Connoisseurs and artists say that nothing like this has been given in Prague," reported a contemporary journal. The last of these three collaborations was COSÌ FAN TUTTE, first given in Vienna on Jan. 26, 1790. Considered a failure, the opera was given only ten performances.

The year of 1791, the last of Mozart's life, brought no end to the composer's personal misfortunes. While he had finally been given a permanent post as court composer and chamber musician (in succession to Gluck) he received such a small salary that it neither relieved him of his debts nor provided for the necessities of life. Impoverished, sick in body and spirit, Mozart gave way to despair. Yet his last year was a period of wonderful creation, yielding two operas—LA CLEMENZA DI TITO and *The Magic Flute*—and the *Requiem*. *The Magic Flute* (*Die Zauberflöte*) and the *Requiem* were the results of commissions. The first was ordered by Johann Emanuel SCHIKANEDER, who wanted a popular German opera for his THEATER-AUF-DER-WIEDEN. He supplied his own libretto. The opera was introduced on Sept. 30 and in time became so popular that it was given a hundred performances. The *Requiem* had a dramatic history. A stranger appeared at Mozart's house and engaged him to write the work on condition that Mozart make no attempt to learn the identity of his patron. Actually the stranger was a representative of Count Franz von Walsegg, an amateur musician who used to order music and present it as his own. Unaware of this, tortured by poverty and failing health, Mozart realized that he was penning his own requiem. And so it proved. The afternoon before he died Mozart summoned three friends and with them sang portions of the composition. At the beginning of the "Lacrimosa" he was so overcome with sorrow he had to put the music aside. After Mozart's death, incidentally, Count Walsegg copied the *Requiem* in his own hand and claimed the authorship when he had it performed.

Mozart completed twenty-five works for the stage, counting serenatas, intermezzi, operettas, comedies and plays with music, and comic and serious operas. Two, *The Abduction from the Seraglio* and *The Magic Flute,* were the first important operas written to German texts, consequently the foundation on which all later German operas were built. Mozart's other operas, settings of Italian texts, for the most part conformed to prevailing Italian styles and tastes. But even here Mozart wrote a special chapter in opera history. His greatest Italian operas, *The Marriage of Figaro, Don Giovanni, Così fan tutte,* may be within formal patterns of Italian opera, but something decidedly new was added. No composer before Mozart had his gift for musical characterization: a sudden accent, the injection of a rhythmic figure, a change of orchestral color, the introduction of a new melodic idea—and we suddenly get a new insight into the idiosyncrasies and hidden motivations of the characters. No one before Mozart had his amazing gamut of musical expression: from levity to grandeur and nobility, from malice to the most eloquent outbursts of feeling and passion. Mozart's operas: *Bastien und Bastienne* (1768) ; *La finta semplice* (1768) ; *Mitridate, Rè di Ponto* (1770) ; *Ascanio in Alba* (1771) ; *Il sogno di Scipione* (1772) ; *Lucio Silla* (1772) ; *La finta giardiniera* (1774) ; *Idomeneo, Rè di Creta* (1781) ; *Die Entführung aus dem Serail* (*The Abduction from the Seraglio,* 1782) ; *Der Schauspieldirektor* (1786) ; *Le nozze di Figaro* (*The Marriage of Figaro,* 1786) ; *Don Giovanni* (1787) ; *Così fan tutte* (1790) ; *Die Zauberflöte* (*The Magic Flute,* 1791) ; *La clemenza di Tito* (1791).

Mozart is the central character of a two-act opera by RIMSKY-KORSAKOV, *Mozart and Salieri,* based on Alexander PUSHKIN's dramatic poem. The theme is the historic rivalry between these two composers and the rumor, based on Salieri's deathbed confession, that he had poisoned Mozart.

See also DON PEDRO.

Much Ado About Nothing, a comedy by William SHAKESPEARE, revolving around the confusions and misunderstandings complicating the love affair of Claudio and Hero, natives of Messina. *See* BÉATRICE ET BÉNÉDICT.

Muck, Karl, conductor. Born Darmstadt, Ger., Oct. 22, 1859; died Stuttgart, Mar. 3, 1940. One of the foremost conductors of his generation, Muck was particularly eminent as an interpreter of WAGNER. He received an extensive academic education in classical philology at the universities of Heidelberg and Leipzig before he specialized in music. His musical training took place at the Leipzig Conservatory. After serving as chorusmaster at the ZÜRICH OPERA, he conducted in smaller Austrian opera houses. In 1886 he became principal conductor of the Angelo Newman Opera Company in Prague. Three years later he attracted attention with his performances of the Wagnerian music dramas in Russia. In 1892 he was appointed first conductor of the Berlin Opera, and it was here that he first became famous throughout Europe for his searching and fastidiously prepared performances. Further triumphs were gathered in COVENT GARDEN in 1899, at BAYREUTH beginning in 1901 (he appeared regularly at Bayreuth until 1931), and in Vienna. In 1906 Muck visited the United States for the first time, making his American debut as conductor of the Boston Symphony Orchestra on Oct. 12, 1906. After returning to Berlin, he was made musical director of the Berlin Royal Opera

(BERLIN STATE OPERA). The twenty years of his regime was one of the most resplendent periods in the history of that institution. In that time Muck directed 1,071 performances of 103 different operas, including 35 novelties. He set an artistic standard for Berlin that was rarely equaled elsewhere.

In 1912 Muck returned to Boston to become permanent conductor of the Boston Symphony Orchestra. When America entered World War I, his position in this country became increasingly embarrassing. It was known he was a friend of the Kaiser, from whom he had received many honors, and his sympathies had been publicized as resting with his countrymen. On Mar. 25, 1918, Muck was arrested. He remained a political prisoner several months, after which he was deported. Back in Europe, Muck continued to conduct in Berlin, Bayreuth, and other major German opera houses. From 1922 to 1933 he was the musical director of the Hamburg Philharmonic Orchestra. After 1933 he lived in retirement in Stuttgart.

muette de Portici, La (also known as *Masaniello*), opera in five acts by AUBER. Libretto by Eugène SCRIBE and Germaine Delavigne. Premiere: Paris Opéra, Feb. 29, 1828. American premiere: Park Theater, New York, Nov. 9, 1829. In seventeenth-century Naples, Fanella, the mute sister of Masaniello, is imprisoned by Alfonso, son of the Viceroy of Naples (tenor). Masaniello (tenor) heads an army in a successful revolt against Alfonso, and is given the crown of Naples. Poisoned by a former friend, Masaniello goes mad, a development enabling Alfonso to quell the revolt. Masaniello is killed, and his sister commits suicide. This opera had far-reaching political repercussions when it was introduced in Brussels in 1830. Its theme—political revolution—made such a profound impression on the Belgians that it sparked their revolt against Dutch rule, resulting in the constitution of Belgium as an independent state. The overture and the BARCAROLLE in Act II are favorites of salon and pop orchestras. Perhaps the most celebrated vocal number is the duet of Masaniello and Fanella in Act IV, known as the "Air du sommeil" or "Slumber Song." Also distinctive are the third-act choral prayer, "Saint bien heureux," and Masaniello's fourth-act CAVATINA, "Du pauvre seul ami fidèle."

Muff, a comedian (tenor) in SMETANA's THE BARTERED BRIDE.

Mugnone, Leopoldo, conductor. Born Naples, Sept. 29, 1858; died there Dec. 22, 1941. His music study took place at the Naples Conservatory. In 1874 he was appointed conductor of the TEATRO LA FENICE in Venice, but he first achieved major recognition at the TEATRO COSTANZI in Rome, where he led the world premiere of CAVALLERIA RUSTICANA in 1890. He then became principal conductor of LA SCALA, where in 1893 he conducted the premiere of FALSTAFF. He was equally distinguished in the Italian and Wagnerian repertories and was one of the earliest advocates of WAGNER in Italy. In 1905 he led successful performances at COVENT GARDEN, an opera house he frequently returned to, leading there the first English performances of FEDORA (in 1906) and IRIS (in 1919). Mugnone also conducted at the SAN CARLO in Naples, the Augusteo in Rome, and in the United States. He wrote several operas, the best known being *Il Biricchino* (1892) and *Vita brettona* (1905).

Müller, Maria, soprano. Born Leitmoritz, Bohemia, Jan. 29, 1898; died Bayreuth, Mar. 13, 1958. She studied singing at the Prague Conservatory and with Max Altglass in New York. Her debut took place in 1919 in Linz, Austria, as ELSA. From 1921 to 1923 she appeared with the PRAGUE OPERA and in 1923–24 with the MUNICH OPERA. On Jan. 21, 1925, she made her American debut at the METROPOLITAN OPERA as SIEGLINDE. She stayed at the Metropolitan eleven years, scoring her greatest successes in the German repertory, and starring in such important premieres and revivals as ALFANO's *Madonna Imperia,* MONTEMEZZI's *Giovanni Gallurese,* PIZZETTI's

FRA GHERARDO, and WEINBERGER'S ŠVANDA. While a member of the Metropolitan she appeared extensively throughout Europe, including COVENT GARDEN, the BERLIN OPERA, the VIENNA STATE OPERA, and the festivals in BAYREUTH and SALZBURG.

Munich Opera (Munich Bayreische Staatsoper), the leading opera house in Munich and one of Germany's major opera companies. The building was erected in 1818 on the site of a Franciscan convent. It burned down in its initial year, was rebuilt with funds provided by King Ludwig I and reopened on Jan. 2, 1825, at which time it was named Hof und Nationaltheater. Here some of WAGNER's most important music dramas were introduced: TRISTAN UND ISOLDE in 1865; DIE MEISTERSINGER in 1868; DAS RHEINGOLD in 1869; and DIE WALKÜRE in 1870. Later premieres up into the World War II period included the following: *The Beloved Voice* (WEINBERGER) ; CAPRICCIO; LE DONNE CURIOSE; DER FRIEDENSTAG; *Das Herz* (PFITZNER) ; *Komoedie des Todes* (MALIPIERO) ; DER MOND; THE MOTHER; PALESTRINA; *Samuel Pepys* (Albert Coates) ; I QUATTRO RUSTEGHI; and THE SECRET OF SUZANNE.

Principal conductors of the opera house up to 1943 included (chronological order) Franz Lachner (under whose direction, begun in 1852, the opera house first acquired its prestige) , Hans von BÜLOW, Hermann LEVI, Richard STRAUSS, Felix MOTTL, Bruno WALTER, Hans KNAPPERTSBUSCH, and Clemens KRAUSS.

The Hof und Nationaltheater was bombed in 1943, during World War II. The activities of the Munich Opera resumed in 1945 under the artistic direction of Günther RENNERT at the Prinzregententheater, which had been rebuilt as a Wagner festival theater and reopened on Aug. 28, 1901, with *Die Meistersinger.* Performances continued there until 1963 under the following conductors: Clemens Krauss, Ferdinand Leitner, Georg SOLTI, Rudolf KEMPE, Ferenc FRICSAY, and Joseph KEILBERTH.

The Nationaltheater was rebuilt and reopened in Nov., 1963, its first week celebrated with the world premiere of EGK's *Die Verlobung in San Domingo.* Rudolf HARTMANN was made general manager. In 1967–68 Rennert returned to his old post as artistic director, replacing Hartmann. Since its reopening in 1945, the Munich Opera has given performances of numerous twentieth-century operas including the following: ANTIGONAE; DIE BERNAUERIN; BLUEBEARD'S CASTLE; CARDILLAC (new version) ; CARMINA BURANA; THE CONSUL; DANTONS TOD; *Don Juan de Mañara* (Tomasi) ; ELEGY FOR YOUNG LOVERS; DIE HARMONIE DER WELT; IRISCHE LEGENDE; JEANNE D'ARC AU BÛCHER; DIE KLUGE; PEER GYNT (Egk) ; PROMETHEUS; *Soldaten* (Bernd Alois Zimmermann) ; WOZZECK; DIE ZAUBERGEIGE.

In 1965 the Munich Opera performed at the EDINBURGH FESTIVAL.

Munich Opera Festival, an annual summer festival of opera presented in July and August by the Munich Opera. The festival was originally intended to concentrate on WAGNER and MOZART—Wagner performed in the Hof und Nationaltheater, and the more intimate Mozart operas in the rococo theater of the Residenz. Since the opening of the festival, its program has expanded greatly. The operas of Richard STRAUSS have assumed equal importance with those of Wagner and Mozart. The repertory was further enriched with performances of Italian masterworks, with revivals of rarely heard older operas, with twentieth-century operas, some of them world premieres. The more elaborate operas are now given at the new Nationaltheater, while the more intimate ones are generally produced at the Cuvilliestheater in the Altes Residenztheater (the old rococo theater of the Residenz, which had been reconstructed, and which reopened in June, 1958) .

The following are some of the novelties heard at the festival through the years: AGRIPPINA; CARDILLAC (new version); DEIDAMIA; DOKTOR UND APOTHEKER; ELEGY FOR YOUNG LOVERS; GIULIO CESARE;

L'infedeltà delusa (HAYDN); IPHIGÉNIE
EN TAURIDE; JEANNE D'ARC AU BÛCHER;
LULU; OBERON; PARIDE ED ELENA; LA
PIETRA DEL PARAGONE; THE RAKE'S PROG-
RESS; *Die Verlobung in San Domingo*
(EGK).

Munsel, Patrice, soprano. Born Spo-
kane, Wash., May 14, 1925. She began
to study voice when she was twelve.
After an additional period of training,
with William P. Herman in New York,
she won the METROPOLITAN AUDITIONS OF
THE AIR in 1943. Her debut at the MET-
ROPOLITAN OPERA took place on Dec. 4,
1943, as Philine in MIGNON. She was
then the youngest leading singer ever
to become a member of the company.
She remained with the company through
the 1957–58 season. Meanwhile in 1948
she made her European debut at the
Copenhagen Opera. In 1952 she appeared in a motion-picture dramatiza-
tion of the life of Nellie MELBA. She has
also frequently been heard in recitals,
and over radio and television.

Muratore, Lucien, tenor. Born Marseilles, Aug. 29, 1876; died Paris, July
16, 1954. He was first a dramatic actor
in Paris and Monte Carlo, appearing
in leading roles with Rejane at the
Odéon. Albert CARRÉ, director of the
OPÉRA-COMIQUE, induced him to leave
the dramatic stage for opera. After a
period of preparation at the Paris Conservatory, he made his debut at the
Opéra-Comique on Dec. 16, 1902, in the
world premiere of HAHN's *La Carmélite*.
He was so successful at the Opéra-
Comique that in 1905 he was engaged
by the PARIS OPÉRA as principal tenor.
For the next half dozen years he was one
of the most highly acclaimed singers in
France. MASSENET selected him to appear in the world premiere of ARIANE
in 1906 and in the premieres of his later
operas *Bacchus* and *Roma*. Muratore
also created the leading tenor roles in
FÉVRIER's MONNA VANNA, Georges Huë's
Le Miracle, and SAINT-SAËNS's *Déjanire*.
He made his American debut in 1913
with the BOSTON OPERA. He then joined
the CHICAGO OPERA where, except for
a single season when he saw action
in the French Army during World

War I, he remained a principal tenor
through the 1921–22 season. After his
retirement from opera he devoted himself to teaching singing in Europe, becoming a member of the faculty of the
American Conservatory in Fontainebleau in 1938. Muratore was married
to the prima donna Lina CAVALIERI
in 1913; it was his second marriage.

Murder in the Cathedral, *see* ASSASSINIO
NELLA CATTEDRALE, L'.

Muse, The, a character (soprano) in
OFFENBACH's THE TALES OF HOFFMANN.

Musetta, Marcel's sweetheart (soprano)
in PUCCINI's LA BOHÈME.

Musetta's Waltz, *see* QUANDO M'EN VO'
SOLETTA.

musette, a simple pastoral melody in
moderate tempo, usually associated with
a drone effect, especially popular in
France in the seventeenth and eighteenth centuries. The music derives its
name from the instrument for which
it was originally intended, the musette
being a small, sweet-toned member of
the bagpipe family. Compositions entitled musettes are found in many sev-
enteenth- and eighteenth-century operas.
Noteworthy examples include the musettes in Act IV of GLUCK's ARMIDE, in
RAMEAU's *Acanthe et Céphise* and *Les
Fêtes d'Hebé,* and HANDEL's *Il pastor
fido.*

**musical quotations and interpolations
in opera.** There are numerous instances
in opera where composers resort to
quotation, sometimes from the works of
other composers, sometimes from their
own creations; sometimes with serious
intent, but most often for comic effect.
Here are some examples: ALBERT HER-
RING (the love-potion theme from TRIS-
TAN UND ISOLDE); ANDREA CHÉNIER ("La
Carmagnole" and the "Marseillaise");
ARLECCHINO (from THE DAUGHTER OF THE
REGIMENT); THE BEAR (Walton occasionally parodies the style of his own opera
TROILUS AND CRESSIDA and his *Viola Con-
certo*); THE BOATSWAIN'S MATE (open-
ing measures of BEETHOVEN's *Fifth
Symphony*); BOULEVARD SOLITUDE (from
MANON); CAPRICCIO (STRAUSS quotes co-
piously in this opera from GLUCK's rival
PICCINNI and from Gluck's IPHIGÉNIE EN

AULIDE, from MOZART's piano concertos, DIE MEISTERSINGER, and OTELLO, and from his own ARIADNE AUF NAXOS and songs); *Daughter of the Regiment* ("Ça ira"); DON GIOVANNI (from MARTÍN's UNA COSA RARA and from Mozart's own THE MARRIAGE OF FIGARO, "NON PIÙ ANDRAI"); FEUERSNOT (from DER FLIEGENDE HOLLÄNDER, and from Strauss's preceding opera, *Guntram*); INTERMEZZO (from FAUST, from SCHUMANN's *Spring Symphony,* from PARSIFAL, and from Strauss's own *Ein Heldenleben*); BEESON's *My Heart's in the Highlands* (from FIDELIO); ORPHEUS IN THE UNDERWORLD ("Che farò senza Euridice" from Gluck's ORFEO ED EURIDICE); LEONORE 40/45 (from *Fidelio,* also excerpts from WAGNER, SCHOENBERG, STRAVINSKY, LEONCAVALLO, and LISZT); MADAMA BUTTERFLY ("The Star-Spangled Banner"); *Die Meistersinger* (from Wagner's own *Tristan und Isolde*).

musica parlante, literally "speaking music"—a term used by the first Florentine composers of opera to describe the recitative style of their vocal writing.

music drama, a term used by Richard WAGNER and some of his successors to designate an opera of serious nature in which the close integration of text and music departed from the older, more formal concepts of opera.

Musset, Alfred de, poet and playwright. Born Paris, Nov. 11, 1810; died there May 1, 1857. Many of Musset's plays have been adapted for operas, including: *Carmosine* (FÉVRIER); *La Coupe et les lèvres* (PUCCINI's EDGAR); *Fantasio* (Ethel SMYTH); *Fortunio* (MESSAGER); *Namouna* (BIZET's DJAMILEH); *On ne Badine pas avec l'Amour* (PIERNÉ); *La Rosiera* (Gnecchi); *Les Caprices de Marianne* (Chausson).

Mussorgsky, Modest, composer. Born Karevo, Russia, Mar. 21, 1839; died St. Petersburg, Mar. 28, 1881. A member of the Russian nationalist school, Mussorgsky created the most distinguished folk opera to come out of Russia, BORIS GODUNOV. The son of a wealthy landowner, Mussorgsky was originally directed by his parents to the army. While in uniform he met the composers DARGOMIZHSKY and Balakirev, who stim-

ulated his latent musical interests. After a brief period of study with Balakirev, Mussorgsky decided, in 1858, to give up the army for music. His debut as composer took place in 1860 with an orchestral work performed in St. Petersburg. He now began planning and writing more ambitious works, including a symphony and an orchestral fantasy. From 1860 on he was a passionate advocate of musical nationalism, in which ideal he associated himself with Balakirev, CUI, RIMSKY-KORSAKOV, and Borodin in a group since known as the FIVE. The abolition of serfdom in 1861 put an end to Mussorgsky's financial security. The necessity of earning a living made him accept a clerkship in the Ministry of Transport in 1863. For the next seventeen years (virtually to the end of his life) he worked as a clerk, relegating musical composition to the status of an avocation. The death of his mother in 1865 was a shattering blow. Previously having revealed unmistakable symptoms of nervous disorders and melancholia, Mussorgsky now became a victim of alcoholism. He was to suffer physically and mentally for the remainder of his life, but this suffering only seemed to strengthen his creative resources. He planned and outlined an opera, THE MARRIAGE, in which he tried to introduce a new concept of musical realism with melodies patterned after the inflections of human speech. He abandoned this project after finishing a single act but only because a new and greater venture began to absorb him completely: the opera *Boris Godunov,* completed in 1870. Unorthodox in approach and style, *Boris* was at first turned down by the BOLSHOI THEATER of St. Petersburg. But after the work was revised along somewhat more formal lines, three scenes were presented there on Feb. 17, 1873. A complete performance of the opera followed on Feb. 8, 1874, and was more or less a failure.

After 1873 Mussorgsky's physical and moral disintegration became complete. He sometimes existed as a beggar might, and there were periods when he was in a state of intoxicated stupefaction. Yet in his periods of mental clarity he produced several remarkable works, including the opera KHOVANTCHINA. In 1879 he undertook a concert tour of southern Russia with the singer Daria Leonova. Back in St. Petersburg he returned to his old ways. Just before his death, he gave indications of losing his mind.

His colleagues sometimes looked upon his music with condescension because, having been incompletely trained, he was guilty of harmonic and instrumental crudities. But he possessed one of the greatest talents of his day, and his best music is marked with a vitality that was hardly matched by that of his contemporaries. Mussorgsky's aim was not exclusively the creation of a national art. He also sought truth, the identification of music with life. His most significant innovations are found in his operas, in his efforts to bring opera closer to life through melodic recitatives in which the lyricism approximated speech. "What I want to do," he once said, "is to make my characters speak on the stage as they would in real life and yet write music that is thoroughly artistic." In this quest, his music often avoided the more traditional concepts of beauty, giving way to ugly discords, primitive rhythms, abrupt transitions, strange chord sequences. Many of these effects, we realize today, were not due to ignorance but to a calculated attempt by Mussorgsky to broaden the expressiveness of his music. This fact was not clear to Mussorgsky's colleagues when, after his death, they edited his works and tried to remove the imperfections. Mussorgsky's operas: SALAMMBÔ (unfinished); *The Marriage* (unfinished); *Boris Godunov* (1870); *Khovantchina* (1873), completed by Rimsky-Korsakov; THE FAIR AT SOROCHINSK (1874), different versions completed by César Cui, Nikolai TCHEREPNIN, and Vissarion Shebalin.

Mustafa, Bey of Algiers (bass) in ROSSINI'S L'ITALIANA IN ALGERI.

Must winter come so soon?, Erika's bleak aria in Act I of BARBER'S VANESSA.

Mutter, Die, *see* MOTHER, THE.

Muzio, Claudia, soprano. Born Pavia, Italy, Feb. 7, 1889; died Rome, May 24, 1936. Her father was stage manager at COVENT GARDEN, then at the METROPOLITAN OPERA. The young singer received her vocal training with Mme. Casaloni, after which she made her opera debut in Arezzo on Feb. 7, 1912, in the title role of MANON LESCAUT. Numerous appearances followed in leading Italian opera houses. She made her American debut at the Metropolitan Opera on Dec. 4, 1916, as TOSCA. She remained with the Metropolitan six years, during which time she created the role of Giorgetta in IL TABARRO and appeared in many notable American premieres and revivals, including L'AMORE DEI TRE RE, ANDREA CHÉNIER, DIE LORELEY, and EUGENE ONEGIN. After leaving the Metropolitan Opera, she became a member of the CHICAGO OPERA COMPANY; later, she returned to the Metropolitan for the single season of 1933–34.

Mylio, Rozenn's childhood sweetheart (tenor), who is also loved by Rozenn's sister Margared, in LALO'S LE ROI D'YS.

My man's gone now, Serena's grief-stricken lament at the death of her husband Robbins, in Act I of GERSHWIN'S PORGY AND BESS.

Myrtale, a slave girl (mezzo-soprano) in MASSENET'S THAÏS.

Mystère de la nativité, Le (The Mystery of the Nativity), an oratorio by Frank MARTIN that is sometimes staged as an opera (as happened at the SALZBURG FESTIVAL in 1960). The text consists of a dozen incidents surrounding Christ's birth as told in a fifteenth-century mystery play. Martin wrote this composition on commission from the Geneva Radio, which introduced it on Dec. 24, 1959. The music has a medieval character through its simulation of Gregorian chant and use of church modes.

Mytyl, a child (soprano) in WOLFF'S THE BLUE BIRD.

N

Nabucco (or **Nabucodonosor**), opera in four acts by VERDI. Libretto by Temistocle Solera. Premiere: La Scala, Mar. 9, 1842. American premiere: Astor Opera House, Apr. 4, 1848.

Characters: Abigaille, reputedly Nabucco's elder daughter (soprano); Fenena, Nabucco's daughter (soprano); Ismaele, a nephew of the King of Jerusalem (tenor); Nabucco, King of Babylon (baritone); Zaccaria, High Priest of Jerusalem (bass); High Priest of Babylon (bass); Abdallo, officer in Nabucco's army (tenor); Anna, Zaccaria's sister (soprano). The action takes place in ancient Jerusalem and Babylon.

Act I. Levites are grieving over their defeat at the hands of Nabucco, King of Babylon, but the priest, Zaccaria, urges them to have faith in God ("Sperate, o figli"). Fenena, a hostage of the Jews, and Ismaele are in love. Abigaille also loves Ismaele. She enters with some Babylonian soldiers and promises Ismaele freedom for himself and his people if he will return her love, but Ismaele refuses. Nabucco, heading his troops, arrives and mocks the defeated Jews ("Tremin gl'insani"). Zaccaria's attempt to kill Fenena fails, due to Ismaele's intervention. His anger aroused, Nabucco then orders the temple to be destroyed.

Act II. With Nabucco once again off to the wars, Fenena becomes regent. Abigaille finds a document proving that she is not Nabucco's daughter but a slave, and she determines to bring ruin on everyone. Zaccaria now brings Abigaille the news that the Jewish prisoners are being freed by Fenena and urges her to take over power. The priest

then prays God for guidance ("Tu sul labbro"). Just as Abigaille is about to seize the crown from Fenena, Nabucco returns and places it on his own head, proclaims himself god, and orders Zaccaria and Fenena (who has become a Jewess) to worship him. A thunderclap throws the crown off his head, creating consternation among the people. Regarding himself a victim of persecution, Nabucco goes mad and Abigaille seizes his crown.

Act III, Scene 1. Abigaille is regent. She orders the death of the Jews, including Fenena.

Scene 2. On the banks of the Euphrates, Jewish slaves lament their fate in the most famous number in the opera, the chorus, "Va, pensiero." Zaccaria prophesies the fall of Babylon.

Act IV. In his prison cell, Nabucco hears the people crying for Fenena's death. His mind clearing, he prays to Jehovah, the Jewish god, to save her ("Dio di guida"). One of Nabucco's officers effects his escape and enables him to rush out and try to save his daughter. At the place of execution, a funeral march is being performed for Fenena. Nabucco's arrival saves her life. The idols are destroyed. Zaccaria once again assumes his high religious station. When Abigaille appears, the people rejoice, but they are unaware that she had previously taken poison. She dies begging God to be forgiven and Zaccaria promises new glories to Nabucco as a devotee of Jehovah.

Nabucco was Verdi's first triumph. As Francis Toye wrote: "*Nabucco* is probably the most satisfactory of all the early Verdi operas .... not until RIGOLETTO did the composer produce again an opera so satisfactory as an artistic whole." The first successful revival of the opera in the twentieth century took place at the FLORENCE MAY MUSIC FESTIVAL on Apr. 22, 1933, followed later the same year by performances at LA SCALA. This opera reopened the rebuilt auditorium of La Scala in 1946, and it opened the season of the METROPOLITAN OPERA on Oct. 24, 1960.

Nachbaur, Franz, tenor. Born Weiler Giessen, Württemberg, Ger., Mar. 25, 1835; died Munich, Mar. 21, 1902. After studying singing with Johann Baptist Pischek in Stuttgart, he made opera appearances in Mannheim, Hanover, Prague, and Vienna. In 1866 he was appointed principal tenor of the MUNICH OPERA, remaining here until his retirement a quarter of a century later. He created several Wagnerian roles, including that of WALTHER in 1868 and of FROH in 1869.

Nachtlager von Granada, Das (The Night Camp at Granada), opera in two acts by Conradin KREUTZER. Libretto by Karl Johann Braun, based on a play by Friedrich Kind. Premiere: Josefstadt Theater, Vienna, Jan. 13, 1834. American premiere: Hoboken, N.J., Nov., 1853. The setting is Spain in the sixteenth century. The Crown Prince, disguised as a hunter, makes love to the shepherdess Gabriele. His rivals plot to kill him, but Gabriele saves his life. In gratitude, the Prince unites Gabriele with Gomez, the man of her choice.

Nadir, a pearl fisher (tenor) in love with Leila, in BIZET'S LES PÊCHEURS DE PERLES.

Naiad, a character (soprano) in Richard STRAUSS'S ARIADNE AUF NAXOS.

Naina, a witch and siren (mezzo-soprano) in GLINKA'S RUSSLAN AND LUDMILLA.

Nancy, Lady Harriet's maid and friend (contralto) in FLOTOW'S MARTHA.

Nannetta, Ford's daughter (soprano) in VERDI'S FALSTAFF.

Napoleon Bonaparte, Emperor of France (baritone) in GIORDANO'S MADAME SANS-GÊNE.

Nápravník, Eduard, conductor and composer. Born Beischt, Bohemia, Aug. 24, 1839; died St. Petersburg, Russia, Nov. 23, 1916. He studied privately with local teachers and with Jan Bedřich Kittel and at the Modern School and the Organ School, both in Prague. He went to Russia in 1861 and in 1869 was appointed principal conductor of the St. Petersburg Opera, where he had been assistant conductor since 1863. For forty years or so he was one of the most significant opera conductors in Russia, responsible for making the St. Petersburg Opera one of the finest in that country. He directed more than three thousand performances, many of them of Russian operas. Nápravník also wrote several operas: *The Citizens of Nizhni* (1868); *Harold* (1886); *Dubrovsky* (1895); *Francesca da Rimini* (1903).

Naqui all' affano, Cinderella's rondo in the closing scene of ROSSINI'S LA CENERENTOLA.

Narraboth, captain of the guards (tenor) in Richard STRAUSS'S SALOME.

Natasha, heroine (soprano), fiancée of Andrei and Anatol's beloved, in PROKOFIEV'S WAR AND PEACE.

National Broadcasting Company Television Opera (NBC Opera), see OPERA PERFORMANCE (5).

National Opera Company, an opera company organized in New York in 1886 to succeed the recently defunct American Opera Company. With Theodore THOMAS, Gustav HINRICHS, and Arthur Mees as conductors, the company toured the country during its initial season. The following season it presented opera performances at the METROPOLITAN OPERA, remaining the resident company until 1889. The company then dissolved, to be reorganized as the Emma JUCH Grand Opera Company, which toured the United States, Canada, and Mexico until 1891.

Natoma, opera in three acts by HERBERT. Libretto by Joseph Redding. Premiere: Philadelphia, Feb. 25, 1911. The setting is early California. Natoma, an Indian princess (soprano), is in love with Lieutenant Merrill (tenor); her rival is a young Spanish girl, Barbara (soprano). When the princess overhears the plot of Alvarado (baritone) to kidnap Barbara, she is willing to sacrifice her own happiness for that of the man she loves. She kills Alvarado, then atones for this crime by entering a convent. The Dagger Dance for orchestra is still played. The "Vaqueros Song," Natoma's lullaby that opens the third act, and Alvarado's serenade to Barbara in the first act are among the better vocal pages.

naturalism, a movement in twentieth-century opera attempting to portray life as authentically as possible. It was preceded by the VERISMO school in Italian opera. The outstanding apostles of naturalism were CHARPENTIER and BRUNEAU.

Nature, Amour, Pollux's air in which he is torn between love and duty, in RAMEAU'S CASTOR ET POLLUX.

Nature immense (L'Invocation à la nature), Faust's invocation to nature, in Part IV of BERLIOZ' THE DAMNATION OF FAUST.

Naudin, Emilio, tenor. Born Parma, Italy, Oct. 23, 1823; died Bologna, May 5, 1890. He received his vocal training in Milan, then in 1843 made his operatic debut in Cremona in PACINI's *Saffo*. Between 1863 and 1872 he was a principal tenor at COVENT GARDEN, where he created for London the part of DON CARLOS. Meanwhile, in Paris in 1865, he created the role of Vasco DA GAMA. He also appeared in such Wagnerian roles as LOHENGRIN and TANNHÄUSER in the English provinces and in Moscow.

Navarraise, La (The Girl from Navarre), opera in two acts by MASSENET. Libretto by Jules Claretie and Henri Cain, based on Claretie's story, *La Cigarette*. Premiere: Covent Garden, June 20, 1894. American premiere: Metropolitan Opera, Dec. 11, 1895. In Spain, during the Carlist war, Anita (soprano) is in love with Araquil (tenor), but his father opposes the marriage since the girl has no dowry. To gain the money, Anita helps General Garrido (bass) of the Royalist troops capture and kill his Carlist enemy, Zuccaraga. Araquil is horrified to learn of this, and is killed when he follows Anita to Zuccaraga's camp. Anita loses her mind out of grief. An orchestral nocturne; the tenor aria, "O ma bien aimée"; and the nocturne, "Mariez donc son coeur," are of interest.

nave, La (The Ship), opera in three acts by MONTEMEZZI. Libretto by Tito Ricordi, based on D'ANNUNZIO's tragedy of the same name. Premiere: La Scala, Nov. 3, 1918. American premiere: Chicago, Nov. 18, 1919. The text is a plea for a unified Italy, with Italy represented by a ship about to be launched; the play is filled with other symbols of church and state.

Nay, Maccus, lay him down, Eadgar's aria in the concluding scene of TAYLOR's THE KING'S HENCHMAN.

NBC Television Opera Theatre, *see* OPERA PERFORMANCE (5).

Ne brochez pas, soyez gentille, Lescaut's warning to Manon about the ways of the world, in Act I of MASSENET's MANON.

Nedda, Canio's wife (soprano) in LEONCAVALLO's PAGLIACCI.

Ned Travis, an ex-soldier (baritone) in Dame Ethel SMYTH'S THE BOATSWAIN'S MATE.

Neipperg, Count, an Austrian nobleman (tenor) in GIORDANO's MADAME SANS-GÊNE.

Nella, Gherardo's wife (soprano) in PUCCINI's GIANNI SCHICCHI.

Nel riposo, Lycomede's bass aria in Act II of HANDEL's DEIDAMIA.

Nelusko, a slave (baritone) in MEYERBEER'S L'AFRICAINE.

Nemio della patria?, Gérard's monologue in Act III of GIORDANO's ANDREA CHÉNIER, in which he looks into his own past and is horrified by what he sees. He was once an honest and noble man, but in the name of revolution and freedom he became a murderer.

Nero, the tyrannical emperor of Rome, persecutor of the Christians, is the central character in various operas. BOITO, MASCAGNI, and RUBINSTEIN each composed an opera entitled either *Nero* or

Nerone, and Nero is a central character in MONTEVERDI'S L'INCORONAZIONE DI POPPEA.

Nerone (Nero), opera in four acts by BOITO. Libretto by the composer. Left unfinished but completed posthumously by Arturo TOSCANINI. Premiere: La Scala, May 1, 1924. Nero has murdered his mother and comes to bury her ashes. When this is done, the snakecharmer, Asteria, appears and confesses to Simon Magus, an agent of Nero's, that she loves the Emperor. Together they try to win Nero's confidence, but Nero believes Asteria is a fury risen to avenge the murder and sends her away; he also imprisons Simon. To effect his escape, Simon has the city set afire. As it burns, the Christians are doomed, and Simon perishes in the flames.

Nerto, *see* MISTRAL, FRÉDÉRIC.

Nerval, Gérard de (born Gérard Labrunie), poet, dramatist, translator. Born Paris, May 22, 1808; died there Jan. 25, 1855. His French translation of GOETHE'S *Faust* was used for BERLIOZ' THE DAMNATION OF FAUST. Claude Arrieu's *Les Deux Rendezvous,* FRANÇAIX'S LA MAIN DE GLOIRE, and GOUNOD'S LA REINE DE SABA are operas derived from Nerval's poetic dramas.

Nessler, Victor, composer. Born Baldenheim, Alsace, Jan. 28, 1841; died Strassburg, May 28, 1890. He planned to enter the church, but the success of his first operetta, *Fleurette,* in 1864 convinced him to become a composer for the stage. He held various musical posts, including that of choral director of the Leipzig Stadttheater, beginning in 1870, and conductor of the Caroltheater, also in Leipzig, after 1879. His most successful operas were: *Dornröschens Brautfahrt,* a fairy opera (1868); *Der Rattenfänger von Hameln* (1879); *Der wilde Jäger* (1881); DER TROMPETER VON SÄKKINGEN (1884); *Otto der Schütz* (1886); *Die Rose von Strassburg* (1890).

Nessun dorma, Calaf's aria expressing concern over Turandot's distress at failing to uncover his identity and his resolve to relieve her anguish, in Act III, Scene 1, of PUCCINI'S TURANDOT.

N'est-ce plus ma main que cette main presse?, Manon's eloquent avowal of love for Des Grieux that wins him back to her, in Act III, Scene 2, of MASSENET'S MANON.

Neuendorff, Adolf, conductor. Born Hamburg, Ger., June 13, 1843; died New York City, Dec. 4, 1897. He came to the United States in his twelfth year. After studying music with J. Weinlich and G. Matzka, he became in 1867 the conductor of the New York Stadttheater. There, on Apr. 15, 1871, he led a visiting European troupe in the American premiere of LOHENGRIN. In 1872 he helped direct a season of Italian opera at the Academy of Music; he returned there in 1875 for a season of German opera. In 1876 he attended the first BAYREUTH FESTIVAL as a correspondent for the New York *Staats-Zeitung.* A year later he led a WAGNER festival in New York that featured the American premiere of DIE WALKÜRE on Apr. 2, 1877. He wrote four comic operas: *The Rat Charmer of Hamelin* (1880); *Don Quixote* (1882); *Prince Woodruff* (1887); *The Minstrel* (1892).

Neues vom Tage (News of the Day), comic opera in three parts by HINDEMITH. Libretto by Marcellus Schiffer. Premiere: Kroll Opera, Berlin, June 8, 1929. American premiere: Santa Fe Opera, N.M., Aug. 12, 1961. This racy, comic, often absurd little opera is an example of ZEITKUNST ("contemporary art"), a movement, popular in Germany in the late 1920's, in which operas combined popular musical idioms (musichall tunes, jazz, etc.) with texts on contemporary themes. Laura and Eduard, a young married couple, quarrel and decide to separate. When Herr and Frau M. try to effect a reconciliation between the two, they get embroiled in a fight with each other, with the result that they themselves get divorced—the attractive Herr Hermann serving as corespondent. At a museum, Laura meets Herr Hermann. Eduard also happens to be there, and seeing his separated wife with Herr Hermann throws him into such a fit that he smashes a statue and is jailed. Laura, having arranged to meet Herr Hermann at the Savoy Hotel, is taking a bath there. Frau M. arrives, creates a scandal, and in doing so attracts the interest of the whole hotel—and the newspapers after that—to Laura and Eduard. They get offers to appear on stage and screen, become rich and famous. They would now very much like to resume their former marital status but are incapable of doing so since the public expects them to go through with their divorce.

Hindemith kept tongue in cheek in composing the music. He wrote a bathtub aria and a hymn to hot water. While most operas have a love duet, this one has a hate duet. Where some operas have wedding marches, this one has a divorce ensemble. A chorus of stenographers is accompanied by the sound of clicking typewriters, while other sounds (such as the breaking of crockery) are simulated realistically in the orchestra.

Neumann, Angelo, tenor and impresario. Born Vienna, Aug. 18, 1838; died Prague, Dec. 20, 1910. He abandoned a mercantile career to become an opera singer. After studying with Stilke-Sessi, he made his opera debut in 1859, after which he sang in various European theaters. From 1862 to 1876 he was principal tenor of the VIENNA OPERA. In 1876 he became the director of the Leipzig Opera, a post he held for six years. He then organized a traveling company that presented the WAGNER music dramas throughout Europe, a significant force in popularizing Wagner. From 1882 to 1885 he was director of the Bremen Opera and, from 1885 until his death, director of the Landestheater in Prague. He wrote a volume of reminiscences of Wagner, *Erinnerungen an R. Wagner* (1907).

Nevada, Emma (born Wixom), soprano. Born Alpha, Cal., Feb. 7, 1859; died Liverpool, Eng., June 20, 1940. She visited Europe in her fifteenth year and decided to stay there for concentrated vocal training. She studied with Mathilde MARCHESI in Vienna from 1877 on and on May 17, 1880, made her debut at HER MAJESTY'S THEATRE in London as AMINA. It was on this occasion that she assumed her stage name of Nevada. She next went to Italy, where she sang successfully in several cities. VERDI heard her and arranged for her to appear at LA SCALA. On May 27, 1887, she appeared for the first time at the OPÉRA-COMIQUE. In 1884 she returned to America and appeared with MAPLESON'S company at the Academy of Music, singing on alternate evenings with PATTI. A year later she married a London physician, Raymond Palmer. In 1885 and 1889 she appeared in opera festivals in Chicago. After retiring from the stage she devoted herself to teaching. Alexander MACKENZIE wrote his opera *Rose of Sharon* for her, and she created the title role at COVENT GARDEN in 1884. Her daughter, Mignon Nevada (born 1886), made successful appearances as a soprano at Covent Garden, La Scala, and other major European opera houses.

Nevers, Count de, (1) *see* ADOLAR.

(2) Catholic nobleman (baritone) in MEYERBEER'S LES HUGUENOTS.

New Opera Company (London), *see* CAMBRIDGE UNIVERSITY MUSICAL SOCIETY.

Neway, Patricia, soprano. Born Brooklyn, N.Y., Sept. 30, 1919. She studied voice at the Mannes College of Music and at the Berkshire Music Center at Tanglewood. Her opera debut took place at the CHAUTAUQUA Festival in 1946 as Fiordiligi in COSÌ FAN TUTTE, and in 1948 she made her first New York City operatic appearance in the role of the Female Chorus of THE RAPE OF LUCRETIA. She came into prominence in 1950 when she created the role of Magda in THE CONSUL, a role in which she appeared both in America and Europe over five hundred times. She also created the part of the Mother in MARIA GOLOVIN at the Brussels World's Fair in 1958. At the NEW YORK CITY OPERA she appeared in the world premiere of THE DYBBUK in 1951 and subsequently distinguished herself there in numerous modern operas, including WOZZECK. Besides appearing with European opera companies and at foreign festivals, she was heard in several performances with her own opera company which she founded in New York.

New York City Opera Company, one of the most significant and progressive opera companies in the United States, second in importance in New York to the METROPOLITAN OPERA. It was organized in 1943 as a unit of the City Center of Music and Drama (the first cultural center in the United States) in order to provide good opera at popular prices. The original company was made up of fifteen singers, two conductors, and one stage director; scenery was borrowed from the St. Louis Municipal Opera. The opening performance was TOSCA on Feb. 21, 1944; the first music director was László HALÁSZ. Eight performances of three operas were given the first season: CARMEN, MARTHA, and *Tosca*. Sixteen performances were given the following season. The first production which was entirely designed and mounted by the new company was ARIADNE AUF NAXOS, in the fall of 1946, a presentation receiving critical acclaim. Other productions during the Halász regime commanding admiration were SALOME, THE TALES OF HOFFMANN, PELLÉAS ET MÉLISANDE, THE MEDIUM, and perhaps most significantly, an excellent revival of PROKOFIEV's THE LOVE FOR THREE ORANGES in 1949. The world premiere of David Tamkin's THE DYBBUK took place in 1951.

Halász resigned in 1952, and for the next four years the company was under the musical direction of Joseph ROSENSTOCK. A highlight of his first season was the American premiere of BLUEBEARD's CASTLE, while another artistic achievement during the period of Rosenstock's musical directorship was a revival of CAPRICCIO. The first staged production of THE TAMING OF THE SHREW (GIANNINI) was also given.

Erich LEINSDORF took over the musical direction of the company in the fall of 1956, presenting in his first and only season there the world premiere of HE WHO GETS SLAPPED (or *Pantaloon*) and the American premieres of THE TEMPEST and DER MOND, together with the first professional presentation of SUSANNAH.

Julius RUDEL took over the musical and artistic directorship in 1957. It was under him that the New York City Opera developed into a company of first importance, with a consistently vital repertory, alive with premieres of American and European operas and with exciting presentations of the contemporary repertory (an area in which it surpassed the efforts of the Metropolitan Opera). When the New York City Opera entered the LINCOLN CENTER FOR THE PERFORMING ARTS to perform at the New York State Theatre, it initiated its new home with the American premiere of one of the more significant operas of the twentieth century, DON RODRIGO, on Feb. 22, 1966. Another highlight of that initial season was a revival of GIULIO CESARE, an artistic event of the first importance.

In a period spanning a quarter of a century, the New York City Opera has presented almost two thousand two hundred performances of about one hundred forty productions, both at home and on tour. Many were world premieres of American operas, including the following: THE CRUCIBLE; *The Dybbuk* (David Tamkin); *Gentlemen Be Seated* (Jerome Moross); *The Golem* (Abraham Ellstein); THE GOOD SOLDIER SCHWEIK; *He Who Gets Slapped*, or *Pantaloon*; LIZZIE BORDEN; MISS JULIE; *Natalia Petrovna* (Lee Hoiby); *Nine Rivers from Jordan* (WEISGALL); THE PASSION OF JONATHAN WADE; *The Servant of Two Masters* (GIANNINI); *Six Characters in Search of an Author* (WEISGALL); THE TENDER LAND; WINGS OF THE DOVE; and WUTHERING HEIGHTS.

In 1970 the New York City Opera offered the first complete staged production in New York of THE MAKROPOULOS AFFAIR and a significant revival of DONIZETTI's *Roberto Devereux*, with Beverly SILLS.

New York Music Critics' Circle Awards (for opera). The New York Music Critics' Circle was organized in 1941, comprising all New York critics who wrote signed criticisms in New York publications. During its twenty-year existence its aim was to select and give citations to the best compositions of each season in various categories. By the time it disbanded, it had given citations to the following operas: THE BALLAD OF BABY DOE, 1962; CARMINA BURANA, 1959; COMEDY ON THE BRIDGE, 1952; THE CRUCIBLE, 1961; LES DIALOGUES DES CARMÉLITES, 1958; THE GAMBLER, 1957; MOTHER OF US ALL, 1947 (special citation); SUSANNAH, 1956; TAMING OF THE SHREW by GIANNINI, 1954 (special award).

Nibelheim, the abode of the Nibelungs in WAGNER'S DAS RHEINGOLD.

Nibelung Ring, The, see RING DES NIBELUNGEN, DER.

Nibelung Saga, The (Das Nibelungenlied), an epic of ancient Teutonic times, the source of WAGNER'S DER RING DES NIBELUNGEN. Several other operas were derived from this saga, among them Heinrich Dorn's *Die Nibelungen* (1854); Felix Draeske's *Gudrun* (1884); and REYER'S SIGURD (1884).

Nicias, a voluptuary (tenor) in MASSENET'S THAÏS.

Nicklausse, Hoffmann's friend (mezzo-soprano) in OFFENBACH'S THE TALES OF HOFFMANN.

Nicolai, Carl Otto, composer and conductor. Born Königsberg, Ger., June 9, 1810; died Berlin, May 11, 1849. The composer of the delightful comic opera, THE MERRY WIVES OF WINDSOR, studied music with Carl Friedrich Zelter and Bernhard Klein. Settling in Berlin, between 1830 and 1833 he completed several works for orchestra and for chorus. In 1834 he went to Italy, where he was employed as organist in the Prussian Embassy in Rome and where he became vitally interested in opera. His first opera was a failure. His second, *Il templario,* was acclaimed at its premiere in Turin in 1840; after that it was heard in leading European cities and in New York. Meanwhile, in 1837, he was appointed principal conductor of the KÄRNTNERTHORTHEATER in Vienna. In 1841 he became principal conductor of

the VIENNA (Royal) OPERA. A year later he helped found the Vienna Philharmonic. After six years of distinguished services as conductor in Vienna he was appointed KAPELLMEISTER of the BERLIN OPERA; two years after this, on Mar. 9, 1849, his masterwork, *The Merry Wives of Windsor,* was introduced there. Though seriously ill, he conducted the first four performances. He died of apoplexy the day he was elected a member of the Berlin Academy. His operas: *Rosmonda d'Inghilterra* (1839); *Il templario* (1840); *Odoardo e Gildippe* (1841); *Die Heimkehr des Verbannten* (1844); *Die lustigen Weiber von Windsor (The Merry Wives of Windsor)* (1849).

Nicolette, a princess hidden in an orange (mezzo-soprano) in PROKOFIEV'S THE LOVE FOR THREE ORANGES.

Nicolini (born Nicola Grimaldi), CASTRATO soprano. Born Naples, Apr., 1673; died there Jan. 1, 1732. His first appearance in opera took place in Naples when he was only twelve. By 1690 he was acknowledged the best soprano in all Naples, and he was engaged for the royal chapel. While holding this post, he appeared with outstanding success in opera houses in Naples, Rome, and Venice; in the last-named city he was decorated with the Order of St. Mark. In 1708 he went to England, making his debut in London on Dec. 14 in Alessandro SCARLATTI'S *Pirro e Demetrio.* He sang in England for some years, scoring particularly in HANDEL'S RINALDO in 1711 and Handel's *Amadigi* in 1715. In 1717 he returned to Italy, where he again appeared extensively, particularly in Venice. In 1731 he returned to his native city to appear in PERGOLESI'S first opera, *Salustia,* but he fell ill during rehearsals and died before the premiere.

Nielsen, Alice, soprano. Born Nashville, Tenn., June 7, 1876; died New York City, Mar. 8, 1943. Her debut on the musical stage took place with the Boston Opera company in *The Mikado.* Success came in operetta, particularly in HERBERT'S *The Fortune Teller* in 1898. Determined to make her way in opera, she went to Italy for further study and then made her opera debut at the Bellini Theater in Naples on Dec. 6, 1903, as MARGUERITE. In the spring of 1904 she appeared for the first time at COVENT GARDEN. Her role was ZERLINA. Back in the United States, she was heard in New York City in 1905 in DON PASQUALE. In 1908 she appeared with the Henry RUSSELL SAN CARLO OPERA COMPANY in New Orleans and from 1909 to 1913 with the Boston Opera. Her first appearance at the METROPOLITAN OPERA took place on Nov. 19, 1909, in LA BOHÈME. After abandoning opera, she returned to operetta and was starred in Friml's *Kitty Darlin'* in 1917.

Niemann, Albert, tenor. Born Erxleben, Ger., Jan. 15, 1831; died Berlin, Jan. 13, 1917. In 1849 he sang in the chorus and appeared in minor parts at the Dessau Opera. After a protracted period of study with Friedrich Schneider, Nusch, and Gilbert DUPREZ, he appeared in smaller German opera theaters. In 1860 he was engaged as principal tenor of the HANOVER OPERA. Six years later he joined the BERLIN OPERA, where he appeared with outstanding success in tenor roles up to the time of his retirement in 1889. WAGNER selected him to create for Paris the role of TANNHÄUSER in 1861, and that of SIEGMUND for BAYREUTH in 1876. On Nov. 10, 1886, Niemann made his American debut at the METROPOLITAN OPERA as Siegmund. While appearing at the Metropolitan he created for America the roles of TRISTAN (1887) and Siegfried in GÖTTERDÄMMERUNG (1888). His correspondence with Wagner was published in 1924.

Nie werd' ich deine Huld verkennen, concluding chorus of MOZART'S THE ABDUCTION FROM THE SERAGLIO, in which Belmonte and the people hymn the praise of the Pasha for his generosity.

Nightingale, The, *see* ROSSIGNOL, LE.

Nikisch, Arthur, conductor. Born Lébényi Szent Miklos, Hungary, Oct. 12, 1855; died Leipzig, Jan. 23, 1922. A child prodigy, he entered the Vienna Conservatory when he was eleven. Two years after leaving the conservatory he became a conductor of the Leipzig Opera, making his bow there on Feb. 11, 1878. He rose to the post of principal conductor in 1882, and for seven years his distinguished performances attracted attention throughout Germany. From 1889 to 1893 Nikisch was principal conductor of the Boston Symphony. In 1893 he assumed the post of principal conductor of the BUDAPEST OPERA, where he remained two years. After 1895, though he made intermittent guest appearances in various European opera houses, he specialized in conducting symphonic music, particularly in his posts as principal conductor of the Leipzig Gewandhaus and the Berlin Philharmonic orchestra. From 1902 to 1907 he was also director of the Leipzig Conservatory. In 1912 he toured the United States with the London Symphony Orchestra.

Nikolaidi, Elena, contralto. Born Smyrna, Turkey, June 13, 1909. She entered the Athens Conservatory when she was fifteen and during her last year there made her debut as soloist with the Athens State Orchestra under Dimitri MITROPOULOS. She became a member of the Athens Lyric Theater, where she was heard in CARMEN, SAMSON ET DALILA, and other operas. In Vienna, where she went for further study, she won an international vocal competition, entitling her to a recital at the Konzerthaus. Engaged by Bruno WALTER for the VIENNA STATE OPERA, she made her debut there on the opening night of the 1936 season, singing Princess Eboli in DON CARLOS. She became so successful in Vienna that in 1947 she received the honorary title of KAMMERSÄNGERIN. Subsequently appearing throughout Europe, she then made her American debut in a New York recital on Jan. 20, 1949. On the opening night of the SAN FRANCISCO OPERA season in 1950 she appeared as AMNERIS. It was in the same role that she made her METROPOLITAN OPERA debut on the opening night of the season in 1951. She has since appeared in leading contralto roles there. A special act of Congress conferred on her the right to remain a permanent resident of the United States.

Nilakantha, Brahman priest (bass), father of Lakmé, in DELIBES'S LAKMÉ.

Nilsson, Birgit, soprano. Born West Karup, Sweden, May 17, 1922. She studied singing at the Royal Academy of Music in Stockholm. In 1947 she became a member of the STOCKHOLM ROYAL OPERA, where she made her debut as Agathe in DER FREISCHÜTZ. The following season she scored a major success as Lady MACBETH in VERDI's opera. From 1947 to 1951 she made guest appearances at the GLYNDEBOURNE FESTIVAL. In 1954 her performance as ELSA at BAYREUTH was acclaimed, as was her interpretation of ISOLDE in 1957 and 1959. During this period she also made her debut at LA SCALA and on Oct. 5, 1956, in the United States with the SAN FRANCISCO OPERA as Brünnhilde in DIE WALKÜRE. She appeared there in the major Wagnerian soprano roles, as well as with the CHICAGO LYRIC OPERA and, in 1957, as Brünnhilde at COVENT GARDEN in the RING cycle. Her debut at the METROPOLITAN OPERA took place on Dec. 18, 1959, as Isolde. She has remained with that company since then, as well as singing at other major opera houses, recognized universally as the most significant Wagnerian soprano since Kirsten FLAGSTAD. She has also appeared as SALOME, Leonore in FIDELIO, and in the Italian repertory. She has sung both Elisabeth and Venus in the same performance of TANNHÄUSER. In 1969 she received the honorary title of KAMMERSÄNGERIN from the Austrian government.

Nilsson, Christine, soprano. Born Wexiö, Sweden, Aug. 20, 1843; died Stockholm, Nov. 22, 1921. She studied singing with Franz Berwald and Baroness Leuhusen in Sweden and with Pierre François Wartel and Enrico delle Sedie in Paris. Her debut took place at the THÉÂTRE LYRIQUE in Paris on Oct. 27, 1864, her role being VIOLETTA. She remained a principal soprano there for three years, afterward appearing with the PARIS OPÉRA. Here, her performance of Marguerite in a revival of FAUST, ten

years after its premiere, was a determining factor in establishing the success of that opera. Between 1870 and 1872 she toured the United States. Between 1872 and 1877 she appeared annually at the DRURY LANE THEATRE, creating for England the principal soprano roles in LOHENGRIN, MEFISTOFELE, and BALFE's *Talismano.* On Oct. 27, 1883, she appeared at the METROPOLITAN OPERA in the performance of *Faust* which opened that opera house. She went into retirement in 1891.

Ninetta, heroine (soprano) in ROSSINI's LA GAZZA LADRA.

Ninette, a princess hidden in an orange (soprano) in PROKOFIEV's THE LOVE FOR THREE ORANGES.

Niun mi tema, Otello's speech before killing himself in Act IV of VERDI's OTELLO.

Nobil acciar, nobili e santi, *see* GLAIVES PIEUX, SAINTES ÉPÉES.

Nobles seigneurs salut (Lieti signori, salute), the Page's salute to Count Raoul de Nangis in Act I of MEYERBEER's LES HUGUENOTS.

Noëmi, Cinderella's stepsister (soprano) in MASSENET's CENDRILLON.

Noi siamo zingarelle, the chorus of the gypsies opening Act II, Scene 2, of VERDI's LA TRAVIATA.

Nolan, Philip, principal character (tenor) in DAMROSCH's THE MAN WITHOUT A COUNTRY.

Non disperar, Cleopatra's aria in Act I, Scene 2, of HANDEL's GIULIO CESARE, as she consoles herself for having good fortune in love even at the price of losing her kingdom.

Non imprecare, umiliati, trio of Padre Guardiano, Leonora, and Don Alvaro in the closing scene of VERDI's LA FORZA DEL DESTINO, as Leonora begs Alvaro to seek salvation in religion and the Padre commands Alvaro to beg God for forgiveness.

Non la sospiri la nostra casetta, love duet of Tosca and Cavaradossi in Act I of PUCCINI's TOSCA.

Non mi dir, Donna Anna's aria in Act II, Scene 4, of MOZART's DON GIOVANNI, informing Don Ottavio that, because of her grief at the death of her father, she cannot marry him.

Non mi resta che il pianto, Suzel's rapturous aria in Act III of MASCAGNI'S L'AMICO FRITZ.

Nonnes qui reposez, Bertram's summons to the dead nuns to rise from their graves in Act II of MEYERBEER'S ROBERT LE DIABLE.

Nono, Luigi, composer. Born Venice, Jan. 29, 1924. He is in the vanguard of today's avant-garde composers. After studying with Bruno Maderna and Hermann SCHERCHEN, he began composing works using TWELVE-TONE TECHNIQUES. His style became so controversial that performances of his works incited riots. His opera INTOLLERANZA 1960 is not only ultramodern in its techniques and materials but is also radical in its political and social concepts. Its premiere in Venice in 1961 created a scandal. When Nono arrived in the United States in 1965 for the American premiere of *Intolleranza 1960* he was at first denied admission because of his avowed Communist affiliation but eventually was admitted. There were no demonstrations at the American premiere in Boston in 1965. *A floresta e jovem a chea de vida (The Forest Is Young and Vital)*—the title is a quotation from an Angolan guerrilla—was introduced at the International Festival of Contemporary Music in VENICE in 1966. Another opera, *The Red Mantle,* was introduced by the ZÜRICH OPERA in 1966–67. Nono is married to SCHOENBERG's daughter.

Non piangere, Liù, Calaf's words of consolation to Liù for her distress at his endangering his life to win Turandot, in Act I of PUCCINI'S TURANDOT.

Non più andrai, Figaro's mocking instructions on how to behave as a soldier, in Act I of MOZART'S THE MARRIAGE OF FIGARO. Mozart has Don Giovanni's private band play a portion of this aria as the Don eats supper in the **Non più di fiori,** Vitellia's rondo aria, one of the most famous vocal excerpts climactic scene in DON GIOVANNI.

in MOZART'S LA CLEMENZA DI TITO, in the final scene.

Non più mesta accata al fuoco, Cinderella's coloratura aria in ROSSINI'S LA CENERENTOLA, Act II.

Non, sans toi, je ne puis vivre, Admetos' refusal to accept Alceste's sacrifice of her life to save his own, insisting he cannot live without her, in Act II of GLUCK'S ALCESTE.

Non sapete, Rafaele's facetious reply to the Camorrists when asked what he sees to love in Maliella, in Act III of WOLF-FERRARI'S THE JEWELS OF THE MADONNA.

Non sapete quale affetto, Violetta's initial defiant refusal to Alfredo's father to give up Alfredo, in Act II of VERDI'S LA TRAVIATA.

Non sei mia figlia, Amonasro's angry condemnation of Aida when at first she refuses to betray Radames and help her own country, Ethiopia, in its war against Egypt, in Act III of VERDI'S AIDA.

Non siate ritrosi, Guglielmo's passionate but frustrated wooing of Fiordiligi in Act I, Scene 3, of MOZART'S COSÌ FAN TUTTE.

Non so più cosa son, Cherubino's song about love, inspired by one of the Countess' ribbons, in Act I of MOZART'S THE MARRIAGE OF FIGARO.

No, Pagliaccio non son!, Canio, stepping out of his role as Pagliaccio, crying out to Nedda (impersonating Columbine) that he is Pagliaccio no longer but Canio, Nedda's husband, in the play-within-a-play sequence in Act II of LEONCAVALLO'S PAGLIACCI.

No! pazzo son! guardate, Des Grieux's plea to the sea captain to permit him to accompany Manon to her exile, in Act III of PUCCINI'S MANON LESCAUT.

Nordica, Lillian (born Norton), soprano. Born Farmington, Me., May 12, 1857; died Batavia, Java, May 10, 1914. One of the most celebrated Wagnerian sopranos of her generation, she began music study with John O'Neal at the New England Conservatory in Boston and continued in Milan with Antonio Sangiovanni. On Mar. 8, 1879, she made her debut at the Manzoni Theater in Milan in DON GIOVANNI, using the stage name of Nordica. Numerous performances followed in Italy, Russia, and Germany, leading to her successful debut at the PARIS OPÉRA on Apr. 22, 1882, as MARGUERITE. Her American debut took place at the Academy of Music in New York on Nov. 23, 1883, once again as Marguerite. For the next four seasons she appeared in New York and other American cities under Colonel MAPLESON's direction. After making her COVENT GARDEN debut on Mar. 27, 1887, she appeared in London each season until 1893, either at Covent Garden or DRURY LANE. Back in America, she made her bow at the METROPOLITAN OPERA on Mar. 27, 1890, in IL TROVATORE.

In 1894 she appeared in BAYREUTH as ELSA. Her success was so striking that then and there she decided to specialize in Wagnerian roles. After a period of study with Julius Kriese in Bayreuth, she appeared for the first time as ISOLDE in 1895 at the Metropolitan Opera. Henceforth she appeared in all the principal soprano roles of the Wagnerian music dramas, acclaimed for her stirring interpretations of the three BRÜNNHILDE roles, Isolde, and KUNDRY. She was an actress of outstanding magnetism who brought nobility to each of her characterizations; and her voice combined beauty with dramatic force. Her last appearance at the Metropolitan took place on Dec. 8, 1909, in the role of Isolde. For a while she appeared with other opera companies in America. A nervous breakdown compelled her to leave the stage, and she concentrated for a while on recitals. In the fall of 1913 she embarked on a tour of the world, planning it as her farewell to a professional career. Her ship was wrecked in the Malay archipelago. Taken to Java, Nordica died there.

At one period in her life Nordica was fired with the ambition to create an American Bayreuth at Harmon-on-the-Hudson, New York. The project never grew beyond the planning stage. In 1927 the Nordica Memorial Association was organized to buy and renovate her birthplace in Maine and make it a museum for mementos of her career.

Noréna, Eidé (born Kaja Hansen Eidé), soprano. Born Horten, Norway, Apr. 26, 1884; died Switzerland, Nov. 19, 1968. She began her career as concert singer after a period of music study in Oslo. Her opera debut took place with the Oslo Opera in GLUCK's ORFEO ED EURIDICE. She then returned to more study of singing in Weimar, London, Italy, and Paris. A successful audition with TOSCANINI brought her a contract for LA SCALA, where she made her debut in RIGOLETTO; it was for this occasion that she permanently assumed the stage name of Eidé Noréna. After appearances at La Scala, COVENT GARDEN, and the PARIS OPÉRA, she came to the United States and for six years was a member of the CHICAGO OPERA. On Feb. 9, 1933, she made her debut at the METROPOLITAN OPERA in LA BOHÈME. She remained at the Metropolitan through the 1937–38 season, after which she returned to Europe to sing at the Paris Opéra and other leading opera houses.

Norina, a young widow (soprano) in DONIZETTI's DON PASQUALE, a role created by Giulia GRISI.

Norma, opera in four (originally two) acts by BELLINI. Libretto by Felice ROMANI, based on a tragedy by L. A. Soumet. Premiere: La Scala, Dec. 26, 1831. American premiere: Park Theater, New York City, Feb. 25, 1841.

Characters: Norma, high priestess of the Druid Temple of Esus (soprano), a role created by Giuditta PASTA; Oroveso, the Archdruid, her father (bass); Clotilda, her confidante (soprano); Adalgisa, virgin of the Temple of Esus (mezzo-soprano); Pollione, Roman proconsul (tenor); Flavio, his centurion (tenor); priests; warriors; virgins of the temple; the two children of Norma and Pollione. The setting is Gaul during the Roman occupation, about 50 B.C.

Act I. Night in the Druid's sacred forest. Norma performs a sacred rite as the Gallic soldiers and Druid priests implore the gods for aid in destroying the Roman oppressors ("Dell' aura tua profetica"). When the Druids depart, Pollione reveals to Flavio that Norma has violated her holy vow by bearing him two sons. Pollione further confesses that he is in love with Adalgisa ("Meco all' altar di Venere"). At the sudden return of the Druids, Pollione and Flavio conceal themselves. Norma appeals to her people not to revolt, for the time is not yet ripe. She then prays for peace ("Casta diva") and laments privately that the hatred of her people for the Romans must inevitably mean hatred for her beloved Pollione ("Ah! bello a me ritorna"). When she departs, followed by the Druids, Adalgisa appears. Tormented by her love for Pollione, she begs the gods to rescue her ("Deh! proteggimi, o Dio!"). Pollione approaches her. At first she resists him, but he is persuasive ("Va, crudele") and she cannot resist him. She rushes into his arms, and they decide to escape to Rome.

Act II. Norma's dwelling. Norma reveals to Clotilda that Pollione is about to return to Rome, a development that causes her no little anxiety. Adalgisa, unaware of Norma's love for Pollione, comes to confess that she has fallen in love and must therefore desert the temple. Norma is sympathetic ("Ah si, fa core, abbracciami"). When Pollione appears, Norma and Adalgisa realize that they love the same man. Norma curses the proconsul for his treachery, while Adalgisa begs for some explanation ("O! di qual sei tu"). Pollione entreats Norma to direct her anger solely against him. Norma is summoned to the temple for the performance of her rites, and Pollione rushes away.

Act III. Norma's dwelling. Tortured by Pollione's infidelity, Norma decides to kill him and their children and then to destroy herself on a funeral pyre. She is, however, incapable of summoning the strength to kill the children. She begs Adalgisa to take care of them after her own death ("Deh! con te li prendi"). Adalgisa entreats Norma not to commit suicide but to be influenced by her maternal instincts and love ("Mira, o Norma"). Further, she insists that she will renounce Pollione and urge him to return to the mother of his children.

Act IV. In the woods, near the temple. The Gallic warriors and Druids have gathered to plan military action against the Romans. Clotilda informs Norma that Pollione has refused Adalgisa's request that he return to Norma. Aroused, Norma calls on her people to wage relentless war on the Romans, and the people respond with cries of vengeance ("Guerra! le Galliche selve!"). Pollione is brought to Norma. She snatches a dagger and advances toward him, claiming that now he is in her power ("In mia mano alfin tu sei"). But she is unable to kill the man she loves. She promises him his freedom if he renounces Adalgisa. He refuses to do so. Norma now turns to her people and confesses that she had desecrated her vows and must be sacrificed. To Pollione she repeats her love vows, and her confidence that they will be reunited in death ("Qual cor tradisti"). Profoundly moved, Pollione now asks to die with Norma. Norma takes his hand and leads him onto the funeral pyre.

Of all Bellini's operas, *Norma* is the public's favorite. It was also the composer's favorite. He once said: "If I were shipwrecked at sea, I would leave all the rest of my operas and try to save *Norma*." While the work has scenes of pageantry and moments of ringing grandeur, it rises to its greatest heights in its lyricism, as in the justly celebrated "Casta diva" of Norma, and the poignant opening scene of the third act. The simplicity and directness of Bellini's art led WAGNER to express enthusiasm for *Norma*, which reminded him "of the dignity of the Greek tragedy. . . . The music is noble and great, simple and grandiose in style." *Norma* was a failure at its premiere, but LA SCALA kept on performing the work until it became a triumphant success.

Normanno, Lord Ashton's follower (tenor) in DONIZETTI'S LUCIA DI LAMMERMOOR.

Nose, The, comic opera in two acts by SHOSTAKOVICH. Libretto by Zamiatin, Ionin, Preiss, and Shostakovich, based on a story by GOGOL. Premiere: Leningrad, Jan. 13, 1930. American premiere: Santa Fe Opera, N.M., August 11, 1965. This was Shostakovich's first opera. When initially produced it was a failure and was set aside for many years. Significant revivals in the 1960's, however—notably by the Düsseldorf Opera on June 27, 1963, and by the STAATSOPER in East Berlin on Feb. 23, 1969—have placed this satire among Shostakovich's significant works. The score is described by James Helme Sutcliffe as "athletic and sharply etched in acidulous instrumental tones, with long stretches for percussion alone and even a jew's harp solo—the amazing self-creation of a twenty-two-year-old. The musical style is less subjective than the 'reform' symphonies and has none of the turgid 'back to TCHAIKOVSKY' sound of those works." The comical text deals with Platon Kovalyev losing his nose while shaving, his efforts to place an advertisement in the papers for it, and his final successful attempt to retrieve it from a government official on whom it was found.

Nothung! Nothung! Neidliches Schwert!, Siegfried's narrative while forging his sword in Act I of WAGNER'S SIEGFRIED.

Nothung! so nenn ich dich, Schwert, Siegmund's apostrophe to the sword, as he removes it from the trunk of the tree in Hunding's house at the end of Act I of WAGNER'S DIE WALKÜRE.

Notre Dame de Paris, novel by Victor HUGO, the source of operas by DARGOMIZHSKY, William Henry Fry, Felipe Pedrell, Franz Schmidt, and Arthur Goring Thomas, among others.

Notte e giorno, Leporello's angry denunciation of his employer, Don Giovanni, for working him night and day, in the opening of MOZART'S DON GIOVANNI.

Nouguès, Jean, composer. Born Bordeaux, Apr. 25, 1875; died Paris, Aug. 28, 1932. He wrote his first opera, *Le Roi du Papagey,* when he was only sixteen. After a period of music study in Paris he completed his first mature opera, *Yannha,* performed in Bordeaux in 1897. In 1904 he produced *Thamyris.* The greatest success of his career was QUO VADIS, his finest work, introduced in Nice on Feb. 9, 1909, and soon after acclaimed in Paris, London, Milan, Philadelphia, and New York. His other operas: *La Mort de Tintagiles* (1905); *Chiquito* (1909); *L'Auberge rouge* (1910); *La Vendetta* (1911); *L'Aigle* (1912); *L'Eclaircie* (1914).

Nourrit, Adolphe, tenor. Born Paris, Mar. 3, 1802; died Naples, Mar. 8, 1839. The creator of principal tenor roles in some of the outstanding French operas of the early nineteenth century, he was the son of Louis Nourrit, a leading tenor of the PARIS OPÉRA. After some study with Manuel GARCÍA, Adolphe made his opera debut at the Paris Opéra on Sept. 10, 1821, in GLUCK'S IPHIGÉNIE EN TAURIDE. In 1826 he succeeded his father as principal tenor of the Opéra. Within the next decade he appeared in numerous world premieres, many of these operas being written for him. Among the roles he created were the leading tenor parts in LA MUETTE DE PORTICI, LA JUIVE, ROBERT LE DIABLE, LES HUGUENOTS, MOÏSE (revised French version), and WILLIAM TELL. It was on Nourrit's advice that HALÉVY interpolated into *La Juive* ELÉAZAR's celebrated aria, with Nourrit himself writing the text; Nourrit also suggested to MEYERBEER the abrupt ending to the popular duet in *Les Huguenots.* When, in 1836, the Paris Opéra engaged Gilbert DUPREZ as a principal tenor, Nourrit regarded it as a personal affront and tendered his resignation. He appeared at the Opéra for the last time on Apr. 1, 1837. He then went to Italy to study the Italian style and traditions with

DONIZETTI and to make appearances at LA SCALA and in Naples. The immense popularity of Duprez in Paris embittered him, a feeling that was heightened by his feeling that he did not receive in Italy the acclaim he deserved. His depression led to his suicide in Naples. In the years before he left France, Nourrit taught at the Paris Conservatory. He also wrote scenarios for ballets performed by Fanny Elssler and Maria Taglioni.

Nous vivrons à Paris, duet of Manon and Des Grieux, concluding Act I of MASSENET'S MANON, as they plan to flee to Paris.

Novák, Vítěszlav, composer. Born Kamenitz, Bohemia, Dec. 5, 1870; died Skuteč, Slovakia, July 18, 1949. He combined the study of law with that of music, the latter at the Prague Conservatory. His teacher in composition, Antonin DVOŘÁK, induced him to specialize in music. After 1900 Novák began writing music with a strongly Bohemian character. In this style he completed his first opera, *The Sprite of the Castle* (1914). Later operas: *Karlstein* (1916); *The Lantern* (1922); *John the Fiddler* (1925). From 1909 to 1925 he was professor of composition at the Prague Conservatory. In 1918 he became professor at the Master School there and in 1919, director. In 1946 he received the honorary title of National Artist from the Republic of Czechoslovakia.

Novotna, Jarmila, soprano. Born Prague, Sept. 23, 1907. She was fifteen when she sang for Emmy DESTINN, who encouraged her to study music seriously. After a year of training, Novotna made her operatic debut at the National Theater in Prague on June 27, 1926, in LA TRAVIATA. She then went to Milan for additional study and for appearances in various Italian opera houses. In 1928 she was engaged by the BERLIN STATE OPERA, with which she toured Austria, Paris, and Salzburg. From 1933 to 1938 she was a principal soprano of the VIENNA STATE OPERA. On Oct. 18, 1939,

she made her American debut with the SAN FRANCISCO OPERA in MADAMA BUTTERFLY. Her METROPOLITAN OPERA debut took place on Jan. 5, 1940, in LA BOHÈME. She remained at the Metropolitan through the 1950–51 season and after that made intermittent appearances there. An exceptionally beautiful woman, she has also made occasional appearances in nonsinging dramatic roles on the stage, in motion pictures, and in television.

Noye's Fludde, a miracle play in one act with music by BRITTEN. Libretto based on the Chester miracle play of the same name. Premiere: Aldeburgh Festival, 1958. American premiere: New York City, Mar. 16, 1959. The text is a retelling in Chaucerian English of the Biblical story of Noah. Britten planned it as a church pageant, involving a children's orchestra and chorus to supplement adult performers and to permit the congregation to join in the performance from time to time. One of the most moving moments is the prayer to God by the children and adults aboard the ark that they be saved from the storm. "It was a marvelous moment," wrote Ross Parmenter. "And ... one felt the miracle that had ended the storm. At the same time, one marveled at Benjamin Britten's imagination in conceiving anything so dramatic and touching that could be presented in a church mostly with amateur forces."

nozze di Figaro, Le, *see* MARRIAGE OF FIGARO, THE.

nozze di Teti e di Peleo, Le (The Wedding of Thetis and Peleus), opera by CAVALLI. Libretto by Orazio Perisiani. Premiere: Teatro San Cassiano, Venice, 1639. This is the first work in operatic history specifically called an "opera." The composer's designation was *opera scenica*. All preceding musicodramatic works had been called DRAMMA PER MUSICA.

Nuit d'hyménée, love duet of Roméo and Juliette just before their final parting in Act IV of GOUNOD'S ROMÉO ET JULIETTE.

Nuitter, Charles Louis (born Truinet), writer on music, librettist, and translator. Born Paris, Apr. 24, 1828; died there Feb. 24, 1899. A prolific writer and a devotee of the theater, he wrote librettos for nine of OFFENBACH'S OPÉRAS COMIQUES. For performances at the THÉÂTRE LYRIQUE and the PARIS OPÉRA he translated into French many operas, including AIDA, LOHENGRIN, THE MAGIC FLUTE, OBERON, RIENZI, and TANNHÄUSER. He also revised the libretto of VERDI'S MACBETH for French presentation. In 1865 he was appointed archivist of the Opéra. He wrote several books of operatic interest, including *Le Nouvel Opéra* (1875), *L'Histoire et description au nouvel opéra* (1884), and, with Ernest Thoinon, *Les Origines de l'opéra français* (1886).

Nume, custode e vindice, Ramfis' scene with chorus in Act I, Scene 2, of VERDI'S AIDA, praying for divine protection.

Nun eilt herbei, Mrs. Ford's aria in Act II of NICOLAI'S THE MERRY WIVES OF WINDSOR.

Nuns' Chorus, The, see AH, SE L'ERROR T'INGOMBRA.

Nun sei bedankt, mein lieber Schwan, Lohengrin's farewell to his swan in Act I of WAGNER'S LOHENGRIN.

Nureddin, young man (tenor) in love with Margiana in CORNELIUS' THE BARBER OF BAGDAD.

Nuri, a village girl (soprano) in D'ALBERT'S TIEFLAND.

O

O amore, o bella luce, Fritz's song when he realizes he loves Suzel, in Act III of MACAGNI'S L'AMICO FRITZ.

O amor! sguardo di stella, Falstaff's hymn to the beauty of Mistress Ford, with whom he is contemplating a rendezvous, in Act I, Scene 1, of VERDI'S FALSTAFF.

O beau pays de la Touraine (O vago suol della Turrena), Marguerite de Valois's rhapsody over the beauty of the Touraine countryside, in Act II of MEYERBEER'S LES HUGUENOTS.

Obéissons quand leur voix appelle, Manon's GAVOTTE in which she espouses the philosophy that life is meant for dance and song, in Act III of MASSENET'S MANON.

Oberon, opera in three acts by WEBER. Libretto by James Robinson Planché, based on Sotheby's translation of Wieland's poem *Oberon*. Premiere: Covent Garden, Apr. 12, 1826. American premiere: Park Theater, New York City, Oct. 9, 1828.

Characters: Oberon, King of the fairies (tenor); Titania, his queen (speaking part); Puck, his attendant (contralto); Harun-al-Rashid, Caliph of Bagdad (bass); Rezia, his daughter (soprano); Fatima, her attendant (mezzo-soprano); Sir Huon de Bordeaux (tenor); Sherasmin, his squire (baritone); Babekan, a Persian prince (baritone); Mesrour, chief of the harem guards (acting part); Almanzor, Emir of Tunis (baritone); Charlemagne (bass); Droll (contralto); Abdallah, a corsair (baritone); Roschana, Almanzor's wife (contralto); elves, nymphs, sylphs, mermaids, spirits; ladies, gentlemen, servants; Moors and pirates. The action takes place in France, Bagdad, and Tunis at the beginning of the ninth century.

The overture is a favorite in the symphonic repertory. It opens with a horn call and proceeds with a pastoral episode dominated by a melody for cellos. In the main body of the overture, the first theme is energetic and feverish, the second is a song for solo clarinet, and the third an excerpt from Rezia's aria, "Ocean, thou mighty monster."

Act I, Scene 1. Oberon's palace. The scene opens with the chorus of elves, "Light as fairy feet." After a quarrel, Queen Titania vows never to return to her husband until he finds two lovers who will remain true in spite of every obstacle. Puck suggests a candidate to Oberon: Sir Huon de Bordeaux, knight of Charlemagne's court, who is in disgrace for having killed Charlemagne's son. For his penance, Huon is sent to Bagdad to kill the man who sits at the Caliph's right hand and then claim the Caliph's daughter, Rezia, as bride. Oberon conjures a vision of Rezia for Huon; at the same time he gives Rezia a vision of Huon. The two fall in love. To aid Huon in his quest, Oberon provides him with a magic horn. Huon is then transported to Bagdad, expressing his delight in the *romanza* "From boyhood trained."

Scene 2. The Caliph's harem. Rezia refuses to consider Prince Babekan as a husband, since she is in love with Huon. Fatima announces the arrival of Huon, who is ready to save Rezia from the Prince.

Act II, Scene 1. The Caliph's palace. Prince Babekan is sitting at the Caliph's side. Huon forces his way into the palace, finds Rezia, and takes her in his arms ("Ruler of this awful hour"). Prince Babekan opposes him and is killed. Sounding his magic horn, Huon is able to escape.

Scene 2. The palace garden. Sherasmin and Fatima vow to love each other. Oberon comes to help Huon and Rezia escape from Bagdad. He warns them against being unfaithful. After the flight, Fatima sings a nostalgic air, "A lonely Arab maid." They arrive at the harbor from which the lovers can proceed to Greece ("Over the dark blue waters").

Scene 3. A cave on a desolate island.

Oberon must now test the fidelity of his lovers. Puck orders the spirits to wreck the ship ("Spirits of earth and sea"). Huon carries Rezia ashore. While Huon is searching for help, Rezia voices her awe at the might of the ocean ("Ocean, thou mighty monster"). Pirates capture Rezia and sell her to the Emir of Tunis. Since Huon has lost his magic horn, he is unable to save her.

Act III, Scene 1. Garden of the Emir's palace. Fatima, now a slave of the Emir, is joined by her beloved Sherasmin. They inform Huon that Rezia is also a slave and advise him to assume the disguise of a gardener in order to save her. Before leaving, Huon's delight is expressed in a rondo, "I revel in hope and joy again."

Scene 2. A hall in the palace. Rezia is grief-stricken at her fate ("Grieve my heart"). The Emir forces his love on Rezia, but she is saved by the sudden appearance of Huon.

Scene 3. The Emir's palace. Huon and Rezia are to be burned alive. But Sherasmin has found Huon's magic horn. When Huon blows on it, his enemies become spellbound and motionless. Oberon and Titania, now reconciled, appear and save the lovers, blessing them for their fidelity. Huon and Rezia are then transported back to the court of Charlemagne, where the ruler forgives Huon.

While *Oberon* is a cornerstone on which German Romantic opera rests, it is a work more often discussed than performed. The sad truth is that it is incapable of sustaining interest, however well it is presented. It has magnificent pages: the remarkable overture, which invoked for Romanticism a new fairy world; the vocal scena, "Ocean, thou mighty monster," surely one of the finest pages of dramatic writing before WAGNER; such delightful examples of Romantic song as Huon's aria, "From boyhood trained." But for all these intermittent flights toward greatness, the score as a whole does little to lift the absurd and cumbersome play above a prevailing level of mediocrity. Yet the premiere of *Oberon* was the crowning triumph of Weber's career. He wrote it on a commission from COVENT GARDEN (which explains why it has an English text). Weber himself conducted the premiere and received an unprecedented acclaim, "an honor which no composer had ever before obtained in England," he wrote. It was his last taste of success; less than two months later he was dead.

Oberthal, Count, ruler of Dordrecht (baritone) in MEYERBEER'S LE PROPHÈTE.

Oberto, Conte di Bonifacio (Oberto, Count of Bonifacio), opera in two acts by VERDI. Libretto by Piazza and Solera. Premiere: La Scala, Nov. 17, 1839. American premiere: Chicago, Oct., 1903 (concert version). This was Verdi's first opera. The main characters are the Count Oberto, his daughter Leonora, and the man who has seduced her, Riccardo. Riccardo kills Oberto in a duel and leaves Italy forever. As the final curtain falls we find Leonora in the depths of despair at having lost both her father and her lover.

Verdi's first opera was so successful that he received commissions to write three more. But he was a long way from realizing himself creatively. Francis Toye notes that "there is little trace of the power of characterization so noticeable in the later operas." Toye, however, does single out two of Riccardo's arias as worthy of attention, "the second, with its beautiful phrase deploring the death of Oberto, being particularly good." The opera is rarely given except to commemorate Verdi anniversaries, as happened in 1939 in Busseto and at LA SCALA in 1951.

Obigny, *see* D'OBIGNY.

O Carlo, ascolta, Rodrigo's dying farewell to Don Carlos in Act IV, Scene 2, of VERDI'S DON CARLOS.

Ocean, thou mighty monster, Rezia's aria in Act II, Scene 3, of WEBER'S OBERON, as she contemplates the fearsome grandeur of the ocean.

Ochs, Baron, the Marschallin's cousin (bass) in Richard STRAUSS'S DER ROSEN-KAVALIER.

O ciel, dove vai tu?, *see* O CIEL, OÙ COUREZ-VOUS?

O ciel, où courez-vous? (O ciel, dove vai tu?), duet of Raoul and Valentine as they vow eternal love to each other, in Act IV of MEYERBEER'S LES HUGUENOTS.

O cieli azzurri, the opening words of Aida's aria, "O patria mia," in Act III of VERDI'S AIDA.

O Colombina, Harlequin's Serenade in Act II of LEONCAVALLO'S PAGLIACCI.

Octavian, a young gentleman (mezzo-soprano), the Cavalier of the Rose, in Richard STRAUSS'S DER ROSENKAVALIER, who is carrying on a love affair with the Marschallin but finally marries Sophie.

O Dei, che smania è questo, the dramatic recitative of Sextus in MOZART'S LA CLEMENZA DI TITO. Though Sextus is a male role it is sung today by a mezzo-soprano, since the part was originally written for a CASTRATO.

O del mio dolce ardor, Paris' song of love in Act I of GLUCK'S PARIDE ED ELENA.

Ode to the Evening Star, *see* O DU MEIN HOLDER ABENDSTERN.

O Dieu! de quelle ivresse, Hoffmann's expression of passion for Giulietta in Act II of OFFENBACH'S THE TALES OF HOFFMANN.

O Dieu, Dieu de nos pères, the Passover Scene sung by Eléazar, Rachel, and chorus in Act II of HALÉVY'S LA JUIVE.

O! di qual sei tu, trio of Norma, Pollione, and Adalgisa, in which Norma curses Pollione for betraying her for Adalgisa, while Adalgisa also begs Pollione for some explanation, in Act II of BELLINI'S NORMA.

O dolci mani, tender duet of Tosca and Cavaradossi in Act III of PUCCINI'S TOSCA, as they meet in Cavaradossi's prison cell.

O don fatale, the most famous aria in VERDI'S DON CARLOS (Act IV, Scene 2), in which Princess Eboli bewails the fact that her beauty has caused so much harm to those she loves.

O du mein holder Abendstern, Wolfram's Ode to the Evening Star in Act III of WAGNER'S TANNHÄUSER.

Odyssey, The, *see* HOMER.

Oedipe, a lyric tragedy in four acts by Georges Enesco. Libretto by Edmond Fleg, based on SOPHOCLES. Premiere: Paris Opéra, Mar. 10, 1936. One of the interesting technical features of Enesco's powerful score is its occasional excursions into MICROTONAL writing.

Oedipus, the subject of two tragedies by SOPHOCLES, *King Oedipus* and *Oedipus at Colonus*. The first is here summarized. Oedipus, King of Thebes, discovers that Laius, whom he has murdered, was actually his own father; also that he, Oedipus, is married to his own mother, Jocasta. In his horror, Oedipus plucks out his eyes while Jocasta hangs herself. *King Oedipus* has been made into operas by Georges Enesco, LEONCAVALLO, and ORFF. STRAVINSKY'S OEDIPUS REX is an opera-oratorio.

Oedipus der Tyrann (Oedipus the Tyrant), opera in three acts by ORFF. Libretto based on Friedrich Hölderlin's translation of the SOPHOCLES drama. Premiere: Württemberg State Opera, Stuttgart, Dec. 11, 1959. This is the second of Orff's trilogy of music dramas based on tragedies of Sophocles and AESCHYLUS. The first was ANTIGONAE in 1949. *Oedipus der Tyrann* was written between 1957 and 1959. The last was PROMETHEUS in 1968. In *Oedipus der Tyrann,* as in the other two musical dramas, the composer is more concerned with spiritual than dramatic values. Some of the score is sung, a good deal of it is song reduced almost to speech, and a few fragments are actually spoken. "The sung portions," says Conrad L. Osborne, "consist primarily of chantlike repetitions of the same note, emphatically accented in the rhythms or broken into oft-repeated little patterns of alternated intervals." As in most of his operas, Orff makes extensive use of percussive effects with various types of drums, tam-tam, xylophones, cymbals, and the piano used percussively. Woodwinds and brass are used sparingly, and there are no stringed instruments played with bows.

Oedipus Rex (Oedipus the King), opera-oratorio in two acts by STRAVINSKY. Libretto by Jean Cocteau, based on the SOPHOCLES drama translated into Latin by Danielou. Premiere: Paris, May 30, 1927 (as oratorio); Vienna, Feb. 23, 1928 (as opera). American premiere: Boston, Feb. 24, 1928 (as oratorio); Metropolitan Opera in Philadelphia, Apr. 10, 1931 (as opera). It is frequently presented in the concert hall as an oratorio and in the opera house as an opera.

O fänd' ich Jubelweisen, chorus of the people of Brabant hailing Lohengrin as victor in his contest with Telramund, at the close of Act I of WAGNER'S LOHENGRIN.

Offenbach, Jacques (born Eberst), composer. Born Cologne, June 20, 1819; died Paris, Oct. 4, 1880. A master of French comic opera (OPÉRA BOUFFE), he also produced an outstanding serious opera, THE TALES OF HOFFMANN. The son of a synagogue cantor, his musical talent led to his being enrolled in the Paris Conservatory, the rule forbidding admission to foreigners being waived for his benefit. Offenbach was unhappy with the discipline at the conservatory and remained there only a year. He continued to study privately: cello with Pierre Norblin, composition with Jacques HALÉVY. His studies ended, he began playing in the orchestra of the OPÉRA-COMIQUE. In 1850 he was appointed musical director of the Comédie-Française, continuing in this capacity for five years. During this period he began writing comic operas. Unable to get them performed, he decided to open a theater of his own. This was the Bouffes-Parisiens, which opened on July 5, 1855, with his musical satire, *Les Deux Aveugles.* Offenbach wrote for his theater twenty-five musical satires, farces, and comic operas within a three-year period. He became an idol of Parisian theater-goers. In 1858 his greatest *opéra bouffe,* ORPHEUS IN THE UNDERWORLD

(*Orphée aux Enfers*), was introduced. The public did not at first respond favorably to this satire on the Olympian gods. But when the critic Jules Janin attacked it for blasphemy and profanation, curiosity was piqued and the opera began playing to crowded houses. After 1861 Offenbach gave up his own theater but continued writing outstandingly successful works for other managers, including LA BELLE HÉLÈNE (1865), *La Vie parisienne* (1866), and LA PÉRICHOLE (1868). In 1872 Offenbach opened a new theater, the Gaîté, which failed three years later, overwhelming Offenbach with debts. To satisfy his creditors he allocated to them all his income for the next few years; when this did not prove sufficient to pay his bills, he undertook an American tour in 1876, which was helpful. Back in Paris, he continued writing comic operas; but the old touch was no longer there, and none of them found favor. Offenbach now avoided the society of his one-time friends and admirers and lived in comparative seclusion. He began working on a serious opera for the first time in his life: *The Tales of Hoffman.* He lived to complete all but the orchestration of the last two acts and the epilogue, which was carried out by Ernest GUIRAUD; but he died four months before the opera's premiere at the Opéra-Comique on Feb. 10, 1881.

Essentially a composer of music in the lighter vein, Offenbach had the gifts of verve, spontaneity, wit, satire, and a ready flow of lovable melodies. But his one serious opera gave proof that he might also have been one of France's foremost writers of grand opera.

O fiori, Angelica's air as she gathers the herbs and flowers from which she extracts the poison for her suicide, in PUCCINI'S SUOR ANGELICA.

Of Mice and Men, opera in three acts by FLOYD. Libretto by the composer, based on the novel by John Steinbeck. World premiere: Seattle Opera, Jan. 20, 1970. The central characters of the opera are two ranch laborers, George and his half-witted friend, Lennie. They dream of the time when they can buy a ranch of their own but are frustrated when the simpleton, Lennie, commits murder and George, out of compassion for his friend, shoots him rather than have him face the law.

In explaining his musical treatment, Floyd said in *Opera News:* "The subject is a difficult one to handle, because it naturally suggests a specific locale and very earthy characters, but you obviously can't sustain an opera for two and a half hours with ranch music. I've tried to distinguish between the most emotionally expressive music for the two main characters, George and Lennie, and the music that comments on the drama or underscores the action. George's and Lennie's is essentially simpler, though sufficiently stylized. . . . Yes, there are some folklike elements, such as a ballad first heard after the death of Candy's dog in Act I, which foreshadows George's ultimate mercy-killing of Lennie. I use this as a kind of loneliness motif that recurs and is heard for the last time in the end, whistled by the ballad singer. It is the kind of dramatic and musical comment that can probably exist only in opera."

O gioia, o gioia, Uberto's air expressing delight in getting his servant, Serpina, to marry him, in PERGOLESI'S LA SERVA PADRONA.

O gioia la nube leggera, Suzanne's expression of delight at the joys of smoking in WOLF-FERRARI'S THE SECRET OF SUZANNE.

O giovinetto, chorus of the people protesting the imminent execution of the Persian prince, in Act I of PUCCINI'S TURANDOT.

O grandi occhi, Fedora's love song to Vladimir as she looks at his photo in Act I of GIORDANO'S FEDORA.

O grido di quest' anima, Enzo's duet with Barnaba in Act I of PONCHIELLI'S LA GIOCONDA when he learns that Laura is still in love with him.

Oh! de' verd'anni miei, Don Carlos' soliloquy after overhearing that Ernani and Silva are plotting against him, in Act III of VERDI'S ERNANI.

Ohimè! morir mi sento, Amneris' expression of despair at realizing she was the cause of Radames' destruction, in Act IV, Scene 1, of VERDI'S AIDA.

O holdes Bild, the rapturous love duet or "dove duo" of Nureddin and Margiana, in Act II of CORNELIUS' THE BARBER OF BAGDAD.

Oh! qu'est-ce que c'est? . . . tes cheveux, Pelléas' apostrophe to Mélisande's hair as it covers his face, in Act III, Scene 1, of DEBUSSY'S PELLÉAS ET MÉLISANDE.

Oh vecchio cor che batti, the Doge's aria in Act I of VERDI'S I DUE FOSCARI, one of the best known vocal excerpts from this rarely performed opera.

O inferno, Amelia qui!, Gabriele's aria in Act II of VERDI'S SIMON BOCCANEGRA, revealing his torments and doubts when ordered to kill Boccanegra.

Oiseau blue, L', *see* BLUE BIRD, THE.

oiseaux dans la charmille, Les (Doll Song), coloratura aria sung to entertain the company by Olympia, a mechanical doll, in Act I of OFFENBACH'S TALES OF HOFFMANN.

O Isis und Osiris, Sarastro's invocation in Act II, Scene 1, of MOZART'S THE MAGIC FLUTE, entreating the gods to grant the lovers the power and courage to meet their coming tests and trials.

Olczewska, Maria (born Marie Berchtenbreitner), mezzo-soprano. Born Augsburg, Ger., Aug. 12, 1892; died Baden, Austria, May 17, 1969. She began her vocal career in operetta, where she was heard by the conductor Arthur NIKISCH who engaged her in 1920 for the Leipzig Opera. After three years there, she appeared for thirteen years with the VIENNA STATE OPERA. At the same time, between 1924 and 1932, she was principal mezzo-soprano at COVENT GARDEN and with the CHICAGO OPERA. On Jan. 16, 1933, she made her debut at the METROPOLITAN OPERA as Brangäne in TRISTAN UND ISOLDE. She remained with the Metropolitan for two seasons, following which she continued her career in Europe. She distinguished herself particularly in the Wagnerian repertory, but she was also heard in French and Italian roles. In 1947 she was appointed professor of voice at the Vienna Conservatory.

Old Maid and the Thief, The, one-act comic opera by MENOTTI. Libretto by the composer. Premiere: NBC network, Apr. 22, 1939 (radio version); Philadelphia Opera Company, Feb. 11, 1949 (staged). Menotti wrote this opera expressly for radio presentation (it had been commissioned by the National Broadcasting Company). Miss Todd, an old maid, welcomes a tramp into her home as a permanent lodger. She treats him royally, but in her efforts to satisfy his ever-increasing needs, she resorts to stealing. When neighbors suspect the tramp of being the thief, Miss Todd urges him to escape. But the tramp insists that since he is innocent he will remain and that Miss Todd must pay for her crimes. Disillusioned, Miss Todd goes to the police with her sad story. While she is gone, the tramp escapes with Miss Todd's maid, carrying away everything portable. Thus (as the subtitle of the opera remarks) "a virtuous woman makes a thief of an honest man."

O légère hirondelle, Mireille's waltz aria in Act I of GOUNOD'S MIREILLE, expressing her joy in loving Vincent.

Olga, (1) a princess (soprano), heroine in RIMSKY-KORSAKOV'S IVAN THE TERRIBLE.

(2) Tatiana's sister (contralto) in TCHAIKOVSKY'S EUGENE ONEGIN.

O liberté, ma vie!, Jean's paean to liberty on being told he must enter a monastery, in Act I of MASSENET'S LE JONGLEUR DE NOTRE DAME.

Olivero, Magda, soprano. Born Saluzzo, Italy, 1914. She made her debut in Turin as Lauretta in GIANNI SCHICCHI in 1933. This was followed by appearances in major Italian opera houses in various Italian roles in which she revealed a prodigious vocal technique and extraordinary dramatic powers. Following her marriage in 1941 she went into retirement, from which she emerged in 1950–51 to appear as Adriana in ADRIANA LECOUVREUR, having promised its composer she would do so. Further appearances revealed there had been no deterioration in the quality of either her singing or acting during her long period of withdrawal from the stage. In the fall of 1967 she made a sensational American debut in DALLAS as MEDEA in CHERUBINI's opera, which led one critic to say "frankly I am at a loss to document the many miracles of heart and mind she accomplished with this thundering part." Her first appearance in the Eastern United States took place on Oct. 18, 1969, in Hartford, Conn., in *Adriana Lecouvreur*.

Olivier, a poet (baritone), in love with the Countess, in Richard STRAUSS's CAPRICCIO.

O Lola, Turiddu's off-stage SICILIANA (sung before the prelude ends) in MASCAGNI's CAVALLERIA RUSTICANA, praising his former sweetheart, Lola, now Alfio's wife.

O luce di quest' anima, Linda's aria in Act I of DONIZETTI's LINDA DI CHAMOUNIX, in praise of love.

Olympia, a mechanical doll (soprano), one of Hoffmann's loves, in OFFENBACH's THE TALES OF HOFFMANN, Act I.

Olympians, The, opera in three acts by BLISS. Libretto by J. B. Priestley. Premiere: Covent Garden, Sept. 29, 1949. Olympian gods are compelled to come down to earth as traveling actors but are permitted to return one night a year to their godly abode. Highlights of Bliss's score include a prayer to Venus, Mercury's dance, the off-stage chorus of the Bacchantes, and a bridal chorus with which the opera ends.

O ma femme! O ma bien aimée!, Roméo's lament at her tomb over the "death" of Juliette, in Act V of GOUNOD's ROMÉO ET JULIETTE.

O malheureuse Iphigénie, Iphigenia's lament closing Act II of GLUCK's IPHIGÉNIE EN TAURIDE.

O ma lyre immortelle, Sapho's aria about her art at the end of GOUNOD's SAPHO.

Ombra mai fù, the aria in HANDEL's SERSE that is known today as "Handel's Largo." *See* LARGO, HANDEL'S.

Ombre légère (Ombra leggiera), Dinorah's Shadow Dance aria in Act II of MEYERBEER's DINORAH, in which, having lost her sanity, she mistakes her shadow on a moonlit night as a welcome friend and proceeds to dance with it to the accompaniment of her singing.

Ombre palide, Alcina's air invoking the supernatural spirits, in HANDEL's ALCINA.

O Mimi, tu più non torni, Rodolfo's duet with Marcello in Act IV of PUCCINI's LA BOHÈME, in which Rodolfo recalls former happier days with Mimi.

O mio bambino caro, Lauretta's plea to her father to find a way for her to marry Rinuccio in PUCCINI's GIANNI SCHICCHI.

O mio Fernando, Leonora's air in Act III of DONIZETTI's LA FAVORITA, announcing her willingness to make any sacrifice required to save her beloved Fernando.

O mon cher amant, je te jure, the most celebrated air in OFFENBACH's LA PÉRICHOLE and one of his most famous melodies. It is the "letter song" in Act I sung by La Périchole as she writes a farewell note to Paquillo, with whom she is in love.

O mon enfant, Louise's father's song of consolation to his daughter after she has quarreled with her mother about giving up Julien, in Act I of CHARPENTIER's LOUISE.

O monumento, Barnaba's soliloquy in Act I of PONCHIELLI's LA GIOCONDA, gloating over his powers as a spy.

O Nadir, tendre ami de mon coeur, Zurga's lament over the disruption of his friendship with Nadir, in Act III of BIZET's LES PÊCHEURS DE PERLES.

O namenlose Freude!, the joyous duet of Florestan and Leonore in BEETHOVEN's FIDELIO, Act II, Scene 1, when they discover that the arrival of the Prime Minister at the prison is imminent and with it, Florestan's freedom.

O nature, Werther's invocation to nature in Act I of MASSENET's WERTHER.

Onegin, *see* EUGENE ONEGIN.

Onégin, Sigrid (born Hoffmann), contralto. Born Stockholm, June 1, 1891; died Magliasco, Switzerland, June 16, 1943. After studying singing with Resz, E. R. Weiss, and Di Ranieri, she made her opera debut in STUTTGART in 1912 as CARMEN. She was so successful that she was given twelve starring roles that season. In 1919 she was engaged by the MUNICH OPERA, where she was acclaimed in the WAGNER repertory. Her American opera debut took place at the METRO-POLITAN OPERA on Nov. 22, 1922, in AIDA. She remained at the Metropolitan through the 1923–24 season. From 1926 to 1933 she was principal contralto of the BERLIN STATE OPERA. She returned to the United States in 1934 for several opera and concert appearances.

135th Street, one-act opera by GERSHWIN. Libretto by Buddy De Sylva. Premiere: New York City, Aug. 29, 1922. The precursor by more than a decade of Gershwin's Negro folk opera, PORGY AND BESS, this one-act Negro jazz opera, originally entitled *Blue Monday,* received only a single performance in its first year—on opening night of the *Scandals of 1922,* the Broadway revue of which it was a part. It was removed from the revue because the producer regarded it as too gloomy. Though it contains two or three effective blues arias, the opera was too primitive, both in text and music, to survive very vigorously; but it did receive a number of revivals after 1922, including one on a coast-to-coast television broadcast.

O'Neill, Eugene, dramatist. Born New York City, Oct. 16, 1888; died Boston, Nov. 27, 1953. He won the Nobel Prize for literature in 1936 and the PULITZER PRIZE for drama three different times. Several of his plays have been made into operas: *Before Breakfast* (a MONODRAMA by Erik CHISHOLM, renamed *Dark Sonnet*); *The Emperor Jones* (GRUEN-BERG, Miroslav Ponc); *The Moon of the Caribbees* (LUALDI's *La luna dei Caraibi*); *Mourning Becomes Electra* (Marvin David Levy).

On me nomme Hélène, Hélène's invocation in OFFENBACH's LA BELLE HÉLÈNE, Act I, one of the most famous airs in the OPÉRA BOUFFE.

On me proposait d'être enflammé, Paquillo's air in Act III, Scene 1, of OFFEN-BACH's OPÉRA BOUFFE LA PÉRICHOLE, in which, imprisoned, he broods over his misery.

On ne Badine pas avec l'Amour, *see* MUSSET, ALFRED DE.

O nuit d'amour, second part of the love duet of Marguerite and Faust in Act III of GOUNOD's FAUST.

O nuit divine, love duet of Roméo and Juliette in Act II of GOUNOD's ROMÉO ET JULIETTE.

O nuit, étends sur eux ton ombre, Méphistophélès' invocation to the night that the lovers, Faust and Marguerite, be united, in Act III of GOUNOD's FAUST.

O padre mio, Manfredo's joyous aria upon his victorious homecoming from battle, in Act I of MONTEMEZZI's L'AMORE DEI TRE RE.

O Paradis (O paradiso), Vasco da Gama's rapturous tribute to the island of Madagascar, in Act IV of MEYERBEER's L'AFRICAINE.

O pastore, a pastoral chorus sung by the guests at a party given by Countess de Coigny, in Act I of GIORDANO's ANDREA CHÉNIER.

O patria mia, Aida's aria nostalgically recalling her Ethiopian homeland, in Act III of VERDI's AIDA.

opera, a dramatic performance, with costumes, scenery, and action, wholly or mostly sung to an orchestral accompaniment. In some operas the music is interrupted by passages of spoken dialogue; in others it is continuous, consisting of recitatives, arias, duets, trios and other ensemble numbers, choruses and ballets; in still others the music continues without definite demarcation into numbers. Opera represents a collaboration of text and music in which storytelling is combined with music's power to arouse emotions and create mood and atmosphere. Together they can achieve an expression which neither can achieve alone. At times in the history of opera the play has served merely as an excuse for the music—a convenient hook on which the composer hung his vocal and instrumental numbers—but in general the evolution of opera shows a continuous attempt to realize the musico-dramatic ideal of an integrated, artistic unity of good theater and music.

Origins of Opera. Though opera was formally born in 1597 with the performance of PERI'S DAFNE in Florence, the new art form was actually the creation of several men, a group including the noblemen BARDI and CORSI, the poet RINUCCINI, and the composers Vincenzo Galilei, Peri, and CAVALIERI. This group, known as the CAMERATA ("those who meet in a chamber"), aspired to restore the forms of Greek drama, including the dramatic use of music. A major problem was that the music of the Camerata's day was chiefly polyphonic. Giving equality to a group of voices, it was not suited for singing by a solo voice. Also, the complex texture of the music made clear articulation of the words difficult. The Camerata finally realized that (according to Giovanni Battista Doni, a seventeenth-century Florentine) "means must be found in the attempt to bring music closer to that of classical times, and to bring out the chief melody prominently so that the poetry could be clearly understandable." Obviously, a new form of music had to be created. Going for guidance to the Greeks, the Camerata came upon a treatise by Aristoxenus that said song should be patterned after speech. In Plato they read: "Let music be first of all language and rhythm, and secondly tone, and not vice versa." Gradually, the members of the group evolved a single-voiced melody, the *stilo rappresentativo,* or RECITATIVE. In 1590 Cavalieri used the new style in a series of musical scenes or pastorals. Soon after, Galilei created settings of the *Lamentations of Jeremiah.* To Peri went the assignment of using the new style in a dramatic presentation restoring the Greek drama. In 1597 he completed *Dafne,* which he described as a DRAMMA PER MUSICA. As the first stage work to be set to music from beginning to end, *Dafne* is the first opera ever written. But since the music of *Dafne* has been lost, musical historians usually point to Peri's second *dramma per musica,* EURIDICE, as the first opera. *Euridice* was introduced in Florence on Feb. 9, 1600, to acclaim. The Camerata felt that its restoration of classic Greek drama was successful; it did not realize that it had evolved a new art form. CACCINI followed Peri's lead in writing works in the new form. Their operas consisted of a continuous flow of recitatives: that is, the poetic lines of the text were sung with exaggerated inflections and were accompanied by a small orchestra of lutes, gambas, and harpsichord or organ. Occasionally, brief choruses and ballets were introduced to provide variety. Though the music was often impressive in its declamation, the use of the recitative style throughout an opera inevitably resulted in monotony.

Early Developments in Italy. After the Florentine originators, MONTEVERDI was the first significant composer of operas. His L'ORFEO, first heard in Mantua in 1607, is the earliest opera still occasionally performed. Monteverdi brought an expressiveness and dramatic impact to opera that it had not known before. His innovations are discussed in this volume in his biographical entry. Monteverdi's presence in Venice, where he settled in 1612, made that city the operatic center of Italy. The next notable figure of the Venetian school was CAVALLI (Monteverdi's pupil), the first composer to use the term *opera* for one of his productions. About 1685 a new school of opera composers emerged in Italy, the Neapolitan school, whose influence predominated until 1750. Its founder and guiding spirit was Alessandro SCARLATTI, and its most significant members were DURANTE, LEO, JOMMELLI, GALUPPI, and PICCINNI. In the typical opera of this school the play was based on episodes from history and legend. The songs, or ARIAS, became the major musical element, and the Neapolitans established the importance of the DA CAPO ARIA. The virtuoso singer was glorified as composers outdid each other in writing decorative melodies for displays of vocal dexterity. Ensemble music was also emphasized, and the OVERTURE acquired increasing importance. In Naples, too, a new type of opera was cultivated: the OPERA BUFFA, or "comic opera," opposed to the OPERA SERIA, or "serious opera." PERGOLESI was the first important composer of this new type.

The Golden Age of Italian Opera. The popularity of Neapolitan opera spread throughout Europe, and its traditions became everywhere firmly rooted. The Italian poet and dramatist METASTASIO was one of the most influential forces in the dominance of the Neapolitan style, chiefly through the overwhelming popularity of his numerous librettos. While certain specific abuses in Italian opera—the outlandish absurdity of many of the texts, the exaggerated importance of singer and song, the excessive ornamentation of melodies—were modified by the reforms of GLUCK, Italian composers generally continued to conform to established patterns. Within their limits, they produced works of unquestioned genius, dressing their stories with musical inspiration of a high order. ROSSINI and DONIZETTI brought to both their comic and serious operas—and BELLINI exclusively to serious operas—a wealth of melodic beauty and a freshness of musical thought that often lifted the humdrum librettos to works of stature. Melodic beauty and freshness of musical thought were combined with the demands of effective theater in the operas of VERDI, the greatest operatic figure produced by Italy, a genius who dominated the world of opera for half a century. Verdi brought the century-old traditions of Italian opera to their highest stages of technical and artistic development, at the same time introducing a dramatic vigor previously unknown. In his last two operas, OTELLO and FALSTAFF, he abandoned many of the more formal Italian patterns to create a synthesis of music and drama never before achieved by an Italian. With MASCAGNI's CAVALLERIA RUSTICANA (1890) a new movement entered Italian opera—VERISMO, or "realism"—emphasizing a more realistic sort of drama and greater naturalism in the music. Followers of this movement included LEONCAVALLO and the most successful Italian opera composer after Verdi, PUCCINI.

Beginnings of French Opera. LULLY, Italian by birth, was the first major figure in French opera. He made several significant departures from the Italian style, placing greater emphasis on ballet and the activity on the stage, giving a new importance to the recitative while simplifying the aria, enriching the harmonic and instrumental writing. These tendencies were further developed by the next outstanding composer of French opera, RAMEAU. In his search for dramatic truth and his indefatigable efforts to extend the horizons of harmony and orchestration, Rameau precipitated an acrimonious debate between the partisans of French opera and Italian. Rameau's ultimate victory was a major step in the advance of French opera. Eleven years after Rameau's death, however, the basic issues of the argument were still contested, this time centering around the personalities of Gluck and Piccinni. The decisive triumph of Gluck's operas was a vindication of Rameau's esthetics.

Gluck's Reforms. The most significant break with the formulas of Italian opera was made by Gluck, a development discussed in more detail in his biographical entry in this volume. Arriving at a new humanity, simplicity, dramatic truth, and realizing a closer bond between text and music than had been previously achieved, Gluck brought a new age for opera with works like ORFEO ED EURIDICE, ALCESTE, and IPHIGÉNIE EN AULIDE. His was a major revolution, setting the stage for Weber and Wagner.

Advances in French Opera. Despite the recognition in France of the validity of the kind of operas written by Rameau and Gluck, the Italians continued to prosper there for many years. The new operas in vogue in Paris were those written by such highly favored Italians as CHERUBINI and SPONTINI. These works catered to the French appetite for grandiose scenes, ceremonials, ballets, melodrama. Spectacle and melodrama were emphasized in the works of MEYERBEER, a German composer who achieved such popularity in France that his works became the models for subsequent French operas in the grand manner. But it should be noted that the operas with which Meyerbeer impressed France—ROBERT LE DIABLE, LES HUGUENOTS, L'AFRICAINE—combined Italian styles and techniques with French temperament and tastes. French grand opera became an institution with the advent of Meyerbeer. There now appeared a number of composers writing in a similar style, though with the economy and restraint imposed on them by their French temperament. A new kind of lyricism—more refined and delicate than the Italian—a growing interest in characterization, and a mounting concern for human emotions now prevailed in French operas. The climax of this trend was reached in the works of HALÉVY, GOUNOD, MASSENET, BIZET, and SAINT-SAËNS, to mention only the leading figures. Naturalism came to French opera in 1900 with Gustave CHARPENTIER's LOUISE and the operas of BRUNEAU—works which stressed a close identification with the problems of everyday life. At the same time there appeared a musical style called impressionism. The first impressionist opera, DEBUSSY's PELLÉAS ET MÉLISANDE, influenced not only French opera but that of the rest of the world. Paralleling the growth of serious French opera were the developments of OPÉRA COMIQUE and OPÉRA BOUFFE, discussed elsewhere under these headings.

Development of German Opera. SCHÜTZ's DAFNE, composed in 1627, was the first opera written in the German language. It was a long time later, however, that a distinctly German tradition came into being. Italian opera meanwhile remained supreme in the courts of Germany and Austria. The Italian style was slavishly imitated by such leading German composers as KEISER, GRAUN, and HASSE. When in Austria Gluck parted company with the Italians, he was laying the groundwork for German opera, which was to be distinguished by its pronounced dramatic interest, enriched musical resources, poetic expressiveness, and intimate connection of music and libretto. But even Gluck's *Orfeo ed Euridice* and *Alceste* were settings of Italian texts, as were nearly all the major operas of MOZART, Gluck's most significant follower in the German school. DON GIOVANNI and THE MARRIAGE OF FIGARO are offsprings of Italian *opera seria* and *opera buffa*. Both operas, however, show such a marked step forward in the musicodramatic concept and such an advance in musical characterization that they are key works in the shaping of the German style. The right of Mozart to belong with the German school is enhanced by the fact that he was the first eighteenth-century composer to write operas to German texts. His THE ABDUCTION FROM THE SERAGLIO (1782) is the oldest German comic opera still performed. It was followed, in 1791, by THE MAGIC FLUTE. Both these works derive their character not from the Italian *opera buffa* but from a German variety of popular musical theater known as the SINGSPIEL. They must, then, be considered the beginnings of German comic opera, a genre that subsequently yielded such works as THE BARBER OF BAGDAD, DIE MEISTERSINGER, and DER ROSENKAVALIER. BEETHOVEN's FIDELIO was another offspring of the *singspiel,* containing, as it does, spoken dialogue. But *Fidelio* is a powerful music drama, the first such in the German language. The accent is on intense emotional and psychological conflicts, and the music acquires a poetic expressiveness not found even in Mozart. Beethoven's single opera was the transition from Mozart to WEBER, with whom German folk opera came into existence. Both the texts and the music of DER FREISCHÜTZ and EURYANTHE drew copiously from German folk sources; in both, German Romanticism came to flower. WAGNER was the climactic figure in German opera. In his works the ideal of the German music drama is finally realized. Wagner's esthetics and achievements are discussed in greater detail in his biographical entry. Here it is only essential to recall that Wagner conceived an operatic form and style incomparable for spaciousness and sublimity. Wagner's effect on operatic music was cataclysmic: once and for all the center of the opera world shifted from Italy to Germany. Inevitably, many German composers began using his language and esthetics. Of his immediate successors the most important was Richard STRAUSS: in his masterworks, SALOME and ELEKTRA, the shadow of the mighty Wagner is in evidence. The *Wagnerzauber* also prevailed in the operas of HUMPERDINCK and PFITZNER.

Nationalism in Opera. The negative reaction to Wagner was reflected in several ways, including the impressionism of Debussy and the expressionism of SCHOENBERG. It was also to be seen in the national movement that arose in Russia among a group of composers sometimes referred to as The FIVE. Inspired by examples set by GLINKA and DARGOMIZHSKY, the composers Balakirev, BORODIN, MUSSORGSKY, CUI, and RIMSKY-KORSAKOV opposed making their music a reflection of Western music, especially that of Germany. In their quest for individuality, they arrived at a style that had its roots deep in Russian idiom and folk sources. Thus, they created a kind of music that can be mistaken for that of no other country. Outstanding in the work of these composers are three folk operas: Borodin's PRINCE IGOR, Mussorgsky's BORIS GODUNOV, and Rimsky-Korsakov's SADKO. The success of The Five inspired composers in other countries to create a national art. Notable examples of these aspirations are to be seen in such diverse works as SMETANA'S THE BARTERED BRIDE (Bohemia), JANÁČEK'S JENUFA (Moravia), MONIUSZKO'S HALKA (Poland), KODÁLY'S HÁRY JÁNOS (Hungary), and VAUGHAN WILLIAMS' HUGH THE DROVER (England).

Opera in England. The Siege of *Rhodes* (1656) was the first play in England to be set throughout to music. No less than five composers were responsible for the score: Henry Lawes, Matthew Locke, Thomas Cooke, Edward Coleman, and George Hudson. The first great English opera composer was not long in appearing: PURCELL, who, about 1690, wrote the first significant English opera, DIDO AND AENEAS, a work so remarkable in dramatic and musical content that it is still capable of moving audiences today. The next great figure in English opera was not a native son but the Saxon-born HANDEL. He lived in England from 1712 to the end of his life, and his many operas written during this period, all representative of the Italian school, were the most important ones of their era. Reaction against the dominant Italian style was manifested in the tremendous popularity of the BEGGAR'S OPERA (1728), one of the first BALLAD OPERAS, a form that was to be in vogue for the rest of the century. In the middle nineteenth century the ballad opera became the inspiration of such opera composers as BALFE, BENEDICT, and William Vincent Wallace. More in the Italian grand opera style, but with the infiltration of English personality, were operas by the later composers. MACKENZIE and STANFORD, HOLST and Vaughan Williams are later composers who wrote operas in the late nineteenth and early twentieth centuries that were unmistakably English in origin. Since World War II a new generation of opera composers has arisen in England to pose that country for the first time since Purcell as a significant rival to other nations. Among these new English voices in opera are BRITTEN, WALTON, and TIPPETT.

Opera in America, see AMERICAN OPERA COMPOSERS AND OPERAS.

Ultramodern Opera. It is to be expected that some of the basic new techniques, idioms, methods, and approaches in music that created a break with past traditions should have also affected twentieth-century opera. Opera, too, found its iconoclasts who parted with accepted procedures by introducing new techniques, structures, and even esthetics. ORFF, in reducing opera to its essentials, adopted a neoprimitive style that was mainly rhythmic declamation, frequently unaccompanied, often made up of continually repeated notes or phrases; rhythm, rather than melody, became the core of his technique, with the result that he employed a huge and varied percussion section. In this same search for elementals, Orff consciously reduced scenery and costuming to the barest essentials (frequently leaving them to the discretion of the producer).

ATONALITY achieved significance with BERG'S WOZZECK and with it the substitution of *sprechstimme* for melody and unresolved discords for harmony. The TWELVE-TONE TECHNIQUES (or dodecaphony) developed by Arnold SCHOENBERG and his disciples were used not only by the Schoenberg school (by Berg in LULU and Schoenberg in MOSES UND ARON) but by many other composers as well, including DALLAPICCOLA, FORTNER, HENZE, KRENEK, LIEBERMANN, Frank MARTIN, and Roger Sessions. Serialism, or SERIAL TECHNIQUES, an outgrowth of twelve-tone techniques, is found in operas by GINASTERA, NONO, and SCHULLER, among many others. DIRECTIONAL music, MICROTONAL MUSIC, or ELECTRONIC MUSIC have been used effectively in such operas as BADINGS' MARTIN KORDA, D.P., BLOMDAHL'S ANIARA, HÁBA'S THE MOTHER, and Schuller's THE VISITATION, to mention only a few representative works.

Opéra, L' (Académie de Musique), the oldest opera house in France and the most celebrated. It is subsidized by the French government. In 1669 a grant was given by Louis XIV to Pierre Perrin, Robert Cambert, and the Marquis de Sourdéac to organize a theater in Paris for opera and ballet performances. On Mar. 19, 1671, the Académie de Musique was launched at the Jeu de Paume with a pastoral by Cambert, POMONE, now accepted as the first French opera. When Perrin was put in debtors' prison, LULLY bought out the

license and took over the direction and supervision of the Académie in 1672. A year later, when MOLIÈRE'S death left the theater at the Palais Royal vacant, the opera company transferred there, remaining ninety years until the theater was destroyed by fire in 1763. Lully headed the opera company until his death in 1687 and created the first significant period in the history of the Paris Opéra; during his regime some twenty of his operas and BALLET-OPERAS were introduced, exerting a far-reaching influence on the early evolution of French opera. The second great period in the history of the Opéra came between 1737 and 1760, when many of the outstanding operas of RAMEAU were given. From 1773 to 1779 the Opéra was dominated by the personality and genius of GLUCK, then visiting from Vienna, a visit climaxed by the victory of his operas over those of the Italian opposition. In 1794 the Académie de Musique moved to the Rue de Richelieu and temporarily became known as the Théâtre des Arts. After the French Revolution, the new regime removed from the repertory many works considered too aristocratic, substituting new operas by MÉHUL, GOSSEC, MONSIGNY, and PHILIDOR. The Empire helped restore many of the prohibited operas, but the ballet-operas of the preceding century had now lost their audience and were replaced by French historical operas. In 1821 the Académie occupied the Salle Favart, and a year later it moved to a theater in Rue le Peletier, where operas by ROSSINI, WEBER, DONIZETTI, and MOZART were added to the repertory. When this theater burned down, a movement was launched to build a permanent home for the Académie. In 1861 the foundation for the new building, designed by Charles Garnier, was finally laid; the building itself, erected at the head of the Avenue de l'Opéra, was not completed for fourteen years. It opened on Jan. 5, 1875, with an orchestral concert. The first opera performed there was LA JUIVE, three days later. The first opera new to the repertory, *Jeanne d'Arc* by Auguste Mermet, was given on Apr. 5, 1876.

The artistic directors of the Opéra included Pierre GAILHARD, Jacques Rouche, Maurice Lehmann, Georges Hirsch, Jacques IBERT, A. M. Julien, Georges AURIC, André Chabaud, and René Nicoly, who was appointed in 1969.

In 1939 the Opéra and the OPÉRA-COMIQUE were merged under a single administration, the Réunion des Théâtres Lyriques Nationaux. Between 1955 and 1967 a single artistic director served for both institutions, first Jacques Ibert, then A. M. Julien, then Georges Auric. When André Chabaud became Auric's successor, the Opéra-Comique once again acquired its own director (Eugène Germain). The company completed its 1968–69 season at the Palais de Chaillot while the building of the Paris Opéra was undergoing alterations. The company returned to its regular home to open the 1969–70 season on Nov. 19 with BERLIOZ' LES TROYENS.

Since its beginnings as the Académie de Musique, the Paris Opéra has presented well over a thousand different works. Many of the premiere performances have been of some of the foremost operas written in France. They included: LES ABENCÉRAGES; ANACRÉON; ARMIDE ET RENAUD; *Atys* (LULLY); BENVENUTO CELLINI; *Bolivar* (MILHAUD); CASTOR ET POLLUX; LE CID; DARDANUS; *Démophoon* (CHERUBINI); HENRY VIII; HIPPOLYTE ET ARICIE; LES INDES GALANTES; *La Juive;* MIREILLE; MONNA VANNA; LA MUETTE DE PORTICI; LE ROI DE LAHORE; LE ROI D'YVETOT; SAPHO; THAÏS; WERTHER.

Among the significant premieres of operas by non-French composers have been: L'AFRICAINE; *Andromaque* (GRÉTRY); ARMIDE; LE COMTE ORY; DON CARLOS; LA FAVORITA; LES HUGUENOTS; IPHIGÉNIE EN AULIDE; IPHIGÉNIE EN TAURIDE; LE PROPHÈTE; ROBERT LE DIABLE; THE SICILIAN VESPERS; WILLIAM TELL.

MENOTTI became the first American to be commissioned by the Paris Opéra to write a work for it. That opera (THE LAST SAVAGE), however, was introduced not at the Opéra, as originally intended, but at the Opéra-Comique.

opéra bouffe, a French comic opera—light, trivial, and frequently farcical in character. It was an outgrowth of the OPÉRA COMIQUE of the middle nineteenth century which then acquired a more serious and artistically ambitious character. The term *opéra bouffe* came from the theaters in which these pieces were played, called *bouffes.* Thus, when OFFENBACH opened his theater for musical satires and farces he called it the Bouffes-Parisiens. Offenbach was the foremost exponent of the *opéra bouffe,* and his ORPHEUS IN THE UNDERWORLD is a classic in this genre.

opera buffa, an Italian comic opera, with dialogue in *recitativo secco* (RECITATIVE). It is distinguished from the more serious variety of Italian opera (OPERA SERIA) in its use of a comic rather than serious subjects. But there are other basic differences. The *opera seria* generally used historical or legendary characters; the *opera buffa* preferred human beings in everyday situations, human-interest stories filled with farcical situations. The *opera buffa* is usually concerned with love intrigues involving cuckolds, deceiving wives, and scheming servants. The *opera seria* utilized complex, highly ornamented arias to exploit the virtuosity of individual singers; the *opera buffa* preferred simple melodies and tunes. The *opera seria* emphasized massive scenes of pageantry; the *opera buffa* required only a few characters moving against a simple setting. Musically the *opera buffa* popularized certain stylistic devices by which it was to be identified: the swift alternation of light and shade for contrast; the use of rhythmic, staccato passages to emphasize coquettish moods; the exploitation of patter songs; the extended finales concluding each act.

The *opera buffa* developed from the INTERMEZZO, a brief comic scene set to music, popular in Italy in the late seventeenth and early eighteenth centuries.

A special theater was opened in 1709 in Naples to perform these *intermezzi,* whose texts were in the Neapolitan dialect. Such figures of the Neapolitan school as Alessandro SCARLATTI and Nicola LOGROSCINO were among the most popular writers of these comic pieces. Another Neapolitan, PERGOLESI, wrote *intermezzi;* and in 1733 he completed a more extended work in a similar style which can be regarded as the first *opera buffa* in history: LA SERVA PADRONA, introduced in Naples on Aug. 28, 1733. Actually, this delightful little work consists of two *intermezzi* performed, respectively, between the first and second and the second and third acts of Pergolesi's *opera seria* entitled *Il prigionier superbo. Il prigionier* was a failure and quickly forgotten, but its *intermezzi,* usually performed continuously as one act, went on to develop a vigorous life of their own. Pergolesi's comic opera not only established the form, style, and esthetic approach which subsequent works in the *opera buffa* genre were to assume, its tremendous popularity in Italy inspired composers there to produce works in a similar vein, thus bringing universal acceptance to the new medium. In Italy, Pergolesi's immediate successors were CIMAROSA (IL MATRIMONIO SEGRETO), GALUPPI (IL FILOSOFO DI CAMPAGNA), PAISIELLO (THE BARBER OF SEVILLE), and PICCINNI (LA CECCHINA). These composers represent the natural transition from Pergolesi to one of the greatest of all *opera-buffa* composers, ROSSINI, whose masterwork, THE BARBER OF SEVILLE, was the model followed by all later composers of *opera buffa.* Of Rossini's successors, the most notable was DONIZETTI (L'ELISIR D'AMORE and DON PASQUALE), while WOLF-FERRARI carried the style into the twentieth century with THE SECRET OF SUZANNE. The first opera of the American composer MENOTTI is also in the *opera buffa* tradition—AMELIA GOES TO THE BALL.

opéra comique, a type of French opera utilizing spoken dialogue. Its present-day meaning is not—as a literal translation of the name might imply—a comic opera. Many celebrated works in this genre are tragic, for example, CARMEN. The form was evolved early in the eighteenth century. At that time the Académie de Musique (or Paris Opéra, as it is now known) had a monopoly on all opera performances. To circumvent this monopoly, a new type of opera was evolved: a light form of theatrical entertainment utilizing singing. These musical plays, with spoken dialogue, were first seen at Paris fairs. It was at the Foire St. Germain, in 1715, that the term *opéra comique* was used for the first time. Originally, the *opéra comique* was true to its name by being a work of humorous character, simple in appeal, designed exclusively as entertainment. The first of these works were often parodies of the serious operas given at the Académie de Musique.

A powerful stimulus to French composers was the performance in Paris of LA SERVA PADRONA in 1752. Frenchmen set out to write works in a similar style. In the same year of 1752 Jean Jacques ROUSSEAU, the philosopher and musician, completed and had performed a delightful little *opéra comique,* LE DEVIN DU VILLAGE, which he confessed was in frank imitation of the PERGOLESI opera. A twenty-three-year-old composer, MONSIGNY, was so moved by *La serva padrona* that he decided henceforth to write only comic operas. GRÉTRY was another composer who was similarly influenced. In time, these two were succeeded by the triumvirate who made the *opéra comique* an institution: BOIELDIEU, ADAM, and AUBER.

In the middle of the nineteenth century the character of the *opéra comique* changed radically. The term was henceforth applied to operas, frequently tragic in theme, in which there were passages of spoken dialogue. The works formerly designated as *opéras comiques* now became known as *opéras bouffes.* The OPÉRA-COMIQUE became the principal home for this new type of opera.

Opéra-Comique, L' (Théâtre National

de l'Opéra-Comique), one of the two national lyric theaters of France (the other being the Académie de Musique or, as it is now known, L'OPÉRA), situated on the Rue Favart in Paris. It was established in 1715 after a special agreement with the Académie de Musique that it would present only operatic works with spoken dialogue. Originally, the Opéra-Comique gave its performances at the Foire St. Germain, where it was so successful that rival theater managers combined to have it closed in 1745. When the Opéra-Comique resumed operations in 1752, it combined with the Comédie-Italienne in presenting performances at the Mauconseil. In 1783 the Opéra-Comique moved to the Rue Favart, but it did not stay there long. A competitive company was organized on the Rue Feydeau in 1791. With audiences divided between the theaters, both suffered financial reverses and had to close in 1801. They then combined forces and gave opera performances on the Rue Feydeau until 1829, from 1829 to 1832 at the Théâtre Ventadour, and from 1832 to 1840 at the Théâtre des Nouveautés. This was the period that saw the premieres of operas by AUBER, BOIELDIEU, and MÉHUL. In 1840 the Opéra-Comique moved to its present site on the Rue Favart, where DONIZETTI'S THE DAUGHTER OF THE REGIMENT and THOMAS'S MIGNON received their world premieres. The building burned down in 1887, and, until a new one was erected on the same site a few years later, the company performed at the Sarah Bernhardt Theatre. The new building opened on Dec. 7, 1898, with Albert CARRÉ as artistic director. It was during Carré's regime that the Opéra-Comique entered upon one of its greatest eras, with the premieres of such French masterworks as PELLÉAS ET MÉLISANDE, LOUISE, ARIANE ET BARBE-BLEUE, and L'HEURE ESPAGNOLE. Following Carré, the artistic directors included Gheusi, Isola, Masson, Rouche, D'Ollone, Wolff, Malherbe, Bondeville,

Agostini, and Lamy. In 1939 the Opéra-Comique was placed with the Paris Opéra under a single administration, the Réunion des Théâtres Lyriques Nationaux. Between 1955 and 1967 a single artistic director was placed at the head of both institutions: Jacques IBERT, then A. M. Julien, and after that Georges AURIC. When Auric resigned in 1967, he was replaced by Eugène Germain, who in 1969 was succeeded by Jean Giraudeau.

The list of world premieres at the Opéra-Comique includes some of the most celebrated works of the French lyric theater: *Ariane et Barbe-bleue;* CARMEN; *Le Carrosse du Saint Sacrement* (Henri Busser); CENDRILLON; DJAMILEH; FRA DIAVOLO; GRISÉLIDIS; LA HABANERA; JOSEPH; LE JUIF POLONAIS; LAKMÉ; LALLA ROUKH; *Louise;* LES MAMELLES DE TIRÉSIAS; MANON; MÂROUF; *Mignon; Les Noces de Jeannette* (MASSÉ); LE PAUVRE MATELOT; *Pelléas et Mélisande;* LE POSTILLON DE LONGJUMEAU; LE ROI D'YS; LE ROI D'YVETOT; LE ROI MALGRÉ LUI; SAPHO; THE TALES OF HOFFMANN.

Operas by foreign composers introduced at the Opéra-Comique have included: DINORAH; *Macbeth* (Bloch); THE LAST SAVAGE.

It should be pointed out that many works now performed at the Opéra-Comique are traditional in form; the company has abandoned its original policy of confining its activities exclusively to operas with spoken dialogue.

Opera Company of Boston, The, the leading opera company in Boston, founded on Apr. 11, 1958, by the Opera Group of Boston with Mrs. David Black as president and Sarah Caldwell as artistic director. In the spring of 1958, the company gave its first performance as part of the Boston Arts Festival, a revival of the rarely given and little known OFFENBACH OPÉRA BOUFFE, *The Voyage to the Moon* (which the company took on a coast-to-coast tour in 1960). Making its home on Norway

Street at the Fine Arts Theatre, re-named The Little Opera House, the Opera Company of Boston inaugurated its first full season on Jan. 29, 1959, with LA BOHÈME. Since then under Miss Caldwell's direction the company has given over fifty productions ranging from HIPPOLYTE ET ARICIE (first American staged presentation) to MOSES UND ARON, INTOLLERANZA 1960, MONTEZUMA (all three American premieres), and LULU (East Coast premiere). The 1968–69 season found the company at a new home, the refurbished Shubert Theatre, which opened on Jan. 10, 1969, with the first presentation in the United States of the entire BARTÓK trilogy of works for the stage: BLUEBEARD'S CASTLE, *The Wooden Prince*, *The Miraculous Mandarin*. Other notable performances by the company have included the world premiere of Robert Middleton's *Command Performance* (1961), the American premiere of the original version of BORIS GODUNOV (1965), the first production in America of the original version of VERDI'S MACBETH (1969), and the world premiere of SCHULLER's opera for children, *The Fisherman and His Wife*. In 1967 the company gave a private performance of *The Voyage to the Moon* at the White House. When the METROPOLITAN OPERA National Company dissolved in the spring of 1967, the Opera Company of Boston filled the breach with a national tour during which it presented *Lulu*.

Opéra de Monte Carlo, L', an opera company founded in 1879 in an opera house designed by Charles Garnier. Its heyday took place under the artistic direction of Raoul Gunsbourg between 1890 and 1954. During this period there took place the world premieres of L'AIGLON, DON QUICHOTTE, L'ENFANT ET LES SORTILÈGES, LE JONGLEUR DE NOTRE DAME, JUDITH (HONEGGER), PÉNÉLOPE (FAURÉ), and LA RONDINE, among other operas. Since Gunsbourg, its artistic directors have included Maurice Besnard, who was succeeded by Louis Ducreux. Its season extends usually from January to April, performances now taking place in the auditorium of the Casino.

opera performance, (1) *Europe*. The first operas by members of the Florentine CAMERATA and their immediate successors were performed privately in the palaces of Italy's nobility. The first public opera house came into existence in 1637, when one of Venice's noblest families, the Trons, opened the TEATRO SAN CASSIANO with a performance of an opera by a now forgotten composer: Francesco Manelli's *Andromèdie*. The boxes were rented annually by Venetian nobility and foreign princes; the general public gained admission to the spacious parterre by paying approximately twenty cents. This new theater was a tremendous success, and many operas were given there. Between 1641 and 1649, for example, thirty different works were performed, including several by MONTEVERDI.

By the end of the seventeenth century, opera was such a favored form of entertainment that there were sixteen different opera houses in Venice alone, each run by a different Venetian family. An opera theater opened in Naples in 1684, the Teatro San Bartolomeo, where works by Alessandro SCARLATTI were performed and where LA SERVA PADRONA was introduced. The most celebrated of all Italian opera houses, LA SCALA, in Milan, was opened in 1776. In Rome, where opera was long forbidden by papal edict, performances were restricted to the homes of royalty.

An opera theater was inaugurated in London as early as 1656, but not until the Restoration, four years later, when the Puritan ban on theatrical entertainment was removed, did opera begin to flourish. The first major opera house in London, DRURY LANE THEATRE, opened in 1696, followed by HER MAJESTY'S THEATRE in 1705 and COVENT GARDEN in 1732. However, when HANDEL's first opera to be performed in England was given in 1711 (RINALDO), it was given in a smaller house, the Queen's Theatre, in Haymarket. Handel helped found and was artistic director of his own opera company in 1721, the Royal Academy of Music; when that failed, he organized still another company in 1729 at the King's Theatre.

An opera house came into existence in Hamburg in 1678. From 1695 to 1705 it was directed by Reinhard KEISER, who was responsible for making Hamburg the first major operatic center of Germany. It was here that Handel made his bow as an opera composer. The Paris OPÉRA, or Académie de Musique, was organized in 1669. The first opera house in Prague opened in 1725, the first in Berlin in 1742. In Vienna, the BURG-THEATER came into existence in 1741 with a performance of Carcano's AMLETO, and soon became a home for operas by GLUCK and MOZART.

The history of opera performances is to be found in the history of the world's leading opera houses. For additional material in the present volume, consult entries on individual opera houses and on major opera festivals.

(2) *United States.* The first opera performance in the Colonies took place in a courtroom in Charleston, S.C., on Feb. 8, 1735. The production was an English BALLAD OPERA, *Flora*. Ballad operas continued to be the only operas performed in the New World up to 1791. In that year an opera troupe, under the direction of Louis Tabery, visited New Orleans and presented French operas in private homes. A year later a theater was built for this group, the Théâtre le Spectacle de Rue St. Pierre. This was the first of several opera theaters in New Orleans. In the FRENCH OPERA HOUSE, opened in 1859, most of the famous French operas of the eighteenth and nineteenth centuries were introduced to the United States.

The first Italian opera heard in America was PAISIELLO'S THE BARBER OF SEVILLE, sung in Baltimore in 1794 (in an English translation). ROSSINI'S THE BARBER OF SEVILLE, also sung in English, was given in New York City in 1819. In 1825 the same work was sung in Italian,

the first Italian language performance in America. In the same year, Manuel GARCÍA visited New York with an Italian opera company and performed several Rossini operas new to this country. García's collaborator in this venture was Lorenzo DA PONTE who, with a French tenor named Montrésor, organized another season of Italian operas in New York a year later. Lorenzo da Ponte was a primary force in the erection of the first permanent opera house in New York, the ITALIAN OPERA HOUSE. The Astor Place Opera, opening in 1847, and its successor, the ACADEMY OF MUSIC, opening in 1854, carried on the major operatic activity in New York City until the METROPOLITAN OPERA was founded in 1883. German opera in the original tongue was heard for the first time in New York in 1845—DER FREISCHÜTZ. The first WAGNER opera heard in the United States was TANNHÄUSER at the Stadt-theater in New York in 1859. Attempts to present opera in the English language were made in 1885 with the founding of the American Opera Company by Theodore THOMAS and again in 1895, when Henry W. SAVAGE presented opera in English at Castle Garden, but neither venture was successful. In 1906 the Metropolitan Opera acquired a formidable rival in the MANHATTAN OPERA COMPANY. Decades after the latter went out of existence, the most significant opera performances in New York, supplementing those presented by the Metropolitan Opera, were those given by the NEW YORK CITY OPERA, founded in 1943, and the AMERICAN OPERA SOCIETY, created in 1951.

The first opera heard in Philadelphia, in 1845, was also the first grand opera by an American: William H. Fry's LEONORA. It was in Philadelphia at the Academy of Music that the American premiere of AIDA took place in 1873. Opera first came to Chicago with a performance of LA SONNAMBULA in 1850. Nine years later Chicago had its first opera season under the direction of Maurice STRAKOSCH, and in 1865 the first opera house in Chicago was erected, the Crosby Theatre. Opera came fully into its own in Chicago with the formation of the CHICAGO OPERA COMPANY in 1910, which was succeeded by the CHICAGO LYRIC OPERA in 1954. Opera was heard for the first time in San Francisco in 1852, when the Pellegrini Opera Troupe gave *La sonnambula*. San Francisco, however, did not become a major center of operatic activity until 1923, when the SAN FRANCISCO OPERA was formed.

The history of opera performances in America and Europe is told in greater detail in the individual articles on the various opera houses of America and Europe. *See:* UNITED STATES. Academy of Music; American Opera Society; Baltimore Opera; Chicago Lyric Opera; Chicago Opera Company; Cincinnati Zoo Opera; Dallas Civic Opera; Damrosch Opera Company; Fort Worth Opera; French Opera House; Italian Opera House; Manhattan Opera; Metropolitan Opera; National Opera Company; New York City Opera; Opera Company of Boston; Philadelphia Lyric Opera Company; San Carlo Opera Company; San Francisco Opera; Seattle Opera.

ELSEWHERE. Berlin Deutsche Staatsoper; Berlin State Opera; Bolshoi Theater; Budapest State Opera; Burgtheater; Cambridge University Musical Society; Cologne Opera; Covent Garden; Dresden Opera; Drury Lane Theatre; English Opera Group; Frankfurt Opera; Geneva Opera; Hamburg State Opera; Hanover Opera; Her (*or* His) Majesty's Theatre; Komische Oper; Mannheim Opera; Munich Opera; L'Opéra (Paris); Opéra-Comique; Opéra de Monte Carlo; Prague Opera; Sadler's Wells; Stockholm Royal Opera; Stuttgart Opera; Teatro alla Pergola; Teatro alla Scala; Teatro Colón; Teatro Communale (Bologna); Teatro Communale (Florence); Teatro dell' Opera (Rome); Teatro la Fenice; Teatro Lirico; Teatro Regio (Parma); Teatro Regio (Turin); Teatro San Carlo; Teatro San Cassiano; Teatro San Moïse; Teatro SS Giovanni

e Paolo; Theater-an-der-Wien; Theater-auf-der-Wieden; Théâtre de la Monnaie; Théâtre Lyrique; Vienna State Opera; Weimar Opera; Zürich Opera.

See also FESTIVALS.

Any survey of opera productions in America must take into account the significant work done throughout the country by colleges, universities, and conservatories. It has been estimated that in 1970 there were about three hundred such operatic groups, giving about two thousand performances of the standard repertory, and two hundred performances of modern works. Many American operas owe their world premieres to such amateur productions, of which the following is merely a representative list: AMAHL AND THE NIGHT VISITORS, first American staged production (Indiana U.); AMELIA GOES TO THE BALL (Curtis Institute); *The Bell Tower* by KRENEK (U. of Illinois); BILLY BUDD, first American staged production (Indiana U.); CARRY NATION (U. of Kansas); *Dark Waters* by Krenek (U. of Southern California); DOWN IN THE VALLEY (Indiana U.); THE JUMPING FROG OF CALAVERAS COUNTY (Indiana U.); THE MEDIUM (Columbia U.); THE MOTHER OF US ALL (Columbia U.); *A Night at the Inn* by DELLO JOIO (Indiana U.); PANFILO AND LAURETTA (Columbia U); *Pieces of Eight* by Bernard Wagenaar (Columbia U.); HE WHO GETS SLAPPED (Columbia U.); *The Rehearsal* by GIANNINI (Juilliard); *The Ruby* by Dello Joio (Indiana U.); *The Scarlet Mill* by Eugene Zador (Brooklyn College); *Six Characters in Search of an Author* by WEISGALL (Columbia U.); SUSANNAH (Florida State U.); *Tarquin* by Krenek (Vassar); *The Trial of Lucullus* by SESSIONS (U. of California, Berkeley); TROUBLE IN TAHITI (Brandeis U.); *The Veil* by Bernard Rogers (Indiana U.); *Venus in Africa* by ANTHEIL (U. of Denver); VOLPONE (U. of Southern California); *The Wife of Martin Guerre* by William Bergsma (Juilliard).

American premieres of foreign operas

given in universities also form a distinguished list, among which are the following: L'ABANDON D'ARIANE (U. of Illinois); ABSTRAKTE OPER NO. 1 (Boston U.); *Amadigi* by HANDEL (Princeton); ANTIGONE by HONEGGER (Juilliard); DIE BERNAUERIN (U. of Missouri); LA BOHÈME by LEONCAVALLO (Columbia U.); CASTOR ET POLLUX (Vassar); IL COMBATTIMENTO DI TANCREDI E CLORINDA (Smith); *The Country Doctor* by HENZE (Northwestern U.); LA DÉLIVRANCE DE THÉSÉE (Iowa State U.); LE DOCTEUR MIRACLE (Yale); ELEGY FOR YOUNG LOVERS (Juilliard); L'ÉTOILE, new version (Mannes School); DER FRIEDENSTAG (U. of Southern California, Los Angeles); *La guerra* by ROSSELLINI (Peabody); L'INCORONAZIONE DI POPPEA (Smith); L'ORFEO (Smith); LE PAUVRE MATELOT (Curtis Institute); IL PRIGIONIERO (Juilliard).

Colleges, universities, and conservatories have also been responsible for reviving many a long forgotten opera, thereby often uncovering a long neglected gem. The following is a sampling: ARNE's *Cooper* (Southern Oregon College); BLOMDAHL's ANIARA (Indiana U.); CAVALLI's *Erismena* (U. of California, Berkeley) and ORMINDO (Oberlin); Cesti's *Orontea* (Cornell U.); GRÉTRY's *L'Amant jaloux* (California State College) and *Silvain* (Xavier U.); HANDEL's DEIDAMIA (Indiana U.); *Imeneo* (Princeton), and SUSANNA (U. of California, Berkeley); HAYDN's ORFEO ED EURIDICE (M.I.T.) and *Orlando Paladino* (U. of California at Santa Barbara); MOZART's *Lucio Silla* (Manhattan School of Music); PAISIELLO's THE BARBER OF SEVILLE (Southern Mississippi U.); and Telemann's *Pimpinone* (Northern Illinois U.). The first staged revival of GRANADOS' GOYESCAS since its world premiere was given at the Manhattan School of Music in 1969.

See also ASPEN MUSIC FESTIVAL; BERKSHIRE MUSIC FESTIVAL.

(3) *Radio.* Even while radio was in its earliest experimental stages it was interested in opera. In the early 1900's, Lee De Forest broadcast from the stage of the MANHATTAN OPERA an aria from CARMEN sung by Mariette Mazarin. On Jan. 13, 1910, there took place an experimental broadcast from the stage of the METROPOLITAN OPERA; parts of CAVALLERIA RUSTICANA, with Emmy DESTINN and Riccardo MARTIN, and PAGLIACCI, with Enrico CARUSO and Pasquale AMATO. This broadcast was picked up by some fifty radio amateurs in or near New York City, and by the *S.S. Avon* at sea. On Jan. 6, 1923, the first European broadcast of a complete opera took place from the stage of COVENT GARDEN—HANSEL AND GRETEL.

In 1925 WEAF (New York) began weekly broadcasts of operas, sung in their original languages by professional performers, directed by Cesare SODERO. This was the first time a series of operas came to radio, and the program was continued successfully for several years. On Sept. 7, 1925, the first stage performance of a regular opera performance was broadcast by a commercial radio station when WJZ transmitted AIDA as given by the Boston Civic Opera at the Manhattan Opera House in New York.

When the first radio network came into existence on Nov. 15, 1926, the National Broadcasting Company network, the event was celebrated with a performance by two opera stars, Mary GARDEN singing in Chicago and Titta RUFFO in New York. The first broadcast of an American opera took place on Sept. 18, 1927—TAYLOR's THE KING'S HENCHMAN—through the facilities of the Columbia Phonograph Broadcasting System (later the Columbia Broadcasting System).

On Jan. 21, 1928, excerpts from opera performances at the Chicago Auditorium became a regular radio feature. Soon after the first broadcast (the Garden Scene from FAUST), a manufacturer of radio supplies sponsored these broadcasts; complete acts were henceforth transmitted through nineteen associated stations.

A new day dawned for opera broadcasting on Mar. 16, 1930, when a performance of FIDELIO was transmitted to

America from the stage of the DRESDEN OPERA, the first transatlantic broadcast of an opera. In 1931 a performance was relayed to America from Covent Garden. During the next few years, through the facilities of the radio networks, opera performances were broadcast to America from the BAYREUTH and SALZBURG festivals, including TOSCANINI's performances of *Fidelio*, DIE MEISTERSINGER, and FALSTAFF relayed from the Salzburg Festival in 1936 through the facilities of the National Broadcasting Company.

The Metropolitan Opera became affiliated with radio in 1931. GATTI-CASAZZA, the manager, consented to a trial broadcast, the quality of which would influence his decision as to whether Metropolitan performances should be broadcast regularly. A performance of MADAMA BUTTERFLY was privately relayed to Gatti-Casazza and his musical staff in an NBC studio. Gatti-Casazza was so impressed that he consented to the transmission of *Hansel and Gretel* from the stage of the Metropolitan on Christmas Day, 1931. This led to the weekly Saturday-afternoon broadcasts from the Metropolitan, first over the NBC network, subsequently over the ABC. For six years these broadcasts were a sustaining feature. During the next three years various sponsors were associated with the broadcasts. In 1940 the Texas Company became the permanent sponsor. In the first quarter-of-a-century of broadcasting, over four hundred and fifty performances of more than seventy-five different operas were heard. Of historic significance was the broadcast of the world premiere of BARBER'S ANTONY AND CLEOPATRA on opening night of the new auditorium of the Metropolitan Opera at the LINCOLN CENTER FOR THE PERFORMING ARTS on Friday evening, Sept. 16, 1966.

While the NBC Symphony was in existence, giving regular symphony concerts over the NBC network, extraordinary concert performances of operas were presented in the 1940's and 1950's under Toscanini's direction, including *Aida*, UN BALLO IN MASCHERA, LA BOHÈME, *Falstaff*, *Fidelio*, ORFEO ED EURIDICE, OTELLO, and LA TRAVIATA. Mention must also be made of the broadcast of a cycle of MOZART operas from the studios of WOR (New York), with Alfred Wallenstein conducting. This took place in the 1940's at a time when some of these operas were little known to the general public.

In 1933 radio in America recognized its responsibility to opera in general and the American composer in particular by commissioning the first opera ever written directly for radio, *The Willow Tree* by CADMAN, broadcast over the NBC network on Oct. 3. Previously on Apr. 17, 1930, NBC had given the world premiere of Charles Skilton's one-act Indian opera, *Sun Bride*. In 1937, CBS began commissioning operas. Among these were: *Flora, Beauty and the Beast,* and *Blennerhasset,* all three by GIANNINI, and GRUENBERG's *Green Mansions*. In 1939 NBC commissioned MENOTTI's THE OLD MAID AND THE THIEF and in 1943, MONTEMEZZI's *L'incantesimo*. But since then radio has resigned from this activity, and whatever commissions for broadcast opera came thereafter were for television transmission.

The Saturday afternoon live broadcasts from the Metropolitan Opera, sponsored by Texaco, have remained the only coast-to-coast transmission of opera from the stage in America. Local stations sometimes broadcast live performances (or performances reproduced on tape) from their own cities. But, throughout the country, the principal source of opera entertainment (apart from the Metropolitan Opera broadcasts) comes from local radio (usually FM) stations transmitting regular programs of complete operas by means of recordings.

In Europe, however, broadcasting of opera performances from the stages of its leading opera houses is a regular feature of radio programing. Significant, too, is the frequency with which the major radio companies of Europe commission leading composers to write operas for radio broadcasting, with most of the premieres given over the radio, though sometimes these operas are introduced within an opera house before they are broadcast. These are some of the operas that have been commissioned by European radio institutions: A TALE OF TWO CITIES; ABSTRAKTE OPER NO. 1; DIE FLUT; IL PRIGIONIERO; EGK's *Columbus* and *Weihnacht;* Niels-Erich Fougstedt's *The Tinderbox;* L'APOSTROPHE; HENZE's *The Country Doctor* and ELEGY FOR YOUNG LOVERS; IBERT's *Barbe-Bleue;* MONSIEUR DE POURCEAUGNAC; LE MYSTÈRE DE LA NATIVITÉ; COMEDY ON THE BRIDGE; Gosta Nystroem's *The Blind;* SUTERMEISTER's *Die schwarze Spinne;* TROILUS AND CRESSIDA.

(4) *Recordings.* Opera singers and excerpts from operas played a prominent role in the early history of recorded music. The phonograph was born on Dec. 15, 1877, when Thomas A. Edison filed a patent application for a reproducing machine. The records for this primitive instrument were cylindrical. In the 1890's several prominent opera stars recorded arias, among them CALVÉ, MAUREL, NORDICA, and TAMAGNO. Meanwhile, in 1887, the disk record was invented by Emile Berliner. The Berliner Gramophone Company issued recordings by some lesser opera singers in 1895. By 1900 the disk had replaced the cylinder, and the recording industry was ready to go into high gear. In 1898 the Gramophone Company was organized in Europe. Soon after the turn of the century it embarked on an ambitious program to record great music in outstanding performances. In 1901 it dispatched engineers to Russia to record eminent singers of the Imperial Opera, including CHALIAPIN. In Mar., 1902, the same company contracted CARUSO to record ten numbers; and soon after this, Calvé, BATTISTINI, RENAUD, and PLANÇON joined the company.

In 1903 the Columbia Phonograph Company of New York introduced the Grand Opera Series with stars of the METROPOLITAN OPERA, including ADAMS, Edouard DE RESZKE, SCHUMANN-HEINK, SEMBRICH, and SCOTTI. The venture was a failure and was temporarily abandoned, but it spurred the Victor Talking Machine Company (incorporated in 1901) to competition. In 1903 Victor set up a recording studio in Carnegie Hall. The first record made with the now-famous Red Seal Label was "Caro mio ben," sung by Ada Crossley. CAMPANARI, HOMER, Plançon, and Scotti were soon making records for Victor; at the same time Victor was issuing in America the best releases of the European Gramophone Company. Lacking an outstanding tenor on its list, Victor signed Caruso to an exclusive contract in 1903. Caruso recorded ten numbers early in 1904 at a fee of four hundred dollars a record. These records proved so popular that after a second recording session, in 1905, Caruso's fee was raised to a thousand dollars a record. The records made at the third session, in 1906, were re-released by RCA Victor in its Treasury Series. FARRAR, GLUCK, and MCCORMACK were other leading singers added to the Victor list after 1907. Influenced by Victor's success, the Columbia company revived its program by engaging GARDEN, Nordica, FREMSTAD, and BONCI, among others.

Despite the high price for some of these records—one single twelve-inch disk, recorded on only one side, the Sextet from LUCIA, cost as much as seven dollars—sales soared. Within a decade the assets of Victor rose to over eight million dollars; in two decades this figure doubled. Caruso's income from his recordings eventually amounted to more than two million dollars.

The early recordings were made acoustically. The artist would sing into a horn which would gather the sound and give it sufficient power to cut a track on a wax disk. This method did not permit much clarity of reproduction. In the 1920's a revolution took place. The radio introduced new techniques and implements, among them the electric microphone. The artist's voice was now amplified and registered electrically. From the field of radio, too, the phonograph acquired a new type of loud-speaker in which amplification was achieved through radio tubes. Electricity brought an altogether new fidelity to recordings. A boom now took place in the sale of phonographs and records. Recordings themselves became more ambitious: for the first time in the United States an entire opera was recorded when in 1928 Victor issued RIGOLETTO. In 1929 Columbia followed suit with its own first complete opera, CARMEN. For some years European companies were the dominant makers of operatic records, but a change came in 1947 when Columbia announced a contract with the Metropolitan Opera to record parts of operas or complete operas from the stage of that house. The first of these recordings was the LIEBES-NACHTMUSIK from TRISTAN UND ISOLDE, sung by TRAUBEL, GLAZ, and RALF, with BUSCH conducting. The first complete opera was HANSEL AND GRETEL in English, followed soon thereafter by COSÌ FAN TUTTE, also in English. But this arrangement between Columbia and the Metropolitan Opera was of short duration, ending in 1955.

The next major development in the recording of operas came in 1948 when Columbia Records announced its long-playing record. Twenty to twenty-five minutes of music could now be put on one side of a record. This innovation was soon adopted by all the other major American companies. Europe followed suit in 1952, when a few minor companies in England issued their first long-playing disks; but it was not long before all the major European companies began producing them. The long-playing record made it possible to record entire operas—even those of the monumental length of the Wagnerian music dramas —on from two to five records. The improvement in the quality of recorded sound and the concomitant reduction in the price for full-length operas led to a tremendous increase in record-buying. In the first full year of long-playing record sales (1949), the total sales amounted to over two million dollars, which proved a pittance compared to the figures that followed in ensuing years. Numerous new companies came into existence, and each year the output of operatic releases increased.

A significant innovation in recording long-playing records came with the invention of magnetic tape, which became the matrix from which the records were made. Magnetic tape could be skillfully edited so that one could remove from it any blemishes and imperfections and substitute more desirable replacements. Thus a type of perfection impossible in a live stage performance could be realized.

The sound quality of recorded music took another major leap forward in 1958 with stereophonic sound. This, and some of the factors described above, brought about an unprecedented boom in the opera-recording market. In 1954, for example, RCA Victor announced that since 1949 it had sold four hundred fifty thousand opera albums at a total price of eight and a half million dollars. The growing demand for more and more opera recordings made it possible for the companies to expand their activities extensively. The basic operatic repertory was now made available in many different versions by some of the world's greatest companies and with the world's most renowned artists. Long forgotten and unknown operas by the masters helped to expand the repertory of available opera recordings. Composers and operas whose names had previously been known only to historians and musicologists now became familiar territory to the record buyer, as the recording industry began penetrating more and more deeply into *terra incognita* for its output. In the 1970 catalogue there were over three hundred recorded operas listed, with the more famous operas boasting of anywhere from five to ten different releases. It would be impossible to estimate the number of opera albums now sold each year the world over by such companies as Columbia, RCA Victor, Angel, Deutsche-Gramaphon, London, and other giant organizations. But there is no question that the figures go well into the millions. With the output and the market growing each succeeding year, it is possible to have not one but two remarkable recordings of the entire RING cycle, one conducted by SOLTI and the other by KARAJAN; and, perhaps more remarkable still, it was possible to acquire in a single year two different recordings of LULU, since modern and even avant-garde opera is by no means neglected. An average of between sixty and seventy new opera releases on records each year for the past few years has made it possible for the opera lover to acquire on disks virtually any opera of historic or esthetic interest.

(5) *Television.* While experiments in televising opera took place in London as early as 1936 and opera was televised by the BBC in 1937–38, it was not until 1941 that opera came to television in the United States. On Mar. 10, 1941, there took place the first American opera telecast: a tabloid version of PAGLIACCI, transmitted from Radio City with METROPOLITAN OPERA performers. The next major event in televised opera took place on Nov. 29, 1948, when the Metropolitan Opera transmitted its opening-night performance (OTELLO) over NBC. Subsequent opening-night performances that the Metropolitan televised were: DER ROSENKAVALIER (1949) and DON CARLOS (1950).

In 1950 a weekly program devoted to abridged operas (on film), entitled "Opera Cameos," was begun on WPIX, produced by Carlo Vinti. This series has since then been televised over a network.

An interesting experiment was undertaken on Dec. 11, 1952, when an actual subscription performance of CARMEN at the Metropolitan Opera was televised over a closed circuit to thirty-one theaters in twenty-seven cities. It was estimated that some seventy thousand persons paid over one hundred thousand dollars in admissions to hear this performance. This was the first time that an actual stage production of any kind was transmitted to different parts of the country. In the fall of 1954 the Metropolitan Opera signed a three-year agreement with the Theater Network Television to televise on a closed circuit its opening-night performances. The first transmission under this agreement took place on the opening night of the 1954–55 season when for the first time in Metropolitan Opera history the attraction was acts from four different operas, instead of a complete opera. But the venture was a failure, and the plan to televise further opening nights on a closed circuit was dropped.

A significant advance in televising opera was made in 1949 with the formation of the NBC Television Opera Theatre, with Samuel Chotzinoff as producer and Peter Herman ADLER as musical and artistic director. The first presentation was WEILL'S DOWN IN THE VALLEY on Jan. 14, 1950; the last new production was LUCIA DI LAMMERMOOR on Jan. 19, 1964. In those fourteen years the company made history in several ways. It commissioned Americans to write operas expressly for TV: DELLO JOIO (THE TRIAL AT ROUEN) ; FOSS (GRIFFELKIN) ; Leonard Kastle (*Deseret*) ; MENOTTI (AMAHL AND THE NIGHT VISITORS, MARIA GOLOVIN, and THE LABYRINTH) . *Amahl and the Night Visitors* was the first opera ever written for the television medium directly, introduced on Christmas Eve, 1951. Since the program was sponsored, *Amahl* became the first opera whose world premiere had been sponsored by a commercial company. For many years, *Amahl and the Night Visitors* was a regular Yuletide feature over the NBC network.

To these world premieres, the NBC Television Opera Theatre added some others of operas it had not commissioned, such as Stanley Hollingsworth's *La Grande Bretache* and MARTINU'S THE MARRIAGE. It presented the first professional performance of TROUBLE IN TAHITI. American premieres of important European operas included BILLY BUDD and WAR AND PEACE. Besides drawing from the familiar repertory, its productions through the years included numerous novelties, among which were LES DIALOGUES DES CARMÉLITES, *Maria Golovin, R.S.V.P.* (OFFENBACH), THE SAINT OF BLEECKER STREET, SUOR ANGELICA, IL TABARRO, and THE TAMING OF THE SHREW (GIANNINI). All foreign-language works were given in new English translations commissioned for this purpose.

Other television networks in the United States offered opera from time to time, though much less frequently than NBC. CBS telecast MOORE's *Gallantry* and Menotti's MARTIN'S LIE (the latter commissioned by CBS); and AMRAM wrote *The Final Ingredient* for ABC. FLOYD's THE SOJOURNER AND MOLLIE SINCLAIR, while written for television, was first produced on the stage, a performance that was taped and then transmitted through a Southern network.

On Feb. 1, 1953, the Metropolitan Opera was presented by the Omnibus program of the FORD FOUNDATION in DIE FLEDERMAUS; the Metropolitan later returned to Omnibus with a performance of LA BOHÈME, in a new English translation. Subsequently Omnibus presented a revival of GERSHWIN's one-act opera 135TH STREET, the American premiere of RESPIGHI's *The Sleeping Beauty,* and the world premiere of Alec Wilder's *Chicken Little.*

Opera was televised in color for the first time on Oct. 31, 1953, with an NBC presentation of *Carmen.* Soon after this, *Amahl and the Night Visitors* and *The Taming of the Shrew* were also given in color.

Significant contributions on a noncommercial basis have been made by NET (National Education Television), which distributed tapes of numerous opera performances to its hundred and more affiliate stations. The repertoire is a varied one ranging from basic works to revivals of such rarely performed operas as DIDO AND AENEAS, LA FINTA GIARDINIERA, RITA, *La scala di seta,* and LA SERVA PADRONA. Modern opera, such as BLUEBEARD'S CASTLE; American opera, such as LIZZIE BORDEN; and avant-garde opera, such as INTOLLERANZA 1960 fea-

tured prominently in its activities. In 1969 under a grant from the Ford Foundation, NET founded a subsidiary opera-producing organization called NET Opera under the artistic and musical direction of Peter Herman Adler. In its 1969–70 season it produced, for United States, Canadian, and British telecasts, the United States premiere of FROM THE HOUSE OF THE DEAD, the world premiere of *My Heart's in the Highlands,* and THE ABDUCTION FROM THE SERAGLIO.

What is believed to be the first opera by an Englishman written exclusively for TV is Richard Arnell's *Love in Transit,* telecast in 1955. Since then BBC-TV has commissioned operas from English composers and telecast their premieres, of which BENJAMIN's *Mañana* and BLISS's *Tobias and the Angel* are two examples. BRITTEN has been commissioned to write his first opera for television, *Owen Wingrave,* based on a ghost story by Henry JAMES. Alexander TCHEREPNIN was commissioned to write *Ivan the Terrible,* telecast in 1968. Other European television companies also have commissioned operas for this medium. Among these works are BADINGS' *Salto of Andros,* KRENEK's *Ausgerechnet und Verspielt,* and SUTERMEISTER's *The Ghost of Canterville* (the last of which received first prize in 1965 as the best television opera in Europe for the year following its premiere over a Salzburg channel).

In 1968 a performance of THE BARBER OF SEVILLE by the Metropolitan Opera was taped for television, in black and white for European distribution and in color for Japan. In 1969 Martha MÖDL was starred in THE RISE AND FALL OF THE CITY MAHAGONNY in a European taped performance for color-TV transmission.

In Europe opera is occasionally televised live from the stage of an opera house or festival, as was the case with LE COMTE ORY and THE RAKE'S PROGRESS, televised directly from GLYNDEBOURNE over a European network. But most televised operas in Europe are studio-produced, live or taped. In either case it has often been the practice in Italy and Germany to prerecord the singing while having attractive-looking performers and talented actors go through the motions of singing. England is partial to live transmission, though in one of its telecasts, that of SALOME, the dance was prefilmed and inserted into the production.

(6) *Motion Pictures*. Even during the era of silent motion pictures, one or two efforts were made to bring opera to the screen. Geraldine FARRAR appeared in CARMEN in an American-made film, while a German company compressed the RING cycle into a two-hour production. In each instance the music was exclusively instrumental, played by an orchestra in the pit, with the scores greatly compressed. The first time "talking pictures" were used commercially, opera played a passing role through several arias sung by Giovanni MARTINELLI, Marion Talley, and Anna Case. This was in New York City on Aug. 6, 1926, when the first half of the program was devoted to a screen concert. Soon after that, in 1928, a pioneer attempt was made by Fortuno GALLO to use the talking screen for opera with a production of PAGLIACCI. But it was many years before opera received any serious consideration as film entertainment.

When the breakthrough finally came, efforts were made to film actual performances on the stage and present these films in theaters. This occurred, for example, with several performances at the SALZBURG FESTIVAL, including DON GIOVANNI, DER ROSENKAVALIER, and COSÌ FAN TUTTE. A better method, however, was still to confine opera basically to the limitations of a stage but to add the mobility of action and scenery permitted by the camera. ZEFFIRELLI's production of LA BOHÈME, with KARAJAN conducting and Mirella FRENI as Mimi, proved a notable example of this technique. In such a way a good many operas were made available on film. Tito GOBBI starred in movie versions of RIGOLETTO, LA FORZA DEL DESTINO, THE BARBER OF SEVILLE, and *Pagliacci* in productions made in Italy. THE TALES OF HOFFMANN under BEECHAM (in which Bruce Dargavel sang all the roles of the evil geniuses) and BORIS GODUNOV, made in the Soviet Union, proved distinguished screen as well as operatic fare. The Soviet Union also made a film version of KATERINA ISMAILOVA, released in the United States in 1969. Renata TEBALDI appeared in LOHENGRIN, a motion picture produced in Italy, and she sang on the sound track but did not appear in another Italian-made production, that of AIDA. Walter FELSENSTEIN, the brilliant director of the KOMISCHE OPER in East Berlin, directed the filming of two operas, OTELLO and *The Tales of Hoffman*. Among other operas that have been filmed are the Karajan productions of *Pagliacci* and the entire *Ring* cycle; Grace BUMBRY in *Carmen,* also conducted by Karajan; Anna MOFFO in LA TRAVIATA; and the 1959 Salzburg Festival performance of *Don Giovanni*. The Karajan and some other recent productions have been made in anticipation of transference to cassettes for home use.

A festival of operatic films took place at the LINCOLN CENTER FOR THE PERFORMING ARTS in New York in July, 1970. The event was inaugurated with films performed by the HAMBURG STATE OPERA (DIE MEISTERSINGER, THE MARRIAGE OF FIGARO, DER FREISCHÜTZ, ZAR UND ZIMMERMANN, and ELEKTRA). This was followed by motion pictures performed by various other festivals and opera companies, including the Salzburg Festival and LA SCALA, the other operas presented being *Carmen, Così Fan Tutte,* CAVALLERIA RUSTICANA, *Pagliacci,* and *Don Giovanni*.

opera seria, a serious or tragic opera, as opposed to an OPERA BUFFA, or comic opera. The term was usually applied to Italian operas of the seventeenth and eighteenth centuries or operas resembling them, including those of HANDEL and such works as IDOMENEO.

operetta (or **light opera**), a romantic play containing songs, musical numbers, and dances. An operetta differs from musical comedy in that the musical score is of a more ambitious character.

Ophelia, Polonius' daughter (soprano), in love with Hamlet, in THOMAS's HAMLET.

Ophelia's Mad Scene, *see* PARTAGEZ-VOUS MES FLEURS!

O prêtres de Baal, Fidès' aria in the Prison Scene where she prays for the destruction of her own son, who has repudiated her, in Act V, Scene 1, of MEYERBEER'S LE PROPHÈTE.

O pur bonheur!, quartet of Juliette, Roméo, Friar Laurence, and Gertrude expressing their joy at the marriage of Roméo and Juliette, in Act III, Scene 1, of GOUNOD'S ROMÉO ET JULIETTE.

O qual soave brivido, love duet of Ricardo and Amelia in Act II of VERDI's UN BALLO IN MASCHERA.

Oracolo, L' (The Oracle), one-act opera by LEONI. Libretto by Camilio Zanoni, based on *The Cat and the Cherub,* a story by Chester Bailey Fernald. Premiere: Covent Garden, June 28, 1905. American premiere: New York City, Feb. 4, 1915. In the Chinese section of San Francisco, about 1900, the New Year is being celebrated. Win-Shee, a learned doctor (bass), consults his books and finds that tragedy awaits Hoo-Chee, son of a wealthy merchant. Chim-Fen, owner of an opium den (baritone), overhears this prophecy and decides to help destiny by kidnaping the boy. Win-Shee's son (tenor) follows the boy to the opium den, where Chim-Fen kills him. Win-Shee avenges the death of his son by strangling the murderer, after the kidnaped boy is returned to his father.

Ora a noi, Sharpless' attempt to warn Cio-Cio-San that Pinkerton has deserted her, in Act II of PUCCINI'S MADAMA BUT-TERFLY.

Ora dolci e divina, Magda's recollection of her past happy life and of a man she once met but whose identity she could not discover, in Act I of PUCCINI'S LA RONDINE.

Ora e per sempre addio, Otello's fare-well to his peace of mind, in Act II of VERDI's OTELLO.

Ora soave, sublime ora d'amore, love duet of Andrea Chénier and Madeleine, in Act II of GIORDANO'S ANDREA CHÉNIER.

Or che più non vedro, Jason's aria in CHERUBINI'S MÉDÉE.

Or co' dadi, *see* SQUILLI, ECHEGGI LA TROMBA GUERRIERA.

Or dammi il braccio tuo, Osaka's romantic appeal to Iris for her love, in Act II of MASCAGNI'S IRIS.

Ordgar, Thane of Devon (bass) in TAYLOR'S THE KING'S HENCHMAN.

Oréstie, L', a trilogy of dramatic works with music by MILHAUD, based on AES-CHYLUS, comprising *Agamemnon,* LES CHOËPHORES, and *Les Euménides.* The world premiere of the entire trilogy took place at the BERLIN FESTIVAL in Apr., 1963. *See* ORESTES.

Orestes, (1) in Greek legend, the son of Clytemnestra and Agamemnon and brother of Electra. He avenges the murder of his father by killing his mother and her lover, Aegisthus. The fates, or Erinnyes, torment him until a trial absolves him. The dramatist AESCHYLUS wrote a trilogy with Orestes as the central character, and these have been made into numerous operas. Richard STRAUSS'S ELEKTRA was based on SOPH-OCLES' tragedy on the same subject; GLUCK'S IPHIGÉNIE EN TAURIDE and KRENEK'S DAS LEBEN DES OREST were derived from EURIPIDES' treatment of the Orestes story.

(2) Son of Klytemnestra and Aga-memnon (baritone) in Richard Strauss's *Elektra.*

(3) Iphigenia's brother (baritone) in Gluck's *Iphigénie en Tauride.*

Orest! es rührt sich niemand!, Recognition Scene in Richard STRAUSS'S ELEKTRA, in which Elektra recognizes an apparent stranger as her brother Orestes.

Orfeo (Orpheus), a Thracian musician, husband of Euridice (Eurydice). He is the principal male character in GLUCK's ORFEO ED EURIDICE, a role created by GUADAGNI. He is also a principal character in PERI's *Euridice,* the earliest opera still to survive. Subsequent operas in which he is the hero include those by J. C. BACH; CACCINI (*Euridice*); CASELLA (*La favola d'Orfeo*); GRAUN; HAYDN; KRENEK; MALIPIERO (*L'Orfeide*, a trilogy); KEISER; MILHAUD (LES MALHEURS D'ORPHÉE); OFFENBACH's OPÉRA BOUFFE, ORPHEUS IN THE UNDERWORLD; and MONTEVERDI'S L'ORFEO.

Orfeo, L', FAVOLA PER MUSICA in prologue and five acts by MONTEVERDI. Libretto by Alessandro Striggio. Premiere: Mantua, Feb. 22, 1607 (private performance); Court Theater, Mantua, Feb. 24, 1607 (public performance). American premiere: New York, Apr. 14, 1912 (concert version); Northampton, Mass., May 12, 1929 (staged). The libretto follows the familiar legend of Orpheus and Eurydice (of which the most celebrated operatic version is GLUCK's *Orfeo ed Euridice*). For the plot *see* ORFEO ED EURIDICE.

Monteverdi's opera is a vibrant work of art. The tentative vocal writing of such earlier composers as PERI and CACCINI has been superseded. Melody emerges for the first time in such moving arias as "Ecco purch'a voi ritorno," which opens the second act and in the same act, "Ahi! caso acerbo," and "Vi ricordo o boschi ombrosi"; also in "Tu se' morta," where Orpheus later expresses grief over his wife's death and in his affecting plea to Charon, "Possente spirto." Monteverdi employed a larger, more varied orchestra than had been used previously, and the instrumental portions of the score project atmosphere and dramatic effect. "Monteverdi turned the aristocratic spectacle of Florence into modern musical drama, overflowing with life and bearing in its mighty waves of sounds the passions which make up the human soul," wrote Henri Prunières.

What is believed to be the first modern staged version was given in Paris on May 2, 1911. Since then the opera has been intermittently revived, notably at the FLORENCE MAY MUSIC FESTIVAL in 1949, the NEW YORK CITY OPERA in 1960, at the AIX-EN-PROVENCE festival in 1965, and at the HOLLAND FESTIVAL and BERLIN OPERA in 1967. When heard today, the opera is often given in an edited version, usually that of MALIPIERO, or RESPIGHI, or ORFF, the last of whom made not one but three different adaptations.

Orfeo ed Euridice (Orpheus and Eurydice), (1) opera in four acts by GLUCK. Libretto by Raniero de CALZABIGI, based on the Greek legend. Premiere: Burgtheater, Vienna, Oct. 5, 1762. American premiere: the Winter Garden, New York City, May 25, 1863.

Characters: Orfeo, Greek musician (contralto); Euridice, his wife (soprano); Amor, god of love (soprano); Happy Shade (soprano); Blessed Spirits; Furies; shepherds, shepherdesses; heroes and heroines. The setting is legendary Greece.

Act I. The tomb of Euridice. Shepherds, shepherdesses, and nymphs are mourning ("Ah! se intorno a quest' urna funesta"), and Orfeo mourns with them. Amor, touched by his grief, instructs him to descend to the lower world and lead Euridice back to earth. But he is to do this only on the condition that he does not look at her.

Act II. Tartarus. The Furies confront Orfeo, demanding to know who dares enter their realm. They perform a demoniac dance to frighten him. Orfeo pleads for mercy ("Deh placatevi con me") and wins them over. The gates of the lower world open. Orfeo passes through and the Furies continue their infernal dance (Dance of the Furies).

Act III. The Elysian Fields. The Blessed Spirits perform a serene and radiant dance (Dance of the Blessed Spirits). Euridice and the Spirits describe the peace and beauty of Elysium ("E quest' asilo ameno e grato"). When Orfeo arrives, he too is spellbound by the heavenly beauty ("Che puro ciel"). Finding his beloved Euridice, he entreats her to follow him; as she does so, he refuses to look back at her.

Act IV. A forest. Euridice is heartbroken, for she interprets Orfeo's failure to look at her as an indication that he loves her no more. She renews her entreaties until Orfeo can resist no longer.

He takes his wife passionately into his arms; as he does so, she dies. Orfeo is grief-stricken ("Che farò senza Euridice"). Amor once again comes to his aid, reviving Euridice and allowing the pair to return safely to earth. In the Temple of Love, Orfeo sings the praises of Amor. Dances of rejoicing take place. Then Orfeo, Euridice, and Amor sing a hymn to true love ("Trionfi, Amore").

Orfeo ed Euridice is the first opera in which Gluck purposefully departed from the stilted formulas, the meretricious texts, the sawdust historical characters, and the ornate music of the Italians; for these he substituted simplicity, economy, and deep human feeling. To this day, *Orfeo* remains a vital and poignant work of art. There is probably no opera in the repertory that accomplishes so much with so few means. There are only two main characters and only four solo voices in all; very little happens throughout the four acts; there are no elaborate scenes or overpowering climaxes. Yet the opera never fails to have dramatic appeal, never fails to touch the heart. As remarkable as its simplicity is its dramatic truth. Text and music are wonderfully integrated as Gluck portrays the terrors of Hell with acrid dissonances and recreates the rapture of Elysium with some of the most beatific music ever written.

When originally given in Vienna in Italian, the part of Orfeo was sung by, as it was written for, a contralto CASTRATO, Gaetano GUADAGNI. But the French did not tolerate castrati on their stages, and so for its premiere a few years later at the OPÉRA in Paris, Gluck revised the score and the part was sung by a tenor. It is the general custom today to perform the original Italian version with a female contralto as Orfeo.

(2) Opera by HAYDN. Libretto by Bedini. Premiere: Florence May Music Festival, May, 1951. American premiere: Cambridge, Mass., May 1, 1965. This is Haydn's finest opera. He completed it in 1791 for performance in London during his visit to that city, but due to managerial difficulties it was not then produced. The score was subsequently dismembered, and the work was known only through excerpts. Haydn scholars reassembled the various parts, and the work was performed for the first time in Vienna in 1950 for a phonograph recording. Its first stage performance took place a half year later.

Orff, Carl, composer. Born Munich, July 10, 1895. He graduated from the Akademie der Tonkunst in Munich in 1914. For four years he worked as coach and conductor in several German theaters. In 1921 he returned to study as a pupil of Heinrich Kaminski. In 1925 he received recognition through his first adaptation of MONTEVERDI'S L'ORFEO. After 1925 he taught at the Gunther School of Music, which he had founded, and conducted the Bavarian Theater orchestra.

In 1935 Orff rejected all the works he had written up to then and began writing operas exclusively—operas in which the paraphernalia of costuming, scenery, and staging were discarded for a return to basic essentials. His first opera (or "scenic cantata," as he called it) in this new style was CARMINA BURANA, based on anonymous medieval poems. It was first presented in Frankfurt in 1937 and has since become his most frequently played work, mostly in concert performances. *Carmina Burana* was the first work in a trilogy that eventually included CATULLI CARMINA and TRIONFO DI AFRODITE. The entire trilogy, TRIONFI, was introduced at LA SCALA early in 1953. These and some of his later operas are based on texts that reach into the remote past, not only to medieval poetry, but also to old Bavarian legends and literature of ancient Greece. ANTIGONAE was introduced at the 1949 SALZBURG FESTIVAL, DIE BERNAUERIN at the 1950 MUNICH FESTIVAL, OEDIPUS DER TYRANN and *Ludus de Natio Infante Mirificus* at the Württemberg Opera in 1959 and 1960 respectively, and PROMETHEUS at the STUTTGART OPERA in 1968. The works mentioned above dispense with traditional lyricism, substituting a kind of rhythmic declamation, sometimes unaccompanied by instruments. Considerable emphasis is placed on rhythm, so that Orff enlists large percussion forces. His is essentially a neoprimitive style, though when he sets folk tales to music his manner becomes lighter, more assimilable, and at times even comic. In July, 1962, Orff visited Canada to serve as chairman of a conference on music education at the University of Toronto's Royal Conservatory of Music. He has been decorated with the *Pour le Merité* for arts and sciences by the West German government. Besides the works already mentioned, Orff has written DER MOND (1936, revised 1945); *Die Kluge* (1942); *Astutuli* (1946); *Ein Sommernachtstraum; Comoedia de Christi Resurrectione* (1956).

Orford, Ellen, schoolmistress (soprano) in love with Peter Grimes in BRITTEN'S PETER GRIMES.

O riante nature, Baucis's aria in Act II of GOUNOD'S PHILEMON ET BAUCIS.

O Richard, o mon roi!, Blondel's aria in GRÉTRY'S RICHARD COEUR DE LION.

Orlando furioso, one of the masterpieces of Renaissance literature, an epic of Roland, by Lodovico ARIOSTO.

Orlofsky, Prince, a nobleman, usually sung by a mezzo-soprano, in Johann STRAUSS'S DIE FLEDERMAUS.

Ormindo, opera in three acts by CAVALLI. Libretto by Faustini. Premiere: Teatro San Cassiano, Venice, Carnival of 1644. American premiere: New York City, Apr. 24, 1968. The plot involves two young officers in love with a queen, who reciprocates their love. Her husband, the king, eventually forgives the lovers, one of whom finds consolation with an Egyptian princess. A chorus, representing the servants, is used with amusing effect in commenting upon these amatory complications.

Orombello, the hero (tenor), in love with Beatrice, in BELLINI'S BEATRICE DI TENDA.

Orovesco, chief of the Druids (bass) in BELLINI'S NORMA.

Orpheus, *see* ORFEO.

Orpheus in the Underworld (Orphée aux Enfers), OPÉRA BOUFFE by OFFEN-BACH. Libretto by Hector Crémieux. Premiere: Bouffes-Parisiens, Paris, Oct. 21, 1858. American premiere: Stadttheater, New York, Mar., 1861. This is a burlesque on the Olympian gods and, incidentally, on the legend of Orpheus and Eurydice. Orpheus, a teacher of music in Thebes, is the husband of Eurydice. Both find their love elsewhere. Orpheus is attracted to Chloe, a shepherdess, while Eurydice loves the shepherd Aristeus, actually Pluto in disguise. When Eurydice elopes to Hades with Aristeus, Orpheus is delighted, but convention decrees that he try to reclaim her. He calls upon Jupiter for help. Jupiter commands Pluto to surrender Eurydice to her husband. Orpheus is ordered not to look at his wife until he has passed the Styx. Now it is Jupiter who falls in love with Eurydice. He hurls a bolt of lightning at Orpheus which so frightens the musician that he momentarily looks at his wife, thus losing her. Jupiter takes Eurydice as a Bacchante, and Orpheus happily returns to Chloe.

The overture is a staple in the repertory of salon orchestras and pop concerts. It opens briskly, then progresses to its first subject, a light, gay tune for the strings. The core of the overture is the second melody, a sentimental song heard first in solo violin, then repeated by full orchestra.

These are some of the best known vocal excerpts in this *opéra bouffe:* in Act I, "Ah, seigneur, ah quel supplice," in which Eurydice prays for deliverance from her husband, and "La mort m'apparait souriante," Eurydice's invocation to death; in Act III, John Styx's autobiographical song, "Quand j'étais roi de Boétie," and the so-called Flea Duet, "Il me semble sur mon épaule," between Eurydice and Jupiter, the latter transformed into a flea; in Act IV, Eurydice's hymn to Bacchus, "Evohé, Bacchus m'inspire."

When introduced, *Orpheus in the Underworld* was not well received and seemed doomed to failure. There was much to cause shock: the way in which Offenbach quotes satirically the famous air from GLUCK'S ORFEO ED EURIDICE, "Che farò senza Euridice"; the juxtaposition of a staid minuet and a scandalous cancan; the discordant accompaniment simulating the snoring of the gods for songs by Cupid and Venus; and the overall sacrilegious treatment of the Olympian gods and their outrageous goings-on. But when the critic Jules Janin attacked it as a profanation of "holy and glorious antiquity," he aroused so much curiosity that the work suddenly attracted capacity audiences. It stayed on for two hundred and twenty-eight performances, and closed only because the cast needed a rest.

Orsini, Maffio, young nobleman (contralto) in DONIZETTI'S LUCREZIA BORGIA.

Orsini, Paolo, head of the house of Orsini (bass) in WAGNER'S RIENZI.

Or son sei mesi, Dick Johnson's aria revealing to Minnie his past and the circumstances that led him to become a criminal, in Act II of PUCCINI'S THE GIRL OF THE GOLDEN WEST.

Ortensio, the Countess of Berkenfeld's servant (bass) in DONIZETTI'S THE DAUGHTER OF THE REGIMENT.

Ortrud, Telramund's wife (mezzo-soprano) in WAGNER'S LOHENGRIN.

O ruddier than the cherry, Polyphemus' aria in Part II of HANDEL'S ACIS AND GALATEA.

Orzse, childhood sweetheart (soprano) of Háry János in KODÁLY'S HÁRY JÁNOS.

Osaka, rich libertine (tenor) in love with Iris in MASCAGNI'S IRIS.

O sancta justitia, *basso buffo* aria of Van Bett, as he makes his first entrance, in Act I of LORTZING'S ZAR UND ZIMMERMANN.

O signore, dal tetto natio, the war chorus of the Crusaders in Act IV of VERDI'S I LOMBARDI.

O sink' hernieder, Nacht der Liebe, *see* LIEBESNACHT.

Osmin, overseer of the Pasha's house (bass) in MOZART'S THE ABDUCTION FROM THE SERAGLIO.

O soave fanciulla, love duet of Mimi and Rodolfo, closing Act I of PUCCINI'S LA BOHÈME.

O sole! Vita! Eternità, chorus of the people, hailing love in the closing scene of PUCCINI'S TURANDOT.

O sommo Carlo, trio of Elvira, Ernani, and Don Carlo with chorus in praise of the Emperor Charles V for having given his blessings to the union of Ernani and Elvira, in Act III of VERDI'S ERNANI.

O Souverain! O Juge! O Père, Rodrigo's prayer in Act III of MASSENET'S LE CID.

Ossian, *see* MACPHERSON, JAMES.

Otello (Othello), opera in four acts by VERDI. Libretto by BOITO, based on the SHAKESPEARE tragedy. Premiere: La Scala, Feb. 5, 1887. American premiere: Academy of Music, New York, Apr. 16, 1888.

Characters: Otello, a Moor, general in the Venetian army (tenor), a role created by TAMAGNO; Iago, his aide (baritone); Cassio, Otello's lieutenant (tenor); Roderigo, a Venetian gentleman (tenor); Lodovico, ambassador of the Venetian Republic (bass); Montano, Otello's predecessor as governor of Cyprus (bass); Desdemona, Otello's wife (soprano); Emilia, Iago's wife (mezzo-soprano); a herald (bass); soldiers; sailors; Venetians; Cypriots. The setting is a seaport of Cyprus toward the end of the fifteenth century.

Act I. Outside Otello's castle. A celebration honors the arrival of Otello, the people hailing his victory over the Turkish fleet ("Esultate!"). Among those present is Iago, who is resentful that Otello had chosen Cassio as his lieutenant. Cassio is here, too, in the company of Roderigo, who is in love with Otello's wife. Iago advises Roderigo to be patient, for surely Desdemona will tire of her husband. A festive bonfire is now lit, hailed by the people ("Fuoco di gioia!"). As the fire burns, Iago sings a drinking song (BRINDISI: "Inaffia l'ugola!"). He induces Cassio to drink wine. When Cassio becomes inebriated, Iago provokes him to fight a duel with Montano, in which the latter is wounded. A riot develops, quelled only by the arrival of Otello. Otello punishes Cassio by removing him from his command. After the crowd disperses, Otello is joined by his wife. Tenderly they recall how they came to fall in love ("Già nella notte densa").

Act II. A hall in the castle. Bent on destroying Otello, Iago philosophizes that God is a cruel being who meant man to be cruel ("Credo in un Dio crudel"). He encourages Cassio to address Desdemona; then, when Otello appears, he fans the latter's jealousy by pointing out how Cassio and Desdemona are in consultation in the nearby garden. Desdemona appears in the company of women and children, who sing her praises in "Dove guardi splendono." To test his suspicions, Otello questions his wife about Cassio, and he is made still uneasier when Desdemona insists that Cassio is innocent of all wrongdoing. When Desdemona wipes her brow with a handkerchief which Otello had previously given her as a gift, he throws it passionately on the ground. This handkerchief is passed on by Emilia to Iago, who contrives to use it in his plot against Otello. Meanwhile, Otello bids farewell to his tranquillity of mind and his hopes for the future ("Ora e per sempre addio"). Iago comes ostensibly to console Otello but actually to arouse him further. He confides that he has found Desdemona's handkerchief in Cassio's room. He also tells Otello that he overheard Cassio talking of his love for Desdemona in a dream ("Era la notte"). Frantic with anger, Otello falls on his knees and swears to seek revenge ("Si, pel ciel marmoreo giuro!").

Act III. The great hall of the castle. On further questioning, Desdemona insists to Otello that both she and Cassio are innocent ("Dio ti giocondi"). She insists that Otello is the sole man she loves ("Esterrefatta fisso io sguardo tuo tremendo"). Otello asks Desdemona for her handkerchief, but the one she offers him is not the one he wants, and he sends her off to her room to fetch it. While she is gone, he bitterly laments that all his illusions have been shattered ("Dio! mi potevi scagliar"). Iago appears and urges Otello to secrete himself behind a column. When Otello does so, Iago accosts Cassio and induces him to

boast about a love affair, which Otello assumes is with Desdemona. Cassio reveals to Iago that he has found Desdemona's handkerchief in his room and wonders how it came there. The sight of the handkerchief is the final proof to Otello that his wife is guilty; he determines to kill her. Lodovico, the Venetian ambassador, arrives to tell Otello that he must return to Venice and turn over his place in Cyprus to Cassio. As Otello imparts this news to Desdemona, he becomes blind with rage and hurls her angrily to the ground. Desdemona bewails the fact that she has lost her husband's love forever ("A terra! si, nel livido"). Otello himself becomes so overwrought that he falls fainting to the ground.

Act IV. A brief orchestral prelude projects an ominous atmosphere. Desdemona's bedroom. As Emilia prepares Desdemona for bed, Desdemona tells her of a song she learned in childhood (Canzone del Salce, "Willow Song": "Salce! Salce!"). After Emilia departs, Desdemona falls on her knees to pray to the Madonna for protection ("Ave Maria"). Otello arrives, once again to subject her to relentless questioning about Cassio. Her insistence that she is innocent arouses his fury. Mad with rage he chokes and kills his wife. Emilia and Lodovico burst into the room to find Desdemona dead. It is only now that Otello learns the truth: that Iago had created the fiction of Desdemona's infidelity in order to destroy him. Otello mourns the sad fate of his wife, then kills himself with his dagger (Otello's Death: "Niun mi tema").

With *Otello,* Verdi broke a self-imposed silence as composer for the stage that had lasted fifteen years, since 1871, when he had completed AIDA. The stimulus sending him back to opera was the powerful and moving libretto that Boito had fashioned from Shakespeare's tragedy. It was a far different Verdi who wrote *Otello* from the one who had gained fame with RIGOLETTO, LA TRAVIATA, IL TROVATORE, and *Aida.* Since his libretto called for a different musical approach and since Verdi had assimilated WAGNER's music dramas, he emerged in *Otello* as a supreme musical dramatist, whose music was continually the handmaid to the play, serving it completely. There was no attempt to imitate Wagner, but there was a conscious effort to bring to Italian lyricism a greater expressiveness, a deeper psychological insight into characters, and a greater dramatic force and truth. Verdi's score was of an integrated, indivisible texture—no longer a collation of attractive sections.

The premiere of *Otello* attracted wide attention. Verdi himself was uncertain of his opera's worth, and he had reserved the right to withdraw it if he found it unsatisfactory in rehearsal. A thunder of applause greeted the composer when the opera ended, and he had to take over twenty curtain calls. Some in the audience wept. Verdi's carriage was dragged by his admirers to his hotel. Until five in the morning, his public continued to shout: "Viva, Verdi!"

Otello, il moro di Venezia (Othello, the Moor of Venice), opera in three acts by ROSSINI. Libretto by Francesco di Salsa, based on the Shakespeare tragedy. Premiere: Teatro del Fondo, Naples, Dec. 4, 1816. American premiere: Park Theater, New York, Feb. 7, 1826. The plot is essentially that of the opera discussed above. The first American revival of a staged performance since 1826 was given by the AMERICAN OPERA SOCIETY in 1968, followed a few weeks later by performances at the LAKE GEORGE OPERA FESTIVAL in New York.

Otello's Death, *see* NIUN MI TEMA.

O temple magnifique (O tempio sontuoso), Selika's aria in Act V of MEYERBEER's L'AFRICAINE.

O Teresa, vous que j'aime, the ecstatic love duet of Teresa and Benvenuto Cellini in Act I of BERLIOZ' BENVENUTO CELLINI.

O terra, addio, the duet of Aida and Radames, their farewell to the world, in Act IV, Scene 2, of VERDI's AIDA.

Othello, a Moor, general in the Venetian army, in ROSSINI's OTELLO, IL

MORO DI VENEZIA and VERDI's OTELLO. In both operas the role is for a tenor.

O transport, O douce extase (Dove son? o qual gioia), love duet of Vasco da Gama and Selika, in Act IV of MEYERBEER's L'AFRICAINE.

Ottavia, wife (soprano) of Nero in MONTEVERDI's L'INCORONAZIONE DI POPPEA.

Ottavio, (1) Donna Anna's beloved (tenor) in MOZART's DON GIOVANNI.

(2) A wealthy Venetian (bass) in WOLF-FERRARI's LE DONNE CURIOSE.

Ottokar, Prince of Bohemia (baritone) in WEBER's DER FREISCHÜTZ.

Ottone, the beloved (tenor) of Ottavia in MONTEVERDI's L'INCORONAZIONE DI POPPEA.

O tu che in seno, Alvaro's aria in which he nostalgically remembers Leonora, whom he believes to be dead, in Act III, Scene 1, of VERDI's LA FORZA DEL DESTINO.

O tu Palermo, Procrida's salute to his native city upon returning home from exile, in Act II of VERDI's THE SICILIAN VESPERS.

Oui, je veux par le monde, Wilhelm Meister's happy-go-lucky philosophy of life, in Act I of THOMAS's MIGNON.

Our arms entwined, Vanessa's aria in Act II of BARBER's VANESSA.

Ourrias, Mireille's suitor (bass) in GOUNOD's MIREILLE.

Où va la jeune Hindoue?, Lakmé's celebrated Bell Song in Act II of DELIBES's LAKMÉ.

O vago suol della Turrena, *see* O BEAU PAYS DE LA TOURAINE.

Over the dark blue waters, quartet of Rezia, Huon, Sherasmin, and Fatima in Act II, Scene 2, of WEBER's OBERON, as they reach the harbor from which Huon and Rezia can proceed to Greece.

overture, an instrumental preface or prelude to an opera. The earliest operas did not have instrumental overtures but began with extended vocal prologues. The use of brief instrumental preludes was soon begun, the early Italian composers calling these pieces sinfonias or toccatas. It was early in the eighteenth century that Alessandro SCARLATTI introduced what has since been called the Italian overture, henceforth employed extensively by the Neapolitan school and its imitators. This type of overture comprised three sections: the first fast, frequently in fugal style; the second slow; the third fast. In France, LULLY popularized a different kind of overture, now known as the French overture. It began with a majestic slow section, followed by a fast part, generally in fugal style, and concluded with a popular dance, such as a minuet.

GLUCK was the first composer to stress a relationship of mood between the overture and the opera. In his ALCESTE and IPHIGÉNIE EN AULIDE, for example, the overture establishes the atmosphere of the opera, and its concluding bars lead directly into the opening scene. MOZART was one of the first composers to use materials from his opera in some of his overtures (DON GIOVANNI, THE MAGIC FLUTE), while in other operas he followed Gluck's lead to use the overture to project the mood or atmosphere of the drama that follows. This effort by Gluck and Mozart to create an intimate bond between overture and opera was furthered by BEETHOVEN, WEBER, and WAGNER. The overtures of these composers were frequently miniature tone poems expressing the dramatic and emotional substance of the opera. Some of Wagner's overtures are called preludes to emphasize their role in creating the emotional setting for the opening scene, and his preludes lead directly into the opening action without pause. Meanwhile, in the nineteenth century, many Italian composers continued the practice of producing overtures that were thoroughly independent of their operas, so much so that it was sometimes the practice of composers like ROSSINI to use the overture of one opera for another. VERDI, who was partial to short orchestral prefaces, makes the overture such a basic part of the scene that follows that with only a few exceptions (LA FORZA DEL DESTINO, THE SICILIAN VESPERS) they cannot be performed at symphony concerts. Some of his overtures quote material from the operas. Some are fragmentary: the prelude to OTELLO comprises just four measures of violent music before the rise of the curtain. With PUCCINI and some other major twentieth-century composers, overtures have been eliminated. A few measures in the orchestra suffice to set the drama into motion. Richard STRAUSS's SALOME and ELEKTRA begin without any orchestral preliminaries.

O vin, dissipe la tristesse (Chanson bachique), Hamlet's drinking song in Act II of THOMAS's HAMLET.

O wär ich schon mit dir vereint, Marcellina's expression of love for Leonore (disguised as a man), in Act I of BEETHOVEN's FIDELIO.

O welche Lust!, the Prisoners' Chorus as, emerging from their dark cells into the sunlight, they sing a paean to freedom, in Act I, Scene 2, of BEETHOVEN's FIDELIO.

O Wunden, wunderveiler heiliger Speer, Gurnemanz' recital to his squires about the history of Amfortas' wound, in Act I, Scene 1, of WAGNER's PARSIFAL.

Ozean, du Ungeheuer! See OCEAN, THOU MIGHTY MONSTER.

O zitt're nicht, mein lieber Sohn, the recitative and aria of the Queen of the Night telling Tamino he can have Pamina as wife if he saves her from imprisonment at the hands of a tyrant, in Act I, Scene 1, of MOZART's THE MAGIC FLUTE.

P

Pacchierotti, Gasparo, soprano and contralto CASTRATO. Born Fabriano, Italy, May, 1740; died Padua, Oct. 28, 1821. After studying at St. Mark's in Venice with Bertoni, he began singing secondary roles in Venice, Vienna, and Milan before he was sixteen and principal roles from 1769 on. He enjoyed extraordinary success in leading opera houses in Italy. In 1778, again between 1780 and 1784, and in 1790 he achieved triumphs in London. Pacchierotti's singing made an even profounder impression on the musicians of his day than FARINELLI's, and in addition he was a fine actor. His range of three octaves extended from C below middle C to the soprano high C. He sang at the openings of two famous Italian opera houses still standing, LA SCALA in Milan and the FENICE in Venice, the latter inauguration taking place in 1792, when Pacchierotti, aged fifty-two, retired in Padua.

Pace e gioia, Almaviva's sardonic greeting to Bartolo in Act II of ROSSINI's THE BARBER OF SEVILLE.

Pace, pace, mio Dio!, Leonora's prayer to God to relieve her of her tortured memories and dreams, in Act IV, Scene 2, of VERDI's LA FORZA DEL DESTINO.

Pace t'imploro, Amneris' plea to Isis for peace, in the closing scene of VERDI's AIDA.

Pacini, Giovanni, composer. Born Catania, Sicily, Feb. 17, 1796; died Pescia, Italy, Dec. 6, 1867. He was a prolific opera composer, who had over seventy operas produced in leading Italian theaters, most of them in the style of ROSSINI. He studied with MARCHESI and Padre Mattei at Bologna and with Furlanetto at Venice. His first opera, *Annetta e Lucinda,* was produced in Venice in 1813. He continued writing operas until 1835, when the failure of *Carlo di Borgogna* at Venice sent him into temporary retirement as a composer. He then settled in Viareggio, where he founded a school of music, which he subsequently transferred to near-by Lucca. When he returned to operatic composition, he created *Saffo* in twenty-eight days, which turned out to be his masterwork and enjoyed a major success when introduced in Naples on Nov. 29, 1840. He completed some forty operas after that, the most significant being MEDEA, heard first at Palermo in 1843; *La regina di Cipro,* introduced in Turin in 1846; and *Niccolo de' Lapi,* first given posthumously in Florence in 1873. He was the author of several treatises and a book of reminiscences, *La mie memorzie artistiche* (Florence, 1865).

Paco, a gypsy (tenor) in FALLA's LA VIDA BREVE.

Padmâvatî, BALLET-OPERA in two acts by ROUSSEL. Libretto by Louis Laloy. Premiere: Paris Opéra, June 1, 1923. This opera, the composer's most important, is based on an event in Indian history. In the thirteenth century Alaoudin, the Mogul sultan, is willing to conclude an alliance with the King of Tchitor on the condition that the king turn over to him his wife, Padmâvatî. After this deal has been consummated, war breaks out anyway between Alaoudin's country and Tchitor, in which the King of Tchitor is defeated. Padmâvatî then kills Alaoudin, for which she suffers death on his funeral pyre.

Padre Guardiano, see GUARDIANO, PADRE.

Paer, Ferdinando, composer. Born Parma, June 1, 1771; died Paris, May 3, 1839. After studying with Gasparo Ghiretti, he wrote his first opera, *La locanda dei vagabondi*, produced in Parma in 1789. He now wrote other operas, both comic and serious, all in the traditional Italian style, but after settling in Vienna in 1797 and becoming acquainted with MOZART's operas, his style became more refined, richer in content, with increasing dramatic interest. In 1802 he was appointed court KAPELLMEISTER in Dresden. During this period he wrote *Leonora*, based on the same story as BEETHOVEN's FIDELIO and introduced in Dresden Oct. 3, 1804, thirteen months before Beethoven's opera was first heard in Vienna. In 1807 Paer went to Paris, where he became MAÎTRE DE CHAPELLE to the court of Napoleon and conductor at the OPÉRA-COMIQUE. In 1812 he succeeded SPONTINI as director of the Théâtre des Italiens, holding this post for fifteen years. In 1832 he was appointed conductor of royal chamber music. He wrote forty-three operas, all of them now forgotten. The most popular were: *I molinari* (1793); *La Griselda* (1796); *Achille* (1801); *Leonora* (1804); *Sofonisba* (1805); *Didone abbandonata* (1810); AGNES (1819); *Le Maître de chapelle* (1821).

Pagano, Arvino's brother (baritone) and his rival for Violanda in VERDI's I LOMBARDI.

Page, husband (baritone) of one of Sir John Falstaff's prospective loves in NICOLAI's THE MERRY WIVES OF WINDSOR. When the opera is sung in its original language, German, Page is known as Herr Reich.

Page, Mistress, (1) one of Sir John Falstaff's prospective loves (mezzo-soprano) in NICOLAI's THE MERRY WIVES OF WINDSOR. Wife of above.

(2) The same (soprano) in VERDI's FALSTAFF.

Page's Song, *see* NOBLES SEIGNEURS, SALUT.

Pagliacci, I, opera in prologue and two acts by LEONCAVALLO. Libretto by the composer. Premiere: Teatro dal Verme, Milan, May 21, 1892. American premiere: New York City, June 15, 1893.

Characters: Canio, head of a theatrical troupe (tenor); Nedda, his wife (soprano); Tonio, a clown (baritone); Beppe, an actor (tenor); Silvio, a villager (baritone); peasants; villagers. The setting is Montalto, a village in Calabria, on the Feast of the Assumption.

Prologue. A vivacious orchestral prelude describes the gaiety attending a village festival. Tonio steps before the curtain to explain that the play about to be witnessed is a real story with real people ("Si può").

Act I. Entrance to the village of Montalto. It is the day of the Feast of the Assumption, August 15. The villagers hail the arrival of an itinerant theatrical company ("Viva Pagliaccio"). Canio announces a performance for that evening. Just before entering the inn, he invites Tonio to accompany him. When the clown refuses, a villager suggests slyly that perhaps Tonio wants to stay behind so that he can be alone with Canio's wife, Nedda. For a moment Canio is disturbed, but he brushes away his anxiety, maintaining one should not confuse life with the theater ("Un tal gioco"). As the church bells ring, the villagers assemble for vespers (Coro delle campane, Chorus of the Bells: "Din, don, suona vespero"). The crowd departs, and Nedda is alone, at first troubled by Canio's momentary display of jealousy, but then dispelling her troubles with thoughts about the carefree flight of birds (BALLATELLA: "Stridono lassù"). Tonio appears and tries to make love to her, but she is repelled by the ugly, deformed clown and drives him away with a whip. A villager, Silvio, is more pleasing to Nedda, and she is receptive to his lovemaking ("Decidi il mio destin"). They are overheard by the clown, who quickly summons Canio to witness the scene; but before Canio can identify his rival, Silvio escapes. When Nedda refuses to divulge the identity of her lover, Canio attacks her with a dagger, but she is saved by Beppe. Overwhelmed by the realization that his wife is unfaithful, Canio sobs bitterly and remarks on his tragic plight, appearing in a comic play while his heart is breaking ("Vesti la giubba").

Act II. The same scene. There is a short intermezzo before the rise of the curtain. Villagers gather before the little traveling theater to witness the evening's performance. The curtain rises on a play which, by unhappy coincidence, concerns a situation similar to that involving the principal performers. Harlequin (played by Beppe) serenades Columbine (Nedda) outside her window, while her husband is away ("O Colombina"). Taddeo (Tonio) enters and tries to make love to Columbine ("È casta al par di neve!"), but he is soon driven away by Harlequin, who enters through the window. Harlequin and Columbine are interrupted in their tryst by the sudden appearance of Columbine's husband, Pagliaccio (Canio). Harlequin makes his escape through the window. All at once, Canio forgets he is playing a part in a play. He exclaims he is no longer Pagliaccio ("No, Pagliaccio non son") and demands the name of Nedda's lover. When she refuses to give it, he kills her with his dagger. From the audience, Silvio rushes to the stage to help Nedda, but it is too late. He, too, is slain by Canio, who then sobs out to the horrified audience: "La commedia è finita," "The comedy is ended."

I Pagliacci belongs to the VERISMO school of Italian opera, which presented everyday characters in everyday situations. This new school of realism had been introduced by MASCAGNI'S CAVALLERIA RUSTICANA only two years earlier; and Leoncavallo's opera contributed handsomely to popularize its aims.

It is customary to speak of I Pagliacci and Cavalleria rusticana in the same breath: the two operas are usually performed on the same bill. They have striking points of similarity in musical style and in the emotional turmoil of their stories. But it is important to notice their points of difference. To his op-era Leoncavallo brought a refinement of writing and a poetic feeling, as well as occasional comic relief not found in Mascagni's Cavalleria.

Victor MAUREL, who created the role of Tonio, brought more than his vocal artistry to bear in making I Pagliacci a sensational success at its premiere, for it was he who suggested to the composer the idea of the prologue, an afterthought that Leoncavallo turned into one of the opera's finest arias.

Paillasses, Les, the title by which I PAGLIACCI is known in France.

painters and paintings in opera. The following operas were inspired by paintings: GOYESCAS by the paintings of Goya; AMAHL AND THE NIGHT VISITORS by Hieronymous Bosch's *The Adoration of the Magi;* Josef Rheinberger's *Die sieben Raben* by a set of paintings by Moritz von Schwind; MONA LISA by Da Vinci's masterpiece of the same name; FRIEDENSTAG by Velasquez' *The Surrender of Breda;* and THE RAKE'S PROGRESS by William Hogarth's series of paintings of the same title.

The following painters are central characters in operas: Cellini (Berlioz' BENVENUTO CELLINI and Franz Lachner's CELLINI); Dürer (Waldemar von Baussnern's *Dürer in Venice*); Gainsborough (COATES's opera of the same name); Gauguin (John Gardner's *The Moon and Sixpence*); Matthias Grünewald (Hindemith's MATHIS DER MALER); Michelangelo (Nicolo Isouard's *Michel-Ange*); Rembrandt (BADINGS, KLENAU in operas of the same name).

Paisiello, Giovanni, composer. Born Taranto, Italy, May 8, 1740; died Naples, June 5, 1816. For nine years he attended the Conservatorio San Onofrio in Naples, beginning in 1754, his teachers including Francesco DURANTE and Geronimo Abos. For a while he specialized in writing choral music, but in 1763 he wrote a comic intermezzo that was so successful when introduced at the conservatory that he received a commission for an opera, *La pupilla,* a preeminent success when introduced in Bologna in 1764. During the next dozen years Paisiello wrote over fifty operas many of them extensively performed; he became one of the most celebrated opera composers in Italy. In 1776 he was invited to Russia by Catherine II. He remained in St. Petersburg eight years, acting as the Empress' music master. It was during this period that he wrote and had produced his best and most popular work, the OPERA BUFFA THE BARBER OF SEVILLE. Paisiello returned to Naples in 1784. For the next fifteen years he was MAESTRO DI CAPPELLA for Ferdinand IV, writing such successful operas as *L'Olimpiade* (1786), *La molinara* (1788), and *Nina* (1789).

When a republican government was temporarily established in Naples in 1799, Paisiello became associated with the new regime as Composer to the Nation. After the Restoration, the court refused to reinstate him because of his republican associations. For two years Paisiello remained in Naples without employment. Then he was called to Paris by Napoleon to serve as MAÎTRE DE CHAPELLE. Because of his wife's poor health, Paisiello returned to Naples two years later where once again he was the object of honor and acclaim, and was reinstated as *maestro di cappella*. His good fortune terminated when Ferdinand IV returned to Naples. From then on, Paisiello suffered neglect and poverty.

In all, Paisiello wrote over a hundred operas. The best abound in pleasing, graceful melodies and ingratiating comedy and at times contain unusual instrumental and dramatic effects. His most successful operas were: *La pupilla* (1764); *Demetrio* (1765); *Don Chisciotte* (1769); *Achille in Sciro* (1778); *La finta amante* (1780); *Il barbiere di Siviglia* (1782); *Andromeda* (1784); *Il re Teodoro in Venezia* (1784); *L'Olimpiade* (1786); *La molinara* (1788); *Nina* (1789); *Proserpina* (1803).

Palemon, an old monk (bass) in MASSENET'S THAÏS.

Palestrina, opera in three acts by PFITZNER. Libretto by the composer. Premiere: Munich Opera, June 12, 1917. This is the composer's most famous opera, and one of the last products of German Romanticism. The theme is the legendary saving of the art of contrapuntal music from banishment by the Church in the sixteenth century through the success of Palestrina's most celebrated composition, the *Missa Papae Marcelli*. In the opera, Palestrina is told by Cardinal Borromeo that all sacred music except the Gregorian plain song is to be prohibited by the Council of Trent. Refusing to fight the edict, Palestrina vows he will never compose again. But he is visited by the spirits of nine composers who prevail on him to return to composition; and an angel sings him a theme which becomes part of the *Missa Papae Marcelli*. Palestrina falls asleep as he writes his music; his son and his pupil gather the manuscript pages. The Mass is shown to the Pope, who is profoundly impressed. Thus, contrapuntal music is saved.

Though originally highly successful and given frequent performances, *Palestrina* has virtually passed out of the permanent repertory, except in Germany. The reasons for this are its lack of love interest (there are no female characters), archaic flavor, and its long stretches of dullness. Occasionally, the three orchestral preludes, each prefacing an act, are heard at symphony concerts.

Pamela, *see* CECCHINA, LA.

Pamina, the Queen of the Night's daughter (soprano) in MOZART'S THE MAGIC FLUTE.

Pandolphe, Cinderella's father (bass), in MASSENET'S CENDRILLON.

Panfilo and Lauretta (or **El amor propiciado**), opera in three acts by Carlos Chávez. Libretto by KALLMAN, based on a tale by BOCCACCIO. Premiere: New York City, May 9, 1957. The text describes the actions of four people of the fourteenth century, who, to escape the plague, find a retreat in a Tuscan villa. The work actually comprises four plays in which each character lives out his real desires. Among the effective musical episodes are the closing chorus to Act I; Venus's final aria, "Look on love with no disguise"; and the concluding chorus, "Time, that closes every eye." When this opera was given its first performance in Mexico on Oct. 28, 1959, it appeared under the title *El amor propiciado*.

Pang, the General Purveyor (tenor) in PUCCINI'S TURANDOT.

Panizza, Ettore, conductor. Born Buenos Aires, Aug. 12, 1875; died Milan, Nov. 29, 1967. Of Italian parents, Panizza was sent to Italy to study at the Milan Conservatory, from which he graduated in 1900. After a rigorous apprenticeship as conductor of symphony orchestras and opera companies throughout Italy, he was appointed principal conductor of Italian operas at COVENT GARDEN in 1907; he held this post six years. In 1916 he made his debut at LA SCALA, and in 1921 he assisted TOSCANINI there as principal conductor. His first appearance in America took place with the Chicago Civic Opera, where he served for several years, meantime also taking many engagements in South America, as he continued to do through the rest of his career. When Tullio SERAFIN resigned as conductor of Italian operas at the METROPOLITAN OPERA, Panizza was chosen as his successor. He made his debut at the Metropolitan Opera on Dec. 22, 1934 (opening night), with AIDA, remaining there through the 1941–42 season, during which period he led the world premieres of *In the Pasha's Garden* and *The Island God,* and the New York premiere of AMELIA GOES TO THE BALL. During World War II, he returned to Buenos Aires, where he went into retirement in 1954. He wrote the following operas: *Il fidanzato del mare* (1897); *Medio Evo Latino* (1900); *Aurora* (1908); *Bisanzio* (1939).

Pantalone, a club member (baritone) in WOLF-FERRARI'S LE DONNE CURIOSE.

Pantasilea, a courtesan (mezzo-soprano) in GINASTERA'S BOMARZO.

Panza, Sancho, Don Quixote's squire (baritone) in MASSENET'S DON QUICHOTTE.

Paolino, a lawyer (tenor), the secret husband of Carolina, in CIMAROSA'S IL MATRIMONIO SEGRETO.

Papagena, Papageno's sweetheart (soprano) in MOZART'S THE MAGIC FLUTE.

Papageno, bird catcher (baritone), Tamino's attendant, in MOZART'S THE MAGIC FLUTE.

Papi, Genarro, conductor. Born Naples, Dec. 21, 1886; died New York City, Nov. 29, 1941. After completing studies at the Naples Conservatory he held various posts as chorus master and conductor. He came to the United States in 1913 and joined the conducting staff of the METROPOLITAN OPERA as TOSCANINI's assistant. After Toscanini left the Metropolitan, Papi became a principal conductor, making his debut in that capacity on Nov. 16, 1916, with MANON LESCAUT. From 1916 to 1927 he conducted at the Metropolitan, resigning to become first conductor of the Chicago Civic Opera. In 1935 he returned to his old post at the Metropolitan. He died just before he was to conduct a performance of LA TRAVIATA. Another conductor was found, but the news of Papi's death was withheld from the cast until the performance ended. (This was a performance, broadcast by radio, in which Jan PEERCE was making his debut.)

Paquillo, street singer (tenor), partner and sweetheart of La Périchole, in OFFENBACH'S OPÉRA BOUFFE LA PÉRICHOLE.

Paquiro, a toreador (baritone) in GRANADOS' GOYESCAS.

Paradise Lost, *see* MILTON, JOHN.

Parassia, Tcherevik's daughter (soprano) in MUSSORGSKY'S THE FAIR AT SOROCHINSK.

Pardon de Ploërmel, Le, *see* DINORAH.

Paride ed Elena (Paris and Helen), opera in five acts by GLUCK. Libretto by Raniero de CALZABIGI. Premiere: Burgtheater, Vienna, Nov. 3, 1770. American premiere: New York City, Jan. 15, 1954 (concert version). The libretto is based on the Greek mythological tale in which Paris, son of the King of Troy, sets sail for Greece. There he meets Helen, wife of Menelaus; he takes her off to Troy, an act that precipitates the Trojan War. In Gluck's opera, Helen is not married to Menelaus, and the central interest is in the passionate love of Helen and Paris. Paris' aria in Act I, "O del mio dolce ardor," is one of the most beautiful Gluck wrote.

Paride ed Elena was the third of Gluck's operas in his later, fully developed style (ORFEO ED EURIDICE and ALCESTE were the preceding ones). Its failure in Vienna led Gluck to leave that city and go to Paris.

Parigi, o cara, duet of Alfredo and Violetta in Act III of VERDI's LA TRAVIATA.

Paris, (1) a nobleman (baritone) in GOUNOD's ROMÉO ET JULIETTE.

(2) King Priam's son (tenor), lover of Helen, in OFFENBACH's OPÉRA BOUFFE LA BELLE HÉLÈNE.

(3) English form of the name of Elena's lover in GLUCK's PARIDE ED ELENA.

Paris Opéra, *see* OPÉRA, L'.

Parker, Horatio William, composer. Born Auburndale, Mass., Sept. 15, 1863; died Cedarhurst, L.I., Dec. 18, 1919. His music study took place in Boston with Stephen Emery, John Orth, and George W. Chadwick and in Munich with Josef Rheinberger and Ludwig Abel. After returning to the United States in 1885 he became director of musical instruction in the schools of St. Paul and St. Mary in Garden City, L.I.; after this he served as organist in various New York churches, and as a teacher of counterpoint at the National Conservatory of Music, then under the direction of DVOŘÁK. In 1894 he became a professor of music at Yale University, a position he retained until his death. Considerable recognition came to him a year earlier when his oratorio *Hora novissima* was first heard. It was soon performed in a number of cities in the United States and England. In 1911 Parker won a ten thousand dollar prize offered by the METROPOLITAN OPERA for an American opera. His opera was MONA, introduced by the Metropolitan on Mar. 14, 1912, played four times to favorable response, and then dropped from the repertory. Two years later Parker won another ten thousand dollar prize, offered by the National Federation of Women's Clubs, with his opera *Fairyland,* produced in Los Angeles on July 1, 1915.

Park Theater, a theater in Park Row, New York City, where the first season of Italian opera in the United States was given by Manuel GARCÍA in 1820. The original theater bearing this name had been built in 1798 as a home for spoken drama but burned down in 1820. It was in a new building on the same site that García's company offered its production. This theater was also destroyed by fire in 1848.

parlando (or **parlante**), Italian for "speaking." In vocal music the term is an indication for the singer to imitate the sound of speech.

Parle-moi de ma mère, duet of Don José and Micaëla, in which he inquires about and receives news of his mother, in Act I of BIZET's CARMEN.

Par le secour, air from LULLY's opera *Roland.*

Parmi les fleurs, Valentine's aria in Act IV of MEYERBEER's LES HUGUENOTS.

Parmi veder le lagrime, the Duke's aria in Act II (or, in some versions, Act III) of VERDI's RIGOLETTO.

Parpignol, a toy vendor (tenor) in PUCCINI's LA BOHÈME.

Parsifal, a "stage-consecrating festival drama" in three acts by WAGNER. Libretto by the composer, based on a medieval legend and a poem by Wolfram von Eschenbach. Premiere: Bayreuth, July 26, 1882. American premiere: Metropolitan Opera, Dec. 24, 1903.

Characters: Titurel, former King of the Knights of the Grail (bass); Amfortas, his son and successor (baritone); Gurnemanz, another Knight of the Grail (bass); Parsifal, a "guileless fool" (tenor), a role created by Hermann WINKELMANN; Kundry, half-woman, half-sorceress (mezzo-soprano); Klingsor, a magician (bass) ; Knights of the Grail; flower maidens; squires; boys. The setting is in and about the Castle of Monsalvat in the Spanish Pyrenees in the Middle Ages.

Act I, Scene 1. A forest near Monsalvat. An orchestral prelude establishes the spiritual atmosphere of the opera; it is built from several of the drama's motives, beginning with the Last Supper and continuing with the Grail, Faith, and Lance motives.

Gurnemanz and his young squires kneel in prayer. Gurnemanz then tells the squires that the ailing Amfortas must be helped when he comes to bathe his spear wound in the lake. Kundry, a servant of the Grail Knights, gives Gurnemanz a vial of oil for the King's wound. When Amfortas is brought in on a litter, he expresses his despair of ever being cured. After he has gone to bathe, Gurnemanz tells his squires the history of the King's wound ("O Wunden, wunderveiler heiliger Speer"). Amfortas had been enticed into the garden of Klingsor, the magician who has determined to secure both the HOLY GRAIL and the Spear that had pierced the body of Jesus. Wresting the Spear from Amfortas, Klingsor had wounded the King with it. Amfortas' wound, it is believed, can be healed only by recovery of the sacred Spear, and the one destined to make this recovery must be a "guileless fool." As Gurnemanz ends his narrative a wild swan falls to the ground, slain by an arrow. Parsifal appears, bow in hand. To Gurnemanz' queries, he reveals all that he knows about himself: the forest is his home, and his mother is named Herzeleide ("Heart's Sorrow"). Gurnemanz, recognizing the boy as the "guileless fool," conducts him to Monsalvat. The scene changes to the stately music of the Transformation Scene.

Scene 2. The hall of the Holy Grail. When Gurnemanz and Parsifal arrive, the hall is empty, but soon the Knights of the Holy Grail appear, singing as they file in ("Zum letzten Liebesmahle"). Amfortas is then brought in

as the boys' chorus chants "Den sündigen Welten." As the Knights partake of Communion, Amfortas uncovers the Holy Grail. The Knights describe the Last Supper in "Blut und Leib der heil'gen Gabe." Parsifal watches the spectacle but is unmoved, uncomprehending. Disgusted at his stupidity, Gurnemanz rudely drives him away.

Act II, Scene 1. A tower atop Klingsor's castle. The world of the magician is evoked in a brief prelude that includes the Enchantment and Kundry motives. Klingsor summons Kundry and orders her to seduce Parsifal so that he may be eliminated as the magician's opponent. Since Kundry is under Klingsor's spell, she yields helplessly to his command.

Scene 2. Klingsor's magic garden. Klingsor's flower maidens dance enticingly about Parsifal (Flower Maidens' Scene). Kundry appears, no longer a hag but a beautiful woman. She reveals to Parsifal that it was she who gave him his name, and she tells him of his parents and his birth ("Ich sah das Kind an seiner Mutter Brust"). Moved, Parsifal at first yields to Kundry's kisses and embraces. But he remembers Amfortas ("Amfortas! Die Wunde"), and he senses that it was in just such a garden as this that, tempted by a woman's beauty, the King received his wound. He pushes Kundry away. Kundry tries to win Parsifal's sympathy by revealing she has been victimized by a curse ("Seit Ewigkeiten harre ich deiner"). When Kundry calls on Klingsor for help, the magician hurls the sacred Spear at Parsifal. Protected by magic powers, Parsifal is unharmed: the Spear remains suspended in midair. Parsifal grasps the weapon, makes the sign of the cross with it, and declares Klingsor's power ended. Kundry falls to the ground with a cry of anguish, and Klingsor's castle collapses in ruin.

Act III, Scene 1. A hermit's hut near Monsalvat. A brief prelude depicts the gloom surrounding the Knights of the Grail; the main motives are those of

Kundry, Spear, Grail, Promise, and Enchantment. Years have passed. Now an aged hermit, Gurnemanz encounters the repentant Kundry. Parsifal, now an armored knight, appears carrying the sacred Spear. He describes his search for the Grail ("Der Irrnis und der Leiden pfade"). Gurnemanz recognizes him and tells him of the present sad state of the Knighthood. He sprinkles water on Parsifal's head; Kundry bathes Parsifal's feet and dries them with her hair. The countryside becomes radiant: it is Good Friday (Charfreitagszauber, Good Friday Spell). Tolling bells summon the Knights to prayer. Parsifal proceeds with Kundry and Gurnemanz to Monsalvat.

Scene 2. The great hall at Monsalvat. The Knights enter with the bier of Titurel, who has died in despair of having the Grail ceremony restored as of old. The ailing Amfortas is helped to his throne. In the depths of his misery he vows never again to uncover the Grail; he implores the Knights to kill him and end his suffering. Parsifal appears, touches Amfortas' wound with the Spear, and heals him ("Nur eine Waffe taugt"). Parsifal then sinks in prayer before the Grail. The Grail glows with holy light. A beam of light descends upon Parsifal, and a dove flutters above his head. Kundry, absolved of her sins, dies at Parsifal's feet. Gurnemanz and Amfortas bow before Parsifal as he raises the Holy Grail in a renewal of consecration.

Parsifal, Wagner's last drama, had a special significance for him. He insisted, because of its religious content, that it never be presented in an ordinary opera house but confined to BAYREUTH, where it should be presented as a kind of religious service. The theme of this religious drama was "enlightenment coming through conscious pity by salvation." Salvation had been the theme of some of Wagner's earlier works, but in them salvation had come through love, sacred and profane. In *Parsifal,* salvation comes through compassion, renunciation, and suffering.

There is no question that *Parsifal* is a moving and at times inspiring spectacle; but it cannot be said that it is a great music drama. The play is too static, the characters are too often lifeless, the monologues too numerous and attenuated. The work is most effective in its spiritual sections, less so in its more human and earthy scenes. It remains, as Wagner intended it to be, a great religious spectacle, but it is not great musical theater.

For several years after its premiere *Parsifal* remained Bayreuth's exclusive property. Concert versions were permitted, and these took place throughout the music world after Wagner's death, but Wagner's widow was scrupulous about not permitting *Parsifal* to be presented on any stage outside Bayreuth. The first such presentation away from Bayreuth took place at the Metropolitan Opera in 1903. For the dramatic circumstances surrounding this performance, *see* METROPOLITAN OPERA.

Partagez-vous mes fleurs!, Ophelia's Mad Scene in Act IV of THOMAS's HAMLET.

Parto, parto, aria of Sextus (and one of the most celebrated episodes) from MOZART'S LA CLEMENZA DI TITO. Though the role of Sextus is male, it is today sung by a mezzo-soprano, since the part was written for a CASTRATO.

Pasero, Tancredi, bass. Born Turin, Jan. 11, 1893. After studying voice with Pessina he made his opera debut in Vicenza in 1917 as Rodolfo in LA SONNAMBULA. Between 1926 and 1952 he was a principal bass at LA SCALA. On Nov. 1, 1929, he made his first appearance at the METROPOLITAN OPERA as Alvise in LA GIOCONDA; he remained with the company until 1933. He achieved major successes in leading opera houses of Europe and South America in an extensive and varied repertory and in the 1930's was acclaimed in performances of MOZART'S operas at the SALZBURG FESTIVAL. His has been described as "a sonorous, smooth *basso cantante* voice," combined with an "authoritative style, vivid dramatic presence, and extraordinary technique."

Pasha, The, see SELIM PASHA.

Pasquale, Don, an old bachelor (bass) in DONIZETTI'S DON PASQUALE, a role created by LABLACHE.

passacaglia, a dance of Spanish origin dating from the early seventeenth century. In stately triple time, it is characterized by a theme played in the bass and repeated throughout the composition, while the upper parts provide variations on the theme. Passacaglias were ordinarily so similar to chaconnes in form and style that the names were used interchangeably in the seventeenth and eighteenth centuries. For occurrences in opera see CHACONNE.

passepied, a lively dance of French origin, similar to the minuet, though played considerably faster. It was used in early French ballets and is occasionally found in operas of the late seventeenth and early eighteenth centuries. There are notable examples of this dance in GLUCK's IPHIGÉNIE EN AULIDE, MOZART's IDOMENEO, and PAISIELLO's *Proserpina*.

Passion of Jonathan Wade, The, opera in three acts by FLOYD. Libretto by the composer. Premiere: New York City Opera, Oct. 11, 1962. The setting is America's South during the Reconstruction period following the Civil War. The hero is the commander of Northern occupation troops in South Carolina, where his idealism finds some admirers and friends and a sweetheart in Celia. But the bitterness of the South in defeat also creates for him powerful enemies. During his marriage to Celia, the ceremony is interrupted by a Ku Klux Klan raid, which subsequently is responsible for Jonathan Wade's murder.

The text is impressive for its vivid characterizations and for the way in which moral, social, and political issues are raised by the plot development. The score is a mixture of expressive declamation and fully developed melodies, the last including a Negro spiritual and an eloquent love duet.

Passo a sei (Dance in Six), a dance in Act I of ROSSINI's WILLIAM TELL.

Passover Scene, see O DIEU, DIEU DE NOS PÈRES.

Pasta, Giuditta (born Negri), soprano. Born Saronno, Italy, Apr. 9, 1798; died Como, Italy, Apr. 1, 1865. One of the most celebrated sopranos of the early nineteenth century, for whom BELLINI wrote the roles of NORMA and AMINA, she entered the Milan Conservatory in her fifteenth year, where she studied with Bonifacio Asioli. Two years later she started appearing in the smaller Italian opera houses. In 1817 she sang in London, where she met and married the tenor Pasta. After an additional period of study with Scappa in Italy, she returned to the opera stage in Venice in 1819. Her brilliant career, however, did not begin to unfold until 1822 in Paris, where she created a sensation. Her voice was faulty in quality and production, but she had such a remarkable range, expressiveness, and dramatic power that her shortcomings were disregarded. She repeated her Parisian triumph in London in 1824 in a series of ROSSINI operas. After her return to Italy she appeared in PACINI's *Niobe,* which the composer wrote for her. In the early 1830's she created the principal soprano roles in *Norma,* LA SONNAMBULA, and ANNA BOLENA, all written expressly for her. By 1837 her voice suffered complete deterioration; nevertheless, she continued to appear in London and St. Petersburg. She went into retirement in 1850, devoting herself to teaching a few select pupils at her Como estate.

pasticcio, Italian for "pie." The word was applied to a form of operatic entertainment popular throughout Europe in the eighteenth century. A *pasticcio* was made up of parts from several different operas, sometimes the operas of a single composer, but frequently of different composers. The intention was to give audiences the maximum number of familiar or exceptional songs in one performance. New words might be fitted to the songs to give coherence to the whole. A case in point is GLUCK's ORFEO ED EURIDICE. When this work was introduced in London in 1770, it was given the "benefit" of additional choruses, recitatives, and arias composed by J. C. BACH to words by Pietro Guglielmi, the program book calling attention to this pair's "enrichment" of the opera. In this case, the basic structure of Gluck's opera was preserved; in other instances, wholly new operas were concocted from the writings of half a dozen or more composers. The term *pasticcio* was also extended to collaborations of several composers. *Muzio Scevola* (1721) was such an opera, its first act by Filippo Amadei, its second by BONONCINI, its third by HANDEL, each act preceded by its own overture.

pastorale, a term in use between the fifteenth and eighteenth centuries for a dramatic work on a pastoral and often mythological subject, frequently allegorical in treatment. At various times pastorales were made up of arias, recitatives, choruses, and ballets. As such, they were one of the forerunners of opera. Especially popular in France, they continued to be written by such composers as Robert Cambert and LULLY well after the establishment of opera as a distinctive form.

Patria oppressa, chorus of the Scottish exiles bewailing the tyranny that has seized their country, in Act IV of VERDI's MACBETH.

patter song, an aria, usually in OPERA BUFFA, where humor is achieved through the rapidity with which the words are sung. Notable examples are the "Largo al factotum" in ROSSINI's THE BARBER OF SEVILLE and "Madamina!" in DON GIOVANNI.

Patti, Adelina (born Adela Patti), soprano. Born Madrid, Feb. 10, 1843; died Brecknock, Wales, Sept. 27, 1919. One of the most celebrated coloratura sopranos of all time, she was the daughter of the Italian singer Salvatore Patti and Caterina Barili. While still a child, she was brought to the United States, where she made her first public appearance when she was only seven. From 1851 to 1855 she concertized extensively under

the management of Maurice STRAKOSCH (who became her brother-in-law). At the age of twelve she ceased singing in public and began intensive study of music; her voice teachers were Ettore Barili and Strakosch. On Nov. 24, 1859, she made her opera debut in New York as LUCIA; on this occasion she was billed as "the little Florinda." She was acclaimed. Her London debut took place on May 14, 1861, in LA SONNAMBULA. Her popularity in England was such that it rivaled that of the sensational Giulia GRISI. Patti appeared at COVENT GARDEN for twenty-three years and for another two years at HER MAJESTY'S THEATRE, throughout this quarter of a century the idol of the English opera public. She duplicated her London successes in Paris in 1862 and at LA SCALA in 1877. She appeared in about forty roles and scored her greatest successes in operas by BELLINI, DONIZETTI, MEYERBEER, and ROSSINI. She was not exceptional either as a musician or an actress, but no one could rival the beauty, purity, and sweetness of her singing.

She withdrew from opera in 1895 and for another decade appeared extensively in concerts. Her last concert took place in London in 1906, her last appearance in public (at a London Red Cross benefit) in 1914. Her older sister, Carlotta Patti (1835–1889), was also a successful singer, though not of her sister's stature. Due to a chronic infirmity of lameness, Carlotta's appearances were intermittent, but after her concert debut in 1861 she made successful appearances in Europe and the United States.

Patzak, Julius, tenor. Born Vienna, Apr. 9, 1898. He attended the Vienna University and School of Music. His debut took place at the Reichenberg State Opera on Apr. 3, 1926. After appearances at the Brno Opera, he became principal tenor of the Munich State Opera in 1928. During the next two decades (except for an interval during World War II) he distinguished himself, particularly in MOZART's operas, in Munich, Berlin, Vienna, COVENT GARDEN, LA SCALA, and the

SALZBURG FESTIVALS. In 1946 he was the first Austrian singer to be engaged by the British Broadcasting Corporation following the war. In 1947 he appeared in the world premiere of DANTONS TOD in Salzburg. He made his American debut at the Cincinnati Music Festival in May, 1954.

Paul, the principal character (tenor) in KORNGOLD'S DIE TOTE STADT.

Paul et Virginie, a novel by Bernardin de St. Pierre, the source of operas by Pietro Carlo Guglielmi, Jean-François LESUEUR, and Victor MASSÉ. The setting is Africa in the eighteenth century, where the lovers, Paul and Virginia, are separated when Virginia is sent home to France. Her ship is wrecked, and her body is washed ashore, to be found by the disconsolate Paul.

Pauline, Lisa's companion (contralto) in TCHAIKOVSKY'S PIQUE DAME.

Pauly, Rosa, soprano. Born Eperjes, Hungary, Mar. 15, 1895. After studying with Rosa Papier in Vienna, she made her debut in Hamburg as AIDA in 1918. From Hamburg she went to sing in Cologne. From 1927 to 1931 she appeared at the KROLL OPERA in Berlin in many major roles and in virtually every significant premiere. During this period she was also heard in guest appearances in Budapest and Paris. After 1931 she appeared with outstanding acclaim at the VIENNA STATE OPERA (hailed for her performances in dramas by WAGNER and Richard STRAUSS and receiving the honorary title of KAMMERSÄNGERIN), the SALZBURG FESTIVALS, and all the major opera houses of Italy. In Italy she was regarded so highly as an actress that she became known as the "German Duse," and her portrait was hung in the Hall of Fame at the Verdi Opera House, between those of Duse and Moissi. Her American debut took place with the New York Philharmonic Symphony in 1937 in a concert version of ELEKTRA. On Jan. 7, 1938, she made her American opera debut at the METROPOLITAN OPERA, once again as Elektra. Pauly remained at the Metropolitan until 1940. After World War II she appeared at COVENT GARDEN, and in Germany and Austria, following which she made her home in Israel.

Paur, Emil, conductor. Born Czernowitz, Austria, Aug. 29, 1855; died Mistek, Moravia, June 7, 1932. After attending the Vienna Conservatory, he began his career in Königsberg in his twenty-first year. In 1880 he was appointed conductor of the MANNHEIM OPERA, and from 1891 to 1893 he conducted opera performances at the Leipzig Stadttheater. He came to America in 1893 to succeed NIKISCH as conductor of the Boston Symphony orchestra. In 1899–1900 he directed performances of the WAGNER music dramas at the METROPOLITAN OPERA, making his debut there on Dec. 23, 1899, with LOHENGRIN. In the spring of 1900 he conducted German operas at COVENT GARDEN. In 1904 he became principal conductor of the Pittsburgh Symphony, holding this post six years. In 1912 he succeeded KARL MUCK as musical director of the BERLIN OPERA, but due to a dispute with the Intendant, he held this post only two months. He remained in Berlin, directing symphony concerts for the rest of his career.

Pauvre Matelot, Le (The Poor Sailor), one-act opera by MILHAUD. Libretto by Jean Cocteau. Premiere: Opéra-Comique, Dec. 12, 1927. American premiere: Philadelphia, Apr. 1, 1937. The libretto was inspired by a newspaper account of an actual event. A sailor returns home after a prolonged absence and is not recognized by his wife. He decides to test her fidelity by telling her he is her husband's rich friend; then he tries to win her love. Late at night, while he is asleep, his wife murders him so that she may have his money to bring her husband home. Though a failure when first produced, *Le Pauvre Matelot* has become its composer's most frequently performed opera, receiving performances in some twenty cities in Germany, as well as in Vienna, Salzburg, Prague, Barcelona, and New York. Henri Prunières has written that Milhaud's lyricism "constantly calls to mind ancient songs and folklore."

Pavarotti, Luciano, tenor. Born Modena, Italy, 1935. He was only four when he began taking singing lessons with his father and twenty-six when he started appearing in opera performances. Success came in 1964 when he made his debut at LA SCALA in KARAJAN'S production of LA BOHÈME. In 1965 he appeared in L'ELISIR D'AMORE in Australia and in 1966 in THE DAUGHTER OF THE REGIMENT at COVENT GARDEN, on both occasions opposite Joan SUTHERLAND. His performance of the latter opera was particularly eventful, since he became the first tenor since DONIZETTI's time to sing Tonio's first-act aria and CABALETTA in its original key. Subsequent appearances in major opera houses, including those with the Rome Opera and the SAN FRANCISCO OPERA, added to his rapidly growing reputation. On Dec. 12, 1968, he made his debut at the METROPOLITAN OPERA in *La Bohème,* and in 1969 he helped open the season of the Rome Opera in a revival of I LOMBARDI. A master of BEL CANTO, he is particularly distinguished for his performances in operas by Donizetti and BELLINI; he made an outstanding recording of Bellini's rarely heard BEATRICE DI TENDA with Joan Sutherland.

Pearl Fishers, The, *see* PÊCHEURS DE PERLES, LES.

Pears, Peter, tenor. Born Farnham, Eng., June 22, 1910. He attended the Royal College of Music, following which he studied voice privately with Elena Gerhardt. After appearing in the chorus at the GLYNDEBOURNE FESTIVAL he made his opera debut in 1942 in London in THE TALES OF HOFFMANN. Between 1943 and 1946 he appeared at SADLER'S WELLS, where, in 1945, he created the role of PETER GRIMES. Since 1946 he has been a member of the ENGLISH OPERA GROUP, and since 1947 he has made numerous guest appearances at COVENT GARDEN, where in 1951 he created the part of Captain Vere in BILLY BUDD. He has particularly distinguished himself in operas by BRITTEN, although he has also been heard in the Italian repertory, in THE MAGIC FLUTE, THE BARTERED BRIDE, and other familiar operas.

Peasants' Ballet, the ballet in Act III of MONIUSZKO'S HALKA.

Peasants' Waltz, a waltz in Act I of BOITO'S MEFISTOFELE.

Pease, James, bass-baritone. Born Franklin, Ind., Jan. 9, 1916; died New York City, Apr. 26, 1967. Music study took place at the Academy of Vocal Arts in Philadelphia, following which he made his opera debut in 1941 as GOUNOD'S MÉPHISTOPHÉLÈS with the PHILADELPHIA OPERA COMPANY. He remained with the company several years in a varied repertory that included the world premiere of TAYLOR'S RAMUNTCHO in 1942. In 1943 he won the METROPOLITAN AUDITIONS OF THE AIR, but was unable to appear with the Metropolitan Opera because of his enlistment in the Army Air Corps. In 1945 he made his debut with the NEW YORK CITY OPERA in the role of SPARAFUCILE, remaining with that company for many years. At TANGLEWOOD, in Lenox, Mass., he appeared in the late 1940's in the American premieres of PETER GRIMES and ALBERT HERRING and in a revival of PIQUE DAME. He joined the HAMBURG STATE OPERA in 1953, specializing in the Wagnerian repertory, which he also performed in Vienna and in 1954 at the BAYREUTH FESTIVAL; in 1956 he was heard in DIE WALKÜRE at Tanglewood. He returned to the New York City Opera in 1959 and 1960.

Pêcheurs de perles, Les (The Pearl Fishers), opera by BIZET. Libretto by Michel Carré and Eugène Cormon. Premiere: Théâtre Lyrique, Paris, Sept. 30, 1863. American premiere: Philadelphia, Aug. 25, 1893. In Ceylon in early times a new tribal chieftain, Zurga (baritone), is chosen by the fishermen. A veiled priestess comes to pray for the people; Zurga promises the priestess a priceless pearl if she remains chaste, but death if she violates her purity. This priestess is Leila (soprano), whom Zurga and his friend Nadir (tenor) had loved as youths. Nadir and Leila recognize each other, and their one-time love is revived.

When Zurga discovers Nadir and Leila embracing he orders both to die. But Zurga is still in love with Leila. To save her, he sets the homes of his people aflame, causing them to run from the place of execution. Nadir and Leila escape in a boat, but one of the fishermen avenges the arson by stabbing Zurga in the back.

One of Bizet's most famous tenor arias appears in this opera: Nadir's ROMANCE, "Je crois entendre encore" in Act I. Other familiar excerpts include the duet of Nadir and Zurga in Act I, "Au fond du temple"; in Act II, Leila's CAVATINA, "Comme autrefois dans le nuit sombre," and Nadir's serenade, "De mon amie fleur endormie"; and in Act III Zurga's lament, "O Nadir, tendre ami de mon coeur."

Pedrillo, Belmonte's servant (tenor) in MOZART'S THE ABDUCTION FROM THE SERAGLIO.

Pedro, (1) a shepherd (tenor) in D'ALBERT'S TIEFLAND.

(2) Pilar's bridegroom (tenor) in LAPARRA'S LA HABANERA.

(3) A burlesquer (soprano) in MASSENET'S DON QUICHOTTE.

See also DON PEDRO.

Peerce, Jan (born Jacob Perelmuth), tenor. Born New York City, June 3, 1904. After studying the violin and playing in jazz bands, he was engaged in 1932 as a singer for the Radio City Music Hall. For five years his singing was a major attraction; he appeared nearly twenty-five hundred times on the stage and many times in radio programs originating at the theater. Presently, he became a star of his own radio program, "Great Moments in Music," and in 1936 was selected by a national poll as the leading male radio singer. Eager to embark on more serious musical endeavors, he began a period of study with Giuseppe Boghetti. In 1938 he sang in BEETHOVEN'S *Ninth Symphony* conducted by TOSCANINI. In 1939 he made his first concert tour, and his bow in opera with the Columbia Opera Company, appearing as the Duke in RIGOLETTO. His debut at the METROPOLITAN OPERA took place on Nov. 29, 1941, as Alfredo in LA TRAVIATA. Peerce has since been a principal tenor of the Metropolitan Opera, distinguishing himself particularly in the French and Italian repertory. Toscanini selected him to sing in radio performances of several operas including *La traviata*, LA BOHÈME, and UN BALLO IN MASCHERA. In 1956 he was the first significant American singer to appear in the Soviet Union since World War II. He has been heard with most of the leading opera companies of the world.

Peer Gynt, (1) a poetic drama by Henrik IBSEN, the source of operas by EGK (*see* below), Leslie Heward, and Viktor Ullmann. Peer Gynt, a lustful, impetuous youth, is the symbol of moral degeneration. He abducts and then abandons the beautiful Solveig. Roaming to foreign lands, he makes love to the daughter of the Troll King. He returns home to be at the bedside of his dying mother, Ase, but then is off for further adventures and escapades. He returns home, old and wasted, to die in Solveig's arms.

(2) Opera in three acts by Egk. Libretto by the composer, based on Ibsen's poetic drama. Premiere: Berlin State Opera, Nov. 24, 1938. American premiere: Hartford, Conn., Feb. 23, 1966. When this opera was introduced, the Nazi press condemned it as unfit "for the National Socialist outlook on the world." When Hitler saw it, however, he expressed his enthusiasm: the official reaction to the opera changed overnight. It received a government prize of ten thousand marks and was performed extensively throughout Germany.

Pèlerins de la Mecque, Les, *see* RENCONTRE IMPRÉVUE, LA.

Pelléas et Mélisande, opera in five acts by DEBUSSY. Libretto is MAETERLINCK'S poetical drama of the same name. Premiere: Opéra-Comique, Apr. 30, 1902. American premiere: Manhattan Opera House, Feb. 19, 1908.

Characters: Arkel, King of Allemonde (bass); Geneviève, his daughter-in-law (soprano); Golaud, her older son (baritone); Pelléas, his brother (tenor); Mélisande, a princess (soprano); Yniold, young son of Golaud (soprano); blind beggars; servants; a physician. The setting is a legendary land in legendary times.

Act I, Scene 1. A forest. Golaud comes upon Mélisande, who is weeping. She answers his questions vaguely, refuses to reveal her identity, and will not allow him to recover the crown she has lost in a spring. Golaud persuades her to follow him to a place of shelter.

Scene 2. A hall in Arkel's castle. Six months have passed. Geneviève reads the blind Arkel a letter from Golaud telling of his marriage to Mélisande (Duo de la lettre: "Voici ce qu'il écrit"). Pelléas comes to ask permission to visit a sick friend. But the king reminds Pelléas that his own father is also sick and needs his attention. Arkel now orders Pelléas to show a signal lamp for the returning Golaud.

Scene 3. A terrace before the castle. When Geneviève goes to look after little Yniold, Pelléas and Mélisande are left alone. Pelléas reveals that he must leave the following day, news that brings Mélisande a stab of pain.

Act II, Scene 1. A fountain in the park. Pelléas and Mélisande come to a deserted fountain which is believed to have the power of opening the eyes of the blind. The fountain exerts its magic by opening the eyes of Pelléas and Mélisande to their love (Duo de la fontaine). As Mélisande playfully tosses her wedding ring into the air, it falls into the depths of the fountain. She is distraught. Pelléas urges her to tell Golaud the truth of its loss.

Scene 2. Golaud's chamber. At the moment Mélisande lost her ring in the fountain, Golaud, hunting, was thrown from his horse. He is in bed, recovering. Mélisande, tending to him, bursts into tears. When he takes her into his arms he notices she is not wearing her wedding ring. As Golaud becomes more insistent in his questioning, Mélisande finally tells him she lost it in a grotto near the sea. Golaud orders her to go with Pelléas to look for it.

Scene 3. A grotto by the sea. It is night. Pelléas and Mélisande have come on their mock search for the ring. A sudden flood of moonlight reveals three blind beggars huddled in a corner of the cave. Mélisande is terrified, and Pelléas leads her back to the castle.

Act III, Scene 1. A tower of the castle. As she combs her hair at a window, Mélisande sings an ancient song ("Saint Daniel et Saint Michel"). Upon Pelléas' arrival on the path below, she gets him to promise not to leave on the morrow. As a reward for this promise, she extends her hand for Pelléas to kiss. Her long hair falls and covers Pelléas' face. The touch of her hair makes him ecstatic (Scène des cheveux: "Oh! qu'est-ce que c'est? . . . tes cheveux"). Golaud discovers them and scolds them for behaving like children.

Scene 2. The castle vaults. Golaud conducts Pelléas to a stagnant pool where the stench is one of death. Pelléas grows apprehensive at Golaud's strange behavior. The two leave the vaults in tense silence.

Scene 3. A terrace. Pelléas emerges from the caverns, sighing with relief ("Ah! je respire enfin"). Golaud warns him not to participate in any more childish games with Mélisande nor to disturb her in any way, since she is about to become a mother.

Scene 4. Before the castle. Suspicious of the conduct between Pelléas and Mélisande, Golaud cautiously questions Yniold about their behavior. When the child is vague, Golaud's suspicions increase. A light appears in Mélisande's window. Golaud lifts his son to the window to see whether Pelléas is inside. When Yniold reveals that this is so, Golaud is sure that his worst suspicions are well founded.

Act IV, Scene 1. A room in the castle. Pelléas tells Mélisande he is going away; they arrange a last rendezvous near the fountain. After they separate, Arkel appears. He is overjoyed that Pelléas' father has recovered, for he feels that the gloom of the castle will now be dispelled

("Maintenant que le père de Pelléas est sauvé"). Golaud appears. He is looking for his sword; there is blood on his brow. The innocence in Mélisande's eyes arouses his anger to a fever pitch. He seizes her by the hair and drags her across the floor until stopped by the entreaties of Arkel.

Scene 2. The park. Waiting at the fountain, Pelléas muses on the strange destiny that has made him fall in love with his brother's wife. When Mélisande appears, all his doubts vanish. They embrace ecstatically ("Viens ici, ne reste pas au bord du clair de lune"). Mélisande hears a sound in the shadows. Golaud, who has been concealed there, rushes at Pelléas and kills him. He then pursues the fleeing Mélisande with drawn sword.

Act V. Mélisande's chamber. Mélisande, who has given birth to a daughter, lies in bed, grievously ill. Golaud is with her, penitent and forgiving ("Mélisande, as-tu pitié de moi?"). Mélisande forgives him. She cannot deny she loved Pelléas, but she insists that their love had been innocent. Arkel brings Mélisande her child. The servants file into the room. Suddenly, they fall on their knees: they sense that Mélisande is dead. The grief-stricken Arkel and Golaud leave the chamber with the motherless infant, who must now live in Mélisande's place.

Romain ROLLAND wrote that the premiere of Pelléas et Mélisande "is one of the three or four red-letter days in the calendar of our lyric theater." For this was a new kind of opera. The action was static; there were few emotional climaxes and no big scenes; the entire effect arose from subtle impressions. The music was as seemingly amorphous as the play, which was set in a dream world filled with symbolic suggestions and peopled with characters who were like shadows. Debussy's music caught the essence of Maeterlinck's drama. He wrote no arias or ensemble numbers, but a continual flow of declamation that resembled speech. This was set against a rich but restrained orchestral background that played as important a role in creating the over-all effect as the singing. The result was a fusion of play and music so complete that there are few equals in operatic literature.

Debussy took ten years to write his only opera. If the composition did not come easily, the production was also destined to bring him anguish. Maeterlinck's greatest interest in the opera lay in the decision of both poet and composer to feature Georgette Leblanc, at that time Maeterlinck's common-law wife, as Mélisande. But Albert CARRÉ, director of the OPÉRA-COMIQUE, had other plans. He sensed that Mary GARDEN, who had come to stardom in the role of LOUISE two years earlier, would be the ideal Mélisande. Without consulting Maeterlinck, he announced her for the part. Suspecting that Debussy was responsible for the decision, Maeterlinck threatened to beat him, and even thought of challenging him to a duel. Now an avowed enemy of Debussy, Carré, the Opéra-Comique, and the new opera, he did everything he could to discredit the work. He wrote a letter to Le Figaro before the premiere denouncing the management of the Opéra-Comique and expressing the wish for the "immediate and emphatic failure" of the opera. He was probably responsible for a malicious parody of the play which was distributed outside the theater before the dress rehearsal, calculated to reduce the opera to ridicule. Thus, scandal preceded the premiere. To make matters still worse, the rehearsals went badly. The men in the orchestra had trouble deciphering their parts, prepared by a careless copyist. There were difficulties with scene designers, who insisted that the many changes were not feasible. A small portion of the opera was censored by a government official.

The public's reaction to this strange and revolutionary work was mixed. Hisses and guffaws mingled with applause and cheers. The critical opinion was also divided. Some thought the work was "without life . . . a continual dolorous melopoeia . . . deliberately shunning all semblance of precision." Others, such as Gustave Bret and André Corneau, did not hesitate to call the opera a masterwork. Of one thing there was no question: Mary Garden was the perfect Mélisande. From the very beginning she made the role her own, and as long as she sang it, both in Europe and America, she had no rivals. Notable Mélisandes after Garden were Maggie TEYTE and Lucrezia BORI.

Peneios, a fisherman (bass), father of Daphne, in Richard STRAUSS's DAPHNE.

Pénélope, (1) lyric drama in three acts by FAURÉ. Libretto by René Fauchois, based on an episode from HOMER's *Iliad*. Premiere: Monte Carlo, Mar. 4, 1913. American premiere: Cambridge, Mass., Nov. 29, 1945. Fauré called this work a "lyric poem"; it is his most celebrated work for the stage. The story of Ulysses' return to Pénélope to find she has been faithful to him through the years received from Fauré a restrained musical treatment in which there is little action or characterization but only a sustained flow of lyricism. The overture is in the symphonic repertory. It consists of two motives, the first representing Pénélope (strings) and the second Ulysses (horns).

(2) "Opera semiseria" in two acts by LIEBERMANN. Libretto by Heinrich Strobel. Premiere: Salzburg Festival, Aug. 17, 1954. In this work the story of Ulysses and Penelope takes place in two times: in classical antiquity and during World War II, when Penelope is remarried to a wealthy man after she has become convinced that her first husband is dead. At the end of the opera, Ulysses returns and makes a plea for pacifism. The world of antiquity and the twentieth century become one. The opera closes with a hymn to art. The antiquity sequences are treated in an OPERA-BUFFA style; those in the twentieth century in the style of OPERA SERIA, with the techniques basically dodecaphonic.

Pensa alla patria, Isabella's mock heroic coloratura aria, in Act II of ROSSINI's L'ITALIANA IN ALGERI.

Penthesilea, *see* KLEIST, HEINRICH WILHELM VON.

Pepa, Paquiro's sweetheart (contralto) in GRANADOS' GOYESCAS.

Pepusch, Johann Christoph (or **John Christopher**), composer. Born Berlin, 1667; died London, July 20, 1752. After holding a Prussian court post from 1681 to 1697, he moved to London in 1700. From 1712 to 1718 he was HANDEL's predecessor as organist and composer to the Duke of Chandos, and after 1713 he was for many years music director of the LINCOLN'S INN FIELDS THEATRE. He wrote the music for several masques performed at this establishment: *Venus and Adonis* (1715); *Apollo and Daphne* (1716); *The Death of Dido* (1716); *The Union of Three Sisters* (1723). In 1718 Pepusch married the wealthy singer Marguerite de l'Epine. Ten years later he arranged the music for John GAY's sensationally successful BALLAD OPERA, THE BEGGAR'S OPERA. The following year he arranged music for two more ballad operas, *The Wedding* and POLLY, the latter a sequel to *The Beggar's Opera*. From 1737 until his death he was the organist at the Charter House.

Perchè ciò volle il mio voler possente, Gérard's aria to Madeleine telling her that fate has bound them together, in Act III of GIORDANO's ANDREA CHÉNIER.

Perchè mai se son tradito, an air in which Narciso, a lesser character, sings about the cruelty of love, in Act I of ROSSINI's IL TURCO IN ITALIA.

Perchè, perchè, non m'ami più?, Michele's poignant query to Giorgietta, inquiring why she loves him no longer, in PUCCINI's IL TABARRO.

Perchè v'amo, *see* DEPUIS L'INSTANT OÙ DANS MES BRAS.

Percy, Anna Bolena's one-time lover (tenor) in DONIZETTI's ANNA BOLENA.

Perdon, perdon, Gabriele's plea to Simon Boccanegra to forgive him for having tried to poison him, in the close of Act II of VERDI's SIMON BOCCANEGRA.

Perfect Fool, The, comic opera in one act by HOLST. Libretto by the composer. Premiere: British National Opera Company, London, May 14, 1923. American premiere: Wichita, Kan., Mar. 20, 1962. This opera, an allegory in Elizabethan style, parodies opera conventions, particularly those of WAGNER and VERDI. The Wizard, the Troubadours, and the Traveler all try to win the heart and hand of the Princess, but she rejects them. But the Fool, with the aid of a magic potion which he expropriates from the Wizard, wins the Princess and annihilates the Wizard when he comes to seek revenge.

Pergamon, Europe's suitor (baritone) in MILHAUD's *opéra minute* L'ENLÈVEMENT D'EUROPE.

Pergola, *see* TEATRO ALLA PERGOLA.

Pergolesi, Giovanni Battista, composer. Born Jesi, Italy, Jan. 4, 1710; died Pozzuoli, Italy, Mar. 16, 1736. The composer of LA SERVA PADRONA studied music with Francesco Santini and Francesco Mondini, after which he entered the Conservatorio dei Poveri di Gesù Cristo in Naples in his sixteenth year. There, his teachers included Gaetano Greco, Francesco DURANTE, and Francesco Feo. His first major work, a sacred drama, *La conversione di San Guglielmo d'Aquitania,* was so successful when introduced in Naples in 1731 that he received a commission from the court for a new opera, *La Salustia,* performed the same year. Several of Pergolesi's next operas were comic interludes, or INTERMEZZI, designed to be played between the acts of serious operas. In 1733 Pergolesi wrote an intermezzo that was soon performed independently and within a few months became an Italian favorite. This was *La serva padrona.* The first important OPERA BUFFA, *La serva padrona* established the traditions for later works in this form. Among Pergolesi's other operas, comic and serious, were: *Lo frate inamorato* (1732); *Il prigionier superbo* (1733); *Adriano in Siria* (1734); *L'Olympiade* (1735); *Flaminio* (1735). All these works and others were finished within a brief period of creative activity before Pergolesi died of consumption at the age of twenty-six. In his serious works as well as his comic ones, Pergolesi's style was characterized by elegance and grace as well as lyric beauty. His best melodies often remind one of MOZART's in their aristocratic beauty, and on occasion (in *La serva padrona,* for example) we find something of Mozart's gift for creating characterizations and pointing up incidents by musical means.

Peri, Jacopo, composer. Born Rome (or Florence), Aug. 20, 1561; died Florence, Aug. 12, 1633. As a member of the CAMERATA which created opera, he wrote DAFNE, the first opera in musical history. Born to a noble Florentine family, he received his musical training from Cristoforo Malvezzi. At different periods of his life he served as music master at the courts of Ferdinando I and Cosimo II de' Medici. When the Florentine Camerata evolved a musicodramatic form calculated to revive ancient Greek drama (*see* OPERA), Peri wrote *Dafne* in 1597 to a text by Ottavio RINUCCINI. Though described by its composer as a DRAMMA PER MUSICA, Dafne is the first opera ever written, since it is the first play which is set throughout to music. *Dafne* was received so enthusiastically when introduced in Florence that in 1600 Peri wrote a second opera, EURIDICE, performed in conjunction with the marriage ceremonies of Henry IV of France and Maria de' Medici. Later Peri operas: *Tetide* (1608); *Guerra d'amore,* a collaboration (1615); *Adone* (1620); *La precedenza delle dame* (1625). In 1608 Peri wrote the recitatives for *Arianna,* for which MONTEVERDI wrote the arias; and in 1628 he provided music for the part of Clori in Marco da Gagliano's *Flora.* Though Peri wrote a considerable amount of music, most of it has been lost, including that of the history-making *Dafne.*

Périchole, La, OPÉRA BOUFFE in three acts by OFFENBACH. Libretto by Henri Meilhac and Ludovic Halévy, based on MÉRIMÉE's *Le Carrosse du Saint-Sacrement.* Premiere: Théâtre des Variétés, Paris, Oct. 6, 1868. American premiere: New York City, Jan. 4, 1869. The setting is eighteenth-century Peru. La Périchole (soprano) is a gypsy street singer in love with her singing partner,

Paquillo (tenor). The Viceroy becomes interested in her and takes her to his palace as lady-in-waiting. When Paquillo discovers that his sweetheart has become the Viceroy's favorite, he denounces her; by the final curtain, however, the lovers are reconciled and have received the Viceroy's blessings. One of Offenbach's most celebrated melodies is found in this opera: La Périchole's letter song to Paquillo, "O mon cher amant, je te jure." Another eloquent air by La Périchole is "Tu n'es pas beau" in Act III, Scene 1. Three significant airs are assigned to Paquillo: "Je dois vous prévenir" (Act I); "Et la maintenant" (Act II); and "On me proposait d'être enflammé" (Act III, Scene 1). La Périchole was revived brilliantly by the METROPOLITAN OPERA on Dec. 21, 1956, in a new English translation.

Per lui che adoro, Isabella's aria with quartet, voicing her love for Lindoro, in Act II of ROSSINI's L'ITALIANA IN ALGERI.

Per me giunto e il di supremo, Rodrigo's farewell to the imprisoned Don Carlos, in Act IV of VERDI's DON CARLOS.

Per me ora fatale, Count di Luna's aria in which he tells his followers he cannot live without Leonora, in Act II, Scene 2, of VERDI's IL TROVATORE.

Permettez, astre du jour, Huascar's air in the second *entrée* in RAMEAU's LES INDES GALANTES.

Per pietà, ben mio perdona, Fiordiligi's disturbed reaction upon realizing she is not immune to temptation, in Act II, Scene 2, of MOZART's COSÌ FAN TUTTE.

Perrault, Charles, poet and writer of fairy tales. Born Paris, Jan. 12, 1628; died there May 16, 1703. His collection of fairy tales, *Les Contes de ma mère l'oye (Mother Goose)* (1697) is world famous. A number of operas have come from these stories: Nicolo Isouard's *Cendrillon,* MASSENET's CENDRILLON, ROSSINI's LA CENERENTOLA, WOLF-FERRARI's *La Cenerentola*—all these adaptations of *Cinderella;* Louis Aubert's *La Forêt bleue;* Georges Huë's *Riquet à la houppe;* Wolf-Ferrari's *Das Himmelskleid;* RESPI-

GHI's *La bella addormentata;* PHILIDOR's *Le Bûcheron;* MALIPIERO's *La bella e il mostro;* HUMPERDINCK's *Dornröschen;* Wheeler Beckett's *The Magic Mirror.*

Perrin, Emile Césare, impresario. Born Rouens, France, Jan. 19, 1814; died Paris, Oct. 8, 1885. One of the most significant opera impresarios of his time, he became manager of the OPÉRA-COMIQUE in 1848, holding this post until 1857. During this period he was also manager of the THÉÂTRE LYRIQUE for the single season of 1854–55. Under his management of the Opéra-Comique such notable singers as Léon CARVALHO, Jean-Baptiste FAURÉ, and GALLI-MARIÉ were introduced. From 1862 to 1870 Perrin was the manager of the PARIS OPÉRA, where he introduced such outstanding operas as L'AFRICAINE, DON CARLOS, and HAMLET, and the distinguished singer Christine NILSSON. From 1870 until his death he was the manager of the Théâtre-Français.

Persiani, Fanny (born Tacchinardi), soprano. Born Rome, Oct. 4, 1812; died Neuilly, France, May 3, 1867. Her father, Niccolò Tacchinardi, taught her singing, and in her eleventh year she sang in opera performances in a little theater built by her father for his students. When she was eighteen she married an opera composer, Giuseppe Persiani, and two years afterward made her formal opera debut in Leghorn in Emile Fournier's *Francesca da Rimini.* Engagements in leading Italian opera houses followed. DONIZETTI was so impressed by the crystalline perfection of her voice that he wrote LUCIA DI LAMMERMOOR with her in mind; she created the role of Lucia in Naples on Sept. 26, 1835. In 1837 she made her first appearance in Paris, as Lucia, and in 1838 she made her London debut, as AMINA. For the next decade she was a favorite in both cities. In 1850 she toured Holland and Russia. She made her farewell appearance at the DRURY LANE THEATRE in 1858, then went into retirement.

Persians, The, see AESCHYLUS.

Per te d'immenso giubilo, wedding

chorus in Act III, Scene 2, of DONIZETTI's LUCIA DI LAMMERMOOR.

Pertile, Aureliano, tenor. Born Montagnana, near Padua, Italy, Nov. 9, 1885; died Milan, Jan. 11, 1952. For four years he studied singing with Vittorio Oretice, after which he made his opera debut in Vicenza in MARTHA in 1911. An additional period of study in Milan with Manlio Bavagnoli preceded his first major success in the Italian premiere of NOUGUÈS's QUO VADIS at the Teatro dal Verme in Milan in 1912. For one season during 1921–22, he was a member of the METROPOLITAN OPERA Company, making his debut there on Dec. 1, 1921, in TOSCA. Two years later TOSCANINI engaged him for LA SCALA where, during the next decade and a half, he scored some of his greatest triumphs, notably in IL TROVATORE, MANON, and in BOITO's MEFISTOFELE and NERONE. He made his farewell appearance on the operatic stage in 1940 in OTELLO, and five years after that became professor of singing at the Milan Conservatory, retaining this post until the time of his death.

Pescator, affonda l'esca, Barnaba's BARCAROLLE in Act II of PONCHIELLI's LA GIOCONDA, as he appears disguised as a fisherman.

Peter, a broommaker (baritone), father of Hansel and Gretel, in HUMPERDINCK's HANSEL AND GRETEL.

Peter I, Czar of Russia (baritone) in LORTZING's ZAR UND ZIMMERMANN.

Peter Grimes, opera in prologue and three acts by BRITTEN. Libretto by Montagu Slater, based on *The Borough*, a poem by George Crabbe. Premiere: Sadler's Wells, London, June 7, 1945. American premiere: Berkshire Music Center, Lenox, Mass., Aug. 6, 1946.

Characters: Peter Grimes, a fisherman (tenor), a role created by Peter PEARS; John, his apprentice (mime); Ellen Orford, schoolmistress and widow in love with Grimes (soprano); Captain Balstrode, retired merchant skipper (baritone); Auntie, landlady of The Boar (contralto); two "nieces," attractions at

The Boar (sopranos); Robert Boles, fisherman (tenor); Swallow, mayor of The Borough (bass); Mrs. Nabob Sedley, widow of an East Indian Company agent (mezzo-soprano); Rev. Horace Adams, rector (tenor); Ned Keene, apothecary (baritone); Dr. George Crabbe, doctor (mime); Jim Hobson (bass); townspeople; fisherfolk.

The action takes place in a small fishing village in England—The Borough —in the early part of the nineteenth century.

Prologue. The Meeting Place. Peter Grimes's apprentice has died, and Peter is being tried for having murdered him. Though Peter is unpopular with his neighbors, he is found innocent. He is warned not to hire another apprentice until at the same time he gets a woman to take care of the boy. Ellen Orford, a schoolmistress in love with Peter, is willing to be that woman, but Peter cannot think of marriage until he has restored himself completely to good standing in the community.

Act I, Scene 1. A street. Between the prologue and Act I an orchestral ENTR'ACTE, "Dawn," gives a picture of a bleak fishing village and seascape. A storm is threatening. Auntie invites the villagers into The Boar after they have pulled in their boats. Only Captain Balstrode and Ned Keene are willing to help Peter in this task. Keene informs Peter he has found for Peter a new apprentice, a fact that meets with the loud disapproval of the townspeople. Captain Balstrode suggests that Peter leave The Borough in view of the hostility he has aroused, but Peter Grimes is determined to win back his self-respect; also he is eager to marry Ellen. Everybody has gone into The Boar, leaving Grimes by himself. As the storm is beginning to erupt, Grimes sings, "What harbor shelters peace?"

Scene 2. An orchestral prelude, "The Storm," now depicts the fury of the rapidly mounting storm. Grimes comes into The Boar to seek shelter, singing a strange ditty as he enters ("Now the

Great Bear and the Pleiades"). Some of the people in the tavern are sure he has gone mad; others, that the devil has taken possession of Grimes's soul. Balstrode urges the people in the tavern to strike up a song, which they do. When this is finished, Ellen arrives with Peter's new apprentice, John.

Act II, Scene 1. Outside the church. A prelude, "Sunday Morning," suggests the peace of a village on Sunday morning with church bells calling the villagers to prayer. Several Sundays have passed. Ellen is outside the church knitting. Peter arrives, demanding that his apprentice, John, come to work for him that day even if this is the Sabbath. When Ellen objects, Grimes strikes her and drags John away. Upon leaving the church, the townspeople learn of this episode. They are so angered they are determined to follow Grimes to see how he is treating John.

Scene 2. In Peter Grimes's hut. Peter pushes his apprentice into the hut, inside of which Peter reflects on his ambition to become rich, marry Ellen, and raise children of his own. When he hears the approaching sounds of angry townspeople, he suspects that his apprentice has instigated them. He pushes the boy out of the house, then follows him. The boy falls over a cliff and is drowned.

Act III, Scene 1. A tranquil orchestral prelude, "Moonlight," brings us a placid nocturnal street scene. Several evenings later at The Boar, the townspeople are dancing a polka, then a waltz. Mrs. Sedley now tries to convince Keene that Grimes has murdered his apprentice, who has disappeared mysteriously. Grimes himself has been gone for two days, a fact that worries both Ellen and Balstrode. The discovery of John's wet shirt on the shore arouses the people in the tavern. Hobson is appointed as policeman to lead several men to the shore to investigate the situation.

Scene 2. The same. A vigorous, frenetic prelude shows how the agitation of the people in The Borough is mount-

ing. A few hours have passed. Grimes is by his boat, singing a chant about the sea, when he hears and is disturbed by the shouts of the people as they explore the shoreline. Ellen and Balstrode try to calm him. But Balstrode, fully aware of the town's fury and hate, urges Grimes to go out to sea and drown himself. As though mesmerized, Peter goes into his boat as Balstrode leads the weeping Ellen Orford away. Having failed to locate Grimes, the townsfolk return. The fishermen are taking down their nets, when word comes from the coast guard that a ship has sunk in the sea. A new day is beginning for the fisherfolk of The Borough without their realizing that Peter Grimes has committed suicide.

Peter Grimes made Britten internationally famous and placed him in the front rank of contemporary opera composers. Its premiere was a gala event. The war in Europe had just ended, SADLER'S WELLS was being reopened for the first time since 1940, and *Peter Grimes* was the first new English opera in several years. All these circumstances combined to provide excitement. A line appeared in front of the theater twenty-four hours before curtain time. By the time the curtain rose, tickets for all scheduled performances had been sold. Notables from the world of music and correspondents from the world's foremost newspapers attended. The tension mounted during the performance itself and erupted into pandemonium at the final curtain. Showers of bouquets descended on the stage. *Peter Grimes* was soon heard throughout the world of opera, translated into eight different languages, and wherever it was given was acclaimed as one of the major operas of the twentieth century. Its premiere at the METROPOLITAN OPERA took place on Feb. 12, 1948.

Though Britten used many different elements—sea chanteys, polytonal duets, simple jigs, broad arias, stark recitatives, realistic tone painting in the orchestra —integration was not sacrificed. With the skill of a master, Britten fused his diverse material into a gripping psychological drama of man's cruelty to man, one of the composer's favorite themes.

Peter Ibbetson, opera in three acts by TAYLOR. Libretto by the composer in collaboration with Constance Collier, based on the novel of the same name by George Du Maurier. Premiere: Metropolitan Opera, Feb. 7, 1931. This was Taylor's second opera, completed four years after THE KING'S HENCHMAN. Peter Ibbetson (a role created by Edward JOHNSON) is victimized by a tyrant uncle and finds relief in dreams. He kills his uncle and is imprisoned for life. In prison, he again succumbs to dreams. These bring up his past and his childhood sweetheart, Mary. After thirty years in prison, Ibbetson learns that Mary is dead. Dreams no longer serve him; he has lost the will to live. He dies; the prison walls disintegrate. Peter is young again, and Mary is waiting for him.

Its most distinguished pages are for orchestra, including the first-act waltzes, the inn music in the second act, and the dream music in the third act.

The opera proved so successful that it was given sixteen times in the next four seasons, one of which was the opening-night performance of the 1933–34 METROPOLITAN OPERA season. The opera was successfully revived at the Empire State Festival in New York in 1961.

Peter Ivanov, a Russian renegade (tenor) in love with Marie in LORTZING'S ZAR UND ZIMMERMANN.

Peters, Roberta, soprano. Born New York City, May 4, 1930. She received her vocal training from William Pierce Herman, her only teacher. Her opera debut was an unscheduled appearance, when she substituted for Nadine CONNER as Zerlina in a performance of DON GIOVANNI at the METROPOLITAN OPERA in 1950. She has remained with the company since then, establishing her reputation in leading soprano roles in the Italian and French repertories and in several MOZART operas. Her first European opera engagement came in 1951 at COVENT GARDEN in a gala performance

of THE BOHEMIAN GIRL conducted by BEECHAM. She was heard at the SALZBURG FESTIVAL in 1963 and through the years at other major European music festivals, as well as in leading opera houses.

Petrarch (born Francesco di Petracco), poet. Born Arezzo, Italy, July 20, 1304; died Arqua, near Padua, July 19, 1374. This celebrated figure of the Middle Ages is the central character in two operas: Enrique GRANADOS' *Petrarca* and Johann Cristoph Kienlen's *Petrarca und Laura.*

Petroff, Ossip, basso. Born Elisavetgrad, Russia, Nov. 15, 1807; died St. Petersburg, Mar. 14, 1878. He was singing at a market fair in Kursk, in 1830, when the director of the St. Petersburg Opera heard him and engaged him. His debut took place that year as SARASTRO. Recognition was immediate. To the end of his life, Petroff was without a rival, either histrionic or vocal, on the Russian stage. He created the leading bass roles in many Russian operas, including BORIS GODUNOV, A LIFE FOR THE CZAR, THE MAID OF PSKOV, RUSSALKA, RUSSLAN AND LUDMILLA, and THE STONE GUEST. His last appearance took place four days before his death.

Petrovich, a captain (baritone) in TCHAIKOVSKY'S EUGENE ONEGIN.

Petruchio, nobleman of Verona (baritone) in GOETZ'S THE TAMING OF THE SHREW.

Pfitzner, Hans, composer. Born Moscow, May 5, 1869; died Salzburg, Austria, May 22, 1949. His parents, who were German, took him to their native land when he was a child. There he studied with his father (director of the Frankfurt Municipal Theater), and at the Hoch Conservatory. For a while he taught piano, conducted, and composed; in 1893 there took place in Berlin a successful concert devoted to his works. Two years later his first opera, *Der arme Heinrich,* was outstandingly successful when introduced in Mainz; it was heard in many major German opera houses during the next decade. In 1897 he settled in Berlin and was engaged as professor of the Stern Conservatory.

From 1903 to 1906 he was the KAPELL-
MEISTER at the Theater des Westens;
in 1907–08 he conducted the Kaim Orchestra in Munich; in 1908 he was
appointed director of the Strasbourg
Conservatory and in 1910 director of
the Strasbourg Opera. Meanwhile, his
second opera, *Die Rose vom Liebesgarten,* was introduced in Elberfeld in
1901, and his third opera, *Christelflein,*
was produced in Munich, Dec. 11, 1906.

Pfitzner settled temporarily in Munich in 1916, and it was here that he
completed his masterwork, the opera
PALESTRINA, first given on June 12, 1917,
to great acclaim. It was sent on tour
throughout Germany (despite travel restrictions imposed by World War I),
and it had many revivals after the war,
particularly at the MUNICH FESTIVALS.

In 1920 Pfitzner returned to Berlin,
where he served as director of the master class in composition at the Academy
of Fine Arts. He spent the last two
decades of his life in Munich, where
he was one of the city's major musical
figures, distinguished as teacher, conductor, and composer. Pfitzner societies
were formed in different parts of Europe to promote his works. When the
Nazis came to power, Pfitzner enthusiastically allied himself with the new
order and became one of its musical
spokesmen. After the German defeat,
Pfitzner became poverty-stricken. He was
found in a Munich home for the aged
by the President of the Vienna Philharmonic, who had him brought to
Austria, where he was supported by the
orchestra.

Pfitzner wrote only one opera after
Palestrina (though he revised his
Christelflein in 1917). This was *Das
Herz,* completed in 1931, and intro-
duced simultaneously by the BERLIN
OPERA and the MUNICH OPERA on Nov.
12 of that year.

Phanuel, a young Jew (tenor) in MAS-
SENET'S HÉRODIADE.

Phèdre, (1) Ariane's sister (soprano)
in MILHAUD'S *opéra minute* L'ABANDON
D'ARIANE.

(2) Thésée's wife (soprano) in Milhaud's *opéra minute* LA DÉLIVRANCE DE
THÉSÉE.

Philadelphia Lyric Opera Company, an
outgrowth of the Philadelphia Civic
Opera, which had been founded in
1923 and existed for seven years under
the musical direction of Alexander
SMALLENS. It presents fifteen performances of ten operas annually, with
Aurelio Fabiani as general manager.
Besides drawing from the traditional
repertory, the Lyric Opera occasionally
digresses to novelties as it did in its
revivals of MEFISTOFELE in 1965, NORMA
with Joan SUTHERLAND in 1968, and
I CAPULETTI ED I MONTECCHI with Renata
SCOTTO on opening night in 1968.

Philémon et Baucis, opera by GOUNOD.
Libretto by Jules BARBIER and Michel
Carré, based on Ovid. Premiere: Théâtre Lyrique, Paris, Feb. 18, 1860. The
setting is Phrygia in mythical times.
An old couple, Philémon (tenor) and
Baucis (soprano), provide hospitality
to two strangers, who are really Vulcan
(bass) and Jupiter (baritone) come to
punish Phrygia. The Phrygians are visited by a storm, but Jupiter saves Philémon and Baucis. Complications set
in when Jupiter restores the youth of
his benefactors, only to fall in love with
the now beautiful Baucis. Touched by
her devotion to Philémon, he finally
permits the pair to enjoy their restored
youth. Two arias from this work are
popular: Vulcan's song in Act I, "Au
bruit des lourds marteaux," and Baucis'
aria in Act II, "O riante nature."

Philidor, François André Danican, composer. Born Dreux, France, ·Sept. 7,
1726; died London, Aug. 24, 1795. One
of the most prolific and successful composers of OPÉRAS COMIQUES of his time,
he came from a family which for generations had been professional musicians. After studying music with André
Campra, Philidor turned to chess and
became a master of the game, leaving
a name that is well known to chess
players of the present day. After 1754
Philidor combined his activity in chess

with composition, and in 1759 his first *opéra comique*, *Blaise le Savetier*, was a brilliant success. His later works, all extremely popular, included: *Le Triomphe du temps* (1761); *Tom Jones* (1764); *L'Amant déguisé* (1769); *Le Bon Fils* (1773); *Zémire et Mélide* (1773); *Les Femmes vengées* (1775); *Persée* (1780); *Thémistocle* (1786); *La Belle Esclave* (1787). Philidor's reputation in London was only second to his fame in Paris. In 1767 he wrote a serious opera, *Ernelinde*. A success when introduced, it was revised two years later, renamed *Sandomir*, and performed again.

Philine, an actress (soprano) in THOMAS'S MIGNON.

Philip II, King of Spain (bass) in THOMAS'S MIGNON.

Philip II, King of Spain (bass) in VERDI'S DON CARLOS.

Phillips, Adelaide, contralto. Born Stratford-on-Avon, Eng., 1833; died Carlsbad, Bohemia, Oct. 3, 1882. She was brought to the United States as a child of seven, where she appeared in several stage productions. Her voice teacher, Sophie ARNOULD, directed her to opera. Jenny LIND heard the young singer and suggested study with her own teacher, Manuel GARCÍA. After two years with García in London, Phillips made her debut in Milan on Dec. 17, 1854, as ROSINA. After successful appearances in Italy she returned to the United States and made her American debut at the Academy of Music in New York on Mar. 17, 1856, as AZUCENA. She remained at the Academy of Music five years. In 1861 she toured Europe, making her Paris debut as Azucena at the Théâtre des Italiens. Subsequently she appeared in the United States with a company directed by CARL ROSA and with the Boston Ideal Opera Company. She then formed the Adelaide Phillips Opera Company. It toured the United States and was a financial failure. After a farewell appearance in Cincinnati in 1881 she went to Europe to recover her health, dying several months later.

Philomela, opera by Henrik Andriessen.

Libretto by Jan Engelman, based on an episode in Ovid's *Metamorphoses*. Premiere: Holland Music Festival, Amsterdam, June 23, 1950. Sweet-singing Philomela is seduced by her brother, Tereus, who then cuts out her tongue to prevent her from betraying him. Philomela revenges herself by killing Tereus' child and serving it to his father at a feast. Through the intervention of the gods, all three principals in this gruesome tale are transformed into birds; now a nightingale, Philomela can sing again.

Phoebus and Pan (Der Streit zwischen Phoebus und Pan), secular cantata in one act by Johann Sebastian Bach. Libretto by Piccaver. Premiere: Leipzig, 1731. American premiere: Brooklyn, N.Y., Feb. 11, 1929 (concert version). This cantata is sometimes given an operatic stage presentation. It is a satirical work (based on the Greek legend of the song contest between Phoebus and Apollo) in which Bach satirizes and at times parodies the pretentious music then being written for operas and mocks his contemporary Johann Adolph Schiebe.

phonograph recordings, *see* OPERA PERFORMANCE (4).

Piangerò la sorte mia, Cleopatra's aria in HANDEL'S GIULIO CESARE IN EGITTO.

Piangi, piangi, Luisa's celebrated aria in Act III of VERDI'S LUISA MILLER.

Piango si voi, quartet of Maria, Gabriele, Fiesco, and Boccanegra with chorus, in Act III of VERDI'S SIMON BOCCANEGRA.

Piave, Francesco Maria, librettist. Born Mureno, Italy, May 18, 1810; died Milan, Mar. 5, 1876. An intimate friend of Giuseppe VERDI, he wrote the librettos of nine of his operas, including ERNANI, LA FORZA DEL DESTINO, MACBETH, and RIGOLETTO.

Piccaver, Alfred, tenor. Born Long Sutton, Eng., Feb. 15, 1884; died Vienna, Sept. 23, 1958. His vocal studies took place in New York, Milan, and Prague. During this period he made his opera debut as ROMÉO in Prague in 1907. Between 1910 and 1937 he was a principal tenor at the VIENNA (Royal) STATE

OPERA, where he appeared in the Austrian premieres of IL TABARRO and THE GIRL OF THE GOLDEN WEST. Between 1923 and 1925 he was a member of the CHICAGO OPERA and in 1925 he appeared at COVENT GARDEN. After leaving the VIENNA STATE OPERA he devoted himself to teaching in London. He returned to the Vienna State Opera in 1955 as a guest performer. From then on he confined his teaching activity to Vienna.

Piccinni, Nicola (sometimes **Niccolo**), composer. Born Bari, Italy, Jan. 16, 1728; died Passy, France, May 7, 1800. His operas were matched against those of GLUCK during the esthetic war between Paris' "Gluckists" and "Piccinnists." Piccinni entered the Conservatorio San Onofrio in Naples in 1742, remaining there twelve years. His teachers included Francesco DURANTE and Leonardo LEO. After leaving the conservatory, he was sponsored by the Prince of Ventimiglia, who arranged to have his first opera, *Le donne dispettose,* produced in Naples in 1754. The opera was such a triumph that envious composers instigated cabals to discredit Piccinni. In spite of their efforts, his next operas continued to enjoy success; one of them, *Il curioso del proprio danno,* first heard in 1755, had several highly successful revivals. In 1758 Piccinni went to Rome to produce there his new opera, *Alessandro nell' Indie.* He now became one of the most celebrated composers in that city. In 1760 he produced a comic opera, LA CECCHINA, which was not only an instantaneous success but was one of the finest comic operas before those of ROSSINI. In 1762 Piccinni wrote six operas that were performed simultaneously by six leading theaters. His esteemed position in Rome was suddenly lost in 1773 with the rise in popularity of his pupil, Pasquale Anfossi. This eclipse so embittered Piccinni that his health broke down, and for a while he refused to compose. When he recovered, he vowed never again to write an opera for the Roman public. He returned to Naples, where his popularity was still at its

height and where his next opera, *I viaggiatori,* was acclaimed. In 1776 he was invited to Paris to write operas for the French stage. He enjoyed high favor at Versailles and was engaged to give singing lessons to the queen. The first opera he produced in Paris was *Roland* (using a libretto which had also been set by GLUCK). This marked the beginning of the bitter feud between the followers of Piccinni and those of Gluck. Recognizing the publicity value of this rivalry, the director of the PARIS OPÉRA commissioned both composers to write music for the same libretto, IPHIGÉNIE EN TAURIDE. Gluck's opera was performed first, in 1779, and was received so enthusiastically that Piccinni tried to withdraw his own work. Piccinni's opera, received less well than Gluck's, nevertheless had seventeen consecutive performances. Still, there could no longer be a question in Paris as to the victory of Gluck's principles and esthetics over those of his Italian rival. However, when Gluck left Paris in 1780, Piccinni once again occupied the center of public interest. But three years later a new Italian composer came into fashion, Antonio SACCHINI, and this led to a sharp decline in the popularity of Piccinni's operas. After the outbreak of the French Revolution, Piccinni returned to Naples, where he received a commission from the king, and where several of his older operas were successfully revived. He lost favor when he was suspected of Republican leanings. For four years he was a virtual prisoner in his own house. In 1798 he was allowed to return to Paris, where he received a government pension and shortly before his death was made an inspector at the conservatory.

Piccinni wrote well over a hundred operas. His best works had a rich fund of pleasing melodies combined with skillfully written ensemble numbers and dramatic finales. Besides operas already mentioned, his most successful works were: *Le gelosie* (1755); *Il re pastore* (1760); *Berenice* (1764); *L'Olimpiade* (1768, revised 1774); *Didone abbando-*

nata (1770); *Antigono* (1771); *Atys* (1780); *Didon* (1783); *Le faux lord* (1783).

Piccola, Scala, La, a CHAMBER-OPERA theater inside the famed LA SCALA in Milan, but with its own entry on another street. It opened in Dec., 1955. Here chamber operas of past and present are given, including such works as IL MATRIMONIO SEGRETO, LA CECCHINA, IL CAMPANELLO DI NOTTE, DON PASQUALE, and so forth. The world premiere of CHEDINI's *L'ipocrita felice* was here given in 1956 and of Giacomo Manzoni's *Atomtod* in 1965.

Picture of Dorian Gray, The, *see* WILDE, OSCAR.

Piège de Méduse, Le, *see* SATIE, ERIK.

Pierné, Gabriel, composer. Born Metz, France, Aug. 16, 1863; died Ploujean, France, July 17, 1937. He attended the Paris Conservatory, where his teachers included Jules MASSENET and César FRANCK and where he received the PRIX DE ROME in 1882. After his return to Paris from Rome he succeeded Franck as organist of Sainte-Clotilde, holding this post eight years. After 1903, he devoted himself to conducting, serving as musical director of the Colonne Orchestra (Paris) for a quarter of a century. As a composer he first achieved recognition with an oratorio, *The Children's Crusade,* in 1902, which won the City of Paris prize. He also wrote several operas: *La Coupe enchantée* (1895, revised 1901); *Vendée* (1897); *La Fille de Tabarin* (1901); ON NE BADINE PAS AVEC L'AMOUR (1910); *Sophie Arnould* (1927).

Pierotto, a villager (contralto) in DONIZETTI's LINDA DI CHAMOUNIX.

Pietà, rispetto amore, Macbeth's revery as he contemplates the tragedy engulfing him, in Act IV of VERDI's MACBETH.

Pietoso al par d'un Nume, Leonora's plea to Fernando to forgive her, in the closing scene in Act IV of DONIZETTI's LA FAVORITA.

pietra del paragone, La (The Touchstone), comic opera in two acts by ROSSINI. Libretto by Luigi Romanelli. Premiere: La Scala, Sept. 26, 1812. Rossini's first opera for LA SCALA concerns the efforts of Count Asdrubale to get married. To test the love of three widows, each of whom is interested in him, he forges a document proving he is bankrupt. Only one of them, Clarice, remains loyal. Now it is her turn to test the Count by disguising herself as her brother and threatening to prevent the marriage. The tests ended, the Count and Clarice finally get married. A successful revival of the opera was given at the GLYNDEBOURNE FESTIVAL on July 22, 1965.

Pilar, Pedro's bride (soprano) in LAPARRA's LA HABANERA.

Pilgrims' Chorus, the chorus of the pilgrims on their journey to and from Rome in Acts I and III of WAGNER's TANNHÄUSER.

Pilgrim's Progress, The, a musical "morality" play in prologue, four acts, and epilogue by VAUGHAN WILLIAMS. Libretto by the composer, based on John BUNYAN's allegory of the same name. Premiere: Covent Garden, Apr. 26, 1951. This is not an opera in the accepted meaning of the term, since it consists of a series of picturesque tableaux frequently suggesting a religious ritual. The prologue shows Bunyan writing his book in Bedford Gaol, where the Pilgrim appears to him. The work then describes the history of the Pilgrim as he goes through the City of Destruction, the Valley of Humiliation, Vanity Fair, the Delectable Mountains, to the Golden Gate of the Celestial City. In the fourth act, Vaughan Williams incorporated a one-act opera, THE SHEPHERDS OF THE DELECTABLE MOUNTAINS, which he had written in 1922. There are a few recurrent musical themes throughout the musical play: a trumpet call describing the Pilgrim's Way, a valor motive which is predominant in Act II, and a hymn which Bunyan sings in both the prologue and the epilogue.

Pilou, Jeannette, soprano. Born Alexandria, Egypt. Born of Greek parents, she decided to become an opera singer after hearing LA BOHÈME. She studied voice for three years in Milan and in 1959 made her debut in that city as VIOLETTA. Following appearances in various European cities, she received a call from the VIENNA STATE OPERA to substitute for an indisposed singer as MIMI. Her performance proved a triumph, and she has remained with that company as a principal soprano since. In 1967–68 she made her debut with the METROPOLITAN OPERA, following her appearances there with performances at the SAN FRANCISCO OPERA, the SALZBURG FESTIVAL, and the June Festival Weeks in Vienna, where she created the role of Oda in Ivan Eröd's *Seidenraupen*.

Pimen, a monk (bass) in MUSSORGSKY'S BORIS GODUNOV.

Pinellino, a shoemaker (bass) in PUCCINI'S GIANNI SCHICCHI.

Ping, the Grand Chancellor (baritone) in PUCCINI'S TURANDOT.

Pinza, Ezio, bass. Born Rome, May 18, 1892; died Stamford, Conn., May 9, 1957. He originally planned to be a civil engineer, but abandoned engineering in his seventeenth year to become a professional bicycle racer. When he was eighteen he started studying singing with Ruzza and continued his studies with Vizzani at the Bologna Conservatory. After service in the artillery during World War I, he made his debut at the Teatro Reale in Rome in 1921 in the role of KING MARK. After two seasons in Rome and another in Turin, he was engaged by LA SCALA, where he appeared three seasons; during this period he appeared in the world premiere of BOITO'S NERONE, in 1924.

Pinza made his American debut at the METROPOLITAN OPERA on Nov. 1, 1926, in SPONTINI'S LA VESTALE, when Olin Downes described him as "a majestic figure on the stage" and a bass "of superb sonority and impressiveness." For the next quarter of a century Pinza was the principal bass of the Metropolitan, appearing in an extensive repertory, and achieving triumphs in such varied roles as BORIS GODUNOV, Figaro (in THE MARRIAGE OF FIGARO), DON GIOVANNI,

Frère Laurent, King DODON, OROVESCO, and LOTHARIO. A dominating figure, he combined powerful characterizations with a voice remarkable for texture, range, volume, and flexibility. While a member of the Metropolitan, Pinza made numerous appearances throughout the world of opera; his interpretations of Don Giovanni and Figaro in *The Marriage of Figaro* were major attractions at the SALZBURG FESTIVALS before World War II.

In 1949 Pinza withdrew from opera to appear in motion pictures and in Broadway musical plays. He scored such a sensation in *South Pacific* that he became a matinee idol. He subsequently appeared in *Fanny*. He also made numerous radio and television appearances. His daughter by his first marriage, Claudia Pinza, is also an opera singer. She made her debut in a SAN FRANCISCO OPERA production of FAUST, appearing with her father (Sept. 21, 1947). She made her debut at the Metropolitan Opera as MICAËLA on Nov. 18, 1947, remaining with the company a single season.

Pipe of Desire, The, one-act opera by CONVERSE. Libretto by George Edward Burton. Premiere: Boston, Jan. 31, 1906. This was the first opera by an American to be performed at the METROPOLITAN OPERA (Mar. 18, 1910). It received the David BISPHAM MEDAL. The Pipe of Desire, owned by the Elf King (bass), has magic powers. Because the peasant youth Iolan (tenor) makes selfish use of the pipe, he brings doom upon himself and his beloved Naoia (soprano). The Elf King seizes the pipe from Iolan and plays on it. As he plays, Naoia is drawn toward the pipe from her sickbed and falls dead at Iolan's feet. The Elf King plays again. This time Iolan dies, and his soul goes forth to meet that of his beloved.

Pique Dame (The Queen of Spades), opera in three acts by TCHAIKOVSKY. Libretto by Modest Tchaikovsky, based on a story by PUSHKIN. Premiere: Maryinsky Theater, St. Petersburg, Dec. 19,

1890. American premiere: Metropolitan Opera, Mar. 5, 1910.

Characters: Herman, an officer of the Hussars (tenor); Count Tomsky, his friend (baritone); Prince Yeletsky, Lisa's betrothed (bass); the Countess (mezzo-soprano); Lisa, her granddaughter (soprano); Pauline, her friend (contralto); a governess (mezzo-soprano); Masha, a chambermaid (soprano); four Russian officers and noblemen; guests; soldiers; masqueraders; and so forth. The action takes place in St. Petersburg at the end of the eighteenth century.

Act I, Scene 1. A public summer garden in St. Petersburg. Count Tomsky wonders about the change that has come over his friend, Herman. The latter explains he has met a girl whose identity he does not know but with whom he has fallen in love ("Once I knew happiness"). Prince Yeletsky arrives with the good news that he is about to get married. When his sweetheart, Lisa, arrives in the company of her grandmother, the Countess, Herman realizes that this is the girl he loves. Tomsky now tells the strange history of the grandmother ("It chanced at Versailles"), a woman obsessed with gambling and come to be known as "The Queen of Spades." She acquired a winning system by having an affair with Count St. Germain but has kept her system a secret. Herman suddenly realizes that if he ever acquired that secret he would be able to amass enough money to win Lisa from the Prince.

Scene 2. Lisa's room. Lisa, her friend Pauline, and several other girls are entertaining themselves by singing "Already the shades of night," following which Pauline contributes a lively peasant song, "Dear friends for whom I sing." They all join in a Russian dance. After the others leave, Herman appears through the window, declaring to Lisa his great love ("Forgive me, bright celestial visions") and receiving in return an ardent response.

Act II, Scene 1. A reception room. A ball is taking place during which Yelet-sky tells Lisa of his great love for her in "I love you, dear." Following a pastoral play, performed for the guests, Lisa secretly passes to Herman the key to her apartment.

Scene 2. The bedroom of the Countess. To reach Lisa's apartment, Herman must pass through the grandmother's bedroom. When the Countess enters with her maids, he hides behind a curtain. When she is left alone, Herman steps out, demands that she give him the secret formula for winning at cards, and when she makes no response, threatens her with a pistol. Terrified, the Countess drops dead of shock. Lisa bursts in, sees her grandmother is dead, and, despite his denials, is convinced that Herman is guilty; that his sole interest in Lisa had been to gain the grandmother's secret.

Act III, Scene 1. A soldiers' barracks. Herman has received a letter from Lisa forgiving him and accepting his explanation. But Herman's conscience is troubled. He sees the ghost of the Countess, which reveals the three cards necessary for winning.

Scene 2. The banks of the Neva. Having arranged a rendezvous with Herman, Lisa is waiting for him (" 'Twill soon be midnight"). When Herman arrives, they fall in each other's arms. But the lust for gambling and winning is greater than his love. Herman deserts her to go off to the gaming house as Lisa commits suicide by jumping from a precipice into the river.

Scene 3. A gambling house. Though not a gambler, Prince Yeletsky has come to try his luck since, as he says, he has been unlucky in love. Tomsky entertains those present with a tune, "Darling maidens." At this point, Herman enters, gambles, and begins to win heavily. Prince Yeletsky now becomes his rival. When the stakes are at their maximum, the losing card turns up for Herman—the Queen of Spades. The ghost of the Countess suddenly arises to haunt Herman. This leads him to stab himself. Before he dies, he begs the Prince to forgive him.

This opera, though a classic in Russia and extremely popular throughout Central Europe, has never been in great favor in the English-speaking world, though it was revived at COVENT GARDEN in 1950 (in an English translation) and then was given there for a few more seasons. The METROPOLITAN OPERA revived it after several decades on Sept. 28, 1965, but without any sustained success.

pirata, Il (The Pirate), opera in two acts by BELLINI. Libretto by Romani. Premiere: La Scala, Oct. 27, 1827. American premiere: New York City, Dec. 5, 1832. In an attempt to save the life of her father, Imogene marries a man she does not love and abandons the one she does. After her husband accuses her of adultery, her lover kills him and is doomed to die. These disastrous developments lead Imogene to insanity. This was the first Bellini opera to be heard in London (April 17, 1830). Long in discard, *Il pirata* suddenly acquired a new lease on life in 1958, when it opened the season of the Teatro Massimo at Palermo and later brought a triumph to Maria CALLAS at LA SCALA. She was heard in this opera at a performance of the AMERICAN OPERA SOCIETY in New York in 1959.

Pistol, Falstaff's henchman (bass) in VERDI'S FALSTAFF.

Pitt, Percy, conductor. Born London, Jan. 4, 1870; died there Nov. 23, 1932. His studies took place at the Leipzig Conservatory and with Josef Rheinberger in Munich. He returned to England in 1893 and after holding various posts as organist and chorus master was appointed chorus master at COVENT GARDEN in 1906. A year later he became an assistant conductor there and in 1908 principal conductor. He remained at Covent Garden until 1915. From 1915 to 1920 he was a conductor with the Beecham Opera Company and from 1920 to 1924, director of the BRITISH NATIONAL OPERA. He returned to Covent Garden as principal conductor in 1924. Two years later he became general musical director of the British Broadcasting Corporation, holding this post until succeeded by Sir Adrian Boult in 1930.

Pittichinaccio, Giulietta's admirer (tenor) in OFFENBACH'S THE TALES OF HOFFMANN, Act II.

Pizarro, governor of the prison of Seville (baritone) in BEETHOVEN'S FIDELIO.

Pizzetti, Ildebrando, composer. Born Parma, Sept. 20, 1880; died Rome, Feb. 13, 1968. He entered the Parma Conservatory in his sixteenth year. In 1901 he was engaged as assistant conductor of the Parma Opera. He had always been interested in the drama and even as a student had begun composing operas but had no success before his late twenties. In 1907 he joined the faculty of the Parma Conservatory. A year later he became professor of theory and composition at the Florence Conservatory, where he was appointed director in 1917 and remained until 1924, when he became director of the Milan Conservatory.

In 1905 Pizzetti had entered the first significant phase of his creative career, a period when he was affected by the writings of his friend, the poet-dramatist Gabriele D'ANNUNZIO. Many of his works were settings of D'Annunzio's writings. His major creation, the opera FEDRA, was introduced at LA SCALA on Mar. 20, 1915. While not initially successful, it subsequently proved one of the most popular of Pizzetti's works.

In his second phase, Pizzetti was influenced by the Bible. The major opera of this period, DEBORA E JAELE, was given at La Scala on Dec. 16, 1922. His last creative period was inspired mostly by Italian history and background, and from these influences came FRA GHERARDO, introduced at La Scala on May 16, 1928. For all these operas he wrote his own librettos.

Pizzetti was essentially a dramatic rather than a lyric composer. His operas are characterized by expressive declamations molded after the inflections of the text and are particularly notable for their choral pages.

In 1930 Pizzetti visited the United States and appeared as pianist and conductor in his own works. In 1936 he became professor of composition at the Santa Cecilia Academy in Rome (in succession to RESPIGHI), where he soon rose to the position of director. He resigned his directorial post in 1952. In 1950 he won the international Italia prize for a one-act radio opera, *Ifigenia.* He achieved a major success with the opera L'ASSASSINIO NELLA CATTEDRALE, text based on T. S. Eliot's *Murder in the Cathedral,* introduced at La Scala in 1958. His last opera, *Clitennestra,* was produced at La Scala in 1965.

His operas: *Fedra* (1912); *Debora e Jaele* (1921); *Lo straniero* (1925); *Fra Gherardo* (1927); *Orseolo* (1935); *L'oro* (1942); *Vanna Luppa* (1947); *Ifigenia* (1950); *Cagliostro* (1952); *La figlia di Jorio* (1954); *Assassinio nella cattedrale* (1958); *Lo stivale d'argento* (1960); *Il calzar d'argento* (1961); *Clitennestra* (1965).

Plaisirs, ramenez-vous, Venus, Cupid's eloquent song to Venus in Act I of RAMEAU'S CASTOR ET POLLUX.

Plançon, Pol-Henri, bass. Born Fumay, France, June 12, 1854; died Paris, Aug. 11, 1914. Trained for a career in business, he turned instead to music. After studying with Gilbert Louis DUPREZ and Giovanni SBRIGLIA, Plançon made his debut in Lyons in 1877 as ST. BRIS. Two seasons later, on Feb. 11, 1880, he made his debut in Paris at the Théâtre de la Gaieté. Three years afterward he became a member of the PARIS OPÉRA. He was a sensation as Méphistophélès in FAUST, a role he sang over a hundred times in a decade. On June 3, 1891, he made his debut in London, as Méphistophélès, and became an instant favorite; he returned to London each season until 1904. On Nov. 29, 1893, he made his American debut at the METROPOLITAN OPERA as Jupiter in PHILÉMON ET BAUCIS. He remained at the Metropolitan through the 1907–08 season, one of the stars of the golden age of great casts. He retired from the stage in 1908, having appeared in many world premieres, including MANCINELLI'S *Ero e Leandro,* MASSENET'S *Ascanio,* LE CID, and LA

NAVARRAISE, and STANFORD'S *Much Ado About Nothing.*

Planquette, Jean-Robert, composer. Born Paris, July 31, 1848; died there Jan. 28, 1903. A successful composer of OPÉRAS COMIQUES, the most famous being *Les Cloches de Corneville (The Chimes of Normandy),* he attended the Paris Conservatory, after which he earned his living writing songs for cafés. His first stage work was a one-act opera, *Paille d'avoine,* in 1874. Success followed in 1877 with *Les Cloches de Corneville,* introduced at the Folies-Dramatiques, where it had a run of four hundred performances. It was almost equally successful for many years in England, the United States, and a half dozen other countries. Among his many other works may be mentioned: RIP VAN WINKLE (1882); *Surcouf* (1887); *Paul Jones* (1889); *Le Talisman* (1892); *Panurge* (1895); *Mam'zelle Quat' Sous* (1897).

Pleurez, pleurez, mes yeux, Chimène's aria in Act III of MASSENET'S LE CID.

Plunkett, a wealthy farmer (bass) in FLOTOW'S MARTHA.

Plus blanche que la blanche hermine (Bianca al par hermine), Raoul's *romanza* in Act I of MEYERBEER'S LES HUGUENOTS. It calls for an obbligato by a viola d'amore.

Plus j'observe, Renaud's air in Act II of LULLY'S penultimate opera, ARMIDE ET RENAUD, after Renaud has awakened from his sleep at the banks of a river, whose natural beauties he rhapsodizes.

Poe, Edgar Allan, poet and story writer. Born Boston, Jan. 19, 1809; died Baltimore, Oct. 7, 1849. Adriano LUALDI'S *Il diavolo nel campanile* was derived from Poe's tale *The Devil in the Belfry* and Vieri Tosatti's *Il sistema della dolcezza* was based on another of Poe's stories. After 1908, Claude DEBUSSY worked intermittently on an opera to his own libretto, based on *The Fall of the House of Usher,* but the work was never completed and only fragments of it exist. An opera on this story and bearing its title was written by Morris Hutchen Rugar. SCHREKER prepared a libretto, *Der rote Tod,* after Poe's *The*

Masque of the Red Death, but abandoned the work after he wrote the music.

Pogner, a goldsmith (bass), father of Eva, in WAGNER'S DIE MEISTERSINGER.

Poisoned Kiss, The, opera in three acts by VAUGHAN WILLIAMS. Libretto by Evelyn Sharp, based on *The Poison Maid,* a story by Richard Garnett. Premiere: Cambridge, Eng., May 12, 1936. American premiere: New York City, Apr. 21, 1937. The composer described his opera as a "romantic extravaganza." It is a fantasy in which Tormentilla, daughter of a sorcerer, has been raised on poisons. When she meets Amaryllus, the son of the empress, she is to kill him with her kiss, but her true love is stronger than the designs of the sorcerer. The score contains pages that satirize various musical styles.

Polacco, Giorgio, conductor. Born Venice, Apr. 12, 1875; died New York City, Apr. 30, 1960. His musical schooling took place at the Liceo Benedetto Marcello in Venice and at the Milan Conservatory. He began his career as conductor at the Shaftsbury Theatre in London, then presenting a season of opera. He subsequently directed opera performances in Italy, Portugal, Belgium, Poland, and Russia, and was acclaimed for his WAGNER performances. After four seasons as principal conductor at the Teatro Colón in Buenos Aires and seven more in Rio de Janeiro, he returned to Italy to become principal conductor at LA SCALA. There he directed the Italian premiere of PELLÉAS ET MÉLISANDE. In 1906 he directed several performances for the SAN FRANCISCO OPERA COMPANY. On Nov. 11, 1912, he made his METROPOLITAN OPERA debut with MANON LESCAUT. Three years later, when TOSCANINI left the Metropolitan, he became one of the leading conductors. He resigned from the Metropolitan in 1917 and for the next several years conducted opera performances in South America, Havana, and Paris. When the Chicago Civic Opera was organized in 1922, Polacco was engaged as its music director and principal conductor, retain-

ing this post until 1930, when ill health sent him into retirement.

Polish Jew, The, *see* JUIF POLONAIS, LE.

Poliuto, opera in four acts by DONIZETTI. Libretto by SCRIBE, based on POLYEUCTE, a tragedy by CORNEILLE. Premiere: Paris Opéra, Apr. 10, 1840, under the title *Les Martyrs.* American premiere: Théâtre d'Orleans, New Orleans, Mar. 24, 1846. This opera has had a turbulent history. Donizetti wrote it originally for Naples, with the intention of having NOURRIT sing the principal male role; this version had a three-act libretto by CAMMARANO. When censors refused to permit its performance, a new four-act version of the text was prepared by Scribe. Under the title of *Les Martyrs,* the opera was produced in Paris. This French text was then translated into Italian and as *I martiri,* the opera was produced in Lisbon on Feb. 15, 1843. The original three-act version, with the Cammarano text, was finally mounted in Naples on Nov. 30, 1848. The opera was revived by LA SCALA in 1960 with a cast headed by CORELLI and CALLAS.

polka, a fast Bohemian dance in duple time, usually with an accent on the second beat and a rest for the second half-beat. There is a celebrated polka in the first act of SMETANA'S THE BARTERED BRIDE. Other operas containing polkas are Smetana's THE KISS and *Two Brides,* and WEINBERGER'S ŠVANDA.

Polkan, a general (bass) in RIMSKY-KORSAKOV'S LE COQ D'OR.

Pollack, Egon, conductor. Born Prague, May 3, 1879; died there June 14, 1933. He attended the Prague Conservatory and began his musical career as chorus master of the Prague Landestheater. In 1905 he was appointed first conductor of the Bremen Opera, where he remained five years. Between 1910 and 1912 he was first conductor of the Leipzig Opera and from 1912 to 1917, of the FRANKFURT OPERA. In 1914 he was invited to COVENT GARDEN to direct the WAGNER music dramas. Beginning in 1915 he was the principal conductor of the Wagner dramas with the CHICAGO OPERA. From 1917 to 1933 he was music director of the HAMBURG OPERA. He was acclaimed not only for his Wagner performances but also for his interpretations of the Richard STRAUSS operas. He died of a heart attack while directing a performance of FIDELIO.

Pollione, (1) proconsul (tenor) in love with Adalgisa, but loved by Norma and father of her children, in BELLINI's NORMA.

(2) King of Eos (tenor) and father of Danae in Richard STRAUSS's DIE LIEBE DER DANAE.

Pollux, Castor's twin brother (baritone) in RAMEAU's CASTOR ET POLLUX.

Polly, BALLAD OPERA in three acts, dialogue and verses by GAY, the music (ballads and popular songs) arranged by PEPUSCH. Premiere: Haymarket Theatre, London, June 19, 1777. American premiere: New York City, Oct. 10, 1925. Written in 1729 as a sequel to the extraordinarily popular BEGGAR'S OPERA, *Polly* was kept from the stage, apparently as a reprisal for the satires of the earlier work. Gay had *Polly* printed, and in this form the ballad opera was widely admired, though not staged till nearly a half century later, with six extra songs by Samuel Arnold. Like *The Beggar's Opera, Polly* has been successfully performed in the twentieth century.

polonaise, a Polish processional dance in triple time, characterized by accents on the second beat. Philine's aria, "Je suis Titania," in Act II of MIGNON is a polonaise; polonaises also appear in Act III of BORIS GODUNOV, Act III of EUGENE ONEGIN, and Scene 2 of WAR AND PEACE.

Polonius, Chancellor of Denmark (baritone) in THOMAS's HAMLET.

Polovtsian Dances, dances of the Polovtsian slaves before Prince Igor in Act II of BORODIN's PRINCE IGOR.

Polyeucte, a drama by Pierre CORNEILLE, the source of operas by DONIZETTI (POLIUTO) and GOUNOD (*Polyeucte*). Polyeucte, though deeply in love with his wife Pauline, refuses to recant his Christian vows and instead accepts martyrdom.

Polyphemus, the Cyclops (bass) in HANDEL's ACIS AND GALATEA.

Pomone, pastoral opera in five acts by Robert Cambert. Libretto by P. Perrin. Premiere: Paris Opéra, Mar. 3, 1671. This is the earliest French opera of which parts (prologue and first act) have survived. This was also the opera with which the PARIS OPÉRA (Académie Royal de Musique) was opened.

Pompeo, a character (baritone) in BERLIOZ' BENVENUTO CELLINI.

Ponchielli, Amilcare, composer. Born Paderno, Italy, Aug. 31, 1834; died Milan, Jan. 16, 1886. The composer of LA GIOCONDA, he entered the Milan Conservatory in his ninth year and stayed there nine years. While still a student he wrote an operetta, *Il sindaco babbèo,* in collaboration with three other students. His studies ended, he became an organist in Cremona and after that bandmaster in Piacenza. During this period he wrote his first opera, *I promessi sposi,* based on MANZONI's great novel and introduced in Cremona in 1856. For the opening of the Teatro dal Verme in Milan in 1872, Ponchielli was commissioned to write an opera. For this occasion he revised *I promessi sposi,* and it was now acclaimed. His next opera, *Le due gemelle,* produced by LA SCALA in 1873, was also well received. Ponchielli became world-famous with *La Gioconda,* introduced at La Scala on Apr. 8, 1876. The opera was a triumph at its premiere, and it was outstandingly successful when heard throughout Europe. None of the operas Ponchielli wrote after *La Gioconda* was able to repeat either the popular success or the consistently high level of dramatic and musical interest of that work.

In 1881 Ponchielli was appointed MAESTRO DI CAPPELLA of the Bergamo Cathedral, and from 1883 on he was professor of composition at the Milan Conservatory. His operas: *I promessi sposi* (1856); *La Savoiarda* (1861, revised as *Lina,* 1877); *Roderico* (1863); *La stella del monte* (1867); *Le due gemelle* (1873); *I Lituani* (1874, revised as *Alduna,* 1884); *La Gioconda* (1876); *Il figliuol prodigo* (1880); *Marion Delorme* (1885); *Bertrando de*

Bornio (composed 1867 but not produced) ; *I mori di Valenza* (completed by A. Cadora and produced posthumously, 1914) .

Pong, the Chief Cook (tenor) in PUCCINI'S TURANDOT.

Pons, Lily, soprano. Born Cannes, France, Apr. 12, 1904. She entered the Paris Conservatory in her thirteenth year as a student of piano. Plans for a virtuoso career were abandoned after a serious illness, following which she turned to singing. After World War I she appeared in minor singing roles at the Théâtre des Varietés in Paris. Her first husband, whom she married in 1923, became convinced of her talent and engaged Alberti di Gorostiaga to teach her. In 1928 Pons made her debut at the Mulhouse Opera in Alsace as LAKMÉ. After appearances in smaller French opera houses, she made her debut at the METROPOLITAN OPERA on Jan. 3, 1931, in LUCIA DI LAMMERMOOR. Up through the season of 1960–61 she was a leading soprano there, acclaimed in the coloratura roles of the French and Italian repertories. Several operas were revived by the Metropolitan for her, including THE DAUGHTER OF THE REGIMENT, LINDA DI CHAMOUNIX, MIGNON, and LA SONNAMBULA. In singing the role of Lakmé, she became the first singer in a half century to render the high F in the BELL SONG that DELIBES had originally intended. On Jan. 3, 1956, a gala performance celebrating the twenty-fifth anniversary of her debut there took place at the Metropolitan Opera. Her personal charm, capacity to invest each of her roles with engaging warmth, and brilliant coloratura range (two and a half octaves) made her an outstanding drawing card in the major opera houses of the world. She sang frequently on radio and television and was starred in a motion picture, *I Dream Too Much.* She became an American citizen in 1940.

Ponselle, Carmela (born Ponzillo), mezzo-soprano. Born Schenectady, N.Y., June 7, 1892. The older sister of the celebrated soprano Rosa PONSELLE, she began studying singing after her sister had become successful. Her opera debut took place in New York City in 1923 in AIDA. On Dec. 5, 1925, she made her debut at the METROPOLITAN OPERA in the same opera. She remained at the Metropolitan until 1928, then returned in 1930 for an additional five seasons. On Apr. 23, 1932, she appeared for the first time in an opera performance with her sister. The opera was LA GIOCONDA. They sang it in Cleveland; in Dec. of the same year the sisters again appeared in the same opera, this time at the Metropolitan in New York. Carmela left the Metropolitan in 1935 when GATTI-CASAZZA denied her permission to accept a radio contract. She specialized in radio appearances and teaching for several years.

Ponselle, Rosa (born Rose Ponzillo), soprano. Born Meriden, Conn., Jan. 22, 1894. She began singing early, and in her youth appeared in church choirs and as soloist in motion-picture theaters and vaudeville houses. She began to study intensively with William Thorner. CARUSO became interested in her and gained her an audition at the METROPOLITAN. She made her debut there on Nov. 15, 1918, in LA FORZA DEL DESTINO, when her voice was described by James Huneker as "vocal gold, with its luscious lower and middle tones, dark, rich, and ductile; brilliant and flexible in the upper register." The following month she was heard in a revival of OBERON and later the same season in the world premiere of Joseph Breil's *The Legend.* In 1927 she achieved one of the outstanding triumphs of her career, singing the title role in a revival of NORMA. In 1930 she achieved another major success as Donna ANNA, and in 1933 she was acclaimed at the FLORENCE MAY MUSIC FESTIVAL in LA VESTALE. In 1935 she gratified her life's ambition by appearing for the first time as CARMEN, singing the role at the Metropolitan; but Carmen was never one of her best parts.

After marrying Carle A. Jackson in

1936, she decided to retire from opera, even though she was then at the height of her fame. Her last appearance at the Metropolitan took place on Feb. 15, 1937, in *Carmen;* her voice—as remarkable for its richness and expressiveness as for its flexibility and range—had lost none of its magnetism or beauty.

In 1954, after a public silence of nearly seventeen years, Miss Ponselle made a recording of sixteen selected songs. She has served as artistic director of the BALTIMORE CIVIC OPERA Company, which celebrated her seventy-fifth birthday on Mar. 10, 1969, with a gala performance of *La forza del destino.*

Ponte, Lorenzo da, *see* DA PONTE, LORENZO.

Poppea, leading female character (soprano), beloved of the Emperor Nero, in MONTEVERDI'S L'INCORONAZIONE DI POPPEA.

Porgi amor, the lament of the Countess Almaviva over the Count's no longer loving her, in Act II of MOZART'S THE MARRIAGE OF FIGARO.

Porgy, a cripple (baritone), the principal male character in GERSHWIN'S PORGY AND BESS.

Porgy and Bess, opera in three acts by GERSHWIN. Libretto by Du Bose Heyward and Ira Gershwin, based on the play *Porgy* by Du Bose and Dorothy Heyward. Premiere: Boston, Sept. 30, 1935.

Characters: Porgy, a cripple (baritone); Bess, his girl (soprano); Crown (baritone); Sportin' Life (tenor); Robbins (tenor); Serena, his wife (soprano); Clara (soprano); Jake, her husband (baritone); Frazier, a lawyer (baritone); natives; hucksters; policemen. The setting is the Negro section of Charleston, S.C., in the 1930's.

Act I, Scene 1. Catfish Row, a Negro tenement street. Clara is singing a lullaby to her child ("Summertime") while a crap game is in progress. In the course of the game, Crown quarrels with Robbins and kills him. Crown escapes. Sportin' Life, who has always had an eye for Crown's girl, Bess, now feels free to invite her to New York. She turns him down, having found refuge in the home of the cripple, Porgy, who loves her unselfishly and devotedly.

Scene 2. Serena's room. There is a wake for Robbins. Neighbors gather to drop coins in a saucer for his burial. Serena is distraught at her husband's death ("My man's gone now").

Act II, Scene 1. Catfish Row. Bess, completely reformed, is living with Porgy, who sings of the happiness that is his ("I got plenty o' nuthin'"). They express their love for each other ("Bess, you is my woman now").

Scene 2. Kittiwah Island. During a lodge picnic, Sportin' Life entertains his friends with his cynical attitude toward religion ("It ain't necessarily so"). Crown, who has been hiding on the island, confronts Bess and persuades her to stay with him.

Scene 3. Catfish Row. A few days later, Bess returns to Porgy. She is sick and delirious. Porgy nurses her back to health. They tenderly reassure each other of their love ("I loves you, Porgy").

Scene 4. Serena's room. A hurricane blows up, and the women of Catfish Row are troubled over their men who have gone out fishing. Clara is particularly upset since she senses that her husband, Jake, is in danger. No one in Catfish Row can save Jake until Crown arrives unexpectedly and offers to do so, ridiculing the crippled Porgy for his inability to be of help.

Act III. Catfish Row. Crown has returned after saving Jake; he is looking for Bess. Afraid of losing the woman he loves, Porgy reaches out his window and chokes his rival to death. The police are unable to discover the murderer, but since they suspect Porgy they take him off to jail. While Porgy is away, Sportin' Life finally persuades Bess to go off with him to New York, tempting her with a packet of dope ("There's a boat dat's leavin' soon for New York"). Back from jail a few days later, Porgy finds Bess gone. Heartbroken but undaunted, he sets out after her ("Oh, Lawd, I'm on my way").

Porgy and Bess was Gershwin's last serious work, and his only full-length opera. It possesses that richness, vitality, and variety of melody, that vigor of rhythm, that spontaneity and freshness we associate with Gershwin's best music. It has much more, too. Of all Gershwin's serious works, it is the only one to reveal compassion, humanity, and a profound dramatic instinct. Rich in materials derived (but never quoted) from spirituals, shouts, and street cries, *Porgy and Bess* is truly a folk opera. Its roots are in the soil of the Negro people, whom it interprets with humor, tragedy, penetrating characterizations, dramatic power, and sympathy. Gershwin wrote his opera for the Theatre Guild, which organization produced it in New York in 1935 after a Boston tryout. It was not at first successful. Some critics thought it was neither an opera nor a musical comedy, but a hybrid. Later revivals impressed audiences and critics alike with the beauty and originality of this work, and it was at length accepted as one of the finest operas written by an American. A return to Broadway in 1942 resulted in the longest run known up to then by a revival, and it was at this time singled out for special praise by the NEW YORK MUSIC CRITICS' CIRCLE. The European premiere took place during World War II at the Danish Royal Opera in Copenhagen (in a Danish translation) on Mar. 27, 1943. Because of Gestapo antagonism to a successful American opera—Denmark was then occupied by the Nazis—the run had to end abruptly. In 1952 an American company began a several-year tour of *Porgy and Bess* in Europe and the Near East. The success of the work has been greater than that of any other American opera played abroad. In Feb., 1955, the company appeared at LA SCALA, and thus *Porgy and Bess* became the first opera by a native American to be heard in that theater. The same company began a Latin American tour on July 7, 1955. On Dec. 26, 1955, it made its historic debut in the Soviet Union in Leningrad, following this with engagements in Moscow and in other places in Eastern Europe. European opera houses have also produced the work with their own companies: the VOLKSOPER in Vienna in 1965, the Göteborg Opera in Sweden in 1966, the Oslo Opera in 1967, between 1967 and 1969 several opera houses in France as well as in Turkey and Bulgaria, and the KOMISCHE OPER in East Berlin in 1970. The opera was made into a motion picture produced in the United States by Samuel Goldwyn with virtually an all-Negro cast, released in 1959. During the summer of 1970, *Porgy and Bess* was given its first performance in Charleston, South Carolina, the setting of the opera. An all-Negro cast presented it as part of the three-hundredth anniversary of the founding of the city. Both the theater and the lavish party following the performance were desegregated for the first time in Charleston's history.

Porpora, Niccolò, singing teacher and composer. Born Naples, Aug. 19, 1686; died there Feb., 1766. While attending the Conservatorio di San Loreto in Naples he wrote his first opera, AGRIPPINA, produced in Naples in 1708. A major success came ten years later in Rome with *Berenice*. He held various court posts as music director before establishing in Naples, in 1712, a school of singing that became famous throughout Europe for the development of such singers as Caffarelli, SENESINO, and FARINELLI. In 1715 Porpora became singing master at the Conservatorio di San Onofrio in Naples. He held similar posts with two conservatories in Venice, after which he visited London in 1729, where for the next few years his operas were produced in competition with those by HANDEL. Handel's popularity finally overwhelmed him, and he returned to Venice to become director of the Ospedale degli Incurabili (for girls). In 1747 he settled in Dresden as conductor and teacher, and beginning with 1752 he spent two years in Vienna, where HAYDN became his pupil and lackey. In 1760 he became choirmaster of the Naples Cathedral and director of the Conservatorio di San Onofrio. In the closing years of his life his fame suffered such a decline that he died a pauper. He wrote about fifty operas. The most successful were: *Flavio Anicio Olibrio* (1711); *Berenice* (1718); *Faramondo* (1719); *Eumene* (1721); *Semiramide riconosciuta* (1724); *Siface* (1725); *Tamerlano* (1730); *Ferdinando* (1734); *Temistocle* (1742); *Partenope* (1742).

portamento, Italian for "carrying." In vocal music it is an indication for the singer to progress smoothly from one note to the next, thus achieving a sliding effect.

Portrait de Manon, Le, opera in one act by MASSENET. Libretto by Georges Boyer. Premiere: Opéra-Comique, May 8, 1894. American premiere: New York City, Dec. 13, 1897. This is a sequel to the composer's famous opera MANON. Des Grieux, now an old man, is in New Orleans where he meets a girl who bears a resemblance to the portrait of Manon he carries with him. The girl turns out to be Manon's daughter. The opera survived for ten years in the OPÉRA-COMIQUE repertoire and was briefly introduced on many other stages but is today almost forgotten.

Possente, Phthà!, Ramfis' prayer at the temple of Vulcan for Egypt's victory in battle in Act I, Scene 2, of VERDI's AIDA.

Possente spirito, Orpheus' successful plea to Charon in MONTEVERDI's L'ORFEO, an air remarkable not only for its emotion but also for its musical embellishments.

Postillon de Longjumeau, Le (The Postilion of Longjumeau), OPÉRA COMIQUE in three acts by Adolphe ADAM. Libretto by Adolphe de Leuven and Leon L. Brunswick. Premiere: Opéra-Comique, Oct. 13, 1836. American premiere: Park Theater, New York, Mar. 30, 1840. Chapelou, a postilion (tenor), becomes famous as a singer under the

name of St. Phar. As a postilion, he had been married to Madeleine (soprano). After his rise to fame, he falls in love with the wealthy Mme. de Latour, who turns out to be Madeleine, whom he had abandoned. The most celebrated aria is Chapelou's first-act postilion song, "Mes amis, écoutez l'histoire." Also of interest are his second-act ROMANCE, "Assis au pied d'un hêtre," and two arias sung by Madeleine, in the first act, "Mon petit mari," and in the second, "Je vais donc le revoir." This *opéra comique,* its composer's most famous work for the stage, was revived by the OPÉRA-COMIQUE on May 17, 1936, to celebrate the centenary of its world premiere. In 1968 it was revived in Germany by the Duisburg Opera and the Düsseldorf Opera.

Poulenc, Francis, composer. Born Paris, Jan. 7, 1899; died Jan. 30, 1963. He studied the piano with Ricardo Viñes and composition with Charles Koechlin. He first became known toward the end of World War I when the French critic Collet linked his name with those of MILHAUD, Louis Durey, HONEGGER, AURIC, and Germaine Tailleferre in proclaiming these composers a new school of French music, henceforth identified as Les SIX. Poulenc wrote music in every form. He first became famous for concert works filled with ironic statements and witty ideas, but many of his later works have great intensity and expressiveness and at times deep religious feeling. He is perhaps the most significant French song composer of the twentieth century. His opera LES DIALOGUES DES CARMÉLITES scored a major success when introduced at LA SCALA on Jan. 26, 1957, after which it was performed by major opera companies in Europe and the United States and in 1957 was televised in the United States over the NBC network. Other operas: *Le Gendarme incompris* (1920); LES MAMELLES DE TIRÉSIAS (1947); LA VOIX HUMAINE (1959).

Poupelinière, Alexandre-Jean-Joseph le Riche de la, music patron. Born Paris, 1692; died there Dec. 5, 1762. La Poupelinière was RAMEAU'S patron, and through his influence Rameau was able to produce some of his most important operas, beginning with HIPPOLYTE ET ARICIE in 1733. For several years, from about 1727, Rameau lived in his palace, directed his orchestra, and taught him music. Rameau incorporated some of La Poupelinière's ariettas in his own operas. The composer used La Poupelinière's influence to have François Joseph GOSSEC appointed as music director of the palace concerts in 1751, after which these concerts became celebrated throughout France.

Pour Bertha, moi, je soupire, John's aria, in which he reveals how much he loves Bertha and his determination to marry her, in Act II of MEYERBEER'S LE PROPHÈTE.

Pour la Vierge, Boniface's aria glorifying the Virgin Mary, in Act I of MASSENET'S LE JONGLEUR DE NOTRE DAME.

Pour les couvents c'est fini (Finita è per frati), the "Chanson Huguenote," Marcel's aria prophesying the ultimate victory of the Huguenots over the monks and priests, in Act I of MEYERBEER'S LES HUGUENOTS.

Pourquoi me reveiller?, the love duet of Werther and Charlotte in Act III of MASSENET'S WERTHER.

Poveri fiori, Adriana's reaction at a gift of violets that are shriveled, an omen of disaster, in Act IV of CILÈA'S ADRIANA LECOUVREUR.

Prague Opera (Landestheater; Stavovské Divadlo), one of the most venerable theaters in Prague. It was built in 1784 by Count Anton von Nostitz-Rieneck for the presentation of Italian operas. It was here that MOZART directed the premiere of DON GIOVANNI in 1787. In 1807, when the repertory became exclusively German, the house became known as the Deutsches Landestheater. WEBER conducted here from 1813 to 1816. In 1888 this theater became the home for plays, though *Don Giovanni* returned to its stage in 1937 to honor the one hundred and fiftieth anniversary of its premiere.

In 1881 the National Theater for the presentation of Bohemian operas was founded. It opened with the premiere of SMETANA'S LIBUŠE. This theater burned down two months after its opening but was rebuilt in 1883 and reopened once again with *Libuše*. Since then this opera house (now identified as Narodni Divadlo) has placed considerable emphasis on Bohemian operas, with significant world premieres of works by SMETANA, DVOŘÁK, FIBICH, Foerster, and JANÁČEK (among many others), though the standard repertory is not slighted. Among its most significant conductors have been Otakar Ostřčil (1920–1935) and Václav Talich (1935–1944 and 1947–1948).

The theater acquired a new home in 1887 and flourished under the musical direction of such famous conductors as SEIDL, MAHLER, KLEMPERER, SZELL, and Rankl. In 1948 it was renamed the Smetana Theater, and now houses the second most important opera company in Prague.

Pratella, Francesco, composer. Born Lugo di Romagna, Italy, Feb. 1, 1880; died Ravenna, May 18, 1955. He attended the Liceo Rossini in Pesaro, then studied with Pietro MASCAGNI, under whose guidance he wrote a one-act opera, *Lilia,* which won honorable mention in the Sonzogno competition in 1903. After completing a second opera, *La sina d'Vargöun,* produced in Bologna in 1909, he allied himself with the futurist movement in Italy, headed by F. T. Marinetti and Luigi Russolo. Pratella now began writing futurist operas, the first being on the subject of aviation, *L'aviatore Dro,* produced in Lugo on Sept. 4, 1920. His later operas: *Il dono primaverile* (1923); *La ninna nanna della Bambola,* a children's opera (1923); *Fabiano* (1939). From 1926 he was director of the Instituto Musicale di Lugo and from 1927 to 1945, director of the Liceo Musicale of Ravenna.

Pré aux clercs, Le (The Meadow of the Scholars), OPÉRA COMIQUE in three acts by HÉROLD. Libretto by François Antoine Eugène de Planard, based on a story by MÉRIMÉE. Premiere: Opéra-Comique, Dec. 15, 1832. American premiere: Baltimore, Oct. 14, 1833. This *opéra comique* is based on a historical subject: the successful effort of Mergy, a Bernese gentleman, to win the heart and hand of Isabella, maid-of-honor to the Queen of Navarre, in spite of the king's opposition. Principal musical episodes include Mergy's aria, "Ce soir" and Isabella's second-act ROMANCE, "Jours de mon enfance."

Précieuses ridicules, Les, *see* PREZIOSE RIDICOLE, LE; MOLIÈRE.

Preislied (Prize Song), *see* MORGENLICH LEUCHTEND IM ROSIGEN SCHEIN.

prelude (German, *vorspiel*), a term frequently used in place of overture. WAGNER and many later composers conceived of the prelude as suggesting the mood and content of the scene to follow, the prelude leading into the scene without a formal ending.

Prenderò quel brunettino, duet of Dorabella and Fiordiligi, in which they decide to be partial to their suitors (who in actuality are their betrotheds in disguise), in Act II, Scene 1, of MOZART's COSÌ FAN TUTTE.

Prendre le dessin d'un bijou, Gérald's aria as he is about to make a drawing of Lakmé's jewels, in Act I of DELIBES's LAKMÉ.

Presago il core della tua condanna, duet of Aida and Radames in Act IV, Scene 2, of VERDI's AIDA, after Aida has entered the tomb to suffer death with Radames.

Près des ramparts de Séville (SEGUIDILLA), Carmen's invitation to Don José to meet her at the tavern Lillas Pastia, in Act I of BIZET's CARMEN.

Prêtre, Georges, conductor. Born Waziers, France, Aug. 14, 1924. Following his studies at the Douai and Paris conservatories and privately with André Cluytens, he made his professional conducting debut with SAMSON ET DALILA in Marseilles. After three years in Marseilles and performances in various other French opera houses, he became the musical director of the Toulouse Opera. In 1956 he made his debut at the OPÉRA-COMIQUE in Paris, following which he was invited to make guest appearances with major European orchestras. His American debut took place in 1959 with the CHICAGO LYRIC OPERA, and in 1963 he returned to the United States to conduct at the SAN FRANCISCO OPERA. Meanwhile he was appointed permanent conductor at the VIENNA STATE OPERA. His debut at the METROPOLITAN OPERA took place on Oct. 17, 1964, with *Samson et Dalila*. Since then Prêtre has conducted performances at the Metropolitan Opera, besides appearing with leading orchestras and opera houses in the United States and Europe.

Preussisches Märchen (Prussian Fairy Tales), BALLET-OPERA by BLACHER. Libretto by Heinz von Cramer, based on *Der Hauptmann von Köpenick*, a play by Zuckmayer. Premiere: Städtische Oper, Berlin, Sept. 22, 1952. This satire on Prussian military bureaucracy was based on an actual event in Prussian history in 1900, when a servant of Wilhelm II, with the aid of a uniform and by forging the payroll became a captain in the army.

Previtali, Fernando, conductor. Born Adria, Italy, Feb. 16, 1907. Upon completing his music study at the Conservatory of Turin, he helped Vittorio GUI organize the FLORENCE MAY MUSIC FESTIVAL and direct it between 1928 and 1936. In 1942–43 and again between 1946 and 1948 he was a principal conductor of LA SCALA. He subsequently directed many notable performances of opera over the Rome radio, including a cycle of VERDI operas in 1951. In Italian opera houses he was responsible for the world premieres of operas by GHEDINI and DALLAPICCOLA, among others, and for the revival of BUSONI's TURANDOT and DOKTOR FAUST. He is probably better known as a symphony conductor, in which capacity he made his American debut with the Cleveland Orchestra on Dec. 15, 1957. He has served as guest conductor of leading orchestras in America and Europe.

Prévost, Abbé (Antoine François Prévost d'Exiles), novelist. Born Hesdin, France, Apr. 1, 1697; died Chantilly, France, Nov. 23, 1763. He was the author of the celebrated romance *L'Histoire du chevalier des Grieux et de Manon Lescaut,* the source of the following operas: AUBER's *Manon Lescaut;* Henze's BOULEVARD SOLITUDE; Massenet's MANON and LE PORTRAIT DE MANON; Puccini's MANON LESCAUT; and Richard Kleinmichel's *Das Schloss de l'Orme.*

Prey, Hermann, baritone. Born Berlin, July 11, 1929. He attended the Berlin Hochschule für Musik. In 1952 he received first prize among two thousand contestants in the Meistersinger competition sponsored by the United States Army. This led to an American tour. Upon returning to Europe, Prey was engaged by the HAMBURG OPERA. Appearances at other leading European opera houses (including LA SCALA and the VIENNA STATE OPERA) and at major European festivals (including SALZBURG, VIENNA, and BAYREUTH) followed. On Dec. 17, 1960, he made his debut at the METROPOLITAN OPERA as Wolfram in TANNHÄUSER. In 1969 he appeared in a filmed version of COSÌ FAN TUTTE, Karl BOEHM conducting, for presentation over German TV.

preziose ridicole, Le (The Ridiculous Smart Women), opera in one act by Felice LATTUADA. Libretto by Arturo Rossata, based on MOLIÈRE's *Les Précieuses ridicules.* Premiere: La Scala, Feb. 9, 1929. American premiere: Metropolitan Opera, Dec. 10, 1930. The text is a satire on the affectations and precious language of the so-called intelligentsia of French society. Otakar Zich's opera *Les Précieuses ridicules* was derived from the same Molière play.

Preziosilla, a gypsy (mezzo-soprano) in VERDI's LA FORZA DEL DESTINO.

Price, Leontyne, soprano. Born Laurel, Miss., Feb. 10, 1927. She studied singing at the Juilliard School of Music for four years, mainly with Florence Page Kimball. For two years she played Bess in PORGY AND BESS during the opera's tour of Europe and the United States. In 1954 she initiated a successful career on the concert stage, and in 1955 she was starred in a performance of TOSCA telecast over the NBC network. Her grand opera debut took place in 1957 with the SAN FRANCISCO OPERA in LES DIALOGUES DES CARMÉLITES. In 1958 she made an outstandingly successful opera debut in Europe by appearing in AIDA at the VIENNA STATE OPERA. On Jan. 27, 1961, she was acclaimed for her Leonora in IL TROVATORE at her METROPOLITAN OPERA debut. On Oct. 22, 1961, she became the first Negro singer to appear in a starring role on opening night of the Metropolitan Opera season. The opera was THE GIRL OF THE GOLDEN WEST. She was also the leading soprano in the world premiere of ANTONY AND CLEOPATRA which opened the new auditorium of the Metropolitan Opera House at the LINCOLN CENTER FOR THE PERFORMING ARTS on Sept. 16, 1966. Besides her appearances at the Metropolitan Opera, she has been heard with the world's great opera companies and at major European festivals, acclaimed everywhere as one of the foremost operatic sopranos of our time.

prigioniero, Il (The Prisoner), one-act opera with prologue by DALLAPICCOLA. Libretto by the composer, based on a short story by Villiers de l'Isle Adam, *La Torture par l'espérance.* Premiere: Turin Radio, Nov. 30, 1949; Teatro Communale, Florence, May 20, 1950 (staged). American premiere: New York City, Mar. 15, 1951. This is Dallapiccola's first successful opera, expressing his hatred of tyranny in any form and his passion for human liberty and dignity. During the reign of Philip II, a Flemish Protestant political prisoner is jailed and tortured. After the prisoner fails in an attempt to escape, a sadistic guard, who calls himself "Brother," torments him to madness. As he is being conducted to the stake, the prisoner can mutter only a single word: "Freedom." Dallapiccola has employed TWELVE-TONE TECHNIQUES for this opera, without sacrificing either dramatic strength or a wealth of feeling and humanity.

prima donna, Italian for "first lady," a term used since the end of the seventeenth century for the leading female singer in an opera or opera company.

The term *prima donna assoluta* ("absolute prima donna") was very much in vogue in the nineteenth century, with many female singers fighting over this designation.

prima uomo, Italian for "first man." In early Italian operas this term was used for the performer of the leading male character or for the CASTRATO taking the leading female part.

Prince de Bouillon, a prince (bass) in CILÈA'S ADRIANA LECOUVREUR, a role created by Giuseppe DE LUCA.

Prince Igor, opera in prologue and four acts by BORODIN (completed by RIMSKY-KORSAKOV and Glazunov). Libretto by Vladimir Stassov, based on an old Russian chronicle. Premiere: Imperial Opera, St. Petersburg, Nov. 4, 1890. American premiere: Metropolitan Opera, Dec. 30, 1915. In the twelfth century, the Polovtzi, a Tartar race of Central Asia, capture Prince Igor (baritone) and his son, Vladimir (tenor). Khan Kontchak (bass), the Polovtsian leader, assures Prince Igor that he is a guest and not a captive and entertains him with a lavish feast and oriental dances. He offers him his freedom if he is ready to promise not to fight the Polovtzi. Igor cannot do this. He effects his escape and returns to his own people, where he is received with ceremony. His son, in love with Kontchakovna (mezzo-soprano), the Khan's daughter, refuses to flee and is accepted by the Khan as a son-in-law.

The OVERTURE to Act I—which uses melodic material from the opera, including Igor's famous second-act aria and themes identifying the Khan and his daughter—is familiar. Even more so are the Polovtsian Dances for chorus and orchestra, with which, in Act II, the Khan entertains the Prince. In the choreography of Michel Fokine, the first dance presents the procession of the royal captives through an oriental-type melody; then comes the dance of the savage men, its main theme in the clarinet, followed by the dance of the boys, in which war games are simulated, and the dance of the young girls with its sensuous oriental melody. The dances conclude with brilliant music in which the dancers salute the Khan.

Two of the memorable vocal numbers are the nocturne of Kontchakovna, "Now the daylight dies," and Igor's celebrated air in Act II, "No sleep, no rest."

Prince of Persia, The, a character (baritone) in PUCCINI'S TURANDOT.

Princesse de Bouillon, wife (mezzo-soprano) of the Prince de Bouillon, in rivalry with Adriana for the love of Maurizio, in CILÈA'S ADRIANA LECOUVREUR.

Princess Eboli, *see* EBOLI, PRINCESS.

Princess on the Pea, The, *see* ANDERSEN, HANS CHRISTIAN.

Princess von Werdenberg, the Marschallin (soprano) in Richard STRAUSS'S DER ROSENKAVALIER.

Printemps qui commence, Dalila's spring song to lure Samson, in Act I of SAINT-SAËNS'S SAMSON ET DALILA.

Prinzivalle, commander of the Florentine army (tenor) in FÉVRIER'S MONNA VANNA.

Prinz von Homburg, Der (The Prince of Hamburg), opera in three acts by HENZE. Libretto by Ingeborg Bachmann, based on Heinrich von KLEIST'S drama of the same name. Premiere: Hamburg Opera, May 22, 1960. This was its composer's third opera but his first on a German subject. The hero is a prince accused of treason—though he has been victorious in battle—for having neglected his military duties for a love affair with Princess Natalie. He is sentenced to be executed but is finally pardoned by the Emperor and permitted to reassume his command. The music is both lyrical and dramatic, with a simplicity of approach not often encountered in Henze's operas. The first performance outside Germany took place during the summer of 1960 at the FESTIVAL OF TWO WORLDS in Spoleto, Italy.

Prise de Troie, La, *see* TROYENS, LES.

Prisoner, The, *see* PRIGIONIERO, IL.

Prisoners' Chorus, *see* O WELCHE LUST!

Pritchard, John, conductor. Born London, Feb. 5, 1921. He has been one of the principal conductors at the GLYNDE-

BOURNE FESTIVAL since 1951, where he received his apprenticeship under Fritz BUSCH as coach and chorus master. Besides MOZART's operas, he has led there distinguished performances of ARIADNE AUF NAXOS and the English premiere of ELEGY FOR YOUNG LOVERS, among many other operas. He conducted the opening performance of the season at COVENT GARDEN in 1952—a new production of UN BALLO IN MASCHERA. In the ensuing years he has led at Covent Garden the world premieres of GLORIANA, MIDSUMMER MARRIAGE, and KING PRIAM, together with distinguished revivals of WOZZECK, LES TROYENS, and several operas in the Russian repertory. He has also appeared at other significant opera houses, including the VIENNA STATE OPERA.

Prix de Rome, a prize instituted in France by Louis XIV in 1666, providing its winner three years of residence at the Academy of Fine Arts in Rome, a branch of the Institut de France. Some of France's major opera composers have been recipients of this award, including BERLIOZ, BIZET, CHARPENTIER, DEBUSSY, HALÉVY, MASSENET, and THOMAS.

Prize Song (Preislied), *see* MORGENLICH LEUCHTEND IM ROSIGEN SCHEIN.

Probe, German for "rehearsal."

Procession of the Knights, procession in Act III, Scene 2, of WAGNER's PARSIFAL, as the knights file into the great hall of Monsalvat carrying the bier of Titurel.

Procession of the Mastersingers, procession in Act III, Scene 2, of WAGNER's DIE MEISTERSINGER, as they enter a field beside the Pegnitz River where the song contest is to be held.

Prodaná nevěsta, Czech title of SMETANA's THE BARTERED BRIDE.

Prodigal Son, The, a "church parable" in one act by BRITTEN. Libretto by William Plomer. Premiere: Aldeburgh Festival, Eng., June, 1968. American premiere: Caramoor Festival, Katonah, N.Y., June 29, 1969. This is Britten's third church parable, the earlier two being CURLEW RIVER and THE BURNING FIERY FURNACE. As in the earlier works, this one opens with a procession of monks into the church to perform a mystery play, in which a Tempter breaks up a happy country family comprised of a patriarch and two sons. The family is reunited in the end. The mystery play over, the monks file out of the church.

Prokofiev, Serge, composer. Born Sontsovka, Russia, Apr. 23, 1891; died Moscow, Mar. 5, 1953. He was exceptionally precocious, completing the writing of three operas by the time he was twelve years old. He entered the St. Petersburg Conservatory in his thirteenth year, remaining there a decade; his teachers included RIMSKY-KORSAKOV, Nikolai TCHEREPNIN, and Anatol Liadov. He graduated in 1914 with the Rubinstein Prize for his *Second Piano Concerto.* During World War I, Prokofiev was exempt from military service, being the only son of a widow. He now completed his first significant works, including the *Classical Symphony* and the ballet *Chout;* he also wrote an opera, THE GAMBLER.

Soon after the outbreak of the Russian Revolution, Prokofiev came to the United States, where he appeared as pianist and conductor in performances of his own works. He was commissioned by the CHICAGO OPERA COMPANY to write a new opera. That work, THE LOVE FOR THREE ORANGES, was produced in Chicago on Dec. 30, 1921, and was a failure; when next presented—by the NEW YORK CITY OPERA in 1949—it was a resounding artistic and box-office success.

Prokofiev next settled in Paris, where he remained for a half dozen years, completing many major orchestral works and ballets. In 1933 he returned to his native land, remaining there (except for an occasional tour) the rest of his life, identifying himself more or less with the Soviet ideology and trying to write works in line with socialist realism. Though acknowledged by Soviet leaders and the press to be one of the great creative figures in the Soviet Union (he won the Stalin Prize for his *Seventh Piano Sonata*), Prokofiev became in 1948 the object for violent attack by the General Committee of the Communist Party. The charge against Prokofiev (and other leading Soviet composers) was that Soviet music had become too esoteric and cerebral, that the musical thinking had grown decadent, representing "a negation of the basic principles of classical music." Prokofiev apologized publicly and promised to mend his ways. His first peace offering was an opera, THE TALE OF A REAL MAN, but this, too, was condemned for its modernistic and antimelodic writing. However, Prokofiev was eventually able to re-establish his honored position in Soviet music. In 1951 he won the Stalin Prize again, and a concert of his works was given to honor his sixtieth birthday. He died of a stroke two years later.

His principal operas: *The Gambler* (1917, revised 1928); *The Love for Three Oranges* (1919); THE FLAMING ANGEL (1923); *Simeon Kotko* (1939); *The Duenna* (1940); WAR AND PEACE (1946); *The Tale of a Real Man* (1948).

Promesse de mon avenir, Scindia's arioso in Act III of MASSENET'S LE ROI DE LAHORE.

promessi sposi, I (The Betrothed), a romantic novel by Alessandro MANZONI. Its background is life in seventeenth-century Italy during the Spanish domination. The composers Enrico Petrella, PONCHIELLI, and Franz Gläser have derived opera libretti from it.

Prometheus, opera in one act by ORFF. Libretto is the original Greek text of the play, usually called *Prometheus Bound* in English translation, by AESCHYLUS. Premiere: Stuttgart Opera, Mar. 23, 1968. American premiere: Brooklyn, N.Y., Oct. 30, 1969 (concert version). This is the last of three Greek tragedies set to music by Orff, the other two being ANTIGONAE and OEDIPUS DER TYRANN. It is the only one in which the composer uses the original Greek text as his libretto. Thomas Scherman, who directed the American premiere with the Little Orchestra Society, explains: "More than any other surviving Greek play, it is the furthest removed from the twentieth century and Christianity. It is not about human beings at all. The play is about gods against gods and very difficult to

understand. Orff's interpretation is exciting because it is as basic and as stark as Aeschylus." The accompanying small orchestra requires twelve percussion players and eight pianists at four pianos. The percussion performers are called upon to play on seventy-eight instruments, seventy onstage and eight offstage.

prompter, an offstage person, usually concealed in a compartment before the stage, who provides opera singers with cues or lines. In France and Germany he is known as *souffleur;* in Italy as *maestro suggeritore.*

Prophète, Le (The Prophet), opera in five acts by MEYERBEER. Libretto by Eugène SCRIBE, based on the historical episode of the Anabaptist uprising in Holland in the sixteenth century. Premiere: Paris Opéra, Apr. 19, 1849. American premiere: New Orleans, Apr. 2, 1850.

Characters: John of Leyden, prophet and leader of the Anabaptists (tenor); Fidès, his mother (mezzo-soprano); Bertha, his sweetheart (soprano); Count Oberthal, ruler of the Dordrecht region (baritone); Zacharias, an Anabaptist preacher (bass); Jonas, another Anabaptist preacher (tenor); Mathisen, a third preacher (basso); nobles; peasants; citizens; soldiers; prisoners. The action takes place in Holland and Germany in 1534.

Act I. A suburb of Dordrecht. Bertha comes to Count Oberthal to ask his permission to marry the innkeeper, John of Leyden. Before she gains admission, the castle is visited by three Anabaptists chanting the hymn "Ad nos, ad salutem," who are bent on rousing the people to rebellion. They are driven away soon after the Count makes his appearance. Bertha arrives with a CAVATINA on her lips at the expectation of soon meeting with John ("Mon coeur s'élance"). The Count finds Bertha so attractive that he wants her for himself. He denies her permission to marry John and imprisons John's mother, Fidès, who had accompanied her.

Act II. An inn in the suburbs of

Leyden. The three Anabaptists are struck by the resemblance of the inn-keeper John to a likeness of King David. They beg him to be the leader of their movement. John tells them of a dream in which he was venerated by a crowd before the cathedral ("Sous les vastes arceaux"). This is further proof to the Anabaptists that John is their destined leader. But John turns them down, since he is interested only in marrying Bertha ("Pour Bertha, moi, je soupire"). Bertha arrives, having escaped from the Count. The Count soon appears and warns John that unless he surrenders Bertha, his mother will be put to death. John reluctantly gives up his claim to Bertha. Released from prison, Fidès expresses her gratitude and love for her son ("Ah, mon fils!"). John is now ready to join the Anabaptist movement. To assure the success of their mission, the Anabaptists leave behind the impression that the innkeeper has been killed.

Act III. The camp of the Anabaptists. The people rally under John as their Prophet. Several prisoners are brought to the camp; one of them is the Count, who discloses to John that Bertha has escaped from him and is now in Mün-ster. When the three Anabaptists are about to kill the Count, John intervenes and saves him; he wants Bertha to pass judgment and sentence on him. An element of John's following deserts him to attack Münster on its own. It is defeated. John now rallies the rest of his people and leads them to a victorious assault on Münster.

Act IV, Scene 1. A square in Münster. Fidès, reduced to beggary, meets Bertha and tells her the sad news that John is dead. Not knowing that John lives as the leader of the Anabaptists, Bertha is convinced that the death of her beloved was caused by the Prophet. She vows revenge.

Scene 2. The Münster Cathedral. Victorious, John enters Münster in triumph and is crowned king. The royal procession advances into the cathedral with magnificent pomp (Marche du couronne-ment, Coronation March). Hiding behind a pillar, Fidès recognizes her son and rushes toward him tenderly. Since his followers believe him to be of divine origin, John must denounce Fidès as a fraud. He accuses her of being insane. To protect her son, Fidès confesses she was mistaken.

Act V, Scene 1. A crypt. John's soldiers have imprisoned Fidès. She bewails the fact that her son has repudiated her and begs the gods to destroy him (Prison Scene: "O prêtres de Baal"). John appears. He throws himself at his mother's feet and begs her forgiveness. At first Fidès is bitter. But she softens when John promises to give up his role and return to Leyden. Bertha suddenly makes her appearance. Seeing John, she is overjoyed to find him alive. But when she discovers that he is the Prophet, she curses him and kills herself with a dagger.

Scene 2. The great hall of the palace where a celebration is taking place ("Versez, que tout respire l'ivresse et le délire"). John has been betrayed: the Anabaptists have begun to turn against him, and the Emperor's troops, led by Count Oberthal, have invaded the palace. John orders the palace gates secured. Then a holocaust is set. As the flames mount, Fidès arrives to join her son in death.

Le Prophète is one of the most colorful, stirring, and spectacular of Meyerbeer's operas. He completed it in 1849, eighteen years after ROBERT LE DIABLE and thirteen after LES HUGUENOTS. It is of particular interest because the composer gave the mother's role such prominence. It was necessity rather than artistic compulsion that led him to do this. At the time the opera was introduced there were no tenors at the PARIS OPÉRA capable of doing justice to the role of John. Meyerbeer decided to balance this deficiency by casting one of the outstanding mezzo-sopranos of the day, Pauline VIARDOT-GARCÍA, as Fidès; and he built up the role to starring proportions. The two principal arias in the opera, among Meyerbeer's finest, are sung not by John or Bertha, but by Fidès: "Ah, mon fils!" and "O prêtres de Baal."

Proserpine (Persephone). In Roman or Greek mythology she is the daughter of Jupiter (Zeus) and Ceres (Demeter). Pluto (Hades) abducts her to make her his wife and help him rule over the shades. Ceres, however, will not allow the earth to be fructified until Mercury (Hermes) has rescued Proserpine. Mercury achieves this mission, but Proserpine still must return to the underworld several months a year. She has come to symbolize the seed corn in the ground, which when fructified nourishes men and animals. The theme has been used as a text for operas by LULLY, MONTEVERDI, PAISIELLO, and SAINT-SAËNS among many others.

Protagonist, Der (The Protagonist), one-act opera by WEILL. Libretto by Georg KAISER. Premiere: Dresden Opera, Mar. 27, 1926. This was Weill's first opera, written in his twenty-fourth year. The central figure of Kaiser's expressionist drama is an actor who confuses the stage with reality and commits suicide while enacting a play.

Protegga il giusto cielo, trio of Donna Anna, Donna Elvira, and Don Ottavio, in which they quietly pray for help in their quest for vengeance against Don Giovanni, in Act I, Scene 4, of MOZART'S DON GIOVANNI.

Prozess, Der, see TRIAL, THE.

Prunier, a poet (tenor) in PUCCINI'S LA RONDINE.

Prynne, Hester, principal female character in Walter DAMROSCH'S THE SCARLET LETTER and Vittorio GIANNINI'S *The Scarlet Letter*. In both operas she is a soprano. In the Damrosch opera, the role was created by GADSKI; in Giannini's, by his sister, Dusolina GIANNINI.

Prynne, Roger, Hester's husband (baritone), in DAMROSCH'S THE SCARLET LETTER.

Pskovityanka, see IVAN THE TERRIBLE.

Publius, leader (bass) of King Titus' bodyguards in MOZART'S LA CLEMENZA DI TITO.

Puccini, Giacomo, composer. Born Lucca, Italy, Dec. 22, 1858; died Brussels, Belgium, Nov. 29, 1924.

The Puccini family had for several generations held musical posts in Lucca. As a boy, Giacomo was enrolled at the Instituto Musicale as a pupil of Carlo Angeloni. His musical progress was rapid, and he was soon able to fill the post of organist in near-by churches, and to write two ambitious choral works enthusiastically received by the townspeople. Now something of a local celebrity, Puccini procured a small subsidy from Queen Margherita which, supplemented by additional funds from a great uncle, enabled him to go to Milan in 1880 for further study. He attended the Milan Conservatory, where his teachers included Antonio Bazzini and Amilcare PONCHIELLI. The latter aroused Puccini's love for the stage and directed him toward writing operas. He had a friend provide Puccini with a suitable libretto, then urged him to set it to music and submit it in the Sonzogno contest for one-act operas. Thus, Puccini completed his first opera, LE VILLI. It did not win the prize, but when introduced at the Teatro dal Verme in Milan on May 31, 1884, it was so successful that LA SCALA accepted it for the following season and RICORDI published the score. Ricordi also commissioned a second opera, EDGAR, a failure when given at La Scala on Apr. 21, 1889. But his third opera was a triumph—MANON LESCAUT, introduced in Turin on Feb. 1, 1893. Puccini found himself famous. His LA BOHÈME in 1896 and TOSCA in 1900 brought him universal recognition as VERDI'S successor.

In 1903 Puccini was seriously hurt in an automobile accident, but confinement to an invalid's chair for eight months did not keep him from writing a new opera, MADAMA BUTTERFLY, produced at La Scala on Feb. 17, 1904. At its premiere, *Madama Butterfly* was the greatest failure Puccini experienced; but in less than a year it turned out to be one of his best-loved and most widely performed works.

In 1907 Puccini came to America to assist at a METROPOLITAN OPERA presentation of *Madama Butterfly*. Commissioned to write an opera for the Metropolitan, he produced a work with an American setting, THE GIRL OF THE GOLDEN WEST. It was introduced by the Metropolitan Opera on Dec. 10, 1910, in one of the most exciting premieres ever held by that house, the composer being present to receive an ovation.

During the next decade Puccini wrote several more operas: a light opera, LA RONDINE; a trilogy of one-act operas collectively entitled IL TRITTICO; and an opera with an oriental setting, TURANDOT. He did not live to complete the last work. Suffering from a cancer of the throat, Puccini underwent an operation in Brussels. A heart attack following the operation was fatal.

Puccini once said of himself that "the only music I can make is of small things." What he meant is that he was never intended by his talent or temperament to produce works in a large design or ambitious in artistic purpose in the manner of WAGNER and VERDI. But if his world was comparatively a small one, he was its lord and master. In the writing of dramas appealing to the heart, filled with tenderness and beauty, he had few equals. He had a dramatic instinct that never failed him, a consummate knowledge of the demands of the stage, and a pronounced feeling for theatrical effect. His writing both for voice and orchestra was the last word in elegance, and his highly personal lyricism had incomparable sweetness, gentleness, and poignancy. His harmonic writing and instrumental colorations were often daring.

His operas: *Le villi* (1884) ; *Edgar* (1889) ; *Manon Lescaut* (1893) ; *La Bohème* (1896) ; *Tosca* (1900) ; *Madama Butterfly* (1904) ; *La fanciulla del west* (*The Girl of the Golden West*) (1910) ; *La rondine* (1917) ; *Il trittico*, consisting of IL TABARRO, SUOR ANGELICA, and GIANNI SCHICCHI (1918) ; *Turandot* (completed by Franco Alfano) .

puce gentille, Une, Méphistophélès' amusing ditty about a flea who, adopted by a king, is dressed in royal fineries and made into a pet, while the courtiers are unable to scratch for fear of killing it. It is found in Part II of BERLIOZ' THE DAMNATION OF FAUST. The flight of the insect is picturesquely simulated in the accompaniment.

Puck, Titania's attendant (contralto) , in WEBER'S OBERON.

Puente, Giuseppe del, *see* DEL PUENTE, GIUSEPPE.

Pulitzer prize (for music) . Pulitzer prizes had been instituted in 1918 in various fields of American literary and journalistic endeavor. The prize for American music was created in 1943, its first recipient being William Schuman for his cantata *A Free Song*. The first opera to win the award was THE CONSUL in 1950. A year later Douglas MOORE received the Pulitzer prize for his opera GIANTS IN THE EARTH. Later operas to win the Pulitzer prize were THE SAINT OF BLEECKER STREET in 1955, VANESSA in 1958, and THE CRUCIBLE in 1963.

puppet opera, *see* MARIONETTE OPERA.

Purcell, Henry, composer. Born London (?) , c. 1659; died Dean's Yard, Westminster, Nov. 21, 1695. One of England's greatest composers, his DIDO AND AENEAS is a landmark in the early history of opera. His father was a Gentleman of the Chapel Royal. In 1669 Purcell became a chorister of the Chapel Royal, studying music with John Blow. In 1673 he left the choir and became "keeper of the instruments." Four years later he was appointed composer of the King's band and in 1679 organist at Westminster Abbey. In 1682 he became one of three organists of the Chapel Royal. In the course of his brief life he composed a considerable amount of important instrumental and sacred music, secular songs, and incidental music and songs to plays of the day. His finest stage work was his opera *Dido and Aeneas*. While some of the plays for which he wrote music have been classed as operas, it is only *Dido and Aeneas* that, strictly speaking, deserves the term.

Puritani, I (The Puritans), opera in three acts by BELLINI. Libretto by Count

Carlo Pepoli, based on the play *Têtes rondes et cavaliers* by François Ancelot and Xavier Boniface Saintine, which, in turn, is based partly on Sir Walter SCOTT's novel, *Old Mortality*. Premiere: Théâtre des Italiens, Paris, Jan. 25, 1835. American premiere: Philadelphia, July 22, 1843.

Characters: Lord Walter Walton, a Puritan leader (bass); Sir George Walton, his brother (bass); Elvira Walton, Lord Walton's daughter (soprano); Sir Richard Forth, a Puritan and suitor of Elvira's (baritone); Henrietta, widow of King Charles I (mezzo-soprano); Lord Arthur Talbot (tenor), a Cavalier and in love with Elvira. The action takes place near Plymouth, Eng., in the year 1649 when the Puritan followers of Cromwell finally defeated the Cavalier faction supporting the Stuarts in the Great Rebellion.

Act I. In Lord Walton's castle, he and his brother, Sir George, have finally given consent to Elvira's marrying Lord Arthur Talbot even though the Waltons are fighting for Cromwell and Talbot is a Cavalier. Elvira expresses her pleasure in the aria "Son vergin vezzosa." When Talbot arrives for the wedding, he finds that the woman he regards as his queen, King Charles' widow, is being held prisoner in the castle and that she is about to be sent to London, presumably to share her husband's fate on the execution block. By disguising Queen Henrietta in Elvira's wedding veil, Talbot manages to spirit her away. Forth, though a Puritan, assists the refugees, for he hopes that with Talbot out of the way, he may win Elvira's hand. But Elvira, when she discovers the apparent last-minute desertion, loses her mind.

Act II. Most of this act is devoted to Elvira's celebrated Mad Scene, "Qui la voce sua soave," a scene quite as difficult, quite as lovely, and even more dramatic than the most famous mad scene of all, the one in LUCIA DI LAMMERMOOR, which was first heard ten months after this one. The act closes with an unusual and stirring duet for two basses, "Suoni la tromba," in which the brothers Walton swear to fight to the death for the Puritan cause.

Act III. Lord Arthur Talbot, having delivered his charge to safety, is now a fugitive hunted by the Puritan soldiery. Nevertheless, he has sneaked back to Elvira's home and overhears her singing a sad ballad, "A una fonta afflito e solo." She appears and recognizes him, as her mind seems to return, in a long and very difficult love duet ("Vieni fra questa braccia") during which he explains the excellent reason for his apparent desertion. They are discovered, however, by the Puritans, and despite the protection the Waltons try to give Talbot, he is about to be executed on the spot when news arrives of Cromwell's victory and his granting of a general amnesty. And so Elvira, who had been shocked back into insanity when the soldiers appeared, once more regains her senses, and the opera ends happily.

When Bellini composed this opera, he had the original cast in mind—Giulia GRISI as Elvira, RUBINI as Talbot, and TAMBURINI and LABLACHE as the Walton brothers. So successful were these great singers in their roles, that they became known all over Europe as "the Puritani Quartet." This was Bellini's last opera, and like his other major works, it remained a part of the standard repertoire as long as there were singers who could master its difficulties, that is, until around the turn of the century. In the fifties it was again revived for two modern mistresses of BEL CANTO, Maria CALLAS and Joan SUTHERLAND.

Pushkin, Alexander, poet. Born Moscow, June 6, 1799; died St. Petersburg, Feb. 10, 1837. Russia's foremost literary figure was the author of many narratives that were made into operas. Among the composers indebted to Pushkin are: Boris Assafiev (*The Bronze Horseman* and *A Feast in Time of Plague*); CUI (*The Captive in the Caucasus* and *A Feast in Time of Plague*); DARGOMIZHSKY (RUSSALKA and THE STONE GUEST); GLINKA (RUSSLAN

AND LUDMILLA) ; Arthur Lourié (*A Feast in Time of Plague*) ; MALIPIERO (*Don Giovanni*) ; MUSSORGSKY (BORIS GODU-NOV) ; NÁPRAVNÍK (*Dubrovsky*) ; RACH-MANINOFF (ALEKO and *The Miserly Knight*) ; Florizel von Reuter (*Post-meister Wyrin*) ; RIMSKY-KORSAKOV (THE LEGEND OF THE CZAR SALTAN, LE COQ D'OR,

and *Mozart and Salieri*) ; STRAVINSKY (MAVRA) ; TCHAIKOVSKY (EUGENE ONEGIN, MAZEPPA, and PIQUE DAME) .

Pu-tin-Pao, executioner (baritone) in PUCCINI'S TURANDOT.

Pylades, Orestes' companion (tenor) in GLUCK'S IPHIGÉNIE EN TAURIDE.

Q

quadrille (or **quadrille de contredanse**), a French dance that made its first oper-atic appearance in RAMEAU'S *Les Fêtes de Polymnie*, in 1745. In the nineteenth century there was a tremendous vogue for quadrilles as social dances, and they appeared in numerous OPÉRAS BOUFFES and operettas. Usually, the music of these later quadrilles was not original but consisted of opera melodies fitted to the five distinct sections of a typical quadrille. Emmanuel CHABRIER carried the practice to its farthest development when he wrote a satirical quadrille on melodies from TRISTAN UND ISOLDE.

Qual cor tradisti, final duet in Act IV of BELLINI'S NORMA, in which Norma repeats her love vows to Pollione and expresses the conviction they will be reunited after death.

Qual' occhio al mondo?, Tosca's aria revealing her suspicions to Cavaradossi that he has had secret meetings with a woman, in Act I of PUCCINI'S TOSCA.

Quand apparaissent les étoiles, Don Quixote's serenade to Dulcinea in Act I of MASSENET'S DON QUICHOTTE.

Quand du Seigneur le jour luira, the church chorus about Judgment Day, in Act IV, Scene 2, of GOUNOD'S FAUST.

Quand'ero paggio del Duca di Nor-folk, Falstaff's boast that once, as a page to the Duke of Norfolk, he had

been slim and handsome, in Act II, Scene 2, of VERDI'S FALSTAFF.

Quand j'étais roi de Boétie, John Styx's autobiographical song with which he en-tertains Eurydice, as he guards her out-side her cell, in Act III of OFFENBACH'S OPÉRA BOUFFE ORPHEUS IN THE UNDER-WORLD.

Quand le destin au milieu (Quando fanciulla ancor l'avverso), Marie's aria expressing her sentiments over the dis-approval of her mother to Marie's mar-riage to Tonio, in Act II of DONIZETTI'S THE DAUGHTER OF THE REGIMENT.

Quando di primavera, Fiorilla's song about springtime in Act II of ROSSINI'S IL TURCO IN ITALIA.

Quando le sere al placido, the most celebrated aria in VERDI'S LUISA MILLER (Act II) , in which Rodolfo gives way to heartbreak at reading the letter in which Luisa insists she is in love with Wurm and not with him.

Quando m'en vo' soletta, Musetta's famous WALTZ in Act II of PUCCINI'S LA BOHÈME, boasting of her appeal to men.

Quando rapita in estasi, Lucia's aria concerning her love for Edgardo, in Act I, Scene 2, of DONIZETTI'S LUCIA DI LAMMERMOOR.

Quanto amore!, duet of Adina and Dulcamara in Act II of DONIZETTI'S L'ELISIR D'AMORE, expressing dismay at the way in which Adina's lover, Nemorino, is being wooed by the village girls. Quanto è bella!, Nemorino's aria expressing his love for Adina, in Act I of DONIZETTI'S L'ELISIR D'AMORE.

quarter-tone opera (microtonal opera), see MICROTONAL MUSIC.

quattro rusteghi, I (The Four Ruffians), OPERA BUFFA in four acts by WOLF-FERRARI. Libretto by Giuseppe Pizzolato, based on a comedy by GOLDONI. Premiere: Munich Opera, Mar. 19, 1906. American premiere: New York City Opera, Oct. 18, 1951. The four ruffians in the title are four Venetian merchants who treat their women harshly. The most notorious of them is Lunardo (bass), who refuses to allow his daughter, Lucieta (soprano), to see her future husband, Filipeto (tenor), before their wedding. This is a marriage Lunardo has arranged, and neither Lucieta nor Filipeto have even seen each other. Filipeto, however, outwits Lunardo by putting on a woman's garb and invading Lunardo's house. Lucieta and Filipeto fall in love at first sight. Violently outraged that he has been outwitted, Lunardo tries to cancel the marriage. The wives of the other three ruffians go to work on their respective husbands, who finally convince Lunardo of the folly of his action. Two orchestral episodes (the overture and the intermezzo preceding the second act) and Filipeto's rapturous air, "Lucieta è un bel nome," are some of the delights of a light and merry score.

Queen Ice-heart, a character (mezzo-soprano) in WEINBERGER'S ŠVANDA.

Queen of Sheba, The (Die Königen von Saba), opera in four acts by GOLDMARK. Libretto by Salomon Hermann MOSENTHAL, based on the Old Testament story. Premiere: Vienna Royal Opera, Mar. 10, 1875. American premiere: Metropolitan Opera, Dec. 2, 1885.

Characters: Queen of Sheba (mezzo-soprano); King Solomon (baritone); High Priest (bass); Sulamith, his daughter (soprano); Assad, betrothed to Sulamith (tenor); Baal Hanan, overseer of the palace (baritone); Astaroth, the Queen's slave (soprano). The setting is Jerusalem and the Syrian desert during the reign of King Solomon.

Act I. Solomon's palace. Assad is to marry Sulamith, but he confides to King Solomon that he has fallen in love with an unknown woman he encountered while she was bathing in a stream. When the Queen of Sheba appears before Solomon, Assad recognizes her as that woman, but she ignores him.

Act II, Scene 1. The palace garden. Assad has a secret meeting with the Queen of Sheba. She is now receptive to his love-making. When she learns that he is to marry Sulamith, she urges him to run away with her.

Scene 2. The Temple. After the wedding of Assad and Sulamith is celebrated, Assad impulsively throws his wedding ring at the Queen's feet. But the Queen insists that Assad is a stranger to her. Assad, furious, curses Jehovah. For this he is condemned to death. The Queen intervenes and persuades King Solomon at least to spare his life.

Act III. The palace. A sumptuous ballet is seen during a reception honoring the Queen. The Queen begs Solomon to release Assad. When he refuses to do so, she angrily leaves him. Sulamith now comes to plead for Assad, promising to dedicate her life to God if he is freed.

Act IV. The desert. King Solomon has freed Assad, and he has become a wandering pilgrim. He is found by the Queen of Sheba. She pleads for his love, but he now feels only hate for her. During a sandstorm, Sulamith appears. Assad pleads for her forgiveness, obtains it, then, spent and exhausted, dies in her arms.

The most famous part of the opera is the sensuous ballet music in Act III. Among the better-known arias are those of Assad, "Magische Töne" in Act I; Solomon, "Blick' empor zu jene Räumen," in Act II; and Sulamith with chorus, "Doch eh' ich in des Todes Tal," in Act III. Otherwise the opera is most effective for its pageantry and ceremonial and storm scenes.

See also REINE DE SABA, LA.

Queen of Shemakha, a queen (soprano) who seduces and wins King Dodon, in RIMSKY-KORSAKOV'S LE COQ D'OR.

Queen of Spades, The, *see* PIQUE DAME.

Queen of the Night, Pamina's mother (soprano) in MOZART'S THE MAGIC FLUTE.

Que fais-tu, blanche tourterelle, Stephano's mocking serenade in Act III, Scene 2, of GOUNOD'S ROMÉO ET JULIETTE, as he looks for his master, Roméo.

Quel bonheur!, Zerlina's aria in Act II of AUBER'S FRA DIAVOLO, speaking of her happiness in loving Lorenzo.

Que l'esclave soit brune ou blonde, duet of Haroun and Splendiano in BIZET'S OPÉRA COMIQUE DJAMILEH.

Quel guardo il cavaliere, Norina's reflections about love and her confidence that she is well schooled in the subtle art of winning a man's heart, in Act I of DONIZETTI'S DON PASQUALE.

Quelle est cette belle?, choral episode in BIZET'S OPÉRA COMIQUE DJAMILEH, concerning Djamileh's allure.

Quel mesto gemito, first-act finale in ROSSINI'S SEMIRAMIDE, which some musicologists feel influenced VERDI in writing the "Miserere" in IL TROVATORE.

Quel plaisir, quelle joie!, the joyous chorus of the crowd awaiting the punishment of Eléazar and Rachel by boiling in oil, in Act V of HALÉVY'S LA JUIVE.

Quentin Durward, *see* SCOTT, SIR WALTER.

Questa cosa accordar, Carolina's attempt to convince her wealthy suitor (who does not know she is secretly married) that she is unworthy of him, in Act I of CIMAROSA'S IL MATRIMONIO SEGRETO.

Questa è la quercia, Falstaff's prayer for protection, when he is suddenly besieged by eerie noises and sounds he believes come from supernatural forces, in Act III, Scene 2, of VERDI'S FALSTAFF.

Questa o quella, the Duke's flippant commentary about inconstancy in Act I of VERDI'S RIGOLETTO.

Questo è quel pezzo, Despina's incantation with a magnet as a mock doctor, as she revives the supposedly dead Ferrando and Guglielmo, in Act I, Scene 4, of MOZART'S COSÌ FAN TUTTE.

Questo sol è il soggiorno, *see* C'EST ICI LE SÉJOUR.

Quickly, Dame, an earthy servant of Dr. Caius (mezzo-soprano) in VERDI'S FALSTAFF.

Quick music's best when the heart is oppressed, the gentle air of the Earl of Essex, sung to Queen Elizabeth I to his own lute accompaniment, in Act I, Scene 2, of BRITTEN'S GLORIANA.

Quiet Don, The (or **Quiet Flows the Don**), opera in four acts by DZERZHINSKY. Libretto by Leonid Dzerzhinsky, based on the novel of the same name by Mikhail Sholokov. Premiere: Leningrad, Oct. 22, 1935. American premiere: Detroit, Mar. 25, 1945. The opera covers the period in Cossack history from 1914 to 1917. It centers around a Cossack, Gregor, who, upon returning home from war in 1914, finds his wife has become the mistress of a nobleman. He kills his rival, abandons his family and former masters, and leads the peasants in revolt.

The tremendous success of this opera came at a time when the Soviet press and political leaders were denouncing SHOSTAKOVICH'S LADY MACBETH OF MZENSK as "formalistic" and "degenerate." (By a curious paradox, Dzerzhinsky's opera was dedicated to Shostakovich.) The authorities used *The Quiet Don* as an example of what true Soviet opera should be; and it is largely as a result of this official blessing that the opera was acclaimed and extensively performed throughout the Soviet Union.

Qui la voce sua soave, Elvira's Mad Scene in Act II of BELLINI'S I PURITANI.

Quinault, Philippe, poet and librettist. Born Paris, June 3, 1635; died there Nov. 26, 1688. Regarded as the creator of French lyric tragedy, he was LULLY'S librettist. Among the operas by Lully for which he wrote the texts were AL-CESTE, AMADIS, *Armide, Atys, Cadmus* *et Hermione, Isis, Persée, Phaëton,* PROSERPINE, *Roland,* and THÉSÉE. A number of his librettos were used by opera composers of a century later, notably J. C. BACH, GLUCK, and PICCINNI.

Qui posa il fianco, trio of Giselda, Oronte, and Arvino, in which they contrive Pagano's exile, in Act III of VERDI'S I LOMBARDI.

Qui sola, vergin rosa, *see* LAST ROSE OF SUMMER, THE.

Quo Vadis, opera in five acts by NOUGUÈS. Libretto by Henri Cain, based on the novel of the same name by Henryk Sienkiewicz. Premiere: Nice, Feb. 9, 1909. American premiere: Metropolitan Opera (in Philadelphia), Mar. 25, 1911. The setting is Rome in the age of Nero. Vincius is in love with the Christian hostage Lygia (soprano). At Nero's palace, when Vincius (tenor) speaks to Lygia of his love, she rejects him because of their different religions. Nero (tenor) orders a giant barbarian to fight a savage animal with Lygia strapped to his back. The barbarian wins the fight, and he and Lygia are freed. But Nero soon repents this act of mercy and sends Lygia to her doom.

R

Rabaud, Henri, composer and conductor. Born Paris, Nov. 10, 1873; died there Sept. 11, 1949. He attended the Paris Conservatory, where his teachers included Jules MASSENET and André Gédalge and where he won the PRIX DE ROME in 1894. As a conductor, he distinguished himself with performances at the OPÉRA between 1908 and 1914 and the OPÉRA-COMIQUE in 1920; he also was conductor of the Concerts du Conservatoire and in 1918 of the Boston Symphony Orchestra. He achieved his first success as a composer with a tone poem, *La Procession nocturne,* in 1899. His most famous work was a comic opera, MÂROUF, introduced at the Paris Opéra on May 15, 1914. In 1920 Rabaud became director of the Paris Conservatory. His other operas: *La Fille de Roland* (1904); *Le Premier Glaive* (1908); *Antoine et Cléopâtre* (1917); *L'Appel de la mer* (1922); *Rolande et le mauvais garçon* (1933); *Le Jeu de l'amour et du hasard* (1948).

Rabelais, François, physician and satirist. Born, probably in Chinon, France, about 1494; died, probably in Paris, about 1553. His masterwork was *Gargantua and Pantagruel,* a picture of the life, thought, and customs of the Renaissance. It was the source of several operas, including: GRÉTRY'S *Panurge;* Antoine Mariotte's *Gargantua;* MASSENET'S *Panurge;* MONSIGNY'S *L'Île sonnante;* SUTERMEISTER'S *Seraphine;* and Claude Terrasse's *Pantagruel.*

Rachel, Eléazar's daughter (soprano) in HALÉVY'S LA JUIVE, a role created by Marie-Cornélie FALCON.

Rachel, quand du Seigneur, Eléazar's moving aria (the most famous in the opera) describing his inner struggle between permitting his adopted daughter, Rachel, to be killed for being a Jewess, and saving her life by revealing that she is really Cardinal Brogny's daughter, in Act IV of HALÉVY'S LA JUIVE.

Rachmaninoff, Sergei, composer, pianist, conductor. Born Onega, Russia, Apr. 1, 1873; died Beverly Hills, Cal., Mar. 28, 1943. Early in his career, after studying at the St. Petersburg and Moscow conservatories, he wrote three operas, none of them adding appreciably to his stature as a composer, and none of them performed today. His first, ALEKO, written when he was only nineteen, was favorably received when introduced at the Moscow Opera on May 9, 1893. The other two were *The Miserly Knight* (1905) and *Francesca da Rimini* (1905). He worked on a fourth opera, *Monna Vanna*, between 1906 and 1908 but abandoned it.

For a period, Rachmaninoff was a conductor of opera. He made his debut in this field soon after 1900 when he directed A LIFE FOR THE CZAR for the Mamontov Opera Company, with which organization he remained a year. In 1905 he was appointed conductor of the BOLSHOI Theater in Moscow, making his debut there with RUSSALKA; during his year at the Bolshoi he conducted his *The Miserly Knight* and *Francesca da Rimini*.

Racine, Jean Baptiste, poet and dramatist. Born La Ferté-Milon, France, Dec., 1639; died Paris, Apr. 26, 1699. Several of his dramas, which are basic works of the classical, French theater, were made into operas; notably: *Andromaque* (opera by GRÉTRY, and ROSSINI's *Ermione*); *Iphigénie en Aulide* (operas by GRAUN and GLUCK); *Mitridate* (MOZART); *Phèdre* (opera by LEMOYNE); *Bérénice* (Albéric Magnard). Hervé's comic opera *Le Nouvel Aladin* is a parody of Racine's *Bajazet*.

Radames, captain of the guards (tenor), in love with Aida, in VERDI's AIDA.

Radames, è deciso il tuo fato, the priests' chorus as they pronounce the death sentence of Radames, in Act IV, Scene 1, of VERDI's AIDA.

radio and opera, *see* OPERA PERFORMANCE (3).

Rafaele, leader of the Camorrists (baritone) in WOLF-FERRARI's THE JEWELS OF THE MADONNA.

Raimondo, chaplain (bass) in DONIZETTI's LUCIA DI LAMMERMOOR.

Raïsa, Rosa (born Rose Burstein), soprano. Born Bialystok, Poland, May 30, 1893; died Los Angeles, Cal., Sept. 28, 1963. She studied singing with Eva Tetrazzini and with Barbara Marchisio at the Naples Conservatory. Her opera debut took place in Parma on Sept. 6, 1913, in VERDI's OBERTO. After appearances at the TEATRO COSTANZI and COVENT GARDEN, she made her American debut at the CHICAGO OPERA on Nov. 28, 1914, as AIDA. Soon afterward, she became one of the most adulated sopranos of that city. Besides appearing in the Italian, French, and (occasionally) German repertories, she was seen in the world premiere of Franke Harling's *A Light of St. Agnes* and in the American premieres of MASCAGNI's *Isabeau* and MONTEMEZZI's LA NAVE. At LA SCALA she created the role of Asteria in BOITO's NERONE, as well as TURANDOT, in the PUCCINI opera. In 1938 she created for America the role of Leah in ROCCA's THE DYBBUK.

Rake's Progress, The, opera in three acts and epilogue by STRAVINSKY. Libretto by W. H. AUDEN and Chester KALLMAN, inspired by Hogarth's series of lithographs of the same name. Premiere: Venice Festival, Sept. 11, 1951. American premiere: Metropolitan Opera, Feb. 14, 1953.

Characters: Truelove, a country squire (bass); Anne, his daughter (soprano); Tom Rakewell, her beloved (tenor); Nick Shadow (baritone); Mother Goose, keeper of a brothel (mezzo-soprano); Baba the Turk, a circus bearded lady (mezzo-soprano); Sellem, an auctioneer (tenor); Keeper of the Madhouse (bass); boys; servants; citizens; madmen; whores; and so forth. The action takes place in eighteenth-century England.

Act I, Scene 1. Garden in Trulove's country home. The orchestral prelude is a brief fanfare. Tom Rakewell, engaged to Anne, does not conform to Anne's father's conception of what a respectable son-in-law should be. The father has found an office job for Tom, which the young man turns down, preferring to depend for his fortune on Lady Luck ("Since it is not by merit we rise or we fall"). Suddenly there appears Nick Shadow with the news that a "forgotten uncle" has bequeathed a fortune to Tom. Nick Shadow informs Tom he must go to London to settle the matter of the inheritance and offers to accompany him as a servant for a salary to be decided upon in a year and a day. When Tom leaves, Nick announces: "The progress of a rake begins!"

Scene 2. Mother Goose's brothel in London. The scene opens with a vigorous chorus sung by the whores and roisterers. Nick has brought Tom here. After Tom recalls his vows of love to Anne, he goes off with Mother Goose to her room. The chorus gaily sings "Lanterloo," an old British song.

Scene 3. Garden in Trulove's country home. In a recitative and aria, Anne sings about how she misses Tom, about whom she has not heard a word. In a CABALETTA, which comes close to being a parody of a grand-opera aria, she expresses her determination to go to London ("I go, I go to him").

Act II, Scene 1. Tom's home in London. Tom is weary of debauchery; he can think only of Anne. Nick the Shadow appears with a picture of the circus bearded lady, Baba the Turk, and convinces Tom that it would be both fun and folly were Tom to marry her.

Scene 2. Outside Tom's house. Anne is waiting for Tom, who arrives in a sedan chair with Baba the Turk. Tom confesses to Anne he has married the circus freak and urges Anne to go back home. After Anne has left, the crowd cheers Baba as she removes a veil from her face and reveals her beard.

Scene 3. A room in Tom's house. Tom is disgusted with Baba, with her appearance, her continual jabbering, and the way she has cluttered up his home with her possessions. Baba goes into a tantrum, which leads Tom to cover her face with his wig, and then to find escape in sleep. As he sleeps, Nick the Shadow arrives with a machine able to make bread from stones. Awakening, Tom is sure he has been dreaming about that invention and is delighted to find that Nick has in his possession a machine that is certain to make a fortune for him.

Act III, Scene 1. A room in Tom's house. Baba is still in the room, her face covered by Tom's wig, when Sellem, an auctioneer, comes to auction off Tom's furniture and possessions (to the tune of a maudlin waltz). He is about to dispose of one of the objects when, removing the wig, it turns out to be Baba. She informs the crowd that she is returning to the circus. At the same time she advises Anne, who has come seeking Tom, to find and reform him. Anne repeats her mock aria, "I go, I go to him," as the voices of Tom and Nick are heard offstage.

Scene 2. A churchyard. Nick informs Tom that the payment he seeks for his services is not money but Tom's soul. The only way Tom can escape the horrors of hell is to beat Nick in a game of cards. When Tom wins, Nick strikes Tom, who goes insane. Then Nick sinks into a grave. At dawn, Tom is found sitting on a tombstone, sprinkling grass on his head and singing a meaningless ballad ("Adonis").

Scene 3. Bedlam. Surrounded by the inmates of the asylum, Tom insists that he is Adonis, who will soon get a visit from Venus. When Anne arrives, Tom greets her as Venus. They sing a love duet, after which Anne rocks him to sleep with a touching lullaby. When Tom has fallen asleep, Anne leaves with her father. Upon awakening, Tom raves that Venus has visited him. When his fellow inmates refuse to believe him, he collapses and dies.

Epilogue. Anne, Tom, Baba, and Trulove appear before the curtain to explain the moral of the weird story that has just been told: "For idle hands and hearts and minds the devil finds a work to do."

The Rake's Progress, Stravinsky's only full-length opera, was his last composition in the neoclassical style he had been favoring since the early 1920's (in subsequent works he would embrace dodecaphony). He intentionally gave his opera an eighteenth-century personality, with its traditional sequence of arias, recitatives, ensemble numbers, and choruses. His models were HANDEL, GLUCK, but mainly MOZART; much of the music has Mozartean simplicity, economy, and affecting lyricism. In reverting to eighteenth-century procedures, Stravinsky uses a chamber orchestra and a harpsichord to accompany the recitatives.

Rákóczy March (Hungarian March), the stirring march, based on a Hungarian folk melody, in Act I of BERLIOZ' THE DAMNATION OF FAUST. The interpolation of a Hungarian march in the Faust legend is justified by having Faust wander in Hungary.

Ralf, Torsten, tenor. Born Malmö, Sweden, Jan. 2, 1901; died Stockholm, Apr. 27, 1954. After attending the Stockholm Conservatory he completed his music study in Berlin. He made his debut in Stettin as CAVARADOSSI in 1930. After two years with the FRANKFURT OPERA, he became a principal tenor of the DRESDEN OPERA in 1935, where he remained nine years and created the role of Apollo in Richard STRAUSS'S DAPHNE. Between 1935 and 1939 and again in 1948 he appeared at COVENT GARDEN. He made his debut with the METROPOLITAN OPERA on Nov. 26, 1945, in the title role of LOHENGRIN. He remained three seasons with the Metropolitan Opera, after which he continued his career in Europe. Though he was most distinguished in the Wagnerian repertory, he was also an outstanding interpreter of VERDI operas, particularly such heroic roles as RADAMES and OTELLO.

Rambaldo, (1) a minstrel (tenor) in MEYERBEER'S ROBERT LE DIABLE.

(2) A wealthy Parisian (baritone) in PUCCINI'S LA RONDINE.

Rameau, Jean-Philippe, composer and theorist. Born Dijon, France, Sept. 25, 1683; died Paris, Sept. 12, 1764. The first French-born master in opera, he was the son of a church organist. As a child he was taught the harpsichord, organ, and violin. In 1701 he traveled through northern Italy, earning his living as an organist and violinist. When he returned to France, he served as organist in Avignon and Clermont-Ferrand. During this period he began writing music

for the harpsichord. About 1705 he settled in Paris, where he studied the organ with Louis Marchand and devoured every book on theory he could find. He published his first volume of harpsichord pieces a year later. Rameau first achieved prominence as a musical theorist, publishing in 1722 his monumental *Traité de l'harmonie,* even today a valuable work. Four years later he published a second volume, *Nouveau Système de musique théorique.* He now came to the attention of the powerful patron, Riche de la POUPELINIÈRE, becoming the conductor of his private orchestra and his organist. Meanwhile, in 1723, Rameau began writing music for the stage. Recognition as an opera composer came in 1733 when his HIPPOLYTE ET ARICIE was performed at the OPÉRA. Rameau was soon accused of sacrificing melody for the sake of harmony and orchestration and of placing too much emphasis on mere drama. With his subsequent operas—notably LES INDES GALANTES (1735), CASTOR ET POLLUX (1737), and DARDANUS (1739)—the opposition grew increasingly hostile. Jean Jacques ROUSSEAU, a believer in the Italian methods, wrote of Rameau that "the French airs are not airs at all, and the French recitative is not recitative." The musicians of the Opéra jeered at Rameau's complex orchestration. Friedrich GRIMM derided Rameau for his excessive use of the ballet. Yet there were also those who acknowledged the composer's genius. "Rameau has made of music a new art," wrote VOLTAIRE, and André CAMPRA said, "He will eclipse us all."

The struggle between Rameau's followers and his enemies was climaxed in 1752 with a squabble known as the "guerre des bouffons." On Aug. 1 a visiting Italian troupe performed PERGOLESI'S LA SERVA PADRONA. Rameau's opponents proclaimed Pergolesi's opera the ideal opera, while violently condemning Rameau's operas for their intricacy and cerebralism. In the other camp were those who felt that Rameau was laying the foundations for a French operatic art. By the end of his life, Rameau was partially vindicated and was recognized as a master. Full vindication came after his death with the victory in Paris of GLUCK's operas over the Italian operas of Nicola PICCINNI.

The following are the most significant of Rameau's operas and BALLET-OPERAS: *Hippolyte et Aricie* (1733); *Les Indes galantes* (1735); *Castor et Pollux* (1737); *Dardanus* (1739); *Les Fêtes de Polymnie* (1745); *Les Fêtes de l'Hymen et de l'Amour* (1747); *Zoroastre* (1749); *Platée* (1749); *Acanthe et Céphise* (1751); *Zephire* (1754); *Anacréon* (1754); *Les Paladins* (1760).

Ramerrez, *see* JOHNSON, DICK.

Ramfis, High Priest of Egypt (bass) in VERDI's AIDA.

Ramiro, a muleteer (baritone) in RAVEL's L'HEURE ESPAGNOLE.

Ramon, (1) a wealthy farmer (bass) in GOUNOD's MIREILLE.

(2) Pedro's brother and slayer (bass) in LAPARRA's LA HABANERA.

Ramuntcho, opera in three acts by TAYLOR. Libretto by the composer, based on the novel of the same name by Pierre Loti. Premiere: Philadelphia, Feb. 10, 1942. In the Basque village of Etchezar, in the early part of the present century, Gracieuse is ready to marry Ramuntcho, the smuggler, if he promises to give up his profession. Ramuntcho must first serve a three-year term in the army. His letters to Gracieuse are intercepted and destroyed by her mother. Convinced that her beloved has forgotten her, Gracieuse enters a convent. When Ramuntcho returns from the army, he discovers what has happened. Despite his pleadings, Gracieuse refuses to leave the convent, insisting that she is now God's bride. Taylor's score makes extensive use of Basque folksongs.

Rance, Jack, sheriff (baritone) in PUCCINI's THE GIRL OF THE GOLDEN WEST, a role created by Antonio Scotti.

ranz des vaches, a call played on the Alpine horn by Swiss herdsmen to summon their cattle. The call has numerous variations. A number of them appear in ROSSINI's WILLIAM TELL, the *ranz des vaches* (for English horn) in the overture being the best known. KIENZL wrote an opera entitled *Ranz des vaches*.

Raoul de Nangis, Huguenot nobleman (tenor) in MEYERBEER's LES HUGUENOTS, a role created by Adolphe NOURRIT.

Rape of Lucretia, The, opera in two acts by BRITTEN. Libretto by Ronald Duncan, based on a play by André Obey, *Le Viol de Lucrèce.* Premiere: Glyndebourne Festival, July 12, 1946. American premiere: Chicago, June 1, 1947. This is a CHAMBER OPERA of modest proportions. There are two choruses, each consisting of a single person: one a man, one a woman. The cast is made up of six principals. The orchestra has only twelve instruments. The music is lean and concise, deriving much of its power from its concentration. The subject is the same as that of SHAKESPEARE's narrative poem. The Roman prince, Tarquinius (baritone), hears accounts in camp of the infidelity of the wives of the Roman officers, with the exception of Lucretia (contralto), wife of Collatinus (bass). Tarquinius leaves camp for Rome to test her fidelity. Since she resists him he is driven to rape her. Disgraced, Lucretia commits suicide in the presence of her husband, who had been hurriedly summoned home. Tarquinius' second-act lullaby, "Within this frail crucible of light" is one of its most effective arias.

rappresentazione di anima e di corpo, La (The Representation of the Soul and the Body), oratorio (or "morality play with music") by CAVALIERI. Libretto by Agostino Manni. Premiere: Rome, Feb., 1600. Often described as the first oratorio ever written, this work is also regarded as an early example of opera, since it was given in a staged presentation, and is the first musicodramatic composition in three acts. The first published score gives specific instruction on how the work is to be staged. The text is an allegory in which Time, Body, Soul, Pleasure, Intellect, and Life are personified.

Raskin, Judith, soprano. Born New York City, June 21, 1932. She studied voice with Anna Hamlin, her only teacher. In 1957 she toured with the NBC TELEVISION OPERA THEATRE, appearing as Susanna in THE MARRIAGE OF FIGARO. This was followed by a telecast of LES DIALOGUES DES CARMÉLITES by the NBC Opera, in which she assumed the role of Sister Constance. She continued appearing in televised performances of opera for several years. During the summer of 1958 she sang with the SANTA FE OPERA, and between 1959 and 1964 she made numerous appearances with the AMERICAN OPERA SOCIETY in such novelties as MÉDÉE, HANDEL's *Samson,* THE RAKE's PROGRESS, and IL TURCO IN ITALIA (in the last, assuming the leading soprano role). She made her debut with the NEW YORK CITY OPERA in 1959, where she specialized in MOZART operas. Her debut at the METROPOLITAN OPERA took place on Feb. 23, 1962, as Susanna. As one of the principal sopranos of this company, she has been heard not only in Mozart's operas, which have become her specialty, but also in ZEFFIRELLI's production of FALSTAFF, conducted by Leonard BERNSTEIN, and as Sophie in DER ROSENKAVALIER, among other operas. During the summer of 1963 she made her first appearance at the GLYNDEBOURNE FESTIVAL.

Raskolnikoff, opera in two acts by SUTERMEISTER. Libretto by Peter Sutermeister, based on DOSTOYEVSKY's CRIME AND PUNISHMENT. Premiere: Stockholm Opera, Oct. 14, 1948. This opera, like the Dostoyevsky novel, emphasizes the psychology of a poor student who turns to murder and finds expiation in the love of a streetwalker. He finally gives himself up to the police to be exiled to Siberia. Gerhart von Westerman points out that the composer's style in this opera differs from that he had previously used, turning to "neo-naturalism, sketching a situation or evoking an atmosphere in a few strokes, with invariably compelling effect." The chorus, which is often heard offstage, is used with extraordinary effect to point up the "alter ego" of the hero, particularly in the second act.

rataplan, a term used for either solos or ensemble numbers in opera in which the sound of a drum is simulated, usually for army scenes. It appears in THE DAUGHTER OF THE REGIMENT, LES HUGUENOTS, and LA FORZA DEL DESTINO.

Ratmir, Ludmilla's suitor (contralto) in GLINKA's RUSSLAN AND LUDMILLA.

Räuber, Die, *see* SCHILLER, FRIEDRICH.

Ravel, Maurice, composer. Born Ciboure, France, Mar. 7, 1875; died Paris, Dec. 28, 1937. He received his musical training at the Paris Conservatory, and first attracted attention in 1902 with his piano pieces, *Pavane pour une infante défunte* and *Jeux d'eau.* During the next few years he twice became the object of critical attention in Paris: first, in 1905, for having failed for the fourth time to win the PRIX DE ROME; in 1907, when he was unjustly accused of being an imitator of Claude DEBUSSY. But he was soon acknowledged a master of contemporary French music. His one-act opera, L'HEURE ESPAGNOLE, was introduced at the OPÉRA-COMIQUE on May 19, 1911. Ravel later wrote another opera, L'ENFANT ET LES SORTILÈGES (1925), calling for pantomime, ballet, and singing.

Ravenswood, *see* EDGARDO.

Rebikov, Vladimir, composer. Born Krasnoyarsk, Siberia, May 31, 1866; died Yalta, Crimea, Dec. 1, 1920. His music study took place at the Moscow Conservatory, in Berlin, and in Vienna. In 1894 he attracted attention with his opera IN THE STORM, produced in Odessa. He evolved a personal theory in which music was "the language of emotion." He explained that, "Our feelings have no prepared and conventional forms and terminations," and that music should "give them corresponding expression." In line with this thinking, he wrote in an unorthodox style abounding in strange harmonies. Sometimes called the "father of Russian modernism," he was one of the first composers to make extensive use of the WHOLE-TONE SCALE. He described some of his operas—most of them very short—as musicopsychological dramas, notably, *Arachne; The Abyss* (1910); *Alpha and Omega* (1911); and *The Woman with the Dagger* (1911). Other operas were: *In the Storm* (1894); *The Christmas Tree,* a children's opera (1903); *Prince Charming,* a fairy opera.

re cèrvo, Il, *see* KÖNIG HIRSCH.

recitative (Italian, *recitativo*), the term denoting the declamatory portions of an opera (or kindred work), used principally to advance the narrative. A "dry" recitative (Italian, *recitativo secco*) has little or no melodic interest and simply follows the normal accentuation of the words. Though it impedes the flow of the music, it is particularly effective to help advance the action. It is accompanied by a few fundamental chords played by harpsichord or piano, though in MANON, for example, such chords are provided by strings. An accompanied recitative (*recitativo accompagnato* or *stromentato*) is more developed musically speaking and has an orchestral accompaniment that may be simple or elaborate and leads more easily into song. Since WAGNER and DEBUSSY, both forms of recitatives have been dispensed with by most operas in favor of a continuous flow of melody. STRAVINSKY, however, revived the *recitativo secco* in THE RAKE'S PROGRESS.

Recondita armonia, Cavaradossi's aria rhapsodizing Tosca's beauty, in Act I of PUCCINI'S TOSCA.

recordings and opera, *see* OPERA PERFORMANCE (4).

Re dell' abisso, Ulrica's incantation over her cauldron in Act I, Scene 2, of VERDI'S UN BALLO IN MASCHERA.

Regina, musical play in prologue and two acts by BLITZSTEIN. Libretto by the composer, based on Lillian Hellman's play *The Little Foxes.* Premiere: Boston, Oct. 11, 1949. The play (a great success on Broadway with Tallulah Bankhead in the leading role) deals with the rapacious Hubbard family in America's South (Alabama in 1900), most of whose members are driven only by lust,

hate, greed, deceit, and theft until they destroy each other and themselves. *Regina* was first seen in an opera house on Apr. 2, 1953, performed by the NEW YORK CITY OPERA, which has since revived it intermittently. Previously it had been staged on Broadway as a musical play. Musical highlights include an aria by Regina recalling her past and describing her suffering, and one by her daughter, Alexandra, which ends the play; also Addie's song, "Night," and the vocal quartet, "Listen to the sound of the rain." The musical episodes are combined with some spoken dialogue.

régisseur, French for "producer" or "director" of an opera production, with oversight of every phase of the production.

Regnava nel silenzio, Lucia's aria describing an apparition she has witnessed of a woman's murder by one of the Ravenswoods, in Act I, Scene 2, of DONIZETTI'S LUCIA DI LAMMERMOOR.

Reich, name for Page in the original German-language version of NICOLAI'S THE MERRY WIVES OF WINDSOR. *See* PAGE.

Reichardt, Johann Friedrich, composer and conductor. Born Königsberg, Ger., Nov. 25, 1752; died Giebichenstein, Ger., June 27, 1814. A pioneer writer of SINGSPIELE, he studied philosophy at the universities of Königsberg and Leipzig, music with C. G. Richter and Franz Adam Veichtner. Between 1775 and 1794 he was court conductor and composer for Frederick the Great and his successor, Friedrich Wilhelm II. In 1783 he founded the Concerts Spirituels for the performance of new music. He visited Paris in 1785 and was commissioned by the OPÉRA to write two works, *Tamerlan* and *Panthée.* When he was suddenly recalled to the court of Frederick the Great, the production of both operas was abandoned. In 1791 he was accused by Friedrich Wilhelm II of sympathy with the French Revolution and was suspended from his court post for three years, a period in which he traveled extensively. In 1794 the Emperor dismissed him permanently. He settled in Giebichenstein, where he became inspector of the Halle salt works. In 1808 he was appointed director of the Cassel Opera. In the same year he visited Vienna, where some of his *singspiele* were performed; because he overstayed his leave, he was dismissed from his post in Cassel. Besides being a composer and conductor, Reichardt was a distinguished writer on musical subjects and an editor of several music publications. His most important operas and *singspiele: Tamerlan* (1786); *Andromeda* (1787); *Protesilao* (1788); *Brenno* (1789); *L'Olimpiade* (1791); *Jery und Bätely* (1801).

Reichmann, Theodor, baritone. Born Rostock, Ger., Mar. 15, 1848; died Marbach, Lake Constance, Switzerland, May 22, 1903. His music study took place in Berlin with Eduard Mantius, in Prague with Luise Ress, and in Milan with Francesco Lamperti. He made his opera debut in 1869 in Magdeburg. After appearing in various opera theaters in Germany and Holland, he was engaged by the MUNICH OPERA in 1874, where he distinguished himself in the Wagnerian repertory. In 1882, in BAYREUTH, he created the role of AMFORTAS. For the next ten years he appeared regularly at the Bayreuth Festivals, but because of differences with the WAGNER family, he did not appear there during the decade 1892–1902. From 1882 to 1889 he was a member of the VIENNA OPERA. On Nov. 27, 1889, he made his American debut at the METROPOLITAN OPERA in DER FLIEGENDE HOLLÄNDER. He remained at the Metropolitan through the 1890–91 season. In 1893 he returned to the Vienna Opera.

Reine de Saba, La (The Queen of Sheba), opera in four acts by GOUNOD. Libretto by Jules BARBIER and Michel Carré. Premiere: Paris Opéra, Feb. 28, 1862. American premiere: French Opera House, New Orleans, Jan. 12, 1889. The Hebrew sculptor Adoniram (tenor) is in love with Balkis, the Queen of Sheba (soprano). Balkis leaves King Solomon (bass) to elope with Adoniram, but by the time she reaches him he has been murdered by one of his own men. Significant excerpts include the second-act march for orchestra; the first-act bass CAVATINA, "Sous les pieds"; the third-act soprano aria, "Plus grand dans mon obscurité"; and the tenor aria, "Inspirez-moi, race divine."

Reine Fiammette, La (Queen Fiammette), opera in four acts by LEROUX. Libretto by Catulle MENDÈS, based on his own play. Premiere: Opéra-Comique, Dec. 23, 1903. American premiere: Metropolitan Opera, Jan. 24, 1919. The setting is the fictional Kingdom of Bologna during the late Renaissance. Cardinal Sforza, conspiring to get rid of Queen Fiammette because of her interest in the teachings of Martin Luther, persuades Danielo to wield the assassin's knife, but Danielo recognizes the Queen as a young woman he had formerly loved. For his failure to kill the Queen, he is condemned to death. When he makes an attempt on the life of the wicked Sforza, both he and the Queen are beheaded.

Reiner, Fritz, conductor. Born Budapest, Dec. 10, 1888; died New York, Nov. 15, 1963. He attended the National Academy in Budapest, after which in 1909 he became chorus master of the BUDAPEST OPERA. In 1910 he was engaged as conductor of the Laibach National Opera and in 1911 of the People's Opera in Budapest. He was appointed first conductor of the DRESDEN OPERA in 1914. When the war broke out, Reiner directed opera performances in Rome and Barcelona. In 1922 he was appointed music director of the Cincinnati Symphony, where he remained eight seasons. In 1930 he became head of the orchestra department of the Curtis Institute of Music. During this period he appeared as guest conductor of leading American orchestras and with several major opera companies. During the 1936 Coronation festivities in London, he scored a major success with performances of the WAGNER music dramas. In 1938 he began a ten-year period as musical director of the Pittsburgh Symphony. After leaving Pittsburgh, Reiner became a principal conductor of the

METROPOLITAN OPERA, making his debut there on Feb. 4, 1949, with SALOME. He resigned from the Metropolitan in 1953 to become the music director of the Chicago Orchestra. In 1955 he was invited to conduct at the reopening of the VIENNA STATE OPERA. In 1963 he was planning a return to the Metropolitan Opera and was deep at work preparing GÖTTERDÄMMERUNG, when he was stricken by a fatal illness.

Reiss, Albert, tenor. Born Berlin, Feb. 22, 1870; died Nice, June 20, 1940. He appeared on the dramatic stage until 1897, when the opera impresario Bernhard Pollini urged him to turn to opera. Reiss's debut took place in Königsberg on Sept. 28, 1897, in ZAR UND ZIMMERMANN. He made his American debut at the METROPOLITAN OPERA on Dec. 23, 1901, as the young sailor in TRISTAN UND ISOLDE. During the same season he was acclaimed for his interpretations of David in DIE MEISTERSINGER and Mime in SIEGFRIED; for many years, these interpretations were considered a standard. He remained with the Metropolitan Opera through the 1919–20 season, creating there the roles of Nick in THE GIRL OF THE GOLDEN WEST, the Broommaker in DIE KÖNIGSKINDER, Nial in MONA, and Richard II in THE CANTERBURY PILGRIMS. He was considered one of the finest tenor COMPRIMARIOS of his day—and something higher when he performed brilliantly as a mezzo in the role of HANSEL AND GRETEL's Witch.

He became an opera producer in 1916 when he presented, and appeared in, BASTIEN UND BASTIENNE and THE IMPRESARIO, both by MOZART. His success led him to direct a two-week season at the Lyceum Theater in the spring of 1916 and to organize the Society of American Singers in 1917. After leaving the Metropolitan, he appeared for a decade with the Charlottenburg Opera in Berlin. He was a frequent guest at WAGNER festivals and at COVENT GARDEN. He retired from opera in 1930.

Rembrandt van Rijn, painter. Born Leyden, Netherlands, July 15, 1607; died Amsterdam, Oct. 4, 1669. The famous artist is the central character in two operas, both entitled *Rembrandt van Rijn,* one by BADINGS, the other by KLENAU.

Remendado, Le, a smuggler (tenor) in BIZET's CARMEN.

Renard, CHAMBER OPERA or BALLET-OPERA in one act by STRAVINSKY. Libretto by the composer, based on Russian folk tales. Premiere: Paris Opéra, June 3, 1922. American premiere: New York City, Dec. 2, 1923 (concert version); New York, Jan. 13, 1947 (staged). The composer explains: *"Renard* is to be played by buffoons, dancers, or acrobats, preferably on a trestle stage, with the orchestra placed behind. The players do not leave the stage. They enter together to the accompaniment of the little march that serves as an introduction and their exit is managed in the same way. The roles are dumb. The voices (two tenors and two basses) are placed in the orchestra." The fable concerns two attempts on the part of Renard the fox to abduct the cock; the attempts are frustrated by the cat and the ram. The fox is finally conquered by the barnyard animals. A feature of Stravinsky's score is the inclusion of a cimbalom, an instrument found chiefly in Hungarian gypsy orchestras.

Renato, the king's secretary (baritone) and husband of Amelia in VERDI's UN BALLO IN MASCHERA.

Renaud, Maurice, baritone. Born Bordeaux, France, July 24, 1861; died Paris, Oct. 16, 1933. His musical training took place in the conservatories of Paris and Brussels. He made his opera debut at the THÉÂTRE DE LA MONNAIE in 1883. Until 1890 he was a leading baritone of that company, creating the title role in REYER's SIGURD and the role of Hamilcar in the same composer's SALAMMBÔ. On Oct. 12, 1890, he made his Paris debut at the OPÉRA-COMIQUE in LE ROI D'YS, and on July 17, 1891, his debut at the OPÉRA in L'AFRICAINE. He was a principal baritone of the Opéra for over a decade. In 1897 he made his first appearance at COVENT GARDEN, in a performance honoring Queen Victoria's Golden

Jubilee. His American debut took place on Jan. 4, 1893, at the FRENCH OPERA HOUSE in New Orleans in SAMSON ET DALILA. A decade later he was contracted by Maurice GRAU to appear at the METROPOLITAN OPERA, but when Heinrich CONRIED took over the direction, Renaud abrogated his contract. He was heard with the MANHATTAN OPERA COMPANY between 1906 and 1910, scoring triumphs in such roles as ATHANAEL (which he created for America), DON GIOVANNI, and SCARPIA. After the Manhattan Opera disbanded, he sang for a season with the CHICAGO OPERA. On Nov. 25, 1910, he made his bow at the Metropolitan Opera in RIGOLETTO, remaining with the company two years. Thereafter, he sang only in Europe.

Rencontre imprévue, La, ou Pèlerins de la Mecque, Les (The Unforeseen Meeting, or The Pilgrims to Mecca), comic opera in three acts by GLUCK. Libretto by L. H. Dancourt, based on a French vaudeville by Lesage and D'Orneval. Premiere: Burgtheater, Vienna, Jan. 7, 1764. American premiere: Cleveland, June 8, 1951. Believing his mistress Princess Rezia is dead, Prince Ali and his servant Osmi wander about aimlessly until they reach Cairo. There the Prince discovers that Rezia is alive and is a member of the Sultan's harem. When Rezia discovers that the Prince is in Cairo, she decides to test his love by sending several harem girls to tempt him. Ali proves his unwavering devotion to Rezia by resisting them, which leads Rezia to welcome him back passionately.

Rennert, Günther, stage director and intendant. Born Essen, Ger., Apr. 1, 1911. He served his apprenticeship in various German theaters as stage director for both dramatic presentations and operas. In 1942 he became stage director of the BERLIN STATE OPERA. In 1945 he directed the performance of FIDELIO which reopened the MUNICH OPERA. From 1946 to 1956 he was intendant of the HAMBURG OPERA, which he helped make one of Germany's leading opera companies. For a number of years after leaving Hamburg he was a free lance, working as a producer for most of the leading European opera houses, as well as at the SALZBURG, EDINBURGH, and GLYNDEBOURNE festivals. He directed his first opera at the METROPOLITAN OPERA, VERDI'S NABUCCO, on opening night of the 1960–61 season. In 1967 he returned to the Munich Opera as intendant, where he was responsible for a highly successful production of the WAGNER RING cycle in 1969. In the spring of 1968 he produced a week of Czech operas at the STUTTGART OPERA.

re pastore, Il (The Shepherd King), DRAMMA PER MUSICA in two acts by MOZART. Libretto by METASTASIO. Premiere: Salzburg, Apr. 23, 1775. Metastasio's text is an allegory in which Alexander the Great is glorified and in which two pairs of lovers respectively symbolize love and the state. Separated from each other by Alexander's political plans, one pair of lovers refuses to sacrifice their love while the other pair is ready to make the sacrifice for the sake of the state. Alexander the Great is so deeply moved by this sacrifice that he revokes his former orders and vows to conquer a second kingdom, which he plans to turn over to the heroic pair. The opera boasts a remarkable soprano aria in "L'amerò, sarò costante" and a stirring duet, "Vanne, vanne à regnar," that closes the first act. Mozart's overall style is half heroic and half pastoral, much of it conceived in terms of the orchestra rather than of voices.

répétiteur, French for "repeater." In opera he instructs or cues the singers in their parts and may also serve as prompter.

répétition, a French term meaning "rehearsal." A *répétition générale* denotes a dress rehearsal attended by critics and invited guests.

rescue opera, a genre of French opera enjoying a brief span of popularity during the French Revolution. The typical libretto shows the hero or heroine being saved after many vicissitudes. CHERUBINI'S LES DEUX JOURNÉES is such an opera.

Residenztheater, an intimate opera house in Munich, built in rococo style, attached to the palace. It was opened in 1753. In 1781 it was the scene for the premiere of MOZART'S IDOMENEO. In recent times the theater has often been used for performances of Mozart's operas at the annual MUNICH FESTIVALS.

Resnik, Regina, soprano and mezzo-soprano. Born New York City, Aug. 20, 1922. She studied voice in New York with Rosalie Miller. She made her debut as LADY MACBETH in 1942 with the New Opera Company in New York. In 1944 she won the METROPOLITAN AUDITIONS OF THE AIR, and on Dec. 6, 1944, made her debut at the METROPOLITAN OPERA in IL TROVATORE. During the next decade she sang principal soprano roles at the Metropolitan. There she created the role of Delilah in *The Warrior* by Bernard Rogers and became America's first ELLEN ORFORD. In July, 1953, she made her first appearance at BAYREUTH as SIEGLINDE. In 1955 she gave up soprano roles and became a mezzo-soprano, making her debut in this new range at the CINCINNATI ZOO OPERA as AMNERIS. She made her first Metropolitan Opera appearance as mezzo-soprano in the role of Marina in BORIS GODUNOV in 1956 and in 1958 created the role of the Baroness in VANESSA. In 1957 she made her first appearance at COVENT GARDEN, where she subsequently gave numerous performances. Her specialty has been colorful roles such as CARMEN, HÉRODIAS, and Dame QUICKLY. On June 19, 1970, she celebrated her twenty-fifth anniversary as a member of the Metropolitan Opera in a gala presentation of *Carmen*. During her long affiliation with the Metropolitan Opera, she was heard one hundred ninety-six times in thirty-seven roles both as soprano and mezzo. In 1971 she became a stage director for the first time by producing *Carmen* for the HAMBURG STATE OPERA and ELEKTRA for Venice.

Respighi, Ottorino, composer. Born Bologna, Italy, July 9, 1879; died Rome, Apr. 18, 1936. He graduated from the Bologna Liceo in 1899, after which he studied with RIMSKY-KORSAKOV in St. Petersburg and Max BRUCH in Berlin. He first attracted attention as a composer with an opera, *Re Enzo,* introduced in Bologna in 1905. While Respighi became famous for his orchestral music and was a leading figure in the Italian movement to turn from opera to symphonic and chamber music, he did not abandon the stage. His first major operatic success came with *Belfagor,* given at LA SCALA on Apr. 26, 1923. His most important opera, LA CAMPANA SOMMERSA, was introduced in Hamburg in 1927 and was given at the METROPOLITAN OPERA a year later.

Respighi became professor of composition at the Santa Cecilia Academy in Rome in 1913. A decade later he was appointed director, holding this post two years. In 1932 he was appointed to the Royal Academy of Italy. He visited the United States in 1925, 1928, and 1932.

His operas: *Re Enzo* (1905); *Marie Victoire* (1909); *La bella addormentata* (1909); *Semirama* (1910); *Belfagor* (1923); *La campana sommersa* (1927); *Maria Egiziaca* (1932); *La fiamma* (1933); *Lucrezia* (completed by his wife).

Reste, repose-toi, the BERCEUSE of Louise's father to Louise in Act IV of CHARPENTIER'S LOUISE.

Resurrection, The, see RISURREZIONE, LA.

Reszke, see DE RESZKE.

retablo de Maese Pedro, El (Master Peter's Puppet Show), CHAMBER OPERA for puppets in one act by FALLA. Libretto by the composer, based on a scene from Part II of CERVANTES' *Don Quixote.* Premiere: Seville, Mar. 23, 1923 (concert version); Paris, June 25, 1923 (staged). American premiere: New York City, Dec. 29, 1925. This chamber opera is a play within a play. Don Quixote and Sancho Panza are members of an audience watching a play in which the story of Melisandra is being enacted by young Master Peter's puppets. The confused Don Quixote, believing the puppet show to be a live episode, leaves his place in the audience to do battle with the puppets, thereby destroying the performance. The composer gave instructions that two sets of puppets be used: large puppets for the audience and Master Peter, small ones for the players. An alternative method was also suggested: actors wearing masks might replace the large puppets. The singers are placed with the orchestra in the pit. When it was produced at the FESTIVAL OF TWO WORLDS in Spoleto in 1969, however, live children were used on the stage in place of puppets.

Rethberg, Elizabeth (born Sättler), soprano. Born Schwarzenburg, Ger., Sept. 22, 1894. Her musical education took place at the Dresden Conservatory. Her debut took place in 1915 with the DRESDEN OPERA in THE GYPSY BARON. She remained a principal soprano of that company for seven seasons, at the same time making guest appearances at LA SCALA, the VIENNA STATE OPERA, and the BERLIN OPERA. Her American debut took place at the METROPOLITAN OPERA on Nov. 22, 1922, in AIDA. For two decades she was a principal soprano of the Metropolitan, appearing in the French, Italian, and German repertories. She was heard in the American premiere of LA CAMPANA SOMMERSA and in such major revivals as THE BARBER OF BAGDAD, DER FREISCHÜTZ, IRIS, and THE MAGIC FLUTE. During her association with the Metropolitan, she was heard with the Chicago Civic Opera, the SAN FRANCISCO OPERA, COVENT GARDEN, the Dresden Opera, and the SALZBURG FESTIVALS. In 1928 she created the title role in Richard STRAUSS's DIE AEGYPTISCHE HELENA; two years later a Rethberg week was celebrated by the Dresden Opera, an occasion on which she was given honorary membership in all the state theaters of Saxony.

She left the Metropolitan Opera in 1942 after differences with the management over her contract. Her last appearance there took place on Mar. 6, 1942, in *Aida*. She has also been prominent as a concert singer and soloist in oratorios. In 1936 and 1938 she toured in joint recitals with Ezio PINZA. She received her American citizenship in 1939.

Rêve, Le, *see* EN FERMANT LES YEUX.

Revisor, Der (The Inspector General), comic opera in five acts by EGK. Libretto by the composer, based on GOGOL's play of the same name. Premiere: Schwetzingen, Ger., May 9, 1957. American premiere: New York City Opera, Oct. 19, 1960. The time is the middle of the nineteenth century; the place, a small Russian town. Rumor has it that a government inspector will arrive from St. Petersburg to make an inspection. When a stranger, Khlestakov, appears, he is believed to be the inspector; and so, he is treated ceremoniously and is given full liberty to borrow huge sums of money, to make love to the wife of a captain, and to enjoy the freedom of the town. It is not long before, through an intercepted letter, the townspeople discover that Khlestakov is not the inspector. Then the real inspector arrives—and the curtain descends. In treating this comical subject, Egk employs a PARLANDO style in place of lyricism to permit the dialogue and action to move briskly. There are, however, a number of set numbers, ensembles, and dances, even a few quotations from Russian folk songs and dances, including one from "A birch tree stood in the field," which TCHAIKOVSKY quoted in his *Fourth Symphony*.

Reyer, Ernest (born Louis Ernest Etienne Rey), composer. Born Marseilles, Dec. 1, 1823; died Levandou, France, Jan. 15, 1909. When he was sixteen he went to Algiers to live with an uncle, where he studied music (mostly by himself) and started composition. His extended stay in Algiers was responsible for his lifelong interest in oriental subjects. In 1848 he returned to Paris, where his first major work, *Le Sélam,* for orchestra, was introduced two years later. In 1854 a one-act opera, *Maître Wolfram,* was given at the THÉÂTRE LYRIQUE. It won praise from HALÉVY and BERLIOZ. Even more successful were a ballet-pantomime,

Sacountala, given by the OPÉRA in 1858, and a comic opera, *La Statue,* produced at the Théâtre Lyrique in 1861. BIZET regarded *La Statue* as the most important new French opera in a quarter of a century. Between 1865 and 1875 Reyer wrote music criticism for French journals and was a vigorous voice in support of WAGNER and the younger French composers. His journalism was collected in two books: *Notes de musique* (1875) and *Quarante Ans de musique* (1909). In 1876 he was appointed to the Institut de France in succession to Ferdinand David. Eight years later his most important work, the opera SIGURD (on which he had been working for a decade), was successfully given at the THÉÂTRE DE LA MONNAIE, and soon after performed at COVENT GARDEN and the Paris Opéra. Reyer's last major work was the opera SALAMMBÔ, introduced at the Théâtre de la Monnaie in 1890. From 1866 on Reyer was the librarian of the Paris Opéra. Besides the operas mentioned above, he composed *Érostate* (1862).

Rezia, the Caliph of Bagdad's daughter (soprano) in WEBER's OBERON.

Rezniček, Emil von, composer. Born Vienna, May 4, 1860; died Berlin, Aug. 2, 1945. He combined the study of music with that of law. His friendship with Ferruccio BUSONI and Felix WEINGARTNER led him to choose music. He entered the Leipzig Conservatory. After completing his studies he conducted theater orchestras in Austria and Germany for several years. All this while, he was composing, but success did not come until 1894 when his opera DONNA DIANA was triumphantly introduced in Prague. Within a short period this opera was performed throughout Germany. From 1896 to 1899 Rezniček was the KAPELLMEISTER of the Court Theater in Mannheim. He settled in Berlin in 1901, where he founded a chamber orchestra and where, in 1906, he became a professor at the Scharwenka Conservatory. In 1907–08 he was principal conductor of the Warsaw Opera and from 1909 to 1911 of the KOMISCHE OPER in Berlin. From 1920 to 1926 he was professor of composition at the Staatliche Hochschule in Berlin. He wrote eleven operas: *Die Jungfrau von Orleans* (1886); *Satanella* (1887); *Emmerich Fortunat* (1888); *Donna Diana* (1894, revised 1908 and 1933); *Till Eulenspiegel* (1902); *Eros und Psyche* (1917); *Ritter Blaubart* (1920); *Holofernes* (1923); *Satuala* (1927); *Spiel oder Ernst?* (1930); *Der Gondolier des Dogen* (1931).

Rheingold, Das, *see* RING DES NIBELUNGEN.

Rhine maidens, three characters who appear in WAGNER's DAS RHEINGOLD and GÖTTERDÄMMERUNG. They are Flosshilde (contralto), Wellgunde (soprano), and Woglinde (soprano).

Riccardo, (1) the Count of Chalais (tenor), lover of Maria di Rohan, in DONIZETTI's MARIA DI ROHAN.

(2) Governor of Boston or King of Sweden (tenor) in VERDI's UN BALLO IN MASCHERA.

rice aria, *see* DI TANTI PALPITI.

Richard Coeur de Lion (Richard the Lion-hearted), opera in three acts by GRÉTRY. Libretto by Michel Jean Sedaine. Premiere: Comédie-Italienne, Paris, Oct. 21, 1784. American premiere: Boston, Jan. 23, 1793. For years, Blondel, Richard's minstrel, wanders about disguised as a blind singer. He discovers that his king is imprisoned, and with the aid of an exiled English knight and Marguerite of Flanders, he effects Richard's escape. A familiar aria is that of Blondel, "O Richard, o mon roi!" BEETHOVEN wrote a set of piano variations (Op. 184) on another air from this opera, "UNE FIÈVRE BRULANTE."

Richardson, Samuel, novelist. Born Derbyshire, Eng., 1689; died London, July 4, 1761. His most famous novel, *Pamela, or Virtue Rewarded,* dealing with the social and sexual pitfalls confronting a virtuous servant, was made into several operas, including: PICCINNI's *La buona figliuola;* Pietro Generali's *Pamela nubile;* Tommaso Traetta's *La* *buona figliuola maritata.* Another Richardson novel, *Clarissa Harlowe,* was made into an opera by BIZET.

Richepin, Jean, poet, novelist, playwright. Born Médéa, Algiers, Feb. 4, 1849; died Paris, Sept. 12, 1926. He adapted his own novel *Miarka* as a libretto for an opera by Alexandre Georges, and *Le Mage* for an opera by MASSENET. Other Richepin works used for operas include *Le Chemineau* (LEROUX), *Le Filibustier* (CUI) and *La Glu* (Gabriel Dupont).

Richter, Hans, conductor. Born Raab, Hungary, Apr. 4, 1843; died Bayreuth, Dec. 5, 1916. One of the most celebrated Wagnerian conductors, he began his career as a choirboy at the Vienna court. From 1860 to 1865 he attended the Vienna Conservatory. In 1866 he went to live with WAGNER at Lucerne. Here he copied the score of DIE MEISTERSINGER and played the organ and piano for Wagner. On Wagner's recommendation, he became chorus director of the MUNICH OPERA, and on Mar. 22, 1870, he directed the first Brussels performance of LOHENGRIN. From 1871 to 1875 he was a conductor of the BUDAPEST OPERA. In 1875 he was appointed principal conductor of the VIENNA OPERA, becoming music director in 1893. In 1876 he was invited by Wagner to direct the first complete performance of the RING at BAYREUTH. When the festival ended he was decorated with the Order of Maximilian by the King of Bavaria and the Falkenorder by the Duke of Weimar. He remained a principal conductor at Bayreuth up to the time of his retirement.

In 1877 he visited London and alternated with Wagner in directing a festival of Wagner's music. His second visit to London, in 1879, was such a success that the Richter Concerts were established, and they continued for almost twenty years. In 1882 he led at DRURY LANE the first performances in England of *Die Meistersinger* and TRISTAN UND ISOLDE. After 1897 he was the principal conductor of the Hallé Orchestra. He led his last symphony concert with that orchestra on Apr. 11, 1911, and his last opera performance a year later with the Vienna Opera *(Die Meistersinger)*. He then went into retirement in Bayreuth.

Ricki, leading female character (soprano) in FRANCHETTI'S GERMANIA.

Ricordi & Company, the leading music publishers of Italy. The house was founded in 1808 by Giovanni Ricordi, who originally made his own engravings. As a friend of ROSSINI, Ricordi (1785–1853) acquired the publishing rights to his operas. He recognized VERDI's genius when that composer was still largely unknown. Over the years the house of Ricordi had a far-reaching influence in establishing the reputations of other Italian composers. As friends and advisers, Giovanni Ricordi's direct descendants Tito (1811–1888) and Guilio (1840–1912) were especially important in the careers of Verdi and PUCCINI. The Ricordi archives contain the manuscripts of over five hundred operas which the company has published. An American branch of the company was established in 1897.

Ride of the Valkyries, The, music accompanying the flight of the Valkyries on their steeds in the opening of Act III of WAGNER'S DIE WALKÜRE.

Riders to the Sea, opera in one act by VAUGHAN WILLIAMS. Libretto is John Millington SYNGE's drama of the same name. Premiere: London, Dec. 1, 1937 (amateur); Cambridge, Feb. 22, 1938 (professional). American premiere: Cleveland, Feb. 26, 1950. The setting is a seacoast town of Ireland, where the sea destroys the husband and all the sons of Mauyra. The opera was revived in New York in a concert presentation on Jan. 27, 1970.

Rienzi, the Last of the Tribunes, opera in five acts by WAGNER. Libretto by the composer, based on the novel of the same name by BULWER-LYTTON. Premiere: Dresden Opera, Oct. 20, 1842. American premiere: Academy of Music, New York, Mar. 4, 1878. In Rome in the fourteenth century, Irene (soprano), sister of Cola di Rienzi (tenor, a role created by Joseph TICHATSCHEK), is abducted by the Orsinis and is rescued by Adriano Colonna (mezzo-soprano), of a rival faction. After a struggle between the Orsinis and the Colonnas, Rienzi appears, decrying the degradation of Rome and the despotism of the nobles. He contrives the overthrow of the nobles at the hands of the people. Peace now prevails, with Rienzi the ruler of Rome. But Paolo Orsini (bass) and Steffano Colonna (bass) plot Rienzi's death. Their plot is frustrated and Rienzi nobly forgives them. Now acquiring the support of the Church, the followers of Orsini and Colonna stir the people to revolt. The Capitol is set afire and the heroic Rienzi and his sister perish, joined in death by Adriano, who loves but cannot save Irene.

Rienzi is the earliest of Wagner's operas which is still occasionally performed. He completed it in 1840, in his twenty-seventh year. When introduced in Dresden, the opera was an outstanding success. It became the most popular opera in the repertory that year and made Wagner's name known throughout Germany for the first time. The stirring overture is frequently performed. It contains material from the opera itself, including the people's prayer at the end of Act I, "Gegrüsst sei hoher Tag," Rienzi's battle hymn in Act III, "Sancto spirito cavaliere," and Rienzi's fifth-act prayer, "Allmächt'ger Vater, blick' herab." Other distinguished excerpts are the march and ballet music in the second act; the song of the messenger of peace, "Ich sah die Stadts," which opens the second act; and Adriano's SCENA in the third act, "Gerechter Gott."

rigaudon, a lively dance, probably of Provençal origin, in either 2/4 or 4/4 time. It appears in eighteenth-century operas, for example, in HANDEL's ALMIRA and RAMEAU's DARDANUS and *Platée*.

Rigoletto, opera in three acts (usually given as four) by VERDI. Libretto by Francesco PIAVE, based on Victor HUGO's play, *Le Roi s'amuse*. Premiere: Teatro la Fenice, Mar. 11, 1851. American premiere: Academy of Music, Feb. 19, 1855.

Characters: Rigoletto, hunchback jester to the Duke of Mantua (baritone), a role created by Felice VARESI; Gilda, his daughter (soprano); Giovanna, her nurse (mezzo-soprano); Duke of Mantua (tenor); Sparafucile, a hired assassin (bass); Maddalena, his sister (contralto); Count Ceprano, a courtier (bass); Countess Ceprano, his wife (mezzo-soprano); Count Monterone (baritone); Borsa, a courtier (tenor); Marullo, another courtier (baritone); courtiers; ladies; gentlemen; servants. The action takes place in Mantua in the sixteenth century.

Act I, Scene 1. The Duke's palace. There is a brief orchestral prelude, making use of the curse motive. During a party, the Duke confides to one of his courtiers that he is attracted to a girl who frequents a nearby church but whose identity is unknown to him. He also finds the beautiful Countess Ceprano alluring, and to the courtier, Borsa, he speaks flippantly of love (Ballata: "Questa o quella"). As the Duke's orchestra strikes up a minuet, the Duke dances with the Countess Ceprano, arousing the jealousy of her husband. Rigoletto, the deformed jester, cruelly comments on the jealousy; at the same time he is the butt of mockery by the courtiers, who hint he is concealing a young girl in his house. The Duke tells his jester he would like to get rid of the Count. Rigoletto's sarcastic suggestions of imprisonment and murder anger the Duke, just as Rigoletto's remarks arouse the anger of the courtiers ("Vendetta del pazzo"). Count Monterone makes a sudden appearance, denouncing the Duke for ruining his daughter. The Duke orders his arrest. As the Count is led away, Rigoletto taunts him. Monterone turns to the hunchback and curses him so violently that Rigoletto recoils in horror.

Scene 2. A deserted street. Rigoletto is stopped by Sparafucile, an assassin for hire. But Rigoletto is not interested. Sparafucile departs, leaving Rigoletto to muse on his objectionable employment with the Duke and his unpleasant duty of having to find mistresses for him ("Pari siamo"). He now enters his own courtyard, and his daughter Gilda comes to greet him. She begs him to tell her of her dead mother, and Rigoletto complies ("Deh! non parlare al misero"). He then warns her that they are surrounded by enemies and that she must be ever on her guard. Hearing a sound in the street, Rigoletto runs out to investigate. The Duke, disguised as a student, slips into the courtyard to woo Gilda, for it is she whom he has admired at her church. Rigoletto now takes leave of his daughter, unaware of the Duke's presence. Gilda is apprehensive at the appearance of the stranger, but he soothes her with a love song ("É il sol dell' anima"). Believing the Duke's word that he is a humble student, Gilda falls in love, and after the Duke leaves, she dreams of him ("Caro nome"). Some of the Duke's courtiers, headed by Ceprano, now come to avenge themselves on Rigoletto for his cruel taunts. Believing Gilda to be Rigoletto's mistress, they plan to abduct her. When Rigoletto returns, he is told by the masked men that they wish to abduct Ceprano's wife for the Duke's pleasure. Slyly, they enlist Rigoletto's help, tie a cloth over his eyes, and place a ladder against the jester's house, Rigoletto believing that the house is Count Ceprano's across the street. The courtiers abduct Gilda ("Zitti, zitti moviamo a vendetta") and vanish. The jester removes the bandage from his eyes, discovers how he has been tricked, and realizes with horror that Monterone's curse of a father upon another father has begun to work its evil.

Act II. The Duke's palace. The Duke is upset, for, having visited Gilda again, he has found her gone ("Parmi veder le lagrime"). His courtiers try to amuse him with the story of their abduction of Rigoletto's "mistress," whom they have brought to the palace. The Duke goes to meet the "mistress." Rigoletto arrives, disheveled and distraught. He tries to force his way past the courtiers

to the Duke's private chambers, denouncing them bitterly ("Cortigiani, vil razza dannata"), and crying that Gilda is his daughter. Gilda enters in tears, having yielded to the Duke. She rushes into her father's arms. But to her father's amazement, she is not distressed, but rapturous, since after her harrowing abduction she has been united with her admirer of the courtyard. As Rigoletto realizes the hideous treachery that has been worked upon him, he swears vengeance upon the Duke.

Act III. Sparafucile's inn. The Duke appears, disguised as a soldier. He calls for wine, cynically commenting on the fickleness of all women ("La donna è mobile"). He then attempts to make a conquest of Maddalena, Sparafucile's sister, who has been the means of luring him to this out-of-the-way spot. Rigoletto and Gilda watch the scene from outside, the jester desiring his daughter to see for herself the sort of man she has cherished. While Rigoletto speaks of his imminent revenge, and Gilda bitterly remarks on her lover's infidelity, Maddalena, within, skillfully leads the Duke on (Quartet: "Bella figlia dell' amore"). Rigoletto now sends his daughter off to shelter in Verona, after which he meets Sparafucile and gives him half his fee to deliver the Duke's body in a sack at midnight. But Maddalena has now become fond of the Duke, and she entreats her brother to spare him. Sparafucile, a man of his word, insists that the hunchback is entitled to a corpse, but he agrees to kill another man in the Duke's place —should another turn up before midnight. Gilda, having crept back to the inn to see her perfidious lover, overhears this evil agreement and sees in it the means of saving the Duke's life as well as ending her own disgrace and sorrow. Dressed as a cavalier for her intended journey to Verona, she enters Sparafucile's inn at the height of a thunderstorm, and in the flickering light, is mistaken for a man. Soon, Rigoletto returns, pays the assassin the rest of his fee, and starts dragging the heavy sack toward the river. At this moment, within the inn, the Duke resumes his lighthearted song about women ("La donna è mobile"). Rigoletto tears open the sack and finds within it his daughter, dying. Grief-stricken, he takes her in his arms; father and daughter bid one another a last farewell ("Lassù in cielo"). The curse of Monterone has been realized.

Verdi wrote fifteen operas before *Rigoletto,* the first of his works destined to occupy a permanent place in the repertory of every leading opera house. *Rigoletto* was also the first of his operas to indicate the range of his lyric genius; it overflows with wonderful arias, duets, and ensemble numbers, one following the other in a seemingly endless procession of melodic beauty. Riches found in this score include one of the most celebrated tenor arias in all opera ("La donna è mobile") one of the most brilliant of all coloratura arias ("Caro nome"), and one of the greatest vocal quartets ever written ("Bella figlia"). But *Rigoletto* has interest apart from its wonderful melodies. This is the first of Verdi's operas in which the composer strikingly revealed his impressive sense of drama and trenchant musical characterization.

Rimsky-Korsakov, Nikolai, composer. Born Tikhvin, Novgorod, Russia, Mar. 18, 1844; died St. Petersburg, June 21, 1908. A leading figure of the Russian national school, and the composer of several distinguished operas, Rimsky-Korsakov was trained for a naval career. A meeting with Mili Balakirev fired him with musical enthusiasm, and he began writing a symphony, despite his inadequate knowledge. In the fall of 1862 he set out on a two-and-a-half year cruise as naval officer that brought him to the United States in 1864 and returned him to Russia in 1865. While stationed in St. Petersburg, he became intimate with Balakirev and his circle and plunged into a vigorous course of self-instruction, making himself easily the ablest theoretician and orchestrater of the FIVE. (Eventually he wrote the standard text

on orchestration used at the turn of the century in most conservatories of the Western world.) He now completed the symphony he had begun a few years earlier. Introduced under Balakirev's direction on Dec. 19, 1865, it was well received. The composer now planned several ambitious works, national in style and idiom, including the *Antar* symphony and his first opera, THE MAID OF PSKOV. The opera was completed in 1872 and was acclaimed when introduced at the Maryinsky Theater on Jan. 13, 1873. The work's success led the government to relieve Rimsky-Korsakov of most of his naval duties so that he could concentrate on music. The special post of Inspector of Naval Bands was created for him. During the next few years he not only led the band concerts but distinguished himself as a conductor of the Free Music Society and the Russian Symphony Concerts. He also became a professor at the St. Petersburg Conservatory. Between 1878 and 1881 Rimsky-Korsakov completed two operas, MAY NIGHT and THE SNOW MAIDEN. For several years after 1881 he applied himself to the task of editing works by GLINKA and MUSSORGSKY. In 1887 he was again productive as a composer, completing some of his most famous orchestral works (including *Scheherezade*) and the opera *Mlada.* Fatigue and inertia attacked him in 1891. For more than two years he was incapable of writing music. When this mental torpor passed, he completed an opera, CHRISTMAS EVE, in 1894. Of the numerous stage works that followed, the two best were SADKO (1896) and LE COQ D'OR (1907).

In 1905 Rimsky-Korsakov was dismissed from his conservatory post for siding with the students in some protests against administrative and regulative practices. He was later reinstated, after the conservatory had effected some needed reforms. Three years later the composer died of a heart attack.

While he is now best known for his orchestral music, it is in his operas that Rimsky-Korsakov made his most imaginative and original contributions. His operas differed radically from those of his colleagues. Mussorgsky was the realist; BORODIN, the Oriental. Rimsky-Korsakov created a make-believe world in which, as Gerald Abraham said, reality was "inextricably confused with the fantastic, naivete with sophistication, the romantic with the humorous, and beauty with absurdity."

His operas: *The Maid of Pskov* (or IVAN THE TERRIBLE) (1873, revised 1878 and 1893); *May Night* (1880); *The Snow Maiden* (1882); *Mlada* (1892); *Christmas Eve* (1895); *Sadko* (1898); *Mozart and Salieri* (1898); *Boyarina Vera Sheloga,* originally a prologue to *The Maid of Pskov,* but subsequently made into an independent opera (1898); *The Czar's Bride* (1899); THE LEGEND OF THE CZAR SALTAN (1900); *Servilia* (1902); *Kastchei the Immortal* (1902); *Pan Voyevoda* (1904); THE LEGEND OF THE INVISIBLE CITY OF KITEZH (1907); *Le Coq d'or* (1907).

Rinaldo, (1) opera by HANDEL. Libretto by Giacomo Rossi, after an episode in TASSO'S JERUSALEM DELIVERED. Premiere: Haymarket Theatre, London, Feb. 24, 1711. This was the first opera Handel produced in England. It was a major success, and its melodies and dances were heard throughout London. The aria "Cara sposa" became a favorite harpsichord piece, and the march was adopted as a regimental number by the London Life Guards. This march was also used for the highwaymen's chorus in THE BEGGAR'S OPERA. The contralto aria "Lascia ch'io pianga" is still frequently heard. GLUCK's opera ARMIDE is based on the same Tasso episode.

(2) A knight (tenor), leader of the Crusades, in GLUCK'S ARMIDE.

Ring des Nibelungen, Der (The Ring of the Nibelung), a cycle of four music dramas (called by the composer a trilogy, the first drama being considered a prelude to the remaining three), comprising DAS RHEINGOLD, DIE WALKÜRE, SIEGFRIED, and GÖTTERDÄMMERUNG. Premiere (of entire cycle): Bayreuth, Aug. 13, 14, 16, and 17, 1876. American pre-

miere (of entire cycle): Metropolitan Opera, Mar. 4, 5, 8, 11, 1889.

(1) **Das Rheingold (The Rhinegold),** prelude (*vorabend*) in one act (four scenes). Premiere: Hof-und-National-Theater, Munich, Sept. 22, 1869. American premiere: Metropolitan Opera, Jan. 4, 1889.

Characters: Wotan, ruler of the gods (bass-baritone); Donner, thunder god (bass); Froh, god of joy (tenor); Loge, fire god (tenor); Fricka, Wotan's wife (mezzo-soprano); Freia, goddess of beauty and youth, sister of Fricka (soprano); Erda, earth goddess (contralto); Fasolt, giant (bass); Fafner, giant (bass); Alberich, king of the Nibelungs (baritone); Mime, Alberich's brother (tenor); Woglinde, a Rhine maiden (soprano); Wellgunde, Rhine maiden (soprano); Flosshilde, Rhine maiden (contralto). The settings are the bottom of the Rhine, mountain summits near the Rhine, and the caverns of Nibelheim in legendary times.

Scene 1. The bottom of the Rhine. A one hundred thirty-six-measure prelude, based on the E-flat chord, grows and expands to suggest the flow of the Rhine. Three Rhine maidens guard a treasure of magic gold. He who gains the gold and fashions it into a ring may rule the world, but only if before making the ring, he renounces love. Alberich, a misshapen dwarf, shouts his renunciation of love and makes off with the gold. The Rhine maidens bewail their loss.

Scene 2. A mountaintop. Wotan and Fricka learn that the new palace built for them by the giants Fasolt and Fafner is finished. Fricka reminds Wotan that the giants must be paid, and the payment promised is her sister, Freia. Wotan insists he was jesting when he had suggested Freia as the price. When the giants come for Freia, Loge suggests a substitute payment: the gold and the ring that Alberich has molded. The giants are willing to accept the gold.

Scene 3. Alberich's cave. Mime, Alberich's brother, has fashioned a helmet, the Tarnhelm, which will give its wearer any form he desires. Wotan and Loge enter the cave and through guile are able to get Alberich to put on the Tarnhelm and transform himself into a toad. He is then easily captured and taken to Valhalla.

Scene 4. A mountain slope near Valhalla. Alberich is compelled to bring up from his caverns all the wealth of the Nibelungs. When the gods insist that he also turn over the golden ring, he curses them. The ring, he cries, will bring disaster to its owner. When Fasolt and Fafner come for their payment, Erda rises from the earth to warn Wotan to surrender the ring (Erda's Warning: "Weiche, Wotan, weiche!"), for Alberich's curse is upon it. So Wotan hurls the ring at the giants. They fight over it, and Fasolt is killed: already the ring is fulfilling Alberich's curse. The gods now enter their new abode ("Entrance of the gods into Valhalla"), to majestic music developed from the motives of Donner, the Rainbow, and Valhalla.

(2) **Die Walküre (The Valkyrie)**, music drama in three acts. Premiere: Munich, Hof-und-National-Theater, June 26, 1870. American premiere: Academy of Music, New York, Apr. 2, 1877.

Characters: Wotan, ruler of the gods (bass-baritone); Fricka, his wife (mezzo-soprano); Brünnhilde, his daughter (soprano); Siegmund, a Wälsung, son of Wotan by a mortal woman (tenor); Sieglinde, a Wälsung, Siegmund's twin sister (soprano); Hunding, her husband (bass); Valkyries.

Act I. Interior of Hunding's house. A brief prelude describes a raging storm. Siegmund bursts into the house, seeking refuge. Exhausted, he stretches wearily before the fire. Sieglinde finds him there, brings him water, and urges him to be a guest. Upon Hunding's arrival, Siegmund is invited to partake of their meal, during which Siegmund tells his hosts all he knows about himself: during a hunt with his father, their house burned down and his twin sister disappeared; subsequently, his father disappeared, and he himself is fated to be a lonely wanderer. Hunding recognizes Siegmund as his enemy, one of the tribe

of Wälsungs, but the laws of hospitality dictate that Siegmund be unharmed as long as he is under Hunding's roof. When Siegmund is left alone he laments the fact that he is in his enemy's house unarmed and that a promise made by his father that he would find a powerful sword has not been kept ("Ein Schwert verhiess mir der Vater"). When Hunding is asleep, Sieglinde comes to Siegmund. She reveals how she was forced to marry Hunding and how, at the wedding feast, a one-eyed stranger plunged a sword into the tree around which Hunding's house is built, prophesying that a hero-warrior would someday remove it. Siegmund exclaims that he will withdraw the sword and avenge Sieglinde. Before he can do so, the door swings open and moonlight floods the room. Siegmund and Sieglinde embrace in a sudden recognition of their love for each other. He tells her of his love ("Winterstürme wichen dem Wonnemond"), and Sieglinde responds with equal ardor ("Du bist der Lenz"). They now know that they are Wälsungs, twin brother and sister, and that it was their father, Wotan, who left the sword in the tree. Siegmund withdraws the sword ("Nothung! so nenn ich dich, Schwert") and escapes with Sieglinde into the night.

Act II. A mountain pass. Brünnhilde, standing on a rocky peak, gives her battle cry ("Ho-jo-to-ho!"). Fricka is angered that Siegmund is to be helped, insisting that the unholy lovers must be punished. Wotan argues in favor of protecting Siegmund so that he can fulfill his mission ("Der alte Sturm"), but in the end gives in to Fricka. Now ordered to deny protection to Siegmund and Sieglinde, Brünnhilde retires in despair. Fleeing from Hunding, Siegmund and Sieglinde reach the rocky declivity, and as Sieglinde takes a badly needed nap, Brünnhilde apears before Siegmund to warn him that his sword has lost its power and that in the coming fight with Hunding he must die (Todesverkündigung: "Siegmund! sieh' auf mich!"). Siegmund maintains he will kill both himself and Sieglinde rather than permit their separation. This so moves Brünnhilde that she decides, in spite of her father's orders, to help him. When Hunding's horn is heard in the distance, Siegmund goes forth to meet him in battle. Brünnhilde tries to protect him. But Wotan intervenes and brings about Siegmund's death. Lifting Sieglinde and the pieces of Siegmund's broken sword, Brünnhilde hastens away. Wotan now destroys Hunding and wrathfully vows to punish his rebellious daughter.

Act III. The summit of a mountain. The curtain rises to the Ride of the Valkyries (Walkürenritt) as the Valkyries on their magic steeds ride and call to each other. Brünnhilde appears with Sieglinde, and tells her sisters how she has incurred their father's anger. The Valkyries are sympathetic but cannot help. Giving Sieglinde the pieces of her brother's sword, Brünnhilde sends her away to bear his child, destined one day to become a hero. Wotan appears. Brünnhilde pleads with her father: Has her sin after all, been so grievous? (Brünnhilde's Plea: "War es so schmälich?"). Wotan's anger now turns to pity and love for his favorite daughter. But she must be punished. Deprived of her godhood, she will be put to sleep, protected by a circle of flame; the first man penetrating the fire and awakening her will become her husband. Embracing Brünnhilde, Wotan bids her a tender farewell (Wotan's Farewell: "Leb' wohl, du kühnes, herrliches Kind"). He places her on a rock, covers her with her shield, and orders Loge, god of fire, to surround her with flames (Feuerzauber, Magic Fire Scene). The fire gradually surrounds the rock as Wotan sadly departs.

(3) **Siegfried,** music drama in three acts. Premiere: Bayreuth, Aug. 16, 1876. American premiere: Metropolitan Opera, Nov. 9, 1887.

Characters: Siegfried, son of Siegmund and Sieglinde (tenor); Mime, a Nibelung (tenor); Alberich, his brother (baritone); Wotan (bass-baritone); Brünnhilde, his daughter (soprano); Erda, earth goddess (con-

tralto); Forest Bird (soprano); Fafner, giant transformed into a dragon (bass).

Act I. Mime's cave. A short prelude comprises the motives of Mime and the Sword. Mime is working at an anvil, trying to forge the broken sword, Nothung, which Sieglinde had left for her son, Siegfried. He becomes impatient as he fails to mend the parts ("Zwangvolle Plage!"), for he knows that if Nothung can be made whole, he will have a weapon that could slay the dragon Fafner, permitting recovery of the gold which the dragon guards. As the dwarf continues with his futile labors, Siegfried enters, leading a bear by a rope. Siegfried, who detests Mime, frightens him with the bear. Since Siegfried knows that Mime is not his father, he questions him about his origin. Terrified, Mime answers Siegfried by telling him that he is the son of Sieglinde, who died when giving birth to him and who left him the broken pieces of Nothung that, when mended, will be an invincible weapon; also, that he, Mime, has raised Siegfried in the forest. Ordering Mime to mend the sword, Siegfried leaves the cave. Wotan appears, disguised as a mortal who calls himself the Wanderer, and Mime learns that only a man without fear can forge Nothung; also, that he who forges the sword will demand Mime's head as a prize. After Wotan leaves, Mime discovers to his horror that Siegfried has never heard the word or experienced the emotion of fear. And his terror mounts when Siegfried goes to work at the anvil to forge the sword himself (Forge Song: "Nothung! Nothung!"). Mime stealthily prepares a poison to destroy Siegfried after Fafner is overcome. The sword is finally forged ("Ho-Ho! Schmiede, mein Hammer"); Siegfried triumphantly leaves with it.

Act II. Fafner's cave. Alberich, awaiting Siegfried at Fafner's cave, is told by Wotan that Siegfried will capture the magic ring; Wotan urges Alberich to convince Fafner to give up the ring before it is too late. Upset by these developments, Alberich departs, vowing to avenge himself against Wotan. Siegfried appears, followed by Mime, urging him on to destroy Fafner. While Mime waits at a nearby spring, Siegfried stretches out under a tree, enjoying the beauty of the forest and the songs of the birds (Waldweben, Forest Murmurs). Then, sounding his horn, he rouses Fafner. After he has killed the dragon, some of its blood burns his hand. Instinctively, Siegfried raises his hand to his lips. The blood has magic powers, and the taste of it enables Siegfried to understand the language of the birds. Listening to their songs, which tell him of the Tarnhelm and the ring ("Göntest du mir wohl"), he learns that the cave contains the treasures. While Siegfried is in the cave, seeking them, Alberich and Mime appear, quarreling as to which shall now have Fafner's treasures. When Siegfried appears with the ring and the Tarnhelm, Alberich hurries away. Mime tries to cajole Siegfried, but Siegfried is now able to understand Mime's true intentions. When Mime hands him a drinking horn containing poison, Siegfried slays him. He then lies to rest under a tree. The song of the Forest Bird reveals to him that Brünnhilde lies asleep on a rock, waiting to be awakened by a hero. Siegfried entreats the Bird to lead him to her.

Act III, Scene 1. A wild glen. Wotan summons Erda to tell her he no longer fears doom, since destiny lies in the hands of the hero, Siegfried. He then orders Erda back into the bowels of the earth. When Siegfried approaches, Wotan (still wearing mortal guise) queries his grandson about Mime, the dragon, and the sword. Impatient with this colloquy and angered at the way the mysterious Wanderer blocks his way, Siegfried shatters Wotan's spear with his sword. Then, blowing his horn, he advances toward the sleeping Brünnhilde.

Scene 2. Brünnhilde's rock. Siegfried passes through the flames that ring the sleeping maiden. He bends down to kiss her on her lips. Brünnhilde awakens and greets the hero ecstatically ("Siegfried, seliger Held"). They embrace ("Heil dir, Sonne!"), and are transfigured by love ("Leuchtende Liebe! lachender Tod!").

(4) **Götterdämmerung (The Twilight of the Gods),** music drama in three acts and a prologue. Premiere: Bayreuth, Aug. 17, 1876. American premiere: Metropolitan Opera, Jan. 25, 1888.

Characters: Brünnhilde (soprano); Siegfried (tenor); Alberich (baritone); Gunther, chief of the Gibichungs (bass); Gutrune, his sister (soprano); Hagen, Gunther's half brother (bass); Waltraute, a Valkyrie (mezzo-soprano); three Norns; Rhine maidens; vassals; warriors; women.

Prologue. Brünnhilde's rock. The three Norns are spinning the fate of the world. When the thread breaks, they realize that doom is at hand. At dawn, Brünnhilde and Siegfried appear. Brünnhilde is leading her horse, Grane, while Siegfried is dressed in full armor. She is sending the hero off to seek adventure ("Zu neuen Thaten, theurer Held"). Siegfried bids her farewell, vowing to love her forever; as a token of his love, he leaves her the ring. Taking Grane and carrying the Tarnhelm and Nothung, Siegfried sounds his horn and sets forth (SIEGFRIED'S RHINE JOURNEY).

Act I, Scene 1. The hall of the Gibichungs. Concerned over the future of the Gibichungs, Hagen tells his half brother, Gunther, that he must marry Brünnhilde, and Siegfried must marry Gunther's sister, Gutrune. Hagen has a scheme to bring this about: when Siegfried comes to the hall, Hagen will make him drink a potion bringing on forgetfulness; Siegfried will then fall in love with Gutrune and help them gain Brünnhilde for Gunther. The sound of Siegfried's horn announces the arrival of the hero. After Siegfried is welcomed, he drinks the potion, instantly loses his memory, and falls in love with Gutrune. Gunther promises Siegfried he can have Gutrune but only if he will help him get Brünnhilde. After an oath of brotherhood ("Blühenden Lebens labendes Blut"), Gunther and Siegfried set forth.

Scene 2. Brünnhilde's rock. Waltraute comes to tell Brünnhilde that Wotan and the gods face a doom that can be prevented only if Brünnhilde returns Siegfried's ring to the Rhine maidens (Waltraute's Narrative: "Seit er von dir geschieden"). Brünnhilde refuses to give up this symbol of Siegfried's love. After Waltraute goes, Siegfried arrives. Brünnhilde is shocked to see a stranger: for through the magic of the Tarnhelm, Siegfried has transformed himself into Gunther. He tears the ring from her finger and seizes her.

Act II. Before the hall of the Gibichungs. Alberich informs Hagen that he must secure the ring ("Schläfst du, Hagen") and Hagen assures him that he will. Siegfried has come back to claim Gutrune as his bride. Hagen sounds the call for his vassals and invites them to a marriage feast. The vassals acclaim Gunther when he arrives with his bride-to-be, Brünnhilde. When Brünnhilde sees Siegfried (now in his own form), she is overwhelmed with gloomy thoughts. The sight of the ring on his finger convinces her that he has abandoned her for Gutrune. She is appalled when Siegfried acts as if he did not know who she was and when he makes an oath on his spear that Brünnhilde is not his wife ("Helle Wehr"). When she learns that Hagen and Alberich are planning to kill Siegfried, she becomes their ally.

Act III, Scene 1. The bank of the Rhine. The Rhine maidens beg Siegfried, who has become separated from his hunting party, for the ring. When he refuses to give it up, the maidens prophesy his doom. Gunther, Hagen, and their vassals catch up with Siegfried. The hero is given a potion that restores his memory of Brünnhilde. As Siegfried rapturously recalls his awakening of her, Hagen plunges his spear into Siegfried's back. With his dying breath the hero bids the absent Brünnhilde farewell ("Brünnhilde! heilige Braut!"). His body is lifted and borne in a solemn procession (Siegfrieds Tod, Siegfried's Funeral Music).

Scene 2. The hall of the Gibichungs. Gutrune watches with horror as the vassals bring in Siegfried's body. At first Gunther says that Siegfried was killed by a wild boar, but he finally names Hagen as the murderer. Hagen kills Gunther in a dispute over the ring. When Hagen reaches for Siegfried's hand to tear off the ring, the dead hand rises threateningly. Brünnhilde now orders a funeral pyre built. She sets it aflame, hails Siegfried and reaffirms her love for him ("Wie Sonne lauter strahlt mir sein Licht"), mounts her horse, and rides to her death in the flames (Immolation Scene: "Starke Scheite schichtet mir dort"). The Rhine rises, and out of its crest swim the Rhine maidens to retrieve the ring. Hagen, attempting to save the ring, is seized and carried beneath the flood. The river subsides. In the distance, Valhalla crumbles in flames, destroying the gods.

Wagner finished the texts of his four Ring dramas in reverse order. In 1848 he began sketching a single drama which he called Siegfrieds Tod. He found that it needed a second play to provide prefatory material; consequently, he began writing Der junge Siegfried. He then felt the need for a third, then a fourth, text for background explanations. Thus, Götterdämmerung (the original Siegfrieds Tod) was written first, and Das Rheingold last. By 1853 the four texts were published. A year later, Wagner began writing the music for Das Rheingold; that for Götterdämmerung was at last completed in 1874. The Ring cycle, then, occupied Wagner for a quarter of a century, a period that also saw the completion and performance of TRISTAN UND ISOLDE and DIE MEISTERSINGER. Wagner did not think he would live to see The Ring performed. He knew that a work requiring four full evenings for performance and demanding tremendous musical and stage forces would not find a sympathetic response from impresarios. Yet, even with the belief that his manuscript might lie untouched, he kept on composing, for The Ring represented the summit toward which he had all the time been climbing, his ultimate goal as a creative artist. The Ring was not only Wagner's most ambitious work, it was the one in which he most completely realized his theories about the music drama. Nowhere was he more adventurous in projecting his ideas about stage direction and scene design. Nowhere was his music a more continuous flow of expressive melody. Nowhere was he more prodigal in his use of musical resources. The LEITMOTIV technique appears in his other dramas, but in *The Ring* the leading motives are the spine and sinew of the musical texture.

The Ring was also Wagner's chief musical embodiment of his ethical and social thinking. In the pursuit of golden treasure, gods as well as men were destroyed. Siegfried was Wagner's conception of the Nietzschean Superman, come to redeem the world from avarice and fear.

Rinuccini, Ottavio, poet and librettist. Born Florence, Italy, Jan. 20, 1562; died there Mar. 28, 1621. As a member of the Florentine CAMERATA he wrote the librettos for the earliest operas: CACCINI's EURIDICE; Gagliano's DAFNE; MONTEVERDI's *Arianna* and *Il ballo delle ingrate;* PERI's *Dafne* and *Euridice.*

Rinuccio, Zita's nephew (tenor) in PUCCINI's GIANNI SCHICCHI.

Rip Van Winkle, (1) a story by Washington IRVING, originally published in *The Sketch Book.* The tale concerns the twenty-year enchanted sleep of the hero in the Catskills; he awakens an old man, the world around him completely changed. George Frederick Bristow's *Rip Van Winkle* was one of the first operas by an American on a native subject. The French composer of OPÉRAS BOUFFES Jean-Robert PLANQUETTE also wrote a work on this theme.

(2) Opera in three acts by DE KOVEN. Libretto by Percy MacKaye, based on the Washington Irving story. Premiere: Chicago Opera Company, Jan. 2, 1920. In this adaptation, Rip Van Winkle is the victim of a sleeping potion, and instead of a nagging wife, he has a sweetheart.

Rise and Fall of the City Mahagonny, The (Aufsteig und Fall der Stadt Maha-gonny), opera in three acts by WEILL. Libretto by Bertolt BRECHT. Premiere: Leipzig Opera and Frankfurt Opera simultaneously, Mar. 9, 1930. American premiere: New York City, Feb. 23, 1952 (concert version) ; New York City, Mar. 4, 1970 (staged). In 1927 Weill and Brecht had written a one-act "song play" called *Mahagonny,* made up of sprightly choruses and lyrics, embracing jazz, music-hall tunes, folksongs, and marching songs. Introduced at the Baden-Baden Festival in Germany, it proved a shock to audiences come to hear something avant-garde and confronted with popular music. After THE THREEPENNY OPERA proved a triumph, Weill and Brecht decided to expand their one-act musical into a full-length opera. Its simultaneous premiere caused a furor, with Nazis provoking riots and with fights breaking out within the theaters between those who liked it and those who considered it degenerate. There was a good deal in Brecht's text to cause shock. The setting is a fictional town in Alabama in the United States—Mahagonny. Three ex-convicts decide to build here a new society where people can do whatever they wish without a thought to morality or ethics, where everything is pardonable except the lack of money. Society in Mahagonny disintegrates as Brecht lays bare the hypocrisy, corruption, and decadence of modern materialism. An economic crash and a devastating hurricane nearly bring about the destruction of Mahagonny. But Mahagonny withstands them just as it has withstood the vices of its citizens. The final irony comes when Trinity's Moses tries to consign the degenerates of Mahagonny to Hell and finds he cannot do so because the people are already living in a hell. Weill's score includes popular tunes, music-hall melodies, the blues and ragtime, together with dissonant modernism of its own time. A hit number (indeed one of Germany's leading song hits in the early 1930's) was the "Alabamy Song," presented by the heroine, Jenny, with a chorus of six girls. This song has an English title because the lyric is in gibberish English. A lively men's chorus, "Erstens, vergesst nicht, kommt den Fressen," reminds the people of Mahagonny that first in importance comes eating, then love, then boxing, then drinking, and that in this town people are permitted to do anything they wish. *The Rise and Fall of the City Mahagonny* was revived in 1965 at the Stratford Summer Festival in Ontario, Canada, in 1969 by the COLOGNE OPERA and at the EDINBURGH FESTIVAL, and in 1970 in Brussels and New York City.

risurrezione, La (Resurrection), opera in four acts by Franco ALFANO. Libretto by Cesare Henau, based on Leo TOLSTOY's novel. Premiere: Turin, Nov. 30, 1904. American premiere: Chicago, Dec. 31, 1925. Prince Dimitri, about to leave with his regiment, meets and falls in love with Katusha. She becomes pregnant, but the Prince is unaware of this. Her life ruined, Katusha, after her child's death, commits a murder and is sentenced to exile in Siberia. The Prince meets her in St. Petersburg just before her exile and is overwhelmed to learn that he is the cause of her downfall. In Siberia Dimitri is finally able to gain her pardon, but she no longer loves him, having found a devoted lover in the convict Simonson. Among the notable arias is one for soprano, "Dieu de Grace," and another for tenor, "Pleure, oui, pleure."

Rita, ou Le Mari battu (Rita, or The Beaten Husband), comic opera in one act by DONIZETTI. Libretto by Vaëz. Premiere: Opéra-Comique, May 7, 1860. American premiere: New York City, May 14, 1957. This is one of its composer's last operas, having been completed in 1840. It was not performed until twelve years after the composer's death. Though rarely heard for many decades, *Rita* has been enjoying significant revivals since the 1950's, notably in Berlin, Buenos Aires, at the PICCOLA SCALA in 1957, and in Turin in 1958. It has since been performed by a number of semiprofessional and university opera laboratories in the United States.

Ritorna vincitor!, Aida's prayer for the safe return from battle of Radames, in Act I, Scene 1, of VERDI'S AIDA.

ritornello, Italian for "little repetition." In early Italian operas, a *ritornello* was a brief instrumental passage played between scenes, or between the vocal portions of a song.

ritorno d'Ulisse in patria, Il (Ulysses' Return to His Country), opera in prologue and five acts by MONTEVERDI. Libretto by Badoaro. Premiere: Venice, Feb., 1641. American premiere: New York City, May 15, 1956 (three scenes). DALLAPICCOLA, the modern Italian dodecaphonist, has made a new arrangement of this opera, which was first heard at the FLORENCE MAY MUSIC FESTIVAL in 1942. In a revised version, this Dallapiccola adaptation was heard at the HOLLAND FESTIVAL in 1962. The ROYAL OPERA OF COPENHAGEN revived it in May, 1969.

Robbins, Serena's husband (baritone) in GERSHWIN'S PORGY AND BESS.

Robert le diable (Robert the Devil), opera in five acts by MEYERBEER. Libretto by Eugène SCRIBE and Germain Delavigne. Premiere: Paris Opéra, Nov. 21, 1831. American premiere: Théâtre Orleans, New Orleans, Dec. 24, 1836. The action takes place in thirteenth-century Palermo. Robert, the Duke of Normandy (tenor), is the son of a mortal woman and a devil. That devil disguises himself as a man and assumes the name of Bertram (bass). He follows his son with the hope of gaining his soul. In Sicily Robert falls in love with the princess Isabella (soprano), and hopes to win her hand in a tournament. But the stratagems of the devil keep him from winning. Thinking that his cause is lost, Robert is willing to use diabolical means to win the woman he loves. At a midnight revel with ghosts, Robert acquires a magic branch with which he gains access to Isabella and with which he hopes to win her against her will. Isabella pleads with him to break the branch, which he finally does, destroying its magic. He is about to sign a contract with his father for the consignment of his soul to hell when he is dissuaded by his foster sister, Alice (soprano). Robert denounces his father, who returns to the lower regions. The redeemed Robert and Isabella are now united in marriage. The role of Robert was created by NOURRIT and that of the Abbess, a nonsinging part, by Taglioni, one of the greatest ballerinas of her day.

When Chopin attended the premiere, he wrote: "If ever magnificence was seen in the theater, I doubt it reached the level of splendor shown in *Robert le diable*. . . . It is a masterpiece. . . . Meyerbeer has made himself immortal." Nevertheless, the opera has achieved virtual mortality.

Robert Storch, *see* STORCH, ROBERT.

Robert, toi que j'aime, Isabella's avowal of love for Robert, in Act IV of MEYERBEER'S ROBERT LE DIABLE.

Robin Hood, opera in three acts by MACFARREN. Libretto by John Oxenford. Premiere: Her Majesty's Theatre, London, Oct. 11, 1860.

Operas on the subject of Robin Hood were also written by the early American composer James Hewitt, produced at the PARK THEATER in New York on Dec. 24, 1800, and by the eighteenth-century English composer W. Shields, presented in Charleston, S.C., on Feb. 16, 1793. DE KOVEN'S *Robin Hood* is an operetta, first produced in Chicago on June 9, 1890. From this work comes the song now so frequently heard at weddings, "Oh promise me!"

Robinson, Count, rich suitor (bass) of first Elisetta and then Carolina in CIMAROSA'S IL MATRIMONIO SEGRETO.

Rocca, Lodovico, composer. Born Turin, Nov. 29, 1895. He attended the Milan Conservatory and Turin University. His first opera, *La morte di Frine,* was produced in 1921. Success came in 1934 with *Il dibuk* (THE DYBBUK), which won first prize in a contest sponsored by LA SCALA and was produced in Milan the same year. Rocca subsequently received the MacCormack Competition and Milan Triennale prizes for the opera *In terra di leggenda.* His

other operas: *La corona di Re Gaulo* (1923); *Monte Ivnor* (1939); *L'uragano* (1952). Between 1940 and 1956 he was the director of the Turin Conservatory.

Rocco, (1) a jailer (bass) in BEETHOVEN'S FIDELIO.

(2) A Camorrist (bass) in WOLFFERRARI'S THE JEWELS OF THE MADONNA.

Rodelinda, opera in three acts by HANDEL. Libretto by Nicolo Haym. Premiere: King's Theatre, Haymarket, London, Feb. 13, 1725. American premiere: Northampton, Mass., May 9, 1931. Rodelinda, queen of the Lombards, is threatened by Grimoaldo, who has usurped power: if she is not receptive to his love, he will kill her child. The exiled king, Bertarido, returns to the palace secretly, overthrows Grimoaldo's rule, and reassumes the throne. The baritone aria "Dove sei amato bene" is popular. The dungeon scene with Bertarido is sometimes mentioned in connection with the somewhat similar scene in BEETHOVEN'S FIDELIO. After GIULIO CESARE, *Rodelinda* was Handel's most popular opera.

Roderigo, a Venetian gentleman (tenor) in VERDI'S OTELLO.

Rodolfo, (1) a count (bass) in BELLINI'S LA SONNAMBULA.

(2) A poet (tenor), in love with Mimi, in PUCCINI'S LA BOHÈME.

(3) Son of a count (tenor), in love with Luisa Miller, in VERDI'S LUISA MILLER.

Rodrigo, (1) Marquis of Posa (baritone) in VERDI'S DON CARLOS.

(2) The Cid, principal male character (tenor) in MASSENET'S LE CID.

Rodrigue, the Cid. *See* above, RODRIGO.

Rodzinski, Artur, conductor. Born Split, Yugoslavia, Jan. 2, 1894; died Boston, Nov. 27, 1958. Though most often identified as a conductor of symphonic music, Rodzinski gave distinguished performances of operas as well. He completed his training as conductor with Franz SCHALK in Vienna, following which he made his debut in Lwow in 1921. For five seasons he led Polish operas in Warsaw. Between 1929 and 1933 he was the permanent conductor of the Los Angeles Philharmonic. As the principal conductor of the Cleveland Orchestra, an appointment received in 1933, he frequently led operas in concert version, including PARSIFAL, ELEKTRA, and the American premiere of LADY MACBETH OF MZENSK in 1935. He subsequently held the posts of permanent conductor with the New York Philharmonic and the Chicago Orchestra. He also gave operatic performances at LA SCALA, at the FLORENCE MAY MUSIC FESTIVAL (where he conducted WAR AND PEACE in its first presentation outside the Soviet Union), and in 1958 at the CHICAGO LYRIC OPERA.

Roi de Lahore, Le (The King of Lahore), opera in five acts by MASSENET. Libretto by Louis Gallet, based on the MAHABHARATA. Premiere: Paris Opéra, Apr. 27, 1877. American premiere: French Opera House, New Orleans, Dec., 1883. Alim, King of Lahore (tenor), and his minister, Scindia (baritone), are rivals for the love of Sita (soprano). Scindia kills Alim, ascends the throne, and is about to marry Sita. The god Indra (bass) allows Alim to return to earth disguised as a beggar. He visits his palace and is recognized by Sita. She kills herself so that she may join Alim in paradise. The ballet music in Act III and Scindia's arioso, "Promesse de mon avenir," are the best-known excerpts.

Roi d'Ys, Le (The King of Ys), lyric drama in three acts by LALO. Libretto by Édouard Blau, based on a Breton legend. Premiere: Opéra-Comique, May 7, 1888. American premiere: New Orleans, Jan. 23, 1890. The legend from which this opera was derived was also the inspiration of DEBUSSY's piano prelude *La Cathédrale engloutie*. Mylio (tenor) is in love with Rozenn (soprano), daughter of the King of Ys (bass), but he is also loved by Rozenn's sister, Margared (mezzo-soprano). On the wedding night, Margared is led by her jealousy to open the sea gates and flood the town of Ys. The panic-stricken townspeople rush to the hills for safety. Conscience-stricken, Margared commits suicide. Corenten (bass), the patron saint of Ys, saves the city. The overture, which quotes principal melodic material from the opera and summarizes the main action, is a familiar concert number. The more familiar vocal excerpts include Rozenn's and Margared's duet in Act I, "En silence pourquoi souffrir?" Margared's aria, "Lorsque je t'ai vu," in Act II, and Mylio's AUBADE in Act III, "Vainement, ma bien aimée."

Roi d'Yvetot, Le (The King of Yvetot), comic opera in four acts by IBERT. Libretto by Jean Limzon and André de la Tourrasse, based on a ballad by Pierre Jean de Beranger. Premiere: Opéra-Comique, Jan. 15, 1930. American premiere: Tanglewood, Lenox, Mass., Aug. 7, 1950. The King of Yvetot is deprived of his rule by his freedom-loving subjects. The men of his realm must now assume command, and they no longer have time for love or work. The women band together to bring back their king. The King falls in love with a servant girl, and when he returns to the throne he makes her queen.

Roi l'a dit, Le (The King Said So), OPÉRA COMIQUE in three acts by DELIBES. Libretto by Edmond Gondinet. Premiere: Opéra-Comique, May 24, 1873. American premiere: Iowa City, Apr. 29, 1967. This was Delibes's first opera. The Marquis de Montecontour, in a moment of confusion, tells Louis XIV that he has a son, when actually he is the father of four daughters. Commanded to bring his son to court, the Marquis is forced to adopt a peasant boy and pass him off as a nobleman. The boy makes the most of his situation, to the dismay of the Marquis, who now contrives a method by which he can be rid of him. All turns out well when the Marquis is made a duke to console him for the loss of his "son," and the adopted boy marries the maid with whom he is in love. The opera's duet for two sopranos, "Dejà les hirondelles," used to be popular as a concert number; so was the overture. Noteworthy arias include Mitou's couplets, "Il vous contre fleurette," and Javotte's "Ah! je n'avais qu'un courage."

Roi malgré lui, Le (The King in Spite

of Himself), OPÉRA COMIQUE in three acts by CHABRIER. Libretto by Émile de Najac and Paul Burani, based on a comedy by F. Ançelot. Premiere: Opéra-Comique May 18, 1887. The action takes place in sixteenth-century France. Henri de Valois, about to be crowned king of France, learns from his beloved, Minka, that a conspiracy to kill him has been hatched by Polish noblemen. Henri disguises himself as his friend de Nangis and joins the band of conspirators, offering them his services as the murderer. When de Nangis comes to the conspirators' camp, he is mistaken for Henri and is in danger of his life. The conspiracy fails. The lives of both de Valois and de Nangis are spared, and Henri de Valois is finally crowned king of France and Poland.

Among the best-known vocal pages are Minka's ROMANCE, "L'amour se devint maître," in Act I; and in Act II, the gypsy song, "Il est un vieux chant de Bohème," the aria of de Nangis, "Je suis roi," and the *Danse slave* and *Fête polonaise.*

This opera represented for its composer a sharp departure in style from his earlier opera, GWENDOLINE (1883). *Gwendoline* had been influenced by WAGNER, while *Le Roi malgré lui* is thoroughly French in its lightness of touch, in its beautifully proportioned melodies, in its grace and charm, and at times in its wit and mockery.

Rolland, Romain, novelist, critic. Born Clamecy, France, Jan. 29, 1866; died Vézelay, France, Dec. 30, 1944. Winner of the Nobel Prize in 1915 for his novel about a musician, *Jean Christophe,* Rolland was educated at the École Normale Supérieure in Paris and the Ecole Française in Rome. He received his doctorate with a thesis on the early history of opera, *Les Origines due théâtre lyrique moderne,* which received the Prix Kastner-Bourgault in 1896. Later books by Rolland also contain significant material on the early history of opera and its composers. These include *Musiciens d'autrefois* (1908), published in the United States as *Some Musicians of Former Days,* and *Voyage musicale au pays du passé* (1909) (*A Musical Tour Through the Land of the Past*). In 1900 Rolland organized the first international congress for the history of music. Three years later he became president of the musical section of the École des Hautes Études Sociales. He resigned in 1909 to devote himself to writing. From 1913 to 1938 he resided in Switzerland. Besides books already mentioned, he wrote a biography of HANDEL (1910), several volumes about BEETHOVEN, an autobiography, *Journey Within* (1947), and an essay on seventeenth-century Italian opera in Lavignac's *Encyclopédie.* His novel *Colas Breugnon* was adapted as an opera by KABALEVSKY.

Roller, Alfred, scene designer. Born Vienna, Feb. 10, 1864; died there June 21, 1935. In 1903 he was engaged by Gustav MAHLER to design new sets for many productions of the VIENNA OPERA, including the RING, TRISTAN UND ISOLDE, FIDELIO, and DON GIOVANNI. He subsequently designed the scenery for the major productions of the annual SALZBURG FESTIVAL. He was also director of the Vienna School of Commercial and Technical Arts.

romance (Italian, *romanza*), in operatic use, a designation for an aria of nondramatic nature, generally expressive of personal sentiments or devoted to setting forth a narrative.

Romance d'Antonia, *see* ELLE A FUI, LA TOURTERELLE.

Romani, Felice, librettist. Born Genoa, Italy, Jan. 31, 1788; died Moneglia, Italy, Jan. 28, 1865. Though trained to be a lawyer, he turned to literature, writing librettos for over a hundred operas and becoming the most significan Italian librettist of his day. Among the operas for which he wrote the texts: BELLINI's NORMA, IL PIRATA, and LA SONNAMBULA; BIZET's *Parisina;* DONIZETTI's L'ELISIR D'AMORE and LUCREZIA BORGIA; MERCADANTE's *Normanni a Parigi;* MEYERBEER's *Margherita d'Anjou* and *L'esule de Granata;* ROSSINI's IL TURCO IN ITALIA; VERDI's *Un giorno di regno.*

Later in life, becoming blind, Romani received a government pension.

Roméo, hero (tenor) and beloved of Juliette in GOUNOD'S ROMÉO ET JULIETTE, a role created by Jean DE RESZKE; and also the hero in BELLINI'S I CAPULETTI ED I MONTECCHI, in which the part is sung by a contralto, having been written for a female voice, and was created by Giuditta GRISI, playing opposite her sister Giulia Grisi, appearing as Juliette.

Romeo and Juliet, tragedy by SHAKESPEARE, the source of many operas, the most famous being GOUNOD'S (see below). The first opera written on this drama was *Romeo und Julia* by BENDA, produced at Gotha on Nov. 25, 1776.

Roméo et Juliette, opera in five acts by GOUNOD. Libretto by Jules BARBIER and Michel Carré, based on SHAKESPEARE. Premiere: Théâtre Lyrique, Paris, Apr. 27, 1867. American premiere: Academy of Music, Nov. 15, 1867.

Characters: Roméo, a Montague (tenor); Juliette, daughter of Capulet (soprano); Capulet, a nobleman (bass); Tybalt, Capulet's nephew (tenor); Paris, kinsman of Capulet (baritone); Gregorio, another kinsman (baritone); Stephano, Roméo's page (soprano); Gertrude, Juliette's nurse (mezzo-soprano); Benvolio, Roméo's friend (tenor); Mercutio, another friend (baritone); Friar Laurence (bass); Duke of Verona (bass); Capulets; Montagues; retainers; guests. The setting is Verona in the fourteenth century.

Act I. Capulet's ballroom. An atmosphere of dire foreboding is projected by an overture-prologue that includes a chorus. This chorus is a French translation of the Shakespeare lines beginning "Two households, both alike in dignity," and spoken, in the play, by a single actor denominated Chorus. A plaintive passage in the orchestra then suggests the tragedy of Romeo and Juliet.

Capulet is giving a ball in honor of Juliette. The masked guests include two uninvited ones from the rival house of Montague, Roméo and Mercutio, Juliette's entrance inspires an enthusiastic response from the guests ("Ah,

quelle est belle"). Mercutio tells of a dream he has had (Ballad of Queen Mab: "Mab, la reine des mensonges"). Roméo forgets the danger of being in the house of his enemy when he catches sight of Juliette and falls in love as she voices her desire to experience life's pleasures (Juliette's Waltz: "Je veux vivre. dans ce rêve"). Approaching the girl, whom he has not yet identified, Roméo begins to pay court and finds Juliette not unreceptive ("Ange adorable"). Their colloquy is interrupted by Tybalt, who recognizes Roméo. Capulet intervenes and prevents a fight. Roméo and Mercutio leave, Roméo having learned that he has lost his heart to Capulet's daughter. Capulet and his guests resume their merrymaking.

Act II. Capulet's garden. The orchestral prelude is in the style of a BARCAROLLE. Roméo serenades Juliette below her balcony ("Ah! lève-toi, soleil"). When Juliette appears, the lovers exchange tender sentiments ("O nuit divine"), decide to get married, and part ("Ah! ne fuis pas encore"). Juliette retires; Roméo lingers a few moments, musing on his passion.

Act III, Scene 1. Friar Laurence's cell. Roméo and Juliette are secretly married by Friar Laurence, who pronounces a prayer ("Dieu, qui fit l'homme ton image"). The three, joined by Juliette's nurse, Gertrude, give voice to their happiness ("O pur bonheur!").

Scene 2. A street. Stephano, seeking Roméo, sings a mocking serenade ("Que fais-tu, blanche tourterelle?"). Rudely awakened, Gregorio, a Capulet, rushes out of his house to attack the Montague page. Mercutio and Tybalt, passing by, are involved in the fight. Mercutio is wounded. Believing that Mercutio is dying, Roméo kills Tybalt. The Duke of Verona, apprised of the situation, banishes Roméo.

Act IV. Juliette's room. Roméo, having secretly spent the wedding night with his bride, bids farewell at dawn. Once again they speak of their love ("Nuit d'hyménée"). When Roméo has gone, Friar Laurence brings the news that the girl's marriage has been arranged. He counsels her to drink a potion which will induce a deathlike sleep; then, believing her dead, her family will place her in the family tomb, from which she can escape to join her lawful husband. Upon the approach of Paris and Capulet. Juliette drains the Friar's potion and falls into a trance.

Act V. Juliette's tomb. Outside the tomb, Friar Laurence learns to his horror that his message about Juliette's simulated death has not reached Roméo. Roméo arrives to mourn the death of his wife. Spellbound by her beauty ("Salut, tombeau! sombre et silencieux") and lamenting her death ("O ma femme! O ma bien aimée!"), he joins her in her supposed death by drinking poison. Just before the poison takes effect, Roméo sees his wife stir. He realizes that she is not dead after all, but it is too late: Roméo is dying. Now it is Juliette's turn to die. She pierces her breast with a dagger, and the lovers die melodiously in one another's arms.

Roméo et Juliette, coming six years after Gounod's most famous opera, FAUST, was such an extraordinary success that it was heard a hundred times in its first year. But the new opera never became as popular as its predecessor. It is not the sustained masterwork that *Faust* is, yet it has a refinement and delicacy that are less evident in *Faust.* When Arthur Hervey wrote that Gounod "created a musical language of his own, one of extraordinary sweetness," he must have had *Roméo et Juliette* in mind. Juliette's waltz in the first act, Roméo's serenade in the second act, and his radiant aria "Salut, tombeau!" in the last are among the finest examples of French lyricism. The opera may lack dramatic tension and variety of mood; but its finest moments make it a rewarding experience.

Romeo und Julia, (1) opera in one act by BLACHER. Libretto by the composer, based on the SHAKESPEARE drama. Premiere: Salzburg, 1947 (concert version); Salzburg, 1950 (staged). American premiere: Bloomington, Ind., Jan. 14, 1953.

Blacher called this work a "scenic oratorio," intending it primarily for concert performance. But it has been staged as an opera. It calls for only two solo voices (soprano and tenor), a small chorus, and chamber orchestra.

(2) Opera in three acts by SUTERMEISTER. Libretto by the composer, based on the SHAKESPEARE drama. Premiere: Dresden, Apr. 13, 1940. This was the composer's first opera, and it brought him international recognition. In it he concentrates on the love interest and permeates his musical writing with emotion and compelling lyricism. Soon after this opera received its world premiere, it was produced in twenty-two opera houses in Europe.

Romeo und Julia auf dem Dorfe, *see* VILLAGE ROMEO AND JULIET, A.

Romerzählung, *see* INBRUNST IM HERZEN.

Ronald, Sir Landon (born Russell), conductor. Born London, June 7, 1873; died there Aug. 14, 1938. He was the son of Henry Russell, the song composer, one of whose other sons, also named Henry RUSSELL, was an opera impresario. Landon Ronald received his training at the Royal College of Music in London. In 1891 be became accompanist and coach at COVENT GARDEN under Luigi Mancinelli. For two seasons he was conductor of the Italian Opera Company, directed by Augustus HARRIS. He then directed a season of English opera at DRURY LANE. In 1894 he toured the United States as Nellie MELBA's conductor and accompanist, and in 1895 he directed opera performances at Covent Garden. Afterward he specialized in symphonic music, appearing as conductor with most of the great orchestras of the world. For a quarter of a century he was the principal of the Guildhall School of Music. He was knighted in 1922.

Ronde du Postillon, *see* MES AMIS, ÉCOUTEZ L'HISTOIRE.

rondine, La (The Swallow), opera in two acts by PUCCINI. Libretto by Giuseppe Adami, based on a German libretto by A. M. Willner and H. Reichert. Premiere: Monte Carlo, Mar. 27, 1917.

American premiere: Metropolitan Opera, Mar. 10, 1928. During the second French Empire, Magda (soprano), mistress of Rambaldo, a wealthy banker (bass), is entertaining her guests. One of them is the poet Prunier (tenor), who suggests that sentimental love is returning to fashion. This encourages Magda to tell her friends about a romance she once had with a student she met in a dance hall, Le Bal Bullier. The poet then tells Magda's fortune: like a swallow she has left her home, and like a swallow she will return. A young man from the country, the son of an old friend of Rambaldo, expresses a desire to visit Le Bal Bullier. Magda has a sudden impulse to follow him. The young man, Ruggero (tenor), is as attracted to Magda as she is to him. They take a villa on the Riviera, and all goes well until Ruggero seeks his mother's permission to marry Magda. At this point, Magda's discretion prompts her to abandon her young lover and return to Rambaldo. Two of Magda's arias in the first act have particular interest: "Che il bel sogno di Doretto" and "Ora dolci e divina."

Rooy, Anton, *see* VAN ROOY, Anton.

Rorem, Ned, composer. Born Richmond, Ind., Oct. 23, 1923. His music study took place at the Curtis Institute in Philadelphia, the Berkshire Music Center at Tanglewood, the Juilliard School of Music, and privately with Aaron COPLAND and Virgil THOMSON. He first attracted attention with a short orchestral work that received the Gershwin Memorial Award in 1948. He won the Lili Boulanger Award in 1950 and in 1951 received a Fulbright Fellowship. While in Europe, where he lived between 1951 and 1955, he completed his first opera, *A Childhood Miracle,* for six voices and thirteen instruments; it was introduced in New York City on May 10, 1955. His second opera, *The Robbers,* was mounted in New York on Apr. 14, 1958, while his most important opera, MISS JULIE, was given by the NEW YORK CITY OPERA on Nov.

4, 1965. He is, however, best known for his songs and his instrumental compositions.

Rosa, Carl (born Rose), impresario. Born Hamburg, Mar. 21, 1842; died Paris, Apr. 30, 1889. He attended the conservatories of Leipzig and Paris, after which he made tours as a violinist and played in various orchestras. In 1866 he toured the United States, where he married the singer Euphrosyne Parepa. They formed an opera company that toured the United States. After his wife died in England in 1874, Rosa founded and directed the CARL ROSA OPERA COMPANY, which gave performances in English and became one of England's major operatic organizations.

Rosalinde, Baron von Eisenstein's wife (soprano) in Johann STRAUSS's DIE FLEDERMAUS.

Rosa Mamai, a girl from Arles (mezzo-soprano) of supposedly questionable reputation, with whom Federico is in love, in CILÈA's L'ARLÉSIANA.

Rosario, a lady of rank (soprano) in GRANADOS' GOYESCAS.

Rosaura, Ottavio's daughter (soprano) in WOLF-FERRARI's LE DONNE CURIOSE.

Rosbaud, Hans, conductor. Born Graz, Austria, July 22, 1895; died Lugano, Italy, Dec. 30, 1962. After completing his music study at the Hoch Conservatory in Frankfurt and holding various operatic posts, he served as principal conductor of the AIX-EN-PROVENCE FESTIVAL between 1947 and 1959. In 1948 he was also appointed music director of Baden-Baden. He made notable appearances at major European opera houses and festivals, mainly in performances of modern operas, scoring a major success at the HOLLAND FESTIVAL in 1958 with ERWARTUNG and VON HEUTE AUF MORGEN.

Roschana, Almanzor's wife (contralto) in WEBER's OBERON.

Rose, Ellen's friend (mezzo-soprano) in DELIBES's LAKMÉ.

Rosenberg, Hilding, composer. Born Bosjökloster, Sweden, June 21, 1892. He did not receive systematic musical training until, in his twenty-fourth year, he entered the Stockholm Conservatory. Travels to Dresden and Paris introduced him to modern idioms, and he now turned from romanticism to modernism. In this vein he wrote some chamber and orchestral music. In 1932 he completed his first opera, *Journey to America*. He subsequently completed several more operas, the most ambitious being a cycle of four opera-oratorios entitled *Joseph and His Brethren* (1949), whose text was derived from Thomas MANN's novel of the same name. On May 21, 1970, his opera *House with a Double Door* was given its premiere by the STOCKHOLM ROYAL OPERA. His other operas: *The Marionettes* (1939); *The Two Princesses; The Island of Bliss* (1945); *The Portrait* (1956).

Rosenkavalier, Der (The Cavalier of the Rose), a "comedy for music" in three acts, by Richard STRAUSS. Libretto by Hugo von HOFMANNSTHAL. Premiere: Dresden Opera, Jan. 26, 1911. American premiere: Metropolitan Opera, Dec. 9, 1913.

Characters: The Feldmarschallin, Princess von Werdenberg (soprano); Baron Ochs von Lerchenau, her cousin (bass); Octavian, a young nobleman (mezzo-soprano); Herr von Faninal, a wealthy merchant (baritone); Sophie, his daughter (soprano); Marianne, Faninal's housekeeper (soprano); Valzacchi, an intriguing Italian (tenor); Annina, his accomplice (contralto); a singer, flute player, notary, milliner, widow, innkeeper; orphans, waiters, musicians, guests; a major domo, and a Negro servant boy to the Princess. The settting is Vienna during the reign of Maria Theresa.

Act I. The Princess's bedroom. A passionate orchestral prelude is built from motives identifying the Marschallin and Octavian. Young Octavian tells the Princess von Werdenberg (the Marschallin) how much he loves her. He is interrupted and sent into hiding by the sudden arrival of the Princess's cousin, Baron Ochs. The lecherous Baron has come with the news that he is about to marry Sophie von Faninal. Octavian, disguised as a maid, emerges from concealment. It is not long before the Baron attempts to arrange a rendezvous with "her." The Baron then explains to his cousin that custom dictates that a silver rose, the pledge of love, be sent to his future bride; he begs the Princess to provide him with a suitable emissary. The major domo now announces that the Princess must attend to her various interviews of the day. As she does so, a tenor entertains her with an Italian serenade ("Di rigori armato"). When the room is emptied of all servants and visitors and the Baron and Octavian have departed, the Princess reflects on her love affair with Octavian. In a poignant monologue ("Kann ich mich auch an ein Mädel erinnern") she laments the passing of her youth, and sadly ponders on how futile it is for her to try to hold on to the love of one so young as Octavian. She then calls to her servant and sends Baron Ochs's silver rose to Octavian so that he may act as the Rose Cavalier.

Act II. Faninal's house. Sophie prays that she may prove worthy as the wife of so exalted a man as the Baron Ochs ("In dieser feierlichen Stunde"). Octavian enters. With great dignity he presents the silver rose (Presentation of the Rose). The young people exchange meaningful glances; at that moment they realize how attracted they are to each other. The Baron arrives. Loud and vulgar, he repels Sophie. He tries to embrace her and repeatedly tells her how fortunate she is to gain him for a husband. When Octavian and Sophie are left alone, they confide to each other their inmost feelings. Returning suddenly, the Baron catches them in an embrace. Enraged, he challenges Octavian to a duel. Scratched in the course of it, Ochs growls and bellows as if he had been mortally wounded. He forgets his pains when a perfumed note arrives proposing a rendezvous with the Princess's "maid"; the note has been sent, of course, by Octavian. The famous waltz music dominates the ending of the scene as Baron Ochs boasts that for any woman who spends the time with him no night is long ("Mit mir").

Act III. A private chamber in a disreputable hotel. Disguised as the maid, Octavian comes to keep his rendezvous. The Baron follows, full of delicious anticipation. But a series of pranks, arranged by Octavian, harasses him. Strange faces appear in the windows. A distraught woman enters, followed by a brood of children who, she claims, belong to Ochs. Such a hubbub is raised that the police appear. They are about to arrest the Baron when the Princess makes her entrance. Octavian puts aside his disguise, and the Baron discovers how thoroughly he has been duped. With dignity, the Princess gives Octavian her blessing to love Sophie ("Hab' mir's gelobt, ihn lieb zu haben"). Octavian and Sophie embrace and give voice to their love ("Ist ein Traum, kann nicht wirklich sein").

Der Rosenkavalier represented a remarkable change of style for its composer, who had previously become famous with such lurid tragedies as ELEKTRA and SALOME. In *Der Rosenkavalier* the touch is light and the mood consistently gay. Having always had a profound admiration for MOZART's comic operas and a love for Johann STRAUSS's operettas, Richard Strauss wrote an opera that combined the best qualities of both composers: the infectious gaiety of the operetta composer, the penetrating wit and the contrasting humanity of Mozart. The wedding of Strauss's score, which traverses the gamut from broad burlesque to moving compassion, and Hugo von Hofmannsthal's libretto, one of the finest in all opera, resulted in a work which well deserves a place with the greatest comic operas of all time.

Rosenstock, Joseph, conductor. Born Cracow, Poland, Jan. 27, 1895. He attended the Vienna Conservatory, then studied privately with Franz SCHREKER. In 1920 he became conductor of the Darmstadt Opera, rising to the position of general music director five years later. From 1925 to 1927 he was the principal conductor of the Wiesbaden Opera. On Oct. 30, 1929, he made his American debut at the METROPOLITAN OPERA, conducting DIE MEISTERSINGER, but he remained only a single season. From 1930 to 1933 he was music director of the MANNHEIM OPERA, and after this he conducted opera performances in Berlin and concerts in Tokyo. In the fall of 1951 he succeeded László HALÁSZ as artistic director and principal conductor of the NEW YORK CITY OPERA COMPANY. He resigned as artistic director of the New York City Opera in 1955 but remained one of the conductors of that company. In 1958 he became music director of the COLOGNE OPERA. He returned as a permanent and principal conductor of the Metropolitan Opera on Jan. 31, 1961, with TRISTAN UND ISOLDE.

Rosina, Bartolo's ward (soprano), in love with Almaviva, in both PIASIELLO's and ROSSINI's THE BARBER OF SEVILLE.

Rosing, Vladimir, tenor and impresario. Born St. Petersburg, Jan. 23, 1890; died Los Angeles, Nov. 24, 1963. After studying music with various teachers, including Giovanni SBRIGLIA and Jean DE RESZKE, he made his opera debut in St. Petersburg in 1912 in EUGENE ONEGIN. A year later he went to London, studied with George Powell, and made his London debut in PIQUE DAME. In 1915 he directed a season of opera at the London Opera House. He became successful in London both in opera and as a recitalist. In 1923 he appeared in the United States for the first time, singing recitals. The same year he organized the AMERICAN OPERA COMPANY, which for six years toured the United States, presenting operas in English. During this period he was also head of the opera department at the Eastman School of Music. The American Opera Company disbanded in 1929. Ten years later Rosing founded and directed the Southern California Opera Association and subsequently joined the staff of the NEW YORK CITY OPERA as consultant and stage director. Between 1950 and 1960 he staged a number of pageants in California.

Rossellini, Renzo, composer. Born Rome, Feb. 2, 1908. He is the brother of Roberto Rossellini, the distinguished Italian motion-picture producer. After studying composition with Sallustion and Setaccioli, he devoted himself to teaching, first at the Liceo Musicale in Pesaro and then at the Conservatory of Rome. He also wrote music criticism and music for films, including several produced by his brother. His first opera was *Aucassino e Nicolette,* completed in 1930. *Il Vortice* was commissioned by the SAN CARLO OPERA, which introduced it on Feb. 8, 1958. His most famous opera is *Uno sguardo del ponte,* based on Arthur Miller's play *A View from the Bridge.* Following its world premiere in Rome on Mar. 11, 1961, it was heard in Germany, Spain, Yugoslavia, and Bulgaria; its American premiere took place in Philadelphia on Oct. 17, 1967. Other operas: *La guerra* (1956); *Le campane,* for television (1959); *Il linguaggio dei fiori* (1963); *Leggenda del ritorno* (1966).

Rossi, Gaetano, librettist. Born Verona, Italy, 1780; died there Jan. 27, 1855. As the official playwright of the TEATRO LA FENICE, he wrote over a hundred opera librettos. They were set to music by many composers, including DONIZETTI, MEYERBEER, NICOLAI, and ROSSINI. The most famous of these operas are Rossini's SEMIRAMIDE and TANCREDI.

Rossignol, Le (The Nightingale), opera in three acts by STRAVINSKY. Libretto by Stepan Mitusov and the composer, based on a story by Hans Christian ANDERSEN. Premiere: Paris Opéra (Diaghilev Ballet Russe), May 26, 1914. American premiere: Metropolitan Opera, Mar. 6, 1926. Since its premieres in Europe and the United States, this opera has been given important performances by LA SCALA (1926), Teatro Colón (1927), the HOLLAND FESTIVAL (1952), and in Washington, D.C., under the composer's direction (1960). The text is set in legendary times, when a Chinese emperor acquires a nightingale whose beautiful singing moves him to tears. When three ambassadors from Japan bring the Emperor a gift of a mechanical nightingale, the live one disappears. The Emperor, on his deathbed, is magically cured when the real nightingale returns to sing for him. The courtiers, expecting to find him dead, discover him in the best of health. Stravinsky made three different uses of this story. This opera was the first. He then converted the opera into a ballet which was produced by Serge DIAGHILEV's Ballet Russe on Feb. 2, 1920. Meanwhile, Stravinsky developed the musical material of the last two acts into a symphonic poem.

Rossi-Lemeni, Nicola, bass. Born Constantinople, Nov. 6, 1920. He studied law, and after receiving his degree, planned to enter diplomatic service. While in the Italian army during World War II, he sang for the troops, and it was then that he decided to become a professional musician. After a short period of study he made his concert debut in Verona, and shortly after that made his operatic debut at the TEATRO LA FENICE as Varlaam in BORIS GODUNOV (1946). Appearances in other major opera houses, Italian and Latin American, followed. His American debut took place at the SAN FRANCISCO OPERA on Oct. 2, 1951, in the role of Boris Godunov. His debut at COVENT GARDEN followed in 1952, and on Nov. 16, 1953, he made his first appearance at the METROPOLITAN OPERA as Méphistophélès in FAUST. He remained only a single season at the Metropolitan Opera. In 1958 he created the role of Thomas à Becket in PIZZETTI's L'ASSASSINIO NELLA CATTEDRALE, and in 1967 he appeared in the American premiere of ROSSELLINI's *Uno sguardo del ponte (A View from the Bridge).*

Rossini, Gioacchino Antonio, composer. Born Pesaro, Italy, Feb. 29, 1792; died Passy, France, Nov. 13, 1868. A highly musical child and the only son of a horn player and a prima donna, he entered the Liceo Musicale in Bologna at age fifteen, and was an exceptional student; however, he was soon obliged to leave because of his family's financial difficulties. He wrote his first opera, *Demetrio e Polibio* at fourteen, though it was not produced till 1812. His second, LA CAMBIALE DI MATRIMONIO, was produced in 1810 in Venice. He wrote a third in 1811 and three more in 1812 before achieving his first substantial success. This came with LA PIETRA DEL PARAGONE, introduced by LA SCALA in 1812 and given fifty times in its first season. TANCREDI and L'ITALIANA IN ALGERI, both introduced in Venice in 1813, were even greater triumphs. Though only twenty-one, Rossini was already the idol of the Italian opera public.

In 1815 he was engaged by Domenico BARBAJA to direct two opera companies in Naples and write new works for them. His first opera under this arrangement was *Elisabetta,* written expressly for the popular prima donna Isabella Colbran. Rossini was later to write several more operas for her. Since his contract permitted him to accept outside commissions, Rossini wrote his masterwork, THE BARBER OF SEVILLE, not for his companies in Naples but for production in Rome. It was introduced at the Teatro Argentina on Feb. 20, 1816. A combination of unhappy circumstances spelled disaster for the premiere, but on the second evening the opera was acclaimed, and with each successive performance it gained new admirers.

In 1822, after marrying Isabella Colbran, Rossini left Italy for the first time, going to Vienna, where he and his operas became the rage. Two years later he went to Paris to direct the Théâtre des Italiens. Rossini's popularity in Paris was so great that Charles X gave him a ten-year contract to write and produce a new opera every other year; at the expiration of the contract he was to receive a generous pension for life. Under the terms of this agreement, Rossini wrote WILLIAM TELL, introduced at the PARIS OPÉRA on Aug. 3, 1829. It was the only opera written under that contract, as Charles X was forced to abdicate in 1830. Though dis-criminating musicians and some critics acclaimed it, the general public did not favor it, and the opera was a failure.

Though Rossini was only thirty-seven years old when he completed *William Tell* and lived for another thirty-nine years, he never again wrote an opera. He was at the height of his creative powers and a world-renowned figure, yet in the next four decades he produced only some sacred music, a few songs, some instrumental and piano pieces. This sudden withdrawal from the world of opera inspired many conjectures. Some said that Rossini's indolence had got the better of him now that he was a wealthy man. Others said that the failure of *William Tell* had embittered him. Still others found Rossini's neurasthenia, which became serious after 1830, the major cause. Whatever the reason, the most famous opera composer of his generation preferred to remain silent after his thirty-eighth opera.

During the next two decades or so, Rossini's life was complicated by prolonged legal battles over his contract with Charles X, by his neurasthenia, by his emotional attachment to Olympe Pélissier, whom he had loved for years but could not marry until his first wife had died. After 1855 his life became easier. Now married to Olympe, he lived in a luxurious Paris apartment and in a summer villa in Passy, entertaining his friends in the grand manner and being a major figure in the social and cultural life of the city. His death was brought about by complications following a heart attack. He was buried in Père Lachaise cemetery in Paris, but at the request of the Italian government his body was removed to Florence and buried in the Santa Croce Church.

Rossini was a remarkably productive composer. He completed an average of two operas a year for nineteen years, in some years writing as many as four. This rate was made possible by an amazing creative facility, but what helped increase his output was his capacity for making compromises. He did not hesitate to use poor material when fresher and more original ideas required painstaking effort. He often borrowed whole numbers from his older operas. He even permitted other composers to interpolate numbers of their own in his works. But though he had the temperament of a hack, he was also a genius who could bring the highest flights of inspiration to his writing. A bold experimenter, he innovated in ways that changed opera procedures. He perfected what is today called the Rossini crescendo: a brief phrase in rapid tempo repeated over and over with no variation save that of volume. He was one of the first composers to write out ornaments and cadenzas instead of allowing the singer to improvise them. He was a pioneer in accompanying recitatives with strings instead of harpsichord or piano. And he was one of the first Italian composers after MONTEVERDI to use orchestral effects and colors with such expressiveness and variety.

Rossini's most important operas were *La scala di seta* (1812); *La pietra del paragone* (1812); IL SIGNOR BRUSCHINO (1813); *Tancredi* (1813); *L'Italiana in Algeri* (1813); *Elisabetta* (1815); *Il barbiere di Siviglia* (*The Barber of Seville*) (1816); *Otello* (1816); LA CENERENTOLA (1817); LA GAZZA LADRA (1817); ARMIDA (1817); MOSÈ IN EGITTO (1818); *La donna del lago* (1819); *Zelmira* (1822); SEMIRAMIDE (1823); LE SIÈGE DE CORINTHE (1826); LE COMTE ORY (1828); *Guillaume Tell* (*William Tell*) (1829).

The centenary of Rossini's death was celebrated during the 1968–69 season by various opera companies with revivals or new stagings of some of Rossini's less familiar operas. These operas included *Le Siège de Corinthe* at La Scala; *La cambiale di matrimonio* at the Piccolo Teatro Musical in Pesaro; *Le comte Ory* at the OPÉRA-COMIQUE; *Equivoco stravagante* at the Wexford Festival in Ireland; *L'Italiana in Algeri* at the Finnish National Opera; *Il Turco in Italia* at the MUNICH OPERA. Also in commemora-

tion of this centenary, the Juilliard Opera in New York gave a bilingual production of *The Barber of Seville*, in Italian on one night and in English on the following evening.

Roswaenge, Helge, tenor. Born Copenhagen, Aug. 29, 1897. Following his debut at Neustrelitz as DON JOSÉ in 1921 and appearances with several opera companies, including the Leipzig Opera, he became a member of the BERLIN STATE OPERA in 1924. During his twenty-one-year affiliation with his company and his many years with the VIENNA STATE OPERA, which began in 1936, he achieved renown as a lyric dramatic tenor, particularly in MOZART's operas and in such roles as CALAF, FLORESTAN, and HUON. For two seasons, between 1934 and 1936, he appeared as PARSIFAL at the BAYREUTH FESTIVAL, and from 1933 to 1939 he was heard regularly at the SALZBURG FESTIVAL. His American debut took place at a recital in New York in 1963. The critics found him at sixty-six still a fine artist.

Rothier, Léon, bass. Born Rheims, France, Dec. 26, 1874; died New York City, Dec. 6, 1951. He was trained as a violinist, but in his seventeenth year the director of the Paris Conservatory urged him to turn to singing. Rothier attended the conservatory from 1894 to 1899. On Oct. 1, 1899, he made his opera debut at the OPÉRA-COMIQUE in PHILÉMON ET BAUCIS. Half a year later he appeared in the world premiere of LOUISE. Rothier remained with the Opéra-Comique until 1903, afterward appearing with opera companies in Marseilles, Nice, and Lyons. He made his American debut at the METROPOLITAN OPERA on Dec. 10, 1910, in FAUST. For over a quarter of a century he was a principal bass of that company, heard in over a hundred different roles. He appeared in the world premiere of PETER IBBETSON and the American premieres of ARIANE ET BARBE-BLEUE, BORIS GODUNOV, and L'OISEAU BLEU. His last appearance at the Metropolitan was in MANON on Feb. 25, 1939.

Rothier also distinguished himself as

a teacher and opera coach. In 1944 he appeared in a Broadway play, *A Bell for Adano*. In 1949 he celebrated his fiftieth anniversary as a singer with a New York recital. He received numerous honors, among them those of Chevalier of the Legion of Honor (France), Officier de l'Instruction Publique (France), and Chevalier of the Belgian Order of Leopold.

Rothmüller, Marko, baritone. Born Trnjani, Yugoslavia, Dec. 31, 1908. He attended the Zagreb Music Academy, then went to Vienna and studied composition with Alban BERG and singing with Fritz Steiner. His opera debut took place with the HAMBURG OPERA in 1932. After two seasons with the Zagreb Opera, he became a member of the ZÜRICH OPERA, where he remained for thirteen years. He first became famous as a member of the New London Opera Company in England, which he joined in 1947, distinguishing himself in such roles as RIGOLETTO, SCARPIA, and JOKANAAN. In 1946 he was engaged by the VIENNA STATE OPERA, where he was a leading baritone for many years. He made his debut at COVENT GARDEN in 1939, and he appeared there regularly between 1948 and 1955 and was acclaimed in 1951 for his performance in WOZZECK, with Erich KLEIBER conducting. In 1948 he made his American debut with the NEW YORK CITY OPERA. While a member of this company for five years, he appeared at the EDINBURGH and GLYNDEBOURNE festivals between 1949 and 1952. On July 22, 1959, his debut at the METROPOLITAN OPERA took place in DIE MEISTERSINGER. He remained with this company through the 1960–61 season and returned in 1964–65.

Rothwell, Walter Henry, conductor. Born London, Sept. 22, 1872; died Los Angeles, Mar. 12, 1927. His musical education was obtained at the Vienna Conservatory, and in Munich with Ludwig Thuille and Max von SCHILLINGS. He began his professional career as a concert pianist, but abandoned this for conducting in 1895, when he was engaged as Gustav MAHLER's assistant at the HAMBURG OPERA. He then conducted operas in various German theaters and directed a season of German operas in Amsterdam in 1903–04. In 1904 he was engaged by the SAVAGE opera company to direct PARSIFAL (in English) in the United States. He remained with the company until 1908, during which period he led the American premiere of MADAMA BUTTERFLY. After 1908 he devoted himself to symphonic music, serving as conductor of the St. Paul Symphony and the Los Angeles Philharmonic.

Rôtisserie de la Reine Pédauque, La, *see* FRANCE, ANATOLE.

Roucher, Andrea's friend (bass) in GIORDANO'S ANDREA CHÉNIER.

Rousseau, Jean Jacques, philosopher, musical theoretician, and composer. Born Geneva, June 28, 1712; died Ermenonville, France, July 2, 1778. The celebrated philosopher was also an influential musician and an active participant in operatic activities. For some years he earned his living by copying music. He contributed articles on music to Diderot's *Encyclopédie,* and proposed some refinements in the system of musical notation. In 1747 he wrote his first opera, *Les Muses galantes.* When PERGOLESI'S LA SERVA PADRONA was introduced in Paris in 1752, Rousseau was so enchanted with it that he wrote a comic opera in a similar vein, LE DEVIN DU VILLAGE, an outstanding success for many years. The controversy that arose over the differing merits of Pergolesi's comic opera and the more dramatic operas of Jean Philippe RAMEAU—the GUERRE DES BOUFFONS—found Rousseau in the Italian camp. His *Lettre sur la musique française,* published in 1753, proved such a bitter attack that Rousseau was hanged in effigy by the artists of the OPÉRA. Rousseau's *Dictionnaire de musique,* which became internationally popular, was published in 1768. The composer worked on a third opera, *Daphnis et Chloé,* but did not finish it. He collected his vocal duets and romances in a volume entitled *Les Consolations des misères de ma vie* (1781). His drama *Pygmalion* was the source for an opera by Giambattista Cimador, for which he himself wrote part of the music, while MOZART'S BASTIEN UND BASTIENNE was based on a parody of Rousseau's *Le Devin du village*.

Roussel, Albert Charles, composer. Born Tourcoing, France, Apr. 5, 1869; died Royan, France, Aug. 23, 1937. He attended the Schola Cantorum, where his teachers included Vincent d'INDY. He first became famous with a ballet, *Le Festin de l'araignée*. His BALLET-OPERA *Padmâvatî*, inspired by a visit to India, was successfully given at the PARIS OPÉRA on June 1, 1923. Roussel, also known for his instrumental music and his songs, wrote two operas: *La Naissance de la lyre* (1924); *Le Testament de la tante Caroline* (1933).

Rouvel, Baron, Fedora's friend (tenor) in GIORDANO'S FEDORA.

Roxanne, Cyrano's beloved in CYRANO DE BERGERAC, an opera by Franco ALFANO and an opera by Walter DAMROSCH. In both she is a soprano.

Royal Hunt and Storm, orchestral episodes from BERLIOZ' LES TROYENS. They are heard in Part II of this opera (*Les Troyens à Carthage*). The music describes first a hunting scene, then a storm during which a frenzied dance is performed by fauns and satyrs in a forest.

Royal Opera House, Covent Garden, *see* COVENT GARDEN.

Royal Opera House of Copenhagen, an opera company founded in 1874 which has distinguished itself for premieres of Danish operas (including Hakon Borrensen's *Royal Guest,* Jean Baptiste Du Puy's *Youth and Folly,* Johann Hartmann's *Little Kirsten,* and Peter Arnold Heise's *King and Marshall*). During the Nazi occupation of Denmark, it gave in Danish the first presentation outside the United States of GERSHWIN'S PORGY AND BESS; its success led the Gestapo to compel the company to withdraw the work from its repertory. Lauritz MELCHIOR made his debut here. The opera house is also used regularly for drama and ballet.

Royal Palace, The, one-act opera by WEILL. Libretto by Ivan Goll. Premiere: Berlin Opera, Mar. 2, 1927. American premiere: San Francisco Opera, Oct. 5, 1968 (adapted by Gunther SCHULLER). The opera combines play, pantomime, and motion pictures. At the Royal Palace, on the shores of an Italian lake, a fashionable woman is surrounded by three men: her rich husband, who bores her; her shallow lover of a former day; her romantic lover of the future. The husband sends her on a trip through Europe, but this fails to cure her depression, and she drowns herself.

Roze, Marie (born Ponsin), soprano. Born Paris, Mar. 2, 1846; died there June 21, 1926. She attended the Paris Conservatory, where she won two first prizes. Her debut took place at the OPÉRA-COMIQUE on Aug. 16, 1865, in the title role of HÉROLD's *Marie*. She remained at the OPÉRA-COMIQUE three years. After additional study with Pierre François Wartel she appeared at the PARIS OPÉRA on Jan. 2, 1870, as MARGUERITE and scored a major success. After 1872 she appeared in London and was a great favorite. From 1883 to 1889 she was a member of the CARL ROSA OPERA COMPANY. In 1890 she settled in Paris as a teacher of singing. Though she made her farewell tour in 1894, she appeared intermittently on the concert stage until 1903.

Rozenn, daughter (soprano) of the King of Ys, sister of Margared, her rival for Mylio's love, in LALO'S LE ROI D'YS.

Rubini, Giovanni-Battista, tenor. Born Romano, Italy, Apr. 7, 1794; died there Mar. 2, 1854. One of the most celebrated opera singers of the early nineteenth century, he studied singing with Rosio in Bergamo and Andrea Nozzari in Naples, then began his career by appearing in minor roles with traveling companies. His increasing success brought him to the attention of Domenico BARBAJA, who engaged him for his Naples company in 1816. He remained here many years, particularly distinguishing himself in ROSSINI's operas. During this period he made his first triumphant appearances in Vienna and Paris. Between 1831 and 1843 he appeared alternately in Paris and London, outstandingly successful in operas of BELLINI, DONIZETTI, and Rossini. In 1843 he made a tour of Holland and Germany with Franz LISZT, then went on alone to St Petersburg, where he was idolized, Czar Nicholas I appointing him Colonel of the Imperial Music. He retired in 1845 after having amassed a fortune. Rubini is remembered not only for the beauty of his singing but for his excessive use of such devices as the vocal sob (often called, in disparagement, the Rubini sob), contrasts between soft and loud, and vibrato.

Rubinstein, Anton, composer and pianist. Born Vykhvatinets, Russia, Nov. 28, 1829; died Peterhof, Russia, Nov. 20, 1894. Taught the piano in childhood, he entered upon a concert career in his tenth year. In 1848 he began an eight-year period of intensive study and composition. Four years later his opera *Dmitri Donskoi* was produced in St. Petersburg and was such a success that the Grand Duchess Helen became his patron. In 1857 he again toured as a pianist, now establishing himself as one of the world's leading concert artists. After a series of sensational piano recitals in St. Petersburg, he was appointed imperial concert director there in 1862. He helped found and for five years he directed the St. Petersburg Conservatory. His activity on the concert stage continued with little interruption; in 1872-73 he made a triumphant tour of the United States. After 1890 he lived principally in Germany. He was the recipient of many honors, including the Order of Vladimir from the Czar, the Knighthood of the Prussian Order of Merit, and the title of Imperial Russian State Councilor. He wrote an autobiography in 1889 to commemorate his fiftieth anniversary as concert pianist; and in 1892 he issued a volume of essays on music, *Die Musik und ihre Meister,* translated into English as *A Conversation on Music.*

As a composer Rubinstein belonged to the German Romantic school. Few of his once popular works are now played.

His most celebrated opera was THE DEMON, which during the first fifty years of its life made its way throughout the operatic world and was produced in ten different languages. For a long time it was in the regular repertory of several leading Russian opera companies. His operas: *Dmitri Donskoi* (1852); *Feramors* (1863); *The Demon* (1875); *The Maccabees* (1875); *Nero* (1879); *Sulamith* (1883); *Christus* (1888); *Moses* (1894).

Rudel, Julius, conductor and opera manager. Born Vienna, Mar. 6, 1921. He attended the Vienna Academy of Music, where he studied composition. By the time he was sixteen he had written two short operas. With the annexation of Austria by Nazi Germany, he emigrated to the United States in 1938. During the next few years he continued his music study at the Greenwich House Music School and the David Mannes School of Music. He received an appointment as rehearsal pianist and coach with the NEW YORK CITY OPERA when it was founded. It was there that he made his debut as conductor in 1944 in Johann STRAUSS'S THE GYPSY BARON. He continued conducting there until 1957, when he was promoted to the post of musical director. During this period he directed the Third Street Music School between 1945 and 1952 and was musical director of the New York City Light Opera Company. In 1956 he directed Cole Porter's musical comedy *Kiss Me, Kate* at the VOLKSOPER in Vienna, where it was a major success. As musical director of the New York City Opera, he was largely responsible for elevating it to a place of first importance among American opera companies, distinguishing himself for his passionate espousal of contemporary operas in general and American operas in particular and presenting many American or world premieres (those of works by, among others, BRITTEN, WALTON, SHOSTAKOVICH, FLOYD, WARD, EINEM, WEISGALL, and MOORE). In addition to his affiliation with the New York City Opera, he was head of the CHAUTAUQUA

OPERA ASSOCIATION in 1958–59, directed the newly founded Gilbert and Sullivan Company in 1960–61, and made guest appearances at SPOLETO and at the CARA-MOOR FESTIVAL in Katonah, N.Y. He has served as a member of the United States Information Agency and in 1965 was named to the Lincoln Center Council at the LINCOLN CENTER FOR THE PER-FORMING ARTS in New York City. He received the DITSON PRIZE in 1958, the Newspaper Guild's Page One Award in music in 1959, and a decoration from the Austrian government in 1961. In 1968 he established the Julius Rudel Award to provide young conductors with experience in performing the artistic and administrative duties of an opera house, this training taking place at the New York City Opera. He was appointed music director of the Cincinnati May Festival for 1971–72.

Rudolf, Max, conductor. Born Frankfurt, June 15, 1902. After completing his music study at the Hoch Conservatory in his native city, he became an opera conductor in Freiburg in 1922. For thirteen years he conducted opera performances in Germany and Czechoslovakia and for five years orchestral concerts in Sweden. He came to the United States in 1940 and five years later became a conductor at the METRO-POLITAN OPERA, making his debut on Jan. 13, 1946, in a benefit concert. He conducted his first opera there, DER ROSENKAVALIER, on Mar. 2. In the same year he also became an American citizen. Besides conducting operas at the Metropolitan Opera, distinguishing himself particularly in the MOZART repertory, he served as its assistant manager between 1950 and 1958. Between 1958 and 1970 he was musical director of the Cincinnati Symphony Orchestra. In 1970 he became head of the newly formed opera department at the Curtis Institute of Music in Philadelphia. He published a treatise, *The Grammar of Conducting,* in 1950.

Ruffo, Titta (born Ruffo Cafiero Titta), baritone. Born Pisa, Italy, June 9, 1877; died Florence, July 6, 1953. After at-

tending the Santa Cecilia Academy in Rome he studied privately with Cassini in Milan. He made his debut at the TEATRO COSTANZI in 1898 as the Herald in LOHENGRIN. His American debut took place with the Chicago-Philadelphia Opera in RIGOLETTO on Nov. 4, 1912. He remained with this company two seasons. During World War I he served as a mechanic in the Italian air force. After the war he returned to the Chicago-Philadelphia company, where he was now acclaimed as one of the most significant opera singers of the time. On Jan. 19, 1922, he made his debut at the MET-ROPOLITAN OPERA in one of his most brilliant roles, that of Figaro in THE BARBER OF SEVILLE. He remained with the Metropolitan until 1929, acclaimed in such roles as AMONASRO, GÉRARD, and BARNABA. Ruffo retired from opera in 1929 and entered the field of motion pictures. His last public appearance took place in 1932 at the opening of the Radio City Music Hall. After 1929 he lived mostly in Italy. Since he was an anti-Fascist (the Socialist deputy Giacomo Matteotti, murdered by the Fascists, was his brother-in-law), he lived in disfavor until the overthrow of Mussolini.

Ruggero, Magda's love (tenor) in PUC-CINI'S LA RONDINE, a role created by Tito SCHIPA.

Ruggiero, (1) chief bailiff (baritone) in HALÉVY'S LA JUIVE.

(2) Principal male character (tenor) in HANDEL'S ALCINA.

Ruhlmann, François, conductor. Born Brussels, Jan. 11, 1868; died Paris, June 8, 1948. He completed his music study at the Brussels Conservatory. After holding various minor conductorial posts, he was engaged by the THÉÂTRE DE LA MON-NAIE in 1908, where he remained until 1914. Before this period, on Sept. 6, 1905, he had made his debut at the OPÉRA-COMIQUE in Paris with CARMEN; a year later he became a principal conductor of that company, holding the post until 1914. In 1914 he was engaged by the PARIS OPÉRA, where he achieved recognition as one of France's leading opera conductors. Among the world and French premieres he conducted were those of ARIANE ET BARBE-BLEUE, L'HEURE ESPAGNOLE, MÂROUF, MAXIMILIEN, and LA VIDA BREVE.

Ruiz, a soldier (tenor), in Manrico's service, in VERDI'S IL TROVATORE.

Rule, Britannia, see ARNE, THOMAS.

Ruler of this awful hour, Huon's prayer for Rezia's recovery, in Act II, Scene 1, of WEBER'S OBERON.

Rusalka, opera in three acts by DVOŘÁK. Libretto by Jaroslav Kvapil. Premiere: Prague National Opera, May 31, 1901. American premiere: Chicago, Mar. 10, 1935. Rusalka, a water sprite (soprano), falls in love with a Prince (tenor) and enlists the help of Ježibaba, a witch (contralto). The witch transforms the sprite into a beautiful but mute woman. The Prince falls in love with Rusalka, but finding her cold and dumb he marries a young Princess instead, which results in Rusalka being changed back into a sprite. When the Princess betrays him, the Prince seeks Rusalka and finds her in a lake. He kisses her and dies in her arms. Among the most notable pages are Rusalka's aria, "O moon in the deep sky," and the Prince's aria, "I know you are a phantom," in Act I; the ballet music in Act II; and the witch's aria, "You must wash it away with blood," in Act III.

Russalka, opera in four acts by DARGOMIZHSKY. Libretto by the composer, based on a play by PUSHKIN. Premiere: St. Petersburg, May 18, 1856. American premiere: New York City, Dec. 1902 (concert version); Seattle, Wash., Dec. 23, 1921 (staged). This is one of the two best-known operas by Dargomizhsky, the other one being THE STONE GUEST. It is also one of his first to fulfill his nationalistic ideals. The central character is Natasha (soprano), daughter of a miller (bass). Betrayed by a Prince (tenor), she commits suicide in a stream. She becomes transformed into a water sprite, Russalka, who lures men to their death. When the Prince marries a woman of his own class, he hears the wail of the water sprite each time he tries to embrace his beloved. One day, wandering near the sprite's stream, he meets a child who tells him she is his daughter. Natasha's father, crazed by his misfortunes, throws the Prince into the stream, where he is reunited with his onetime sweetheart and their child. Noteworthy excerpts include the miller's aria, "Ah, you young girls," in Act I; the Slavic and Gypsy Dance for orchestra in Act II; Olga's aria, "Once a husband asked his wife," and the Prince's CAVATINA, "Some unknown power," both in Act III.

Russell, Henry, impresario. Born London, Nov. 14, 1871; died there Oct. 11, 1937. The son of Henry Russell, an eminent writer of songs, he was the brother of a noted conductor (see RONALD, SIR LANDON).

Russell planned to be a doctor but turned to music after a permanent injury to his eye. After studying singing at the Royal College of Music, he joined its faculty and achieved considerable renown as a teacher of singing. Through his knowledge of anatomy, he was able to originate a new method of voice production praised by Nellie MELBA, Eleanora Duse, and others. His extensive association with singers enabled him to procure an appointment as manager of the COVENT GARDEN opera season in 1903 and 1904. In 1905 he toured the United States with his own opera company. Four years later he became director of the newly founded BOSTON OPERA COMPANY, holding this post until the dissolution of the company in 1914. In the spring of 1914 he took his own company to Paris for a two-month season at the THÉÂTRE DES CHAMPS ELYSÉES. He then settled in London but returned to the United States in 1921 to manage a lecture tour for Maurice MAETERLINCK.

Russlan and Ludmilla, opera in five acts by GLINKA. Libretto by the composer, V. F. Shirkov, K. B. Bakhturin, and others, based on a poem by Alexander PUSHKIN. Premiere: Imperial Theater, St. Petersburg, Dec. 9, 1842. American premiere: New York City, Dec. 26, 1942 (concert version).

Characters: Svietosar, Grand Duke of Kiev (bass) ; Ludmilla, his daughter (soprano) ; Russlan, a knight in love with Ludmilla (baritone) ; Ratmir, a second suitor of Ludmilla (contralto) ; Farlaf, a third suitor (bass) ; Gorislava, young lady in love with Ratmir (soprano) ; Finn, a sorcerer (tenor) ; Tchernomor, a dwarf; Naina, a witch (mezzo-soprano) ; Bayan, a bard (tenor). The setting is legendary Russia.

Act I. The court of Svietosar. The familiar overture, which opens with vigorous chords, is made up of a lively tune for strings and woodwinds and a Russian folksong-type of theme for violas, cellos, and bassoon. The Grand Duke is entertaining Ludmilla's three suitors. A bard is prophesying the future for Ludmilla in "There is a desert country." Ludmilla favors Russlan and, aware she is soon to be married, sings a CAVATINA to her father, "Soon I must leave thee." When festivities are at their height, Ludmilla mysteriously disappears. Svietosar promises his daughter to the suitor who finds her.

Act II. Finn's cave. Russlan learns from the sorcerer that Ludmilla has been abducted by the dwarf Tchernomor; he is also warned about the witch Naina, who is Farlaf's ally. Farlaf, meanwhile, visits the witch for help, singing a *buffo* rondo, or PATTER SONG, "The happy day is done." Her advice is to allow Russlan to find Ludmilla and then to kidnap her. The scene changes to a battlefield, where Russlan, looking at the quiet fields, delivers the air "O say, ye fields." Through the mist appears a gigantic, mysterious head (whose part is sung by a chorus inside it). Russlan subdues the head with his spear; and under the head there lies a magic sword, which Russlan is told how to use.

Act III. Naina's domain. To help Farlaf, Naina uses her wiles to divert his rival by having Persian virgins sing a sad but seductive chorus, "The evening shadows." Gorislava reflects on her love for Ratmir in the romance-cavatina "O my Ratmir." Ratmir is imprisoned after he succumbs to one of Naina's sirens,

rhapsodizing her in "The wondrous dream of love." Russlan is about to experience the same fate when he is saved by Finn.

Act IV. Tcheronomor's house. Tcheronomor arrives to the strains of a celebrated march, the most famous instrumental episode in the opera besides the overture. The dwarf has imprisoned Ludmilla. He has arranged a ballet of oriental dances to amuse her, but she is bored. When Russlan comes to save his beloved, the dwarf puts Ludmilla to sleep. Russlan defeats the dwarf with his magic sword by cutting off his beard, in which his strength resides. Unable to rouse Ludmilla, Russlan carries her away.

Act V. The court of Svietosar. With a magic ring, Finn again comes to Russlan's help, and Ludmilla is roused from her profound sleep. Svietosar happily gives his daughter to Russlan to wed. The people rejoice.

Russlan and Ludmilla was Glinka's second and last opera. In his first, A LIFE FOR THE CZAR, he made his initial experiments in creating a truly Russian opera. That opera had been a success chiefly because it was simply a Russianized Italian opera, and audiences could respond to its Bellinian melodies. But in *Russlan* Glinka grew bolder in his attempts to achieve nationalism. He departed completely from the Italian style to produce an opera authentically Russian in spirit and music. *Russlan and Ludmilla* was revolutionary for its day and when first heard was a failure. Not until its revival in 1859 did it receive the recognition it deserved. From then on it was accepted in its native land as one of the most significant of all Russian operas. There was hardly a Russian composer after 1860 who was not influenced by it.

Rustic Chivalry, *see* CAVALLERIA RUSTICANA.

Rutledge, Mary, Philip Nolan's sweetheart (soprano) in Walter DAMROSCH's THE MAN WITHOUT A COUNTRY, a role created by Helen TRAUBEL.

Rysanek, Leonie, soprano. Born Vienna,

Nov. 12, 1926. After studying voice at the Vienna Conservatory, mainly with Alfred JERGER, she made her opera debut in Innsbruck in 1949 as Agathe in DER FREISCHÜTZ. She continued her vocal studies at Innsbruck with Rudolf Grossman, whom she subsequently married. From 1950 to 1952 she appeared in opera performances at Saarbrücken, and in 1951 she was heard as SIEGLINDE in the first postwar festival at BAYREUTH. In 1952 she became a member of the MUNICH OPERA and in 1954 a principal soprano of the VIENNA STATE OPERA. From 1953 on she appeared intermittently at COVENT GARDEN for many years. She scored a major success in her American debut with the SAN FRANCISCO OPERA on Sept. 18, 1956, as SENTA. In 1958 and 1959 she was acclaimed at Bayreuth, and on Feb. 5, 1959, she made a remarkable debut as LADY MACBETH at the METROPOLITAN OPERA, a company with which she has since remained a principal soprano.

S

Saamschedine, Princess, the Sultan's daughter (soprano) in RABAUD's MÂROUF.

Sabata, Victor de, conductor and composer. Born Trieste, Apr. 10, 1892; died Santa Margherita, Italy, Dec. 11, 1967. He graduated from the Milan Conservatory in 1911 and soon afterward became known as an orchestral composer through performances in Italy, France, Belgium, and Russia. He scored an even greater success with an opera, *Il macigno,* introduced at LA SCALA on Mar. 30, 1917. He subsequently wrote two more operas, *Lysistrata* and *Mille e una notte.* Sabata also distinguished himself as one of the foremost conductors in Europe. After World War I he was appointed first conductor of the MONTE CARLO OPERA, where he remained a dozen years. For the next twenty years he was first conductor of La Scala. He also conducted opera performances with other leading European companies and at BAYREUTH, SALZBURG, and the FLORENCE MAY MUSIC FESTIVAL. He first visited the United States in 1927 as guest conductor of several major orchestras and subsequently returned a number of times, principally as a guest conductor of the New York Philharmonic in the 1940's. He was appointed artistic director of La Scala in 1951 and retired three years later.

Sacchini, Antonio, composer. Born Florence, June 14, 1730; died Paris, Oct. 6, 1786. He attended the Conservatorio Santa Maria di Loreto in Naples, where he wrote an INTERMEZZO, *Fra Donato,* which was acclaimed in 1756. In 1762 he achieved a major triumph in Rome with his opera *Semiramide;* he remained in Rome several years, rivaling the popularity of Nicola PICCINNI. After the successful performance of his *Alessandro nell' Indie* in Venice, he was appointed director of the Conservatorio dell' Ospedaletto. Between 1770 and 1772 he lived in Germany, and from 1772 and 1782 he was in London, where his operas were in vogue. Financial difficulties compelled him to flee to Paris in 1782. There he received royal patronage and was favored by the general public. In Paris he wrote two new operas in which he assimilated some of the progressive ideas and style of GLUCK; one of these operas, *Oedipe à Colone,* his masterwork, received over six hundred performances between 1786 and 1844. He wrote over sixty operas, the most important being: *Semiramide* (1762); *L'Olimpiade* (1767); *Alessandro nell' Indie* (1768); *Ezio* (1770); *Tamerlano* (1771); *Armida e Rinaldo* (1772); *La Colonie* (1775); *Dardanus* (1784); *Oedipe à Colone* (1786).

Sachs, Hans, poet, composer, playwright. Born Nuremberg, Nov. 5, 1494; died there January 19, 1576. The most celebrated of the MASTERSINGERS, Sachs became the central character of WAGNER'S DIE MEISTERSINGER and of LORTZING'S HANS SACHS. Some of the poet's dramatic pieces were later the source of operas, including Joseph Forster's *Der dot Mon,* Bernhard Paumgartner's *Das heisse Eisen,* and Werner Wehrli's *Das heisse Eisen.*

Sachse, Leopold, stage director. Born Berlin, Jan. 5, 1880; died Englewood Cliffs, N.J., Apr. 4, 1961. He attended the Cologne Conservatory, then studied singing with Benno Stolzenberg and Blanche Selva. In 1907 he became director of the Münster Stadttheater and in 1915 intendant of the HAMBURG OPERA. After a period of staging musical productions in Paris, Sachse came to the United States. In 1935 he was appointed stage director of the METROPOLITAN OPERA and a year later teacher of stage techniques at the Juilliard School of Music. Subsequently he became a stage director of the NEW YORK CITY OPERA.

Sacra la scilta, aria of Luisa's father when he refuses to be a tyrant and order his daughter to marry a man she does not love, in Act I of VERDI'S LUISA MILLER.

Sacrifice, The, opera in three acts by CONVERSE. Libretto by the composer and John Macy. Premiere: Boston Opera House, Mar. 3, 1911. In California—the year is 1846, and Mexico and the United States are at war—Bernal, a Mexican officer, is Captain Burton's rival for the love of Chonita. When the American officer realizes the extent of Chonita's love for the Mexican, he sacrifices his life to save theirs.

Sadko, opera in seven tableaux (three or five acts) by RIMSKY-KORSAKOV. Libretto by the composer and V. I. Bielsky. Premiere: Moscow, Jan. 7, 1898. American premiere: Metropolitan Opera, Jan. 25, 1930. In medieval Novgorod, Sadko (tenor) bets the local merchants that he can catch a net of goldfish, the wager being his life against their wealth. Foreign visitors are spectators. One of them is a Hindu merchant (tenor), who, singing of his home, presents the most celebrated aria in the opera, "Song of India"; another visitor, a Norseman (bass), contributes a second popular aria, "Song of the Viking Guest," while a third, a Venetian (baritone), renders a BARCAROLLE, "Song of the Venetian Guest" (all three arias come in Scene 4). After Sadko wins his wager with the cooperation of the beautiful Volkhova, daughter of the Sea King (soprano), he sets sail. In the face of danger he is willing to sacrifice his own life to the King of the Sea (bass) to save ship and men. Coming to the bottom of the sea, he meets Volkhova, whom he marries. But she becomes a river, and Sadko goes home to his wife in Novgorod, where he is welcomed back as a hero.

Other interesting vocal excerpts are two arias by Sadko, "O ye dark forests" in Scene 1, and "Farewell, my friends," in Scene 5; and Volkhova's cradle song in Scene 7, "Sleep went along."

Sadler's Wells Opera, a London opera company, the only permanent opera repertory theater in England dedicated to performances of opera in English. The original Sadler's Wells Theatre was built in the eighteenth century in north London and was used for plays, pantomimes, and musical productions. After about a century of use, the building was abandoned. In 1926 it was acquired by Lilian Baylis and other lovers of drama and opera as a branch for the Old Vic Theatre, which had been producing dramas and operas since 1914. After 1934, all the Old Vic's opera performances were given at Sadler's Wells. A famous ballet company developed at Sadler's Wells, originally under the direction of Ninette de Valois, which gave performances of its own besides being seen in the opera productions. In addition to the usual French, Italian, and German operas, Sadler's Wells produced, up to the time of World War II, such novelties as BORIS GODUNOV (the composer's original version); *The Devil Take Her* (BENJAMIN); DON CARLOS (first performance in English); EUGENE ONEGIN; HUGH THE DROVER; THE LEGEND OF THE CZAR SALTAN; MACBETH (Arthur Collingwood); SIR JOHN IN LOVE; THE SNOW MAIDEN; *The Travelling Companion* (STANFORD). In 1939–40 the company moved to the auditorium on Rosebery Avenue, where it was directed by Sir Tyrone Guthrie. The opera house closed down during World War II, but the company traveled and produced many operas under the directorship of its prima donna, Joan Cross. The house reopened in 1945 with the world premiere of PETER GRIMES. From 1948 to 1953 Norman Tucker was codirector and after 1953 sole director of the company. He was succeeded by Stephen Arlen. Since the end of World War II its musical directors have been James Robertson, Alexander Gibson, Colin Davis, Bryan Balkwill, and Mario Bernandi. After World War II the company offered the following novelties, among others: THE CONSUL; THE CUNNING LITTLE VIXEN; DER FREISCHÜTZ; FROM THE HOUSE OF THE DEAD (first London staging); GLORIANA (first revival since its world premiere); KAT'A KABANOVA; *The Moon and Sixpence* (Gardner, a world premiere); *Nelson* (Berkeley, a world premiere); ORPHEUS IN THE UNDERWORLD; LES PÊCHEURS DE PERLES; I QUATTRO RUSTEGHI (British premiere); RIDERS TO THE SEA; THE RISE AND FALL OF THE CITY MAHAGONNY; ROMEO UND JULIA (SUTERMEISTER); RUSALKA (DVOŘÁK); ŠVANDA; *A Tale of Two Cities* (BENJAMIN, a world premiere). In 1955 Camilla Williams became the first Negro singer to appear at Sadler's Wells, seen as CIO-CIO-SAN. In 1965 the company visited the Prague Spring Festival in performances of THE RAKE'S PROGRESS.

The company moved from Rosebery Avenue to the Coliseum near Trafalgar Square in 1968, inaugurating its new home on Aug. 21 with a performance of DON GIOVANNI.

Saffi, heroine (soprano), and beloved of Sandor Barinkay, in Johann STRAUSS'S THE GYPSY BARON.

Sai cos' ebbe cuore, Madama Butterfly's little song to her son, Trouble, in Act II of PUCCINI'S MADAMA BUTTERFLY.

Sailors' Chorus, *see* STEUERMANN! LASS DIE WACHT!

St. Bris, Count de, Catholic nobleman (bass) in MEYERBEER'S LES HUGUENOTS.

Saint Daniel et Saint Michel, Mélisande's ancient song at the opening of Act III of DEBUSSY'S PELLÉAS ET MÉLISANDE.

Saint-Georges, Jules Henri Vernoy de, novelist and librettist. Born Paris, Nov. 7, 1801; died there Dec. 23, 1875. One of the most significant and prolific French librettists after Eugène SCRIBE, he produced over a hundred librettos, which were set to music by ADAM, AUBER, BIZET, FLOTOW, HALÉVY, HÉROLD, and many others. Operas with his librettos include THE DAUGHTER OF THE REGIMENT (a collaboration with Alfred Bayard); Auber's *Les Diamants de la couronne;* HALÉVY'S *L'Eclair* (a collaboration with F. A. E. Planard); LA JOLIE FILLE DE PERTH (libretto a collaboration with Jules Adenis). THE BOHEMIAN GIRL was founded on Saint-Georges's ballet-pantomime *The Gypsy.*

Saint Julien l'Hospitalier, *see* FLAUBERT, GUSTAVE.

Saint of Bleecker Street, The, a "music drama" in three acts by MENOTTI. Libretto by the composer. Premiere: Broadway Theater, New York, Dec. 27, 1954. The setting is New York's Italian quarter. Annina, a passionate religious mystic, receives the stigmata upon her palms, provoking the frenzied devotion of the Catholic neighborhood. Michele, her brother, a troubled agnostic, uses argument and force in his futile attempts to draw Annina away from what he regards as superstition and ignorance. At the same time he manifests a devotion to the sickly girl that prevents any decisive move. Desideria, Michele's worldly minded sweetheart, taunts him with being in love with his sister. In the furious quarrel that follows, Michele kills Desideria with a knife and becomes a hunted man. Later, he creeps back to Bleecker Street to watch his sister taking her vows to enter the novitiate. The emotional tension of the elaborate ceremony proves too much for the frail Annina, and she dies in her moment of greatest joy. For this gripping play, Menotti provided a score that is frequently high-tensioned and dramatic, vivid in its realism. But contrast is injected with arias of a PUCCINI-like sweetness and lyricism, comic episodes, and light dance tunes. The opera had a run of some ninety performances in New York and received the PULITZER PRIZE, the Drama Critics' Award, and the NEW YORK MUSIC CRITICS' CIRCLE AWARD. It was given its first performance in Italy at LA SCALA on May 8, 1955, and in 1956 was telecast in England over the BBC.

Saint-Pierre, Jacques Henri Bernardin de, writer. Born Le Havre, France, Jan. 19, 1737; died Eragny-sur-Oise, France, Jan. 21, 1814. His romantic novel PAUL ET VIRGINIE, a French classic, was made into operas by Pietro Guglielmi, Rodolphe KREUTZER, Jean-François LESUEUR, and Victor MASSÉ.

Saint-Saëns, Camille, composer. Born Paris, Oct. 9, 1835; died Algiers, Dec. 16, 1921. He was exceptionally precocious in music, began lessons when he was only three, and made his first public appearance as pianist when he was four and a half. Further study took place with Camille Stamaty and Pierre Maleden and later at the Paris Conservatory. In 1857 Saint-Saëns became organist of the Madeleine Church, remaining twenty years and achieving recognition as one of the foremost organists of his day. He also attracted attention as a composer, with his *Second Symphony,* which won first prize in a contest sponsored by the Société Sainte-Cécile. His first opera, *La Princesse jaune,* was given by the OPÉRA-COMIQUE on June 12, 1872.

Five years later, his second, *Le Timbre d'argent,* was produced at the THÉÂTRE LYRIQUE. His SAMSON ET DALILA was not accepted for performance in Paris because opera directors considered it too Wagnerian and too severe. It found an advocate in Franz LISZT, who used his influence to get it performed in Weimar, 1877. Not until thirteen years later, after it had been acclaimed in most of the rest of Europe, was it heard in France.

Saint-Saëns continued composing prolifically in every branch of musical composition for the remainder of his life. He had other activities, too: as concert pianist, conductor, organist, professor of piano at the Ecole Niedermeyer, editor, writer, and as founder of the Société Nationale de Musique. He also indulged his passion for travel. He visited the United States twice, in 1906 and 1916. His last appearance as a pianist was in Dieppe on Aug. 6, 1921. Two weeks later he led his last orchestral concert. He died suddenly while on a visit to Algiers.

His operas: *La Princesse jaune* (1872); *Le Timbre d'argent* (1877); *Samson et Dalila* (1877); *Etienne Marcel* (1879); HENRY IV (1883); *Gabriella di Vergy* (1885); *Proserpine* (1887); *Ascanio* (1890); *Phryné* (1893); *Les Barbares* (1901); *Hélène* (1904); *L'Ancêtre* (1906); *Déjanire* (1910).

Sakuntala, a Sanskrit drama by KALIDASA, written in the fifth century. Several operas were derived from this drama, including ALFANO's *La leggenda di Sacuntala,* Louis Coerne's *Sakuntala,* Ignace Jan Paderewski's *Sakuntala,* and WEINGARTNER's *Sakuntala.*

Salammbô, opera in five acts by REYER. Libretto by Camille du Locle, based on FLAUBERT's novel of the same name. Premiere: Théâtre de la Monnaie, Feb. 10, 1890. American premiere: French Opera House, New Orleans, Jan. 25, 1900. In an army camp outside ancient Carthage, Matho (tenor) steals a magic veil (zaimph) that covers a holy statue at the shrine of the goddess Tanit. When Salammbô, daughter of the general

Hamilcar (soprano), tries to recover the veil, Matho forces his love upon her. The Carthaginians seize Matho, imprison him for the theft, and condemn him to execution. To Salammbô, who has saved the veil, goes the honor of executing him. Salammbô uses the sword intended for Matho to commit suicide. Matho takes the dying Salammbô in his arms and kills himself with her sword.

MUSSORGSKY began an opera on this story about 1860 but abandoned the project. The contemporary composer Josef Matthias Hauer has made Flaubert's novel into an opera that employs TWELVE-TONE music.

Salce! Salce!, Desdemona's Willow Song, a song she had learned as a child, in Act IV of VERDI'S OTELLO.

Salieri, Antonio, composer and conductor. Born Legnano, Italy, Aug. 18, 1750; died Vienna, May 7, 1825. He attended the San Marco singing school in Venice. In 1766 he was taken to Vienna, where he continued his music study. Four years later he conducted the premiere of his first opera, *Le donne letterate*. Between 1770 and 1774 nine of his operas were produced at court. In 1774 he succeeded Florian Gassmann as conductor of Italian opera and chamber composer. Four years later he returned to Italy, writing operas for performance there. LA SCALA opened its doors (Aug. 3, 1778) with one of his new operas: *Europa riconosciuta*. In 1784 Salieri was in Paris, where several of his new operas, strongly influenced by those of GLUCK, were given successfully. Back in Vienna, he continued writing operas prolifically and became director of the opera; on one occasion he had five new ones produced in a single year.

He was one of the most influential musicians in Vienna. At different periods he was a teacher of BEETHOVEN, SCHUBERT, and LISZT, all of whom admired and liked him. But he was a rival and enemy of MOZART, and as court KAPPELMEISTER he intrigued successfully against the younger man. An unfounded rumor was circulated after Mozart's death that he had been poisoned by Salieri; this persistent legend was the basis of RIMSKY-KORSAKOV's opera *Mozart and Salieri*.

After half a century of service at the Viennese court, Salieri retired in 1824 on a pension. Of his fifty or so operas, these were the most successful: *Armida* (1771); *Don Chisciotte alle nozze di Gamace* (1771); *La fiera di Venezia* (1772); *La secchia rapita* (1772); *Semiramide* (1782); *Les Danaïdes* (1784); *La grotta di Trofonio* (1785); *Tarare* (1787); *Il pastor fido* (1789); *Palmira* (1795); *Falstaff* (1799); *Angiolina* (1800); *Cesare di Farmacusa* (1800); *Die Neger* (1804); *Cyrus und Astyages* (1818).

Salignac, Eustase Thomas, tenor and teacher of singing. Born Generac, France, Mar. 29, 1867; died Paris, 1945. He studied singing at the Marseilles and Paris conservatories. In 1893 he made his opera debut at the OPÉRA-COMIQUE. After two seasons there he came to the United States, making his American debut at the METROPOLITAN OPERA on Dec. 11, 1896, singing the role of DON JOSÉ. He remained there seven consecutive seasons, appearing in all the principal tenor parts of the French repertory. During this period he also appeared at COVENT GARDEN. After returning to France in 1903, he joined the Opéra-Comique, remaining there ten seasons. In 1913 he was appointed director of the Nice Opera. A decade later he returned to the Opéra-Comique, and in 1926 he was director of an opera company that toured Canada and appeared in New York. In 1923 he became a professor of singing at the Fontainebleau Conservatory and in 1924 professor of elocution at the Paris Conservatory. In 1933 and 1937 he organized competitions to discover new French singers. He created the role of MÂROUF in RABAUD's opera of the same name (1918) and appeared in world premieres of operas by MASSENET, LAPARRA, and MILHAUD, among others.

Salle Favart, see OPÉRA-COMIQUE.

Salome, one-act music drama by Richard STRAUSS. Libretto is the play by Oscar WILDE, in a German translation by Hedwig Lachmann. Premiere: Dresden Opera Dec. 9, 1905. American premiere: Metropolitan Opera, Jan. 22, 1907.

Characters: Herod, Tetrarch of Judea (tenor); Herodias, his wife (mezzo-soprano); Salome, her daughter (soprano), a role created by Marie WITTICH; Jokanaan, the prophet (baritone); Narraboth, a captain of the guards (tenor); Page of Herodias (mezzo-soprano); Jews; Nazarenes; soldiers. The setting is a terrace of Herod's palace in Galilee about A.D. 30.

During a banquet of Herod's, Jokanaan (John the Baptist), from depths where he is held prisoner, proclaims the coming of the Messiah ("Nachmer wird Einer kommen"). Salome orders that the prophet be brought before her. When he arrives, he curses Herod and Herodias and denounces them. He commands Salome not to imitate her mother's dissolute life ("Tochter der Unzucht"). When Salome tries to entice Jokanaan by saying she yearns for his body and is hungry for his kisses ("Ich will deinen Mund küssen"), he returns to his prison. Herod, seeking diversion, begs Salome to dance for him. She promises to do so, but only if the Tetrarch will then reward her by granting any wish she may have. She performs the Dance of the Seven Veils, then demands the head of Jokanaan. The horrified Tetrarch finally acquiesces, and the severed head is brought to Salome. She addresses it passionately ("Ah! Du wolltest mich nicht deinen Mund küssen lassen!"), after which she kisses the dead lips. Revolted by the spectacle, Herod orders his soldiers to crush Salome beneath their shields.

Wilde's play was perfectly matched by Strauss's sensuous and erotic music. The result was an opera that shocked many an audience in the early 1900's. A premiere planned in Vienna had to be canceled when the censors stepped in. In Berlin, the Kaiser at first forbade its performance; when it was allowed, it inspired such adjectives as "repulsive" and "perverse." The London premiere was prevented by censors. In America, the premiere created a storm of protest that is described elsewhere (*see* METROPOLITAN OPERA HOUSE). But time has cushioned the shock, and it is now conceded that *Salome* is a drama of unforgettable impact, as well as a remarkably successful example of fusion of text and music.

A French composer, Antoine Mariotte, also wrote an opera on Wilde's play. Though he completed it before Strauss wrote his opera, it was not introduced until 1908 in Lyons. Strauss had to give Mariotte written permission to have the latter's opera produced, waiving his rights to the exclusive use of the Wilde text. After the premiere of Mariotte's opera, Strauss had to issue a public denial that he had ever demanded that Mariotte destroy his manuscript, as rumor insisted that he did.

Salomé, the principal female character (soprano) in MASSENET'S HÉRODIADE.

Salud, a gypsy girl (soprano) in FALLA'S LA VIDA BREVE.

Salut à la France, finale of DONIZETTI'S THE DAUGHTER OF THE REGIMENT, as the entire ensemble pays a stirring tribute to France.

Salut à toi, soleil, *see* HYMN TO THE SUN.

Salut! demeure chaste et pure, Faust's CAVATINA saluting Marguerite's peaceful abode, in Act III of GOUNOD'S FAUST.

Salut, tombeau! sombre et silencieux, Roméo's aria in Act V of GOUNOD'S ROMÉO ET JULIETTE as he contemplates the beauty of his supposedly dead wife, Juliette, in her tomb.

Salvezza alla Francia, *see* SALUT À LA FRANCE.

Salzburg Festival, one of the most significant of Europe's festivals. It was created in the summer of 1920 through the combined efforts of Hugo von HOFMANNSTHAL, Max Reinhardt, Franz SCHALK, and Richard STRAUSS. In 1926 a festival theater (Festspielhaus) was built for opera and symphonic performances.

Up to the time of World War II, a pattern of activity was established which continued with only minor deviations. Since Salzburg was the birthplace of MOZART, his music predominated. The festival, which lasted approximately a month, beginning the last week in July, embraced operas and orchestral, chamber, and choral music. The opera performances, invariably of the highest caliber, enlisted singers for the most part from the VIENNA STATE OPERA, together with the opera house orchestra and chorus. Guest singers and conductors were invited to participate from all parts of the world. Though Mozart's operas were the core of the repertory, operas of Richard Strauss, GLUCK, WEBER, VERDI, WAGNER, BEETHOVEN, and ROSSINI were given. Among the many famous conductors who led performances were TOSCANINI, Richard Strauss, Schalk, FURTWÄNGLER, BÖHM, SERAFIN, and WEINGARTNER.

The festival suspended activity during World War II. It resumed operations on Aug. 1, 1946, with the cooperation of the United States Army. Since World War II the festival has once again been given for a month, beginning the last week in July. Opera performances are given not only in the Festspielhaus but also in the open-air Felsenreitschule (a historic quarry that later became an arena for tournaments) and in the new Grosses Festspielhaus, which opened on July 26, 1960, with DER ROSENKAVALIER. The programing still emphasizes Mozart, including now many of his rarely heard operas (such as *Ascanio in Alba*, BASTIEN UND BASTIENNE, LA FINTA GIARDINIERA, LA FINTA SEMPLICE, and so forth) as well as his familiar masterworks. Richard Strauss's works also still play a prominent role in the repertory. But the activity has been greatly expanded to embrace not only non-German and non-Austrian operas such as BORIS GODUNOV, CARMEN, DON CARLOS, Verdi's MACBETH, but also rare novelties of the past and a considerable number of new operas, including premieres. Among the world premieres heard at Salzburg since the end of World War II are: ANTIGONAE (ORFF); DIE BASSARIDEN; DANTONS TOD; IRISCHE LEGENDE;

Julietta (Heimo Erbse); DIE LIEBE DER DANAE; *Penelope* (LIEBERMANN); DER PROZESS. Other modern operas given there include LE MYSTÈRE DE LA NATIVITÉ (first staged performance); SCHOOL FOR WIVES (European premiere); VANESSA (European premiere, and the first American opera ever given at the festival); LE VIN HERBÉ. Characteristic of the interest of the festival in rarely given old operas was the inclusion in the program for 1969 of LA RAPPRESENTAZIONE DI ANIMA E DI CORPO and LA SERVA PADRONA. Among the conductors heard in opera performances have been ABBADO, Antal Dorati, KARAJAN (who was artistic director of the festival for several years), MEHTA, Seiji Ozawa, PRITCHARD, and SAWALLISCH. The festival commemorated its fiftieth anniversary in 1970, opening with a new production of FIDELIO in the restored and remodeled Felsenreitschule; also included was a new production of OTELLO, conducted by Karajan.

The Salzburg summer festival should not be confused with the Salzburg Easter Festival, which was initiated in 1967, and at which the monumental production of the RING cycle under the musical, artistic, and stage direction of Karajan, was first seen: DIE WALKÜRE in 1967; DAS RHEINGOLD in 1968; SIEGFRIED in 1969; and GÖTTERDÄMMERUNG in 1970. Each of these productions was scheduled to be brought to the Metropolitan the year of its premiere, was recorded, and was filmed for distribution in theaters and over television.

Sa main, sa douce main, Marguerite's song of joy as, in prison, she hears Faust's voice, in Act V, Scene 2, of GOUNOD's FAUST.

Samiel, the Black Huntsman (speaking part) in WEBER's DER FREISCHÜTZ.

Sammarco, Mario, baritone. Born Palermo, Dec. 13, 1868; died Milan, Jan. 24, 1930. His vocal instruction took place mainly with Antonio Cantelli. In 1888 he made his opera debut in Palermo as VALENTIN. He appeared in major Italian opera houses, including LA SCALA, beginning with 1896, and in 1905 he was so highly acclaimed at his debut in COVENT GARDEN as SCARPIA that he made appearances there every season up to the time of World War I. His American debut took place at the MANHATTAN OPERA HOUSE in New York City on Feb. 1, 1908, as TONIO. He stayed with this company two seasons, following which he was a member of the CHICAGO OPERA COMPANY for one. He was heard in the world premieres of ZAZA, GERMANIA, and NATOMA, among other operas.

Samoset, an Indian chief (bass) in HANSON'S MERRY MOUNT.

Samson, leader of the Israelites, the central character in Bernard Rogers' *The Warrior* and SAINT-SAËNS's SAMSON ET DALILA. In both operas the role is for a tenor.

Samson et Dalila (Samson and Delilah), opera in three acts by SAINT-SAËNS. Libretto by Ferdinand Lemaire, based on the Biblical story. Premiere: Weimar, Dec. 2, 1877. American premiere: New Orleans, Jan. 4, 1893.

Characters: Samson, leader of the Israelites (tenor); Dalila, a Philistine, priestess of the Temple of Dagon (mezzo-soprano); High Priest of Dagon (baritone); Abimelech, Satrap of Gaza (bass); an old Hebrew (bass); Messenger of the Philistines (tenor); Hebrews; Philistines; people of Gaza; dancers. The setting is Gaza, Palestine, about 1150 B.C.

Act I. A public square. The Hebrews, in bondage to the Philistines, lament their lot. Samson, their muscular leader, tries to hearten them by urging them to praise God and not to complain ("Arrêtez, ô mes frères"). Abimelech begins to harass Samson, until the latter kills him with his own sword. The High Priest emerges from the temple to call the Philistines to avenge the Satrap's death ("Maudite à jamais soit la race"). Rallying under Samson's leadership, the Hebrews attack the Philistines. They sing a hymn of victory ("Hymne de joie") as the Philistines disperse, carrying away Abimelech's body. From the temple come Dalila and her maidens, bearing garlands for the Hebrews and singing a tribute ("Voici le printemps"). Coquettishly, Dalila approaches Samson to lure him. She sings a song of spring ("Printemps qui commence"). Bewitched by her beauty, Samson prays to heaven for the strength to resist her.

Act II. Before Dalila's house. Dalila invokes the magic of love to aid her in overpowering Samson ("Amour! viens aider ma faiblesse"). The High Priest urges Dalila to use her beauty to uncover the source of Samson's physical strength. When Samson arrives, a storm is brewing. Dalila lavishes her love on him ("Mon coeur s'ouvre à ta voix"), then begs him to disclose the secret of his strength. Samson denounces her as a temptress. Dalila goes inside her house. Samson follows, succumbing to her wiles. Within the house, Dalila cuts Samson's hair, which is the source of his power, and then calls to the Philistine soldiers to enter and seize him.

Act III, Scene 1. The mill of Gaza. Samson is a prisoner of the Philistines. His eyes have been plucked out, and he is in chains. As he turns the Philistine's mill, he begs God to have mercy on him ("Vois ma misère, hélas!"). In the distance are heard the voices of the Hebrews denouncing Samson for having betrayed them. ("Samson, qu'as-tu fait du Dieu de tes pères?").

Scene 2. The Temple of Dagon. The Philistines are celebrating their victory over the Hebrews with revelry ("BACCHANALE"). Samson, in chains, is led into the temple by a child. He is mocked by the Philistines, particularly by Dalila. Samson asks to be led between the two great pillars supporting the temple roof. He then prays to God for a brief return of his former strength ("Souviens-toi de ton serviteur"). His prayer is answered. Samson sends the pillars over, and the roof crashes down, burying Samson and his enemies.

Because of its Biblical subject and its wealth of choral music, *Samson et Dalila* used sometimes to be given as an oratorio. Its sound musical values, its highly effective mingling of French lyricism with Hebraic chants and oriental dances, make it a rewarding experience however it is performed. But it is unquestionably more effective in a stage production, since it is a consistently striking visual spectacle. In view of its dramatic and musical merits, it now seems strange that the opera had to wait so long for success. When one act was given in a concert version in Paris in 1875, critics complained about its "absence of melody" and "an instrumentation which nowhere rises above the level of the ordinary." There were no opera directors in Paris interested in the work, and it was finally introduced in Weimar in German, several years after its completion, on Dec. 2, 1877. It was first heard in France in Rouen in 1890 and in Paris in 1892 in a performance by the OPÉRA. By then the work had been acclaimed throughout Europe. Thus, paradoxically, France was one of the last nations in Europe to recognize one of the best-loved of French operas. It entered the repertory of the METROPOLITAN OPERA on Feb. 8, 1895, with Francesco TAMAGNO as Samson, and it has frequently been revived there since.

The American composer Bernard Rogers also wrote an opera in one act, *The Warrior*, on the theme of Samson and Delilah, with a libretto by Norman Corwin. It was introduced at the Metropolitan Opera on Jan. 11, 1947, but was soon withdrawn.

Samson, qu'as-tu fait du Dieu de tes pères?, chorus of the Hebrews denouncing Samson, in Act III, Scene 1, of SAINT-SAËNS's SAMSON ET DALILA.

San Antonio Grand Opera Festival, a festival founded in 1951 in San Antonio, Texas, by Max Reiter. Each spring it presents one performance each of four operas on successive weekends, conducted by Victor ALESSANDRO and with leading singers recruited from major opera companies. Among the less usual operas performed through the years have been BORIS GODUNOV, LE COQ D'OR, ELEKTRA, MARTHA, NABUCCO, and SALOME. The festival celebrated its eighteenth

anniversary on Mar. 1, 1969, with a new production of FAUST staged in the theater of the Performing Arts Center.

San Carlo Opera (Naples), *see* TEATRO SAN CARLO.

San Carlo Opera Company, an American company named after the celebrated Neapolitan house. It was organized in 1909 by Fortuno GALLO. From then up to the time of its demise in 1955, it toured the United States in popular-priced opera performances. It was an unsubsidized, self-supporting company. While it had for the most part included young and unknown singers (some of whom later became famous, including Eugene Conley, Dorothy KIRSTEN, and Jean MADEIRA), it also occasionally featured such famous performers as BONELLI, BORI, JERITZA, MARTINELLI, RUFFO, and SCHIPA.

Sancho Panza, *see* PANZA, SANCHO.

S'ancor si piange in cielo, the aria of the Queen seeking consolation at the tomb of Charles V in the opening of Act V of VERDI's DON CARLOS.

Sancto spirito cavaliere, Rienzi's battle hymn in Act III of WAGNER's RIENZI.

Sand, Georges (born Amadine Aurore Dupin), novelist. Born Paris, July 1, 1804; died Nohant, France, June 8, 1876. Her novel *Consuelo* was made into operas by Giovanni Gordigiani, Vladimir Kashperov, Giacomo Orefice, and Alfonso Rendano. Other operas based on Sand's novels include Julius Benedict's *The Red Beard* and Augusto Machado's *Laureana*.

Sanderson, Sybil, soprano. Born Sacramento, Cal., Dec. 7, 1865; died Paris, May 15, 1903. MASSENET wrote several operas for her, including THAÏS. She went to Paris when she was nineteen and attended the Conservatory, where her teachers included Mathilde MARCHESI and Giovanni SBRIGLIA. Her debut took place at The Hague in 1888 in the title role of MANON. She was acclaimed, and the Paris Exposition of 1889 engaged Massenet to write an opera expressly for her. The work was *Esclarmonde,* and Sanderson made her Parisian debut in the title role at the OPÉRA-COMIQUE on May 14, 1889. The opera was one of her triumphs; within a short period she appeared in it a hundred times in Paris, as well as in Brussels and St. Petersburg. Massenet now regarded her as the ideal interpreter of his female roles. She was next acclaimed as Thaïs, another role written for her. On Jan. 16, 1895, she made her American debut at the METROPOLITAN OPERA in *Manon*. However, she failed to duplicate her striking European successes in this country. In 1902 she returned to Paris.

Sandman, a character (soprano) in HUMPERDINCK'S HANSEL AND GRETEL.

Sandman's Lullaby, see DER KLEINE SANDMANN BIN ICH.

Sandor Barinkay, landowner and principal character (tenor) in Johann STRAUSS'S THE GYPSY BARON.

Sandys, Lady Marigold, Sir Gower Lackland's fiancée (soprano) in HANSON'S MERRY MOUNT.

San Francisco Opera Company, one of the leading opera companies in the United States. It was organized by Gaetano MEROLA in 1923. Principal singers were recruited from the METROPOLITAN OPERA, while minor roles and chorus parts were taken by local singers; the orchestra was the San Francisco Symphony. Performances of the initial season took place in the Civic Auditorium. The repertory embraced ANDREA CHÉNIER, LA BOHÈME, MEFISTOFELE, ROMÉO ET JULIETTE, TOSCA, and IL TRITTICO. The principal singers included DE LUCA, DIDUR, GIGLI, and MUZIO. In 1924 the company was incorporated as a nonprofit organization with Merola as general director and Robert I. Bentley as president. A campaign for funds yielded enough to assure a regular season. In 1932, on the completion of the War Memorial Opera House, the company was transferred to its permanent home, inaugurating it with a performance of *Tosca* on Oct. 15.

In its first quarter of a century the company gave five hundred forty-eight performances of seventy-four operas. Gaetano Merola died only two weeks before the opening of the 1953 season, but there was no postponement. Kurt Herbert ADLER, formerly Merola's assistant, became artistic director, a post he has since then held. One of the crowning successes of the 1969 season was this company's first staging of ROSSINI'S LA CENERENTOLA, with Teresa BERGANZA.

Under the Merola regime the following novelties were given, together with favorites from the regular repertory: *Anima allegra* (Vittadini); LE COQ D'OR; L'ENFANT ET LES SORTILÈGES; FRA DIAVOLO; L'HEURE ESPAGNOLE; MÂROUF; MARTHA; *Il trittico;* and WERTHER.

Under Kurt Herbert Adler the opera company expanded both its activities and its repertory. Its world premieres have included DELLO JOIO'S *Blood Moon* and MOORE'S CARRY NATION. American premieres included: CHRISTOPHE COLOMB (first American staging); LES DIALOGUES DES CARMÉLITES; DIE FRAU OHNE SCHATTEN; JEANNE D'ARC AU BÛCHER; KATERINA ISMAILOVA; *The Little Portuguese Inn* (CHERUBINI); THE MAKROPOULOS AFFAIR; MÉDÉE (Cherubini); A MIDSUMMER NIGHT'S DREAM; THE ROYAL PALACE; TROILUS AND CRESSIDA.

Among the novelties offered have been: CAPRICCIO; CARMINA BURANA; *La cenerentola;* THE CRUCIBLE; ERWARTUNG; L'ITALIANA IN ALGERI; JENUFA; DIE KLUGE; LULU; LES PÊCHEURS DE PERLES; PIQUE DAME; I PURITANI; THE RAKE'S PROGRESS; LES TROYENS; THE TURN OF THE SCREW; THE VISITATION; WOZZECK.

In 1961 a Spring Opera was founded to present popular-priced performances with young American singers. Four years later there was established the WESTERN OPERA THEATER, under the musical direction of Herbert Grossman, to become the touring arm of the San Francisco Opera. During its first season it gave thirty-five performances in the Pacific Coast and Mountain states. In 1968–69, under the musical direction of Richard Woitach, it gave about one hundred fifty performances. The regular company in addition has presented seasons of opera in Los Angeles and San Diego.

sanglot, French for "sob," a term implying the interpolation of an exclamation, or emotional accent, in a vocal part.

Santa Fe Opera, an opera company founded in 1957 in Santa Fe, N.M., under the artistic direction of John Crosby. Its first presentation, MADAMA BUTTERFLY, took place on July 3, 1957, in an outdoor auditorium built on a seventy-five-acre ranch just outside the city, seating about five hundred; the seating capacity was subsequently increased to twelve hundred with the addition of a balcony in 1965. The season lasts through July and August, presenting annually about eight different works. A strong accent has been placed on world and American premieres. The former included FLOYD'S WUTHERING HEIGHTS, Marvin David Levy's *The Tower,* and SCHOENBERG's *Die Jacobsleiter* (an oratorio staged as an opera). Among the American premieres were: DIE BASSARIDEN; BOULEVARD SOLITUDE; CARDILLAC (new version); DAPHNE (Richard STRAUSS); THE DEVILS OF LOUDON; HELP, HELP, THE GLOBOLINKS!; KÖNIG HIRSCH; LULU; NEUES VOM TAGE; THE NOSE; *Persephone* (STRAVINSKY, first American staging).

The company visited Berlin and Belgrade in 1961, its presentations including THE BALLAD OF BABY DOE. On the early morning of July 27, 1967—only a few hours after the American premiere of the new version of HINDEMITH's *Cardillac*—the opera house burned to the ground. Within thirty-six hours, the company continued its season in the Sweeney Gymnasium of the Santa Fe High School without missing a single performance. A new theater was bulit, opening on July 2, 1968, with *Madama Butterfly.*

Sante, a servant (silent part) in WOLF-FERRARI'S THE SECRET OF SUZANNE.

Santuzza, a village girl (soprano) in love with Turiddu in MASCAGNI'S CAVALLERIA RUSTICANA, a role created by Gemma BELLINCIONI.

Sapho, (1) opera in three or four acts by GOUNOD. Libretto by Émile Augier. Premiere: Paris Opéra, Apr. 16, 1851. This was Gounod's first opera, written for the prima donna Pauline VIARDOT, who created the title role. Though enthusiastically praised in BERLIOZ' review, the opera was a comparative failure and received only six performances in the first season. It was later revised, once in two acts and once in four, but never really caught on. The central character is the Greek poetess of Lesbos. The concluding aria, "O ma lyre immortelle," is familiar.

(2) Opera in five acts by MASSENET. Libretto by Henri Cain and Arthur Bernède, based on the novel of the same name by Alphonse DAUDET. Premiere: Opera-Comique, Nov. 27, 1897. American premiere; Manhattan Opera House, Nov. 17, 1909. Jean Gaussin, a simple country fellow, falls in love with Fanny, who has served as an artist's model of Sapho. Later, learning of her loose life, he leaves her but eventually returns because he cannot live without her. While he is asleep, Fanny disappears, convinced that she and Jean can never be happy together. Jean's aria in Act I, "Ah! qu'il est loin," is the best-known vocal excerpt.

S'apra il ciel, Clorinda's dying air, in which she sees heaven opening up for her. It closes MONTEVERDI's opera IL COMBATTIMENTO DI TANCREDI E CLORINDA.

saraband, a sedate dance, probably of Spanish origin, in triple time, with the phrase beginning on the first beat, that is, without an upbeat. Sarabands appear in some seventeenth- and eighteenth-century operas. An aria found in HANDEL's RINALDO, "Lascia ch'io pianga," is set to an instrumental saraband from his earlier opera ALMIRA.

Sarastro, priest of Isis (bass) in MOZART's THE MAGIC FLUTE.

Sarastro's invocation, *see* O ISIS UND OSIRIS.

Sardou, Victorien, playwright. Born

Paris, Sept. 7, 1831; died there Nov. 8, 1908. His dramas and comedies, among the most popular produced in France in the nineteenth century, were often used for operas. The most famous was PUCCINI's TOSCA. Others derived from Sardou's plays or for which Sardou wrote the text were: BIZET's GRISÉLIDIS; FÉVRIER's *Gismonda;* GIORDANO's FEDORA and MADAME SANS-GÊNE; LEROUX's *Cléopâtre* and *Théodora;* Emile Paladhile's *La Patrie;* PIERNÉ's *La fille du Tabarin;* SAINT-SAËNS's *Les Barbares;* and Nikolai Soloviev's *Cordelia.*

Sargent, Sir Malcolm, conductor. Born Stamford, Eng., Apr. 29, 1895; died London, Oct. 3, 1967. He studied organ at the Royal College of Organists in London and piano with Benno Moiseiwitsch. His conducting debut took place at a Promenade Concert in 1921. In 1924 he became a conductor of the BRITISH NATIONAL OPERA COMPANY, where he led the world premieres of HUGH THE DROVER and AT THE BOAR'S HEAD; from 1926 to 1928 and again in 1951 he led the D'Oyly Carte Company; and in 1936 and again in 1954 he directed performances at COVENT GARDEN, including the premiere of TROILUS AND CRESSIDA. However, his principal significance lay in the fields of symphonic and choral music. Between 1950 and 1957 he was the principal conductor of the BBC Symphony. He was knighted in 1947.

Sarka, opera in three acts by FIBICH. Libretto by Aňezka Schulzova. Premiere: National Theater, Prague, Dec. 28, 1897. The Bohemian legend that inspired this opera was also the subject of one of SMETANA's tone poems in the *My Country (Má Vlast)* cycle. Sarka is a Bohemian folk heroine who slew the knight Ctirad. The overture, the soprano aria "You are lovely as a summer night," the tenor aria "I am not afraid, cold death," and the duet by soprano and tenor, "How lovely you are," are of special interest.

Sarti, Giuseppe, composer. Born Faenza, Italy, Dec. 1, 1729; died Berlin, July 28, 1802. After studying with Padre Martini in Bologna he became organist

of the Faenza Cathedral in 1748. His first opera, *Pompeo in Armenia,* was successfully given in his native city in 1752. IL RE PASTORE, in 1753, made him famous. In the same year he was called to Copenhagen to direct an Italian opera troupe. During his prolonged stay in Denmark he wrote some twenty operas, many of them acclaimed in Italy. From 1775 to 1779 he was director of the Ospedaletto Conservatory in Venice. From 1779 to 1784 he was MAESTRO DI CAPPELLA of the Milan Cathedral, and from 1784 to 1802, court conductor to Catherine II in Russia. He died in Berlin on his way back to Italy from Russia. The most famous of his more than fifty operas were *Il re pastore* (1753); *Ciro riconosciuto* (1756); *Armida* (1759); *Didone abbandonata* (1768); *Achille in Sciro* (1779); *Giulio Sabino* (1781); *I due litiganti* (1782); *Castore e Polluce* (1786). MOZART in his DON GIOVANNI has the Don's band entertain him with a melody from *I due litiganti.*

Satie, Erik, composer. Born Honfleur, France, May 17, 1866; died Paris, July 1, 1925. This extreme individualist, noted for his tender and humorous music, his whimsical titles, and his peculiar instructions to performers, composed a "symphonic drama" for four sopranos and chamber orchestra which is sometimes staged as a serious one-act opera. It is based on three Platonic dialogues and entitled SOCRATE (1920). In addition he composed an operetta for puppets, *Geneviève de Brabant* (1899), and two operettas for live singers, *Pousse d'amour* (1905) and *La Piège de Méduse* (1913).

Sauguet, Henri, composer. Born Bordeaux, France, May 18, 1901. His music study took place with local teachers and with Charles Koechlin in Paris. He then allied himself with several young musicians who, as the "School of Arcueil," sought the inspiration of Erik SATIE. Sauguet's first major work was an OPÉRA BOUFFE, *Le Plumet de Colonel,* given in Paris in 1924. After achieving success with several ballets,

SAUVÉE! 618

he wrote music criticism for various Parisian journals and helped found the literary magazines *Candide* and *Revue Hebdomadaire*. He visited the United States in 1953. His operas: *La Contrabasse* (1930) ; LA CHARTREUSE DE PARME (1939) ; *La Gageure imprévue* (1944) ; *Les Caprices de Marianne* (1954) ; LA DAME AUX CAMÉLIAS (1957).

Sauvée! Christ est ressuscité!, closing chorus, hailing Marguerite's redemption, in Act V, Scene 2, of GOUNOD'S FAUST.

Savage, Henry Wilson, impresario. Born Alton, N.H., Mar. 21, 1859; died Boston, Nov. 29, 1927. Originally a real-estate promoter, when he was compelled to take over the Castle Theater in Boston, he decided to use it as a home for opera. Without previous musical experience, he organized a company in 1897, presenting grand and light operas. In 1900 he founded the English Grand Opera Company, which that year gave opera in English at the METROPOLITAN OPERA HOUSE in New York. In 1904 he organized a touring company to present PARSIFAL (in English) throughout the United States. On Oct. 15, 1906, his company gave the American premiere of MADAMA BUTTERFLY in Washington, D.C. His company toured the country again in 1911 with THE GIRL OF THE GOLDEN WEST (in English). The company also gave the American premieres of such celebrated operettas as Franz Lehár's *The Merry Widow* and Oscar Straus's *The Waltz Dream*.

Savitri, chamber opera in one act by HOLST. Libretto by the composer, based on an episode in the MAHABHARATA. Premiere: London, Dec. 5, 1916. American premiere: Chicago, Jan. 23, 1934. Death (bass) comes to claim the woodcutter Satyavan (tenor) ; but he is saved when his wife, Savitri (soprano), wins Death over through love and reason.

Sawallisch, Wolfgang, conductor. Born Munich, Aug. 26, 1923. During World War II he studied piano with Wolfgang Ruoff, theory with Hans Sachsse, and conducting at the Munich Conservatory.

In 1947 he became a coach at the Augsburg Opera. In 1950–51 he conducted operettas, and in 1953 operas with that company. Between 1953 and 1957 he served as general music director in Aachen. From 1957 to 1959 he was the principal conductor of the Wiesebaden Opera and from 1959 to 1963 general music director in Cologne. Meanwhile, in 1957 he had a triumph at the BAYREUTH FESTIVAL with a new production of TRISTAN UND ISOLDE. He also conducted new productions there of DER FLIEGENDE HOLLÄNDER in 1959 and TANNHÄUSER in 1961. He made frequent appearances at other music festivals, including those in Vienna, EDINBURGH, and Montreux. He toured the United States in 1964 with the Vienna Symphony Orchestra. He has since held the post of music director of the Cologne Municipal Theater and has headed a class in conducting at the Cologne Academy of Music. In 1969 he was appointed principal conductor of the MUNICH OPERA in succession to Joseph KEILBERTH.

Sayao, Bidu, soprano. Born Rio de Janeiro, Brazil, May 11, 1902. After preliminary study in her native city, she went to France and became a pupil of Jean DE RESZKE. Returning to Brazil, she made her concert debut in 1925 and her opera debut as ROSINA a year after that. She was now engaged by the OPÉRA-COMIQUE in Paris, where she appeared for several years. In 1935 she made her American debut in a recital in New York. On Feb. 14, 1937, she made her bow at the METROPOLITAN OPERA in MANON and was hailed. She remained a permanent member of that company for the next decade and a half and was particularly successful in such roles as those of GILDA, VIOLETTA, MIMI, JULIETTE, Rosina, and Manon. After leaving the Metropolitan, she sang in South America and Europe. She made her last appearances in opera in Rio de Janeiro in 1958. She now lives in retirement in Maine.

Sbriglia, Giovanni, tenor and teacher of singing. Born Naples, Italy, June 23, 1832; died Paris, Feb. 20, 1916. After attending the Naples Conservatory, he made his debut with the SAN CARLO OPERA in his twenty-first year. He then appeared throughout Italy. Max MARETZEK engaged him for the Academy of Music in New York. He appeared in opera in Havana, Mexico, and United States until 1875, when he settled in Paris as a teacher. He re-formed the voice of Jean DE RESZKE from baritone to tenor, and also helped train Édouard and Josephine DE RESZKE. His many famous pupils included Lillian NORDICA, Pol PLAÇON, and Sybil SANDERSON. In 1890 he was appointed a member of the Royal Academy in Florence. He was also an officer of the French Academy.

Scala, La, *see* TEATRO ALLA SCALA.

Scalchi, Sofia, contralto. Born Turin, Italy, Nov. 29, 1850; died Rome, Aug. 22, 1922. After studying with Augusta Boccabadati, she made her debut in Mantua in 1866 in UN BALLO IN MASCHERA. She scored her first major success when she made her bow at COVENT GARDEN on Nov. 5, 1868, as AZUCENA. She appeared at Covent Garden each season thereafter until 1890. Meanwhile, in 1882 she came to the United States with the MAPLESON company. She made her debut at the METROPOLITAN OPERA as SIEBEL in the performance of FAUST that opened that opera house on Oct. 22, 1883. In 1884 she returned to the Mapleson company for four years; in 1891 she was back at the Metropolitan for five seasons. After appearing in the American premieres of ANDREA CHÉNIER, FALSTAFF, LA GIOCONDA, and OTELLO, she went into retirement in 1896.

Scaria, Emil, bass-baritone. Born Graz, Austria, Sept. 18, 1838; died Blasewitz, Ger., July 22, 1886. His music study took place at the Vienna Conservatory. In 1860 he made his opera debut in Pest as ST. BRIS. He was such a failure that he abandoned the stage for further study, selecting Manuel GARCÍA as his teacher. He returned to the opera stage in Dessau but realized his first success at the Crystal Palace in London in 1862. In 1863 he appeared with the Leipzig Opera and in 1864 with the DRESDEN OPERA. In 1872 he was engaged by the VIENNA OPERA. He created the role of Gurnemanz when PARSIFAL was introduced in BAYREUTH in 1882. He began revealing signs of mental disturbance by forgetting whole pages from operas in which he was appearing. He was last heard in TANNHÄUSER, and during the second act, he inquired of the prompter what opera they were giving and had to be led from the stage. After that he broke down completely and went insane.

Scarlatti, Alessandro, composer. Born Palermo, Sicily, May 2, 1660; died Naples, Italy, Oct. 24, 1725. He was the founder and leading figure of the Neapolitan school that developed many of the techniques and traditions of Italian opera. After studying with Giacomo Carissimi in Rome, he completed his first opera, *L'errore innocente,* which attracted considerable interest. In 1682 Scarlatti settled in Naples, his home for the next twenty years. There he became MAESTRO DI CAPPELLA to the Viceroy. He wrote prolifically for the stage, and his operas enjoyed immense favor both with royalty and the general public. Political disturbances in Naples sent Scarlatti to Rome in 1702. Through the influence of Cardinal Ottoboni, he was appointed assistant *maestro di cappella* of the church of Santa Maria Maggiore in 1703; four years later he became the *maestro.* In 1709 Scarlatti returned to Naples to resume his old post with the Viceroy. Except for occasional visits to Rome, he remained in Naples for the rest of his life. His pupils included Francesco DURANTE, Johann Adolph HASSE, and Nicola LOGROSCINO —all later famous as composers.

The popularity of Scarlatti's operas, and the influence of his personality, shifted the center of Italian operatic activity from Venice to Naples. In Naples such characteristic forms as the Italian OVERTURE, the ARIA DA CAPO, and the accompanied RECITATIVE were developed; a new importance was given to ensemble numbers, the chorus, and the orchestra. So widely were Scarlatti's operas imitated that Charles Burney, writing in the 1770's, declared: "I find part of his property among the stolen goods of all the best composers of the first forty or fifty years of the eighteenth century." The most celebrated of Scarlatti's hundred and some operas were: *Teodora* (1693); *Pirro e Demetrio* (1694); *L'Eraclea* (1700); *Mitridate Eupatore* (1707); *La principessa fedele* (1710); *Il Tigrane* (1715); IL TRIONFO DELL' ONORE (1718); *Telemaco* (1718); *Griselda* (1721); *La virtù negli amori* (1721).

Alessandro's son Domenico Scarlatti (1685–1757) is now remembered only for the five hundred and fifty sonatas he composed for the harpsichord. These fascinating works were all composed relatively late in Scarlatti's life. In his early years he wrote a dozen or so operas, all appreciated in their day. The most important were: *Ifigenia in Aulide* (1713); *Amleto* (1715); and *Narciso* (1720).

Scarlet Letter, The, (1) novel by Nathaniel HAWTHORNE, the source of operas by Walter DAMROSCH and Vittorio GIANNINI. The setting is Boston in the seventeenth century. Hester Prynne is condemned to be an outcast and wear the scarlet letter "A" (for Adulteress) when she refuses to reveal the identity of her child's father. The father proves to be a young minister, Arthur Dimmesdale, who confesses and then dies. Hester's husband, Robert Chillingworth, who had known the secret, becomes mentally unstable, but Hester and her daughter, Pearl, live on. The operatic adaptations differ somewhat.

(2) Opera in three acts by Walter Damrosch. Libretto by George Parsons Lathrop, based on the Hawthorne novel. Premiere: Damrosch Opera Company, Boston, Feb. 10, 1896.

(3) Opera in two acts by Vittorio Giannini. Libretto by the composer, based on the Hawthorne novel. Premiere: Hamburg State Opera, June 2, 1938.

Scarpia, chief of police (baritone) in PUCCINI'S TOSCA.

scena, Italian for "scene," a term used in opera for a vocal number (generally, but not always, for one singer) more extended and of a dramatic character than an aria.

Scène des cheveux, *see* OH! QU'EST-CE QUE C'EST? . . . TES CHEVEUX.

Scène infernale, orchestral excerpt from PROKOFIEV'S THE LOVE FOR THREE ORANGES.

Schalk, Franz, conductor. Born Vienna, Austria, May 27, 1863; died Edlach, Austria, Sept. 2, 1931. His music study took place in Vienna with Anton Bruckner, among other teachers. In 1888 he conducted in Reichenbach. After appearances in Graz and Prague, he made his bow at COVENT GARDEN in 1898. On Dec. 14, 1898, he made his American debut at the METROPOLITAN OPERA, conducting DIE WALKÜRE. In 1900 he was engaged by the VIENNA OPERA, where he remained a principal conductor till the end of his life; from 1918 on he was the institution's musical director (in collaboration with Richard STRAUSS between 1919 and 1924). He helped found the SALZBURG FESTIVAL in 1920 and was one of its major conductors.

Schatzerwalz (Treasure Waltz), *see* HA, SEHT, ES WINKT.

Schau her, das ist ein Taler, Pedro's wolf narrative (Wolfserzählung) in Act I of D'ALBERT'S TIEFLAND.

Schaunard, a musician (baritone) in PUCCINI'S LA BOHÈME.

Schauspieldirektor, Der (The Impresario), one-act comedy with music by MOZART. Libretto by Gottlieb Stephanie. Premiere: Schönbrunn, Austria, Feb. 7, 1786. American premiere: New York City, Nov. 9, 1870. The original play, as written on commission for performance at a party given by the Emperor Joseph II, was a rather long one-act farce with opportunity for only five musical numbers: an overture, two soprano arias, a trio, and a finale. There were ten characters, only four of whom had to sing at all; and of these, only two—the sopranos—had to sing music of any difficulty. The story has to do with Frank, the impresario of a troupe that has failed in Vienna, and his efforts to get another group of players together to try again in Salzburg. In the end he is so disgusted with the selfish motives of the applicants and their lack of artistic ideals that he walks out on them; but his stage manager, Buff, takes over with the backing of a banker named Eiler. In an extensively revised text by Louis Schneider, first produced in 1845, and still often used with revisions, five of the nonsinging characters were completely omitted, and the play reduced to its most amusing and musical sections. Buff is renamed "Mozart," Frank is renamed "SCHIKANEDER" (librettist and impresario for THE MAGIC FLUTE), and the two sopranos, "Madame Lange" (Mozart's sister-in-law, who sang in the premiere) and "Madame Cavalieri" (another well-known soprano, also in the premiere). Eiler is amusingly embarrassed when both show up for auditions as leading lady, for one is a mistress he is trying to discard (she's a little long in the tooth) and the other is a young girl whom he has just picked up in the part that morning. (Incidentally, both prima donnas were precisely twenty-five when they sang at the premiere.) The impasse is resolved by finding roles for both women and by Eiler's paying both salaries. When Mozart received the commission for the music, he was part way through composing THE MARRIAGE OF FIGARO, and at least two of the numbers, the overture and a trio for the two sopranos and Buff (Mozart), are worthy of that masterpiece. The little jewel, in versions based on Schneider's condensation, is frequently performed by opera workshops; but the tendency nowadays is to revert to the original names of the characters. Possibly this is because we do not like to see the divine Mozart represented as a low-comedy conniver.

Scheff, Fritzi, soprano. Born Vienna, Aug. 30, 1879; died New York City, Apr. 8, 1954. While she achieved her greatest successes on the Broadway stage, particularly in Victor HERBERT's operettas, she first received recognition in opera. Her mother, Hortense Scheff, was a member of the VIENNA OPERA. Fritzi Scheff attended the Hoch Conservatory in Frankfurt, then made her debut in that city in 1897 in ROMÉO ET JULIETTE. She made her American debut at the METROPOLITAN OPERA on Dec. 28, 1900, as Marcellina in FIDELIO. She was then heard in the lighter-voiced roles of the Italian and French repertories, as well as in WAGNER and MOZART operas. She abandoned opera in 1903 to appear in Victor Herbert's *Babette,* and in 1906 she achieved a triumph in Herbert's *Mlle. Modiste.* She had a long and successful career in operettas, musical comedies, and vaudeville.

Scherchen, Hermann, conductor. Born Berlin, June 21, 1891; died Florence, June 12, 1966. Self-taught in music, he played the viola with the Berlin Philharmonic before becoming a conductor. He had a long and distinguished career as a symphony conductor at modern music festivals, mainly in Winterthur, Switzerland. He made his American debut as conductor late in life, at Philharmonic Hall in New York in Nov., 1964. A staunch advocate of modern music, he led the premieres of several significant new operas, including IL PRIGIONIERO in 1950 and KÖNIG HIRSCH. He was also responsible through his performances for the belated recognition of MOSES UND ARON. Other modern operas heard under his leadership included ABSTRAKTE NO. 1, THE GAMBLER, HIN UND ZURÜCK, MAVRA, and SALOME. He adapted Webern's second cantata as a stage work, presenting it for the first time in Naples in 1958 under the title *Il Cuore.* He was conducting a performance of MALIPIERO's opera *Orpheus* in Florence when he suffered a fatal heart attack.

Scherz, List, und Rache (Jest, Cunning,

and Revenge), *see* GOETHE, JOHANN WOLFGANG VON.

Schikaneder, Johann Emanuel, actor, singer, playwright, and impresario. Born Straubing, Austria, Sept. 1, 1748; died Vienna, Sept. 21, 1812. He was a member of a company of strolling players before settling in Vienna in 1784. Six years later he commissioned MOZART (whom he had previously befriended in Salzburg) to write an opera for his THEATER-AUF-DER-WIEDEN. The opera, for which Schikaneder supplied the libretto, WAS THE MAGIC FLUTE. Schikaneder created the role of Papageno. Later, opening another house, the THEATER-AN-DER-WIEN, he placed a statue of himself as Papageno on the roof. It was for this theater that the impresario commissioned BEETHOVEN'S FIDELIO. Long successful, the talented Schikaneder ultimately died in poverty.

Schiller, Friedrich von, poet and dramatist. Born Marbach, Ger., Nov. 10, 1759; died Weimar, May 9, 1805. An outstanding figure in German Romantic literature, his many poetical dramas were a bountiful source of opera texts, among them: *Die Braut von Messina* (FIBICH'S *The Bride of Messina* and Nicola Vaccai's *La sposa di Messina*), *Die Bürgschaft* (operas by George Hellmesberger and Franz Lachner), *Don Carlos* (operas by Michael Costa and VERDI), *Fiesco* (LALO'S *Fiesque*), *Die Jungfrau von Orleans* (BALFE'S *Joan of Arc*, REZNIČEK'S *Die Jungfrau von Orleans*, TCHAIKOVSKY'S THE MAID OF ORLEANS, Nicola Vaccai's *Giovanna d'Arco*, and Verdi's *Giovanna d'Arco*), *Kabale und Liebe* (Verdi's LUISA MILLER), *Das Lied von der Glocke* (D'INDY'S *Le Chant de la cloche*), *Die Räuber* (KLEBE'S *Die Räuber*, MERCADANTE'S *I briganti,* Verdi's *I masnadieri*), *Der Taucher* (opera by REICHARDT); *Wallenstein* (operas by August von Adelburg and WEINBERGER), *Wilhelm Tell* (Benjamin Carr's *The Archers,* ROSSINI'S WILLIAM TELL).

Schillings, Max von, conductor and composer. Born Düren, Ger., Apr. 19, 1868; died Berlin, July 23, 1933. Trained for a career in science, he also studied music. While attending the Munich University, he was influenced by Richard STRAUSS and Ludwig Thuille to specialize in music. In 1892 he became an assistant conductor at the BAYREUTH FESTIVAL, and a decade later chorus master. From 1908 to 1918 he was general music director of the city of Stuttgart; when, in 1912, a new opera house was opened, Schillings was given the honorific "von" by the king of Württemberg. In 1919 he succeeded Richard Strauss as musical director of the BERLIN STATE OPERA. He resigned in 1925 after a dispute with the Prussian Ministry of Fine Arts. When the Nazis came into power in 1933, just before his death, he was appointed principal conductor of the Städtische Oper in Berlin (BERLIN DEUTSCHE STAATSOPER).

Schillings visited the United States for the first time in 1924, appearing as a conductor of German operas. He returned in 1931 as principal conductor of the German Grand Opera Company. His first opera, *Ingwelde,* was produced in Karlsruhe in 1894. It was more than two decades before he achieved a major success as a composer; it came with his opera MONA LISA, given in Stuttgart on Sept. 26, 1915, and soon thereafter performed extensively in Europe and the United States. Schillings' style was strongly influenced by WAGNER. Besides the two operas already mentioned, he wrote *Der Pfeifertag* (1899, revised 1931) and *Moloch* (1906).

In 1923 Schillings married the prima donna of the Berlin Opera, Barbara Kemp. She had created the title role in his *Mona Lisa.*

Schipa, Tito, tenor. Born Lecce, Italy, Jan. 2, 1889; died New York City, Dec. 16, 1965. He attended the Lecce Conservatory, received his first vocal lesson in his fifteenth year, and when he was twenty-one studied voice with Emilio Piccoli in Milan. His debut took place in 1911 in Vercelli in LA TRAVIATA. Success came in Rome, after which he appeared in leading opera houses of Europe and South America. In 1919 he was engaged by the CHICAGO OPERA, where he remained until 1932. On Nov. 23, 1932, he made his debut at the METROPOLITAN OPERA in L'ELISIR D'AMORE. He remained at the Metropolitan until 1935, and returned during the 1940–41 season. During this period he was often heard at LA SCALA and other major European opera houses. He made a concert tour of the United States in 1947. In 1955 he was a representative of the Italian government in an Italian opera festival held in the principal cities of Belgium. He retired in 1962, after an extensive concert tour undertaken at the age of seventy-three.

Schippers, Thomas, conductor. Born Kalamazoo, Mich., Mar. 9, 1930. His musical training took place at the Curtis Institute, Yale University, and the Juilliard School of Music. He made his conducting debut in New York City with the Lemonade Opera in 1949. One year later he conducted the premiere of THE CONSUL. On Apr. 9, 1952, he made his NEW YORK CITY OPERA debut with AMAHL AND THE NIGHT VISITORS. He conducted various performances at the New York City Opera for the next three years, including the world premiere of THE TENDER LAND. In 1954 he led the world premiere of THE SAINT OF BLEECKER STREET in New York. In May, 1955, he made a successful debut at LA SCALA. On Dec. 24 of the same year, he made his first appearance at the METROPOLITAN OPERA, conducting DON PASQUALE. Since then he has directed distinguished opera performances at La Scala, the Metropolitan Opera, the FESTIVAL OF TWO WORLDS in Spoleto, and with various other opera companies and at major festivals. In June, 1962, he conducted the first staged presentation of L'ATLANTÍDA at La Scala. He succeeded Max RUDOLF as music director of the Cincinnati Symphony in 1970.

Schlafe wohl! und mag dich reuen (Dormi pur), the Good-Night Quartet of Lionel, Plunkett, "Martha," and "Julia," in Act II of FLOTOW's MARTHA.

Schläfst du, Hagen, Alberich's description to Hagen of the curse of the ring in the opening of Act II of WAGNER's GÖTTERDÄMMERUNG.

Schlemil, Giulietta's lover (bass) in OFFENBACH's THE TALES OF HOFFMANN.

Schlusnus, Heinrich, baritone. Born Braubach, Ger., Aug. 6, 1888; died Frankfurt, June 19, 1952. He studied singing in Berlin with Louis Bachner and in 1915 made his opera debut in Hamburg. From 1915 to 1917 he was a member of the Nuremberg Opera and from 1917 on a principal baritone of the BERLIN OPERA. He also made many guest appearances in European opera houses, including BAYREUTH, and· with the CHICAGO OPERA. He was a noted concert artist.

Schmedes, Erik, tenor. Born Gjentofte, Denmark, Aug. 27, 1866; died Vienna, Mar. 23, 1931. He was trained as a pianist, but in 1888 Pauline VIARDOT-GARCÍA heard him sing and advised him to specialize in singing. After studying with N. Rothmühl in Berlin and Désirée ARTÔT in Paris, he made his debut in Wiesbaden on Jan. 11, 1891, in the baritone role of the Herald in LOHENGRIN. In 1894 he was engaged as first baritone of the Nuremberg Opera. After an additional period of study with Luise Ress in Vienna, he became a member of the DRESDEN OPERA in 1896. He was advised by Bernhard Pollini to change the range of his voice to tenor. After training with A. Iffert in Dresden, he made his debut as tenor at the VIENNA OPERA on Feb. 11, 1898, as SIEGFRIED. He remained a principal tenor of the Vienna Opera until 1924. During this period he made many guest appearances in leading European opera houses and at the BAYREUTH FESTIVAL. On Nov. 18, 1908, he made his American debut at the METROPOLITAN OPERA as SIEGMUND; he remained there only a single season.

Schmeling, Gertrud Elisabeth, see MARA, GERTRUD.

Schmelzlied, see NOTHUNG! NOTHUNG!

Schmidt-Isserstedt, Hans, conductor. Born Berlin, May 5, 1900. He studied composition with Franz SCHREKER in Berlin but was influenced to become a conductor by hearing performances by NIKISCH, WEINGARTNER, and MUCK. After appointments in opera houses in Wuppertal, Rostock, and Darmstadt, he became principal conductor of the HAMBURG STATE OPERA in 1935 and the BERLIN DEUTSCHE STAATSOPER in 1943. Though principally a symphonic conductor, both with the North German Radio Symphony in Hamburg since 1945 and the Stockholm Philharmonic since 1955, he has given notable operatic performances at GLYNDEBOURNE, COVENT GARDEN, and the Hamburg State Opera, including premieres. He made his American debut as guest conductor of the Philadelphia Orchestra in Nov. of 1961.

Schmiedlied, *see* HO-HO! SCHMIEDE, MEIN HAMMER.

Schnorr von Carolsfeld, Ludwig, tenor. Born Munich, July 2, 1836; died Dresden, July 21, 1865. He created the role of TRISTAN. After attending the Leipzig Conservatory, and studying privately with Eduard Devrient, he made his debut at the Karlsruhe Opera in MÉHUL'S JOSEPH. After a brief period there he was engaged by the DRESDEN OPERA in 1860, where he remained five years. During this period, in 1862 he returned to the Karlsruhe Opera to appear in LOHENGRIN, making such an impression on WAGNER that the latter decided to have him create the role of Tristan. Thus, Schnorr von Carolsfeld appeared in the world premiere of *Tristan und Isolde* in Munich on June 10, 1865, an occasion upon which his wife, Malwina Garrigues-Schnorr (1825–1904), created the part of ISOLDE. He died a little more than a month afterward of rheumatic fever.

Schoeck, Othmar, composer and conductor. Born Brünnen, Switzerland, Sept. 1, 1886; died Zürich, Mar. 8, 1957. He was the son of Alfred Schoeck, a famous painter, and for a while considered following in his father's footsteps. He decided on music in his seventeenth year. After studying at the Zürich Conservatory and with Max Reger in Leipzig, he conducted various choral and orches-

tral groups in Switzerland. His first opera, *Don Ranudo,* was introduced in 1919. Subsequent compositions included several operas: *Venus* (1922); PENTHE-SILEA (1927); *Massimilla Doni* (1937); *Das Schloss Durande* (1943). There was a Schoeck Festival in Berne, Switzerland, in Apr., 1934.

Schoeffler, Paul, bass baritone. Born Dresden, Sept. 15, 1897. After attending the Dresden Conservatory, he studied singing with various teachers, including Mario SAMMARCO in Milan. Fritz BUSCH heard him sing in 1925 and engaged him for the DRESDEN STATE OPERA, where he appeared for the next twelve years. In 1937 he became a permanent member of the VIENNA STATE OPERA and he was also heard at the BAYREUTH and SALZBURG festivals, at COVENT GARDEN, and in the principal opera houses of Paris, Prague, Budapest, Brussels, Amsterdam, Milan, Rome, and Naples, being particularly successful in the roles of BORIS GODUNOV, KURWENAL, IAGO, FIGARO (in *The Marriage of Figaro*), DON GIOVANNI, and AMFORTAS. He appeared in the world premieres of CARDILLAC, ŠVANDA, CAPRICCIO, DANTONS TOD, and SLY. He made his American debut at the METROPOLITAN OPERA on Jan. 26, 1949, as Jokanaan in SALOME and was acclaimed for his characterization as well as for his singing. He last appeared at the Metropolitan in 1956.

Schoenberg, Arnold, composer. Born Vienna, Sept. 13, 1874; died Brentwood, Cal., July 13, 1951. The father of atonal music wrote several works for the stage. He began music study at the Realschule in Vienna and continued it privately with Alexander ZEMLINSKY. His earliest works inspired a hostile reaction in Vienna in 1900. He began writing in an atonal style after 1908, and in this forbidding idiom he produced such iconoclastic works as ERWARTUNG (1909), a monodrama, and the drama with music DIE GLÜCKLICHE HAND (1913). He began developing TWELVE-TONE TECHNIQUES in 1915 and by 1925 had codified a system which he espoused with the fervor of a prophet. The most important of his disciples in the field of opera composition were BERG and WELLESZ.

Schoenberg left Europe immediately after the rise of Hitler and settled permanently in the United States, becoming an American citizen in 1941. In 1935–36 he was a professor at the University of California, and from 1936 to 1944 at the University of California in Los Angeles; after 1944 he taught a small, select group of students privately. In 1947 he received the Special Award of Merit from the National Institute of Arts and Letters. His seventieth and seventy-fifth birthdays were celebrated with commemorative concerts and Schoenberg cycles in America and Europe. Besides the two stage works previously mentioned, Schoenberg wrote a one-act opera, VON HEUTE AUF MORGEN (1921), and an uncompleted two-act Biblical opera, MOSES UND ARON (1932), which achieved considerable international attention after the composer's death.

Schoen-René, Anna, teacher of singing. Born Coblenz, Ger., Jan. 12, 1864; died New York City, Nov. 13, 1942. Her music study took place at the Berlin Royal Academy and privately with Pauline VIARDOT-GARCÍA. In 1887 she made her debut at the Saxon-Altenburg Opera. She came to the United States in 1895 to appear at the METROPOLITAN OPERA, but a serious illness prevented this, and she made no further stage appearances. After an additional period of study with Manuel GARCÍA in England, she concentrated on teaching singing, first in Minneapolis, and afterward for many years at the Juilliard School of Music. She was the author of *America's Musical Inheritance* (1941).

School for Wives, OPÉRA-COMIQUE in one act by LIEBERMANN. Libretto by Heinrich Strobel, based on MOLIÈRE's *L'école des femmes*. Premiere: Louisville, Ken., Dec. 3, 1955. The setting is a square in the suburbs of Paris during the reign of Louis XIV. Arnolphe, a wealthy old man, is contemptuous of all women.

Nevertheless, he wants to get married to a girl who will devote herself completely to him. He selects his own ward, Agnes, a country girl, and has her raised in a convent to protect her from the outside world. By the time he brings her home to marry her, Agnes has fallen in love with a young neighbor named Horace. The bitter rivalry of the old man and the younger one is resolved when Agnes' father reveals that he long ago betrothed Agnes to the son of one of his old friends; and that old friend turns out to be the father of Horace. The opera ends as the entire cast reminds Arnolphe of a BEAUMARCHAIS epigram: "If you wish to make a foolish woman resourceful, lock her up."

Schorr, Friedrich, baritone. Born Nagyvárad, Hungary, Sept. 2, 1888; died Farmington, Conn., Aug. 14, 1953. He combined the study of law with that of music, attending the University of Vienna and studying singing privately with Adolph Robinson. During a brief visit to the United States in 1911 he appeared in minor roles with the CHICAGO OPERA. His official debut in opera took place the same year in Graz, when he appeared as WOTAN. After five years in Graz, he appeared with the National Opera in Prague and the COLOGNE OPERA. In 1923 he was engaged as principal baritone of the BERLIN STATE OPERA where, during the next decade, he established his reputation as one of the foremost Wagnerian baritones of his day. Meanwhile, in 1923 he returned to the United States as a member of the Wagnerian Opera Company, then touring America. On Feb. 14, 1924, he made his bow at the METROPOLITAN OPERA as WOLFRAM. He remained the principal German baritone of the Metropolitan for the next two decades. His last appearance at the Metropolitan took place on Mar. 2, 1943, as Wotan.

Schorr appeared at several BAYREUTH FESTIVALS, beginning in 1925, and at various times he made guest appearances with most of the major opera companies of Europe. In Sept., 1938, he was appointed vocal advisor to the WAGNER department of the Metropolitan Opera; in this capacity he guided many young Americans in Wagnerian traditions and style. After his retirement from the stage, he taught at the Hartt School of Music in Hartford, Conn., where he established an opera workshop. In 1950 he became advisor on German operas at the NEW YORK CITY OPERA COMPANY.

Besides his performances in all the principal baritone roles of the Wagnerian repertory, Schorr was heard at the Metropolitan Opera in the American premieres of JONNY SPIELT AUF and ŠVANDA.

Schott, Anton, tenor. Born Schloss Staufeneck, Bavaria, June 24, 1846; died Stuttgart, Jan. 6, 1913. Before embracing music, he was an army officer. He began studying singing with Agnes Schebest-Strauss in 1871 and at the end of the same year made his debut at the MUNICH OPERA. In 1872 he was engaged as a leading tenor of the BERLIN OPERA. In 1880 he made a successful London debut as RIENZI, and in 1882 he appeared in Italy with the Angelo NEUMANN troupe in the WAGNER dramas. On Nov. 17, 1884, he made his American debut at the METROPOLITAN OPERA as TANNHÄUSER (the opening night of Leopold DAMROSCH's first season of German opera). He remained at the Metropolitan until 1887 and was subsequently heard in special guest performances in opera in Europe and South America and on the concert stage.

Schreker, Franz, composer. Born Monaco, Mar. 23, 1878; died Berlin, Mar. 21, 1934. He attended the Vienna Conservatory, and his first opera, *Flammen,* was written when he was only twenty. His failure to get it performed was so discouraging that for a while he abandoned composition for other musical activities. In 1911 he founded the Berlin Philharmonic Choir, with which he performed many new, provocative works; his espousal of the most advanced tendencies in music brought about his dismissal from the faculty of the Academy of Prussian Arts in 1913.

His first opera to be performed was *Der ferne Klang,* given in Frankfurt in 1912. It was a failure, denounced for it vigorous modern style and stark realism. Another opera, *Das Spielwerk und die Prinzessin,* created such a scandal when given in Vienna in 1913 that it had to be dropped. Recognition finally came with DIE GEZEICHNETEN, introduced in Frankfurt in 1918. An ever greater success followed in 1920, *Der Schatzgäber.* From this time on, Schreker's operas were given in leading European opera houses; there were over two hundred performances of his stage works in Austria and Germany before 1924. Schreker's musical style combined Wagnerian traits with a Debussyan impressionism. His texts, written by himself, ranged from naturalism to mysticism and were strongly concerned with sexual psychology.

In 1920 Schreker became director of the Akademische Hochschule für Musik in Berlin, where his influence as a teacher was profound. He resigned this post in 1933 when the Nazis came to power. After *Der Schatzgäber,* Schreker wrote the following operas: *Irrelohe* (1924); *Der singende Teufel* (1928); *Christophorus* (1932); *Der Schmied von Gent* (1932).

Schröder-Devrient,   Wilhelmine, soprano. Born Hamburg, Dec. 6, 1804; died Coburg, Ger., Jan. 26, 1860. She was guided to the stage from her childhood on, making public appearances until her seventeenth year, when she retired to concentrate on vocal study with J. Mazatti in Vienna. In 1821 she made a successful singing debut at the BURGTHEATER in Vienna as PAMINA. After appearances in Prague and Dresden, she scored a sensation as Leonore in FIDELIO in Vienna (1822). In 1823 (the year she married her first husband, Karl Devrient, an actor) she was engaged as principal soprano of the DRESDEN OPERA. She remained with this company for almost a quarter of a century. She appeared in the world premieres of three WAGNER operas, creating the roles of Adriano in RIENZI, SENTA, and VENUS. During this period she was also acclaimed in other European opera houses, making her Paris debut in 1830, her London debut in 1832. After leaving the opera stage, she made concert appearances throughout Germany.

Schubert, Franz Peter, composer. Born Vienna, Jan. 31, 1797; died Vienna, Nov. 19, 1828. The first of the great German Romantics and the father of the lied was surprisingly ineffectual in opera. Most of his works designated as operas were actually SINGSPIELE or operettas—plays with incidental songs. The few that can be characterized as operas were not performed in Schubert's lifetime and have rarely been heard since; they were burdened by ridiculous librettos and the composer's inability to bring to them any of the soaring inspiration found in other works. Schubert wrote the following complete operas: *Des Teufels Lustschloss* (1814); *Alfonso und Estrella* (1822); *Fierrabras* (1823). The following operas were not completed and exist only in fragments: *Die Bürgschaft* (1816); *Adrast* (1819); *Sakuntala* (1820). All Schubert's other stage works—*Die Zwillingsbrüder* (1820); *Die Zauberharfe* (1820), *Rosamunde* (1823), and a few more—are either *singspiele,* or plays with incidental music. Alfred Orel suggests the following explanation for Schubert's failure in opera: "The stage demands far and away coarser means of expression than the song, and these were unknown to Schubert. The dramatic accents of his works for the stage grow too much out of the lyrical; they do not breathe out the essential hot life of the dramatist. . . . Seen at the far greater distance of the theater audience, the delicate colors in which Schubert here works grow pale." This sounds like a reasonable explanation of the fact that none of the post-mortem productions of the operas has been very successful. Yet there is no dearth of critics to tell us that the scores contain much beautiful and dramatic music.

Schubert attended the school of the court chapel, after which for a while he earned his living as a schoolmaster. He produced his first masterpieces in the song form in his seventeenth year. He then abandoned teaching for composition, and for the remainder of his life was partly dependent upon the generosity of his friends for life's necessities. He lived in obscurity and poverty, in spite of which his musical production was prodigious. Universal recognition of his true stature as a composer did not come until many years after his death.

Schuch, Ernst von, conductor. Born Graz, Austria, Nov. 23, 1846; died Dresden, May 10, 1914. He was a child prodigy who appeared on the concert stage both as violinist and pianist. After completing his music study in Vienna with Otto Dessoff, he was appointed in 1872 first conductor of the DRESDEN OPERA, a post he held until the end of his life; in 1882 he was elevated to the position of musical director. He maintained the Dresden Opera on the highest artistic level throughout his regime and was responsible for many significant premieres, including those of most of the famous operas of Richard STRAUSS, DOHNÁNYI'S *Tante Simona,* Paderewski's *Manru,* and WOLF-FERRARI'S L'AMORE MEDICO. He was also responsible for introducing PUCCINI's operas to Germany. In 1897 he received a patent of nobility from the Emperor of Austria. In the spring of 1900 he visited the United States and led three concerts and a performance of LOHENGRIN at the METROPOLITAN OPERA.

Schuller, Gunther, composer. Born New York City, Nov. 22, 1925. He attended the Manhattan School of Music, following which he played the horn with the Cincinnati Symphony Orchestra and first horn with the orchestra of the METROPOLITAN OPERA. In 1964 he was appointed associate professor of music at Yale University; the following year he succeeded Aaron COPLAND as head of the composition department at the Berkshire Music Center; and since 1966 he has been president of the New England Conservatory in Boston. He has produced a considerable amount of concert music in avant-garde techniques, developing an idiom he called "third stream music," which combines the rhythm and improvisations of jazz with such advanced methods of twentieth-century music as serialism. This technique, together with other advanced styles, is found in his first opera, THE VISITATION, whose premiere took place in Hamburg on Oct. 12, 1966. His opera for children, *The Fisherman and His Wife*, libretto by John Updike, based on a fairy tale by the Grimms, was given its world premiere in Boston by the Opera Company of Boston on May 8, 1971.

Schuloper, German term for "school opera." This is a form of contemporary German opera which has an educational function. HINDEMITH's *Wir bauen eine Stadt* is such an opera.

Schumann, Elisabeth, soprano. Born Merseburg, Ger., June 13, 1885; died New York City, Apr. 23, 1952. Her only teacher in singing was Alma Schadow in Hamburg. In 1910 she made her debut at the HAMBURG OPERA as the shepherd in TANNHÄUSER. For the next seven years she appeared with that company in the German and Italian repertories. On Nov. 20, 1914, she made her American debut at the METROPOLITAN OPERA as Sophie in DER ROSENKAVALIER, one of her most celebrated roles. Schumann remained only a single season at the Metropolitan. At the recommendation of Richard STRAUSS, she was engaged by the VIENNA STATE OPERA in 1919. She appeared there for the next two decades, a favorite of Viennese opera-goers. She appeared regularly at the SALZBURG and MUNICH festivals, as well as in leading European opera houses, achieving triumphs in operas by MOZART and Richard Strauss. She was decorated by the Danish government with the High Order for Art and Science and was made an honorary member of the Vienna Philharmonic Orchestra. She combined her career in the opera house with one on the concert stage, where she was acclaimed as one of the foremost interpreters of *lieder* of her generation.

When Austria was annexed by Germany, she established her home permanently in the United States, becoming a citizen in 1944. In 1938 she became a faculty member of the Curtis Institute of Music and at the time of her death was the head of the voice department.

Schumann, Robert, composer. Born Zwickau, Ger., June 8, 1810; died Endenick, Ger., July 29, 1856. Like SCHUBERT, Schumann was a giant figure in German Romantic music whose contribution to opera was slight. He wrote only a single opera, GENOVEVA. Introduced in Leipzig on June 25, 1850, it received three performances. The opera had many other productions, none too successful, in the nineteenth century, and a revival at the FLORENCE MAY MUSIC FESTIVAL of 1951 failed to stir new interest in it.

Schumann-Heink, Ernestine (born Ernestine Rossler), contralto. Born Lieben, near Prague, June 15, 1861; died Hollywood, Cal., Nov. 16, 1936. She studied with Marietta von Leclair in Graz. Her concert debut took place when she was fifteen in a performance of BEETHOVEN's *Ninth Symphony* in Graz. On Oct. 13, 1878, she made her opera debut at the DRESDEN ROYAL OPERA as AZUCENA. Additional study now took place with Karl Krebs and Franz Wüllner. After marrying her first husband, Ernst Heink, in 1882, she was engaged by the HAMBURG OPERA, where she remained sixteen years, outstanding in the Wagnerian repertory. In 1892 she made her London debut as ERDA. From 1896 to 1906 (except for 1904) she appeared regularly at the BAYREUTH FESTIVAL in the RING cycle. From 1897 to 1900 she was heard at COVENT GARDEN. In 1898 she signed a ten-year contract with the Berlin Royal Opera (BERLIN STATE OPERA). It gave her a leave of absence to appear in America, and on Nov. 7, 1898, she made her American debut in Chicago as ORTRUD. On Jan.

9, 1899, she made her first appearance at the METROPOLITAN, once again as Ortrud. So great was her American success that when her leave of absence expired, she bought out her contract so that she might continue to appear at the Metropolitan. She remained at the Metropolitan until 1904. After leaving the Metropolitan, she appeared in leading German opera houses. In 1909 she created the role of Klytemnestra in Richard STRAUSS's ELEKTRA. She now made periodic returns to the Metropolitan Opera: in 1909–10, 1911–13, 1915–1917, 1925–26, 1928–29, and 1931–32. Her last Metropolitan appearance was as Erda on Mar. 11, 1932. She had become an American citizen in 1908.

In 1926, the fiftieth anniversary of her Graz debut was celebrated at Carnegie Hall. This was followed by her last concert tour of the United States. In 1935 she appeared in a motion picture, *Here's to Romance*. Her opera repertory embraced some one hundred fifty roles, to which she brought not only exceptional vocal power and expressiveness but a profound musicianship, pronounced dramatic feeling, and a striking temperament.

Schütz, Heinrich, composer. Born Köstritz, Saxony, Oct. 8, 1585; died Dresden, Nov. 6, 1672. His significance rests chiefly in his choral music; he was a towering figure in German music before the day of Johann Sebastian Bach. Schütz wrote one opera, *Dafne*, partly based on a translation of the RINUCCINI libretto which had previously been used by the early Florentine opera composers. Although the score is lost, this opera has historic importance: it is the first with a German-language text and is consequently the first German opera. Schütz wrote it in 1627 for the ceremonies attending the marriage of the daughter of the Saxon Elector to the Landgrave of Hesse-Darmstadt.

Schützendorf, Gustav, baritone. Born Cologne, 1883; died Berlin, Apr. 27, 1937. He was born to a musical family; four of his brothers became opera singers. After music study in Cologne and Munich he made his debut in Düsseldorf in DON GIOVANNI in 1905. He then appeared extensively in German opera houses. On Nov. 17, 1922, he made his American debut at the METROPOLITAN OPERA in the role of FANINAL. He remained with the Metropolitan until 1935, distinguishing himself in German roles, particularly as BECKMESSER and ALBERICH.

Schwanda, *see* ŠVANDA THE BAGPIPER.

Schwarzkopf, Elisabeth, soprano. Born Jarotschin, Poland, Dec. 9, 1915. She attended the Berlin Hochschule für Musik, studying singing with Maria IVOGÜN. Her debut took place on Easter Day, 1938, when she appeared as the first Flower Maiden in PARSIFAL at the Berlin Städtische Oper (BERLIN DEUTSCHE STAATSOPER). She continued singing minor roles with that company until 1942. After a period of additional study with Maria Ivogün, she established her reputation as a *lieder* singer following a successful concert debut in Vienna in Nov., 1942. She then appeared in several guest performances in MOZART's operas at the VIENNA STATE OPERA. Highly praised, she was engaged as a principal singer. Her triumphs in Vienna were duplicated at COVENT GARDEN, LA SCALA, and at the BAYREUTH and SALZBURG festivals. In 1951 she created the role of Anne Trulove in THE RAKE'S PROGRESS in Venice, and in 1953 she appeared in the world premiere of ORFF's TRIONFI at La Scala. She made her American debut as a *lieder* singer, then in 1955 made her first American appearance in opera with the SAN FRANCISCO OPERA as the MARSCHALLIN, the role in which she made her METROPOLITAN OPERA debut on Oct. 13, 1964. Whether in the concert hall or in the opera house, she is one of the foremost sopranos of the twentieth century and has achieved world acclaim in spite of the antagonism toward her in many countries on account of her close associations with the leaders in Nazi Germany during World War II.

schweigsame Frau, Die (The Silent Woman), comic opera in three acts by Richard STRAUSS. Libretto by Stefan

Zweig, based on Ben JONSON's *Epicoene*. Premiere: Dresden Opera, June 29, 1935. American premiere: New York City Opera, Oct. 7, 1958. The central character, Sir Morosus (bass), is a rich, lonely old man who is persuaded by Schneidebart, his barber (baritone), that he needs a nice, quiet young wife. When Sir Morosus' long-lost nephew, Henry (tenor), shows up, he is first delighted to see him, then angrily threatens to disinherit him for having become the leader of a troupe of actors of which Henry's wife, Aminta (soprano) is a member. Learning from the barber of his uncle's marital intentions, Aminta, against her inclinations, is persuaded to disguise herself as a sweet, quiet, loving innocent. She wins the old man; a mock marriage is gone through, with one of the actors disguised as a minister; and immediately Aminta turns into a noisy shrew. When she has tortured her "husband" almost out of his mind, the imposture is explained to him, and greatly relieved, he welcomes his nephew and Aminta back into his good graces. William Mann points out that "Morosus is musically very much the hero of the opera; all the best music goes to him . . . in the duet "Ja, das wär schön" . . . and later in the closing scene of the opera."

Schweig und tanze, Elektra's rapturous aria in the finale of Richard STRAUSS's ELEKTRA, as she dances to her death on her father's grave.

Schwelton, the German equivalent of MESSA DI VOCE.

Schwetzingen, a festival inaugurated in 1956 in Schwetzingen, Germany, where performances are given in the rococo theater of the castle. Novelties (such as IL MATRIMONIO SEGRETO and ROSSINI's *La Scala di seta*) are performed together with contemporary works. Among the world premieres given here have been ELEGY FOR YOUNG LOVERS, *In seinem Garten liebt Don Perlimplin Belisa* (FORTNER), and DER REVISOR.

Sciarrone, a gendarme (bass) in PUCCINI's TOSCA.

Scindia, the King's minister (baritone) in MASSENET's LE ROI DE LAHORE.

Scintille diamant, Dapertutto's description of the magic powers of the diamond on his ring, in Act II of OFFENBACH's THE TALES OF HOFFMANN.

Scott, Norman, bass. Born New York City, Nov. 30, 1920; died there Sept. 22, 1968. He attended the Juilliard School, where, in 1946, he appeared in LE DONNE CURIOSE. Between 1947 and 1952 he was a member of the NEW YORK CITY OPERA. He made his debut with the METROPOLITAN OPERA on Nov. 15, 1951, as MONTERONE. During his seventeen seasons with this company, he was heard over six hundred fifty times in forty-five roles. Besides performing with other American opera companies, he appeared at the VOLKSOPER in Vienna in 1956 and the TEATRO COLÓN in 1960–61. He was also heard in America in radio broadcasts of AIDA, UN BALLO IN MASCHERA, and FALSTAFF conducted by TOSCANINI.

Scott, Sir Walter, poet and novelist. Born Edinburgh, Aug. 15, 1771; died Abbotsford, Sept. 21, 1832. Scott wrote novels and long narrative poems that have been used for many operas, these being the most important: *The Bride of Lammermoor* (Michele Carafa's *La Fiancée de Lammermoor*, DONIZETTI's LUCIA DI LAMMERMOOR, Alberto Mazzucato's *La fidanzata di Lammermoor*); *The Eve of St. John* (opera by Mackenzie); *The Fair Maid of Perth* (BIZET's LA JOLIE FILLE DE PERTH); *Guy Mannering* (opera by Henry Bishop, and BOIELDIEU's LA DAME BLANCHE); *The Heart of Midlothian* (opera by Henry Bishop, Michele Carafa's *La Prison d'Edimbourg*, Federico Ricci's *La prigione d'Edimburgo*); *Ivanhoe* (opera by Sir Arthur SULLIVAN, NICOLAI's *Il templario*, MARSCHNER's DER TEMPLER UND DIE JÜDIN); *Kenilworth* (AUBER's *Leicester*, DE LARA's *Amy Robsart*, DONIZETTI's *Il castello di Kenilworth*); *The Lady of the Lake* (ROSSINI's *La Dame du lac*); *Maid Marian* (DE KOVEN's ROBIN HOOD); *Montrose* (opera by Henry Bishop); *Old Mor-*

tality (BELLINI'S I PURITANI); *Quentin Durward* (operas by Aleck Maclean and François Gevaert); *Rob Roy* (operas by FLOTOW and De Koven); *The Talisman* (opera by BALFE); *Waverly* (opera by Franz Holstein).

Scotti, Antonio, baritone. Born Naples, Jan. 25, 1866; died there Feb. 26, 1936. After completing his studies with Mme. Trifari-Payanini and Vincenzo Lombardi, he made his debut in Malta in 1889 as AMONASRO. Numerous appearances in Italy, Spain, Russia, Poland, and South America followed. He made his debut at LA SCALA in 1898 as HANS SACHS. In the fall of 1899 he made his American debut in Chicago, and on Dec. 27 of the same year he made his first appearance at the METROPOLITAN OPERA as DON GIOVANNI. During the next thirty-five years Scotti was one of the principal members of the Metropolitan Opera company, outstandingly successful in such roles as SCARPIA (which he created for America), Don Giovanni, Amonasro, SHARPLESS, DR. MALATESTA, MARCELLO, FALSTAFF, and RIGOLETTO. He appeared in the American premieres of ADRIANA LECOUVREUR, LE DONNE CURIOSE, FEDORA, L'ORACOLO, TOSCA, and DE LARA'S *Messaline*. He was featured in such significant Metropolitan premieres and revivals as DON CARLOS, L'ELISIR D'AMORE, *Falstaff*, IRIS, LUCREZIA BORGIA, and THE SECRET OF SUZANNE. He was in the cast of *Rigoletto* when CARUSO made his American debut; and he was the Scarpia for fifteen different Toscas.

Soon after World War I, Scotti formed his own company, the Scotti Opera Company, which he managed for four seasons in tours of the United States. On Jan. 1, 1924, celebrating his twenty-fifth year at the Metropolitan, he appeared in a gala performance of *Tosca*. His last appearance at the Metropolitan took place on Jan. 20, 1933, as Chim-Fen in *L'Oracolo,* a role he had created in 1905.

Scotto, Renata, soprano. Born Savona, Italy, Feb. 24, 1934. Completing her vocal studies in Milan with Llopart

and Ghirardini, she made her opera debut at the Teatro Nazionale in Milan as VIOLETTA in 1953. In the same year she was engaged by LA SCALA, where she first achieved wide recognition. Her performance as Amina in LA SONNAMBULA at the EDINBURGH FESTIVAL in 1957 (where she replaced CALLAS at the final performance) won her European renown. She has also been heard intermittently at COVENT GARDEN, as well as other European opera houses, and on Oct. 13, 1965, she made her debut at the METROPOLITAN OPERA as CIO-CIO-SAN.

Scratch, the human form assumed by the devil (tenor) in MOORE'S THE DEVIL AND DANIEL WEBSTER.

Scribe, August-Eugène, dramatist and librettist. Born Paris, Dec. 24, 1791; died there Feb. 20, 1861. The most significant and at the same time most prolific of French librettists, Eugène Scribe wrote librettos that fill twenty-six volumes, while his more than three hundred plays require fifty volumes. The following are the most notable of the many operas for which he furnished librettos: AUBER'S FRA DIAVOLO and LA MUETTE DE PORTICI; BELLINI'S LA SONNAMBULA; BOIELDIEU'S LA DAME BLANCHE; CILÈA'S ADRIANA LECOUVREUR; DONIZETTI'S LA FAVORITA; HALÉVY'S LA JUIVE; MEYERBEER'S LES HUGUENOTS, LE PROPHÈTE, ROBERT LE DIABLE, and L'AFRICAINE; ROSSINI'S LE COMTE ORY; VERDI'S THE SICILIAN VESPERS. The librettos of Donizetti's L'ELISIR D'AMORE and Verdi's UN BALLO IN MASCHERA were based on plays by Scribe. In 1836 Scribe was made a member of the French Academy.

Scuoti quella fronda di ciliegio, Cio-Cio-San's and Suzuki's Flower Duet in Act II of PUCCINI'S MADAMA BUTTERFLY, as they decorate the house with cherry blossoms to await the arrival of Pinkerton.

Se al volto mai ti senti, terzetto of Vitellia, Sextus, and Publio in Act II of MOZART'S LA CLEMENZA DI TITO, in which Sextus takes leave of his beloved, Vitellia, after being arrested by Publio.

Searle, Humphrey, composer. Born Oxford, Eng., Aug. 26, 1915. He studied music with John Ireland and R. O. Morris at the Royal College of Music in London and in Vienna with Anton Webern, who interested him in TWELVE-TONE TECHNIQUES. After service in the British Army during World War II, he was employed on the music staff of BBC between 1946 and 1948. He produced a good deal of instrumental music in an expressionist style that brought him recognition. A one-act opera, *The Diary of a Madman,* was produced at the BERLIN MUSIC FESTIVAL on Oct. 3, 1958; it was given its American premiere at the Aspen School Opera Workshop on Aug. 17, 1967. This was followed by *The Photo of the Colonel,* premiered in Frankfurt, on June 3, 1964, and *Hamlet,* introduced by the HAMBURG OPERA on Mar. 6, 1968.

Seattle Opera, an opera company founded in Seattle, Wash., in 1964, presenting in its first season two performances each of CARMEN and TOSCA. It has expanded its program of activity to present each season five performances each of five operas, under the artistic direction of Glynn Ross. In its second season it inaugurated the practice of first giving productions with international stars and then, for a single performance at half price, employing lesser known and usually local performers. Seventy-five thousand seats are annually sold for the five operas, in addition to thirty thousand students' seats provided by the Supplementary Secondary and Elementary Education Act of 1965. Among the less familiar works given have been STRAVINSKY's *L'Histoire du soldat,* conducted by the composer, and THE CRUCIBLE. OF MICE AND MEN received its world premiere on Jan. 22, 1970.

Sebastian, George, conductor. Born Budapest, Aug. 17, 1903. He studied composition with KODÁLY in Budapest and conducting with Bruno WALTER in Germany. After serving as a coach under Walter at the MUNICH OPERA, he became the conductor of the Leipzig Opera, where he appeared between 1924 and 1927. From 1927 to 1931 he conducted at the Berlin Städtische Oper (BERLIN DEUTSCHE STAATSOPER), from 1944 to 1947 at the SAN FRANCISCO OPERA, and since 1947 he has been a principal conductor of the PARIS OPÉRA.

Sebastiano, a rich landowner (baritone) in D'ALBERT's TIEFLAND.

Secondate, aurette amiche, duet of Ferrando and Guglielmo in Act II, Scene 2, of MOZART's COSÍ FAN TUTTE, as, disguised as Albanians, they serenade Dorabella and Fiordiligi.

Second Hurricane, The, a children's opera in two acts by Aaron COPLAND. Libretto by Edward Denby. Premiere: New York City, Apr. 21, 1937. The opera combines spoken scenes with songs and was intended for performance by high-school children. The story concerns the efforts of four boys and two girls to bring flood victims food and aid. There is no curtain: a chorus drifts upon the stage, with it the principal characters. The head of the school appears to explain to the audience what is about to take place, and the opera begins.

Secret Marriage, The, *see* MATRIMONIO SEGRETO, IL.

Secret of Suzanne, The (Il segreto di Susanna), one-act opera (or INTERMEZZO) by WOLF-FERRARI. Libretto by Enrico Golisciani. Premiere: Munich Opera, Dec. 4, 1909. American premiere: Philadelphia-Chicago Opera Company, playing in New York, Mar. 14, 1911. The characters are the Countess Suzanne (soprano), Count Gil (baritone), and Sante, a servant (silent role). The setting is a living room in Piedmont around the turn of the century. Count Gil is disturbed, since every time he returns home he detects the odor of cigarette smoke. His suspicions that his wife in entertaining a lover mount as she evades answering his questions. In a fit of anger he smashes some furniture. His wife calms him by suggesting that he visit his club. The Count goes but decides to spy on his wife through a window. Thus he learns the truth: that Suzanne, entirely faithful to him, is a secret smoker. Joyfully he rushes into the room and joins her in a cigarette.

An astonishing contrast to the composer's tragic opera THE JEWELS OF THE MADONNA, *The Secret of Suzanne,* with its fresh and witty score, is the most successful of Wolf-Ferrari's several comic works for the stage.

The sprightly, vivacious little overture has been a concert favorite, as has a charming orchestral intermezzo. The better-known arias include two by Suzanne, "O gioia la nube leggera" and "Via! così non mi lasciate," and one by Gil, "Il dolce idillio."

Sedaine, Michel Jean, playwright and librettist. Born Paris, July 4, 1719; died there May 17, 1797. He published his first book in 1750, a volume of fables and songs; six years later he wrote his first opera libretto. Some of the best-known operas of his day were written to his librettos: GLUCK's *Le Diable à quatre;* GOSSEC's *Les Sabots et le cerisier;* GRÉTRY's AUCASSIN ET NICOLETTE, *Guillaume Tell, Raoul Barbe-Bleue,* and RICHARD COEUR DE LION; MONSIGNY's *Aline, Le Déserteur, Félix, Le Roi et le fermier,* and *Rose et Colas;* PHILIDOR's *Blaise, le savetier* and *Le Diable à quatre.* At least one composer of the twentieth century has written an opera to a libretto by Sedaine: Henri SAUGUET in his *La Gageure imprévue.* Sedaine was elected to the French Academy in 1786.

Sedie, Enrico delle, *see* DELLE SEDIE, ENRICO.

Sedley, Mrs., a scandalmonger (contralto) in BRITTEN's PETER GRIMES.

Seefried, Irmgard, soprano. Born Köngetried, Ger., Oct. 9, 1919. She attended the Augsburg Conservatory and made her opera debut in her eleventh year as GRETEL. Her first operatic engagement as a mature artist was with the Aachen Opera, where she proved so successful between 1939 and 1943 that in 1943 she was engaged by the VIENNA STATE OPERA. She made her debut there as EVA and became an immediate favorite. In 1944 Richard STRAUSS selected her to sing the role of the Composer in

ARIADNE AUF NAXOS for the celebration of his eightieth birthday. She now appeared extensively in Europe, notably at the Vienna State Opera, where she was a principal soprano, and at the SALZBURG and EDINBURG festivals, where she distinguished herself particularly in Mozartean roles. She made her American debut with the Cincinnati Symphony in 1951 and her opera debut with the METROPOLITAN OPERA on Nov. 20, 1953, as Susanna in THE MARRIAGE OF FIGARO. In later years she has devoted herself more to concert appearances than to opera performances.

segreto di Susanna, Il, *see* SECRET OF SUSANNE, THE.

seguidilla, a Spanish song and dance in triple time, usually in fast tempo, often accompanied with castanets. Carmen's aria, "Près des ramparts de Séville," in Act I of BIZET's CARMEN is a typical seguidilla.

Seht da den Herzog von Brabant, Lohengrin's address to his people after restoring Gottfried from a swan to a human form, in the closing scene of WAGNER's LOHENGRIN.

Seidl, Anton, conductor. Born Budapest, Hungary, May 7, 1850; died New York City, Mar. 28, 1898. One of the most noted of Wagnerian conductors, Seidl directed the American premieres of several WAGNER music dramas. He attended the Leipzig Conservatory, after which Hans RICHTER engaged him as chorus master of the VIENNA OPERA and introduced him to Wagner. In 1872 Seidl worked for Wagner in BAYREUTH, copying the RING cycle. He stayed with Wagner until 1876, assisting at the first Bayreuth festival. On Wagner's recommendation he became conductor of the Leipzig Opera in 1879, holding this post three years. He then became principal conductor of the Angelo NEUMANN company, which presented Wagner's works throughout Europe until 1883. In that year he became principal conductor of the Bremen Opera.

Upon the sudden death of Leopold DAMROSCH in 1885, Seidl was invited to the United States to take over the

German repertory at the METROPOLITAN OPERA. He made his American debut on Nov. 23, 1885, with LOHENGRIN. He remained a principal conductor of German operas at the Metropolitan until his death (except for the three-year period, beginning in 1892, when German opera took a secondary place in the repertory). During this time he led the American premieres of DIE MEISTERSINGER, TRISTAN UND ISOLDE, DAS RHEINGOLD, SIEGFRIED, and GÖTTERDÄMMERUNG, as well as the first cyclic performance of the *Ring*. From 1891 until his death he was also conductor of the New York Philharmonic Orchestra. In the spring of 1897 he directed at COVENT GARDEN and in the summer of the same year he returned to Bayreuth after a prolonged absence. He died unexpectedly at the height of his career.

Seien wir wieder gut, the composer's aria in Richard STRAUSS's ARIADNE AUF NAXOS.

Se il mio nome, the serenade of Count Almaviva (assuming the guise of the impoverished Lindoro), lamenting to Rosina that he can give her only love and not wealth, in Act I, Scene 1, of ROSSINI's THE BARBER OF SEVILLE.

Se il padre perdei, Ilia's aria in Act II of MOZART's IDOMENEO.

Seit er von dir geschieden (Waltraute's Narrative), plea to Brünnhilde to give up the ring and thus save the gods from doom, in Act I, Scene 2, of WAGNER's GÖTTERDÄMMERUNG.

Seit Ewigkeiten harre ich deiner, Kundry's confession to Parsifal she is a victim of a curse, in Act II, Scene 2, of PARSIFAL.

Selig, wie die Sonne, the quintet of Walther, Eva, Sachs, David, and Magdalena, in which Walther sings a part of his dream song while the others express their reactions, in Act III of DIE MEISTERSINGER.

Selika, African queen (soprano), the captive of Vasco da Gama, in MEYERBEER's L'AFRICAINE.

Selim Pasha, Sultan of Turkey (speaking part) in MOZART's THE ABDUCTION FROM THE SERAGLIO.

Selim, Sultan, Sultan of Turkey (bass), in love with Fiorilla, a Neapolitan lady, in ROSSINI's IL TURCO IN ITALIA.

Sellem, an auctioneer (tenor) in STRAVINSKY's THE RAKE's PROGRESS.

Sembrich, Marcella (born Marcelline Kochanska), soprano. Born Wisniewczyk, Poland, Feb. 18, 1858; died New York City, Jan. 11, 1935. From her father, a concert violinist, she received her first music lessons when she was only four. Additional music study took place for four years at the Lemberg Conservatory. Upon Franz LISZT's advice, she decided to devote herself to singing, and studied with Viktor Rokitansky in Vienna and Francesco LAMPERTI in Milan. After marrying Wilhelm Stengel, one of her teachers at the Lemberg Conservatory, she went to Athens, where on June 3, 1877, she made her opera debut in I PURITANI. Following more study, with Richard Lewy in Vienna, she made her German debut in Dresden in Oct., 1878, in one of her most brilliant roles, LUCIA. On June 12, 1880, she made her London debut at the Royal Italian Opera, once again as Lucia, and was so successful that she was invited back for four successive seasons. On Oct. 24, 1883, she made her American debut at the METROPOLITAN OPERA, singing the role of Lucia, and was highly acclaimed. From 1884 to 1898 she sang in the leading opera houses of Europe, and from 1898 to 1909 she was a principal soprano of the Metropolitan Opera. Her last appearance at the Metropolitan took place on Feb. 6, 1909, when she appeared in acts from several operas. She now retired from the stage and devoted herself to teaching, first at the Curtis Institute of Music, later at the Juilliard School of Music. To her finest roles—ROSINA, VIOLETTA, NORINA, Lucia, GILDA, DINORAH, MIMI, aud ZERLINA—she brought a surpassing beauty of tone and a brilliant technique. She was also a notable singer of *lieder*.

Semele, (1) a secular oratorio, sometimes staged as an opera, by HANDEL. Libretto is an adaptation of Congreve's drama. Premiere: London, Feb. 10, 1744. One of Handel's noblest tenor arias comes from this work, "Wher'er you walk." The story involves Jupiter and his beloved Semele. Juno, jealous of Jupiter, tells Semele she can gain immortality by having Jupiter appear before her in his full divinity; Semele is destroyed by the blaze of glory that follows. She leaves behind her a son, Bacchus.

(2) The Queen (soprano) in Richard STRAUSS'S DIE LIEBE DER DANAE.

Semiramide, OPERA SERIA in two acts by ROSSINI. Libretto by Gaetano ROSSI, based on VOLTAIRE's drama. Premiere: Teatro la Fenice, Feb. 3, 1823. American premiere: New Orleans, May 1, 1837. Semiramis is very roughly the Babylonian equivalent of Klytemnestra, and Ninus the Babylonian equivalent of Agamemnon. Semiramis, Queen of Babylon (soprano), murders her husband, King Ninus (bass), with the help of her lover, Assur (baritone). She subsequently falls in love with a handsome young warrior whom she believes to be a Scythian, but who is actually her son Arsace (contralto). When she discovers his identity, she saves his life by receiving Assur's dagger blow intended for her son. Arsace then kills Assur and ascends the throne. Rossini, who usually made his overtures independent of his operas, composed the overture of this opera from themes that are used in the body of the work. Principal themes in the overture, a concert favorite, include a majestic melody first given by four horns, then amplified by woodwinds accompanied by plucked strings; a light and vivacious tune for the strings; and an equally jaunty episode for the woodwinds. The overture ends dramatically with a typical Rossini crescendo.

Some of Rossini's most notable ensemble numbers are found in this opera, two in particular: "Ebbène, a te ferisci," a duet of Arsace and Semiramis; and "Quel mesto gemito," in the first-act finale, which some musicologists feel influenced VERDI in writing the Miserere

for IL TROVATORE. Two arias are of particular interest: Semiramis' "Bel raggio lusinghier," and Arsace's "Ah! quel giorno."

The role of Semiramis was a particular favorite of Adelina PATTI's. After a sixty-nine year absence of *Semiramide* from the American operatic scene, it was revived early in 1964 by the AMERICAN OPERA SOCIETY with Joan SUTHERLAND.

The legendary Babylonian Semiramis was a favorite heroine of the seventeenth and eighteenth centuries. Among the composers who made operas of her story were CALDARA, GALUPPI, GLUCK, GRAUN, HASSE, MEYERBEER, PORPORA, SACCHINI, A. SCARLATTI, and VIVALDI. RESPIGHI was also attracted to the legend, composing an opera *Semirama* in 1910.

semiseria, Italian for "semi-serious," differentiating an opera with comic interludes from an OPERA SERIA.

Sempre libera, Violetta's exultant expression of determination to live only for pleasure and freedom, in Act I of VERDI's LA TRAVIATA. It is the CABALETTA to her aria "Ah! fors' è lui."

Sempronio, an apothecary (bass) who seeks to marry his ward, Grilletta, in HAYDN's comic opera LO SPEZIALE.

Senesino (born Francesco Bernardi), contralto castrato. Born Siena, Italy, about 1680; died there about 1750. His stage name was derived from that of his native city. He studied with Antonio BERNACCHI in Bologna, after which he appeared at the DRESDEN OPERA. HANDEL heard him there and engaged him for London, where Senesino appeared for the first time in Nov., 1720, in BONONCINI's *Astarto*. He was a sensation. For the next fifteen years he was the idol of the London opera public, creating in that time the principal roles in numerous Handel operas. He continued singing for Handel until 1733, when he quarreled with the composer-impresario and joined a rival company headed by Niccolò PORPORA. He returned to Italy a wealthy man in 1735.

Senta, Daland's daughter (soprano) in WAGNER'S DER FLIEGENDE HOLLÄNDER.

Senta's Ballad, *see* TRAFT IHR DAS SCHIFF.

Senza mamma, Angelica's Lament, the best-known aria in PUCCINI'S SUOR ANGELICA.

Se pietà, Cleopatra's aria after having successfully convinced Caesar to flee from a conspiracy against him, in Act I, Scene 3, of HANDEL'S GIULIO CESARE IN EGITTO.

Serafin, Tullio, conductor. Born Rottanova, Italy, Dec. 8, 1878; died Rome, Feb. 2, 1968. He attended the Milan Conservatory. After playing the violin in the orchestra of LA SCALA, he was engaged as a conductor of the Teatro Communale in Ferrara in 1900. In 1903 he conducted at the Teatro Regio in Turin and in 1909 was engaged by La Scala, where he distinguished himself not only in the Italian repertory but also in operas by WAGNER, WEBER, and GLUCK. His American debut took place at the METROPOLITAN OPERA on Nov. 3, 1924, with AIDA. He remained at the Metropolitan a decade, directing the Italian repertory, two Wagner operas, and the world premieres of THE EMPEROR JONES, THE KING'S HENCHMAN, MERRY MOUNT, and PETER IBBETSON. He also conducted the American premieres of LA CENA DELLE BEFFE, THE FAIR AT SOROCHINSK, *Giovanni Gallurese* (Montemezzi), SIMON BOCCANEGRA, TURANDOT, and LA VIDA BREVE. He left the Metropolitan in 1934 after a dispute with the management. Returning to Italy, he served as principal conductor and aritistic director of the TEATRO DELL' OPERA in Rome from 1934 to 1943 and as principal conductor of La Scala in 1939–40. In 1942 he conducted the first Italian performance of WOZZECK. He returned to America in the fall of 1952 to conduct the NEW YORK CITY OPERA, and between 1956 and 1958 he was conductor at the CHICAGO OPERA. In 1962 he became artistic adviser of the Teatro dell' Opera in Rome, where, in his eighty-fourth year, he conducted four operas, including ROSSINI'S OTELLO.

Serafina, heroine (soprano) in DONIZETTI'S IL CAMPANELLO DI NOTTE, married to the aged apothecary, Don Annibale.

Seraglio, *see* ABDUCTION FROM THE SERAGLIO, THE.

Serena, (1) Robbins' wife (soprano) in GERSHWIN'S PORGY AND BESS.

(2) A Camorrist (soprano) in WOLF-FERRARI'S THE JEWELS OF THE MADONNA.

serenade (Italian, *serenata*), most often, in operatic usage, a love song under a lady's window. Among the most famous operatic serenades are: "Im Mohrenland gefangen war" (THE ABDUCTION FROM THE SERAGLIO); "Ecco ridente in cielo" (THE BARBER OF SEVILLE); "Deh, vieni alla finestra" (DON GIOVANNI); "Vous qui faites l'endormie" (FAUST); "Aprila, o bella" (THE JEWELS OF THE MADONNA); "Dans la cité lointaine" (LOUISE); "O Colombina" (PAGLIACCI); "Ah! lève-toi soleil" (ROMÉO ET JULIETTE); "Di rigori armato" (DER ROSENKAVALIER); "Deserto sulla terra" (IL TROVATORE).

Serge, Katerina's beloved (tenor) in SHOSTAKOVICH'S KATERINA ISMAILOVA (*Lady Macbeth of Mzensk*).

serial techniques, a development of the TWELVE-TONE system to embrace not only pitch but also rhythm, tone color, dynamics, and so forth. Several important avant-garde operas have used these techniques. Among them are BOMARZO, DON RODRIGO, INTOLLERANZA 1960, and THE VISITATION.

Serov, Alexander, composer. Born St. Petersburg, Jan. 23, 1820; died Feb. 1, 1871. He studied to be a lawyer but his friendship with Mikhail GLINKA made him turn to music. After 1850 he wrote vigorous music criticism in the Russian press. In 1857 he traveled to Germany and became an ardent Wagnerian. When he returned to Russia he posed himself as a vigorous opponent of musical nationalism. His first opera, *Judith,* produced in May, 1863, in St. Petersburg, was a major success and did much to win support for Serov's musical position. His second opera, *Rogneda,* produced in 1865, was an even greater success, gaining the composer a handsome government pension.

While the style and esthetic approach of these operas were obviously Wagnerian, neither was, strictly speaking, a music drama in WAGNER's sense of the term. The writing of such a work was now Serov's goal. In 1867 he started *The Power of Evil*, but did not live to complete it; the last act was finished by N. T. Soloviev. The opera was produced on Apr. 19, 1871, and for a while was very popular. Like Wagner, Serov wrote his own librettos.

Serpina, Uberto's maid (soprano) in PERGOLESI'S LA SERVA PADRONA.

Serse (Xerxes), comic opera in three acts by HANDEL. Librettist unknown. Premiere: King's Theatre, London, Apr. 15, 1738. American premiere: Northampton, Mass., May 12, 1928. Handel's forty-third opera, this is the only one by him in an exclusively comic vein. Xerxes and Arsamene, brothers (castrato sopranos), are in love with Romilda (soprano). Xerxes uses his royal power to win her but fails. In the end he must satisfy himself with her sister, Atalanta (soprano). This is the opera in which the famous so-called Largo is heard. It is the opening aria, "Ombra mai fù" —Xerxes' apostrophe to a shade tree. Within the opera this andante aria has satirical elements, but slowed down in various transcriptions to "Largo" it becomes a pompous melody with "religious" overtones. Though this opera is set in ancient Persia, Handel included the tunes of London street cries.

serva padrona, La (The Servant Mistress), INTERMEZZO or OPERA BUFFA in two acts by PERGOLESI. Libretto by G. A. Federico. Premiere: Teatro San Bartolomeo, Naples, Aug. 28, 1733. American premiere: Baltimore, June 14, 1790.

Characters: Uberto, a bachelor (bass); Serpina, his maid (soprano); Vespone, Uberto's valet (silent role). The setting is Naples in the early eighteenth century.

Act I. A room in Uberto's house. Uberto is upset because Serpina has delayed bringing his chocolate. His anger grows when Serpina tells him she is in no hurry to obey his order ("Stizzoso, mio stizzoso"). Uberto now wants to take a walk, but Serpina announces firmly that if he does so she will lock him out of the house. His servant's effrontery convinces him that his house

needs a mistress. Serpina agrees, insisting that she will become his wife. She enlists the aid of Uberto's valet.

Act II. The same scene. Serpina hides the valet in a closet. When Uberto appears, she tells him sadly that she has found another man and will no longer disturb Uberto with her marital designs. Uberto is curious about her lover, but her only reply is a lament that, surely, he will forget her completely when he himself gets married ("A Serpina penserete"). In an aside to the audience, Serpina expresses her belief that her intrigue is working. When Uberto is skeptical ("Son imbrogliato io gia"), Serpina produces her supposed lover: Vespone disguised as a captain. Uberto is now convinced that all along he has wanted Serpina as a wife. Even after the identity of the captain is disclosed, Uberto is pleased at the turn of events.

La serva padrona is an intermezzo, but it introduces so many of the stylistic elements afterward found in the Italian *opera buffa* that it may be considered the progenitor of this form. It is a work of exquisite perfection, the music catching every shade of comedy and burlesque, sentiment and poignancy, in its sparkling solos and duets. The work was tremendously popular in its day, and it exerted a wide influence on composers of comic operas. It is still often performed, being an effective work for groups of limited resources.

Setti, Giulio, choral conductor. Born Traviglio, Italy, Oct. 3, 1869; died Turin, Oct. 2, 1938. After serving as chorus master in various opera houses in Italy, Cairo, Cologne, and Buenos Aires, he came to the United States in 1908 and was engaged as chorus master of the METROPOLITAN OPERA. He remained in this post twenty-seven years, until his retirement in 1935, when he returned to Italy.

Settimana Musicale Chigiana, a festival founded in 1939 and held every September in Siena, Italy. It is particularly notable for its revival of less familiar works by seventeenth- and eighteenth-century Italian composers, including

CHERUBINI, Rinaldo da Capua, GALUPPI, Giuseppe Orlandini, SACCHINI, Alessandro SCARLATTI, and VIVALDI, among others. Performances take place at the Teatro dei Rozzi and since 1950 also at the Teatro dei Rinnovati. In 1951 the program of revival was temporarily set aside to permit performances of several VERDI operas to commemorate the fiftieth anniversary of the master's death.

Se vuol ballare, Figaro's aria in which he lightly explains to Susanna that he knows well how to handle his master, the Count, if the latter makes advances to her, in Act I of MOZART'S THE MARRIAGE OF FIGARO.

Sextus, Vitellia's lover in MOZART'S LA CLEMENZA DI TITO. Though a male role, it is today sung by a mezzo-soprano because the part had been written for a CASTRATO.

Shadow Dance, *see* OMBRE LÉGÈRE.

Shakespeare, William, poet and dramatist. Born Stratford-on-Avon, Apr., 1564; died there Apr. 23, 1616. His comedies and tragedies have provided the material for a great number of operas, the following being the most significant (where opera titles are not given, they are the same as the play).

All's Well That Ends Well: CASTELNUOVO-TEDESCO.

Antony and Cleopatra: BARBER, MALIPIERO.

As You Like It: Francesco Veracini's *Rosalinda.*

The Comedy of Errors: Isa Krejci's *The Revolt at Ephesus;* Stephen Storace's *Gli quivoci.*

Coriolanus: August Baeyens.

Cymbeline: Arne Eggen; also, KREUTZER'S *Imogene,* Edmond Missa's *Dinah,* Eduard Sobolevski's *Imogene.*

Hamlet: Giuseppe Carcano, Luigi Caruso, FACCIO, Francesco Gasparini, Aristide Hignard, MARATZEK, MERCADANTE, SEARLE, Sandor Szokolay, THOMAS, and Mario Zafred.

Henry IV: SAINT-SAËNS.

Julius Caesar: HANDEL, KLEBE, Malipiero.

King Lear: Alberto Ghislanzoni, Vito Frazzi.

Macbeth: Dennis Arundell, BLOCH, Lawrence Collingwood, Nicholas Gatty, Karl Taubert, VERDI, and Lauro Rossi's *Biorn.*

Measure for Measure: WAGNER'S DAS LIEBESVERBOT.

The Merchant of Venice: Fernand Brumagne, Castelnuovo-Tedesco, HAHN, Ciro Pinsuti; also, Flor Alpaerts' *Shylock,* J. B. Foerster's *Jessica,* Otto Taubmann's *Porzia.*

The Merry Wives of Windsor: DITTERSDORF, NICOLAI, Peter Ritter; also, ADAM'S *Falstaff,* BALFE'S *Falstaff,* PHILIDOR'S *Herne le chasseur,* SALIERI'S *Falstaff,* VAUGHAN WILLIAMS' SIR JOHN IN LOVE, Verdi's FALSTAFF (with material from *Henry IV).*

A Midsummer Night's Dream: Dennis Arundell, BRITTEN, MANCINELLI, ORFF, Thomas, Victor Vreuls; also, Marcel Delannoy's *Puck,* Georges Huë's *Titania,* PURCELL'S THE FAIRY QUEEN, John Christopher Smith's *The Fairies.*

Much Ado About Nothing: Arpad Doppler, STANFORD, and BERLIOZ' BÉATRICE ET BÉNÉDICT.

Othello: ROSSINI, Verdi.

Richard III: Gaston Salvayre.

Romeo and Juliet: BENDA, BLACHER, GOUNOD, Pietro Carlo Guglielmi, Filippo Marchetti, Malipiero, SUTERMEISTER, Nicola Vaccai, ZANDONAI; also, BELLINI'S I CAPULETTI ED I MONTECCHI, Conrado del Campo's *Los amantes de Verona,* Richard d'Ivry's *Les Amants de Verone.*

The Taming of the Shrew: GIANNINI, Shebalin; also, Renzo Bossi's *Volpino il calderio,* GOETZ'S *Der Widerspänstigen Zähmung,* Alick Maclean's *Petruccio,* WOLF-FERRARI'S SLY.

The Tempest: Atterberg, FIBICH, Nicholas Gatty, C. A. Gibbs, HALÉVY, LATTUADA, MARTIN, Purcell, REICHARDT, John Christopher Smith, Sutermeister's *Der Zauberinsel,* Johann Zumsteeg.

Twelfth Night: AMRAM; also, SMETANA'S *Viola* (unfinished), Karl Taubert's *Cesario,* Karel Weis's *Viola.*

A Winter's Tale: GOLDMARK; also, Bruch's *Hermione,* Josef Nesvera's *Perdita.*

Shaklovity, a boyar (baritone) in MUS- SORGSKY'S KHOVANTCHINA.

Shaliapin, Feodor, *see* CHALIAPIN.

Shanewis (The Robin Woman), opera in two acts by CADMAN. Libretto by Nelle Richmond Eberhart. Premiere: Metropolitan Opera, Mar. 23, 1918. Mrs. Everton, a wealthy Californian (contralto), finances the musical career of the Indian girl Shanewis (contralto) in New York. Shanewis meets and falls in love with Lionel Rhodes (tenor), fiancé of Mrs. Everton's daughter Amy (soprano). Lionel wants to marry Shanewis. The girl is willing, if Lionel will first visit her on her reservation. After Shanewis returns to her tribe, Lionel follows and is fascinated by Indian customs. When Mrs. Everton and her daughter follow Lionel, Shanewis hears for the first time of his previous betrothal. She proudly rejects him. Finding Shanewis grief-stricken, her foster brother believes Lionel has deserted her. He kills Lionel with an arrow.

Filled with melodies and rhythms suggestive of Indian music, *Shanewis* is an early example of an American opera with an American setting. It is also the first American opera that survived more than a single season at the METRO- POLITAN OPERA.

Sharpless, the United States Consul (baritone) in PUCCINI'S MADAMA BUTTER- FLY, a role created by Giuseppe DE LUCA.

Shepherds of the Delectable Mountains, The, one-act opera by VAUGHAN WIL- LIAMS. Libretto by the composer, based on an episode in BUNYAN's *The Pilgrim's Progress.* Premiere: London, July 11, 1922. American premiere: Cincinnati, Dec. 16, 1949. Vaughan Williams subsequently incorporated this work into his opera THE PILGRIM'S PROGRESS.

Sherasmin, Sir Huon de Bordeaux's squire (baritone) in WEBER'S OBERON.

Sheridan, Richard Brinsley, dramatist. Born Dublin, Oct. 30, 1751; died London, July 7, 1816. A number of operas were based upon three of his plays: *The Critic* (opera by STANFORD); *The Duenna* (operas by Ferdinando Bertoni,

Robert Gerhard, Thomas Linley, and PROKOFIEV'S BETROTHAL IN A CONVENT); *The School for Scandal* (opera by KLENAU).

Shirley, George, tenor. Born Indianapolis, Ind., Apr. 18, 1934. He graduated from Wayne University with a bachelor of science degree in music, then studied voice with Themy S. Georgi. In 1959 he made his opera debut in Woodstock, N.Y., in DIE FLEDERMAUS. After sharing the second prize in the Italian Concorso di Vercelli, he made his Italian opera debuts in 1960 as RODOLFO at the Teatro Nuovo in Milan and at the TEATRO ALLA PERGOLA in Florence. One year later he was the winner of the METRO- POLITAN AUDITIONS OF THE AIR, which brought him a debut with the METRO- POLITAN OPERA on Oct. 24 as Ferrando in COSÌ FAN TUTTE. That same year he also appeared with the NEW YORK CITY OPERA, the SAN FRANCISCO OPERA, the SANTA FE OPERA, and at the FESTIVAL OF TWO WORLDS in Spoleto. He has remained with the Metropolitan Opera since then, appearing in over twenty roles. He has also been heard at GLYNDEBOURNE, CO- VENT GARDEN, the Scottish Opera, and the BERKSHIRE MUSIC FESTIVAL. His extensive repertory has enabled him to appear in the American premiere of KÖNIG HIRSCH, the New York premieres of LES INDES GALANTES and VERDI's *Ardolo*, and in such other rarely heard works as ANNA BOLENA and DAPHNE. Besides the regular traditional Italian and French repertory, he has also been heard in operas by MOZART and in LULU, DER FLIEGENDE HOLLÄNDER, DIE MEISTERSINGER, SALOME, and DER ROSENKAVALIER.

Shostakovich, Dmitri, composer. Born St. Petersburg, Sept. 25, 1906. He attended the Glasser School of Music and the St. Petersburg Conservatory. Upon his graduation from the conservatory, he completed his *First Symphony,* a work that made him famous throughout the world of music. Several failures followed this substantial success. One of these was an opera, THE NOSE, based on a GOGOL story, which, after its premiere in

1930, was officially denounced as "bourgeois" and "decadent." But several later compositions revived Shostakovich's popularity and added to his reputation; these include a ballet, *The Bolt,* and a concerto for piano and orchestra. On Jan. 22, 1934, his opera LADY MACBETH OF MZENSK was introduced in Moscow. It was a triumph and for two years played to capacity houses. Then a violent attack was leveled against it from official quarters. For a time it almost seemed that this might be the end of the composer's career. But in 1937 Shostakovich succeeded in rehabilitating his position in Soviet music with his *Fifth Symphony.* In 1940 he won the Stalin Prize for his *Piano Quintet.* During World War II, as a defense worker in Leningrad, he was a public hero. He glorified the struggle of the Soviet people in several large works, among them his *Seventh Symphony.* But again Shostakovich became the object for official denunciation when, in 1948, the Central Committee of the Communist Party described some of his works as "formalistic" and "decadent." And once again he returned to grace, this time with an oratorio, *The Song of the Forests,* which won the Stalin Prize in 1949. In Mar., 1949, he briefly visited New York as a cultural emissary of the Soviet Union. He returned to the United States in 1959 on a cultural exchange plan. In 1963 his extensive revision of *Lady Macbeth of Mzensk*—now called KATERINA ISMAILOVA—was a success when introduced in Moscow. Besides receiving the Stalin (or Lenin) Prize five times and the Order of Lenin twice, he was given on his sixtieth birthday the highest honor the Soviet Union can bestow on a composer, the title of Hero of Socialist Labor. He also received the International Sibelius Prize in 1958 and the Silver Insignia of Honor from the Austrian Republic in 1967. His operas: *The Nose* (1930) ; *Lady Macbeth of Mzensk* (1934), revised as *Katerina Ismailova* (1956) ; *Moskova Tcheremushki* (1958) .

Shuisky, a prince (tenor) in MUSSORGSKY'S BORIS GODUNOV.

Sia qualunque delle figlie, Don Magnifico's joyous air, as he imagines himself a rich and powerful man should one of his daughters marry the Prince, in Act II of ROSSINI'S LA CENERENTOLA.

Siberia, opera in three acts by GIORDANO. Libretto by F. Civinni. Premiere: La Scala, Dec. 19, 1903. American premiere: French Opera House, New Orleans, Jan. 13, 1906. Stephana, mistress of Prince Alexis, loves and is loved by Vassili. In a fit of jealousy, Alexis challenges Vassili to a duel and is wounded. For this Vassili is exiled to Siberia. Stephana goes there to join him and share his fate. During an attempt at flight, Stephana is fatally wounded and Vassili is caught. Before she dies, Stephana is able to persuade the commandant of the post to free her beloved. The second-act orchestral intermezzo and *Cena di Pasqua,* the tenor arias "Orride steppe" and "T'incontrai per la via!", and the soprano aria "Qual vergogna" are of interest.

Si, che un tuo solo accento, Fernando's expression of satisfaction on becoming an officer in the King's army when he realizes Leonora is inaccessible to him, in Act I of DONIZETTI'S LA FAVORITA.

siciliana, originally a Sicilian dancesong; in later times a vocal or instrumental piece in 12/8 or 6/8 time, generally in a minor key, and of moderate speed. A number of HANDEL's finest arias are basically sicilianas. A classic example of an instrumental siciliana is to be found in GLUCK's ARMIDE. The aria "O fortune, à ton caprice," in the finale of Act I of MEYERBEER'S ROBERT LE DIABLE, was designated a siciliana. Turiddu's "O Lola," in the opening of CAVALLERIA RUSTICANA is another siciliana.

Sicilian Vespers, The (Les Vêpres Siciliennes; I vespri siciliani), opera in five acts by VERDI. Libretto by Eugène SCRIBE and Anne Honoré Duveyrier. Premiere: Paris Opéra, June 13, 1855. The setting is thirteenth-century Sicily, where the population rises in revolt against the occupying French. Against such a background, Elena (soprano) , a

Sicilian noblewoman and patriot, is in love with a commoner, Arrigo (tenor). But Arrigo turns out to be the son of Monforte (baritone), governor of Sicily, who is on the side of the French. When the governor consents to the marriage of Elena and Arrigo, she uses the wedding bells as the signal for the Sicilians to rise and massacre the French. The overture, made up of three principal themes from the opera, is the most popular part of the score. The first theme is associated in the opera with the massacre of the French garrison; the second, the farewell of Elena and Arrigo; and the third, the duet of Monforte and Arrigo. Also outstanding are the bass aria, "O tu Palermo," and the Ballet of the Seasons in Act II; as well as Elena's BOLERO, "Mercè, diletti amiche," and Arrigo's air, "La brezza aleggia," in Act V.

Siebel, young man (mezzo-soprano) in love with Marguerite in GOUNOD'S FAUST.

Siège de Corinthe, Le (L'assedio di Corinto; The Siege of Corinth), opera in three acts by ROSSINI. Libretto by L. A. Soumet and G. L. Balochi. Premiere: Paris Opéra, Oct. 9, 1826. American premiere: Italian Opera House, New York, Feb. 6, 1835. This opera is a revision of an earlier Rossini opera in two acts, MAOMETTO II, which he had written in 1820 and which had been introduced at the SAN CARLO OPERA in Naples on Dec. 3 of the same year. This opera had never been given in France. When Rossini became Premier Compositeur du Roi and was required to write operas expressly for the French stage, he had Louis Alexandre Soumet and Guiseppe Balochi adapt the libretto of *Maometto II* for French consumption. Renamed *Le Siège de Corinthe,* and produced with a cast headed by NOURRIT, it was a tremendous success. The text concerns a Greek girl, the Christian daughter of the Governor of Corinth, and her love for a Mohammedan prince. The Prince leads an attack on Corinth and lays waste to the city. The daughter chooses to die with her father rather than marry the con-queror. The subject was close to the hearts of Frenchmen—one of the main reasons why the opera proved so successful—for at that time sophisticated Frenchmen were deeply involved in the Greek struggle for independence. Realizing that the acclaim given the opera at its premiere was for the theme of the text rather than the music, Rossini refused to take a bow. "Nevertheless," says Francis Toye, "there can be no doubt that the music did make a great impression on its own account. Nothing quite like it had been heard at the OPÉRA before; in particular the dramatic vigor of the finales and the emotional excitement of the last-act chorus, in which the Greeks vow to die on the battlefield, drove the audience wild with enthusiasm. . . . Grand opera [as opposed to OPERA SERIA] had been born." One of the none-too-frequent revivals of this opera was given at LA SCALA in 1969, Thomas SCHIPPERS conducting.

Siegfried, (1) son (tenor) of Siegmund and Sieglinde in WAGNER'S SIEGFRIED and GÖTTERDÄMMERUNG.

(2) The third music drama in WAGNER'S DER RING DES NIBELUNGEN.

Siegfried, seliger Held, Brünnhilde's ecstatic greeting to Siegfried as she awakens from her deep sleep upon being kissed by the hero, in the closing scene of WAGNER'S SIEGFRIED.

Siegfried's Funeral Music (Siegfrieds Tod), in Act III of WAGNER'S GÖTTERDÄMMERUNG. It opens with a roll of the timpani followed by the death motive in the lower strings. There follow a number of motives associated with Siegfried: Heroism of the Walsungs (brass); Sympathy (horns and woodwinds); Love (oboes); Sword (trumpets); Glorification of Death (full orchestra); and Brünnhilde (clarinets and English horns). The return of the Death motive and the roll of drums bring the music to its conclusion.

Siegfried's Rhine Journey (Siegfrieds Rheinfahrt), orchestral interlude between the prologue and Act I of WAGNER'S GÖTTERDÄMMERUNG. It is a musical projection of Siegfried's journey down the Rhine as he sets forth for heroic exploits. This music begins with the motives of Decision to Love (strings and clarinets) and Siegfried (horns). Motives connected with the life and achievements of the hero are woven into an integrated symphonic fabric. Among these motives are the Magic Fire (strings); Rhine (brass); Ring (woodwinds and strings); Power of the Ring (oboes). The last part of this orchestral episode anticipates some of the action in the ensuing scenes of the music drama.

Sieglinde, Hunding's wife (soprano), sister of Siegmund, in WAGNER'S DIE WALKÜRE.

Sieglinde's love song, *see* DU BIST DER LENZ.

Siegmund, Sieglinde's brother (tenor) in WAGNER'S DIE WALKÜRE, a role created by Heinrich VOGL.

Siegmund! sieh' auf mich!, Brünnhilde's greeting to Siegmund, before revealing that he must die, in Act II of WAGNER'S DIE WALKÜRE.

Siegmund's love song, *see* WINTERSTÜRME WICHEN DEM WONNEMOND.

Sieh die Freudentränen fliessen, love duet of Belmonte and Constanze after having devised a method of escape, in Act II of MOZART'S THE ABDUCTION FROM THE SERAGLIO.

Siepi, Cesare, bass. Born Milan, Feb. 10, 1923. After study with Chiesa, he won first prize in a national singing contest in 1941. Three months later he made his opera debut as SPARAFUCILE in Schio, near Venice. The war interrupted his career. His second debut took place in 1946 in NABUCCO, the performance which reopened LA SCALA. He then sang throughout Italy and was acclaimed in the title role of MEFISTOFELE, conducted by TOSCANINI. In 1950 he made his debut at both COVENT GARDEN and the METROPOLITAN OPERA, the appearance at the latter opera house taking place on the opening night of the 1950–51 season, in DON CARLOS. He has been a principal bass at the Metropolitan Opera since then, distinguishing himself as BORIS GODUNOV and DON GIOVANNI, as well as

in the VERDI repertory. Between 1953 and 1958 he appeared at the SALZBURG FESTIVAL, where his performance as Don Giovanni was filmed. He has made frequent television appearances in America and in 1962 made his bow in the Broadway musical theater in *Bravo, Giovanni!*

Sie sind ein Charlatan, comic duet of the doctor and the apothecary in DITTERSDORF'S THE DOCTOR AND THE APOTHECARY.

Sigismund, Polish king (bass) in GLINKA'S A LIFE FOR THE CZAR.

Signore, ascolta, Liù's plea to Calaf not to risk his life by trying to win Turandot, in Act I of PUCCINI'S TURANDOT.

Signor Bruschino, Il, one-act comic opera by ROSSINI. Libretto by Giuseppe Foppa. Premiere: Teatro San Moise, Venice, late Jan., 1813. American premiere: Metropolitan Opera, Dec. 9, 1932. In eighteenth-century Italy, Sofia (soprano), ward of Gaudenzio (bass), is about to be forced to marry Bruschino's son (baritone), even though she loves Florville (tenor). When Bruschino's son is imprisoned for debt, Florville impersonates him and is able to win Gaudenzio's consent to his marriage. Two of Gaudenzio's buffo arias reveal Rossini's uncommon gift for comedy: "Nel teatro del gran mondo" and "Hola testa." Beautiful lyricism is found in Sofia's song, "Ah, voi condur volette alla disperazio." The vivacious overture is occasionally heard at symphony concerts. Rossini here exploits an unusual effect by having the violinists tap the music stands with their bows in one section.

Sigurd, opera in four acts by REYER. Libretto by Camille Du Locle and Alfred Blau. Premiere: Théâtre de la Monnaie, Jan. 7, 1884. American premiere: French Opera House, New Orleans, Dec. 24, 1891. The text, like that of WAGNER'S RING cycle, is based on the Nibelung sagas.

Si io penso alla tortura, Madeleine's complaint about the discomforts suffered by a young lady who must be dressed fashionably, in Act I of GIORDANO'S ANDREA CHÉNIER.

Si la rigueur et la vengeance, Cardinal Brogny's plea to the people to replace hatred with tolerance, in Act I of HALÉVY'S LA JUIVE.

Sills, Beverly, (born Belle Silverman), soprano. Born New York City, May 25, 1929. As a child she appeared in motion pictures and regularly on a radio network program. After receiving vocal training from Estelle LIEBLING, she made her opera debut when she was seventeen as Micaëla in CARMEN with the Philadelphia Civic Opera. This was followed by two seasons of coast-to-coast tours with the Charles Wagner Opera. In 1953 she was a member of the SAN FRANCISCO OPERA, where she was heard as Elena in MEFISTOFELE and as Donna ELVIRA. She joined the NEW YORK CITY OPERA COMPANY in 1955–56. Her performances as the Queen of Shemakha in LE COQ D'OR and especially as Cleopatra in HANDEL'S GIULIO CESARE attracted national attention. In 1965 she appeared in all the three leading female roles in THE TALES OF HOFFMANN, and in 1966–67 she sang the roles of all three heroines in PUCCINI'S IL TRITTICO. She was also starred in the world premieres of THE WINGS OF THE DOVE and WEISGALL'S Six Characters in Search of an Author, and in the New York premiere of THE BALLAD OF BABY DOE. With the Opera Company of Boston she appeared in the American premiere INTOLLERANZA 1960. She has also appeared successfully at the TEATRO COLÓN, the VIENNA STATE OPERA, COVENT GARDEN, and LA SCALA. She made her debut at the last-named opera house in 1969 in a revival of ROSSINI'S LE SIÈGE DE CORINTHE. In Oct., 1970, she made a triumphant appearance as Queen Elizabeth in a revival of DONIZETTI'S Roberto Devereux by the New York City Opera.

Silva, Don Ruy Gomez de, Spanish grandee (bass) in VERDI'S ERNANI.

Silvana, see WALDMÄDCHEN, DAS.

Silvio, a villager (baritone) in LEONCAVALLO'S PAGLIACCI.

Si, me ne vo contessa, Gérard's aria in which he announces publicly his sympathy with the poor and the downtrodden, in Act I of GIORDANO'S ANDREA CHÉNIER.

Simionato, Giulietta, mezzo-soprano. Born Forli, Italy, Dec. 15, 1910. After studying voice with Ettore Lucatello in Rovigo, she received first prize in a BEL CANTO competition in Florence in 1933. She appeared in minor roles with opera companies in Florence, Milan, and Padua before joining the LA SCALA company, where she assumed major roles. When TOSCANINI directed a La Scala concert performance of BOITO'S NERONE in 1947, he selected Simionato for the part of Asteria. In the same year her performance as Cherubino in THE MARRIAGE OF FIGARO was acclaimed at the EDINBURGH FESTIVAL. In Palermo, in 1954, BELLINI'S rarely heard I CAPULETTI ED I MONTECCHI was revived for her. By the time she made her American debut, she had become known to American opera lovers through her many fine recordings. That debut took place in 1954 with the CHICAGO LYRIC OPERA. In 1955 she was heard with the SAN FRANCISCO OPERA, and in 1957 she made her New York debut in a concert performance of DONIZETTI'S ANNA BOLENA. Her debut at the METROPOLITAN OPERA took place on Oct. 26, 1959, as Azucena in IL TROVATORE. She remained with the Metropolitan Opera through the 1960–61 season, then appeared with major European opera companies. Some of her greatest successes came in such less familiar roles as Jane Seymour in Anna Bolena, Romeo in I Capuletti ed i Montecchi, and in the leading mezzo-soprano roles in various operas by ROSSINI, such as Rosina and LA CENERENTOLA.

Simon Boccanegra, opera in prologue and three acts by VERDI. Libretto by Francesco Maria PIAVE (later revised by BOITO), based on a play by Antonio García Gutierrez. Premiere: Teatro la Fenice, Mar. 12, 1857 (original version); La Scala, Mar. 24, 1881 (revised version). American premiere: Metropolitan Opera, Jan. 28, 1932.

Characters: Simon Boccanegra, Doge of Genoa (baritone) ; Maria Boccanegra (known also as Amelia Grimaldi), his illegitimate daughter (soprano) ; Jacopo Fiesco, her grandfather, a patrician (bass) ; Gabriele Adorno, a young patrician (tenor) ; Paolo Albiani, a courtier of the Doge (baritone) ; Pietro, a courtier (bass) ; Amelia's maidservant (mezzo-soprano) ; senators; commoners; soldiers; seamen; and so forth. The action takes place in the middle of the fourteenth century in and near Genoa.

Prologue. A square in Genoa, outside Fiesco's palace. Simon Boccanegra, whom the commoners plan to elect as Doge, comes to the palace for news of Fiesco's daughter, Maria, whom he expects to marry and with whom he has had a daughter. He learns she is a prisoner in the palace. Fiesco emerges from the palace lamenting the death of his beloved daughter, Maria ("Il lacerato spirito"). He and Simon Boccanegra have a fiery exchange ("Qual cieco fato") in which Boccanegra informs Fiesco that Maria's daughter has disappeared. Then Boccanegra learns of Maria's death; his grief is not assuaged when he is proclaimed Doge.

Act I, Scene 1. Fiesco's gardens, outside Genoa. Twenty-four years have passed. Without knowing she is his granddaughter, Fiesco has raised Boccanegra's daughter, whom he has named Amelia Grimaldi. She is in love with Gabriele Adorno, a young nobleman politically opposed to Boccanegra. Upon appearing, she looks into the distant horizon and recalls her childhood ("Come in quest' ora bruna"). She is troubled, for the Doge—Boccanegra— wants her to marry Paolo. To convince her, Boccanegra pays her a visit. A locket with her mother's picture discloses to Boccanegra that she is his own daughter ("Figlia! a tal nome palpito"). Boccanegra extracts from her a vow to keep this fact a secret. He then goes to Paolo to tell him that Amelia will not marry him.

Scene 2. The council chamber in the Doge's palace. Outside the palace the people are shouting their disapproval of the patricians. Fiesco and Gabriele are dragged into the council room. Gabriele is accused of having tried to kill a man of unknown identity who attempted to abduct Amelia. Convinced that the man is Boccanegra, Gabriele rushes toward him with his sword, but Amelia intervenes and saves her father. At the same time she accuses Paolo of the crime. Although he is really guilty, Paolo denies the crime, whereupon Boccanegra, as guardian of the people's honor, commands that he must curse the guilty one. Cornered and horrified, Paolo must, in effect, curse himself, "Sia maledetta!", and the effective close of the scene has the whole court repeating the curse in whispers: "Sia maledetta!"

Act II. The Doge's palace. Paolo now swears vengeance on the Doge and sets out a poisoned cup of wine for him. Next he summons Fiesco and Gabriele to persuade them to join in his plot. Fiesco refuses to stoop to assassination, but Gabriele is won over when Paolo claims that Amelia is even now in the palace and that Boccanegra intends to seduce her. Amelia pleads on behalf of her good friend the Doge, but before she can tell who he is, Boccanegra comes in, and Gabriele hides. Boccanegra, tired out, sinks into his chair, takes the poisoned refreshment, and falls asleep. Gabriele springs out with lifted dagger, but Amelia saves her father just in time. The Doge, learning now that his political enemy is his daughter's beloved, magnanimously offers to release the young man to fight on the other side; and Gabriele is so much moved by this that he swears to fight on the side of the man he now expects to become his father-in-law.

Act III. The palace. The people are acclaiming the Doge's victory over the threatened revolt instigated by Paolo. For this Paolo is sentenced to die. Led away for execution, he confides to Fiesco that the Doge will die with him, for the poison in the wine works slowly but surely. The dying Boccanegra finally discloses to Fiesco that Amelia is his daughter; then he proclaims Gabriele his successor as Doge.

Of all of Verdi's baritone roles, that of Boccanegra is the most demanding both vocally and histrionically and one of the most impressive. As the Earl of HAREWOOD wrote, it is the character of Boccanegra which is "the most remarkable thing about the opera, a puissant character and amongst Verdi's greatest creations; all the way through one cannot help but be impressed by the amazing consistency of the characterization. . . . Boccanegra is a mature creation, whose insight and integrity are expressed in music as well as drama."

Simone, Donati's cousin (bass) in PUCCINI'S GIANNI SCHICCHI.

Si, morir ella de, Alvise's aria in which he plans the murder of his wife, Laura, for loving another man, in Act III of PONCHIELLI'S LA GIOCONDA.

Singher, Martial, baritone. Born Oloron-Sainte-Marie, France, Aug. 14, 1904. He attended the Paris Conservatory. In 1930 he made his debut at the PARIS OPÉRA, where he remained a principal baritone until 1939. During this period he was a guest of major European opera companies. He made a successful American debut at the METROPOLITAN OPERA on Dec. 10, 1943, as DAPERTUTTO. In a later appearance in THE TALES OF HOFFMANN he was cast in all the leading baritone parts. He remained with the Metropolitan until 1959, acclaimed particularly in the French repertory. He is the only singer to have sung the role of Pelléas as well as that of Golaud in PELLÉAS ET MÉLISANDE. He has appeared at the TEATRO COLÓN, COVENT GARDEN, and several times at the FLORENCE MAY FESTIVAL. He has also distinguished himself as a concert artist.

Singspiel, an early German form of comic opera, established in the middle of the eighteenth century by Johann Adam HILLER. Its chief characteristic is the use of spoken dialogue instead of recitatives. Hiller derived the form from the French comic theater, giving it a German personality by making German popular and folk songs an element of his music. Early *singspiel* composers were Johann Mattheson and Johann Friedrich REICHARDT. The tradition was carried on by MOZART in his THE ABDUCTION FROM THE SERAGLIO and THE MAGIC FLUTE, and to a certain degree by BEETHOVEN in his FIDELIO.

Sì, pel ciel marmoreo giuro!, Otello's and Iago's vow of vengeance against Cassio for allegedly having become Desdemona's lover, in Act II of VERDI'S OTELLO.

Si può, the opening words of Tonio's prologue in LEONCAVALLO'S PAGLIACCI, in which he explains to the audience that the emotions about to be portrayed are real emotions felt by real people.

Sir John in Love, opera in four acts by VAUGHAN WILLIAMS. Libretto by the composer, based on SHAKESPEARE'S *The Merry Wives of Windsor.* Premiere: London, Mar. 21, 1929, American premiere: New York City, Jan. 20, 1949, The score makes notable use of English folksongs, including "Greensleeves."

Sirval, Marchioness de, Charles's mother (mezzo-soprano) in DONIZETTI'S LINDA DI CHAMOUNIX.

Sisera, King (tenor) of the Kenites, the enemy of the Hebrews, who becomes a fatal victim at the hands of Jael, in PIZZETTI'S DEBORA E JAELE.

Sister Angelica, *see* SUOR ANGELICA.

Sita, the woman (soprano) loved by the King of Lahore in MASSENET'S LE ROI DE LAHORE.

Si tu m'aimes, Carmen, love duet of Escamillo and Carmen in Act IV of BIZET'S CARMEN.

Six, Les (The Six), a group of six French composers who emerged to fame just after World War I. They were Georges AURIC, Louis Durey, Germaine Tailleferre, Arthur HONEGGER, Darius MILHAUD, and Francis POULENC. The last three have made significant contributions to the art of opera. The name for the group was suggested by the critic Henri Collet in the periodical *Comoedia,* issue of Jan. 16, 1920, when he reviewed the composers' album of piano pieces and likened the composers to the Russian school known as the FIVE.

Sleepwalking scene, *see* LADY MACBETH; SONNAMBULA, LA.

Slezak, Leo, tenor. Born Mährisch-Schönberg, Moravia, Aug. 18, 1873; died Egern-on-Tegernsee, Bavaria, June 1, 1946. Described as "the second TAMAGNO," he was one of the most celebrated tenors of the early twentieth century. He planned to become an engineer but, while engaged in technical studies, decided to develop his voice. He took only a few lessons before joining the chorus of the Brno Opera. He made his debut at the Brno Opera in LOHENGRIN on Mar. 17, 1896. After appearances at the BERLIN OPERA and at COVENT GARDEN, he received from the VIENNA OPERA a seven-year contract, making his debut there in WILLIAM TELL. For a quarter of a century, Slezak was a principal tenor of the Vienna Opera, the idol of the Viennese. In 1908 he temporarily retired to study with Jean DE RESZKE. He returned to the opera stage triumphantly in London in May, 1909, as OTELLO. It was in this role that he made his American debut at the METROPOLITAN OPERA on Nov. 17, 1909. Slezak remained at the Metropolitan through the 1912–13 season, outstandingly successful in the WAGNER repertory. He also distinguished himself on the concert stage. He was appearing in recitals in Russia when World War I broke out. He escaped to Germany, where he joined the army and saw action. After the war, he continued his career at the Berlin Opera and the Vienna State Opera. After retiring from opera, he continued to appear as a concert singer. He was the author of several volumes of reminiscences, one of which was published in English as *Song of Motley* (1938). His son, Walter Slezak, has been successful on the American musical-comedy stage and in motion pictures.

Sly, opera in three acts by WOLF-FERRARI. Libretto by Forzano, based on the introduction to SHAKESPEARE's *The Taming of the Shrew.* Premiere: La Scala, Dec. 29, 1927. It received a notable revival over the BBC in London on Dec. 11, 1954, Rudolf KEMPE conducting.

Smallens, Alexander, conductor. Born St. Petersburg, Jan. 1, 1889. His musical training took place at the Institute of Musical Art in New York and at the Paris Conservatory. In 1911 he became assistant conductor of the Boston Opera company, and soon after, first conductor of another company, the Boston National Opera. For two years he conducted the Anna Pavlova ballet troupe, touring the United States and South America. During this period he became the first North American conductor to direct operas at the TEATRO COLÓN. In 1919 he was appointed first conductor of the CHICAGO OPERA. He remained four seasons, conducting the premieres of DE KOVEN's RIP VAN WINKLE and PROKOFIEV's THE LOVE FOR THREE ORANGES. During this period he also conducted opera in Europe. In 1924 he became musical director of the Philadelphia Civic Opera; in 1934 he began leading opera performances in Lewisohn Stadium in New York. He conducted the premiere of PORGY AND BESS (1935), a work with which he was identified for many years. Between 1952 and 1956 he led the American Negro company that presented GERSHWIN's opera in a triumphant tour of Europe, the Near East, the Soviet Union, and other countries behind the Iron Curtain. Smallens also led the American premieres of Richard STRAUSS's ARIADNE AUF NAXOS and FEUERSNOT. Other novelties given under his direction include FOUR SAINTS IN THREE ACTS, HIN UND ZURÜCK, MAVRA, and *Sette canzoni* (MALIPIERO). After conducting in Holland in 1956–57 he was compelled to give up his career because of neuritis of his hands. He went into total retirement in Taormina, Sicily.

Smanie implacabili, Dorabella's lament

because her beloved is supposedly being recalled to his troops, in Act I, Scene 3, of MOZART'S COSÌ FAN TUTTE.

Smetana, Bedřich, composer. Born Litomischl, Bohemia, Mar. 2, 1824; died Prague, May 12, 1884. The most significant composer of Bohemian national operas, he had little systematic musical training until his nineteenth year, though he interested himself in musical activities from childhood on. In his nineteenth year he fell in love with Katharina Kolař, who convinced him that he should turn to music seriously. He went to Prague in 1843 and became a pupil of Josef Proksch. A year later he was engaged as music teacher by Count Leopold Thun, holding this post four years. In 1848 he helped organize the first significant music school in Prague. In 1849 he married Katharina Kolař. A year later he was appointed pianist to the former Emperor of Austria, Ferdinand I, then residing in Prague. At the same time he began writing orchestral and chamber works. From 1856 to 1861 he lived in Gothenburg, Sweden, where he taught, played the piano, and conducted the city's orchestra. He interrupted his stay in 1859 with a return to Bohemia. His wife died during this trip. Remarrying in Prague, he returned to Gothenburg for an additional two years.

In 1861, again in his native land, Smetana assumed a dominating position in its musical life. He became director of the music school in Prague, led an important orchestra and chorus, wrote music criticism in which he espoused the cause of Bohemian music, founded and directed a dramatic school for the Bohemian Theater in Prague, helped organize the Society of Artists. He did not neglect composition. In 1863 he completed his first opera, *The Brandenburgers in Bohemia,* which may be considered Bohemia's first major national opera. Produced in Prague on Jan. 5, 1866, it was highly successful. His second opera, THE BARTERED BRIDE, is one of the greatest folk operas. At its premiere (May 30, 1866) it was not well received, but after its third performance it was acclaimed. Smetana later wrote two other excellent folk operas: DALIBOR (1868) and LIBUŠE (1871).

After 1874 Smetana was afflicted with deafness. Despite this infirmity he continued producing important music, including his cycle of national tone poems entitled *My Country (Má Vlast),* one of which is *The Moldau.* He also wrote the following operas: *Two Widows* (1874); THE KISS (1876); *The Secret* (1878); *The Devil's Wall* (1882); and *Viola* (unfinished). His last complete opera, *The Devil's Wall,* was severely criticized at its premiere (though it later became popular), a disappointment which precipitated the composer's breakdown. Becoming insane in 1883, he was confined, dying a year later.

Smeton, Anna Bolena's page (mezzo-soprano) in DONIZETTI'S ANNA BOLENA.

Smithers, Henry, a cockney trader (tenor) in GRUENBERG'S THE EMPEROR JONES.

Smyth, Dame Ethel, composer. Born London, Apr. 23, 1858; died Woking, Eng., May 8, 1944. She attended the Leipzig Conservatory and soon after her graduation received recognition for her chamber music and a mass. A one-act opera, *Der Wald (The Forest)* was produced in Dresden in 1901. A three-act opera, THE WRECKERS (*Les Naufrageurs*) was introduced in Leipzig in 1906. Her most famous work, THE BOATSWAIN'S MATE, was produced in London in 1916. These works placed her in the front rank of English opera composers of the early twentieth century. She also wrote the following operas: *Fantasio* (1898); *Fête galante* (1923); *Entente cordiale* (1925). An authoritative conductor of her own works, she also became known as a leader of the woman-suffrage movement. In 1920 she was made Dame of the British Empire. She wrote several autobiographical volumes, the best known being *Impressions That Remained* (1919).

Snow Maiden, The (Snegurochka),

opera in prologue and four acts by RIMSKY-KORSAKOV. Libretto by the composer, based on a play by Alexander Ostrovsky, in turn derived from a fairy tale. Premiere: Maryinsky Theater, St. Petersburg, Feb. 10, 1882. American premiere (probable): Metropolitan Opera, Jan. 23, 1922. The composer subtitled this opera "A Legend of Springtime." The setting is the land of Berendeys in prehistoric times. The Snow Maiden (soprano) is safe from death by the sun's rays only so long as she is innocent of love. She wants to live the life of a mortal and is encouraged to do so by Tsar Berendey (tenor), who wants her to discover love. She is placed in the care of two villagers. There her life is complicated by the fact that the merchant Mizguir (baritone) falls in love with her, deserting his sweetheart. Ultimately, the Snow Maiden falls in love with Mizguir. The sun touches her and she disappears. Grief-stricken, Mizguir throws himself into a lake. The Dance of the Tumblers (or Buffoons) in Act III is a well-known orchestral excerpt; so is the introduction to Act I. Noteworthy vocal excerpts: in Act I, the Snow Maiden's aria, "How painful," and "In the fields a lime tree stood," for chorus; in Act II, Tsar Berendey's CAVATINA, "Full of wonders"; in Act III, Tsar Berendey's aria, "Joyous day departs"; and in Act IV, the Snow Maiden's death, "And yet I faint."

So anch'io la virtù magica, Norina's aria in Act I, Scene 2, of DONIZETTI's DON PASQUALE, boasting she knows all the tricks for winning a man's love.

Socrate, a "symphonic drama" in three parts by SATIE. Libretto by the composer, derived from the *Dialogues* of Plato, translated by Victor Cousin. Premiere: Paris, Feb. 14, 1920. American premiere: New York City, Jan. 6, 1965. Though basically a concert work, *Socrate* has enough dramatic interest to warrant occasional staging as an opera. It is in a single act, divided into three parts: "Portrait of Socrates"; "By the Banks of Ilyssus"; and "Death of Socrates." Each part is based on one of three of Plato's *Dialogues: The Symposium, Phaedrus,* and *Phaedo.* The work is scored for four sopranos and chamber orchestra, with the writing for voices mainly recitative, and the orchestra moving independently of the voices to achieve a technique that approximates and anticipates linear writing. The work is at times deeply reflective, and at times, as in the third part, it rises to great peaks of eloquence. Rollo H. Myers has written that throughout the work Satie achieved "something that no one had hitherto attempted in music—the weaving of a kind of tapestry of sound to carry a long, melodic narration entrusted to four different voices, succeeding one another like runners in a relay race."

Sodero, Cesare, conductor. Born Naples, Aug. 2, 1886; died New York City, Dec. 16, 1947. He studied with Giuseppe Martucci and graduated from the Naples Conservatory when he was only fourteen. After touring Europe as cellist, he came to the United States in 1906 and for seven years directed various American opera companies, including the CHICAGO OPERA. From 1913 to 1925 he was general music director of the Edison Phonograph Company. He turned to radio in 1925 and achieved significance as a pioneer in broadcasting operas. In 1926 he directed a series of fifty-three operas in tabloid form for NBC. From 1926 to 1934 he conducted several hundred symphony concerts over NBC. He then became musical director of the Mutual network. In 1942 he became a principal conductor of the METROPOLITAN OPERA, making his debut there on Nov. 28 with AIDA. He remained with the Metropolitan until his death. He wrote an opera, *Ombre russe,* broadcast by NBC in 1929 and given its stage premiere in Venice in 1930.

So Do They All, see COSÌ FAN TUTTE.

So elend und treu, Saffi's air in praise of the loyalty of the gypsies, in Act I of Johann STRAUSS's THE GYPSY BARON.

Sofia, Gaudenzio's ward (soprano) in ROSSINI's IL SIGNOR BRUSCHINO.

Sogno soave e casto, Ernesto's aria condemning his friend Malatesta for having betrayed him, in Act I, Scene 1, of DONIZETTI'S DON PASQUALE.

Sojourner and Mollie Sinclair, The, opera in one act by FLOYD. Libretto by the composer. Premiere: Raleigh, N.C., Dec. 2, 1963. This opera was intended for television broadcast, but its world premiere was staged, then taped for television transmission. The work was commissioned by the Carolina Charter Tercentenary Committe to help celebrate the three hundredth anniversary of North Carolina. The opera is set in Cape Fear River Valley in the middle of the seventeenth century, and the characters are Scottish Highlanders, who are torn by their conflict of allegiance to North Carolina, their new homeland, and their native land, Scotland.

Sola, perduta, abbandonata, Manon's cry of terror in the darkness of a desolate plain near New Orleans, toward the close of Act IV of PUCCINI'S MANON LESCAUT.

Soldiers' Chorus, (1) *see* GLOIRE IMMORTELLE DE NOS AÏEUX.

(2) *See* SQUILLI, ECHEGGI LA TROMBA.

Solenne in quest' ora, duet of Carlo and Alvaro, in which Alvaro entreats Carlo to destroy a packet of letters so that he can die in peace, in Act III, Scene 2, of VERDI'S LA FORZA DEL DESTINO.

Solingo, errante e misero, Ernani's plea to Don Silva to spare his life, in Act IV of VERDI'S ERNANI.

Solomon, the Hebrew King (baritone) in GOLDMARK'S THE QUEEN OF SHEBA.

Solti, Georg, conductor. Born Budapest, Oct. 21, 1912. He graduated from the Hochschule für Musik in Budapest in 1930 with diplomas in conducting, piano, and composition. He made his debut conducting THE MARRIAGE OF FIGARO at the BUDAPEST OPERA in 1936, and in 1937 and 1938 he assisted TOSCANINI in preparing his opera performances at the SALZBURG FESTIVAL. During World War II he lived in Switzerland, where he directed performances of the Swiss Radio Orchestra. From 1947 to 1951, while serving as general music

director in Munich, he conducted distinguished performances for the MUNICH OPERA. From 1951 to 1961 he was the director-general of music in Frankfurt, musical director of the FRANKFURT OPERA, and conductor of the Museum concerts in that city. He was largely responsible for lifting the Frankfurt Opera to a significant place among German opera companies. During this period he made highly successful appearances at the EDINBURGH and GLYNDEBOURNE festivals. His American debut took place with the SAN FRANCISCO OPERA on Sept. 25, 1953, conducting Richard STRAUSS'S ELEKTRA. He conducted for the Chicago Opera in 1956–57, then made his debut at the METROPOLITAN OPERA on Dec. 17, 1960, with TANNHÄUSER. He made his debut at COVENT GARDEN in Dec., 1959, leading DER ROSENKAVALIER. In Sept., 1961, he was appointed musical director of Covent Garden. He resigned in 1969 to become music director of the Chicago Symphony. He combined this post with that of music director of the Orchestre de Paris in 1971. In both symphonic music and opera he is one of the foremost and most versatile conductors of the twentieth century.

Sombre destine, Dinorah's legend about the treasure, in Act II of MEYERBEER'S DINORAH.

sommeil, French for "sleep"—in old French operas, a term signifying a quiet instrumental piece accompanying a scene of slumber or dreaming. An example occurs in RAMEAU'S DARDANUS.

Sommi dei, tenor aria invoking the gods to protect the broken heart, in HANDEL's *Radamisto.*

Son geloso del zeffiro errante, duet of Elvino and Amina in which he tells her he is jealous even of the breeze that caresses her, in Act I of BELLINI'S LA SONNAMBULA.

Song of India, the Hindu aria in Scene 4 of RIMSKY-KORSAKOV'S SADKO.

Song of Roxane, Roxane's aria in Act II of SZYMANOWSKI'S KING ROGER. It has become popular in Paul Kochanski's transcription for violin and piano.

Song of the Flea, *see* PUCE GENTILLE, UNE.

Song of the Gnat, the little ditty sung by the Nurse for Xenia and Feodor, Boris' children, in Act II, Scene 2, of MUSSORGSKY'S BORIS GODUNOV.

Song of the Rat, *see* THE DAMNATION OF FAUST, Part II, Scene 3.

Song of the Venetian Guest, song in Scene 4 of RIMSKY-KORSAKOV'S SADKO.

Song of the Viking Guest, song in Scene 4 of RIMSKY-KORSAKOV'S SADKO.

song-speech, *see* SPRECHSTIMME.

Son imbrogliato io gia, Uberto's expression of skepticism that Serpina has a lover, in Act II of PERGOLESI'S LA SERVA PADRONA.

sonnambula, La (The Sleepwalker), opera in two acts by BELLINI. Libretto by SCRIBE. Premiere: Teatro Carcano, Milan, Mar. 6, 1831. American premiere: Park Theater, New York, Nov. 13, 1835.

Characters: Amina, an orphan (soprano); Teresa, her foster mother (mezzo-soprano); Lisa, mistress of an inn (soprano); Alessio, a peasant, her suitor (bass); Elvino, Amina's fiancé (tenor); Count Rodolfo (bass); a notary (tenor); peasants. The action takes place in a Swiss village in the early nineteenth century.

Act I, Scene 1. The village green. The betrothal of Amina and Elvino is being celebrated by the village people ("Tutto e gioia"). When Amina arrives she expresses her gratitude to her foster mother and gives expression to her joy ("Come per me sereno"). A stranger—who actually is Count Rodolfo, son of the late lord of the manor, and who is believed to have died—arrives, recalling nostalgically the days of his youth ("Vi ravviso"). He arouses Elvino's jealousy by telling Amina how beautiful she is. With the approach of dusk, Teresa warns the people to go home, since this is the time when a mysterious phantom comes to haunt the village. When they leave and when the stranger enters the inn, Elvino tells Amina he envies even the breeze that caresses her and bids her goodnight ("Son geloso del zeffiro errante").

Scene 2. Count Rodolfo's room in the inn. Lisa comes to Rodolfo to tell him that he has been recognized by the villagers, who are coming to pay him homage. As she takes her leave, she drops a handkerchief that Rodolfo places on his bed. Amina, a sleepwalker, now enters Rodolfo's room, calling Elvino's name, and falls into Rodolfo's bed in a sound sleep. Elvino, finding her there, draws the wrong conclusion. When she awakens, he denounces her fiercely and, despite her protestations of innocence, breaks their engagement.

Act II, Scene 1. The woods near the inn. Amina's friends have come to the Count to seek his help in clearing Amina's reputation. Amina is with them, lamenting her lost happiness. When Elvino appears, the villagers try to convince him of Amina's innocence, but he refuses to listen. Nevertheless he confesses that he does not hate her and will never forget her ("Ah! perche non posso odiarti").

Scene 2. By the mill. Now that Elvino has rejected Amina, Lisa is about to marry him. Rodolfo insists to the still skeptical Elvino that Amina is not guilty of wrongdoing. Suddenly Amina appears. She is walking in her sleep on the mill roof, grief-stricken that she will never marry Elvino ("Ah! Non credea mirarti"). She looks at the withered flowers that Elvino had given her and compares them to her own decayed love. Elvino, now convinced, kneels before her, begging for forgiveness. Amina awakens and is overjoyed to discover that Elvino still loves her ("Ah! non giunge").

Though extraordinarily popular in the nineteenth century, particularly as a vehicle for such celebrated coloratura sopranos as MALIBRAN, SEMBRICH, PATTI, Jenny LIND, and TETRAZZINI, among others, *La sonnambula* lapsed into comparative neglect in the first decades of the present century. *La sonnambula* is only as good as the prima donna who sings the leading role. It is due mainly to the talent of such celebrated coloratura sopranos as Lily PONS, Renata

SCOTTO, Anna MOFFO, and most significantly, Joan SUTHERLAND that *La sonnambula* has within the past quarter of a century or so once again become a favorite with opera audiences everywhere.

Sonnez, clairons, que vos chants de victoire, the chorus of homage to Prince Léopold, in Act III of HALÉVY'S LA JUIVE.

Son pochi fiori, Suzel's hymn to spring, in Act I of MASCAGNI'S L'AMICO FRITZ.

Son sessant' anni, Gérard's bitter denunciation of aristocracy, in Act I of GIORDANO'S ANDREA CHÉNIER.

Sonst spielt' ich mit zepter, romantic aria by Peter, one of the important vocal numbers in LORTZING'S ZAR UND ZIMMERMANN.

Sontag, Henriette (born Gertrud Walburga Sonntag), soprano. Born Coblenz, Ger., Jan. 3, 1806; died Mexico City, June 17, 1854. The daughter of actors, she made her stage debut at the age of six. After attending the Prague Conservatory, she made her opera debut in her fifteenth year as a last-minute replacement for an indisposed prima donna in Prague. In 1822 she appeared in German and Italian roles at the VIENNA OPERA. WEBER was so impressed by her that he engaged her for EURYANTHE, in which opera she created the title role in 1823 with outstanding success. She sang the soprano parts in the premieres of BEETHOVEN'S *Ninth Symphony* and *Missa Solemnis*. On Aug. 13, 1825, she made her debut in Berlin in L'ITALIANA IN ALGERI. Soon after she made her bows in Paris and London in THE BARBER OF SEVILLE.

After marriage to Count Rossi, a Sardinian diplomat in 1830, she was obliged to retire from the stage for the dignity of his office, but she continued to appear in concerts. Her husband eventually resigned his post and followed his wife as she resumed her career. Sontag was once again acclaimed in the leading opera houses of London, Paris, and Germany. In 1852 she made a triumphal tour of the United States.

She was singing in Mexico when she was fatally stricken with cholera.

Son vergin vezzosa, Elvira's jubilant aria speaking of her joy in having her father's and uncle's consent to her marriage to Talbot, in Act I of BELLINI'S I PURITANI.

Sonzogno, Edoardo, publisher. Born Milan, Apr. 21, 1836; died there Mar. 14, 1920. He founded the music publishing house of Sonzogno in 1874, after inheriting his father's printing plant and bookstore. This house became celebrated in the field of opera by sponsoring contests for one-act operas, the first in 1883; CAVALLERIA RUSTICANA won the prize in 1888. The house specialized in publishing cheap editions of old Italian music. From 1861 to 1909 Sonzogno was the owner and director of the newspaper *Il Secolo*. In 1894 he established a theater in Milan, the Lirico Internazionale.

Sophie, (1) Charlotte's sister (mezzo-soprano) in MASSENET'S WERTHER.

(2) Janusz' beloved (contralto) in MONIUSZKO'S HALKA.

(3) Herr von Faninal's daughter (soprano) in Richard STRAUSS'S DER ROSENKAVALIER.

Sophocles, poet and dramatist. Born Colonus, Greece, c. 496 B.C.; died, place unknown, 406 B.C. One of the great tragic poets and dramatists of ancient Greece. Operas were derived from a number of dramas by Sophocles, notably *Antigone* (operas by HONEGGER, ORFF, Menelaos Pallantios, Ljubomir Pipkov, Niccolò Zingarelli), *Electra* (operas by Johann Haeffner, Jean LEMOYNE, Richard STRAUSS), *Oedipus at Colonus* (operas by Charles Radoux-Rogier, SACCHINI, Zingarelli), *Oedipus Tyrannus* (operas by Georges Enesco, LEONCAVALLO, Orff, STRAVINSKY). PIZZETTI'S *Clitennestra* is based partly on Sophocles' *Electra* and partly on AESCHYLUS' *Oresteia*.

soprano, the highest female voice, normally ranging a little more than two octaves upward from the B-flat below middle C. Soprano voices are classified as dramatic, lyric, and coloratura; the last, besides possessing an agility not required of the other types, requires a compass of two octaves and a fourth above middle C. The term "soprano" was also applied to the higher male voices that used to sing women's parts in operas of the seventeenth and eighteenth centuries (see CASTRATO).

soprano acuto, Italian for "high soprano."

soprano Falcon, a type of dramatic soprano associated with such operatic roles as RACHEL and VALENTINE. It was named after the singer Marie-Cornélie FALCON.

soprano leggiero, a light, or agile, soprano.

soprano sfogato, a high, thin soprano.

Sorel, John, Magda's husband (baritone) in MENOTTI's THE CONSUL.

Sorgeva il dì del bosco in seno, see JOUR NAISSAIT DANS LE BOCAGE, LE.

Sorochinski Fair, see FAIR AT SOROCHINSK, THE.

Sorte amica, chorus of Sicilian knights in Act I of MEYERBEER's ROBERT LE DIABLE.

sortita, Italian for "coming out," an eighteenth-century operatic term referring to the initial appearance and initial aria of a singer.

sotto voce, Italian for "under the voice," in vocal music a direction to sing barely audibly, or in an undertone.

soubrette, a French term referring in opera to a young comedienne (frequently a lady's maid in comic operas), usually petite and coquettish and with a light soprano voice. Typical soubrette roles are those of Serpina in LA SERVA PADRONA, Despina in COSÌ FAN TUTTE, Susanna in THE MARRIAGE OF FIGARO, Adele in DIE FLEDERMAUS. The Italian equivalent is *servetta*.

Sous le ciel tout étoilé, Lakmé's gentle song as she nurses Gérald back to health, in Act III of DELIBES's LAKMÉ.

Sous les vastes arceaux, John's description of his dream in which he saw himself venerated in front of the cathedral by crowds, in Act II of MEYERBEER's LE PROPHÈTE.

Souviens-toi de ton serviteur, Samson's prayer to God to restore his lost strength, in Act III, Scene 2, of SAINT-SAËNS's SAMSON ET DALILA.

Souzay, Gerald (born Gérard Marcel Tisserand), baritone. Born Angers, France, Dec. 8, 1920. Though basically a concert singer (one of the outstanding interpreters of French art songs), he has given some distinguished performances in opera. His vocal studies took place with Pierre Bernac, Claire Croiza, Vanni Marcoux, Lotte LEHMANN, and at the Paris Conservatory, from which he graduated with honors. He made his recital debut in 1945 and his American concert debut in 1950. He soon achieved worldwide recognition as a recitalist in a repertory ranging from LULLY and GLUCK to modern composers, from French art songs to German *lieder*. He made his American opera debut with the NEW YORK CITY OPERA in MONTEVERDI's L'ORFEO on Sept. 29, 1960. On Jan. 18, 1962, he appeared at the Rome Opera as Golaud in PELLÉAS ET MÉLISANDE, and on Jan. 21, 1965, he made his debut at the METROPOLITAN OPERA as Count Almaviva in MOZART's THE MARRIAGE OF FIGARO. He has also made operatic appearances at various European festivals, including those of FLORENCE, EDINBURGH, SALZBURG, and GLYNDEBOURNE.

So war es mit Pagliazzo, Zerbinetta's aria describing her love life in Richard STRAUSS's ARIADNE AUF NAXOS. This is preceded by a remarkable dramatic recitative, GROSS-MÄCHTIGE PRINZESSIN.

Spalanzani, scientist and inventor (tenor) in OFFENBACH's THE TALES OF HOFFMANN.

Sparafucile, an assassin (bass) in VERDI's RIGOLETTO.

Spargi d'amaro pianto, Lucia's aria in Act III, Scene 2, of DONIZETTI's LUCIA DI LAMMERMOOR in which she begs that a flower be placed on her grave and that no tears be shed over her death.

Sperate, o figli, Zaccaria's aria in which he tries to support the morale of his people by urging them to have faith in God, in the opening of Act I of VERDI's NABUCCO.

speziale, Lo (Der Apotheker, The Apothecary), comic opera in three acts by HAYDN. Libretto by Carlo GOLDONI. Premiere: Esterház, Austria, autumn of 1786. American premiere: New York, Mar. 16, 1926.

Sempronio, an apothecary (bass), wants to marry his ward, Grilletta (soprano), but she is in love with Mengono (tenor). To be near his sweetheart, Mengono gets a job in Sempronio's shop, where they can exchange kisses and tender words while his employer is away. Sempronio catches them one day in the act of kissing and announces firmly that he will marry Grilletta without further delay. Mengono and another rival for Grilletta's love, Volpino (soprano), disguise themselves as notaries; each draws up the necessary marriage contract but makes sure to insert his own name in place of Sempronio's. When this maneuver fails, Volpino returns disguised as a Turk, maintaining that he represents the Pasha for the purchase of Sempronio's complete stock of drugs. But forthwith the "Pasha" appears, who is actually Mengono in disguise. Things get out of hand when Volpino threatens to kill Sempronio with a dagger. Saved by Mengono, Sempronio is ready and willing to give up Grilletta to his rival.

Karl Geiringer regards the second-act finale as "one of the most effective ensemble numbers in the pre-Mozart opera buffa," calling attention to the "repeated changes of tempo and the introduction of roguish but also affectionate mirth." There are a number of arias that find Haydn at his lyrical best, such as that of Mengono, "Per quel che ha mal di stomaco," and that of Volpino, "Amore nel mio petto," in Act I, and Grilletta's aria in Act II, "A fatti tuoi badar tu puoi."

Spinelloccio, the doctor (bass) in PUCCINI's GIANNI SCHICCHI.

Spinning Chorus, see SUMM' UND BRUMM'.

Spira sul mare, Cio-Cio-San's aria introducing Pinkerton to her relatives, in Act I of PUCCINI's MADAMA BUTTERFLY.

Spirito del Nume sovra noi discendi,

the offstage chorus of the priests beseeching the gods for a just punishment for Radames, in Act IV, Scene 1, of VERDI's AIDA.

Spirito gentil, the aria in which Fernando recalls his lost love, in Act IV of DONIZETTI's LA FAVORITA.

Spirits of earth and sea, Puck's orders to the spirits to wreck the ship on which Huon and Rezia are sailing, in Act II, Scene 3, of WEBER's OBERON.

Splendiano, the Prince's secretary and Djamileh's ally (tenor) in BIZET's OPÉRA COMIQUE, DJAMILEH.

Splendon più belle in ciel, aria of Baltasar with chorus of monks commenting on the splendors of a religious life, in Act IV of DONIZETTI's LA FAVORITA.

Spohr, Ludwig, violinist, composer, conductor. Born Brunswick, Ger., Apr. 5, 1784; died Cassel, Oct. 22, 1859. He received violin instruction from his seventh year, and in 1802 he began concertizing in Germany, achieving recognition as a virtuoso two years later. In 1805 he became conductor of the ducal orchestra at Gotha, beginning an eventful career as a conductor. In 1817 he went to Frankfurt to direct opera performances and while there led the premieres of two of his own operas: *Faust* and *Zemire und Azore.* In 1820, as a guest conductor of the Royal Philharmonic in London, he made conducting history by directing the orchestra with a baton; earlier performances of that orchestra had been led either by the concertmaster (while playing his violin) or by the continuo player.

In 1822 Spohr became the director of the Cassel Court Theater, where he remained thirty-five years. A champion of WAGNER, he led performances of DER FLIEGENDE HOLLÄNDER in 1842 and TANNHÄUSER in 1853. He had earlier directed the premiere of his own most important opera, JESSONDA, in 1823. *Jessonda* has historical importance as one of the earliest German operas to use accompanied recitatives throughout instead of spoken dialogue. His operas: *Die Prüfung* (1806); *Alruna* (1808); *Die Eulenkönigin* (1808); *Der Zweikampf mit der*

Geliebten (1811); *Faust* (1816, revised 1852); *Zemire und Azore* (1819); *Jessonda* (1823); *Der Berggeist* (1825); *Pietro von Abano* (1828); *Der Alchimist* (1830); *Der Kreuzfahrer* (1845).

Spoleto Festival, see FESTIVAL OF TWO WORLDS.

Spoletta, a police agent (tenor) in PUCCINI'S TOSCA.

Spontini, Gasparo, composer. Born Majolati, Italy, Nov. 14, 1774; died there Jan. 24, 1851. His parents intended him for the priesthood, but he preferred music. In 1793 he entered the Conservatorio de' Turchini in Naples. He showed such promise as a student that the director of the Argentina Theater in Rome commissioned him to write an opera, *I puntigli delle donne,* which was a success. He left Naples for Rome and continued to write operas, many of them comic. Among the most successful of these was *L'eroismo,* performed in many Italian theaters.

In 1803 Spontini went to Paris. His association with leading French composers led him to abandon his light style for a more serious one. On Dec. 6, 1807, he was acclaimed for LA VESTALE, which had taken him three years to write, and which leading French musicians hailed as a masterwork; it won a prize for dramatic composition, the unanimous decision of the judges. The opera immediately became a fixture in the repertory of the PARIS OPÉRA, receiving over two hundred performances by 1830; as early as 1828 it was given in the United States. To this day it remains the most frequently revived of Spontini's operas. Another substantial success followed on Sept. 28, 1809, *Fernand Cortez.* A year later Spontini became conductor of Italian operas at the Théâtre de l'Impératrice; he was dismissed in 1812 because of differences with the director. In 1814 he became court composer for Louis XVIII, a post in which he wrote several operas glorifying the restoration of the Bourbons.

The failure of his *Olympie* in 1819 was such a blow to his pride that he left Paris for Berlin, where he was appointed general music director by Friedrich Wilhelm III. His operas in Berlin were not successful. Increasingly bitter, Spontini became involved in altercations with his patrons and co-workers. He was finally compelled to resign his post in 1841. For a while he lived in Paris, but on an invitation from WAGNER, he went to Dresden in 1844 to direct *La vestale.* Toward the end of his life, Spontini lived in his native city, devoting himself to charity. His last years were marked by failing memory and hearing. He was the recipient of many honors, including the title of Conte de Sant' Andrea from the Pope, the knighthood of the Prussian Order of Merit, and membership in the Berlin Academy and the French Institute. His best operas, after those already mentioned, were: *La finta filosofa* (1799); *La fuga in maschera* (1800); *Milton* (1804); *Nurmahal* (1822); *Alcidor* (1825); *Agnes von Hohenstaufen* (1827, revised 1837).

Sportin' Life, dope peddler (tenor) in GERSHWIN'S PORGY AND BESS.

Spose del grande Osiride, address of the Persian king to Isis in ROSSINI'S *Aureliano in Palmira.* This melody was borrowed by the composer subsequently for his famous serenade, "Ecco ridente," in THE BARBER OF SEVILLE.

Sprechstimme, German for "speech voice," a kind of song-speech developed by Arnold SCHOENBERG and used by some of the composers of the atonal school. The words are half sung, half spoken, with their pitch not exactly notated. *Sprechstimme* is an important feature of WOZZECK and LULU. *Sprechgesang,* "speech song," is the term used for the music sung in a *sprechstimme.*

Springer, manager of a theatrical troupe (bass) in SMETANA'S THE BARTERED BRIDE.

Squilli, echeggi la tromba guerriera, the soldiers' hymn to war and victory at the opening of Act III, Scene 1, of VERDI'S IL TROVATORE.

Staatsoper (Dresden), see DRESDEN OPERA.

Stabile, Mariano, baritone. Born Palermo, May 12, 1888; died Milan, Jan. 11, 1968. Born to Sicilian nobility, he attended the Santa Cecilia in Rome and received his vocal training from Antonio Cotogni. He made his debut in 1909 at the Teatro Biondo in Palermo as Marcello in LA BOHÈME. For the next decade he appeared in various Italian opera houses without attracting much attention. Fame came on Dec. 26, 1921, when he appeared as FALSTAFF at the personal invitation of TOSCANINI, who was beginning the first of eight seasons as musical director of LA SCALA. He won an ovation in this role, and it became one of his outstanding characterizations; he made more than a thousand appearances in the part. Remaining a principal baritone of La Scala, Stabile appeared with outstanding success at COVENT GARDEN and at the GLYNDEBOURNE and SALZBURG festivals. His finest roles besides that of Falstaff included DON PASQUALE, SCARPIA, GIANNI SCHICCHI, and RIGOLETTO. After an appearance at the TEATRO LA FENICE in 1960, he went into retirement as a singer, devoting himself after that to lecturing on opera.

Städtische Oper (Berlin), *see* BERLIN DEUTSCHE STAATSOPER.

Stag King, The, *see* KÖNIG HIRSCH.

Standin' in the need of prayer, Brutus Jones's prayer to God for forgiveness and protection, in Act II of GRUENBERG'S EMPEROR JONES. Though in the style of a Negro spiritual, the melody is original with Gruenberg and should not be confused with the spiritual of the same name.

Stanford, Charles Villiers, composer, conductor, and teacher. Born Dublin, Sept. 30, 1852; died London, Mar. 29, 1924. He studied music privately in Dublin and London, after which he attended Queen's College, Cambridge, on an organ scholarship. In 1873 he became organist of Trinity College. After an additional two-year period of study in Germany with Carl Reinecke and Friedrich Kiel, he made his debut as a composer with incidental music to Tennyson's *Queen Mary,* written at the request of the poet, and performed in London in 1876. His first opera, *The Veiled Prophet of Khorassan,* was in-

troduced in Hamburg in 1881. In 1883 he became a professor of composition at the Royal College of Music and in 1887 professor of music at Cambridge; he held both posts for the rest of his life. His students included Ralph VAUGHAN WILLIAMS, Gustav HOLST, Frank Bridge, and John Ireland. He was knighted in 1901, and in 1904 he became the first Englishman elected to the Berlin Academy of Arts. After *The Veiled Prophet of Khorassan* he wrote the following operas: *Savonarola* (1884); THE CANTERBURY PILGRIMS (1884); *Shamus O'Brien* (1889); *Much Ado About Nothing* (1901); *The Critic* (1916); *The Travelling Companion* (1917). He wrote several volumes of reminiscences, including *Pages from an Unwritten Diary* (1914) and *Interludes* (1922).

Starke Scheite schichtet mir dort, Brünnhilde's Immolation Scene at the close of WAGNER'S GÖTTERDÄMMERUNG as, hailing Siegfried, she rides on her mount to her death through the flames of his funeral pyre.

Star trompetti, Tagliaferro's *buffo* aria in PICCINNI'S LA CECCHINA.

Steber, Eleanor, soprano. Born Wheeling, W. Va., July 17, 1916. She attended the New England Conservatory of Music and studied singing privately with William Whitney and Paul Althouse. In 1940 she won the METROPOLITAN OPERA AUDITIONS OF THE AIR. On Dec. 7, 1940, she made her debut at the METROPOLITAN OPERA as Sophie in DER ROSENKAVALIER. She remained a principal soprano of that company for almost two decades, appearing in the French, Italian, and German repertory and creating the role of VANESSA in 1958; she also assumed the part of the Marschallin in *Der Rosenkavalier.* During this period she made successful appearances at the GLYNDEBOURNE, EDINBURGH, and BAYREUTH festivals. She subsequently devoted herself principally to concert appearances and to teaching voice at the Institute of Music in Cleveland.

Steersman, The, a sailor (tenor) in WAGNER'S DER FLIEGENDE HOLLÄNDER.

Steersman's Song, see MIT GEWITTER UND STURM.

Steffani, Agostino, composer. Born Castelfranco, Italy, July 25, 1654; died Frankfurt, Feb. 12, 1728. His music study took place in Munich and Rome. In 1675 he was appointed court organist in Munich. Three years later he visited Paris, where he came under LULLY's influence. In 1680 he decided to enter the church, and in 1682 he became Abbot of Leipzig. Meanwhile, in 1680, his first opera, *Marco Aurelio,* was produced in Munich. This was followed by five more operas given in the same city. He went to Hanover in 1688 to become court KAPELLMEISTER. His opera *Henrico Leone* opened a new opera house there in 1689. This work is particularly noteworthy for its advances in orchestration. In the next nine years Steffani completed nine more operas that were popular in Hanover.

Before the end of the century, he became involved in diplomacy, serving as special envoy to the German courts. He participated in the complex negotiations resulting in the creation of a ninth Elector for Brunswick. His success brought him an appointment as Bishop of Spiga. Subsequently he was privy councilor and Papal Protonotary at Düsseldorf. In 1711 he resigned his post as *kapellmeister* in Hanover (which he had retained even while engaged in diplomacy) and turned it over to HANDEL, whom he had met in Italy.

His most important operas were: *Marco Aurelio* (1681); *Solone* (1685); *Servio Tullio* (1686); *Henrico Leone* (1689); *La lotta d'Ercole con Achelao* (1689); *La superbia d'Alessandro* (1690, revised 1691); *Orlando generoso* (1691); *I Baccanali* (1695); *Briseide* (1696); *Arminio* (1707); *Tassilone* (1709).

Steffano Colonna, a Roman patrician (bass) and rival to Orsini in WAGNER's RIENZI.

Stein, Gertrude, writer. Born Allegheny, Pa., Feb. 3, 1874; died Neuilly, France, July 27, 1946. One of the leading experimental writers of her time, much of whose work struck many readers as being nonsensical, Miss Stein provided Virgil THOMSON with the texts for two operas: FOUR SAINTS IN THREE ACTS and THE MOTHER OF US ALL.

Stein, Horst, conductor. Born Elberfeld, Ger., 1928. He completed his music studies at the Hochschule für Musik in Cologne, following which he held minor conductorial posts in Mannheim and Wuppertal. From 1951 to 1955 and again from 1961 to 1963 he was a conductor at the HAMBURG STATE OPERA and from 1955 to 1961 at the BERLIN STATE OPERA. He made his American debut in 1964 with the SAN FRANCISCO OPERA and remained a principal conductor of it for several years. In 1698 he became a principal conductor of the VIENNA STATE OPERA. He has made guest appearances in major opera houses in Europe and at the TEATRO COLÓN.

Steinberg, William (born Hans Wilhelm Steinberg), conductor. Born Cologne, Aug. 1, 1899. He was graduated in 1920 from the Cologne Conservatory, where he received the Wuellner Prize for conducting. After serving as assistant to Otto KLEMPERER at the COLOGNE OPERA, he became principal conductor there in 1924. From 1925 to 1929 he held a similar post with the German Opera in Prague and from 1929 to 1933 with the FRANKFURT OPERA. With the rise of the Nazis to power, Steinberg left Germany for Palestine, where he helped to organize the Palestine Orchestra (subsequently become the Israel Philharmonic) and prepared it for its first concert under TOSCANINI. At Toscanini's invitation he came to the United States, where he made his debut as guest conductor of the NBC Symphony. From 1945 to 1952 he was the music director of the Buffalo Philharmonic, and since 1952 he has been music director of the Pittsburgh Symphony. In 1968 he divided his activity between the Pittsburgh Symphony and the Boston Symphony, having been appointed music director of the latter orchestra in succession to Erich LEINSDORF. Though concentrating on symphonic music, he has occasionally given performances of operas in America, having made his American debut as an opera conductor with the SAN FRANCISCO OPERA on Oct. 16, 1944, with FALSTAFF and his debut at the METROPOLITAN OPERA with AIDA on Jan. 2, 1965.

Stella, (1) an opera singer (soprano) in OFFENBACH'S THE TALES OF HOFFMANN.

(2) A Camorrist (soprano) in WOLF-FERRARI'S THE JEWELS OF THE MADONNA.

Stella del marinar, Laura's prayer to God to forgive her, in Act II of PONCHIELLI'S LA GIOCONDA.

Stephana, Prince Alexis' mistress (soprano) in GIORDANO'S SIBERIA.

Stephano, Roméo's page (soprano) in GOUNOD'S ROMÉO ET JULIETTE.

Steuermann! Lass die Wacht!, Sailors' Chorus in Act III of WAGNER'S DER FLIEGENDE HOLLÄNDER.

Steuermannslied, see MIT GEWITTER UND STURM.

Stevens, Risë, contralto. Born New York City, June 11, 1913. She was a student at the Juilliard School of Music from 1932 to 1935, and her study was completed in Salzburg with Marie GUTHEIL-SCHODER and Herbert GRAF. Her debut took place in Prague as MIGNON in 1936, and her success brought her an engagement with the VIENNA STATE OPERA. Her American debut took place in Philadelphia on Nov. 22, 1938, in the title role of DER ROSENKAVALIER during a visit to that city of the METROPOLITAN OPERA; a month later she appeared with the Metropolitan in New York in *Mignon*. She appeared there in the principal contralto roles of the French and Italian repertories up through 1960–61.

In 1939 she became the first American singer to appear at the GLYNDEBOURNE FESTIVAL in England; in 1949 she appeared at the PARIS OPÉRA; and in 1953 she was invited to LA SCALA to create the leading role in a new Italian opera, Virgilio Mortari's *La figlia del diavolo*. This was her first appearance in Italy. She has been seen in several motion pictures, including *The Chocolate Soldier* and *Going My Way,* and she has frequently sung on radio and television. Between 1965 and 1967 she was co-manager of the short-lived Metropolitan Opera National Company.

Stewa, Jenufa's cousin (tenor), father of her child, in JANÁČEK'S JENUFA.

Stewart, Thomas, baritone. Born San Saba, Texas, Aug. 29, 1928. He graduated from Baylor University in Waco in 1953, where he was trained in electronics before redirecting himself to music. There followed vocal study with Mack HARRELL at the Juilliard School. He appeared there in CAPRICCIO and met and married the young soprano Evelyn LEAR. His professional debut took place with the NEW YORK CITY OPERA, where he remained one season. After appearing in Chicago as ASHTON to Maria CALLAS' LUCIA, he went to Germany in 1957, where he was a permanent member of the BERLIN DEUTSCHE STAATSOPER for five years and earned the honorary title of KAMMERSÄNGER. During this period he made guest appearances at COVENT GARDEN. His first Wagnerian roles were assumed in BAYREUTH in 1960, where he was heard as DONNER and as GUNTHER. He subsequently appeared at the Bayreuth Festival as AMFORTAS, the DUTCHMAN, and WOTAN. The last-named role was also assumed in KARAJAN's productions of DIE WALKÜRE and SIEGFRIED at the SALZBURG Easter FESTIVAL in 1967 and 1968, as well as in Paris, Berlin, and at the METROPOLITAN OPERA in New York, where he made his debut on Mar. 9, 1966, as Ford in FALSTAFF. He has been heard with some of the world's foremost opera companies and at major festivals. In the Karajan production of GÖTTERDÄMMERUNG at the 1970 Salzburg Easter Festival, he assumed the role of Gunther. Besides appearing in Wagnerian roles, Stewart has distinguished himself as DON GIOVANNI, ESCAMILLO, ALMAVIVA, AMONASRO, and IAGO.

Stich-Randall, Teresa, soprano. Born West Hartford, Conn., Dec. 24, 1927.

She was a scholarship student at the Hartford School of Music in Connecticut. While attending Columbia University, where she specialized in music, she appeared in the world premieres of THOMSON's THE MOTHER OF US ALL and Otto Luening's EVANGELINE, as well as in other operas. TOSCANINI selected her to sing roles in his NBC Symphony performances of AIDA and FALSTAFF. In 1951 she went to Europe on a Fulbright Fellowship. There she received first prize in the Concours International for opera singers in Lausanne, Switzerland. In Aug., 1952, she made her European debut as Violetta in LA TRAVIATA at the VIENNA STATE OPERA. Her performances as a permanent member of that company were supplemented by many significant guest appearances at leading European festivals and major European opera houses. On Nov. 13, 1955, she made her debut at the CHICAGO LYRIC OPERA in RIGOLETTO, and on Oct. 24, 1961, she appeared for the first time at the METROPOLITAN OPERA, in COSÌ FAN TUTTE. She has since remained a principal soprano of that company, besides appearing in other major opera houses of the world, distinguishing herself particularly in the Mozartean repertory.

Stiedry, Fritz, conductor. Born Vienna, Oct. 11, 1883; died Zürich, Aug. 9, 1968. He attended Vienna University and the Vienna Conservatory. Gustav MAHLER recommended him for the post of assistant conductor at the DRESDEN OPERA in 1907. After one season there and several seasons in other European opera houses, he was engaged in 1914 as a principal conductor of the BERLIN (Royal) OPERA. Because of the outbreak of war, he was unable to assume this office until two years later. In 1924 he became principal conductor of the VOLKSOPER in Vienna, and in 1929 he succeeded Bruno WALTER as musical director of the Municipal Opera in Berlin. When the Nazis came to power, Stiedry went to the Soviet Union. For several years he was musical director of the Leningrad Philharmonic. He came to the United States in 1938, making it his permanent home. On Nov.

15, 1946, he made his debut at the MET-ROPOLITAN OPERA, conducting SIEGFRIED. He remained there until 1958, achieving particular distinction in the German repertory. He subsequently went into retirement in Majorca to devote himself to composition, then moved to Switzerland, where he died.

Stignani, Ebe, contralto. Born Naples, July 10, 1907. She graduated from the Naples Conservatory in 1925, then made her opera debut with the TEATRO SAN CARLO in the same year as AMNERIS. TOSCANINI engaged her for LA SCALA, where she was a principal contralto between 1925 and 1956. During this period she made frequent appearances at COVENT GARDEN. She made her American debut with the SAN FRANCISCO OPERA on Oct. 17, 1938, as SANTUZZA, returning to that company a decade later. Subsequent appearances took place in leading European opera houses. She has been acclaimed in the principal contralto roles in the Italian repertory.

stile concitato, see COMBATTIMENTO DI TANCREDI E CLORINDA, IL.

Still, William Grant, composer. Born Woodville, Miss., May 11, 1895. He attended the Oberlin Conservatory and the New England Conservatory, after which he studied privately with Edgard Varèse in New York. He first achieved recognition as a composer with orchestral works, including the *Afro-American Symphony,* written in 1931. Three years later he received a Guggenheim Fellowship and a Rosenwald Fellowship. He has written the following operas: *Blue Steel* (1935); THE TROUBLED ISLAND (1938); *A Bayou Legend* (1940); *A Southern Interlude* (1942); *Costaso* (1949); *Highway No. 1; Mota; Minette Fontaine. The Troubled Island* was given by the NEW YORK CITY OPERA in 1949; *Highway No. 1* was introduced in Miami in 1963.

Stizzoso, mio stizzoso, Serpina's aria in Act I of PERGOLESI's LA SERVA PADRONA, in which she tells her employer she is in no haste to follow his orders.

Stockholm Royal Opera, principal opera company in Stockholm, Sweden. Its history goes back to 1773, when the old Ball House was remodeled on orders by Gustavus III, and it opened with Uttini's *Thetis och Pelee* (text by the King), regarded now as Sweden's first grand opera. In its first season this company performed GLUCK'S ORFEO ED EURIDICE. An important national opera, *Gustav Vasa* by J. G. Naumann, was produced in 1786. Meanwhile a new house had opened on Sept. 30, 1782, with Naumann's *Cora och Alonzo,* the composer conducting. This theater survived until 1890. The opera house now in use was built on the same site and opened on Apr. 8, 1899, with Andreas Hallén's *Waldmarsskatten,* written for the occasion.

Between 1924 and 1939 John Forsell was artistic director. He was succeeded by Harald Andre (1939–1949), Joel Berglund (1949–1954), Set SVANHOLM (1954–1963), and Goeran GENTELE. Among its most significant conductors have been Leo Blech, Issai DOBROWEN, and Silvio VARVISO.

Throughout the years, the Stockholm Royal Opera has given a hearing to works by Sweden's leading composers, including Vilhelm Stenhammer, Andreas Hallén, Hilding ROSENBERG, and Karl BLOMDAHL. In the single season of 1969–70, premieres were given of the following Swedish operas: Bengt Hallberg's *Girl Alone at Home;* Rosenberg's *House with a Double Door;* and Lars John Werle's *Journey.* But the opera house also became famous for its Wagnerian performances and for developing such distinguished Wagnerian singers as LARSEN-TODSEN, THORBORG, Svanholm, BERGLUND, Sigurd and Jussi BJÖRLING, and Birgit NILSSON. The company visited the EDINBURGH FESTIVAL in 1959, COVENT GARDEN in 1960, and Montreal for Expo 67 in 1967.

Stokowski, Leopold, conductor. Born London, Apr. 18, 1882. Although his career has been identified primarily with symphonic music—particularly by virtue of his brilliant career as music director of the Philadelphia Orchestra—Stokowski has periodically distinguished himself in opera. In 1929 he led the American premiere of BORIS GODUNOV in its original version as MUSSORGSKY wrote it; this was a concert performance. On Mar. 19, 1931, he directed the American premiere of WOZZECK in a staged presentation. In recent years Stokowski has identified himself more closely than ever with opera. Between 1959 and 1961 he was a guest conductor at the NEW YORK CITY OPERA, where he led memorable performances of such novelties as CARMINA BURANA, L'ORFEO, and IL PRIGIONIERO. He made his debut at the METROPOLITAN OPERA on Feb. 24, 1961, with TURANDOT. He was one of the guest performers at the farewell presentation at the Metropolitan Opera House on Apr. 16, 1966, with which the company left the auditorium it had occupied since its beginnings.

Stolz, Rosine (born Victorine Noël), mezzo-soprano. Born Paris, Feb. 13, 1815; died there July 28, 1903. After studying at Alexandre Choron's school in Paris, she made her opera debut in Brussels in 1832. She was first acclaimed for her singing of Rachel in LA JUIVE, as a result of which she was engaged by the PARIS OPÉRA, where she made her debut on Aug. 25, 1837, once again as Rachel. For a decade she was the idol of the Parisian opera public. Several operas were written for her, including DONIZETTI's *Don Sebastian* and LA FAVORITA and HALÉVY's *La Reine de Chypre.* Her last appearance in opera took place in 1860, after which she went into retirement.

Stolz, Teresa (born Teresina Stolzová), soprano. Born Elbe Kosteletz, Bohemia, June 2, 1834; died Milan, Aug. 23, 1902. After attending conservatories in Prague and Trieste, she made her opera debut in Tiflis. Between 1865 and 1879 she became one of the outstanding sopranos in Italy. She was a friend of VERDI, and she scored some of her greatest successes in his operas. She created the role of Leonora in LA FORZA DEL DESTINO, and she appeared in the Italian premiere of AIDA. Her last public appearance was as soloist in Verdi's *Requiem* in 1879.

Stolzing, Walther von, Franconian knight (tenor) in WAGNER'S DIE MEISTER-SINGER.

Stone, Jabez, a New England farmer (bass) in MOORE'S THE DEVIL AND DANIEL WEBSTER.

Stone, Mary, Jabez Stone's wife (mezzo-soprano) in MOORE'S THE DEVIL AND DANIEL WEBSTER.

Stone Guest, The, opera in three acts by DARGOMIZHSKY (completed by CUI and RIMSKY-KORSAKOV). Libretto is PUSHKIN'S play of the same name. Premiere: St. Petersburg, Feb. 28, 1872. American premiere: Evanston, Ill., Dec. 3, 1968 (scenes). In this version of the DON JUAN story, as in the DA PONTE-MOZART version, the stone guest is a statue of the Commandant, slain in a duel by the Don. Mockingly, the Don invites the statue to be his guest at dinner. The statue keeps the appointment and consigns the Don to the fires of hell. This was the composer's last opera and the one in which he brought his lifelong nationalist ambitions to fruition. Cui referred to it as "the very keystone of the new Russian opera." It was written almost entirely in a dramatic recitative style.

Storch, Christine, wife (soprano) of composer Robert Storch in Richard STRAUSS'S INTERMEZZO.

Storch, Robert, a composer (baritone) in Richard STRAUSS'S INTERMEZZO.

Story of a Real Man, The, *see* TALE OF A REAL MAN, THE.

Stracciari, Riccardo, baritone. Born Casalecchio, Italy, June 26, 1875; died Rome, Oct. 10, 1955. Completing his studies in Bologna, he made his debut in that city as MARCELLO in 1898. He was a member of LA SCALA in 1904–05 and of COVENT GARDEN in 1905. On Dec. 1, 1906, he made his debut at the METROPOLITAN OPERA as the elder Germont in LA TRAVIATA; he remained with the company for two seasons. In 1918–19 he appeared with the CHICAGO OPERA and in 1925 with the SAN FRANCISCO OPERA. After that he appeared in Italy's leading opera houses until 1942. His interpretation of the role of Figaro in ROSSINI'S

THE BARBER OF SEVILLE (in which he was heard almost a thousand times) was world famous. He was also acclaimed in the VERDI repertory.

Stradella, Alessandro, composer. Born Naples, about 1642; died Genoa, Feb. 28, 1682. The romantic and only partly documented story of Stradella's life runs as follows. As a youth he became famous as a singer, violinist, and composer and was invited to Venice to write an opera for the carnival season. The Venetian senator Alvise Contarini engaged him to teach singing to his mistress, Hortensia. Stradella fell in love with her, and they fled from Venice. The senator engaged two assassins to pursue him. Legend would have us believe that the assassins caught up with Stradella in Rome but were so moved by one of his oratorios that they warned him that his life was in danger. The pair now fled to Turin, where they acquired the protection of the Duchess of Savoy. One night Stradella was waylaid on the street and stabbed, but not fatally. The Duchess arranged for Stradella and Hortensia to get married and live at her palace. But a year after that, on a visit to Genoa, Stradella was murdered. This largely unsubstantiated biography was the inspiration for FLOTOW'S opera ALESSANDRO STRADELLA. Stradella was a composer who brought to operatic lyricism a new expressiveness and dramatic feeling, entitling him to a place in musical history as a precursor of the Neapolitan school represented by Alessandro SCARLATTI. His operas: *Corispera* (1665); *Orazio Cocle sul ponte* (1666); *Trespoulo tutore* (1667); *La forza del amore paterno* (1678); *La Doriclea* (undated manuscript discovered in the twentieth century).

Strakosch, Maurice, impresario. Born Gross-Seelowitz, Moravia, 1825; died Paris, Oct. 9, 1887. He attended the Vienna Conservatory, after which he toured Europe as a concert pianist. In 1848 he came to America, where for about a dozen years he was active as a teacher and pianist. His first venture as an opera impresario took place in New

York in 1857, when he managed a season of Italian operas; two years later he took his troupe to Chicago. In 1873 and 1874 he managed opera performances in Paris, and in 1884 and 1885 he collaborated with his brother Max in directing opera performances at the Teatro Apollo in Rome. He wrote two operas which were produced in New York, *Giovanni di Napoli* and *Sardanapalus*. His wife was the soprano Carlotta Patti, sister of Adelina PATTI. He served as manager for Adelina Patti's concert tours in Europe. His autobiography, *Souvenirs d'un impresario*, appeared in 1887.

Strauss, Johann, the Younger, composer. Born Vienna, Oct. 25, 1825; died there June 3, 1899. His father, Johann Strauss, was internationally famous as a composer of dance music and conductor of Viennese orchestras. Johann Strauss the Younger made his debut as a composer and conductor of light music on Oct. 15, 1844. With the composition of such waltzes as "The Beautiful Blue Danube," "Tales from the Vienna Woods," and "Wine, Women and Song," Strauss's popularity grew to prodigious proportions; he became the Waltz King, the idol of Vienna, the voice and symbol of Hapsburg Austria. His first operetta, *Indigo and the Forty Thieves, or A Thousand and One Nights,* was produced at the THEATER-AN-DER-WIEN on Feb. 10, 1871. DIE FLEDERMAUS (*The Bat*) was seen at the same theater on Apr. 5, 1874. At first, it was a failure. But in Berlin, where it was produced soon after the premiere in Vienna, it was a sensation; its international popularity soon followed. *Der Zigeunerbaron* (THE GYPSY BARON) was introduced eleven years after *Die Fledermaus*, on Oct. 24, 1885, and was one of the triumphs of the composer's career. Meanwhile, in 1876, Strauss came to the United States to appear in concerts commemorating the centenary of American independence. In 1894 the fiftieth anniversary of his debut as a conductor was celebrated for an entire week in Vienna. Though Strauss's stage works were operettas, intended primarily for the popular theater, they have often been produced in major opera houses. In addition to those mentioned, his most important stage works were *Cagliostro* (1875) and *A Night in Venice* (1883).

Strauss, Richard, composer and conductor. Born Munich, June 11, 1864; died Garmisch-Partenkirchen, Ger., Sept. 8, 1949. Strauss's father, the leading horn player of the MUNICH OPERA, gave Richard WAGNER practical help in the perfection of Siegfried's horn call in his opera SIEGFRIED. Strauss's mother was was the daughter of a prosperous brewing family. Exceptionally precocious, Strauss was given piano lessons when he was four. At six he began composition. While receiving musical instruction from August Tombo and Benno Walter, he gained his academic education at the University of Munich. In 1880 three of his songs were performed in Munich; a year later his first symphony was introduced by Hermann LEVI. In 1885 Strauss became the assistant of Hans von BÜLOW with the Meiningen Orchestra; the following year he succeeded Bülow as principal conductor. His friendship with the poet-musician Alexander Ritter (who was married to Wagner's niece) brought about in Strauss a re-evaluation of his music and the adoption of new principles. Ritter, a passionate Wagnerite, convinced Strauss that he should write music of a dramatic and programatic nature, within forms more flexible than the traditional symphony and suite. Forsaking his classic inclinations and freeing himself from the influence of Brahms, Strauss began the writing of the tone poems which were to make him one of the most provocative musical figures of his day: *Don Juan, Death and Transfiguration, Till Eulenspiegel's Merry Pranks,* and their successors. He was also fertile in the field of the song, producing after 1883 some of the finest songs since those of SCHUMANN and Brahms.

His first opera, GUNTRAM, produced in Weimar in 1894, was a slavish imitation of Wagner and was a failure. His second, FEUERSNOT, produced in 1901, was also poorly received. But with SALOME, first given in Dresden on Dec. 9, 1905, he created a work that once again made him one' of the most controversial and highly publicized figures in music. *Salome* was followed by another opera that excited enthusiasm and produced shock: ELEKTRA, first performed in Dresden on Jan. 25, 1909. *Elektra* was the first opera in which Strauss collaborated with the Austrian poet and dramatist Hugo von HOFMANNS-THAL, an arrangement that continued for the next quarter of a century, until Hofmannsthal's death. With DER ROSEN-KAVALIER, a comedy, given in Dresden on Jan. 26, 1911, Strauss confirmed his position as the foremost German opera composer after Wagner. After World War I Strauss's productivity remained unabated. He continued composing operas until 1941, producing two masterworks well deserving a place with his earlier great operas: DIE FRAU OHNE SCHATTEN in 1917 and ARABELLA in 1932. In 1952, three years after his death, came the last premiere of one of his operas, DIE LIEBE DER DANAE, at the SALZBURG FESTIVAL.

Besides his eminence as a composer, Strauss had a worldwide reputation as a conductor. He was particularly noteworthy in his own works and in the operas of MOZART and Wagner. The conductor at the Weimar court. In 1898 in 1889 and 1894 he was the first conductor at the Weimar Court. In 1898 he became musical director of the BER-LIN (Royal) OPERA, remaining there for twelve years. From 1919 to 1924 he was principal conductor and co-music-director of the VIENNA STATE OPERA. Later he conducted frequently at music festivals in Munich, BAYREUTH, and Salzburg, as well as in major European opera houses. He visited the United States twice, in 1904 and 1921, but only as an orchestral conductor in programs devoted largely to his own music.

With the rise of the Nazis in Germany, Strauss at first identified himself closely with the new regime, becoming President of the Third Reich Music Chamber. He willingly substituted for Bruno WALTER when Walter, a Jew, was removed as conductor of the Leipzig Gewandhaus; and he replaced TOSCANINI at the Bayreuth Festival when the maestro refused to come to Nazi Germany. But Strauss soon came into conflict with government officials when he collaborated with the Jewish writer Stefan Zweig on DIE SCHWEIGSAME FRAU. After 1939, when Strauss violently opposed the Nazi invasion of Poland, he was for a short period placed under house arrest at his home in Garmisch-Partenkirchen. The fact that his son married a Jewess further made Strauss *persona non grata* with the Nazis. During the war years Strauss lived partly in Switzerland, but mainly at Garmisch-Partenkirchen, where he died.

The centenary of Strauss's birth was commemorated in Munich between Feb. 23 and mid-March, 1964, with the production of eleven of his operas conducted by Karl BÖHM, together with the performance of other Strauss works.

His operas: *Guntram* (1893, revised 1940); *Feuersnot* (1901); *Salome* (1905); *Elektra* (1908); *Der Rosenkavalier* (1910); ARIADNE AUF NAXOS (1912, revised 1916); *Die Frau ohne Schatten* (1917); INTER-MEZZO (1923); DIE AEGYPTISCHE HELENA (1927); *Arabella* (1932); *Die schweigsame Frau* (1935); *Friedenstag* (1936); DAPHNE (1937); *Die Liebe der Danae* (1940); CAPRICCIO (1941).

Stravinsky, Igor, composer. Born Oranienbaum, Russia, June 17, 1882. The son of an opera singer at the Maryinsky Theater in St. Petersburg, Igor Stravinsky studied music privately while preparing for a legal career. In his twentieth year he met RIMSKY-KORSAKOV, who encouraged him to undertake composition. After two years of study with Rimsky-Korsakov, Stravinsky completed several orchestral works that came to the notice of Serge DIAGHILEV, the impresario of the Ballet Russe. Diaghilev engaged Stravinsky to write music for his company. The resulting works, beginning with *The Firebird* in 1910 and including *Petrouchka, The Rites of*

Spring, and *Les Noces,* made the composer one of the most celebrated figures in the world of music. *Les Noces,* while strictly speaking a cantata, is sometimes performed as an opera. Stravinsky also wrote two operas during this period, *The Nightingale* (LE ROSSIGNOL) (1914), and RENARD (1917), the last a CHAMBER OPERA.

In 1910 Stravinsky settled in France, his home for the next decade and a half. Here he wrote the comic opera MAVRA (1922) and an oratorio, OEDIPUS REX (1927), a work that has sometimes been staged as an opera.

Stravinsky paid the first of several visits to the United States in 1925, appearing as a guest conductor in programs largely of his own works. He settled permanently in this country in 1939, becoming a citizen. Among his major works composed after coming to America is THE RAKE'S PROGRESS, an opera introduced at the VENICE FESTIVAL on Sept. 11, 1951, and soon after heard in most of the leading opera houses, including the METROPOLITAN OPERA. Where his first two earlier operas are in the neo-primitive style Stravinsky had favored in the 1910's, *The Rake's Progress* is a neo-classic work, in fact the last composition in that style before the composer experimented with TWELVE-TONE and SERIAL TECHNIQUES. He has not written any operas in these avant-garde idioms.

Streit zwischen Phoebus und Pan, Der, *see* PHOEBUS AND PAN.

Streltsy, the, a band of Russian radicals conspiring to overthrow Peter the Great, in MUSSORGSKY'S KHOVANTCHINA.

Strepponi, Giuseppina, soprano. Born Lodi, Italy, Sept. 18, 1815; died Busseto, Italy, Nov. 14, 1897. She was Giuseppe VERDI'S second wife. After attending the Milan Conservatory, she made her opera debut in Trieste in 1835. She became celebrated in tragic roles. On Feb. 22, 1842, she made her debut at LA SCALA in DONIZETTI'S *Belisario;* in the same year she created the role of Abigaille in Verdi's NABUCCO. By 1849 she had retired from the stage, taken up a teaching career in Paris, and become Verdi's

mistress. That year she also became the mistress of his country estate in Busseto, and ten years later they were married.

Stretti insiem tutti tre, *see* TOUS LES TROIS RÉUNIS.

Stretto, Italian for "drawn together." In opera it connotes the part of an aria or finale in which the accents are drawn together, or quickened, to create excitement.

Stride la vampa, Azucena's aria recollecting the episode in the past when her mother was burned as a witch, in Act II, Scene 1, of VERDI'S IL TROVATORE.

Stridono lassù, Nedda's BALLATELLA, describing the flight of birds, in Act I of LEONCAVALLO'S PAGLIACCI.

Strindberg, August, novelist and dramatist. Born Stockholm, Jan. 22, 1849; died there May 14, 1912. Several of his plays have been made into operas. These include CHISHOLM'S *Simoon;* MEYEROWITZ' *Simoon;* Ture Rangström's *Kronbruden;* Julius Roentgen's *Samum;* ROREM'S MISS JULIE; Edward Staempfli's *Ein Traumspiel;* Julius Weissmann's *Die Gespenstersonata, Schwanenweise,* and *Ein Traumspiel.*

Stromminger, Wally's father (bass) in CATALANI'S LA WALLY.

Stückgold, Grete (born Schmeidt), soprano. Born London, July 6, 1895. She attended the Hochschule für Musik in Munich and studied singing privately with Jacques Stückgold, whom she married. Her opera debut took place in Nuremburg in 1913. She was then engaged by the BERLIN OPERA, where she appeared for several seasons. Her American debut took place at the METROPOLITAN OPERA on Nov. 2, 1927, in DIE MEISTERSINGER. She remained with the Metropolitan until 1931, returning for two additional periods: 1932–34 and 1938–39. Besides her appearances at the Metropolitan, she performed at COVENT GARDEN, with the Chicago Civic Opera, and with other major companies. She distinguished herself primarily in the Wagnerian repertory, but also was successful in the French and Italian repertories. Her second husband was Gustav SCHÜTZENDORF (1883–1937), who was a leading baritone with the Metropolitan Opera from 1922 to 1935. Having retired from the stage, Mme. Stückgold opened an opera school in New York in 1953.

Sturm, Der, *see* TEMPEST, THE.

Stuttgart Opera (Württembergisches Staatstheater), an important German opera company in Baden-Württemberg, Germany. While opera performances took place in Stuttgart from the sixteenth century on, the history of the present-day Stuttgart Opera can be said to have begun in 1912, when a new opera house was opened with the premiere of Richard STRAUSS'S ARIADNE AUF NAXOS. The house closed down during World War II for a season (1944–45). It reopened after the war and in Dec., 1946, gave the first performance in Germany of MATHIS DER MALER and six months later the premiere of ORFF'S DIE BERNAU-ERIN. It developed into a major company under the general musical direction of Ferdinand Leitner, who had been appointed in 1947, particularly with its performances of the works of WAGNER, MOZART, and Richard STRAUSS as well as of contemporary operas. In the spring of 1968 it presented a week of Czech operas, including JENUFA, produced by Günther RENNERT. The company has performed in Paris, London, and Edinburgh, among other European cities.

styrienne, a slow dance tune usually in 2/4 time. Mignon's aria, "Je connais un pauvre enfant," in Act II of THOMAS'S MIGNON is a styrienne.

Sucher, Rosa (born Hasselbeck), soprano. Born Velburg, Ger., Feb. 23, 1849; died Eschweiler, Ger., Apr. 16, 1927. After attending the Munich Akademie, she began her opera career in Treves. She then appeared in principal German opera houses. In 1877 she married the opera conductor Josef Sucher (1843–1908). In 1879 she became a principal soprano of the HAMBURG OPERA, where she was acclaimed in Wagnerian roles. She appeared at the BAYREUTH FESTIVALS between 1886 and 1899. From 1888 to 1899 she was principal soprano at the BERLIN OPERA, where her husband

was a principal conductor; she frequently sang in performances conducted by her husband. Her American debut took place at the METROPOLITAN OPERA on Feb. 25, 1895, as ISOLDE. Her farewell to the opera stage took place in Berlin on Nov. 3, 1903, as SIEGLINDE. After 1908 she lived in Vienna, where she taught singing. Her autobiography, *Aus meinem Leben,* appeared in 1914.

Su! del Nilo al sacro lido!, The King of Egypt's exhortation to his people to go forth to battle, in Act I, Scene 1, of VERDI'S AIDA.

Suicidio!, aria of La Gioconda in Act IV of PONCHIELLI'S LA GIOCONDA, as she contemplates suicide.

Sukarev, Olga, a countess (soprano) in GIORDANO'S FEDORA.

Sulamith, the High Priest's daughter (soprano) in GOLDMARK'S THE QUEEN OF SHEBA.

Sulla vetta tu del monte, madrigal of the musicians in Act II of PUCCINI'S MANON LESCAUT.

Sulle tue mani l'anima, duet of Enzo and Laura expressing gratitude to La Gioconda and bidding her farewell, in Act IV of PONCHIELLI'S LA GIOCONDA.

Sullivan, Sir Arthur, composer. Born London, May 13, 1842; died there Nov. 22, 1900. He is most famous as W. S. Gilbert's collaborator in writing comic operas. He wrote one grand opera, IVANHOE, in 1891. It was the initial production of the newly founded Royal English Opera Company on Jan. 31, 1891. A failure at its premiere, it has since been virtually forgotten.

Sullivan received his musical education at the Royal Academy of Music in London and at the Leipzig Conservatory. After writing some serious instrumental and choral works he wrote his first comic opera, *Cox and Box,* in 1867. His fruitful collaboration with Gilbert began in 1875 with *Trial by Jury* and continued until 1896.

Sulpizio, Sergeant of the French 21st Regiment (bass) in DONIZETTI'S THE DAUGHTER OF THE REGIMENT.

Summertime, Clara's lullaby in Act I of GERSHWIN'S PORGY AND BESS.

Summ' und brumm', the Spinning Chorus in Act II of WAGNER'S DER FLIEGENDE HOLLÄNDER.

Sunken Bell, The, *see* CAMPANA SOMMERSA, LA.

Suor Angelica (Sister Angelica), one-act opera by PUCCINI. Libretto by Gioacchino Forzano. Premiere: Metropolitan Opera, Dec. 14, 1918. This is the second of the three one-act operas that comprise IL TRITTICO (the others are GIANNI SCHICCHI and IL TABARRO). The setting is a convent in the seventeenth century. Sister Angelica (soprano, a role created by Geraldine FARRAR) has sought refuge to expiate an old sin. When her aunt, the Princess (contralto), visits her, Angelica inquires about the fate of the child that she abandoned before taking vows. The Princess replies that the child has been dead for two years. Angelica prays for forgiveness and commits suicide by drinking poison. But before she dies the Madonna, leading Angelica's child by the hand, miraculously appears to signal forgiveness. An orchestral intermezzo, Anglica's Lament, "Senza mamma," and her arioso, "O fiori," are among the best-known excerpts.

Suore, che riposate, Bertram's invocation in Act III of MEYERBEER'S ROBERT LE DIABLE.

Supervia, Conchita, mezzo-soprano. Born Barcelona, Spain, Dec. 8, 1899; died London, March 30, 1936. At the age of fourteen she made her opera debut at the TEATRO COLÓN in Buenos Aires. A year later she appeared in Italy, scoring a great success at LA SCALA, where she was heard in the Italian premiere of L'HEURE ESPAGNOLE. The wide range, flexibility, and brilliance of her voice made her particularly effective in operas by ROSSINI, notably THE BARBER OF SEVILLE, L'ITALIANA IN ALGERI, and LA CENERENTOLA. She was also acclaimed at the PARIS OPÉRA, the OPÉRA-COMIQUE, and at the THÉÂTRE DES CHAMPS ELYSÉES where in 1929 she was heard in a season of Rossini operas. In 1932–33 she was a member of the Chicago Civic Opera company. In 1934 she made her first

appearance at COVENT GARDEN. She was also a noted concert artist.

Suppé, Franz von (born Francesco Suppe Demelli), composer. Born Spalato, Yugoslavia, Apr. 18, 1819; died Vienna, May 21, 1895. A composer of operettas for the popular theater, Suppé wrote some works of sufficient stature to be performed in opera houses. In this respect his stage writings are comparable to those of Johann STRAUSS THE YOUNGER. After attending the University of Padua, Suppé studied music at the Vienna Conservatory. He then conducted various theater orchestras until 1862, when he was appointed conductor of the THEATER-AN-DER-WIEN. Three years later he became conductor of the Leopoldstadt Theater, also in Vienna, holding this post till the end of his life. His first operetta, *Das Mädchen vom Lande*, was introduced in 1847 and was a huge success. He completed some one hundred and fifty similar pieces, the most famous being: *Die schöne Galatea* (*The Beautiful Galatea*, 1864), *Fatinitza* (1876), *Boccaccio* (1879), *Donna Juanita* (1880). *Donna Juanita* and *Boccaccio* were given by the METROPOLITAN OPERA, the first in 1931, the second in 1932.

Suppliants, The, *see* AESCHYLUS.

Sur mes genoux, fils du soleil (In grembo a me), Selika's lullaby to Vasco da Gama in Act II of MEYERBEER'S L'AFRICAINE.

Susanin, Ivan, a peasant (bass) in GLINKA'S A LIFE FOR THE CZAR.

Susanna, Figaro's betrothed (soprano) in MOZART'S THE MARRIAGE OF FIGARO.

Susannah, "musical drama" in two acts by FLOYD. Libretto by the composer. Premiere: Tallahassee, Fla., Feb 24, 1955. This opera's central theme is, in the composer's own words, "persecution and the concomitant psychological ramifications." The time is the present; the place a farm in New Hope Valley in the Tennessee mountains. Susannah is victimized by the gossip of her townspeople. When Reverend Blitch calls on her to help her, he is so moved by her agony—and so sympathetic to her beauty —that he makes advances to her. He is discovered by Susannah's brother, who kills him in cold blood. The crowd now descends on Susannah to vent on her its fury but is kept at bay by her menacing shotgun. As the curtain descends, Susannah is standing in the doorway of her farm, a forlorn and lonely creature. This opera scored a major success at the NEW YORK CITY OPERA in 1956, when it received the NEW YORK MUSIC CRITICS' CIRCLE AWARD. In the summer of 1958 it was produced at the Brussels Exposition in Belgium. It has since acquired a permanent place in the repertory of American operas. It was the first work performed by the short-lived Metropolitan Opera House National Company— in Indianapolis on Sept. 20, 1965.

Su, su, marinar, see HOLÀ! MATELOTS.

Sutermeister, Heinrich, composer. Born Feuerthalen, Switzerland, Aug. 12, 1910. He studied philology in Paris and Basel and music with ORFF, Walter Courvoisier, and PFITZNER. In 1934–35 he served as coach and conductor at the Municipal Theater in Berne, Switzerland. He remained in Berne to concentrate on composition. The first time he attracted international attention was with his first opera, ROMEO UND JULIA, produced in 1940; following this was *Der Zauberinsel* (based on SHAKESPEARE'S *The Tempest*), introduced in Dresden on Oct. 30, 1942. After World War II he settled in Vaux-sur-Morges, Lake Geneva, where he completed RASKOLNIKOFF, based on DOSTOYEVSKY'S *Crime and Punishment;* following its premiere in 1948, he once again achieved international renown. His other stage operas: *Niobe* (1946); *Der rote Stiefel* (1951); *Titus Feuerfuchs* (1958); *Seraphine* (1959); *Madame Bovary* (1967). He also wrote several radio operas, one of which, *Fingerhütchen,* was also staged; and a television opera, *Das Gespenst von Canterville.* Since 1963 he has taught a class in composition at the Hanover Hochschule für Musik in Germany.

Sutherland, Joan, soprano. Born Sydney, Australia, Nov. 7. 1929. She was a student at the Sydney Conservatory, where she made her opera debut in 1950 in

GOOSSENS' *Judith.* In 1952 she joined the company of COVENT GARDEN. During her first season there she was heard in operas by MOZART and VERDI, and in the world premiere of GLORIANA. In 1955 she created the leading female role in THE MIDSUMMER MARRIAGE. In 1956 she became the first British artist to sing the role of the Countess in THE MARRIAGE OF FIGARO at GLYNDEBOURNE, and in 1959 she caused a sensation at Covent Garden in LUCIA DI LAMMERMOOR. Her American debut took place in Dallas, Texas, on Nov. 17, 1960, in HANDEL'S ALCINA. On Feb. 21, 1961, she made her first appearance in New York, in a concert version of BELLINI'S BEATRICE DI TENDA. She was received with the greatest enthusiasm at her first appearance with the METROPOLITAN OPERA. This took place on Nov. 26, 1961, when she sang Lucia. In 1961 she was made Commander of the British Empire by Queen Elizabeth. Equally distinguished in coloratura and dramatic roles, she has become universally recognized as one of the leading sopranos of the twentieth century, not only in the traditional repertory but also in less familiar works of Handel, ROSSINI, Bellini, and DONIZETTI, where her BEL CANTO singing has seldom been equaled.

Suzanne, Count Gil's wife (soprano) in WOLF-FERRARI'S THE SECRET OF SUZANNE.

Suzel, a farmer's daughter (soprano) in MASCAGNI'S L'AMICO FRITZ, a role created by Emma CALVÉ.

Suzel, buon di, duet of Fritz and Suzel, often identified as the "Duet of the Cherries," in Act II of MASCAGNI'S L'AMICO FRITZ.

Suzuki, Cio-Cio-San's servant (mezzo-soprano) in PUCCINI'S MADAMA BUTTERFLY.

Švanda the Bagpiper (Švanda Dudak; Schwanda der Dudelsackpfeifer), folk opera in two acts by WEINBERGER. Libretto by Miloš Kareš and Max BROD, based on a folk tale by Tyl. Premiere: Prague, Apr. 27, 1927. American premiere: Metropolitan Opera, Nov. 7, 1931. Babinsky (tenor) covets Dorota, wife of Švanda (soprano). He induces Švanda (baritone) to try to win the heart of the wealthy Queen Ice-heart (contralto) with his magic pipings. Švanda follows Babinsky's urging and wins the Queen; but when the latter discovers he is married, she orders his execution. Švanda is able to elude death with his music and with the aid of Babinsky's magic. In consequence of a rash oath, Švanda is consigned to hell, from which he is rescued by Babinsky when the latter wins him in a card game with the devil. Babinsky finally recognizes that he can never win Dorota, and the married couple are happily reunited. The polka and fugue from this opera are well-known concert numbers. Operas about Švanda had already been composed by Adalbert Hřimaly (1896), Karel Weis (1905), and Karel Bendl (1907), but none approached the success of Weinberger's.

Svanholm, Set, tenor and opera director. Born Västeras, Sweden, Sept. 2, 1904; died Saltsjoe-Duvnaes, Sweden, Oct. 4, 1964. After attending the Stockholm Conservatory from 1927 to 1929, he studied singing with John Forsell. He made his opera debut as a baritone in the role of SILVIO at the STOCKHOLM ROYAL OPERA in 1930. He continued to appear in baritone roles for a half-dozen years, then began appearing as a tenor at the Stockholm Royal Opera, scoring major successes in the Wagnerian repertory. He appeared in other European opera houses and at the BAYREUTH and SALZBURG festivals before making his American debut. This took place at the METROPOLITAN OPERA on Nov. 15, 1946, in the title role of SIEGFRIED. He remained with this company through 1955–56, besides appearing at COVENT GARDEN and in Brussels and Copenhagen. He was appointed singer to the Swedish court in 1946. Between 1954 and 1963 he was artistic director of the Stockholm Royal Opera.

Svietosar, Grand Duke of Kiev (bass) in GLINKA'S RUSSLAN AND LUDMILLA.

Swallow, The, see RONDINE, LA.

Swarthout, Gladys, mezzo-soprano. Born Deepwater, Mo., Dec. 25, 1904; died La Ragnaia, Italy, July 6, 1969. She attended the Bush Conservatory in Chicago and was prepared for opera by Leopoldo MUGNONE in Italy. Her debut took place with the Chicago Civic Opera in 1924 as the shepherd boy in TOSCA. During her initial season with this company she appeared in over half its performances in minor roles. On Nov. 15, 1929, she made her debut at the METROPOLITAN OPERA as LA CIECA. Two months later she was featured in the American premiere of SADKO and in 1934 in the premiere of MERRY MOUNT. She remained with the Metropolitan until 1938, returning for three additional periods: 1939–41, 1942–43, and 1944–45. She subsequently appeared in concerts and motion pictures and on radio.

Synge, John Millington, dramatist and poet. Born Rathfarnham, Ireland, Apr. 16, 1871; died Dublin, Mar. 24, 1909. The following of his plays dealing with Irish peasant life have been made into operas: *The Playboy of the Western World* (Leonid Polovinkin's *The Irish Hero*); *Riders to the Sea* (RABAUD'S *L'Appel de la mer;* VAUGHAN WILLIAMS' RIDERS TO THE SEA) ; and *The Shadow of the Glen* (Arrigo Pedrollo's *La Veglia*).

Szell, George, conductor. Born Budapest, June 7, 1897; died Cleveland, July 30, 1970. His music study took place with Eusebius Mandyczewski, J. B. Forster, Richard Robert, and Max Reger. In 1917 he was recommended by Richard STRAUSS for a post as conductor of the Strassburg Municipal Opera. After conducting in Prague and Düsseldorf, Szell was engaged as principal conductor of the BERLIN OPERA, where he remained from 1924 to 1929. From 1929 to 1937 he was the principal conductor of the German Opera in Prague. His American debut took place on Aug. 16, 1940, when he led a Hollywood Bowl concert. In 1942 he was engaged by the METROPOLITAN OPERA, making his debut there on Dec. 9 with SALOME. He remained with that company four years, specializing in the German repertory but also directing such operas as BORIS GODUNOV and OTELLO. He left the Metropolitan in 1946 to become music director of the Cleveland Orchestra, a post he held with outstanding distinction until his death. He returned to the Metropolitan Opera for some guest appearances in 1953, but a few months later he announced his decision to terminate his contract due to differences with the management over artistic procedures. From 1949 on he made numerous appearances as conductor of MOZART'S operas at the SALZBURG FESTIVAL, and he conducted the world premieres of IRISCHE LEGENDE, PENELOPE, and SCHOOL FOR WIVES.

Szenkar, Eugen, conductor. Born Budapest, Apr. 9, 1891. He attended the Budapest Conservatory and in 1912 was engaged as chorus master and assistant conductor of the Landestheater in Prague. From 1913 to 1915 he was a principal conductor of the Landestheater and the Budapest Volksoper. In 1923 he was engaged as musical director of the Berlin Volksoper, succeeding Otto KLEMPERER. A year later he became principal conductor of the COLOGNE OPERA, remaining with this organization until 1933. Afterward, he conducted concerts in the United States, Europe, and Palestine. In 1939 he settled in Rio de Janeiro as conductor of the Brazilian Symphony Orchestra. After World War II he appeared as a guest conductor of major orchestras in England, Austria, Israel, and Egypt. In 1950–51 he was principal conductor of the MANNHEIM OPERA, and from 1952 to 1956 he served as general music director in Düsseldorf.

Szymanowski, Karol, composer. Born Timoshovka, Russia, Oct. 6, 1882; died Lausanne, Switzerland, Mar. 29, 1937. The son of Polish parents, he studied with Sigismund Noskowski in Warsaw. Writing in an oriental idiom, he composed his first opera, HAGITH, in 1913. His second opera, one of his major works, came a decade later: KING ROGER, introduced at the Warsaw Opera on June 19, 1926. His writing in this opera was influenced by the folk songs and dances of Poland. This national style is found in other of his works, including the ballet *Harnasie.* In 1926 Szymanowski became director of the Warsaw Conservatory. Bad health, of which he had been a victim all his life, compelled him to resign in 1929. Later he became president of the Warsaw Academy of Music. He left a large body of compositions in practically every form, most of them marked by a strong individuality and the whole entitling him to a position as the outstanding Polish composer of his time.

T

tabarro, Il (The Cloak), one-act opera by PUCCINI. Libretto by Giuseppe Adami, based on a play by Didier Gold, *La Houppelande.* Premiere: Metropolitan Opera, Dec. 14, 1918. This is one of three one-act operas making up the trilogy IL TRITTICO (the others are GIANNI SCHICCHI and SUOR ANGELICA). The setting is a barge on the Seine River. Michele, a skipper (baritone), suspects his wife, Giorgietta (soprano), of being unfaithful and tries to win back her love by reminding her how he used to protect her under his cloak. Giorgietta remains cold to him. She arranges a rendezvous with her longshoreman lover, Luigi (tenor), using as a signal a lighted match. But when Michele lights his pipe, Luigi takes it for his signal. Michele forces a confession from him, chokes him to death, and covers his body with his cloak. When Giorgietta appears, Michele snatches the cloak from the body and hurls his wife on her dead lover. Principal vocal excerpts: the arias of Giorgietta ("È ben altro il mio sogno") and Michele ("Perchè, perchè, non m'ami più?") and the duet of Giorgietta and Luigi ("Ma chi lascia sobborgo").

Tabor, Augusta, Horace Tabor's divorced wife (mezzo-soprano), in MOORE'S THE BALLAD OF BABY DOE, a role created by Frances BIBLE.

Tabor, Horace, Mayor of Leadville, Col., and principal character (baritone) in MOORE'S THE BALLAD OF BABY DOE, a role created by Walter CASSELL.

Tacea la notte placida, Leonora's aria revealing that she has been serenaded by a mysterious troubadour, in Act I, Scene 2, of VERDI'S IL TROVATORE.

Taddei, Giuseppe, baritone. Born Genoa, June 26, 1916. He made his opera debut in Rome in 1936. After appearing in Italian opera houses he was a member of the VIENNA STATE OPERA between 1946 and 1949. In subsequent appearances at LA SCALA, the Rome Opera, COVENT GARDEN, the SALZBURG FESTIVAL, he distinguished himself as an outstanding interpreter of both dramatic and buffo roles. He made his American operatic debut with the SAN FRANCISCO OPERA on Oct. 15, 1957, as SCARPIA.

Tagliaferro, Cecchina's master (bass), and subsequently her husband, in PICCINNI'S LA CECCHINA.

Tagliavini, Ferruccio, tenor. Born Reggio, Italy, Aug. 14, 1913. After attending the Parma Conservatory, he won first prize in a national singing contest conducted by the FLORENCE MAY MUSIC FESTIVAL in 1938. A year later he made his opera debut at the TEATRO COMMUNALE in Florence as RODOLFO. Successful appearances in major Italian opera houses followed, including LA SCALA, SAN CARLO, and the TEATRO REALE in Rome. In 1946 he made an extensive tour of South America. On Jan. 10, 1947, he was acclaimed as Rodolfo at his debut at the METROPOLITAN OPERA.

Between 1946 and 1954 he appeared in principal tenor roles there, besides singing in recitals throughout the United States, and over the radio. After leaving the Metropolitan he appeared in most of the major European opera houses, including La Scala between 1955 and 1956, and was starred in several motion pictures in Italy. A master of BEL CANTO, he has distinguished himself particularly in such roles as ELVINO and Nemorino in L'ELISIR D'AMORE.

Tajo, Italo, bass. Born Pinerolo, Italy, Apr. 25, 1915. Upon completing his vocal studies in Turin, he made his opera debut in that city as FAFNER in 1935. At the festivals at EDINBURGH and GLYNDEBOURNE and in leading Italian opera houses, he established his reputation in buffo roles during the post–World War II period. He made his American debut with the SAN FRANCISCO OPERA on Sept. 23, 1948, as Colline in LA BOHÈME. He made numerous appearances in major rolls with that company during the next six years. Meanwhile, on Dec. 28, 1948, he made his debut at the METROPOLITAN OPERA as Basilio in THE BARBER OF SEVILLE. His appearances in Europe have been extensive in leading bass roles of the Italian and French repertories, as BORIS GODUNOV, and especially in the MOZART operas.

Talbot, Lord Arthur, a Cavalier (tenor) in love with Elvira in BELLINI'S I PURITANI.

Tale of a Real Man, The, opera in three acts by PROKOFIEV. Libretto by Myra Mendelson (the composer's wife). Premiere: Kirov Opera, Leningrad, Dec. 3, 1948 (preview performance); Bolshoi Opera, Moscow, Oct., 1960. Prokofiev wrote this opera to rehabilitate himself with the Soviet authorities after a devastating attack on him by the General Committee of the Communist Party in 1948. "In my new opera," the composer explained at the time, "I intend to use trios, duets, and contrapuntally developed choruses for which I will make use of some interesting northern folk songs." The text was also intended to appeal to Soviet officials, since the central character is a brave Soviet airplane pilot who loses both his legs but insists on remaining in the service. But this opera failed to restore Prokofiev to the good graces of Soviet officialdom (this was to come later, with other works). *Sovietskaya Musica* wrote: "Prokofiev goes to all the negative and repulsive usages present in the music of the period of reckless infatuation with modernistic trickery."

Tale of the Czar Saltan, The *see* LEGEND OF THE CZAR SALTAN, THE.

Tale of the Invisible City of Kitezh, The, *see* LEGEND OF THE INVISIBLE CITY OF KITEZH, THE.

Tale of Two Cities, A, opera in prologue and three acts by BENJAMIN. Libretto by Cedric Cliffe, based on the novel of the same name by DICKENS. Premiere: BBC network, London, Apr. 17, 1953; London, July 23, 1957 (staged). American premiere: San Francisco, Apr. 2, 1960. This opera, whose text closely follows the plot of the Dickens novel, won first prize during the Festival of Britain in 1953.

Tales of Hoffmann, The (Les contes d'Hoffmann), opera in three acts, with prologue and epilogue, by OFFENBACH. Libretto by Jules BARBIER and Michel Carré, based on their play derived from stories by E. T. A. HOFFMANN. Premiere: Opéra-Comique, Feb. 10, 1881. American premiere: New York City, Maurice Grau's French Opera Company, Oct. 16, 1882.

Characters: Hoffmann, a poet (tenor); Nicklausse, his friend (mezzo-soprano); Olympia, one of Hoffmann's loves (soprano); Giulietta, another love (soprano); Antonia, a third love (soprano); Coppélius, a magician, also appearing in the guises of Dr. Miracle and Dapertutto (baritone); Pittichinaccio. Giulietta's admirer (tenor); Lindorf, a Nuremberg councilor (baritone); Stella, an opera singer (soprano); Andrès, her servant (tenor); Hermann, a student (baritone); Nathaniel, another student (tenor); Schlemil, Giulietta's lover (bass); Spalanzani, a scientist and inventor (tenor); Cochenille, his servant (tenor); Crespel, Antonia's father (bass); Frantz, his servant (tenor): Luther, a tavern keeper (bass); the Muse (soprano; Voice of Antonia's mother (mezzo-soprano); the Muse of Poetry (soprano). The action takes place in Nuremberg, Venice, and Munich in the nineteenth century.

Prologue. The taproom of Luther's tavern in Nuremberg. Lindorf intercepts a love note addressed to Hoffmann; it is an invitation for the poet to visit Stella after her performance in the opera house adjoining the tavern. Lindorf makes it plain that the poet will not keep the rendezvous. Hoffmann and a group of students enter the taproom during an intermission of Stella's opera. The students ask the poet for a song. Though dejected, he complies with a ballad about a hunchback jester at the Eisenach court (Légende de Kleinzach: "Il était une fois à la cour d'Eisenach"). But all at once Hoffmann abandons his ugly subject to speak of the beauty of a woman. The students twit him for being in love. The poet insists that he is through with love, having had three unfortunate experiences. Encouraged by a bowl of punch, he sets about describing them.

Act I. Spalanzani's drawing room. Spalanzani has collaborated with the magician Coppélius to create Olympia, a mechanical doll almost human in appearance. Hoffmann has seen Olympia from a distance and has fallen in love with her, as he reveals in the aria, "Ah, vivre deux." When he confides to Nicklausse about his love, his friend tells a story about a mechanical doll that fell in love with a mechanical bird ("Une poupée aux yeux d'émail"). Hoffmann refuses to heed the story's warning. Spalanzani now entertains his guests by winding up Olympia so that she sings (Doll Song, Air de la poupée: "Les oiseaux dans la charmille"). More in love with her than ever, Hoffmann invites the doll to dance with him (Waltz). The dance becomes frenetic, and Hoffmann falls in a faint. Coppélius (an incarnation of Lindorf, Hoffmann's rival) now enters. He rages at Spalanzani because the latter has paid for Olympia with a worthless check. For revenge, he smashes the doll to pieces. It is only now that Hoffmann discovers he has been in love with clockwork.

Act II. The gallery of Giulietta's palace in Venice. A minuet is the entr'-acte between Acts I and II. The voices of Nicklausse and Giulietta are heard extolling the beauty of the night and the power of love (BARCAROLLE: "Belle nuit, o nuit d'amour"). Hoffmann finds the barcarolle melancholy, and he offers a happier tune ("Amis, l'amour tendre et rêveur"). Hoffmann loves Giulietta without realizing she is in the power of a magician, Dapertutto (another embodiment of Hoffmann's rival). Dapertutto points to a diamond on his finger and explains its powers ("Scintille diamant"). After Hoffmann gives ardent expression to his love for Giulietta ("O Dieu! de quelle ivresse"), Schlemil, also in love with Giulietta, begins to quarrel with Hoffmann. In the ensuing duel, Schlemil is killed. But Hoffmann discovers that he cannot hope to win Giulietta's love—for the magician's slave throws herself into the arms of another admirer and disappears in a gondola.

Act III. A room in Crespel's house, Munich. Hoffmann is in love with Crespel's daughter, Antonia. Seated at her piano, she sings a lament about her lover who has gone away (Romance d'Antonia: "Elle a fui, la tourterelle"). Her song over, she almost faints. Crespel, her father, comes to her aid, reminding her she is a victim of consumption and that she must never again tax her health with singing. When Hoffmann arrives, he and Antonia confide their love for each other ("J'ai le bonheur dans l'âme"). But the power of Dr. Miracle (once again, Lindorf) is again triumphant. He evokes the ghost of Antonia's mother, who entreats the girl to sing. Unable to resist her dead mother's wish, Antonia sings, collapses, and dies in her father's arms.

Epilogue. Luther's Tavern. An INTERMEZZO is based on the melody from the BARCAROLLE. As Hoffmann finishes his remarkable story, Nicklausse suggests that his three women are in reality one —the singer Stella. He proposes a toast to her. Hoffmann angrily shatters his glass and falls into a drunken stupor. The students troop out, and the Muse of Poetry briefly appears to Hoffmann to console him with the philosophy that one may be made great through love but even greater through tears. Hoffmann drunkenly rises, repeats the passionate avowals he had made to Giulietta, and then sinks back in his chair, completely unconscious. When Stella appears, the triumphant Lindorf bears her off. But though the poet has failed her, Stella makes a friendly, sentimental gesture: just before she and Lindorf disappear, she throws a flower at Hoffmann's feet.

Genius of OPÉRA BOUFFE, Offenbach ended his triumphant career with a serious opera, the only one he ever wrote. The wonder is that with this single effort he was able to produce so successful a work. Responding sensitively to the libretto, he created a score in which E. T. A. Hoffmann's world of dreams and fantasies comes delightfully and movingly to life.

Seriously ill when he began *The Tales of Hoffmann*, Offenbach sensed that he had begun a race with death. His greatest hope was to complete what he felt would be his greatest composition. He did not live to see it performed. While making some minor revisions in the score he fainted; two days later he was dead. The opera, introduced a few months after his death, was such a huge success that it was given over a hundred performances during its first year.

Offenbach had hoped that a single baritone would be used for the four evil geniuses, and a single soprano for the three heroines, but this practice has rarely been followed. In 1937 at the METROPOLITAN OPERA, Lawrence TIBBETT sang all the evil geniuses, and so did Martial SINGHER twenty years later. Bruce Dargavel did the same thing in the English motion-picture adaptation conducted by Sir Thomas BEECHAM. At the world premiere, Adele Isaac was heard in all the leading soprano parts, a feat accomplished in the 1960's by Anna MOFFO and Beverly SILLS.

Talvela, Martti, bass. Born Hiitola, Finland, Feb. 4, 1935. He recieved his vocal training in Stockholm, then made his opera debut with the STOCKHOLM ROYAL OPERA in 1961. After two seasons with that company he became a member of the BERLIN DEUTSCHE STAATSOPER, where he was heard by Wieland WAGNER, who invited him to appear at BAYREUTH as TITUREL in 1962. He subsequently made other appearances at Bayreuth, as well as at LA SCALA, the Rome Opera, and with other major European companies. He was selected by KARAJAN to sing the part of Hunding in his production of DIE WALKÜRE, first at the SALZBURG Easter Festival, then at the METROPOLITAN OPERA in 1968.

Tamagno, Francesco, tenor. Born Turin, Dec. 28, 1850; died Varese, Italy, Aug. 31, 1905. His music study took place at the Turin Conservatory. After a period of military service and further study with Carlo Pedrotti, he made his opera debut in Palermo in 1873 in UN BALLO IN MASCHERA. Seven years later he was so successful at LA SCALA, particularly in the role of ERNANI, that he was engaged to tour South America. Returning to Italy, he appeared in the major opera houses. Because of the exceptional power and brilliance of his voice and his pronounced histrionic ability, VERDI selected him to create the title role in the premiere of his OTELLO. Tamagno's performance was a triumph, and contributed to the over-all success of the production; it became the standard by which later interpretations were measured. On Mar. 24, 1891, he made his American debut at the METROPOLITAN OPERA, again as Otello. He appeared at the Metropolitan through the 1894–95 season. He then continued his European career and retired in 1902.

Tamara, heroine (soprano) in Anton RUBINSTEIN's THE DEMON.

tambourin, a lively dance in 2/4 time, originating in Provence, accompanied by a tambourin, a rectangular stringed instrument played by hitting the strings with padded sticks. The characteristic drumming beat is suggested in tambourins composed for other instruments. The famous *Tambourin* found in RAMEAU's harpsichord *Suite in E* was drawn from the composer's opera *Les Fêtes d'Hébé*. Other operatic instances of tambourins are those in Rameau's *Platée* and LES INDES GALANTES, HANDEL's ALCINA, GLUCK's IPHIGÉNIE EN AULIDE, and PAISIELLO's *Prosperina*.

Tamburini, Antonio, baritone. Born Faenza, Italy, Mar. 28, 1800; died Nice, Nov. 9, 1876. As a boy he received vocal lessons from Aldobrando Rossi and sang in the opera chorus in his native city. He made his debut in Cento in Pietro Generali's *La contessa di colle erboso*. Appearances in other Italian cities followed, including two years in Rome, where he was heard in ROSSINI's MOSÈ IN EGITTO. For four years he sang for the impresario Domenico BARBAJA in Naples, Milan, and Vienna, becoming one of the most highly acclaimed baritones of his time. In Vienna he and the tenor RUBINI were the first foreigners since the Duke of Wellington to receive the Order of the Savior. For almost a decade, beginning in 1832, he was an idol of the opera public in London and Paris. In 1841 he returned to Italy, a year later beginning a ten-year stay in Russia. In 1843 he created the role of Dr. Malatesta in DON PASQUALE in Paris. After 1852 he sang in London, Holland, and Paris, even though his voice had greatly deteriorated. He made his last opera appearance in London in 1859, after which he went into retirement in Nice.

Taming of the Shrew, The, (1) a comedy by William SHAKESPEARE in which Petruchio, by amusing stratagems, drives his wife, Katherine, to distraction and thus cures her of her terrible tempers and obstinacy.

(2) Comic opera (*Der widerspänstigen Zähmung*) in four acts by GOETZ. Libretto by J. V. Widmann, based on the SHAKESPEARE comedy. Premiere:

Mannheim, Oct. 11, 1874. American premiere: Academy of Music, New York, Jan. 4, 1886.

(3) Opera in three acts by Vittorio GIANNINI. Libretto by Dorothea Fee and the composer, based on the SHAKESPEARE comedy, with material from ROMEO AND JULIET and the sonnets. Premiere: Cincinnati, Ohio, Jan. 31, 1953. It was successfully revived at the LAKE GEORGE OPERA FESTIVAL in New York on Aug. 21, 1965.

Tamino, a prince (tenor) in love with Pamina in MOZART'S THE MAGIC FLUTE.

T'amo, si, t'amo, e in lagrime, duet of Riccardo and Amelia, bidding each other permanent farewell, in Act III, Scene 2, of VERDI'S UN BALLO IN MASCHERA.

Tancredi, (1) a Christian knight (bass) in MONTEVERDI'S IL COMBATTIMENTO DI TANCREDI E CLORINDA.

(2) OPERA SERIA in two acts by ROSSINI. Libretto by Gaetano ROSSI, based on VOLTAIRE'S *Tancrède,* derived from TASSO. Premiere: Teatro la Fenice, Feb. 6, 1813. This was one of Rossini's greatest successes before THE BARBER OF SEVILLE, which it preceded by three years; it was also his first serious opera. The setting is Syracuse during the conflicts of the Christians and Moslems, and the story engages the hero and heroine in an assortment of trials and misunderstandings before they find true love. The opera contains one of Rossini's most beautiful love songs, "Di tanti palpiti." The overture was taken by the composer from one of his earlier operas, LA PIETRA DEL PARAGONE. The orchestration in this opera was once considered so advanced that Stendhal remarked that it represented "an art of expressing by means of instruments that portion of their sentiments which the characters could not convey to us."

Tanglewood, *see* BERKSHIRE MUSIC FESTIVAL.

Tannhäuser, opera in three acts by WAGNER. Libretto by the composer. Premiere: Dresden Opera, Oct. 19, 1845. American premiere: Stadt Theater, New York, Apr. 4, 1859 (first Wagner opera produced in the United States).

Characters: Hermann, Landgrave of Thuringia (bass); Elisabeth, his niece (soprano); Tannhäuser, minstrel knight (tenor), a role created by Joseph TICHATSCHEK; Wolfram von Eschenbach, his friend (baritone); Venus (soprano or mezzo-soprano); a young shepherd (soprano); minstrel knights; nobles; ladies; bacchantes; nymphs; pilgrims. The setting is Thuringia and the Wartburg at the beginning of the nineteenth century.

The overture begins with the Pilgrims' Chorus and contains the Venusberg music and Tannhäuser's hymn to Venus.

Act I, Scene 1. The Hill of Venus. Venus is reclining on a couch. Before her is the minstrel-knight Tannhäuser, a fugitive from the world, now her partner in the enjoyment of sensual pleasures and revelry. Bacchantes are dancing (BACCHANALE). When they finish, Tannhäuser sings a hymn to Venus ("Dir töne Lob!"). But he longs to return to his own world. Venus tries to reawaken his ardor ("Geliebter, komm"). Rejected, she is enraged, insisting that the world will never forgive him. Tannhäuser, however, puts his trust in the Virgin Mary. As he pronounces her name, Venus disappears, and darkness engulfs her realm.

Scene 2. A valley. Tannhäuser finds himself in a valley below the Castle Wartburg. A young shepherd passes, singing a pastoral tune, hailing the Goddess of Spring ("Frau Holda kam aus dem Berg hervor"). Now is heard the chant of pilgrims on their way to Rome (Pilgrims' Chorus). As they file past Tannhäuser, he falls on his knees in prayer. The sound of horns brings to the scene a group of minstrel knights; Wolfram recognizes Tannhäuser and welcomes him warmly after his year's absence. Tannhäuser is reluctant to rejoin his old friends, but when Wolfram tells him how Elisabeth has been grieving over his absence ("Als du im kühnem sange"), he decides to return with them to the Wartburg ("Ha, jetzt erkenne ich sie wieder").

Act II. The Hall of Minstrels in Wartburg Castle. Elisabeth, overjoyed that Tannhäuser is returning, sings a hymn to the hall ("Dich, teure Halle"). When Tannhäuser appears, she questions him about his absence; his answers are evasive. After they reassure each other of their love ("Gepreisen sei die Stunde"), the knights file in (March), followed by the nobles, ladies, and attendants ("Freudig begrüssen wir die edle Halle"). A song contest is about to take place, the prize to be Elisabeth's hand in marriage. The Landgrave announces that the subject of the songs will be love. Wolfram sings a hymn to pure and unselfish love ("Blick' ich umher"). He is acclaimed. Tannhäuser sings a rhapsody to Venus ("Dir Göttin der Liebe"), glorifying sensual pleasures and carnal love. His audience is horrified. The ladies rush out of the hall, while some of the knights menace Tannhäuser with their swords. Elisabeth protects Tannhäuser, crying out that she will pray for his soul, and begs for his right to seek salvation ("Zurück von ihm!"). Tannhäuser, contrite, promises to atone for his sins and begs for forgiveness. But the Landgrave banishes him, suggesting that he join the pilgrims and seek absolution from the Pope. Tannhäuser falls on his knees and kisses the hem of Elisabeth's garment. He then rushes out to join the pilgrims.

Act III. The valley of the Wartburg. The act is preceded by a prelude entitled *Tannhäuser's Pilgrimage,* woven out of themes suggesting in turn Tannhäuser's penitence, Elisabeth's intercession, and Tannhäuser's suffering. A reminder of the Pilgrims' Chorus is followed by the Heavenly Grace motive in the brass. The prelude ends with a suggestion of Tannhäuser's salvation.

Tannhäuser has been gone for several months. Elisabeth is waiting for his return. Pilgrims return from Rome, but Tannhäuser is not with them. Falling to her knees before a shrine, Elisabeth prays that Tannhäuser's sin may be forgiven (Elisabeth's Prayer: "Allmächt'ge Jungfrau"). After she leaves, the valley grows dark. Wolfram asks the evening star to guide Elisabeth and protect her (Ode to the Evening Star: "O du mein holder Abendstern"). Now he sees Tannhäuser stumbling toward him; the haggard knight is in rags. Tannhäuser tells him that the Pope has refused absolution, saying that his soul could never be reborn, just as the staff in the Pope's hand could never sprout leaves (Rome Narrative: "Inbrunst im Herzen"). Doomed, Tannhäuser can only hope to return to Venus, who appears briefly on the mountain, singing seductively. But once again, when Wolfram mentions the name of Elisabeth, Tannhäuser rejects the temptress. A funeral procession draws near. Minstrels and pilgrims are bearing the bier on which lies the dead Elisabeth. Sinking beside the bier, Tannhäuser also dies. As the morning dawns, more pilgrims arrive from Rome: they bear the Pope's staff, which has miraculously put forth leaves.

Tannhäuser, written between 1843 and 1845, belongs to Wagner's first creative period, in which he was still more or less subservient to tradition. The opera contains formal arias, ensemble numbers, choruses, scenes of pageantry, marches, and even a ballet. The musicodramatic concept of his later dramas was not yet his ideal. Yet there is much in *Tannhäuser* to suggest the mature Wagner. There is a tentative, at times highly effective, use of leitmotifs, as in the recurrent use of themes designating the pilgrims, Venusberg, sensual love, and pure love. One also finds the first examples of the kind of narratives which would abound in his later works; for example, the Rome Narrative.

The version of *Tannhäuser* most often heard today is not the one introduced in Dresden in 1845, but a revision prepared by Wagner for the Paris premiere in 1861. To meet Parisian partiality for ballet, Wagner interpolated an elaborate bacchanale in the opening scene, besides making other alterations The Paris premiere was a fiasco, largely brought about by Wagner's enemies, but the Paris version is the one most audiences now prefer.

Tanz und Musik steh'n im Bann des Rhythmus, Olivier's air maintaining that dance and music are both the servants of rhythm, in Richard STRAUSS's CAPRICCIO.

Taras Bulba, see GOGOL, NIKOLAI.

Tarquinius, Etruscan prince (baritone), seducer of Lucretia, in BRITTEN's THE RAPE OF LUCRETIA.

Tartuffe, see MOLIÈRE.

Tasso, Torquato, poet. Born Sorrento, Italy, Mar. 11, 1544; died Rome, Apr. 25, 1595. Tasso's epic poems have been made into many operas. His magnum opus was *La Gerusalemme liberata,* which was made into operas as ARMIDA by DVOŘÁK, HAYDN, ROSSINI, SACCHINI, SALIERI, and TRAETTA; as ARMIDE by GLUCK; as ARMIDE ET RENAUD by LULLY; under its original title by Carlo Pallavacini and Vincenzo Righini; and as RINALDO by HANDEL. Other operas based on this epic were Johann Haeffner's *Renaud;* Sebastiano Moratelli's *Erminia ne' boschi* and *Erminia al campo;* Luis Persius' *Jérusalem délivrée;* Michel Angelo Rossi's *Erminia sul giordano;* and Niccolò Zingarelli's *La distruzione di Gerusalemme.*

Tasso's other epics were the source of such operas as André CAMPRA's *Tancrède;* MONTEVERDI's IL COMBATTIMENTO DI TANCREDI E CLORINDA; Vincenzo Righini's *La selve incantata.* Tasso appears as a central character in ROSSINI's *Torquato Tasso* and DONIZETTI's *Torquato Tasso.*

Tatiana, Mme. Larina's daughter (soprano), in love with Eugene Onegin, in TCHAIKOVSKY's EUGENE ONEGIN.

Tauber, Richard (born Ernst Seiffert), tenor. Born Linz, Austria, May 16, 1892; died London, Jan. 8, 1948. He attended the Hoch Conservatory in Frankfurt and studied singing with Carl Beines. He made his opera debut in Chemnitz as TAMINO in 1913. He was immediately engaged by the DRESDEN OPERA, where for a decade he appeared in leading tenor roles of the German, Italian, and French repertories. Meanwhile, in 1915, he also became a member of the BERLIN (Royal) OPERA. After World War I, he appeared frequently as a guest in major European opera houses, distinguishing himself particularly in operas of MOZART.

Tauber became even more famous in operetta, particularly in the operettas of Franz Lehár. He was the idol of theatergoers in Germany, Austria, England, and France. He was also distinguished on the concert stage. He made his American debut on Oct. 28, 1931, in a New York song recital, and fifteen years later appeared on the Broadway stage in Lehár's *The Land of Smiles,* renamed *Yours Is My Heart.* He also appeared in numerous motion pictures. After the rise of Hitler, Tauber settled permanently in England, where he became a British citizen and married the British actress Diana Napier.

Taylor, Deems, composer and music critic. Born New York City, Dec. 22, 1885; died there, July 3, 1966. He began to study the piano in his eleventh year. Later, he studied composition and orchestration with Oscar Coon. While attending college, Taylor wrote music for student shows, one of which, *The Echo,* was produced on Broadway. After leaving college, Taylor acted in vaudeville, then became an editor, translator, and journalist. In 1919 he achieved recognition as a composer with his suite for orchestra *Through the Looking Glass.* Two years later he became the music critic of the *New York World,* but resigned after four years to devote himself to composition. In 1926, on a commission from the METROPOLITAN OPERA, he completed his first opera, THE KING's HENCHMAN. It was introduced at the Metropolitan on Feb. 17, 1927. Its success led the Metropolitan to commission a second opera: PETER IBBETSON, seen on Feb. 7, 1931, and so well liked that it was given sixteen times in four seasons, and opened the 1933–34 season. Taylor's third opera, RAMUNTCHO, was produced by the Philadelphia Opera Company on Feb. 10, 1942. His last opera was a fantasy based on a play by Lady Gregory, *The Dragon*, introduced in New York on Feb. 6, 1958. Taylor also distinguished himself as an author, program annotator, and master of ceremonies on radio programs and in films.

Tchaikovsky, Peter Ilyich, composer. Born Votinsk, Russia, May 7, 1840; died St. Petersburg, Nov. 6, 1893. He attended the School for Jurisprudence in St. Petersburg, after which he became a clerk in the Ministry of Justice. However, he had been fond of music from childhood on, and in 1862 he resigned from his post with the Ministry and enrolled in the newly founded St. Petersburg Conservatory. After graduation, he became professor of harmony at the new Moscow Conservatory. During this period he completed his first symphony, performed in 1868, and an opera, *The Voyevoda*, performed in Moscow on Feb. 11, 1869, and given five times. Tchaikovsky himself was dissatisfied with the opera and subsequently he destroyed the score; in recent times, however, the score has been reconstructed from the orchestral and vocal parts. Two more operas followed in the next few years: *Undine* in 1869, and *Oprichnik* in 1872. A third opera, *Mandragora,* was never finished. During this period Tchaikovsky also produced his first orchestral masterwork, the symphonic poem *Romeo and Juliet*.

In 1877 Tchaikovsky embarked on a marriage which was unhappy from the first day. He did not love Antonia Miliukova either before or after he married her. It is possible that he used this alliance to conceal his homosexual tendencies. In any event this unfortunate step upset his nervous system, and he tried to commit suicide. He then fled from his wife and traveled throughout Europe for a year. He never returned to her. Despite these emotional and physical upheavals, he completed several major works, one of which was his most important opera, EUGENE ONEGIN, introduced in Moscow in 1879.

While traveling about Europe, Tchaikovsky learned that a wealthy patron, Nadezhda Filaretovna von Meck, stood ready to provide him with a handsome annual pension. This marked the beginning of a strange relationship between Madame von Meck and Tchaikovsky, carried on exclusively through correspondence. These letters were often passionate in their avowal of love, yet their authors never met. The reason for this condition, laid down by the patron, has never been satisfactorily explained. In any event, it is a curious fact that the great love affair of Tchaikovsky's life was carried on exclusively by letter. Financially independent and stimulated by the outpouring admiration of his patron, he produced a succession of masterworks. Then in 1890, after thirteen years, the strange friendship came to a sudden end. While in the Caucasus, he received word that Madame von Meck's financial reverses compelled her to terminate the pension. Since Tchaikovsky was now financially secure, he hastened to tell her he was no longer in need of her generosity and to express the hope that their friendship might continue. This letter and later ones were not answered. When he returned to Moscow, Tchaikovsky discovered that his patron had not suffered reverses but had used this as an excuse to break off a relationship that had begun either to bore or to embarrass her. The realization that she had thus discarded him was a blow from which the composer never completely recovered.

In 1891 Tchaikovsky visited the United States, conducting four concerts in New York, one in Baltimore, one in Philadelphia. Back in Russia he became a victim of emotional instability. In such a mood he completed his last symphony, appropriately named by his brother the *Pathétique*. The composer died less than two weeks after conducting the premiere of this work.

Though not heard as frequently as his other works, Tchaikovsky's best operas, while not consistent masterpieces, are filled with some of his finest melodic inspiration and often have compelling dramatic power. His operas: *The Voyevoda* (1868) ; *Undine* (1869) ; *Oprichnik* (1872) ; VAKULA THE SMITH (1874, revised 1885) ; *Eugene Onegin* (1878) ; THE MAID OF ORLEANS (*Joan of Arc*) (1879, revised 1882) ; MAZEPPA (1883) ; *The Enchantress* (1887) ; PIQUE DAME (The *Queen of Spades*) (1890) ; *Iolanthe* (1891) .

Tchekov, Anton, *see* CHEKHOV.

Tcherepnin, Alexander, composer. Born St. Petersburg, Jan. 20, 1899. The son of Nicolai TCHEREPNIN, Alexander studied with his father, then attended the conservatories of St. Petersburg and Paris. He attracted attention with a piano concerto, but real success came with an opera, *01-01*, introduced in Weimar on Jan. 31, 1928. In 1933 he toured as a composer-pianist, making his first visit to the United States in 1934. From 1934 to 1937 he lived in the Orient. In 1948 he settled permanently in the United States. He was a member of the music faculties of the San Francisco Music and Art Institute and from 1949 to 1964 of the DePaul University Music School in Chicago. He became an American citizen in 1958. After 1964 he gave up teaching completely to concentrate exclusively on music, dividing his permanent residence between New York and Paris. His wife, Lili Shiannmin, is a Chinese musician with whom he has appeared in concerts of Chinese music. The Russian and oriental influences in Tcherepnin's life are revealed in the exotic atmosphere and vivid colors of many of his works. A distinguishing technical trait is the use of a nine-tone scale; another is a contrapuntal method he has designed as interpoint. His operas: *01-01* (1925) ; *Die Hochzeit der Sobeide* (1930) ; *The Farmer and the Fairy,* whose world premiere took place at Aspen, Col. on Aug. 13, 1952; and *Ivan the Terrible,* commissioned by the BBC in London and introduced over that television network on Christmas Eve of 1968.

Tcherepnin Nicolai, composer. Born St. Petersburg, May 14, 1873; died Issy-les-Moulineaux, France, June 26, 1945. He was a pupil of RIMSKY-KORSAKOV. For five years beginning in 1909, he was the conductor of Serge DIAGHILEV's Ballet Russe in Paris. Just before World War I he returned to Russia, but after the Revolution he settled permanently in Paris, where he devoted himself principally to writing music for the stage. His style was primarily influenced by the techniques and approaches of the Russian national school. He wrote three operas: *The Marriage Broker; Poverty Is Not a Crime;* and *Ivan the Chancellor.* He completed MUSSORGSKY's THE FAIR AT SOROCHINSK, a version introduced at the MONTE CARLO OPERA in 1923 and seven years later produced at the METROPOLITAN OPERA.

Tcherevik, a peasant (bass) in MUSSORGSKY's THE FAIR AT SOROCHINSK.

Tchernomor, a dwarf in GLINKA's RUSSLAN AND LUDMILLA.

Teatro alla Pergola, an opera house in Florence, named after the street on which it is located. It was built in 1657 by the Medici as a home for spoken drama. On its site, the first opera, PERI's DAFNE, had been performed in 1597. Opera was presented at the Teatro alla Pergola for the first time in 1738. Here took place the world premieres of DONIZETTI's *Parisana,* MEYERBEER's *Il crociato in Egitto,* and VERDI's MACBETH. Through the years it offered significant Italian premieres, including those of THE MARRIAGE OF FIGARO in 1788, DON GIOVANNI in 1792, and THE ABDUCTION FROM THE SERAGLIO in 1935; also of DINORAH, LES HUGUENOTS, LE PROPHÈTE, and ROBERT LE DIABLE. The auditorium is now used mainly during the FLORENCE MAY MUSIC FESTIVAL, though occasionally an operatic production is given there during the winter season. The principal opera performances in Florence in winter, however, take place at the TEATRO COMMUNALE.

Teatro alla Scala (La Scala), the leading opera house in Italy, and one of the most important opera houses of the world. It was built in Milan in 1776 on the old site of the church of Santa Maria alla Scala, by order of Empress Maria Theresa, replacing a theater which had burned. Designed by Piermarini of Fogliano, it was the finest and costliest theater of its day. It opened on Aug. 3, 1778, with SALIERI's *Europa riconosciuta*.

The theater was extensively remodeled in 1867. In 1872 it became the property of the municipality of Milan, administered by a commission elected by the city council and the theater's box owners. Throughout the nineteenth century, La Scala helped shape Italian operatic history by performing numerous world premieres by the pre-eminent and significant composers of the period, including BELLINI, DONIZETTI, ROSSINI, and VERDI. This is a partial list: ANDREA CHÉNIER; *Edgar* (PUCCINI) ; FALSTAFF; LA GAZZA LADRA; LA GIOCONDA; I LOMBARDI; LUCREZIA BORGIA; MEFISTOFELE; NABUCCO; NORMA; OBERTO, CONTE DI SAN BONIFACO; OTELLO; LA PIETRA DI PARAGONE; IL PIRATA; IL TURCO IN ITALIA; LA WALLY.

In 1897 in a wave of economy the city administration stopped the funds for the opera house, and it had to close. Such resentment was expressed by the Milanese that the city had to restore its financial support. Between 1898 and 1903 TOSCANINI was the principal conductor. It was during this period that the music dramas of WAGNER first gained prominence in the repertory (La Scala gave the Italian premieres of DIE WALKÜRE and SIEGFRIED) ; the repertory was further freshened with the introduction of other German, as well as French and Russian, operas (La Scala gave the first Italian performances of SALOME, LOUISE, and PELLÉAS ET MÉLISANDE) . Following the first Toscanini regime, the important premieres at La Scala before Toscanini's return included L'AMORE DEI TRE RE, FEDRA, and MADAMA BUTTERFLY.

The house closed down again during the years of World War I. In 1920 a group of patrons provided the funds to reopen the theater. The building was completely modernized. It reopened with Toscanini as its artistic director, with full power over every phase of production. The Toscanini era between 1921 and 1929 restored to La Scala its former glory with luminous performances of the standard repertory with few parallels in the world. It reopened on the evening of Dec. 26, 1921, with Toscanini conducting FALSTAFF. In the ensuing years German operas were once again given their rightful place in the repertory (Wagner, MOZART, FIDELIO, DER FREISCHÜTZ) , and so were the French and Russian (there was a historic presentation of BORIS GODUNOV) . The world premieres included the following: RESPIGHI's *Belfagor*, LA CENA DELLE BEFFE, DEBORA E JAELE, FRA GHERARDO, ALFANO's *La leggenda di Sacuntala*, NERONE, TURANDOT.

Following Toscanini's resignation in 1929, high standards were generally maintained under the musical direction of Victor de SABATA, who served from 1931 to 1954.

The theater closed again during World War II and was later severely bombed. After partial restoration, it reopened on May 11, 1946, with Toscanini conducting an orchestral concert, the first of ten to raise funds for the completion of the reconstruction. The first new opera performed at La Scala after the company resumed operations was PIZZETTI's *L'Oro*, on Jan. 1, 1947.

With the resignation of de Sabata in 1954, Gianandrea Gavazzeni became artistic director. In 1969 he was succeeded by Luciano Chailly.

Since its reopening following World War II, La Scala has presented the world premieres of, among other works: L'ASSASSINIO NELLA CATTEDRALE; L'ATLANTÍDA, staged version; *Le Bacanti* (GHEDINI) ; *Clitennestra* (Pizzetti) ; I CORDOVANO (Goffredo Petrassi) ; DAVID; LES DIALOGUES DES CARMÉLITES; *Donna è mobile* (MALIPIERO) ; *Job,* staged version (DALLAPICCOLA) ; TRIONFO DI AFRODITE.

Many notable revivals, novelties, and Italian premieres have also been given since the end of World War II. Among them have been ANNA BOLENA; IL CAMPANELLO DI NOTTE; LA CECCHINA; THE CONSUL; *Crescendo* (CHERUBINI) ; THE FLAMING ANGEL; GIULIO CESARE; *Hercules*

(HANDEL); L'INCORONAZIONE DI POPPEA; A LIFE FOR THE CZAR; *Macbeth* (Ernest Bloch); MARIA DI ROHAN; MÉDÉE; MINES OF SULPHUR; *Mitridate Eupatore* (A. SCARLATTI); L'ORFEO; *Il Pirata*; RITA; LE SIÈGE DE CORINTHE; TROILUS AND CRESSIDA; ULISSE.

The company performed in COVENT GARDEN in 1950, at the EDINBURGH FESTIVAL in 1957, and in Montreal at Expo 67 in 1967.

See also PICCOLA SCALA.

Teatro Colón, the leading opera house of South America, located in Buenos Aires, Argentina. It opened in 1857, but the present auditorium did not open until May 25, 1928. From the early twentieth century on it did yeoman service in presenting world premieres of South American operas by composers such as Felipe Boero, Raul Espile, Gilardo Gilardi, and Juan Bautista Massa, among many others, none of which have been performed outside South America. The international prestige of the Teatro Colón can be said to date from 1930, when the composer Juan José Castro became its musical director, a post he filled for many years. The foremost opera stars have appeared on its stage in thoroughly polished performances and in as highly varied a repertory as can be encountered anywhere. The season of 1955–56, for example, included Castro's *Bodas de sangre*, BORIS GODUNOV, SAUGUET's *Caprices de Marianne*, ERWARTUNG, RESPIGHI's *Fiamma*, KHOVANTCHINA, THE MEDIUM, DER ROSENKAVALIER, together with operas by MOZART, VERDI, and GOUNOD. The 1965 season offered THE DAMNATION OF FAUST, LES DIALOGUES DES CARMÉLITES, DIE FRAU OHNE SCHATTEN, L'INCORONAZIONE DI POPPEA, LULU, and WERTHER, together with the standard repertory. In 1964 the theater gave the world premiere of DON RODRIGO; in 1968 it offered I QUATTRO RUSTEGHI for the first time in Venetian dialect since 1927; and in 1969 its repertory embraced LA CLEMENZA DI TITO, DOKTOR FAUST, DER FREISCHÜTZ, MÉDÉE, NORMA, VOLO DI NOTTE, and WOZZECK, among other presentations. Since Castro, the musical direction passed to Juan B. Montero, and after that to Enzio Valenti Ferro.

Teatro Communale, Bologna, an opera company that opened in 1763 in what has been described as "one of the most magnificent opera houses in the world" (designed by Antonio Galli Bibiena). The opera house began to achieve significance in the third quarter of the nineteenth century: in 1875 in the first production of MEFISTOFELE following its fiasco at LA SCALA; between 1871 and 1877 in performances of WAGNER's dramas under the direction of Angelo Mariani. Its season extends from November or December to March and emphasizes the Italian repertory with outstanding guest artists.

Teatro Communale, Florence, one of two opera houses in Florence, Italy (the other being TEATRO ALLA PERGOLA). Built in 1864 (without a roof, which was added in 1883), it was originally called Teatro Politeama Fiorentino Vittorio Emmanuele. It acquired its present name in 1932, when it came under the jurisdiction of the city government. In 1959–60 the theater was modernized, reopening in 1961. It has a regular winter season, its repertory frequently incorporating performances from the annual FLORENCE MAY MUSIC FESTIVAL. IL PRIGIONIERO received its world premiere here in 1950.

Teatro Costanzi, *see* TEATRO DELL' OPERA.

Teatro dell' Opera, the leading opera house in Rome, Italy. When it opened on Nov. 27, 1880, with SEMIRAMIDE, it was called Teatro Costanzi in a new auditorium designed by A. Sfondrini. (The theater was renovated in 1926 and 1960.) Among the more significant world premieres presented during the 1890's were L'AMICO FRITZ, CAVALLERIA RUSTICANA, IRIS, and TOSCA. When the opera house acquired a subsidy from the state, it was renamed Teatro Reale dell' Opera, opening on Feb. 28, 1928, with NERONE. It retained this name until 1947, when it assumed its present one. Since 1938 the company has given outdoor summer performances in the ruins of the Carcalla Baths. Between June 22 and July 6, 1968, the company gave performances at the METROPOLITAN OPERA House, the first time since the nineteenth century that a full-scale Italian company visited New York City. The 1969–70 season provided the world premiere of Luciano Chailly's *Idiota* (Feb. 14, 1970), the Italian premiere of Rolando Penerai's *Dantons Tod* (Apr. 30, 1970), and a new production of BELLINI's *La straniera* with Renata SCOTTO. Massimo Bogianckino served as artistic director from 1963 to 1969, when he was succeeded by Mario Zafred. Among the more significant premieres, revivals, and novelties heard at the Teatro dell'Opera during the past quarter of a century have been *Alzira* (VERDI); *Ballo delle ingrate* (MONTEVERDI); BOULEVARD SOLITUDE; IL CAVALIERI DI EKEBU (ZANDONAI); CHRISTOPHE COLOMB; LA CLEMENZA DI TITO; *Clitennestra* (PIZZETTI); *Contratto* (Virgilio Mortari); *Dantons Tod* (Rolando Penerai); *Il dibuk* (Lodovico Rocca); *Ecube* (MALIPIERO); *La figlia del Jorio* (DONIZETTI); THE FLAMING ANGEL; THE GAMBLER; GIULIO CESARE; *Idiota* (Luciano Chailly); *Margherita de Cortona* (Licinio Refice); MOSES UND ARON; OEDIPUS REX; *Organo di bambù* (Ennio Porrino); OTELLO (ROSSINI); IL PRIGIONIERO; *Romulus* (Allegra); *Il sistèma della dolcezza* (Vieri Tosatti); *La straniera* (Bellini); IL TURCO IN ITALIA; and THE YOUNG LORD, conducted by the composer.

Teatro la Fenice, the leading opera house in Venice, and one of Italy's greatest operatic institutions. Its construction began in 1790, but before the building was completed it was destroyed by fire. Living up to its name (in English, The Phoenix), it was rebuilt, opening on May 16, 1792, with PAISIELLO's *I giucho d'Agrigento.* Fire once again destroyed the auditorium in 1836, and a new house was built on the same site, opening on Dec. 26, 1837. Many significant world premieres have taken place at La Fenice, including: BEATRICE DI TENDA; I CAPULETTI ED I MONTECCHI; *La donna del lago* (ROSSINI); L'ITALIANA IN

ALGERI; THE RAKE'S PROGRESS; RIGOLETTO; SEMIRAMIDE; *Sigismondo* (Rossini); SIMON BOCCANEGRA; TANCREDI; LA TRAVIATA; THE TURN OF THE SCREW. HANDEL'S ALCINA was revived in 1960, produced by ZEFFIRELLI and starring Joan SUTHERLAND. In 1969 DONIZETTI's *Belisario* (written for this opera house, introduced in 1836, but not performed there since 1841) was a significant revival.

Teatro Lirico Internazionale, an opera house in Milan built by Edoardo SONZOGNO, the publisher, to replace the Teatro Cannobiana, where opera had been given between 1779 and 1894. The Teatro Lirico opened in 1894 with Spiro Samara's *La martire.* Among the operas introduced there were ANDREA LECOUVREUR, CILÈA's L'ARLÉSIANA (in which CARUSO made his debut in Milan), FEDORA, and ZAZA. Italian premieres included LOUISE, LA PRISE DE TROIE, THAÏS, and WERTHER. In 1938 the theater was destroyed; it was rebuilt a year later. When LA SCALA was bombed during World War II, it gave its performances for several seasons in the auditorium of the Teatro Lirico. Opera no longer is produced there.

Teatro Reale dell' Opera, *see* TEATRO DELL' OPERA.

Teatro Regio, Parma, the principal opera house in Parma, Italy. It opened in May, 1829, with BELLINI's *Zaira,* and was renovated in 1853. Since VERDI was born near Parma, this opera house is primarily identified with his works. Almost two thousand performances have been given of twenty-four of his twenty-six operas, including works like *Stiffelio,* which had not been performed in a century. The company is also partial to the French repertory and particularly to BERLIOZ, having given numerous performances of THE DAMNATION OF FAUST, as well as other Berlioz operas. Italo CAMPANINI often conducted here, and TOSCANINI played the cello in the opera orchestra before he became a conductor.

Teatro Regio, Turin, the principal opera house in Turin, Italy. It opened in 1741 on Via Rossini. TOSCANINI served a significant apprenticeship as conductor here (1886, 1889–1891, 1895–1898). Among the world premieres performed here were LA BOHÈME, *Francesca da Rimini* (ZANDONAI), and MANON LESCAUT. The opera house was destroyed by fire in 1936 and was not rebuilt until 1970. Performances by the Teatro Regio during this interim were given at the Teatro Nuovo.

Teatro San Carlo, the leading opera house in Naples, and one of Italy's most historic and significant operatic organizations. It was built (in two hundred seventy days) to replace the St. Bartholomew Theater and opened with Sarro's *Achille in Siro* on Nov. 4, 1737. The theatre was enlarged in 1777. Here the most significant works of the Neapolitan school of composers were introduced—operas by CIMAROSA, JOMMELLI, PAISIELLO, PERGOLESI, PICCINNI, Alessandro SCARLATTI, and SPONTINI. From 1810 to 1839 it was under the artistic direction of Domenico BARBAJA, becoming at that time one of the world's great opera houses. The theater was further enlarged in 1812, but was destroyed by fire in 1816. It was rebuilt and in 1844 remodeled; in 1929 the stage was modernized and a new foyer added. During World War II it was bombed, but not sufficiently to prevent productions. During the war the opera company was managed by the British occupation forces, and in 1946 the San Carlo was invited to London to give performances at COVENT GARDEN. After the war the opera house was once again remodeled. Under the artistic direction of Pasquale di Costanzo, who has remained its general manager since then, the company embarked on a progressive program that included first performances in Italy of works by such composers as HANDEL, HAYDN, RIMSKY-KORSAKOV, and ROUSSEL. In 1969–70, the San Carlo Opera played host to the Bulgarian Opera, which offered performances of BORIS GODUNOV. The resident company opened the season with ROSSINI's MOSÈ IN EGITTO and subsequently starred Beverly SILLS in LA TRAVIATA, Elena Sulitosi in NORMA, and Grace BUMBRY in SALOME. Among the world premieres given here have

been *Adina* (ROSSINI); *Aladdin and the Magic Lamp* (Rota); ARMIDA (ROSSINI); *La donna del lago* (Rossini); *Elizabetta, regina d'Inghilterra* (Rossini); *La guerra* (ROSSELLINI); LUCIA DI LAMMERMOOR; LUISA MILLER; *Mosè in Egitto* (Rossini); OTELLO (Rossini); *Tess* (ERLANGER); *Vivi* (Manini); *Zelmira* (Rossini). In 1966 the company commemorated the centenary of CILÈA with gala performances of ANDREA LECOUVREUR and the less familiar *Mess Mariant*. In 1968–69 it revived DONIZETTI's *Maria Stuarda* and PIZZETTI's *Lo straniero*. Its artistic director is Rubino Profeta.

Teatro San Cassiano, the first public opera house in history. It opened in Venice in 1637 with Francesco Mannelli's *Andromeda* and continued to present operas until 1800.

Teatro San Moïse, one of the oldest public opera houses in history, opening in Venice in 1640 and offering productions regularly till 1818. Five ROSSINI operas received their world premieres here, including his first produced opera, LA CAMBIALE DI MATRIMONIO, and *La Scala di Seta* and IL SIGNOR BRUSCHINO.

Teatro Santi Giovanni e Paolo, second oldest public opera house in history, opening in Venice in 1639. MONTEVERDI's L'INCORONAZIONE DI POPPEA was given its world premiere here in 1642.

Tebaldi, Renata, soprano. Born Pesaro, Italy, Feb. 1, 1922. For ten years she attended the conservatories of Pesaro and Parma, where she at first specialized in the piano. When she decided to become a singer, she took private lessons from Carmen Mellis and dramatic coaching from Giuseppe Pais. She made her debut at the Rivigo Theater as Elena in MEFISTOFELE in 1944. Success came when TOSCANINI heard her and engaged her to sing at one of his concerts with which LA SCALA was reopened in 1946. Appearances with various Italian opera companies led to an engagement with La Scala, where she was a principal soprano between 1949 and 1954. In 1950 she was heard at COVENT GARDEN and at the EDINBURGH FESTIVAL. She made her American debut at the SAN FRANCISCO OPERA on

Sept. 26, 1950, as AIDA. On Jan. 31, 1955, she appeared for the first time at the METROPOLITAN OPERA, singing the role of DESDEMONA. She has remained with that company since and has also made appearances with many of the world's other major opera companies. The extraordinary quality and virtuosity of her singing, together with her dramatic power, have placed her with the foremost opera stars to emerge since the end of World War II, particularly in the operas of VERDI and PUCCINI. She appeared in a motion-picture version of LOHENGRIN filmed in Italy and sang for (but did not appear in) an Italian film version of *Aida*.

Télaire, Pollux' beloved (soprano) in RAMEAU'S CASTOR ET POLLUX.

Telephone, The, one-act opera by MENOTTI. Libretto by the composer. Premiere: New York City, Feb. 18, 1947. Ben, trying to propose to Lucy, is continually interrupted by Lucy's passion for telephone conversations. In desperation he rushes out to a phone booth, telephones his proposal, and is accepted.

Television of opera, *see* OPERA PERFORMANCE (5).

Tell, *see* WILLIAM TELL.

Te lo rammenti, Mimi's tender aria recalling Rodolfo and their onetime happiness together, in Act IV of PUCCINI'S LA BOHÈME.

Telramund, Frederic of, Count of Brabant, Elsa's guardian (baritone), in WAGNER'S LOHENGRIN.

Telva, Marion, contralto. Born St. Louis, Mo., Sept. 26, 1897; died Norwalk, Conn., Oct. 23, 1962. She began studying singing seriously on the advice of Ernestine SCHUMANN-HEINK. On Dec. 31, 1920, she made her debut at the METROPOLITAN OPERA as the Italian singer in MANON LESCAUT. She remained at the Metropolitan for a decade, distinguishing herself in leading roles in both Italian operas and the Wagnerian repertory. She was seen in several important premieres and revivals, including those of DIE AEGYPTISCHE HELENA, NORMA, PETER IBBETSON, and THE SNOW MAIDEN. She went into retirement

after the 1930–31 season. Re-engaged in 1935, she was unable to perform because of poor health.

Tempest, The (Der Sturm), opera in nine scenes and epilogue by Frank MARTIN. Libretto by the composer, based on SHAKESPEARE, as translated into German by Schlegel. Premiere: Vienna, June 17, 1956. American premiere: New York City Opera, Oct. 11, 1956. In this, its composer's first opera, he uses the Shakespeare text except for a few minor deletions and changing Ariel's part into a dancing role (the vocal portions heard offstage from a single voice or chorus). The composer has explained that he tried to emphasize the different worlds of Ariel, Prospero, Miranda, and Ferdinand, the courtiers, the drunkards, and Caliban, "each requiring music entirely different from the others." Ballet and pantomime play integral parts in the production, so much so that the opera sometimes gives the impression of being a scenic oratorio. Declamation is preferred to fully developed arias, and the voice is given considerable preference over the orchestra.

Templer und die Jüdin, Der (The Templar and the Jewess), opera in three acts by MARSCHNER. Libretto by W. A. Wohlbrück and the composer, based on Sir Walter SCOTT'S IVANHOE. Premiere: Leipzig Opera, Dec. 22, 1829. American premiere: Stadt Theater, New York, Jan. 29, 1872. Robert SCHUMANN quoted the aria "Wer ist der Ritter hoch geehrt" in the final variation of his *Études symphoniques* for piano.

Tender Land, The, opera in three acts by Aaron COPLAND. Libretto by Horace Everett. Premiere: New York City Opera, Apr. 1, 1954 (original version); Oberlin, Ohio, May 20, 1955 (revised). This opera was written on a commission from Richard Rodgers and Oscar Hammerstein II to help celebrate the thirtieth anniversary of the League of Composers in New York. The setting is the Midwest; the time, the early 1930's. Laurie, a farm girl, and Martin, a young harvester, fall in love and make plans to elope. Martin loses heart and flees from the area. Heartbroken and deserted, Laurie abandons the security of her family and home to go in search of Martin. Copland makes skillful use of American folk-music elements, such as square-dance music and a quotation from the folksong "Courtin' Time." Nevertheless, his writing is basically in a modern vein with exploitation of dissonance and polytonality for dramatic effect. The opera ends with an outstanding piece of vocal-ensemble writing, the quintet "The promise of living."

Tennyson, Alfred Lord, poet. Born Somersby, Eng., Oct. 6, 1809; died Haslemere, Eng., Oct. 6, 1892. He became poet laureate of England in 1850. His *Idylls of the King,* a poetic adaptation of the Arthurian legend, was made into operas by Herman Bemberg *(Elaine)*, Walter Courvoisier *(Lanzelot und Elaine)*, and Odon Michalovich *(Edin)*. His *Enoch Arden* was adapted as an opera by Rezsö Raimann, also by Eduardo Sanchez de Fuentes *(Naufrago)*.

tenor, the highest range of the adult male voice, when produced naturally. Normally, it extends about two octaves upward from the C an octave below middle C. A lyric tenor is one with a brilliant, bright, easy-flowing voice (for roles like RODOLFO and ALFREDO), while a dramatic tenor has a resonant, dynamic, and vibrant voice (especially for roles in the Wagnerian music dramas, where he is referred to as a *Heldentenor*).

tenuto, Italian for "held," an indication for performers to hold notes longer than their complete value.

Ter Arutunian, Rouben, scenic and costume designer. Born Tiflis, Russia, July 24, 1920. He is of Armenian descent. He planned to become a concert pianist but was diverted to painting and designing in 1938 after seeing performances of the Ballets de Colonel de Basil. Between 1939 and 1944 he attended art schools and universities in Berlin and Vienna. His apprenticeship as a costume designer took place in 1940 with the BERLIN STATE OPERA. In 1943 he designed costumes for THE BARTERED BRIDE

produced by the DRESDEN OPERA, and in 1944, for SALOME at the VIENNA STATE OPERA. Following the termination of World War II he spent three years attending the École Nationale Superieure des Beaux-Arts in Paris. He came to the United States in 1951. For three years he was staff designer for CBS-TV, winning an Emmy Award in 1957 for his contribution to a production of *Twelfth Night*. He also worked with the NBC OPERA COMPANY on its television productions of THE ABDUCTION FROM THE SERAGLIO, THE MAGIC FLUTE, and GRIFFELKIN. Between 1953 and 1959 he was a member of the NEW YORK CITY OPERA COMPANY. In 1961 he designed the production of DELLO JOIO's *Blood Moon* for the SAN FRANCISCO OPERA, and in 1968 he designed productions of MADAMA BUTTERFLY and DIE BASSARIDEN for the SANTA FE OPERA. He has also done scenic and costume designing for Broadway productions.

Teresa, (1) a mill owner and foster mother of Amina (mezzo-soprano) in BELLINI'S LA SONNAMBULA.

(2) Belducci's daughter (soprano) in BERLIOZ' BENVENUTO CELLINI.

T'eri un giorno, duet of Gennaro and his mother, Carmela, in which, fearful of the consequences of Gennaro's love for Maliella, the mother pleads for him to go to church and pray, in Act I of WOLF-FERRARI's THE JEWELS OF THE MADONNA.

Ternina, Milka, soprano. Born Belgisč, Croatia, Dec. 19, 1863; died Zagreb, May 18, 1941. She studied singing with Ida Winterberg in Zagreb and Joseph Gänsbacher in Vienna. Her debut took place in 1882 in Angram, while she was still studying in Zagreb, in the role of Amelia in UN BALLO IN MASCHERA. On Anton SEIDL's recommendation she was selected to succeed Katharina KLAFSKY as principal soprano of the Bremen Opera. In 1890 she was engaged by the MUNICH ROYAL OPERA, where for a decade she distinguished herself as one of the outstanding Wagnerian sopranos of her time. Her American debut took place in Boston in 1896 with the DAM-

ROSCH OPERA COMPANY; she sang the role of Brünnhilde in DIE WALKÜRE. She made her London debut as ISOLDE in 1898 and her first appearance at BAYREUTH as KUNDRY in 1899. On Jan. 27, 1900, she made her METROPOLITAN OPERA debut as ELISABETH. During her association with the Metropolitan she created for America the role of Kundry; for participating in this performance, given against the wishes of the WAGNER family, she was denounced and never again invited to Bayreuth. Ternina also created for America the role of TOSCA. She went into retirement in 1906 at the height of her career after an attack of paralysis. For a year she taught singing at the Institute of Musical Art in New York, after which she taught singing privately in Zagreb. There she was credited with the discovery of Zinka MILANOV.

Teschek, bedien' dich, Mandryka's generous offer to Count Waldner to help himself to the contents of Mandryka's purse, in Act I of Richard STRAUSS's ARABELLA.

Teschemacher, Marguerite, soprano. Born Cologne, March 3, 1903; died Tegernsee, May 19, 1959. She created the roles of DAPHNE in Richard STRAUSS's opera of the same name and Miranda in SUTERMEISTER's *Zauberinsel.* She made her debut in COLOGNE as MICAËLA in 1924. After being a member of the MANNHEIM and STUTTGART opera companies she was a principal soprano of the DRESDEN OPERA between 1935 and 1946, where she sang the part of the Countess in the Dresden premiere of Richard Strauss's CAPRICCIO. From 1948 to 1952 she sang with the Düsseldorf Opera. She also appeared at COVENT GARDEN in 1931 and 1936.

Te souvient-il du lumineux voyage, duet of Thaïs and Athanaël in the closing scene of MASSENET's THAÏS, as Thaïs lies dying.

tessitura, Italian for "texture," the prevailing level or range of a singer's part.

Tetrazzini, Luisa, soprano. Born Florence, June 29, 1871; died Milan, Apr. 28, 1940. One of the greatest coloratura sopranos of the twentieth century, she studied first with her sister Eva, a dra-

matic soprano, and then at the Musical Institute in Florence. Her debut took place in Florence in 1890 in the role of INEZ. After many appearances in Italy and South America, she scored her first major triumphs with a new company touring Mexico in 1905. The company later appeared in San Francisco, where she was a sensation. She made her COVENT GARDEN debut on Nov. 2, 1907, as VIOLETTA. On Jan. 15, 1908, she made her first appearance with the MANHATTAN OPERA COMPANY, again as Violetta. She became such a favorite in New York that in her first season with the Manhattan Opera she appeared twenty-two times instead of the fifteen originally scheduled. She remained with the company until its dissolution. On Dec. 27, 1911, she made her bow at the METROPOLITAN OPERA as LUCIA. She stayed only a single season at the Metropolitan. For the next few years she toured the United States in recitals, and in 1913 she appeared with the CHICAGO OPERA. After World War I she returned to America for several concert tours; her last appearance in this country was in 1931. She then devoted herself to teaching singing in Milan. Her older sister, Eva, made successful opera appearances in Europe and America, retiring when she married the opera conductor Cleofonte CAMPANINI.

Teufel von Loudon, Die, see DEVILS OF LOUDON, THE.

Teyte, Maggie (born Tate), soprano. Born Wolverhampton, Eng., Apr. 17, 1888. After attending the Royal College of Music in London she studied privately for four years with Jean DE RESZKE. Her debut took place at the OPÉRA-COMIQUE in 1908 as MÉLISANDE. A year later in Munich she created the role of Suzanne in THE SECRET OF SUZANNE. On Nov. 4, 1911, she made her American opera debut in Philadelphia as CHERUBINO. For three seasons she was a permanent member of the CHICAGO OPERA, and from 1915 to 1917 she appeared with the BOSTON OPERA. After World War I she toured extensively in song recitals, becoming an outstanding interpreter of French songs. She returned to opera on Mar. 25, 1948, singing Mélisande with the NEW YORK CITY OPERA COMPANY, and in 1951 she appeared with Kirsten FLAGSTAD in a performance of DIDO AND AENEAS in London. For her services to French music during World War II, she was decorated with the Croix de Lorraine in 1945.

Thaïs, opera in three acts by MASSENET. Libretto by Louis Gallet, based on the novel of the same name by Anatole FRANCE. Premiere: Paris Opéra, Mar. 16, 1894. American premiere: Manhattan Opera House, New York, Nov. 25, 1907.

Characters: Thaïs, a courtesan (soprano), a role created by Sybil SANDERSON; Athanaël, a cenobite monk (baritone); Nicias, a wealthy Alexandrian (tenor); Crobyle, his slave (soprano); Myrtale, another slave (mezzo-soprano); Palemon, an old monk (bass); La Charmeuse, a dancer (soprano); Albine, an abbess (mezzosoprano); cenobites; actors; dancers; citizens of Alexandria. The setting is Egypt in the fourth century.

Act I, Scene 1. A cenobite community. A peaceful overture depicts night over the Nile River. Back from Alexandria, Athanaël tells his associates about the evil prevailing in that city, and the destructive influence of the courtesan Thaïs. Athanaël dreams that Thaïs is performing a sensual dance. He awakens with horror. Now determined to convert Thaïs and refusing to be dissuaded by Palemon's arguments, he sets out for Alexandria.

Scene 2. Nicias' house in Alexandria. Athanaël arrives in the city ("Hélas! l'enfant encore") and laments that it should have become so degenerate ("Voilà donc la terrible cité"). When Nicias appears, Athanaël welcomes his old friend warmly. Nicias is cynical when Athanaël tells him he has come to convert Thaïs, but for the sake of his friendship—and despite his own infatuation with the courtesan—he offers to help. With the help of two attractive slave girls, he fits out the monk in handsome clothes. When Thaïs arrives,

Athanaël is at first stunned by her beauty. She learns from Nicias that Athanaël is a philosopher who voluntarily lives in the desert and who has come to save her soul. Athanaël explains further that his teachings embrace the rejection of the flesh. Thaïs mockingly replies that her religion is that of love. Provocatively she suggests to the monk that he try the delights she offers. Athanaël, horrified, rushes from the house.

Act II, Scene 1. Thaïs' house. Thaïs meditates on her world-weariness ("Ah! je suis seule"). She begs her mirror to tell her again that she is beautiful (Air of the Mirror: "Dis-moi que je suis belle"). Athanaël interrupts her reveries. While marveling at her beauty, he remains inflexible in his resolve to save her. When Thaïs tries to lure him into making love to her, Athanaël reveals that he is really a monk and will be her savior. A sudden fear seizes Thaïs, she falls on her knees and begs for mercy. Exultant, the monk promises her a new joy as the bride of Christ. From a distance comes Nicias' voice, calling to her. Recovered from her temporary fear, Thaïs exclaims she is and always will be a courtesan and has no use for God.

Scene 2. Before Thaïs' house. Preceding the rise of the curtain, the orchestra plays the celebrated Meditation, the beautiful melody symbolic of Thais' spiritual regeneration. Weary and spent from a night of revelry, Thaïs approaches Athanaël and confesses to him that her life has been wasted. She is ready to follow Athanaël, but begs that she may take with her a statue of Eros ("L'amour est une vertu rare"). When the monk learns that this statue was a gift from Nicias, he smashes it; then, entering the courtesan's house, he destroys all the other symbols of physical pleasures. Meanwhile Nicias and his friends appear, continuing their revelry. Voluptuous dances are performed, including one by La Charmeuse. When Athanaël and Thaïs emerge from the house, they announce that the old Thaïs is dead and that a new spiritual woman has arisen in her place. Learning that the monk intends to take Thaïs away, the crowd rushes at Athanaël to kill him. Nicias saves the situation by throwing gold coins. In the mad scramble for them, the people forget Thaïs.

Act III, Scene 1. A desert oasis. An orchestral prelude depicts the suffering of Thaïs and Athanaël during their arduous trek across the desert. Thaïs is in a state of exhaustion, but the monk urges her on, insisting she must mortify her flesh. But at the sight of her bleeding feet, Athanaël is filled with pity. He bathes her feet and brings her fruit and water. Thaïs now enters a state of exaltation. When nuns appear, Athanaël tells them he has brought them a sinner. The Abbess Albine and her sisters conduct Thaïs to a cell in their convent. At her departure Athanaël is tortured by the thought that he will never again see Thaïs.

Scene 2. The cenobite community. Athanaël confesses to Palemon that in saving Thaïs he has lost his soul. He cannot drive Thaïs from his mind ("En vain j'ai flagellé ma chair"). When Palemon leaves, Athanaël prays, but as he does so he sees Thaïs in a vision, sensuous and irresistible. Voices now proclaim that Thaïs must die. Horrified, Athanaël rushes away, determined to see her again.

Scene 3. The convent garden. A repetition of the Meditation marks the change of scene. Thaïs is dying, surrounded by nuns. When Athanaël arrives, the nuns leave the monk and Thaïs alone. The monk pleads for Thaïs to return to Alexandria with him. Gently Thaïs recalls their spiritual regeneration through the long journey in the desert; she has finally found peace (Death of Thaïs: "Te souvient-il du lumineux voyage"). Athanaël now tries to convince her that the only truth lies in physical pleasures. Thaïs raises herself, seeing a vision of Paradise ("Deux seraphins aux blanches ailes"). Athanaël begs her not to leave him. She falls back dead. The monk is inconsolable in his grief.

In adapting France's novel, Louis Gallet made a compromise between prose and poetry by using a free-flowing rhythmic prose. Massenet's music adapted itself to Gallet's style. As Ernest Newman pointed out, the composer "cut his melodic periods to the size and shape of those of his librettist," making "his musical phrase-divisions, in the main, at the same points. The mood and feeling of play and music are also at one." The Gallet text, though it passes from sensual to spiritual love and back, from physical voluptuousness to religious exaltation, places greater emphasis on spiritual than physical joy. And Massenet's music, in its over-all sweetness and radiance, is more soulful than passionate.

Thale dampfen, Die, the Hunters' Chorus in Act III, Scene I, of WEBER'S EURYANTHE.

Thanatos, god of death (bass) in GLUCK'S ALCESTE.

Theater-an-der-Wien, one of the most important theaters in Vienna, founded by Emanuel SCHIKANEDER with funds provided by the merchant Zitterbach. Schikaneder had a statue placed on the roof of the building representing himself in the role of PAPAGENO, which he had created ten years earlier. The theater was intended to rival the Burgtheater and to replace the THEATER-AUF-DER-WIEDEN. It opened on June 13, 1801, with *Alexander,* a play by Schikaneder, with music by the theater's KAPELLMEISTER, Franz Teyber. For a while, the productions were mainly spectacles, but before long, operas were introduced. In 1803 CHERUBINI'S LODOÏSKA and *Der Bernardsberg* were performed. It was for this theater that Schikaneder commissioned BEETHOVEN to write his only opera, FIDELIO, introduced in 1805. SCHUBERT'S *Die Zauberharfe* was produced there in 1820. In 1821 Domenico BARBAJA became director of the theater, which now distinguished itself with performances of ROSSINI'S operas. Jenny LIND appeared there in 1846. The Theater-an-der-Wien then became a home for operettas, and it was there that such classics as DIE FLEDERMAUS, THE GYPSY BARON, and *The Merry Widow* were introduced. THE BARTERED BRIDE was produced there (its first performance in German) in 1893 and LA BOHÈME (the first PUCCINI opera heard in Vienna) in 1897. Between 1945 and 1954 the auditorium was used by the VIENNA STATE OPERA, while the main opera house was being rebuilt following its bombing during World War II. In 1961 the city of Vienna purchased the Theater-an-der-Wien, and on May 30, 1962, it opened under these new auspices with THE MAGIC FLUTE. The house is now used mainly for dramatic productions and operattas. But on May 24, 1970, *Fidelio* returned to the theater (conducted by Leonard BERNSTEIN) to commemorate the bicentennial of Beethoven's birth.

Theater-auf-der-Wieden, a theater built in Vienna in 1787 by Emanuel SCHIKANEDER, endowed with special privileges by the Emperor. It was here that THE MAGIC FLUTE was introduced. The theater closed in 1801.

Théâtre de la Monnaie, the leading opera house in Belgium. Modeled after Italian opera houses, it opened in Brussels in 1700, presenting works by LULLY and RAMEAU. The original theater was destroyed in 1820, and a larger one was built ten years later on the same site. Soon after reopening, the first performance in Belgium of LA MUETTE DE PORTICI had profound consequences, touching off the revolt against Dutch rule that resulted in Belgium's constitution as an independent state. The present building opened in 1856. The first significant era in the history of this company came between 1875 and 1899, when Lapissida was artistic director. This was the period that saw the premieres of MASSENET'S HÉRODIADE and REYER'S SALAMMBÔ and SIGURD. It was at this opera house that CARMEN, with Minnie HAUK singing the title role, achieved its first major success. In the last half century or so, the repertory has given prominence to operas by Belgian and French composers: for example, in a thirty-five-year period beginning with 1918 it presented forty-one new operas by Belgians, twenty-four by Frenchmen,

and only fifteen by other composers. Corneille du Thorant was director for many years, followed by Joseph Rogatschewsky (1953–1959). During Rogatschewsky's regime the premieres, unusual revivals, and novelties included AMELIA GOES TO THE BALL; *Atlantide* (Tomasi) ; THE BLUE BIRD; CARMINA BURANA; COMEDY ON THE BRIDGE; DAVID (MILHAUD) ; IVAN THE TERRIBLE; *Mozart and Salieri* (RIMSKY-KORSAKOV) ; OEDIPE (Enesco) ; LES PÊCHEURS DE PERLES; and *Tel fils* (Tichepin). Maurice Huismann, who succeeded Rogatschewsky, has been director since 1959. He inaugurated a new era for the theater by disbanding the company, initiating a program of inviting foreign companies to perform at the theater, and engaging prominent French and Belgian singers to perform in specific productions.

Among the notable world premieres given by the Théâtre de la Monnaie have been *Antigone* (HONEGGER) ; LES CHOËPHORES, staged version; *L'Étranger* (D'INDY) ; *Fervaal* (d'Indy) ; THE GAMBLER; GWENDOLINE; LES MALHEURS D'ORPHÉE; LA REINE FIAMMETTE.

Théâtre des Champs Elysées, a significant theater in Paris, frequently the home for opera performances. It opened in 1913 with presentations of BENVENUTO CELLINI and DER FREISCHÜTZ conducted by WEINGARTNER. In 1913 the house was used by DIAGHILEV for a season of Russian operas; Russian operas were also performed there intermittently in the 1920's and 1930's. In 1924 the theater offered a season of MOZART operas, and in 1929 it provided the auditorium for the visiting BAYREUTH FESTIVAL ensemble. Between Nov., 1936, and Feb., 1937, while the PARIS OPÉRA was being renovated, its company performed here. Opera performances have been presented from time to time since World War II.

Théâtre Lyrique, an opera house inaugurated in Paris on Sept. 21, 1851, under the direction of Edmond Souveste. It achieved its greatest significance as an operatic institution under the managership of Léon Carvalho between 1856 and 1860 and from 1862 to 1868. Rebuilt between 1860 and 1862, it reopened in the latter year. Carvalho was succeeded by Pasdeloup, who remained director until 1870. Rebuilt in 1874, the theater was renamed the Théâtre des Nations; the company of the OPÉRA-COMIQUE performed there between 1887 and 1898. In 1899 it acquired its present name of Théâtre Sarah Bernhardt and basically became a home for dramatic productions and occasionally for visiting foreign opera companies. Among the celebrated French operas introduced there were FAUST, LA JOLIE FILLE DE PERTH, LE MÉDECIN MALGRÉ LUI, MIREILLE, LES PÊCHEURS DE PERLES, PHILÉMON ET BAUCIS, ROMÉO ET JULIETTE, and LES TROYENS.

Théâtre National de l'Opéra-Comique, *see* OPÉRA-COMIQUE, L'.

Thebom, Blanche, mezzo-soprano. Born Monessen, Pa., Sept. 19, 1919. She received her training from Edyth Walker, MATZENAUER, and Lothar WALLERSTEIN. After making several concert appearances she made her opera debut at the METROPOLITAN OPERA on Nov. 28, 1944 (during its visit to Philadelphia), as Fricka in DIE WALKÜRE. For over twenty-five years she remained a principal soprano of the Metropolitan in the Wagnerian, French, and Italian repertories. She was also heard at the STOCKHOLM ROYAL OPERA, COVENT GARDEN, the SAN FRANCISCO OPERA, and at other major houses. In 1955 at the Metropolitan Opera, she created for America the role of Adelaide in ARABELLA. After supervising a performance of AIDA at the Municipal Theater in Atlanta, Ga., in 1967, she was appointed in 1968 manager of the short-lived Atlanta Opera Company.

Thésée, (1) young man (tenor) in love with Ariane but pursued by Phèdre, in MILHAUD's *opéra minute* L'ABANDON D'ARIANE.

(2) Phèdre's husband (tenor), loved by Aricie, in MILHAUD's *opéra minute* LA DÉLIVRANCE DE THÉSÉE.

Thill, Georges, tenor. Born Paris, Dec. 14, 1897. After attending the Paris Conservatory, he studied privately with Fernando de Lucia in Naples and Ernest Dupré in Paris. In 1924 he made his debut at the PARIS OPÉRA in THAÏS. He became an outstanding favorite at the Opéra, at COVENT GARDEN, LA SCALA, and the THÉÂTRE DE LA MONNAIE. On Mar. 20, 1931, he made his American debut at the METROPOLITAN OPERA in ROMÉO ET JULIETTE. He was unable to duplicate in America his European successes, and he stayed at the Metropolitan only two seasons. After leaving, he returned to sing in France. He starred with Grace MOORE in a motion-picture adaptation of LOUISE that was filmed in France.

Thomas, Ambroise, composer. Born Metz, France, Aug. 5, 1811; died Paris, Feb. 12, 1896. He attended the Paris Conservatory, where he won many prizes, including the PRIX DE ROME. In Rome he wrote several choral, orchestral, and chamber works. After returning to Paris in 1836 he concentrated on music for the stage. He completed his first opera in 1837, *La Double échelle*, produced at the OPÉRA-COMIQUE. He wrote a number of other operas for the Opéra-Comique and some ballets for the OPÉRA before achieving his first major success, with *Mina*, given at the Opéra-Comique in 1843. A succession of operas continued to flow from his pen, all of them performed at the Opéra-Comique, culminating with MIGNON, introduced on Nov. 17, 1866. *Mignon* was Thomas's triumph. In less than thirty years it was given over a thousand performances; on the occasion of its thousandth performance (1894) Thomas was honored with the Grand Cross of the Legion of Honor. After *Mignon,* his most important opera was HAMLET (1868), his first work since 1840 that was a grand opera rather than an OPÉRA COMIQUE. Introduced by the Paris Opéra, it was a major success.

In 1851 Thomas became a member of the Institut de France. Five years later he was appointed a professor of composition at the Paris Conservatory. In 1871 he succeeded AUBER as the director of the conservatory. His most important operas were *Mina* (1843); *Le Caïd* (1849); *Le Songe d'une nuit d'été* (1850); *Raymond* (1851); *Psyché* (1857); *Le Carnaval de Venise* (1857); *Mignon* (1866); *Hamlet* (1868); *Françoise de Rimini* (1882).

Thomas, Jess, tenor. Born Hot Springs, S.D., Apr. 8, 1927. While studying for his doctorate in educational psychology at Stanford University in Palo Alto, Cal., he was persuaded by Otto Schulman, professor of voice at the university, to consider opera as a career. In 1956 Thomas began studying voice with Schulman, following which he took lessons in Germany with Emmy Seiberlich. His opera debut, meanwhile, had taken place in 1957 with the SAN FRANCISCO OPERA, where he was heard as Malcolm in VERDI's MACBETH. For three years Thomas was a member of the Baden State Theater, making his German debut in the title role of LOHENGRIN at Karlsruhe. He appeared as Bacchus in ARIADNE AUF NAXOS in Württemberg and at the MUNICH FESTIVAL of 1960. In the summer of 1961 he sang the role of PARSIFAL at the BAYREUTH FESTIVAL, and in the fall of the same year he appeared as Radames in Wieland WAGNER's production of AIDA that opened the new German Opera House in Berlin. He returned to the United States to make his debut at the METROPOLITAN OPERA on Dec. 11, 1962, as Walther in DIE MEISTERSINGER. He has been prominently featured in the Wagnerian repertory at the Metropolitan Opera, the VIENNA STATE OPERA, other European opera houses, and at festivals; but he has also appeared successfully in various other operas, including DIE FRAU OHNE SCHATTEN, EUGENE ONEGIN, FIDELIO, and SAMSON ET DALILA.

Thomas, John Charles, baritone. Born Meyersdale, Pa., Sept. 6, 1891; died Apple Valley, Cal., Dec. 13, 1960. After completing music study at the Peabody Conservatory, he appeared extensively in operettas and musical comedies, achieving great success in Sigmund Romberg's *Maytime*. Thomas made his concert debut in 1918. Six years later he appeared in opera for the first time in a performance of AIDA in Washington, D.C. He went to Europe in 1925 and was acclaimed for his performance in HÉRODIADE at the THÉÂTRE DE LA MONNAIE. Thomas remained three years with that company, singing fifteen major roles; he appeared in the world premiere of LES MALHEURS D'ORPHÉE. After other successful appearances in London, Berlin, and Vienna, he returned to the United States in 1930 and sang with the Chicago Civic Opera. On Feb. 2, 1934, he made his debut at the METROPOLITAN OPERA in LA TRAVIATA. He remained with the Metropolitan through the 1942–43 season. In 1940 he appeared in the motion picture *Kingdom Come*. Successful also in concerts and on radio, Thomas subsequently served as executive director of the Santa Barbara (Cal.) Music Academy, and after that as manager of a radio station.

Thomas, Theodore, conductor. Born Essen, Ger., Oct. 11, 1835; died Chicago, Jan. 4, 1905. This pioneer in the development of musical culture in America made his conductorial debut in the opera house. As concertmaster of the orchestra at the ACADEMY OF MUSIC in New York in 1858, he took over a performance of LA JUIVE, when the regular conductor became indisposed. Though Thomas was known chiefly as a conductor of concerts, in 1885 he became conductor of the newly formed American Opera Company. Despite some brilliant performances, the company was a failure and collapsed after a single season. When it was succeeded by the NATIONAL OPERA COMPANY, Thomas continued as one of the conductors for a single season.

Thomas à Becket (Tommaso Becket), the Archbishop (bass) in PIZZETTI's L'ASSASSINIO NELLA CATTEDRALE, a role created by Nicola ROSSI-LEMENI.

Thomson, Virgil, composer, critic, and writer on music. Born Kansas City, Mo., Nov. 25, 1896. He took courses in music at Harvard University. After his graduation (1922), he continued his music study in Paris with Nadia Boulanger. He remained in Paris until 1932, devoting himself to composition. His first major work was a provocative opera, FOUR SAINTS IN THREE ACTS, the text by Gertrude STEIN. The work was introduced in Hartford, Conn., in 1934. Thomson's second opera, THE MOTHER OF US ALL (once again with text by Gertrude Stein) was commissioned by the Alice M. DITSON FUND and introduced in New York in 1947. Two decades later he completed a third opera, *Lord Byron*. Between 1940 and 1957 he was the chief music critic of the New York *Herald Tribune*. He has written scores for several motion pictures; one of these, *Louisiana Story*, won the PULITZER PRIZE for music in 1949. In 1966 he received the Gold Medal from the National Institute of Arts and in 1968 the Creative Arts Medal from Brandeis University. He was visiting professor of music at the University of Buffalo in 1965 and at the Carnegie Institute of Technology in 1966. Thomson has also written a number of books, including an autobiography entitled *Virgil Thomson* (1966).

Thorborg, Kirsten, mezzo-soprano. Born Venjan, Kopparbergslän, Sweden, May 19, 1896; died Falun, Sweden, Apr. 12, 1970. Vocal study took place at the opera school of the STOCKHOLM ROYAL OPERA, with which she made her debut as ORTRUD in 1924. From 1924 to 1930 she was a member of that company. She appeared with the BERLIN STATE OPERA between 1933 and 1935, the VIENNA STATE OPERA from 1935 to 1938, at the SALZBURG FESTIVAL between 1935 and 1937, and at COVENT GARDEN from 1936 to 1939. Her success in the RING dramas at Covent Garden in 1936 brought her a contract with the METROPOLITAN OPERA, where she made her debut on Dec. 21, 1936, as Fricka in DIE WALKÜRE. She remained with the Metropolitan until 1950 and was regarded as one of the leading Wagnerian mezzo-sopranos of her time. She was also acclaimed for her performances as Klytemnestra in

ELEKTRA and as Orfeo in Gluck's ORFEO ED EURIDICE. In 1944 she was appointed singer to the Swedish court.

Thousand and One Nights, *see* ARABIAN NIGHTS.

Threepenny Opera, The (Die Dreigroschenoper), comic opera in prologue and eight scenes by WEILL. Libretto by Bertolt BRECHT. Premiere: Berlin, Aug. 31, 1928. American premiere: New York City, Apr. 13, 1933. This cynical modern descendant of GAY's THE BEGGAR's OPERA was founded on the popular eighteenth-century work, which it follows only freely. The authors used *The Beggar's Opera* to point up the social, political, and moral decay of Germany in the late 1920's. In the prologue, a Soho street musician sings "Moritat," or "Mack the Knife" (the history of the highwayman Macheath), a song that became extremely popular in the United States in the 1950's. The plot then describes the marriage of Macheath and Polly; Macheath's conviction, imprisonment, and sentencing for execution; and his pardon by the Queen at the zero hour. The score is filled with popular tunes (a shimmy, blues, Tin Pan Alley-type ballads) together with classical-type arias, canons, and chorales. Besides "Moritat," the more popular numbers include the "Zuhälterballade," the "Kanonensong," and the closing chorale, "Verfolgt das Unrecht nicht zu sehr."

When first produced the opera had a run of some four-thousand performances in about one hundred and twenty German theaters. It was also made into a German motion picture. In 1952, the American composer Marc BLITZSTEIN brought Weill's opera up to date by writing new lyrics and adapting the text, but with no changes in the score. This new version had a six-year off-Broadway run and two national companies touring the United States.

Tibbett, Lawrence (born Tibbet) baritone. Born Bakersfield, Cal., Nov. 16, 1896; died New York City, July 15, 1960. He did not begin to study singing seriously until after he had made many church and light-opera appearances. His principal study took place with Frank La Forge and Basil Ruysdael. He made his debut at the METROPOLITAN OPERA on Nov. 23, 1923, as a monk in BORIS GODUNOV. He continued appearing in minor roles until there took place an event that has been described as "without precedent in the annals of the Metropolitan." On Jan. 2, 1925, at a revival of FALSTAFF, Tibbett had to serve as a last-minute replacement for the singer scheduled to appear as FORD. His exciting performance, both vocally and histrionically, elicited one of the most stirring ovations in the history of the opera house. That evening lifted Tibbett to stardom, and from then on he was seen in the principal baritone roles of many Italian and French operas; he sang in the world premieres of THE EMPEROR JONES, THE KING'S HENCHMEN, and PETER IBBETSON and in the Metropolitan premieres of JONNY SPIELT AUF, PETER GRIMES, KHOVANTCHINA, and SIMON BOCCANEGRA. He remained with the Metropolitan Opera company until 1950, a period in which he was also heard in London, Paris, Vienna, and Prague. At COVENT GARDEN he was heard in the world premiere of Eugene GOOSSENS' Don Juan de Mañara. Among his most celebrated roles were IAGO and SCARPIA. In 1937 at the Metropolitan Opera, he assumed all the evil-genius roles in THE TALES OF HOFFMANN. He made numerous appearances on radio programs and was starred in several motion pictures, including The Rogue Song and The New Moon.

Tichatschek, Joseph (born Tichacek), tenor. Born Ober-Weckseldorf, July 11, 1807; died Dresden, Jan. 18, 1886. WAGNER esteemed him so highly that he chose him to create the roles of RIENZI and TANNHÄUSER. He studied medicine before becoming a singer. He began his career as a member of the chorus of a small opera company, from which he graduated into singing minor roles. He began appearing in major parts in Graz and Vienna, but his reputation was established with the DRESDEN OPERA while he was a member of its company (between 1837 and 1870). In 1841 he appeared at the DRURY LANE THEATRE in London as ROBERT LE DIABLE and ADOLAR.

Tiefland, opera in prologue and three acts by D'ALBERT. Libretto by Rudolph Lothar, adapted from Terra Baixa, a Spanish play by Angel Guimera. Premiere: Prague, Nov. 15, 1903. American premiere: Metropolitan Opera, Nov. 23, 1908 (abridged). Pedro (tenor), a shepherd who lives atop a mountain in the Pyrenees, dreams that he will be sent a bride. The landowner Sebastiano (baritone) gives him Martha (soprano), on condition that he live in the lowland. The reason for the condition becomes clear to Pedro when he learns that Sebastiano has betrayed Martha. Her shame revealed, Martha begs the shepherd to kill her, but his love is too great. When Sebastiano tries to detain the girl, Pedro overcomes him in a fight with bare hands and then returns to his mountain with Martha. The most celebrated aria is the Wolfserzählung of Pedro in Act I, "Schau her, das ist ein Taler," describing a battle with a wolf.

Tiefland first became successful when it was given in an abridged form at the METROPOLITAN OPERA in 1908. After that it was acclaimed in England and throughout Germany. It was in this work that Kirsten FLAGSTAD made her opera debut in Oslo in 1913, and with it she also inaugurated her career as director of the National Opera in Oslo in 1959. It was revived by the NEW YORK CITY OPERA in 1948.

Tietjen, Heinz, conductor, opera producer, and administrator. Born Tangier, Morocco, June 24, 1881; died Bayreuth, Nov. 1, 1967. He began conducting opera performances in Treves in 1904, where he remained almost two decades, becoming the opera company's artistic director in 1907. After 1919 he held the post of artistic director with the Saarbrücken Opera and the Breslau Opera. From 1927 to 1943 he was the director of the Berlin Städtische Oper (BERLIN DEUTSCHE STAATSOPER), and from 1931 to 1944, artistic director of the BAYREUTH FESTIVAL. Between 1956 and 1959 he was affiliated with the HAMBURG OPERA, and in 1958 he returned to Bayreuth to conduct LOHENGRIN. He also staged Wagnerian performances at COVENT GARDEN in 1950 and 1951.

Tippett, Sir Michael, composer. Born London, Jan. 2, 1905. He attended the Royal College of Music, then came to the fore with various instrumental works that were Romantic in style and strongly influenced by Sibelius. He later developed his own idiom, in which Romanticism was combined with polyphony. His first opera, THE MIDSUMMER MARRIAGE, was produced at COVENT GARDEN in 1955 and returned there in a new production in 1968. This was followed by the opera KING PRIAM, produced at Coventry Cathedral in England on May 29, 1962, then performed at Covent Garden in June of the same year. In Dec., 1970, his opera *Knot Garden* was introduced at Covent Garden. He visited the United States in 1965 and again in 1967–68; during the latter period he appeared as guest conductor of the St. Louis Symphony. He was knighted by the Queen in June of 1966.

Ti rincora, amata figlia, *see* AU SECOURS DE NOTRE FILLE.

Tisbe, one of Cinderella's stepsisters (mezzo-soprano) in ROSSINI's LA CENERENTOLA.

Titania, queen of the fairies (speaking role) in WEBER's OBERON.

Titurel, retired king of the Knights of the Grail (bass), father of Amfortas, in WAGNER's PARSIFAL.

Titus, Roman emperor (tenor) in MOZART's LA CLEMENZA DI TITO.

Toby, Madame Flora's servant (mute) in MENOTTI's THE MEDIUM.

Toch, Ernst, composer. Born Vienna, Dec. 7, 1887; died Los Angeles, Oct. 1, 1964. The winning of the Mozart Prize in 1909 enabled him to attend the Hoch Conservatory in Frankfurt. Recognition of his talent came quickly. In 1910 he received the Mendelssohn

Prize and for four consecutive years the Austrian State Prize for chamber-music works. During World War I he served in the Austrian army. He emerged as an important composer after the war, with major orchestral and chamber works and a delightful CHAMBER OPERA, *The Princess on the Pea,* produced at Baden-Baden on July 17, 1927, and given in America for the first time on June 9, 1936, in New York. In 1932 he visited the United States for the first time, appearing as pianist with the Boston Symphony in a program including several of his works. After the rise of Hitler, Toch settled in the United States and became a citizen. He wrote music for motion pictures and taught at the University of Southern California. In 1954 he was visiting composer at the Berkshire Music Center at Tanglewood; in 1956 he received the PULITZER PRIZE for his *Third Symphony;* in 1957 the West German Republic honored him with its Grand Cross of Merit; and in 1963 he received the Austrian Cross of Honor for Science and Art. His operas: *Wegwende* (1925); *Die Prinzessin auf der Erbse* (*The Princess on the Pea,* 1927); *Egon und Emilie* (1928); *Der Fächer* (1930); *The Tale Is Told.*

Todd, Miss, the old maid (contralto) in MENOTTI's THE OLD MAID AND THE THIEF.

Tokatyan, Armand, tenor. Born Plovdiv, Bulgaria, Feb. 12, 1899; died Pasadena, Cal., June 12, 1960. He appeared in operettas in Paris before studying singing seriously in Milan with Nino Cairone. In 1921 he made his opera debut in Milan in MANON LESCAUT. In the same year he came to the United States and appeared with the SCOTTI Opera Company. On Feb. 14, 1923, he made his METROPOLITAN OPERA debut in the American premiere of Franco Vittadini's *Anima allegra.* He remained at the Metropolitan a decade, returning for three additional periods: 1935–37, 1938–42, and 1943–46. He appeared in other American premieres: those of LE PREZIOSE RIDICOLE, IL SIGNOR BRU-

SCHINO, and LA VIDA BREVE. He also made concert and radio appearances. After leaving the Metropolitan in 1946, he continued to sing in Europe.

To leave, to break, to find, to keep, a five-voice canon near the close of BARBER'S VANESSA.

Tolstoy, Leo, novelist. Born Tula, Russia, Aug. 28, 1828; died Astapovo, Russia, Nov. 20, 1910. Three of his novels have been made into operas: *Anna Karenina* by HUBÁY, *Resurrection* by ALFANO, and *War and Peace* by PROKOFIEV.

Tomb Scene, *see* FRA POCO A ME RICOVERO.

Tommaso Becket, *see* THOMAS À BECKET.

Tom Rakewell, Anne Truelove's sweetheart (tenor) in STRAVINSKY'S THE RAKE'S PROGRESS.

Tomsky, a count (baritone), friend of Herman, in TCHAIKOVSKY'S PIQUE DAME.

Ton coeur n'as pas compris, the love duet of Leila and Nadir in Act II of BIZET'S LES PÊCHEURS DE PERLES.

Töne, Töne, the trio of the nymphs in Richard STRAUSS'S ARIADNE AUF NAXOS.

Tonio, (1) Marie's lover (tenor) in DONIZETTI'S THE DAUGHTER OF THE REGIMENT.

(2) A clown (baritone) in LEONCAVALLO'S PAGLIACCI, a role created by Victor MAUREL.

Toreador Song, *see* VOTRE TOAST.

Torquemada, a clockmaker (tenor) in RAVEL'S L'HEURE ESPAGNOLE.

Tosca, opera in three acts by PUCCINI. Libretto by Giuseppe Giacosa and Luigi ILLICA, based on Victorien SARDOU's drama *La Tosca*. Premiere: Teatro Costanzi, Rome, Jan. 14, 1900. American premiere: Metropolitan Opera, Feb. 4, 1901.

Characters: Floria Tosca, an opera singer, (soprano), a role created by Hariclea Darclee; Mario Cavaradossi, a painter (tenor); Baron Scarpia, chief of police (baritone); Cesare Angelotti, a political plotter (bass); Spoletta, a police agent (tenor); Sciarrone, a gendarme (bass); a sacristan (bass); a jailer (bass); and executioner (silent); a shepherd (mezzo-soprano); towns-people; guards. The setting is Rome in 1800.

Act I. The Church of Sant' Andrea della Valle. The curtain rises after three chords always associated with Scarpia. Angelotti, fleeing from the police, hides in the church, unseen by anybody. Shortly afterward Mario Cavaradossi enters to take up work on a portrait of one of the worshipers who has caught his eye. He is unaware that his model is Angelotti's sister. In love with Tosca, Cavaradossi removes her miniature from his pocket and becomes rhapsodic over her beauty ("Recondita armonia"). As he starts painting again, he is accosted by Angelotti, his old friend, who asks for and gets his help. At the sound of Tosca's voice, Angelotti conceals himself. Tosca appears. The lovers exchange ardent sentiments ("Non la sospiri la nostra casetta"). She is concerned because, having heard whispering voices, she suspects that her lover has been having a secret meeting with a woman. Cavaradossi manages to calm her, and they make an assignation for the evening at his house. When Tosca leaves, Cavaradossi guides Angelotti out of the church to his own home, where he is to hide. Scarpia arrives, searching for Angelotti. The police chief comes upon a fan belonging to Angelotti's sister. When Tosca returns to spy on Cavaradossi, Scarpia shows her the fan and readily arouses her jealousy by suggesting it belongs to the woman of Cavaradossi's portrait. The church services now begin ("Te Deum"). As Scarpia kneels, he thinks of his forthcoming destruction of Cavaradossi and conquest of Tosca.

Act II. Scarpia's apartment. Scarpia is sending a message to Tosca, confident that he can win her love and jubilant over that prospect ("Ella verra"). Then he gets news that Angelotti cannot be found. Cavaradossi, who is brought in by the police, hotly disclaims any knowledge of the refugee's whereabouts. When Tosca appears, she rushes to her love, but Cavaradossi is led to an adjoining room so that the information may be forced out of him. Scarpia opens the door so that Tosca may hear her lover's anguished cries as he is being tortured. Unable to stand the cries, Tosca reveals that Angelotti can be found in Cavaradossi's garden. As Cavaradossi is brought back, the news comes that Napoleon has won a great victory at Marengo. Cavaradossi shouts with joy, but Scarpia surreptitiously orders him led to jail to be executed next morning. Now Scarpia tries to win Tosca's love. With anguish, Tosca muses on how cruelly fate has treated her, she who has devoted her life to art, love, and prayer ("Vissi d'arte"). Spoletta then brings tidings that Angelotti has killed himself at the moment of his capture. Scarpia suggests that Cavaradossi will be the next to die, unless Tosca wishes to save him. Tosca promises to give herself to Scarpia if Cavaradossi's life is spared. Scarpia summons Spoletta and orders a mock execution for the prisoner, secretly adding a counterorder. He now approaches Tosca to claim his reward. Tosca, believing that she has preserved her lover's life, plunges a dagger into Scarpia's heart.

Act III. The terrace of the prison castle. Cavaradossi, in his cell, prepares for death by bidding his memory of Tosca farewell ("E lucevan le stelle"). Tosca arrives. They touch each other's hands lovingly ("O dolci mani") and speak of their love. She shows her lover the passport she obtained from Scarpia before she took his life, explaining that Cavaradossi must fall as if dead when blank cartridges are fired at him. Cavaradossi is led to the wall and shot—not with blanks. Tosca is stunned as she discovers Scarpia's final treachery. Spoletta and soldiers come to arrest her. She evades them by climbing the parapet and hurling herself into space.

Sardou's blood-and-thunder drama attracted two other composers before Puccini set it to music. One was VERDI, who decided he was too old to undertake the assignment. The other was FRANCHETTI, who signed a contract with Sardou giving him exclusive rights to the play. Puccini became impressed with the operatic possibilities of the drama when he saw Sarah Bernhardt act it, but not until a decade later, when he read that Franchetti had acquired the opera rights, did he actively want to set the play. There followed a discreditable intrigue involving not only Puccini, but also Franchetti's librettist, ILLICA, and the publisher Ricordi. The conspirators were finally successful in convincing Franchetti not to write the opera. When Franchetti gave up his contract, Puccini made his own with Sardou. Understandably, Franchetti never forgave Puccini.

Tosca did not at first seem the kind of drama that suited Puccini's talent which, up to now, had been at its best in tender and sentimental plays. *Tosca* was lurid, filled with horror, sadism, murder, and suicide. However, with a true dramatist's instinct, Puccini changed his style to meet the demands of the play. His beautiful lyricism, however, was far from forgotten. The over-all effect of *Tosca* is one of compelling drama, but several of its arias are among the most memorable that Puccini ever wrote.

Toscanini, Arturo, conductor. Born Parma, Italy, Mar. 25, 1867; died New York City, Jan. 16. 1957. For over half a century he was a giant figure in opera performances at LA SCALA, the METROPOLITAN OPERA, BAYREUTH, and SALZBURG. He attended the Parma Conservatory from which he graduated in 1885 with the highest ratings. For a while he played the cello in various opera orchestras. The conductor of a touring company resigned just before a performance of AIDA in Rio de Janeiro on June 26, 1886. Toscanini left his seat in the orchestra and took over the baton. Without opening the score, he directed with such authority and brilliance that he was given an ovation. From that night on, Toscanini was the company's conductor; during the remainder of the tour he directed eighteen different operas, all of them from memory.

Back in Italy, he returned to the cello for a while but soon began to conduct opera performances with such distinction that he was acclaimed the most brilliant of the younger conductors. In 1898 he was given the most important operatic post in Italy: that of principal conductor and artistic director of La Scala. After his debut there on Dec. 26, 1898, leading DIE MEISTERSINGER, Toscanini helped write one of the most brilliant chapters in the history of La Scala. He enriched the repertory through the introduction of many rarely heard or new German, French, and Russian operas. He instituted rigorous rehearsals, and made exacting demands on every department. Such a standard of performance was realized that La Scala under Toscanini became one of the greatest of the world's opera houses.

During this period Toscanini remained only three seasons at La Scala. His regime came to an end with dramatic suddenness when at a performance of UN BALLO IN MASCHERA the audience refused to comply with his rule against encores. When the audience persisted in its cries for a repetition of an aria, Toscanini left the opera house in the middle of the performance and refused to conduct again. In 1906 he returned to La Scala, after promises had been made that every artistic demand would be adhered to. This time he stayed two seasons.

When Giulio GATTI-CASAZZA was engaged as one of the managers of the Metropolitan Opera in 1908, he induced Toscanini to come with him. Disturbed by his frequent clashes with La Scala officials, Toscanini welcomed a change of scene. On Nov. 16, 1908, he made his first appearance at the Metropolitan Opera, conducting *Aida*, "the finest performance of *Aida* ever given in New York," as one of the critics wrote. A month later he directed his first WAGNER performance in America,

GÖTTERDÄMMERUNG. Toscanini's performances at the Metropolitan set new criteria. He conducted twenty-nine different operas, including the world premieres of THE GIRL OF THE GOLDEN WEST and MADAME SANS-GÊNE, and such novelties as L'AMORE DEI TRE RE, ARIANE ET BARBE-BLEUE, GLUCK's *Armide,* and BORIS GODUNOV.

Toscanini resigned from the Metropolitan after the 1914–15 season. He had been involved in a Herculean struggle to achieve perfect performances, and he was weary of struggles with temperamental singers. When in 1920 plans were made to reopen La Scala after its period of darkness during the war, a group of wealthy patrons offered to pay all the bills if Toscanini would return as artistic director. Toscanini consented on the condition that his word would be the law. He now had a free hand in matters of repertory, number of rehearsals, selection of singers. Limitless financial and artistic resources were placed at his command. On Dec. 26, 1921, La Scala reopened with Toscanini directing FALSTAFF. Toscanini remained at his directorial post for eight years, a period that was another of La Scala's greatest. He resigned in 1929 because he felt he no longer had the physical strength to carry the crushing burdens of an opera house. His career was now devoted primarily to symphonic music. He became musical director of the New York Philharmonic and after that of the NBC Symphony Orchestra, which had been founded for him. On special occasions he returned to the theater: at the Bayreuth Festivals in 1930 and 1931, where he was the first Italian conductor, and at the Salzburg Festivals. He also led distinguished radio performances of operas (*Aida, Un Ballo in Maschera,* LA TRAVIATA, Act 2 of Gluck's ORFEO ED EURIDICE, *Falstaff,* among others) with the NBC Symphony. He led his last concert with the orchestra on Apr. 4, 1954—an all-Wagner program, following which he went into retirement, except for the making of a recording of *Aida.*

He died in his sleep. Following funeral services in New York his body was returned to Milan where on Feb. 18, 1957, it was put to rest in the family tomb at the city's central cemetery.

The one-hundredth anniversary of his birth was celebrated in Italy with gala performances in Florence, Parma, and at La Scala. The house where he was born was purchased by his children to be made into a Toscanini library and museum.

tote Stadt, Die (The Dead City), opera in three acts by KORNGOLD. Libretto by Paul Schott, based on a play by Georges Rodenbach. Premiere: Hamburg Opera and Cologne Opera (simultaneously), Dec. 4, 1920. American premiere: Metropolitan Opera, Nov. 19, 1921. This is its composer's most famous opera. The three acts are described as pictures, and are filled with dream sequences. Paul (tenor) is a widower who lives in the past with haunting memories of his dead wife. He meets Marietta (soprano), a dancer who is the image of his dead wife, and he falls in love with her; but he loves in her only that which reminds him of his wife. Marietta is determined to have Paul love her for herself alone. When she desecrates the memory of the dead woman by putting on her hair, which Paul has saved and cherished, Paul strangles her. But the murder turns out to be one of his dreams. He now realizes that he must forget his wife for good.

The opera was given highly successful revivals in Munich in 1956 and at the Vienna VOLKSOPER in 1967.

To this we've come, Magda's outburst following her frustrated efforts to gain an audience with the consul of a totalitarian state in MENOTTI'S THE CONSUL.

Tourel, Jennie, mezzo-soprano. Born Montreal, June 18, 1910. After studying with Anna El-Tour in Paris, and adopting as her own name an anagram of her teacher's, she made her debut as CARMEN at the OPÉRA-COMIQUE in 1933. The exceptional range of her voice enabled her to appear there during the next seven years in a great variety of roles. She made her American debut with the CHICAGO OPERA in 1936 and her METROPOLITAN OPERA debut on May 15, 1937, in MIGNON. This was the sole appearance she made at the Metropolitan in this period. In 1942 she was selected by TOSCANINI to sing in a performance of BERLIOZ' ROMÉO ET JULIETTE with the New York Philharmonic. She returned to the Metropolitan Opera in 1943 and for the next four seasons appeared there successfully in many roles, including that of Rosina in THE BARBER OF SEVILLE, which Metropolitan Opera audiences heard for the first time as ROSSINI wrote it, for coloratura mezzo-soprano. While a member of the Metropolitan she made guest appearances with the NEW YORK CITY OPERA during its initial season in 1944. After leaving the Metropolitan she sang in South America, at the Opéra-Comique, and at festival performances in HOLLAND, EDINBURGH, and Venice, creating the role of Baba in THE RAKE'S PROGRESS in Venice in 1951. She has also appeared extensively in recitals and as soloist with orchestras.

Tous les trois réunis (Stretti insiem tutti tre), trio expressing the joy of Marie, Tonio, and Sulpizio at their reunion, in Act II of DONIZETTI'S THE DAUGHTER OF THE REGIMENT.

Toye, Geoffrey, conductor and opera director. Born Winchester, Eng., Feb. 17, 1889; died London, June 11, 1942. After completing his music study at the Royal College of Music, he became a conductor of various musical theaters. From 1931 to 1934 he was the director of the SADLER'S WELLS OPERA and from 1934 to 1936 of COVENT GARDEN. He resigned from the latter following differences with Sir Thomas BEECHAM. He was the composer of an opera, *The Red Pen*, which was broadcast in London on Feb. 7, 1927.

Tozzi, Giorgio, bass-baritone. Born Chicago, Jan. 8, 1923. Following an extended period of vocal study with Giacomo Rimini and John Daggett Howell, he made his opera debut on Dec. 29, 1948, in the American premiere of THE RAPE OF LUCRETIA. Further vocal study then took place in Milan at the Conservatorio Giuseppe Verdi, the Scuola

Musicale di Milano, and privately with Giulio Lorando. In 1950 he made four appearances in LA SONNAMBULA at the Teatro Nuovo in Milan. He then made numerous appearances in various European opera houses and festivals, making his debut at LA SCALA in 1954 in LA WALLY. On Mar. 9, 1955, he made his debut at the METROPOLITAN OPERA in LA GIOCONDA. As one of the leading bass-baritones of that company since then, he has distinguished himself in such roles as SARASTRO, PLUNKETT, ARKEL, FIGARO, and HANS SACHS, as well as in the traditional Italian repertory, and he created the role of the Doctor in VANESSA. In 1961 he was heard in a coast-to-coast telecast of BORIS GODUNOV with the NBC OPERA company. He has also appeared with the SAN FRANCISCO OPERA and with the foremost opera companies of Europe. In the summer of 1957 he was starred opposite Mary Martin in a production of *South Pacific* on the West Coast; he also sang for movie actor Rossano Brazzi on the soundtrack of the motion picture.

Traetta, Tommaso, composer. Born Bitonto, Italy, Mar. 30, 1727; died Venice, Apr. 6, 1779. He was a pupil of Durante at the Conservatorio di Loreto in Naples. His first opera, *Il Farnace* (produced at the SAN CARLO OPERA on Nov. 4, 1751) was so successful that it brought him commissions to write six more operas. From then on he was a highly productive composer, completing almost fifty operas. Among the most important were two staged in Vienna: ARMIDA on Jan. 3, 1761, and IFIGENIA IN TAURIDE on Oct. 4, 1763. Between 1765 and 1768 he was director of the Conservatorio dell' Ospedaletto, and from 1768 to 1775 he worked at the court in St. Petersburg (successor to GALUPPI), where he staged many of his operas. Though pursuing a traditional course in the writing of his operas, he anticipated GLUCK in the dramatic strength of some of his scenes and in some of his methods.

Traft ihr das Schiff, Senta's Ballad about the legend of the Flying Dutchman, in Act II of WAGNER'S DER FLIEGENDE HOLLÄNDER.

Tränen, Tränen, sollst du nicht vergiessen, duet of Abu Hassan and his wife, Fatima, in WEBER'S one-act comic opera ABU HASSAN.

Transatlantic, opera in three acts by ANTHEIL. Libretto by the composer. Premiere: Frankfurt Opera, May 25, 1930. This was one of the first grand operas by an American to receive its premiere in Europe (it was sung in German). A JAZZ opera, it deals with an American Presidential candidate and his hunt for a beautiful woman. Most of the setting is in modern New York, with some of the scenes taking place in a Childs' restaurant, in the New York harbor into which a liner is entering, in a moving elevator, and in a bathroom where a lady sings an aria while taking a bath. The opera was thoroughly American in style and approach, utilizing what Antheil described as a "moving-picture technique": rapid action with events and incidents piling upon one another in rapid succession. The last act was subdivided into thirty scenes upon a "kind of constructivist stage, parts of which could be blacked out or lighted as they were needed."

Transformation Scene, the music accompanying the change of scene in Act I of WAGNER'S PARSIFAL from the forest to the castle of Monsalvat. After a march-like subject, the work reaches a climax with the penitence motive of Amfortas and ends with the love feast motive.

Transposed Heads, The, opera in six scenes by Peggy GLANVILLE-HICKS. Libretto by the composer, based on Thomas MANN'S novel of the same name. Premiere: Louisville, Ky., Apr. 3, 1954. In making the adaptation from Thomas Mann, the composer explains that "with the exception of a few connecting phrases here and there every line of the text is original Mann writing. . . . It was my aim to create grand opera on a chamber-music scale. The work is essentially a virtuoso piece for singers, the whole form and pacing coming from the vocal element as does the shape of a Baroque concerto from the solo elaboration. . . . Many of the tunes throughout the work are taken freely and in some cases directly from Hindu folk sources." The opera is set in India, where her husband and her lover are rivals for the love of Sita. They behead themselves. Commanded by the gods to replace the heads on the bodies, Sita puts the head of her husband on her lover's body, and the head of her lover on her husband. The problem of which of the two men is her legal husband becomes so complex that the three commit suicide.

Traubel, Helen, soprano. Born St. Louis, June 20, 1899. She began to study singing when she was thirteen with her first and only teacher, Vetta Kerst. Three years later she made her debut as soloist with the St. Louis Symphony. Though she was offered a contract by the METROPOLITAN OPERA in 1926, she turned it down, feeling she was not yet ready. She continued studying for the next eight years, preparing roles and singing in churches and synagogues. When she appeared as soloist with the St. Louis Symphony in an all-WAGNER program conducted by Walter DAMROSCH, the conductor was so impressed that he asked her to appear in the leading female role of his new opera, THE MAN WITHOUT A COUNTRY. When Traubel made her debut at the Metropolitan Opera on May 12, 1937, it was in the role of Mary Rutledge in Damrosch's opera.

After making many successful concert appearances, Traubel returned to the Metropolitan Opera on Dec. 28, 1939, appearing in her first WAGNER role, that of SIEGLINDE. She was such a success that for two years she divided the leading Wagnerian soprano roles with Kirsten FLAGSTAD. When Flagstad left the Metropolitan Opera in 1941, Traubel became the principal Wagnerian soprano of the company. Within a few years her reputation as one of the great Wagnerian sopranos of our time was firmly established. Traubel resigned from the Metropolitan after the 1952–53 season, following a disagreement over her right to appear in night clubs. Since then she has appeared in concerts, night clubs, on

radio and television, in motion pictures, and on Broadway in the Rodgers and Hammerstein musical *Pipe Dream* in 1955.

Traveling Companions, The, see ANDERSEN, HANS CHRISTIAN.

traviata, La (The Lost One), opera in three acts (but usually given as four) by VERDI. Libretto by Francesco Maria PIAVE, based on Alexandre DUMAS's *La Dame aux camélias*. Premiere: Teatro la Fenice, Mar. 6, 1853. American premiere: Academy of Music, Dec. 3, 1856.

Characters: Violetta Valery, a courtesan (soprano); Annina, her maid (soprano or mezzo-soprano); Giuseppe, her servant (tenor); Alfredo Germont, her lover (tenor); Flora Bervoix, her friend (mezzo-soprano); Giorgio Germont, Alfredo's father (baritone); Baron Douphol, Alfredo's rival (baritone); Gastone, Viscount of Létorières (tenor); Marquis d'Obigny, a nobleman (bass); Dr. Grenvil, a physician (bass); servants, ladies, gentlemen. The setting is in and around Paris, about 1840.

Act I. Violetta's house. A brief prelude contains two themes from the opera, one connected with Violetta's illness, the other with her poignant farewell to Alfredo. At a party Alfredo Germont is introduced to the hostess, Violetta, who invites him to sing a drinking song as the guests drink a toast. He complies, and she and the guests join in the refrain (BRINDISI: "Libiamo, libiamo"). When the guests leave the room, Violetta is seized by a fainting spell. Alfredo offers his assistance; he grows solicitous over her delicate health. He then confesses that he has loved her for over a year ("Un dì felice"). Violetta protests that she is not worthy of his love, but Alfredo grows more passionate. The guests now return to bid their hostess good night. When Violetta is alone, she muses about Alfredo's love and her own sympathetic reaction to it ("Ah! fors' è lui"). Then she proudly exclaims she lives only for pleasure and freedom ("Sempre libera").

Act II, Scene 1. A country house. Violetta and Alfredo are living together. He is overjoyed that she has renounced for his sake her former life, and he is grateful that she has taught him the meaning of love ("De' miei bollenti spiriti"). Annina confides that Violetta has been selling her jewels to support him. Enraged, he rushes off to Paris to raise some money. While he is gone, his father comes to denounce Violetta. He finds her to be a charming and generous woman, but even this does not keep him from trying to break off the liaison. He tells Violetta that his daughter, about to marry a nobleman, is threatened with desertion if the scandal surrounding the name of Germont is not terminated. Violetta first protests she cannot give up the man she loves ("Non sapete quale affetto"). Then, poignantly, she realizes that her affair with Alfredo must ultimately destroy not only all those related to him but Alfredo himself. She decides to yield to the demands of the old man ("Dite alla giovine"). She writes a letter of farewell to the man she loves. But before she can run away—and while the elder Germont is out of the house—Alfredo returns. She lies, telling him she is off to Paris to gain the consent of the elder Germont for the marriage, bidding him a tender farewell at the same time ("Amami, Alfredo"). Only after she leaves does Alfredo come upon her farewell letter. Believing she deserted him because she does not love him any longer and is lonesome for the gaiety of Paris, Alfredo is heartsick. His father reappears and tries to console him with reminders of their happy home in the Provence ("Di Provenza il mar"). But Alfredo is inconsolable.

Scene 2. Flora Bervoix's house in Paris. At a party women gypsies are dancing and singing ("Noi siamo zingarelle"). Alfredo is gambling and winning. Violetta is also a guest, having come with Baron Douphol. When Violetta and Alfredo meet, he ignores her and continues his gambling. But when the guests drift into the dining salon, Violetta approaches him and implores

him to leave the house before he gets into trouble. Alfredo promises to leave only if Violetta goes with him. She insists she is unable to do so since she is bound by a promise. Convinced that she will not go with him because of her tie to Baron Douphol, Alfredo calls loudly to the guests to return. Before their eyes he hurls his money at Violetta. The Baron challenges him to a duel. Alfredo's father appears and denounces his son for his outrageous behavior.

Act III. Violetta's bedroom. Dying of tuberculosis, Violetta reads a letter from the elder Germont in which he promises that Alfredo will be allowed to return to her. But Violetta knows it is too late. She bids the world farewell ("Addio del passato"). Alfredo arrives. He falls on his knees and begs Violetta to forgive him, for he has learned the truth about Violetta's renunciation of him. He promises her they will return to their idyllic home near Paris ("Parigi, o cara"). Violetta listens, then sinks back in her bed, exhausted. The elder Germont comes with a physician, but both are too late. Violetta emits a cry of anguish and dies.

An early biographer of Verdi, misled by a letter of the composer's, claimed that the premiere of La traviata was a fiasco, and almost every writer on the subject since has repeated this error. The reasons given for the failure, to quote the first edition of the present encyclopedia, were: "First, the opera was produced in contemporary costumes and scenery, and the novelty of seeing an opera in the dress of the day jarred the audience. Second, the principal tenor had a cold and was in poor voice. Third, the play was regarded as immoral. Fourth, the sight of a buxom soprano pretending to die of a wasting disease was ludicrous. The opera was withdrawn." This report is herewith withdrawn; for in 1964 an article in *Opera News* by Mary Jane Matz reported what she found out in Venice by searching through the files of LA

FENICE and the newspapers of the day, that the opera was costumed, according to the playbills and the still extant costume designs, in the period of Louis XIV; the tenor may have had an off day, but the soprano was vastly admired; the opera was highly praised; the composer took bows and was roundly applauded after every act; the opera was given ten times in a comparatively short season. Verdi may have been disappointed that *La traviata* was not the immediate thunderous hit that IL TROVATORE had been a few months earlier, but it was certainly no fiasco. And today, with the possible exception of AIDA, *La traviata* has enjoyed—or suffered—more performances in the great opera houses of the world than any other opera by the most frequently produced opera composer of them all. And on smaller stages it outstrips even *Aida*'s record, for it requires neither elephants nor brass bands to produce, but just fine singing.

The American composer, Hamilton Forrest, also wrote an opera based on Dumas's *La Dame aux camélias: Camille,* produced in Chicago on Dec. 10, 1930.

Tra voi, belle, Des Grieux's mocking serenade to all womankind, in Act I of PUCCINI's MANON LESCAUT.

Treasure Waltz, *see* HA, SEHT, ES WINKT.

Tremin gl' insani, Nabucco's mockery of the defeated Jews, in Act I of VERDI's NABUCCO.

Treulich geführt, the Bridal Chorus in Act III, Scene 1, of WAGNER's LOHENGRIN.

Trial, The (Der Prozess), opera in two acts by EINEM. Libretto by Boris BLACHER and Heinz von Cramer, based on the novel of the same name by Franz KAFKA. Premiere: Salzburg Festival, Aug. 17, 1953. American premiere: New York City Opera, Oct. 22, 1953. The two acts are subdivided into nine "pictures," carrying the following titles: The Arrest; Fräulein Buerstner; The Summons; The First Hearing; The Whipper; The Advocate; The Manufacturer; The Painter; In the Cathedral. "My object," the composer explained, "was to find a form that would be adequate to the course of the dramatic events. Neither an illustrating, VERISMO technique, nor a symphonic one, nor numbers seemed advisable. The single scenes represented unities which develop according to musical not literary principles." Joseph K., a respectable bank employee, is arrested for unexplained reasons. A chain of nightmarish incidents follows, until he is finally led to court and condemned, though still unable to uncover the crime he is accused of. A unifying element in the score is a series of recurrent rhythmic patterns. Some of the performers fill several different roles in order to emphasize the fact that "these Kafka characters are not so much separate beings as the embodiment of more general figures." One singer, therefore, is required to represent the three characters of Fräulein Buerstner, Leni, and the wife of the Law Court, and a single singer represents the individuals connected with the Court.

The American composer Gunther SCHULLER also wrote an opera based on Kafka's *The Trial*—THE VISITATION.

Trial at Rouen, The, *see* TRIUMPH OF ST. JOAN, THE.

Trial of Lucullus, The, (1) opera in one act by Dessau. Libretto by Bertolt BRECHT. Premiere: Berlin State Opera, Mar. 17, 1950. For a brief summary of the plot see below.

(2) Opera in one act by Roger Sessions. Text by Bertolt Brecht. Premiere: Berkeley, Cal., Apr. 18, 1947. In the realm of the dead, the shade of the Roman general, Lucullus, must stand trial before a jury of humble people before he can enter Elysium. Lucullus pleads his case by citing his military achievements. The jury, however, sees in his case only the dead, the wounded, and the pillaged lands that were the result of his victories, and they condemn him. Sessions' opera is almost entirely in a declamatory style.

Brecht had written the text originally in 1939 for radio performance as an indictment of Hitler.

Trinke, Liebchen, trinke schnell, the

drinking duet of Alfred and Rosalinde in Act I of Johann STRAUSS'S DIE FLEDER-MAUS.

Trionfi, a trilogy of three operas or "scenic cantatas" by ORFF. Premiere of complete trilogy: La Scala, Feb. 13, 1953. The three works are CARMINA BURANA, CATULLI CARMINA, and TRIONFO DI AFRODITE.

trionfo dell' onore, Il, OPERA BUFFA in three acts by Alessandro SCARLATTI. Libretto by Francesco Antonio Tullio. Premiere: Teatro dei Fiorentini, Nov. 26, 1718. American premiere: New York City, Nov. 11, 1954. This is one of the earliest comic operas in history, preceding PERGOLESI'S LA SERVA PADRONA by fifteen years. The central character, Riccardo, is a rake who makes love to and abandons two women, Leonora and Doralice. His escapades involve him in a duel in which he is wounded. This leads him to repent his ways and to marry Leonora. This work is a typical example of the Neapolitan school of opera composers, with its three-part Italian OVERTURE, DA CAPO arias, and *secco* and *stromentato* RECITATIVES.

Trionfo di Afrodite (The Triumph of Aphrodite), opera or "scenic cantata" by ORFF. Libretto by the composer, based on poems by Catullus, Sappho, and EURIPIDES. Premiere: La Scala, Feb. 13, 1953. American premiere: Houston, Tex., Apr. 2, 1956 (concert version).

This is the third of a trilogy of stage works collectively entitled *Trionfi* which includes CARMINA BURANA and CATULLI CARMINA. The *Trionfo di Afrodite* is more a description of a ritual than a dramatic composition. A young couple is being led to the wedding tent for their marriage ceremony in an impressive procession. There they submit to Aphrodite's laws. Upon the appearance of Aphrodite, the entire assemblage sings a hymn of praise to the goddess.

Triquet, a Frenchman (tenor) in Tchaikovsky's EUGENE ONEGIN.

Tristan und Isolde, music drama in three acts by WAGNER. Libretto by the composer. Premiere: Munich Opera,

June 10, 1865. American premiere: Metropolitan Opera, Dec. 1, 1886.

Characters: Tristan, a Cornish knight (tenor), a role created by Ludwig SCHNORR VON CAROLSFELD; King Mark of Cornwall, his uncle (bass); Isolde, Princess of Ireland (soprano); Brangäne, her attendant (mezzo-soprano); Kurwenal, Tristan's servant (baritone); Melot, King Mark's courtier (tenor); a shepherd (tenor); a helmsman (baritone); sailors; knights. The action takes place aboard ship, in Cornwall, and in Brittany in legendary times.

The prelude is made up of basic motives from the opera, principally the themes of the Love Potion, Tristan's Love Glance, and finally the so-called Deliverance by Death. The prelude is a sustained crescendo followed by a decrescendo, suggesting the growing passions of the lovers and their tragic fate.

Act I. Tristan's ship. Off-stage the song of a sailor is heard singing about an Irish girl traveling westward ("Westwärts schweift der Blick"). Isolde is upset, for although she is being taken to Cornwall to become King Mark's bride, she has fallen in love with Tristan, the King's nephew and representative aboard ship. When she sends for Tristan, he refuses to see her but sends Kurwenal instead. Bitterly Isolde recalls how she spared Tristan's life after he had slain her beloved Morold ("Wie lachend sie mir Lieder singen"). Aware that her love can never be satisfied, she directs Brangäne to prepare a death potion. Brangäne prepares a love potion instead. When Tristan finally appears, Isolde begs him to share with her a cup of peace. Though filled with foreboding, Tristan consents. They drink. As the love potion works its magic, they look at each other with overwhelming love, then cling to one another as the ship arrives at Cornwall.

Act II. A garden before Isolde's chamber. Though Isolde is now married to King Mark, the passion consuming her and Tristan has not abated. King Mark leaves for a hunting trip, but Melot is suspicious and intends to guide the hunters back and catch the lovers off guard. Brangäne guesses his intent, but Isolde is deaf to advice and warnings: she can think only of her reunion with Tristan. When he appears, they embrace passionately and give voice to their ecstasy ("Bist du mein?"), then succumb to their limitless love ("O sink' hernieder, Nacht der Liebe"). From a distance, Brangäne warns them to take heed ("Habet Acht!"). But they are conscious only of their overwhelming emotions. A scream of terror by Brangäne ("Rette dich Tristan") precedes the sudden arrival of Kurwenal, hurrying to warn Tristan and Isolde that King Mark is coming. The King appears, followed by Melot. King Mark is so grief stricken at this visible proof of Isolde's infidelity that he is incapable of anger ("Wozu die Dienste"). He asks Isolde if she is ready to follow Tristan wherever he chooses to go. When Isolde replies quickly in the affirmative ("Als für ein fremdes Land"), Melot draws his sword and challenges Tristan. Tristan makes no effort to defend himself and is seriously wounded.

Act III. The courtyard of Tristan's castle in Brittany. A brief prelude provides a somber tonal picture of the garden near the sea. Kurwenal is tenderly nursing the stricken Tristan. A shepherd passes, playing a reed pipe. When Tristan regains consciousness, Kurwenal explains how he has been brought here, insisting that Isolde will surely follow. Feverishly Tristan begs Kurwenal to scan the horizon for the sight of her ship ("Das Schiff! siehst du noch nicht?"). The pipings of the shepherd suddenly grow quick and gay. Kurwenal looks over the rampart and joyfully announces the approach of a ship. Tristan, wild with joy, struggles to his feet. The reunion is brief: as Isolde clasps her lover, he dies in her arms. A second ship brings King Mark, come to forgive Tristan and to allow the lovers to go their way together. Kurwenal, unaware of this, draws his sword and is slain by Melot. Isolde now bids her dead lover farewell (Liebestod,

"Love Death": "Mild und leise wie er lächelt"), then falls dead on his body.

Wagner completed *Tristan und Isolde* in 1859 in what might be called a breathing spell from the harrowing labors of composing his monumental RING cycle. *Tristan* itself is a work as vast in concept and design, as bold in execution, as revolutionary in its approach to operatic traditions, and as exacting in its demands on singers and orchestra as any of the *Ring* dramas. Wagner's thinking about the esthetics of the musical drama, his LEITMOTIV technique, and his new melodic and orchestral speech are as mature in *Tristan* as in the *Ring* and are realized with equal mastery. Indeed from certain points of view *Tristan* is a finer work than any of the succeeding dramas, with the possible exception of DIE MEISTERSINGER. There is in *Tristan* greater integration, dramatic unity, and clarity of design. Music and drama are one, as the single theme of human passion unfolds with shattering effect in both play and score.

The opera was not immediately recognized as the masterpiece it is. It waited six years for its premiere in Munich, when it was received so coldly that it was discarded after three performances. Actually it would have been dropped after one presentation had it not been for the influence of Wagner's patron, King Ludwig. Meanwhile, a projected premiere in Vienna had been abandoned after fifty-seven rehearsals; singers and orchestra insisted that Wagner's music was unsingable and unplayable. Yet time has placed *Tristan und Isolde* high on the list of enduring operas, largely because of all Wagner operas and music dramas it is one of the most appealing and affecting.

MARTIN'S LE VIN HERBÉ is a twentieth-century adaptation of the Tristan and Isolde legend.

Tristes apprêts, Télaire's air to Pollux in Act I of RAMEAU'S CASTOR ET POLLUX.

Tristram, Sir, *see* MICKLEFORD.

trittico, Il (The Triptych), trilogy of one-act operas by PUCCINI. Premiere: Metropolitan Opera, Dec. 14, 1918. The operas are: IL TABARRO, SUOR ANGELICA, and GIANNI SCHICCHI.

Triumph of St. Joan, The, opera in two acts by DELLO JOIO. Libretto by the composer. Premiere: NBC-TV, Apr. 8, 1956, under the title *The Trial at Rouen;* New York City Opera, Apr. 15, 1959, under the definitive title of *The Triumph of St. Joan* (first staged performance).

The composer wrote *two* operas under the title of *The Triumph of St. Joan.* The first with a text by Joseph Machlis, completed in 1949, was discarded as an opera, some of its material being appropriated for a symphony. The second is an entirely different work both in text and music, originally intended for television, then rewritten for the stage. The text is devoted mainly to Joan's trial at Rouen, with Friar Julien partial to Joan and Bishop Cauchon determined to destroy her. In her cell Joan refuses to follow the Friar's advice to submit to the authority of the Church. During the trial, which consumes the entire second act, Joan is condemned to die after she has proudly reviewed her military achievements. The opera ends with Joan burned at the stake. Following its staged premiere the opera received the NEW YORK MUSIC CRITICS' CIRCLE AWARD.

Troilus and Cressida, opera in three acts by WALTON. Libretto by Christopher Hassall, based on the poem by CHAUCER. Premiere: Covent Garden, Dec. 3, 1954. American premiere: San Francisco Opera, Oct. 7, 1955.

Characters: Calkas, High Priest of Pallas (bass); Antenor, Captain of Trojan Spears (baritone); Troilus, Prince of Troy (tenor); Pandarus, Calkas' brother (tenor); Cressida, Calkas' daughter (soprano); Evadne, her servant (mezzo-soprano); Horaste, Pandarus' friend (baritone); Diomede, Prince of Argos (baritone); priests; priestesses; Trojans; Greeks. The action takes place in Troy in or about the twelfth century B.C.

Act I. Before the Temple of Pallas in Troy. Trojan citizens are complaining of the futility of prayer and sacrifice in the winning of the ten-year war against the Greeks. Calkas, the high priest of Pallas, advises a negotiated peace, but the angry citizens drive him away. When the crowd disperses, Prince Troilus reveals his love for Calkas' daughter, Cressida. When Cressida appears, she rejects Troilus' bid for her love. Pandarus, Calkas' brother, offers to help Troilus win Cressida, but he needs little help. For when Cressida is alone she betrays the fact that she is truly in love with Troilus but fears to disclose her feelings out of shame for her father, whom she regards as a traitor. Calkas, indeed, deserts to the enemy, but Troilus is too much in love with Cressida for this to destroy his feelings.

Act II, Scene 1. The home of Pandarus. Cressida is being prepared for bed at her uncle's home. Troilus arrives. A passionate love duet between the two lovers follows.

Scene 2. The home of Pandarus. A brief orchestral prelude describes the turbulent emotions of the lovers. It is morning. Greek soldiers invade the household, and Troilus and Cressida go into hiding. The leader, Diomede, has come to claim Cressida and to use her as an exchange for Trojan prisoners. When he sees her, he is stunned by her beauty. Since the exchange agreement had been signed by King Priam, Cressida is compelled to fulfill her mission. She bids Troilus a tender farewell.

Act III. The camp of the Greeks. Ten weeks have gone by. Cressida is pining for Troilus, from whom she has not heard a word. Her father convinces her to marry Prince Diomede. Just before her marriage, Troilus appears and urges her to escape with him, but she refuses. An impressive sextet then reflects the emotions of each of the principal characters involved, those of Diomede, Troilus, Cressida, Pandarus, Calkas, and Cressida's servant, Evadne. Troilus condemns all women, attacks Diomede with his sword but is killed by Calkas, who stabs him in the back. Diomede now has a change of heart about Cressida. He orders her to be kept in the camp as a harlot, with Calkas returned to Troy in chains. Cressida bids her dead lover, Troilus, a final farewell, then stabs herself with his sword.

Once considered one of the most important operas by an Englishman in the twentieth century, *Troilus and Cressida* was commissioned by BBC-TV and had originally been intended for television transmission. Its world premiere, however, was given at COVENT GARDEN with the permission of BBC. The opera finds the composer at the height of his creative powers, and it proved a phenomenal success. Its strong suit is its eloquent lyricism, which prevails throughout the work, particularly in the passionate love music.

Trojan March, march music from BERLIOZ' LES TROYENS. In Part I of this opera (*La Prise de Troie*), it is triumphal music; in Part II (*Les Troyens à Carthage*), it is transformed into a dirge.

Trompeter von Säkkingen, Der (The Trumpeter of Säkkingen), opera in four acts by NESSLER. Libretto by Rudolph Bunge, based on the poem of the same name by Joseph Victor von Scheffel. Premiere: Wiesbaden, May 4, 1884. American premiere: Metropolitan Opera, Nov. 23, 1887. Just after the Thirty Years' War, the trumpeter Werner (baritone) is in love with the noble lady Maria (soprano), but her parents want her to marry Damian, a nobleman (tenor). During a peasants' attack, Werner proves himself a hero, while his rival betrays his cowardice; at the same time, Werner turns out to be of noble birth after all. The marriage of Werner and Maria now gets the blessings of her parents. Werner's aria in Act II, "Behüt dich Gott," is the best-known excerpt.

Troubled Island, The, opera in three acts by STILL. Libretto by Langston Hughes, based on his play *The Drums of Haiti*. Premiere: New York City Opera, Mar. 31, 1949. The hero is Jean Jacques Dessalines, who helped establish Haitian independence.

Trouble in Tahiti, one-act opera by BERNSTEIN. Libretto by the composer.

Premiere: Waltham, Mass., June 12, 1952. This comedy in seven scenes centers around the domestic bickerings of a typical American couple in a typical American suburb. Following a bitter exchange between husband and wife at the breakfast table, the husband goes off to his business and then to a gymnasium, while the wife goes to town to consult her psychiatrist and see a movie entitled *Trouble in Tahiti*. The couple continue to quarrel that same evening but after dinner decide to end their misunderstanding by going off together to see *Trouble in Tahiti*. The opera has had a number of presentations: during the BERKSHIRE MUSIC FESTIVAL at Tanglewood, Mass., on television (1952), and as part of a Broadway theatrical offering, *All in One* (1955).

trovatore, Il (The Troubadour), opera in four acts by VERDI. Libretto by Salvatore CAMMARANO, based on a play by Antonio García Gutierrez. Premiere: Teatro Apollo, Rome, Jan. 19, 1853. American premiere: Academy of Music, May 2, 1855.

Characters: Leonora, lady-in-waiting to the Queen (soprano); Inez, her attendant (soprano); Manrico, an officer serving the Prince of Biscay (tenor); Ruiz, a soldier in his service (tenor); Count di Luna, a nobleman (baritone); Ferrando, his captain of the guards (bass); Azucena, a gypsy (contralto); soldiers; nuns; gypsies; attendants; jailers. The action takes place in Biscay and Aragon in the middle of the fifteenth century.

Act I ("The Duel"), Scene 1. The palace at Aliaferia. Ferrando regales the soldiers of the Queen with the story of Count di Luna and his long-lost brother ("Di due figli vivea"): A gypsy, burned by the Count's father as a witch was avenged by her daughter, who kidnaped Count di Luna's younger brother. This happened many years ago, and it is believed that the stolen child was thrown into the flames that consumed the gypsy. As Ferrando finishes his gruesome story, a clock strikes midnight.

Scene 2. The palace gardens. Leonora reveals to Inez that a mysterious knight she had once crowned as victor in a tournament has recently been serenading her and that she has fallen in love with him ("Tacea la notte placida"). Inez fears that the troubadour will bring her lady misfortune. When the ladies leave the garden, Count di Luna appears. In love with Leonora, he has come to tell her of his feelings. In the distance he hears the serenade of the troubadour ("Deserto sulla terra"). Leonora has also heard the song and mistaking the Count for the troubadour she rushes to him ardently. When she recognizes her mistake, the Count becomes enraged and rushes into the shadows to challenge the troubadour to a duel. He proves to be Manrico, leader of a rival army. As Count di Luna and Manrico cross swords, Leonora faints.

Act II ("The Gypsy"), Scene 1. A gypsy camp in Biscay. Gypsies, working at anvils, sing as they swing their hammers (Anvil Chorus: "Vedi! le fosche notturne spoglie"). Nearby, Azucena recalls the time when her mother was burned as a witch ("Stride la vampa"). Some of the gypsies try to console her, but Azucena is bitter and urges Manrico, who is with her, to avenge this cruel murder ("Mi vendici"). When the gypsies leave to the strains of the Anvil Chorus, she tells Manrico the rest of the story: how she stole the infant brother of Count di Luna in order to kill him but instead, in her madness, threw her own babe into the fire. The story raises in Manrico's mind doubts about his own origin, but Azucena insists that he is rightfully hers, since she found him dying on a battlefield and brought him back to health. Manrico now reveals to Azucena that when he recently fought a duel with Count di Luna, for some inexplicable reason he spared the Count's life ("Mal reggendo all' aspro assalto"). The tale infuriates Azucena; she fiercely urges Manrico to strike down the Count ruthlessly. Ruiz arrives with words that Manrico must return to his troops. Man-

rico also learns that Leonora, believing that he has died in battle, is about to enter a convent. Azucena tries to restrain him from leaving, but Manrico pushes her aside.

Scene 2. The convent near Castellor. Count di Luna and his men have come to abduct Leonora. He speaks of his great love for her ("Il balen del suo sorriso"), then tells his followers he cannot live without her ("Per me ora fatale"). With a background of the voices of nuns in the Nuns' Chorus ("Ah, se l'error t'ingombra"), Leonora appears. The Count and his men seize her. Manrico and a band of henchmen arrive before the abduction. Leonora is ecstatic to discover that Manrico is alive ("E deggio e posso crederlo"). Manrico rescues her and bears her off.

Act III ("The Gypsy's Son"), Scene 1. A military encampment. Manrico has taken Leonora to Castellor, which is about to be attacked by Count di Luna and his men. The Count's soldiers sing a hymn to war and victory ("Squilli, echeggi la tromba guerriera"). Bitter that the woman he loves is with another man, Count di Luna vows to avenge himself. Ferrando now brings him the news that the gypsy Azucena has been captured. When the Count subjects her to questioning, she tells him of her past ("Giorno poveri vivea"). She tells him she is Manrico's mother. When he suspects that she is guilty of his brother's death, he condemns her to death by burning.

Scene 2. The fortress of Castellor. Manrico and Leonora are about to be married. Manrico promises he will be true till death ("Ah si, ben mio"). Ruiz brings information about Azucena's imprisonment and forthcoming execution. Manrico vows to save her ("Di quella pira"). His soldiers shout their allegiance.

Act IV ("The Penalty"), Scene 1. The palace at Aliaferia. Captured, Manrico waits in a cell. Leonora comes in disguise, hoping to catch a glimpse of her beloved. She prays that her love for him will sustain him through his suffering ("D'amor sull' ali rosee"). A bell tolls. Within the castle voices intone a prayer for the doomed prisoners (Miserere: "Ah! che la morte ognora") ; the solemn chanting impels Leonora to express her own concern for Manrico ("Tu vedrai che amore in terra"). When Count di Luna appears, she hides, to emerge boldly when she overhears him giving orders concerning the executions. Leonora offers herself in return for Manrico's life. When the Count accepts the bargain, she secretly takes poison.

Scene 2. Manrico's cell. Azucena, tormenting herself with recollections of her mother's death, is soothed by Manrico. They console each other with the hope that some day they may return to their happy mountain land ("Ai nostri monti"). After Azucena falls asleep, Manrico welcomes Leonora, who has come to tell him he is free to go. When she refuses to accompany him, Manrico learns the price of his freedom. While he denounces her for betraying their love, she sinks to the ground in agonizing pain. Manrico takes her in his arms. Learning that she has poisoned herself, he begs her to forgive him. Count di Luna enters the cell, takes in the situation, and orders Manrico's immediate execution. Manrico bids his mother a poignant farewell ("Ah, madre addio"). When the Count forces Azucena to watch the execution from the window, the gypsy, crazed with grief, cries out that Count di Luna has just killed his own brother ("Egli era tuo fratelli").

Though the Tiber River overflowed its banks the day that *Il trovatore* was first heard and Roman opera-goers had to wade through water and mud to reach the Teatro Apollo, the premiere was a triumph. "The public listened to every number with religious silence and broke out with applause at every interval," reported the *Gazzetta Musicale,* "the end of the third act and the whole of the fourth arousing such enthusiasm that their repetition was demanded." To this day the score brings undiluted plea-

sure to the listener. Verdi's genius gave him the wings to soar above the confusion of an involved libretto, the inspiration for some of the most celebrated pages in all Italian opera.

Troyens, Les (The Trojans), opera in five acts by BERLIOZ, divided into two operas (I. *La Prise de Troie;* II. *Les Troyens à Carthage*). Text by the composer, based on VIRGIL's *Aeneid.* Premiere of complete opera: Karlsruhe, Ger., Dec. 6, 1890. American premiere: Part I, New York City, May 6, 1882 (concert version) ; Part II, New York City, Jan. 13, 1877 (concert version) ; both parts, slightly abridged, Boston, May 27, 1955 (staged) ; both parts, complete, New York City, Dec. 29, 1959 (concert version). The complete *Les Troyens,* requiring five and a half hours for full performance, was heard for the first time as Berlioz conceived it in Sept., 1969, at COVENT GARDEN, under the direction of Colin DAVIS.

The first of the two operas, *La Prise de Troie (The Capture of Troy)*, retells the story of Troy's conquest by means of the wooden horse. The spirit of Hector then dispatches Aeneas to Italy to found a new kingdom.

The second opera, *Les Troyens à Carthage (The Trojans in Carthage)*, details the celebrated love story of Dido and Aeneas, which Henry PURCELL had also made into an opera some two centuries earlier. However, to Ernest Newman the main theme of this second opera is not the love affair but "the *Trojans*—the long drawn-out working out by the rival gods and goddesses of the irreconcilable destinies of Troy and Carthage and Augustan Rome."

One of the most celebrated vocal excerpts is the love duet, text taken from Shakespeare's *The Merchant of Venice,* "In such a night as this," from Part II. Often given at symphony concerts are the orchestral excerpts of the Trojan March, heard in both parts, and the Royal Hunt and Storm from Part II.

Tsar Berendey, the Czar (tenor) of the mythical land of the Berendeys, who encourages the Snow Maiden to go out and seek love in RIMSKY-KORSAKOV'S THE SNOW MAIDEN.

Tsar Saltan, The Legend of, *see* LEGEND OF THE CZAR SALTAN, THE.

Tsar's Bride, The, *see* CZAR'S BRIDE, THE.

Tu che la terra adora, *see* DIEU, QUE LE MONDE RÉVÈRE.

Tu che la vanita conoscesti del mondo, Princess Eboli's recollections of the joys she once knew as the beloved of Don Carlos, in Act V of VERDI'S DON CARLOS.

Tucker, Richard, tenor. Born Brooklyn, N.Y., Aug. 28, 1913. He studied with Paul Althouse, then served as cantor at the Brooklyn Jewish Center in New York and as leading tenor of the Chicago Theater of the Air. He made his debut at the METROPOLITAN OPERA on Jan. 25, 1945, as Enzo in LA GIOCONDA. Since then he has been a principal tenor of the Metropolitan Opera, besides appearing in other major opera houses, including LA SCALA, VIENNA STATE OPERA, TEATRO COLÓN, and COVENT GARDEN. He has appeared in over thirty principal tenor roles mostly in the Italian and French repertory, in which he has been generally acclaimed as one of the foremost tenors of our time. In 1949 TOSCANINI selected him to sing the role of Radames in the concert performance of AIDA he conducted with the NBC Symphony. Tucker is the brother-in-law of Jan PEERCE, another distinguished Metropolitan Opera tenor.

Tu la mia stella sei, Cleopatra's famous aria in HANDEL'S GIULIO CESARE IN EGITTO.

Tu m'as donné le plus doux rêve, duet of Lakmé and Gérald in Act III of DELIBES'S LAKMÉ, Gérald expressing horror as Lakmé is content to accept death.

Tu n'es pas beau, La Périchole's plea to Paquillo to escape from prison, in Act III, Scene 1, of OFFENBACH'S LA PÉRICHOLE.

Tu puniscimi, o signore, Luisa's despairing cries when compelled to write a letter in which she falsely confesses she loves Wurm and not Rodolfo, in Act II of VERDI'S LUISA MILLER.

Turandot, (1) a play by Carlo GOZZI that has been made into operas by numerous composers.

(2) Opera in two acts by BUSONI. Libretto by the composer, based on the Gozzi play. Premiere: Zürich, May 11, 1917. American premiere: Brooklyn, N.Y., Mar. 19, 1958 (concert version); New York City Opera, Mar. 25, 1962 (staged). Busoni originally wrote incidental music for Max Reinhardt's production of Karl Vollmoeller's version of the Gozzi play, given at the Deutsches Theater on Oct. 27, 1911. He then expanded his score into an opera.

(3) Opera in three acts by PUCCINI. Libretto by Giuseppe Adami and Renato Simoni, based on Gozzi's play in an adaptation by Johann Friedrich von SCHILLER. Premiere: La Scala, Apr. 25, 1926. American premiere: Metropolitan Opera, Nov. 16, 1926.

Characters: The Emperor Altoum (tenor); Princess Turandot, his daughter (soprano), a role created by Rosa RAÏSA; Timir, dethroned king of the Tartars (bass); Prince Calaf, the Unknown Prince, his son (tenor); Liù, a slave girl (soprano); Ping, Grand Chancellor (baritone); Pang, the General Purveyor (tenor); Pong, the Chief Cook (tenor); Pu-tin-Pao, executioner (baritone); a mandarin (baritone); Prince of Persia (baritone); priests; mandarins; people of Peking; imperial guards; eight wise men; slaves. The setting is Peking in legendary times.

Act I. Before the Imperial Palace in Peking. Princess Turandot has announced she will marry any man of noble blood who can answer three riddles; but he who tries and fails must die. The people listen to a mandarin pronounce the death sentence for a Persian prince who has failed his opportunity. In the crowd is an old man, Timur, who has been thrown to the ground. He is helped by Liù and by his son, Calaf. When the Persian prince is led to his execution the crowd cries out for mercy ("O giovinetto"). Turandot's appearance silences the crowd, which now falls to its knees. But Calaf remains standing; he condemns the Princess for her cruelty. He is also so moved by her beauty that he offers to try answering her riddles. Liù, who loves him, begs him to desist from this folly ("Signore, ascolta"), reminding him that the only thing that sustained her during his exile was her memory of him. Calaf consoles her ("Non piangere, Liù") but remains stubborn in his desire to win Turandot.

Act II, Scene 1. A pavilion of the palace. Ping, Pang, and Pong read the names of Turandot's victims and pray that she may desist from her game and find true love. A trumpet fanfare announces that a new candidate is ready for the test.

Scene 2. A square outside the palace. Turandot explains to a large assemblage the reason for her strange decree. Her grandmother had met an unhappy fate at the hands of Tartars. Turandot, consequently, has sworn to avenge this cruelty on all who aspire to love her. She now warns the Unknown Prince, about to be a contestant for her love ("In questa reggia") that he will be destroyed if he fails the test. Calaf accepts the conditions. One by one the riddles are presented, and one by one they are answered. The crowd acclaims Calaf ("Gloria, o vincitore"). Now faced with the necessity of marrying Calaf, Turandot begs him to release her from her promise. He offers to do so, but only if, by the following dawn, she can uncover his true identity. The people sing the praises of the Emperor ("Ai tuoi piedi ci prostriamo").

Act III, Scene 1. The palace gardens. The Emperor's heralds are scouring the city, trying to learn the identity of the Unknown Prince. There has been a royal edict that no one in Peking will sleep until this is accomplished. Calaf comments on this, then muses on how the Princess is troubled and how he plans to resolve her problems with a kiss ("Nessun dorma"). Timur and Liù are brought to the palace and ordered to reveal the Unknown Prince's name. Liù insists that she alone knows it and that not even the threat of death will com-

pel her to divulge it. When the executioner comes to seize her, Liù stabs herself and dies. Calaf now approaches Turandot and boldly takes her in his arms and kisses her. Turandot bursts into tears ("Del primo pianto") realizing she loves him and is awed when, for the sake of his own love for her, he is willing to accept death and free her of her promise. When he reveals his name, Turandot discovers that he is the prince of the hated Tartars and insists upon his death.

Scene 2. The pavilion of the palace. The Emperor is surrounded by his court. Turandot tells the Emperor that she has learned the prince's name. Turning to Calaf she jubilantly announces that it is—Love. Turandot and Calaf embrace and the people sing a hymn to love ("O sole! Vita! Eternità!").

Turandot was Puccini's last opera, and he died before he could finish it. Puccini's score ends shortly after Liù's suicide. The composer Franco Alfano completed the opera by adding a duet and the concluding scene, the version in which the opera is now performed. However, when TOSCANINI directed the world premiere at LA SCALA two years after Puccini's death, he insisted on performing the opera as Puccini had left it. Toscanini was carrying out Puccini's wish, made just before his death: "If I do not succeed in finishing the opera, someone will come to the front of the stage and say, 'At this point the composer died.'" When the music stopped, Toscanini turned to the audience and said, "Here the Maestro put down his pen."

Besides being his last, *Turandot* was also Puccini's most original opera. Never had his musical thinking been so advanced. Unorthodox scales, dissonances, timbres permeate the score, yet the tender and affecting Puccini lyricism is not sacrificed. His last opera proved that the composer was growing artistically all the time, that he had the courage to tap new veins in his indefatigable search for greater artistic truth.

Turco in Italia, Il (The Turk in Italy), opera in two acts by ROSSINI. Libretto by

Felice ROMANI. Premiere: La Scala, Aug. 14, 1814. American premiere: Park Theater, New York, Mar. 14, 1826. This is a kind of companion opera to L'ITALIANA IN ALGERI, with which the composer had enjoyed a tremendous success one year earlier.

The setting is Naples during the eighteenth century. A Turkish ship sails into the harbor of Naples. Its commander, Sultan Selim of Turkey (bass), falls in love with. Fiorilla (mezzo-soprano), a Neapolitan lady married to Don Geronio (bass). She is also attracted to him and entertains him at her home. When Geronio discovers them together, she admits her infatuation with the Sultan. Fiorilla and the Sultan plan to elope, but Fiorilla has a rival in the gypsy girl Zaide (soprano), which complicates matters. The girls fight over who is to get the Sultan, who proves more partial to Fiorilla, and he is willing to pay Geronio a handsome price for her. Geronio not only spurns the offer but threatens to kill the Sultan. But the latter is determined to get the woman he loves. At a masked ball the Sultan mistakes the disguised Zaide for Fiorilla and makes plans with her for elopement. When he discovers that "Fiorilla" is actually Zaide he appears more satisfied than disheartened. And Fiorilla, with a sudden change of heart, vows henceforth to remain true to her husband, the only man she really loves.

The principal arias include two by Fiorilla ("Chi servir non brama amor" and "Quando di primavera") and one by Don Narciso (tenor), a minor character in love with Fiorilla ("Perchè mai se son tradito").

Il Turco in Italia, long neglected, has enjoyed numerous significant performances in Europe following a highly successful revival in Rome in 1950 with CALLAS and STABILE. The MANNHEIM OPERA gave it a significant presentation in Jan., 1969.

Turgenev, Ivan, author. Born Orel, Russia, Nov. 9, 1818; died Bougival, France, Sept. 3, 1883. Turgenev's stories have been made into the following operas: Ippolitov-Ivanov's Asa, Alexander Kastalsky's Clara Militch, and Antoine Simon's The Song of Love Triumphant. The prima donna Pauline VIARDOT-GARCÍA wrote three operettas to Turgenev's librettos.

Turiddu, a soldier (tenor) in MASCAGNI's CAVALLERIA RUSTICANA.

Turiddu's farewell, see MAMMA, QUEL VINO È GENEROSO.

Turner, Claramae, contralto. Born Dinuba, Cal., Oct. 28, 1920. She studied voice in San Francisco with Nino Comel, Giacomo Spadoni, and Kurt Herbert ADLER. After appearing in several Gilbert and Sullivan operettas, she was engaged for a season by the SAN FRANCISCO OPERA in 1944–45. On May 8, 1946, she created the title role in THE MEDIUM in New York. This led to an engagement with the METROPOLITAN OPERA, where she made her debut as AMNERIS on Dec. 4, 1946. During the next four seasons she was heard at the Metropolitan Opera mostly in the French and Italian repertory, though occasionally in German operas, including SALOME. Between 1947 and 1955 and again in 1957–58 she was a principal contralto of the San Francisco Opera where, on Sept. 26, 1952, she sang in all three operas of PUCCINI's trilogy, IL TRITTICO. She has sung with other major companies in Europe, Canada, and Latin America, her repertory embracing some seventy-five roles. In 1955 she appeared in the motion-picture adaptation of the Rodgers and Hammerstein musical play Carousel.

Turner Eva, soprano. Born Oldham, Eng., Mar. 10, 1892. She attended the Royal Academy of Music in London for four years, following which in 1915 she made her debut with the CARL ROSA COMPANY, with which she remained nine years, rising from chorus member to leading roles. After additional study with Richard Broad, she was engaged by TOSCANINI to sing FREIA at LA SCALA in 1924. Beginning with 1928 she was frequently heard at COVENT GARDEN over a period of two decades. She also made appearances with the Chicago Civic Opera between 1928 and 1930, in Buenos

Aires, and various European cities. A remarkable vocal range combined with dramatic power brought her success in dramatic soprano roles in VERDI and WAGNER and in TURANDOT. Between 1950 and 1959 she taught voice at the University of Oklahoma in the United States and from 1959 to 1966 at the Royal Academy of Music in London. She was created Dame of the British Empire in 1962.

Turn of the Screw, The, opera in prologue and two acts by BRITTEN. Libretto by Myfawny Piper, based on the novel of the same name by Henry JAMES. Premiere: Venice, Sept. 14, 1954. American premiere: New York City, Mar. 19, 1958 (amateur performance); New York City Opera, Mar. 25, 1962. The text concerns the curse of evil that afflicted two children in the charge of a neurotic governess. They live in a house haunted by the ghosts of two former servants. One of the children, the girl, becomes a victim of terror, while the other, a boy, meets his death. In declamatory style, Britten's score is throughout dramatically gripping and high-tensioned. The acts are divided into sixteen scenes, before each of which an orchestral prelude serves to set the mood. Each prelude is constructed on a twelve-note theme based on intervals of fourths and fifths.

Tu se' morta, Orpheus' anguished lament upon Eurydice's second death, after he has yielded to her pleas to look at her, in MONTEVERDI's L'ORFEO.

Tu sul labbro, Zaccaria's prayer to God for guidance, in Act II of VERDI's NABUCCO.

Tutcha (or Toucha), a burgher (tenor) in love with the Princess Olga, daughter of Ivan the Terrible, in RIMSKY-KORSAKOV's IVAN THE TERRIBLE.

Tutta su me ti sposa, Manon's aria of regret at having brought disaster to the life of her lover, Des Grieux, in Act IV of PUCCINI's MANON LESCAUT.

Tutto nel mondo è burla, closing chorus of VERDI's FALSTAFF, commenting upon the fact that all the world is a joke.

Tu, tu, piccolo iddio!, Cio-Cio-San's farewell to her son before she stabs herself, in Act III of PUCCINI's MADAMA BUTTERFLY.

Tu vedrai che amore in terra, Leonora's expression of anguish over Manrico, having overheard that Count di Luna plans his execution, in Act IV, Scene 1, of VERDI's IL TROVATORE.

Tu vergine santa in voco, Giselda's prayer in Act I of VERDI's I LOMBARDI.

Twelfth Night, opera in two acts by David AMRAM. Libretto by the composer based on SHAKESPEARE's comedy. Premiere: Lake George, N.Y., Aug. 1, 1968. This opera had been commissioned to help celebrate the four hundredth anniversary of Shakespeare's birth (1564) by the Joseph Papp Shakespeare productions in New York. The venture fell through when the opera was half done and was put aside by the composer. He completed it on a second commission, this time from the LAKE GEORGE OPERA company. Amram's score is in a conventional idiom, neatly pointing up the comic elements in Shakespeare's play and made up for the most part of recitatives and arias. In her review in *Musical America,* Shirley Fleming singled out several excerpts for special attention: the bravura aria for viola, "Make me a willow cabin at your gate"; the expressive song for one of the clowns, "She never told her love"; and "a quite haunting setting of 'The wind and the rain' (which, incidentally, is the orchestra's opening statement and serves as one of the unifying motives throughout the opera)."

twelve-tone techniques, a system of musical composition developed and made famous by Arnold SCHOENBERG and used by him and other composers of the atonal school for operas and other compositions. This method calls for the construction of a work from a preconceived row of twelve different tones according to certain rigid rules. The following are some of the operas utilizing this idiom either in whole, in part, or in some variation: LULU; IL PRIGIONIERO; ULISSE; FORTNER's *In seinem Garten liebt Don*

Perlimplin Belisa; Josef Hauer's SA-LAMMBÔ and *Die schwarze Spinne;* BOULE-VARD SOLITUDE; KÖNIG HIRSCH; KRENEK'S *Karl V;* LIEBERMANN'S LEONORE 40/45 and PENELOPE; MOSES UND ARON; MONTE-ZUMA; and Sandor Szokolay's HAMLET. *See also* SERIAL TECHNIQUES.

Twilight of the Gods, The, *see* GÖTTER-DÄMMERUNG.

Two daughters of the aged stream are we, song of the two sirens in Act IV of PURCELL'S KING ARTHUR, as they try un-successfully to lure King Arthur.

Two Foscari, The, *see* BYRON, GEORGE NOEL GORDON, LORD.

Tybalt, Juliette's cousin (tenor) in GOUNOD'S ROMÉO ET JULIETTE.

Tyl, Father, a woodcutter (baritone) in WOLFF'S THE BLUE BIRD.

Tyl, Grandfather, Father Tyl's father (bass) in WOLFF'S THE BLUE BIRD.

Tyl, Grandmother, Father Tyl's mother (contralto) in WOLFF'S THE BLUE BIRD.

Tyl, Mother, Father Tyl's wife (con-tralto) in WOLFF'S THE BLUE BIRD.

U

Ubaldo, a knight (baritone) in GLUCK'S ARMIDE.

Über seine Felder, Arabella's simple folk tune, with which she amuses herself in the opening of Act III of Richard STRAUSS'S ARABELLA.

Uberto, principal male character (bass) in PERGOLESI'S LA SERVA PADRONA.

Udite, udite, o rustici, Dr. Dulcamara's aria in praise of his own genius, in Act I of DONIZETTI'S L'ELISIR D'AMORE.

Uhde, Hermann, baritone. Born Bremen, Ger., July 20, 1914; died Copenhagen, Oct. 10, 1965. Completing his vocal studies in Bremen, he made his de-but in that city in 1936 as Titurel in PARSIFAL. He was engaged by the MUNICH OPERA in 1942, where he remained two seasons. He returned as principal bari-tone in 1951 and distinguished himself in the German repertory. Between 1955 and 1961 he was a member of the METROPOLITAN OPERA, making his debut there on Nov. 18, 1955, as TELRAMUND. He was also heard in other major Euro-pean opera houses and at leading festi-vals, notably BAYREUTH, where he was especially admired as WOTAN. In 1949 he created the role of Creon in ORFF'S

ANTIGONAE at the SALZBURG FESTIVAL. He died of a heart attack on the stage of the Royal Opera in Copenhagen while performing the leading role in Niels Viggo Bentzon's new opera, *Faust 3.*

Ulisse (Ulysses), (1) Greek hero (tenor) in MONTEVERDI'S IL RITORNO D'ULISSE IN PATRIA.

(2) Opera in prologue and two acts by DALLAPICCOLA. Libretto by the com-poser, based on HOMER. Premiere: Berlin Deutsche Staatsoper, Sept. 29, 1968. It took the composer sixteen years to com-press Homer's epic into a workable libretto that comprises eleven scenes. James Helme Sutcliffe has called the opera a "think piece . . . about a man's search for himself and his discovery of (strangely) a Christian God." He sum-marizes the text as follows: "The opera opens with Calypso's lament after Ulys-ses' departure and continues with the hero's discovery by Princess Nausicaa and his arrival at the court of King Alcinous, where by flashbacks he tells of his adventures in the land of the Lotus Eaters, with Circe, and in Hades." The score is dodecaphonic, "derived from a single row, varied with hexa-

chordal permutations and substituting major sevenths for octave doublings."

Ulrica, a fortuneteller (contralto) in VERDI'S UN BALLO IN MASCHERA.

Una cosa rara (A Rare Thing), opera in two acts by MARTÍN Y SOLER. Libretto by Lorenzo DA PONTE, based on the story of the same name by Luis Velez de Guevara. Premiere: Burgtheater, Vienna, Nov. 17, 1786. This charming little opera was applauded by MOZART'S enemies (including Antonio SALIERI) as a check to the mounting success of THE MARRIAGE OF FIGARO. *Una cosa rara* was so successful that the Viennese public forsook Mozart's opera, which closed after nine performances. Mozart made an amusing quotation from this opera in DON GIOVANNI, where an orchestra entertains the Don with music and Leporello comments: "Hurrah!" That's *cosa rara.*" This opera by Martín contains one of the earliest successful Viennese waltzes. *The Siege of Belgrade,* an opera by Stephen Storace, written in 1791, was an adaptation of *Una cosa rara. Der Fall ist noch weit seltener!,* produced in Vienna on May 10, 1790, was a sequel to *Una cosa rara;* its music was by Schack and its text by SCHIKANEDER.

Una donna a quindici anni, Despina's coy description of the joys and art of love, in Act II, Scene 1, of MOZART'S COSÌ FAN TUTTE.

Una furtiva lagrima, Nemorino's aria in Act II of DONIZETTI'S L'ELISIR D'AMORE, in which he is moved to find tears in his beloved Adina's eyes, a sign to him that she loves him.

Una macchia è qui tutt'ora, Lady Macbeth's sleepwalking scene in Act IV, Scene 2, of VERDI'S MACBETH, where she is tortured by a guilty conscience for the murders she has committed to further her husband's ambitions.

Una povera ragazza, a famous aria from PICCINNI'S LA CECCHINA. In it the heroine, Cecchina, laments that she is just a poor, greatly misunderstood child.

Un' aura amorosa, Ferrando's aria sentimentalizing over the course of true love, in Act I, Scene 3, of MOZART'S COSÌ FAN TUTTE.

Un autre est son époux, Werther's air of desolation upon seeing his beloved Charlotte with her husband Albert, in Act II of MASSENET'S WERTHER.

Una vergine, un angel di Dio, Fernando's *romanza* confessing to Baltasar that he has fallen in love with an unidentified woman who passes regularly beneath his window, in Act I, Scene 1, of DONIZETTI'S LA FAVORITA.

Una voce poco fa, Rosina's aria as she reads a love letter from Lindoro in Act I of ROSSINI'S THE BARBER OF SEVILLE.

Una volta c'era un re, Cinderella's ballad as she prepares coffee, in which she recounts the tale of a king weary of single blessedness, in the opening of ROSSINI'S LA CENERENTOLA.

Un bel dì, vedremo, Cio-Cio-San's poignant aria expressing her belief that some day Pinkerton will return to her, the most famous aria in Act II of PUCCINI'S MADAMA BUTTERFLY.

Und du wirst mein Geliebter, duet of Arabella and Mandryka, expressing their interest in each other, in Act II of Richard STRAUSS'S ARABELLA.

Under the willow tree, a folklike tune sung by Erika and Vanessa in Act II of Samuel BARBER'S VANESSA.

Un dì all'azzurro spazio, a love poem by Andrea Chénier, which he delivers to the guests at the Chateau de Coigny, in Act I of GIORDANO'S ANDREA CHÉNIER.

Un dì, ero piccina, Iris' narrative to Osaka, repeating the idea told her by a priest that pleasure and death are one, in Act II of MASCAGNI'S IRIS.

Un dì felice, the love duet of Alfredo Germont and Violetta in Act I of VERDI'S LA TRAVIATA.

Undine, opera in four acts by LORTZING. Libretto by the composer, based on the story of the same name by Friedrich de la Motte-Fouqué. Premiere: Magdeburg Opera, Apr. 21, 1845. American premiere: Niblo's Garden, New York, Oct. 9, 1856. This was Lortzing's first serious opera and it was a major success. The knight Hugo von Ringstetten (tenor) marries Undine, daughter of a fisherman (soprano). He then discovers that she is a water fairy who can win herself a soul and immortality through the love of a faithful man. When Hugo is unfaithful with Berthalda (soprano), Undine returns to her watery realm, but on the day Hugo marries Berthalda, Undine appears and lures him to his death beneath the water. Significant arias: Undine's "Ich scheide nun" (Act I) and "Nun ist's vollbracht" (Act III), and Hugo's second-act ROMANCE, "Es wohnt am Seegestade."

Several other composers have made operas from the legend of Undine, the water sprite, including E. T. A. HOFFMANN, whose *Undine* was produced in Berlin on Aug. 3, 1816.

Und ob die Wolke sie verhülle, Agathe's prayer for heavenly protection as she is about to marry Max in Act III, Scene 1, of WEBER'S DER FREISCHÜTZ.

Une fée, un bon ange, Lady Angela's aria in Act I of AUBER'S LE DOMINO NOIR.

Une fièvre brulante, an air from André GRÉTRY'S RICHARD COEUR DE LION that BEETHOVEN used as a theme for his *Eight Variations in C* for piano, Op. 184.

Une Nuit de Cléopâtre, *see* GAUTIER, THÉOPHILE.

Une poupée aux yeux d'émail, Nicklausse's song about a mechanical doll that fell in love with a mechanical bird, in Act I of OFFENBACH'S THE TALES OF HOFFMANN.

Une voix mystérieuse, Irma's rhapsody over love and Paris in Act II, Scene 2, of CHARPENTIER'S LOUISE.

Unger, Caroline, contralto. Born Vienna, Oct. 28, 1803; died Florence, Mar. 23, 1877. She studied in Italy with various teachers, including Domenico Ronconi. In 1821 she made her debut in Vienna as DORABELLA. Three years later she sang the contralto parts in the first performance of BEETHOVEN'S *Ninth Symphony* and *Missa solemnis*. She appeared extensively in opera performances in Italy, where many operas were written for her, including BELLINI'S *La straniera,* DONIZETTI'S *Maria di Rudenz* and *Parisana,* MERCADANTE'S *Le due illustre rivali,* and PACINI'S *Niobe.* In 1833 she was an outstanding success at the Théâtre des Italiens in Paris. After marrying Fran-çois Sabatier in 1841 she went into retirement.

Unis dès la plus tendre enfance, Pylades's tender aria in Act II of GLUCK'S IPHIGÉNIE EN TAURIDE.

Un mari sage est en voyage, Helen's dramatic air in Act II of OFFENBACH'S LA BELLE HÉLÈNE.

Un matrimonio nobile, Geronimo's expression of delight upon learning that his daughter, Elisetta, is to marry a wealthy count, in CIMAROSA'S IL MATRIMONIO SEGRETO.

Un pauvre petit Savoyard, Antonio's ROMANCE, one of the outstanding arias in CHERUBINI'S THE WATER CARRIER. This number is the protoype of romances and ballads found in many other operas, such as Senta's Ballad in WAGNER'S DER FLIEGENDE HOLLÄNDER.

Un rat plus poltron, the gay ditty about a rat sung by the student, Wagner, in Act II of GOUNOD'S FAUST. It remains unfinished as Méphistophélès interrupts after a few lines.

Un tal gioco, Canio's aria maintaining that the theater and life are not the same and that his wife, Nedda, and any potential suitor for her love should not succumb to such a belief, in Act I of LEONCAVALLO'S PAGLIACCI.

Unter blühenden Mändelbäumen, Adolar's *romanza* recalling his beloved Euryanthe, in Act I, Scene 1, of WEBER'S EURYANTHE.

Uppman, Theodor, baritone. Born San José, Cal., Jan. 12, 1920. He studied voice with Steuart Wilson at the Curtis Institute in Philadelphia and with EBERT at the University of California. His debut took place at Stanford University in 1946 as PAPAGENO. He appeared at COVENT GARDEN in 1951–52, where he created the title role of BILLY BUDD, which he also performed in the NBC OPERA THEATRE version. He made his debut at the METROPOLITAN OPERA on Nov. 27, 1953, as PELLÉAS, and he has since been a leading baritone there in a wide variety of roles. He created the title role in THE PASSION OF JONATHAN WADE.

Urbain, Marguerite's page (mezzosoprano) in MEYERBEER'S LES HUGUENOTS.

Urban, Joseph, scene designer. Born Vienna, May 26, 1872; died New York City, July 10, 1933. He studied architecture in Vienna. In 1901 he came to the United States, where he subsequently designed for the Boston Opera company and, for many years, for some of the most successful productions at the METROPOLITAN OPERA. He also designed sets for COVENT GARDEN and the VIENNA STATE OPERA.

Urlus, Jacques, tenor. Born Hegenrath, Ger., Jan. 9, 1867; died Noordwijk, Holland, June 6, 1935. He was trained to be an engineer, but in 1887 he began to study singing seriously in Utrecht. After attending the Amsterdam Conservatory, he made his debut in Amsterdam on Sept. 20, 1894, in PAGLIACCI. He subsequently distinguished himself as a Wagnerian tenor, being acclaimed at BAYREUTH, the THÉÂTRE DE LA MONNAIE, and COVENT GARDEN. He made his American debut in Boston on Feb. 12, 1912, as TRISTAN and made his first appearance at the METROPOLITAN OPERA, once again as Tristan, on Feb. 8, 1913. He remained at the Metropolitan Opera through the 1916–17 season. His last important appearance took place at Covent Garden in 1924 under the direction of Bruno WALTER.

Ursuleac, Viorica, soprano, Born Czernowitz, Rumania, Mar. 26, 1899. Her principal vocal study took place with Lilli LEHMANN, who prepared her for the operatic stage. After making her debut at the VIENNA STATE OPERA in 1924, she was a member of the FRANKFURT OPERA between 1927 and 1930, the Vienna State Opera from 1930 to 1934, and the BERLIN STATE OPERA between 1933 and 1945. She also appeared at the SALZBURG FESTIVALS between 1930 and 1934 and again in 1942. She was so highly regarded by Richard STRAUSS that he chose her to create the roles of ARABELLA, Danae in DIE LIEBE DER DANAE, Maria in FRIEDENSTAG, and the Countess in CAPRICCIO. She also appeared successfully in several Wagnerian roles (notably SENTA and SIEGLINDE) and in operas by VERDI. She was the wife of the conductor Clemens KRAUSS.

V

Va, crudele, Pollione's air pleading for Norma's love, in Act I of BELLINI'S NORMA.

Vado, corro, duet of Norinda and Malatesta, in which they conspire against Pasquale by proposing to introduce him to the nonexistent beautiful sister of Malatesta, in Act I of DONIZETTI'S DON PASQUALE.

V'adoro, pupille, Cleopatra's air in HANDEL'S GIULIO CESARE.

Vainement, ma bien aimée, Mylio's AUBADE with choral accompaniment in Act III of LALO'S LE ROI D'YS pleading for his right to visit Rozenn on her wedding day.

Vaisseau fantôme, Le (The Phantom Vessel), opera by DIETSCH. Libretto by Benedict Henri Révoil and Paul Henri Foucher, based on Richard WAGNER'S scenario for DER FLIEGENDE HOLLÄNDER. Premiere: Paris Opéra, Nov. 9, 1842. Wagner wrote his scenario, intending to use it himself for an opera to be produced by the PARIS OPÉRA. But the Opéra's interest did not extend as far as his music. It bought only the scenario, turning it over to Dietsch. Wagner consented to this arrangement because of his poverty and because it did not preclude his writing his own opera later. Dietsch's opera was not successful. **Vakula the Smith,** opera in four acts by TCHAIKOVSKY. Libretto by Yakov Polonsky, based on GOGOL's story CHRISTMAS EVE. Premiere: St. Petersburg, Dec. 6, 1876 (original version); Moscow, Jan. 31, 1887 (revised version under the title *Tcherevicky,* or *Little Shoes*). American premiere: New York City, May 26, 1922 (revised). This was Tchaikovsky's fourth opera, preceding EUGENE ONEGIN by four years. It was a particular favorite with the composer, as is proved by the fact that he returned to it eleven years after having written it to make extensive revisions. The text follows the plot of Gogol's story more or less faithfully. Commenting on his revision, Tchaikovsky wrote: "I have composed some completely new scenes; all that was bad I threw out. What is good I have left, lightening the massiveness and weightiness of the harmonies." The revisions made a success out of what Tchaikovsky himself termed "a brilliant failure" when the first version was produced.

Va! laisse-les couler mes larmes, Charlotte's song of tears in Act III of MASSENET's WERTHER.

Valdengo, Giuseppe, baritone. Born Turin, May 24, 1914. His vocal studies took place in Turin and his debut in Parma in 1936 as Figaro in ROSSINI's THE BARBER OF SEVILLE. In 1939 he was engaged by LA SCALA and from 1946 to 1948 he was a member of the NEW YORK CITY OPERA. He made his debut at the METROPOLITAN OPERA as Tonio in PAGLIACCI on Dec. 19, 1947, remaining with the company until 1954. During this period he was also heard as Iago and Amonasro in performances of OTELLO and AIDA conducted by TOSCANINI over NBC and at the GLYNDEBOURNE FESTIVAL in 1955.

Valentin, Marguerite's brother (baritone) in GOUNOD's FAUST.

Valentine, St. Bris's daughter (soprano) in MEYERBEER's LES HUGUENOTS.

Valentino, Francesco (born Francis Valentine Dinhaupt), baritone. Born New

York City, Jan. 6, 1907. His principal music study took place in Milan, following which he made his debut in Parma as GERMONT in 1927. Between 1937 and 1940 he appeared at LA SCALA and between 1938 and 1939, and again in 1947, at the GLYNDEBOURNE FESTIVAL. He made his debut at the METROPOLITAN OPERA as Enrico in LUCIA DI LAMMERMOOR on Dec. 9, 1940, remaining with the company until 1961 and distinguishing himself in the French and Italian repertory.

Valery, Violetta, a courtesan (soprano), the heroine in VERDI's LA TRAVIATA.

Valhalla, the abode of the gods, in WAGNER's DER RING DES NIBELUNGEN.

Valkyrie, The (Die Walküre), *see* RING DES NIBELUNGEN, DER.

Valleria, Alwina (born Schoening), soprano. Born Baltimore, Oct. 12, 1848; died Nice, France, Feb. 17, 1925. She was the first American-born singer to appear in principal roles at the METROPOLITAN OPERA. After attending the Royal Academy of Music in London, she made her opera debut in St. Petersburg in 1871. Appearances followed in Germany, at LA SCALA, and at DRURY LANE in London. She was a favorite in London and was heard at HER MAJESTY'S THEATRE in 1877–78 and at COVENT GARDEN from 1879 to 1882. She made her American debut on Oct. 22, 1879, with the MAPLESON company at the Academy of Music in FAUST. On Oct. 26, 1883, she made her debut at the Metropolitan Opera, singing the role of Leonora in IL TROVATORE. In 1884 she joined the CARL ROSA COMPANY, being heard in the world premieres of MACKENZIE's *The Troubadour* and Arthur Goring Thomas' *Nadeshda.* She retired from the stage in 1886.

Valletti, Cesare, tenor. Born Rome, Dec. 18, 1922. His vocal training came from local teachers. Following his debut at Bari in 1947, he appeared at COVENT GARDEN in 1950 and in the same year was engaged by LA SCALA, where he remained for over a decade. On Dec. 10, 1953, he made his debut at the METROPOLITAN OPERA as Ottavio in DON GIO-

VANNI; he remained with the company until 1960. Though he went into retirement in 1967, he performed the role of Nero in MONTEVERDI's L'INCORONAZIONE DI POPPEA at the CARAMOOR FESTIVAL at Katonah, N.Y., on June 22, 1968.

Valzacchi, an intriguing Italian (tenor) in Richard STRAUSS's DER ROSENKAVALIER.

Valzer del bacio, waltz from the third act of CATALANI's LA WALLY. It has become a semiclassical repertory piece.

Vampyr, Der (The Vampire), opera in two acts by MARSCHNER. Libretto by Wilhelm August Wohlbrück, based on a French melodrama by Nodier, Carmouche, and De Jouffroy, in turn derived from a story by John William Polidori. Premiere: Leipzig, Mar. 29, 1828. Lord Ruthven (baritone), a Scottish criminal, escapes doom at the hands of the spirits for three years, on the condition that each year he bring a pure maiden for sacrifice. A vampire in disguise, he makes Ianthe (soprano) and Emmy (soprano) his victims before he is discovered and destroyed by a bolt of lightning.

Van Bett, Burgomaster (bass) in LORTZING's ZAR UND ZIMMERMANN.

van Dyck, Ernest, tenor. Born Antwerp, Apr. 2, 1861; died Berlaer-Lez-Lierre, Belgium, Aug. 31, 1923. After studying both law and journalism, he decided to become a singer. He studied with Saint Yves-Bax in Paris, then made his opera debut at the Théâtre Eden on May 3, 1887, in the French premiere of LOHENGRIN. After an intensive period of study with Felix MOTTL, he appeared as PARSIFAL at BAYREUTH in 1888 with outstanding success. He was immediately engaged by the VIENNA OPERA, where he remained a decade. He also made frequent guest appearances in other leading European opera houses; he was featured in the world premiere of *Der Evangelimann* in London in 1897. On Nov. 29, 1898, he made his American debut at the METROPOLITAN OPERA as TANNHÄUSER. He stayed at the Metropolitan through the 1901–02 season, acclaimed not only in the WAGNER dramas but also in the French repertory. In 1907 he managed a season of German operas at COVENT GARDEN, and in 1914 he appeared in the first performance in Paris of *Parsifal.*

Vanessa, opera in four acts by BARBER. Libretto by Gian Carlo MENOTTI. Premiere: Metropolitan Opera, Jan. 15, 1958.

Characters: Vanessa, a baroness (soprano), a role created by Eleanor STEBER; Erika, her niece (mezzo-soprano), a role created by Rosalind ELIAS; the old baroness, Vanessa's mother (mezzo-soprano); Anatol, a young man (tenor), a role created by Nicolai GEDDA; the old doctor (bass), a role created by Giorgio TOZZI; Nicholas, majordomo (baritone); a footman (tenor); a pastor (mime); servants; peasants; guests. The action takes place in or about 1905 in Vanessa's castle in a northern country.

Act I. Drawing room. Vanessa is impatiently waiting for a guest to arrive. She orders that the tower bell be rung to help the guest through a raging snowstorm, then asks her mother, the old baroness, and her niece, Erika, to leave the room so that she may be alone when the guest arrives. At long last a young man appears whom Vanessa, keeping her back to him, calls "Anatol" with deep emotion. Without turning around, she reveals that she has waited twenty years for her former lover, always confident he would return. She also entreats him to leave the house this very night if he cannot say he loves her. When the visitor, speaking for the first time, says that he believes he can love her, Vanessa whirls around to look at the owner of this youthful voice, and in violent rage she calls him a fraud. Feeling faint with shock, she calls for her niece, who assists her off to bed. While the women are gone, the young man examines the rich furnishings, and when Erika returns he explains that while he is not the Anatol whom Vanessa had expected, he is another Anatol—the son of the Anatol, now dead, whom Vanessa had loved twenty years before. He adds that he is sure that if Vanessa knew who he is, she would permit him to stay in the castle on such a bad night. Erika acquiesces in this idea; and Anatol, carefully observing Erika's youthful charm, calmly sits down to the dinner that had been laid out for his father.

Act II. The drawing room. A month has passed. Erika confesses to her grandmother that she had an affair with Anatol the night he arrived but that she does not love him. In fact she knows that Vanessa has fallen in love with him. Vanessa and Anatol return from skating in a happy mood, a mood intensified when a visiting doctor tries to teach Vanessa and Erika some dancing steps and encourages Vanessa and Erika to sing a folk tune, "Under the willow tree." Later Vanessa expresses the ambition to marry Anatol, even though the grandmother feels that Anatol should become Erika's husband. Upon severe questioning from the grandmother, Anatol finally expresses his readiness to marry Erika even though he does not love her. Perhaps, he says, love will come later. Left alone, Erika breaks down and insists to herself that it is Vanessa Anatol must accept as wife since Vanessa has been waiting for so many years.

Act III. Entrance hall. At a New Year's Eve ball, the engagement of Anatol and Vanessa is to be announced. Peasants are dancing, and the ballroom, off-stage, is heard to be alive with gaiety and music. While this is going on, Erika comes down the steps staggering, muttering that Anatol's child must not be brought into life. She rushes out of the house, while the dancing and the music continue in the ballroom.

Act IV, Scene 1. Erika's bedroom. Erika, having been found unconscious in a ravine outside the castle, is being carried into her bedroom. She has suffered a miscarriage, as she reveals to her grandmother, and is comforted by the belief that neither Vanessa nor Anatol is aware of what has happened or of her former condition.

Scene 2. The drawing room. Two weeks have gone by. Vanessa and Anatol have just been married and prepare to leave for Paris. The five characters reflect on what has happened in the canonic quintet, "To leave, to break, to find, to keep, to stay, to wait, to hope, to dream, to weep and remember" (Vanessa, Erika, the baroness, Anatol, and the doctor). When the wedding couple depart, Erika is left alone. She orders all mirrors draped and the gate shut to visitors. "Now it is my turn to wait," she says to herself.

Though *Vanessa* is Barber's first opera, it is a work of his full creative maturity, which reveals itself throughout in the mastery of his technique, in his uncommon gift of projecting the most subtle or elusive moods and atmosphere, in his dramatic power, and in many pages of soaring lyricism. In addition to "Under the willow tree" and the closing five-voice canon mentioned in the plot summary, Barber's score includes such notable pages as Erika's air in the first act, "Must winter come so soon?", Vanessa's love song in the second act, "Our arms entwined," and an orchestral intermezzo originally heard in the fourth act but now given in the third.

Vanessa was such a success when introduced that it returned to the METROPOLITAN OPERA repertory for several seasons after that, besides becoming the first American opera ever performed at the SALZBURG FESTIVAL (its European premiere, in 1958), where, however, it was less cordially received.

Vanna, Guido, commander of the Pisan army (tenor) in FÉVRIER'S MONNA VANNA.

Vanne, disse, Alice's ROMANCE in Act I of MEYERBEER'S ROBERT LE DIABLE.

van Rooy, Anton, baritone. Born Rotterdam, Jan. 1, 1870; died Munich, Nov. 28, 1932. After studying with Julius Stockhausen in Germany, he made his opera debut at BAYREUTH in 1897 as Wotan in the RING cycle. In 1898 he made his debuts in Berlin and London and on Dec. 14, 1898, his American debut at the METROPOLITAN OPERA as Wotan in DIE WALKÜRE. He remained at the

Metropolitan until 1908, heard in all the leading baritone roles of the WAGNER repertory, including that of Titurel in the American premiere of PARSIFAL. During these years he also sang regularly at Bayreuth and COVENT GARDEN. After leaving the Metropolitan, he became the leading Wagnerian baritone of the FRANKFURT OPERA. He also distinguished himself as a concert singer and a soloist in oratorio performances.

Vanya, Ivan Susanin's adopted son (contralto), in GLINKA'S A LIFE FOR THE CZAR.

van Zandt, Marie, soprano. Born New York City, Oct. 8, 1861; died Cannes, France, Dec. 31, 1919. She created the role of LAKMÉ. Her mother, Jennie van Zandt, sang at LA SCALA and at the Academy of Music in New York. Marie studied with Francesco LAMPERTI in Milan and in 1879 made her debut in Turin as ZERLINA. Successful appearances followed, particularly at COVENT GARDEN in 1879 and at the OPÉRA-COMIQUE in 1880. DELIBES wrote *Lakmé* for her, and she appeared in its first performance in 1883. An organized opposition at the Opéra-Comique contributed to discredit her at this time; on one occasion, the false rumor was circulated that she appeared on the stage while inebriated. On Dec. 21, 1891, she made her debut at the METROPOLITAN OPERA as AMINA; she stayed at the Metropolitan only one season. In 1896 she returned to the Opéra-Comique and revived there her earlier successes. Soon after this she married and went into retirement.

Va, pensiero, chorus of the Jews lamenting their fate, in Act III of VERDI'S NABUCCO.

Varesi, ,Felice, baritone. Born Calais, 1813; died Milan, Mar. 13, 1889. He created the roles of GERMONT, MACBETH, and RIGOLETTO in VERDI'S operas. His debut took place in Varese in 1834, following which he appeared in major Italian opera houses and in London in 1864.

Varlaam, a drunken monk (bass) in MUSSORGSKY'S BORIS GODUNOV.

Varlaam's Song, *see* IN THE TOWN OF KAZAN.

Varnay, Astrid, soprano. Born Stockholm, Sweden, Apr. 25, 1918. Her father, a stage manager, founded the first opera company in Oslo; her mother was a coloratura soprano. She came to the United States when she was five and later became a citizen. She joined the METROPOLITAN OPERA company in 1941. When Lotte LEHMANN was unable to appear as SIEGLINDE on Dec. 6, 1941, Varnay stepped in as a last-minute replacement. Six days later she made another unscheduled appearance, this time substituting for Helen TRAUBEL as Brünnhilde, again in DIE WALKÜRE. Until 1956 she appeared at the Metropolitan in leading soprano roles, not only in the Wagnerian repertory, in which she excels, but also in Richard STRAUSS'S SALOME and ELEKTRA and in Italian and French operas. She also appeared in the world premiere of MENOTTI'S *The Island God.* In 1947 she sang in the first performance of WAGNER'S entire RING cycle given at the TEATRO COLÓN in Buenos Aires. Her European debut took place in 1951 at the FLORENCE MAY MUSIC FESTIVAL, when she sang in VERDI'S MACBETH. The same summer she sang at the BAYREUTH FESTIVAL—the first of many such appearances. She was the first American artist to sing Brünnhilde at Bayreuth. She has sung in other opera houses of Europe and South America. In 1951 she was selected by the United States State Department to appear at the BERLIN OPERA in the Allied Festival of the Arts.

Varviso, Silvio, conductor. Born Zürich, Feb. 26, 1924. He studied conducting at the Zürich Conservatory, following which he led performances at St. Gallen and Basel in Switzerland. Between 1958 and 1961 he was a guest conductor of the BERLIN DEUTSCHE STAATSOPER. He made his American debut with the SAN FRANCISCO OPERA on Sept. 15, 1959, in GLUCK'S ORFEO ED EURIDICE, remaining with the company two seasons. After making his debut at the METROPOLITAN OPERA on Nov. 26, 1961, in LUCIA DI LAMMERMOOR, he remained one of the permanent conductors of the company.

Vassilenko, Sergei, composer. Born Moscow, Mar. 30, 1872; died there Mar. 11, 1956. He attended the Moscow Conservatory, his teachers including Sergei Taneiev and Ippolitov-Ivanov. As his graduation exercise in 1900 he wrote an opera-oratorio, *The Legend of the Great City of Kitezh,* a subject used by RIMSKY-KORSAKOV two years later. In 1906 he became a professor at the Moscow Conservatory, where he remained over thirty years. His earlier works, most of them for orchestra, were national in feeling and style. He then became interested in the folk music of oriental people, and this influence prevails in his later works. In this vein he wrote his opera, *Son of the Sun,* about the Boxer Rebellion; it was introduced in Moscow on May 23, 1929. His other operas: *Christopher Columbus* (1933); *Buran,* in collaboration with Mukhatar Ashrafi (1938); *The Grand Canal* (1940); *Suvorov* (1941).

Vassili, Prince Alexis' rival (baritone) for Stefana's love, in GIORDANO'S SIBERIA.

Vaughan Williams, Ralph, composer. Born Down Ampney, Eng., Oct. 12, 1872; died London, Aug. 26, 1958. His academic education took place at Charterhouse and Trinity College, Cambridge; his study of music at the Royal College of Music in London, with Max BRUCH in Berlin, and in 1908 with Maurice RAVEL in Paris. Meanwhile he had become acquainted with English folksongs. This music exerted such a fascination on him that he joined the Folk-Song Society and devoted himself to research in the field of folk music. His artistic development was profoundly affected; henceforth his compositions showed folk influences. His many orchestral works have placed him in the front rank of contemporary English composers. In 1914 he completed his first opera, HUGH THE DROVER, in which the influence of English backgrounds and folk music is again in evidence.

During World War I, Vaughan Williams served in the Territorial Royal Army Military Corps and also saw active service in the Artillery. After the war he became professor of composition at the Royal College of Music, a post he held with distinction for over three decades. He also completed many major works, among them THE SHEPHERDS OF THE DELECTABLE MOUNTAINS (1922), an opera-oratorio, and SIR JOHN IN LOVE (1929), an opera dealing with Falstaff. Some years later Vaughan Williams incorporated the first of these works in his opera THE PILGRIM'S PROGRESS.

In 1935 the composer received the Order of Merit and in 1942 and 1952 his seventieth and eightieth birthdays were celebrated throughout England with concerts of his works. Vaughan Williams visited the United States for the first time in 1922 to direct a program of his music at the Norfolk Music Festival. He made two later visits, one in 1932, another in 1954.

His operas: *Hugh the Drover* (1914); *The Shepherds of the Delectable Mountains* (1922); *Sir John in Love* (1929); *Job,* a masque (1930); THE POISONED KISS (1936); RIDERS TO THE SEA (1937); *The Pilgrim's Progress* (1951).

Va, vecchio John, Falstaff's boastful air about his powers over women, in Act II, Scene 1, of VERDI'S FALSTAFF.

Vedi, io piango, Loris' reminder to Fedora that he is being hounded by spies, in Act II of GIORDANO'S FEDORA.

Vedi! le fosche notturne spoglie, the celebrated Anvil Chorus of the gypsies, in Act II, Scene 1, of VERDI'S IL TROVATORE.

Vedrai, carino, Zerlina's consolation of Masetto after he has been thrashed by Don Giovanni, in Act II, Scene 1, of MOZART'S DON GIOVANNI.

Vedrommi intorno, Idomeneo's aria in Act I, Scene 2, of MOZART'S IDOMENEO.

Velluti, Giovanni Battista, CASTRATO soprano. Born Monterone, Ancona, Italy, Jan. 28, 1780; died Bruson, Feb., 1861. He was the last of the celebrated castrati. He achieved enormous successes in Italian opera houses early in his career. In 1812 he appeared in Vienna and in 1825 in London. Since by 1825 the vogue for castrati had long since passed, his London appearance (in MEYERBEER'S IL CROCIATO IN EGITTO) was a failure.

Vendetta del pazzo, chorus of the courtiers expressing their anger at Rigoletto, in Act I, Scene 1, of VERDI's RIGOLETTO.

Vendulka, beloved (soprano) of Lukas, in SMETANA's THE KISS.

Vengeance Duet, see KOMM, DENN UNSER LEID ZU RACHEN.

Venice Festival of Contemporary Music (Festivo internazionale di musica contemporanea), a significant festival held in Venice in September once every two years in conjunction with the Venice *biennale*. Its first artistic director was Nando Balli, who was succeeded by Mario Labroca. Opera performances are given at the TEATRO LA FENICE. Among the operas receiving their world premieres here have been THE RAKE'S PROGRESS in 1951; THE TURN OF THE SCREW in 1954; INTOLLERANZA 1960 in 1961; and MALIPIERO's *Metamorfosi di Bonaventura* in 1966.

Venite, inginocchiatevi, Susanna's amusing lesson to Cherubino on how to behave like a lady, after dressing him up in women's clothes, in Act II of MOZART's THE MARRIAGE OF FIGARO.

Venus, Goddess of Love (soprano) in WAGNER's TANNHÄUSER.

Venusberg Music, the BACCHANALE in Act I of WAGNER's TANNHÄUSER.

Venus descendeth, see JOUR NAISSAIT DANS LE BOCAGE, LE.

Venus d'Ille, La, see MÉRIMÉE, PROSPER.

Vêpres siciliennes, Les, see SICILIAN VESPERS, THE.

Verachtet mir die Meister nicht, Hans Sachs's admonition to the victorious Walther in the singing contest that discipline and rules are important in the development of art, in the closing scene of WAGNER's DIE MEISTERSINGER.

Verdi, Giuseppe, composer. Born Le Roncole, Italy, Oct. 10, 1813; died Milan, Jan. 27, 1901. He was given his first music lessons by a local organist and by Ferdinando Provesi, town organist of Busseto. The Busseto townspeople recognized Verdi's talent and in 1832 raised a fund for him to go to the Milan Conservatory. Verdi, however, was denied admission there because he was too old and too poorly trained. Instead he studied privately with Vincenzo Lavigna. In 1833 he returned to Busseto, where he remained on and off for five years. He was appointed conductor of the Busseto Philharmonic Society, and in 1836 he married Margherita Barezzi. In Busseto he also completed his first opera, OBERTO. In 1838 he returned to Milan where on Nov. 17, 1839, *Oberto* was produced at LA SCALA and acclaimed. The young composer received from La Scala a commission to write three new operas, and the publishing house of Ricordi accepted *Oberto*.

The first of the new operas was a comedy, UN GIORNO DI REGNO. Given in 1840, it was a distressing failure, but its successor, NABUCCO, introduced on Mar. 9, 1842, was such a triumph that overnight Verdi became an idol. Dishes and items of wearing apparel were named after him; he could demand and get the highest fees for future commissions. In the decade between 1842 and 1851 he completed a dozen operas, the most important being I LOMBARDI, ERNANI, MACBETH, and LUISA MILLER.

Though he was now the most popular opera composer in Italy, he had not yet hit his full stride. A new creative period began in 1851 with RIGOLETTO. Verdi proved that his earlier operas had merely been the apprenticeship of a master, who now produced a series that became the most extensively performed and the best loved Italian operas of all time. *Rigoletto* was followed by IL TROVATORE, SIMON BOCCANEGRA, UN BALLO IN MASCHERA, LA FORZA DEL DESTINO, DON CARLOS, and AIDA. What distinguished these operas was not only their exceptional lyricism (each had an apparently inexhaustible fund of melodies and ensemble numbers) but their pronounced dramatic quality. Verdi was an artist who knew the theater: how to meet its demands through music, characterization, climax, and at times a profound humanity.

Becoming rich as well as world famous, Verdi bought a large farm at Sant' Agata, and here he spent his summers almost to the end of his life. His first wife having died in 1840, he married again in 1859. His wife was Giuseppina Strepponi, a singer who had appeared in his *Nabucco*. She retired from the stage after her marriage to devote herself completely to her famous husband. Indicative of his tremendous popularity was the fact that when Cavour instituted the first Italian parliament, Verdi was elected a deputy.

The last opera in Verdi's rich second period, *Aida*, was commissioned by the Khedive of Egypt to inaugurate a new opera house commemorating the opening of the Suez Canal. *Aida* was introduced in Cairo under magnificent auspices in 1871. For the next fifteen years Verdi wrote no more operas, though he made several attempts to write a *King Lear*. He finally became convinced that he was through as a composer, that the new age which Richard WAGNER had initiated made his kind of opera old-fashioned.

He was drawn out of his long, seemingly permanent retirement by an eloquent libretto that Arrigo BOITO fashioned from SHAKESPEARE'S *Othello*. The premiere of OTELLO at La Scala in 1887 was an event attracting world attention, and the opera was one of the greatest triumphs of Verdi's long career. The audience, coming to pay homage to a master, did not fail to recognize that he had soared to new heights.

Verdi wrote one more opera, once again to a libretto by Boito, adapted from Shakespeare. This time it was a comedy, FALSTAFF. Introduced at La Scala in 1893, it was no less a triumph than *Otello* had been, and it proved no less significant in revealing that the seventy-nine-year-old master was still growing artistically.

With the death of his wife in 1897, Verdi lost his will to live. He could no longer bear staying at his beloved Sant' Agata, and he took rooms in a Milan hotel. His sight and hearing began to fail, and after that (as he once complained) "all my limbs no longer obey me." One day he suffered a paralytic

stroke; six days later he was dead. All Italy mourned the death of her national hero. At his funeral a quarter of a million of his admirers crowded the streets to pay him their last respects. During the procession TOSCANINI led a chorus from *Nabucco*. The same night Toscanini led it again at La Scala as a last tribute.

Verdi's operas: *Oberto* (1836); *Un giorno di regno* (1840); *Nabucco* (or *Nabuccodonosor*) (1842); *I Lombardi* (1843); *Ernani* (1844); I DUE FOSCARI (1844); *Giovanna d'Arco* (1845); *Alzira* (1845); ATTILA (1846); *Macbeth* (1847); *I masnadieri* (1847); *Il corsaro* (1848); *La battaglia di Legnano* (1849); *Luisa Miller* (1849); *Stiffelio* (1850); *Rigoletto* (1851); *Il trovatore* (1853); LA TRAVIATA (1853); *I vespri siciliani*, or THE SICILIAN VESPERS (1855); *Simon Boccanegra* (1857); *Aroldo* (1857); *Un ballo in maschera* (1859); *La forza del destino* (1862); *Don Carlos* (1867); *Aida* (1871); *Otello* (1887); *Falstaff* (1893).

Verdi prati, Ruggiero's air, one of the finest in HANDEL'S ALCINA.

Vere, captain of the British Navy (tenor) in BRITTEN'S BILLY BUDD, a role created by Peter PEARS.

Vergil, *see* VIRGIL.

verismo, a naturalistic movement in Italian opera launched with CAVALLERIA RUSTICANA. The emphasis was on librettos with everyday characters and situations, usually among working classes, a complete departure from costume plays and episodes from history or legend. Dramatic arias became preferable to florid ones, and stress was placed on naturalistic recitatives, choruses that set a mood, and on orchestral tone painting. The *verismo* movement is found in some of the operas of LEONCAVALLO, MASCAGNI, GIORDANO, PUCCINI, and ZANDONAI. In France its counterpart is found in the naturalistic operas of BRUNEAU and in CHARPENTIER'S LOUISE.

verkaufte Braut, Die, *see* BARTERED BRIDE, THE.

Verranno a te sull' aure, the love and

farewell duet of Lucia and Edgardo, in Act I, Scene 2, of DONIZETTI'S LUCIA DI LAMMERMOOR.

Verrett, Shirley, mezzo-soprano. Born New Orleans, La., in or about 1933. She was operating a real-estate office in Los Angeles when she decided to become a singer. After a period of voice study with Anna Fitziu, she attended the Juilliard School of Music for six years, where she received her vocal training from Marian Szekely-Freschl. She made her debut in 1957 at the Antioch College Shakespeare Festival in Yellow Springs, Ohio, in THE RAPE OF LUCRETIA. This was followed a year later by her professional debut at the NEW YORK CITY OPERA in WEILL's *Lost in the Stars*. Her first concert appearance, in New York City in 1958, was followed by recitals elsewhere, as well as appearances with major symphony orchestras: in 1962 she was heard with the New York Philharmonic in a concert presentation of the first act of ROSSINI's LE COMTE ORY. In July, 1962, she was acclaimed for her performance as CARMEN at the FESTIVAL OF TWO WORLDS in Spoleto, a performance she repeated at the BOLSHOI THEATER in Moscow, where she received a twenty-minute ovation. She subsequently appeared in the same role with the New York City Opera (1964) and LA SCALA (1966). On May 11, 1966, she made her first appearance in London at COVENT GARDEN as Ulrica in UN BALLO IN MASCHERA. Among her operatic appearances in 1969 were those at the FLORENCE MAY MUSIC FESTIVAL (as AMNERIS), the EDINBURGH FESTIVAL (in DONIZETTI's *Maria Stuarda*), and over the Italian Radio (LES TROYENS). On Jan. 8, 1970, she appeared at La Scala in a new production of SAMSON ET DALILA and in June of the same year in a TV production in Paris of NORMA with Montserrat CABALLÉ.

Versez, que tout respire l'ivresse et le délire, the drinking song during the palace festivities in the last scene of MEYERBEER's LE PROPHÈTE.

Vespone, Uberto's valet (silent role) in PERGOLESI's LA SERVA PADRONA.

vespri siciliani, I, *see* SICILIAN VESPERS, THE.

vestale, La (The Vestal), opera in three acts by SPONTINI. Libretto by Étienne de JOUY. Premiere: Paris Opéra, Dec. 15, 1807. American premiere: Théâtre d'Orleans, New Orleans, Feb. 17, 1828. This is its composer's most famous opera, a work of historical importance in that it is a transition in opera development from the operas of GLUCK to those of MEYERBEER. The setting is Rome during the Roman empire. Licinius (tenor), a young general, back from a campaign in Gaul, discovers that his beloved Giulia (soprano) has become a vestal virgin. He penetrates the temple and revives her love for him. In their passionate exchange, Giulia forgets that she must watch the holy fires; she allows them to be extinguished. For this sacrilege she is stripped of her veil and condemned to be buried alive. As she is being led to her death, a bolt of lightning relights the fires. The Romans take this as a sign that Giulia has been forgiven by the gods, and she is spared from death. The opera was revived by the METROPOLITAN OPERA on Nov. 12, 1925. In 1933 it was handsomely mounted at the FLORENCE MAY MUSIC FESTIVAL, and since that time has been produced from time to time to star Maria CALLAS.

Vesti la giubba, Canio's aria (the most famous in the opera) lamenting the necessity of his appearing in a comic play while his heart is breaking because his wife has been unfaithful, in the close of Act I of LEONCAVALLO's PAGLIACCI.

Vestris, Lucia Elizabeth (born Bartolozzi), contralto. Born London, Jan. 3 or Mar. 2, 1787; died there Aug. 8, 1856. She created the role of Fatima in WEBER's OBERON. After studying voice with Corri, she made her debut at the KING's THEATRE in London in July, 1815, in Peter von Winter's *Il ratto di Proserpina*. She sang regularly there between 1821 and 1825, as well as at the Théâtre Italien in Paris. She subsequently managed COVENT GARDEN and other opera companies in London and appeared in the English versions of several operas including NORMA and THE MARRIAGE OF FIGARO. Because of the rich texture of her low tones, she was also able to appear as DON GIOVANNI and as Macheath in THE BEGGAR'S OPERA.

Via! così non mi lasciate, Suzanne's plea for affection from her husband as she sends him off to his club, in WOLF-FERRARI'S THE SECRET OF SUZANNE.

Viardot-García, Pauline, mezzo-soprano and teacher of singing. Born Paris, July 18, 1821; died there May 18, 1910. Daughter of the tenor and singing teacher Manuel del Popolo GARCÍA, she was the sister of the prima donna MALIBRAN and the singing teacher Manuel García. She began to study music with her parents, later studying the piano with Franz LISZT, composition with Anton Reicha. In 1837 she made her debut as a singer in Brussels. She then appeared extensively throughout Europe. In 1839 she was a member of the Théâtre des Italiens in Paris, where, two years later, she married the theater's manager, Louis Viardot. As the principal soprano of the PARIS OPÉRA, she appeared in the world premiere of LE PROPHÈTE (1849), creating the role of Fidès. For a decade, beginning in 1848, she was a favorite with London and Paris opera-goers. In Paris she appeared as Orfeo in GLUCK'S ORFEO ED EURIDICE, arranged by BERLIOZ (1859), and in the title role of ALCESTE (1861). She made her last appearance in 1863. During her retirement, in Paris, she wrote plays, poems, and several operettas: one of the latter, CENDRILLON (which had its premiere in Paris in 1904), was revived at the Newport, R.I., Festival in 1969. She was the mistress of the famous Russian author Ivan TURGENEV, whose writings provided her with the texts for three operettas. From 1871 to 1875 she taught singing at the Paris Conservatory.

Via resti servita, duet of Marcellina and Susanna, in which Susanna expresses her suspicions about Marcellina's contract with Figaro wherein he had promised to marry her if he could not repay

a financial debt, in Act I of MOZART'S THE MARRIAGE OF FIGARO.

Vicar of Wakefield, The, see GOLDSMITH, OLIVER.

Vicino a te s'acqueta, duet of Chénier and Madeleine in Act IV of GIORDANO'S ANDREA CHÉNIER, as (about to die) they exchange expressions of ardent devotion.

Vickers, Jon, tenor. Born Prince Albert, Canada, Oct. 29, 1926. While employed as manager of a chain of Woolworth stores in Canada, Vickers made an appearance in a Gilbert and SULLIVAN operetta. A scholarship brought him to the Royal Conservatory in Toronto, where he studied voice with George Lambert. After his graduation he made important concert appearances in Canada. In 1956 he was heard in New York in a concert version of FIDELIO. On Apr. 27, 1957, he made his debut at COVENT GARDEN in UN BALLO IN MASCHERA. As a principal tenor of that company he played the leading role in a revival of BERLIOZ' LES TROYENS, as well as in the more traditional repertory. In the summer of 1958 he sang the role of SIEGMUND at BAYREUTH, where he proved so impressive that he was contracted to appear as PARSIFAL. There followed major appearances in Europe and America, including the DALLAS CIVIC OPERA (where he appeared opposite Maria CALLAS in CHERUBINI'S MÉDÉE in 1958), the VIENNA STATE OPERA (where he made his debut in Jan., 1959), the SAN FRANCISCO OPERA (his debut taking place on Sept. 11, 1959, as RADAMES), and LA SCALA. On Jan. 17, 1960, he made his debut at the METROPOLITAN OPERA as CANIO. Since then he has come to be regarded as the most important HELDENTENOR since MELCHIOR, but he is no less significant in the Italian and French repertory.

vida breve, La (Life Is Short), opera in two acts by FALLA. Libretto by Carlos Fernandez-Shaw. Premiere: Nice, France, Apr. 1, 1913. American premiere: Metropolitan Opera, Mar. 6, 1926. This was Falla's first major work, in which his pronounced leanings toward nationalist music first became evident. The gypsy girl Salud (soprano) is in love with Paco (tenor) ; but though the latter keeps up a pretense that he is in love with her, he is actually about to marry somebody else. Salud discovers the truth at the wedding. She curses Paco, but the sight of him again transforms her anger to tenderness. Broken in heart, she falls dead at his feet. The opera's two Spanish dances are its most familiar excerpts, particularly the first one, which is frequently heard in Fritz Kreisler's transcription for violin and piano. Gilbert Chase has noted that in these dances "Falla achieves a higher degree of artistry and ethnic authenticity than is to be found in any previous manifestation of Spanish lyric drama."

Viene la sera, the love duet of Cio-Cio-San and Pinkerton, in Act I of PUCCINI's MADAMA BUTTERFLY.

Vieni, amor mio, Amneris' aria in Act II, Scene 1, of VERDI's AIDA, as she thinks of and pines for her beloved Radames.

Vieni fra questa braccia, the ecstatic love duet of Elvira and Arthur after Elvira recovers her sanity, at the close of BELLINI's I PURITANI.

Vieni, o diletta, Aida's expression of sorrow at the sad fate facing her native Ethiopia, in Act I, Scene 1, of VERDI's AIDA.

Vieni, t'affretta, the Letter Scene in Act I, Scene 2, of VERDI's MACBETH, in which Lady Macbeth reads a communication from her husband telling her of the witches' prophecy.

Vien, Leonora, a' piedi tuoi, an aria in which King Alfonso speaks of his love for Leonora, in the opening of Act II of DONIZETTI's LA FAVORITA.

Vienna Festival Weeks, a festival of the first importance, initiated in Vienna in 1951, organized under the auspices of the Vienna municipality. The festival usually begins the last week in May and continues through June, recruiting each of the city's leading cultural organizations. It also features distinguished visiting performers, orchestras, chamber-music groups, and opera companies. All facets of music are covered, as well as drama and ballet.

The VIENNA STATE OPERA and the VOLKSOPER provide most of the operatic activity, drawing major productions from their regular winter repertory, but often also featuring important premieres, novelties, revivals, and new productions. Through the years the State Opera has emphasized the works of MOZART, WAGNER, and Richard STRAUSS, together with some of the masterworks of the French and Italian repertory, sometimes in new productions. In 1959 it offered a new production of ARABELLA; in 1960, its repertory included L'ASSASSINIO NELLA CATTEDRALE; in 1965 it presented the first Viennese performance of SHOSTAKOVICH's THE NOSE and his KATERINA ISMAILOVA; in 1966, the world premiere of Alfred Uhl's *Der mysteriose Herr X* was given, as well as the first staged production of Josef Hauer's *Die schwarze Spinne*; in 1969 it commemorated the centenary of the Vienna State Opera with festive new performances of operas by Mozart, Wagner, and Strauss, as well as presentations of LULU, WOZZECK, and DANTONS TOD. The two-hundredth anniversary of BEETHOVEN's birth was commemorated on June 9, 1970, with a performance of FIDELIO, conducted by Leonard BERNSTEIN. The Volksoper, while concentrating on operettas and the more familiar works from the basic opera repertory, has over the years also contributed unusual productions and novelties, including EINEM's *Der Zerissine*; a significant revival of DIE TOTE STADT; DVOŘÁK's RUSALKA; and THE MAKROPOULOS AFFAIR.

Visiting opera groups have included SADLER's WELLS in PETER GRIMES in 1965; the PRAGUE OPERA and the Brno Opera in 1967 in MARTINU's *Julietta* and SMETANA's DALIBOR respectively; the BERLIN DEUTSCHE STAATSOPER in EGK's *La tentation de St. Antoine* and a revival of WEILL's *The Seven Deadly Sins* in 1968; and other celebrated foreign companies in productions of their native operas.

Vienna State Opera (Staatsoper), the leading opera house of Austria and one of the great operatic institutions of the world. Before World War I it was known as the Vienna Royal Opera (Hofoper). It was opened on the Ring in Vienna on May 25, 1869, with DON GIOVANNI. J. F. von Herbeck was its first artistic director, a post he retained until 1875. During his regime there took place the world premieres of GOETZ's *Der widerspäntigen Zähmung,* as well as of THE QUEEN OF SHEBA and GENOVEVA; also the first Viennese performance of AIDA. Herbeck was followed by Franz Janner (1875–1880) and Hans RICHTER (1880–1896). With Richter it became one of Europe's major opera houses with remarkable performances of the RING cycle, as well as of other Wagnerian music dramas; SAMSON ET DALILA; and in 1892 the world premiere of WERTHER. With Gustav MAHLER as artistic director between 1896 and 1907, the Vienna Royal Opera became a world-renowned institution, consistently maintaining a standard of performance and a variety of repertoire matched by few companies anywhere. It was during this period that THE BARTERED BRIDE first became famous as conducted by Mahler and that Mahler initiated the practice in FIDELIO of using the *Leonora Overture No. 3* between scenes in Act II. During the Mahler regime, restudied productions of the basic productions (and most notably of the works of MOZART and WAGNER) became the rule. The CLAQUE was eliminated. Latecomers could not be seated during the performance. A revolving stage was used for the first time (in a production of COSÌ FAN TUTTE). Every performer was driven mercilessly to give the best of which he or she was capable. Among the novelties produced during this decade were: CAVALLERIA RUSTICANA (first Vienna performance); DER CORREGIDOR; DALIBOR; THE DEMON; DJAMILEH; EURYANTHE; FALSTAFF; FEUERSNOT; *Das Heimchen am Herd* (GOLDMARK); *Iolanthe* (TCHAIKOVSKY); *Lobetanz* (Thuille); LOUISE; OBERON; RIENZI; *Rose vom Liebesgarten* (PFITZNER); LO SPEZIALE; and ZAIDE.

With Hans Gregor as director between 1911 and 1918, the Vienna Opera witnessed the world premiere of ARIADNE AUF NAXOS and the first performances in that city of THE GIRL OF THE GOLDEN WEST, PELLÉAS ET MÉLISANDE, and DER ROSENKAVALIER. In 1918 the title of Royal Opera was officially changed to State Opera, with Franz SCHALK as artistic and musical director. He retained this position until 1929, but shared it with Richard STRAUSS between 1920 and 1924. This was the period in which Vienna first witnessed BORIS GODUNOV, DIE FRAU OHNE SCHATTEN (world premiere), IL TRITTICO, and TURANDOT.

Between 1929 and 1934, Clemens KRAUSS was artistic director, followed by Felix WEINGARTNER (1934–1936) and Bruno WALTER (1936–1938). When the Nazis invaded Austria, they smashed the bust of Mahler which stood in the vestibule of the opera house and changed the artistic program of the company to meet their own standards. With many of its leading performers either dismissed or refusing to appear in a Nazi-dominated opera house, the standards of the Vienna State Opera suffered marked deterioration. Karl BÖHM was made artistic director in 1943, but the tenure of his office was brief. By order of Göring, the opera house closed down, its last performance being GÖTTERDÄMMERUNG, conducted by Böhm, on June 30, 1944. On Mar. 12, 1945, the opera house was severely damaged by bombs.

When performances were resumed on May 1, 1945, with THE MARRIAGE OF FIGARO, Josef KRIPS conducting, the opera was seen at the VOLKSOPER. The following October the company presented *Fidelio* at the THEATER-AN-DER-WIEN. For a decade, the Vienna State Opera used both auditoriums, the "State Opera at the Theater-an-der-Wien" directed by Franz Salmhofer, and the "State Opera at the Volksoper" directed by H. Juch. During this period the original opera house on the Ring was being reconstructed. It reopened on Nov. 5, 1955, with *Fidelio.* Böhm was made artistic director, but once again his regime was brief. In 1956 he was succeeded by

KARAJAN, whose regime was marked by the new prominence given to Italian operas (without, of course, neglecting the German repertory). The Karajan era was a brilliant one, a restoration of the glory the opera company had known in earlier years, but his dictatorial methods and sometimes unreasonable demands led to bitter disagreements with Egon HILBERT, the general director, which finally led to Karajan's resignation in 1964. Hilbert remained sole director up to the time of his death in 1969, when he was succeeded by Heinrich Reif-Gintl; in 1969 Horst STEIN was made principal conductor. In 1970 it was announced that Rudolf Gamsjäger would succeed Reif-Gintl as director in 1972.

In 1967 the Vienna State Opera appeared in the Western Hemisphere for the first time with performances at Expo 67 in Montreal, Canada. It visited the Soviet Union in 1971. In 1969 it celebrated its centenary with performances of most of the forty-seven works then in its permanent repertory. Festivities began on May 2 with a new production of ARABELLA. On the afternoon of May 25 Leonard BERNSTEIN conducted BEETHOVEN's *Missa solemnis* in the auditorium of the Vienna State Opera; that same evening Böhm led *Fidelio*. The centennial celebration featured cycles of Mozart, Wagner, and Richard Strauss, and a cycle entitled "The Musical Theater of the 20th Century," which included DANTON'S TOD, KATERINA ISMAILOVA, LULU, *Pelléas et Mélisande,* and WOZZECK.

Since the reopening of the rebuilt opera house, the Vienna State Opera has presented the following premieres and novelties among others: CAPRICCIO; CARMINA BURANA; CATULLI CARMINA; *Das Christelflein* (Pfitzner) ; THE CONSUL; *Dantons Tod;* GIULIO CESARE; INTERMEZZO; JEANNE D'ARC AU BÛCHER; *Katerina Ismailova; Lulu;* THE NOSE; PALESTRINA; DER PROZESS; THE RAKE'S PROGRESS; DER STURM, a world premiere; TRIONFO D'AFRODITE.

The history of the post–World War II period would not be complete without at least a mention of the triumph accorded Leonard Bernstein when he conducted *Falstaff, Der Rosenkavalier,* and *Fidelio.*

Viens, gentille dame, a CAVATINA sung by the Laird of Avenell, calling for "the white lady" to make an appearance, in Act I of BOIELDIEU's LA DAME BLANCHE.

Viens ici, ne reste pas au bord du clair de lune, love duet of Pelléas and Mélisande in Act IV, Scene 2, of DEBUSSY's PELLÉAS ET MÉLISANDE.

View from the Bridge, A, *see* ROSSELLINI, RENZO.

Vigny, Alfred de, author, poet, dramatist. Born Loches, France, Mar. 27, 1799; died Paris, Sept. 17, 1863. His historical novel *Cinq-Mars* was made into an opera of the same name by Charles GOUNOD, and his drama *Chatterton* was the source of LEONCAVALLO's first opera.

Village Romeo and Juliet, A, an opera in prologue and three acts by DELIUS. Libretto by the composer in collaboration with his wife, based on Gottfried KELLER's story *Romeo und Julia auf dem Dorfe.* Premiere: Komische Oper, Berlin, Feb. 21, 1907 (as *Romeo und Julia auf dem Dorfe*) . Described by the composer as a "lyric drama in six pictures," this opera is centered around a feud between two households, with the son of one falling in love with the daughter of another. The lovers run away and end up committing suicide. An orchestral interlude, "The Walk to the Paradise Garden," has become independently popular. Delius wrote it five years after completing his opera, inserting it as an ENTR'ACTE between the fifth and sixth "pictures."

villi, Le (The Witches) , opera in two acts by PUCCINI. Libretto by Ferdinando Fontana. Premiere: Teatro dal Verme, Milan, May 31, 1884 (one-act version) ; Teatro Regio, Turin, Dec. 26, 1884 (two-act version) . American premiere: Metropolitan Opera, Dec. 17, 1908. This was Puccini's first opera. He entered it in the Sonzogno competition but failed to gain even an honorable mention. It did, however, make an impression on

BOITO, who raised a fund to finance its production. That performance was so successful that LA SCALA accepted the opera for the following season and Ricordi published it and commissioned a new work from the composer. The setting is the Black Forest, where the betrothal of Robert (tenor) and Anna (soprano) is celebrated. Going to seek his fortune before marrying, Robert forgets his beloved in the pleasures of the city, and Anna dies of grief. Broken in spirit and fortune, Robert returns expecting to find Anna waiting for him, but confronts only an apparition who denounces him for his desertion. Witches dance around him until he falls dead at their feet.

Villon, François (born François de Montcorbier), poet. Born Paris, 1431; died there about 1463. The poet is the central character of NOUGUÈS's opera *Une Aventure de Villon.*

Vinay, Ramón, tenor and baritone. Born Chillan, Chile, Aug. 31, 1912, of a French father and an Italian mother. He spent his boyhood in France, where he studied engineering. After a period of music study he joined a traveling company in 1934 with which he made his opera debut as a baritone in Mexico City as Count di Luna in IL TROVATORE. His second debut, this time as a tenor, took place with the National Opera Company of Havana in June, 1944, when he appeared in the title role of OTELLO. One year later, in the fall of 1945, he made his North American debut with the NEW YORK CITY OPERA as DON JOSÉ and on Feb. 22, 1946, made his METROPOLITAN OPERA debut in the same role. He scored a great personal success at the Metropolitan on Dec. 9, 1946, when, on ten hours' notice, he substituted for Torsten RALF in the title role of *Otello.* He sang this role, too, in a concert performance by the NBC Symphony conducted by TOSCANINI. Vinay left the Metropolitan Opera in 1961, but before then he had appeared at the BAYREUTH FESTIVAL between 1952 and 1957 and at LA SCALA between 1953 and 1960. He was also heard at the SALZBURG

and HOLLAND FESTIVALS and in leading opera houses of Europe and South America. In 1962 at the Bayreuth Festival he assumed the baritone role of TELRAMUND and thereafter added other baritone roles to his repertoire but retaining the tenor roles as well.

Vincent, Mireille's suitor (tenor) in GOUNOD's MIREILLE.

V'inganni, ma fu l'inganno, Don Alfonso's air that closes MOZART's COSÌ FAN TUTTE and in which he philosophizes that everything that had transpired in the opera turned out for the best for the four principal characters.

Vin herbé, Le, a cantata for solo voices, chorus, and orchestra by Frank MARTIN sometimes produced as an opera, as happened at the SALZBURG FESTIVAL in 1948. The text is the legend of Tristan and Isolde as adapted by Joseph Bedier in 1900, of which Martin used three chapters. Martin's musical style is more strongly suggestive of DEBUSSY than of WAGNER. The world premiere (concert version) took place in Zürich on Mar. 26, 1942; the American premiere (also a concert version), in New York City on Feb. 26, 1961.

Vin ou bière, chorus of the soldiers and villagers, opening Act II of GOUNOD's FAUST.

Violanda, Arvino's wife (soprano) in VERDI's I LOMBARDI.

Violetta, *see* VALERY, VIOLETTA.

Vi ravviso, Rodolfo's recollections of his childhood upon returning to his home in a Swiss village, in Act I of BELLINI's LA SONNAMBULA.

Virgil (or **Vergil**), poet. Born Andes, Cisalpine Gaul, Oct. 15, 70 B.C.; died Brundisium, Italy, Sept. 21, 19 B.C. His Latin epic *Aeneid* provided the material for several operas. The most famous is PURCELL's DIDO AND AENEAS. Others include: ARNE's *Dido and Aeneas;* BERLIOZ' LES TROYENS; Pascal Colasse's *Enée et Lavinie;* Joseph Martin Kraus's *Aeneas i Carthago;* Nikolai Lissenko's *The Aeneid.*

Vi ricordo o boschi ombrosi, Orfeo's air in Act II of MONTEVERDI's L'ORFEO.

Visconti, Luchino, designer and producer. Born Milan, Nov. 2, 1906. After working in motion pictures he was impelled to become an opera producer upon hearing CALLAS in NORMA in 1954. He became affiliated with LA SCALA, where he produced for Callas a number of operas, including LA VESTALE, LA TRAVIATA, ANNA BOLENA, LA SONNAMBULA, and IPHIGÉNIE EN TAURIDE. He also designed and produced operas at COVENT GARDEN, the FESTIVAL OF TWO WORLDS at Spoleto, Teatro Massimo in Palermo, and various other opera houses and festivals.

Vishnevskaya, Galina, soprano. Born Leningrad, Oct. 25, 1926. Following her debut in 1950 in Strelnikov's *Kholopka,* she joined the BOLSHOI OPERA in 1952, where she has been heard in the French, Italian, and Russian repertory. Meanwhile, on Nov. 6, 1961, she made her debut as AIDA at the METROPOLITAN OPERA, where she remained for one season. In 1962 she made her debut at COVENT GARDEN. Her husband is the cellist Mstislav Rostropovich.

Vision fugitive, Herod's aria extolling the beauty of Salomé and expressing his passion for her, in Act II of MASSENET'S HÉRODIADE.

Visitation, The, opera in three acts by SCHULLER. Libretto by the composer, based on KAFKA's *The Trial.* Premiere: Hamburg Opera, Oct. 12, 1966. American premiere: Hamburg Opera (in New York City), June 28, 1967. In making his adaptation of Kafka's *The Trial* (previously made into an opera by EINEM—DER PROZESS), Schuller transferred the setting to the Southern part of the United States and transformed the hunted Joseph K. of Kafka's play into an American Negro university student, Carter Jones. Thus the opera deals strongly and directly with the racial problems in the United States, with Carter despised by his own people because he is moving in the world of white people and rejected by white people because he is a Negro. He becomes the victim of racial persecution when he is accused of a crime that he did not commit. He is hunted down, found

guilty in a kangaroo court, and lynched. Schuller's score is a combination of JAZZ and SERIAL TECHNIQUES, an idiom for which the composer devised the term "third stream music." The opera opens with a recording of the blues, "Nobody knows you when you're down," as sung by Bessie Smith. While a full symphony orchestra is used for the serial music, a seven-man ensemble is employed for the jazz passages, sometimes as background music for the singers and sometimes in conjunction with the regular orchestra.

This opera was commissioned by the HAMBURG OPERA, where it created a sensation at its premiere, critics and audiences hailing it as a masterwork. However, at its American premiere in New York, the reaction went to the opposite extreme, with sharp denunciation of both the text and the music. When produced later by the SAN FRANCISCO OPERA, it was considered far better than it had been judged to be in New York, though not the masterwork Germany had regarded it.

Vissi d'arte, Tosca's aria expressing her dedication to her art, in Act II of PUCCINI'S TOSCA.

Vitellia, daughter (soprano) of a former Roman emperor and the heroine in MOZART's opera LA CLEMENZA DI TITO.

Vitellius, Roman proconsul (baritone) in MASSENET'S HÉRODIADE.

Viva il vino, Turiddu's drinking song in MASCAGNI'S CAVALLERIA RUSTICANA.

Vivaldi, Antonio, composer. Born Venice, c. 1675; died Vienna, July 27, 1741. His music study took place with his father and with Giovanni Legrenzi in Venice, but he was prepared not for music but for the Church. In 1703 he became a priest. His musical career began in 1709, when he became a teacher of the violin at the Ospedale della Pietà in Venice, rising to the post of music director seven years later. About 1720 he left Venice to become KAPELLMEISTER to Prince Philip of Hesse in Mantua. After a period of touring Europe as violin virtuoso, he returned to Italy, where he now became outstandingly popular for his operas. Though a dominant figure in the musical world of his time, he suffered poverty and neglect at the end of his life and went to a pauper's grave when he died. Though he is known today chiefly for his instrumental music, of which he wrote an astonishing amount, he also composed some forty operas. The most successful were: *Nerone fatto Cesare* (1715); *L'Arsilda regina di Ponto* (1716); *L'incoronazione di Dario* (1716); *Armida al campo d'Egitto* (1718); *La crèola* (1723); *L'inganno trionfante in amore* (1725); *Farnace* (1726); *La fida ninfa* (1732); *Montezuma* (1733); *L'Olimpiade* (1734); *Griselda* (1735); *Rosmira* (1738); *Feraspe* (1739).

Viva Pagliaccio, chorus of the villagers hailing the arrival of the theatrical troupe, in the opening scene of LEONCAVALLO'S PAGLIACCI.

Vivetta, goddaughter (soprano) of Rosa Mamai in CILÈA'S L'ARLÉSIANA.

Vivi du, Percy's aria in DONIZETTI'S ANNA BOLENA.

Vladimir, Prince Igor's son (tenor) in BORODIN'S PRINCE IGOR.

Voce di donna, La Cieca's aria in Act I of PONCHIELLI'S LA GIOCONDA, as, in gratitude for having been saved by Laura, she presents her with a rosary.

voce di gola, Italian for "throat voice" or guttural voice.

Voce fatal, Chevreuse's aria in DONIZETTI'S MARIA DI ROHAN.

voce velata, Italian for "veiled voice," a muffled quality produced intentionally.

Vogl, Heinrich, tenor. Born Au, Ger., Jan. 15, 1845; died Munich, Apr. 21, 1900. After studying with Franz Lachner he made his debut at the MUNICH OPERA in 1865. He became a permanent member of that company, and it was here that he scored his first major successes in the Wagnerian repertory. When SCHNORR VON CAROLSFELD died in 1865, Vogl became the outstanding interpreter of TRISTAN. In 1869 he appeared in the world premiere of DAS RHEINGOLD as Loge, and a year later he sang Siegmund in the premiere of DIE WALKÜRE. He appeared at BAYREUTH in 1876 and in 1882 toured Germany and Austria.

In 1868 he married the soprano Theresa Thoma, then the principal soprano of the Munich Opera, creator of the role of SIEGLINDE, and for many years a significant interpreter of ISOLDE.

Voi, che mie fide ancelle, Cleopatra's air in HANDEL'S GIULIO CESARE IN EGITTO.

Voi che sapete, Cherubino's aria questioning the meaning of love, in Act II of MOZART'S THE MARRIAGE OF FIGARO.

Voici ce qu'il écrit, the duet of Geneviève and Arkel, in which Geneviève reads to the blind Arkel a letter from Golaud revealing his marriage to Mélisande, in Act I, Scene 2, of DEBUSSY'S PELLÉAS ET MÉLISANDE.

Voi ci diffuse nell' aria, Lucinda's opening aria in Act I of WOLF-FERRARI'S L'AMORE MEDICO.

Voici le printemps, the song of Dalila and her priestesses as they bring garlands to the victorious Hebrews, in Act I of SAINT-SAËNS'S SAMSON ET DALILA.

Voilà donc la terrible cité, Athanaël's lament on the degeneration of Alexandria, in Act I, Scene 2, of MASSENET'S THAÏS.

Voi lo sapete, Santuzza's aria in MASCAGNI'S CAVALLERIA RUSTICANA, confiding to Lucia her love affair with Turiddu.

Vois ma misère, hélas! Samson's plea to God in Act III, Scene 1, of SAINT-SAËNS'S SAMSON ET DALILA to relieve his misery after having been put in chains and having had his eyes plucked out.

Voix humaine, La, opera in one act by POULENC. Libretto by Jean Cocteau. Premiere: Opéra-Comique, Feb. 9, 1959. American premiere: New York City, Feb. 21, 1960. This is a one-character opera. An unnamed young woman (soprano) is parting, over the telephone, from her lover, who is about to marry another woman. The libretto, originally a play, consists of recollections of the affair she had enjoyed, plans for her future, and her varying emotional responses to the apparently sympathetic responses of her lover. The vocal line is almost entirely declamatory; the orchestra is used principally to fill in the pauses while the man is speaking to her. The little opera (which takes about forty minutes to perform) was successfully presented at the AIX-EN-PROVENCE FESTIVAL in 1960 and after that by the AMERICAN OPERA SOCIETY in New York.

Volkhova, the Princess of the Sea (soprano) who marries Sadko on the ocean bottom in RIMSKY-KORSAKOV'S SADKO.

Volksoper, the second most important opera house in Vienna. It opened on the Gürtel (the secondary Ring) on Dec. 14, 1898, as the Kaiser-Jubilaeums Stadttheater (celebrating Emperor Francis Joseph I's jubilee) with a presentation of Heinrich von KLEIST'S drama, *Hermannsschlacht.* For a number of years only dramas were presented there. The first opera to be heard at the Volksoper was DER FREISCHÜTZ on Sept. 15, 1904, Alexander ZEMLINSKY conducting. Under the direction of Rainer Simons, opera with popular appeal and at modest admission prices was given regularly. The Simons era lasted until 1917. Felix WEINGARTNER was musical director between 1919 and 1924, followed by Fritz STIEDRY in 1924–25, and Leo BLECH in 1925–26. A. Baumann was general director between 1938 and 1945, when the company was officially named People's Opera (Municipal Städtische Volksoper), subsidized by the city, with its organization assumed by the VIENNA STATE OPERA. In 1945 the theater became the temporary home of the Vienna State Opera until that company shared its performances between the auditoriums of the Volksoper and the THEATER-AN-DER-WIEN, while its main opera house (bombed during World War II) was being rebuilt. When the Volksoper once again became an independent organization in 1955, Franz Salmhofer was made director, remaining until 1963, when he was succeeded by Albert Moser. Besides presenting delightful performances of operettas and highly competent presentations of the familiar operatic fare, the Volksoper has continually given numerous important novelties and revivals. These included: BLUEBEARD'S CASTLE; LA CENERENTOLA; DALIBOR; DER EVANGELI-MANN; HALKA; HÁRY JÁNOS; THE MAKRO-POULOS AFFAIR; LE ROSSIGNOL; RUSALKA; DIE TOTE STADT; DIE ZAUBERGEIGE; *Der Zerissine* (EINEM). Operas by ORFF and MENOTTI have also been given. One of the innovations of the Volksoper was to interpolate in its regular repertory notable examples of the American musical theater under the artistic direction of Marcel Prawy. These have included Cole Porter's *Kiss Me Kate,* PORGY AND BESS, and BERNSTEIN's *West Side Story,* all three distinct successes.

Volo di notte (Night Flight), opera in one act by DALLAPICCOLA. Libretto by the composer, based on *Vol de nuit,* a novel by St. Exupéry. Premiere: Florence, May 18, 1940. American premiere: Palo Alto, Cal., Mar. 1, 1962. This was the composer's first opera; it has been extensively performed in Europe.

Volpino, a young man (soprano), one of the three rivals for Grilletta, in HAYDN'S LO SPEZIALE.

Volpone, opera in three acts by ANTHEIL. Libretto by Albert Perry, freely adapted from Ben JONSON's comedy of the same name. Premiere: Los Angeles, Cal., Apr. 9, 1953 (original version); New York City, July, 1953 (revised). This is its composer's best-known opera, with music as well as text in an engagingly satirical vein. Volpone is a wily Venetian who pretends he is dying to gather gifts from his prospective legatees. The original version took four hours to produce; following the world premiere, composer and librettist cut down the opera to two hours' performance time. Francis Burt, John Coombs, and Louis GRUENBERG are other composers who wrote operas on this subject.

Voltaire (born François Marie Arouet), philosopher and author. Born Paris, Nov. 21, 1694; died there May 30, 1778. His writings were the source of the following operas: *Alzira* (operas by VERDI and Niccolò Zingarelli); *La Belle Arsène* (opera by MONSIGNY); *Candide* (Lev Knipper); *La Fée urgèle* (Egidio Dune, Ignaz Pleyel); *Le Huron* (GRÉTRY); *Isabelle et Gertrude* (Grétry); *Maometto II* (ROSSINI); *Mérope* (GRAUN); *Olympie*

(SPONTINI) ; *Semiramide* (Rossini) ; *Tancredi* (Rossini, using also material from TASSO) ; *Zaira* (BELLINI) . Voltaire wrote the librettos for the following operas by Jean-Philippe RAMEAU: *Pandore; La Princesse de Navarre; Le Temple de gloire; Les Fêtes de Ramire; Samson.*

Volta la terrea, the plea of Oscar the page to save Ulrica from exile, in Act I, Scene 1, of VERDI'S UN BALLO IN MASCHERA.

Von Heute auf Morgen (From Day to Day), opera in one act by SCHOENBERG. Libretto by the composer's wife, using the pseudonym of Max Blonda. Premiere: Frankfurt, Feb. 1, 1930. This is one of the few comic operas using TWELVE-TONE TECHNIQUES, and the composer's only one in a comic mode. The central character is a shrewd woman who uses guile and maneuvers to keep her husband from deserting her. The opera was revived in Naples in 1953 and at the HOLLAND FESTIVAL in 1958; a taping of the latter performance was televised in England over the BBC.

Vorspiel, German for "prelude." *See* PRELUDE.

Votre toast (Toreador Song) , the song with which Escamillo, the toreador, describes the thrills of his profession, in Act II of BIZET'S CARMEN.

Vous ne savez pas, the duet at the fountain of Pelléas and Mélisande, opening Act II of DEBUSSY'S PELLÉAS ET MÉLISANDE.

Vous qui du Dieu vivant outragez la puissance, the Cardinal's excommunication of Prince Léopold, in Act III of HALÉVY'S LA JUIVE.

Vous qui faites l'endormie, Méphistophélès' mocking serenade of Marguerite, in Act IV, Scene 3, of GOUNOD'S FAUST.

Voyez sur cette roche, Zerlina's aria in Act I of AUBER'S FRA DIAVOLO, telling the "Marquis" about the infamous Fra Diavolo, the "Marquis" being Fra Diavolo in disguise.

Vulcan, a god (bass) in GOUNOD'S PHILÉMON ET BAUCIS.

W

Wach' auf, es nahet gen den Tag, chorus acclaiming Hans Sachs in Act III, Scene 2, of WAGNER'S DIE MEISTERSINGER.

Wagner, (1) a student (tenor) in BOITO'S MEFISTOFELE.

(2) A student (baritone) in GOUNOD'S FAUST.

Wagner, Cosima, second wife of Richard WAGNER. Born Bellaggio, Italy, Dec. 25, 1837; died Bayreuth, Apr. 1, 1930. She was the daughter of Franz LISZT. Her first husband, whom she married in 1857, was the celebrated pianist, conductor, and Wagner enthusiast Hans von BÜLOW. Married to Wagner, she helped him prepare the first BAYREUTH FESTIVAL, and after Wagner's death she maintained an autocratic rule over the Bayreuth performances. She wrote a memoir of her father, *Franz Liszt: Gedenkblatt von seiner Tochter* (1911) .

Wagner, Johanna, soprano. Born Hanover, Ger., Oct. 13, 1826; died Würzburg, Ger., Oct. 16, 1894. The niece of Richard WAGNER, she created the role of ELISABETH. She received her musical training from her father, a professional singer. After making various concert appearances, she became in 1844 a principal soprano of the DRESDEN OPERA, where she appeared in the first performance of TANNHÄUSER (1845). For two years she studied in Paris with Pauline VIARDOT-GARCÍA, then between 1850 and 1852 be-

came the principal soprano of the BER-
LIN (Royal) OPERA. Losing her singing
voice in 1861, she became an actress.
From 1882 to 1884 she taught singing
at the Royal School of Music in Munich.
Wagner-Régény, Rudolf, composer. Born
Regen, Transylvania, Aug. 28, 1903;
died Berlin, Sept. 18, 1969. He attended
the Leipzig Conservatory and the Hochschule für Musik in Berlin. Before
World War II he was employed as conductor in various theaters and motion-
picture houses. He was director of the
Hochschule für Musik in Rostock between 1947 and 1950 and in 1950 became
director of the State Conservatory in
East Berlin. He was a prolific composer
of operas. The most significant of these
were *Die Bürger von Calais* (Berlin,
Jan. 28, 1939); *Johanna Balk* (Vienna,
Apr. 4, 1941); *Prometheus* (Cassel, Sept.
12, 1959); and *Das Bergwerk zu Falun*
(Salzburg, Aug. 16, 1961).

Wagner, Richard, composer. Born Leipzig, May 22, 1813; died Venice, Feb. 13,
1883.

It was long thought that Wagner was
the son of Karl Friedrich Wagner, a
Leipzig police official, but it is now generally believed that the actor Ludwig
Geyer, a close friend of his mother, was
his father. In any event, Karl Friedrich
Wagner died a half year after Richard
was born. About a year afterward Richard's mother married Geyer. A cultured
man, Geyer instilled in Richard a love
for the arts, particularly literature. As a
boy Richard nursed the ambition to become a writer; when he was eleven he
wrote a four-act political drama in the
style of Shakespeare.

Richard was enrolled in the Thomasschule in Leipzig, where he was so lax
that he was expelled. Subsequently he
entered the University of Leipzig, where
once again he was indifferent to his
studies. Only one serious interest absorbed him: music. He began his mastery of the art by studying a book on
theory. In 1829 he wrote an overture
that was performed in Leipzig. Two
years later he studied theory for six
months with Theodor Weinlig. He now

completed a symphony (performed in
Leipzig and Prague in 1833) and tried
writing a first opera, *Die Hochzeit*. His
first complete opera was DIE FEEN, written in 1834; it was not performed in the
composer's lifetime. DAS LIEBESVERBOT,
based on SHAKESPEARE's *Measure for
Measure,* followed in 1836.

Meanwhile, in 1834, he became the
conductor of the Magdeburg Opera,
where he made his debut leading DON
GIOVANNI. On Mar. 29, 1836, he introduced there his *Das Liebesverbot*. It was
such a fiasco that the company (never
too solvent) had to go into bankruptcy.
He found a new post in Königsberg; it
was there he met Minna Planer and
married her on Nov. 24, 1836. Between
1837 and 1839 he conducted operas in
Riga. Heavily involved in debts, he was
summarily dismissed and had his passport confiscated. To avoid imprisonment
he had to flee from Riga by a smuggler's
route.

He arrived in Paris on Sept. 17, 1839,
with bright hopes for the future. He had
letters of introduction to MEYERBEER,
then one of the most influential composers in the city; he also had parts of
his new opera, RIENZI. But his three
years in Paris proved a period of agonizing hardships and frustrations. Nevertheless, he completed *Rienzi* in 1840 and
DER FLIEGENDE HOLLÄNDER in 1841.

A change of fortune came in 1842
with an outstandingly successful performance of *Rienzi* at the DRESDEN OP-
ERA. While *Der fliegende Holländer*
given by the same company a year later
was a failure, Wagner's reputation had
grown to such proportions that in 1843
he was appointed the KAPELLMEISTER of
the Dresden Opera. During the next six
years he elevated the artistic standards
of the opera company to new heights.
Wagner completed two new operas in
Dresden. The first was TANNHÄUSER,
given in Dresden in 1845 and a failure.
The second, LOHENGRIN, had to wait for
performance until Franz LISZT accepted
it for WEIMAR, introducing it there on
Aug. 28, 1850. *Lohengrin* soon became
popular throughout Germany. Wagner

had not attended the premiere because by then he was a political exile; having become involved in the revolutionary movement of 1848–49 in Saxony, he had avoided arrest by fleeing from the country.

After a visit to Paris, he established his permanent home in Zürich. It was now that he began clarifying his new ideas about opera and to expound them in essays and pamphlets. He had become impatient with the methods and patterns that for so long a time had constricted composers. He conceived opera as a synthesis of the theatrical arts (poetry, music, acting, scenery, drama). Old practices had to be discarded. The formal demarcations between recitative and aria had to make way for a continuous flow of melody. Such irrelevant elements as ballets had to be eliminated. Dramatic expressiveness was to be intensified by bringing symphonic breadth to orchestral and vocal writing. To realize his ideal of an inseparable text and score, he developed the technique of the leading motive (LEITMOTIV): a melodic idea or phrase associated with a character, situation, or idea. The ideal opera would be unified by a structure of these recurring motives. To put these theories into practice, Wagner outlined a vast musicodramatic project based on the NIBELUNG legends. Originally he planned a single music drama, as he called his new form, but he ended writing four: DAS RHEINGOLD, DIE WALKÜRE, SIEGFRIED, and GÖTTERDÄMMERUNG. This tetralogy was named DER RING DES NIBELUNGEN. Wagner finished writing the texts and published them in 1852. The score of the last drama was completed in 1874. Thus, the creation of the *Ring* absorbed him for a quarter of a century, a period that also saw the composition and performance of two of his other music dramas: TRISTAN UND ISOLDE (1859) and DIE MEISTERSINGER VON NÜRNBERG (1867).

While these Herculean labors were occupying him, his personal life was becoming complicated. His marriage to Minna had been unhappy and explosive, and he found solace in the love of other women, usually the wives of his benefactors. A ruthless egotist, he used people for his own needs and was unconcerned about the pain he caused. Thus in 1853 he had an extended and passionate affair with Mathilde Wesendonck, even though her husband had provided him with a home in Zürich and had financed several of his concerts. The affair inspired him to write *Tristan und Isolde*. Several years later he fell in love with the wife of another intimate friend, Hans von BÜLOW. She was Cosima, daughter of Franz Liszt. Though Bülow dedicated himself to the promotion of Wagner's music, Wagner did not hesitate to take advantage of Cosima's fascination with him. Far from attempting to conceal the relationship, he insisted upon calling their first child, born in 1865, Isolde. After a second daughter was born to them, Wagner and Cosima set up their own home on Lake Lucerne; a year after their third child, Siegfried, was born, Wagner and the now-divorced Cosima were married. Wagner remained devoted to her for the rest of his life.

The struggles of his artistic life were also to be resolved in victory. After being pardoned for his radical activities, Wagner returned to Saxony in 1862. Two years later he acquired a wealthy and powerful patron in Ludwig II, King of Bavaria. Under Ludwig's patronage, *Tristan und Isolde* was introduced in Munich in 1865, *Die Meistersinger* in 1868, *Das Rheingold* in 1869, and *Die Walküre* in 1870. But getting his dramas performed did not completely satisfy Wagner. He nursed an ambition to have a special theater built where they could be performed according to his own ideas of staging. He overcame seemingly insurmountable obstacles to make his dream a reality. On Aug. 13, 1876, his vision became a fact. In a theater built according to his specifications in BAYREUTH, his *Ring* tetralogy was given its first complete performance, with the great of the world attending.

Wagner completed one more drama, the consecrational play PARSIFAL, introduced in Bayreuth on July 26, 1882. After the harrowing task of bringing this work to performance, Wagner went with Cosima on a vacation to Venice. He suffered a heart attack there and died. His body was brought back to Bayreuth to be buried in the garden of his home, Villa Wahnfried.

His operas: *Die Feen* (1834); *Das Liebesverbot* (1836); *Rienzi* (1840); *Der fliegende Holländer* (1841); *Tannhäuser* (1845); *Lohengrin* (1848); *Das Rheingold* (1854); *Die Walküre* (1856); *Tristan und Isolde* (1859); *Die Meistersinger von Nürnberg* (1867); *Siegfried* (1871); *Götterdämmerung* (1874); *Parsifal* (1882).

For *Das Rheingold, Die Walküre, Siegfried,* and *Götterdämmerung* see RING DES NIBELUNGEN, DER.

Wagner, Siegfried, conductor and composer. Born Triebschen, Lucerne, Switzerland, June 6, 1869; died Bayreuth, Aug. 4, 1930. The only son of Richard and Cosima WAGNER, he was educated as an architect but turned to music, studying with HUMPERDINCK and Julius Kniese. In 1894 he became an assistant conductor at BAYREUTH and from 1896 on conducted there regularly. From 1909 until his death he supervised all the productions at Bayreuth. He visited the United States in 1923–24, conducting several concerts of his father's music to raise funds for the reopening of the Bayreuth Theater after World War I. He married Winifred Williams in 1915; after his death, she became the guiding hand at the Bayreuth Festivals until the beginning of World War II.

Siegfried Wagner wrote fourteen operas, all to his own texts. The following were the most successful: *Der Kobold* (1904); *Sternengebot* (1908); *Der Heidenkönig* (1915); *Der Friedensengel* (1915); *Schwarzschwanenreich* (1918); *Sonnenflammen* (1918); *Der Schmied von Marienburg* (1920).

Wagner tuba, a wind instrument devised by Richard WAGNER to fill the gap between horns and the ordinary tubas to achieve darker colors and more brusque sound qualities than either instrument is capable of. Wagner used four such tubas in DER RING DES NIBELUNGEN—two tenor tubas in B-flat and two bass tubas in F.

Wagner, Wieland, designer and producer. Born Bayreuth, Jan. 5, 1917; died Munich, Oct. 16, 1966. He was the son of Siegfried WAGNER, the grandson of Richard WAGNER, and brother of Wolfgang WAGNER. He became a stage and scenic designer at BAYREUTH, his first production being PARSIFAL in 1939. After the resumption of the Bayreuth Festival following the end of World War II, he collaborated with his brother, Wolfgang, in assuming the artistic and business direction of the festival activities. He revolutionized the staging of the Wagnerian music dramas by reducing scenery, props, and stage action to essentials, while depending upon lighting for dramatic effect. Besides his work at Bayreuth, he staged and directed operatic performances according to his esthetic ideas in Hamburg, Stuttgart, Brussels, Rome, and elsewhere in a repertory that besides Wagner included such operas as ELEKTRA, SALOME, FIDELIO, and CARMEN. He had planned to come to the United States in 1966 to stage and produce LOHENGRIN for the METROPOLITAN OPERA. He died less than two months before that production was given.

Wagner, Wolfgang, designer and producer. Born Bayreuth, Aug. 30, 1919. He was the son of Siegfried WAGNER, grandson of Richard WAGNER, and brother of Wieland WAGNER. With his brother he served as business and artistic administrator at the BAYREUTH FESTIVAL after World War II. He helped stage and direct performances in which his brother's modern innovations were introduced, many of which he opposed. Though he retained some of his brother's productions and methods after Wieland's death, Wolfgang returned to a more traditional format and procedures in his newer productions.

Wahn! Wahn! Überall Wahn!, Hans Sachs's monologue lamenting the sad state into which the world has fallen, in

Act III, Scene 1, of WAGNER'S DIE MEISTERSINGER.

Waldmädchen, Das (The Dumb Girl of the Woods), opera in two acts by WEBER. Libretto by Carl Franz Goulfinger, Ritter von Steinsberg. Premiere: Freiberg, Saxony, Nov. 24, 1800. This was Weber's first opera to get a performance, having been written before he was fourteen. A few days after its premiere it was produced in Chemnitz (as *Das stumme Waldmädchen*) and subsequently in Vienna. Some years later, Franz Karl Hiemer completely revised the libretto in three acts, and Weber wrote an almost entirely new score in a more mature style. Under the title of *Silvana,* this work had its premiere in Frankfurt on Sept. 16, 1810. It was a distinct success and became the first of Weber's operas to be translated and produced outside of Germany. The heroine, being a dumb maiden, was played in pantomime while a cello or an oboe spoke for her.

Waldner, Count, Arabella's father (bass) in Richard STRAUSS'S ARABELLA.

Waldweben (Forest Murmurs), a scene in Act II of WAGNER'S SIEGFRIED, in which Siegfried, lying under a tree, is enjoying the beauty of the forest and the song of the birds.

Walker, Edyth, mezzo-soprano. Born Hopewell, N.Y., Mar. 27, 1867; died New York City, Feb. 19, 1950. She studied voice with Orgeni in Dresden before making her opera debut in Berlin in 1894 as FIDÈS. While a member of the VIENNA STATE OPERA between 1895 and 1903, she continued her voice studies with Marianne Brandt. Meanwhile on Nov. 30, 1903, she made her debut as AMNERIS with the METROPOLITAN OPERA, with which she remained three seasons. Between 1906 and 1912 she sang with the HAMBURG OPERA and between 1912 and 1917 with the MUNICH OPERA. She also made appearances as KUNDRY and ORTRUD at the BAYREUTH FESTIVAL in 1908 and was heard at COVENT GARDEN in 1900, 1908, and 1910. Following her retirement from the stage, she devoted herself to teaching voice for three years

at the American Fontainebleau Conservatory in France and then privately in New York.

Walk to the Paradise Garden, The, orchestral ENTR'ACTE between the fifth and sixth "pictures" of DELIUS' A VILLAGE ROMEO AND JULIET. This gentle orchestral episode describes the mood of two lovers as they pause at Paradise Garden at a village fair during their elopement.

Walküre, Die, *see* RING DES NIBELUNGEN, DER.

Walkürenritt, *see* RIDE OF THE VALKYRIES, THE.

Wallace, Jake, traveling camp minstrel (baritone) in PUCCINI'S THE GIRL OF THE GOLDEN WEST.

Wallenstein, *see* SCHILLER, FRIEDRICH.

Wallerstein, Lothar, stage director. Born Prague, Nov. 6, 1882; died New Orleans, Nov. 13, 1949. He studied to be a doctor but abandoned medicine for music. From 1910 to 1914 he was conductor and stage director of the Posen Opera. From 1918 to 1922 he held a similar position with the Breslau Opera and from 1924 to 1927 with the FRANKFURT OPERA. In 1927 he was appointed stage director of the VIENNA STATE OPERA, where he remained eleven years and staged over seventy-five new works. During this period he also staged operas at LA SCALA and the SALZBURG FESTIVALS. He came to the United States just before World War II and in 1949 was appointed resident stage director of the New Orleans Opera Association.

Wallmann, Margherita, producer. Born Vienna, June 22, 1904. She was trained to be a dancer and was a member of the VIENNA STATE OPERA ballet corps when an accident compelled her to give up her profession. In 1936 Bruno WALTER invited her to produce GLUCK'S ORFEO ED EURIDICE at the SALZBURG FESTIVAL. She proved herself so adept at her new profession that she was called upon by leading European opera houses for her services. At LA SCALA she staged the world premieres of L'ASSASSINIO NELLA CATTEDRALE, MILHAUD'S *David,* and LES DIALOGUES DES CARMÉLITES, as well as revivals of ALCESTE, MÉDÉE, and NORMA. She produced CARMEN for the CHICAGO OPERA in 1959 and directed a new production of LUCIA DI LAMMERMOOR at the METROPOLITAN OPERA in 1964.

Wally, La, opera in four acts by CATALANI. Libretto by Luigi ILLICA, based on *Die Geyer-Wally,* a novel by Wilhelmine von Hilbern. Premiere: La Scala, Jan. 20, 1892. American premiere: Metropolitan Opera, Jan. 6, 1909. In nineteenth-century Switzerland Wally (soprano), daughter of Stromminger (bass), refuses to marry Gellner (baritone), as she is in love with Hagenbach. Gellner tries to murder Hagenbach (tenor), which only brings the lovers closer together. But the lovers finally meet their doom in an avalanche. The preludes to Acts III and IV, the Valzer del bacio in Act III, and Wally's aria "Ebben? ne andrò lontana" in Act I are the best-known excerpts.

Walpurgis Night, ballet music in Act IV, Scene 3, of GOUNOD'S FAUST.

Walter, a count (bass), father of Rodolfo, in VERDI'S LUISA MILLER.

Walter, Bruno (born Schlesinger), conductor. Born Berlin, Sept. 15, 1876; died Beverly Hills, Cal., Feb. 17, 1962. After receiving his musical education at the Stern Conservatory in Berlin, he served his apprenticeship in various small German opera houses. Gustav MAHLER engaged him as assistant conductor of the VIENNA OPERA in 1901. Walter worked under Mahler for eleven years and developed into a mature artist. In 1914 Walter was engaged as general music director of the MUNICH OPERA in succession to Felix MOTTL. His performances there of MOZART and WAGNER gained him an international reputation. In 1923 Walter made his American debut as guest conductor of the New York Symphony Society. After that he appeared extensively in the United States as a conductor of its major orchestras.

Walter's long association with the SALZBURG FESTIVAL began in 1922. He appeared at COVENT GARDEN for the first time in 1924; for the next seven years he was one of this institution's principal conductors of Wagner and Mozart. In 1925 he was appointed principal conductor of the Charlottenburg Opera (BERLIN DEUTSCHE STAATSOPER) in Berlin and in 1930 principal conductor of the Leipzig Gewandhaus Orchestra. He had to resign his posts in Germany and leave the country when the Nazis came to power. When Felix WEINGARTNER resigned as musical director of the Vienna State Opera in 1936, Bruno Walter replaced him by holding the offices of principal conductor and musical advisor. When Hitler took over Austria, Walter made his home in Paris. During World War II he continued conducting opera and symphony performances throughout the free world. At the same time he transferred his permanent home to California, where he lived for the rest of his life; he also became an American citizen. On Feb. 14, 1941, he made his debut at the METROPOLITAN OPERA in FIDELIO. Until 1957 Walter concentrated his conducting efforts mainly on the New York Philharmonic and the Metropolitan Opera. When World War II ended he also performed in Europe. He was given a hero's welcome when he paid his first return visit to the Vienna State Opera in *Fidelio.* A heart attack in 1957 compelled him to curtail his activities. After that and until his death, he was active in the field of recording, recreating some of his most famous interpretations of symphonic masterworks in stereophonic sound.

Walter Fürst, a Swiss patriot (bass) in ROSSINI'S WILLIAM TELL.

Walther, *see* STOLZING, WALTHER VON.

Walton, Lord Gaultiers, Elvira's father (bass), in BELLINI'S I PURITANI.

Walton, Sir William, composer. Born Oldham, Eng., Mar. 29, 1902. He received his musical training at the Christ Church Cathedral Choir School, Oxford, and first attracted attention as a composer in 1922 with *Façade,* a provocative setting of some spirited dadaistic poems by Edith Sitwell. Walton did not write an opera until late in his career, after he had established himself as one of the outstanding English composers of his day. The opera, an important work, was

TROILUS AND CRESSIDA, introduced in London in 1954. He was knighted in 1951 and in 1953 wrote a *Te Deum* for the coronation of Queen Elizabeth II. Soon after the end of World War II, he began a career as conductor of his own works, making his first American appearance in 1955 and later directing an all-Walton program at the Lewisohn Stadium in New York City on Aug. 8, 1963.

Waltraute, a valkyrie (mezzo-soprano) in WAGNER'S DIE WALKÜRE and GÖTTER-DÄMMERUNG.

waltz, an Austrian dance of peasant origin, it acquired its polish and its fame in Vienna in the late eighteenth century, then spread throughout the world. One of the earliest examples of a typical Viennese waltz is found in MARTÍN's opera UNA COSA RARA, produced in Vienna in 1785. The following operas are notable for containing waltzes: LA BOHÈME (Musetta's Waltz, Act II); EUGENE ONEGIN (Act II); FAUST ("Ainsi que la brise," Act II); HANSEL AND GRETEL (Gingerbread Waltz, Act III); ME-FISTOFELE (Peasants' Waltz, Act I); ROMÉO ET JULIETTE ("Je veux vivre dans ce rêve," Act I); LA WALLY ("Valzer del bacio," Waltz of the Kiss, Act III); WAR AND PEACE (Scene 2). Johann STRAUSS's DIE FLEDERMAUS and Richard STRAUSS's DER ROSENKAVALIER are works that might be called waltz-inspired.

Wanderer, The, the god Wotan, in mortal guise, in WAGNER'S SIEGFRIED.

Wann hörst du auf, Gotthold's aria in DITTERSDORF'S THE DOCTOR AND THE APOTHECARY.

War and Peace, opera in prologue and thirteen scenes by PROKOFIEV. Libretto by the composer and Mira Mendelson (Prokofiev's wife), based on the novel by Leo TOLSTOY. Premiere: Maly Theater, Leningrad, June 12, 1946 (eight scenes only); Florence May Music Festival, 1953 (entire work). American premiere: NBC-TV, Jan. 13, 1957 (abridged).

Characters: Andrei, Prince Bolkonsky (baritone); Nicolai, his father (bass); Princess Marie, Andrei's sister (mezzo-soprano); Ilya, Count Rostov (bass); Natasha, his daughter (soprano); Sonya, her cousin (mezzo-soprano); Princess Akhrosimova (soprano); Pierre, Prince Bezukov (tenor); Hélène, his wife (mezzo-soprano); Anatol, Prince Kuragin, Hélène's brother (tenor); Dolokhov, Anatol's friend (baritone); Michael, Prince Kutuzov, Field Marshal of the Russian Army (bass); Napoleon Bonaparte (baritone); Vassili Denisov, Pierre's friend (baritone); Platon Karateyev, a soldier (tenor); Balaga, a coachman (bass); peasants; soldiers; Cossacks; Russian aristocracy; members of Napoleon's staff; partisans. The action takes place in Russia between 1809 and 1812.

Scene 1. A garden at Count Rostov's estate. Prince Andrei, a visitor, is gloomily contemplating the night scene, despondent about life. Natasha and Sonya appear at a window above him, rhapsodizing over the beauty of the spring night. Andrei cannot see Natasha but is so deeply moved by the sound of her voice that his will to enjoy life returns.

Scene 2. A ballroom in a palace at St. Petersburg. It is New Year's Eve, 1810. A gay party is taking place; the guests are dancing a POLONAISE. Count Pierre Bezukov, a friend of the Rostov family, urges Andrei to dance with Natasha. As they dance a waltz, Andrei recognizes her as the girl whose voice had so fascinated him. On an odd impulse he determines to make her his wife if, after the dance, Natasha goes to her cousin Sonya. This she does.

Scene 3. An anteroom in Prince Bolkonsky's palace. Having asked for Natasha's hand in marriage, Andrei is accepted by the girl and her father. But Andrei's father is opposed to the match and has sent him abroad for a year. When Natasha and her father call on the old Prince, he treats them rudely.

Scene 4. A salon in Prince Bezukov's palace. Hélène, wife of Pierre, is giving a party for her friends. Among those present is Natasha. Though Hélène knows that Natasha is betrothed to the departed Andrei, she nevertheless tries to interest Natasha in Anatol Kuragin, Hélène's brother. Anatol falls in love with her at sight and implores her to elope with him. Natasha, deeply moved by Anatol's ardor, becomes interested in him.

Scene 5. A study in Dolokhov's home. Dolokhov is trying to convince his friend Anatol not to go through with the mad plan to elope with Natasha, especially as he already has a secretly married wife. Anatol, however, is deaf to his arguments and vows to give up his dissolute life for the sake of Natasha and to abandon his mistress, a gypsy girl.

Scene 6. A room in the home of Princess Akhrosimova. The Rostovs, leaving on a trip, have entrusted Natasha to the care of the aged Princess Akhrosimova. Natasha, however, is making plans to elope with Anatol, but when he arrives, he is refused entry by a footman, for the Princess had learned about the planned elopement from Sonya, and she now takes Natasha severely to task for betraying her parents and her fiancé. Natasha explains that she has broken off her engagement with Andrei secretly, that she loves Anatol, who, she insists, is a most honorable man. But she is disenchanted by Pierre, Anatol's brother-in-law, who reveals to Natasha the full extent of Anatol's escapades. Natasha bursts into tears for she now realizes her mistake in having abandoned her fiancé for Anatol. Her grief affects Pierre to the point where he confesses that were he free he would propose to Natasha.

Scene 7. Pierre's study. Hélène is entertaining some friends and Anatol. When Pierre arrives he orders Anatol to leave Moscow, which Anatol promises to do. Pierre is in a state of utter despair over the amoral climate existing in his household when Denisov, an army lieutenant, brings him the news that Napoleon is mobilizing his army on the Russian front. Pierre leaves hurriedly to join the Russian forces.

Scene 8. The hills near Borodino. Partisans and guerilla fighters are awaiting a French attack. Andrei is with them, upset by Natasha's betrayal of their engagement and his frustrated love. When Pierre arrives, Andrei, about to take over the command of his regiment, bids his friend a tender farewell. Pierre now joins the army as a common soldier. When Marshal Kutuzov arrives, the army passes in a grand review. The Marshal summons Andrei to ask him to become a member of his staff, but Andrei insists his place is at the front, where the battle has finally begun.

Scene 9. Napoleon's camp at Shevardinsky Redoubt. Confident of victory, Napoleon pictures in his mind his march into captured Moscow. Messengers, however, bring him only news of defeat, of disastrous French losses. Napoleon cannot understand why victory is no longer in his grasp.

Scene 10. A hut near Fili. Marshal Kutuzov calls a council of war to decide whether to defend or abandon Moscow. Despite the advice of his staff, Kutuzov decides on abandoning the city, convinced as he is that the people will stand firm against the occupying French and ultimately drive them out.

Scene 11. A street in Moscow. Moscow is being abandoned by the Russians, among them the Rostovs, who have taken along some wounded officers. Though Natasha is unaware of it, Andrei is one of those officers. Pierre hears the news from the Rostov servants and plots to assassinate Napoleon. Moscow is in flames. When Pierre and a peasant soldier, Platon Karateyev, are rounded up by the French and accused of arson, they proudly reiterate their conviction that in the end Russia will emerge triumphant. The same feeling is found among the Russians who had remained in the city, a fact that impresses Napoleon when he arrives in Moscow with his staff.

Scene 12. A hut outside Moscow. Andrei is wounded and delirious. When Natasha appears, he thinks her to be a vision of his delirium. Once he is made aware that it is truly she and not a hallucination, they fall into each other's arms and recall their happy days together. Natasha begs for his forgiveness, which he gives, while reaffirming his great love for her. Then he lapses back into delirium and dies.

Scene 13. The road to Smolensk. The French are in full retreat. With them as prisoners are Pierre and Platon; the latter, sick and unable to go on, is shot by his captors. A band of Russian partisans successfully attack the French column, and free Pierre, who learns that the French army is being routed and that Moscow is once again free. Czarist troops appear, headed by Marshal Kutuzov, who praises the people for their courage. The people in turn raise their voices to hymn the praises of Kutuzov, who, they say, was responsible for this great Russian victory.

When in 1941 Prokofiev and his wife first conceived of this epic opera, it was to be done in two parts, the first ending at Scene 7 in the account given above. But until he died in 1953, the composer kept tinkering with both score and libretto and never came to a final, definitive version. The synopsis here given is based on the version used by the Bolshoi Opera on Aug. 11, 1967, at Expo 67 in Montreal, the first staged performance in the Western Hemisphere.

Prokofiev's opera is of giant dimensions, demanding an enormous cast and, in its spectacular scenes, the most elaborate staging. In those episodes where huge masses are deployed, the score is notable for its stirring choral writing. But subtle character delineation also is a strong element in the music, particularly the portrayals of Andrei, Anatol, and Natasha. When the emphasis is on love scenes, Prokofiev can be soaringly lyrical, just as he can be subtly and sensitively atmospheric in his orchestral tone portraits.

Ward, Robert, composer. Born Cleveland, Sept. 13, 1917. He attended the Eastman School of Music, the Juilliard School, and the Berkshire Music Center. He first attracted attention as a composer with several orchestral works, including two symphonies. Between 1949

and 1951 he received Guggenheim Fellowships. In 1955 he became president of the American Composers Alliance and a year later was appointed vice president and managing editor of the Galaxy Music Corporation. His first opera, HE WHO GETS SLAPPED, was introduced in New York in 1956. In 1962 he received the PULITZER PRIZE in music for THE CRUCIBLE, an opera based on the play of the same name by Arthur MILLER, its premiere taking place in New York in 1961. This was followed by THE LADY FROM COLORADO, introduced in Central City, Col., in 1964.

War es so schmälich?, Brünnhilde's plea to Wotan to forgive her, in Act III of WAGNER'S DIE WALKÜRE.

Warren, Leonard, baritone. Born New York City, Apr. 21, 1911; died there, Mar. 4, 1960. He engaged in business activities until 1933, when he decided to become a professional singer. His vocal studies took place with Sidney Dietch in New York, and subsequently with Giuseppe de LUCA and others in Milan. After singing with the chorus of the Radio City Music Hall, he won the METROPOLITAN AUDITIONS OF THE AIR. As a result he made his opera debut at the METROPOLITAN OPERA on Jan. 13, 1939, as Paolo in SIMON BOCCANEGRA. He was first a COMPRIMARIO but soon a principal baritone of that company, besides making highly successful appearances in Mexico, South America, Puerto Rico, Italy, and Canada. In 1953 he was acclaimed at LA SCALA, and in 1958 he toured the Soviet Union. He was generally regarded as one of the leading baritones of his time, particularly in VERDI operas. He also appeared over radio, television, and in the motion picture *When Irish Eyes Are Smiling*. He died on the stage of the Metropolitan Opera during a performance of LA FORZA DEL DESTINO.

Wartburg, the castle of the minstrel-knights in Thuringia, in WAGNER'S TANNHÄUSER.

Was bluten muss?, Elektra's ecstatic threat to her mother following the murder of Agamemnon, in Richard STRAUSS's ELEKTRA.

Was gleicht wohl auf Erden, the Huntsmen's Chorus in Act III, Scene 2, of WEBER's DER FREISCHÜTZ.

Wasps, The, *see* ARISTOPHANES.

Water Carrier, The (Der Wasserträger; Les Deux Journées), opera in three acts by CHERUBINI. Libretto by Jean-Nicolas Bouilly. Premiere: Théâtre Feydeau, Paris, Jan. 16, 1800. This is a notable example of a category come to be known as "the rescue opera," of which BEETHOVEN's FIDELIO is another representative. When, in seventeenth-century France, Count Armand (tenor) falls into disfavor with Mazarin, Michèle, the water carrier (bass), arranges for the Count's escape from Paris in a water barrel. The Count and his wife (soprano) are seized by soldiers, but before they are taken back to Paris, Michèle comes with the news that the King has forgiven the Count and restored to him his former high station. One of its principal arias is Antonio's ROMANCE, "Un pauvre petit Savoyard." The soldiers' chorus which opens the second act and the third-act bridal chorus are distinguished ensemble numbers. The overture is occasionally performed at symphony concerts.

Waters, Mrs., a landlady (soprano) whom Harry Bennis is seeking to marry, in Dame Ethel SMYTH's THE BOATSWAIN'S MATE.

Weathers, Felicia, soprano. Born St. Louis, Aug. 13, 1937. She studied voice with Charles KULLMANN and Dorothee Manski at Indiana University. Following graduation from the university, she was declared laureate in the International Competition of Young Singers at Sofia, Bulgaria. Her opera debut took place at the ZÜRICH OPERA, where she was discovered by Rudolf HARTMANN, stage director, who engaged her for the MUNICH OPERA. KARAJAN also became impressed with her talent and engaged her for the VIENNA STATE OPERA. She made her debut with the METROPOLITAN OPERA on Oct. 21, 1965, as Lisa in PIQUE DAME. She has since been a member of the company. She has also appeared with the HAMBURG OPERA, the STOCKHOLM OPERA, and the CHICAGO LYRIC OPERA; with the last company she made a notable appearance in PROKOFIEV's THE FLAMING ANGEL on Dec. 12, 1966.

Weber, Carl Maria von, composer. Born Eutin, Oldenburg, Ger., Nov. 18, 1786; died London, June 5, 1826. He was born a sickly child, with a disease of the hip that gave him a lifelong limp. Despite this infirmity, he had to travel continually with his parents, since his father played the violin in various small orchestras. The father compelled the boy to study music industriously, bent on developing a prodigy. When Carl was eleven, he studied for six months with Michael Haydn in Salzburg. His later study took place in Munich. It was there that he completed his first opera, *Die Macht der Liebe und des Weins.* His second, DAS WALDMÄDCHEN, was performed in 1800 in Freiberg, then in Chemnitz and Vienna. (It was subsequently revised and renamed *Silvana.*)

In 1803 Weber went to Vienna and studied for two years with Abbé Vogler. Upon Vogler's recommendation he received a post as conductor with the Breslau Opera in 1805. His three years in Breslau were unhappy, since he was in perpetual conflict with the management and members of the company, while his dissolute and irresponsible behavior aroused the hostility of the public. He left Breslau and assumed two other musical posts. The second, in Stuttgart, came to a sudden end when he was accused of having stolen some funds. A period of travel followed, during which Weber appeared as a concert pianist and composed several large works, including a comic opera, ABU HASSAN, successful when given in Munich in 1811. Finally in 1813 he settled in Prague and became director of the Opera. Three years later he received his most important conductorial assignment when he was engaged as musical director of the DRESDEN OPERA. His success was so substantial that his post was confirmed for life. His future assured, Weber married the singer Caroline

Brandt. Weber devoted himself to conducting German operas, and this inflamed him with an ideal: he would write a national opera. The task took him three years. The opera, DER FREISCHÜTZ, was introduced in Berlin on Aug. 18, 1821 (his wife appearing as Agathe) and was such a sensation that Weber became the man of the hour. His opera received fifty performances in a year and a half, then duplicated its successes the following year in Dresden and Vienna. German audiences went wild over *Der Freischütz*, in which the romantic tendencies of the times were crystallized and in which German traditions, backgrounds, and culture were glorified.

Weber was now commissioned by the impresario Domenico BARBAJA to write a new opera for Vienna. His EURYANTHE was introduced in that city in 1823 and was acclaimed. His last opera, OBERON, was written for COVENT GARDEN on commission. Though ill at the time, Weber made the arduous journey to London to complete *Oberon* and supervise its production. The premiere in 1826—Weber himself conducted—was such a triumph that Weber described it as "the greatest success of my life." But the supreme effort of completing and producing his new opera undermined his health completely. He died in his sleep, just before he was to make his journey home. He was buried in London. Eighteen years later his body was transferred to Dresden. For this second burial, WAGNER wrote special music and delivered the eulogy.

While Weber's three operatic masterworks—*Der Freischütz, Euryanthe,* and *Oberon*—are no longer in the permanent repertory and are heard only when an opera company undertakes an adventurous revival, their significance cannot be overestimated. They helped to establish a national operatic movement that could rival the then ascendant Italian school. The road from Weber leads directly to Wagner, as Wagner himself conceded. Before Wagner, Weber made tentative use of the LEITMOTIV

method; he gave greater dramatic significance to the recitative and greater symphonic importance to the orchestra than any composer before his time; and he integrated his plays and music more successfully than any composer since GLUCK.

His operas: *Die Macht der Liebe und des Weins* (1798); *Das Waldmädchen* (1800); *Peter Schmoll und seine Nachbarn* (1803); *Rübezahl* (1805); *Silvana* (1810); *Abu Hassan* (1811); *Der Freischütz* (1821); *Die drei Pintos* (unfinished); *Euryanthe* (1823); *Oberon* (1826).

Webster, Daniel, the celebrated American statesman and orator, a principal character (baritone) in MOORE'S THE DEVIL AND DANIEL WEBSTER. He also appears briefly as a character in THOMSON'S THE MOTHER OF US ALL.

Wedekind, Frank, dramatist. Born Hanover, July 24, 1864; died Munich, Mar. 9, 1918. Two of his plays, *Earth Spirit* (*Der Erdgeist*) and *Pandora's Box* (*Die Büchse der Pandora*), were made into a single libretto for LULU. Max Ettinger's *Frühlingserwachen* and WEISGALL's *The Tenor* are based on Wedekind's plays.

Weiche, Wotan, weiche!, Erda's warning to Wotan not to surrender the ring to the two giants, in the final scene of WAGNER'S DAS RHEINGOLD.

Weill, Kurt, composer. Born Dessau, Ger., Mar. 2, 1900; died New York City, Apr. 3, 1950. He attended the Berlin Hochschule für Musik, where his teachers included HUMPERDINCK; he subsequently studied privately with BUSONI. His first opera, DER PROTAGONIST, introduced in Dresden in 1926, made extensive use of popular-music idioms. This element was pronounced in his succeeding operas, making him an outstanding exponent of a German cultural movement known as ZEITKUNST, which glorified contemporary subjects treated in a racy, modern style. In 1928 he wrote his greatest success, a modern adaptation of *The Beggar's Opera:* THE THREEPENNY OPERA (*Die Dreigroschenoper*). Introduced in Berlin on Aug. 31, it enjoyed a sensational success, being given a total of over four thousand performances in some one hundred twenty German theaters. In 1930 came another provocative opera, THE RISE AND FALL OF THE CITY MAHAGONNY (*Aufstieg und Fall der Stadt Mahagonny*). Here Weill perfected his popular-song form and used it to replace the traditional opera aria; one of these numbers, "The Alabamy Song," became a great hit.

Weill's last German opera, *Der Silbersee* (*The Silver Lake*), opened simultaneously in 1933 in eleven different German cities. The following morning the Reichstag was burned. Weill's opera closed and the composer fled to Paris. In 1935 he came to the United States, later becoming a citizen. He soon assumed a leading position in the Broadway musical world, producing a succession of stage triumphs that included *Knickerbocker Holiday, Lady in the Dark,* and *One Touch of Venus.* He also completed a one-act American folk opera, DOWN IN THE VALLEY, introduced at Indiana University on July 15, 1948.

His operas: *The Protagonist* (1926); *The Royal Palace* (1927); THE CZAR HAS HIMSELF PHOTOGRAPHED (1928); *The Threepenny Opera* (1928); *Happy End* (1929); *The Rise and Fall of the City Mahagonny* (1930); *Der Jasager* (1930); *Die Bürgschaft* (1932); *Der Silbersee* (1933); *Down in the Valley* (1948).

Weimar Opera, a significant opera company in Weimar, Ger., which enjoyed its heyday between 1848 and 1859 with LISZT as musical director and Hans von BÜLOW as a principal conductor. It was during this period that there took place in Weimar the world premieres of *Alfonso und Estrella* (SCHUBERT), THE BARBER OF BAGDAD, and LOHENGRIN, as well as such novelties as BENVENUTO CELLINI and GENOVEVA. Liszt was succeeded by Eduard Lassen, who introduced several of his own operas and SAMSON ET DALILA, besides mounting TRISTAN UND ISOLDE when other opera houses refused to do so following its Munich premiere. HAN-

SEL AND GRETEL was given its world premiere and WERTHER its German premiere in 1893 during the period when Richard STRAUSS was musical director. In 1894 he led the world premiere of his first opera, GUNTRAM. Performances were given at the Hoftheater until 1907, when the present theater, the Deutsches Nationaltheater, was constructed.

Weinberger, Jaromir, composer. Born Prague, Jan. 8, 1896; died St. Petersburg, Fla., Aug. 6, 1967. He was a pupil of Vitezslav Novák and Jaroslav Krička at the Prague Conservatory, after which he studied privately with Max Reger in Berlin. In 1922 he came to the United States and taught composition at the Ithaca Conservatory in New York. He returned to Europe four years later, becoming director of opera at the National Theater in Bratislava and head of the Eger School of Music. Success as a composer came with a folk opera, ŠVANDA THE BAGPIPER, first given in Prague on Apr. 27, 1927. Between 1927 and 1931 it was heard over two thousand times in Europe; on Nov. 7, 1931, it was given at the METROPOLITAN OPERA.

With the rise of the Nazi threat to Czechoslovakia, Weinberger escaped to Paris. In 1939 he came to the United States, where he became a citizen and ultimately made his permanent home in St. Petersburg, Fla. In America he wrote a number of instrumental compositions drawing on American historical themes and at times using American idioms. His last work was the *Five Songs from Des Knabens Wunderhorn,* introduced at the VIENNA FESTIVAL WEEKS in 1962. Depression over his failure to get a hearing for his compositions in the United States induced a melancholia that finally led him to commit suicide.

His operas: *Švanda the Bagpiper* (1927); *The Beloved Voice* (1931); *The Outcasts of Poker Flat* (1932); *A Bed of Roses* (1934); *Wallenstein* (1937); *A Bird's Opera* (1941).

Weingartner, Felix, conductor and composer. Born Zara, Dalmatia, June 2, 1863; died Winterthur, Switzerland,

May 7, 1942. His music study began in Graz. In his eighteenth year he entered the Leipzig Conservatory, where he won the Mozart Award. After leaving Leipzig, his first opera, *Sakuntala*, was performed in Weimar in 1884. There he met and became a friend of LISZT, who convinced him that he ought to become a conductor. Through Liszt's recommendation, Weingartner became Hans von BÜLOW's assistant with the Meiningen Orchestra. In 1891 Weingartner was appointed principal conductor of the BERLIN (Royal) OPERA. After a brief period as conductor of the Kaim Concerts in Munich, he was summoned to Vienna in 1908 to succeed Gustav MAHLER as artistic director of the Opera and principal conductor of the Vienna Philharmonic. Weingartner became famous in Vienna for his outstanding performances of the BEETHOVEN symphonies and the WAGNER music dramas. He left Vienna in 1911 and from 1912 to 1914 was principal conductor of the Hamburg Stadttheater and from 1914 to 1919 music director in Darmstadt.

He first came to the United States in 1905 as a guest conductor of the New York Philharmonic Orchestra. In 1912 he made his American debut as opera conductor by directing TRISTAN UND ISOLDE with the BOSTON OPERA.

In 1927 he settled in Basel, Switzerland, to become director of the Conservatory and conductor of symphony concerts. In 1935 he was recalled to Vienna to replace Clemens KRAUSS as artistic director. He remained in this post only until the fall of 1936. He also appeared as guest conductor in most of the major opera houses of the world, and at the SALZBURG FESTIVALS. He wrote several books, including a valuable treatise on conducting (1895) and a history of BAYREUTH (1896). In addition he prepared new editions of several operas, including WEBER's OBERON and MÉHUL's JOSEPH.

His operas were: *Sakuntala* (1884); *Malawika* (1886); *Genesius* (1892); *Orestes,* a trilogy including *Agamemnon, Das Totenopfer,* and *Die Errin-*

nyen (1902); *Kain und Abel* (1914); *Dame Kobold* (1916); *Die Dorfschule* (1920); *Meister Andrea* (1920); *Der Apostat* (1938).

Weisgall, Hugo, composer. Born Ivancice, Czechoslovakia, Oct. 13, 1912. His family settled in Baltimore in 1920, where he attended the Peabody Conservatory. He subsequently studied composition with Rosario Scalero at the Curtis Institute and privately with Roger Sessions. After serving in the army during World War II he devoted himself in Baltimore to teaching music privately and directing several musical organizations, one of which (the Chamber Music Society) he founded in 1949. Between 1953 and 1956 he lectured on music at Johns Hopkins. As a composer he has distinguished himself in opera. His first opera was *The Tenor,* based on a play by WEDEKIND, introduced in Baltimore on Feb. 11, 1952. *The Stronger,* derived from a play by STRINDBERG, was heard in Westport, Conn., on Aug. 9, 1952. His later operas were *Six Characters in Search of an Author* (New York City, Apr. 26, 1959); *Purgatory* (Washington, D.C., Feb. 17, 1961); *Athaliah* (New York City, Feb. 17, 1964); and *Nine Rivers from Jordan,* produced by the NEW YORK CITY OPERA on Oct. 9, 1968. Since 1953 Weisgall has taught at the Juilliard School of Music and since 1960 has been professor of composition at Queens College in New York. From 1952 to 1962 he was also chairman of the faculty at the Cantors Institute and Seminary College of Jewish Music. He received Guggenheim Fellowships in 1955 and 1959.

Welcher Wechsel, Constanze's lament at being separated from her beloved Belmonte, in Act II of MOZART's THE ABDUCTION FROM THE SERAGLIO.

Welche Wonne, welche Lust, Blonde's expression of joy at learning that Belmonte has devised a plan for her escape, in Act II of MOZART's THE ABDUCTION FROM THE SERAGLIO.

Welitch (or Welitsch), Ljuba, soprano. Born Borissova, Bulgaria, July 10, 1913.

She studied singing in Sofia and in Vienna, then joined the Graz Opera Company, where she made her debut as NEDDA. After appearances with several provincial opera companies, during which period she was heard in over forty roles, she became a member of the HAMBURG OPERA. In 1943 she was engaged by the VIENNA STATE OPERA, where she scored her first major successes. Her London debut took place at COVENT GARDEN in 1947 in a performance of Richard STRAUSS's SALOME. She enjoyed a triumphant success. Her American debut, also in *Salome,* was no less a sensation at the METROPOLITAN OPERA on Feb. 4, 1949. During the next few years she was a principal soprano of both Covent Garden and the Metropolitan Opera, besides giving guest performances with leading European opera companies. Since 1955 she has been all but retired from opera but has had a career in motion pictures.

Wellesz, Egon, composer and musicologist. Born Vienna, Oct. 21, 1885. He attended the University of Vienna and studied music privately with Arnold SCHOENBERG. From 1911 to 1915 he taught music history in Vienna. In 1919 he joined the faculty of the Vienna University, where from 1928 on he was a professor of music history. After the annexation of Austria by Germany, he left his native land and settled in England, where he received a research fellowship at Oxford. He visited the United States in 1947 and delivered lectures at Princeton University and Columbia University. He is an authority on Byzantine music, having written a definitive study of it in 1922 and an allied work, *Eastern Elements in Western Chant,* in 1947. In 1948 he was appointed University Reader in Byzantine Music at Oxford. He has also written a study on the early history of opera, *Cavalli und der Stil der venetianischèn Oper* (1913), a biography of Arnold Schoenberg (1921), and *Die Hymnen der Ostkirche* (1962). As a composer, he is represented by a number of operas: *Die Prinzessin Girnara* (1921); *Alkestis* (1924); *Die Op-*

ferung des Gefangenen (1926); *Scherz, List und Rache* (1928); *Die Bacchantinen* (1931); *Incognita* (1951).

Wellgunde, a Rhine maiden (soprano) in WAGNER's DAS RHEINGOLD and GÖTTERDÄMMERUNG.

Wenzel, Micha's bumpkin son (tenor) in SMETANA's THE BARTERED BRIDE.

Werdenberg, *see* PRINCESS VON WERDENBERG.

Wer ein holdes Weib errungen, the closing chorus of BEETHOVEN's FIDELIO, in which Florestan and the people pay tribute to a devoted wife.

Wer ein Liebchen hat gefunden, Osmin's cynical appraisal of women, in Act I of MOZART's THE ABDUCTION FROM THE SERAGLIO.

Werfel, Franz, novelist and dramatist. Born Prague, Sept. 10, 1890; died Beverly Hills, Cal., Aug. 26, 1945. His novel *The Forty Days of Musa Dagh* was the source of Lodovico ROCCA's opera *Monte Ivnor.* MILHAUD's MAXIMILIEN was derived from Werfel's play *Juarez and Maximilian.* A discriminating music lover, Werfel wrote a novel entitled *Verdi: A Novel of the Opera* (1925) and collaborated with Paul Stefan in editing *Verdi: The Man in His Letters* (1942). He also translated the librettos of several of VERDI's operas into German. He married and was divorced from the widow of Gustav MAHLER.

Werner Kirchhofer, the trumpeter (baritone) in NESSLER's DER TROMPETER VON SÄKKINGEN.

Werther, opera (or lyric drama) in four acts by MASSENET. Libretto by Edouard Blau, Paul Milliet, and Georges Hartmann, based on GOETHE's novel *Die Leiden des jungen Werther.* Premiere: Vienna Royal Opera, Feb. 16, 1892. American premiere: Chicago, Mar. 29, 1894. This is one of the few operas by Massenet in which the heroine is not a courtesan but a virtuous woman. In Germany in 1772 Werther (tenor, a role created by Ernest VAN DYCK) falls in love with Charlotte (soprano), who is betrothed to his friend, Albert (baritone). Charlotte, who returns Werther's love but feels duty-bound to marry Albert, urges Werther to leave her forever. When she discovers that he has asked Albert for his pistols, she becomes apprehensive, and rushes to him late one night in a blinding snowstorm. Werther has shot himself, and he dies in her arms. Werther's invocation to nature, "O nature," in Act I; his air of desolation, "Un autre est son époux," and his prayer, "Lorsque l'enfant revient," in Act II; and the duet of Werther and Charlotte, "Pourquoi me reveiller?" and Charlotte's song of tears, "Va! laisse-les couler mes larmes," both in Act III, are among the more familiar vocal excerpts.

Western Opera Theatre, see SAN FRANCISCO OPERA.

Westwärts schweift der Blick, the young sailor's song opening Act I of WAGNER's TRISTAN UND ISOLDE.

When I am laid in earth, Dido's Lament before her death, in Act III of PURCELL's DIDO AND AENEAS.

Wher'er you walk, one of HANDEL's most noble tenor arias. It comes from SEMELE and glorifies the wonder and beauty of the world.

Whitehill, Clarence, baritone. Born Marengo, Iowa, Nov. 5, 1871; died New York City, Dec. 19, 1932. He was employed as a clerk when Nellie MELBA heard him and advised him to study singing. He went to Paris and studied with Giovanni SBRIGLIA and Alfred Auguste Giraudet. His debut took place at the THÉÂTRE DE LA MONNAIE in 1899 in ROMÉO ET JULIETTE. He made such a good impression that he was engaged by the OPÉRA-COMIQUE. In 1900 he returned to the United States and sang with the Henry SAVAGE Opera Company. After an additional period of study in Germany and appearances in minor German opera houses, he made his METROPOLITAN OPERA debut on Nov. 25, 1909, as AMFORTAS, a role for which he became noted. During this period he remained at the Metropolitan only two seasons. After an engagement with the CHICAGO OPERA, he returned to the Metropolitan in 1918, now remaining fourteen years. He was acclaimed for his interpretations of Wagnerian roles, particularly those of Amfortas, HANS SACHS, and WOTAN. He was also heard in French operas including the Metropolitan premieres of LOUISE and PELLÉAS ET MÉLISANDE. He resigned from the Metropolitan after the 1931–32 season because of differences with the management.

White Wings, opera in two acts by MOORE. Libretto is Philip Barry's play of the same name. Premiere: Hartford, Conn., Feb. 9, 1949. "White Wings" is an organization of street cleaners in an unnamed American city in 1895. Archie Inch and Mary Todd are in love, but are kept apart by their differing views on horses. Archie comes from a generation of White Wingers who revere the horse while Mary has faith in the future of the automobile. She grows wealthy when her father becomes a successful automobile manufacturer. After the last horse in town is shot, the now impoverished and humble Archie is able to marry the girl he loves.

whole-tone scale, a seven-note scale in which the intervals are equally spaced, the interval between each note being the same (a full tone). DEBUSSY's PELLÉAS ET MÉLISANDE exploits the use of the whole-tone scale.

widerspenstigen Zähmung, Der, see TAMING OF THE SHREW, THE.

Wie aus der Ferne, Senta's joyous reaction on learning from her father that the Dutchman has asked for her hand, in Act II of WAGNER's DER FLIEGENDE HOLLÄNDER.

Wie fühl ich stolz mein Herz entbrannt, the summons of King Henry to his retinue to prepare for battle in the opening of Act III, Scene 2, of WAGNER's LOHENGRIN.

Wie kann ich Freude noch in meinem Blicken zeigen, Leonore's aria of her frustration in love, in DITTERSDORF's THE DOCTOR AND THE APOTHECARY.

Wie lachend sie mir Lieder singen, Isolde's recital to Brangäne of Tristan's earlier visit to Ireland and of how Isolde had saved his life, in Act I of WAGNER's TRISTAN UND ISOLDE.

Wiesbaden Opera Festival, the second oldest existing opera festival in Europe (the oldest being the BAYREUTH festival). It was inaugurated in 1896 at the command of Kaiser Wilhelm II of Germany with gala performances by the local opera company. Since that time the festival has taken place annually each May. Opera dominates the festival's proceedings. Performances are given by the Wiesbaden State Opera (Hessisches Staatstheater), of which Claus Helmust Dreste is director and Heinz Walburg principal conductor. The festival has acquired an international character with presentations by the leading opera companies of Europe in a varied repertory that, besides including the more familiar repertory, embraces novelties ranging from ARMIDE of LULLY and *Pimpione* by Telemann to PRINCE IGOR, DALIBOR, DAS LEBEN DES OREST, THE GAMBLER, and KATERINA ISMAILOVA. In 1968, for example, the festival played host to the TEATRO LA FENICE and the Bulgarian National Opera; in 1969, to the OPÉRA-COMIQUE and the TEATRO COMMUNALE of Bologna. Performances are given at the opera house occupied during the winter season by the Wiesbaden State Opera since its opening in 1894. The festival suspended operations during World War II, but resumed in 1950, and has been presented annually since.

Wie Sonne lauter strahlt mir sein Licht, Brünnhilde's reaffirmation of her love of Siegfried, in the middle of the Immolation Scene, just before she plunges into the burning funeral pyre in Act III, Scene 2, of WAGNER's GÖTTERDÄMMERUNG.

Wilde, Oscar, poet, dramatist, novelist. Born Dublin, Oct. 16, 1856; died Paris, Nov. 30, 1900. His poetic drama *Salome* (which he wrote in French) was translated into German to make the libretto of Richard STRAUSS's opera of the same name. Another composer, Antoine Mariotte, made an operatic version of Wilde's play at about the same time, causing a conflict (*see* SALOME). Other operas made from Wilde's writings include: Renzo Bossi's *L'usignuolo e la rosa;* CASTELNUEVO-TEDESCO's *The Importance of Being Earnest;* Jaroslav Křička's *The Gentleman in White;* Alexander ZEM-

LINSKY's *Eine florentinische Tragödie* and *Der Zwerg;* William Orchard's *The Picture of Dorian Gray;* Hans Schaeuble's *Dorian Gray.*

Wilder, Thornton, novelist and playwright. Born Madison, Wis., Apr. 17, 1897. His celebrated 1928 Pulitzer Prize novel, *The Bridge of San Luis Rey,* was made into an opera by Hermann Reutter (*Die Brücke von San Luis Rey*). Wilder wrote the text for *Alcestiad,* an opera by Louise Talma, and his play, THE LONG CHRISTMAS DINNER, served as the basis for a libretto for the one-act opera by HINDEMITH.

Wilhelm Meister, *see* GOETHE, JOHANN WOLFGANG VON.

Wilhelm Tell, a poetic drama by Friedrich SCHILLER, the source of operas by Benjamin Carr (*The Archers,* one of the earliest American operas), GRÉTRY, and ROSSINI.

William Ratcliff, a drama by Heinrich HEINE, the source of operas by CUI and MASCAGNI, among others. Mascagni's, a student effort, was later revised.

William Tell (Guillaume Tell), opera in four acts by ROSSINI. Libretto by Étienne de JOUY and Hippolyte Bis, based on the drama by Friedrich SCHILLER. Premiere: Paris Opéra, Aug. 3, 1829. American premiere: Park Theater, New York, Sept. 19, 1831.

Characters: William Tell, a Swiss patriot (bass); Hedwig, his wife (soprano); Jemmy, his son (soprano); Arnold, another Swiss patriot (tenor); Melcthal, his father (bass); Walter Fürst, another Swiss patriot (bass); Gessler, Austrian governor of Schwitz and Uri (bass); Mathilde, his daughter (soprano); Rudolph, captain of Gessler's guards (tenor); Ruodi, a fisherman (tenor); Leuthold, a shepherd (bass); knights; peasants; pages; ladies; hunters; soldiers. The setting is Switzerland in the fourteenth century.

The famous overture is a veritable tone poem, beginning with a description of a Swiss dawn. A storm erupts, followed by a pastoral section. The overture ends with a vigorous march, introduced by a fanfare.

Act I. Tell's chalet on Lake Lucerne. Swiss patriots are conspiring to overthrow the tyrant Gessler. Arnold, one of them, is in love with Gessler's daughter. A marriage celebration is taking place. Shepherds participate in a folk dance (*passo a sei*). The festivities are disturbed when the shepherd Leuthold appears and asks for help: one of Gessler's soldiers has tried to abduct his daughter, and he has killed the man. William Tell starts ferrying Leuthold across the lake. Gessler's soldiers arrive. Since they cannot find Leuthold, they seize Melcthal instead.

Act II, Scene 1. A forest. Mathilde, in love with Arnold, muses on how she prefers a simple life with her beloved to the luxury of her father's palace ("Sombre forêt"). When Arnold appears, the lovers greet each other passionately and curse the destiny that keeps them apart. Mathilde departs as Tell and Walter Fürst come to inform Arnold that his father, Melcthal, has been killed by Gessler. The three patriots swear a mighty oath to overthrow Gessler.

Scene 2. A secret meeting place in a wood. The patriots of the cantons of Schwitz and Uri gather to plan rebellion and are inspired by a rousing speech by William Tell.

Act III, Scene 1. A ruined chapel near Gessler's palace. Arnold comes to bid his beloved Mathilde farewell ("Pour notre amour") because it has become his mission to destroy her father. Mathilde promises to remain true to Arnold.

Scene 2. The market place of Altdorf. Gessler addresses his people on the occasion of the centenary of Austrian rule. The people, in festive mood, celebrate the observance with songs and dances. William Tell and his son Jemmy are present. Noticing that Tell is not paying proper homage to Gessler, the captain of the guards arrests him and brings him to the governor. Hoping to humiliate Tell, Gessler orders him to place an apple on his son's head and split the apple with an arrow. Tell begs his son to remain immobile and put his trust in God ("Sois immobile"). He then takes aim and shoots the apple squarely. Bitterly Tell informs the governor that had he missed his target and hurt his son he would have sent a second arrow into Gessler's heart. The governor orders Tell's arrest.

Act IV, Scene 1. Before Melcthal's house. Arnold recalls the happy days of his youth ("Asile héréditaire"). The patriots appear with the news of Tell's arrest.

Scene 2. The shore of Lake Lucerne. Mathilde tells Hedwig Tell that her husband has escaped. As a storm is brewing, the patriots appear with Tell at their head. Gessler arrives, hunting for Tell. Tell kills him with an arrow. The patriots give voice to their rejoicing, which is further intensified with the news that Gessler's palace has fallen. Switzerland is now free. The patriots sing a hymn of joy.

In writing his last opera, Rossini was consciously--perhaps *too* consciously—creating his crowning masterpiece. He built the work on monumental lines. It requires six hours for a complete performance; it is filled with big scenes and pageantry. All this was new to Rossini, who heretofore had been at his best in light, spontaneous music for comparatively trivial episodes. Also new was the dramatic power, sublimity of expression, psychological insight into character, and symphonic breadth and harmonic richness of the musical writing found in *William Tell*. These elements compensate for the dull stretches and the lapses of inspiration. Audiences have never been wholeheartedly fond of *William Tell*. Students of opera, however, consider it a surpassing creation. BELLINI said it reduced all operas of his day, including his own, to pygmies. WAGNER considered that it anticipated his own revolutions in dramatic thought and stylistic approaches.

Willow Song, *see* SALCE! SALCE!

Willst jenes Tag's du nicht dich mehr entsinnen, Erik's aria rebuking Senta for her alleged faithlessness, in Act III of WAGNER'S DER FLIEGENDE HOLLÄNDER.

Windgassen, Wolfgang, tenor. Born Annemasse, Ger., June 26, 1914. His father, Fritz Windgassen, was leading tenor of the STUTTGART OPERA; his mother, Vally von der Osten, was a coloratura soprano. Wolfgang Windgassen studied with his father and with Maria Ranzow and Alfons Fischer. In 1941 he made his debut in Pforzheim as Alvaro in LA FORZA DEL DESTINO. In 1945 he became a member of the Stuttgart Opera, and beginning with 1951 made frequent appearances at the BAYREUTH FESTIVAL, singing the role of PARSIFAL in the first festival season following the end of World War II. He further established his reputation as an outstanding Wagnerian HELDENTENOR at the VIENNA STATE OPERA, beginning with 1953; at COVENT GARDEN since 1954; and at the METROPOLITAN OPERA, where he made his debut as SIEGMUND on Jan. 22, 1957.

Wings of the Dove, The, opera in two parts (six scenes) by MOORE. Libretto by Ethan Ayer, based on the novel of the same name by Henry JAMES. Premiere: New York City Opera, Oct. 12, 1961. In or about 1900, Milly Theale, a beautiful and wealthy American girl in London, who is mortally ill, has fallen in love with an impoverished journalist, Miles Dunster. His sweetheart, Kate, encourages him to marry Milly for her money so that they can live in style after Milly's death. Learning from an aristocratic suitor of this nefarious plan, Milly collapses physically. After her death Dunster learns that she has left him her fortune in spite of his wickedness, an act of generosity that turns his love for Kate into hate. The opera is in a traditional mold, with set numbers and many lyrical pages. Light dance music (a polka, and a waltz, for example) helps to establish the atmosphere and background of the story. Moore incorporated into his opera an episode, "Masque of Janus," comprising song, dance, and pantomime, presented as entertainment for the guests attending a party at the Palazzo Leporelli in Venice.

Winkelmann, Hermann, tenor. Born Brunswick, Ger., Mar. 8, 1849; died Vienna, Jan. 18, 1912. He created the role of PARSIFAL. After completing his vocal studies in Hanover, he made his debut in Sonderhausen in 1875. Engagements in other opera houses followed, including one with the HAMBURG OPERA, where he created the title role of RUBINSTEIN's *Nero,* and another with the VIENNA (Royal) OPERA, where he was heard as LOHENGRIN and TANNHÄUSER. Hans RICHTER recommended him to WAGNER, who invited him to create the role of Parsifal at the BAYREUTH FESTIVAL in 1882; he continued appearing in that role there until 1888. In London he was the first to sing there the roles of WALTHER and TRISTAN and for Vienna the roles of Tristan and OTELLO. In 1884 he was heard in the United States in Wagner Festival concerts.

Winter's Tale, A, *see* SHAKESPEARE.

Winterstürme wichen dem Wonnemond, Siegmund's Spring Song, in Act I of WAGNER's DIE WALKÜRE.

Wird Philomene trauern, Fatima's aria in WEBER's ABU HASSAN.

Wir winden dir den Jungfernkranz, the chorus of the bridesmaids, at the end of Act III, Scene 1, of WEBER's DER FREISCHÜTZ.

Witch, The, a character (mezzo-soprano) in HUMPERDINCK's HANSEL AND GRETEL.

Witch of Salem, A, opera in two acts by CADMAN. Libretto by Nelle Richmond Eberhart. Premiere: Chicago Civic Opera, Dec. 8, 1926. The background is the witch trials in Salem, Mass., in 1692. Sheila loves Arnold, who perfers Claris. When she cannot win Arnold, she accuses Claris of being a witch. Just before Claris is executed, Sheila confesses to Arnold that she lied and offers herself as a substitute for Claris at the scaffold, but only if he will kiss her once. Arnold does so, and Sheila dies in Claris' place.

Witch's House, The (Das Knusperhäuschen), the prelude to Act III of HUMPERDINCK's HANSEL AND GRETEL.

Witch's Ride, *see* HEXENRITT.

Witch's Song, *see* HURR, HOPP, HOPP, HOPP.

With drooping wings, the concluding chorus, an elegy at the death of Dido, in PURCELL's DIDO AND AENEAS.

Witherspoon, Herbert, bass. Born Buffalo, N.Y., July 21, 1873; died New York City, May 10, 1935. After graduation from Yale University in 1895, he studied music with Gustav Stoeckel, Horatio Parker, and Edward MacDowell. He received instruction in singing from Walter Henry Hall and Max Treumann in New York, Jean-Baptiste FAURÉ and Jacques Bouhy in Paris, and Francesco LAMPERTI in Milan. He made his debut in 1898 with a small opera company in New York. After extensive appearances in concerts and oratorio performances, he made his debut at the METROPOLITAN OPERA on Nov. 26, 1908, as TITUREL. He remained at the Metropolitan Opera until 1914, when he retired from the stage to concentrate on teaching. In 1925 he became president of the Chicago Musical College. In 1930 he was engaged as artistic director of the Chicago Civic Opera and in 1931 as president of the Cincinnati Conservatory. When Giulio GATTI-CASAZZA retired as general manager of the Metropolitan Opera in 1935, Witherspoon was selected as his successor. But before his first season began he died of a heart attack in his office at the Metropolitan.

Within this frail crucible of light, Tarquinius' lullaby in Act II of BRITTEN'S THE RAPE OF LUCRETIA.

Witte, Erich, tenor and producer. Born Bremen, Ger., Mar. 19, 1911. Following his debut in Bremen in 1934, he appeared in several German opera houses, including the WIESBADEN OPERA between 1937 and 1938. On Dec. 1, 1938, he made his debut at the METROPOLITAN OPERA in TANNHÄUSER. After a single season at the Metropolitan Opera, he joined first the VIENNA STATE OPERA and then became a principal tenor of the BERLIN STATE OPERA in 1940, appeared at the BAYREUTH FESTIVAL in 1943 as DAVID and again between 1952 and 1955 as LOGE, and at COVENT GARDEN between 1952 and 1955. He subsequently turned to producing operas, becoming principal producer of the FRANKFURT OPERA in 1961.

Wittich, Marie, soprano. Born Giessen, Ger., May 27, 1868; died Dresden, Aug. 4, 1931. She created the role of SALOME in Richard STRAUSS's opera. Having completed her vocal studies in Würzburg, she appeared in a number of German opera houses before becoming a principal soprano of the DRESDEN OPERA in 1889, where she remained until 1914. During this period she was also heard in principal Wagnerian roles at the BAYREUTH FESTIVAL between 1901 and 1910, as well as with other major European opera companies.

Woglinde, a Rhine maiden (soprano) in WAGNER'S DAS RHEINGOLD and GÖTTERDÄMMERUNG.

Wo ist er dessen Sündenbecher jetzt voll ist?, the bitter denunciation by Jokanaan of Herod and Herodias for their dissolute ways, in Richard STRAUSS's SALOME.

Wolf, Hugo, composer. Born Windischgraez, Austria, Mar. 13, 1860; died Vienna, Feb. 22, 1903. He attended the Vienna Conservatory for a brief period, but for the most part was self-taught. He became a music critic of the Vienna Salonblatt in 1884. Three years later he published his first volumes of the songs for which he is today remembered and admired. His opera DER CORREGIDOR, introduced in Mannheim in 1896, was a failure. He was working on a second opera, Manuel Venegas, when he lost his mind and was confined to a private hospital for the rest of his life.

Wolfserzählung, see SCHAU HER, DAS IST EIN TALER.

Wolf-Ferrari, Ermanno, composer. Born Venice, Jan. 12, 1876; died Venice, Jan. 21, 1948. He was trained to be an artist, but a visit to BAYREUTH turned him to music. He completed his music study in Munich with Josef Rheinberger. In 1899 he made his debut as composer with a Biblical cantata, La Sulamite, a success when performed in Venice. A year later LA CENERENTOLA, his first opera, was introduced at the TEATRO LA FENICE. Success came with an OPERA BUFFA, LE DONNE CURIOSE, given in Munich in 1903. His masterwork in the comic style, THE SECRET OF SUZANNE, was introduced in Munich in 1909. His tragic opera, THE JEWELS OF THE MADONNA, first heard in

Berlin in 1911, was also acclaimed. From 1902 to 1909 he was the director of the Liceo Benedetto Marcello in Venice. In 1912 he visited the United States to supervise the American premiere of *The Jewels of the Madonna* at the CHICAGO OPERA.

His operas: *La cenerentola* (1900); *Le donne curiose* (1903); I QUATTRO RUSTEGHI (1906); *Il segreto di Susanna* (*The Secret of Suzanne*, 1909); *I gioielli della Madonna* (*The Jewels of the Madonna*, 1911); L'AMORE MEDICO (1913); *Gli amanti sposi* (1925); *Veste di Cielo* (1927); SLY (1927); *La vedova scaltra* (1931); IL CAMPIELLO (1936); *La Dama Boba* (1938); *Gli dei a Tebe* (1943).

Wolff, Albert Louis, conductor and composer. Born Paris, Jan. 19, 1884; died there, Feb., 1970. He graduated from the Paris Conservatory. After serving as church organist for four years, he became in 1908 chorus master of the OPÉRA-COMIQUE. His debut as a conductor took place there in 1911 in the world premiere of LAPARRA's *La jota*. For several seasons he conducted at the Opéra-Comique. He made his American bow on Nov. 21, 1919, at the METROPOLITAN OPERA leading FAUST. A month later on Dec. 27, he conducted there the world premiere of his opera *L'Oiseau bleu* (THE BLUE BIRD). He remained at the Metropolitan Opera until 1921, specializing in French operas. In 1922 he returned to the Opéra-Comique, and in 1924 he became artistic director of a new opera company at the THÉÂTRE DES CHAMPS ELYSÉES. He subsequently distinguished himself as conductor of symphonic music.

Wolff, Fritz, tenor. Born Munich, Oct. 28, 1894; died there Jan. 18, 1957. His debut took place at BAYREUTH in 1925 in the role of LOGE. He continued appearing at the festival from 1925 to 1941, while also assuming principal Wagnerian roles with the BERLIN STATE OPERA between 1930 and 1943, COVENT GARDEN between 1929 and 1933, and again in 1937–38, and in Cleveland, Ohio, in 1934–35. Becoming almost blind after World War II, he retired from the stage and became a teacher of voice at the Hochschule für Musik in Munich.

Wolfram von Eschenbach, a minstrel-knight (baritone), Tannhäuser's friend, in WAGNER'S TANNHÄUSER.

Worms, Carlo, Ricki's lover (baritone) in FRANCHETTI'S GERMANIA.

Wotan, ruler of the gods (bass-baritone) in WAGNER'S DAS RHEINGOLD, DIE WALKÜRE, and SIEGFRIED.

Wotan's Farewell, *see* DIE WALKÜRE, Act III.

Wowkle, Billy Jackrabbit's squaw (mezzo-soprano) in PUCCINI'S THE GIRL OF THE GOLDEN WEST.

Wozu die Dienste, King Mark's sorrowful narrative upon discovering that Tristan has betrayed him, in Act II of WAGNER'S TRISTAN UND ISOLDE.

Wozzeck, opera in three acts by BERG. Libretto by the composer, based on the drama of the same name by Georg BÜCHNER, which in turn was based on a real murder in 1824. Premiere: Berlin State Opera, Dec. 14, 1925. American premiere: Philadelphia, Mar. 19, 1931.

Characters: Wozzeck, a soldier (baritone); Marie, his mistress (soprano); her son (soprano); a drum major (tenor); a captain (bass); a doctor (bass); Andres, a friend of Wozzeck's (tenor); Margret, Marie's neighbor (contralto). The setting is a small town in Germany; the time about 1820.

Act I. In the captain's room the captain quizzes Wozzeck about his illicit relationship with Marie and their illegitimate child. He then lectures Wozzeck about morality. When Wozzeck maintains that the poor cannot afford the luxury of virtue, the captain upbraids him for thinking too much. The scene shifts to the open country, where Wozzeck and Andres, a fellow soldier, are chopping wood. Wozzeck is filled with dread at the sound of strange noises and hallucinations. As his friend sings about the life of a huntsman, Wozzeck imagines that the world is being set afire by the sinking sun. We now enter Marie's room, where Marie is holding her child in her arms. A military band passes under her window playing martial music.

Looking out of the window, Marie is impressed by the Drum Major, a fact that her neighbor Margret comments upon, much to Marie's anger. Marie now sings a lullaby to her child (Mädel, was fangst du jetzt an?"). Wozzeck arrives distraught. Then when Marie tries to calm him, he rushes off. And now Wozzeck is in the study of a fanatical doctor, where he is the subject for experiments. Partaking of a special diet prepared for him, Wozzeck begins to see hallucinations. The doctor is delighted, for his experiments are successful, but he soon becomes hot-tempered at Wozzeck's strange explanations of his behavior. Wozzeck cries out for Marie. Back at Marie's room, she once again admires the Drum Major strutting under her window. She begins to flirt with him, then invites him into her house.

Act II. In Marie's room. She is proudly admiring earrings the Drum Major has given her. When Wozzeck arrives, she tries to hide the jewelry but Wozzeck notices this and suspiciously inquires where she got the earrings. She tells him she found them. After Wozzeck has left her his wages, Marie bitterly denounces him but also feels some guilt. In the street, Wozzeck finds the captain and the doctor discussing sickness and death. They taunt Wozzeck about Marie's infidelity. Wozzeck returns to Marie, openly accuses her of having been unfaithful, and strikes her. Marie replies by saying she would prefer a knife in her breast to Wozzeck's hands on her body. This further increases Wozzeck's fury. The scene shifts to a beer garden where Marie and the Drum Major are dancing a waltz. Wozzeck, seeing them, cries out for justice. Andres tries to calm him. A fool tells Wozzeck he smells blood, and as Marie and the Drum Major dance past him, Wozzeck feels that the world is whirling around him madly. Later that night the Drum Major wakens the soldiers sleeping in the barracks and drunkenly boasts about his new conquest. He implies that the girl is Marie, and when this gets no overt response from the much disturbed

Wozzeck, the burly Drum Major wrestles Wozzeck to the floor, threatens to choke him to death, and leaves the barracks as the other soldiers impassively turn over and go back to sleep.

Act III. Repentant, Marie is seeking solace in the Bible in her room. She interrupts her reading by taking her child in her arms and comforting him, but then returns to the Bible to read about Mary Magdalene, whom she identifies with herself. She then consents to take a walk with Wozzeck, who is distraught and incoherent. They walk along a forest path to a pond. When they sit down to rest, Wozzeck kisses her. Then when he sees the rise of the moon, he exclaims that it is the color of blood. He murders Marie with a knife and escapes to the tavern, where he encourages the apprentices and their girls to dance. Margret happens to notice blood on Wozzeck's hands, which causes her to cry out. Wozzeck leaves the tavern to return to the pond to search for his incriminating knife. When he finds it, he wades into the pond in order to get rid of it and in doing so drowns. The captain and the doctor hear his cries for help. The captain wants to investigate but the doctor, superstitious and afraid, prevents him from doing so. In front of Marie's house, children are playing games, and Marie's son is prancing about with a hobbyhorse. The children come to tell him that his mother is dead, but he does not understand what they are saying, and when they run off to see the body, he continues to jump around on his hobbyhorse exclaiming "Hopp-hopp." Then he trots off to follow his playmates.

There are few works in the entire history of opera that are so remarkably original and dramatically effective as *Wozzeck* and that have had such a profound impact on the development of twentieth-century opera. Berg uses a vocal style that is freely declamatory, at some points approaching the sound of exaggerated speech through the use of SPRECHSTIMME. The lyricism is stark, at times strange and exotic, piercing in its intensity, gruesome in its dressing of atonal harmonies—all this reflecting the morbidness of the text with striking success. At first hearing the opera seems to be without shape or form, but this is most certainly not the case. The entire opera is built along the lines of a three-part song form (A-B-A), with the first part, or act, entitled "Exposition," the second, "Denouement," and the third, "Catastrophe." Involved in each are Berg's versions of such traditional musical forms as a passacaglia, a rhapsody, a suite, a sonata, a fantasia and fugue, and a set of inventions. These forms are not necessarily evident to the person hearing *Wozzeck*, and the composer did not intend them to be; they are present for their symbolic appropriateness to various moments of the story. Berg's orchestration is rich and unusual: at various points he calls for a chamber orchestra, a military band, a restaurant orchestra, an accordion, an out-of-tune upright piano, and a bombardon (a kind of tuba).

There are times when Berg makes use of popular materials, such as a lullaby rooted in German folksong, a military march, dance music, and so forth, but these are distorted atonally like images reflected by a cracked mirror. Yet for all the unorthodoxy of Berg's methods, style, and sounds, the opera is filled with moments of compelling dramatic and emotional interest. These include Marie's lullaby to her child; the scene in which Marie reads the story of Mary Magdalene by candlelight; the harrowing sounds describing Wozzeck's terror as he comes to the pond searching for his knife; and the unforgettable closing scene when Marie's child plays on his hobbyhorse, little realizing his mother is dead, though his friends have told him so.

The music world first became acquainted with *Wozzeck* through three excerpts introduced at the Frankfurt Music Festival on June 11, 1924, SCHERCHEN conducting. These pieces created a sensation. In 1925, after one hundred thirty-seven rehearsals, the work was produced in its entirety by the BERLIN STATE OPERA. There were widely divergent opinions. A critic in the *Deutsche Zeitung* "had the sensation of having been not in a public theater but in an insane asylum." Others considered it the greatest opera since PELLÉAS ET MÉLISANDE, an opinion that is now widespread. A booklet was published in Vienna quoting and analyzing these strange differences of critical thought. Regardless of controversy, *Wozzeck* soon established itself as one of the most compelling, as well as influential of modern operas. Within a decade of its premiere it was given over twelve hundred times in twenty-eight European cities. In the period following World War II the opera had a number of significant revivals in the United States as well as in Europe. It was produced in English by the NEW YORK CITY OPERA in 1952 and by the METROPOLITAN OPERA on Mar. 5, 1959. The fortieth anniversary of the opera's premiere was celebrated in Berlin with a gala presentation on Dec. 14, 1965.

Manfred Gurlitt's *Wozzeck* (1926), another opera based on Georg Büchner's drama, has been entirely eclipsed by Berg's masterpiece.

Wreckers, The (Les Naufrageurs), opera in three acts by Dame Ethel SMYTH. Libretto (in French) by H. B. Brewster. Premiere: Leipzig, Nov. 11, 1896. The setting is the Cornish coast in the eighteenth century. The primitive inhabitants regard shipwrecks as gifts from heaven and conspire to bring on many such wrecks. Only Thirza (mezzo-soprano), wife of Pascoe (bass), the headman of the village, is repelled by such savagery and lights warning fires, thus causing near famine. When she is discovered, she and her sympathizing lover, Mark (tenor), are locked into a cave on the shore where the rising tide will drown them.

Wrestling Bradford, the Puritan clergyman (baritone) in HANSON'S MERRY MOUNT.

writers as characters in opera. These are some of the world-famous writers who are principal characters in operas:

Andrea Chénier (GIORDANO) ; Boccaccio (SUPPÉ) ; Byron (THOMSON's *Lord Byron*) ; Chatterton (LEONCAVALLO) ; Dante (GODARD, NOUGUÈS, and Philpot) ; Emily Dickinson (MEYEROWITZ' *Eastward in Eden*) ; Milton (SPONTINI) ; Petrarch (Hippolyte Duprat's *Petrarque;* GRANADOS' *Petrarca;* Johann Christoph Kienlen's *Petrarca und Laura*) ; Sappho (GOUNOD, Hugo Kaun, MASSENET, Anton Reicha) ; Torquato Tasso (DONIZETTI, ROSSINI) .

Wurm, rival (basso) to Rodolfo for the love of Luisa in VERDI'S LUISA MILLER.

Wuthering Heights, opera in prologue and three acts by FLOYD. Libretto by the composer, based on Emily Brontë's novel of the same name. Premiere: Sante Fe Opera, N.M., July 16, 1958 (original version) ; New York City Opera, Apr. 9, 1959 (revised) . In making the transition from novel to opera, the composer pushed forward the time to the nineteenth century and narrated the tragic history of Catherine Earnshaw and Heathcliff through a flashback technique.

X

Xenia, daughter (soprano) of Boris Godunov in MUSSORGSKY'S BORIS GODUNOV.

Xerxes, *see* SERSE.

Y

Yamadori, a Japanese prince (baritone) in love with Cio-Cio-San, in PUCCINI'S MADAMA BUTTERFLY.

Yeats, William Butler, poet and dramatist. Born Dublin, June 13, 1865; died Menton, France, Jan. 28, 1939. Operas based on Yeats's writing include EGK'S IRISCHE LEGENDE; Lou Harrison's *The Only Jealousy of Emer;* Fritz Hart's *The*

Land of Heart's Desire; and Manolis Kalomiris' *The Shadowy Waters.*

Yeletsky, a prince (baritone) , Herman's rival for Lisa's love, in TCHAIKOVSKY'S PIQUE DAME.

Yniold, Golaud's young son (soprano) in DEBUSSY'S PELLÉAS ET MÉLISANDE.

Young Lord, The, *see* JUNGE LORD, DER.

Z

Zaccaria, high priest of Jerusalem (bass) in VERDI'S NABUCCO.

Zacharias, an Anabaptist preacher (bass) in MEYERBEER'S LE PROPHÈTE.

Zaide, (1) a gypsy girl (soprano), rival of Fiorilla for the love of the Sultan Selim of Turkey, in ROSSINI'S IL TURCO IN ITALIA.

(2) SINGSPIEL in two acts (unfinished) by MOZART. Lyrics by Johann Andreas Schachtner. Premiere: Frankfurt, Jan. 27, 1866 (originally composed about 1779). American premiere: Tanglewood, Lenox, Mass., Aug. 8, 1955. The plot is something like the one for Mozart's THE ABDUCTION FROM THE SERAGLIO. When the *singspiel* was first performed, it was given with spoken dialogue by Karl Gollmick, for the original had been lost, and with an overture and finale by Anton André.

Zampa, OPÉRA COMIQUE by HÉROLD. Libretto by MÉLESVILLE. Premiere: Opéra-Comique, May 31, 1831. American premiere: Boston, July 26, 1833 (probable). Zampa (baritone) is a pirate bandit invading the island of Castel Ugano. He compels Camilla (soprano) to abandon her betrothed and marry him instead. During the pirates' celebration of this event, Zampa derisively places a ring on the finger of a statue of Alice, a girl he has betrayed. The statue refuses to release the ring. Camilla now escapes. As Zampa attempts to pursue her, the statue drags him to his death in the sea.

The overture is a favorite of salon orchestras and at pop concerts. One of the best-known vocal excerpts is the third-act duet in the form of a BARCAROLLE, "Pourquoi trembler."

Zandonai, Riccardo, composer. Born Sacco, Italy, May 28, 1883; died Pesaro, Italy, June 5, 1944. His music study took place in Roveredo with V. Gianferrari and at the Pesaro Liceo with MASCAGNI. BOITO introduced him to the publisher RICORDI, who commissioned him to write his first opera, *The Cricket on the Hearth,* introduced in Turin in 1908 with moderate success. He was acclaimed in 1914 for his best opera, *Francesca da Rimini,* first performed that year in Turin and afterward given by many major opera houses. In 1921 he completed another important opera, *Giulietta e Romeo,* introduced at the TEATRO COSTANZI on Feb. 14, 1922. From 1939 to the time of his death he was director of the Liceo Rossini in Pesaro. Besides operas already mentioned, he wrote: *Conchita* (1911); *Melenis* (1912); *La via della finestra* (1919); *I cavalieri di Ekebù* (1925); *Giuliano* (1928); *La farsa amorosa* (1933); *Una partita* (1933).

Zandt, Marie van, *see* VAN ZANDT, MARIE.

Zanelli, Renato (born Morales), baritone and tenor. Born Valparaiso, Chile, Apr. 1, 1892; died Santiago, Mar. 25, 1935. His music study took place in Chile, and as a baritone he made his opera debut at Santiago in 1916 as Valentin in FAUST. On Nov. 19, 1919, he made his debut at the METROPOLITAN OPERA as AMONASRO. He continued singing baritone roles at the Metropolitan Opera until 1923. He then went for additional study to Milan, where he developed himself into a tenor, making his debut as such in Naples in 1924 as RAOUL. He returned annually to sing in Santiago, Chile, and other South American opera houses. In 1928 and again in 1930 he appeared in COVENT GARDEN, being particularly successful as OTELLO in VERDI's opera. He subsequently performed in major Italian opera houses, appearing in the world premiere of PIZZETTI's *Lo straniero* in Rome in 1933 and achieving immense success not only as Otello, but also as SIEGMUND and TRISTAN. His career ended in 1933 due to poor health.

Zaretski, Lensky's friend (baritone) in TCHAIKOVSKY'S EUGENE ONEGIN.

Zar lässt sich photographiren, Der, *see* CZAR HAS HIMSELF PHOTOGRAPHED, THE.

Zar und Zimmermann (The Czar and the Carpenter), comic opera in three acts by LORTZING. Libretto by the composer. Premiere: Leipzig, Dec. 22, 1837. American premiere: Astor Place Opera House, New York, Dec. 9, 1851. Peter I of Russia (baritone) assumes the identity of a carpenter, Peter Michailov, in Sardam. There, a carpenter, Peter Ivanov (tenor), is mistaken for the disguised Czar by foreign envoys seeking to negotiate treaties. The ensuing complications are finally straightened out, the Czar returns to Russia, and Ivanov marries the girl he loves, Marie (soprano). One of the most infectious arias is the entrance song of the Burgomaster, Van Bett (bass), "O sancta justitia," with its catchy refrain, "O, ich bin klug und weise." Also of interest: Marie's lament about the evils of jealousy in the first act, "Die Eifersucht ist eine Plage"; in the second act, the air of the French Ambassador, Chateauneuf (tenor), "Lebe wohl, mein flandrisch' Mädchen," and Peter's celebrated romantic song, "Sonst spielt' ich mit Zepter."

zarzuela, a form of Spanish opera that arose in the seventeenth century and took its name from the Palace of Zarzuela near Madrid, where these entertainments first became popular. A few zarzuelas are entirely sung, but a usual feature of this form is spoken dialogue between the songs. The works are not long, allowing three or four to be given in an evening. Some zarzuelas are tragic or melodramatic; most are of a humorous cast, ranging from satire to burlesque. The form has always retained its popularity and led to the founding of the Teatro de la Zarzuela in Madrid in 1856. Many leading Spanish composers have composed zarzuelas, and the popularity of the form and style continues today.

Zauberflöte, Die, *see* MAGIC FLUTE, THE.

Zaubergeige, Die (The Magic Violin), opera in three acts by EGK. Libretto by the composer and Ludwig Andersen, based on a puppet play by Count Pocci. Premiere: Frankfurt, May 20, 1935 (first version); Stuttgart Opera, May 2, 1954 (revised). In a fairy-tale kingdom, Kaspar, a servant, goes to seek his fortune. His entire fortune is three coins presented him by Gretl. One of these he gives to a beggar, who is Cuperus, king of the spirits in disguise. Cuperus rewards Kaspar's generosity by granting him any wish. Kaspar asks for and receives a magic violin capable of enchanting those who listen to it, but in return he must renounce love. After various adventures with his violin, Kaspar is incapable of resisting the appeal of Ninabella. This not only robs the violin of its power but also dooms Kaspar to death. Cuperus, however, proves forgiving. He spares Kaspar, who, after having surrendered his magic violin, returns to his first love, Gretl. The opera is in a folk style, overflowing with folk tunes and dances of Bavarian origin. This is Egk's first opera, and his first work to gain him recognition.

Zauberoper, *see* MAGIC OPERA.

Zaza, opera in four acts by LEONCAVALLO. Libretto by the composer, based on the play of the same name by Pierre Berton and Charles Simon. Premiere: Teatro Lirico, Milan, Nov. 10, 1900. American premiere: Tivoli Opera House, San Francisco, Nov. 27, 1903. Zaza (soprano) is a cafe singer who is the lover of her stage partner, Cascart (baritone). She soon becomes attracted to Milio Dufresne (tenor) and abandons Cascart to become Dufresne's mistress. Learning that Dufresne is married, she frightens him by threatening to disclose their affair to his wife. Milio suddenly realizes how much his family means to him, and Zaza leaves Milio's home without making a scene. Later she renounces her beloved and sends him back to his family. Familiar vocal excerpts: "Il bacio" (the Kiss Duet) of Zaza and Cascart, and Dufresne's aria "È un riso gentil," both in Act I; Cascart's aria, "Buona Zaza" in Act II; and Cascart's fourth-act aria, "Zaza, piccola zingora." The role of Zaza was created by Rosina Storchio.

Zdenka, Arabella's sister (soprano), who appears throughout the opera disguised as a boy, in Richard STRAUSS'S ARABELLA.

Zeffirelli, Franco (born Corsi), producer, stage director, and designer. Born Florence, Feb. 12, 1923. Zeffirelli was employed in the spoken theater and motion pictures before turning to opera. His first significant assignments in opera came from LA SCALA with L'ITALIANA IN ALGERI in 1952–53 and LA CENERENTOLA a season later. His production of L'ELISIR D'AMORE in 1954 proved a triumph. In 1956 he was invited to Holland to stage FALSTAFF, and in 1957 he began the first of a series of productions for the DALLAS CIVIC OPERA. His international fame as one of the foremost producers, stage directors, and designers of his time began at COVENT GARDEN in 1959 with his productions of LUCIA DI LAMMERMOOR, CAVALLERIA RUSTICANA, and PAGLIACCI. Highly distinguished productions in Dallas added to his rapidly developing fame, notably those of THE BARBER OF SEVILLE, DON GIOVANNI, and THE DAUGHTER OF THE REGIMENT. During the summer of 1961 he was employed at the GLYNDEBOURNE FESTIVAL and in 1961–62 by the CHICAGO LYRIC OPERA. This was followed by spectacular presentations of AIDA at La Scala, TOSCA at Covent Garden, and *Falstaff* at the METROPOLITAN OPERA, where he made his debut on Mar. 6, 1964, and where in 1966 he staged the world premiere of BARBER'S ANTONY AND CLEOPATRA, having first adapted SHAKESPEARE's text in collaboration with the composer. Later distinguished productions included those of *L'elisir d'amore* at the EDINBURGH FESTIVAL in 1967, *Don Giovanni* at the Dallas

Civic Opera in 1969, and *Cavalleria rusticana* and *Pagliacci* at the Metropolitan Opera during the 1969–70 season.

Zeffiretti lusinghieri, Ilia's aria in Act III, Scene 1, of MOZART's IDOMENEO.

Zeitkunst, German for "art of the time," a term used in Germany in the 1920's to describe works dealing with current themes treated in a modern style. The German operas of WEILL and HINDEMITH'S NEUES VOM TAGE and HIN UND ZURÜCK are representative examples.

Zémire et Azor, *comédie-ballet* in four acts by GRÉTRY. Libretto by MARMONTEL, based on *Amour par amour* by La Chaussée. Premiere: Fontainebleau, Nov. 9, 1771 (court performance). American premiere: New York City, June 1, 1787. The text is a version of the familiar fairy tale, *Beauty and the Beast.* Sir Thomas BEECHAM conducted a successful revival of Grétry's opera at the Bath Festival in England in 1955. On Aug. 9, 1968, the opera was given at the Court Theater of Drottningholm, Sweden, with the same settings that were used at its Drottningholm Theater premiere on July 22, 1778.

In the operatic adaptation of the fairy tale, Azor is a prince who is turned into a monster because of his selfishness and vanity, and Zémire is the beautiful woman who restores him into a human being through her love. This version was also made into an opera by SPOHR. Ignaz Umlauf's opera, *Der Ring der Liebe* is a sequel.

Zemlinsky, Alexander, composer and conductor. Born Vienna, Oct. 4, 1872; died New York City, Mar. 16, 1942. He attended the Vienna Conservatory. His first opera, *Sarema,* won the Leopold Award in 1897. It was as a conductor of operas that he first became known. In 1906 he became first conductor of the Vienna VOLKSOPER. Two years later he was engaged as first conductor of the VIENNA OPERA. In 1911 he was appointed musical director of the German Opera in Prague, where he remained sixteen years. From 1927 to 1933 he was principal conductor of the BERLIN STATE OPERA. When the Nazis came to power,

Zemlinsky returned to Vienna. In 1938 he came to the United States, where he died four years later. He was a distinguished teacher, his pupils including Arnold SCHOENBERG, Erich KORNGOLD, and Artur BODANZKY. His operas: *Sarema* (1897); *Es war einmal* (1900); *Kleider machen Leute* (1910); *Eine florentinische Tragödie* (1917); *Der Zwerg* (1921); *Der Kreidekreis* (1933).

Zenatello, Giovanni, tenor. Born Verona, Italy, Feb. 22, 1876; died New York City, Feb. 11, 1949. He attended the Scuola di Canto, after which he studied privately with Giovanni Moretti in Milan. In 1899 he made his debut at the SAN CARLO in Naples as a baritone, singing the role of Silvio in PAGLIACCI. Two years later at the same theater and in the same opera, he sang CANIO, making a sensational debut as a tenor, which he thereafter remained. From 1903 to 1907 he appeared at LA SCALA, where he created the role of Pinkerton in MADAMA BUTTERFLY and that of Vassili in GERMANIA. After successful appearances at COVENT GARDEN, he made his American debut at the MANHATTAN OPERA on Nov. 4, 1907, in LA GIOCONDA. He stayed with the Manhattan Opera two seasons, then appeared for five more with the Boston Opera, and for a single season with the CHICAGO OPERA. He retired from the stage in 1930, devoting himself to teaching singing in New York together with his wife, the Spanish contralto Maria Gay.

Zeno, Apostolo, poet and librettist. Born Venice, Dec. 11, 1668; died there Nov. 11, 1750. He was the most significant opera librettist before METASTASIO. In 1710 he founded in Venice the *Giornale de letterati d'Italia*. Eight years later he settled in Vienna, where he served as court poet. Returning to Venice, he lived there the rest of his life. He wrote over seventy librettos which were set to music by most of the famous composers of his generation, including: BONONCINI (*Astarto*); CALDARA (*Ifigenia in Aulide*); Francesco Gasparini (*Merope*); HANDEL (*Faramondo* and *Scipio*); HASSE (*Lucio Papirio*); Antonio Lotti; JOM-

MELLI; PERGOLESI (*Salustia*); PORPORA (*Temistocle*); SACCHINI; Domenico SCARLATTI; VIVALDI; and Niccolò Zingarelli.

Zerbinetta, a character (soprano) in Richard STRAUSS'S ARIADNE AUF NAXOS.

Zerlina, (1) the innkeeper's daughter (soprano) in AUBER'S FRA DIAVOLO.

(2) Masetto's betrothed (soprano) in MOZART'S DON GIOVANNI.

Ziegler, Edward, opera manager. Born Baltimore, Mar. 25, 1870; died New York City, Oct. 25, 1947. His professional career in music began when he became assistant music critic to James Gibbons Huneker on the *New York Sun*. After holding various other posts as music critic in New York, he became administrative secretary of the METROPOLITAN OPERA in 1916. In 1920 he was engaged as assistant general manager to GATTI-CASAZZA. He remained at the Metropolitan until the end of his life, supervising most of its administrative and financial operations and scouting Europe for new singers. He arranged the broadcasts of the Metropolitan Opera from its stage and in 1940 was one of the leaders of the successful public drive to raise a million dollars for the Metropolitan.

Zigeunerbaron, Der, *see* GYPSY BARON, THE.

Zita, Donati's cousin (mezzo-soprano) in PUCINNI'S GIANNI SCHICCHI.

Zitti, zitti, (1) Fugal trio of Almaviva, Rosina, and Figaro as they prepare to escape from Bartolo's house via the window, in Act II of ROSSINI'S THE BARBER OF SEVILLE.

(2) The chorus of the courtiers pleading for haste as they abduct Gilda, in Act I, Scene 2, of VERDI'S RIGOLETTO.

Zola, Émile, author. Born Paris, Apr. 2, 1840; died there Sept. 29, 1902. The foremost exponent of French literary naturalism profoundly affected the development of the French opera composer Alfred BRUNEAU, who adapted many of Zola's novels for operas, while writing other works to Zola's librettos. Manfred Gurlitt wrote an opera on Zola's *Nana*. Karel Weis used Zola's

Soirées de Medaic for his opera *The Attack on the Mill*. The same story was used by Bruneau for his *L'Attaque du moulin*.

Zuane, a gondolier (bass) in PONCHIELLI'S LA GIOCONDA.

Zukunftsart and **Zukunftsmusik,** German for "the art of the future" and "music of the future." The terms were used by WAGNER to describe his music. For the next half century they were current in the literary battles fought over Wagner's esthetics.

Zum letzten Liebesmahle, chorus of the Knights of the Holy Grail as they file into the hall of the HOLY GRAIL to partake of Communion, in Act I, Scene 2, of WAGNER'S PARSIFAL.

Zu neuen Thaten, Brünnhilde's farewell to Siegfried as he sets forth to seek new deeds and adventures, in the prologue to WAGNER'S GÖTTERDÄMMERUNG.

Zuniga, a captain of the guards (bass) in BIZET'S CARMEN.

Zurga, tribal chieftain (baritone) in BIZET'S LES PÊCHEURS DE PERLES.

Zürich June Festival, an annual festival inaugurated in Zürich, Switzerland, in 1937 under the direction of Hans Zimmermann, who remained in charge until 1956. This festival features drama, ballet, art exhibits, performances of instrumental music and opera, the last in performances by the ZÜRICH OPERA. Under Zimmermann the festival offered the world premieres of JEANNE D'ARC AU BÛCHER, LULU, and MATHIS DER MALER (among other operas), and the first European production of PORGY AND BESS. In 1964 the festival honored the memory of Richard STRAUSS with performances of five of his operas. In 1965 it celebrated the seventieth anniversary of HINDEMITH's birth with a new production of *Mathis der Maler* (among other of his works). In 1969 HENZE's *Il re cèrvo* (KÖNIG HIRSCH) was conducted by the composer, and a cycle of MOZART's operas was performed.

Zürich Opera, the major opera company in Switzerland. It presents an annual season of opera performances at the Stadttheater in Zürich, which opened in 1891. In 1903 this was the first company to give an entirely legal staged production of PARSIFAL outside BAYREUTH. In 1917 it presented the world premiere of ARLECCHINO; in 1937 that of LULU; in 1942 that of LE VIN HERBÉ; in 1957 the first staged presentation of MOSES UND ARON; and in 1961 and 1967 respectively the premieres of MARTINU'S GREEK PASSION and NONO's *The Red Mantle*. Beginning with 1937, the company officiated at the ZÜRICH JUNE FESTIVAL. Hans Zimmermann was director between 1937 and 1956. He was succeeded by Karl Heinz Krahl, Herbert GRAF, and Hermann Juch. Hans ROSBAUD was musical director between 1955 and 1958; the present musical director is Christian Voechtig. Among the more important productions of comparatively unfamiliar and rarely given operas produced by the company since the end of World War II are *Amphion* (HONEGGER); *Aroldo* (VERDI); CARDILLAC; *Füsse in Feuer* (Armin Schibler); *Heimkehr* (Marcel Mihalovici); L'HEURE ESPAGNOLE; A MIDSUMMER NIGHT'S DREAM; RASKOLNIKOFF; RUSALKA; *Venus* (SCHOECK); and DIE ZAUBERGEIGE.

Zurück von ihm!, Elisabeth's declamation, protecting Tannhäuser from the knights and insisting on his right to seek salvation, in Act II of WAGNER'S TANNHÄUSER.

Zwangvolle Plage!, Mime's expression of impatience at being unable to forge the sword, in the opening of Act I of WAGNER'S SIEGFRIED.

Zweite Brautnacht! Zaubernacht, Helen's rapturous aria (the best known in the opera) following her magic flight with Menelaus to a place near the Atlas mountains, in Act II of Richard STRAUSS'S DIE AEGYPTISCHE HELENA.

Zwischenfälle bei einer Notlandung (Incidents in Connection with a Crash Landing), opera in "two phases and fourteen situations" by BLACHER. Libretto by Heinz von Cramer. Premiere: Hamburg Opera, Feb. 4, 1966. The text describes the experiences of eleven survivors following a crash landing of a plane. Significant use is made of ELEC-

TRONIC sounds in this opera, providing "audible backgrounds for scenes illustrating the amazing, sometimes terrifying world of technology," according to James H. Sutcliffe. In describing the text, Sutcliffe calls it "a series of film-like sequences showing the survivors trapped in a strange, sinister, even murderous technical world, through which they wander, stage by stage, trying to escape what seems to be the treadmill of a nightmare." He also points out that the audience is surrounded by "twenty-five separate sources for amplified sound."

Zylis-Gara, Teresa, soprano. Born Vilno, Poland, Jan. 23, 1937. She began her musical training in Lodz when she was fourteen, then won several prizes in local singing contests and made an appearance in Cracow in HALKA. Winning a competition sponsored by the German Radio in Munich in 1960 brought her appearances with a number of minor German opera companies. In 1966 and 1967 she scored major successes at the Düsseldorf Opera in L'INCORONAZIONE DI POPPEA and ANNA BOLENA respectively and with the PARIS OPÉRA as Donna ELVIRA. She followed this with appearances at the festivals at GLYNDEBOURNE and SALZBURG and with such principal European companies as COVENT GARDEN, the VIENNA STATE OPERA, the MUNICH OPERA, and the BERLIN DEUTSCHE STAATSOPER. Her debut at the METROPOLITAN OPERA took place on Jan. 4, 1969, as Donna Elvira, a performance she repeated that same summer at the Salzburg Festival, when it was filmed.